Production & Operations MANAGEMENT

Strategic & Tactical Decisions

FIRST CANADIAN EDITION

JAY HEIZER
Texas Lutheran College

BARRY RENDER
Rollins College

JAMES D. FORRESTER
Ryerson Polytechnic University

KIRK L. BAILEY
Ryerson Polytechnic University

Prentice Hall Canada Inc., Scarborough, Ontario

Keith Davis, teacher, scholar, mentor, and friend, and Albert J. Simone, for always setting the standards for high-quality academics

* * *

Margaret Forrester and Professor C. D'Arcy Dakin, J.D. Forrester's "mentor" in P.O.M.: "Thank you, D'Arcy." Karyl Bailey and Professor Park M. Reilly of the Faculty of Engineering, University of Waterloo, who said "Education should be fun. If it isn't, there's something wrong!" (The best professor/teacher K.L. Bailey has ever encountered at any level)

Canadian Cataloguing in Publication Data

Production and operations management : strategic and tactical decisions

1st Canadian ed.
ISBN 0-13-840638-3

1. Production management. I. Heizer, Jay H.
TS155.P745 1997 658.5 C96-932368-9

Prentice-Hall, Inc., Upper Saddle River, *New Jersey*
Prentice-Hall International (UK) Limited, *London*
Prentice-Hall of Australia, Pty. Limited, *Sydney*
Prentice-Hall Hispanoamericana, S.A., *Mexico City*
Prentice-Hall of India Private Limited, *New Delhi*
Prentice-Hall of Japan, Inc., *Tokyo*
Simon & Schuster Southeast Asia Private Limited, *Singapore*
Editora Prentice-Hall do Brasil, Ltda., *Rio de Janeiro*

ISBN: 0-13-840638-3

Acquisitions Editor: *Sarah Kimball*
Developmental Editor: *Maurice Esses*
Copy Editor: *Rodney Rawlings*
Production Editor: *Marjan Farahbaksh*
Production Coordinator: *Deborah Starks*
Photo Research: *Marijke Leupen*
Art Director: *Mary Opper*
Cover Design: *Monica Kompter*
Cover Image: *Kevin Ghiglione*
Page Layout: *Michael Kelley/Joan Wilson*

Original edition published by Prentice-Hall, Inc., Upper Saddle River, New Jersey

This edition is authorized for sale in Canada only.
1 2 3 4 5 VH 01 00 99 98 97

Printed and bound in USA

FOREWORD

When I first entered a production operation in 1952 the world of business was divided into two parts, like the Red Sea had been. One part made big things out of little things; the other part purchased the little things, found the customers, took care of the money, sold stuff, and complained about the activities of the first part. The two portions of the company had nothing in common and little interest in each other.

Over the years it was discovered that there are no separate parts of an organization. It is a body that requires all components to function together as a unit if a successful life is to be obtained.

However everyone knew that the world was made up of separate parts. Markets were described as domestic and international. The latter was not part of the organization and often had a great deal of difficulty obtaining information about plans, products, and people. Now we have learned that the world of business has no boundaries and there are only domestic markets. We have also learned that we have suppliers and customers who do not speak our language or observe our holidays.

Functional operations used to be responsible for whatever noun was in their title. Manufacturing manufactured, purchasing purchased, personnel personneled, and quality was done by the quality department. When I was a quality manager top management held me personally responsible if a customer received something that was not proper. Everyone else were "bad guys" trying to get stuff by quality, and we were the "good guys." When enough things went wrong the practice was to find a tougher, smarter cop. There was no thought of getting things done right.

When I began preaching the prevention of problems, called quality management, it took a while for people to catch on. The breakthrough came with the determination of the "price of nonconformance." How much did it cost to do things wrong, and then fix them. Most companies came to the realization that it took 25% and more of their revenues to live that way. That was the beginning of the quality revolution.

When I talk to operations management classes each year I am always impressed that the students are learning to look at the world from a platform that did not exist in my early career. The broad scope of this book assures that this will happen. It provides a place to begin the future by reviewing the past. The students always want to know about the "reality" of quality management, which is the general subject of my chat. I tell them that basic concepts are the important part of business management, that there are no "systems" to do the executive's work. Concepts come from understanding, understanding begins with learning, and learning comes from examining credible resources with an open mind.

I know you will enjoy yourself in this course.

PHILIP CROSBY

WEB SITE

Visit the Prentice Hall Canada Web site!
Send us your comments,
browse our catalogues,
and more.

www.phcanada.com

Or reach us through e-mail at

phcinfo_pubcanada@prenhall.com

Brief Contents

CONTENTS

PART THREE STRATEGIC DECISIONS FOR MEETING CUSTOMER NEEDS

PREFACE

The book is intended to provide you with a current, complete, and practical introduction to the field of production/operations management (P/OM). The text can be used at either the undergraduate or the MBA level.

The authors realize that the majority of readers are not P/OM majors. However, we feel that students in management, marketing, finance, economics, accounting, information systems, and engineering will find the material both helpful and useful in learning to appreciate how the P/OM manager enriches their professional lives.

The material is designed so that you will be exposed to technical/engineering issues that have business concerns. This exposure will help you develop skills as a leader, facilitator, and team builder with a vision and focus on critical issues in P/OM.

The focus is on the current and future technological and competitiveness issues that managers face in the global market and their role in providing solutions to those issues. The authors hope that on completing the course, you will appreciate the role of the production/operations manager and consider this area as a possible career path.

FOCUS OF THE FIRST CANADIAN EDITION

Contents

STRATEGIC AND TACTICAL DECISIONS FOR MEETING CUSTOMER NEEDS. We balance the coverage of managerial and strategic issues with a series of decisions for meeting the needs of customers. To provide maximum flexibility, we have included eight chapter supplements that deal with decision-making techniques such as linear programming, queuing, simulation, and learning curves. This allows instructors to spend as much or as little time as needed on each component of the course.

INTERNATIONAL EXAMPLES. As productivity and the world economy are so closely linked with our own, we have made a special effort to include international illustrations in our narrative, problems, cases, and *POM in Action* boxes. This emphasis is also tied to our focus in each chapter on how to achieve world-class standards in performance. We discuss scores of international firms; Volvo, British Airways, Nissan, Toyota, Komatsu, and Siemens are just some of them. Our coverage of P/OM strategy in Chapter 2 discusses issues of international competitiveness.

STATE-OF-THE-ART DEVELOPMENTS. In order to keep up to date, we have included substantial coverage of TQM (total quality management) tools, house of quality, benchmarking, finite scheduling, time-based competition, work cells, animated simulation, keiretsu, virtual organizations, and Japanese layout.

QUALITY MANAGEMENT. Due to its increasingly important role throughout the operations process, we have provided significant coverage of the important issue of quality. This helps us develop an approach for every other P/OM decision. With expanded coverage of European (ISO 9000) and Japanese quality standards, the Baldrige Awards, house of quality, benchmarking, poka-yoke, Kaizen, and fishbone diagrams, we introduce the latest concepts in the quality discipline.

A Balance of Service and Manufacturing Applications. P/OM has a service as well as a traditional manufacturing aspect. This first Canadian edition takes special note of services. Many chapters include service aspects of operations, and others have special sections that note the distinction between service and manufacturing in P/OM. For instance, in the work measurement sections, we have used service jobs as examples. Similarly, office layouts receive emphasis, as do service location issues, quality management, and project management applied to services.

New Appendix D: Learning Curve Coefficients and Cumulative Totals. For the Canadian edition we have added an Appendix D, "Learning Curve Coefficients and Cumulative Totals," that includes all of the units of production up more than 500. And we have expanded the learning curve value sets from 5 to 12. This allows far more range in teaching and explaining learning curves.

Pedagogy

Solved Problems. Solved problems are included in this edition. They are provided as models for students as they work unsolved problems on their own.

Data Base Applications. A feature called "Data Base Applications" appears in chapters on quality control, linear programming, forecasting, location strategy, transportation models, layout, aggregate planning, material requirements planning, short-term scheduling, and project management. These very large problems are intended for analysis by computer. They permit students to spend more time interpreting outputs of realistic problems to supplement problem-solving skills developed with the regular programs.

Cases. We have provided many cases for this first Canadian edition. Most of these have been developed by leading P/OM academics. The cases are generally one to two text pages in length, making them short enough to cover in weekly assignments. But they also deal with situations in a realistic, detailed manner that adds depth to each chapter. Almost all cases are based on real-world companies.

Three Levels of Problems. The number of end-of-chapter problems is substantial, and each is identified as one of three levels: introductory (one dot), moderate (two dots), and challenging (three dots). In addition, these problems focus on problem formulation and interpretation as well as calculation. Many discussion questions have been provided as well.

POM in Action Boxes. Recent examples of P/OM practice, from a variety of sources such as the *Maclean's*, *Wall Street Journal*, *Fortune*, *Harvard Business Review*, *Forbes*, and the World Wide Web, are included in all chapters and supplements. These boxes bring P/OM to life and help drive home the points made in the chapters. These real P/OM issues can spark the students' interest and enliven class discussion. Fifty-six POM *in Action* boxes appear in this edition.

CRITICAL THINKING EXERCISES. Our book is the first P/OM text to provide a new feature that challenges the student to face critical issues of business today. It appears in each chapter and supplement as a "Critical Thinking Exercise." Students working in small groups or teams may be an appropriate way to tackle the subject presented. Many of these exercises deal with ethical issues and decisions or with issues for which no clear answer exists. We hope they lead to lively classroom debate.

WORLD-CLASS PROFILES. We have provided the exciting feature of full-colour tours of world-class organizations. Each of the 18 chapters now begins with a photo essay of a firm chosen for its leadership in the area of P/OM covered in that chapter.

PHOTOS. In addition, to the world-class tours, over 170 full-colour photos appear in this edition, along with detailed captions tying them to the contents of their chapters and to specific components. These photos and captions increase student interest and add a depth not found in other textbooks.

WEB SITES OF INTEREST. We have included some references to the WWW (World Wide Web) throughout the text.

AB:POM SOFTWARE. A microcomputer software package, AB:POM (developed by Howard Weiss, Temple University), is available with the text. This package, the most popular Decision Support Software in college P/OM use, provides both breadth of functions and user-friendliness. It includes more than a dozen P/OM application programs that range from forecasting to queuing to line balancing to project scheduling to MRP. We think most students appreciate the experience of using a computer to solve problems. Instructors, however, can structure the course with or without the use of the software. At the end of each problem-oriented chapter, the student will also find an explanation of how to use the software for that particular application. In addition, detailed instructions for using the software are located in Appendix F. For most effective learning, the software has been structured to closely match the approach, notation, and terms found in this text. STORM and QSOM software are also available at reduced prices, through Prentice Hall, with this book.

SYMBOLIC SPREADSHEET PRINTOUTS. A "symbolic" spreadsheet is one that illustrates the actual formulas used to make calculations. In addition to the "black box" approach of AB:POM, instructors and students can also develop their own formulas via spreadsheet to solve problems in forecasting, simulation, time studies, PERT, and most other application areas. This is one of the first P/OM texts to show this alternative approach. Spreadsheet software is illustrated along with AB:POM printouts at the end of eleven of the chapters and supplements.

CD-ROM AND PRESENTATION GRAPHICS. An exciting new feature in this edition is lecture/classroom material for the course on two colourful media—CD-ROMs and Presentation Graphics disks. Key features from each chapter are highlighted in both. The CD-ROM also includes photographs and video highlights. (At this time, only the U.S. version of this material is available.)

STUDY GUIDE. Another supplement available with the text is a student *Study Guide* that comes complete with alternate narrative, solved problems, and answered review questions on a chapter-by-chapter basis.

NAME INDEX, COMPANY INDEX, AND GENERAL INDEX. Three indices are provided. The name index provides a listing of authors who are noted in the book. The company index illustrates the large number of real-world organizations that are described in the book.

ALSO AVAILABLE TO INSTRUCTORS. A comprehensive *Annotated Instructor's Edition*, as well as a *Test Bank*, *Transparency Masters*, a *DataDisk* that contains problem data, a complete *Solutions Manual*, and a special set of CBC video segments are all available with this edition.

ORGANIZATION OF THE BOOK

We have identified ten decisions that are critical to effective production/operations management. These are divided into strategic and tactical decisions, and are presented in a realistic, global, and dynamic environment. We hope this approach presents P/OM decisions in a way that will assist current and future managers in understanding how to manage operations effectively.

Part One provides an introduction to P/OM productivity, P/OM strategy, and international issues that drive operations decisions.

Part Two focusses on identifying the customer's needs. Its three chapters deal with quality and forecasting. Quality provides an overview, because setting a quality plan is both strategic (Chapter 3) and tactical (Chapter 4) in nature.

Part Three focusses on six strategic management decisions beyond quality for meeting customers needs: product design, process-technology selection, facility locations, facility layout, human resources, and purchasing/JIT.

PART ONE Introduction
Introduction to P/OM (Chap. 1)
Productivity, Operations Strategy, and Global Competition (Chap. 2)

⇓

PART TWO Identifying Customer Needs
Total Quality Management (Chap. 3)
Statistical Quality Control (Chap. 4)
Forecasting (Chap. 5)

⇓

PART THREE Strategic Decisions for Meeting Customer Needs
Product (Chap. 6)
Process (Chap. 7)
Technology (Chap. 8)
Location (Chap. 9)
Layout (Chap. 10)
Human Resource Management (Chap. 11)
Purchasing and JIT (Chap. 12)

⇓

PART FOUR Tactical Decisions for Meeting Customer Needs
Inventory Management (Chaps. 13 and 14)
Scheduling
- Intermediate (Aggregate) (Chap. 15)
- Short-Term (Chap. 16)
- Project (Chap. 17)

Maintenance and Reliability (Chap. 18)

Part Four introduces three tactical decisions of operations management for meeting customer needs. These are scheduling (short-term in Chapter 16, intermediate-term in Chapter 15, and project-oriented in Chapter 17), inventory control, and maintenance. This philosophy of four parts in the book is summarized in the figure.

We have, for the sake of completeness, included a great deal of material in this text. However, to cover all of the topics in a one-semester course would be unusual. Consequently, we developed the organization shown in the figure that allows substantial flexibility for the instructor. Instructors may skip over many of the technical chapter supplements (such as linear programming, learning curves, work measurement, simulation, transportation models, and queuing). On the other hand, those instructors preferring a quantitative treatment will especially appreciate many of the supplements, and the numerous quantitative examples, solved problems, AB:POM software, and the spreadsheet formulations. Those preferring a more qualitative treatment of P/OM may stress the numerous case studies and our unique "Critical Thinking Exercises." We think the result is a text that allows instructors to teach the course in their own way and at their own pace.

ACKNOWLEDGMENTS

We would like to thank the many individuals, listed here in alphabetical order, who were kind enough to assist us in writing this first Canadian edition in 1996. Without the help of these fellow professors and student researchers, we would never have received the feedback needed to put together a teachable text.

Dr. J. Bhadury
Faculty of Administration
University of New Brunswick
P.O. Box 4400
Fredericton, New Brunswick

Rami Guirguis, B.B.M.
Business Management graduate
Ryerson Polytechnic University
Toronto, Ontario

Steve Hammerschmidt, B.B.M.
Business Management graduate
Ryerson Polytechnic University
Toronto, Ontario

Professor C.F. Hobbs
School of Business
Carleton University
Ottawa, Ontario

Professor Michael Piczak
Department of Business Administration
Mohawk College
P.O. Box 2034
Hamilton, Ontario

Dr. Ahmet Satir
Decision Sciences and MIS Department
Concordia University
Montreal, Quebec

Professor Vedat Verter
Faculty of Management
McGill University
Montreal, Quebec

In addition, we appreciate the fine people at Prentice Hall Canada who provided help and encouragement during the preparation of the manuscript: Maurice Esses, who helped shepherd the project through to conclusion; Marjan Farahbaksh who assisted ably with the final production; and especially Ellen Boyington, the best publisher's representative we've ever met, who encouraged us to take on this project.

We also appreciate the efforts of colleagues who have helped to shape the entire learning package that accompanies this text: Professor Howard Weiss (Temple University) developed AB:POM microcomputer software; Ted Ashford (Rollins College) prepared the transparency masters and presentation graphics. Finally, the following professors provided the excellent case studies found in this edition:

Michael Ballot
University of the Pacific

James Evans
University of Cincinnati

Marilyn Helms
University of Tennessee-Chattanooga

Marilyn S. Jones
Winthrop University

Jerry Kinard
Western Carolina University

Curtis P. McLaughlin
University of North Carolina-Chapel Hill

Zbignew H. Przasnyski
Loyola Marymount University

Roger W. Schmenner
Indiana University

Kala Chand Seal
Loyola Marymount University

Bruce Simmons
University of Akron

Victor E. Sower
Sam Houston State University

Ralph M. Stair, Jr.
Florida State University

Richard J. Tersine
University of Oklahoma

Timothy L. Urban
University Of Tulsa

We have been fortunate to have been able to work with all of these people.

We wish you a pleasant and productive introduction to production and operations management.

1

PRODUCTION/OPERATIONS MANAGEMENT

CHAPTER OUTLINE

LEARNING OBJECTIVES

When you complete this chapter you should be able to:

Identify or define:

- Production and productivity
- Production/operations management (P/OM)
- What production/operations managers do
- The three major functions of a business

Describe or explain:

- A brief history of operations management
- Career opportunities in production/operations management
- The future of the discipline

WORLD-CLASS PROFILE: ALCAN CABLE

QUALITY WINS SMALL MANUFACTURING FOR LAPOINTE WORKS, ALCAN CABLE DIVISION

Quality is a journey, not a destination. However, the journey itself often produces tangible results for organizations undertaking it. This is readily apparent at the Lapointe Works, Alcan Cable Division. Built in the 1970s, Lapointe Works is one of seven North American plants of the Alcan Cable Division of Alcan Aluminum Inc. The plant manufactures aluminum rod alloys, which are divided into two categories: mechanical alloys used for products such as protective sheathing for electrical cable, nails, rivets, window screens, etc. and ducting alloys for use in electrical cable for high-tension power lines. In 1990, Alcan Cable committed itself to Quality by establishing a new mission to become "a world-class manufacturer" within four years.

With the arrival of the Canada-U.S. free trade agreement, American producers entered the Canadian market, causing a drop in the price of aluminum. Lapointe's management team realized that to face this stiff new competition, they would have to maintain their dedication to Quality improvement.

Alcan Cable also realized that continual market assessment would be essential to success. By conducting research on future demand, they recognized that mechanical alloys, though difficult to produce, could carve out an important market niche. To succeed, Alcan Cable would have to become more competitive in this area.

Alcan employees conduct a final quality assurance inspection prior to shipment. Complaints from clients have been reduced by 85% for the period 1992–1996.

The taking of molten metal samples before and during production ensures consistent and accurate chemical composition. Improved metal recovery has increased productivity by 15% resulting in a decrease in unit cost.

Source: Adapted from an article by The National Quality Institute of Canada, 1995.

Accordingly, Lapointe Works began manufacturing mechanical alloys. Today they are recognized as a leader in the production of aluminum rod.

These factors spurred Lapointe's Quality improvement program forward. Leadership has been demonstrated in setting missions, vision, and direction for the plant. This leadership fostered commitment from the whole organization to making improvements; continuous learning programs have been put in place to support these initiatives.

As an integral part of an innovative communications approach, the work manager and his or her colleagues hold daily meetings to steer the plant towards its overall objectives, which approximately 80% of employees attend. The meeting's minutes are disseminated to the entire site that same day.

Another integral part of this program is Lapointe Works' customer focus. Customers are regularly asked for their input and taken on site tours by employees. Feedback and internal development ensure that processes and process controls are examined and improved continuously. Suppliers are also given clear instructions on the manufacturing requirements and they consult regularly with plant representatives.

All these activities are covered by the main guidelines of Alcan's mission, which include the health and safety of all employees and respect for the environment.

This is what a Quality journey is all about, and Lapointe Works exemplifies how it should be done. Notable successes have resulted:

- Starting from zero in 1994, Lapointe Works has captured approximately 32% of the market share in the aluminum mesh category.
- From 1990 to 1995, the plant more than doubled its production of value-added alloys, growing from 25% to 56% of its capacity.
- The plant has obtained ISO 9002 certification.
- Customer complaints have been reduced by 85% between 1992 and 1996 and on-time delivery is at 99% efficiency.
- They have not lost one client because of quality problems since 1990.
- They have achieved a 90% participation rate in Ontario in cross-functional teams in 1996.

In 1995 they won the Trophy for Quality—Small Manufacturing from Canada Awards for Excellence.

This photo illustrates cleanliness of the Lapointe works, and the space allotted to the process. Health and safety are first on the agenda at Alcan, with the result being no "lost time accidents" since July 1994 at this location.

Aluminum coils ready for shipping.

It was August 1913 in Detroit and Ford Motor managers Clarence Avery and C. W. Klann struggled to build cars. Men had been building cars for decades, but Avery and Klann wanted to do it faster and cheaper. Their plan was to put the car together while it moved and the men assembling it stood still—a revolutionary change. For centuries, men had moved and the work stood still. Moving work while men stand still is difficult. But they succeeded. In 9 months, they reduced the time spent on assembly from over 12 hours to just 93 minutes. They revolutionized production and before they were through, they put America on wheels with 15 million Model T Fords. ♦

Production

Production management and operations management

In this text, we discuss how managers continue to revolutionize production and how you, too, can manage resources to improve production and our quality of life. **Production** is the creation of goods and services. **Production management and operations management (P/OM)** are activities that transform resources into goods and services. Activities creating goods and services take place in all organizations.

In companies that manufacture goods, the production activities that create those goods are usually quite obvious. For instance, we can watch the creation of a tangible product such as a Sony television set or a Chevy truck. When referring to such activity, we tend to use the term *production management*.

In other organizations that do not create physical products, the production function may be less obvious. The "production" that takes place when your cheque is processed at your bank, or when you make an airline reservation, or when a patient is taken care of in a hospital, is called *operations*. The product that is produced may take some unusual forms, such as placing machine-readable marks on paper, filling an empty seat on an airplane, or prescribing medication. We call the companies that do this type of work *service organizations*. The production activity that goes on in these service organizations is usually referred to as *operations* or *operations management*. The *POM in Action* box "Canada's Borrowing, with Its Fat Fees, Lures Wall Street" provides a brief glimpse at why U.S. financial services flock to Bay Street.

Frederick W. Taylor's *Principles of Scientific Management* revolutionized manufacturing. A scientific approach to the analysis of daily work and the tools of industry frequently increased productivity 400%. For instance, by 1913, Model T Fords were being assembled with less than two hours of labour.

As we progress through the text, we examine exciting examples of production and operations functions, ranging from General Motors to McDonald's. We see how production managers in these firms create the goods and services that enrich our lives. Production/operations managers make the decisions that transform resources into goods and services. In this text we use the words *production and operations*, as well as the combination *production/operations management* (or P/OM), when we discuss this transformation process.

HERITAGE OF OPERATIONS MANAGEMENT

The field of P/OM is relatively young, but its history is rich and interesting. Our lives and the P/OM discipline have been enhanced by the innovations and contributions of numerous individuals. We introduce you to a few of these individuals in this section.

Eli Whitney (1800) is credited with the early popularization of interchangeable parts, which he achieved by standardizing parts and through effective quality control. In a contract he signed with the U.S. government for 10,000 muskets, he was able to command a premium price because the muskets had interchangeable parts.

POM IN ACTION

Canada's Borrowing, with Its Fat Fees, Lures Wall Street

Toronto's financial district located in and around Bay Street occupies just a bit more than 2.5 kilometres of real estate. The street resembles Manhattan, which explains why movie companies looking for Wall Street locations are attracted to it. Filmmakers are not attracted just for the resemblance but also because of the cheap Canadian dollar.

During 1995 many of Wall Street's large investment firms were lured to Bay Street by the large underwriting commissions. Since then, companies like Salomon Brothers, Goldman, Sachs & Company, Smith Barney (part of Travelers), Morgan Stanley Group, and Lehman Brothers have expanded their operations on Bay Street.

Encouraging American investment companies to Canada is helping to sell government bonds. Their presence has also created advisory committees to assist with mergers, acquisitions, and corporate financing. The North American Free Trade Agreement is increasing North American business and benefiting American business. Jamie Kiernan, President of Goldman, Sachs Canada Ltd., has said there is a market for large requirements of debt and equity capital. According to empirical tabulations by London's *Euromoney Magazine*, Ontario ranked fourth in worldwide provincial, state, and municipal borrowers for the year ended June 30, 1994, with $7.5 billion in loans.

The big American drive for Canadian financial business has produced a "lemming effect," since according to David Driscoll, editor of the weekly Toronto investment newsletter *The Investment Reporter*, "if there's money to be made, no one wants to be left behind and everyone follows." Canadians can appreciate the influx of American players doing business in Canada. Greg Clarke, Vice President of the Investment Dealers Association of Canada, said it is more desirable to have well experienced, educated, and "well-capitalized players" in the Canadian marketplace, since it encourages innovation and produces better markets.

Companies like Goldman, Sachs Canada Ltd. have set up large-scale bond trading and investment operations. Morgan Stanley has increased the size of their Toronto office. The Bank of Hong Kong (Canada) has expanded their operations in Bay Street securities firm BBN James Capel.

Source: Adapted from "Canada's Borrowing, With Its Fat Fees, Lures Wall Street," *The New York Times*, April 15, 1995, Late Edition, p. 31.

Frederick W. Taylor (1881) contributed to personnel selection, planning and scheduling, and motion study.[1] One of his major contributions was his belief that management should be much more resourceful and aggressive in the improvement of work methods. Taylor and his colleagues, Henry L. Gantt and Frank and Lillian Gilbreth, were among the first to seek scientifically the best way to produce. Because of his work, Taylor is known as the father of scientific management. Taylor made a distinction between management (for example, those who plan, organize, staff, direct, and control) and labour (those who do the physical work). He believed that management should assume more responsibility for

1. matching employees to the job
2. providing the proper training
3. providing proper work methods and tools
4. establishing legitimate incentives for work accomplished

As suggested earlier, by 1913, Henry Ford had provided the leadership that combined standardized parts with the quasi-assembly lines of the meat-packing and mail-order industries and had added the concept of the modern moving assembly line.

[1]Frederick W. Taylor, *Principles of Scientific Management* (New York: Harper & Brothers, 1911).

Frank and Lillian Gilbreth were interested in finding the one best way to accomplish work tasks. In pursuit of this effort, they invented a wide variety of techniques and devices. One technique was to use cameras to record movement by attaching lights to an individual's arms and legs. In that way they could track the movement of individuals while performing various jobs.

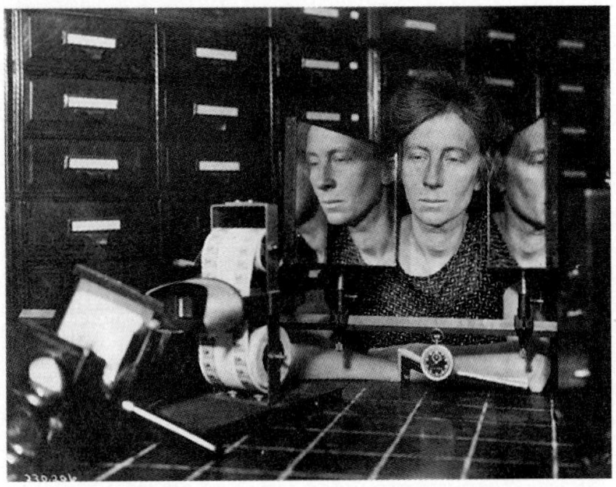

Quality control is another historically significant contribution to the field of P/OM. Walter Shewhart (1924), who understood statistics and the need for evaluating quality, provided the foundations for statistical sampling and quality control. W. Edwards Deming (1950), another leader in quality control, believed, as did Frederick Taylor, that management must do more to improve the work environment and processes so that quality can be improved.

Industrial engineering
Management science

Production/operations management will continue to progress based on contributions from other disciplines, including **industrial engineering** and **management science.** These disciplines, along with statistics, management, and economics, have contributed substantially to greater productivity.

Physical sciences

Innovations from the **physical sciences** (biology, anatomy, chemistry, and physics) have also contributed to advances in P/OM. These advances include new adhesives, chemical processes for printed-circuit boards, gamma rays to sanitize food products, and molten tin tables on which to float a higher-quality molten glass as it cools. The design of products and processes often depend on the biological and physical sciences.

Information sciences

An especially important contribution to P/OM has come from **information sciences.** In a modern organization, information management implies the use of computers that turn raw data into information—and the rapid flow of accurate information is critical to effective management. Information science is a discipline that has grown due to the contributions of a variety of people, including Charles Babbage and John Vincent Atanasoff. Babbage, in 1832, was the first person to design a prototype computer. Ada, the Countess of Lovelace and daughter of the poet Byron, was the first person to design a way to program it. A century later John Atanasoff, while on the faculty of Iowa State, described and built the first digital computer (the ABC computer) in the winter of 1937–1938. These and subsequent contributions to computing and information sciences have provided operations management with an ability to handle problems that previously could not have been addressed and to provide society with a great diversity of goods and services.

Understanding the history of P/OM provides a basis for both studying the discipline today and planning a future in it. In this chapter, we look at the diverse ways you can prepare for a career in production/operations management. Let us first look, though, at how we organize firms to create goods and services.

FIGURE 1.1 ■ Three Functions Required of All Organizations

Organization	Marketing	Operations	Finance/Accounting
Fast food restaurant	Advertise on TV Give away promotional materials Sponsor kids' leagues	Make hamburgers/fries Maintain equipment Design new facilities	Pay suppliers Collect cash Pay employees Pay bank loans
University	Mail catalogues Call on high schools	Research for truth Disseminate truth	Pay faculty/staff Collect tuition
Automobile manufacturer	Advertise on TV, in newspapers, etc. Support auto racing Offer rebates	Design automobiles Manufacture parts Assemble automobiles Develop suppliers	Pay suppliers, employees Prepare budgets Pay dividends Sell stock
Church/temple synagogue	Call on newcomers	Conduct weddings Conduct funerals Conduct services	Count contributions Keep track of pledges Pay the mortgage, other bills

ORGANIZING FOR THE CREATION OF GOODS AND SERVICES

To create goods and services, all organizations perform three functions (see Figure 1.1). These functions are the necessary ingredients not only for production, but also for an organization's survival. The functions are

1. *Marketing*, which generates the demand or, at least, takes the order for a product or service.
2. *Production/operations*, which creates the product.
3. *Finance/accounting*, which tracks how well the organization is doing, pays the bills, and collects the money.

Universities, churches, temples, synagogues, and businesses all perform these functions. Any institution, even a volunteer group such as Scouts Canada, is organized to perform these three basic functions. Figure 1.2 shows how an airline, a bank, and a manufacturing firm organize themselves to perform these functions. The shaded areas of Figure 1.2 show the production and operations in these organizations.

WHY STUDY P/OM?

We study P/OM for four reasons. First, P/OM is one of the three major functions of any organization and is essential to understanding what organizations do. Only by studying P/OM do we understand how people organize themselves for productive enterprise.

FIGURE 1.2 ■ Organization Charts for (a) an Airline, (b) a Bank, and (c) a Manufacturing Organization. The green areas are P/OM tasks.

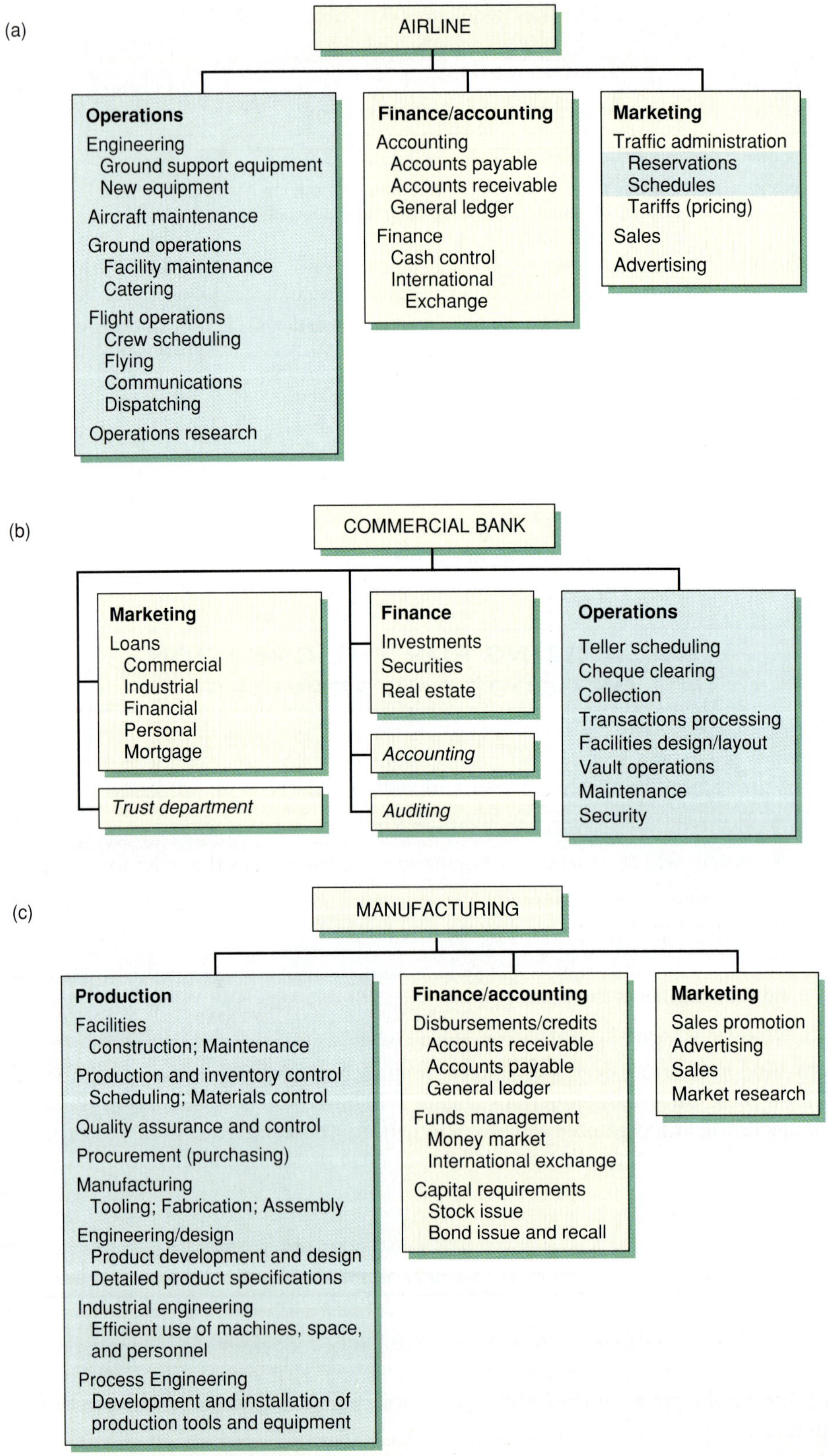

Second, we study P/OM because we want to know how goods and services are produced. The production function is the segment of our society that creates the products we use. Third, we study P/OM because it is one of the most costly parts of any organization. Table 1.1 shows the large percentage of revenue spent in the P/OM functions of selected businesses. This cost makes it a legitimate focus as societies strive to increase productivity. Indeed, P/OM may provide the best opportunity for an organization to improve its profitability as it provides goods or services. Example 1 shows us how a firm might increase its profitability via the production function.

EXAMPLE 1

Landrum Technologies is a small firm that must double its dollar contribution to overhead in order to be profitable enough to purchase the next generation of production equipment. The management has determined that if the firm fails to increase contribution, its bank will not make the loan and the equipment cannot be purchased. If the firm cannot purchase the equipment, the limitations of the old equipment will preclude Landrum Technologies from remaining in business, and the firm will be unable to provide jobs for its employees or goods and services for its customers. The data below show a simple income statement and three strategic options for the firm. The first strategic option is a *marketing option*, where good marketing management may increase sales by 50%. By increasing sales by 50%, contribution will in turn increase 71%. But increasing sales by 50% may be more than difficult; it may even be impossible.

Second is a *finance/accounting* option, where finance costs are cut in half through good financial management. But even a reduction by 50% is inadequate for generating the necessary increase in contribution. Contribution is increased by only 21%.

Third is a *P/OM option*, where management reduces production costs by 20% and increases contribution by 114%!

Given the conditions of our brief example, we now have a bank willing to lend additional funds to Landrum Technologies.

OPTIONS FOR INCREASING CONTRIBUTION

		MARKETING OPTION*	FINANCE OPTION†	PRODUCTION OPTION‡
	CURRENT	INCREASE SALES REVENUE 50%	REDUCE FINANCE COSTS 50%	REDUCE PRODUCTION COSTS 20%
Sales	$100,000	$150,000	$100,000	$100,000
Costs of goods	– 80,000	–120,000	– 80,000	– 64,000
Gross margin	20,000	30,000	20,000	36,000
Finance costs	– 6,000	– 6,000	– 3,000	– 6,000
Contribution§	14,000	24,000	17,000	30,000

*Increasing sales 50% increases contribution by $10,000, or 71.4% (10,000/14,000).
†Reducing finance costs 50% increases contribution by $3,000, or 21.4%.
‡Reducing production costs 20% increases contribution by $16,000, or 114.2% (16,000/14,000).
§Contribution to fixed cost (excluding finance costs) and profit.

The Hawthorne studies began to determine the impact of lighting on productivity. They concluded by recognizing the importance of a social system at the workplace. Shown here is part of the relay assembly room at the Hawthorne plant of Western Electric.

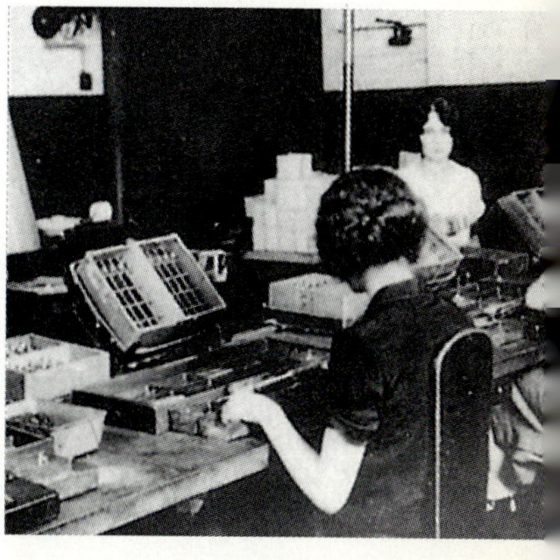

TABLE 1.1 ■ PERCENTAGE OF SALES SPENT ON THE P/OM FUNCTION FOR SELECTED ORGANIZATIONS

	MEAT-PACKING INDUSTRY	FURNITURE MANUFAC-TURING	RESTAURANT	HEAVY EQUIPMENT MANUFACTURING
Production/Operations				
Material	79%	40%	38%	42%
Direct labour	8%	15%	20%	12%
Fringes, supervision, supplies	3%	22%	16%	23%
	90%	77%	74%	77%
Selling, Finance, General, and Administrative	9%	15%	22%	20%
Interest, Extraordinary Items, Taxes, and Profits	1%	8%	4%	3%

Note: All figures are approximate because standardized categories are grouped and rounded.

The production option taken in Example 1 is the successful strategy recently used by Cummins Engine. As you see from the *POM in Action* box "The Yankee Samurai," this strategy was the only one that made sense. The Cummins case is not unusual. An efficient production function has a high payoff for the company and the managers concerned.

The fourth reason for studying P/OM is to understand what production/operations managers do. By understanding what these managers do, you can build the decision-making skills necessary to be such a manager. Such an understanding is integral to exploring the numerous and lucrative career opportunities in P/OM.

WHAT PRODUCTION/OPERATIONS MANAGERS DO

Management process

All good managers perform the basic functions of the management process.[2] The **management process** consists of the following:

1. *Planning.* Managers determine objectives and goals for organizations and develop programs, policies, and procedures that will help organizations attain them. Managers also determine subordinate plans for every department, group, and individual.
2. *Organizing.* Managers develop a structure of individuals, groups, departments, and divisions to achieve objectives.
3. *Staffing.* Managers determine personnel requirements, including the best way to recruit, train, retain, and terminate employees for achieving objectives.
4. *Leading.* Managers lead, supervise, and motivate personnel to achieve objectives.

[2]See Henri Fayol, *General and Industrial Administration* (London: Pitman, 1969); Harold Koontz, *Toward a Unified Theory of Management* (New York: McGraw-Hill, 1964); and J. G. March and H. Simon, *Organizations* (New York: John Wiley, 1958).

POM IN ACTION

The Yankee Samurai

It all began when the first truck engines marked "Komatsu" and "Nissan" appeared on a California dock. Soon after, calls were received from good customers such as Navistar and Freightliner, telling Cummins that they were trying out these Japanese medium-truck engines.

Cummins, a company that held almost 60% of the U.S. heavy-duty diesel-truck engine market, had a lot to lose. After all, if the Japanese were gaining momentum in the medium-engine market, the heavy-engine market could be their next target. To protect themselves, Cummins decided to become more competitive. They cut their prices 10 to 40%. That was the easy part.

Next came cost cutting and simultaneously dealing with inflation. Costs needed to be cut by a minimum of 33%, and this was no easy task.

But Cummins decided to learn from the Japanese and studied their production methods. They found that U.S. accounting systems tended to hide certain costs. Cummins also discovered that by using more flexible machinery, they could reduce their inventory from 60 days' supply down to 3 or 4 days' supply.

Now it was time to tackle their big item, cutting material costs, which represented 50% of the production budget. Cummins turned to their suppliers for suggestions. Could they help? Yes. It turned out that no one had ever asked before. In 3 years, Cummins was able to lower material costs an impressive 18%. Relationships with suppliers have gone from adversarial to cooperative. In Cummins' chairperson's own words, "We're trying to do everything with our suppliers that we want to do with our customers."

Sources: Forbes (July 14, 1986); *Accountancy,* 103 (May 1991): 39–43; *Business Week* (October 2, 1993): 222–224.

5. *Controlling.* Managers develop the standards and communication networks necessary to ensure that the enterprise is pursuing appropriate plans and achieving objectives.

Production/operations managers apply this management process to the decisions they make in the P/OM function. In a complex organization, managers contribute to production and operations through the activities shown in Table 1.2. Each of these activities requires planning, organizing, staffing, directing, and controlling.

The activities shown in the table require that operations managers make decisions. These decisions allocate resources that affect the efficiency and strategy of the firm. In this text, we provide an introduction to the proper way to make these decisions.

WHERE ARE THE P/OM JOBS?

Figure 1.3 shows jobs in Canada by sector. Manufacturing, which has a high portion of P/OM jobs, now constitutes about 15% of all jobs; construction and mining industries, about 7%; and services, the remaining 78%. The service sector includes government, education, food and lodging, trade, utilities, transportation, finance, insurance, real estate, legal, medical, and repair and maintenance. Table 1.3 is a list of firms in these various categories.

TABLE 1.2 ■ ACTIVITIES OF TYPICAL PRODUCTION AND OPERATIONS DEPARTMENTS

DEPARTMENT	ACTIVITY
Research and development (R&D)	Conducts product research, product development.
Product design	Fine-tunes product design to enhance production efficiency.
Process design	Selects or designs and develops production tools, equipment, and processes.
Facilities planning, construction	Plans, constructs, and repairs facilities.
Purchasing	Determines the best source for given specification, delivery, and price.
Industrial engineering (IE)	Determines most efficient use of machines, space, and personnel; work measurement.
Methods and procedures	Directs efforts toward improvement in procedures at the workplace.
Production planning and inventory control (PIC)	Schedules the manufacturing processes; manages inventory.
Management science	Applies the methodology, models, and procedures of mathematics or management information systems to manufacturing operations.
Quality management/quality control	Reviews designs, products, and processes to ensure quality objectives are met.
Maintenance	Focusses on designing systems and procedures that will create and maintain a reliable system.

PREPARING FOR A CAREER IN P/OM?

In the production and inventory control area, entry-level jobs often go to P/OM graduates. A P/OM graduate can enhance his or her qualifications by becoming a certified professional purchaser (CPP). The Purchasing Management Association of Canada (PMAC) offers this certification.[3]

[3]PMAC, 2 Carlton Street, Suite 1414, Toronto, Ontario M5B 1J3; National Association of Purchasing Management (NAPM), P.O. Box 418, Oradell, NJ 07649.

FIGURE 1.3 ■ Jobs in Canada by Sector for 1994

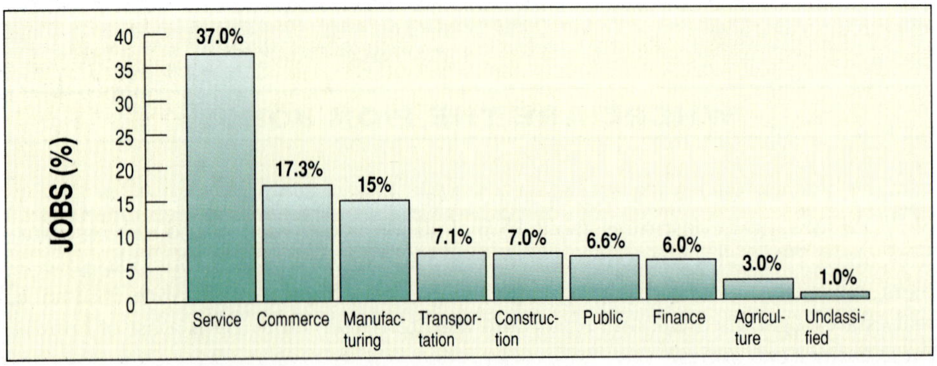

(*Source:* Statistics Canada, *Labour Force Annual Averages*, 1984–1994.)

TABLE 1.3 ■ EXAMPLES OF ORGANIZATIONS IN EACH SECTOR

COMPANY/ORGANIZATION	EXAMPLE
Manufacturing	Canadian General Electric; Stelco
Construction	Tacc Construction
Mining	Hollinger; Inco Ltd.
Service	
Government	Federal; provincial; municipal; metropolitan
Education	Public; private
Food	McDonald's; St. Cinnamon
Lodging	Best Western; Hilton; Holiday Inn
Entertainment	Cineplex; Famous Players
Trade (Retail/Wholesale)	White Rose; Eaton's; Home Hardware
Utilities	B.C. Telephone; Ontario Hydro
Transportation	
Airlines	Air Canada; British Airways
Railroad	Canadian National; Canadian Pacific
Trucking	Atlas Van Lines; Laidlaws
Finance	Royal Bank; Canada Trust
Insurance	London Life; Prudential; Royal
Real Estate	
Development	Kaneff Group; Greenpark
Sales	Coldwell Bankers; Royal LePage
Legal	Fraser Beatty; McCarthy & McCarthy
Medical	Toronto Sick Children's; Shouldice
Repair and Maintenance	IBM Computer Maintenance; Xerox Maintenance

Membership in a student or local chapter of PMAC is also an excellent way to enhance qualifications for positions in this field. Jobs are available in virtually all sectors from hospitals and banks to aircraft maintenance to manufacturing.

Management science is a term used to describe a wide variety of quantitative and computer-related tasks. Consequently, the term encompasses a wide variety of opportunities. Most entry-level positions in this area go to majors in mathematics, quantitative management, information systems, management, or P/OM, depending on the exact nature of the assignment. The Society of Manufacturing Engineers (SME)[4] is one source of information about P/OM careers in manufacturing.

Students with an information science background often possess the necessary skill to get P/OM jobs. These students can carve a niche for themselves by assisting in developing computerized accounting, ordering, inventory control, forecasting, or personnel systems or in creating mathematical models that help the firm make better decisions. Those interested can turn to the local chapter of the Data Processing Management Association (DPMA)[5] or the Canadian Information Processing Society (CIPS).[6]

[4]SME, 17 Coltbridge Court, Scarborough, Ontario M1M 2H6. SME, One SME Drive, P.O. Box 930, Dearborn, MI 48121.

[5]DPMA, see local chapter. DPMA, 505 Busse Highway, Park Ridge, IL 60068.

[6]CIPS, 430 King Street, Toronto, Ontario M5V 1L5.

POM IN ACTION

CFOs: A Profile of Chief Financial Officers

Who are CFOs? Where do they come from? And is there a discernible pattern as to the profile of a CFO?

In 1995 a group of 200 CFOs from America's top 200 companies were analyzed. Biographical information was used to make a collective single identity.

The profile showed that 39% of CFOs were in their 40s, 42% in their 50s, and 19% in their 60s, with an average age of 52.6, mode of 49, and median of 52. The ages at time of appointment were from 26 to 64 with a mean of 46.4, but 66% were under 50 when appointed as CFO.

Not surprisingly due to the nature of the study, 94% were born in the United States and the remainder immigrated from Canada, Cuba, England, France, India, and Germany. Interestingly, 16.7% came from New York followed by Illinois 9.7%, New Jersey 8.3%, and Massachusetts 5.6%. Approximately half of the CFOs came from the northeastern United States followed by the central 27.1%, southern 11.8%, and western 7.6%.

Over 35% held bachelor's degrees, 50% master's, and 10% law degrees; 5% listed doctorates as their highest degree held. Not surprisingly, only one CFO had no degree compared to the 65% that held graduate degrees or better. Fully one-third of the MBAs came from highly noted universities such as Harvard (13.1%), Wharton (7.5%), Columbus and Stanford (4.7%), and Cornell, Michigan, MIT, Northwestern, and NYU (3.7% each). The pattern was similar for law degrees.

With the requirements changing, so did the candidates. Of CFOs under 50, 24.7% held bachelor's degrees and 75.3 advanced degrees, whereas of CFOs over 50, 42.1% percent held bachelor's degrees and 57.9% advanced degrees. The spreads in education were comparable for the education levels at time of appointment as CFO. Younger CFOs seemed to be better educated at time of appointment.

The average tenure was 18.7 years with a median of 18 and mode of 24. The biggest discrepancy was seen in CFOs under 50, who served an average of 8.4 years before appointment as against CFOs over 50, who served an average of 21 years before being appointed.

The executive level had been the domain of the CEO, CFO, and/or COO; but newcomers to this group were the CIO (chief information officer) and CTO (chief technology officer).

Source: Adapted from California State University, Los Angeles, "CFOs: A Profile of Chief Financial Officers," January 1995.

Information on a P/OM career in traffic and transportation can be obtained from the Canadian Institute of Traffic and Transportation (CITT).[7]

The National Quality Institute (NQI)[8] was established with seed money from industry to spearhead the quality movement across Canada. The Excellence Conference and the Canada Awards for Excellence provide an opportunity to enhance Canada's commitment to quality. Details for a career in quality management can be obtained from NQI headquarters in Ottawa.

Students can contact their provincial association of professional engineers, who can advise and guide them in a P/OM career.

Many opportunities exist for individuals with other backgrounds as well. Students in the *physical sciences*, for example, can find opportunities in a wide variety of jobs related to production and operations. These jobs range from protecting the environment to developing new adhesives or production processes.

Whatever the job and career, the task is to transform effectively resources into products and services. This transformation must take place efficiently because the

[7]CITT, 33 Yonge Street, Toronto, Ontario M5E 1G4.

[8]NQI, 360 Albert Street, Suite 1540, Ottawa, Ontario K1R 7X7.

production/operations manager is responsible, more than anyone else in our society, for improving productivity.

THE PRODUCTIVITY CHALLENGE

Productivity

Production, as defined earlier, is the creation of goods and services. **Productivity** is the enhancement of the production process. Enhancement of production means a favourable comparison of the quantity of resources employed (inputs) to the quantity of goods and services produced (outputs) (see Figure 1.4). Productivity can be improved by either reducing *inputs* while keeping *output* constant or increasing *output* while keeping *inputs* constant. Inputs, as defined by economists, are land, labour, capital, and management. Managers combine these inputs in a production system that converts inputs to outputs. Outputs are goods and services, including such diverse items as guns, butter, education, improved judicial systems, and ski resorts.

Productivity allows both firms and countries to maintain their competitiveness. Measurement of productivity is an excellent way to evaluate performance of a firm or a country. Productivity management is also an excellent way to evaluate a firm's or a country's ability to provide an improving standard of living for its people. *Only through increases in productivity can the standard of living improve.* Moreover, only through increases in productivity can labour, capital, and management receive additional payments. If payments to labour, capital, or management are increased without increased productivity, then prices rise. On the other hand, prices tend to drop as productivity increases, because the same inputs are producing more outputs.

Since the 1950s Canada has shown a steady decline in relative international productivity in manufacturing (calculated as a ratio of total physical output to total physical input). At the start of the 1950s Canada was second only to the United States. In the 1980s Canada slipped two positions to fourth behind the United States, Germany, and Italy. During the first half of the 1990s Canada slipped another place to fifth, behind

FIGURE 1.4 ■ The Economic System Transforms Inputs to Outputs. An effective feedback loop evaluates process performance against a plan. It also evaluates customer satisfaction and sends signals to the institutions controlling the inputs and process.

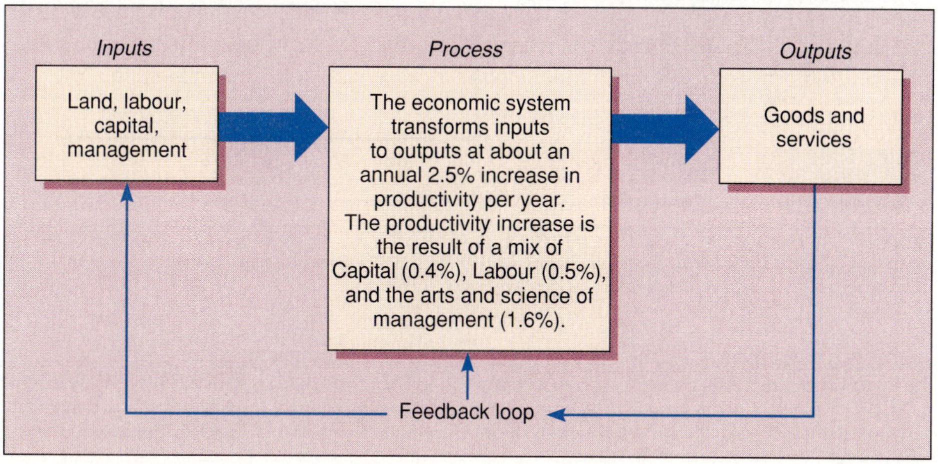

France. But as the *POM in Action* box "Does Canada Compete?" shows, Canada has strengthened in the resource and service sectors. The box also shows that recent productivity gains in Canada are encouraging. When productivity lags, so does improvement in the quality of life. Companies, like countries, must first determine the reasons for low levels of productivity improvement and then address them. In this text, we examine how to improve productivity by studying the strategic and tactical decisions made by operations managers.

Productivity Measurement

Measuring productivity is, in some cases, quite direct. Such is the case when productivity can be measured as labour-hours required per tonne of steel or as the energy (BTUs) necessary to generate a kilowatt of electricity.[9] An example is

$$\text{Productivity} = \frac{\text{units produced}}{\text{input used}}$$

$$= \frac{\text{units produced}}{\text{labour-hours}} = \frac{1{,}000}{250} = 4$$

In many instances, however, substantial measurement problems do exist.[10] Some of these measurement problems are as follows:

1. *Quality* of inputs and outputs may change while the quantity remains constant.

FIGURE 1.5 ■ A Comparison of Productivity in the United States, Japan, and Germany

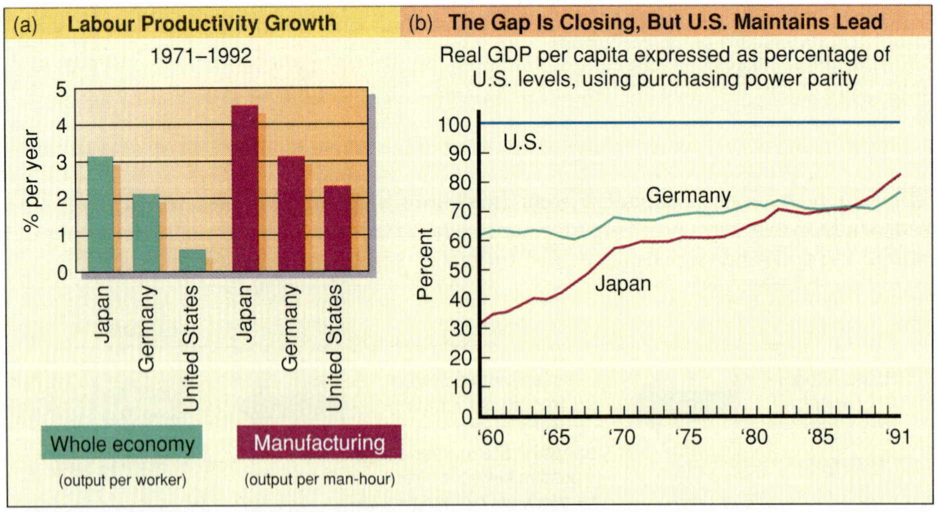

(*Sources:* [a] Adapted from *The Economist* [February 13, 1993]: 67; [b] Bureau of Labour Statistics, based on OECD price calculation, as reported in *Forbes* [September 14, 1992]: 43.)

[9]The quality of units produced and the time period are assumed to remain constant.

[10]See John W. Henrici, "How Deadly Is the Productivity Disease?" *Harvard Business Review*, 59 (November/December 1981): 123–129, for discussion of measurement problems at the national level; and David J. Sumanth, *Productivity Engineering and Management* (New York: McGraw-Hill, 1984), for an excellent discussion at the company level.

POM IN ACTION

Does Canada Compete?

One of the most important questions that Canadians must ask themselves is "Is Canada internationally competitive in production and services?" In 1992, Canada reportedly ranked favourably in the macroeconomics scale for competitiveness, moving from fifteenth to twelfth place. This improvement was due, in part, to a favourable cost of living in comparison with other countries, stringent control of inflation, the end of the recession, and a change in processes used in manufacturing and the provision of services.

With respect to the Canadian financial markets, in which firms operate, there was a dramatic movement in Canada's rank from eleventh to third place. The Canadian financial system was operating very efficiently, and public confidence in it remained relatively stable. Canada had also benefited from low short-term real interest rates, sophisticated capital markets, and a strong banking system that attracts external capital. Canada benefited in terms of infrastructure from the availability of excellent telecommunications and high per capita use of computer systems. It also benefited from good production of primary resources such as coal, crude oil, and hydroelectricity. Science and technology revealed significant promise in raising the competitiveness in the area of basic and applied research, and in 1992 Canada's ranking had improved from seventeenth to sixteenth place.

There was high female participation in the Canadian labour force, equal opportunity employment for minority groups and women, and high secondary and postsecondary enrollment. Canada had many advantages in natural resources, infrastructure, and financial systems.

However, according to the report, Canadians had to address issues regarding skills training and R&D spending in order to strengthen their current and long-term competitiveness, and more emphasis would have to be placed on Canada's manufacturing sector to compete successfully in the international marketplace. Although Canada possessed a strong automobile manufacturing sector, it had to go beyond the American market, which is protected, and penetrate into the international markets.

Source: Adapted from "Does Canada Compete?" CMA—*The Management Accounting Magazine*, 67, no. 8 (October 1993), p. 30.

2. *External elements* may cause an increase or decrease in productivity for which the system under study may not be directly responsible.[11] For instance, a more reliable electric power service may greatly improve production, thereby improving the firm's productivity because of this support system rather than because of managerial decisions made within the firm.
3. *Precise units of measure* may be lacking. Not all automobiles require the same inputs—some cars are subcompacts, and others are Porsches.

The measurement problems noted here are particularly acute in the service sector. We earlier identified the **service sector** as repair and maintenance, government, food and lodging, transportation, insurance, trade, financial, real estate, education, legal, medical, and other professional occupations. Note, for instance, the measurement problems in a law office where each case is different. Every legal case will vary, altering the accuracy of the measure "cases per labour-hour" or "cases per employee." Despite these measurement problems, the operations manager must strive for productivity improvement and the information that documents that progress. Indeed, productivity increases in service firms are just as critical as in manufacturing.

Service sector

[11]These are exogenous variables, that is, variables outside of the system under study that influence it.

Productivity Variables

Productivity variables

Productivity increases exist because of the management of three variables.[12] These **productivity variables** are

1. *labour*, which contributes 0.5% to the increase
2. *capital*, which contributes 0.4% to the increase
3. *management*, which contributes 1.6%

These three factors (Figure 1.6) are critical to productivity improvement. They represent the broad areas in which managers can take action to obtain better productivity.

LABOUR. Historically, the quality of labour contributes about one-half of 1% to productivity improvement each year. Three traditional variables for improved labour productivity have been

1. basic education appropriate for an effective labour force
2. diet of the labour force
3. social overhead that makes labour available, such as transportation and sanitation

Under some conditions, such as a major construction job in an underdeveloped country, the manager may find these three variables important. However, in developed nations, basic education, diet of the labour force, and social overhead do not now appear to be the critical variables to increase productivity. In developed and postindustrialized nations, however, the real challenge to management is *maintaining and enhancing the skills of labour*. This issue is particularly acute in the midst of rapidly expanding technology and knowledge. Indeed, the variations between countries can be substantial. While Germany has outstanding apprenticeship programs, many nations do not. A study reported by *The Financial Post* on December 17, 1993 showed that less than 15% of Ontario's 16-year-olds could add and/or subtract beyond the grade-nine level. When the students' problem-solving abilities were tested using a required minimum ability level, only 3% of students at the senior level passed. This study involved approximately 50,000 13- to 16-year-old Canadian students.

Knowledge society

Education will remain an important high-cost item in postindustrial societies. Most Western societies are postindustrial, or knowledge, societies. A **knowledge society** is one in which much of the labour force has migrated from manual work to work based on knowledge. Consequently, improving the quality of labour in both developing and developed nations remains a challenge. Perhaps improvements can be found not only through increasing the competence of labour, but also via a fifth item, *better-utilized labour with a stronger commitment*. Improvements in labour productivity are possible. However, they can be expected to be increasingly difficult and expensive. What one company does to find workers skilled for today's needs and to aid in the transfer of technology to developing nations is described in the *POM in Action* box, "Bilateral Ties Between Malaysia and Canada Continue to Grow" in this chapter.

[12] See the work of Solomon Fabricant, *A Primer on Productivity* (New York: Random House, 1969); Dale W. Jorgensen, *Productivity and U.S. Economic Growth* (Cambridge, MA: Harvard University Press, 1987); and Angus Maddison, "Growth and Slowdown in Advanced Capitalist Economics: Technique of Quantitative Assessment," *Journal of Economic Literature*, 25, no. 2 (June 1987): 649–698.

FIGURE 1.6 ■ The Contribution of Capital, Labour, and Management to the Annual Increase in Productivity in Canada

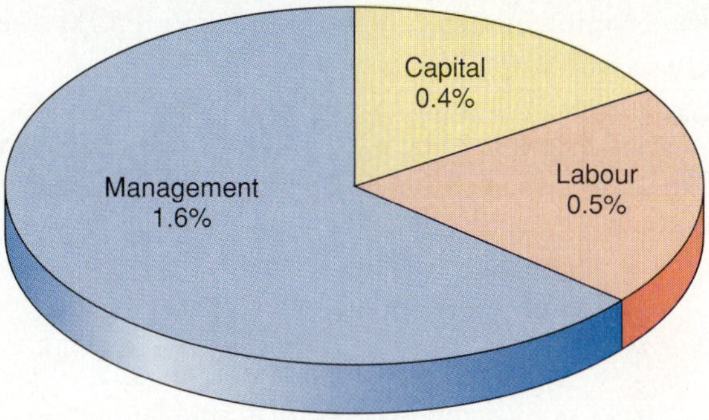

Note: The definitive measure of these three variables for the Canadian experience is open to discussion and not easily determined. However, since the Canadian experience does mirror that of the United States in many ways, the U.S. figures are given as an approximate guideline.

CAPITAL. Human beings are tool-using animals. Capital investment provides those tools. These tools can range from desk computers to complex machinery and new airports. Capital investment has increased in the United States every year except for a few very severe recession periods. Capital investment adds about 0.4% to productivity each year. Annual capital investment in the United States has increased (until recent years) at the rate of 1.5% of the base investment. This means that the amount of capital invested after allowances for depreciation has grown by 1.5% per year.

However, as inadequate depreciation and taxes drive up the cost of capital, capital investment becomes increasingly expensive.[13] When the capital invested per employee drops, as it has in recent years, we can expect a drop in productivity. Production can often be accomplished with some trade-off between labour and capital. That is, if we want to build a road, we can do so with crews of thousands using shovels or we can invest in earth-moving equipment. Using labour rather than capital may reduce unemployment in the short run, but it also makes economies less productive and therefore

Improving the reading, writing, and mathematical capabilities of Canadians so that they can handle more complex jobs is a major concern for the federal government and for industry.

[13]For instance, the U.S. minimum alternative tax in many instances fails to allow companies to recover their investment. *Economic Effects of the Corporate Alternative Minimum Tax* (Washington, DC: American Council for Capital Formation, Center for Policy Research, 1991).

lowers wages in the long run. The trade-off between capital and labour is continually in flux. The more expensive capital is, the more projects requiring capital are squeezed out. Managers adjust their investment plans to changes in capital cost.

In this text, we examine numerous opportunities for P/OM to enhance productivity through improved utilization of capital.

The *POM in Action box* "Bilateral Ties Between Malaysia and Canada Continue to Grow" provides a good example of how Canadians have improved their process in delivering services, making Canada more competitive in the global market.

POM IN ACTION

Bilateral Ties Between Malaysia and Canada Continue to Grow

The relationship between Canada and Malaysia has evolved from one of donor-recipient into that of a partnership, given Malaysia's strong and sustained economic growth over recent years.

The flow of information on opportunities in both countries has been very good, although "we would like more Malaysian businessmen to visit Canada to find out about and avail themselves of the opportunities," added a Canadian representative. He said Canada, which was coming out of recession, had wide experience in infrastructural projects which could benefit a developing country like Malaysia.

Malaysia should view Canada's participation in NAFTA (the North American Free Trade Agreement) as an opportunity to utilize an expanded market. He explained that NAFTA, which also groups the United States and Mexico, would not become a fortress, since there are no plans to increase tariffs. Instead, all steps being taken are aimed at making it a free trade area.

Malaysian companies should consider establishing offices or factories in Canada with a view to exploiting the huge NAFTA market, he said. Education, he pointed out, is a field in which many Malaysians can benefit from Canada. Over 2,000 Malaysians were studying in Canada's 70 government-accredited universities and 205 colleges. So far, between 70,000 and 80,000 Malaysians have graduated from various educational institutions in Canada, and the number is expected to double within the next two years.

The representative said there was growing awareness of the high standard of the Canadian education system and its competitive cost of education and living compared to that of countries which Malaysians traditionally go to for higher studies. Some of the more popular courses Malaysians pursued in Canada were business, engineering, medicine, science, and computer science.

Malaysian interest in Canada and the Canadian education system has increased in recent years as a result of coordinated and concerted efforts undertaken by the Canadian government and individual educational institutions.

Twinning programs already in place are between the University of Calgary and Sunway College; between Mara and Canadian schools including the British Columbia Institute of Technology; six Canadian universities are participating in the International Medical College's medical training program; and three Canadian community colleges (Sheridan, Vancouver, and Cariboo) are involved in the establishment of a Women's Institute of Management.

To further promote Canadian education opportunities among Malaysians, the government set up Education Canada (Malaysia), a counselling and information centre. It provided advice on courses, choice of universities, visa applications, and sociocultural adjustments. The representative said Canada's educational institutions were becoming increasingly interested and involved in helping to meet Malaysia's demand for internationally recognized education.

He added that large Canadian business corporations were also involved in many prestigious projects in Malaysia. Toronto-based Adamson Associates, the lead technical consultant for the Kuala Lumpur City Centre, had been involved in New York's Battery Park, London's Canary Wharf, and an 88-storey building in Shenzen, China.

(Continued)

The Light Rail Transit II system was to use the skytrain technology pioneered by Bombardier Incorporated, a world leader in urban transit systems. SNC-Lavalin Canada was also a major partner in the consortium implementing the project.

Canadian specialists are currently working on two hydroelectric projects. Hydro-Quebec had been appointed as a consultant to Malaysian Resources Corporation Bhd, which had been awarded a contract to lay a 500 kilovolt transmission line through about half the length of peninsular Malaysia.

Teshmont, a Canadian company specializing in high-voltage direct current transmission, was working on an interconnection of Thai and Malaysian power networks. Terra Geotechnics, first exposed to Southeast Asia with a contract in Johor Bahru in 1993, is currently exploring other business opportunities. The mid-sized Vancouver-based company, together with its joint venture partner HSS Integrated, a leading local engineering firm, was looking at some major infrastructure development projects.

The representative said Canada's industries had a strong transfer-of-technology component. Thus, industries involved in computers, software, information technology, oil and gas, architecture, and construction could benefit from them. Canada has invested over RN180 million in Malaysia through development assistance. Through the Canadian International Development Agency (CIDA), the Canadian government has been able to provide support and assistance to Malaysia's industrial and institutional development.

Programs initiated by CIDA included human resource planning and development, economic policy formulation, the environment, women in development, and private sector ventures. Hopefully, there will soon be direct air services between Malaysia and Canada, negotiations for which are already under way, as this would help further improve trade between the two countries.

In 1995 Malaysia Airlines started two direct flights per week from Vancouver to Kuala Lumpur, though as of December 1996 Air Canada and British Airways have not started direct flights to Malaysia.

Source: Adapted from "From Strength to Strength," *Malaysian Business* (June 16, 1995), ad supplement: 56.

MANAGEMENT. Management is a factor of production and an economic resource.[14] Management is responsible for ensuring that labour and capital are effectively used to increase productivity. Management accounts for almost two-thirds of the annual 2.5% increase in productivity. The arts and sciences of management include improvements made by using technology and knowledge. Such improvements require training and education as well as dynamic organizations. However, although Canada is considered a high-technology society, the country invests less in civilian research and development than do any of its major industrial competitors.[15] The research, utilization, and dissemination of knowledge specific to technique and technology may be a current shortcoming of Canada. Moreover, Japan seems to be disseminating information faster and more ably than is Canada.[16]

As we move through the text, we note legal and cultural values that distinguish the Canadian economy from those of other nations. We now live in a world economy, and the production/operations manager must adjust to both the opportunities and the realities of the global economy.

[14]For an excellent discussion of management as an economic resource, see Frederick Harbison and Charles A. Myers, *Management in the Industrial World: International Analysis* (New York: McGraw-Hill, 1959).

[15]"A Time to Dismantle the World Economy," *The Economist* (November 9, 1985): 22.

[16]Robert S. Cuttler, "A Survey of High-Technology Transfer Practices in Japan and in the United States," *Interfaces*, 19, no. 6 (November/December 1989): 62–77.

PRODUCTIVITY ACTIONS OF THE PRODUCTION/OPERATIONS MANAGER. Because society and commerce are changing, education and training requirements continue to increase. For instance, not only did the introduction of computers require added training, but each generation of new computers also requires more training. Each additional management science technique requires education, and new organizational designs require more organizational development. These requirements for more training and education are the inevitable results of the knowledge explosion and the development of a high-technology society. The effective operations manager will *ensure that available knowledge and technology are disseminated and utilized.*

The *more effective utilization* of capital, as opposed to additional capital, is also important. The manager, as a productivity catalyst, is charged with the task of making improvements in the use of capital.

Recent increases in effectiveness in oil exploration, airline scheduling, inventory management, and feedlot operations, for example, show the strides that can be made through the *utilization of management and management science*. Productivity gains in knowledge societies require managers who are comfortable with technology, management science, and management. In this text, we have organized the P/OM aspects of management into ten strategic and tactical decisions. We begin discussion of these ten decisions in Chapter 2.

The productivity challenge is difficult. A country cannot be a world-class competitor with second-class inputs. Poorly educated labour inputs, inadequate capital inputs, and dated technologies are second-class inputs. Low-quality, second-class inputs must be changed to high-quality, first-class inputs. High productivity and high-quality outputs require high-quality inputs.

Productivity and the Service Sector

The service sector provides a challenge to the accurate measurement of productivity and productivity improvement. Productivity of the service sector has proven difficult to improve. This is happening because in the service sector work is

1. typically labour-intensive
2. frequently individually processed
3. often an intellectual task performed by professionals
4. often difficult to mechanize and automate

The more intellectual and personal the task, the more difficult it has been to achieve increases in productivity.

SUMMARY

Production/operations, marketing, and finance/accounting are the three functions basic to all organizations. The production/operations function creates goods and services. Much of the progress of operations management has been made in the twentieth century, but since the beginning of time, humankind has been attempting to improve its material well-being. P/OM is the primary vehicle for making that improvement.

The effective use of labour, capital, and management by production/operations managers increases productivity. Most productivity improvements are available to assertive, innovative, entrepreneurial managers. Production/operations managers function as productivity catalysts. Moreover, improvements in productivity are the responsibility of the professional manager, and professional managers are among the few people in our society who *can* make this improvement. Modern technological society consists of complex organizations that cry out for effective management. The challenge is great but exciting, and the rewards to the manager and to society are substantial.

KEY TERMS

SOLVED PROBLEM

Solved Problem 1.1

Productivity can be measured in a variety of ways, such as labour, capital, energy, material usage, and so on. In this example, Boe Warren, a noted producer of apple pies sold to supermarkets, has been able, with his current equipment, to produce 24 pies per bushel of apples. He currently purchases 100 bushels per day, and each bushel requires 3 labour-hours to process. He believes that he can hire a professional food broker, who can buy a better-quality apple at the same cost. If this is the case, he can increase his production to 26 pies per bushel. His labour-hours will increase by 8 hours per day.

What will be the impact on productivity (pies per labour-hour) if the food broker is hired?

$$\text{Current labour productivity} = \frac{24 \text{ pies} \times 100 \text{ bushels}}{100 \text{ bushels} \times 3 \text{ hours}} = \frac{2{,}400}{300}$$

$$= 8.0 \text{ pies per labour-hour}$$

$$\text{Labour productivity with food broker} = \frac{26 \text{ pies} \times 100 \text{ bushels}}{(100 \text{ bushels} \times 3 \text{ hours}) + 8 \text{ hours}}$$

$$= \frac{2{,}600}{308} = 8.44$$

Using last year (i.e., 8.0) as a base, the increase is 5.5%: 8.44/8.0 = 1.055, or a 5.5% increase over last year.

DISCUSSION QUESTIONS

1. Define production/operations management in your own words. Will your definition accommodate both manufacturing and service operations?
2. Consider the potential contribution of information sciences to P/OM. Why is the management of information of such great importance in the management of "production"?
3. Figure 1.2 outlines the marketing, operations, and finance/accounting function of three organizations. Prepare a chart similar to Figure 1.2 outlining the same functions for
   (a) a large metropolitan newspaper
   (b) a local drugstore
   (c) a college library
   (d) a local service organization (Boy Scouts, Girl Scouts, Rotary International, Lions, Grange, etc.)
   (e) a doctor's or dentist's office
   (f) a jewelry factory
4. Do the preceding assignment for some other enterprise of your choosing, perhaps an organization where you have worked.
5. What is the difference between production and operations?
6. Identify some disciplines that will contribute in a major way to the future development of P/OM.
7. Can you identify the operation function(s) of a past or current employer? Draw an organization chart for the operations function of that firm.
8. What are the three classic functions of a firm?
9. What departments might you find in the P/OM function of a home appliance manufacturer?
10. Productivity increases as the result of change in what three variables?
11. Which of the three variables noted in Question 10 provide the best opportunity for increase in productivity?
12. How did Canadian productivity compare with productivity changes in Germany and Japan between 1971 and 1992?
13. What are the problems in the measurement of productivity?
14. Identify the contributions to P/OM of Eli Whitney, Henry Ford, and W. Edwards Deming.

CRITICAL THINKING EXERCISE

University funding in Canada must be revamped if Canada is to retain its most talented people and ensure its ability to compete effectively on the world stage, said Mr. Peter Godsoe, chairperson and CEO of Scotiabank, in a 1995 speech.

According to Mr. Godsoe, the Canadian education system had overemphasized universal access, and must place equal weight on developing schools and programs that rival the best in the world.

The brain drain is already a reality, he said, citing the World Economic Forum's World Competitiveness Report. It ranked Canada second-lowest among the G7 nations in keeping its well-educated people at work in their home country.

Assuming Mr. Godsoe is right, what are the strengths and weaknesses of the Canadian system? What features would we want to emulate from Japan and Israel, who excel in academic education, from Germany, a leader in apprenticeship programs, or from other nations?

Source: Adapted from Canada NewsWire Ltd., "University Funding Policies Must Change, Says Scotiabank Chairman and CEO," *Financial News* (October 2, 1995).

PROBLEMS

• **1.1** Boe and Ann Warren bake apple pies for resale to local supermarkets. They and their three employees invest 50 hours per day making 150 pies.

a) What is their productivity?

b) They have discussed reassigning work so the flow through the bakery is smoother. If they are correct and they can do the necessary training, they think they can increase apple pie production to 155 per day. What is their new productivity?

c) What is their increase in productivity?

• **1.2** Joan Blasco-Paul produces Christmas tree ornaments for resale at local craft fairs and Christmas bazaars. She is currently working a total of 15 hours per day to produce 300 ornaments.

a) What is Joan's productivity?

b) Joan thinks that by redesigning the ornaments and switching from use of a contact cement to a hot-glue gun she can increase her total production to 400 ornaments per day. What is her new productivity?

c) What is the increase in productivity?

: **1.3** Brewerton's Manitoba Sip'n Whiskey is an extraordinary organization established by John Brewerton shortly after the Treasury Department began using infrared photography to find distillers that showed little interest in purchasing revenue stamps. Because Frank's expenses have gone up, he has a new-found interest in efficiency. Frank is interested in determining the productivity of his organization. He has last year's records and good current data. He would like to know if his organization is maintaining the national average of 2.5% annual increase in productivity. He has the following data:

	LAST YEAR	NOW
Production	1,000	1,000
Labour (hours)	300	275
Corn mash (bushels)	50	45
Capital invested ($)	10,000	11,000
Energy (BTUs)	3,000	2,850

Show the productivity increase for each category and then determine the annual improvement for labour-hours, the typical standard for comparison.

• **1.4** Lackey's, a local bakery, is worried about increased costs—particularly energy. Last year's records can provide a fairly good estimate of the parameters for this year. Charles Lackey, the owner, does not believe things have changed much, but he did invest an additional $3,000 for modifications to the bakery's ovens to make them more energy-efficient. The modifications were supposed to make the ovens at least 15% more efficient, but extra labour-hours were required to become familiar with the process changes. Charles has asked you to check the energy savings of the new ovens and also to look over other measures of the bakery's productivity to see if the modifications were beneficial. You have the following data to work with:

	LAST YEAR	NOW
Production (dozen)	1,500	1,500
Labour	350	325
Capital	15,000	18,000
Energy	3,000	2,750

• **1.5** The approximate figures for service jobs in certain countries are shown. Overall productivity increases are highest in Japan, Germany, and the United States (in that order). What conclusions might you draw about productivity and the percentage of services in the economy?

PERCENTAGE OF JOBS THAT ARE SERVICE JOBS	
United States	78
Japan	57
Germany	62

- **1.6** As a library assignment, find the U.S. productivity rate for the (a) latest quarter and (b) latest year.
- **1.7** As a library assignment, find the U.S. productivity rate (increase) last year for the (a) national economy, (b) manufacturing sector, and (c) service sector.

CASE STUDY

S&P Data

S&P Data of Don Mills, Ontario is a very successful example of Ontario's more than 1,400 call centres. S&P Data came to life in 1986 from a good idea. Since 1987 it has grown from a small, one-room operation into a multifaceted, technologically driven call centre with multinational clients. In fact, in 1994 it was Canada's 24th-fastest-growing company. The owners of S&P Data, Dan Plashkes and Edward Schwartz, attribute the spectacular growth of the company to a number of factors: a commitment to being Canada's most technologically advanced call centre, a drive to be flexible and consistent, responsive client service, and superb operator training and recruiting.

The reasons clients outsource their telemarketing needs to S&P Data vary. For companies wanting to set up a 1-800 number for customer service, the principal attraction is S&P Data's dedicated group of multilingual communicators on staff 24 hours a day, 7 days a week, 365 days a year. These communicators are fully bilingual in Quebecois French, with many speaking other languages such as Cantonese, Italian, Korean, and Spanish. Clients value S&P's ability to operate a 24-hour customer order desk for their products or promotions. Still others value the expertise in generating sales and sales leads via skilled telemarketers. The fact is, S&P Data can handle just about any telemarketing need.

The key to operating a successful call centre is responsiveness, or, in other words, being poised to execute programs within a day's notice. The constant state of readiness requires resources and infrastructure to be in place to turn on a dime, in the areas of both technology and human resources. There can be no question but that the location of S&P Data in Toronto has helped S&P to meet the challenge of providing exceptional levels of service. It places S&P in the middle of a cultural mosaic, facilitating recruitment from a multitude of language groups, translating into a broader overall service offering. Given the importance of bilingualism in the Canadian marketplace, access to a large Quebecois-French-speaking pool of communicators at a time when these language skills are at a premium enhances the desirability of the central location. Another important factor is the ability to recruit personnel with specific skill sets. In the case of a high-technology client, S&P was asked to recruit bilingual operators with a background in computer and software technology. With the large concentration of educated personnel available in Toronto, meeting these specialized demands for a specific project becomes a manageable task, even in cases where they have only 24 hours to set up.

On the technology side, S&P Data recognized the need for intelligent partnering to meet its objective of being the most technologically advanced call centre in Canada. Partnerships with Bell Canada and Northern Telecom, for instance, led to the installation of the first digital telephone system equipped with Bell Canada's Megalink, Meridian Max ACD, and Customer Call Routing (CCR) in July 1993. The switch was again upgraded in February 1995 to an MI Option 81, which not only increased the processing power of the PBX, but also allowed S&P Data to implement a network ACD environment.

(Continued)

With the assistance of yet another outside partner, S&P Data developed a software-based predictive dialing system that incorporates computer telephony integration and skills-based routing within its architecture. The ongoing maintenance and evolution of both its telephone and its systems technology would not be possible without the presence of the necessary support services and ongoing interaction, again made possible by the accessibility of its location in southern Ontario.

S&P Data is a true testament to the opportunities available to Canada's call centre establishment. Ontario possesses the world's largest fibre optic network and can match or exceed any North American jurisdiction in terms of access lines with digital switching and advanced development. Ontario has an experienced, adaptable, and well-educated workforce of more than five million people, almost 40% of Canada's total workforce. In addition, Ontario has a strong college and university network that includes dedicated telemarketing training, Canada's largest concentration of private sector training, and major research universities supporting the latest telecommunications applications. In addition to publicly funded education and apprenticeship programs, Canada and Ontario offer training and skills development programs.

DISCUSSION QUESTIONS

1. How would you measure the productivity of an S&P communicator? List a number of alternatives.
2. What part does culture play in this service?
3. Would you tie salary/wages to productivity? Explain.
4. What skill level/educational background is needed to be an S&P communicator?
5. Should S&P consider relocating to Moncton–St. John, which has become a leading call centre location in Canada?

Source: Adapted from Technology Marketing Corporation,"S&P Data's Technologically Advanced Call Center Thrives in Toronto, Ontario" (June 1995).

BIBLIOGRAPHY

Babbage, C. *On the Economy of Machinery and Manufacturers*, 4th ed. London: Charles Knight, 1835.

CMA — *The Management Accounting Magazine*, 67, no. 8: 30.

Canada Newswire Ltd., *Financial News* (October 2, 1995).

Canadian Papermaker, 46, no. 1: 62.

Drucker, P. F. *The Concept of the Corporation*. New York: Mentor, 1946.

Drucker, P. F. "The New Productivity Challenge." *Harvard Business Review*, 69, no. 6 (November/December 1991): 69.

Fabricant, S. A *Primer on Productivity*. New York: Random House, 1969.

Ferdows, K., and A. De Meyer. "Lasting Improvements in Manufacturing Performance: In Search of a New Theory." *Journal of Operations Management*, 9, no. 2 (April 1990): 168.

Garvin, D. A. *Operations Strategy: Text and Cases*. Englewood Cliffs, NJ: Prentice Hall, 1992.

Harbison, F., and C. A. Myers. *Management in the Industrial World*. New York: McGraw-Hill, 1959.

Hounshell, D. A. *From the American System to Mass Production 1800–1932: The Development of Manufacturing*. Baltimore: Johns Hopkins University Press, 1985.

Malhotra, M. K., D. C. Steele, and V. Grover. "Important Strategic and Tactical Manufacturing Issues in the 1990s." *Decision Sciences*, 25, no. 2 (March/April 1994): 189–214.

McLaughlin, Paul. *Canadian Business*, 61, no. 8: 83–85.

Smith, A. *An Inquiry into the Nature and Causes of the Wealth of Nations*. London: Strahan and Cadell, 1776.

Taylor, F. W. *The Principles of Scientific Management*. New York: Harper & Brothers, 1911.

———. *Shop Management*. New York: Harper & Brothers, 1919.

Technology Marketing Corporation, "S&P Data's Technologically Advanced Call Center Thrives in Toronto, Ontario," June 1995.

Vora, J. A. "Productivity and Performance Measures: Who Uses Them?" *Production and Inventory Management Journal*, 33, no. 1 (First Quarter 1992): 46–49.

Wrege, C. D. *Frederick W. Taylor, the Father of Scientific Management: Myth and Reality*. Homewood, IL: Business One Irwin, 1991.

Wren, D. A. *The Evolution of Management Thought*. New York: Ronald Press, 1994.

WEB SITES OF INTEREST

A site developed by John McKirdy for his POM commerce course at Queen's University, which contains organizational material for courses, sample plant and service tour reports, several cases including (copyrighted) graphics, and assignments.

qusbc.bus.queensu.ca/course/c341_home.html

2

P/OM STRATEGY AND INTERNATIONAL COMPETITION

CHAPTER OUTLINE

LEARNING OBJECTIVES

When you complete this chapter you should be able to:

Identify or define:
- Strategy
- Mission
- Competitive advantage
- World-class

Describe or explain:
- How to establish a mission and strategies
- The contribution of the P/OM function to strategy
- Strategies and tactical decisions of P/OM

WORLD-CLASS PROFILE: KOMATSU

KOMATSU DRESSER MODIFIES ITS STRATEGY TO OBTAIN COMPETITIVE ADVANTAGE

Komatsu, a long-time Japanese manufacturer of construction and mining equipment, competes worldwide in some very competitive markets. Like other organizations, Komatsu must constantly review how to organize its resources for maximum benefit. This review and change of resource allocation means modifications in Komatsu's strategy. Over the years, these modifications have taken many forms.

In the 1960s, Komatsu augmented its product line and reduced development costs by licensing designs and technology from others, such as Cummins Engine and International Harvester. This period also saw a strategic move toward improved quality.

In the 1970s, Komatsu's strategy was to become an international enterprise and build export markets, while reducing costs because of the increasing value of the yen. It expanded into Eastern bloc countries and established subsidiaries in Europe and America, as well as service departments in newly industrializing countries.

In the 1980s, Komatsu responded to an even stronger yen through joint ventures with Dresser Industries (to form the Komatsu Dresser Company) and manufacturing outside of Japan. By the 1990s, the strategy includes the latest in manufacturing technology to improve quality and drive down costs, as well as added focus on electronic engine controls for environmentally friendly engines.

The battle for construction equipment is fierce. World-class competitors such as Caterpillar, John Deere, Champion, and Ingersoll-Rand fight for these markets. But Komatsu's constant strategic adjustments to its environment have allowed Komatsu to be number one or two in a variety of markets throughout the world.

Komatsu Dresser sells products (crawler tractors, loaders, hydraulic excavators, and wheel loaders) to construction and mining markets in North America in direct competition with Caterpillar.

Advanced manufacturing equipment like this welding robot helps Komatsu Dresser turn out some of the highest quality products on the market.

The strategic changes mean more emphasis on environmental issues. Here research is being conducted on exhaust gas emission control for diesel engines to make Komatsu equipment more environmentally friendly.

Komatsu, in its continuing fierce worldwide battle with Caterpillar for the global heavy equipment customer, is building equipment throughout the world as cost and logistics dictate. This worldwide strategy allows Komatsu to move production as markets and exchange rates change.

General Electric is number two in the world, behind Philips, in the light bulb business. Light bulbs are big business, generating over $2 billion in sales for GE in the United States alone. But GE cannot become number one in the world without a strong presence in Europe, where it holds a paltry 2% of the market. GE's European strategy obviously needed help, and GE wanted a foot in the door to Eastern European markets. Therefore, in January, 1990, GE bought a controlling interest in Tungsram Company, the declining state-owned Hungarian light bulb maker. Tungsram has become GE's strategic vehicle to European competition.[1] ♦

The job of GE's production function is to use its resources to produce goods and services effectively and efficiently, and that may mean opening a plant in Hungary. Operations managers are *effective* when they operate a system that supports the firm's strategy and goals. They are *efficient* when that system supports the firm with economical use of resources.

THE P/OM MISSION AND STRATEGY

In this section, we describe how to develop missions (i.e., a firm's purpose) and strategies (i.e., a specific plan for achieving the mission). The operations manager determines missions and strategies for very complex systems; so let us first say a few words about systems.

Systems

System

The word *system* implies order and arrangement. A **system** is a set of interacting variables. The operations manager takes these interacting variables and designs a system to achieve a particular objective or mission. One kind of system designed to achieve a particular objective is a *transformation system* that converts inputs into goods and services. The economy is such a system; the firm is such a system; and the production function is such a system. These systems provide the goods and services of our society. Such systems have inputs, transformations, and outputs. To function properly, such systems also have an information flow, called a feedback loop. Figure 2.1 shows the production system and its particular inputs, transformation, outputs, and feedback loops. This feedback lets the inputs and the transformation process know what the customer thinks of its performance.

Production/operations managers manage a variety of systems *within the P/OM function*. There are many P/OM systems, including inventory and scheduling systems, purchasing systems, and maintenance systems. Production/operations managers also respond to a variety of systems *outside the P/OM function, but within the firm*. Among these systems are marketing and finance systems. Still other systems are *outside the firm*, such as economic systems, a system of world trade, and political systems. Managers who understand both the internal and external systems will be better managers.

[1]John S. McClenahen, "Light in the East," *Industry Week*, 241, no. 5 (March 2, 1992): 14–19; and Richard Bruner, "Tungsram's Leading Light," *International Management*, 47, no. 11 (December 1992): 42–46.

FIGURE 2.1 ■ The Production System Transforms Inputs to Outputs

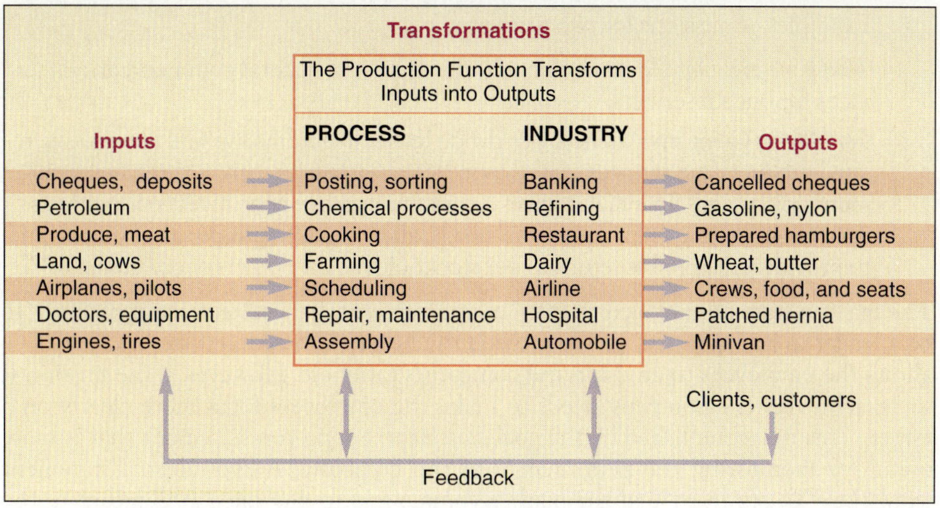

They will be able to coordinate the linkages of people, material, money, and information that are essential for effective and efficient performance.

Viewing the enterprise as a system within other systems allows managers to see the organization in its environment. This insight provides managers a perspective that allows them to design a P/OM system that supports the company's mission and objectives.

SUBSYSTEMS. Complex systems also contain smaller systems. These subsystems sometimes have their own relatively narrow objectives. Therefore, the manager must keep subsystems focused on the goals of the overall system. For example, a finance department may perceive its goal as holding inventory levels close to zero. The sales department, however, may want to keep large stocks of inventory in the hopes that this will help achieve sales goals. When conflicting objectives such as these occur, the larger system (the firm) may not be operating at its best or optimum level. When a system is not operating at its best level, it is said to be **suboptimized**. By understanding the goals of the subsystem and the linkages between systems, the operations manager has an opportunity to avoid suboptimization. Understanding systems, both internal and external, allows the operations manager to make good decisions that improve the productivity of the operations function.

Suboptimized

Mission

To satisfy opportunities in the economic system, managers identify what goods or services the firm will contribute to society. *This contribution is the organization's (or system's) reason for being, that is, its* ***mission***. Establishing a mission ensures a focus on a common purpose, a concept around which the firm can rally. The mission states the rationale for the organization's existence. Developing a good plan is difficult, but is easier if the mission has been well defined. The mission can also be thought of as the intent of the plan—what is to be achieved. Once an organization decides upon its mission, each "functional area" within the firm, namely, marketing, finance/accounting,

Mission

and production/operations, develops its supporting mission. Figure 2.2 provides a hierarchy of sample missions for a manufacturing firm.

Examples of missions for two firms are:

> *Telephone and Data Systems, Inc.*: "to be the finest in total communications services for our subscribers."[2]
>
> *Ford Motor Company:* "to be a worldwide leader in automotive and automotive related products and services as well as in newer industries such as aerospace, communications, and financial services . . . and to improve continually our products and services to meet our customers' needs, allowing us to prosper as a business and to provide a reasonable return to our stockholders, the owners of our business."[3]

The mission statement of a company—a long-run, very general statement such as "To be a leader in the industry" or "To provide the best health care service in Canada"—allows the employees to envision the company's rationale. However, if the mission is to be achieved, the company needs to make the employees focus more clearly on a target. This is accomplished by the **goal** *statement*, a long-run statement that is more useful for monitoring the performance of the company. A typical goal statement would be: "To attain 25% of the market volume and to provide a 20% return to the shareholders by the year 2001." Such a statement is measurable.

Goal statement

The *objective* is an even more focussed statement as to what production, services, marketing, and human resources must do to accomplish the mission/goal of the company. A production objective could be "to introduce a health and safety program to reduce time lost by accidents by 30% with an estimated net savings of $1,000,000 by 1997." Another objective could be "To review the process, machinery, equipment, and personnel used" in the creation of the product or service.

Objective

These brief mission statements provide a rationale and purpose for each firm's existence. Once missions are identified, a plan must be identified to achieve that mission. We call such plans strategies.

Strategy

Strategy

A **strategy** is a plan designed to achieve a mission. Each functional area has a strategy for achieving its mission and for helping the organization reach the overall mission. A strategy should be established in light of the threats and opportunities in the environment and the strengths and weaknesses of the organization.

Only when these external threats/opportunities and internal strengths/weaknesses are understood can the firm begin to build an effective strategy. A brief look at strategic implications of developments in the world economy is presented in Example 1.

EXAMPLE 1

Global Strategy. Postindustrial societies such as those in the European Community (EC) and North America have global as well as local opportunities and threats to consider. Let us take a look at global changes taking place in the economic environment.

[2] Annual report.

[3] *Quality Progress* (October 1989): 49.

First, as we will discuss in Chapter 9, exchange rates, labour rates, productivity, and local attitude and values make a major difference in the location decision. But even with those constraints, we should notice that most of the products made in Canada (or anywhere else) are also made elsewhere in the world. Virtually no product is still available from only one national source. Those other places in the world where Canadian products are likely to be produced are places where high-volume, standardized products can be built by productive low-cost labour with few fringe benefits and a burning desire to sell to affluent Western markets. This desire to sell to the Western world is often augmented by national policies such as low taxes, export credits, and subsidies that support such sales.

Second, although the EC is not a low-labour-cost competitor, it is maturing into one huge market. Volume in this market, and therefore the optimum size of facilities in this market, is increasing. This allows surviving firms in the EC to spread their fixed expenses over more units. Therefore, these firms could very well be low-cost producers even with high labour costs. And depending upon the trade arrangements that develop with Eastern Europe, low labour cost could be available for the next decade.

Third, communication, travel, and shipments between continents are relatively easy, inexpensive, and rapid. This means that both markets and sources are truly global.

Fourth, the affluent world itself is demanding quality, immediate delivery, and options. Affluence allows this market to purchase the latest technology and readily discard the old.

What are the strengths and weaknesses for Western firms in such an environment? What are the potential competitive advantages for Western firms in this changing world? Perhaps sophisticated, flexible production systems that produce high-quality, innovative, option-filled products for wealthy consumers are a reasonable strategy. The products produced would utilize the strengths found in higher skills, technology, and education that are unique to the postindustrialized society. And they would bypass a potential weakness, low labour costs.

Western manufacturing firms that remain in competition with the high-volume, relatively low-technology facilities of the world will be in lean, focussed plants (see Chapter 10, Operations Layout Strategy), utilizing both a high degree of automation (see Chapter 7, Process Strategy and Capacity Planning) and worker commitment (see Chapter 11, Human Resource Strategy).

The U.S. home appliance market is growing annually at 2% or less, about half of that projected for Europe. Therefore, Whirlpool chairman David Whitwam's strategy is to take Whirlpool global. Whirlpool recently acquired a major interest in Inglis Limited of Canada, Vitromatic of Mexico, and a 53% stake in N. V. Philips in the Netherlands. Whirlpool has also moved toward global procurement of 35 strategic materials and components. Appliance giants Maytag, Electrolux, and GE have similarly developed and implemented global strategies to enable them to compete internationally and to be a part of the new European Community. They are also positioned for the next round of tariff reductions, which should result from the recently concluded GATT negotiations.

As Example 1 suggests, firms evaluate their internal strengths and weaknesses and their external opportunities and threats. Mission and strategy development requires that an organization find an opportunity in the environment for which it is uniquely qualified. That is, the company identifies its own unique competencies—its own special capabilities—that fit an opportunity. A firm does not want to attack the market with exactly the same mission and strategy as a competitor. Instead, the firm wants to find those voids or opportunities in the environment that provide a chance for it to mobilize uniquely its resources for a competitive advantage. Many Japanese companies are matching their strengths with opportunities in Southeast Asia, as shown in the *POM In Action* box "Japan Flocks to Southeast Asia to Build Its Products."

The significant role that P/OM can play to support a competitive strategy is evident from a study done by Prof. David Aaker. Of 32 broad categories that contribute

FIGURE 2.2 ■ Sample Mission for a Company, the Production/Operations Function, and the Major Departments in a Production/Operations Function

SAMPLE COMPANY MISSION

To pursue a diversified, growing, and profitable worldwide manufacturing business in electronic components, apparatus, and systems; and to service these products for industry, commerce, agriculture, government, and home.

SAMPLE PRODUCTION/OPERATIONS MANAGEMENT MISSION

To produce products consistent with the company's mission as the worldwide low-cost manufacturer.

SAMPLE P/OM DEPARTMENTAL MISSION

Quality Management	To attain the exceptional quality that is consistent with our company mission and marketing objectives, by close attention to design, procurement, production, and field service opportunities for enhancing design.
Product Design	To lead in research and engineering competencies in all areas of our primary business, designing and producing products and services with outstanding quality and inherent customer value.
Process Design	To determine and design or produce the production process and equipment that will be compatible with low-cost product, high quality, and a good quality-of-work-life for our employees at economical cost.
Layout	To achieve, through skill, imagination, and resourcefulness in plant layout and work methods, production effectiveness and efficiency while supporting a high quality-of-work-life for our employees.
Location	To locate, design, and build efficient and economical facilities that will yield high value to the company, its employees, and the community.
Human Resources	To provide a good quality-of-work-life, with well-designed, safe, rewarding jobs, stable employment, and equitable pay, in exchange for outstanding individual contribution from employees at all levels.
Purchasing	To cooperate with suppliers and subcontractors to develop stable, effective, and efficient sources of supply for those components that are to be procured from outside sources.
Scheduling	To achieve high utilization of manufacturing facilities through effective scheduling.
Inventory	To achieve low investment in inventory consistent with high customer service levels and high facility utilization.
Maintenance	To achieve high utilization of facilities and equipment by effective preventive maintenance and prompt repair of facilities and equipment.

to competitive advantage, 28% fall into the production category that includes product, process, location, and scheduling.[4] From this and similar studies, the major role P/OM can play in strategy development is clear.[5] A list of typical strategies to be supported by P/OM is shown in Figure 2.3.

The production manager's task is to mobilize the resources of P/OM to contribute to a successful strategy. We have identified ten P/OM decisions as critical to this effort.

[4]See David A. Aaker, "Creating a Sustainable Competitive Advantage," *California Management Review* (Winter 1989): 91–106.

[5]Shawnee K. Vickery, Cornelia Droge, and Robert E. Markland, "Production Competence and Business Strategy: Do They Affect Business Performance?" *Decision Sciences*, 24, no. 2 (March/April 1993): 435–455; Robert H. Hayes and Steven C. Wheelwright, *Restoring Our Competitive Edge* (New York: John Wiley, 1984).

FIGURE 2.3 ■ Typical Strategies to Be Supported by P/OM

COMPETITIVE ADVANTAGE	DEFINED AS THE CAPABILITY TO:
Flexibility	
Design	Make rapid design changes and/or introduce new products quickly
Volume	Respond to swings in volume
Quality	
Conformance	Offer consistent quality
Performance	Provide high-performance products
Delivery	
Speed	Deliver products quickly
Dependability	Deliver on time (as promised)
Low price	Compete on price
After-sale service	Provide after-sale service
Broad line	Produce a broad product line

Source: Adapted from Jeffrey G. Miller and Aleda Roth, "A Taxonomy of Manufacturing Strategies," *Management Science*, 40, no. 3 (March 1994): 285–304.

Strategic and Tactical Decisions of P/OM

The 10 strategic and tactical P/OM decisions that support missions and implement strategies are as follows:[6]

1. **Quality Strategy.** The customer's quality expectations must be determined and policies and procedures established to identify and achieve that quality.
2. **Product Strategy.** Product strategy defines much of the transformation process. Production costs, quality and human resource decisions interact strongly with the design of products. Product designs often set the lower limits of cost and the upper limits of quality.
3. **Process Strategy.** Process options are available for a product. Process decisions commit management to basic approaches to technology, quality, human resource utilization, and maintenance. These expense and capital commitments will determine much of the firm's basic cost structure.
4. **Location Strategy.** Facility location decisions for both manufacturing and service organizations may determine the ultimate success of the operation. Errors made at this juncture may overwhelm other efficiencies.
5. **Layout Strategy.** Capacity needs, personnel levels, purchasing decisions, and inventory requirements influence layout. Additionally, the processes and material must be sensibly located in relation to each other.
6. **Human Resource Strategy.** Human resources are an integral and expensive part of the total system design. Therefore, the quality-of-work-life provided, the talent and skills required, and their costs must be determined.
7. **Purchasing and Just-in-Time Strategy.** These decisions determine what is to be made and what is to be purchased. Consideration is also given to quality,

[6]For another perspective see Manoj K. Malhotra, Daniel C. Steel, and Varun Grover, "Important Strategic and Tactical Manufacturing Issues in the 1990s," *Decision Sciences*, 25, no. 2 (March/April 1994): 189–214.

Canadian-owned Wajax Limited sells and distributes heavy mobile equipment. Wajax' strategy is to acquire three heavy mobile equipment distribution companies to cement a major role in the international equipment manufacturers industry, specifically in forestry and construction.

Wajax has taken ownership of Lounsbery Industrial Limited, a company specializing in forestry in the maritime provinces. This purchase is complemented by the acquisition of Timberjack Inc. with locations in Thunder Bay and Kapuskasing. The final acquisition was Telect Canada Inc., a company operating across Canada to distribute mounted aerial devices and digger-derricks for construction purposes.

Wajax plans to improve and increase their core business in the domestic market, and to become competitive in the international market. Based on M. E. Porter's model described in *The Competitive Advantages of Nations*, Wajax' tactical approach should lead to success.

Source: Adapted from Business Wire, "Wajax Announces Three Acquisitions in Heavy Mobile Equipment Distribution Business," February 7, 1996.

POM IN ACTION

Japan Flocks to Southeast Asia to Build Its Products

Joseph Romm's book, *The Once and Future Superpower*, provides a scholarly look at an important new trend in Japanese industry. Romm claims that Japan's strategy, called the New Asian Industrial Development plan, is to gather Asian economies into an economic flock with Japan at the head. It is doing so by targeting Indonesia, Malaysia, the Philippines, Thailand, Vietnam, India, and Bangladesh not only as primary suppliers of basic materials like rubber, oil, and timber, but also as manufacturers of low-value-added products.

Malaysia, for example, has been selected by Japanese investors to become the world's largest manufacturer of window unit air conditioners for the global market. Sony uses Malaysia to build its compact disc players. Overall, Japanese investment in Malaysia has ballooned ($1.5 billion in 1990) with some 550 Japanese manufacturing and service businesses already in place.

Thailand, with a population of 55 million, is even more dramatically affected, with $3.6 billion in Japanese investment in 1989 alone (compared to only $565 million from the United States). Thailand's close economic ties with Japan are also shown by its trade figures. In 1993, for example, 30% of Thailand's imports came from Japan, while only 12% came from the United States. As well, the Japanese have opened many factories in Thailand, a strategy which boosts exports of Japanese VCRs and colour TVs to the United States, while giving the appearance of increased U.S. trade with Thailand.

Elsewhere in Southeast Asia, Sumitomo Electric is moving labour-intensive assembly of auto-wiring systems to Indonesia; Suzuki has opened an auto plant in India; and JVC has contracted with Hanoi Electronics in Vietnam to produce its TVs.

These decisions, reflecting a systematic strategy by world-class Japanese firms, pose new low-labour-cost threats to competitors.

Sources: Joseph Romm, *The Once and Future Superpower* (New York: Morrow, 1992); and *Forbes* (November 23, 1992): pp. 108–112.

delivery, and innovation, at a satisfactory price. An atmosphere of mutual respect between buyer and supplier is necessary for effective purchasing.

8. **Inventory Tactics.** Inventory decisions can be optimized only when considered in light of customer satisfaction, suppliers, production schedules, and human resource planning.
9. **Scheduling Tactics.** Feasible and efficient schedules of production must be developed; the demands on human resources and facilities must be determined and controlled.
10. **Maintenance and Reliability Tactics.** Decisions must be made regarding desired levels of reliability and maintenance. Plans for implementation and control of reliability and maintenance are necessary.

Each of the foregoing decisions discussed is presented in one or more chapters in the text. These 10 areas do not, of course, represent all that operations managers do or all that they should know. For instance, our discussion of organization theory, accounting, staffing, or human behaviour and communication skills is limited, but all are important for the effective operations manager. Moreover, as we shall see in subsequent chapters, these 10 P/OM decision areas interact strongly with each other. When the 10 decisions are not made in such a way as to contribute to the company's strategy, the operations manager has failed.

DEVELOPING A P/OM STRATEGY

The operations manager is an active participant in determining the firm's mission and strategy because so many resources are a P/OM responsibility. Only when operations managers understand the organization's overall strategy can optimal decisions be made. The best utilization of resources requires more than effective marketing and finance. Jazzy ads and new financial leverage schemes do not create better products delivered on time to the customer. Only the production function does that. The production function is a vital element in building a competitive advantage. By

FIGURE 2.4 ■ Developing Operations Strategy

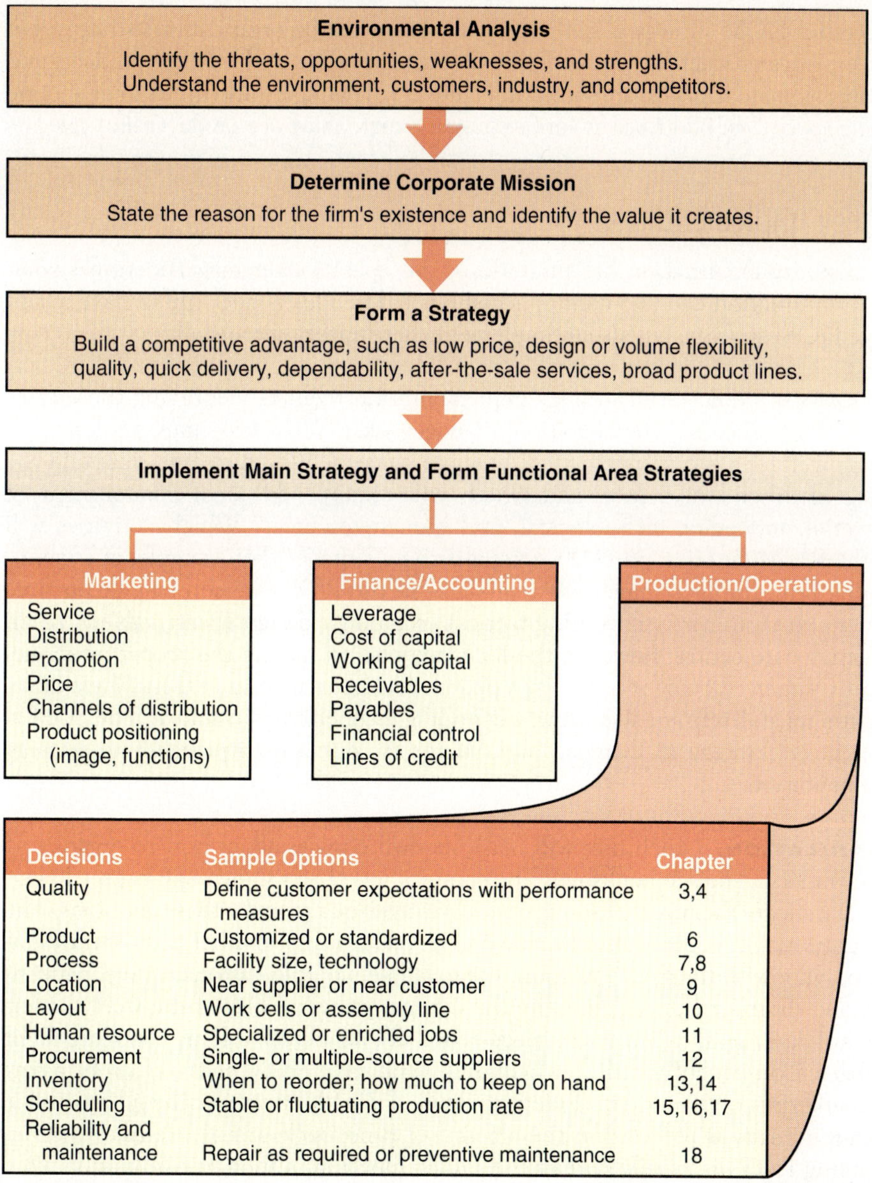

Decisions	Sample Options	Chapter
Quality	Define customer expectations with performance measures	3,4
Product	Customized or standardized	6
Process	Facility size, technology	7,8
Location	Near supplier or near customer	9
Layout	Work cells or assembly line	10
Human resource	Specialized or enriched jobs	11
Procurement	Single- or multiple-source suppliers	12
Inventory	When to reorder; how much to keep on hand	13,14
Scheduling	Stable or fluctuating production rate	15,16,17
Reliability and maintenance	Repair as required or preventive maintenance	18

Competitive advantage

competitive advantage, we mean an advantage that competitors do not have. Johnson Electric, as indicated in the *POM in Action* box "Strategy at Hong Kong's Johnson Electric Is Global," found competitive advantage in speed of manufacture, staying informed of customer needs, and efficient manufacturing.

The production function can contribute to a competitive advantage in a variety of ways. However, P/OM is only one-third of the strategic triad, which also includes marketing and finance/accounting. Figure 2.4 provides a synopsis of strategic options for marketing, finance, and P/OM. These functions, as well as other functions of the firm, make contributions to strategy. In this text, we note a variety of specific examples of how firms do so.

P/OM Strategy Considerations

A successful P/OM strategy is not only consistent with the organization's strategy, but also recognizes product life cycles. Every product has a life cycle. A few products and their approximate life cycle are shown in Figure 2.5. That figure also shows some specific strategic issues to be addressed at various stages in each phase of a product's life cycle.

Strategy Implementation

Because every organization has limitations, the operations manager identifies what the P/OM function can and cannot accomplish. The idea is not only to have a supportive P/OM strategy, but also to implement that strategy successfully.

KEY TASKS. Successful strategy implementation requires identifying those tasks that are key to success. The operations manager asks, "What tasks must be done particularly well for a given operations strategy to succeed? Which elements contain the highest likelihood of failure, and which will require additional commitment of managerial, monetary, technological, and human resources? Which activities will help the P/OM function provide a competitive advantage?" For example, in a manufacturing firm, the most important ingredient in the P/OM mission may be on-time shipment to customers (scheduling tactics) or product design (heart valves). In an emergency care centre, however, the focus may be on having the proper personnel present (human resource strategy) and pharmaceuticals (inventory tactics) available. Each firm must determine its own way of finding competitive advantage. The *POM in Action* box "Strategy at Compaq and Microsoft" discusses approaches to strategy implementation.

ORGANIZATION. Each firm will make its own choices about how to organize so the key tasks can be accomplished. The organization charts shown in Chapter 1 (Figure 1.2) indicate the way that some firms have organized to make these decisions. The organization of the operations function and its relationship to other parts of the organization vary with the P/OM mission. For example, volatile customer travel patterns dominate short-term scheduling in the airline industry. Day-of-the-week preference, holidays, seasonality, and college schedules all play a role in changing flight schedules. Consequently, airline scheduling, although a P/OM activity, can be a part of a marketing organization. (Refer to Figure 1.2(a).) Effective scheduling in the trucking industry is reflected in the amount of time trucks travel loaded. However, scheduling trucks is usually part of the P/OM function, although information from

POM IN ACTION

Strategy at Hong Kong's Johnson Electric Is Global

Patrick Wang, managing director of Johnson Electric Holdings, Ltd., walks through his Hong Kong headquarters with a micromotor in his hand. This tiny motor, about twice the size of his thumb, powers a Dodge Viper power door lock. Although most people have never heard of Johnson Electric, we all have several of their micromotors nearby. This is because Johnson is the world's leading producer of micromotors for cordless tools, household appliances (such as coffee grinders and food processors), personal care items (such as hair dryers and electric shavers), and cars. A luxury Mercedes, with its headlight wipers, power windows, power seat adjustments, and power side mirrors, may use 50 Johnson micromotors per vehicle.

Like all truly global businesses, Johnson spends liberally on communications to tie together its global network of factories, R&D and design centres. For example, Johnson Electric is installing a $20 million videoconferencing system that allows engineers in Cleveland, Ohio, and Stuttgart, Germany, to monitor trial production of their micromotors in China.

Johnson's first strength is speed—13 million motors a month, mostly assembled in China. Its second strength is the ability to stay close to its customers. Johnson has design and technical centres scattered across the United States, Europe, and Japan. "The physical limitations of the past are gone" when it comes to deciding where to locate a new centre, says Patrick Wang. "Customers talk to us where they feel most comfortable, but products are made where they are most competitive."

Sources: Forbes (November 8, 1993): 292–293; and *Asian Business* (February 1993): 12.

POM IN ACTION

Strategy at Compaq and Microsoft

Two world-class companies, Compaq and Microsoft, lead in bringing new products to market with quality and marketability. They share these five traits in doing so:

They focus on one business. For example, Compaq makes only one product, personal computers, and more specifically, business PCs. "We don't spend a lot of time worrying about the home marketing or the educational market ... [but] focus on developing new products to meet the needs of the business PC user," says Michael Swavely, division president.

They are global. Both Microsoft and Compaq are so strong that they are able to compete globally. And they pursue international markets that have stiff competition, which forces them to remain world-class. Compaq is the second leading supplier of business PCs in the U.S., Canadian, and European markets, and has 45% of its sales abroad.

Their senior management is actively involved in defining and improving the product development process. Microsoft's Bill Gates, for example, keeps in contact with his engineers by electronic mail memos, sometimes 30 in a day.

They recruit and retain the top people in their fields. Microsoft is always known for hiring the best and brightest possible. Thousands have become millionaires by staying on and helping the company grow.

They understand that speed to market reinforces product quality. Microsoft's Windows NT, with a staggering 4.3 million lines of code, almost killed the 200 programmers on the project in rushing it to market in 1993. But it redefined the concept of network software and windows software by marrying them. It also reflects Gates' aggressive goals of continuous improvement.

Sources: Wall Street Journal (August 6, 1990): A12; and (May 26, 1993): A1, A12.

FIGURE 2.5 ■ Strategy and Issues During a Product's Life Cycle.

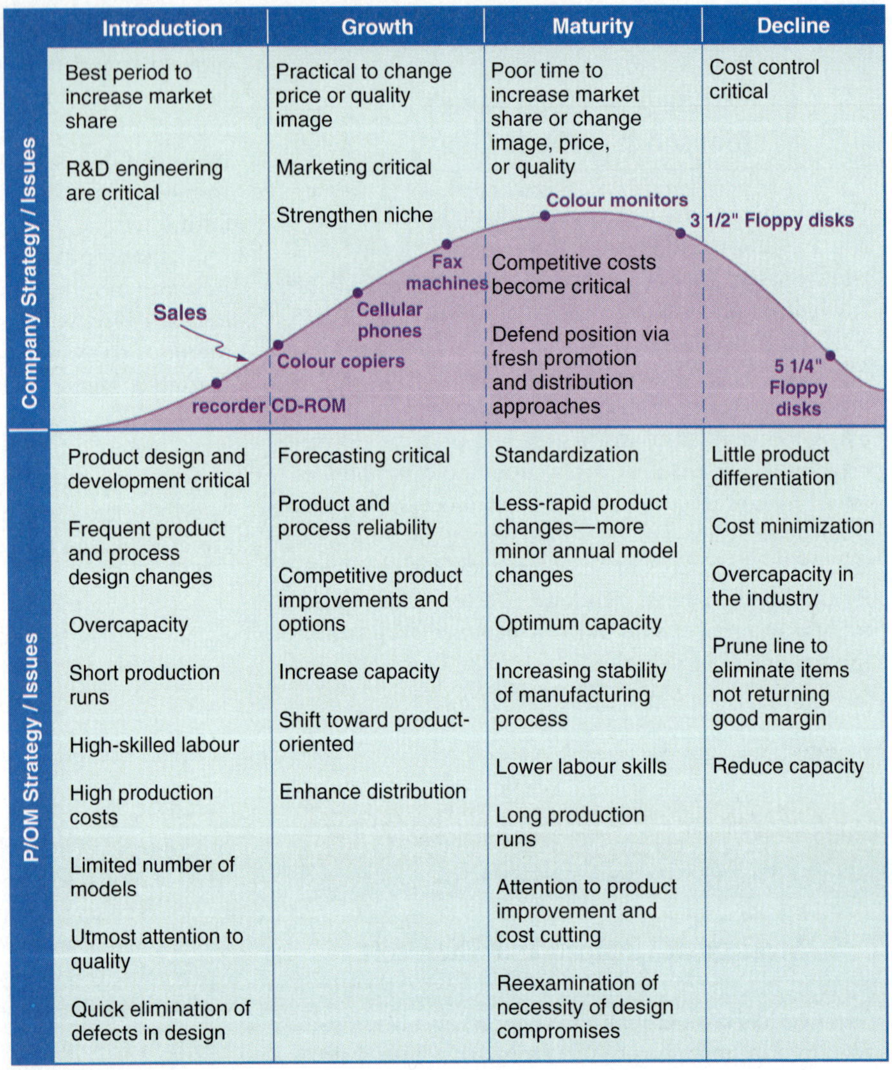

(*Sources:* Various; see, for instance, Michael E. Porter, *Techniques for Analyzing Industries and Competitors* (New York, Free Press, 1980).)

delivery and pickup points, drivers, and other parts of the organization is required. When the organization of the P/OM function results in effective scheduling in the air passenger and commercial trucking industries, a competitive advantage can exist.

The production/operations manager develops strategy, identifies key tasks, groups activities into an organized structure, and staffs with personnel who will get the job done. The manager works with subordinate managers to build plans, budgets, and programs that will successfully implement strategies that achieve missions. When the operations manager has done the foregoing, the basics for an efficient system that transforms inputs into outputs exist. Then the operations manager should be able to implement a P/OM strategy that will increase productivity and provide competitive advantage.

Strategy Dynamics

Strategies change. They change for two reasons. First, *strategy is dynamic because of changes within the organization*. All areas of the firm are subject to change. Changes may be in a variety of areas including purchasing, finance, technology, and product life. All may make a difference in an organization's strengths and weaknesses and therefore its strategy. Figure 2.5 shows possible change in both overall strategy and P/OM strategy during the product's life cycle. Second, *strategy is dynamic because of changes in the environment*. Komatsu, the international manufacturer of large earth-moving equipment shown in this chapter's World-Class Profile, provides an example of how strategy must change as the environment changes. Komatsu, in its worldwide competition with Caterpillar, has had to adopt strategies of quality enhancement, product-line growth, and cost reduction.[7] P/OM strategies are increasingly global.

INTERNATIONAL ISSUES IN P/OM

The world has increasingly turned into one interconnected economy, a *global village*, where the economy of one country is affected by the economies of many others. For example, as other countries have targeted the United States as an export destination, American companies have had to turn more to foreign markets for sales and profits. And, as we saw in the opening quote of this chapter, GE has turned to Hungary for a strategic alliance to produce and market light bulbs.

GE is not alone in its global P/OM strategy. Note that every firm in Table 2.1 generates the majority of its sales outside its home country. An enormous 98% of Nestlé's sales come from beyond its home in Switzerland. It is no wonder that writers such as Alvin Toffler think that international firms will become *stateless*.[8] They are no longer German or Swiss or Canadian. National identities do not matter in many decisions. Decisions are made on economic, not national, merits.

As firms increasingly position their production function in a dynamic global environment, they will also have substantial investments outside their "home" country. Variations in labour skills and cost, capital availability and cost, local infrastructures and markets, and political risk are the challenges firms face.[9]

As a test of *your* knowledge about international companies, try to answer the questions in our quiz in Table 2.2. You will probably be surprised regarding ownership of the eleven famous product lines listed in the first column.

ACHIEVING A WORLD-CLASS P/OM STRATEGY

Firms that compete successfully in the international arena are known as **world-class firms.** A **world-class P/OM function** is one that obtains excellence in meeting customer requirements through continuous improvement. Most world-class firms, whether manufacturing or service, will have P/OM functions that are also world-class.

World-class firms
World-class P/OM function

[7]Gary Hamel and C. K. Prahalad, "Strategic Intent," *Harvard Business Review*, 67, no. 3 (May/June 1989): 63–76.

[8]Lois F. Lunin, "Recipe for Intelligence," *Information Today* (March 1994): 61–63.

[9]See the discussion in M. E. McGrath and R. W. Hoole, "Manufacturing's New Economies of Scale," *Harvard Business Review* (May/June 1992): 94–99.

TABLE 2.1 ■ WORLD-CLASS FIRMS HAVE INTERNATIONAL STRATEGIES

COMPANY	HOME COUNTRY	% SALES OUTSIDE HOME COUNTRY	% ASSETS OUTSIDE HOME COUNTRY
Avon Products	United States	61	48
Bayer	Germany	65	NA
Bell Canada	Canada	59	36
Citicorp	United States	66	51
Colgate-Palmolive	United States	65	47
Daimler-Benz	Germany	61	NA
Dow Chemical	United States	54	45
Gillette	United States	68	66
Hoechst	Germany	77	NA
Honda	Japan	63	36
Honeywell Canada	Canada	50	100
IBM	United States	59	55
ICI	Britain	78	50
Nestlé	Switzerland	98	95
Northern Telecom	Canada	97	82
Philips	Netherlands	94	85
Procter & Gamble	United States	52	41
Siemens	Germany	51	NA
Sony	Japan	66	NA
Unilever	Britain/Netherlands	75	70

NA: Not available.

Sources: Business Week (May 4, 1990): 103; *Forbes* (July 18, 1994): 277; 1995 Bell Canada annual report; 1995 Northern Telecom annual report; Marketing Department, Honeywell (Canada) Ltd.

These firms have been successful in putting together an operations strategy that supports the overall company mission by creating a competitive advantage. Each of the 10 decisions of P/OM in its own way can contribute to this competitive advantage. For each of these 10 decisions, Table 2.3 suggests some characteristics of world-class firms. These characteristics are addressed in their respective chapters. A world-class P/OM function contributes to competitive advantage, making the organization successful today and providing products, services, and jobs for tomorrow.

SUMMARY

P/OM is a major function that can contribute in a significant way to an organization's competitiveness. Organizations must understand their environment and realistically identify their own abilities. Then they implement a strategy that utilizes those abilities within the environment to achieve the mission. Only when all of the above are done well can the organization have a competitive advantage and be a world-class performer. In our global economy, in which companies easily operate and compete across international borders, world-class performance is increasingly required.

TABLE 2.2 ■ INTERNATIONAL QUIZ: CAN YOU MATCH THE PRODUCT WITH THE PROPER PARENT COMPANY AND COUNTRY?

PRODUCT	PARENT COMPANY	COUNTRY OF PARENT
Arrow shirts		
Braun household appliances		
Burger King food		
Firestone tires		
Godiva chocolate		
Haagen-Dazs ice cream		
Jaguar autos		
MGM movies		
Lamborghini autos		
Goodrich tires		
Alpo pet foods		
Meridian Systems communication equipment		

Choose from these parent companies:
a Automobili Lamborghini
b Bidermann International
c Bridgestone
d Campbell Soup
e Credit Lyonnais
f Ford Motor Company
g Gillette
h Grand Metropolitan
i Michelin
j Nestlé
k Northern Telecom

Choose from these countries:
1 France
2 Great Britain
3 Indonesia
4 Japan
5 United States
6 Switzerland
7 Canada

Answers: Arrow: b, 1; Braun: g, 5; Burger King: h, 2; Firestone: c, 4; Godiva: d, 5; Haagen-Dazs: h, 2; Jaguar: f, 5; MGM: e, 1; Lamborghini: a, 3; Goodrich: i, 1; Alpo: j, 6.; Communication equipment, k, 7

TABLE 2.3 ■ WHAT ARE THE CHARACTERISTICS OF WORLD-CLASS FIRMS IN THE STRATEGIC AND TACTICAL AREAS OF P/OM? HERE ARE EXAMPLES OF HOW WORLD-CLASS FIRMS DEAL WITH IMPORTANT P/OM ISSUES.

QUALITY STRATEGY

Improves systems via empowered employees.

Reduces costs and wins orders via quality.

PRODUCT STRATEGY

Produces one or only a few products.

Introduces new products continually.

Links product strategy to market share and product life cycles.

HUMAN RESOURCES STRATEGY

Trains employees to perform a variety of jobs.

Fosters mutual trust and respect, resulting in a high level of morale.

Builds an outstanding staff via effective recruiting, selection, training, and retention.

PROCESS STRATEGY

Develops uniquely efficient equipment or process.

Generates a dollar of sales with low capital requirements relative to the competition.

SCHEDULING TACTICS

Schedules effectively for high utilization.

Wins orders with conformance to delivery promises.

Enhances use of facilities by effective scheduling.

Develops stable production schedules.

LOCATION STRATEGY

Finds locations that yield an advantage in cost, revenue, customer service, and market penetration.

Pursues opportunities internationally.

continued

TABLE 2.3 ■ WHAT ARE THE CHARACTERISTICS OF WORLD-CLASS FIRMS IN THE STRATEGIC AND TACTICAL AREAS OF P/OM? HERE ARE EXAMPLES OF HOW WORLD-CLASS FIRMS DEAL WITH IMPORTANT P/OM ISSUES.

INVENTORY TACTICS

Minimizes investment in inventory.

Uses JIT techniques to control inventory and to ensure consistent quality.

LAYOUT STRATEGY

Uses work cells and flexible facilities.

Streamlines movement of material for efficiency and value.

PROCUREMENT STRATEGY

Evaluates and develops suppliers into world-class performers.

Integrates suppliers into the production system.

MAINTENANCE TACTICS

Performs effective preventive maintenance, reducing product variability.

Trains employees to do equipment inspection and minor preventive maintenance.

KEY TERMS

System (p. 32)
Suboptimized (p. 33)
Mission (p. 33)
Goal statement (p. 34)
Objective (p. 34)
Strategy (p. 34)
Competitive advantage (p. 40)
World-class firms (p. 43)
World-class P/OM function (p. 43)

SOLVED PROBLEM

Solved Problem 2.1

How does a company in the very mature and established meatpacking industry win a competitive advantage?[10] Quebec Beef Packers (QBP) was able to win a strong competitive advantage by restructuring traditional beef-processing operations. In beef packing, traditional operations involved raising cattle on scattered farms and ranches, shipping them live to labour-intensive, unionized slaughtering plants, and then transporting whole sides of beef to grocery retailers whose butcher departments cut them into smaller pieces and packaged them for sale to grocery shoppers.

Solution

Quebec Beef Packers revamped traditional operations with a radically different strategy. Large automated plants employing nonunion labour were built near economically transportable supplies of cattle. Then the meat was partially butchered at the processing plant into smaller, high-yield cuts (sometimes sealed in plastic ready for purchase), boxed, and shipped to retailers. QBP's inbound cattle transportation expenses, traditionally a major cost item, were cut significantly by avoiding major losses that occurred when live animals were shipped long distances. Additionally, major outbound shipping-cost savings were achieved by not having to ship whole sides of beef with their high waste factor. QBP's strategy was so successful that it was, by 1985, the largest Canadian meatpacker, surpassing the former industry leaders, Swift, Wilson, and Armour.

[10]Adapted from information in Michael E. Porter, *Competitive Advantage* (New York: Free Press, 1985), p. 109; Arthur A. Thompson, Jr., and A. J. Strickland III, *Strategy Formulation and Implementation* (Homewood, IL: BPI/Irwin, 1989).

DISCUSSION QUESTIONS

1. Describe the registration system at your university. What are its inputs, transformations, and outputs?
2. Would the complex system in which productions/operations managers operate be different with faster feedback loops?
3. What are the similarities and differences in the transformation process between a fast-food restaurant and a computer manufacturer?
4. Identify the 10 strategic and tactical decisions of operations management.
5. Identify the transformation that takes place in your automobile repair garage. What are the manifestations of the 10 production and operation management (P/OM) decisions at the garage? That is, how is each of the ten decisions accomplished? (Figure 2.4 may be helpful.)
6. Answer Question 5 for some other enterprise of your choosing.
7. Based on what you know of the automobile industry, how has the P/OM strategy of General Motors or Ford changed in the last 10 years?
8. As a library assignment, identify the mission of a firm and the strategy that supports that mission.
9. What is an example of suboptimization?
10. In this chapter, we have identified 10 strategic and tactical decisions of P/OM. What are some strategic and tactical decisions of finance and marketing?
11. What are the implications to North America of Japan's strategy for dominance in Southeast Asia, as described in the *P/OM in Action* box?

CRITICAL THINKING EXERCISE

IBM at one time had a 70% market share in the computer business. Most of that business was in large computers, known as mainframes. Throughout the 1980s and 90s technology and markets favoured computer networks, then PCs, and now computer networks *and* PCs. IBM has had a difficult time adjusting. IBM's sales, employment, and percentage of installed computers have dropped. From a P/OM perspective, how might IBM have matched its strengths and weaknesses with the opportunities and threats of the environment?

PROBLEMS

• **2.1** Find an article in the business literature (*Business Week*, *Wall Street Journal*, *Forbes*, *Fortune*, and so on) that (1) documents an organization's current P/OM strategy and (2) documents a *change* in an organization's P/OM strategy.

⋮ **2.2** Identify how changes in the external environment affect the P/OM strategy for a company. For instance, discuss what impact the following external factors might have on P/OM strategy:

a) major increases in oil prices

b) water- and air-quality legislation

c) fewer young prospective employees entering the labour market in 1985 through 1995

d) inflation vs. stable prices

e) legislation moving health insurance from a benefit to taxable income

⋮ **2.3** Identify how changes in the internal environment affect the P/OM strategy for a company. For instance, discuss what impact the following internal factors might have on P/OM strategy:

a) maturing of a product

b) technology innovation in the manufacturing process

c) changes in product design that move Compaq's disk drives from 3½-in. floppy drives to CD-ROM drives

CASE STUDY

Signature Vacations

Signature Vacations is the first-ever travel company to receive the prestigious Partners in Progress award from Sears Canada Inc. The retail giant annually acknowledges a handful of its suppliers for this award, which is based partly on the views of Sears' front-line selling personnel, but also on service levels, customer satisfaction, quality of product, innovations, and support to Sears staff. As Sears Travel marketing manager Lawrence Macdonald points out, "It's far more than a popularity contest." "I'm delighted that Sears has chosen Signature for its first-ever Partners in Progress award," says Dermot Blastland, Signature president. "We launched Signature in August [1995] and appreciate the recognition that the Sears Travel counsellors have given to our efforts. I have the highest praise for the calibre of service they provide." The awards were presented at a gala dinner in Toronto on May 2, 1996.

Signature Vacations is Canada's largest vacation company, providing holidays for over a million Canadians a year. In 1995, Signature resulted as the rebranding of three existing Canadian tour operators which had been formed as long ago as 1972. Signature is affiliated with Fiesta West of Vancouver and Encore Cruises of Toronto.

DISCUSSION QUESTIONS

1. What is the mission/goal of Signature Vacations?
2. How would you measure productivity in this business? Explain.
3. What are the key operating strategies that Signature uses to obtain competitive advantage?

Source: Adapted from Canada NewsWire Ltd., "Signature Vacations Scores First Ever Partners in Progress Award with Sears Canada," May 16, 1996.

CASE STUDY

Canadian Tire

Citing reduced operating and distribution expenses and an ongoing successful store expansion program, Canadian Tire Corporation president and CEO, Stephen E. Bachand announced in 1996 that Canadian Tire was "working smarter." In an address to shareholders and other guests at the company's annual general meeting, Bachand declared that, overall, the company had achieved very positive financial results in an exceptionally competitive environment.

He outlined three key areas that Canadian Tire has focussed on to meet the needs of its customers and remain the country's largest and most successful hard goods retailer: cutting costs, building new-format stores, and delivering on the company's commitment to provide customer-driven service. "Cost reduction must continue to play an essential role at 'The New Tire' in satisfying the expectations of both our customers and our shareholders," Bachand added. In 1995, Canadian Tire had reduced its operating expenses as a percentage of consolidated gross operating revenue by 29 basis points. Since 1995, Canadian Tire had reduced them by 111 points. Total distribution expenses as a percentage of shipments to associate dealers were also reduced for the third consecutive year.

Bachand described the company's new-format store program as "the most ambitious retail redevelopment plan in Canadian Tire's history." As part of that plan, launched in 1994, 250 existing Canadian Tire stores were to be expanded or replaced with the corporation's new-format stores by the year 2000. As part of this program, the company was to have opened 70 new-format stores by the end of 1996. This included a total of 57 new stores opened or in development in 1996. The new stores feature wider aisles, better signage, and a greater selection of products in the automotive, sports and leisure, and home products categories.

Customer response to the new stores has been significant: customer counts were up 20%, average sales per customer were up 20%, and average total sales had jumped by over 45%. Regarding Canadian Tire's customers, Bachand said, "They are the real ex-

(Continued)

perts in customer service and we are responding to them."

To improve customer satisfaction, the company implemented a price-match guarantee, a hassle-free national warranty and returns policy, and customer service training sessions for staff. New financial services included the Warranty Plus™ and Charge-Gard™ insurance products. Canadian Tire also became the first non-deposit-taking financial institution in Canada to issue a MasterCard with its pilot Canadian Tire Options MasterCard™ program, launched last year. "Our franchise is on solid footing ... and within a 15-minute drive of eight out of every ten Canadians," Bachand summarized. "The strategic agenda continues to prove its worth ... advancing and improving 74-year-old traditions of financial performance and community service."

Canadian Tire Corporation Limited comprises Canadian Tire Acceptance Limited (CTAL), Canadian Tire Retail (CTR), and Canadian Tire Petroleum. CTAL manages related financial services for the corporation. CTR is Canada's largest hard goods retailer, specializing in automotive, sports and leisure, and home products. There are 423 Canadian Tire associate stores serving communities nationwide. Canadian Tire Petroleum has 20 convenience stores and 200 gasoline outlets, and is the largest independent retailer of gasoline in Canada.

DISCUSSION QUESTIONS

1. Suggest a mission statement for Canadian Tire.
2. Provide a SWOT (strengths, weaknesses, opportunities, threats) analysis.
3. Review the ten P/OM decisions discussed in the chapter and determine the reasons behind Canadian Tire's problems/success.
4. What tools/techniques would you use to explain your analysis to top executives?

Source: Adapted from Canada NewsWire Ltd., "The New Tire 'Working Smarter,' Canadian Tire Chief Executive Tells Shareholders," May 9, 1996.

BIBLIOGRAPHY

Barro, R. J. "Economic Growth in a Cross Section of Countries." *Quarterly Journal of Economics*, 106 (May 1991): 407–443.

Canada NewsWire Ltd., "Signature Vacations Scores First Ever Partners in Progress Award with Sears Canada," May 16, 1996.

Chase, R. B., and R. H. Hayes. "Beefing Up Operations in Service Firms." *Sloan Management Review*, 33, no. 1 (Fall 1991): 15–26.

Committee on Analysis of Research. *The Competitive Edge: Research Priorities for U.S. Manufacturing*. Washington, DC: National Academy Press, 1991.

De Long, J. B., and L. H. Summers. "Equipment Investment and Economic Growth." *Quarterly Journal of Economics*, 106 (May 1991): 445–502.

Drucker, P. F. "The Emerging Theory of Manufacturing." *Harvard Business Review* (May/June 1990): 94.

Egelhoff, W. G. "Great Strategy or Great Strategy Implementation—Two Ways of Competing in Global Markets." *Sloan Management Review*, 34, no. 2 (Winter 1993): 37.

Forrester, J. *Industrial Dynamics*. Cambridge: MIT Press, 1964.

Gerwin, D. "Manufacturing Flexibility: A Strategic Perspective." *Management Science*, 39, no. 4 (April 1993): 395–410.

Good, Arthur H., and Stephen Grandosky, *Canadian Business Review*, 22, no. 2: 31.

Hamel, G., and C. K. Prahalad. "Strategy as Stretch and Leverage." *Harvard Business Review*, 71, no. 2 (March/April 1993): 75–84.

Hayes, R. H., and G. P. Pisano. "Beyond World-Class: The New Manufacturing Strategy." *Harvard Business Review*, 72, no. 1 (January/February 1992): 77–86.

Hayes, R. H., S. Wheelwright, and K. B. Clark. *Dynamic Manufacturing*. New York: Free Press, 1988.

Heim, J. A., and W. D. Compton, eds. *Manufacturing Systems: Foundations of World-Class Practice*. Washington, DC: National Academy Press, 1992.

Kiernan, M. J. "The New Strategic Architecture: Learning to Compete in the Twenty-First Century." *The Executive*, 7, no. 1 (February 1993): 7–21.

Kim, Y., and J. Lee. "Manufacturing Strategy and Production Systems: An Integrated Framework." *Journal of Operations Management*, 11, no. 1 (March 1993): 3–15.

Kogut, B., and N. Kulatilaka. "Operating Flexibility, Global Manufacturing, and the Option Value of a Multinational Network." *Management Science*, 40, no. 1 (January 1994): 123–139.

Little, J. D. C. "Tautologies, Models, and Theories: Can We Find 'Laws' of Manufacturing?" *Industrial Research & Development*, 24, no. 3 (July 1992): 7.

National Center for Manufacturing Sciences. *Competing in World-Class Manufacturing: America's 21st Century Challenge*. Homewood, IL: Business One Irwin, 1990.

Ohmae, K. "The Borderless World." *Sloan Management Review*, 32 (Winter 1991): 117.

Peteraf, M. A. "Commitment: The Dynamic of Strategy." *Academy of Management Executive*, 6, no. 3 (August 1992): 97.

Pine, B. J. II, B. Victor, and A. C. Boynton. "Making Mass Customization Work." *Harvard Business Review*, 71, no. 5 (September/October 1993): 108–119.

Porter, M. E. *The Competitive Advantages of Nations*. New York: Free Press, 1990.

Rich, P. "The Organizational Taxonomy: Definition and Design." *The Academy of Management Review*, 17, no. 4 (October 1992): 758.

Rockart, J. F., and J. D. Hofman. "Systems Delivery: Evolving New Strategies." *Sloan Management Review*, 33, no. 4 (Summer 1992): 21.

Schmenner, R. W. "International Factory Productivity Gains." *Journal of Operations Management*, 10, no. 2 (April 1991): 229–254.

Shaw, M. J., J. J. Solberg, and T. C. Woo. "System Integration in Intelligent Manufacturing: An Introduction." *Industrial Engineering Research & Development*, 24, no. 3 (July 1992): 2.

Skinner, W. *Manufacturing: The Formidable Competitive Weapon*. New York: John Wiley, 1985.

Sloan, A. P. *My Years with General Motors*. New York: Doubleday, 1972.

Stephanou, S. *The Manufacturing Challenge from Concept to Production*. New York: Van Nostrand Reinhold, 1991.

Stonebraker, P. W., and G. K. Leong. *Operations Strategy: Focusing Competitive Excellence*. Boston: Allyn & Bacon, 1994.

2 SUPPLEMENT

DECISION-MAKING TOOLS

SUPPLEMENT OUTLINE

Ultra Petroleum Corporation (VSE: NASDAQ) is a Canadian company that concentrates resources in the U.S. for oil drilling exploration projects. With decision tree analysis, Ultra concentrated its strategic efforts on operating low-risk exploration projects. Its objective is to become a reliable company by increasing the rate of cash returns through an increase in barrels of oil obtained per day. Ultra's strategy includes: (1) Using engineering consultants to locate potential drilling fields. (2) Reorganizing around profitability and reliability by: (a) drilling in familiar, low-risk territories to tap into larger reserves, (b) concentrating management strength in areas where their expertise can be exploited, (c) steering investment toward more productive wells, (d) maintaining a low overhead and drilling more wells at lower cost, (e) planning to outsource oil and gas processing to Delhi Gas Pipeline Corporation.[1] ♦

Horsehead pump commonly used in drilling for oil.

[1]*Source*: "Ultra Petroleum Corporation," special report, *Oil and Investor* (February 1996): 30–31.

Operations managers are decision makers. To achieve the goals of their organizations, managers must understand how decisions are made and know what decision-making tools to use. To a great extent, the success or failure of people and companies depends on the quality of their decisions. The manager who insisted on launching the space shuttle *Challenger* (which exploded in 1986), despite being told that it should not be launched, did not rise to power within NASA. The talents of Michael Cowpland, chairperson, president, and CEO of Corel Corporation, have made Corel the leading Canadian developer/manufacturer of software.

Model

In this supplement and throughout the text, we use the term *model* over and over. Models lie at the heart of P/OM decision making. A **model** is a representation of reality. It can be a physical model, such as a scale model of a factory or a model of an airplane for use in a wind tunnel. Or it can be a mathematical model, which is even more common. One simple mathematical model you learned in geometry is the formula Area = length × width. Other models can be much more complex and can even represent the operation of a business. Such a model would have variables to account for production costs, transportation costs, inventory costs, and data-handling costs, as well as a wide variety of other possible inputs and outputs.

Models and the techniques of scientific management can help managers:

1. understand how their own companies work
2. understand how other companies work
3. see a way of reducing, or at least understanding, uncertainty that surrounds business plans and actions

Throughout this book, we introduce you to a broad range of models and tools that help operations managers make better decisions. This supplement first examines the analytic decision-making process, then categorizes the models you will be dealing with, and finally introduces decision theory, which is one of the most popular decision-making tools in use.

THE ANALYTIC DECISION PROCESS

What makes the difference between a good decision and a bad decision? A "good" decision, using analytic decision making, is based on logic and considers all available data and possible alternatives. It also follows these six steps:

1. **Define the problem and the factors that influence it.** The problem to be decided must be stated clearly and concisely, which in many cases is the most important and difficult step.
2. **Establish decision criteria and goals.** Managers must develop specific and measurable objectives. Most firms have more than just a goal of maximizing profit.
3. **Formulate a model or relationship between goals and variables.** In other words, we want to develop a representation of the situation—a model. Most models presented in this book contain one or more variables. A variable, as the name implies, is a measurable quantity that may vary or is subject to change.
4. **Identify and evaluate alternatives.** Managers need to generate as many solutions to the problem as possible (and usually quickly). Most managers like to have a *range* or set of options so they can evaluate each option for its merits and drawbacks.

NASA (the U.S. National Aeronautics and Space Administration) awarded Spar Aerospace Limited the contract to develop two flight robotic workstations that will enable astronauts to operate the international space station's MSS (Mobile Service System).

Reasons for NASA's decision include Spar's expertise in the field of robotics, and specifically in robotic arms. They built the Canadarm used by NASA's space shuttle and the manipulator arm used in underground storage tanks containing radioactive waste.

The photo shows the Canadarm at work. Spar has shown they have the technical ability to compete globally.

Source: Canada NewsWire Ltd., "Spar Wins $30 Million NASA Contract to Supply Robotic Workstations for International Space Station," *Financial News*, February 27, 1996.

5. **Select the best alternative.** This is the alternative that best satisfies and is most consistent with the stated goals.
6. **Implement the decision.** Putting into action the steps of the chosen alternative can be the most difficult phase of decision making. Implementation involves making task assignments and a timetable for their completion.

We should point out that these steps do not always follow one another without some looping back to an earlier step. Modifying one or more steps before the final results are implemented is not unusual. Still, making "good" decisions in operations problems means performing all six steps.

MODELS FOR DECISION MAKING

When applied to operations management decisions, the decision process is closely tied to the use of mathematical models and "quantitative" analysis.

There are advantages and disadvantages of modelling. We use models to try to represent the reality of a real system by duplicating its important features, appearance, and characteristics. Models are not a panacea: Indeed, most models are simplifications of the real world. The emphasis in this book is not on model building per se, but on the use of models to help operations managers make decisions. We think you should know:

1. when a model is appropriate and what its assumptions and limitations are
2. what purpose a model might serve in a particular problem

3. how to use the model and produce results
4. how to interpret, in management terms, the results of the model

Advantages and Disadvantages of Using Models

The mathematical models presented in this book are tools that have become widely accepted by managers for several reasons.

1. They are less expensive and disruptive than experimenting with the real-world system.
2. They allow operations managers to ask "what if" types of questions (that is, questions such as "what if" my inventory cost increases 3% next year—how will profits change?).
3. They are built for management problems and encourage management input.
4. They force a consistent and systematic approach to the analysis of problems.
5. They require managers to be specific about constraints and goals relating to a problem.
6. They can help reduce the time needed in decision making.

The main limitations of models are as follows:

1. They may be expensive and time-consuming to develop and test.
2. They are often misused and misunderstood (and feared) because of their mathematical complexity.
3. They tend to downplay the role and value of nonquantifiable information.
4. They often have assumptions that oversimplify the variables of the real world.

The province of Newfoundland has attracted more than $21 million from companies for the rights to drill for oil on 29 parcels of land. The companies must: (1) begin the bidding process for "work commencement" with the successful bidder paying 20% of the bid value up front; (2) begin further testing and analysis and then decide the maximum depth drilled before the site is abandoned; (3) set up a wildcat drill site that becomes their responsibility if it is unsuccessful.

Newfoundland Hunt Co. and Sandhurst Exploration Ltd. took opposing bidding strategies: Hunt bought only two of the more promising parcels for higher prices, and Sandhurst bought thirteen low-cost sites.

Source: "Newfoundland Frontier Draws Hefty Tract Bids," *Oil & Gas Journal* (April 1, 1996): 28.

DECISION THEORY

Decision theory, an analytic approach to choosing the best alternative or course of action, is one of the most widely used and useful of all decision-making tools. Decision theory can be separated into three decision models. These are based on the degree of certainty of the possible outcomes or consequences facing the decision maker. The three types of decision models are as follows:

1. *Decision making under certainty*—the *decision maker knows with certainty* the consequence or outcome of any alternative or decision choice. For example, a decision maker knows with complete certainty that a $100 deposit in a chequing account will result in an increase of $100 in the balance of that account.
2. *Decision making under uncertainty*—the *decision maker does not know the probability* of occurrence of the outcomes for each choice. For example, the probability that Canada Post will be replaced by home-to-home computer networks is unknown.
3. *Decision making under risk*—the *decision maker knows the probability* of occurrence of the outcomes or consequences for each choice. For instance, Chrysler may not know how many of its successful minivans it will sell next year, but the probability of selling more than 450,000 is 0.30.

Fundamentals of Decision Theory

Regardless of the complexity of a decision, all decision makers are faced with alternatives and states of nature. An *alternative* is a course of action or a strategy that a decision maker might choose. A *state of nature* is an occurrence or a situation over which the decision maker has no control. For example, if the Alaskan weather should be unseasonably warm, a temporary ice island for drilling would melt and thus prove to be a very costly decision.

Decision Tables

Decision tables are, quite simply, charts that help define alternatives. For any alternative and a particular state of nature, there is a consequence or outcome, which, in business, is usually expressed as a monetary value. This is called a conditional value. Note that all of the alternatives in Example S1 are listed down the left side of the table, that states of nature are listed across the top, and that conditional values are in the body of the decision table.

Decision tables

EXAMPLE S1

The Getz Products Company is investigating the possibility of producing and marketing backyard storage sheds. Undertaking this project would require the construction of either a large or a small manufacturing plant. The market for the product produced—storage sheds—could be either favourable or unfavourable. Getz, of course, has the option of not developing the new product line at all. With a favourable market, a large facility would give Getz Products a net profit of $200,000. If the market is unfavourable, a $180,000 net loss would occur. A small plant would result in a net profit of $100,000 in a favourable market, but a net loss of $20,000 would be encountered if the market was unfavourable. The following table shows the decision table based on this information.

DECISION TABLE WITH CONDITIONAL VALUES FOR GETZ PRODUCTS

	STATES OF NATURE	
ALTERNATIVES	FAVOURABLE MARKET	UNFAVOURABLE MARKET
Construct large plant	$200,000	–$180,000
Construct small plant	$100,000	–$ 20,000
Do nothing	$0	$0

In Examples S2 and S3, we see how to use decision tables.

DECISION MAKING UNDER CERTAINTY. This is the easiest situation a manager can face. If, for example, Getz Products, the company in Example S1, knows that the market for storage sheds will be favourable, the firm will build a large plant. If the firm is certain the market will be unfavourable, it will do nothing.

DECISION MAKING UNDER UNCERTAINTY. When there is complete *uncertainty* as to which state of nature in a decision table may occur (that is, when we cannot even assess probabilities for each possible outcome), we rely on three decision methods:

Maximax

1. **Maximax**—this method finds an alternative that *max*imizes the *max*imum outcome for every alternative. First, we find the maximum outcome within every alternative, and then we pick the alternative with the maximum number. Because this decision criterion locates the alternative with the *highest* possible *gain*, it has been called an "optimistic" decision criterion.

Maximin

2. **Maximin**—this method finds the alternative that *max*imizes the *min*imum outcome for every alternative. First, we find the minimum outcome within every alternative, and then we pick the alternative with the maximum number. Because this decision criterion locates the alternative that has the *least* possible *loss*, it has been called a "pessimistic" decision criterion.

Equally likely

3. **Equally likely**—this method finds the alternative with the highest average outcome. First, we calculate the average outcome for every alternative, which is the sum of all outcomes divided by the number of outcomes. We then pick the alternative with the maximum number. The equally likely approach assumes that each state of nature is equally likely to occur.

Example S2 applies each of these approaches to the Getz Products Company.

EXAMPLE S2

Given Getz's decision table of Example S1, determine the maximax, maximin, and equally likely decision criteria.

1. The maximax choice is to construct a large plant. This is the *max*imum of the *max*imum number within each row, or alternative.
2. The maximin choice is to do nothing. This is the *max*imum of the *min*imum number within each row, or alternative.
3. The equally likely choice is to construct a small plant. This is the maximum of the average outcome of each alternative. This approach assumes that all outcomes for any alternative are *equally likely*.

	STATES OF NATURE				
ALTERNATIVES	FAVOURABLE MARKET	UNFAVOURABLE MARKET	MAXIMUM IN ROW	MINIMUM IN ROW	ROW AVERAGE
Construct large plant	$200,000	–$180,000	$200,000 ←	–$180,000	$10,000
Construct small plant	$100,000	–$20,000	$100,000	–$20,000	$40,000 ←
Do nothing	$0	$0	$0	$0 ←	$0
			Maximax	Maximin	Equally likely

DECISION MAKING UNDER RISK. Decision making under risk, a more common occurrence, relies on probabilities. Several possible states of nature may occur, each with an assumed probability. Given a decision table with conditional values and probability assessments for all states of nature, we can determine the **expected monetary value (EMV)** for each alternative. This figure represents the expected value or *average* return for each alternative if we could repeat the decision a large number of times. Picking the alternative that has the maximum EMV is one of the most popular decision criteria.

Expected monetary value (EMV)

The EMV for an alternative is the sum of possible payoffs of the alternative, each weighted by the probability of that payoff occurring.

EMV (Alternative *i*) = (payoff of 1st state of nature) × (probability of 1st state of nature)
+ (payoff of 2nd state of nature) × (probability of 2nd state of nature)
+ . . . + (payoff of last state of nature) × (probability of last state of nature)

Example S3 shows how a sample EMV is calculated.

EXAMPLE S3

Getz Products' P/OM manager believes that the probability of a favourable market is exactly the same as that of an unfavourable market. This is, each state of nature has a 0.50 chance. We can now determine the EMV for each alternative (see the following table).

	STATES OF NATURE	
ALTERNATIVES	FAVOURABLE MARKET	UNFAVOURABLE MARKET
Construct large plant	$200,000	–$180,000
Construct small plant	$100,000	–$20,000
Do nothing	$0	$0
Probabilities	0.50	0.50

1. EMV (large plant) = (0.5)($200,000) + (0.5)(–$180,000) = $10,000
2. EMV (small plant) = (0.5)($100,000) + (0.5)(–$20,000) = $40,000
3. EMV (do nothing) = (0.5)($0) + (0.5)($0) = $0

The maximum EMV is seen in the second alternative, constructing a small plant. Thus, according to the EMV decision criterion, we would build the small facility.

EXPECTED VALUE OF PERFECT INFORMATION (EVPI). If a manager were able to determine which state of nature would occur, then he or she would know which decision to make. Once a manager knows which decision to make, the payoff increases because the payoff is now a certainty, not a probability. Because the payoff will increase if we know which state of nature will occur, this knowledge, or "perfect information," has value. Therefore, we now look at how to determine the value of this information. We call this difference between the payoff under certainty and the payoff under risk the **expected value of perfect information (EVPI)**.

Expected value of perfect information (EVPI)

EVPI = expected value under certainty − maximum EMV

Expected value under certainty

To find the EVPI, we must first compute the **expected value under certainty**, which is the average return based on perfect information. In order to calculate this value, we choose the best alternative for each state of nature and multiply its payoff by the probability for that state of nature.

Expected value under certainty = (best outcome or consequence for 1st state of nature) × (probability of 1st state of nature) + (best outcome for 2nd state of nature) × (probability of 2nd state of nature) + . . . + (best outcome for last state of nature) × (probability of last state of nature)

In Example S4, we use the data and decision table from Example S3 to examine the expected value of perfect information.

EXAMPLE S4

Suppose Getz Products' P/OM manager has been approached by a marketing research firm that proposed to help him make the decision about whether or not to build the plant to produce storage sheds. The marketing researchers claim that their technical analysis will tell Getz with certainty whether or not the market is favourable for the proposed product. In other words, it will change Getz's environment from one of decision making under risk to one of decision making under certainty. This information could prevent Getz Products from making a very expensive mistake. The marketing research firm would charge Getz $65,000 for the information. What would you recommend to Getz? Should the P/OM manager hire the firm to make the marketing study? Even if the information from the study is perfectly accurate, is it worth $65,000? What would it be worth? Determining the value of such *perfect information* can be very useful. It places an upper bound on what Getz would be willing to spend on information.

By referring to the table in Example S3, Getz's manager can calculate the maximum that he or she would pay for information, that is, the EVPI. First, he or she computes the expected value under certainty, and then, using this information, calculates the EVPI. The procedure is outlined as follows.

1. The best outcome for the state of nature "favourable market" is "build a large facility" with a payoff of $200,000. The best outcome for the state of nature "unfavourable market" is "do nothing" with a payoff of $0.

   Expected value under certainty = ($200,000)(0.50) + ($0)(0.50) = $100,000

   Thus, if we had perfect information, we would expect (on the average) $100,000 if the decision could be repeated many times.

2. The maximum EMV is $40,000, which is the expected outcome without perfect information.

$$\text{EVPI} = \text{expected value under certainty} - \text{maximum EMV}$$
$$= \$100{,}000 - \$40{,}000 = \$60{,}000$$

Thus, the *most* Getz Products should be willing to pay for perfect information is $60,000. This, of course, is again based on the assumption that the probability of each state of nature is 0.50.

Decision Trees

Any decision that can be placed in a decision table can also be placed in a decision tree. A **decision tree** is a graphic display of the decision process that indicates decision alternatives, states of nature and their respective probabilities, and payoffs for each combination of alternative and state of nature. Decision trees are most useful for problems that include *sequential* decisions and states of nature. When later decisions depend on the outcomes of prior ones, decision tables are too difficult to structure. Decision trees are *much* easier to visualize.

Decision tree

Two symbols are used in decision trees:

1. □—a decision node from which one of several alternatives may be selected.
2. ○—a state of nature node out of which one state of nature will occur.

In constructing a decision tree, we must be sure that all alternatives and states of nature are in their correct and logical places and that we include *all* possible alternatives and states of nature. Example S5 presents a sample decision tree.

EXAMPLE S5

Figure S2.1 presents a decision tree for Getz Products, using the symbols just introduced.

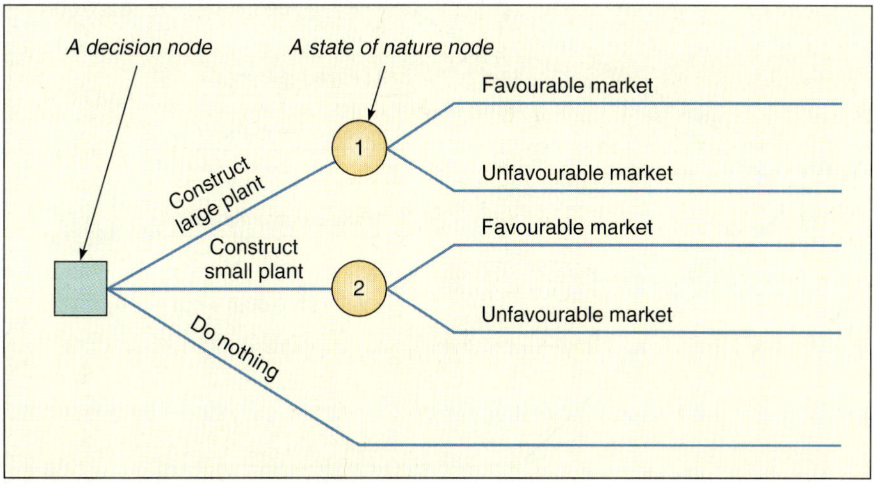

FIGURE S2.1 ■ Getz' Decision Tree

Although all previously discussed decision criteria apply to decision trees, expected monetary value (EMV) is the most commonly used and usually the most appropriate criterion for decision-tree analysis. Early steps in the analysis are to graph the decision tree and to specify the monetary consequences of all possible outcomes on the tree for a particular siuation.

Analyzing problems with *decision trees* involves five steps:

1. Define the problem.
2. Structure or draw the decision tree.
3. Assign probabilities to the states of nature.
4. Estimate payoffs for each possible combination of alternatives and states of nature.
5. Solve the problem by computing monetary values (EMV) for each state of nature node. This is done by working *backward*, that is, by starting at the right of the tree and working back to decision nodes on the left.

EXAMPLE S6

We present a completed and solved decision tree for Getz Products in Figure S2.2. Note that the payoffs are placed at the right-hand side of each of the tree's branches. The probabilities (first used by Getz in Example S3) are placed in parentheses next to each state of nature. The expected monetary values for each state of nature node are then calculated and placed by their respective nodes. The EMV of the first node is $10,000. This represents the branch from the decision node to construct a large plant. The EMV for node 2, to construct a small plant, is $40,000. Building no plant or doing nothing has, of course, a payoff of $0. The branch leaving the decision node leading to the state of nature node with the highest EMV will be chosen. In Getz's case, a small plant should be built.

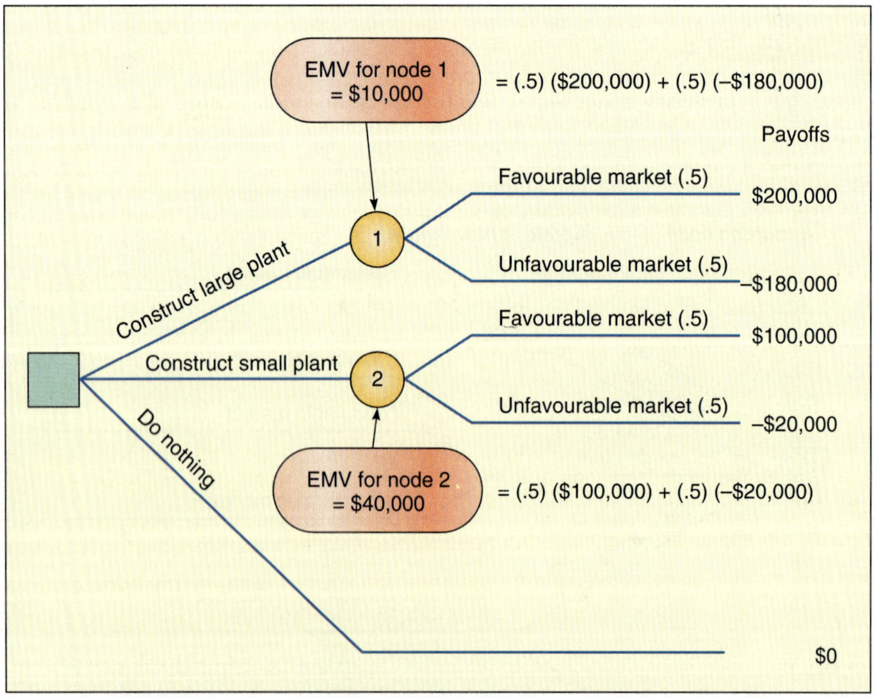

FIGURE S2.2 ■ Completed and Solved Decision Tree for Getz Products

A MORE COMPLEX DECISION TREE. As we mentioned before, when a *sequence* of decisions must be made, decision trees are much more powerful tools than decision tables. Let us say that Getz Products has two decisions to make, with the second decision dependent on the outcome of the first. Before deciding about building a new plant, Getz has the option of conducting its own marketing research survey, at a cost of $10,000. The information from this survey could help the company decide whether to build a large plant or a small plant, or not to build at all. Getz Products recognizes that such a market survey will not provide it with *perfect* information, but may *help* quite a bit nevertheless.

Getz's new decision tree is represented in Figure S2.3 of Example S7. Take a careful look at this more complex tree. Note that *all possible outcomes and alternatives* are included in their logical sequence. This is one strength of using decision trees in making decisions. The manager is forced to examine all possible outcomes, including unfavourable ones. He or she is also forced to make decisions in a logical, sequential manner.

EXAMPLE S7

Examining the tree in Figure S2.3, we see that Getz's first decision point is whether to conduct the $10,000 market survey. If it chooses *not* to do the study (the lower part of the tree), it must decide to build a large plant, a small plant, or no plant. This is Getz's second decision point. The market will either be favourable (0.50 probability) or unfavourable (also 0.50 probability) if it builds. The payoffs for each of the possible consequences are listed along the right-hand side. In fact, this lower portion of Getz's tree is *identical* to the simpler decision tree shown in Figure S2.2.

The upper part of Figure S2.3 reflects the decision to conduct the market survey. State of nature node number 1 has two branches coming out of it. Let us say there is a 45% chance that the survey results will indicate a favourable market for the storage sheds. We also note that the probability is .55 that the survey results will be negative.

The rest of the probabilities shown in parentheses in Figure S2.3 are all *conditional* probabilities. For example, 0.78 is the probability of a favourable market for the sheds *given* a favourable result from the market survey. Of course, you would expect to find a high probability of a favourable market given that the research indicated that the market was good. Do not forget, though, that there is a chance that Getz's $10,000 market survey did not result in perfect or even reliable information. Any market research study is subject to error. In this case, there's a 22% chance that the market for sheds will be unfavourable given that the survey results are positive.

Likewise, we note that there is a 27% chance that the market for sheds will be favourable given that Getz's survey results are negative. The probability is much higher (0.73) that the market will actually be unfavourable given that the survey was negative.

Finally, when we look to the payoff column in Figure S2.3, we see that $10,000—the cost of the marketing study—had to be subtracted from each of the top 10 tree branches. Thus, a large plant with a favourable market would normally net a $200,000 profit. But because the market study was conducted, this figure is reduced by $10,000. In the unfavourable case, the loss of $180,000 would increase to $190,000. Similarly, conducting the survey and building *no plant* now result in a –$10,000 payoff.

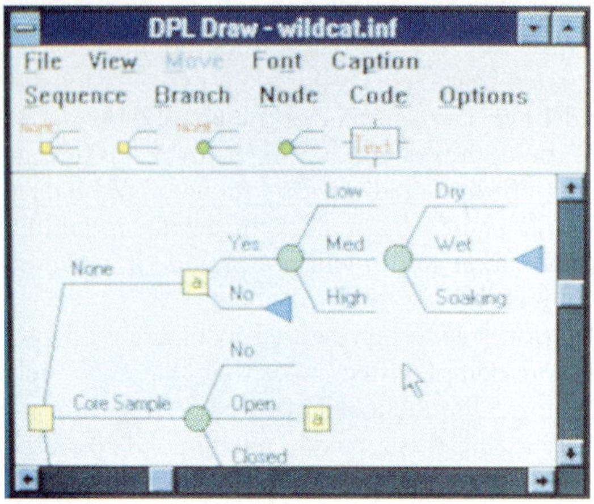

Decision tree software is a relatively new advance that permits users to solve decision analysis problems with flexibility, power, and ease. Programs such as DPL and Supertree allow decision problems to be analyzed with less effort and in greater depth than ever before. Full-colour presentations of options open to managers always have impact. In this photo wildcat drilling options are explored with DPL, a product of Applied Decision Analysis in Menlo Park, CA.

With all probabilities and payoffs specified, we can start calculating the expected monetary value of each of the branches. We begin at the end or right-hand side of the decision tree and work back toward the origin. When we finish, the best decision will be known.

1. Given favourable survey results,

$$\text{EMV(node 2)} = (.78)(\$190{,}000) + (.22)(-\$190{,}000) = \$106{,}400$$

$$\text{EMV(node 3)} = (.78)(\$90{,}000) + (.22)(-\$30{,}000) = \$63{,}600$$

The EMV of no plant in this case is –$10,000. Thus, if the survey results are favourable, a large plant should be built.

2. Given negative survey results,

$$\text{EMV(node 4)} = (.27)(\$190{,}000) + (.73)(-\$190{,}000) = -\$87{,}400$$

$$\text{EMV(node 5)} = (.27)(\$90{,}000) + (.73)(-\$30{,}000) = \$2{,}400$$

The EMV of no plant is again –$10,000 for this branch. Thus, given a negative survey result, Getz should build a small plant with an expected value of $2,400.

3. Continuing on the upper part of the tree and moving backward, we compute the expected value of conducting the market survey.

$$\text{EMV(node 1)} = (.45)(\$106{,}400) + (.55)(\$2{,}400) = \$49{,}200$$

4. If the market survey is *not* conducted,

$$\text{EMV(node 6)} = (.50)(\$200{,}000) + (.50)(-\$180{,}000) = \$10{,}000$$

$$\text{EMV(node 7)} = (.50)(\$100{,}000) + (.50)(-\$20{,}000) = \$40{,}000$$

The EMV of no plant is $0. Thus, building a small plant is the best choice, given the marketing research is not performed.

5. Because the expected monetary value of conducting the survey is $49,200—versus an EMV of $40,000 for not conducting the study—the best choice is to *seek marketing information*. If the survey results are favourable, Getz should build the large plant. But if the research is negative, it should build the small plant.

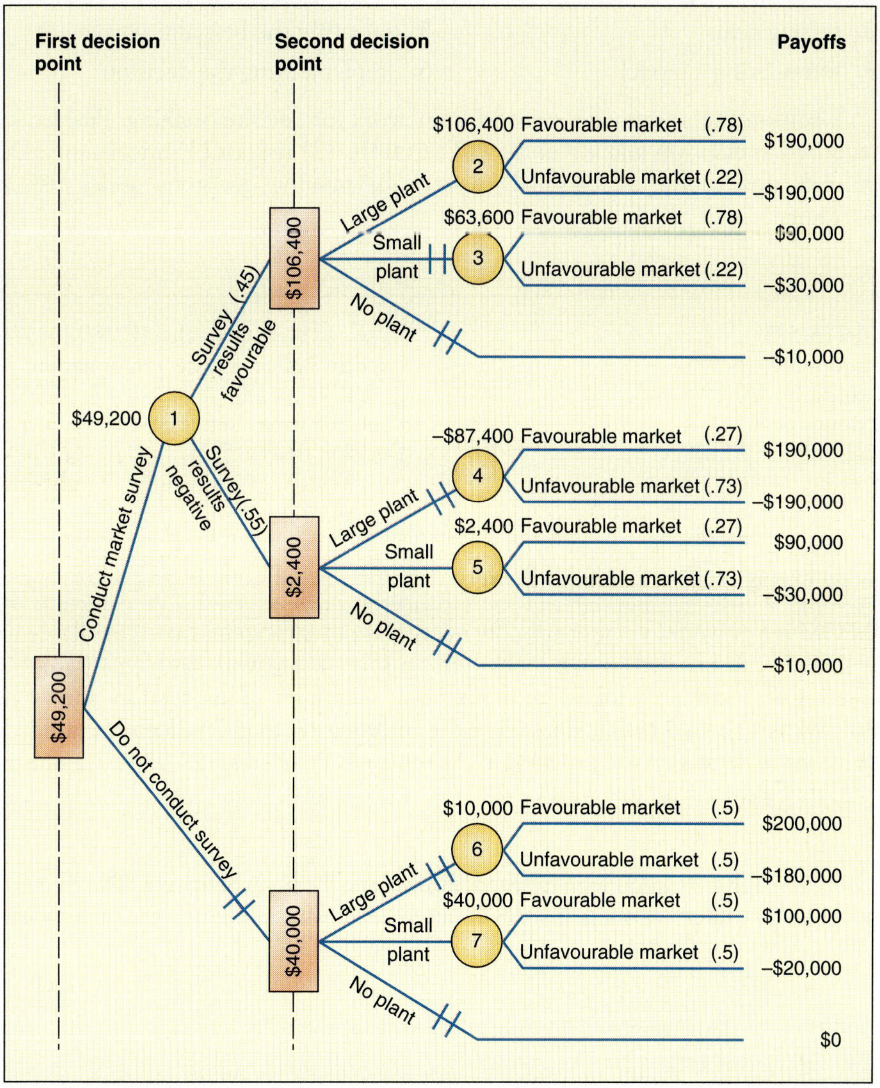

FIGURE S2.3 ■ Getz' Decision Tree with Probabilities and EMVs Shown. The short parallel lines mean "prune" that branch; it is less favourable than another available option and thus can be dropped.

SUMMARY

Operations managers make many important decisions. They must decide on investment levels for product development, for plants and equipment, and for new buildings. They decide what inventory levels are appropriate, when to schedule workers, and when to perform maintenance. Successful decision makers use all the tools available to them, including mathematical models. They also follow a process that involves six steps:

1. defining the problem
2. setting goals
3. formulating a model
4. identifying alternative solutions
5. selecting the best alternative
6. implementing the decision

Decision theory provides a useful framework for decision making. Problems are categorized as decision making under (1) certainty, (2) risk, or (3) uncertainty. Decision trees and tables are especially useful for making decisions under risk and uncertainty.

KEY TERMS

Model (p. 52)
Decision table (p. 55)
Maximax (p. 56)
Maximin (p. 56)
Equally likely (p. 56)
Expected monetary value (EMV) (p. 57)
Expected value of perfect information (EVPI) (p. 58)
Expected value under certainty (p. 58)
Decision tree (p. 59)

USING AB:POM AND SPREADSHEETS TO SOLVE DECISION-THEORY PROBLEMS

Solving Examples S1–S4 with AB:POM

AB:POM is a powerful yet user-friendly microcomputer program that is available with this text. It can be used in many chapters to solve homework problems (which are marked with computer logos) and textbook examples. This section shows how AB:POM can be used to calculate all of the information found in decision tables. We provide more details on the program in Appendix F. Programs S2.1 and S2.2 illustrate how Getz Products can use AB:POM to provide decision-theory calculations.

PROGRAM S2.1 ■ AB:POM's Decision Table Program with Screens Shown for a Three-Alternative, Two States-of-Nature Problem. Once we respond with three alternatives, two states of nature, and maximize profit, the table below appears. In Program S2.2, inputs and outputs are all shown.

Decision Tables

Number of alternatives (2–10) 3 Number of nature states (2–8) 2

Profits -maximize profits

Sample Screen

Probability→	0.000	0.000
	state 1	state 2
alternatv 1	0	0
alternatv 2	0	0
alternatv 3	0	0

PROGRAM S2.2 ■ AB:POM Output for Example S1–S4 (Getz Products). We entered all the shaded data, including the labels "LG. FACILITY," "FAV MKT," and so on. Probabilities must sum to 1.

GETZ PRODUCTS EXAMPLES S2–S5

Probability →	0.500	0.500			
	FAV MKT	BAD MKT	EMV	Row Min	Row Max
LG. FACILITY	200000	-180000	10000	−180000	200000
SM. FACILITY	100000	-20000	40000	−20000	100000
DO NOTHING	0	0	0	0	0
		column maximum →	40000	0	200000

The maximum expected monetary value is 40000 given by SM. FACILITY
The maximin is 0 given by DO NOTHING
The maximax is 200000 given by LG. FACILITY

PERFECT 200000 0 100000←EV under certainty
The expected value of perfect information is 60000

Using a Spreadsheet to Solve Examples S1–S4

An entirely different approach to working with decision-theory calculations is to build your own model, unique to each problem, with a spreadsheet program such as Lotus, Excel, Quattro, Visicalc, or others.

Program S2.3 shows the spreadsheet formulas needed to compute the expected monetary values and EVPI for Getz Products. For example, the formula +$B$12*B8 + $C$12*C8 is used to multiply the probability values times the monetary outcomes to get an EMV of $10,000 for the large facility in cell D8. Note the use of $, which creates an absolute cell. An absolute cell makes copying the general formula in Cell D8 to cells D9 and D10 easier.

Cells D9 and D10 contain EMV values for the other alternatives. Cell D14 computes the maximum EMV with the formula @MAX(D8 . . D10) to be $40,000. Cell D15 computes a value for EVPI using the same type of approach discussed in the chapter.

PROGRAM S2.3 ■ Using a Spreadsheet to Compute EMV Values for Getz Products (Examples S1–S4). This "symbolic" spreadsheet shows Getz' data and the formulas used in calculations.

	A	B	C	D
1	Expected Monetary Value			
2				
3	States	Favourable	Unfavourable	EMV
4	of Nature	Market	Market	Computed
5				
6	Alternatives			
7				
8	Large Facility	200000	−180000	+$B$12*B8+$C$12*C8
9	Small Facility	100000	−20000	+$B$12*B9+$C$12*C9
10	Do Nothing	0	0	+$B$12*B10+$C$12*C10
11				
12	Probabilities	0.5	0.5	
13				
14	Maximum EMV =			@MAX(D8 . . D10)
15	EVPI =			@MAX(B8 . . B10)*B12+ @MAX(C8 . . C10)*C12–D14

SOLVED PROBLEM

Solved Problem S2.1

Daily demand for cases of Tidy Bowl cleaner at Ravinder Nath's Supermarket has always been 5, 6, or 7 cases. Develop a decision tree that illustrates her decision alternatives as to whether to stock 5, 6, or 7 cases.

Solution

The decision tree is shown in Figure S2.4.

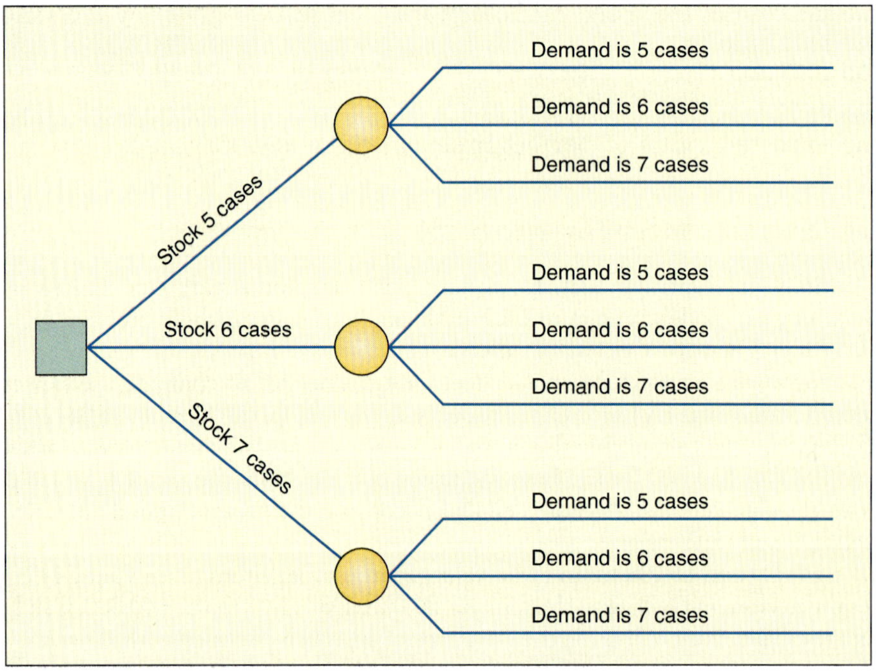

FIGURE S2.4 ■ Demand at Ravinder Nath's Supermarket

DISCUSSION QUESTIONS

1. Describe each step in the decision process.
2. Why do operations managers build models? What kind of models are most useful?
3. Give an example of a good decision you made that resulted in a bad outcome. Also give an example of a bad decision you made that had a good outcome. Why was each decision good or bad?
4. What is an alternative? What is a state of nature?
5. Discuss the differences between decision making under certainty, under risk, and under uncertainty.
6. Jenine Duffey is trying to decide whether to invest in real estate, stocks, or certificates of deposit. How well she does depends on whether the economy enters a period of recession or inflation. Develop a decision table (excluding the conditional values) to describe this situation.
7. Describe the meaning of EMV and EVPI. Provide an example in which EVPI can help a manager.
8. What techniques are used to solve decision-making problems under uncertainty? Which technique results

in an optimistic decision? Which technique results in a pessimistic decision?

9. What is the most conservative method of making a decision under uncertainty? Why?

10. What are the five steps used in analyzing a problem with a decision tree?

11. When is a decision tree preferred over a decision table?

CRITICAL THINKING EXERCISE

A robust 60-year-old male college professor has just been diagnosed as having a defective heart valve. Although he is otherwise healthy, his condition could prove fatal if left untreated. Based on current research, chances of survival *without* surgery would be as follows: a 50% chance of living 1 year, a 20% chance of surviving for 2 years, a 20% rate for 5 years, and a 10% chance of living to age 68. The probability of survival beyond age 68 without an operation is extremely low.

The operation, however, is a serious surgical procedure. Five percent of the patients succumb during the operation or its recovery stage, with an additional 45% dying during the first year after surgery. Twenty percent survive for 5 years, 13% survive for 10 years, and 8%, 5%, and 4% survive for 15, 20, and 25 years, respectively.

How would you evaluate this critical situation if the person described was a close relative? Discuss all the factors to be considered.

PROBLEMS

• **S2.1** Given the following conditional value table, determine the appropriate decision under uncertainty using:

a) maximax

b) maximin

c) equally likely

	STATES OF NATURE		
ALTERNATIVES	VERY FAVOURABLE MARKET	AVERAGE MARKET	UNFAVOURABLE MARKET
Large plant	$275,000	$100,000	–$150,000
Small plant	$200,000	$60,000	–$10,000
Overtime	$100,000	$40,000	–$1,000
Do nothing	$0	$0	$0

• **S2.2** G. W. Willis's company is considering expansion of its current facility to meet increasing demand. If demand is high in the future, the major expansion would result in an additional net profit of $800,000, but if demand is low, there would be a loss of $300,000. If demand is high, the minor expansion will result in an increase in net profits of $200,000, but if demand is low, there is a loss of $100,000. The company has the option of not expanding. If there is a 50% chance the demand will be high, what should the company do to maximize the long-run average profits?

: **S2.3** Foto Colour is a small supplier of chemicals and equipment used by some photographic stores to process 35-mm film. One product that Foto colour supplies is BC-6. Doug Niles, president of Foto Colour, normally stocks 11, 12, or 13 cases of BC-6 each week. For each case that Doug sells, he receives a profit of $35. BC-6, like many photographic chemicals, has a very short shelf life. If a case is not sold by the end of the week Doug must discard it. Since each case costs Doug $56, he loses $56 for every case that is not sold by the end of the week. There is a probability of 0.45 of selling 11 cases, a probability of 0.35 of selling 12 cases, and a probability of 0.2 of selling 13 cases.

a) What is your recommended course of action?

b) If Doug is able to develop BC-6 with an ingredient that stabilizes BC-6 so that it no longer has to be discarded, how would this change your recommended course of action?

S2.4 Young Cheese Company is a small manufacturer of several different cheese products. One product is a cheese spread that is sold to retail outlets. Peg Young must decide how many cases of cheese spread to manufacture each month. The probability that the demand will be 6 cases is 0.1, for 7 cases it is 0.3, for 8 cases it is 0.5, and for 9 cases it is 0.1. The cost of every case is $45, and the price Peg gets for each case is $95. Unfortunately, any cases not sold by the end of the month are of no value as a result of spoilage. How many cases of cheese should Peg manufacture each month?

S2.5 Kamlesh Mehta, chief engineer at Domtar Chemical, Inc., has to decide whether or not to build a new processing facility, using the latest technology. If the new processing facility works, the company could realize a profit of $200,000. If the processing facility fails, the company could lose $150,000. At this time, Mehta estimates there is a 60% chance that the new process will fail.

The other option is to build a pilot plant and then decide whether or not to build a complete facility. The pilot plant would cost $10,000 to build. Mehta estimates there is a 50/50 chance the pilot plant will work. If the pilot plant works, there is a 90% probability that the complete plant, if it is built, will work. If the pilot plant project does not work, there is only a 20% chance that the complete project (if it is constructed) will work. Mehta faces a dilemma. Should he build the plant? Should he build the pilot project and then make a decision? Help Mehta by analyzing this decision-theory problem.

S2.6 Stanley Shader, president of SS Industries, is considering whether or not to build a manufacturing plant in the Maritimes. His decision is summarized in the following table:

ALTERNATIVES	FAVOURABLE MARKET	UNFAVOURABLE MARKET
Build large plant	$400,000	–$300,000
Build small plant	$80,000	–$10,000
Don't build	$0	$0
Market probabilities	0.4	0.6

a) Construct a decision tree.

b) Determine the best strategy, using expected monetary value (EMV).

c) What is the expected value of perfect information (EVPI)?

S2.7 Varzandeh Mfg. Corp. buys on-off switches from two suppliers. The quality of the switches from the suppliers is indicated below:

PERCENT DEFECTIVE	PROBABILITY FOR SUPPLIER A	PROBABILITY FOR SUPPLIER B
1	0.70	0.30
3	0.20	0.40
5	0.10	0.30

For example, the probability of getting a batch of switches that are 1% defective from supplier A is 0.70. Because Varzandeh orders 10,000 switches per order, this would mean that there is a 0.7 probability of getting 100 defective switches out of the 10,000 switches if supplier A is used to fill the order. A defective switch can be repaired for $0.50. Although the quality of supplier B is lower, it will sell an order of 10,000 switches for $37 less than supplier A.

a) Develop a decision tree.

b) Which supplier should Varzandeh use?

: **S2.8** Mary Fischer, a concessionaire for the local arena, has developed a table of conditional values for the various alternatives (stocking decision) and states of nature (size of crowd).

	STATES OF NATURE (SIZE OF CROWD)		
ALTERNATIVES	LARGE	AVERAGE	SMALL
Large inventory	$20,000	$10,000	–$2,000
Average inventory	$15,000	$12,000	$6,000
Small inventory	$9,000	$6,000	$5,000

If the probabilities associated with the states of nature are 0.30 for a large crowd, 0.50 for an average crowd, and 0.20 for a small crowd, determine:

a) the alternative that provides the greatest expected monetary value (EMV)

b) the expected value of perfect information (EVPI)

: **S2.9** Even though independent gasoline stations have been having a difficult time, Susan Helms has been thinking about starting her own independent gasoline station. Susan's problem is to decide how large her station should be. The annual returns will depend on both the size of her station and a number of marketing factors related to the oil industry and demand for gasoline. After a careful analysis, Susan developed the following table.

SIZE OF FIRST STATION	GOOD MARKET ($)	FAIR MARKET ($)	POOR MARKET ($)
Small	50,000	20,000	–10,000
Medium	80,000	30,000	–20,000
Large	100,000	30,000	–40,000
Very large	300,000	25,000	–160,000

For example, if Susan constructs a small station and the market is good, she will realize a profit of $50,000.

a) Develop a decision table for this decsion.

b) What is the maximax decision?

c) What is the maximin decision?

d) What is the equally likely decision?

:S2.10 Using the data in Problem S2.9, develop a decision tree and determine the best decision based on the highest expected monetary value criteria. Assume each outcome is equally likely.

:S2.11 Lynn Heinrichs is hospital administrator for Burnaby Hospital. She is trying to determine whether to build a large wing on the existing hospital, a small wing, or no wing at all. If the population of Burnaby continues to grow, a large wing could return $150,000 to the hospital each year. If the small wing were built, it would return $60,000 to the hospital each year if the population continues to grow. If the population of Burnaby remains the same, the hospital would encounter a loss of $85,000 if the large wing were built. Furthermore, a loss of $45,000 would be realized if the small wing were constructed and the population remains the same. Unfortunately, Lynn does not have any information about the future population of Burnaby.

a) Construct a decision tree.

b) Construct a decision table.

c) Using the equally likely criterion, determine the best alternative.

d) If the likelihood of growth is 0.6 and that of remaining the same is 0.4, and the decision criterion is expected monetary value, what decision should Lynn make?

•S2.12 Jim Higgins is considering opening a bicycle shop in Regina. Jim enjoys biking, but this is to be a business endeavour from which he expects to make a living. Jim can open a small shop, a large shop, or no shop at all. Because there will be a 5-year lease on the building that Jim is thinking about using, he wants to make sure he makes the correct decision. Jim is also thinking about hiring his old marketing professor to conduct a marketing research study to see if there is a market for his services. From the studies conducted, the results could be either favourable or unfavourable. Develop a decision tree for Jim.

:S2.13 Jim Higgins (of Problem S2.12) has done some analysis of his bicycle shop decision. If Jim builds a large shop he will earn $60,000 if the market is favourable, but he will lose $40,000 if the market is unfavourable. The small shop will return a $30,000 profit with a favourable market and a $10,000 loss if the market is unfavourable. At the present time, he believes there is a 50/50 chance that there will be a favourable market. His old marketing professor will charge him $5,000 for the market research. He has estimated that there is a 0.6 probability that the market will be favourable. Furthermore there is a 0.9 probability that the market will be favourable given a favourable outcome of the study. However, the marketing professor has warned Jim that there is a probability of only 0.12 of a favourable market if the marketing research results are not favourable. Expand the decision tree of Problem S2.12 to help Jim decide what to do.

•S2.14 Dick Szecsy is not sure what he should do. He can build either a large video rental section or a small one in his drugstore. He can also gather additional information, or simply do nothing. If he gathers additional information, the results could suggest either a favourable or an unfavourable market, but it would cost him $3,000 to gather the information. Dick believes that there is a 50/50 chance that the information will be favourable. If the rental market is favourable, Dick will earn $15,000 with the large section or $5,000 with the small. With an unfavourable video rental market, however, Dick could lose $20,000 with the large section or $10,000 with the small section. Without gathering additional information, Dick estimates that the probability of a favourable rental market is 0.7. A favourable report from the study would increase the probability of a favourable rental market to 0.9. Furthermore, an unfavourable report from the additional information would decrease the probability of a favourable rental market to 0.4. Of course, Dick could forget all of these numbers and do nothing. What is your advice to Dick?

:S2.15 Bakery Products is considering the introduction of a new line of products. In order to produce the new line, the bakery is considering either a major or a minor renovation of the current plant. The following conditional values table has been developed by the bakery.

ALTERNATIVES	FAVOURABLE MARKET	UNFAVOURABLE MARKET
Major renovation	$100,000	–$90,000
Minor renovation	$40,000	–$20,000
Do nothing	$0	$0

Under the assumption that the probability of a favourable market is equal to the probability of an unfavourable market, determine:

a) the appropriate decision tree showing payoffs and probabilities

b) the best alternative using expected monetary value (EMV)

:S2.16 Assume that the research and development department at BRK Labs, Inc., a small pharmaceutical company, has tentatively found an ointment that grows hair. This discovery adds substantial value to BRK Labs. As president of BRK, you must make a recommendation to the investors. You face three choices: first, to sell the discovery to a larger drug company—it is worth $10 million; second, to begin experimental laboratory testing and *then* make a decision, or third, to arrange financing for an all-out, aggressive marketing program, with the hope that testing and development will go well along the way. The real goal of this third option is to move so fast that the competition is left with little chance of catching up.

The experimental laboratory testing program will cost $5 million, and there is a 50/50 chance that favourable results will be found and survive FDA review prior to a larger company's preempting BRK Labs. Occasionally, even with unfavourable test results, alternative uses for a drug are found; but this occurs only about once in 10 cases, and the value of the formula still drops to only $1 million. On the other hand, if a favourable formulation is found, you estimate the discovery and results are worth $20 million. But because BRK Labs is a small company with limited resources and marketing ability, even with favourable laboratory test results, the chance of BRK Labs successfully getting the product approved and on the market is only about 40%. Even with favourable laboratory test results and a decision to market, costs will include not only $5 million in test costs but also an additional $3 million for marketing.

The third choice for BRK Labs is to proceed aggressively on its own and aim for the marketing coup of the decade. As president, you figure there is only about one chance in five of BRK's doing this. However, the payoff from BRK's doing this successfully is $100 million. (This figure is five times greater than the results mentioned earlier because the $20 million reflects the potential for a competitor to enter the market while BRK is in experimental testing.) Under this third choice, marketing costs are $3 million and testing will cost $5 million. Both of these expenses apply for this option whether the product is ultimately successful or not.

a) Draw the decision tree.

b) Determine the expected monetary value (EMV).

c) What do you recommend to the investors? How might this recommendation differ based on the firm's financial status?

d) How sensitive is this solution to changes in probabilities? Does this change your conclusion?

CASE STUDY

Western Leather Company

The Western Leather Company of Vancouver, B.C., has been producing leather goods for more than 30 years. It purchases prepared hides from tanners and produces leather clothing accessories such as wallets, belts, and handbags. The firm has just developed a new leather product and has prepared a 1-year production and sales plan for it. The new product is best described as a combination billfold, key case, and credit card carrier. As company president Peggy Lane has noted, "It is a super carryall for small this-and-thats." Lane has placed her administrative assistant, Harold Hamilton, in charge of the project.

Hamilton has established that material and variable overhead for the carryall should be about \$1.50 per case over the next year, given a 5-day week and no overtime. Unit labour and machining costs, however, depend on the choice of machine that will be used for production. Hamilton has narrowed the choice down to two specialized pieces of equipment. Machine 1 is a semiautomated machine that will cut the material to the size needed for one unit and also will sew it, install the rings and snaps, and emboss it with two types of designs. This machine costs \$250,000 and will add \$2.50 to the average variable cost for labour and other machine-related costs. This piece of equipment has a production capacity of 640 units per day. However, estimated downtime for maintenance and repairs is 12.5% (1/8 the time).

Machine 2 is fully automated. It cuts, sews, installs rings and snaps, and is capable of embossing the case with three types of designs. This machine costs \$350,000 and will add \$1.75 to the average variable cost for labour and other machine-related costs. Machine 2 has a higher production capacity (estimated at 800 units per day) than the semiautomated machine. However, estimated downtime is 25% (1/4 the time), consistent with its greater complexity.

Marketing estimates for the next year have been more difficult to project than production costs and capacity estimates. However, \$6.00 seems the likeliest selling price for the carryall. This price brings it into line with comparable products on the market, but because it offers more than these products it has the potential to outsell them. Sales volume estimates seem to centre on 140,000 units for the year. Analysis of the potential market has been difficult because this new product is different from similar ones now being sold. Hamilton's best estimates of sales at \$6.00 per unit and the probabilities attached to these volumes are in Table 1.

TABLE 1 ■ THE WESTERN LEATHER COMPANY FIRST-YEAR SALES VOLUME ESTIMATE

SALES VOLUME	PROBABILITY
120,000 units	0.15
130,000 units	0.25
140,000 units	0.40
150,000 units	0.15
160,000 units	0.05

Given these marketing estimates and the machine capacities, the company will have to decide either to modify the machines in order to increase capacity or work overtime if demand is at the higher levels. This decision can be made based on the first week's worth of sales, which are expected to be a good indicator of the annual sales level. Overtime premiums would raise the costs by \$1.20 per case on the semiautomated machine and by \$0.90 on the fully automated machine. Modification of Machine 1, the semiautomatic one, would cost \$15,000 to meet the highest levels of sales. Modifications of Machine 2 would cost \$20,000.

Lane has directed Hamilton to make a decision based on first-year sales, since demand for a product such as this is uncertain after its initial popularity passes. Western operates on a fifty-week year, because the company usually closes down for the holidays.

DISCUSSION QUESTIONS

1. Using a decision tree (show *all* work) based on maximizing expected profit, decide which

(Continued)

machine Western Leather should select. Should overtime be scheduled or should the machine be modified, and under what circumstances?

2. Set up a payoff matrix for the sales volumes given (assume the machines cannot be modified and overtime is used) and assume that the probability of occurrence of the five levels of sales are not known. Then, decide which machine should be purchased using:
   a) the maximax criterion
   b) the maximin criterion
   c) the equally likely criterion

Source: Professor Michael Ballot, University of the Pacific. Modified for the Canadian edition.

BIBLIOGRAPHY

Brown, R. "Do Managers Find Decision Theory Useful?" *Harvard Business Review* (May/June 1970): 78–89.

Brown, R. V. "The State of the Art of Decision Analysis: A Personal Perspective." *Interfaces*, 22, no. 6 (November/December 1992): 5–14.

Canada NewsWire Ltd., "Spar Wins $30 Million NASA Contract to Supply Robotic Workstations for International Space Station," *Financial News*, February 26, 1996.

Dantzig, G. B. "The Diet Problem." *Interfaces*, 20, no. 4 (July/August 1990): 43–47.

Gass, S. I. "Model World: Models at the OK Corral." *Interfaces*, 21, no. 6 (November/December 1991): 80.

Green, A. E. S. "Finding the Japanese Fleet." *Interfaces*, 23, no. 5 (September/October 1993): 62.

Hess, S. W. "Swinging on the Branch of a Tree: Project Selection Applications." *Interfaces*, 23, no. 6 (November/December 1993): 5–12.

Kirkwood, C. W. "An Overview of Methods for Applied Decision Analysis." *Interfaces*, 22, no. 6 (November/December 1992): 28–39.

Lane, M. S., A. H. Mansour, and J. L. Harpell. "Operations Research Techniques: A Longitudinal Update 1973–1988." *Interfaces*, 23, no. 2 (March/April 1993): 63–68.

Lev, B. "Airline Operations Research." *Interfaces*, 20, no. 3 (May/June 1990): 99.

Moore, E. W., Jr., J. M. Warke, and L. R. Gorban. "The Indispensable Role of Management Science in Centralizing Freight Operations at Reynolds Metals Company." *Interfaces*, 21, no. 1 (January/February 1991): 107–129.

Pratt, J. W., H. Raiffa, and R. Schlaifer. *Introduction to Statistical Decision Theory*. New York: McGraw-Hill, 1965.

Raiffa, H. *Decision Analysis: Introductory Lectures on Choices Under Certainty*. Reading, MA: Addison-Wesley, 1968.

Render, B., and R. M. Stair, Jr. *Introduction to Management Science*. Boston: Allyn and Bacon, 1992.

———. *Quantitative Analysis for Management*, 5th ed. Boston: Allyn and Bacon, 1994.

Schlaifer, R. *Analysis of Decisions Under Certainty*. New York: McGraw-Hill, 1969.

3

Total Quality Management

CHAPTER OUTLINE

LEARNING OBJECTIVES

When you complete this chapter you should be able to:

Identify or define:
- Quality
- Canada Awards for Excellence
- Malcolm Baldrige Awards
- Deming, Juran, and Crosby
- Taguchi technique

Explain:
- Why quality is important
- Total quality management (TQM)
- House of quality
- Pareto charts
- Process charts
- Quality robust products
- Inspection

WORLD-CLASS PROFILE: MOTOROLA

Total Quality Management Provides A Competitive Advantage at Motorola

Motorola decided some years ago to be a world leader in quality. Indeed, Motorola is so good that it became the first winner of the Malcolm Baldrige National Quality Award. Motorola believes in total quality management and practises it from the top, specifically from Honorary Chairperson Robert Galvin. It achieves outstanding quality through demonstrated top management commitment that permeates the entire organization.

To make the quality focus work, Motorola did a number of things:

- Aggressively began a worldwide education program to be sure that employees understood quality and statistical process control.
- Established goals, namely its Six Sigma program. The program means that Motorola can expect to have a defect rate of no more than a few parts per million.
- Established extensive employee participation and a competitive system whereby employees vie for awards based on performance of their particular work group. This is a worldwide competition.

Motorola's divisions can expect a quality service review every two years. Five member teams are selected from various parts of the company to perform the review. After the review, the general manager and staff have a session with the teams and go over the review. The strengths and weaknesses are discussed and recommendations are given to the local management about improvements that must be made. The system is working; it gives Motorola uniformity and consistency. Corporate goals receive commitment throughout the organization and that is a powerful quality tool.

Total quality management (TQM) provides a competitive advantage for Motorola.

The development of robust products requires good experimental design and extensive testing. Shown are Motorola's portable phones, in an Accelerated Life Testing (ALT) facility.

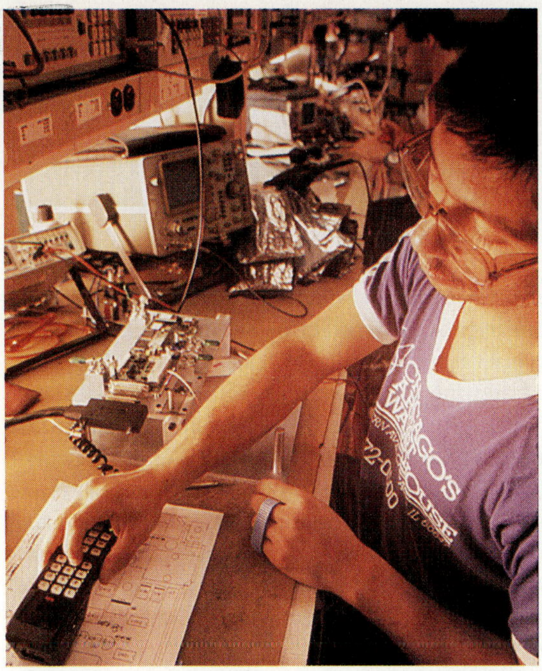

When automated inspection devices work, they are used. However, when manual intervention in the testing process is appropriate, as is shown here, it is used.

Motorola's ALT facility also tests extreme conditions of temperature shock, dust, water, and vibrations. Here cellular phones are undergoing a water test.

With Motorola's strong emphasis on total quality management, Motorola employees are responsible for evaluating their own work, including locating and recording defects. Here employees are evaluating printed circuit boards.

Employee training emphasis has switched from "how to use machinery" to a wide range of personal and technical improvement skills for problem solving. Industry leaders like Kraft General Foods, Ault Foods, Heinz, Campbell, Weston Foods, and Coca-Cola Bottlers have switched to total quality management (TQM).

Employees are trained to function as a group, replacing the traditional hierarchy of worker-supervisor-manager. McCormick Canada Inc. (London, Ontario) emphasizes basic communication training for all production workers. Campbell Soup Company interviews job applicants for suitability in teamwork. Ault Foods has reduced its former eight levels of administration to four, reducing middle management with TQM by having work groups make many decisions. *Good manufacturing practices (GMP)* is another area for basic training to meet government regulation of food production practices. Retraining of disabled or older workers to help them move to a different line of work is becoming important as the Canadian population ages. The Clifford Evans Training Centre (Cambridge, Ontario) is an example of union-management trust fund partnership between Zehrs Markets and the United Food & Commercial Workers. By 1992 all union members donated 15¢ per hour to support courses.[1] ♦

There is no topic in organizations today more important than quality. The future of Milliken, Motorola, and every other firm hinges on its ability to provide quality goods and services for both domestic and international consumption. Determining quality expectations is critical to identifying and meeting customer needs. Quality affects the *entire organization*, from supplier to customer and from product design to maintenance. In this chapter, we deal with two quality issues. We first define *quality* and discuss why it is important. We then present the concept of total quality management (TQM) and its tools. In Chapter 4, we explore the subject of statistical quality control.

DEFINING QUALITY

The National Quality Institute (NQI) defines *quality* as comprising six key elements: (1) leadership, (2) customer focus, (3) planning for improvement, (4) people focus, (5) supplier focus, (6) process optimization.[2] Some definitions are *user-based*. They propose that quality "lies in the eyes of the beholder." Marketing people like this approach, and so do customers. To them, higher quality means better performance, nicer features, and other (sometimes costly) improvements. To production managers, quality is *manufacturing-based*. They believe that quality means conforming to specifications and "making it right the first time." Yet a third approach is the *product-based* definition, which views quality as a precise and measurable variable. This approach views a high-quality ice cream as having high-butterfat content.

In this text, we address all three categories of quality. Quality characteristics are first identified through market research, which identifies what the customer wants (a

[1]Adapted from "Power of the People: Training Creates a More Effective Workforce," *Food in Canada*, 52 (January/February 1992): 26, 28.

[2]*1996 Guide for Canada Awards for Excellence*, sec. 2'

user-based approach to quality). These characteristics are then translated into specific product attributes (a product-based approach to quality). Then the manufacturing process ensures that the products are made precisely to specifications (a manufacturing-based approach to quality). A process that ignores any one of these steps will not result in a product that meets or exceeds the customer's expectations.[3]

"Well, as a last-ditch measure, we could improve the corporate image by improving the product."

Source: *Wall Street Journal*, with permission of Cartoon Features Syndicate.

WHY QUALITY IS IMPORTANT

Quality goods and services are strategically important to firms and to countries. The quality of a firm's products, the prices it charges, and the supply it makes available are all factors that determine demand. In particular, quality affects a firm in four ways:

1. *Costs and market share*. Figure 3.1 shows that improved quality can lead to both increased market share and cost savings. Both can also affect profitability. Likewise, adhering to quality standards means fewer defects and lower service costs. One analysis of air conditioner manufacturers even showed that quality and productivity were positively related. In that study, companies with the highest quality were five times as productive (as measured by units produced per labour-hour) as companies with the poorest quality.[4] Indeed, when the implications of an organization's long-term costs and the potential for increased market share are considered, total costs may well be at a minimum when 100% of the goods or services are perfect and defect-free.
2. *Company's reputation*. An organization can expect its reputation for quality—be

FIGURE 3.1 ■ Two Ways Quality Can Improve Profitability

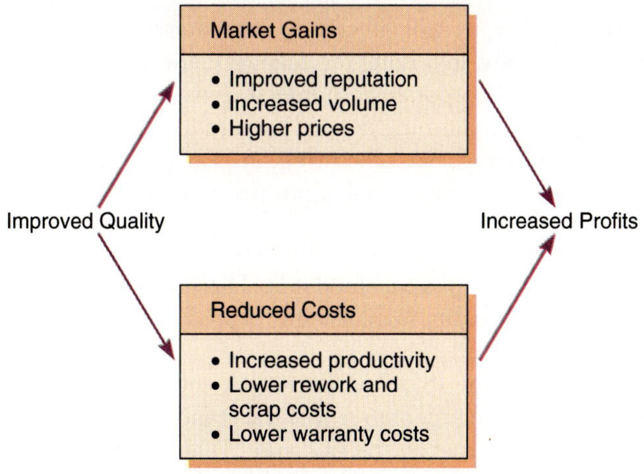

[3] David A. Garvin, "What Does 'Product Quality' Really Mean?" *Sloan Management Review*, 26, no. 1 (Fall 1984): 29.

[4] Garvin, 36.

An emphasis on quality has helped many businesses improve profitability. Mobil Oil's lubricant-blending plant in Bogota, Colombia, attained ISO certification in 1993 and, through a number of quality initiatives, reached record production. Here Luis Pineda monitors a filling machine.

it good or bad—to follow it. Quality will show up in perceptions about the firm's new products, employment practices, and supplier relations. Self-promotion is not a substitute for quality products.

3. *Product liability*. The courts hold organizations that design, produce, or distribute faulty products or services liable for damages or injuries resulting from their use. In Canada the federal government passes acts to protect the consumer; however, generally the consumer needs to check with the federal agency involved to determine if there is an act covering his or her specific problem. For example, in 1996 there were concerns about certain types of venetian blinds that posed a potential health risk; this was the responsibility of Health Canada. For an automobile problem the consumer needs to check with Transport Canada to determine if there is an act to cover it. There is, however, a hazardous products act (1985) administered by the federal government. The reader should also check with his or her provincial government to determine if there is an act covering the consumer.
4. *International implications*. In this technological age, quality is an international, as well as a P/OM, concern. For both a company and a country to compete effectively in the global economy, products must meet global quality and price expectations. Inferior products harm a firm's profitability and a nation's balance of payments.

INTERNATIONAL QUALITY STANDARDS

Quality is so important internationally that a number of quality standards have been developed. Japan, the European Community, the United States, and Canada have all developed their own quality standards.

JAPAN'S INDUSTRIAL STANDARD. The Japanese specification for quality management is published as Industrial Standard Z8101-1981. The standard states:

> Implementing quality control effectively necessitates the cooperation of all people in the company, involving top management, managers, supervisors, and workers in all areas of corporate activities such as market research, research and development, product planning design, preparations for production, purchasing, vendor management, manufacturing, inspection, sales, and afterservices, as well as financial control, personnel administration, and training and education.

ISO 9000

EUROPE'S ISO 9000 STANDARD. The European Community (EC) has developed the **ISO 9000** series of quality standards. The focus of the EC standards is to force the establishment of quality management procedures on firms doing business in the EC.

Several factors make the ISO 9000 series the subject of interest: (1) the standards may achieve worldwide acceptance, (2) the standards are now being applied to some products made or imported by the EC, and (3) adherence to the standards may be necessary for product certification. The *POM in Action* box "Sidus Systems Inc." suggests that ISO 9000 is becoming increasingly important.

AMERICAN STANDARDS. The United States has long had military specifications for defense contracts, and in recent years, the American Quality Control Society has developed specifications equivalent to those of the EC. They are Q90, Q91,

POM IN ACTION

Sidus Systems Inc.

Sidus Systems Inc. (Toronto) is the largest Canadian-owned computer manufacturer.

In 1994, Sidus had considered a strategic alliance with EDS (NYSE: GME) to distribute their desktop system worldwide. EDS operated in 35 countries and had revenues in 1993 reported at $8.6 billion. The alliance did not materialize. Sidus reconsidered their options and decided to distribute their systems themselves. The company has a strong presence in world markets through their own international marketing group and through its work with the Canadian government.

From its ISO 9000–certified manufacturing facility in Toronto, the company tailors computing solutions for an ever-increasing list of public- and private-sector customers in Canada and throughout the world. Sidus is the NO. 1 seller of personal computers to the federal government.

Projected revenues for 1996 were in excess of $200 million and sales since 1992 have grown at an average rate of 30%. Sidus stock is traded on the Toronto stock exchange.

Source: Adapted from PR NewsWire Association Ltd., "Sidus Awards EDS Global Logistics Management Contract" (October 1994).

Q92, Q93, and Q94. Q90 provides an overview and introduction to the other standards, definitions, and concepts related to quality.

Q91 is the general standard for design, development, manufacturing, installation, and servicing of products or services.

Q92 provides more detail than Q91 for organizations involved in production, installation, and servicing of products or services.

Q93 provides more detail than Q91 for organizations specifically involved in inspection and tests and for distributors and value-added contractors.

Q94 provides guidelines for managing and auditing a quality control system.

The international implications of quality are so important that, in 1988, the United States established the *Malcolm Baldrige National Quality Award* for quality achievement. The award is named for the former Secretary of Commerce in the United States. Winners include Motorola (1988); Milliken and Xerox (1989); IBM, Federal Express, and Cadillac (1990); Solectron, Zytec, and Marlow (1991); Ritz-Carlton Hotels, AT&T, and Texas Instruments (1992); Eastman Chemical, Ames Rubber (1993), and GTE; and Wainwright Industries (1994). Figure 3.2 presents the criteria framework for the awards.

CANADIAN STANDARDS. The Canadian market is not big enough to absorb the product/service output of Canadian businesses, and therefore Canadian companies realize that the international market is crucial. However, to be competitive their products and services must meet the Japanese, European, and American standards. The Canadian Standards Association (CSA), located in Toronto, uses the **Can/CSA-ISO 9000** standard for Canada.

Can/CSA-ISO 9000

To be successful in the international market *quality* of product/service is key. The National Quality Institute (NQI) in Ottawa introduced in 1984 the Canada Awards for Excellence in three areas: (1) the quality award, (2) the entrepreneurship award, and (3) the innovation award. Recent award winners include Biothermica International Inc. (Quebec); Instrumar Limited (Newfoundland); Merak Projects Ltd. (Alberta); and Augat Photon Systems Inc. (British Columbia). Two Canadians well recognized for their views on quality are Jim Clemmer, author of *Firing on All Cylinders* and *Pathways to Performance*, and Stan Brown of Coopers & Lybrand, highly regarded in the consulting field.

TOTAL QUALITY MANAGEMENT

(TQM) Total quality management

Total quality management (TQM) refers to a quality emphasis that encompasses the entire organization, from supplier to customer. TQM stresses a commitment by management to have a continuing companywide drive toward excellence in all aspects of products and services that are important to the customer.[5]

FIGURE 3.2 ■ National Quality Institute Awards Criteria Framework

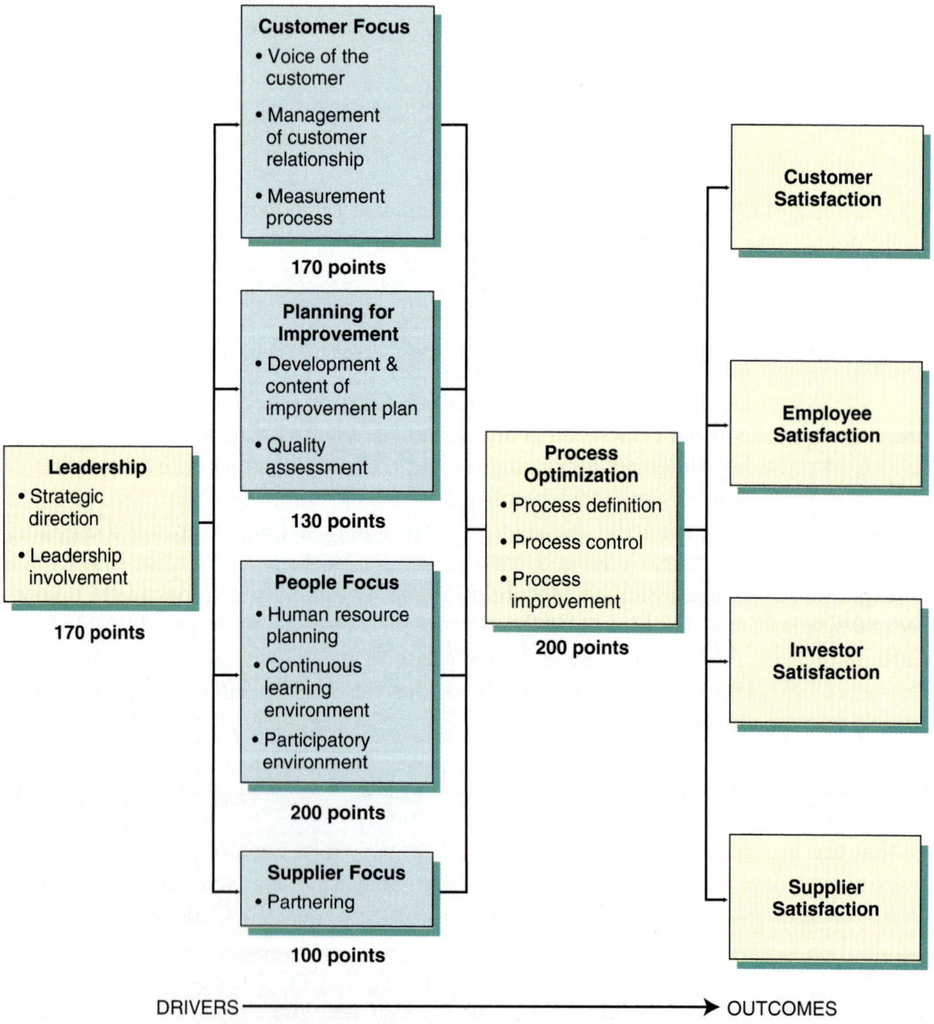

[5]The term *companywide quality control* (CWQC) is sometimes used to describe an organization's commitment to quality; see L. P. Sullivan, "The Seven Stages in Company-Wide Quality Control," *Quality Progress* (May 1986): 78.

TABLE 3.1 ■ DEMING'S 14 POINTS FOR IMPLEMENTING QUALITY IMPROVEMENT

1. Create consistency of purpose.
2. Lead to promote change.
3. Build quality into the product; stop depending on inspections to catch problems.
4. Build long-term relationships based on performance instead of awarding business on the basis of price.
5. Continuously improve product, quality, and service.
6. Start training.
7. Emphasize leadership.
8. Drive out fear.
9. Break down barriers between departments.
10. Stop haranguing workers.
11. Support, help, and improve.
12. Remove barriers to pride in work.
13. Institute a vigorous program of education and self-improvement.
14. Put everybody in the company to work on the transformation.

Source: Deming revised his 14 points a number of times over the years. See W. E. Deming, "Transformation of Western Style of Management," *Interfaces*, 15, no. 3 (May/June 1985): 6–11; W. Edwards Deming, "Improvement of Quality and Productivity Action Through Action by Management," *National Productivity Review* (Winter 1981–1982): 12–22; W. Edwards Deming, "Philosophy Continues to Flourish," *APICS—The Performance Advantage*, 1, no. 4 (October 1991): 20.

TQM is important because quality decisions influence each of the 10 strategic and tactical decisions made by production/operations managers. Every chapter that follows deals with some aspect of identifying and meeting customer expectations. Meeting those expectations requires an emphasis on TQM if a firm is to compete as a leader in world markets. Figure 3.2 shows the criteria used by the National Quality Institute in choosing award recipients.[6]

Quality expert W. Edwards Deming used 14 points (see Table 3.1) to indicate how he implemented TQM.[7] We develop these into five concepts for an effective TQM program: (1) continuous improvement, (2) employee involvement, (3) benchmarking, (4) just-in-time (JIT), and (5) knowledge of tools.

Continuous Improvement

Total quality management (TQM) requires a never-ending process of continuous improvement. The end goal is perfection, which is never achieved but always sought.

Kaizen

The Japanese use the word **Kaizen** to describe this ongoing process of unending improvement—the setting and achieving ever-higher goals. In the United States, *TQM*, *zero defects*, and *six sigma* are used to describe such efforts. Whatever word or phrase is used, P/OM managers are key players in building a work culture that endorses continuous improvement.

Employee Empowerment

Employee empowerment

TQM requires **employee empowerment**, or involving employees in every step of the production process. Consistently, business literature suggests that some 85% of quality

[6]National Quality Institute, *1996 Guide for Canada Awards for Excellence* (Ottawa: 1996).

[7]John C. Anderson, Manus Rungtusanatham, and Roger G. Schroeder, "A Theory of Quality Management Underlying the Deming Management Method," *Academy of Management Review*, 19, no. 3 (1994): 472–509.

problems have to do with materials and processes, not with employee performance. Therefore, the task is to design equipment and processes that produce the desired quality. This is best done with a high degree of involvement by those who understand the shortcomings of the system. Those dealing with the system on a daily basis understand it better than anyone else. When nonconformance occurs, the worker is seldom wrong. Either the product was designed wrong, the system that makes the product was designed wrong, or the employee was improperly trained.[8] Although the employee may be able to help solve the problem, the employee rarely causes it.

Techniques for building employee empowerment include (1) building communication networks that include employees; (2) open, supportive supervisors; (3) moving responsibility from both managerial and staff responsibilities to production employees; (4) building high-morale organizations; (5) and formal techniques such as team building and quality circles.

Quality circle

Teams can be built to address a variety of issues. One popular approach to team building is a focus on quality via quality circles. A **quality circle** is a group of between

Leaders in the Fight for Quality
W. Edwards Deming. (left) The awarding of the Deming Prize for quality control on Japanese TV is a national event. After World War II, Dr. Deming went to Japan to teach quality. And the Japanese learned. In his quality crusade, Deming insisted that management accept responsibility for building good systems. The employee, he believed, cannot produce products that on the average exceed the quality of what the process is capable of producing. Dr. Deming died in 1993.
J. M. Juran. (middle) A pioneer in teaching the Japanese how to improve quality, Juran believes strongly in top management commitment, support, and involvement in the quality effort. He is also a believer in teams that continually seek to raise quality standards. Juran varies from Deming somewhat in focussing on the customer and defining quality as fitness for use, not necessarily the written specifications.
Philip B. Crosby. (right) *Quality Is Free* was Crosby's attention-getting book published in 1979. Crosby's traditional view has been "with management and employee commitment great strides can be made in improving quality." He also believes that in the traditional trade-off between the cost of improving quality and the cost of poor quality, the cost of poor quality is understated. The cost of poor quality should include all of the things that are involved in *not* doing the job right the first time.

[8]See a related discussion in Asher Israeli and Bradley Fisher, "The Worker Is Never Wrong," *Quality Progress* (October 1989): 95.

6 and 12 employees who volunteer to meet regularly to solve work-related problems. The members, all from the same work area, receive training in group planning, problem solving, and statistical quality control. They generally meet about 4 hours per month (usually after work, but sometimes on company time). Although the circle members are not rewarded financially, they do receive recognition from the firm. A specially trained team member, called the facilitator, usually helps train the circle members and keeps the meetings running smoothly. Quality circles have proven to be a cost-effective way to increase productivity as well as quality.

Benchmarking

Benchmarking is another ingredient in an organization's TQM program. **Benchmarking** involves selecting a demonstrated standard of performance that represents the very best performance for processes or activities very similar to yours. The idea is to develop a target at which to shoot and then to develop a standard or benchmark against which to compare your performance. The steps for developing benchmarks are:[9]

Benchmarking

- Determine what to benchmark
- Form a benchmark team
- Identify benchmarking partners
- Collect and analyze benchmarking information
- Take action to match or exceed the benchmark

In the ideal situation, you find one or more similar organizations that have proved to be leaders in the particular areas that you want to study. Then you compare yourself (benchmark yourself) against them. The company need not be in your industry. Indeed, to establish world-class standards, it may be best to look outside of your industry. If one industry has learned how to compete via rapid product development but yours has not, it does no good to study your industry.

As discussed in the *POM in Action* box "Strategy to Foster Environment Industry Growth," the federal government has formed "Centres of Excellence" by which companies can benchmark their R&D efforts. However, competitive data need not be elaborate or sophisticated. Even casually developed data can suggest areas for further investigation. This is the case in Table 3.2, which indicates that in 1995, General Motors only generated sales of $162,700 per employee, while Ford and Chrysler were at $265,400 and $238,800, respectively. This information suggests that a true benchmark study may be warranted.

TABLE 3.2 ■ SALES PER EMPLOYEE, 1995

	SALES $ (BILLIONS)	EMPLOYEES (1000S)	SALES $ PER EMPLOYEE (1000S)
Ford	385.2	347	1,138.9
Chrysler	472.8*	112	4,222.1
General Motors	238.1	709	335.8

*Reflects the effect the GM strike had on Chrysler products.

[9]Adapted from Michael J. Spendolini, *The Benchmarking Book* (New York: AMACOM, 1992).

POM IN ACTION

Strategy to Foster Environment Industry Growth

In 1994, the Canadian government introduced an Environmental Industry Strategy, based on:

- 22 specific initiatives with a budget of $57.5 million
- continuing federal and regional programs and activities
- new federal initiatives by departments providing environmental programs with a mandate for three prime objectives:
  1. federal support that is direct, easily accessible, cost-effective, and in a service-oriented environment
  2. support for the development and commercialization of innovative environmental technology
  3. improvement of access to global and domestic markets for environmental companies

To aid in streamlining the decision process, the federal strategy created an implementation steering committee to represent all parties involved. The programs would set goals on a province-by-province basis. The first priority: to help companies involved in pollution-related technologies and processes exceed environmental standards.

A second phase was to support research in areas of strategic economic importance to Canada and create new opportunities through the formation of Centres of Excellence networks.

The initiative was also designed to help companies enter the international market to use and sell newfound technologies and expertise. It supported the creation of strategic alliances between smaller environmental firms to help them compete internationally.

The Environmental Industry Strategy called for the creation of a national statistical database on environmental standards, critical not only for the industry's growth and for industry benchmarking but also as an aid to the government in making policy decisions.

To promote strategy domestically, the government recommitted itself to green procurement. Further, it pledged to review its practices to ensure it did not inadvertently harm environmental companies.

Source: Adapted from "Strategy to Foster Environment Industry Growth," *Eco-Log Week* (September 30, 1994). For a copy of the Environmental Strategy contact Industry Canada's Environmental Affairs Branch: (613) 954-3080, fax (613) 952-9564.

Benchmarks can and should be established in a variety of areas. Total quality management requires measurable benchmarks.

Just-in-Time (JIT)

The philosophy behind just-in-time (JIT) is one of continuing improvement and enforced problem solving. When implemented, JIT reduces the amount of inventory a firm has on hand by establishing quality and purchasing controls that bring inventory to the firm just-in-time for use. JIT is related to quality in three ways.

First, JIT cuts the cost of quality. This occurs because scrap, rework, inventory investment, and damage costs are directly related to inventory on hand. Because there is less inventory on hand with JIT, costs are lower. Additionally, inventory *hides* bad quality, while JIT immediately *exposes* bad quality.

Second, JIT improves quality. As JIT shrinks lead time, it keeps evidence of errors fresh and limits the number of potential sources of error. JIT creates, in effect, an early warning system for quality problems, both within the firm and with vendors.

Finally, better quality means less inventory and a better, easier-to-employ JIT system. Often the purpose of keeping inventory is to protect against poor production performance resulting from unreliable quality. If consistent quality exists, JIT allows us to reduce all the costs associated with inventory.

Knowledge of TQM Tools

To empower employees and implement TQM as a continuing effort, managers must train everyone in the organization in the techniques of TQM. In the following section, we focus on some of the diverse and expanding tools that are used in the TQM crusade.

TOOLS FOR TQM

Six tools/techniques that aid the TQM effort are (1) quality function deployment (house of quality), (2) Taguchi techniques, (3) Pareto charts, (4) process charts, (5) cause-and-effect diagrams (fish-bone charts), and (6) statistical process control. We will now introduce these tools.

Quality Function Deployment (QFD)

An effective TQM program translates customer desires into specific, designable features. **Quality function deployment (QFD)** refers to both (1) determining what will satisfy the customer and (2) translating those customer desires into the target design.[10] We use QFD early in the production process to help us determine where to deploy quality efforts.

Quality function deployment (QFD)

One of the tools of QFD is the house of quality. The **house of quality** is a graphic technique for defining the relationship between customer desires and product (or service). Only by defining this relationship in a rigorous way can operations managers build products and processes with features desired by customers. Defining this relationship is the first step in building a world-class production system. To build the house of quality, we perform six basic steps:

House of quality

1. Identify customer *wants*.
2. Identify product/service attributes. (Think of attributes as *how* the product/service will meet the *wants*.)
3. Relate the customer *wants* to the product/service *hows*.
4. Conduct an evaluation of competing products.
5. Develop performance specifications for product or service *hows*.
6. Assign (deploy) *hows* to the appropriate place in the transformation process.

Example 1 shows how to construct a house of quality.

EXAMPLE 1

Through extensive market research, Great Cameras, Inc., determined customer *wants*. Those *wants* are shown in the following illustration on the left of the house of quality and are lightweight, easy to hold steady, no double exposures, easy to use, and reliable. Then the product development team determined *how* the organization

[10] See Yoji Akao (ed.), *Quality Function Deployment* (Cambridge, MA: Productivity Press, 1990).

is going to translate those customer *wants* into product design and process attribute targets. These *hows* are entered across the top portion of the house of quality. These attributes are low electricity requirements, aluminum components, auto focus, auto exposure, auto film advance, and ergonomic design.

The product team then evaluated each of the customer *wants* against the *hows*. In the matrix of the house, the team evaluated how well its design will meet customer needs. Similarly, in the "roof" of the house, the product development team developed the relationship between the attributes. Finally, the team developed importance ratings for its design attributes and a ranking of how to proceed with product and process design.

A variety of modifications can be made to the house of quality. For instance, it can be used to evaluate how a competitor meets customer demands.

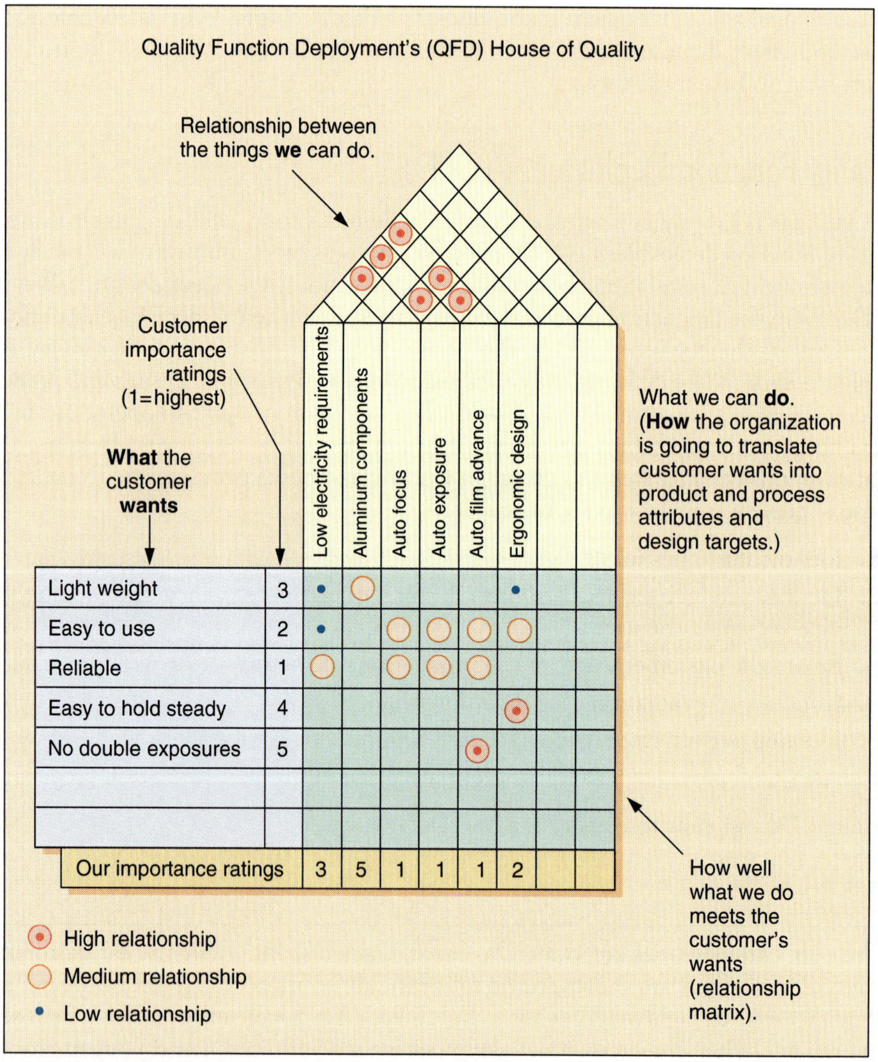

Taguchi Technique

Most quality problems are the result of product and process design. Therefore, tools are needed to address these areas. One of those tools is the **Taguchi technique**, named after Japanese engineer, Genichi Taguchi.[11]

Taguchi technique

TAGUCHI CONCEPTS. Three concepts are important to understanding Taguchi's approach and method. These concepts are *quality robustness*, *quality loss factor*, and *target-oriented quality*.

The Taguchi method calls for making products and processes that are *quality robust*. **Quality robust** products are products that can be produced uniformly and consistently in adverse manufacturing and environmental conditions. Taguchi's idea is to remove the *effects* of adverse conditions instead of removing the causes. Taguchi suggests that removing the effects is often cheaper than removing the causes and more effective in producing a robust product. In this way, small variations in materials and process do not destroy product quality.

Quality robust

Taguchi has also defined what he calls a quality loss function. A **quality loss function (QLF)** identifies all costs connected with poor quality and shows how these costs increase as the product moves away from being exactly what the customer wants. These costs include not just customer dissatisfaction, but also warranty and service costs; internal inspection, repair, and scrap costs; and costs that can best be described as costs to society. Notice that Figure 3.3(a) shows the quality loss function as a curve that increases at an increasing rate. It takes the general form of a simple quadratic formula:

Quality loss function (QLF)

$$L = D^2C$$

where L = loss
D^2 = square of the deviation from the target value
C = cost of avoiding the deviation

All the losses to society due to poor performance are included in the loss function. The smaller the loss, the more desirable the product. The farther the product is from the target value, the more severe the loss.

Taguchi observed that the traditional way of looking at specifications (that is, the product is good until it fails to fall within the tolerance limits) is too simplistic. As shown in Figure 3.3(b), conformance-oriented quality produces more units farther from the target. Therefore, the loss (cost) is higher in terms of customer satisfaction and benefits to society.

Target-oriented quality is a philosophy of continuous improvement to bring the product exactly on target.

Target-oriented quality

Pareto Charts

Pareto charts organize errors, problems, or defects to help production personnel focus on problem-solving efforts. They are based on the work of Vilfredo Pareto, a nineteenth-century economist. Joseph M. Juran popularized Pareto's work when he suggested that 80% of a firm's problems are a result of only 20% of the causes. As the *POM in Action* box "Cleaning Up: Cadet Uniform Uses Teamwork" suggests, Pareto

Pareto charts

[11] R. N. Kackar, "Taguchi's Quality Control, Parameter Design, and the Taguchi Method," *Journal of Quality Technology* (October 1985): 176–188; Lance Ealey, "Taguchi Basics," *Quality* (November 1988): 30–32; and Glen Stuart Peace, *Taguchi Methods* (Reading, MA: Addison-Wesley, 1993).

charts, though simple, can identify problems and focus effort. Pareto analysis, as shown in Example 2, indicates which problems may yield the greatest payoff.

Example 2 indicates that of the five types of defects identified, the vast majority were of one type, scratches; so 20% (1 of 5) of the causes result in 81.3% (61 of 75) of the defects.

EXAMPLE 2

Custom Wine Glasses of Lloydminster, Saskatchewan, has just collected the data from 75 defects from the day's production. The boss decides to prepare a Pareto analysis of the defects. The data provided are scratches 61; porosity 5; nicks 4; contamination 3; and miscellaneous 2.

The Pareto chart shown indicates that about 80% of the defects were the result of one cause, scratches.

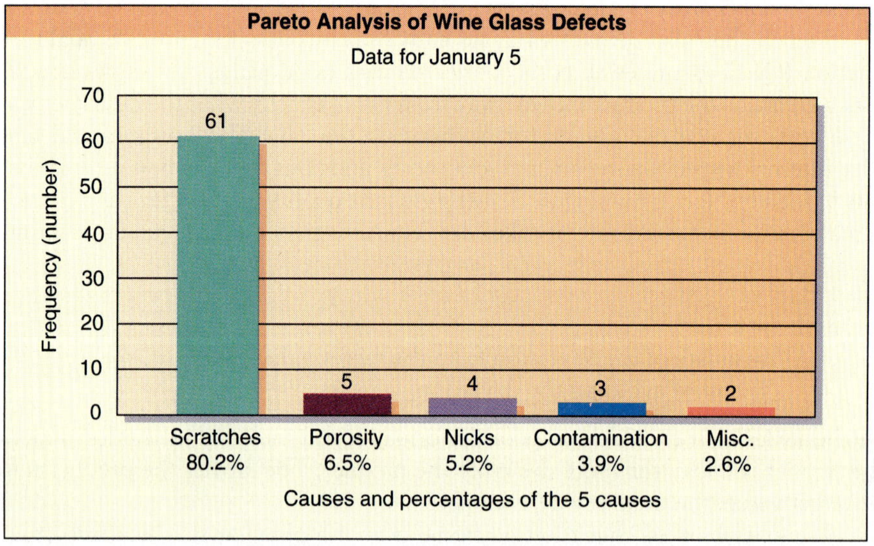

The majority of defects will be eliminated when this one cause is corrected.

Process Charts

Process charts are designed to help us understand a sequence of events (that is, the process) through which a product or service travels. The process flow chart graphs the steps of the process and their relationship. This type of analysis can:

1. help identify the best data collection points;
2. isolate and track the origin of problems;
3. identify the best place for process audits; and
4. identify opportunities for travel distance reduction.

As shown in Example 3, a process chart organizes information about a process in a graphical matter, using five standard symbols and distance. The standard American Society of Mechanical Engineers (ASME) process symbols are O = operation; ⇓ = transportation; □ = inspection; D = delay; ▽ = storage.

Process charts

POM IN ACTION

Cleaning up: Cadet Uniform Uses Teamwork

By 7 A.M. you will see bright orange Cadet vans pulling out of the Cadet plant for their day's uniform deliveries to local firms. The drivers, called customer service representatives, act as salespeople and diplomats and their salaries, which are based on customer satisfaction and income generation, average $53,000 annually.

Cadet has acquired a reputation for innovation over the past decade or so, and in 1992 received a certificate of merit from the Canada Awards for Business Excellence. President Quentin Wahl stated "Cadet's major innovation has been its focus on motivating its team members [the preferred term for employees]. A result has been higher productivity, fewer mistakes, and loyal customers." Though you have to continually improve the quality of your product, said Wahl, the focus is employee motivation in combination with quality improvement programs.

The business proved to be more difficult than Wahl anticipated. Cleaning thousands of identical uniforms for hundreds of customers leads to human errors. The quality program, implemented in 1980, included spending millions of dollars for a bar code reader to keep track of all the uniforms. By 1994, only 1 in 100,000 uniforms went missing or was incorrectly delivered.

Wahl believes in the open book style of management: he places sales, cost, and growth figures on the bulletin board to share the information with his employees. He eliminated a dozen parking spots at the plant for an outdoor lunch area, and frequently holds Friday-afternoon barbecues. In 1994 the average employee turnover rate at Cadet was just 7%, in contrast to the industry average of 65 to 70%. Wahl pointed out that in almost any business, "the lowest-paid, least-recognized employees, and the ones with the highest turnover rates, are the people who meet the customer."

Source: Adapted from "Cleaning Up: Cadet Uniform Uses Teamwork and Motivation to Dominate Its Niche in the Dry Cleaning Sector," *Maclean's* (December 12, 1994).

FIGURE 3.3 ■ (a) Quality Loss Function; (b) Distribution of Product Produced. Taguchi aims for the target, because products produced near the upper and lower acceptable specifications result in higher quality loss function.

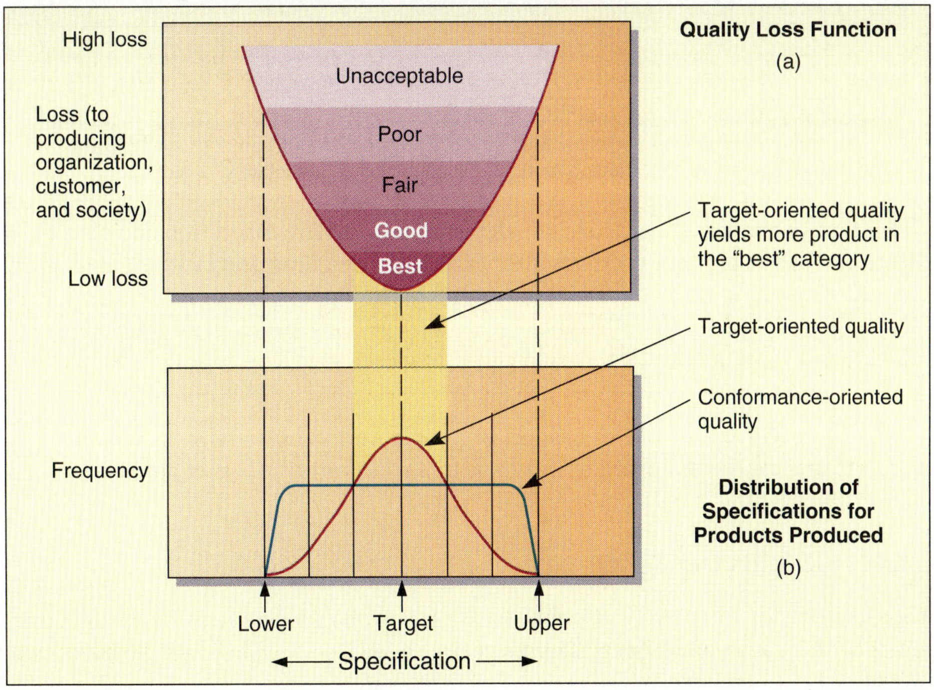

EXAMPLE 3

The WJC Chicken Processing Plant in Moncton, New Brunswick, would like to understand more about its packing and shipping process. After observation of the packing and shipping line and discussion with the operators, you prepare the following process chart:

PROCESS CHART

Present Method [X]
Proposed Method [X]

SUBJECT CHARTED *Packing and Shipping Process* DATE *1/1/96*
CHART BY *HRC*
CHART NO. *1*
DEPARTMENT *Packing and Shipping* SHEET NO. *1* OF *1*

DIST. IN METRES	TIME IN MINS.	CHART SYMBOLS	PROCESS DESCRIPTION
3		○ ⇨ □ D ▽	To Packing Station
—		○ ⇨ □ D ▽	Pack
0.6		○ ⇨ □ D ▽	To Weigh Station
—		○ ⇨ □ D ▽	Weigh
0.6		○ ⇨ □ D ▽	To Airtight Sealing, Weighing, and Labelling
—		○ ⇨ □ D ▽	Automatic Sealing, Weighing, and Labelling
15.2		○ ⇨ □ D ▽	To Quick-Freeze Storage
—		○ ⇨ □ D ▽	Quick-Freeze Storage
7.6		○ ⇨ □ D ▽	To Bulk Packing
—		○ ⇨ □ D ▽	Bulk Packing
12.2		○ ⇨ □ D ▽	To Shipping Dock
		○ ⇨ □ D ▽	Load on Shipping Truck
		○ ⇨ □ D ▽	
		○ ⇨ □ D ▽	
		○ ⇨ □ D ▽	
		○ ⇨ □ D ▽	
			TOTAL

The standard American Society of Mechanical Engineers (ASME) process symbols are ○ = operation; ⇨ = transportation; □ = inspection; D = delay; ▽ = storage

This type of analysis should help you determine (1) where inspection and data collection could take place (perhaps after automatic weighing and labelling and after automatic sealing and after quick-freeze), (2) the opportunities for reducing the distance travelled (perhaps to quick-freeze storage, bulk packing, and the shipping dock), and (3) where to look should certain types of problems arise.

As you will see in our discussion of people and work systems in Chapter 11, process charts can be useful analytical tools in a wide variety of other applications.

Cause-and-Effect Diagram

Cause-and-effect diagram
Ishikawa diagram

Another tool for identifying possible locations of quality problems and inspection points is the **cause-and-effect diagram**, also known as an **Ishikawa diagram** or a

fish-bone chart. Figure 3.4 illustrates a chart (note the shape resembling the bones of a fish) for an everyday quality control problem—a dissatisfied airline customer. Each "bone" represents a possible source of error.

Fish-bone chart

The way to get started on any cause-and-effect diagram is to have four categories: material, machinery/equipment, manpower, and methods. These four M's are the "causes." They provide a good checklist for initial analysis. When such a chart is systematically developed, possible quality problems and inspection points are highlighted.

Statistical Process Control (SPC)

Statistical process control monitors standards, makes measurements, and takes corrective action as a product or service is being produced. Samples of process outputs are examined; if they are within acceptable limits, the process is permitted to continue. If they fall outside certain specific ranges, the process is stopped and, typically, the assignable cause is located and removed.

Statistical process control

FIGURE 3.4 ■ Fish-Bone Chart (or Cause-and-Effect Diagram) for Problems in Airline Customer Service

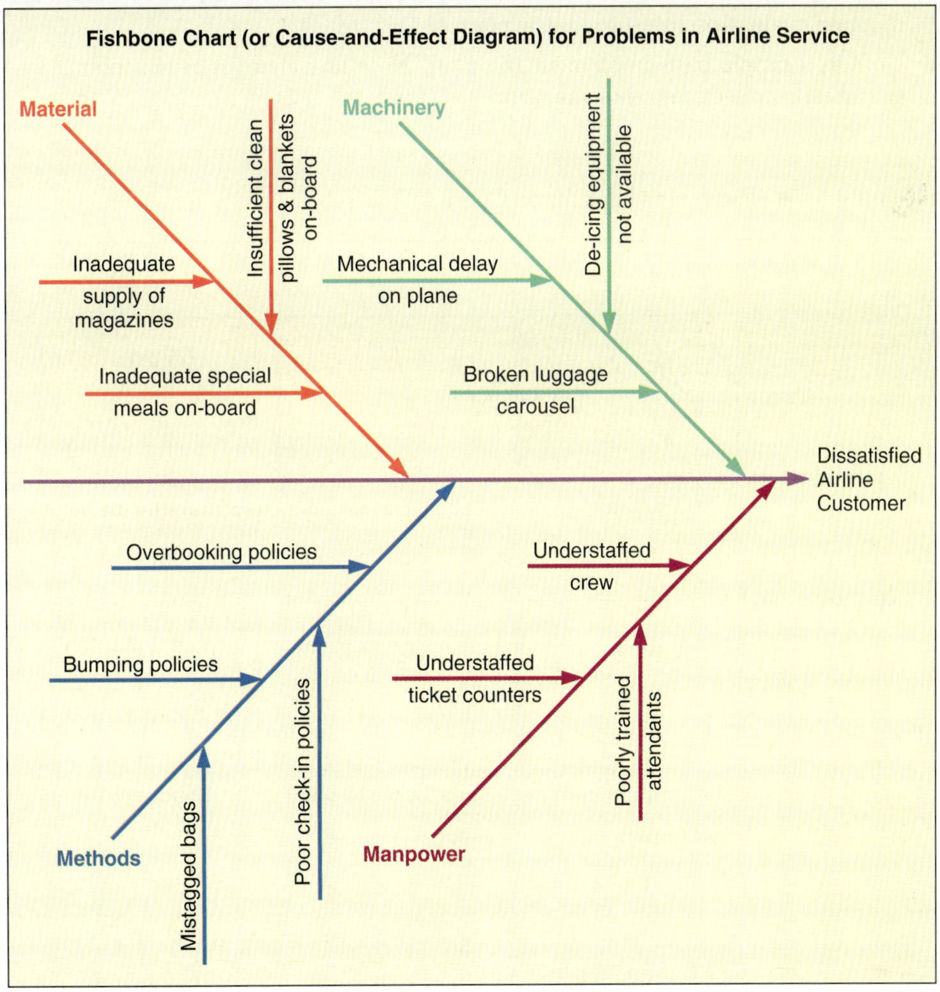

Control charts

Control charts are graphic presentations of data over time that show upper and lower limits for the process we want to control. Control charts are constructed in such a way that new data can be quickly compared to past performance data. We take samples of the process output and plot the average of these samples on a chart that has the limits on it. The upper and lower limits in a control chart can be in units of temperature, pressure, weight, length, and so on.

Figure 3.5 shows the useful information that can be portrayed in control charts. When the average of the samples falls within the upper and lower control limits and no discernible pattern is present, the process is said to be in control. Otherwise, the process is out of control or out of adjustment.

Chapter 4 details how control charts of different types are developed. It also deals with the statistical foundation underlying the use of this important tool.

Plan-Do-Check-Act (PDCA) Wheel

THE PLAN-DO-CHECK-ACT (PDCA) WHEEL. As an aid to management in the continuous improvement process, W. Edwards Deming introduced the **Plan-Do-Check-Act (PDCA) Wheel**. PDCA gave management a workable tool that could easily be used. The steps are as follows:

- *Plan*. Analyze the existing process and standardize it. Collect information on existing problems. Study the problems, develop a plan for addressing them, and determine an evaluation measure for the plan.
- *Do*. On a simple basis implement the plan. Note any changes at this point. Systematically collect data for evaluation.

FIGURE 3.5 ■ Patterns to Look for on Control Charts

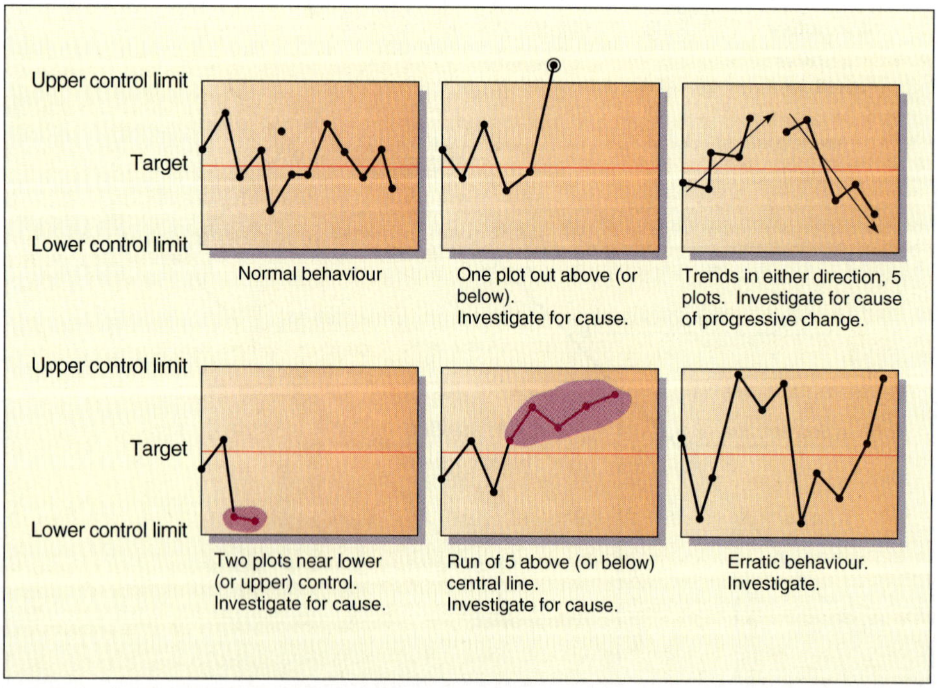

(*Source:* Adapted from Bertrand L. Hansen, *Quality Control: Theory and Applications*, 1991, p. 65. Reprinted by permission of Prentice-Hall, Englewood Cliffs, New Jersey.)

- *Check.* Compare the results of the data collected in the "Do" phase with expectations in the "Plan" phase.
- *Act.* If results meet expectations, implement the new process/system. Communicate the new process/system to those employees that will be associated with it. Training should be provided.

If results are not successful, revise the plan and repeat the process, or stop the project.

Corrective Action Reporting Seminars (CARS). An integrative approach to the problem-solving model has been developed by Professor Michael Piczak of Mohawk College and is used extensively in his **corrective action reporting seminars (CARS)**. CARS consist of eight major stages: (1) problem finding, (2) assembling the CAR team, (3) specifying the trouble, (4) stopping the bleeding, (5) identifying the root causes, (6) developing an improved approach, (7) installing permanent fix and monitoring compliance, and (8) considering preventative action.

Corrective action reporting seminars (CARS)

THE ROLE OF INSPECTION

To make sure a system is producing at the expected quality level, inspection of some or all of the items is needed. This **inspection** can involve measurement, tasting, touching, weighing, or testing of the product (sometimes even destroying it when doing so). Its goal is to detect a bad product immediately. Inspection does not correct deficiencies in the system or defects in the products; nor does it change a product or increase its value. Inspection only finds deficiencies and defects; and it is expensive. Inspection should be thought of as an audit. Audits do not add value to the product. But production/operations managers, like financial managers, need audits and they need to know when and where to audit. So there are two basic issues relating to inspection. They are (1) *when to inspect* and (2) *where to inspect*.

Inspection

When and Where to Inspect

Deciding when and where to inspect depends on the type of process and the value added at each stage. Inspection in manufacturing firms can take place at any of the following six points.

1. Inspect at your supplier's plant while the supplier is producing.
2. Inspect at your plant upon receipt of goods from your supplier.
3. Inspect before costly or irreversible processes.
4. Inspect during the step-by-step production process.
5. Inspect when production is complete.
6. Inspect before shipment from your plant.

A cross-functional team leader inspecting for defects before final assembly.

Pareto charts, process charts, and cause-and-effect diagrams, as discussed in the previous section, are TQM tools to aid in this "when and where" to inspect decision. However, inspection is not a substitute for a robust product produced by a good process. In one well-known experiment conducted by an independent research firm, 100 defective pieces were added to a "perfect" lot of items and then subjected to

100% inspection.[12] The inspectors found only 68 of the defective pieces in their first inspection. It took another three passes by the inspectors to find the next 30 defects. The two last defects were never found. So the bottom line is that there is variability in the inspection process. Additionally, inspectors are only human: they become bored, they become tired, and the inspection equipment itself has variability. Even with 100% inspection, inspectors cannot guarantee perfection.

Source Inspection

Source inspection

The best inspection is inspection at the source. This is called **source inspection** and is consistent with the concept of employee empowerment where individual employees self-check their own work. The idea is that each process and each employee *treat the next step in the process as the customer,* ensuring perfect product to the next "customer." This inspection may be assisted by the use of checklists and controls such as a fail-safe device called a poka-yoke, a name borrowed from the Japanese.

Poka-yoke

A **poka-yoke** is a foolproof device or technique that ensures production of good units every time.[13] These special devices avoid errors and provide quick feedback of problems. A simple example of a poka-yoke device is the diesel or leaded gas pump nozzle that will not fit into the "unleaded" gas tank opening on your car. This same poka-yoke technique is used by airplane fuel service companies at airports. The idea of source inspection and poka-yokes is to ensure that 100% good products or services are provided.

Service Industry Inspection

Service and manufacturing organizations have similar inspection needs. And in both, the when-and-where-to-inspect decision presents many options. However, Pareto charts and process charts prove very useful tools to successfully address these issues. Some specific examples of locations where inspection may prove particularly useful in service organizations are illustrated in Table 3.3. The service manager, like the production manager, must maximize source inspection through employee empowerment and poka-yoke-like techniques such as checklists.

Inspection of Attributes vs. Variables

Attribute inspection

Variable inspection

When inspections take place, quality characteristics may be measured as either *attributes* or *variables*. **Attribute inspection** classifies items as being either good or defective. It does not address the degree of failure. For example, the lightbulb burns or it does not. **Variable inspection** measures such dimensions as weight, speed, height, or strength to see if the item falls within an acceptable range. If a piece of electrical wire is supposed to be 0.5 millimetres in diameter, a micrometer can be used to see if the product is close enough to pass inspection.

Knowing whether attributes or variables are being inspected helps us decide which statistical quality control approach to take.

[12] *Statistical Quality Control* (Springfield, MA: Monsanto Chemical Company, n.d.), p. 19.

[13] For further discussion, see Alan Robinson, *Modern Approaches to Management Improvement: The Shingo System* (Cambridge, MA: Productivity Press, 1990).

TOTAL QUALITY MANAGEMENT IN SERVICES

Quality of services is more difficult to measure than quality of manufactured goods.[14] Generally, though, a user of a service has a few features in mind as a basis for comparison among alternatives. Lack of one feature may eliminate a service firm from consideration. Quality also may be perceived as a bundle of attributes in which many lesser characteristics are superior to those of competitors.

Extensive, in-depth interviews with consumer focus groups identified 10 general attributes or determinants of service quality[15] (see Table 3.4). The same study also drew the following conclusions:

1. *Consumers' perceptions of service quality result from a comparison of their expectations before they receive their actual experience with the service*. In other words, service quality is judged on the basis of whether it meets expectations.
2. *Quality perceptions are derived from the service process as well as from the service outcome*. The way the service is performed can be as important as the actual service from the consumer's point of view.
3. *Service quality is of two types, normal and exceptional*. First, there is the quality level at which the regular service is delivered, such as the bank teller's handling of a transaction. Second, there is the quality level at which "exceptions" or "problems" are handled. This implies that a quality control system must recognize and have prepared a set of alternate plans for less-than-optimal operating conditions. In addition, when a problem occurs, the low-contact firm may suddenly become a high-contact firm. Thus, good customer relations are important in maintaining quality, regardless of the type of service.

Designing a high-quality process that fills these pharmaceutical bottles in sterile conditions is much more fruitful than having an inspector evaluate the bacteria count on bottles filled in a poor system. Good-quality systems focus on quality processes, not after-the-fact inspections.

TABLE 3.3 ■ INSPECTION POINTS IN THREE SERVICE ORGANIZATIONS

TYPE OF ORGANIZATION	SOME POINTS OF INSPECTION	ISSUES TO CONSIDER
Bank	Teller stations	Shortages, courtesy, speed, accuracy
	Loan processing	Collateral, proper credit checks, rates, terms of loans, default rates, loan ratios
	Cheque clearing	Accuracy, speed of entry, percentage of cheques cleared each day
Department store	Stockrooms	Clean, uncluttered, organized, level of stockouts, ample supply, rotation of goods
	Display areas	Attractive, well-organized and stocked, visible goods, good lighting
	Sales counters	Neat, courteous, knowledgeable personnel; waiting time; accuracy in credit checking and sales entry
Restaurant	Kitchen	Clean, proper storage, unadulterated food, health regulations observed, well organized
	Cashier station	Speed, accuracy, appearance
	Dining areas	Clean, comfortable, regular monitoring by personnel

[14]This section is adapted from Robert Murdick, Barry Render, and Roberta Russell, *Service Operations Management* (Boston: Allyn and Bacon, 1990), pp. 421–422.

[15]L. Berry, V. Zeithaml, and A. Parasuraman, "Quality Counts in Services, Too," *Business Horizons* (May/June 1985): 45–46.

TABLE 3.4 ■ DETERMINANTS OF SERVICE QUALITY

Reliability involves consistency of performance and dependability. It means that the firm performs the service right the first time and also means that the firm honours its promises.

Responsiveness concerns the willingness or readiness of employees to provide service. It involves timeliness of service.

Competence means possession of the required skills and knowledge to perform the service.

Access involves approachability and ease of contact.

Courtesy involves politeness, respect, consideration, and friendliness of contact personnel (including receptionists, telephone operators, etc.).

Communication means keeping customers informed in language they can understand and listening to them. It may mean that the company has to adjust its language for different consumers—increasing the level of sophistication with a well-educated customer and speaking simply and plainly with a novice.

Credibility involves trustworthiness, believability, and honesty. It involves having the customer's best interests at heart.

Security is the freedom from danger, risk, or doubt.

Understanding/knowing the customer involves making the effort to understand the customer's needs.

Tangibles include the physical evidence of the service.

Source: Excerpted from A. Parasuraman, Valerie A. Zeithaml, and Leonard L. Berry, "A Conceptual Model of Service Quality and Its Implications for Future Research," *Journal of Marketing* (Fall 1985): 44.

Follow-up interviews with service managers suggest that service quality can be measured by how effectively a service can close the gaps between expectations and the service provided. The *POM in Action* box "CMAs in Telecommunications: The Challenge Ahead" shows how service managers will improve service quality to the customer in the field of telecommunications.

ACHIEVING WORLD-CLASS STANDARDS

Quality is a tremendous competitive weapon. World-class firms such as Lever, Honeywell(Canada), and Motorola achieve outstanding quality performance in a variety of ways. They understand that:

- Top management provides TQM leadership, with an emphasis on doing it correctly the first time.
- Customer requirements are understood and achieved.
- Quality is approached via TQM, not quality inspection systems.
- Systems and procedures are designed to deliver quality products and services.
- Continuous improvement programs are in place to ensure that quality in all phases of the organization is always improving.
- Employees know the cost of quality and are trained in TQM tools.
- Performance measurers for quality are included in manager evaluation.
- Benchmarking procedures are in place and are used.

POM IN ACTION

CMAs in Telecommunications: The Challenge Ahead

Management accountants brought up under the monopoly system of Canadian telecommunications or cable companies are now faced with corporate competition and downsizing, reengineering, TQM, and other new and advanced accounting practices.

Leonard van der Heyden, vice-president of human resources for Bell Canada, says, "From a strategic management perspective, I think what's important is that we have a clearly enunciated policy where we are ultimately going in telecommunications, what the rules of the game are, what kind of game we're playing." Ottawa seems to be favouring free trade over domestically grown businesses by allowing the U.S. conglomerates AT&T and Sprint into Canada, and for this reason Heyden says that there are no more five-year plans, just two-year ones—if you're lucky. The companies seem to be more reactive to the fast-changing market and long-term planning has less meaning now.

The emphasis is on value-added customer service such as marketing, quality customer service, cost containment, and cost reduction. New products ventures will first identify the source of value to the customer, and then incorporate systems and cost and pricing structures. According to Heyden, "That's where management accountants have the edge. Their strength at this point in the history of telecommunications is their overview of the organization and their understanding of the impact on the bottom line."

The problem facing the industry is a limited supply of skilled and qualified workers due to reductions in staff, which will hamper the firms' ability to compete in the future. Heyden stresses the importance of a CMA's skill set with the analytical and disciplined approach to problem solving, but also emphasizes the importance of effective communication. The successful CMA will be able to think on his or her feet and articulate clearly under fire.

Source: Adapted from "CMAs in Telecommunications: The Challenge Ahead," *CMA—The Management Accountant Magazine* (February 1996).

- Quality is a competitive weapon because quality forces so many other things, such as design, processes, inventory, schedules, maintenance, and training to be right.

SUMMARY

Quality is a term that means different things to different people. But it is defined in this chapter as the totality of features and characteristics of a product or service that bear on its ability to satisfy stated or implied needs. Defining quality expectations is critical to effective and efficient operations.

Quality requires building a total quality management (TQM) environment, because quality cannot be inspected into a product. The chapter also addresses five TQM concepts: continuous improvement, employee empowerment, benchmarking, just-in-time, and knowledge of TQM tools. The six TQM tools introduced in this chapter are house of quality, Taguchi method, Pareto charts, process charts, cause-and-effect diagrams, and statistical process control (SPC).

KEY TERMS

ISO 9000 (p. 80)
Can/CSA-ISO 9000 (p. 81)
Total quality management (TQM) (p. 82)
Kaizen (p. 83)
Employee empowerment (p. 83)
Quality circle (p. 84)
Benchmarking (p. 85)
Quality function deployment (QFD) (p. 87)
House of quality (p. 87)
Taguchi technique (p. 89)

Quality robust (p. 89)
Quality loss function (QLF) (p. 89)
Target-oriented quality (p. 89)
Pareto charts (p. 89)
Process charts (p. 90)
Cause-and-effect diagram (p. 92)
Ishikawa diagram (p. 92)
Fish-bone chart (p. 93)
Statistical process control (p. 93)
Control charts (p. 94)
Plan-Do-Check-Act (PDCA) Wheel (p. 94)
Corrective action reporting seminars (CARS) (p. 95)
Inspection (p. 95)
Source inspection (p. 96)
Poka-yoke (p. 96)
Attribute inspection (p. 96)
Variable inspection (p. 96)

DISCUSSION QUESTIONS

1. Provide your own definition of product quality.
2. Name several products that do not require high quality.
3. Do you think the establishment of the *NQI's Canada Awards for Excellence* had much effect on the quality of products actually produced in Canada?
4. How can a university control the quality of its output (that is, its graduates)?
5. What are the major concepts of TQM?
6. Find a recent article on quality circles and summarize its major points. Do you think quality circles will be commonplace in all Canadian firms? Why?
7. How can a firm build a climate of continuous improvement?
8. What are the three basic concepts of the Taguchi method?
9. What are six tools of TQM?
10. What is the "house of quality"?
11. Why is the target-oriented performance better than conformance-oriented performance?
12. What are 10 determinants of service quality?
13. What is the quality loss function (QLF)?
14. What does the formula $L = D^2C$ mean?
15. How would you change the Canada Awards for Excellence criteria?
16. What are the four M's of a cause-and-effect diagram?

CRITICAL THINKING EXERCISE

Canadian Airlines International was formed from the merger of five airlines over the past years. Most were known for their safe and efficient operation rather than their customer-service savvy. During the mergers of 1981, thousands of employees were laid off, morale plummeted, and customer service became incidental.

Eight years later the company implemented a service-quality initiative which, while it was met with heavy skepticism by the employees and unions, also resulted in tremendous support for the possibility of a merger with Air Canada. In response, the Canadian unions agreed to measures to help the company in exchange for (1) a say in how the company would be run, and (2) the end of merger talks with Air Canada, opting, instead, for a merger with American Airlines. The service-quality measures included wage reductions of $250 million over four years, and buying into American Airlines' Sabre reservation system and centralized accounting function.

Again in 1996 Canadian Airlines was faced with financial troubles that had company president Keven Benson calling for a further 10% wage reduction, a downsizing of the domestic Montreal, Ottawa, Toronto routes, and renegotiation of the service contract with American Airlines. With a number of factors in its favour, including one of the youngest aircraft fleets in North America, Canadian has the chance to build a superior company. Continued understanding between labour is the key to realizing that chance.

If wage concessions and domestic reductions were to occur, what strategy would management need to adopt to ensure that quality remains a priority among employees?

Source: Adopted from "Behind the Scenes at Canadian Airlines," CGA *Magazine* 27 no. 6 (June 1993): 30–33.

PROBLEMS

: **3.1** Use quality function deployment's house of quality technique to construct a relationship matrix between customer *wants* and *how* you as a production manager would address them. Consider the *wants* and *hows* of the following:

a) ice cream

b) a soft drink

· **3.2** Conduct an interview with a prospective purchaser of a new bicycle and translate the customer's *wants* into the specific *hows* of the firm.

· **3.3** Use Pareto analysis to investigate the following data collected on a printed-circuit-board assembly line.

a) Prepare a graph of the data.

b) What conclusions do you reach?

DEFECT	NUMBER OF DEFECT OCCURRENCES
Wrong component	217
Components not adhering	146
Excess adhesive	64
Misplaced transistors	600
Defective board dimension	143
Mounting holes improperly positioned	14
Circuitry problems on final test	92

: **3.4** Develop a process chart for one of the following:

a) changing an automobile tire

b) paying a bill in a restaurant

c) making a deposit at your bank

: **3.5** Prepare a process chart for one of the following:

a) a fast-food drive-thru window (single window)

b) a two-station drive-thru window (pay at one, pick up at second)

c) the registration process at your college

⁝ **3.6** Draw a fish-bone chart detailing reasons why a bolt might not be correctly matched to a nut on an assembly line.

⁝ **3.7** Draw a fish-bone chart showing why a typist you paid to prepare a term paper produced a document with numerous errors.

CASE STUDY

Westshore Electrical, Inc.

Westshore Electrical, Inc., is a medium-sized British Columbia manufacturer of wire windings used in making electric motors. Joe Wilson, Operations Manager, has experienced an increasing problem with rejected product found during the manufacturing operation. "I'm not sure where to begin," said Joe at the weekly staff meeting with his boss. "Rejects in the Winding Department have been killing us the past 2 months. Nobody in operations has any idea why. I have just brought in a consultant, Roger Gagnon, to take a look at the situation and make recommendations about how we can find out what is going on. I don't expect Roger to make technical recommendations—just see if he can point us in the right direction."

Gagnon's first stop later that day was the production floor. His discussions with the production supervisors in the Winding Department indicated they had no real grasp of what the problem was or what to do to correct it. A tour of the winding operation indicated that there were three machines that wound wire onto plastic cores to produce the primary and secondary electric motor windings. After inspection by quality control, these windings then went to the Packaging Department. Packaging personnel, Gagnon found, inspect their own work and make corrections on the spot. The problem is that too many windings are found to be defective and require reworking before they can be packaged.

Gagnon's next stop was the Quality Control Department, where he obtained the records for the past month's Winding Department rejects (Table 1).

DISCUSSION QUESTIONS

1. Prepare an outline for Roger Gagnon's report.
2. What charts, graphs, computer printouts, and so forth might be included in the report?
3. Prepare Gagnon's recommendation, with justification, on one page.
4. Prepare the detail necessary to supplement Gagnon's recommendation and justification so Joe Wilson will understand how he arrived at your recommendations.

Source: Professor Victor E. Sower, Ph.D., C.Q.E., Sam Houston State University. Modified for the Canadian edition.

TABLE 1 ■ JANUARY TRANSFORMER REJECT LOG: WINDING PROCESS

			No. of Reject Units by Cause						
Date	No. Inspected	Winder	Bad Wind	Twisted Wire	Broken Leads	Abraded Wire	Wrong Core	Wrong Wire	Failed Electrical Test
1	100	1	1	0	4	1	0	0	1
	100	2	2	1	0	0	1	5	0
	100	3	0	0	0	5	0	0	3
2	100	1	0	1	3	0	0	0	0
	100	2	3	1	0	0	2	3	0
	100	3	0	0	1	6	0	0	0
3	100	1	1	0	0	2	0	0	0
	100	2	0	0	0	0	0	3	0
	100	3	0	0	1	4	0	0	3
4	100	1	0	0	3	0	0	0	0
	100	2	0	0	0	0	0	2	0
	100	3	0	0	0	3	1	0	3
5	100	1	0	1	5	0	0	0	0
	100	2	0	0	0	0	0	2	1
	100	3	0	0	0	3	0	0	2
8	100	1	0	0	2	0	0	0	0
	100	2	0	0	0	0	0	1	0
	100	3	0	0	0	3	0	0	3

(Continued)

TABLE 1 ■ JANUARY TRANSFORMER REJECT LOG: WINDING PROCESS (CONTINUED)

Date	No. Inspected	Winder	No. of Reject Units by Cause: Bad Wind	Twisted Wire	Broken Leads	Abraded Wire	Wrong Core	Wrong Wire	Failed Electrical Test
9	100	1	0	1	2	0	0	0	0
	100	2	0	0	0	0	0	1	0
	100	3	0	0	0	3	0	0	4
10	100	1	0	0	5	0	0	0	0
	100	2	1	0	0	0	1	0	0
	100	3	0	0	0	5	0	0	4
11	100	1	0	0	4	0	0	0	0
	100	2	0	0	0	0	0	0	0
	100	3	0	0	0	4	0	0	4
12	100	1	0	0	3	0	1	0	0
	100	2	1	0	1	0	0	0	0
	100	3	0	0	0	5	0	0	4
15	100	1	0	0	2	0	0	1	0
	100	2	0	0	0	0	0	1	0
	100	3	0	0	0	3	0	0	3
16	100	1	0	0	6	0	0	0	0
	100	2	0	0	0	0	0	0	0
	100	3	0	0	0	3	0	0	3
17	100	1	0	1	1	0	0	0	0
	100	2	0	0	0	0	0	0	1
	100	3	0	0	0	3	0	0	3
18	100	1	1	0	2	0	0	0	0
	100	2	0	0	0	0	0	1	0
	100	3	0	0	0	4	0	0	1
19	100	1	0	0	2	0	0	0	0
	100	2	0	0	0	0	0	0	0
	100	3	0	0	0	3	0	0	1
22	100	1	0	1	4	0	0	0	0
	100	2	0	0	0	0	0	0	0
	100	3	0	0	0	3	0	1	2
23	100	1	0	0	4	0	0	0	0
	100	2	0	0	0	0	0	0	1
	100	3	0	0	0	4	0	0	3
24	100	1	0	0	2	0	0	1	0
	100	2	0	1	0	0	0	0	0
	100	3	0	0	0	4	0	0	3
25	100	1	0	0	3	0	0	0	0
	100	2	0	0	0	1	0	0	0
	100	3	0	0	0	2	0	0	4
26	100	1	0	0	1	0	0	0	0
	100	2	0	1	0	1	0	0	0
	100	3	0	0	0	2	0	0	3
29	100	1	0	0	2	0	0	0	0
	100	2	0	0	1	0	0	0	0
	100	3	0	0	0	2	0	0	3
30	100	1	0	0	2	0	0	0	0
	100	2	0	0	0	0	1	0	0
	100	3	0	0	0	2	0	0	3

Note: Assume that each defective unit was rejected because of one, single defect.

CASE STUDY

Quality Cleaners

The owner of Quality Cleaners has decided that a quality improvement program must be implemented in its dry cleaning service. Customers bring clothes to one of five stores or pickup stations. Orders are then delivered to the cleaning plant twice (morning and afternoon) each day, with deliveries of orders being made to the stores at the same time, allowing for same-day service by customer request.

The stores are opened at 7:00 A.M. by a full-time employee. This person is relieved at 3:00 P.M. by a part-time employee, who closes the store at 6:00 P.M.

When the clothes are received from the customer, a five-ply ticket showing the customer name, phone number, due date, and special requests is prepared. One ply is given to the customer as a claim check and the store keeps one ply (to show what they have in process). The clothes and the remaining plies of the ticket are put in a nylon laundry bag for delivery to the plant.

At the cleaning plant the departments are:

Mark-in. Each order is removed from the bag; items are tagged for identification later and sorted into large buggies according to due date, type of garment, and cleaning requirements. The buggies are moved to the cleaning department as they become full. Also at mark-in, garments are checked for spots, stains, tears, or other special handling. The problem is written on a strip-tag (a 1.3-centimetre-wide paper tape) and attached to the garment with the identification tag.

Cleaning. The buggies are emptied into the cleaning machine one item at a time to allow for inspection. The primary items checked for are spots and stains requiring special attention and foreign objects. For example, an ink pen left in a pocket could ruin the whole load. As items are removed from the cleaning machine, they are placed on hangers and moved by conveyor to the pressing department.

Pressing. There are four presses: one for silks, one for pants, and two general-purpose. On an ordinary day, three of the presses will be operating, but which three of the four are operating will depend upon the total demand and product mix that particular day. As items are pressed, they are placed on a conveyor that delivers them to the assembly department.

Assembly. Cleaned items are grouped into customer orders, bagged, and put in the appropriate queue for delivery to the respective store. At this time, two plies (of the remaining three) of the ticket are attached to the order, and one ply stays at the plant to show this order was completed. When the customer picks up the order, one ply will stay on the order.

The store will retain the last ply and pull the corresponding ply from its work-in-process file to show that this order is complete.

Note: Although Quality Cleaners is a larger-than-average cleaning operation, total annual revenues are approximately $500,000. Therefore, any suggestions must be relatively inexpensive.

At present, a majority of the employees are cross-trained to allow for flexibility. Table 2 indicates the production employees and the positions for which they are trained. P indicates this is the primary duty, or the one they perform most often. A check indicates they are also trained in that function.

For example, one day David may only clean; the next day he cleans awhile and then presses pants. This presents a problem in determining who put a double crease in Mrs. Jones' slacks, but the

TABLE 2

		PRESSES		
EMPLOYEE	CLEANING	GENERAL-PURPOSE	SILKS	PANTS
David	P	✓		✓
Tasha	✓	✓		P
Len	✓	P	✓	
Mary		✓	P	✓
Betty (part-time)	✓	✓		✓
Mike (part-time)	✓	✓		✓

(Continued)

owner believes this flexibility in scheduling is valuable and must be maintained.

DISCUSSION QUESTIONS

1. Design the quality program. Consider the following issues:
   a) Where should inspection(s) occur?
   b) How will accountability be achieved?
   c) What factors (variables, attributes, other considerations) should be checked?
   d) Is statistical process control (SPC) appropriate?
      i. Variable or attribute?
      ii. At what point?
2. What are the cost items for implementing your plan? Give a budget, including equipment, supplies, and labour-hours (divided into types of labour).
3. What records should be kept to measure the success of the program in terms of cost, quality performance, and service to the customer?

Source: Professor Marilyn S. Jones, Winthrop University.

BIBLIOGRAPHY

Akao, Y., ed. *Quality Function Deployment: Integrating Customer Requirements into Product Design*. Cambridge, MA: Productivity Press, 1990.

Berry, L. L., A. Parasuraman, and V. A. Zeithaml. "Improving Service Quality in America: Lessons Learned." *The Academy of Management Executive*, 8, no. 2 (May 1994): 32–52.

Besterfield, D. H. *Quality Control*, 4th ed. Englewood Cliffs, NJ: Prentice Hall, 1994.

Blackburn, R., and B. Rosen. "Total Quality and Human Resources Management: Lessons Learned from Baldrige Award-Winning Companies." *The Academy of Management Executive*, 7, no. 3 (August 1993): 49–66.

Caporaletti, L., E. Gillenwater, and J. Jaggers. "The Application of Taguchi Methods to a Coil Spring Manufacturing Process." *Production and Inventory Management Journal*, 34, no. 4 (Fourth Quarter 1993): 22–27.

Carr, L. P. "Applying Cost of Quality to a Service Business." *Sloan Management Review*, 33, no. 4 (Summer 1992): 72.

Costin, H. *Readings in Total Quality Management*. New York: Dryden Press, 1994.

Crosby, P. B. *Let's Talk Quality*. New York: McGraw-Hill, 1989.

———. *Quality Is Free*. New York: McGraw-Hill, 1979.

———. "Working Like a Chef." *Quality* (January 1989): 24–25.

Deming, W. E. *Out of the Crisis*. Cambridge, MA: Center for Advanced Engineering Study, 1986.

Denton, D. K. "Lessons on Competitiveness: Motorola's Approach." *Production and Inventory Management Journal*, 32, no. 3 (Third Quarter 1991): 22.

DeVor, R. E., T. Chang, and J. W. Sutherland. *Statistical Quality Design and Control: Contemporary Concepts and Methods*. New York: Macmillan, 1992.

Dobyns, L., and C. Crawford-Mason. *Quality or Else: The Revolution in World Business*. New York: Houghton Mifflin, 1991.

Elsayed, E. A., and D. Dietrich. "Quality Control and Its Applications in Production Systems." *Industrial Engineering Research & Development*, 24, no. 5 (November 1992): 2–3.

Evans, J. R., and W. M. Lindsay. *The Management and Control of Quality*, 2d ed. New York: West, 1993.

Feigenbaum, A. V. *Total Quality Control*, 3d ed. New York: McGraw-Hill, 1991.

Forker, L. B. "Quality: American, Japanese, and Soviet Perspectives." *The Academy of Management Executive*, 5, no. 4 (November 1991): 63–73.

Foster, S. T., Jr. "Designing and Initiating a Taguchi Experiment in a Services Setting." *OM Review*, 9, no. 3: 37–50.

Gehani, R. R. "Quality Value-Chain: A Meta-Synthesis of Frontiers of Quality Movement." *The Academy of Management Executive*, 7, no. 2 (May 1993): 29–42.

Hart, M. K. "Quality Tools for Decreasing Variation and Defining Process Capability." *Production and Inventory Management Journal*, 33, no. 2 (Second Quarter 1992): 6.

———. "Quality Control Training for Manufacturing." *Production and Inventory Management Journal*, 32, no. 3 (Third Quarter 1991): 35.

Hauser, J. R. "How Puritan-Bennett Used the House of Quality." *Sloan Management Review*, 34, no. 3 (Spring 1993): 61–70.

Hauser, J. R., and D. Clausing. "The House of Quality." *Harvard Business Review*, 3 (May/June 1988): 63–70.

Hill, R. C. "When the Going Gets Rough: A Baldrige Award Winner on the Line." *The Academy of Management Executive*, 7, no. 3 (August 1993): 75–79.

Juran, J. M. "Made in the U.S.A.: A Renaissance in Quality." *Harvard Business Review*, 14, no. 4 (July/August 1993): 35–38.

Krishnan, R., A. B. Shani, R. M. Grant, and R. Baer. "In Search of Quality Improvement: Problems of Design and Implementation." *The Academy of Management Executive*, 7, no. 4 (November 1993): 7.

Miller, J. G. *Benchmarking*. Homewood, IL: Business One Irwin, 1992.

Nandakumar, P., S. M. Datar, and R. Akella. "Models for Measuring and Accounting for Cost of Conformance Quality." *Management Science*, 39, no. 1 (January 1993): 1–16.

Peace, G. S. *Taguchi Methods: A Hands-On Approach*. Reading, MA: Addison-Wesley, 1993.

Porteus, E. L. "Note: The Impact of Inspection Delay on Process and Inspection Lot Sizing." *Management Science*, 36, no. 8 (August 1990): 999–1007.

Price, F. *Right Every Time: Using the Deming Approach*. New York: Marcel Dekker, 1990.

Ryan, T. P. *Statistical Methods for Quality Improvement*. New York: John Wiley, 1989.

Schonberger, R. J. "Is Strategy Strategic? Impact of Total Quality Management on Strategy." *The Executive*, 6, no. 3 (August 1992): 80.

Tsui, K. "An Overview of Taguchi Method and Newly Developed Statistical Methods for Robust Design." *Industrial Engineering Research & Development*, 24, no. 5 (November 1992): 44–57.

Vaziri, H. K. "Using Competitive Benchmarking to Set Goals." *Quality Progress*, 25, no. 10 (October 1992): 81.

4

STATISTICAL QUALITY CONTROL

CHAPTER OUTLINE

LEARNING OBJECTIVES

When you complete this chapter you should be able to:

Identify or define:

- Assignable causes of variations
- Natural causes of variations
- Central limit theorem
- Attribute inspection
- Variable inspection
- Process control
- $\bar{x}$-charts
- *R*-charts
- LCL and UCL
- $\bar{p}$ and $\bar{c}$ charts
- Acceptance sampling
- OC curve
- AQL and LTPD
- Manufacturer's risk
- Buyer's risk
- AOQ

Explain:

- The role of statistical quality control

Steelmakers Seek Funds for Waste Recycling and Process Control Programs

When, in 1995, steelmakers sought continued government financial support for two steel-related programs at the U.S. Department of Energy, they were turned down by a budget-cutting Congress. Now Acme Steel Co. is seeking private-sector funding for a Waste Recycling Demonstration Program and an Advanced Process Control Program.

The two industry-government partnerships would have cost the U.S. federal treasury about $16.5 million and $4.4 million, respectively, in fiscal 1996. Despite the industry's offer to pick up 50% of the waste recycling program's costs and 30% of the process control program's costs, the House Appropriations subcommittee that oversees Energy Department programs rejected the proposal.

Speaking on behalf of American Iron and Steel Institute (AISI) members, Brian W.H. Marsden, chairperson and chief executive officer of Acme Steel Co., called the ongoing research endeavours "two programs of great vale to our future competitiveness, energy-efficiency, and improved environmental performance." One of the goals is to develop "energy-efficient and environmentally friendly technology to replace the blast furnace/coke oven process."

To advance the technology's implementation, Marsden pointed to a highly successful program that was started in 1994 to "research the production of hot metal from recycled steel plant waste oxides." The AISI has been submitting proposals to private-sector organizations to help with the construction of a demonstration plant producing 226,800 tonnes of hot metal per year from 453,600 tonnes of waste oxides a year. Stelco's Lake Erie Works, on the Canadian side of Lake Erie, is one of the North American steelmills being approached for the site of the demonstration plant.

The Advanced Process Control Program, Marsden said, is actually a set of six ongoing research projects on sensor and control systems, which will allow steelmakers to "see, hear, and feel" the processes in their plants with more precision. The projects involve major national laboratories, and each is sponsored by a steel company. Marsden has suggested that better process controls would also benefit other industries.

Source: Adapted from "Steelmakers Seeking Funds for DOE Efforts," *American Metal Market* 103, no 60 (March 29, 1995):7.

Molten iron being tapped from the pilot scale vessel at a waste oxide recycling plant.

Steelmaking coke ovens.

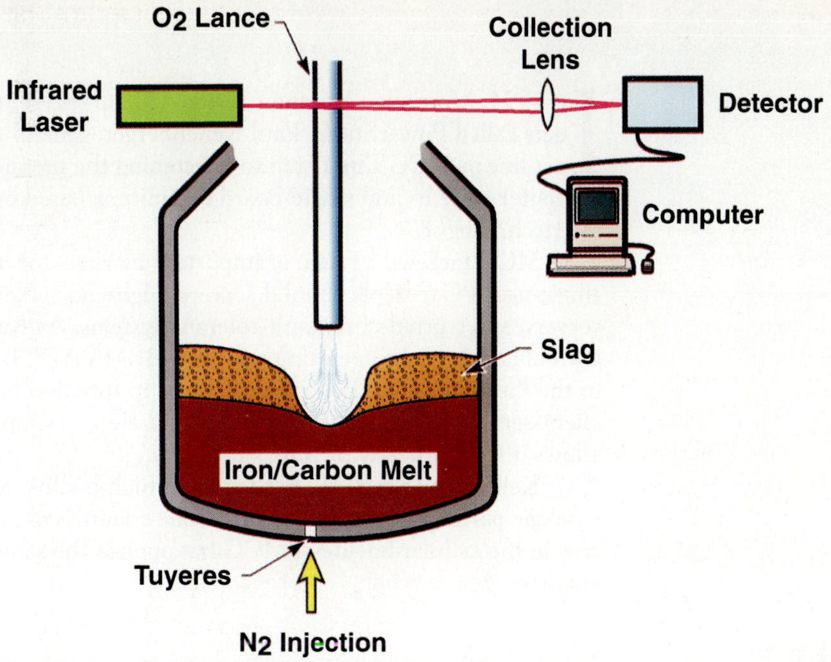

Advanced process control in steelmaking: composition and temperature are monitored using diode laser spectroscopy and computers.

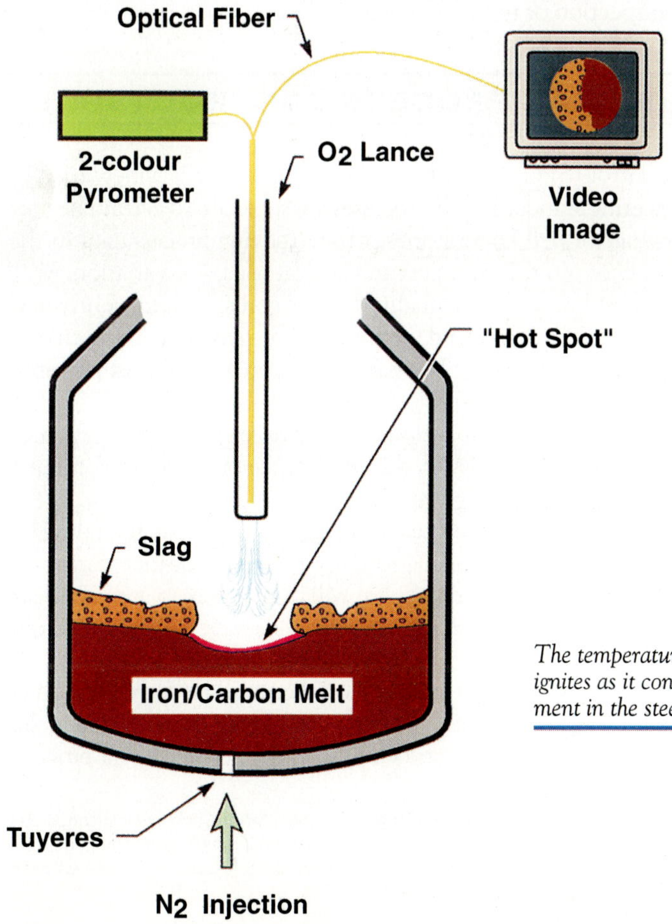

The temperature of the "hot spot" zone where oxygen ignites as it contacts the steel is a critical quality element in the steelmaking process.

In 1994, Motorola Computer Group (MCG) presented a line of computer products called PowerStack. Paul Kellenberger, general manager, described this product line as MCG's first step to "becoming the premier source of a full line of computer systems and single-board computers, based on the PowerPC microprocessor [technology]

MCG targeted a range of important markets for its products—from desktop single-user PC to departmental servers, high-end symmetrical Multi-Processor servers, and trusted-core, fault-tolerant systems. As well, MCG planned to support the industry's major operating systems—IBM's AIX 4.1 and Windows NT—ported to the PowerPC. The PowerPC capacity to function both as a client platform in client-server environments and as a stand-alone personal computer allows it to compete with Intel's Pentium.

Kellenberger sees MCG's focus on high-quality, low-cost manufacturing, strategic partnerships, and dedicated sale channels as responsible for their prior success in the cellular business. MCG has applied the same winning formula to the PC business. ♦

In this chapter, we address statistical process control (SPC)—the same techniques used at Motorola to achieve six sigma. We also introduce acceptance sampling. *Statistical process control* is the application of statistical techniques to the control of manufacturing processes. *Acceptance sampling* is used to determine acceptance or rejection of a lot of material evaluated by inspection or test of a sample.

STATISTICAL PROCESS CONTROL (SPC)

Statistical process control (SPC) is a statistical technique that is widely used to ensure that processes are meeting standards. All processes are subject to a certain degree of variability. Walter Shewhart of Bell Laboratories, while studying process data in the 1920s, made the distinction between the common and special causes of variation. W. Edwards Deming, perhaps the best known of the quality control gurus, had frequently made reference to Shewhart in his own writings and seminars. Many people now refer to these variations as *natural* and *assignable* causes. Shewhart developed a simple but powerful tool to separate the two—the **control chart**.

Control chart

We use statistical process control to measure performance of a process. A process is said to be operating in statistical control when the only source of variation is common (natural) causes.

For example, natural materials such as wood display variances, including both density and colouration, which vary according to the weather conditions during the life of the tree. Even man-made materials such as steel will display some variance (visible with the aid of electron microscopes) due to tiny imperfections such as displaced atoms in the crystal lattice structure.

The process must first be brought into statistical control by detecting and eliminating special (assignable) causes of variation.[1] Then its performance is predictable, and its ability to meet customer expectations can be assessed. The *objective* of a process control

[1]Removing assignable causes is work. As W. Edwards Deming observed, "a state of statistical control is not a natural state for a manufacturing process. It is instead an achievement, arrived at by elimination, one by one, by determined effort, of special causes of excessive variation." See W. Edwards Deming, "On Some Statistical Aids Toward Economic Production," *Interfaces*, 5, no. 4 (1975): 5.

system is *to provide a statistical signal when assignable causes of variation are present.* Such a signal can quicken appropriate action to eliminate assignable causes.

NATURAL VARIATIONS. Natural variations affect almost every production process and are to be expected. **Natural variations** are the many sources of variation within a process that is in statistical control. They behave like a constant system of chance causes. Although individual values are all different, as a group, they form a pattern that can be described as a distribution. When these distributions are *normal,* they are characterized by two parameters. These parameters are

Natural variations

- mean, μ (the measure of central tendency, in this case, the average value)
- standard deviation, σ (variation, the amount by which the smaller values differ from the larger ones)

As long as the distribution (output precision) remains within specified limits, the process is said to be "in control," and the modest variations are tolerated. Variations within these limits are considered acceptable, as they do not affect the proper functioning of the item. A good example would be variations in the gaps at the edges of car doors. If the gaps are *too small,* the door will bind. But too large a gap impairs the function of keeping hostile weather conditions at bay, and detracts from the "good fit" appearance of the doors. That said, the *correct* door dimensions need not be dead precise: a manufacturer must consider a quality/price tradeoff.

Doors for mass-market cars are mass-produced and unavoidably will display some variances in dimensions due to differences in both materials and manufacturing process conditions. To insist on *exact* dimensions for every door would mean that more than 90% of doors produced would be rejected, a rejection rate that would dramatically increase production costs and selling prices. Any manufacturer following a policy of such precision would have to develop a customer base of those willing to pay a very high price for it.

While marketing studies have shown that customers do exist for such high precision and its attendant prices, the number of such customers is extremely small. These few are those who possess virtually unlimited personal resources. The vast majority are far more pragmatic and willing to accept a reasonable price/quality tradeoff as long as a very good, but not necessarily perfect, product can be obtained at a reasonable price.

ASSIGNABLE VARIATIONS. Assignable variation in a process can be traced to a specific reason. Factors such as machine wear, misadjusted equipment, fatigued or untrained workers, or new batches of raw material are all potential sources of **assignable variations**.

Assignable variations

Natural and assignable variations distinguish two tasks for the P/OM manager. The first is to ensure that the process will have only natural variation that is capable of operating under control. The second is, of course, to identify and eliminate assignable variations so that the processes will remain under control.

SAMPLES. Because of natural and assignable variation, statistical process control uses averages of small samples (often of five items or parts) as opposed to data on individual parts. Individual pieces tend to be too erratic to make trends quickly visible.

Figure 4.1 provides a detailed look at the important steps in determining process variation. The horizontal scale can be weight (as in the number of ounces in boxes of cereal), or length (as in fence posts), or any physical measure. The vertical scale is frequency.

FIGURE 4.1 ■ Natural and Assignable Variation

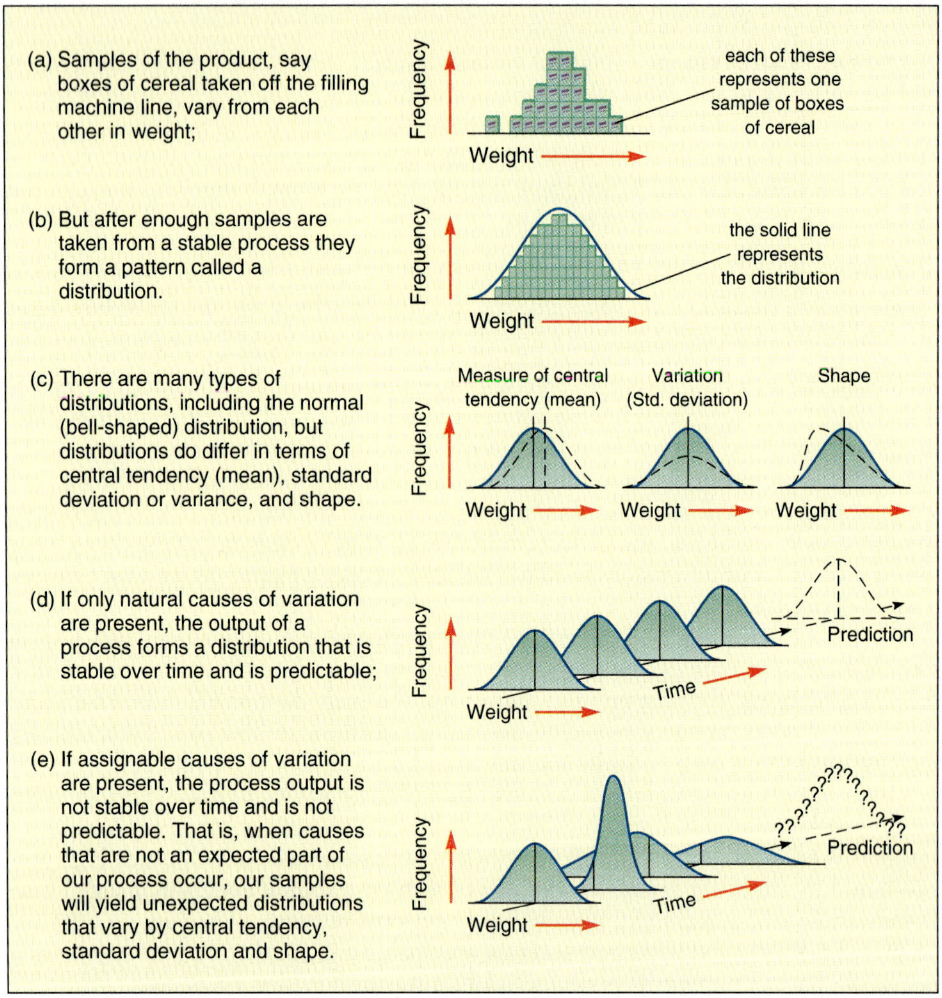

"All quality control does is find our mistakes. I want to start avoiding them."

CONTROL CHARTS. The process of building control charts is based on the concepts presented in Figure 4.2. This figure shows three distributions that are the result of outputs from three types of processes. We plot small samples and then examine characteristics of the resulting data to see if the process is within "control limits." The purpose of control charts is to help distinguish between natural variations and variations due to assignable causes. As seen in Figure 4.2, a process is (a) in control *and the process is capable of producing within established control limits*, (b) in control, *but the process is not capable of producing within established limits*, or (c) out of control. We now look at how to build control charts that help the P/OM manager keep a process under control.

Control Charts for Variables

Variables are characteristics that have continuous dimensions. They have an infinite number of possibilities. Examples are weight, speed, length, or strength. (In most products there is frequently a single measurable dimension most indicative of quality or lack thereof.)

FIGURE 4.2 ■ Process Control: Three Types of Process Outputs

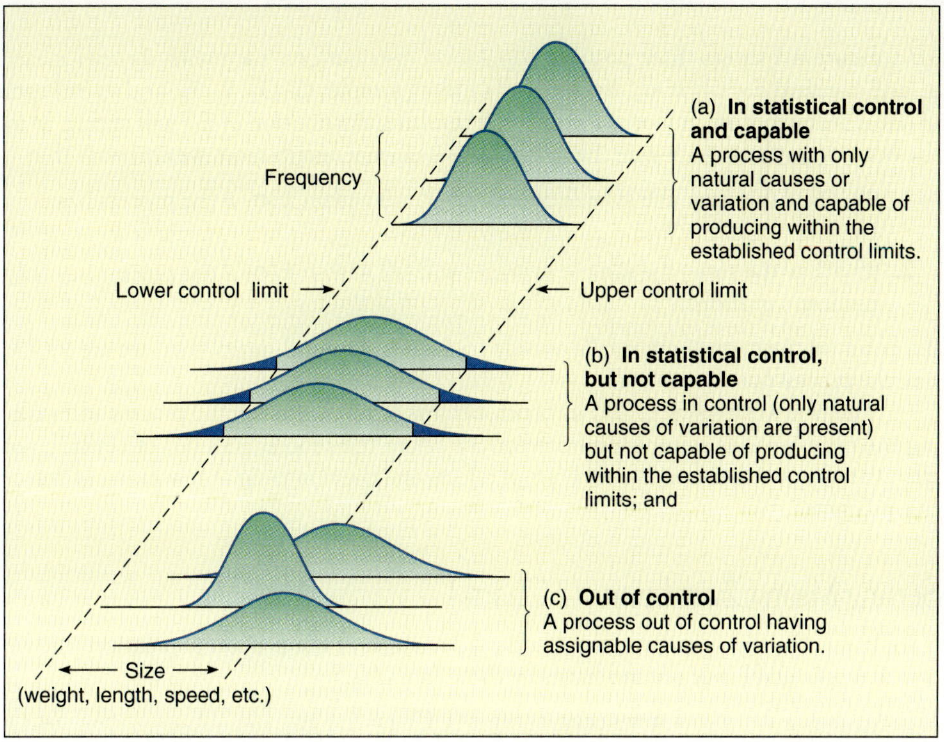

Control charts for the mean, $\bar{x}$, and the range, R, are used to monitor processes that hav continuous dimensions. The **$\bar{x}$- (x-bar) chart** tells us whether changes have occurred in the central tendency of a process. This might be due to such factors as tool wear, a gradual increase in temperature, a different method used on the second shift, or new and stronger materials. The ***R*-chart** values indicate that a gain or loss in uniformity has occurred. Such a change might be due to worn bearings, a loose tool part, an erratic flow of lubricants to a machine, or to sloppiness on the part of a machine operator. The two types of charts go hand in hand when monitoring variables.

$\bar{x}$-chart

***R*-chart**

Both charts *must* be examined before one can determine whether a process is truly "in control." If either chart shows or both show, an out-of-control condition, the process is declared to be "out-of-control."

The Central Limit Theorem

Central limit theorem

The theoretical foundation for $\bar{x}$-charts is the **central limit theorem.** In general terms, this theorem states that regardless of the distribution of the population of all parts or services, the distribution of $\bar{x}$'s (each of which is a mean of a sample drawn from the population) will tend to follow a normal curve as the sample size grows larger. And, fortunately, even if the sample (n) is fairly small (say 4 or 5), the distributions of the averages will still roughly follow a normal curve. The theorem also states that (1) the mean of the distribution of the $\bar{x}$'s (called $\bar{\bar{x}}$) will equal the mean of the overall population (called μ); and (2) the standard deviation of the sampling distribution, $\sigma_{\bar{x}}$, will be the population standard deviation, σ_x, divided by the square root of the sample size, n. In other words,

$$\bar{\bar{x}} = \mu \quad \text{and} \quad \sigma_{\bar{x}} = \frac{\sigma_x}{\sqrt{n}}$$

Figure 4.3 shows three possible population distributions, each with its own mean, μ, and standard deviation σ_x. If a series of random samples ($\bar{x}_1$, $\bar{x}_2$, $\bar{x}_3$, $\bar{x}_4$, and so on) each of size n is drawn from any one of these, the resulting distribution of $\bar{x}_i$'s will appear as in the bottom graph of that figure. Because this is a normal distribution, we can state that

1. 99.7% of the time, the sample averages will fall within $\pm 3\sigma_{\bar{x}}$ if the process has only random variations; and
2. 95.5% of the time, the sample averages will fall within $\pm 2\sigma_{\bar{x}}$ if the process has only random variations.

If a point on the control chart falls outside of the $\pm 3\sigma_{\bar{x}}$ control limits, then we are 99.7% sure the process has changed. This is the theory behind control charts.

The true worth of SPC and its control charts is in monitoring the process and making the necessary adjustments and corrections *before* the process goes out of control, *not after*, thereby saving the enormous costs of rejects and the scrapping or reworking of defective products.

Setting Mean Chart Limits ($\bar{x}$ Charts)

If we know, through past data, the standard deviation of the process population, σ_x, we can set upper and lower control limits by these formulas:

$$\text{Upper control limit (UCL)} = \bar{\bar{x}} + z\sigma_{\bar{x}} \tag{4.1}$$

$$\text{Lower control limit (LCL)} = \bar{\bar{x}} - z\sigma_{\bar{x}} \tag{4.2}$$

where $\bar{\bar{x}}$ = mean of the sample means
z = number of normal standard deviations (2 for 95.5% confidence, 3 for 99.7%)
$\sigma_{\bar{x}}$ = standard deviation of the sample means = $\sigma_x/\sqrt{n}$
n = sample size

Example 1 shows how to set control limits for sample means using standard deviations.

Because process standard deviations are either not available or difficult to compute, we usually calculate control limits on the basis of the average *range* values rather than of

EXAMPLE 1

The weights of boxes of Oat Flakes within a large production lot are sampled each hour. To set control limits that include 99.7% of the sample means, samples of nine boxes are randomly selected and weighed. Here are the results for the past 12 hours (weights are given in grams):

Hour	Avg. of 9 Boxes	Hour	Avg. of 9 Boxes	Hour	Avg. of 9 Boxes
1	513	5	495	9	490
2	504	6	492	10	495
3	435	7	456	11	426
4	444	8	491	12	519

The average mean of all 12 of the samples is easily calculated to be exactly 480 grams and the population standard deviation is calculated to be 30 grams. We therefore have $\bar{\bar{x}} = 480$ grams, $\sigma_x = 30$ gms, $n = 9$, and $z = 3$. The control limits are:

$$UCL_{\bar{x}} = \bar{\bar{x}} + z\sigma_{\bar{x}} = 480 + 3\left(\frac{30}{\sqrt{9}}\right) = 480 + 3\left(\frac{30}{3}\right) = 510 \text{ grams}$$

$$LCL_{\bar{x}} = \bar{\bar{x}} - z\sigma_{\bar{x}} = 480 - 3\left(\frac{30}{\sqrt{9}}\right) = 16 - 3\left(\frac{30}{3}\right) = 450 \text{ grams}$$

standard deviations. Table 4.1 provides the necessary conversion for us to do so. The range is defined as the difference between the largest and the smallest items in one sample. For example, if the heaviest box of Oat Flakes in hour 1 of Example 1 was 570 grams and the lightest was 420 grams, the range for that hour would be 150 grams. We use Table 4.1 and the equations

$$UCL_{\bar{x}} = \bar{\bar{x}} + A_2\bar{R} \tag{4.3}$$

and

$$LCL_{\bar{x}} = \bar{\bar{x}} - A_2\bar{R} \tag{4.4}$$

where $\bar{R}$ = average range of the samples
A_2 = value found in Table 4.1
$\bar{\bar{x}}$ = mean of the sample means

Example 2 shows how to set control limits for sample means using Table 4.1 and the average range.

Acceptable tolerance levels on auto body parts at this New United Motor Manufacturing (NUMMI) plant in Fremont, California, are so small that the company uses computers to see whether the process is in or out of control. Workers at NUMMI (which makes the Toyota Corolla and GM Prizm) are empowered to stop the entire production line by pulling the overhead cord if any quality problems are spotted.

FIGURE 4.3 ■ The Relationship Between Population and Sampling Distributions. Regardless of the population distribution (e.g., beta, normal, uniform), each with its own mean (μ) and standard deviation (σ_x), the distribution of sample means is always normal.

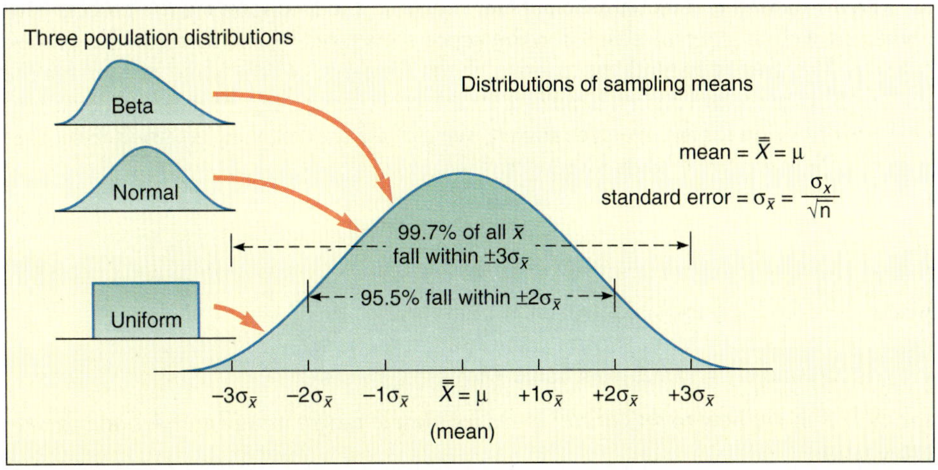

EXAMPLE 2

Super Cola bottles soft drinks labelled "net vol. 1 litre." An overall process average of 1,009 millilitres has been found by taking several batches of samples, in which each sample contained five bottles. The average range of the process is 25 millilitres. Determine the upper and lower control limits for averages in this process.

Looking in Table 4.1 for a sample size of 5 in the mean factor A_2 column, we find the number .577. Thus, the upper and lower control chart limits are

$$\begin{aligned} UCL_{\bar{x}} &= \bar{\bar{x}} + A_2\bar{R} \\ &= 1009 + (.577)(25) \\ &= 1009 + 14.425 \\ &= 16.154 \text{ ounces} \end{aligned}$$

$$\begin{aligned} LCL_{\bar{x}} &= \bar{\bar{x}} - A_2\bar{R} \\ &= 1009 - 14.425 \\ &= 988 \text{ millilitres} \end{aligned}$$

Setting Range Chart Limits (*R* Charts)

In Examples 1 and 2, we determined the upper and lower control limits for the process *average*. In addition to being concerned with the process average, operations managers are interested in the process *dispersion*, or *variability*. Even though the process average is under control, the variability of the process may not be. For example, something may have worked itself loose in a piece of equipment.

Perhaps a nut or bolt designed to hold a part of the production machine at the correct setting may not have been tightened properly and each machine cycle will cause the setting to change. Improper balance of a domestic washing machine will cause vibrations and premature wear to the machine. (In extreme cases, the washing machine will actually "walk" across the floor.) Some manufacturers, fearful of high warranty claims, have installed "tilt" mechanisms to shut down the washing machine to minimize the damage caused by improper levelling or an unbalanced load.

As a result of this variability of the process, the average of the samples may remain the same, but the variation within the samples could be entirely too large. For this reason, P/OM managers use control charts for ranges in order to monitor the process variability, as well as control charts for the process average, which monitor the process average. The theory behind the control charts for ranges is the same as that for the process average control charts. Limits are established that contain ±3 standard deviations of the distribution for the average range $\bar{R}$. We can use the following equation to set the upper and lower control limits for ranges:

$$UCL_R = D_4\bar{R} \quad (4.5)$$

$$LCL_R = D_3\bar{R} \quad (4.6)$$

where UCL_R = upper control chart limit for the range
LCL_R = lower control chart limit for the range
D_4 and D_3 = values from Table 4.1

Example 3 shows how to set control limits for sample ranges using Table 4.1 and the average range.

EXAMPLE 3

The average *range* of a process loading is 5.3 kilograms. If the sample size is 5, determine the upper and lower control chart limits.

Looking in Table 4.1 for a sample size of 5, we find that $D_4 = 2.114$ and $D_3 = 0$. The range control limits are

$$
\begin{aligned}
UCL_R &= D_4\overline{R} \\
&= (2.114)(5.3 \text{ kilograms}) \\
&= 11.2 \text{ kilograms}
\end{aligned}
$$

$$
\begin{aligned}
LCL_R &= D_3\overline{R} \\
&= (0)(5.3 \text{ kilograms}) \\
&= 0
\end{aligned}
$$

TABLE 4.1 ■ FACTORS FOR COMPUTING CONTROL CHART LIMITS

SAMPLE SIZE, N	MEAN FACTOR, A_2	UPPER RANGE, D_4	LOWER RANGE, D_3
2	1.880	3.268	0
3	1.023	2.574	0
4	.729	2.282	0
5	.577	2.114	0
6	.483	2.004	0
7	.419	1.924	0.076
8	.373	1.864	0.136
9	.337	1.816	0.184
10	.308	1.777	0.223
12	.266	1.716	0.284
14	.235	1.671	0.329
16	.212	1.636	0.364
18	.194	1.608	0.392
20	.180	1.586	0.414
25	.153	1.541	0.459

Source: Reprinted by permission of American Society for Testing Materials. Copyright 1951. Taken from Special Technical Publication 15-C, "Quality Control of Materials," pp. 63 and 72.

STEPS TO FOLLOW IN USING CONTROL CHARTS. Five steps are generally followed in using $\overline{x}$- and R-charts:

1. Collect 20 to 25 samples of $n = 4$ or $n = 5$ each from a stable process and compute the mean and range of each.
2. Compute the overall means ($\overline{\overline{x}}$ and $\overline{R}$), set appropriate control limits, usually at the 99.7% level, and calculate the preliminary upper and lower control limits. If the process is not currently stable, use the desired mean, μ, instead of $\overline{\overline{x}}$ to calculate limits.
3. Graph the sample means and ranges on their respective control charts and determine whether they fall outside the acceptable limits.

4. Investigate points or patterns that indicate the process is out of control. Try to assign causes for the variation and then resume the process.
5. Collect additional samples and, if necessary, revalidate the control limits using the new data.

Control Charts for Attributes ($\bar{p}$ and $\bar{c}$ Charts)

Control charts for $\bar{x}$ and R do not apply when we are sampling *attributes*, which are typically classified as defective or nondefective. Measuring defectives involves counting them—for example, the number of defective AAA, AA, B, etc., batteries in a lot (those whose voltage readings fall outside the control limits for stated voltage). Items such as small batteries, household lightbulbs, or fluorescent tubes are far beyond economic rework should they be discovered to be defective. A lightbulb is basically an electric filament enclosed in a glass envelope and a threaded metal ferrule, and either produces an acceptable level of light or not. Such an item, which retails at less than $1, cannot be economically disassembled and repaired, and so if defective must be scrapped at a total loss. Standard wire coat hangers are another example.

Variables, on the other hand, are usually measured for length or weight. There are two kinds of attribute control charts: (1) those that measure the percent defective in a sample—called *p*-charts and (2) those that count the number of defects—called *c*-charts.

p-charts

P-CHARTS. Using ***p*-charts** is the chief way to control attributes. Although attributes that are either good or bad follow the binomial distribution, the normal distribution can be used to calculate *p*-chart limits when sample sizes are large. The procedure resembles the $\bar{x}$-chart approach, which was also based on the central limit theorem.

The formulas for *p*-chart upper and lower control limits follow:

$$UCL_p = \bar{p} + z\sigma_{\hat{p}} \tag{4.7}$$

$$LCL_p = \bar{p} - z\sigma_{\hat{p}} \tag{4.8}$$

where $\bar{p}$ = mean fraction defective in the sample
z = number of standard deviations ($z = 2$ for 95.5% limits; $z = 3$ for 99.7% limits)
$\sigma_{\hat{p}}$ = standard deviation of the sampling distribution

$\sigma_{\hat{p}}$ is estimated by the formula:

$$\sigma_{\hat{p}} = \sqrt{\frac{\bar{p}(1-\bar{p})}{n}} \tag{4.9}$$

where n = size of each sample.

Example 4 shows how to set control limits for *p*-charts for these standard deviations.

C-CHARTS. In Example 4, we counted the number of defective records entered. A defective record was one that was not exactly correct. A bad record may contain more than one defect, however. We use **c-charts** to control the *number* of defects per unit of output (or per insurance record in the preceding case).

c-charts

Control charts for defects are helpful for monitoring processes in which a large number of potential errors can occur but the actual number that do occur is relatively small. Defects may be errors in newspaper words, bad circuits in a microchip, blemishes on a table, or missing pickles on a fast-food hamburger.

The Poisson probability distribution, which has a variance equal to its mean, is the basis for *c*-charts. Because *c* is the mean number of defects per unit, the standard deviation is equal to $\sqrt{\bar{c}}$. To compute 99.7% control limits for $\bar{c}$, we use the formula

$$\bar{c} \pm 3\sqrt{\bar{c}} \qquad (4.10)$$

Example 5 shows how to set control limits for a $\bar{c}$ chart.

Note that although we have discussed process charts and control limits, a focus on the target value, not the limits, is best.

EXAMPLE 4

Data entry clerks at ARCO key in thousands of insurance records each day. Samples of the work of 20 clerks are shown in the table. Two hundred records entered by each clerk were carefully examined to make sure they contained no errors. The fraction defective in each sample was then computed.

Set the control limits to include 99.7% of the random variation in the entry process when it is in control.

Sample Number	Number of Errors	Fraction Defective	Sample Number	Number of Errors	Fraction Defective
1	12	.06	11	12	.06
2	10	.05	12	2	.01
3	0	.00	13	16	.08
4	2	.01	14	14	.07
5	8	.04	15	10	.05
6	4	.02	16	8	.04
7	10	.05	17	22	.11
8	6	.03	18	6	.03
9	6	.03	19	0	.00
10	4	.02	20	8	.04
				160	

$$\bar{p} = \frac{\text{total number of errors}}{\text{total number of records examined}} = \frac{160}{(200)(20)} = .04$$

$$\sigma_{\hat{p}} = \sqrt{\frac{(.04)(1-.04)}{200}} = .014$$

(*Note:* 100 is the size of each sample $= n$)

$$UCL_p = \bar{p} + z\sigma_{\hat{p}} = .04 + 3(.014) = .082$$

$$LCL_p = \bar{p} - z\sigma_{\hat{p}} = .04 - 3(.014) = .002$$

Note: LCL cannot have a negative value, as the lowest possibility for an LCL is zero or *no* defectives. A negative result would imply better than perfect, i.e., zero defectives, which is logically impossible. *Should an LCL calculation result in a negative value, simply set the LCL to zero.*

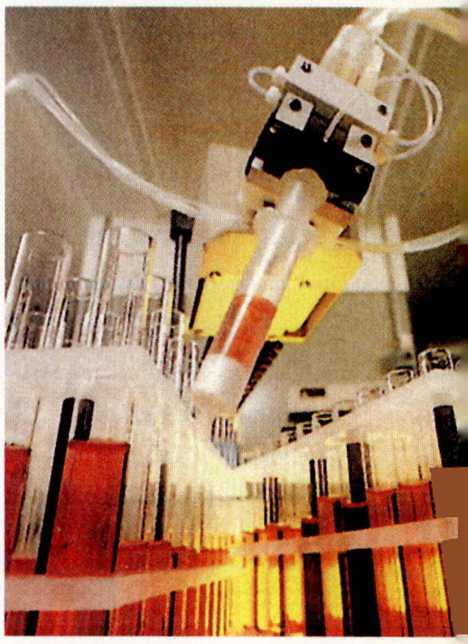

Space-age robotics and computerized analytical equipment are used by Waste Management to protect groundwater. Waste management processing and disposal centers analyze up to 60,000 samples annually in its attempt to assure the highest standards of environmental quality.

When we plot the control limits and the sample fraction defectives, we find that only one data entry clerk (number 17) is out of control. The firm may wish to examine that individual's work a bit more closely to see if a serious problem exists (see Figure 4.4.)

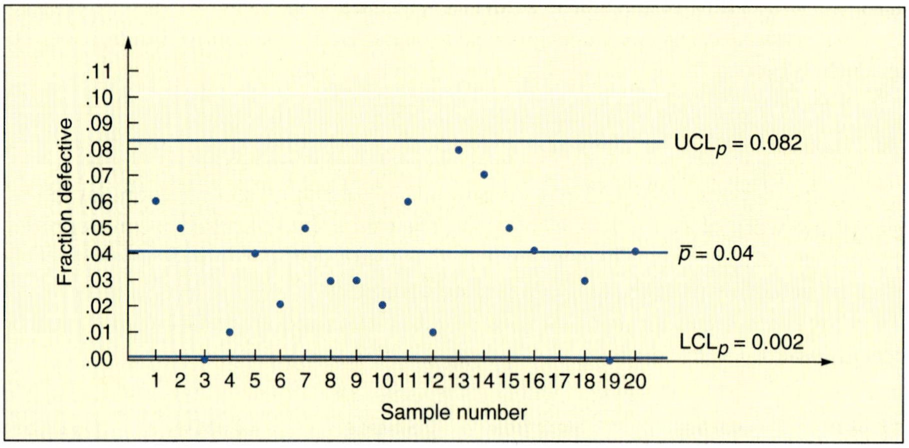

FIGURE 4.4 ■ *p*-Chart for Data Entry for Example 4

POM IN ACTION

ADT Joins with Police to Reduce False Alarms

ADT Security Systems launched a renewed effort to decrease the frequency of false alarms. Approximately 98% of all alarms sounded are false, due mostly to user error, which is of great concern to law enforcement, security alarm companies, and communities.

To promote the reduction of false alarms, ADT undertook public relations and direct mail campaigns and meetings with law enforcement officials. these initiatives included:

- FADE (False Alarm Dispatch Elimination), a global program to eliminate the dispatch of police, fire, and/or medical teams for non-emergency situations
- a $20 million investment to improve technology that reduces false alarms, and strict equipment and quality control standards for their alarm detection devices
- verification of emergencies by CMC (Customer Monitoring Centres) before and after the police are called
- product and procedural training for security personnel and customers, in addition to follow-up training material that focuses on false alarm reduction and local law enforcement policies and procedures for false alarms
- partnership with local law enforcement, government, and community organizations to maintain these and other initiatives

As a result of ADT's efforts, the number of customer false alarms per system in Canada was reduced by an average of 30% in 1995. Verification of alarm calls resulted in the cancellation of over 10,000 false alarms before the police were notified. In 1996 ADT's efforts were rewarded with the lowest false alarm average of all major economic security companies

Source: Adapted from Canada NewsWire Ltd., "ADT Security Systems Working with Law Enforcement Units in an Effort to Reduce False Alarms," June 13, 1996.

Interpreting SPC Run Charts

After run charts have been drawn, they must be interpreted and put to use. Seven sample charts are presented in Figure 4.5.

CHART 1. Displays "normal behaviour" or the expected random variation about the centreline. The CL is, as has been shown above, X or R or *p* or *c* according to the type of

EXAMPLE 5

> Red Top Cab Company receives several complaints per day about the behaviour of its drivers. Over a 9-day period (where days are the units of measure), the owner received the following numbers of calls from irate passengers: 3, 0, 8, 9, 6, 7, 4, 9, 8, for a total of 54 complaints.
>
> To compute 99.7% control limits, we take
>
> $$\bar{c} = \frac{54}{9} = 6 \text{ complaints per day}$$
>
> Thus,
>
> $$UCL_c = \bar{c} + 3\sqrt{\bar{c}} = 6 + 3\sqrt{6} = 6 + 3(2.45) = 13.35$$
>
> $$LCL_c = \bar{c} - 3\sqrt{\bar{c}} = 6 - 3\sqrt{6} = 6 - 3(2.45) = 0$$
>
> After the owner plotted a control chart summarizing these data and posted it prominently in the drivers' locker room, the number of calls received dropped to an average of three per day. Can you explain why this occurred?

run chart being constructed. The random variations shown are, for the most part, variations that are expected due to normal variations in materials, and *not* in the process itself. The points, while varying, cluster quite closely to the centreline, varying back and forth around it, and show no discernible trend in either direction.

CHART 2. While this chart shows the expected "random variations," there is real cause for concern as the variance is too great and the data points are too close to the control limits. An immediate investigation should be carried out to determine why the process displays wider-than-expected variations about the centreline and are so close to the control limits.

CHARTS 3, 4, 5. A point has gone beyond the control limits—either upper or lower or both. If any point exceeds either control limit, the process can be deemed to be out of control and a search should be begun immediately to determine assignable causes. In the case of X and R charts, the process is yielding products outside of the dimensional limits which are therefore "rejects" of unacceptable quality. In the case of *p* and *c* charts, should data points "go below" the lower control limit (LCL), one must investigate to determine why quality has shown a dramatic improvement.

One possible explanation may be different batch numbers of raw materials and/or different suppliers. If the material which produces an unexpectedly low number of rejects is from a different supplier, a process engineer would likely advise the purchasing department of the result and request a change to the better-quality supplier. In this instance, a new set of production samples would be taken from the new supplier's materials and a

FIGURE 4.5 ■ Interpreting SPC Run Charts

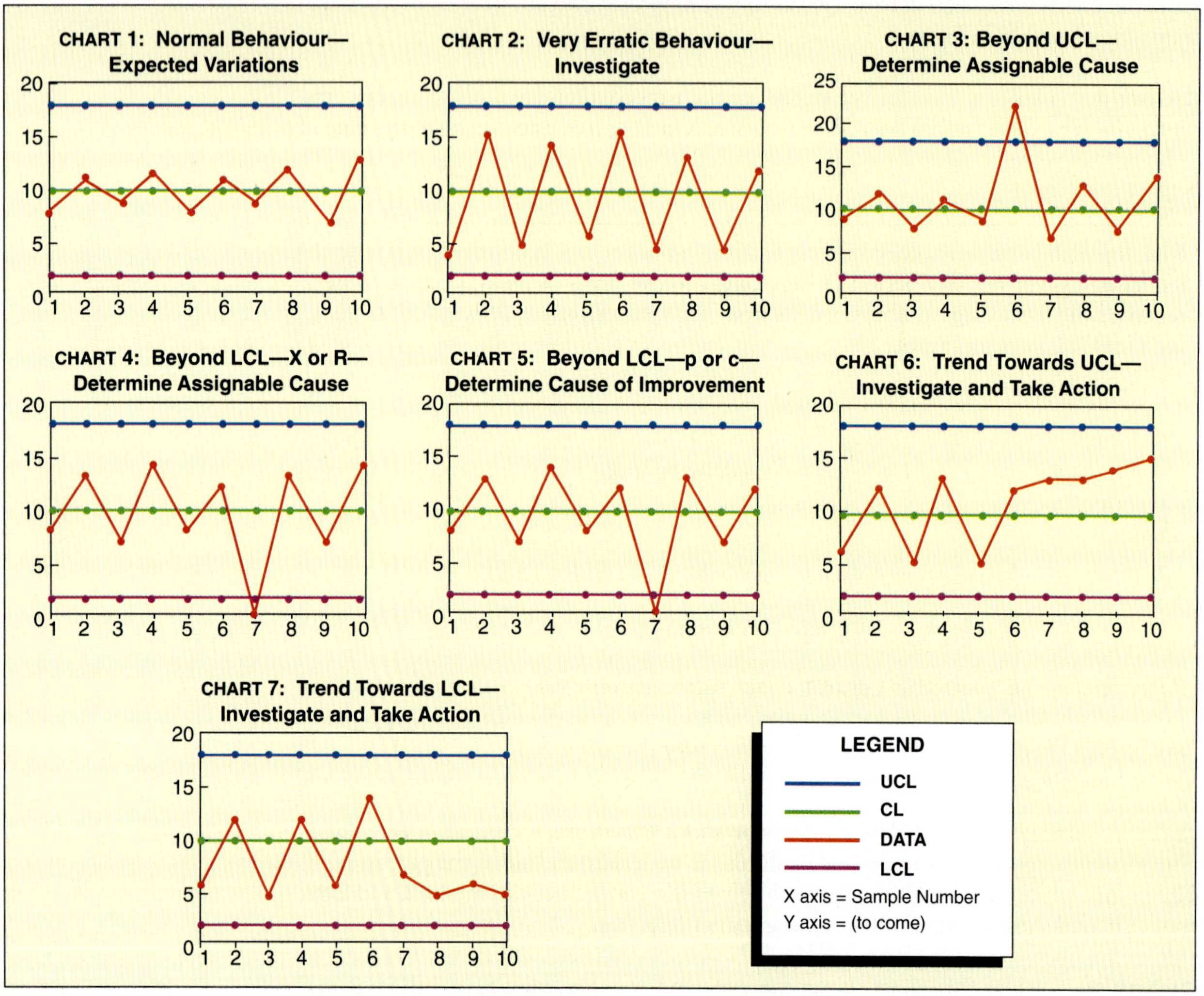

new set of control limits and charts would have to be produced to control the now-changed process.

CHARTS 6 & 7. These charts demonstrate the true essence of SPC as presented by Shewhart of GE, W. Edwards Deming, Joseph Juran, and Philip Crosby. Their major emphasis is that if one is able to sort the quality products from the others *after* these products have been produced then it is *too late*. The true essence of SPC is that trends towards an out-of-control condition can be observed and corrected *before* defective products are produced. The proper use of SPC demands that quality levels be monitored throughout the process from supplier to finished product and at every step in between. It should be absolutely clear from the writings of the four QC gurus noted above that if quality control techniques are used correctly, "zero defects" can be approached, if not achieved.

Both chart 6 and chart 7 show trends towards an out-of-control condition. If acted upon correctly, these are warnings that while the process is not yet out of control, it is certainly moving in that direction. It is clear that the assignable causes must be determined and corrected *before* the process actually does go out of control. Part of the technique of TQM involves not only tools such as SPC "run charts" but also the empowerment of production employees who may shut down the process when a negative trend is noted and not afterwards. In the past 15 years, many of Tom Peters' works have emphasized the point that "out of control" is too late and unacceptable for world-class firms.

ACCEPTANCE SAMPLING

Acceptance sampling is a form of testing that involves taking random samples of "lots" or batches of finished products and measuring them against predetermined standards. Sampling, as mentioned earlier in this chapter, is more economical than 100% inspection. The quality of the sample is used to judge the quality of all items in the lot. Although either attributes or variables can be inspected by acceptance sampling, attribute inspection is more commonly used in business and is illustrated in this section.

Acceptance sampling

Acceptance sampling can be applied when raw materials arrive at a plant during a production process, or in final inspection, but it is usually used to control incoming lots of purchased products. A lot of items rejected, based on an unacceptable level of defects found in the sample, can (1) be returned to the supplier or (2) be 100% inspected to cull out all defects, with the cost of this screening usually billed to the supplier, or (3) reworked in–plant at supplier expense when the defect is minor and easily corrected (this is a common option when a facility such as an automobile manufacturing plant possesses the necessary equipment to correct the problem and when delivery time and freight costs are considered). However, acceptance sampling is not a substitute for adequate process controls. In fact, the current approach is to build statistical quality controls at the supplier level so that acceptance sampling can be eliminated.

Sampling Plans

A lot of items can be inspected in several ways, including the use of single, double, or sequential sampling.

SINGLE SAMPLING. Two numbers specify a **single sampling** plan: They are the number of items to be sampled (n) and a prespecified acceptable number of defects (c). If there are fewer or equal defects in the lot than the acceptance number, c, then the whole batch will be accepted. If there are more than c defects, the whole lot will be rejected or subjected to 100% screening.

Single sampling

DOUBLE SAMPLING. Often a lot of items is so good or so bad that we can reach a conclusion about its quality by taking a smaller sample than would have been used in a single sampling plan. If the number of defects in this smaller sample (of size n_1) is less than or equal to some lower limit (c_1), the lot can be accepted. If the number of defects exceeds an upper limit (c_2), the whole lot can be rejected. But if the number of defects in the n_1 sample is between c_1 and c_2, a second sample (of size n_2) is drawn. The cumulative results determine whether to accept or reject the lot. The concept is called **double sampling**.

Double sampling

SEQUENTIAL SAMPLING. Multiple sampling is an extension of double sampling, with smaller samples used sequentially until a clear decision can be made. When units

Sequential sampling

are randomly selected from a lot and tested one by one, with the cumulative number of inspected pieces and defects recorded, the process is called **sequential sampling**.

If the cumulative number of defects exceeds an upper limit specified for that sample, the whole lot will be rejected. Or if the cumulative number of rejects is less than or equal to the lower limit, the lot will be accepted. But if the number of defects falls within these two boundaries, we continue to sample units from the lot. It is possible in some sequential plans for the whole lot to be tested, unit by unit, before a conclusion is reached.

Selection of the best sampling approach—single, double, or sequential—depends on the types of products being inspected and their expected quality level. A very low-quality batch of goods, for example, can be identified quickly and more cheaply with sequential sampling. This means that the inspection, which may be costly and/or destructive, can end sooner. On the other hand, there are many cases where a single sampling plan is easier and simpler for workers to conduct even though the number sampled may be greater than under other plans.

Operating Characteristic (OC) Curves

Operating characteristic (OC) curve

The **operating characteristic (OC) curve** describes how well an acceptance plan discriminates between good and bad lots. A curve pertains to a specific plan, that is, a combination of n (sample size) and c (acceptance level). It is intended to show the probability that the plan will accept lots of various quality levels.

Naturally, we would prefer a highly discriminating sampling plan and OC curve. If the entire shipment of parts has an unacceptably high level of defects, we hope the sample will reflect that fact with a very high probability (preferably 100%) of rejecting the shipment.

Figure 4.6(a) shows a perfect discrimination plan for a company that wants to reject all lots with more than 2½% defectives and accept all lots with less than 2½% defectives. Unfortunately, the only way to assure 100% acceptance of good lots and 0% acceptance of bad lots is to conduct a full inspection, which is often very costly.

Figure 4.6(b) reveals that no OC curve will be as steplike as the one in Figure 4.6(a); nor will it be discriminating enough to yield 100% error-free inspection. Figure

FIGURE 4.6 ■ (a) Perfect Discrimination for Inspection Plan. (b) OC Curves for Two Different Acceptable Levels of Defects ($c = 1$, $c = 4$) for the Same Sample Size ($n = 100$). (c) OC Curves for Two Different Sample Sizes ($n = 25$, $n = 100$) but Same Acceptance Percentages (4%). Larger sample size shows better discrimination.

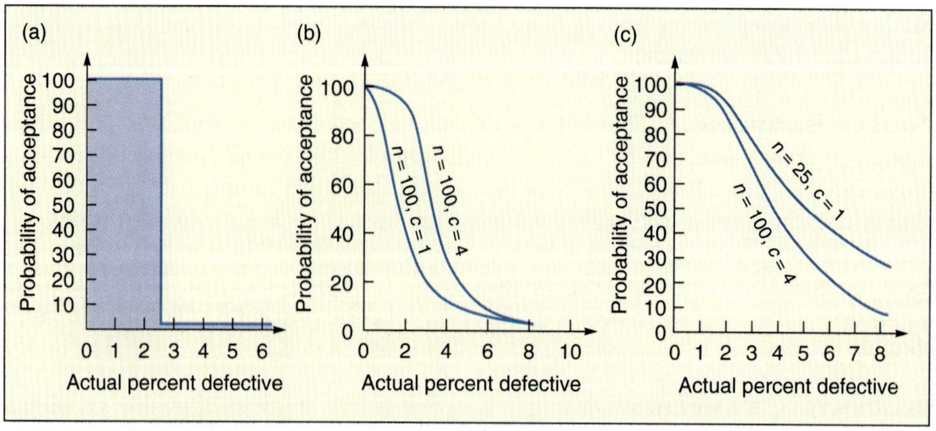

4.6(b) does indicate, though, that for the same sample size (n = 100 in this case), a smaller value of c (of acceptable defects) yields a steeper curve than does a larger value of c. So one way to increase the probability of accepting only good lots and rejecting only bad lots with random sampling is to set very tight acceptance levels.

A second way to develop a steeper, and thereby sounder, OC curve is to increase the sample size. Figure 4.6(c) illustrates that even when the acceptance number is the same proportion of the sample size, a larger value of n will increase the likelihood of accurately measuring the lot's quality. In this figure, both curves use a maximum defect rate of 4% (equal to 4/100 = 1/25). Yet if you take a straightedge or ruler and carefully examine Figure 4.6(c), you will be able to see that the OC curve for $n = 25$, $c = 1$ rejects more good lots and accepts more bad lots than the second plan. Here are a few measurements to illustrate that point.

When the Actual Percentage of Defects in the Lot Is:	Then the Probability (Approximate) of Accepting the Whole Lot Is:	
	For N = 100, C = 4	For N = 25, C = 1
1%	97%	90%
3%	15%	47%
5%	3%	18%
7%	1%	6%

In other words, the probability of accepting a more than satisfactory lot (one with only 1% defects) is 97% for $n = 100$, but only 90% for $n = 25$. Likewise, the chance of accepting a "bad" lot (one with 5% defects) is only 3% for $n = 100$, whereas it is 18% using the smaller sample size.[2] Of course, were it not for the cost of extra inspection, every firm would opt for larger sample sizes.

Manufacturer's and Buyer's Risk

In acceptance sampling, two parties are usually involved: the manufacturer of the product and the buyer of the product. In specifying a sampling plan, each party wants to avoid costly mistakes in accepting or rejecting a lot. The manufacturer wants to avoid the mistake of having a good lot rejected (*manufacturer's risk*) because the lot must usually be replaced. Conversely, the buyer wants to avoid the mistake of accepting a bad lot because defects found in a lot that has already been accepted are usually the responsibility of the buyer (*buyer's risk*). The OC curve shows the features of a particular sampling plan, including the risks of making a wrong decision.

Figure 4.7 illustrates four sampling concepts:

1. The **Acceptable quality level (AQL)** is the lowest level of quality a buyer is willing to accept. If an acceptable quality level is 20 defects in a lot of 1,000 items or parts, then AQL is 20/1,000 = 2% defectives.

Acceptable quality level (AQL)

[2]It bears repeating that sampling always runs the danger of leading to an erroneous conclusion. Let us say in this example that the total population under scrutiny is a load of 1,000 computer chips, of which in reality only 30 (or 3%) are defective. This means that we would want to accept the shipment of chips, because 4% is the allowable defect rate. But if a random sample of $n = 50$ chips were drawn, we could conceivably end up with zero defects and accept that shipment (that is, it is OK) or we could find all 30 defects in the sample. If the latter happened, we could wrongly conclude that the whole population was 60% defective and reject them all.

Lot tolerance percent defective (LTPD)

2. The **Lot tolerance percent defective (LTPD)** is the quality level of a lot a buyer considers bad. The buyer wishes to reject lots that have this level of quality. If it is agreed that an unacceptable quality level is 70 defects in a lot of 1,000, then the LTPD is 70/1,000 = 7% defective.

   To derive a sampling plan, the manufacturer and the buyer must define not only "good lots" and "bad lots" through the AQL and LTPD, but also risk levels.

Manufacturer's risk

3. **Manufacturer's risk** (α) is the probability that a "good" lot will be rejected. This is the risk of taking a random sample that results in a much higher proportion of defects than the population of all items. A lot with an acceptable quality level of AQL still has an α chance of being rejected. Sampling plans are often designed to have the manufacturer's risk set at $\alpha = .05$, or 5%.

Buyer's risk

4. **Buyer's risk** (β) is the probability that a "bad" lot will be accepted. This is the risk of taking a random sample that results in a lower proportion of defects than the overall population of items. A common value for buyer's risk in sampling plans is $\beta = .10$, or 10%.

Type I error
Type II error

In statistics, the probability of rejecting a good lot is called a **Type I error**. The probability of a bad lot being accepted is referred to as a **Type II error**.

Sampling plans and OC curves can be developed by computer (as seen in the computer programs supplied with this text), by published tables such as the U.S. Military Standard MIL-STD-105 or the Dodge-Romig table, or by calculation, using the binomial or Poisson distributions.[3] To help you understand the theory underlying the use of sampling plans, we will illustrate how an OC curve is constructed statistically.

In attribute sampling, where products are determined to be either good or bad, a binomial distribution is usually employed to build the OC curve. The binomial equation is

$$P(x) = \frac{n!}{x!(n-x)!}p^x(1-p)^{n-x} \tag{4.11}$$

where n = number of items sampled (called trials)
p = probability that an x (defect) will occur on any one trial
$P(x)$ = probability of exactly x results in n trials

When the sample size (n) is large and the percent defective (p) is small, however, the Poisson distribution can be used as an approximation of the binomial formula. This is convenient because binomial calculations can become quite complex, and because cumulative Poisson tables are readily available. Our Poisson table appears in Appendix B.

In a Poisson approximation of the binomial distribution, the mean of the binomial, which is np, is used as the mean of the Poisson, which is λ; that is,

$$\lambda = np \tag{4.12}$$

In Example 6, we set n and c values for a sampling plan and then computed the α and β risks to see if they were within desired levels. Often, organizations instead develop an OC curve for preset values and an AQL and then substitute values of n and c until the plan also satisfies the β and LTPD demands.

[3]The two most frequently used tables for acceptance plans are *Military Standard Sampling Procedures and Tables for Inspection by Attributes* (MIL-STD-105D) (Washington, DC: U.S. Government Printing Office, 1963); and H. F. Dodge and H. G. Romig, *Sampling Inspection Tables—Single and Double Sampling*, 2nd ed. (New York: John Wiley, 1959).

FIGURE 4.7 ■ An Operating Characteristic (OC) Curve Showing Manufacturer's and Buyer's Risk. *Note:* A good lot for this particular acceptance plan has less than or equal to 2% defectives. A bad lot has 7% or more defectives.

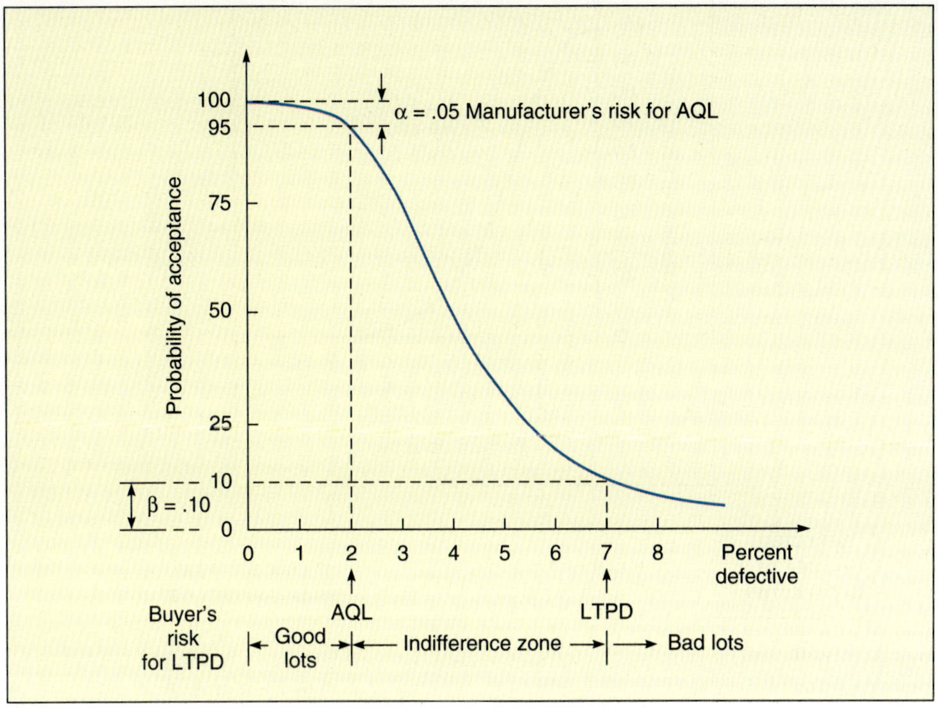

Average Outgoing Quality (AOQ)

In most sampling plans, when a lot is rejected, the entire lot is inspected and all of the defective items are replaced. Use of this replacement technique improves the average

Although we increasingly rely upon automated inspection techniques, much inspection is still done manually. Here, an employee of Bausch & Lomb in Indonesia inspects contact lenses.

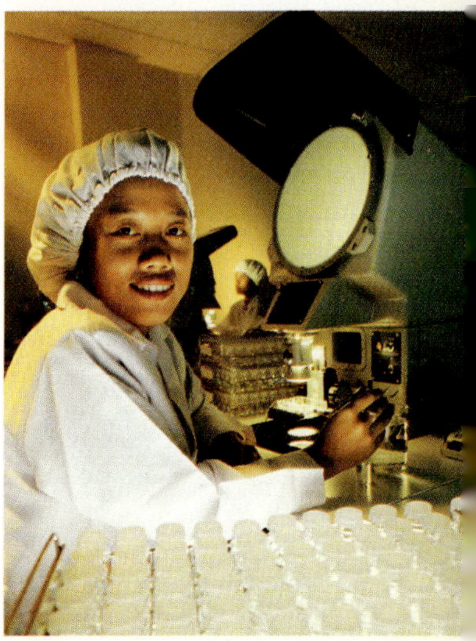

EXAMPLE 6

A shipment of 2,000 portable battery units for microcomputers is about to be inspected by a Malaysian importer. The Korean manufacturer and the importer have set up a sampling plan in which the α risk is limited to 5% at an AQL of 2% defective, and the β risk is set to 10% at LTPD = 7% defective. We want to construct the OC curve for the plan of $n = 120$ sample size and an acceptance level of $c \leq 3$ defectives. Both firms want to know if this plan will satisfy their quality and risk requirements.

To solve the problem, we turn to the cumulative Poisson table in Appendix B, whose columns are set up in terms of the acceptance level, c. We are interested only in the $c = 3$ column for this example. The rows in the table are λ (= np), which represents the number of defects we would expect to find in each sample.

By varying the percent defectives (p) from .01 (1%) to .08 (8%) and holding the sample size at $n = 120$, we can compute the probability of acceptance of the lot at each chosen level. The values for P (acceptance) calculated in what follows are then plotted to produce the OC curve shown in Figure 4.8.

FIGURE 4.8 ■ OC Curve Constructed for Example 6

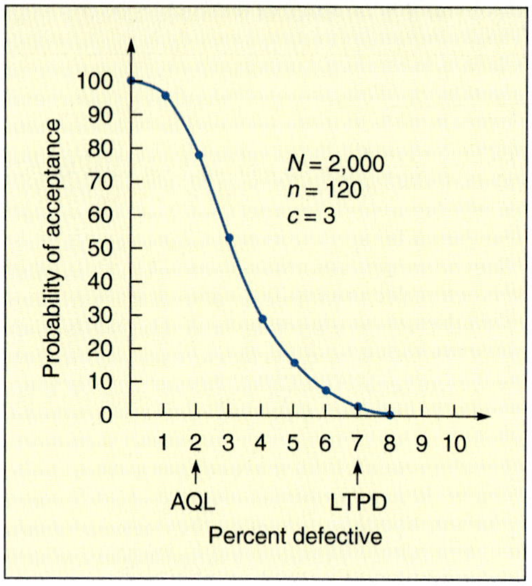

SELECTED VALUES OF % DEFECTIVE	MEAN OF POISSON, $\lambda = np$	P (ACCEPTANCE) FROM APPENDIX B
.01	1.20	.966
.02	2.40	.779 ← $1 - \alpha$ at AQL
.03	3.60	.515
.04	4.80	.294
.05	6.00	.151
.06	7.20	.072
.07	8.40	.032* ← β level at LTPD
.08	9.60	.014*

*Interpolated from value.

Now back to the issue of whether this OC curve satisfies the quality and risk needs of the buyer and manufacturer of the batteries. For the AQL of $p = .02 = 2\%$ defects, the P (acceptance) of the lot = .779. This yields an α risk of $1 - .779 = .221$, or 22.1%, which exceeds the 5% level desired by the manufacturer. The β risk of .032, or 3.2%, is well under the 10% sought by the buyer. It appears that new calculations are necessary with a larger sample size if the α level is to be lowered.[4]

[4]Indeed, as AB:POM's quality control module will verify, the sample size should be 165.

Average outgoing quality (AOQ)

outgoing quality in terms of percent defective. In fact, given (1) any sampling plan that replaces all defective items encountered and (2) the true incoming percent defective for the lot, it is possible to determine the **average outgoing quality (AOQ)** in percent defective. The equation for AOQ is

$$AOQ = \frac{(P_d)(P_a)(N-n)}{N} \tag{4.13}$$

where P_d = true percent defective of the lot
P_a = probability of accepting the lot
N = number of items in the lot
n = number of items in the sample

In most cases, we do not know the value of P_a; we must determine it from the particular sampling plan. The fact that we seldom know the true incoming percent defective presents another problem. In most cases, several different incoming percent defective values are assumed. Then we can determine the average outgoing quality for each value.

EXAMPLE 7

The percent defective from an incoming lot in Example 6 is 3%. An OC curve showed the probability of acceptance to be .515. Given a lot size of 2,000 and a sample of 120, what is the average outgoing quality in percent defective?

$$AOQ = \frac{(P_d)(P_a)(N-n)}{N}$$

$$= \frac{(.03)(.515)(2{,}000-120)}{2{,}000} = .015$$

Thus, an acceptance sampling plan changes the quality of the lots in percent defective from 3% to 1.5% on the average. Acceptance sampling significantly increases the quality of the inspected lots.

EXAMPLE 8

To illustrate the AOQ relationship, let us use the data we developed for the OC curve in Example 6. The lot size in that case was N = 2,000 and the sample size was n = 120. We assume that any defective batteries found during inspection are replaced by good ones. Then using the formula for AOQ given before and the probabilities of acceptance from Example 6, we can develop the following numbers:

P_D	×	P_A	×	$(N - n)/N$	=	AOQ
.01		.966		.94		.009
.02		.779		.94		.015
.03		.515		.94		.015
.04		.294		.94		.011
.05		.151		.94		.007
.06		.072		.94		.004
.07		.032		.94		.002
.08		.014		.94		.001

These numbers are graphed in Figure 4.9 as the average outgoing quality as a function of incoming quality.

FIGURE 4.9 ■ A Typical AOQ Curve Using Data from Example 8

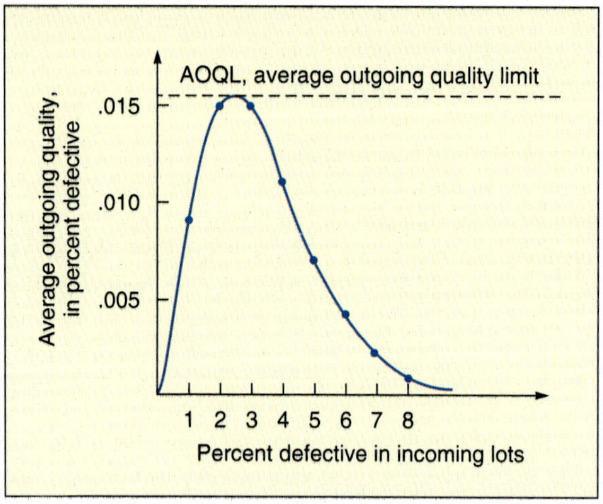

Did you notice how AOQ changed for different percent defectives? When the percent defective of the incoming lots is either very high or very low, the percent defective of the outgoing lots is low. AOQ at 1% was .009, and AOQ at 8% was .001. For moderate levels of the incoming percent defective, AOQ is higher: AOQ at 2–3% was .015. Thus, AOQ is low for small values of the incoming percent defective. As the incoming percent defective increases, the AOQ increases up to a point. Then, for increasing incoming percent defective, AOQ decreases.

The maximum value on the AOQ curve corresponds to the highest average percent defective or the lowest average quality for the sampling plan. It is called the *average outgoing quality limit (AOQL)*. In Figure 4.9, the AOQL is just over 1.5%, meaning the batteries are about 98.4% good when the incoming quality is between 2 and 3%.

Acceptance sampling is useful for screening incoming lots. When the defective parts are replaced with good parts, acceptance sampling helps to increase the quality of the lots by reducing the outgoing percent defective.

ACHIEVING WORLD-CLASS STANDARDS

World-class organizations establish an environment of total quality management (TQM) where employees know and use the tools of TQM. This is accomplished via an aggressive education program. The education to build and maintain a work force comfortable with TQM cannot be overemphasized. World-class Motorola requires that 1.5% of revenue be spent on education. Other world-class organizations require up to 200 hours of training per person per year. Another approach to ensure a major commitment to TQM and its tools is taken at Xerox where each manager is evaluated on quality performance in his or her organization.

Statistical process control (SPC) is one step on the way to quality. SPC requires understanding process capability, control charting, and timely corrections. Processes are designed and maintained so they are capable of producing products that meet customer expectations. Consequently, in world-class organizations, employees are provided facilities, education, and training for TQM and SPC. SPC permeates world-class organizations.

SUMMARY

Statistical process control and acceptance sampling are major statistical tools of quality control. Control charts for SPC help the operations manager distinguish between natural and assignable variations. The $\bar{x}$-chart and the R-chart are used for variable sampling and the p-chart and the c-chart for attribute sampling. Sampling plans and operating characteristic (OC) curves facilitate acceptance sampling and provide the manager with tools to evaluate the quality of a production run or shipment.

A few years ago, IBM Canada Ltd. ordered some parts from a new supplier in Japan. IBM stated in its order that acceptable quality allowed for 1.5% defects—a demanding standard in North America at that time. The Japanese sent the order, with a few parts packaged separately in plastic. *Their letter said: "We don't know why you want 1.5% defective parts, but for your convenience we have packaged them separately."*

KEY TERMS

Control chart (p. 110)
Natural variations (p. 111)
Assignable variations (p. 111)
$\bar{x}$-chart (p. 113)
R-chart (p. 113)
Central limit theorem (p. 113)
p-charts (p. 118)
c-charts (p. 118)
Acceptance sampling (p. 123)
Single sampling (p. 123)
Double sampling (p. 123)
Sequential sampling (p. 124)
Operating characteristic (OC) curve (p. 124)
Acceptable quality level (AQL) (p. 125)
Lot tolerance percent defective (LTPD) (p. 126)
Manufacturer's risk (p. 126)
Buyer's risk (p. 126)
Type I error (p. 126
Type II error (p. 126)
Average outgoing quality (AOQ) (p. 128)

USING AB:POM AND SPREADSHEETS TO SOLVE QUALITY CONTROL PROBLEMS

Solving Example 4 with AB:POM's Quality Control Module

AB:POM's quality control module addresses a number of quality issues through an initial screen that provides these options: (1) $\bar{x}$- and *R*-charts, (2) *p*-charts, (3) *c*-charts, (4) attribute sampling, (5) variable sampling, and (6) OC curves. We illustrate the *p*-chart option in Program 4.1 using the data from Example 4.

PROGRAM 4.1 ■ AB:POM's *p*-Chart Option. AB:POM computes the average percentage of defects (the centre line of the *p*-bar chart), which is displayed as .04 for Example 4 data. Using these data, the program presents the limits for four different control charts at the bottom of the screen. There is one chart with 95% confidence, one with 98%, one with 99%, and one with 3 standard deviations (99.7%) confidence.

Quality Control — Solution

Number of samples (1–99) 20 Sample size (n) (2–9999) 100

ARCO Insurance Records

Sample Number	Number of Defects	Percent Defects	Sample Number	Number of Defects	Percent Defects
1	6	0.0600	13	8	0.0800
2	5	0.0500	14	7	0.0700
3	0	0.0000	15	5	0.0500
4	1	0.0100	16	4	0.0400
5	4	0.0400	17	11	0.1100
6	2	0.0200	18	3	0.0300
7	5	0.0500	19	0	0.0000
8	3	0.0300	20	4	0.0400
9	3	0.0300			
10	2	0.0200			
11	6	0.0600			
12	1	0.0100			

	95%	98%	99%	99.7%
Upper Control Limit	0.0784	0.0857	0.0906	0.0988
Centre Line (p-bar)	0.0400	0.0400	0.0400	0.0400
Lower Control Limit	0.00159	0.0000	0.0000	0.0000

A Spreadsheet Approach to Example 1's $\bar{x}$-Chart

Program 4.2 illustrates how easy it is to compute upper and lower control limits for an $\bar{x}$-chart with spreadsheets. The @STD and @AVG formulas compute the standard deviations (σ_x) and average ($\bar{\bar{x}}$) of the 12 observed sample averages. These are used to compute $\sigma_{\bar{x}}$ (in cell D7) and control limits (in cells D9 and D10).

PROGRAM 4.2 ■ A "Symbolic" Spreadsheet for Computing Upper and Lower Control Chart Limits

	A	B	C	D	E
1	Spreadsheet used to solve Example 1				
2					
3	Sample	Sample			
4	Number	Weight		Sample Size =	9
5	1	17.1		X bar bar = (B19)	
6	2	16.8		Z value =	3
7	3	14.5		Sigma X bar = (B18) /	
@SQRT(E4)		14.8			
8	4	16.5			
9	5	16.4		UCL xbar = (B19+(E6*E7))	
10	6	15.2		LCL xbar = (B19–(E6*E7))	
11	7	16.4			
12	8	16.3			
13	9	16.5			
14	10	14.2			
15	11	17.3			
16	12				
17		-----------			
18		@STD(B5. .B16)		Standard deviation (sigma)	

SOLVED PROBLEMS

Solved Problem 4.1

The manufacturer of precision parts for drill presses produces round shafts for use in the construction of drill presses. The average diameter of a shaft is .56 inch. The inspection samples contain six shafts each. The average range of these samples is .006 inch. Determine the upper and lower control chart limits.

Solution

The mean factor A_2 from Table 4.1, where the sample size is 6, is seen to be .483. With this factor, you can obtain the upper and lower control limits:

$$\begin{aligned} UCL &= .56 + (.483)(.006) \\ &= .56 + .0029 \\ &= .5629 \end{aligned}$$

$$\begin{aligned} LCL &= .56 - .0029 \\ &= .5571 \end{aligned}$$

Solved Problem 4.2

Nocaf Drinks, Inc., a producer of decaffeinated coffee, bottles Nocaf. Each bottle should have a net weight of 100 grams. The machine that fills the bottles with coffee is new, and the operations manager wants to make sure that it is properly adjusted. The operations manager takes a sample of $n = 8$ bottles and records the average and range in ounces for each sample. The data for several samples are in the following table. Note that every sample consists of 8 bottles.

Sample	Sample Range	Sample Average	Sample	Sample Range	Sample Average
A	10.25	100.12	E	14.08	104.25
B	13.75	104.32	F	15.47	98.25
C	11.03	99.75	G	13.89	99.47
D	12.67	100.89	H	11.66	100.25

Is the machine properly adjusted and in control?

Solution

We first find that $\bar{\bar{x}} = 100.91$ and $\bar{R} = 12.85$. Then, using Table 4.1, we find

$$UCL_{\bar{x}} = \bar{\bar{x}} + A_2\bar{R} = 100.91 + (.373)(12.85) = 105.70$$

$$LCL_{\bar{x}} = \bar{\bar{x}} - A_2\bar{R} = 100.91 - (.373)(12.85) = 96.12$$

$$UCL_R = D_4\bar{R} = (1.864)(12.85) = 23.95$$

$$LCL_R = D_3\bar{R} = (.136)(12.85) = 1.75$$

It appears that the process average and range are both in control.

Solved Problem 4.3

Altman Electronics, Inc., makes resistors, and among the last 100 resistors inspected, the percent defective has been 5%. Determine the upper and lower limits for this process for 99.7% confidence.

Solution

$$UCL_p = \bar{p} + 3\sqrt{\frac{\bar{p}(1-\bar{p})}{n}} = .05 + 3\sqrt{\frac{(.05)(1-.05)}{100}}$$

$$= .05 + 3(0.0218) = .1154$$

$$LCL_p = \bar{p} - 3\sqrt{\frac{\bar{p}(1-\bar{p})}{n}} = .05 - 3(.0218)$$

$$= .05 - .0654 = 0 \text{ (because percent defective cannot be negative)}$$

Solved Problem 4.4

In an acceptance sampling plan developed for lots containing 1,000 units, the sample size n is 85 and c is 3. The percent defective of the incoming lots is 2%, and the probability of acceptance, which was obtained from an OC curve, is 0.64.

What is the average outgoing quality?

Solution

$$AOQ = \frac{(P_d)(P_a)(N-n)}{N} = \frac{(.02)(.64)(1{,}000-85)}{1{,}000} = .012 \text{ or } AOQ = 1.2\%$$

DISCUSSION QUESTIONS

1. Why is the central limit theorem so important in statistical quality control?
2. Why must both be produced and examined before conclusions can be drawn?
3. Explain the difference between an $\bar{x}$- and an R-chart.
4. What might cause a process to be out of control?
5. A manufacturer of standard wire clothing hangers has been finding its process to be out of control, producing an unacceptably high number of defectives. The hangers are produced in very large volumes and at very high speeds on automatic machines fed with very large coils of wire of the correct diameter. What are some of the possible *assignable causes* for the high level of defectives?
6. Heath-Satchell Manufacturing produces roof linings for cars and trucks for a number of major automobile and truck manufacturers. The linings must match, in both colour and pattern, other items of interior trim such as door panels and seats. An out of control condition has been noted and the production line stopped. What are some of the possible *assignable causes*?
7. The Old Scots preserves company, co-owned by the Forresters and MacMickings, produces jams and preserves in 250 millilitre containers. The main quality measure is the *fill amount*. The products are dispensed at high temperatures for pasteurization purposes by automatic filling equipment into pre-labelled jars which are then vacuum-sealed with metal tops. The process has just gone out of control. What are some of the possible *assignable causes*?
8. Explain why a process can be out of control even though all samples fall within the upper and lower control limits.
9. What is the difference between variable and attribute sampling?
10. What charts are used for variable sampling?
11. What charts are used for attribute sampling?
12. What do the terms *manufacturer's risk* and *buyer's risk* mean?
13. Define Type I and Type II errors.
14. Explain the difference between single, double, and sequential sampling.
15. Define AQL and LTPD.
16. What is "average outgoing quality"?
17. What is the AOQL?

CRITICAL THINKING EXERCISE

When Nashua Corp., a large paper company, had quality problems, they called noted quality guru W. Edwards Deming. Deming discovered that the Nashua technicians did not understand natural variations. They frequently stopped the paper-coating machinery to make adjustments to the coating head. But by assuming any variation had to be corrected, they were inadvertently *increasing* the variation. What they did was the equivalent of trying to adjust a scale while someone was jumping up and down on it. When they stopped meddling with the machine, it turned out to be in fairly good statistical control. The special (assignable) cause of variation was eliminated. Nashua then went back to work at reducing the common (natural) causes of variation in the machine.[5]

Prepare a brief explanation for forepersons at Nashua Corp. of special (assignable) vs. common (natural) variations.

[5] Adapted from Jeremy Maine, *Quality Wars* (New York: Free Press, 1994), p. 110.

PROBLEMS

• **4.1** The overall average on a process you are attempting to monitor is 75 units. The average range is 6 units. What are the upper and lower control limits if you choose to use a sample size of 10?

• **4.2** The overall average on a process you are attempting to monitor is 50 units. The average range is 4 units. What are the upper and lower control limits if you choose to use a sample size of 5?

• **4.3** Your supervisor, Mike Perman, has asked that you check and report on the output of a machine on the factory floor. This machine is supposed to be producing widgets that have a mean weight of 50 grams, and a range of 3.5 grams. The table contains the data for a sample size of n =10 taken during the past 3 hours:

	Sample Number									
	1	2	3	4	5	6	7	8	9	10
Sample Average	55	47	49	50	52	57	55	48	51	56
Sample Range	3	1	5	3	2	6	3	2	2	3

What are the control limits and what conclusions do you draw?

• **4.4** Food Storage Technologies produces refrigeration units for food producers and retail food establishments. The overall average temperature that these units maintain is 8°C. The average range is –17°C. Samples of 6 are taken to monitor the process. Determine the upper and lower control-chart limits for averages and ranges for these refrigeration units.

• **4.5** Autopitch devices are made for both major- and minor-league teams to help them improve their batting averages. When set at the standard position, Autopitch can throw hard balls toward a batter at an average speed of 96 kilometres per hour. Company executives take samples of 10 Autopitch devices at a time to monitor these devices and to maintain the highest quality. The average range is 5 kilometres per hour. Using control-chart techniques, determine control-chart limits for averages and ranges for Autopitch.

• **4.6** Major Products, Inc., produces granola cereal, granola bars, and other natural food products. Its natural granola cereal is sampled to ensure proper weight. Each sample contains eight boxes of cereal. The overall average for the samples is 510 grams. The range is only 15 grams. Determine the upper and lower control-chart limits for averages for the boxes of cereal.

: **4.7** Small boxes of NutraFlakes cereal are labelled "net weight 400 grams." Each hour, random samples of size $n = 4$ boxes are weighed to check process control. Five hours of observation yielded the following:

	Weights			
Time	Box 1	Box 2	Box 3	Box 4
9 A.M.	392	416	396	414
10 A.M.	404	408	396	392
11 A.M.	396	420	410	404
Noon	388	392	412	411
1 P.M.	385	404	396	396

Using these data, construct limits for $\bar{x}$- and R-charts. Is the process in control? What other steps should the QC department follow at this point?

: **4.8** Sampling four pieces of precision-cut wire (to be used in computer assembly) every hour for the past 24 hours has produced the following results:

	HOUR											
	1	2	3	4	5	6	7	8	9	10	11	12
$\bar{x}$ (cm)	3.25	3.10	3.22	3.39	3.07	2.86	3.05	2.65	3.02	2.85	2.83	2.97
R (cm)	.71	1.18	1.43	1.26	1.17	.32	.53	1.13	.71	1.33	1.17	.40

	HOUR											
	13	14	15	16	17	18	19	20	21	22	23	24
$\bar{x}$ (cm)	3.11	2.83	3.12	2.84	2.86	2.74	3.41	2.89	2.65	3.28	2.94	2.64
R (cm)	.85	1.31	1.06	.50	1.43	1.29	1.61	1.09	1.08	.46	1.58	.97

Develop appropriate control charts and determine whether there is any cause for concern in the cutting process.

• **4.9** In the past, the defect rate for your product has been 1.5%. What are the upper and lower control-chart limits if you wish to use a sample size of 500 and $z = 3$?

• **4.10** In the past, the defect rate for your product has been 3.5%. What are the upper and lower control-chart limits if you wish to use a sample size of 500 and $z = 3$?

: **4.11** You are attempting to develop a quality monitoring system for some parts purchased from Manitoba Manufacturing Co. These parts are either good or defective. You have decided to take a sample of 100 units. Develop a table of the appropriate upper and lower control-chart limits for various values of the fraction defective in the sample taken. The values for p in this table should range from .02 to .1 in increments of .02. Develop the upper and lower control limits for a 99.7% confidence level.

: **4.12** Due to the poor quality of various semiconductor products used in their manufacturing process, Microlaboratories has decided to develop a quality control program. Because the semiconductor parts it receives from suppliers are either good or defective, George Haverty has decided to develop control charts for attributes. The total number of semiconductors in every sample is 200. Furthermore, George would like to determine the upper control-chart limit and the lower control-chart limit for various values of the fraction defective (p) in the sample taken. To allow more flexibility, he has decided to develop a table that lists values for p, UCL, and LCL. The values for p should range from .01 to .1, incrementing by .01 each time. What are the UCLs and the LCLs for 99.7% confidence?

⋮ **4.13** For the last 2 months, Robin Russo has been concerned about the number 5 machine at the West Factory. In order to make sure that the machine is operating correctly, samples are taken, and the average and range for each sample are computed. Each sample consists of 12 items produced from the machine. Recently, 12 samples were taken, and for each, the sample range and average were computed. The sample range and sample average were 1.1 and 46 for the first sample, 1.31 and 45 for the second sample, .91 and 46 for the third sample, and 1.1 and 47 for the fourth sample. After the fourth sample, the sample averages increased. For the fifth sample, the range was 1.21 and the average was 48; for sample number 6 it was .82 and 47; for sample number 7, it was .86 and 50; and for the eighth sample, it was 1.11 and 49. After the eighth sample, the sample average continued to increase, never going below 50. For sample number 9, the range and average were 1.12 and 51; for sample number 10, they were .99 and 52; for sample number 11, they were .86 and 50; and for sample number 12, they were 1.2 and 52.

Although Robin's boss was not overly concerned about the process, Robin was. During installation, the supplier set an average of 47 for the process with an average range of 1.0. It was Robin's feeling that something was definitely wrong with machine number 5. Do you agree?

: **4.14** Pet Products, Inc., caters to the growing market for cat supplies, with a full line of products ranging from litter to toys to flea powder. One of its newer products, a tube of paste that prevents hair balls in long-haired cats, is produced by an automated machine that is set to fill each tube with 63.5 grams of paste.

To keep this filling process under control, four tubes are pulled randomly from the assembly line every 4 hours. After several days, the data shown in the table resulted. Set control limits for this process and graph the sample data for both the $\bar{x}$- and R-charts.

	Sample Number												
	1	2	3	4	5	6	7	8	9	10	11	12	13
$\bar{x}$	63.5	63.6	63.7	63.4	63.0	63.2	63.3	63.7	63.7	63.5	63.3	63.2	63.6
R	2.0	1.0	1.7	0.9	1.2	1.6	1.8	1.3	1.6	1.3	1.8	1.0	1.8

	Sample Number											
	14	15	16	17	18	19	20	21	22	23	24	25
$\bar{x}$	63.3	63.4	63.4	63.5	63.6	63.8	63.5	63.9	63.2	63.3	64.0	63.4
R	1.5	1.7	1.4	1.1	1.8	1.3	1.6	1.0	1.8	1.7	2.0	1.5

· **4.15** The smallest defect in a computer chip will render the entire chip worthless. Therefore, tight quality control measures must be established to monitor these chips. In the past, the percentage defective for these chips for a California-based company has been 1.1%. The sample size is 1,000. Determine upper and lower control-chart limits for these computer chips. Use $z = 3$.

: **4.16** Canadian Supply Company (CSC) manufactures paper clips and other office products. Although inexpensive, paper clips have provided the firm with a high margin of profitability. The percentage defective for paper clips produced by CSC has been averaging 2.5%. Samples of 200 paper clips are taken. Establish upper and lower control-chart limits for this process at 99.7% confidence.

: **4.17** Daily samples of 100 power drills are removed from Drill Master's assembly line and inspected for defects. Over the past 21 days, the following information has been gathered. Develop a 3 standard deviation (99.7% confidence) p-chart and graph the samples. Is the process in control?

Day	1	2	3	4	5	6	7	8	9	10	11
Number of Defective Drills	6	5	6	4	3	4	5	3	6	3	7

(Continued)

DAY	12	13	14	15	16	17	18	19	20	21
Number of Defective Drills	5	4	3	4	5	6	5	4	3	7

: **4.18** A random sample of 100 Modern Art solid maple dining room tables that came off the firm's assembly line is examined. Careful inspection reveals a total of 2,000 blemishes. What are the 99.7% upper and lower control limits for the number of blemishes? If one table had 42 blemishes, should any special action be taken? (*Note*: The finished tables retail at $1,000 each.)

: **4.19** Eighty items are randomly drawn from a lot of 6,000 talking toy animals, and the total lot is accepted if there are $c \leq 2$ defects. Develop an OC curve for this sample plan.

: **4.20** A load of 200 desk lamps has just arrived at the warehouse of Lighting, Inc. Random samples of $n = 5$ lamps are checked. If more than one lamp is defective, the whole lot is rejected. Set up the OC curve for this plan.

: **4.21** Develop the AOQ curve for Problem 4.20.

: **4.22** Each week, Melissa Bryant Ltd. receives a batch of 1,000 popular Swiss watches for its chain of East Coast boutiques. Bryant and the Swiss manufacturer have agreed on the following sampling plan: $\alpha = 5\%$, $\beta = 10\%$, AQL = 1%, LTPD = 5%. Develop the OC curve for a sampling plan of $n = 100$ and $c \leq 2$. Does this plan meet the manufacturer's and the buyer's requirements?

: **4.23** Kristi Conlin's firm in St. John, New Brunswick, has designed an OC curve that shows a ⅔ chance of accepting lots with a true percentage defective of 2%. Lots of 1,000 units are produced at a time, with 100 of each lot sampled randomly. What is the average outgoing quality level?

DATA BASE APPLICATION

: **4.24** Canada Battery Corp. has recently been receiving complaints from retailers that its 9-volt batteries are not lasting as long as other name brands. Silvie Lachance, head of the TQM program at the Chomedy, Quebec, plant, believes there is no problem, because her batteries have had an average life of 50 hours, about 10% longer than competitors' models. To raise the lifetime above this would require a new level of technology not available to Canada Battery. Nevertheless, she is concerned enough to set up hourly assembly line checks. She decides to take 5 samples of 9-volt batteries for each of the next 25 hours to create the standards for control-chart limits (see the table).

CANADA BATTERY DATA—BATTERY LIFETIMES (IN HOURS)

	SAMPLE						
HOUR	1	2	3	4	5	$\overline{X}$	R
1	51	50	49	50	50	50.0	2
2	45	47	70	46	36	48.8	34
3	50	35	48	39	47	43.8	15
4	55	70	50	30	51	51.2	40
5	49	38	64	36	47	46.8	28
6	59	62	40	54	64	55.8	24
7	36	33	49	48	56	44.4	23

(*Continued*)

CANADA BATTERY DATA—BATTERY LIFETIMES (IN HOURS)—CONTINUED

	SAMPLE						
HOUR	**1**	**2**	**3**	**4**	**5**	$\bar{X}$	**R**
8	50	67	53	43	40	50.6	27
9	44	52	46	47	44	46.6	8
10	70	45	50	47	41	50.6	29
11	57	54	62	45	36	50.8	26
12	56	54	47	42	62	52.2	20
13	40	70	58	45	44	51.4	30
14	52	58	40	52	46	49.6	18
15	57	42	52	58	59	53.6	17
16	62	49	42	33	55	48.2	29
17	40	39	49	59	48	47.0	20
18	64	50	42	57	50	52.6	22
19	58	53	52	48	50	52.2	10
20	60	50	41	41	50	48.4	19
21	52	47	48	58	40	49.0	18
22	55	40	56	49	45	49.0	16
23	47	48	50	50	48	48.6	3
24	50	50	49	51	51	50.2	2
25	51	50	51	51	62	53.0	12

With these limits in place, Lachance now takes five more hours of data, shown in the following sample:

	SAMPLE				
HOUR	**1**	**2**	**3**	**4**	**5**
26	48	52	39	57	61
27	45	53	48	46	66
28	63	49	50	45	53
29	57	70	45	52	61
30	45	38	46	54	52

a) Is the manufacturing process in control?

b) Comment on the lifetimes observed.

CASE STUDY

Bayfield Mud Company

In November 1994, John Wells, a customer service representative of Bayfield Mud Company, was summoned to the Barrie warehouse of Wet-Land Drilling, Inc., to inspect three boxcars of mud-treating agents that Bayfield Mud Company had shipped to the Barrie firm. (Bayfield's corporate offices and its largest plant are located in Barrie, Ontario.) Wet-Land Drilling had filed a complaint that the 50-pound bags of treating agents that it had just received from Bayfield were short-weight by approximately 5%.

The light-weight bags were initially detected by one of Wet-Land's receiving clerks, who noticed that the railroad scale tickets indicated that the net weights were significantly less on all three of the boxcars than those of identical shipments received on October 25, 1994. Bayfield's traffic department was called to determine if lighter-weight dunnage or pallets were used on the shipments. (This might explain the lighter net weights.) Bayfield indicated, however, that no changes had been made in the loading or palletizing procedures. Hence, Wet-Land randomly checked 50 of the bags and discovered that the average net weight was 47.51 kilograms. They noted from past shipments that the bag net weights averaged exactly 50.0 kilograms, with an acceptable standard deviation of 1.2 kilograms. Consequently, they concluded that the sample indicated a significant short-weight. (The reader may wish to verify this conclusion.) Bayfield was then contacted, and Wells was sent to investigate the complaint. Upon arrival, Wells verified the complaint and issued a 5% credit to Wet-Land.

Wet-Land's management, however, was not completely satisfied with only the issuance of credit for the short shipment. The charts followed by their mud engineers on the drilling platforms were based on 50-kilogram bags of treating agents. Lighter-weight bags might result in poor chemical control during the drilling operation and might adversely affect drilling efficiency. (Mud-treating agents are used to control the pH and other chemical properties of the cone during drilling operation.) This could cause severe economic consequences because of the extremely high cost of oil and natural gas well-drilling operations. Consequently, special use instructions had to accompany the delivery of these shipments to the drilling platforms. Moreover, the light-weight shipments had to be isolated in Wet-Land's warehouse, causing extra handling and poor space utilization. Hence, Wells was informed that Wet-Land Drilling might seek a new supplier of mud-treating agents if, in the future, it received bags that deviated significantly from 50 kilograms.

The quality control department at Bayfield suspected that the light-weight bags may have resulted from "growing pains" at the Barrie plant. Because of the earlier energy crisis, oil and natural gas exploration activity had greatly increased. This increased activity, in turn, created increased demand for products produced by related industries, including drilling muds. Consequently, Bayfield had to expand from a one-shift (6:00 A.M. to 2:00 P.M.) to a two-shift (2:00 P.M. to 10:00 P.M.) operation in mid-1994, and finally to a three-shift operation (24 hours per day) in the fall of 1996.

The additional night-shift bagging crew was staffed entirely by new employees. The most experienced forepersons were temporarily assigned to supervise the night-shift employees. Most emphasis was placed on increasing the output of bags to meet the ever-increasing demand. It was suspected that only occasional reminders were made to double-check the bag weight-feeder. (A double-check is performed by systematically weighing a bag on a scale to determine if the proper weight is being loaded by the weight-feeder. If there is significant deviation from 50 kilograms, corrective adjustments are made to the weight-release mechanism.)

To verify this expectation, the quality control staff randomly sampled the bag output and prepared the following chart. Six bags were sampled and weighed each hour.

DISCUSSION QUESTIONS

1. What is your analysis of the bag weight problem?
2. What procedures would you recommend to maintain proper quality control?

Source: Professor Jerry Kinard, Western Carolina University. Modified for the Canadian edition.

(Continued)

Time	Average Weight (kilograms)	Range		Time	Average Weight (kilograms)	Range	
		Smallest	Largest			Smallest	Largest
6:00 A.M.	49.6	48.7	50.7	6:00	46.8	41.0	51.2
7:00	50.2	49.1	51.2	7:00	50.0	46.2	51.7
8:00	50.6	49.6	51.4	8:00	47.4	44.0	48.7
9:00	50.8	50.2	51.8	9:00	47.0	44.2	48.9
10:00	49.9	49.2	52.3	10:00	47.2	46.6	50.2
11:00	50.3	48.6	51.7	11:00	48.6	47.0	50.0
12 Noon	48.6	46.2	50.4	12 Midnight	49.8	48.2	50.4
1:00 P.M.	49.0	46.4	50.0	1:00 A.M.	49.6	48.4	51.7
2:00	49.0	46.0	50.6	2:00	50.0	49.0	52.2
3:00	49.8	48.2	50.8	3:00	50.0	49.2	50.0
4:00	50.3	49.2	52.7	4:00	47.2	46.3	50.5
5:00	51.4	50.0	55.3	5:00	47.0	44.1	49.7
6:00	51.6	49.2	54.7	6:00	48.4	45.0	49.0
7:00	51.8	50.0	55.6	7:00	48.8	44.8	49.7
8:00	51.0	48.6	53.2	8:00	49.6	48.0	51.8
9:00	50.5	49.4	52.4	9:00	50.0	48.1	52.7
10:00	49.2	46.1	50.7	10:00	51.0	48.1	55.2
11:00	49.0	46.3	50.8	11:00	50.4	49.5	54.1
12 Midnight	48.4	45.4	50.2	12 Noon	50.0	48.7	50.9
1:00 A.M.	47.6	44.3	49.7	1:00 P.M.	48.9	47.6	51.2
2:00	47.4	44.1	49.6	2:00	49.8	48.4	51.0
3:00	48.2	45.2	49.0	3:00	49.8	48.8	50.8
4:00	48.0	45.5	49.1	4:00	50.0	49.1	50.6
5:00	48.4	47.1	49.6	5:00	47.8	45.2	51.2
6:00	48.6	47.4	52.0	6:00	46.4	44.0	49.7
7:00	50.0	49.2	52.2	7:00	46.4	44.4	50.0
8:00	49.8	49.0	52.4	8:00	47.2	46.6	48.9
9:00	50.3	49.4	51.7	9:00	48.4	47.2	49.5
10:00	50.2	49.6	51.8	10:00	49.2	48.1	50.7
11:00	50.0	49.0	52.3	11:00	48.4	47.0	50.8
12 Noon	50.0	48.8	52.4	12 Midnight	47.2	46.4	49.2
1:00 P.M.	50.1	49.4	53.6	1:00 A.M.	47.4	46.8	49.0
2:00	49.7	48.6	51.0	2:00	48.8	47.2	51.4
3:00	48.4	47.2	51.7	3:00	49.6	49.0	50.6
4:00	47.2	45.3	50.9	4:00	51.0	50.5	51.5
5:00	46.8	44.1	49.0	5:00	50.5	50.0	51.9

CASE STUDY

SPC at the *Gazette*

Of critical importance to a newspaper is accurate typesetting. To assure typesetting quality, a quality improvement team was established in the printing department at the *Gazette* in Salmon Arm, British Columbia. The team developed a procedure for monitoring the performance of typesetters over a period of time. Such a procedure involves sampling output, establishing control limits, comparing the *Gazette*'s accuracy with that of the industry, and occasionally updating the information.

The team randomly selected 30 of the *Gazette*'s newspapers published during the preceding 12 months. From each paper, 100 paragraphs were randomly chosen and were read for accuracy. The number of paragraphs with errors in each paper was recorded, and the fraction of paragraphs with errors in each sample was determined. The table shows the results of the sampling.

Sample	Paragraphs with Errors in the Sample	Fraction of Paragraphs with Errors (per 100)	Sample	Paragraphs with Errors in the Sample	Fraction of Paragraphs with Errors (per 100)
1	2	.02	16	2	.02
2	4	.04	17	3	.03
3	10	.10	18	7	.07
4	4	.04	19	3	.03
5	1	.01	20	2	.02
6	1	.01	21	3	.03
7	13	.13	22	7	.07
8	9	.09	23	4	.04
9	11	.11	24	3	.03
10	0	.00	25	2	.02
11	3	.03	26	2	.02
12	4	.04	27	0	.00
13	2	.02	28	1	.01
14	2	.02	29	3	.03
15	8	.08	30	4	.04

DISCUSSION QUESTIONS

1. Plot the overall fraction of errors (p) and the upper and lower control limits on a control chart using a 95.45% confidence level.
2. Assume the industry upper and lower control limits are .1000 and .0400, respectively. Plot them on the control chart.
3. Plot the fraction of errors in each sample. Do all fall within the firm's control limits? When one falls outside the control limits, what should be done?

Source: Professor Jerry Kinard, Western Carolina University. Modified for the Canadian edition.

BIBLIOGRAPHY

Besterfield, D. H. *Quality Control*, 2nd ed. Englewood Cliffs, NJ: Prentice Hall, 1986.

Boka, Bruce, and M. Suzanne Bocka. *Quality Management*. Homewood, IL: Richard D. Irwin, 1992.

Crosby, Philip B. *Completeness: Quality for the 21st Century*. New York: Dutton, 1992.

Das, T. K., and M. A. Wortman. "Asymmetric Patrolling Repairman Systems with General Repair Time and Walk Time Distributions: Cost Analysis of Service Schedule." *IIE Transactions*, 25, no. 6 (November 1993): 19.

Gabor, Andrea. *The Man Who Discovered Quality: How W. Edwards Deming Brought the Quality Revolution to America*. New York: Penguin Books, 1992.

Gitlow, Howard S., and Shelley J. Gitlow. *Total Quality Management in Action*. Englewood Cliffs, NJ: Prentice Hall, 1994.

Hwarng, H. B., and N. F. Hubele. "X Control Chart Pattern Identification Through Efficient Off-Line Neural Network Training." *IIE Transactions*, 25, no. 3 (May 1993): 27–40.

Kumar, S., and Y. P. Gupta. "Statistical Process Control at Motorola's Austin Assembly Plant." *Interfaces*, 23, no. 2 (March/April 1993): 84–92.

Nemoto, Masao. *Total Quality Control for Management: Strategies and Techniques from Toyota and Toyoda Gosei*. Englewood Cliffs, NJ: Prentice Hall, 1987.

Peters, Tom, and Bob Waterman. *In Search of Excellence*. New York: Warner Books, 1982.

Peters, Tom, and Nancy Austin. *A Passion for Excellence*. New York: Warner Books, 1985.

Runger, G. C., and D. C. Montgomery. "Adaptive Sampling Enhancements for Shewhart Control Charts." *IIE Transactions*, 25, no. 3 (May 1993): 41–51.

Wilkins, Robert H. *The Quality Empowered Business*. Englewood Cliffs, NJ: Prentice Hall, 1994.

See additional references at the end of Chapter 3.

SOFTWARE AND WEB SITES OF INTEREST

1. Quality Council of Alberta's QCA Resource Centre: An excellent listing of videos, books, audiocassettes.

http://www.infostream.ab.ca/qca/rescen.html

2. AT SIGMA PC: Statistical Process Control Software. Powerful software that analyzes data based on statistical process control.

http://www.atsigma.com/SPC-main.htm

3. Improvit for Windows: Statistical process control software.

http://www.pcengineering.com/imp.htm

4. SPC Orchestra: A statistical process control software package that runs in MS Excel. A free, downloadable demo is available.

http://www.spcorch.com/

5. Statistical Process Control Training Materials: The "complete classroom" training kit: books, videos, slides, etc., from SPC&CI, an Ontario-based firm. This product has been used by Ford Motor Co., the U.S. Navy, Motorola, Dow Chemical, and others.

http://www.barint.on.ca/qps/spcmat.html

4 SUPPLEMENT

STATISTICAL TOOLS FOR MANAGERS

SUPPLEMENT OUTLINE

When the ship S.S. *Central America* sank roughly 322 kilometres off the coast of South Carolina in the great hurricane of 1857, some 425 people lost their lives. Also lost to the ocean floor, more than 2,400 metres below, were gold bars and coins worth $400 million. In 1985, the Columbus-America Discovery Group hired Lawrence Stone to develop a series of probability distributions for the location of the gold cargo. Stone's probability maps of several hundred square kilometres of ocean provided estimates of the success of finding the wreck at each grid point. By 1989, the project was successful, recovering about a tonne of gold. Thirty-nine insurance companies filed their claims to the recovered gold, but the Discovery Group won the rights to the gold in every case. Part of the gold recovered from the S.S. *Central America* is shown below.

(*Source:* Adapted from L. Stone, "Search for the *S.S. Central America*," *Interfaces* [January/February 1992]: 32–54.)

Statistics and probabilities are important not only in the search for gold. Statistics applications permeate the subject of operations management because so much of decision making depends on probabilities that are based on limited or uncertain information. This supplement provides you with a review of several important statistical tools that you will find useful in many chapters of the text. An understanding of the concepts of probability distributions, expected values, and variances is needed in the study of decision trees (Chapters 2 Supplement, 6, and 7), quality control (Chapters 3 and 4), forecasting (Chapter 5), queuing models (Chapter 10 Supplement), work measurement (Chapter 11 Supplement), learning curves (Chapter 12 Supplement), inventory (Chapter 13), simulation (Chapter 13 Supplement), project management (Chapter 17), and maintenance (Chapter 18).

DISCRETE PROBABILITY DISTRIBUTIONS

Discrete probability distribution

In this section, we explore the properties of **discrete probability distributions**, that is, distributions in which outcomes are not continuous. When we deal with discrete variables, there is a probability value assigned to each event. These values must be between 0 and 1, and they must sum to 1. Example S1 relates to a sampling of student grades.

EXAMPLE S1

The Dean at York University, Nancy Beals, is concerned about the undergraduate statistics training of new MBA students. In a sampling of 100 applicants for next year's MBA class, she asked each student to supply his or her final grade in the course in statistics taken in the second or third year of their undergraduate program. To translate from letter grades to a numeric score, the Dean used the following system:

5. A **4.** B **3.** C **2.** D **1.** F

The responses to this query of the 100 potential students are summarized in the table below. Also shown is the probability for each possible grade outcome. This discrete probability distribution is computed using the relative frequency approach. Probability values are also often shown in graph form as in Figure S4.1.

PROBABILITY DISTRIBUTION FOR GRADES

GRADE LETTER OUTCOME	SCORE VARIABLE (X)	NUMBER OF STUDENTS RESPONDING	PROBABILITY, P(X)
A	5	10	0.1 = 10/100
B	4	20	0.2 = 20/100
C	3	30	0.3 = 30/100
D	2	30	0.3 = 30/100
F	1	10	0.1 = 10/100
		Total = 100	1.0 = 100/100

FIGURE S4.1 ■ Probability Function for Grades

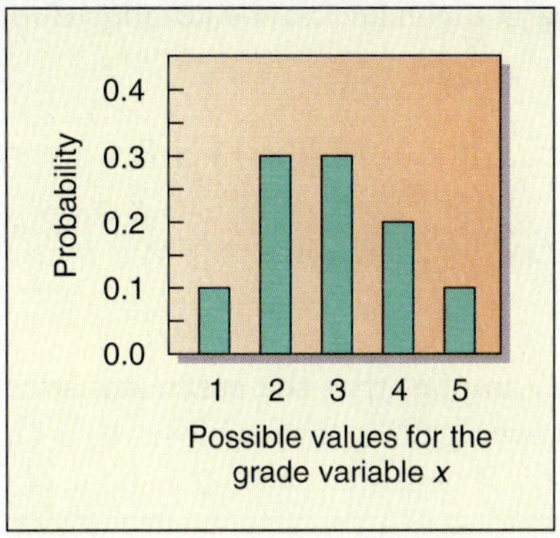

This distribution follows the three rules required of all probability distributions:

1. the events are mutually exclusive and collectively exhaustive
2. the individual probability values are between 0 and 1 inclusive
3. the total of the probability values sum to 1

The graph of the probability distribution in Example S1 gives us a picture of its shape. It helps us identify the central tendency of the distribution (called the expected value) and the amount of variability or spread of the distribution (called the variance). Expected value and variance are discussed next.

Expected Value of a Discrete Probability Distribution

Once we have established a probability distribution, the first characteristic we are usually interested in is the "central tendency" or average of the distribution.[1] We compute the **expected value**, a measure of central tendency, as a weighted average of the values of the variable:

Expected value

$$E(x) = \sum_{i=1}^{n} x_i P(x_i) = x_1 P(x_1) + x_2 P(x_2) + \cdots + x_n P(x_n) \qquad \text{(S4.1)}$$

where x_i = variable's possible values
$P(x_i)$ = probability of each of the variable's possible values

The expected value of any discrete probability distribution can be computed by: (1) multiplying each possible value of the variable x_i by the probability $P(x_i)$ that outcome will occur, and (2) summing the results, indicated by the summation sign, Σ. Example S2 shows such a calculation.

[1]If the data we are dealing with have not been grouped into a probability distribution, the measure of central tendency is called the arithmetic mean, or simply, the average. Here is the mean of the following seven numbers: 10, 12, 18, 6, 4, 5, 15.

$$\text{Arithmetic mean, } \overline{X} = \frac{\Sigma X}{n} = \frac{10 + 12 + 18 + 6 + 4 + 5 + 15}{7} = 10$$

EXAMPLE S2

Here is how the expected grade value can be computed for the question in Example S1.

$$E(x) = \sum_{i=1}^{5} x_i P(x_i) = x_1 P(x_1) + x_2 P(x_2) + x_3 P(x_3) + x_4 P(x_4) + x_5 P(x_5)$$
$$= (5)(.1) + (4)(.2) + (3)(.3) + (2)(.3) + (1)(.1)$$
$$= 2.9$$

The expected grade of 2.9 implies that the mean statistics grade is between D (2) and C (3), and that the average response is closer to a C, which is 3. Looking at Figure S4.1, we see that this is consistent with the shape of the probability function.

Variance of a Discrete Probability Distribution

Variance

In addition to the central tendency of a probability distribution, most decision makers are interested in the variability or the spread of the distribution. The **variance** of a probability distribution is a number that reveals the overall spread or dispersion of the distribution.[2] For a discrete probability distribution, it can be computed using the following equation:

$$\text{Variance} = \sum_{i=1}^{n} (x_i - E(x))^2 P(x_i) \quad \text{(S4.2)}$$

where x_i = variable's possible values
$E(x)$ = expected value of the variable
$P(x_i)$ = probability of each possible value of the variable

To compute the preceding variance, the expected value is subtracted from each value of the variable squared, and multiplied by the probability of occurrence of that value. The results are then summed to obtain the variance.

Standard deviation

A related measure of dispersion or spread is the **standard deviation**. This quantity is also used in many computations involved with probability distributions. The standard deviation, σ, is just the square root of the variance:

$$\sigma = \sqrt{\text{variance}} \quad \text{(S4.3)}$$

Example S3 shows a variance and standard deviation calculation.

[2]Just as the variance of a probability distribution shows the dispersion of the data, so does the variance of ungrouped data, that is, data not formed into a probability distribution. The formula is: Variance = $\Sigma(X - \overline{X})^2 / n$. Using the numbers 10, 12, 18, 6, 4, 5, and 15, we find that $\overline{X} = 10$. Here are the variance computations:

$$\text{Variance} = \frac{(10-10)^2 + (12-10)^2 + (18-10)^2 + (6-10)^2 + (4-10)^2 + (5-10)^2 + (15-10)^2}{7}$$
$$= \frac{0 + 4 + 64 + 16 + 36 + 25 + 25}{7}$$
$$= \frac{170}{7} = 24.28$$

We should also note that when the data we are looking at represent a *sample* of a whole set of data, we use the term $n - 1$ in the denominator, instead of n, in the variance formula.

EXAMPLE S3

Here is how this procedure is done for the statistics grade survey question:

$$\text{Variance} = \sum_{i=1}^{5}(x_i - E(x))^2 P(x_i)$$

$$= (5 - 2.9)^2(.1) + (4 - 2.9)^2(.2) + (3 - 2.9)^2(.3) + (2 - 2.9)^2(.3) + (1 - 2.9)^2(.1)$$

$$= (2.1)^2(.1) + (1.1)^2(.2) + (.1)^2(.3) + (-.9)^2(.3) + (-1.9)^2(.1)$$

$$= .441 + .242 + .003 + .243 + .361$$

$$= 1.29$$

The standard deviation for the grade question is

$$\sigma = \sqrt{\text{variance}}$$

$$= \sqrt{1.29} = 1.14$$

CONTINUOUS PROBABILITY DISTRIBUTIONS

There are many examples of continuous variables. The time it takes to finish a project, the number of kilograms in a barrel of butter, the high temperature during a given day, the exact length of a given type of lumber, and the weight of a railroad car of coal are all examples of continuous variables. Variables can take on an infinite number of values, so the fundamental probability rules must be modified for continuous variables.

As with discrete probability distributions, the sum of the probability values must equal 1. Because there are an infinite number of values of the variables, however, the probability of *each value* of the variable *must be* 0. If the probability values for the variable values were greater than 0, then the sum would be infinitely large.

The Normal Distribution

Normal distribution

One of the most popular and useful continuous probability distributions is the **normal distribution**, which is characterized by a bell-shaped curve. The normal distribution is completely specified when values for the mean, μ, and the standard deviation, σ, are known.

THE AREA UNDER THE NORMAL CURVE. Because the normal distribution is symmetrical, its midpoint (and highest point) is at the mean. Values of the *x*-axis are then measured in terms of how many standard deviations they are from the mean.

The area under the curve (in a continuous distribution) describes the probability that a variable has a value in the specified interval. The normal distribution requires complex mathematical calculations, but tables that provide areas or probabilities are readily available. For example, Figure S4.2 illustrates three commonly

FIGURE S4.2 ■ Three Common Areas Under Normal Curves

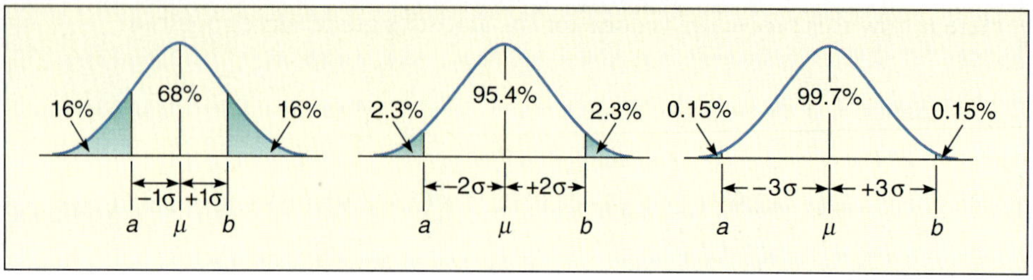

used relationships that have been derived from standard normal tables (a procedure we discuss in a moment). The area from point *a* to point *b* in the first drawing represents the probability, 68%, that the variable will be within 1 standard deviation of the mean. In the middle graph, we see that about 95.4% of the area lies within plus or minus 2 standard deviations of the mean. The third figure shows that 99.7% lies between $\pm 3\sigma$.

Translated into an application, Figure S4.2 implies that if the expected lifetime of an experimental computer chip is $\mu = 100$ days, and if the standard deviation is $\sigma = 15$ days, then we can make the following statements:

1. 68% of the population of computer chips studied have lives between 85 and 115 days (namely, $\pm 1\sigma$).
2. 95.4% of the chips have lives between 70 and 130 days ($\pm 2\sigma$).
3. 99.7% of the computer chips have lives in the range from 55 to 145 days ($\pm 3\sigma$).
4. Only 16% of the chips have lives greater than 115 days (from first graph, the area to the right of $+1\sigma$).

USING THE STANDARD NORMAL TABLE. To use a table to find normal probability values, we follow two steps.

Step 1. Convert the normal distribution to what we call a *standard normal distribution*. A standard normal distribution is one that has a mean of 0 and a standard deviation of 1. All normal tables are designed to handle variables with $\mu = 0$ and $\sigma = 1$. Without a standard normal distribution, a different table would be needed for each pair of μ and σ values. We call the new standard variable z. The value of z for any normal distribution is computed from the equation:

$$z = \frac{x - \mu}{\sigma} \qquad \text{(S4.4)}$$

where x = value of the variable we want to measure
μ = mean of the distribution
σ = standard deviation of the distribution
z = number of standard deviations from x to the mean, μ

For example, if $\mu = 100$, $\sigma = 15$, and we are interested in finding the probability that the variable x is less than 130, then we want $P(x < 130)$.

$$z = \frac{x - \mu}{\sigma} = \frac{130 - 100}{15} = \frac{30}{15} = 2 \text{ standard deviations}$$

FIGURE S4.3 ■ Normal Distribution Showing the Relationship Between z Values and x Values

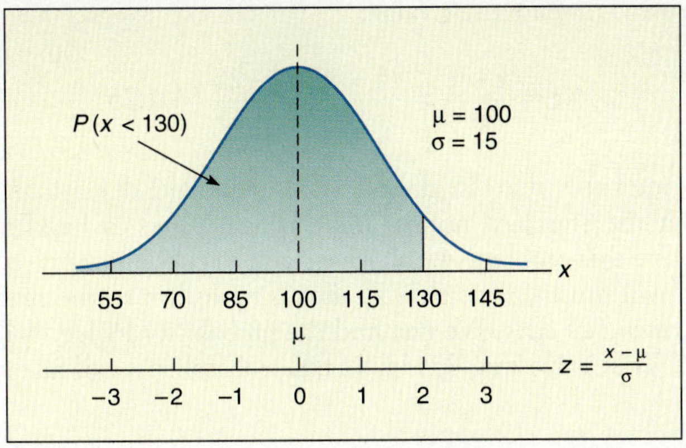

This means that the point x is 2.0 standard deviations to the right of the mean. This is shown in Figure S4.3.

Step 2. Look up the probability from a table of normal curve areas. Appendix A is such a table of areas for the standard normal distribution. It is set up to provide the area under the curve to the left of any specified value of z.

Let us see how Appendix A can be used. The column on the left lists values of z, with the second decimal place of z appearing in the top row. For example, for a value of $z = 2.00$ as just computed, find 2.0 in the left-hand column and .00 in the top row. In the body of the table, we find that the area sought is .97725, or 97.7%. Thus:

$$P(x < 130) = P(z < 2.00) = 97.7\%$$

This suggests that if the mean lifetime of a computer chip is 100 days with a standard deviation of 15 days, the probability that the life of a randomly selected chip is less than 130 is 97.7%. By referring to Figure S4.2, we see that this probability could also have been derived from the middle graph. (Note that 1.0 – .977 = .023 = 2.3%, which is the area in the right-hand tail of the curve.)

Example S4 illustrates the use of the normal distribution further.

EXAMPLE S4

Holden Construction Co. builds primarily three- and four-unit apartment buildings (called triplexes and quadraplexes) for investors, and it is believed that the total construction time in days follows a normal distribution. The mean time to construct a triplex is 100 days, and the standard deviation is 20 days. If the firm finishes this triplex in 75 days or less, it will be awarded a bonus payment of $5,000. What is the probability that Holden will receive the bonus?

FIGURE S4.4 ■ Probability Holden Will Receive the Bonus by Finishing in 75 Days

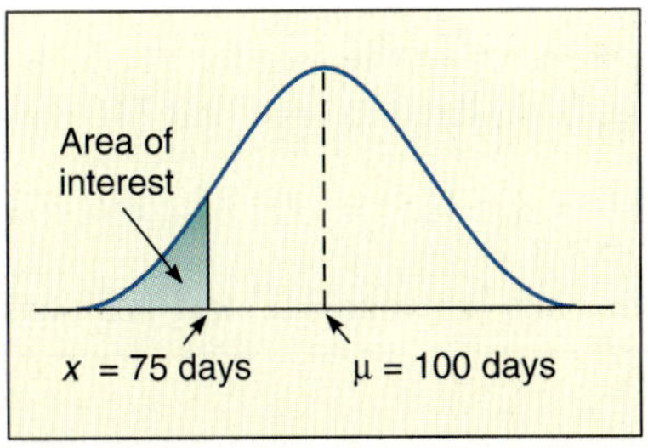

Figure S4.4 illustrates the probability we are looking for in the shaded area. The first step is to compute the z value:

$$z = \frac{x - \mu}{\sigma} = \frac{75 - 100}{20} = \frac{-25}{20} = -1.25$$

This z value indicates that 75 days is −1.25 standard deviations to the left of the mean. But the standard normal table is structured to handle only positive z values. To solve this problem, we observe that the curve is symmetric. The probability Holden will finish in *less than 75 days is equivalent* to the probability it will finish in *more than 125 days*. We first find the probability Holden will finish in less than 125 days. That value was .89435. So the probability it will take more than 125 days is

$$P(x > 125) = 1.0 - P(x < 125) = 1.0 - .89435 = .10565$$

Thus, the probability of completing the triplex in 75 days is .10565, or about 10%.

A second example: What is the probability the triplex will take between 110 and 125 days? We see in Figure S4.5 that

$$P(110 < x < 125) = P(x < 125) - P(x < 110)$$

FIGURE S4.5 ■ Probability of Holden Completion Between 110 and 125 Days

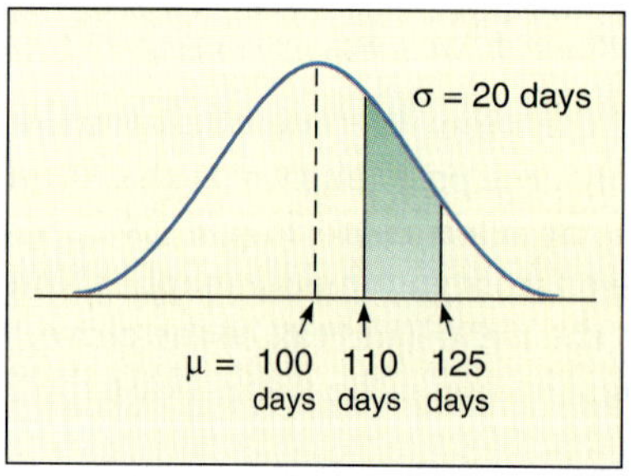

That is, the shaded area in the graph can be computed by finding the probability of completing the building in 125 days or less *minus* the probability of completing it in 110 days or less.

Recall that $P(x < 125 \text{ days})$ is equal to .89435. To find $P(x < 110 \text{ days})$, we follow the two steps developed earlier.

1. $z = \frac{x - \mu}{\sigma} = \frac{110 - 100}{20} = \frac{10}{20} = .50$ standard deviation
2. From Appendix A, we see that the area for $z = .50$ is .69146. So the probability the triplex can be completed in less than 110 days is .69146. Finally,

$$P(110 < x < 125) = .89435 - .69146 = .20289$$

The probability that it will take between 110 and 125 days is about 20%.

SUMMARY

The purpose of this supplement is to assist readers in tackling decision-making issues that involve probabilistic (uncertain) information. A background in statistical tools is quite useful in studying operations management. We examined two types of probability distributions, discrete and continuous. Discrete distributions assign a probability to each specific event. Continuous distributions, such as the normal, describe variables that can take on an infinite number of values. The normal, or bell-shaped, distribution is very widely used in business decision analysis and is referred to throughout this book.

KEY TERMS

Discrete probability distribution (p. 146)
Expected value (p. 147)
Variance (p. 148)
Standard deviation (p. 148)
Normal distribution (p. 149)

USING SPREADSHEETS TO COMPUTE EXPECTED VALUES AND VARIANCES

Program S4.1 shows the formulas used to compute the expected value for Example S1 and the variances for Example S2. If data are not grouped into a probability distribution, the computations are much simpler, because the @avg and @var formulas can be applied directly.

PROGRAM S4.1 ■ A Spreadsheet Approach to Expected Value and Variance Calculations. Examples S1 and S2 are illustrated with formulas.

	A	B	C	D	E
1	Examples S1 and S2				
2				Expected	
3	Test	No. of		Value	Variance
4	Scores	Students	Probability	Calculations	Calculations
5	5	10	+B5/B10	+A5*C5	((A5–D12)^2)*C5
6	4	20	+B6/B10	+A6*C6	((A6–D12)^2)*C6
7	3	30	+B7/B10	+A7*C7	((A7–D12)^2)*C7
8	2	30	+B8/B10	+A8*C8	((A8–D12)^2)*C8
9	1	10	+B9/B10	+A9*C9	((A9–D12)^2)*C9
10		@Sum(B5. .B9)			
11					
12			Expected Value	= @Sum(D5. .D9)	
13			Variance	= @Sum(E5. .E9)	
14			Standard Deviation	= @Sqrt(D13)	

DISCUSSION QUESTIONS

1. What is the difference between a discrete probability distribution and a continuous probability distribution? Give your own example of each.
2. What is the expected value and what does it measure? How is it computed for a discrete probability distribution?
3. What is the variance and what does it measure? How is it computed for a discrete probability distribution?
4. Name three business processes that can be described by the normal distribution.

CRITICAL THINKING EXERCISE

The normal probability distribution is clearly the most widely used and understood continuous distribution in business. Its parameters, as we discuss in this supplement, are μ and σ. Yet there are many other continuous distributions that are not bell-shaped. Find information to describe three of them. What are their parameters and shapes? Describe business applications of each and when they would be more appropriate than the normal distribution.

PROBLEMS

• **S4.1** Rami Guirguis Abbasi Health Food stocks five loaves of Vita-Bread. The probability distribution for the sales of Vita-Bread is listed in the following table. How many loaves will Rami sell on the average?

Number of Loaves Sold	Probability
0	.05
1	.15
2	.20
3	.25
4	.20
5	.15

: **S4.2** What are the expected value and variance of the following probability distribution?

Variable, X	Probability
1	.05
2	.05
3	.10
4	.10
5	.15
6	.15
7	.25
8	.15

• **S4.3** Sales for Hobi-cat, a 17-foot catamaran sailboat, have averaged 250 boats per month over the past 5 years with a standard deviation of 25 boats. Assuming that the demand is about the same as past years and follows a normal curve, what is the probability that sales will be less than 280 boats next month?

: **S4.4** Refer to Problem S4.3. What is the probability that sales will be more than 265 boats during the next month? What is the probability that sales will be under 250 boats next month?

: **S4.5** Precision Parts is a job shop that specializes in producing electric motor shafts. The average shaft size for the E300 electric motor is 1.55 centimetres, with a standard deviation of .32 centimetre. It is normally distributed. What is the probability that a shaft selected at random will be between 1.55 and 1.86 centimetres?

: **S4.6** Refer to Problem S4.5. What is the probability that a shaft size will be greater than 1.86 centimetres? What is the probability that a shaft size will be between 1.52 and 1.70 centimetres? What is the probability that a shaft size will be under 1.25 centimetres?

: **S4.7** An industrial oven used to cure sand cores for a factory manufacturing engine blocks for small cars is able to maintain fairly constant temperatures. The temperature range of the oven follows a normal distribution, with a mean of 232°C and a standard deviation of −4°C. Kamvar Farahbod, president of the factory, is concerned about the large number of defective cores that have been produced in the past several months. If the oven gets hotter than 246°C, the core is defective. What is the probability that the oven will cause a core to be defective? What is the probability that the temperature of the oven will range from 238° to 243°C?

⁝ **S4.8** Steve Hammershmidt, production supervisor for Ontario Fruit Supply, estimates that the average sales of oranges is 4,700 and the standard deviation is 500 oranges. Sales follow a normal distribution.

a) What is the probability that sales will be greater than 5,500 oranges?

b) What is the probability that sales will be greater than 4,500 oranges?

c) What is the probability that sales will be less than 4,900 oranges?

d) What is the probability that sales will be less than 4,300 oranges?

: **S4.9** Lori Becher has been the production manager of Medical Suppliers, Inc. (MSI), for the past 17 years. MSI is a producer of bandages and arm slings. During the past 5 years, the demand for the No-Stick bandage has been fairly constant. On the average, sales have been about 87,000 packages of No-Stick. Lori has reason to believe that the distribution of No-Stick follows a normal curve, with a standard deviation of 4,000 packages. What is the probability sales will be less than 81,000 packages?

BIBLIOGRAPHY

Campbell, S. *Flaws and Fallacies in Statistical Thinking*. Englewood Cliffs, NJ: Prentice Hall, 1974.

Canavos, G. C., and D. M. Miller. *An Introduction to Modern Business Statistics*. Belmont, CA: Duxbury Press, 1993.

Heineke, Janelle N., and Larry C. Miele. *Games and Exercises for Operations Management* (Englewood Cliffs, NJ: Prentice Hall, 1995).

Huff, D. *How to Lie with Statistics*. New York: Norton, 1954.

Levin, R. I., D. S. Rubin, J. P. Stinson, and E. S. Gardner. *Quantitative Approaches to Management*, 8th ed. New York: McGraw-Hill, 1992.

Render, B., and R. M. Stair. *Quantitative Analysis for Management*, 5th ed. Boston: Allyn and Bacon, 1994.

Tsokos, C. *Probability Distributions: An Introduction to Probability Theory with Applications*. North Scituate, MA: Duxbury Press, 1972.

WEB SITES OF INTEREST

1. Econometrics Laboratory Software: EML software packages: TSP, SAS, STRATA, GAUSS, MATLAB, SST (Statistical Software Tools), RATS (Regression and Time Series), MAPLE V, and others.

http://emlab.berkeley.edu/eml/emlsoftware.html

2. The Virtual Mathematics Center at University of California, Irvine. Includes math journals on line, math dictionaries, and encyclopedias, mathematical calculators, statistical calculators, interactive Java applet math tutorials, math courses, and tutorials.

http://www-sci.lib.uci.edu/~martindale/GradMath.html

5

FORECASTING

CHAPTER OUTLINE

LEARNING OBJECTIVES

When you complete this chapter you should be able to:

Identify or define:
- Forecasting
- Types of forecasts
- Time horizons
- Approaches to forecasts

Explain:
- Moving averages
- Exponential smoothing
- Trend projections
- Regression and correlation analysis
- Measures of forecast accuracy

WORLD-CLASS PROFILE: TUPPERWARE INTERNATIONAL

Forecasting Is Critical to Tupperware's Competitive Advantage

Stainless steel alloy molds, each requiring over 1,000 hours of skilled hand-crafting, are the heart of the manufacturing process. Each mold creates the exact shape of a new product: the mold's costs average $100,000 and their weight can be up to 4.5 tonnes. When a specific product is scheduled for a production run, its mold is carefully placed, as we see in the photo, into an injection molding machine.

When many people think of Tupperware, they envision plastic food storage containers sold through home parties. That image is correct, but Tupperware also happens to be a successful global manufacturer with over 80% of its $1.3 billion in sales outside the United States. A household name in nearly 100 countries, the firm has 14 plants: one in Hemingway, S.C., four in Latin America, one in Africa, five in Europe, and three in Asia. Throughout the world, Tupperware stands for quality, providing a lifetime warranty that each of its 400 plastic products will not chip, crack, break, or peel.

Forecasting demand at Tupperware is a critical, never-ending process, with each of its fifty profit centres around the world responsible for computerized monthly, quarterly, and 12-month sales projections. These are aggregated by region and then globally at Tupperware's World Headquarters in Orlando, Florida. The forecasts drive production at each plant.

The variety of statistical forecasting models used at Tupperware includes every technique discussed in this chapter, including moving averages, exponential smoothing, and regression analysis. At world headquarters, huge databases are maintained that map the sales of each product, the test market results of each *new* product (since 20% of the firm's sales come from products less than 2 years old), and where each product is in its own life cycle.

Three factors are key in the sales forecast: (1) the number of "consultants" or sales representatives that are registered, (2) the percentage of these dealers that are currently "active" (this number changes each week and month), and (3) the sales per active dealer, on a weekly basis. Forecasts incorporate historical data, recent events, and promotional events.

Tupperware maintains its edge over strong competitors such as Rubbermaid by using a group process to refine its statistical forecasts. Inputs come from sales, marketing, finance, and produc-

The plastic pellets which are melted at 260°C into Tupperware products are dropped through pipes from second floor bins into the machine holding a mold. After being injected into the water-cooled molds at a pressure up to 1,406 kilograms per square centimetre, the product cools and is removed and inspected.

tion, but final forecasts are the consensus of all participating managers. This final step is Tupperware's version of the "jury of executive opinion" described in this chapter.

Tupperware Canada Ltd. is located in Markham, Ontario, and the Rubbermaid Industries Canada head office is nearby in Mississauga, Ontario. Both firms sell extensively into Canadian markets.

This packing line assembles and packs thousands of products daily. Tupperware's semi-automated order, distribution, and storage system uses a robotic line to automatically "pick" individual orders and place them in plastic cartons. From enormous warehouses, orders are shipped throughout North America.

Tupperware's Manufacturing Process

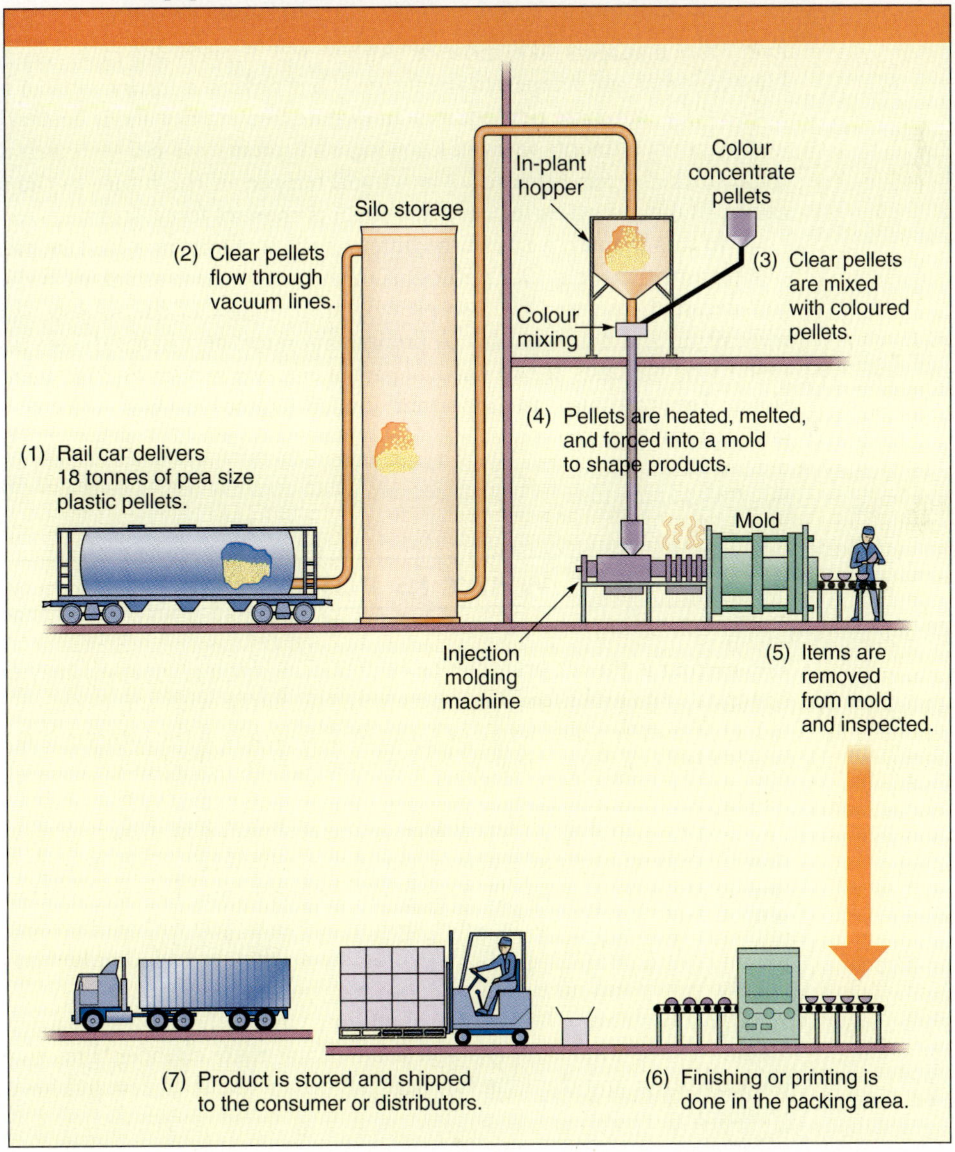

In 1970, Boeing, McDonnell Douglas, and Lockheed, all U.S. firms, dominated the global market for commercial aircraft. To counterbalance these American powerhouses, a group of European countries began to subsidize the European-based Airbus Industries so that it could improve the quality and productivity of its jet production. In 1990, about 85% of the world's airline jets were still made in the United States, but Airbus was capturing one-third of new worldwide contracts. Using forecasting techniques that you will study in this chapter, Airbus predicts that the huge, multibillion dollar investments made in it will see a payoff. Between 1990 and 2008, forecasts are that 11,500 planes, worth $600 billion, will be sold. Airbus, now second in sales to Boeing, predicts a significant increase in that market share. ♦

Every day managers like those at Airbus and Tupperware make decisions without knowing what will happen in the future. They order inventory without knowing what sales will be, purchase new equipment despite uncertainty about demand for products, and make investments without knowing what profits will be. Managers are always trying to make better estimates of what will happen in the future in the face of uncertainty. Making good estimates is the main purpose of forecasting.

In this chapter, we examine different types of forecasts, and we present a variety of forecasting models. Our purpose is to show that there are many ways for managers to forecast the future. We also provide an overview of the subject of business sales forecasting and describe how to prepare, monitor, and judge the accuracy of a forecast. Good forecasts are an *essential* part of efficient service and manufacturing operations. They are also an important modelling tool in both strategic and tactical decision making.

WHAT IS FORECASTING?

Forecasting

Forecasting is the art and science of predicting future events. It may involve taking historical data and projecting them into the future with some sort of mathematical model. It may be a subjective or intuitive prediction of the future. Or it may involve a combination of these, that is, a mathematical model adjusted by a manager's good judgement.

As we introduce different forecasting techniques in this chapter, you will realize that there is seldom one single, superior method. What works best in one firm under one set of conditions may be a complete disaster in another organization, or even in a different department of the same firm. In addition, you will realize that there are limits as to what can be expected from forecasts. They are seldom, if ever, perfect. They are also costly and time-consuming to prepare and monitor.

Few businesses, however, can afford to avoid the process of forecasting by just waiting to see what happens and then taking their chances. Effective planning in both the short and the long run depends on a forecast of demand for the company's products.

Forecasting Time Horizons

Forecasts are usually classified by the future time horizon that they cover.[1] The three categories are as follows:

1. *Short-range forecast.* This forecast has a time span of up to 1 year but is generally less than 3 months. It is used for planning purchasing, job scheduling, workforce levels, job assignments, and production levels.
2. *Medium-range forecast.* A medium-range, or intermediate, forecast generally spans from 3 months up to 3 years. It is useful in sales planning, production planning and budgeting, cash budgeting, and analyzing various operating plans.
3. *Long-range forecast.* Generally 3 years or more in time span, long-range forecasts are used in planning for new products, capital expenditures, facility location or expansion, and research and development.

Medium-range and long-range forecasts have three features that differentiate them from short-range forecasts. First, intermediate and long-run forecasts deal with more comprehensive issues and support management decisions regarding planning and products, plants, and processes. Implementing some facility decisions, such as GM's opening a new Saturn auto manufacturing plant, can take 5 to 8 years from inception to completion. Second, short-term forecasting usually employs different methodologies than do longer-term ones. Mathematical techniques such as moving averages, exponential smoothing, and trend extrapolation (all of which we shall examine shortly) are common to short-run projections. Broader, *less* quantitative methods are useful in predicting such issues as whether a new product, like the optical disk recorder, should be introduced in a company's product line. And third, as you would expect, short-range forecasts tend to be more accurate than longer-range forecasts. Factors that influence demand change every day. Thus, as the time horizon lengthens, it is likely that one's forecast accuracy will diminish. It almost goes without saying, then, that sales forecasts need to be updated regularly in order to maintain their value and integrity. After each sales period, the forecast should be reviewed and revised.

The Influence of Product Life Cycle

Another factor to consider when developing sales forecasts, especially longer ones, is the product's life cycle. Products, and even services, do not sell at a constant level throughout their lives. Most successful products pass through four stages: (1) introduction, (2) growth, (3) maturity, and (4) decline.

Products in the first two stages of their life cycle need longer forecasts than those in the maturity and decline stages. Forecasts are useful in projecting different staffing levels, inventory levels, and factory capacity as the product passes from the first to the last stage. The subject of introducing new products, and their life cycles, is treated in more detail in Chapter 6.

[1]For details, see Peter W. Stonebraker and G. Keong Leong, *Operations Strategy* (Boston: Allyn and Bacon, 1994).

TYPES OF FORECASTS

Organizations use three major types of forecasts in planning the future of their operations.

Economic forecasts

1. **Economic forecasts** address the business cycle by predicting inflation rates, money supplies, housing starts, and other planning indicators.

Technological forecasts

2. **Technological forecasts** are concerned with rates of technological progress, which can result in the birth of exciting new products, requiring new plants and equipment.

Demand forecasts

3. **Demand forecasts** are projections of demand for a company's products or services. These forecasts, also called sales forecasts, drive a company's production, capacity, and scheduling systems and serve as inputs to financial, marketing, and personnel planning.

Economic and technological forecasting are specialized techniques that may be outside the role of the operations manager. The emphasis in this book therefore will be on demand forecasting.

FORECASTING APPROACHES

Quantitative forecasts
Qualitative forecasts

There are two general approaches to forecasting, just as there are two ways to tackle all decision modelling. One is quantitative analysis; the other is a qualitative approach. **Quantitative forecasts** employ a variety of mathematical models that use historical data and/or causal variables to forecast demand. Subjective or **qualitative forecasts** incorporate important factors such as the decision maker's intuition, emotions, personal experiences, and value system in reaching a forecast. Some firms use one approach and some use the other. In practice, a combination or blending of the two styles is usually most effective.

Overview of Qualitative Methods

In this section, we consider four different *qualitative* forecasting techniques.

Jury of executive opinion

1. **Jury of Executive Opinion.** Under this method, the opinions of a group of high-level managers, often in combination with statistical models, are pooled to arrive at a group estimate of demand.

Sales force composite

2. **Sales Force Composite.** In this approach, each salesperson estimates what sales will be in his or her region. These forecasts are then reviewed to ensure they are realistic and then combined at the district and national levels to reach an overall forecast.

Delphi method

3. **Delphi Method.** There are three different types of participants in the Delphi method: decision makers, staff personnel, and respondents. The decision makers usually consist of a group of 5 to 10 experts who will be making the actual forecast. The staff personnel assist the decision makers by preparing, distributing, collecting, and summarizing a series of questionnaires and survey results.

To get a grasp on future trends in the world of medical research, Bristol-Myers Squibb Company questioned 220 well-known research scientists. These leaders made a *jury of executive opinion* suggesting that the future treatment of disease will concentrate on its causes. In other words, rather than treat diseases like cancer through symptom elimination, medical treatment will focus on attacking individual cells of the disease itself. As a result of this qualitative forecasting, Bristol-Myers created the fluorescence-activated cell sorter, which targets antibodies of tumor cells through the use of lasers and computers. The firm's Canadian head office is located in Montreal, Quebec.

The respondents are a group of people, often located in different places, whose judgements are valued and are being sought. This group provides inputs to the decision makers before the forecast is made.

4. **Consumer Market Survey.** This method solicits input from customers or potential customers regarding their future purchasing plans. It can help not only in preparing a forecast, but also in improving product design and planning for new products.

Consumer market survey

Overview of Quantitative Methods

Five quantitative forecasting methods are addressed in this chapter. They are as follows:

1. Naive approach	time-series models
2. Moving averages	
3. Exponential smoothing	
4. Trend projection	
5. Linear-regression causal model	causal model

TIME-SERIES MODELS. **Time-series** models predict on the assumption that the future is a function of the past. In other words, they look at what has happened over a period of time and use a series of past data to make a forecast. If we are predicting weekly sales of lawn mowers, we use the past weekly sales for lawn mowers in making the forecast.

Time series

CAUSAL MODELS. Causal models, such as linear regression, incorporate the variables or factors that might influence the quantity being forecast. For example, a causal model for lawn-mower sales might include factors such as new housing starts, advertising budget, and competitors' prices.

Eight Steps to a Forecasting System

Forecasting always follows the same eight steps, regardless of the method used:

1. Determine the use of the forecast—what objectives are we trying to obtain?
2. Select the items that are to be forecasted.
3. Determine the time horizon of the forecast—is it short-, medium-, or long-term?
4. Select the forecasting model(s).
5. Gather the data needed to make the forecast.
6. Validate the forecasting model.
7. Make the forecast.
8. Implement the results.

These steps present a systematic way of initiating, designing, and implementing a forecasting system. When the system is to be used to generate forecasts regularly over time, data must be routinely collected. Then the actual computations used to make the forecast are usually done by computer. This is the process that virtually every retailer, from Wal-Mart to Sears to Eaton's, follows daily, using point-of-sale computer terminals as the data collection device. The *POM in Action* box "Expert Systems Change the Way Xerox Does Forecasting" describes how that firm developed its current forecasting system.

TIME-SERIES FORECASTING

A time series is based on a sequence of evenly spaced (weekly, monthly, quarterly, and so on) data points. Examples include weekly sales of Nike Air Jordans, quarterly earnings reports of Microsoft stock, daily shipments of Molson's beer, and annual consumer price indices. Forecasting time-series data implies that future values are predicted *only* from past values and that other variables, no matter how potentially valuable, are ignored.

Decomposition of a Time Series

Analyzing time series means breaking down past data into components and then projecting them forward. A time series typically has four components: trend, seasonality, cycles, and random variation.

1. *Trend* is the gradual upward or downward movement of the data over time.
2. *Seasonality* is a data pattern that repeats itself after a period of days, weeks, months, or quarters (the latter being from where the term *seasonality* arose, that is, the seasons, fall, winter, spring, and summer). There are six common seasonality patterns:

3. *Cycles* are patterns in the data that occur every several years. They are usually tied into the business cycle and are of major importance in short-term business analysis and planning.
4. *Random variations* are "blips" in the data caused by chance and unusual situations. They follow no discernible pattern.

PERIOD OF PATTERN	SEASON LENGTH	NUMBER OF SEASONS IN PATTERN
Week	Day	7
Month	Week	4–4½
Month	Day	28–31
Year	Quarter	4
Year	Month	12
Year	Week	52

Figure 5.1 shows a time series and its components.

There are two general forms of time-series models in statistics. The most widely used is a multiplicative model, which assumes that demand is the product of the four components:

$$\text{Demand} = \text{trend} \times \text{seasonality} \times \text{cycle} \times \text{random variation}$$

An additive model provides an estimate by adding the components together. It is stated as:

POM IN ACTION

Expert Systems Change the Way Xerox Does Forecasting

"Expert systems" and "artificial intelligence" are now the most commonly used terms in the corporate boardroom. Becoming increasingly popular, they describe computer systems that use knowledge about a specific complex application area to act as an expert consultant to users. Using this new software, which in effect permits a computer to mimic human reasoning, has made planning at Xerox Corp. much more flexible than ever.

Until 1990, the copier giant's seven-member sales forecasting team used a hodgepodge of forecasting models and methods to do its job. At one extreme, analysts graphed historical data and extrapolated it into the future for each line of copier. These graphs were then distributed within the company. At the other extreme, some analysts used spreadsheet models such as Lotus 1-2-3. This patchwork approach was so labourious and took so long to develop that next year's forecast was started in July of the preceding year. Further, the team could only manage to forecast out the next 12 months.

Now, after 2 years of development, a new forecasting model using expert systems is up and running. Not only can Xerox wait until October to start developing the next forecast, but the firm can now make forecasts for 3 years out. And the new system constantly analyzes actual results versus the forecast, updating its parameters to refine its accuracy. Further, the time saved allows the Xerox team to consider how factors outside the firm, such as inflation or rivals' activities, might affect future sales.

Sources: Business Week (November 2, 1992): 133–136; *CIO* (August 1993): 38–46; and *MIS Quarterly* (September 1990): 323–329.

The Xerox Tower of North American Centre, North York, Ontario. Before 1990, it took Xerox 6 months to produce a 12 month sales forecast. Using expert systems software, Xerox now develops a 3 year forecast in 3 months.

$$\text{Demand} = \text{trend} + \text{seasonality} + \text{cycle} + \text{random variation}$$

In most real-world models, forecasters assume that the random variations are averaged out over time. They then concentrate on only the seasonal component and a component that is a combination of trend and cyclical factors.

Naive Approach

The simplest way to forecast is to assume that demand in the next period is just equal to demand in the most recent period. In other words, if sales of a product, say, Motorola

FIGURE 5.1 ■ Product Demand Charted over 4 Years with Trend and Seasonality Indicated

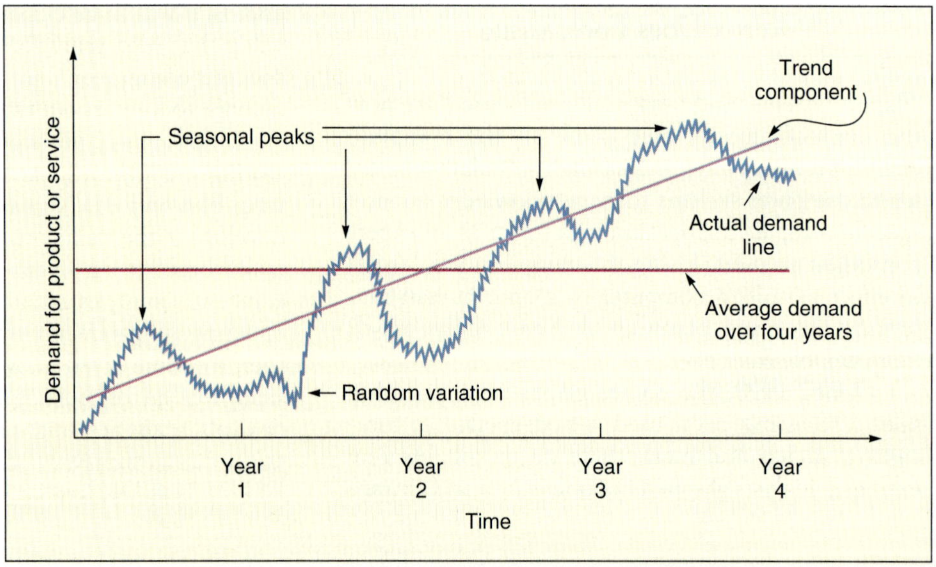

cellular phones, were 68 units in January, we can forecast that February's sales will also be 68 phones. Does this make any sense? It turns out that for some product lines, selecting this **naive approach** is the most cost-effective and efficient objective forecasting model. It at least provides a starting point against which the more sophisticated models that follow can be compared.

Naive approach

Moving Averages

A **moving-average** forecast uses a number of recent actual data values to generate a forecast. Moving averages are useful if we can assume that market demands will stay fairly steady over time. A 4-month moving average is found by simply summing the demand during the past 4 months and dividing by 4. With each passing month, the most recent month's data are added to the sum of the previous 3 months' data, and the earliest month is dropped. This tends to smooth out short-term irregularities in the data series.

Moving averages

Mathematically, the simple moving average (which serves as an estimate of the next period's demand) is expressed as

$$\text{Moving average} = \frac{\Sigma \text{ demand in previous } n \text{ periods}}{n} \tag{5.1}$$

where n is the number of periods in the moving average—for example, 4, 5, or 6 months, respectively, for a 4-, 5-, or 6-period moving average.

Example 1 shows how moving averages are calculated.

When there is a detectable trend or pattern, weights can be used to place more emphasis on recent values. This makes the techniques more responsive to changes because more recent periods may be more heavily weighted. Choice of weights is somewhat arbitrary because there is no set formula to determine them. Therefore,

EXAMPLE 1

Storage shed sales at Donna's Garden Supply are shown in the middle column of the table. A 3-month moving average appears on the right.

MONTH	ACTUAL SHED SALES	3-MONTH MOVING AVERAGE
January	10	
February	12	
March	13	
April	16	$(10 + 12 + 13)/3 = 11\frac{2}{3}$
May	19	$(12 + 13 + 16)/3 = 13\frac{2}{3}$
June	23	$(13 + 16 + 19)/3 = 16$
July	26	$(16 + 19 + 23)/3 = 19\frac{1}{3}$
August	30	$(19 + 23 + 26)/3 = 22\frac{2}{3}$
September	28	$(23 + 26 + 30)/3 = 26\frac{1}{3}$
October	18	$(26 + 30 + 28)/3 = 28$
November	16	$(30 + 28 + 18)/3 = 25\frac{1}{3}$
December	14	$(28 + 18 + 16)/3 = 20\frac{2}{3}$

deciding which weights to use requires some experience and a bit of luck. If the latest month or period is weighted too heavily, the forecast might reflect a large unusual change in the demand or sales pattern too quickly.

A weighted moving average may be expressed mathematically as

$$\text{Weighted moving average} = \frac{\Sigma\,(\text{weight for period } n)\,(\text{demand in period } n)}{\Sigma \text{ weights}} \tag{5.2}$$

Example 2 shows how to calculate a weighted moving average.

EXAMPLE 2

Donna's Garden Supply (see Example 1) decides to forecast storage shed sales by weighting the past 3 months as follows:

WEIGHTS APPLIED	PERIOD
③	Last month
②	Two months ago
①	Three months ago
6	Sum of weights

Forecast for this month =

$$\frac{③ \times \text{sales last mo.} + ② \times \text{sales 2 mos. ago} + ① \times \text{sales 3 mos. ago}}{6 \leftarrow \text{sum of the weights}}$$

The results of this weighted average forecast are as follows:

MONTH	ACTUAL SHED SALES	THREE-MONTH WEIGHTED MOVING AVERAGE
January	10	
February	12	
March	13	
April	16	$[(3 \times 13) + (2 \times 12) + (10)]/6 = 12\frac{1}{6}$
May	19	$[(3 \times 16) + (2 \times 13) + (12)]/6 = 14\frac{1}{3}$
June	23	$[(3 \times 19) + (2 \times 16) + (13)]/6 = 17$
July	26	$[(3 \times 23) + (2 \times 19) + (16)]/6 = 20\frac{1}{2}$
August	30	$[(3 \times 26) + (2 \times 23) + (19)]/6 = 23\frac{5}{6}$
September	28	$[(3 \times 30) + (2 \times 26) + (23)]/6 = 27\frac{1}{2}$
October	18	$[(3 \times 28) + (2 \times 30) + (26)]/6 = 28\frac{1}{3}$
November	16	$[(3 \times 18) + (2 \times 28) + (30)]/6 = 23\frac{1}{3}$
December	14	$[(3 \times 16) + (2 \times 18) + (28)]/6 = 18\frac{2}{3}$

In this particular forecasting situation, you can see that weighting the latest month more heavily provides a much more accurate projection.

Both simple and weighted moving averages are effective in smoothing out sudden fluctuations in the demand pattern in order to provide stable estimates. Moving averages do, however, have three problems. First, increasing the size of n (the number of periods averaged) does smooth out fluctuations better, but it makes the method less sensitive to *real* changes in the data. Second, moving averages cannot pick up trends very well. Because they are averages, they will always stay within past levels and will not predict a change to either a higher or lower level. Finally, moving averages require extensive records of past data.

Figure 5.2, a plot of the data in Examples 1 and 2, illustrates the lag effect of the moving-average models.

Exponential Smoothing

Exponential smoothing is a sophisticated weighted moving-average forecasting method that is still fairly easy to use. It involves very *little* record keeping of past data. The basic exponential smoothing formula can be shown as follows:

Exponential smoothing

$$\text{New forecast} = \text{last period's forecast} + \alpha(\text{last period's actual demand} - \text{last period's forecast}) \quad (5.3)$$

where α is a weight, or **smoothing constant,** chosen by the forecaster, that has a value from 0 and 1. Equation (5.3) can also be written mathematically as

Smoothing constant

$$F_t = F_{t-1} + \alpha(A_{t-1} - F_{t-1}) \quad (5.4)$$

FIGURE 5.2 ■ Actual Demand vs. Moving-Average and Weighted Moving-Average Methods for Donna's Garden Supply

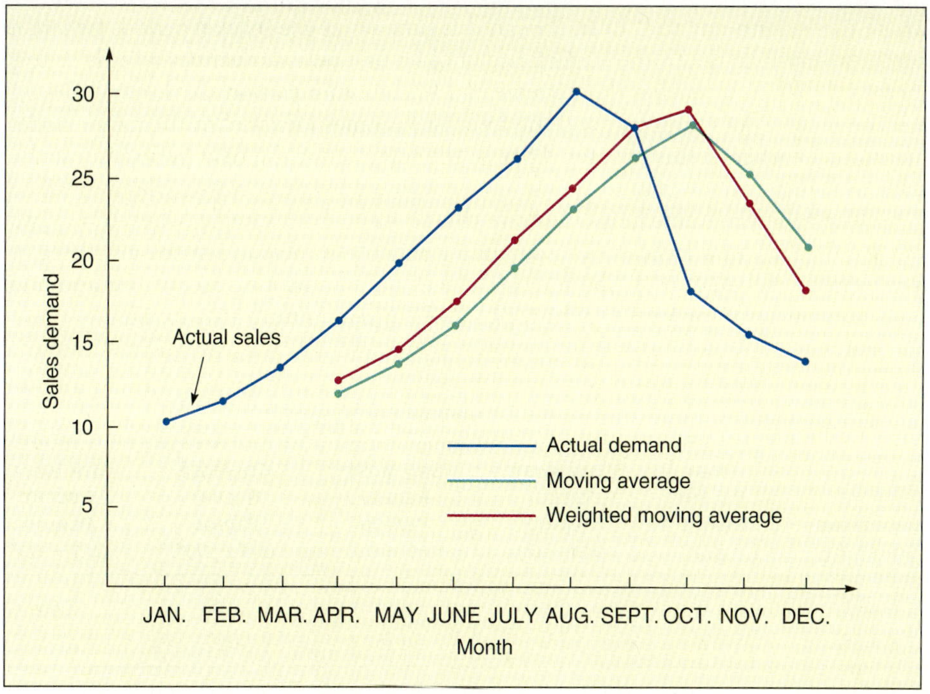

where F_t = new forecast
F_{t-1} = previous forecast
α = smoothing constant ($0 \leq \alpha \leq 1$)
A_{t-1} = previous period's actual demand

The concept is not complex. The latest estimate of demand is equal to our old estimate adjusted by a fraction of the difference between the last period's actual demand and the old estimate. Example 3 shows how to use exponential smoothing to derive a forecast.

EXAMPLE 3

In January, a car dealer predicted a February demand for 142 Ford Mustangs. Actual February demand was 153 autos. Using a smoothing constant chosen by management, of $\alpha = .20$, we can forecast the March demand using the exponential smoothing model. Substituting into the formula, we obtain

$$\text{New forecast (for March demand)} = 142 + .2(153 - 142) = 144.2$$

Thus, the demand forecast for Ford Mustangs in March is rounded to 144.

The *smoothing constant*, α, is generally in the range from .05 to .50 for business applications. It can be changed to give more weight to recent data (when α is high) or more weight to past data (when α is low). To demonstrate this weighting concept, Equation 5.4 can be rewritten algebraically in the form

$$F_t = \alpha A_{t-1} + \alpha(1-\alpha)A_{t-2} + \alpha(1-\alpha)^2 A_{t-3} + \alpha(1-\alpha)^3 A_{t-4} + \cdots + \alpha(1-\alpha)^n A_{t-n} \qquad (5.5)$$

where the weights add to 1. Even though this time series goes back n periods (where n can be a very long time), the importance of older past periods declines quickly as α is increased. When α reaches the extreme of 1.0, then in Equation (5.5), $F_t = 1.0A_{t-1}$. All the older values drop out, and the forecast becomes identical to the naive model mentioned earlier in this chapter. That is, the forecast for the next period is just the same as this period's demand.

The following table helps illustrate this concept. For example, when $\alpha = .5$, we can see that the new forecast is based almost entirely on demand in the last three or four periods. When $\alpha = .1$, the forecast places little weight on recent demand and takes *many* periods (about 19) of historic values into account.

	Weight Assigned To:				
Smoothing Constant	Most Recent Period (α)	2nd Most Recent Period $\alpha(1-\alpha)$	3rd Most Recent Period $\alpha(1-\alpha)^2$	4th Most Recent Period $\alpha(1-\alpha)^3$	5th Most Recent Period $\alpha(1-\alpha)^4$
$\alpha = .1$	.1	.09	.081	.073	.066
$\alpha = .5$	.5	.25	.125	.063	.031

SELECTING THE SMOOTHING CONSTANT. The exponential smoothing approach is easy to use, and it has been successfully applied in virtually every type of business. The appropriate value of the smoothing constant, α, however, can make the difference between an accurate forecast and an inaccurate forecast. In picking a value for the smoothing constant, the objective is to obtain the most accurate forecast. The overall accuracy of a forecasting model can be determined by comparing the forecasted values for past known periods with the actual or observed demand for those periods.

The forecast error is defined as

$$\text{Forecast error} = \text{demand} - \text{forecast}$$

MEAN ABSOLUTE DEVIATION. One measure of the overall forecast error for a model is the **mean absolute deviation (MAD)**. This value is computed by taking the sum of the absolute values of the individual forecast errors and dividing by the number of periods of data (n):

Mean absolute deviation (MAD)

$$\text{MAD} = \frac{\Sigma\,|\text{forecast errors}|}{n} \tag{5.6}$$

Example 4 applies this concept with a trial-and-error testing of two values of α.

EXAMPLE 4

The Port of Toronto has unloaded large quantities of grain from ships during the past eight quarters. The port's operations manager wants to test the use of exponential smoothing to see how well the technique works in predicting tonnage unloaded. He guesses that the forecast of grain unloaded in the first quarter was 175 tons. Two values of α are examined: $\alpha = .10$ and $\alpha = .50$. The following table shows the *detailed* calculations for $\alpha = .10$ only:

QUARTER	ACTUAL TONNAGE UNLOADED	ROUNDED FORECAST USING $\alpha = .10$*	ROUNDED FORECAST USING $\alpha = .50$*
1	180	175	175
2	168	$176 = 175.00 + .10(180 - 175)$	178
3	159	$175 = 175.50 + .10(168 - 175.50)$	173
4	175	$173 = 174.75 + .10(159 - 174.75)$	166
5	190	$173 = 173.18 + .10(175 - 173.18)$	170
6	205	$175 = 173.36 + .10(190 - 173.36)$	180
7	180	$178 = 175.02 + .10(205 - 175.02)$	193
8	182	$178 = 178.02 + .10(180 - 178.02)$	186
9	?	$179 = 178.22 + .10(182 - 178.22)$	184

*Forecasts rounded to the nearest tonne.

To evaluate the accuracy of each smoothing constant, we can compute the absolute deviations and MADs.

Quarter	Actual Tonnage Unloaded	Rounded Forecast with $\alpha = .10$	Absolute Deviation for $\alpha = .10$	Rounded Forecast with $\alpha = .50$	Absolute Deviation for $\alpha = .50$
1	180	175	5	175	5
2	168	176	8	178	10
3	159	175	16	173	14
4	175	173	2	166	9
5	190	173	17	170	20
6	205	175	30	180	25
7	180	178	2	193	13
8	182	178	4	186	4
	Sum of absolute deviations		84		100
	$\text{MAD} = \frac{\Sigma\,\lvert\text{deviations}\rvert}{n}$		10.50		12.50

On the basis of this analysis, a smoothing constant of $\alpha = .10$ is preferred to $\alpha = .50$ because its MAD is smaller.

Most computerized forecasting software includes a feature that automatically finds the smoothing constant with the lowest forecast error. Some software modifies the alpha value if errors become larger than acceptable.

Mean squared error (MSE)

MEAN SQUARED ERROR. The **mean squared error (MSE)** is another way of measuring overall forecast error. MSE is the average of the squared differences between the forecasted and observed values. Its formula is

$$\text{MSE} = \frac{\Sigma\text{ forecast errors}^2}{n} \tag{5.7}$$

Example 5 finds the MSE for the Port of Toronto noted in Example 4.

EXAMPLE 5

Quarter	Actual Tonnage Unloaded	Forecast for $\alpha = .10$	$(\text{Error})^2$
1	180	175	$5^2 = 25$
2	168	176	$8^2 = 64$
3	159	175	$(16)^2 = 256$
4	175	173	$2^2 = 4$
5	190	173	$(17)^2 = 289$
6	205	175	$(30)^2 = 900$
7	180	178	$2^2 = 4$
8	182	178	$4^2 = 16$
			Sum of errors squared = 1,558

$$\text{MSE} = \frac{\Sigma\text{ forecast errors}^2}{n} = 1{,}558/8 = 194.75$$

Is this MSE good or bad? The answer is, it all depends on the MSEs for other values of α. As a practice exercise, find the MSE for $\alpha = .50$. (You should get MSE = 201.5.) This indicates that $\alpha = .10$ is a better choice because we want to minimize MSE. Coincidentally, this confirms the conclusion we reached in Example 4 using MAD.

Exponential Smoothing with Trend Adjustment

As with any moving-average technique, simple exponential smoothing fails to respond to trends. To illustrate a more complex exponential smoothing model, let us consider one that adjusts for trend. The idea is to compute a simple exponential smoothing forecast as before and then adjust for positive or negative lag in trend. The formula is

Forecast including trend (FIT_t) = new forecast (F_t) + trend correction (T_t)

To smooth out the trend, the equation for the trend correction uses a smoothing constant, β, in the same way the simple exponential model uses α. T_t is computed by

$$T_t = (1 - \beta)T_{t-1} + \beta(F_t - F_{t-1}) \tag{5.8}$$

where T_t = smoothed trend for period t

T_{t-1} = smoothed trend for previous period

β = trend-smoothing constant that we select

F_t = simple exponential smoothed forecast for period t

F_{t-1} = forecast for previous period

There are three steps to compute a trend-adjusted forecast.

Step 1. Compute a simple exponential forecast for time period t (F_t).

Step 2. Compute the trend by using the equation

$$T_t = (1 - \beta)T_{t-1} + \beta(F_t - F_{t-1})$$

To start step 2 for the first time, an initial trend value must be inserted (either by a good guess or by observed past data). After that, trend is computed.

Step 3. Calculate the trend-adjusted exponential smoothing forecast (FIT_t) by the formula

$$FIT_t = F_t + T_t$$

Example 6 shows how to use trend-adjusted exponential smoothing.

EXAMPLE 6

A large Winnipeg manufacturer uses exponential smoothing to forecast demand for a pollution-control equipment product. It appears that an increasing trend is present.

MONTH	DEMAND	MONTH	DEMAND
1	12	6	26
2	17	7	31
3	20	8	32
4	19	9	36
5	24		

Smoothing constants are assigned the values of $\alpha = .2$ and $\beta = .4$. Assume the initial forecast for month 1 was 11 units.

Step 1. Forecast for month 2 (F_2) = forecast for month 1 (F_1) + α (month 1 demand – forecast for month 1):

$$\begin{aligned} F_2 &= 11 + .2(12 - 11) \\ &= 11.0 + .2 = 11.2 \text{ units} \end{aligned}$$

Step 2. Compute the trend present. Assume an initial trend adjustment of zero, that is, $T_1 = 0$.

$$\begin{aligned} T_2 &= (1 - \beta)T_1 + \beta(F_2 - F_1) \\ &= 0 + 4(11.2 - 11.0) \\ &= .08 \end{aligned}$$

Step 3. Compute the forecast including trend (FIT_t):

$$\begin{aligned} FIT_2 &= F_2 + T_2 \\ &= 11.2 + .08 \\ &= 11.28 \text{ units} \end{aligned}$$

We will do the same calculations for the third month also.

Step 1. $F_3 = F_2 + \alpha(\text{demand in month } 2 - F_2)$
$= 11.2 + .2(17 - 11.2) = 12.36$

Step 2. $T_3 = (1 - \beta)T_2 + \beta(F_3 - F_2)$
$= (1 - .4)(.08) + .4(12.36 - 11.2) = .51$

Step 3. $FIT_3 = F_3 + T_3$
$= 12.36 + .51 = 12.87$

So the simple exponential forecast (without trend) for month 2 was 11.2 units, and the trend-adjusted forecast was 11.28 units. In month 3, the simple forecast (without trend) was 12.36 units, and the trend-adjusted forecast was 12.87 units. Naturally, different values of T_1 and β can produce even better estimates.

The following table completes the forecasts for the 9-month period. Figure 5.3 compares actual demand, forecast without trend (F_t), and forecast with trend (FIT_t). Note that although FIT_t is better than F_t in this case, it is still not perfect in predicting actual demand. Perhaps a higher value of β would help.

MONTH	ACTUAL DEMAND	FORECAST, F_T (WITHOUT TREND)	TREND	ADJUSTED FIT_T
1	12	11.00	0	—
2	17	11.20	.08	11.28
3	20	12.36	.51	12.87
4	19	13.89	.92	14.81
5	24	14.91	.96	15.87
6	26	16.73	1.30	18.03
7	31	18.58	1.52	20.10
8	32	21.07	1.91	22.98
9	36	23.25	2.02	25.27

FIGURE 5.3 ■ Actual Compared to Forecasts

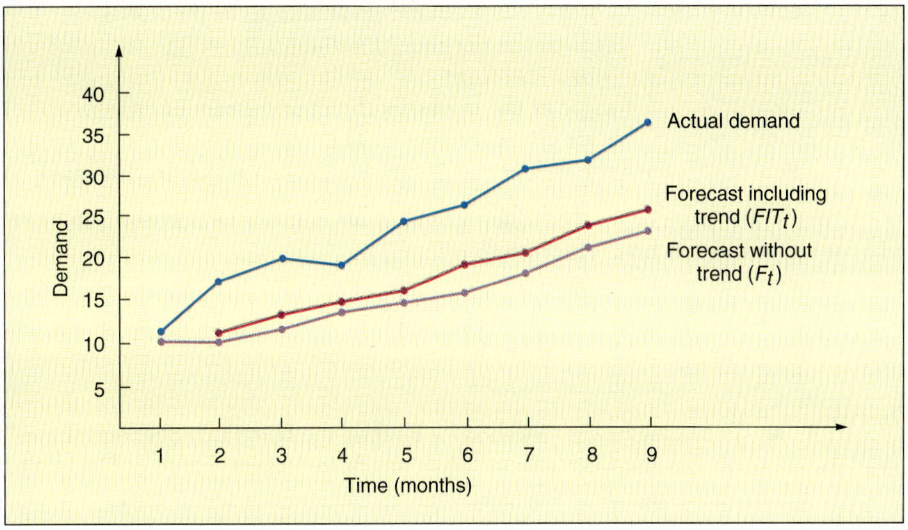

The value of the trend-smoothing constant, β, resembles the α constant because a high β is more responsive to recent changes in trend. A low β gives less weight to the most recent trends and tends to smooth out the present trend. Values of β can be found by the trial-and-error approach, or by using sophisticated commercial forecasting software, with the MAD used as a measure of comparison.

Simple exponential smoothing is often referred to as first-order smoothing, and trend-adjusted smoothing is called second-order, or double, smoothing. Other advanced exponential smoothing models are also in use, including seasonal-adjusted and triple smoothing, but these are beyond the scope of this book.[2]

[2]For more details, see E. S. Gardner, "Exponential Smoothing: The State of the Art." *Journal of Forecasting*, 4, no. 1 (March 1985), or R. Brown, *Smoothing, Forecasting and Prediction* (Englewood Cliffs, NJ: Prentice Hall, 1973).

Trend Projections

Trend projection

The last time-series forecasting method we will discuss is **trend projection**. This technique fits a trend line to a series of historical data points and then projects the line into the future for medium-to-long-range forecasts. Several mathematical trend equations can be developed (for example, exponential and quadratic), but in this section, we will look at *linear* (straight-line) trends only.

If we decide to develop a linear trend line by a precise statistical method, we can apply the *least squares method*. This approach results in a straight line that minimizes the sum of the squares of the vertical differences from the line to each of the actual observations. Figure 5.4 illustrates the least squares approach.

A least squares line is described in terms of its y-intercept (the height at which it intercepts the y-axis) and its slope (the angle of the line). If we can compute the y-intercept and slope, we can express the line with the following equation:

$$\hat{y} = a + bx \tag{5.9}$$

where $\hat{y}$ (called "y hat") = computed value of the variable to be predicted (called the dependent variable)
a = y-axis intercept
b = slope of the regression line (or the rate of change in y for given changes in x)
x = the independent variable (which is *time* in this case)

Statisticians have developed equations that we can use to find the values of a and b for any regression line. The slope b is found by

$$b = \frac{\Sigma xy - n\bar{x}\bar{y}}{\Sigma x^2 - n\bar{x}^2} \tag{5.10}$$

FIGURE 5.4 ■ The Least Squares Method for Finding the Best-Fitting Straight Line, Where the Asterisks Are the Locations of the Seven Actual Observations or Data Points

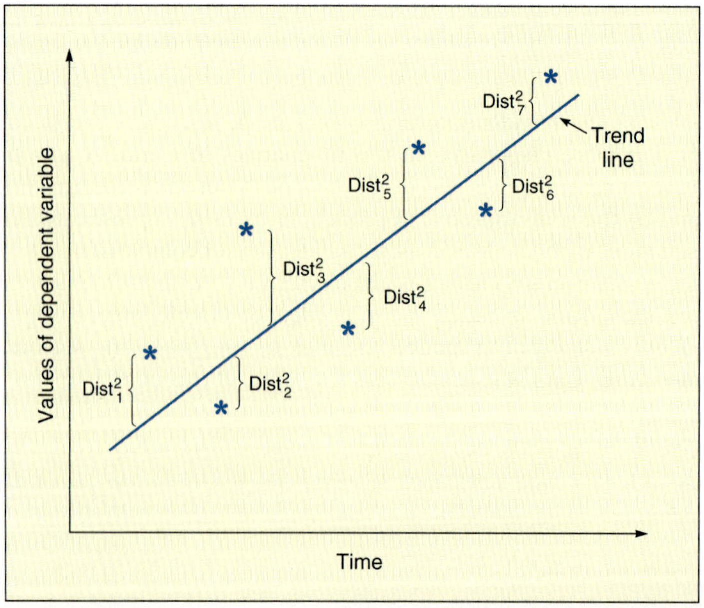

where b = slope of the regression line
Σ = summation sign
x = values of the independent variable
y = values of the dependent variable
$\bar{x}$ = average of the value of the x's
$\bar{y}$ = average of the value of the y's
n = number of data points or observations

We can compute the y-intercept a as follows:

$$a = \bar{y} - b\bar{x} \tag{5.11}$$

Example 7 shows how to apply these concepts.

EXAMPLE 7

The demand for electrical power at Ontario Hydro over the period 1989–95 is shown below, in megawatts. Let us fit a straight-line trend to these data and forecast 1996 demand.

Year	Electrical Power Demand	Year	Electrical Power Demand
1989	74	1993	105
1990	79	1994	142
1991	80	1995	122
1992	90		

With a series of data over time, we can minimize the computations by transforming the values of x (time) to simpler numbers. Thus, in this case, we can designate 1989 as year 1, 1990 as year 2, and so on.

Year	Time Period	Electric Power Demand	x^2	XY
1989	1	74	1	74
1990	2	79	4	158
1991	3	80	9	240
1992	4	90	16	360
1993	5	105	25	525
1994	6	142	36	852
1995	7	122	49	854
	$\Sigma x = 28$	$\Sigma y = 692$	$\Sigma x^2 = 140$	$\Sigma xy = 3{,}063$

$$\bar{x} = \frac{\Sigma x}{n} = \frac{28}{7} = 4 \qquad \bar{y} = \frac{\Sigma y}{n} = \frac{692}{7} = 98.86$$

$$b = \frac{\Sigma xy - n\bar{x}\bar{y}}{\Sigma x^2 - n\bar{x}^2} = \frac{3{,}063 - (7)(4)(98.86)}{140 - (7)(4^2)} = \frac{295}{28} = 10.54$$

$$a = \bar{y} - b\bar{x} = 98.86 - 10.54(4) = 56.70$$

Hence, the least squares trend equation is $\hat{y} = 56.70 + 10.54x$. To project demand in 1996, we first denote the year 1996 in our new coding system as $x = 8$:

$$\text{Demand in 1996} = 56.70 + 10.54(8)$$
$$= 141.02, \text{ or } 141 \text{ megawatts}$$

We can estimate demand for 1997 by inserting $x = 9$ in the same equation:

$$\text{Demand in 1997} = 56.70 + 10.54(9)$$
$$= 151.56, \text{ or } 152 \text{ megawatts}$$

To check the validity of the model, we plot historical demand and the trend line in Figure 5.5. In this case, we may wish to be cautious and try to understand the 1994–1995 swings in demand.

FIGURE 5.5 ■ Electrical Power and the Computed Trend Line

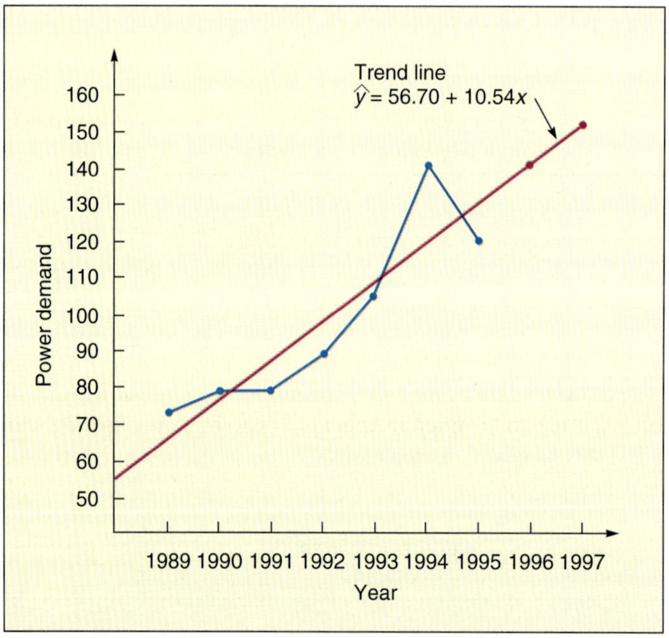

SEASONAL VARIATIONS IN DATA

Time-series forecasting such as that in Example 7 involves looking at the *trend* of data over a series of time observations. As we stated before, however, seasonality sometimes makes adjustment in the trend-line forecast necessary. Demand for coal and fuel oil, for example, usually peaks during cold winter months. Demand for golf clubs or suntan lotion may be highest in summer. Analyzing data in monthly or quarterly terms usually makes it easy for a statistician to spot seasonal patterns. Seasonal indices can then be developed by several common methods. Example 8 illustrates one way to compute seasonal factors from historical data.

EXAMPLE 8

Monthly sales of Compaq Company laptop computers at Reva Computerland are shown below for 1993–1994.

Month	Sales Demand 1993	Sales Demand 1994	Average 1993–1994 Demand	Average Monthly Demand*	Seasonal Index†
Jan.	80	100	90	94	.957
Feb.	75	85	80	94	.851
Mar.	80	90	85	94	.904
Apr.	90	110	100	94	1.064
May	115	131	123	94	1.309
June	110	120	115	94	1.223
July	100	110	105	94	1.117
Aug.	90	110	100	94	1.064
Sept.	85	95	90	94	.957
Oct.	75	85	80	94	.851
Nov.	75	85	80	94	.851
Dec.	80	80	80	94	.851
			Total average demand = 1,128		

*Average monthly demand $= \dfrac{1{,}128}{12 \text{ months}} = 94$

†Seasonal index $= \dfrac{\text{average 1993–94 demand}}{\text{average monthly demand}}$

Using these seasonal indices, if we expected the 1995 annual demand for computers to be 1,200 units, we would forecast the monthly demand as follows:

Month	Demand	Month	Demand
Jan.	$\dfrac{1{,}200}{12} \times .957 = 96$	July	$\dfrac{1{,}200}{12} \times 1.117 = 112$
Feb.	$\dfrac{1{,}200}{12} \times .851 = 85$	Aug.	$\dfrac{1{,}200}{12} \times 1.064 = 106$
Mar.	$\dfrac{1{,}200}{12} \times .904 = 90$	Sept.	$\dfrac{1{,}200}{12} \times .957 = 96$
Apr.	$\dfrac{1{,}200}{12} \times 1.064 = 106$	Oct.	$\dfrac{1{,}200}{12} \times .851 = 85$
May	$\dfrac{1{,}200}{12} \times 1.309 = 131$	Nov.	$\dfrac{1{,}200}{12} \times .851 = 85$
June	$\dfrac{1{,}200}{12} \times 1.223 = 122$	Dec.	$\dfrac{1{,}200}{12} \times .851 = 85$

For simplicity, trend calculations were ignored and only two periods were used for each monthly index in the above example. Example 9 illustrates how indices that have already been prepared can be applied to adjust trend line forecasts.

EXAMPLE 9

Management of Davis's Department Store has used time-series regression to forecast retail sales for the next four quarters. The sales estimates are \$100,000, \$120,000, \$140,000, and \$160,000 for the respective quarters. Seasonal indices for the four quarters have been found to be 1.30, .90, .70, and 1.15, respectively.

To compute a seasonalized or adjusted sales forecast, we just multiply each seasonal index by the appropriate trend forecast:

$$\hat{y}_{\text{seasonal}} = \text{Index} \times \hat{y}_{\text{trend forecast}}$$

Hence for

Quarter I: $\hat{y}_{I} = (1.30)(\$100{,}000) = \$130{,}000$
Quarter II: $\hat{y}_{II} = (.90)(\$120{,}000) = \$108{,}000$
Quarter III: $\hat{y}_{III} = (.70)(\$140{,}000) = \$98{,}000$
Quarter IV: $\hat{y}_{IV} = (1.15)(\$160{,}000) = \$184{,}000$

CAUSAL FORECASTING METHODS: REGRESSION AND CORRELATION ANALYSIS

Unlike time-series forecasting, *causal forecasting* models usually consider *several* variables that are related to the quantity being predicted. Once these related variables have been found, a statistical model is built and used to forecast the item of interest. This approach is more powerful than the time-series methods that use only the historic values for the forecasted variable.

Many factors can be considered in a causal analysis. For example, the sales of IBM PCs might be related to IBM's advertising budget, the price charged, competitors' prices and promotional strategies, or even the economy and unemployment rates. In this case, PC sales would be called the *dependent variable* and the other variables would be called *independent variables*. The manager's job is to develop the best statistical relationship between PC sales and the independent variables. The most common quantitative causal forecasting model is **linear-regression analysis**.

Linear-regression analysis

Using Regression Analysis to Forecast

We can use the same mathematical model we employed in the least squares method of trend projection to perform a linear-regression analysis. The dependent variables that we want to forecast will still be $\hat{y}$. But now the independent variable, x, need no longer be time.

$$\hat{y} = a + bx$$

where $\hat{y}$ = value of the dependent variable, sales here

a = y-axis intercept
b = slope of the regression line
x = independent variable

Example 10 shows how to use linear regression.

EXAMPLE 10

Mazza Construction Company renovates old homes in Hamilton, Ontario. Over time, the company has found that its dollar volume of renovation work is dependent on the Hamilton area payroll. The following table lists Mazza's revenues and the amount of money earned by wage earners in Hamilton during the years 1990–1995.

MAZZA'S SALES ($000,000), Y	LOCAL PAYROLL ($000,000,000), X	MAZZA'S SALES ($000,000), Y	LOCAL PAYROLL ($000,000,000), X
2.0	1	2.0	2
3.0	3	2.0	1
2.5	4	3.5	7

Mazza's management wants to establish a mathematical relationship that will help it predict sales. First, it needs to determine whether there is a straight-line (linear) relationship between area payroll and sales, so it plots the known data on a scatter diagram.

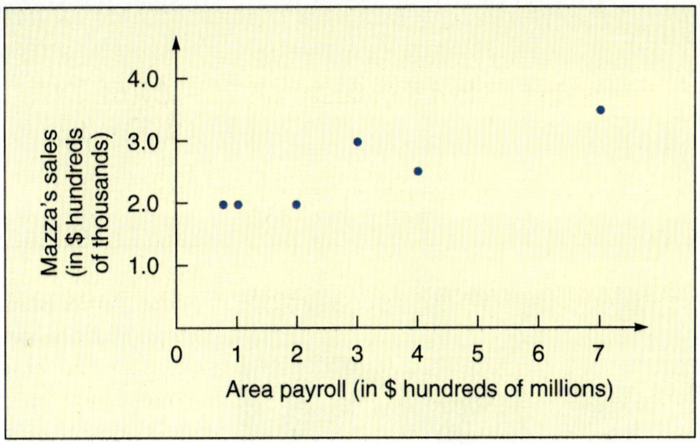

It appears from the six data points that there is a slight positive relationship between the independent variable, payroll, and the dependent variable, sales. As payroll increases, Mazza's sales tend to be higher.

We can find a mathematical equation by using the least-squares regression approach.

SALES, Y	PAYROLL, X	X^2	XY
2.0	1	1	2.0
3.0	3	9	9.0
2.5	4	16	10.0
2.0	2	4	4.0
2.0	1	1	2.0
3.5	7	49	24.5
$\Sigma y = 15.0$	$\Sigma x = 18$	$\Sigma x^2 = 80$	$\Sigma xy = 51.5$

$$\bar{x} = \frac{\Sigma x}{6} = \frac{18}{6} = 3$$

$$\bar{y} = \frac{\Sigma y}{6} = \frac{15}{6} = 2.5$$

$$b = \frac{\Sigma xy - n\bar{x}\bar{y}}{\Sigma x^2 - n\bar{x}^2} = \frac{51.5 - (6)(3)(2.5)}{80 - (6)(3^2)} = .25$$

$$a = \bar{y} - b\bar{x} = 2.5 - (.25)(3) = 1.75$$

The estimated regression equation, therefore, is

$$\hat{y} = 1.75 + .25x$$

or

$$\text{Sales} = 1.75 + .25\ (\text{payroll})$$

If the local chamber of commerce predicts that the Hamilton area payroll will be $6 hundred million next year, we can estimate sales for Mazza with the regression equation:

$$\begin{aligned}\text{Sales (in hundred thousands)} &= 1.75 + .25(6)\\ &= 1.75 + 1.50 = 3.25\end{aligned}$$

or

$$\text{Sales} = \$325{,}000$$

Glidden Paints assembly lines fill thousands of cans per hour. To predict demand for its products, the firm uses causal forecasting methods such as linear regression, with independent variables such as disposable personal income and GDP. Although housing starts would be a natural variable, Glidden found it correlated poorly with past sales. It turns out that most Glidden paint is sold through retailers to customers who already own homes or businesses.

FIGURE 5.6 ■ Distribution About the Point Estimate of $600 Million Payroll

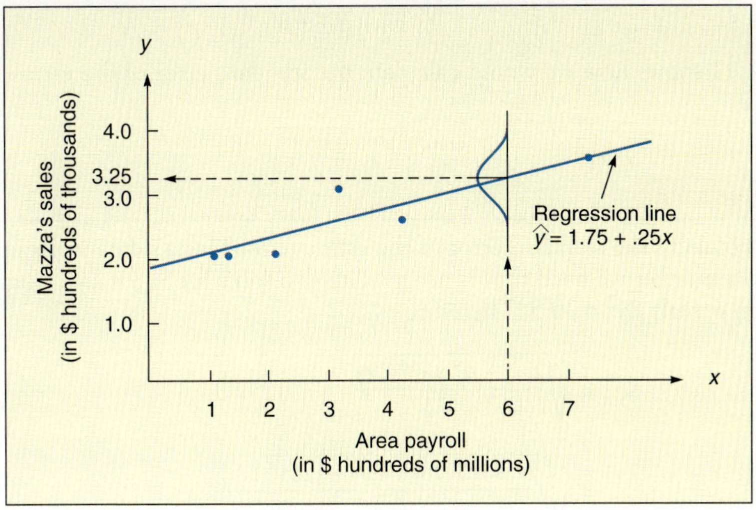

The final part of Example 10 shows a central weakness of causal forecasting methods like regression. Even when we have computed a regression equation, it is necessary to provide a forecast of the independent variable x—in this case, payroll—before estimating the dependent variable y for the next time period. Although this is not a problem for all forecasts, you can imagine the difficulty of determining future values of *some* common independent variables (such as unemployment rates, gross national product, price indices, and so on).

Standard Error of the Estimate

The forecast of $325,000 for Mazza's sales in Example 10 is called a *point estimate* of y. The point estimate is really the mean, or expected value, of a distribution of possible values of sales. Figure 5.6 illustrates this concept.

To measure the accuracy of the regression estimates, we need to compute the **standard error of the estimate**, $S_{y,x}$. This is called the *standard deviation of the regression*. Equation (5.12) is a similar expression to that found in most statistics books for computing the standard deviation of an arithmetic mean:

Standard error of the estimate

$$S_{y,x} = \sqrt{\frac{\Sigma(y - y_c)^2}{n - 2}} \tag{5.12}$$

where y = y-value of each data point
y_c = computed value of the dependent variable, from the regression equation
n = number of data points

Equation (5.13) may look more complex, but it is actually an easier-to-use version of Equation (5.12). The two formulas provide the same answer and can be used in setting up prediction intervals around the point estimate.[3]

[3]When the sample size is large ($n > 30$), the prediction interval value of y can be computed using normal tables. When the number of observations is small, the t-distribution is appropriate. See J. Neter, W. Wasserman, and S. Whitmore, *Applied Statistics*, 3rd ed. (Newton, MA: Allyn & Bacon, 1991).

$$S_{y,x} = \sqrt{\frac{\Sigma y^2 - a\Sigma y - b\Sigma xy}{n-2}} \tag{5.13}$$

Example 11 shows how we would calculate the standard error of the estimate in Example 10.

EXAMPLE 11

Let us compute the standard error of the estimate for Mazza's data in Example 10. The only number we need that is not available to solve for $S_{y,x}$ is Σy^2. Some quick addition reveals $\Sigma y^2 = 39.5$. Therefore,

$$S_{y,x} = \sqrt{\frac{\Sigma y^2 - a\Sigma y - b\Sigma xy}{n-2}}$$

$$= \sqrt{\frac{39.5 - 1.75(15.0) - .25(51.5)}{6-2}}$$

$$= \sqrt{.09375} = .306 \text{ (in \$ hundred thousands)}$$

The standard error of the estimate is then $30,600 in sales.

Correlation Coefficients for Regression Lines

The regression equation is one way of expressing the nature of the relationship between two variables. Regression lines are not "cause-and-effect" relationships. They merely describe the relationship between variables. The regression equation shows how one variable relates to the value and changes in another variable.

Coefficient of correlation

Another way to evaluate the relationship between two variables is to compute the **coefficient of correlation**. This measure expresses the degree or strength of the linear relationship. Usually identified as r, the coefficient of correlation can be any number between +1 and −1. Figure 5.7 illustrates what different values of r might look like.

FIGURE 5.7 ■ Four Values of the Correlation Coefficient

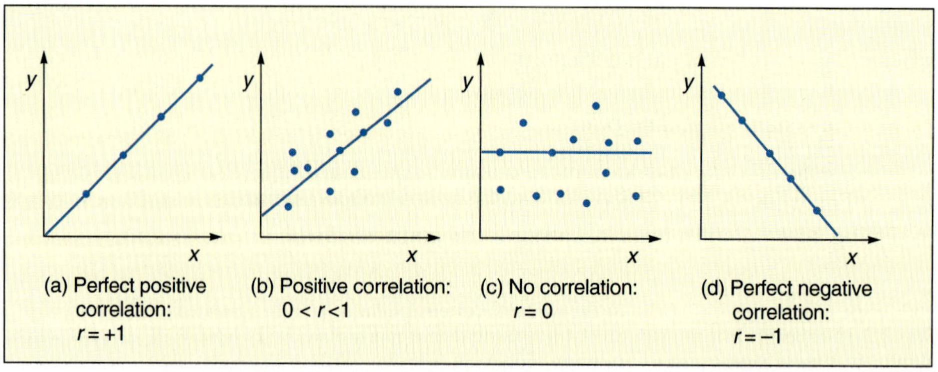

To compute r, we use much of the same data needed earlier to calculate a and b for the regression line. The rather lengthy equation for r is

$$r = \frac{n\Sigma xy - \Sigma x \Sigma y}{\sqrt{[n\Sigma x^2 - (\Sigma x)^2][n\Sigma y^2 - (\Sigma y)^2]}} \tag{5.14}$$

Example 12 shows how to calculate the coefficient of correlation for the data in Examples 10 and 11.

EXAMPLE 12

In Example 10, we looked at the relationship between Mazza Construction Company's renovation sales and payroll in Hamilton. To compute the coefficient of correlation for the data shown, we need only add one more column of calculations (for y^2) and then apply the equation for r.

Y	X	X^2	XY	Y^2	
2.0	1	1	2.0	4.0	
3.0	3	9	9.0	9.0	
2.5	4	16	10.0	6.25	New
2.0	2	4	4.0	4.0	column
2.0	1	1	2.0	4.0	
3.5	7	49	24.5	12.25	
$\Sigma y = 15.0$	$\Sigma x = 18$	$\Sigma x^2 = 80$	$\Sigma xy = 51.5$	$\Sigma y^2 = 39.5$	

$$r = \frac{(6)(51.5) - (18)(15.0)}{\sqrt{[(6)(80) - (18)^2][(6)(39.5) - (15.0)^2]}}$$

$$= \frac{309 - 270}{\sqrt{(156)(12)}} = \frac{39}{\sqrt{1{,}872}}$$

$$= \frac{39}{43.3} = .901$$

This r of .901 appears to be a significant correlation and helps to confirm the closeness of the relationship between the two variables.

Although the coefficient of correlation is the measure most commonly used to describe the relationship between two variables, another measure does exist. It is called the *coefficient of determination* and is simply the square of the coefficient of correlation, namely, r^2. The value of r^2 will always be a positive number in the range of $0 \leq r^2 \leq 1$. The coefficient of determination is the percent of variation in the dependent variable (y) that is explained by the regression equation. In Mazza's case, the value of r^2 is .81, indicating that 81% of the total variation is explained by the regression equation.

Multiple-Regression Analysis

Multiple regression

Multiple regression is a practical extension of the simple regression model we just explored. It allows us to build a model with several independent variables instead of just one variable. For example, if Mazza Construction wanted to include average annual interest rates in its model to forecast renovation sales, the proper equation would be

$$\hat{y} = a + b_1x_1 + b_2x_2 \tag{5.15}$$

where $\hat{y}$ = dependent variable, sales
a = y-intercept
x_1 and x_2 = values of the two independent variables, area payroll and interest rates, respectively
b_1 and b_2 = slopes for the two independent variables

The mathematics of multiple regression becomes quite complex (and is usually tackled by computer), so we leave the formulas for a, b_1, and b_2 to statistics textbooks. However, Example 13 shows how to interpret Equation (5.15) in forecasting Mazza's sales.

EXAMPLE 13

The new multiple-regression line for Mazza Construction, calculated by computer software, is

$$\hat{y} = 1.80 + .30x_1 - 5.0x_2$$

We also find that the new coefficient of correlation is .96, implying the inclusion of the variable x_2, interest rates, adds even more strength to the linear relationship.

We can now estimate Mazza's sales if we substitute values for next year's payroll and interest rate. If Hamilton's payroll will be $600 million and the interest rate will be .12 (12%), sales will be forecast as

$$\begin{aligned}\text{Sales (\$ hundred thousands)} &= 1.80 + .30(6) - 5.0(.12)\\ &= 1.8 + 1.8 - .6\\ &= 3.00\end{aligned}$$

or

$$\text{Sales} = \$300{,}000$$

MONITORING AND CONTROLLING FORECASTS

Once a forecast has been completed, it should not be forgotten. No manager wants to be reminded when his or her forecast is horribly inaccurate, but a firm needs to determine why the actual demand (or whatever variable is being examined) differed significantly from that projected. If the forecaster *is* accurate, that individual usually makes sure that everyone is aware of his or her talents. Very seldom does one read articles in *Fortune*, *Forbes*, or the *Wall Street Journal*, however, about money managers who are consistently off by 25% in their stock market forecasts.

Tracking signal

One way to monitor forecasts to ensure they are performing well is to employ a tracking signal. A **tracking signal** is a measurement of how well the forecast is predicting actual values. As forecasts are updated every week, month, or quarter, the newly available demand data are compared to the forecast values.

The tracking signal is computed as the *running sum of the forecast errors (RSFE)* divided by the *mean absolute deviation (MAD)*:

$$\begin{pmatrix}\text{Tracking} \\ \text{signal}\end{pmatrix} = \frac{\text{RSFE}}{\text{MAD}}$$

$$= \frac{\Sigma(\text{actual demand in period } i - \text{forecast demand in period } i)}{\text{MAD}} \quad (5.16)$$

where

$$\text{MAD} = \frac{\Sigma|\text{forecast errors}|}{n}$$

as seen earlier in Equation (5.6).

Positive tracking signals indicate that demand is greater than forecast. Negative signals mean that demand is less than forecast. A good tracking signal, that is, one with a low RSFE, has about as much positive error as it has negative error. In other words, small deviations are okay, but the positive and negative ones should balance one another so the tracking signal centers closely around zero.

Once tracking signals are calculated, they are compared to predetermined control limits. When a tracking signal exceeds an upper or lower limit, there is a problem with the forecasting method, and management may want to reevaluate the way it forecasts demand. Figure 5.8 shows the graph of a tracking signal that is exceeding the range of acceptable variation. If the model being used is exponential smoothing, perhaps the smoothing constant needs to be readjusted.

How do firms decide what the upper and lower tracking limits should be? There is no single answer, but they try to find reasonable values—in other words, limits not so low as to be triggered with every small forecast error, and not so high as to allow bad forecasts to be regularly overlooked. George Plossl and Oliver Wight, two

A professional economist forecasts the demand for Northern Telecom's products.

inventory control experts, suggested using maximums of ±4 MADs for high-volume stock items and ±8 MADs for lower-volume items.[4] Other forecasters suggest slightly lower ranges. One MAD is equivalent to approximately .8 standard deviations, so that ±2 MADs = ±1.6 standard deviations, ±3 MADs = ±2.4 standard deviation, and ±4 MADs = ±3.2 standard deviations. This suggests that for a forecast to be "in control," 89% of the errors are expected to fall within ±2 MADs, 98% within ±3 MADs, or 99.9% within ±4 MADs.[5]

Example 14 shows how the tracking signal and RSFE can be computed.

EXAMPLE 14

Tom Tucker Bakery's quarterly sales of croissants (in thousands), as well as forecast demand and error computations, are shown below. The objective is to compute the tracking signal and determine whether forecasts are performing adequately.

Quarter	Forecast Demand	Actual Demand	Error	RSFE	|Forecast Error|	Cumulative Error	MAD	Tracking Signal
1	100	90	−10	−10	10	10	10.0	−1
2	100	95	−5	−15	5	15	7.5	−2
3	100	115	+15	0	15	30	10.0	0
4	110	100	−10	−10	10	40	10.0	−1
5	110	125	+15	+5	15	55	11.0	+.5
6	110	140	+30	+35	30	85	14.2	+2.5

$$\text{MAD} = \frac{\Sigma|\text{forecast errors}|}{n} = \frac{85}{6} = 14.2$$

$$\text{Tracking signal} = \frac{\text{RSFE}}{\text{MAD}} = \frac{35}{14.2} = 2.5 \text{ MADs}$$

This tracking signal is within acceptable limits. We see that it drifted from −2.0 MADs to +2.5 MADs.

Adaptive Smoothing

Adaptive smoothing

A lot of research has been published on the subject of adaptive forecasting. Adaptive forecasting refers to computer monitoring of tracking signals and self-adjustment if a signal passes its preset limit. For example, when applied to exponential smoothing, the α and β coefficients are first selected on the basis of values that minimize error forecasts, and then adjusted accordingly whenever the computer notes an errant tracking signal. This is called **adaptive smoothing**.

[4]See G. W. Plossl and O. W. Wight, *Production and Inventory Control* (Englewood Cliffs, NJ: Prentice Hall, 1967).

[5]To prove these three percentages to yourself, just set up a normal curve for ±1.6 standard deviations (z values). Using the normal table in Appendix A, you find that the area under the curve is .89. This represents ±2 MADs. Likewise, ±3 MADs = ±2.4 standard deviations encompass 98% of the area, and so on for ±4 MADs.

FIGURE 5.8 ■ A Plot of Tracking Signals

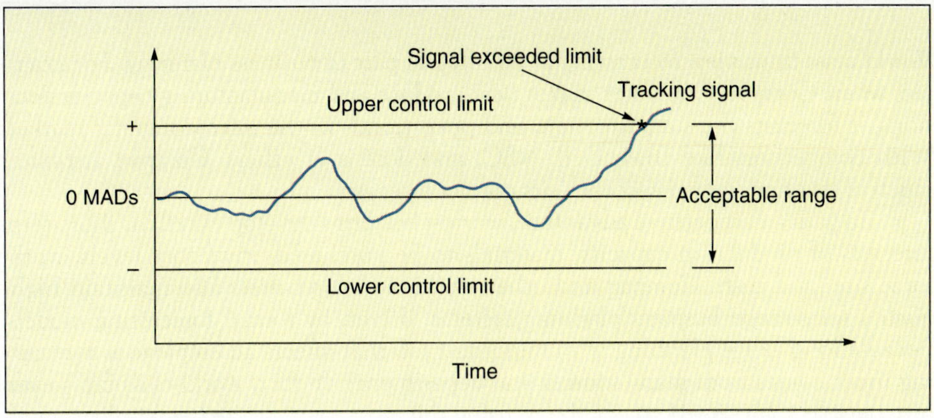

Focus Forecasting

Rather than adapt by choosing a smoothing constant, computers allow us to try a variety of forecasting models. Such an approach is called focus forecasting. **Focus forecasting** is based on two principles. The first is that very sophisticated forecasting models are not always better than simple ones. The second is that there is no single technique that should be used for all products or services.

Focus forecasting

Bernard Smith, inventory manager for American Hardware Supply, is the man who coined the term *focus forecasting*. Smith's job was to forecast quantities for 100,000 hardware products purchased by American's 21 buyers.[6] He found that buyers neither trusted nor understood the exponential smoothing model then in use. They instead used very simple approaches of their own. So Smith developed his new computerized system for selecting forecasting methods.

Smith chose seven forecasting methods to test. They ranged from the simple ones buyers used (such as the naive approach) to some of the more statistical models. Every month, Smith applied the forecasts of all seven models to each item in stock. In these simulated trials, the forecast values were subtracted from the most recent actual demands, giving a simulated forecast error. The forecast method yielding the least error is selected by the computer, which then uses it to make next month's forecast. Buyers still have an override capability, but American Hardware finds that focus forecasting provides excellent results.

The Institute of Business Forecasting in Flushing, New York, has as its mission "to disseminate the knowledge about business forecasting and planning." For more information, the reader may wish to visit IBF's home page on the World Wide Web at **http://www.ibforecast.com/** or e-mail to **forecast@nyiq.net**.

The Computer's Role in Forecasting

As we can see from American Hardware Supply, forecast calculations are seldom performed by hand in this day of computers. Many academic and commercial packaged programs are readily available to handle time-series and causal projections.

Popular commercial packages include General Electric's *Time Series Forecasting* and IBM's IMPACT (Inventory Management Program and Control Technique). Popular university packages available for PCs are SAS, SPSS, STORM, QSB, AB:POM, and Minitab.

[6]Bernard T. Smith, *Focus Forecasting: Computer Techniques for Inventory Control* (Boston: CBI Publishing, 1978).

ACHIEVING WORLD-CLASS STANDARDS

World-class firms view forecasting as an integral part of business planning. For example, when Compaq Computer makes new product and manufacturing capacity decisions, it forecasts the size, direction, and price trends in the microcomputer market. With competitors like IBM, Dell, NEC, and dozens of others, Compaq attributes much of its phenomenal success to its correct forecasts.

To gain a competitive advantage, world-class firms develop excellent short-term forecasts of production capacity, materials to be purchased, inventory levels, workforce size, and cash. Compaq and other world-class forecasters also maintain high-quality long-range business planning systems, driven by formal forecasting models. Because long-range planning is an important job that affects all employees, forecasting input comes from many sources and departments. In fact, world-class firms even hire outside analysts who specialize in using the most sophisticated technology, models, and data bases available to their industry. Sources of useful data outside the firm may include global and industry data gathered by universities, trade associations, consulting firms, and government agencies.

World-class organizations continuously track the accuracy of their forecasts. They want their business plans and management decisions to be based on the latest and most valid data available.

SUMMARY

Forecasts are a critical part of the operations manager's function. Demand forecasts drive the production, capacity, and scheduling systems in a firm and affect the financial, marketing, and personnel planning functions.

There are a variety of qualitative and quantitative forecasting techniques. Qualitative approaches employ judgement, experience, intuition, and a host of other factors that are difficult to quantify. Quantitative forecasting uses historical data and causal relations to project future demands. No forecasting method is perfect under all conditions. And even once management has found a satisfactory approach, it must still monitor and control its forecasts to make sure errors do not get out of hand. Forecasting can often be a very challenging, but rewarding, part of managing.

KEY TERMS

Forecasting (p. 160)
Economic forecasts (p. 162)
Technological forecasts (p. 162)
Demand forecasts (p. 162)
Quantitative forecasts (p. 162)
Qualitative forecasts (p. 162)
Jury of executive opinion (p. 162)
Sales force composite (p. 162)
Delphi method (p. 162)
Consumer market survey (p. 163)
Time series (p. 163)
Naive approach (p. 167)
Moving averages (p. 167)
Exponential smoothing (p. 169)
Smoothing constant (p. 169)
Mean absolute deviation (MAD) (p. 171)
Mean squared error (MSE) (p. 172)
Trend projection (p. 176)
Linear-regression analysis (p. 180)
Standard error of the estimate (p. 183
Coefficient of correlation (p. 184)
Multiple regression (p. 186)
Tracking signal (p. 187)
Adaptive smoothing (p. 188)
Focus forecasting (p. 189)

USING AB:POM AND SPREADSHEETS FOR FORECASTING

Examples of AB:POM in Exponential Smoothing and Regression

AB:POM's forecasting program provides an initial menu screen asking whether you wish to do a time-series forecast or a least squares causal forecast. If time series is selected, you may use (1) moving averages, (2) weighted moving averages, (3) exponential smoothing, (4) exponential smoothing with trend, (5) least squares trend analysis, (6) deseasonalize data, or (7) deseasonalize data then regress. If you select the causal model, you may do simple or multiple regression. We provide two sample printouts in Programs 5.1 and 5.2 to illustrate one of the time-series approaches and linear regression. These programs solve Examples 4 and 10.

PROGRAM 5.1 ■ AB:POM's Exponential Smoothing Program Using Example 4 Data. This program demonstrates the input/output for exponential smoothing, using Example 4's data. We entered (1) the number of data periods, (2) the model desired, (3) alpha, (4) the eight demands, (5) the initial forecast of 175, and (6) the titles for each period (i.e., QTR1, QTR2, and so on).

If you look back to Examples 4 and 5, note that the MAD and MSE are slightly different. This is because AB:POM does not calculate an error for this initial forecast (Period 1). So the error terms are based on seven periods, not the eight we used earlier. Conclusions reached tend to be the same with either approach. Bias, a third type of forecast error, is also provided by AB:POM. Bias is a measure of the *direction* of forecast error. It tells us whether our forecasts tend, on average, to be too high or too low.

Forecasting — Solution

Number of past data periods (2–99) 8

PORT OF TORONTO, EXAMPLE 4

Method –> Exponential Smoothing

alpha (α) 0.100

	Period (x)	Demand (y)	Forecast	Error	|Error|	Error^2
QTR 1	1	180.00	175.00			
QTR 2	2	168.00	175.50	-7.50	7.50	56.25
QTR 3	3	159.00	174.75	-15.75	15.75	248.063
QTR 4	4	175.00	173.175	1.82500	1.82500	3.33061
QTR 5	5	190.00	173.357	16.6425	16.6425	276.97
QTR 6	6	205.00	175.022	29.9783	29.9783	898.70
QTR 7	7	180.00	178.020	1.98042	1.98042	3.92208
QTR 8	8	182.00	178.218	3.78	3.78	14.31
TOTALS	36.00	1439.00		30.9586	77.4586	1501.54
AVERAGE	4.50	0.5625		4.42265	11.0655	214.506
				(Bias)	(MAD)	(MSE)
		Next period's forecast	178.60	Standard error = 17.3294		

F1 = Help F2 = Summary F3 = Graph F9 = Print Esc

PROGRAM 5.2 ■ AB:POM's Linear Regression Program Using Example 10 Data. There is only one independent variable, so this is also called simple regression. Outputs include the regression line, correlation coefficient, and standard error.

In this and other cases, the data points can also be graphed by pressing the F3 function key. This program is accessed off the Forecasting Menu by requesting the "Least Squares" option.

Number of past data periods (2-99) 6 Number of independ. variables (1-6) 1

MAZZA

Method -> Least Squares–Simple and Multiple Regression

	B 0	B 1
Coef ->	1.75	0.25

	SALES	PAYROLL	Forecast	Error	|Error|	Error^2
1990	2.00	1.00	2.00	0.00	0.00	0.00
1991	3.00	3.00	2.50	0.50	0.50	0.25
1992	2.50	4.00	2.75	−0.25	0.25	0.0625
1993	2.00	2.00	2.25	−0.25	0.25	0.0625
1994	2.00	1.00	2.00	0.00	0.00	0.00
1995	3.50	7.00	3.50	0.00	0.00	0.00
TOTALS				0.00	1.00	0.375
AVERAGE				0.00	.166667	0.0625
				(Bias)	(MAD)	(MSE)

Regression line = SALES = 1.75 +0.25*PAYROLL
Correlation coefficient = 0.9013878 Standard error = .3061862

F1 = Help F2 = Summary F3 = Graph F9 = Print Esc

Examples of Spreadsheet Software for Exponential Smoothing and Regression

Program 5.3 uses Example 4's data to illustrate exponential smoothing via spreadsheets. This "symbolic spreadsheet" shows all the formulas used in forecasting in cells D6 through D13. $B$3 is called an "absolute reference" to the value of alpha in B3. Cells E6 through E13 hold the formulas for computing the absolute differences of forecast tonnage in column C and actual in column B. They are also rounded off. The @SUM and @AVG commands in cells E14 and E15, respectively, total the absolute values and then provide their mean (the MAD).

Program 5.4 shows the use of spreadsheets in regression analysis using the /Data Regression (/DR) command. When we press /DR, the following submenu appears:

X-Range Y-Range Output-Range Intercept Reset Go Quit

We first use the x-Range option to select the independent variable(s). We specify B5..B10 (payroll) as our only independent variable in Example 10. We then use the Y-Range option to specify the dependent variable of sales. We enter range A5..A10.

The Output-Range option specifies where to display the regression results. This needs to be an unused area of the spreadsheet and must be at least nine rows long and two columns wider than the number of independent variables. We need only specify the upper left corner of the output range. Because we want the results to appear in the range A12..D20, we specify A12 at the prompt.

PROGRAM 5.3 ■ Using Spreadsheets to Compute the Port of Toronto's Exponential Smoothing Forecast. The symbolic spreadsheet, showing formulas in cells, is provided.

	A	B	C	D	E
1	Port of Toronto Exponential Smoothing Forecast from Example 4				
2					
3	Alpha =	0.1			
4					
5	Quarter	Act.Tons	Frcst	$F_{t-1} + \alpha(A_{t-1} - F_{t-1})$	Abs. Error
6	1	180	175	+C6+$B$3*(B6-C6)	@ROUND(@ABS(B6-C6),0)
7	2	168	+D6	+C7+$B$3*(B7-C7)	@ROUND(@ABS(B7-C7),0)
8	3	159	+D7	+C8+$B$3*(B8-C8)	@ROUND(@ABS(B8-C8),0)
9	4	175	+D8	+C9+$B$3*(B9-C9)	@ROUND(@ABS(B9-C9),0)
10	5	190	+D9	+C10+$B$3*(B10-C10)	@ROUND(@ABS(B10-C10),0)
11	6	205	+D10	+C11+$B$3*(B11-C11)	@ROUND(@ABS(B11-C11),0)
12	7	180	+D11	+C12+$B$3*(B12-C12)	@ROUND(@ABS(B12-C12),0)
13	8	182	+D12	+C13+$B$3*(B13-C13)	@ROUND(@ABS(B13-C13),0)
14	Total				@SUM(E6. .E13)
15	Average				@AVG(E6. .E13)

PROGRAM 5.4 ■ Regression Analysis with Spreadsheet Software and the /Data Regression Command. Mazza's data from Example 11 are shown. The constant value output is the Y-intercept. The X-coefficient is the slope of the independent variable, i.e., payroll.

	A	B	C	D	E	F
1	Mazza Construction Regression Using Example 10 Data					
2						
3	Sales(Y)	Payroll(X)	Regression			
4	($100,000)	($100,000,000)	Line			
5	2	1	+$C$19*$B5+$D$13			
6	3	3	+$C$19*$B6+$D$13			
7	2.5	4	+$C$19*$B7+$D$13			
8	2	2	+$C$19*$B8+$D$13			
9	2	1	+$C$19*$B9+$D$13			
10	3.5	7	+$C$19*$B10+$D$13			
11						
12		Regression Output:				
13	Constant				1.75	
14	Std Err of Y Est				0.306186	
15	R Squared				0.8125	
16	No. of Observations				6	
17	Degrees of Freedom				4	
18						
19	X=coefficients(s)			0.25		
20	Std Err of Coef.		0.0600480577			

SOLVED PROBLEMS

Solved Problem 5.1

Sales of Green Line Jet Skis have grown steadily during the past 5 years (see table). The sales manager had predicted in 1990 that 1991 sales would be 410 air conditioners. Using exponential smoothing with a weight of $\alpha = .30$, develop forecasts for 1992 through 1996.

YEAR	SALES	FORECAST
1991	450	410
1992	495	
1993	518	
1994	563	
1995	584	
1996	?	

Solution

YEAR	FORECAST
1991	410.0
1992	422.0 = 410 + .3 (450 − 410)
1993	443.9 = 422 + .3 (495 − 422)
1994	466.1 = 443.9 + .3 (518 − 443.9)
1995	495.2 = 466.1 + .3 (563 − 466.1)
1996	521.8 = 495.2 + .3 (584 − 495.2)

Solved Problem 5.2

Room registrations in the Toronto Towers Plaza Hotel have been recorded for the past nine years. Management would like to determine the mathematical trend of guest registration in order to project future occupancy. This estimate would help the hotel determine whether a future expansion will be needed. Given the following time series data, develop a regression equation relating registrations to time. Then forecast 1996 registrations. Room registrations are in the thousands:

1987: 17	1988: 16	1989: 16	1990: 21	1991: 20
1992: 20	1993: 23	1994: 25	1995: 24	

Solution

Year	Transformed Year, x	Registrants, y (in thousands)	x^2	xy
1987	1	17	1	17
1988	2	16	4	32
1989	3	16	9	48
1990	4	21	16	84
1991	5	20	25	100
1992	6	20	36	120
1993	7	23	49	161
1994	8	25	64	200
1995	9	24	81	216
	$\Sigma x = 45$	$\Sigma y = 182$	$\Sigma x^2 = 285$	$\Sigma xy = 978$

$$\bar{x} = \frac{45}{9} = 5, \qquad \bar{y} = \frac{182}{9} = 20.22$$

$$b = \frac{\Sigma xy - n\bar{x}\bar{y}}{\Sigma x^2 - n\bar{x}^2} = \frac{978 - (9)(5)(20.22)}{285 - (9)(25)} = \frac{978 - 909.9}{285 - 225} = \frac{68.1}{60} = 1.135$$

$$a = \bar{y} - b\bar{x} = 20.22 - (1.135)(5) = 20.22 - 5.675 = 14.545$$

$$\hat{y}\,(\text{registrations}) = 14.545 + 1.135x$$

The projection of registrations in 1997 (which is $x = 11$ in the coding system used) is

$$\hat{y} = 14.545 + (1.135)(11) = 27.03$$

or 27,030 guests in 1997.

Solved Problem 5.3

Quarterly demand for Jaguar XK8's at a Vancouver auto dealer is forecast with the equation

$$\hat{y} = 10 + 3x$$

where x = quarters, and

Quarter I of 1994 = 0
Quarter II of 1994 = 1
Quarter III of 1994 = 2
Quarter IV of 1994 = 3
Quarter I of 1995 = 4
and so on

and

$$\hat{y} = \text{quarterly demand}$$

The demand for sports sedans is seasonal, and the indices for Quarters I, II, III, and IV are 0.80, 1.00, 1.30, and 0.90, respectively. Forecast demand for each quarter of 1996. Then seasonalize each forecast to adjust for quarterly variations.

Solution

Quarter II of 1995 is coded $x = 5$; Quarter III of 1995, $x = 6$; and Quarter IV of 1995, $x = 7$. Hence, Quarter I of 1996 is coded $x = 8$; Quarter II, $x = 9$; and so on.

$\hat{y}$(1996 Quarter I) = 10 + 3(8) = 34	Adjusted forecast = (.80)(34) = 27.2
$\hat{y}$(1996 Quarter II) = 10 + 3(9) = 37	Adjusted forecast = (1.00)(37) = 37
$\hat{y}$(1996 Quarter III) = 10 + 3(10) = 40	Adjusted forecast = (1.30)(40) = 52
$\hat{y}$(1996 Quarter IV) = 10 + 3(11) = 43	Adjusted forecast = (.90)(43) = 38.7

DISCUSSION QUESTIONS

1. Briefly describe the steps that are used to develop a forecasting system.
2. What is a time-series forecasting model?
3. What is the difference between a causal model and a time-series model?
4. What is a qualitative forecasting model, and when is it appropriate?
5. What is the meaning of least squares in a regression model?
6. What are some of the drawbacks of the moving-average forecasting model?
7. What effect does the value of the smoothing constant have on the weight given to the past forecast and the past observed value?
8. Briefly describe the Delphi technique.
9. What is MAD, and why is it important in the selection and use of forecasting models?
10. Describe the three forecasting time horizons and their use.
11. Name and discuss three *qualitative* forecasting methods.
12. Which of the forecasting techniques can place the most emphasis on recent values? How does it do this?
13. What does it mean to decompose a time series?
14. What is the basic difference between a weighted moving average and exponential smoothing?
15. Describe two popular measures of forecast accuracy.
16. What is the difference between a dependent and an independent variable?
17. Define the meaning of the coefficient of determination in your own words. Provide an example.
18. What is the purpose of a tracking signal?

CRITICAL THINKING EXERCISE

In 1994, the Board of Regents, responsible for all public higher education funding in a Canadian province, hired a consultant to develop a series of enrollment forecasting models, one for each college and university. These models used historical data and exponential smoothing to forecast next year's enrollments. Based on the model, which included a smoothing constant (α) for each school, each college's budget was set by the Board. The head of the Board personally selected each smoothing constant, based on what she called her "gut reactions and political acumen."

What do you think the advantages and disadvantages of this system are? Answer from the perspective of (a) the Board of Regents and (b) the President of each university and college. How can this model be abused and what could be done to remove any biases? How can a *regression model* be used to produce results that favour one forecast over another?

PROBLEMS

• **5.1** Daily high temperatures in the city of Calgary for the last week have been as follows: 27, 30, 28, 31, 33, 26, 29 (yesterday).

a) Forecast the high temperature today, using a 3-day moving average.
b) Forecast the high temperature today, using a 2-day moving average.
c) Calculate the mean absolute deviation based on a 2-day moving average.

• **5.2** For the data below, develop a 3-month moving-average forecast.

MONTH	AUTOMOBILE BATTERY SALES	MONTH	AUTOMOBILE BATTERY SALES
January	20	July	17
February	21	August	18
March	15	September	20
April	14	October	20
May	13	November	21
June	16	December	23

• **5.3** Given the following data, develop a 3-year moving-average forecast of demand.

YEAR	1	2	3	4	5	6	7	8	9	10	11
DEMAND	7	9	5	9	13	8	12	13	9	11	7

• **5.4** Eli Cohen has developed the following forecasting model:

$$\hat{y} = 36 + 4.3x$$

where $\hat{y}$ = demand for Aztec air conditioners and
x = the outside temperature (°F).

a) Forecast demand for the Aztec when the temperature is 70°F.

b) What is demand for a temperature of 80°F?

c) What is demand for a temperature of 90°F?

• **5.5** Data collected on the yearly demand for 23-kilogram bags of grass seed at Bob's Hardware Store are shown in the following table. Develop a 3-year moving average to forecast sales. Then estimate demand again with a weighted moving average in which sales in the most recent years are given a weight of 2 and sales in the other two years are each given a weight of 1. Which method do you think is best?

YEAR	1	2	3	4	5	6	7	8	9	10	11
DEMAND FOR GRASS SEED (THOUSANDS OF BAGS)	4	6	4	5	10	8	7	9	12	14	15

• **5.6** Develop a 2- and a 4-year moving average for the demand for bags of grass seed in Problem 5.5.

• **5.7** In Problems 5.5 and 5.6, four different forecasts were developed for the demand for grass seed. These four forecasts are a 2-year moving average, a 3-year moving average, a weighted moving average, and a 4-year moving average. Which one would you use? Explain your answer.

: **5.8** Use exponential smoothing with a smoothing constant of .3 to forecast the demand for grass seed given in Problem 5.5. Assume that last period's forecast for year 1 is 5,000 bags to begin the procedure. Would you prefer to use the exponential smoothing model or the weighted-average model developed in Problem 5.5? Explain your answer.

• **5.9** Using smoothing constants of .6 and .9, develop a forecast for the sales of Green Line Jet Skis. See Solved Problem 5.1.

• **5.10** What effect did the smoothing constant have on the forecast for Green Line Jet Skis? See Solved Problem 5.1 and Problem 5.9. Which smoothing constant gives the most accurate forecast?

• **5.11** Use a 3-year moving-average forecasting model to forecast the sales of Green Line Jet Skis. See Solved Problem 5.1.

• **5.12** Using the trend-projection method, develop a forecasting model for the sales of Green Line Jet Skis. See Solved Problem 5.1.

: **5.13** Would you use exponential smoothing with a smoothing constant of .3, a 3-year moving average, or trend to predict the sales of Green Line Jet Skis? Refer to Solved Problem 5.1 and Problems 5.11 and 5.12.

⁝ **5.14** Demand for heart transplant surgery at Toronto General Hospital has increased steadily in the past few years, as seen in the following table.

YEAR	1	2	3	4	5	6
HEART TRANSPLANT SURGERIES PERFORMED	45	50	52	56	58	?

The director of medical services predicted 6 years ago that demand in year 1 would be for 41 surgeries.

a) Use exponential smoothing, first with a smoothing constant of .6 and then with one of .9, to develop forecasts for years 2 through 6.

b) Use a 3-year moving average to forecast demand in years 4, 5, and 6.

c) Use the trend-projection method to forecast demand in years 1 through 6.

d) With MAD as the criterion, which of the above four forecasts is best?

• **5.15** A careful analysis of the cost of operating an automobile was conducted by a firm. The following model was developed:

$$Y = 4{,}000 + 0.20X$$

where Y is the annual cost and X is the miles driven.

a) If a car is driven 24,000 kilometres this year, what is the forecasted cost of operating this automobile?

b) If a car is driven 40,000 kilometres this year, what is the forecasted cost of operating this automobile?

c) Suppose that one car was driven 24,000 kilometres and the actual cost of operating this was $6,000, and a second car was driven 40,000 kilometres and the actual operating cost was $10,000. Calculate the mean absolute deviation for this.

• **5.16** Given the following data, use exponential smoothing ($\alpha = 0.2$) to develop a demand forecast. Assume the forecast for the initial period is 5.

PERIOD	1	2	3	4	5	6
DEMAND	7	9	5	9	13	8

5.17 Consulting income at Dr. Thomas W. Jones Associates for the period February–July has been as follows:

MONTH	February	March	April	May	June	July
INCOME (IN THOUSANDS)	70.0	68.5	64.8	71.7	71.3	72.8

Use trend-adjusted exponential smoothing to forecast August's income. Assume that the initial forecast for February is $65,000 and the initial trend adjustment is 0. The smoothing constants selected are $\alpha = .1$ and $\beta = .2$.

5.18 Resolve Problem 5.17 with $\alpha = .1$ and $\beta = .8$. Using MAD, which smoothing constants provide a better forecast?

5.19 Calculate (a) MAD and (b) MSE for the following forecast versus actual sales figures.

FORECAST	100	110	120	130
ACTUAL	95	108	123	130

5.20 Given the following data, use the least squares regression to derive a forecasting equation. What is your estimate of the demand in period 7?

PERIOD	1	2	3	4	5	6
DEMAND	7	9	5	11	10	13

5.21 Given the following data, use least squares regression to develop a relation between the number of rainy summer days and the number of games lost by the Leaside, Ontario, Midget baseball team.

YEAR	1986	1987	1988	1989	1990	1991	1992	1993	1994	1995
RAINY DAYS	15	25	10	10	30	20	20	15	10	25
GAMES LOST	25	20	10	15	20	15	20	10	5	20

5.22 Sales of industrial vacuum cleaners at Gary Williams Supply Co. over the past 13 months are shown below.

MONTH	Jan.	Feb.	March	April	May	June	July
SALES (IN THOUSANDS)	11	14	16	10	15	17	11
MONTH	Aug.	Sept.	Oct.	Nov.	Dec.	Jan.	
SALES (IN THOUSANDS)	14	17	12	14	16	11	

a) Using a moving average with three periods, determine the demand for vacuum cleaners for next February.

b) Using a weighted moving average with three periods, determine the demand for vacuum cleaners for February. Use 3, 2, and 1 for the weights of the most recent, second most recent, and third most recent periods, respectively. For example, if you were forecasting the demand for February, November would have a weight of 1, December would have a weight of 2, and January would have a weight of 3.

c) Evaluate the accuracy of each of these methods.

d) What other factors might Williams consider in forecasting sales?

: **5.23** The operations manager of a musical instrument distributor feels that demand for bass drums may be related to the number of television appearances by the popular rock group Green Shades during the previous month. The manager has collected the data shown in the following table.

DEMAND FOR BASS DRUMS	3	6	7	5	10	8
GREEN SHADES TV APPEARANCES	3	4	7	6	8	5

a) Graph these data to see whether a linear equation might describe the relationship between the group's television shows and bass drum sales.

b) Use the least squares regression method to derive a forecasting equation.

c) What is your estimate for bass drum sales if the Green Shades performed on TV nine times last month?

• **5.24** A study to determine the correlation between bank deposits and consumer price indices in Windsor, Ontario, revealed the following (which was based on $n = 5$ years of data):

$$\Sigma x = 15$$
$$\Sigma x^2 = 55$$
$$\Sigma xy = 70$$
$$\Sigma y = 20$$
$$\Sigma y^2 = 130$$

a) Find the coefficient of correlation. What does it imply to you?

b) What is the standard error of the estimate?

: **5.25** The accountant at Barbara Herdman Coal Distributors, Inc., notes that the demand for coal seems to be tied to an index of weather severity developed by the Canadian Weather Bureau. That is, when weather was extremely cold in Canada over the past 5 years (and hence the index was high), coal sales were high. The accountant proposes that one good forecast of next year's coal demand could be made by developing a regression equation and then consulting the *Farmer's Almanac* to see how severe next year's winter will be. For the data in the following table, derive a least squares regression and compute the coefficient of correlation of the data. Also compute the standard error of the estimate.

COAL SALES, Y (IN MILLIONS OF TONNES)	4	1	4	6	5
WEATHER INDEX, X	2	1	4	5	3

: 5.26 Thirteen students entered the P/OM program at Humber College 2 years ago. The following table indicates what their grade point averages (GPAs) were after being in the program for 2 years and what each student scored on the SAT exam when he or she was in high school. Is there a meaningful relationship between grades and SAT scores? If a student scores a 350 on the SAT, what do you think his or her GPA will be? What about a student who scores 800?

STUDENT	A	B	C	D	E	F	G	H	I	J	K	L	M
SAT SCORE	421	377	585	690	608	390	415	481	729	501	613	709	366
GPA	2.90	2.93	3.00	3.45	3.66	2.88	2.15	2.53	3.22	1.99	2.75	3.90	1.60

• 5.27 Dr. Jerilyn Ross, a New York City psychologist, specializes in treating patients who are agoraphobic (afraid to leave their homes). The following table indicates how many patients Dr. Ross has seen each year for the past 10 years. It also indicates what the robbery rate was in New York City during the same year.

YEAR	1	2	3	4	5	6	7	8	9	10
NUMBER OF PATIENTS	36	33	40	41	40	55	60	54	58	61
CRIME RATE (ROBBERIES) PER 1,000 POPULATION	58.3	61.1	73.4	75.7	81.1	89.0	101.1	94.8	103.3	116.2

Using trend analysis, how many patients do you think Dr. Ross will see in years 11, 12, and 13? How well does the model fit the data?

: 5.28 Using the data in Problem 5.27, apply linear regression to study the relationship between the crime rate and Dr. Ross's patient load. If the robbery rate increases to 131.2 in year 11, how many phobic patients will Dr. Ross treat? If the crime rate drops to 90.6, what is the patient projection?

• 5.29 Accountants at the firm Doke and Reed believed that several travelling executives submit unusually high travel vouchers when they return from business trips. The accountants took a sample of 200 vouchers submitted from the past year; they then developed the following multiple-regression equation relating expected travel cost ($\hat{y}$) to number of days on the road (x_1) and distance travelled (x_2) in miles:

$$\hat{y} = \$90.00 + \$48.50x_1 + \$.40x_2$$

The coefficient of correlation computed was .68.

a) If Bill Tomlinson returns from a 300-mile trip that took him out of town for 5 days, what is the expected amount he should claim as expenses?

b) Tomlinson submitted a reimbursement request for $685. What should the accountant do?

c) Should any other variables be included? Which ones? Why?

• 5.30 In the past, Kelly Gibson's tire dealership sold an average of 1,000 radials each year. In the past 2 years 200 and 250, respectively, were sold in fall, 350 and 300 in winter, 150 and 165 in spring, and 300 and 285 in summer. With a major expansion planned, Ms. Gibson projects sales next year to increase to 1,200 radials. What will the demand be each season?

• **5.31** Suppose the number of auto accidents in a certain region is related to the regional number of registered automobiles in thousands (b_1), alcoholic beverage sales in \$10,000s (b_2), and rainfall in inches (b_3). Furthermore, imagine that the regression formula has been calculated as

$$Y = a + b_1X_1 + b_2X_2 + b_3X_3$$

where Y = number of automobile accidents,
$a = 7.5$, $b_1 = 3.5$, $b_2 = 4.5$, and $b_3 = 2.5$

Calculate the expected number of automobile accidents under the following conditions:

	X_1	X_2	X_3
a)	2	3	0
b)	3	5	1
c)	4	7	2

• **5.32** The following multiple-regression model was developed to predict job performance as measured by a company job performance evaluation index based on a preemployment test score and college grade point average (GPA).

$$Y = 35 + 20X_1 + 50X_2$$

where Y = job performance evaluation index
X_1 = preemployment test score
X_2 = college GPA

a) Forecast the job performance index for an applicant who had a 3.0 GPA and scored 80 on the preemployment score.

b) Forecast the job performance index for an applicant who had a 2.5 GPA and scored 70 on the preemployment score.

: **5.33** City government has collected the following data on annual sales tax collections and new car registrations:

Annual Sales Tax Collections (in millions)	1	1.4	1.9	2	1.8	2.1	2.3
New Car Registrations (in thousands)	10	12	15	16	14	17	20

Determine the following:

a) The least squares regression equation.

b) Using the results of part (a), find the estimated sales tax collections if new car registrations total 22.

c) The coefficients of correlation and determination.

: **5.34** Passenger kilometres flown on Southwest Airlines, a commuter firm serving the London, Ontario, hub, are shown for the past 12 weeks.

WEEK	1	2	3	4	5	6
ACTUAL PASSENGER KILOMETRES (IN THOUSANDS)	17	21	19	23	18	16
WEEK	7	8	9	10	11	12
ACTUAL PASSENGER KILOMETRES (IN THOUSANDS)	20	18	22	20	15	22

a) Assuming an initial forecast for week 1 of 17,000 kilometres, use exponential smoothing to compute kilometres for weeks 2 through 12. Use $\alpha = .2$.

b) What is the MAD for this model?

c) Compute the RSFE and tracking signals. Are they within acceptable limits?

5.35 Bus and subway ridership in Toronto, Ontario, during the summer months is believed to be heavily tied to the number of tourists visiting that city. During the past 12 years, the following data have been obtained:

YEAR	**NUMBER OF TOURISTS (IN MILLIONS)**	**RIDERSHIP (IN MILLIONS)**	**YEAR**	**NUMBER OF TOURISTS (IN MILLIONS)**	**RIDERSHIP (IN MILLIONS)**
1	.7	.15	7	1.6	.24
2	.2	.10	8	1.2	.20
3	.6	.13	9	1.4	.27
4	.4	.15	10	2.0	.44
5	1.4	.25	11	1.5	.34
6	1.5	.27	12	.7	.17

a) Plot these data and decide if a linear model is reasonable.

b) Develop a regression relationship.

c) What is expected ridership if 1 million tourists visit the city in a year?

d) Explain the predicted ridership if there are no tourists at all.

e) What is the standard error of the estimate?

f) What is the model's correlation coefficient and coefficient of determination?

5.36 Emergency calls to the 911 system of Sudbury, Ontario, for the past 24 weeks are shown:

WEEK	1	2	3	4	5	6	7	8	9	10	11	12
CALLS	50	35	25	40	45	35	20	30	35	20	15	40
WEEK	13	14	15	16	17	18	19	20	21	22	23	24
CALLS	55	35	25	55	55	40	35	60	75	50	40	65

a) Compute the exponentially smoothed forecast of calls for each week. Assume an initial forecast of 50 calls in the first week, and use $\alpha = .1$. What is the forecast for week 25?

b) Reforecast each period using $\alpha = .6$

c) Actual calls during week 25 were 85. Which smoothing constant provides a superior forecast? Explain and justify the measure of error used.

: **5.37** Using the 911 call data in Problem 5.36, forecast calls for weeks 2 through 25 with a trend-adjusted exponential smoothing model. Assume an initial forecast for 50 calls for week 1 and an initial trend of zero. Use smoothing constants of $\alpha = .3$ and $\beta = .1$. Is this model better than that of Problem 5.36? What adjustment might be useful for further improvement? (Again, assume actual calls in week 25 were 85.)

: **5.38** Edmonton Power and Light has been collecting data on demand for electric power in its west subregion for only the past 2 years. Those data are shown:

	Demand in Megawatts			Demand in Megawatts	
Month	Last Year	This Year	Month	Last Year	This Year
Jan.	5	17	July	23	44
Feb.	6	14	Aug.	26	41
Mar.	10	20	Sept.	21	33
Apr.	13	23	Oct.	15	23
May	18	30	Nov.	12	26
June	15	38	Dec.	14	17

The utility needs to be able to forecast demand for each month next year in order to plan for expansion and to arrange to borrow power from neighbouring utilities during peak periods. Yet the standard forecasting models discussed in this chapter will not fit the data observed for the 2 years.

a) What are the weaknesses of the standard forecasting techniques as applied to this set of data?

b) Because known models are not really appropriate here, propose your own approach to forecasting. Although there is no perfect solution to tackling data such as these (In other words, there are no 100% right or wrong answers.), justify your model.

c) Forecast demand for each month next year using the model you propose.

: **5.39** Attendance at Toronto's newest theme park, Magicland, has been as follows:

Quarter	Guests (in thousands)	Quarter	Guests (in thousands)
Winter '92	73	Summer '93	124
Spring '92	104	Fall '93	52
Summer '92	168	Winter '94	89
Fall '92	74	Spring '94	146
Winter '93	65	Summer '94	205
Spring '93	82	Fall '94	98

Compute seasonal indices using all of the data.

• **5.40** Claude Simpson, manager of Simpson's Department Store, has used time-series extrapolation to forecast retail sales for the next four quarters. The sales estimates are \$120,000, \$140,000, \$160,000, and \$180,000 for the respective quarters. Seasonal indices for the four quarters have been found to be 1.25, .90, .75, and 1.15, respectively. Compute a seasonalized or adjusted sales forecast.

DATA BASE APPLICATION

: **5.41** Thornton Bank is proud of its long tradition in Waterloo, Ontario. Begun by Angela Thornton 6 years after World War II, the bank has bucked the trend of financial and liquidity problems that has plagued the industry since 1985. Deposits have increased slowly but surely over the years, despite recessions in 1960, 1983, 1988, and 1991. Ms. Thornton believes it necessary to have a long-range strategic plan for her firm, including a 1-year forecast and preferably even a 5-year forecast of deposits. She examines the past deposit data and also peruses Ontario's gross provincial product (GPP) over the same 44 years. (GPP is analogous to gross national product, GNP, but on the provincial level.)

a) Using exponential smoothing, with $\alpha = .6$, then trend analysis, and finally linear regression, discuss which forecasting model fits best for Thornton's strategic plan. Justify why one model should be selected over another.

b) Carefully examine the data. Can you make a case for excluding a portion of the information? Why? Would that change your choice of model?

YEAR	DEPOSITS*	GPP†	YEAR	DEPOSITS*	GPP†	YEAR	DEPOSITS*	GPP†
1952	.25	.4	1967	2.3	1.6	1982	24.1	3.9
1953	.24	.4	1968	2.8	1.5	1983	25.6	3.8
1954	.24	.5	1969	2.8	1.6	1984	30.3	3.8
1955	.26	.7	1970	2.7	1.7	1985	36.0	3.7
1956	.25	.9	1971	3.9	1.9	1986	31.1	4.1
1957	.30	1.0	1972	4.9	1.9	1987	31.7	4.1
1958	.31	1.4	1973	5.3	2.3	1988	38.5	4.0
1959	.32	1.7	1974	6.2	2.5	1989	47.9	4.5
1960	.24	1.3	1975	4.1	2.8	1990	49.1	4.6
1961	.26	1.2	1976	4.5	2.9	1991	55.8	4.5
1962	.25	1.1	1977	6.1	3.4	1992	70.1	4.6
1963	.33	.9	1978	7.7	3.8	1993	70.9	4.6
1964	.50	1.2	1979	10.1	4.1	1994	79.1	4.7
1965	.95	1.2	1980	15.2	4.0	1995	94.0	5.0
1966	1.7	1.2	1981	18.1	4.0			

*In \$ millions.

†In \$ billions.

CASE STUDY

The North-South Airline

In 1994, Northern Airlines* merged with Southeast Airlines to create the fourth-largest U.S. carrier. The new North-South Airline inherited both an aging fleet of Boeing 727-200 aircraft and Stephen Ruth. Ruth was a tough former Secretary of the Navy who stepped in as new President and Chairman of the Board.

Ruth's first concern in creating a financially solid company was maintenance costs. It was commonly surmised in the airline industry that maintenance costs rose with the age of the aircraft. He quickly noticed that historically there has been a significant difference in the reported B727-200 maintenance costs (from ATA Form 41s) in both the airframe and the engine area between Northern Airlines and Southeast Airlines, with Southeast having the newer fleet.

On November 12, 1994, Peg Young, Vice President of Operations and Maintenance, was called into Ruth's office and asked to study the issue. Specifically, Ruth wanted to know (1) whether the average fleet age was correlated to direct airframe maintenance costs and (2) whether there was a relationship between average fleet age and direct engine maintenance costs. Young was to report back with the answer, along with quantitative and graphical descriptions of the relationship, by November 26.

Young's first step was to have her staff construct the average age of Northern and Southeast B727-200 fleets, by quarter, since the introduction of that aircraft to service by each airline in late 1985 and early 1986. The average age of each fleet was calculated by first multiplying the total number of calendar days each aircraft had been in service at the pertinent point in time by the average daily utilization of the respective fleet to total fleet hours flown. The total fleet hours flown was then divided by the number of aircraft in service at that time, giving the age of the "average" aircraft in the fleet.

The average utilization was found by taking the actual total fleet hours flown at September 30, 1993, from Northern and Southeast data, and dividing by total days in service for all aircraft at that time. The average utilization for Southeast was 8.3 hours per day, and the average utilization for Northern was 8.7 hours per day. Because the available cost data were calculated for each yearly period ending at the end of the first quarter, average fleet age was calculated at the same points in time.

The Fleet data are shown in Table 1. Airframe cost data and engine cost data are both shown paired with fleet average age in that table.

DISCUSSION QUESTION

1. Prepare Peg Young's response to Stephen Ruth.

*Dates and names of airlines and individuals have been changed in this case to maintain confidentiality. The data and issues described here are actual.

TABLE 1 ■ NORTH-SOUTH AIRLINE DATA FOR BOEING 727-200 JETS

	Northern Airlines Data			Southeast Airlines Data		
Year	Airframe Cost per Aircraft	Engine Cost per Aircraft	Average Age (Hours)	Airframe Cost per per Aircraft	Engine Cost per Aircraft	Average Age (Hours)
1987	$51.80	$43.49	6,512	$13.29	$18.86	5,107
1988	54.92	38.58	8,404	25.15	31.55	8,145
1989	69.70	51.48	11,077	32.18	40.43	7,360
1990	68.90	58.72	11,717	31.78	22.10	5,773
1991	63.72	45.47	13,275	25.34	19.69	7,150
1992	84.73	50.26	15,215	32.78	32.58	9,364
1993	78.74	79.60	18,390	35.56	38.07	8,259

CASE STUDY

The Akron Zoological Park

During the late 1970s, global changes in consumer preferences for radial tires, inflation, and changes in governmental priorities almost resulted in the permanent closing of the Akron Children's Zoo. Lagging attendance and a low level of memberships did not help matters. Faced with uncertain prospects of continuing, the City of Akron opted out of the zoo business. In response, the Akron Zoological Park was organized as a corporation to contract with the city to operate the zoo.

The Akron Zoological Park is an independent organization that manages the Akron Children's Zoo for the city. To be successful, the zoo must maintain its image as a quality place for its visitors to spend their time. Its animal exhibits are clean and neat. The animals, birds, and reptiles look well cared for. As resources become available for construction and continuing operations, the zoo keeps adding new exhibits and activities. Efforts seem to be working, because attendance increased from 53,353 in 1986 to an all-time record of 133,762 in 1991.

Due to its northern climate, the zoo conducts its open season from mid-April until mid-October. It reopens for 1 week at Halloween and for the month of December. Zoo attendance depends largely on the weather. For example, attendance was down during the month of December 1992, which established many local records for the coldest temperature and the most snow. Variations in weather also affect crop yields and prices of fresh animal foods, thereby influencing the costs of animal maintenance.

In normal circumstances, the zoo may be able to achieve its target goal and attract an annual attendance equal to 40% of its community. Akron has not grown appreciably during the past decade. But the zoo became known as an innovative community resource, and as indicated in Table 2, annual paid attendance has doubled. Approximately 35% of all visitors are adults. Children accounted for one-half of the paid attendance. Group admissions remain a constant 15% of zoo attendance.

The zoo does not have an advertising budget. To gain exposure in its market, then, the zoo depends on public service announcements, the zoo's public television series, and local press coverage of its activities and social happenings. Many of these activities are but a few years old. They are a strong reason that annual zoo attendance has increased.

Although the zoo is a nonprofit organization, it must ensure that its sources of income equal or exceed its operating and physical plant costs. Its continued existence remains totally dependent on its ability to generate revenues and to reduce its expenses.

TABLE 2 ■ ANNUAL ATTENDANCE

YEAR	TOTAL PERSONS	ADMISSION FEE ($)		
		ADULT	CHILD	GROUP
1995	117,874	4.00	2.50	1.50
1994	125,363	3.00	2.00	1.00
1993	126,853	3.00	2.00	1.50
1992	108,363	2.50	1.50	1.00
1991	133,762	2.50	1.50	1.00
1990	95,504	2.00	1.00	.50
1989	63,034	1.50	.75	.50
1988	63,853	1.50	.75	.50
1987	61,417	1.50	.75	.50
1986	53,353	1.50	.75	.50

DISCUSSION QUESTIONS

1. The President of the Akron Zoo asked you to calculate the expected gate admittance figures and revenues for both 1996 and 1997. Would simple linear-regression analysis be the appropriate forecasting technique?
2. Besides admission price, what other factors that influence annual attendance should be considered in the forecast?

Source: Professor F. Bruce Simmons, III, The University of Akron.

BIBLIOGRAPHY

Box, G. E. P., and G. Jenkins. *Time Series Analysis: Forecasting and Control*. San Francisco: Holden Day, 1970.

Brown, R. G. *Statistical Forecasting for Inventory Control*. New York: McGraw-Hill, 1959.

Chambers, J. C., C. Satinder, S. K. Mullick, and D. D. Smith. "How to Choose the Right Forecasting Techniques." *Harvard Business Review*, 49 (July/August 1971): 45–74.

Collopy, F., and J. S. Armstrong. "Rule-Based Forecasting: Development and Validation of an Expert Systems Approach to Combining Time Series Extrapolations." *Management Science*, 38, no. 10 (October 1992): 1094.

Gardner, E. S. "Exponential Smoothing: The State of the Art." *Journal of Forecasting*, 4 (March 1985).

Georgoff, D. M., and R. G. Murdick. "Managers' Guide to Forecasting." *Harvard Business Review*, 64 (January/February 1986): 110–120.

Gips, J., and B. Sullivan. "Sales Forecasting—Replacing Magic with Logic." *Production and Inventory Management Review*, 2 (February 1982).

Murdick, R., B. Render, and R. Russell. *Service Operations Management*. Boston: Allyn and Bacon, 1990.

Murdick, R., and D. M. Georgoff. "Forecasting: A Systems Approach." *Technological Forecasting and Social Change*, 44 (1993): 1–16.

Render, B., and R. M. Stair. *Cases and Readings in Management Science*, 2nd ed. Boston: Allyn and Bacon, 1988.

———. *Quantitative Analysis for Management*, 5th ed. Boston: Allyn and Bacon, 1994.

6

PRODUCT STRATEGY

CHAPTER OUTLINE

LEARNING OBJECTIVES

When you complete this chapter you should be able to:

Identify or define:
- Product life cycle
- Product development team
- Value engineering
- Value analysis
- Group technology
- Configuration management
- Time-based competition

Explain:
- Product-by-value analysis
- Product documentation

PRODUCT STRATEGY PROVIDES COMPETITIVE ADVANTAGE AT REGAL MARINE

Twenty-five years after its founding by potato farmer Paul Kuck, Regal Marine has become a powerful force on the waters of the world. Product design is critical in the highly competitive pleasure boat business, where Regal is one of the largest manufacturers in the United States. "We keep in touch with our customers and we respond to the marketplace," says Kuck. "We're introducing six new models this year alone. I'd say we're definitely on the aggressive end of the spectrum." With changing consumer tastes, compounded by material changes, and ever-improving marine engineering, the design function is under constant pressure. Added to these pressures is the constant issue of cost competitiveness combined with providing good value for customers.

Consequently, Regal Marine is a frequent user of computer-aided design (CAD). New designs come to life via Regal's three-dimensional CAD system, borrowed from automotive technology. Regal's naval architects' goal is to continue to reduce the time from concept to prototype to production. Their latest product, the Rush, is a radical 4.27 metre design that seats four people, operates in shallow water, and can pull a water skier or kneeboarder. The sophisticated CAD system not only has reduced product development time, but also has reduced problems with tooling and production, while resulting in a superior product.

All of Regal's products, from the $9,000 Rush to the $225,000 12.19 metre Commodore yacht, follow a similar production process. Hulls and bows are separately hand-produced by spraying preformed molds with three to five layers of a fibreglass laminate. This product hardens and is removed to become the upper and lower structure of the boat. As this "superstructure" moves to an assembly line and is joined, components are added at each workstation.

Wooden decks, precut in house by computer-driven routers, are

Once a hull has been pulled from the mold, it travels down a monorail assembly path. JIT inventory delivers engines, wiring, seats, flooring, and interiors when needed.

CAD/CAM is used to design the hull of a new product. This process results in faster and more efficient design and production.

delivered on a just-in-time basis for installation at one station. Engines, one of the few purchased components, are installed at another. Racks of electrical wiring harnesses, engineered and rigged in-house, are then installed. An in-house upholstery department delivers the customized seats, beds, dashboards, or other cushioned components. Finally, chrome fixtures are put in place, and the boat is sent to Regal's test tank for watertight, gauge, and system inspection.

At the final stage, boats are placed in this test tank where a rain machine ensures watertight fits.

The Rush, designed and produced in record time, entered the hot new market for small, fast, and powerful pleasure boats.

A computer numerically controlled device (a CNC router) cuts out wood parts (flooring, cabinets, supports) used in a boat. The computer stores each part in memory and allows Regal to maximize cuts for top efficiency.

Experience suggests that when Toyota and General Motors (GM) each design an auto for 1998, Toyota will take 2 years and GM 5. Speed of design will provide Toyota with a number of advantages. First, Toyota will be able to design next year's technology into the car and the production process, but GM will be using 3-year-old technology. Additionally, Toyota will only need to forecast customer needs 2 years into the future, but GM will require a 5-year time horizon. Consequently, GM is more likely to be wrong. And, of course, Toyota's design organization is gaining development experience more than twice as fast as General Motors'.[1] ♦

Product strategy

As Toyota and GM know, the basis for any organization's existence is the product or service it provides society. Companies that meet customer needs with exciting, useful high-quality products or services find customers. Those that do not will not last. So one of the critical decisions for managers in world-class firms is the selection, definition, and design of products. Products and services are diverse: they range from a GE toaster, to an appendectomy, to a KFC chicken nugget dish, or a Bell Canada call waiting service. The objective of a **product strategy** is to meet the demands of the marketplace with a competitive advantage.

The production function itself should have available the necessary managerial ability, technological skills, and financial and human resources. When these abilities, skills, and resources do not support a product with a competitive advantage, the product should probably not be produced or offered.

Product selection and design decisions should involve the entire organization, because they affect the entire organization. Additionally, changing a strategic product commitment can be a lengthy and expensive process. In this chapter, we look at efficiently performing product selection, development, and documentation. Moving a product from idea to market is critical to organizational success.

PRODUCT SELECTION

Product Options

Management has many options in the selection, definition, and design of products. Product selection is choosing the product or service to provide customers or clients. For instance, hospitals specialize in various types of patients and various types of medical procedures. A hospital's management may decide to operate a general-purpose hospital, a maternity hospital, or, as in the case of Shouldice, a hospital specializing in hernias, as shown in the photo. Hospitals select their product when they decide what kind of hospital to be. Numerous other options exist for hospitals, just as they exist for McDonald's or General Motors.

Product decisions are fundamental and have major implications throughout the operations function. The strategy implications are substantial and pervasive. The

[1]See related discussion in James P. Womack, Daniel T. Jones, and Daniel Roos, *The Machine That Changed The World* (New York: Macmillan, 1990), p. 111.

Product selection occurs in services as well as manufacturing. Shown here is Shouldice Hospital, Toronto, Ontario, renowned for its world-class specialization in hernia repair—no emergency room, no maternity ward, no open heart surgery, just hernias. Shouldice became world-class by selecting and then focussing on a product (service) at which it could excel. Discharging its patients 3 days earlier than other hospitals, Shouldice's cost is about one-third that of general-purpose hospitals. Local anesthetics are used; patients enter and leave the operating room on their own; rooms are spartan, discouraging patients from remaining in bed; and all meals are served in a common dining room. As Shouldice has demonstrated, product selection impacts the entire production system.

example that follows indicates the strategic implications of a rather minor design change.

> An appliance maker found that it could extend the life of a product and save \$1.75 per unit in warranty costs by substituting a newly designed part. Against expectations, it turned out that the new part would add more than \$2 to the cost of each unit—hardly an attractive proposition, operationally speaking. But on strategic grounds the move still made excellent sense. By sparing the end user cost and inconvenience over the product's lifetime, it would strengthen the company's sales message and increase the product's value in the customer's eyes. Management's decision to go ahead has since been rewarded by a hefty gain in market share.[2]

Identifying New Product Opportunities

An organization cannot survive without introducing new products. Older products are maturing and others in periods of decline must be replaced. This requires a constant successful introduction of new products and active participation by the operations manager. Successful firms have learned how to turn opportunities into successful products.

Product selection, definition, and design take place on a continuing basis because so many new product opportunities exist.[3] Factors influencing market opportunities include *economic change*, *sociological and demographic change*, *technological change*, and *political change*. In addition, other changes and opportunities may be brought

[2]Reprinted by permission of the *Harvard Business Review*. Excerpt from "Breakthrough Manufacturing," by Elizabeth A. Hass (March/April 1987). Copyright © 1987 by the President and Fellows of Harvard College; all rights reserved.

[3]See, for instance, an interesting article by Tom Peters, "All Markets Are Now Immature," *Industry Week* (July 3, 1989): 14–16.

about through *market practice*, *professional standards*, *suppliers*, and *distributors*. Operations managers must be aware of these factors and be able to anticipate changes in products, product volume, and product mix.

Product Life Cycles

Products are born. They live and they die. They are cast aside by a changing society. It may be helpful to think of a product's life as divided into four phases. Those phases, introduction, growth, maturity, and decline, are illustrated for several products in Figure 6.1. That figure also reveals the relative positions of a number of products.

Product life cycles may be a matter of a few hours (a newspaper), months (seasonal fashions and personal computers), years (Betamax video recorders), or decades Volkswagen beetle). Regardless of the length of the cycle, the task for the operations manager is the same: to design a system that helps introduce new products successfully. If the operations function cannot perform effectively at this stage, the firm may be saddled with losers—products that cannot be produced efficiently and perhaps not at all.

Figure 6.2 shows the four life cycles and the relationship of product sales, costs, and profit over the life cycle of a product. Note that typically a firm has a negative cash flow while it develops a product. When the product is successful, those losses may be recovered. Eventually, the successful product may yield a profit prior to its decline. However, the profit is fleeting. As Figure 6.3 shows, leading companies generate a substantial portion of their sales from products less than 5 years old.

FIGURE 6.1 ■ Examples of Products in Various Life Cycle Stages

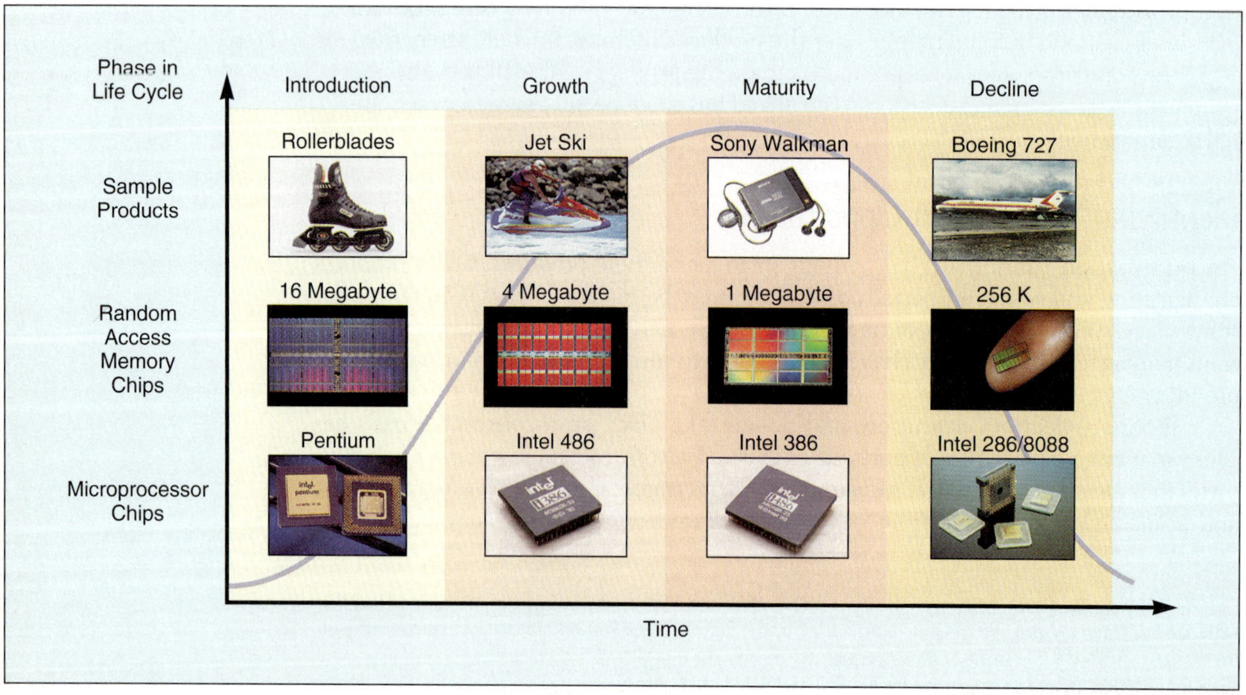

FIGURE 6.2 ■ Product Life Cycle, Sales, Cost, and Profit

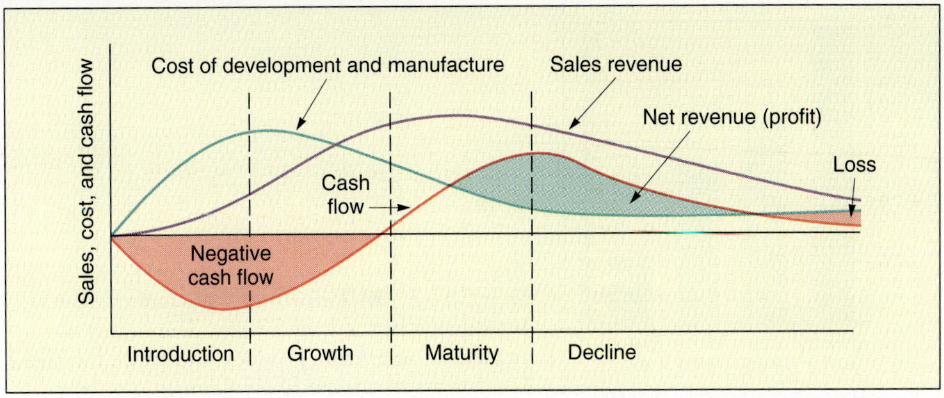

Despite efforts to introduce new products, many new products do not succeed. Consequently, product selection, definition, and design occur frequently. In fact, it is estimated that only 1 out of 25 products introduced actually succeeds! However, many more products go through product development, final production design, and preliminary stages of production but are judged too marginal for further investment. Therefore, they are not introduced.

This means that the number of products that must be reviewed for production and, in some cases, actually produced can be substantial, perhaps as many as 500 for each financially successful product. The relative number of products surviving a given development state is shown in Figure 6.4. Production managers and their organizations must be able to accommodate this volume of new product ideas while maintaining activities to which they are already committed.[4]

Life Cycle and Strategy

Just as operations managers must be prepared to develop new products, they must also be prepared to develop strategies for new and existing products. Periodic examination of products is appropriate to determine their position in the life cycle because *strategies change as products move through their life cycle*. Successful product strategies require determining the best strategy for each product based on its position in its life cycle. A firm, therefore, identifies products or families of products and their position in the life cycle. Let us review some strategy options as products move through their life cycle.

INTRODUCTORY PHASE. Because products in the introductory phase are still being "fine-tuned" for the market, as are their production techniques, they may warrant unusual expenditures for (1) research, (2) product development, (3) process modification and enhancement, and (4) supplier development. For example, when videocassette recorders (VCRs) were first introduced, the features desired by the public were still being determined. At the same time, production managers were still groping for the best manufacturing techniques.

[4]See a discussion of this issue in Rosabeth Moss Kanter, "Swimming in New Streams: Mastering Innovation Dilemmas," *California Management Review*, 31, no. 4 (Summer 1989): 45–69.

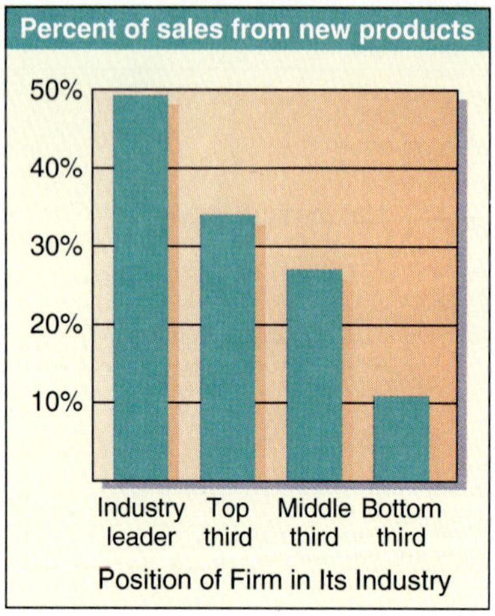

FIGURE 6.3 ■ Percent of Sales from Products Introduced in the Last 5 Years. The higher the percent of sales from products introduced in the last 5 years, the more likely the firm is to be a leader.

FIGURE 6.4 ■ Product Development Yields Few Successes

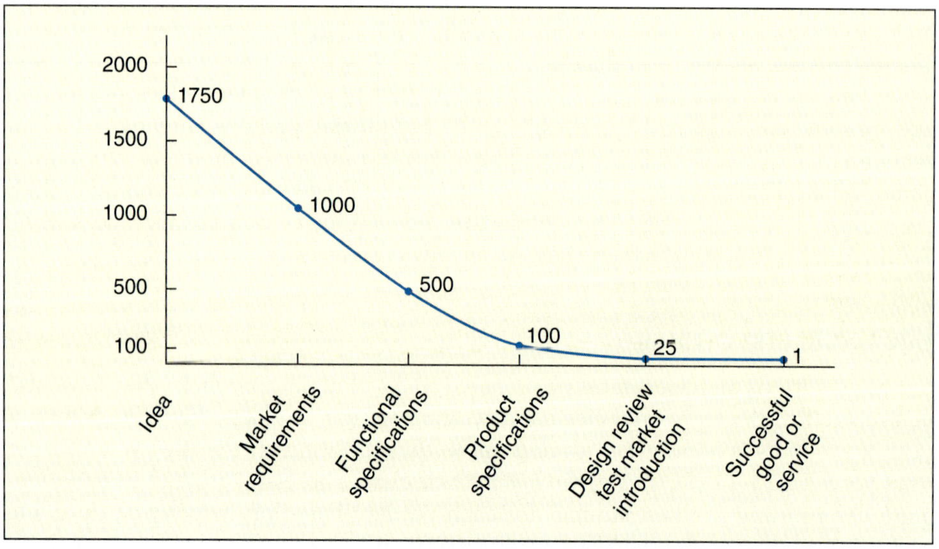

GROWTH PHASE. In the growth phase, product design has begun to stabilize, and effective forecasting of capacity requirements is necessary. Adding capacity or enhancing existing capacity to accommodate the increase in product demand may be necessary.

MATURITY PHASE. With product maturity come competitors, so high-volume, innovative production may be appropriate. Improved cost control, reduction in options, and a paring down of the product line may be effective or necessary for profitability and market share.

PRODUCT DECLINE. Management may need to be ruthless with those products whose life cycle is at an end. Dying products are typically poor products in which to invest resources and managerial talent. Unless dying products make some unique

TABLE 6.1 ■ HOW PRODUCT DEVELOPMENT IS MANAGED MAKES A DIFFERENCE: PRODUCT DEVELOPMENT PERFORMANCE OF REGIONAL AUTO INDUSTRIES

	JAPANESE PRODUCERS	EUROPEAN VOLUME PRODUCERS	AMERICAN PRODUCERS
Average engineering hours per new car (millions)	1.7	2.9	3.1
Average development time per new car (in months)	46.2	57.3	60.4
Number of employees in project team	485.0	904.0	903.0
Number of body types per new car	2.3	2.7	1.7
Average ratio of shared parts	18%	28%	38%
Ratio of delayed products	1 in 6	1 in 3	1 in 2

Source: Adapted from James P. Womack, Daniel T. Jones, and Daniel Roos, *The Machine That Changed the World* (New York: Macmillan, 1990), p. 118. Data are representative of performance in the mid-1980s. The world auto industry has become more competitive in the ensuing decade.

contribution to the firm's reputation or its product line or can be sold with an unusually high contribution, their production should be terminated.[5]

NCR corporation has demonstrated the success of the team approach with their new 2760 electronic cash register. It is assembled with no screws or bolts. The entire terminal consists of just fifteen vendor-produced components. Assembly is so easy that this engineer can put the terminal together blindfolded. NCR has reduced the number of parts by 85%, the number of suppliers by 65, and the time to assemble by 25%.

PRODUCT DEVELOPMENT

Management of the product development process may well determine not only product success, but also the firm's future. Table 6.1 provides a view of six important factors in product development in the automobile industry. In this section, we examine how to be successful at product development.

The Product Development System

Figure 6.5 shows a product development system. In this system, product options go through eight stages, starting with ideas that may be from either internal or external sources, and ending with the evaluation of a new product. The initial stage of successful new product development may put emphasis on factors that are external (market driven) or internal (technology- and innovation- driven) or a combination. Outstanding organizations find the best combination for idea generation. The *POM in Action* box "Vendors Respond to Pressure" discusses how vendors respond to software manufacturers' requirements.

Approaches to Product Development

One approach to overall product development is to assign a product manager to "champion" the product through the product development system and the related organizations. However, the best product development approach seems to be a formal

[5]*Contribution* is defined as the difference between direct cost and selling price. Direct costs are labour and material that go into the product.

POM IN ACTION

Vendors Respond to Pressure

Today's software programs require much more computer capacity to run than those developed six years ago. As software manufacturers continue to create more complex programs, they will increase the demands on the workstation manufacturers to deliver more power to the desktop. Having more microprocessing power will become even more important as the services offered over communications networks expand to include video-on-demand, multimedia transmission, and interactive services. Manufacturers are developing open architectures that provide companies with more flexibility, are not proprietary, and offer more processing power at about one-fifth the price.

Options are becoming vitally important for businesses purchasing equipment to meet their distributed computing requirements. Executives and managers are demanding access to corporate data to develop better business, product development, and marketing strategies. Because data warehousing tools have PC interfaces, businesses want workstation and server architectures that can access and transmit large volumes of data across a network and run from the desktop.

Wireless communications over LANs and WANs, complex geographic information systems, voice/image recognition programs, and OCR technologies are only a few examples of industry drivers that will continue to fuel development of workstation and server technologies.

Source: Adapted from "Vendors Respond to Pressure: Client/Server Processing Power Increases," *Computing Canada*, 21, no. 18 (September 1, 1995): 47.

team approach. Such teams are known variously as product development teams, design for manufacturability teams, and value engineering teams. The Japanese bypass the team issue by not subdividing their organization into research and development, engineering, production, and so forth. Consistently with the Japanese style of group effort and teamwork, these activities are all in one organization. The Japanese culture and management style are more collegial and the organization less structured than in most Western countries. Therefore, they find it unnecessary to have "teams" provide the necessary communication and coordination. However, the typical Western style and the conventional wisdom is to use teams. **Product development teams** are charged with the responsibility of moving from market requirements for a product to achieving a product success (Figure 6.5). Such teams often include marketing, manufacturing, purchasing, quality assurance, and field service personnel. Many teams also include representatives from vendors. Regardless of the formal nature of the product development effort, research suggests that success is more likely to occur in an open, highly participative environment where those with potential contributions are allowed to make them. The objective of a product development team is to make the product or service a success. This includes marketability, manufacturability, and serviceability.

Product development teams

Design for manufacturability and value engineering teams

Design for manufacturability and value engineering teams, on the other hand, have a somewhat narrower charge. They are charged with improvement of designs and specifications at the research, development, design, and production stages of product development. In addition to immediate, obvious cost reduction, design for manufacturability and value engineering may produce other benefits. These include

1. reduced complexity of the product
2. additional standardization of components

FIGURE 6.5 ■ Product Development Stages

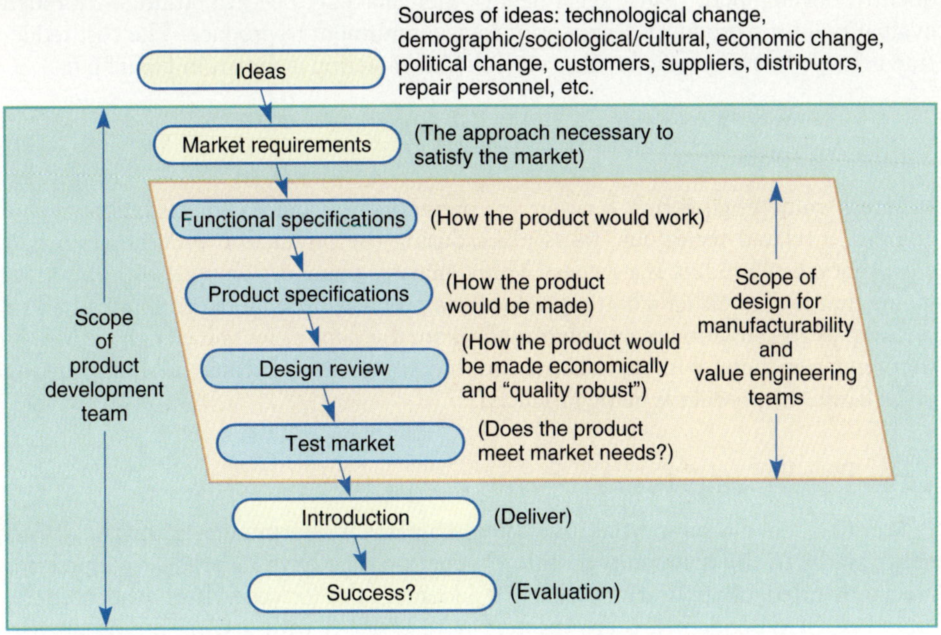

Product concepts are developed from a variety of sources, both external and internal to the firm. Concepts that survive the product idea stage progress through various stages with nearly constant review in a highly participative environment to minimize failure.

The new washer transmission designed by Maytag can switch from slow reciprocal motion of the agitator shaft during the wash cycle to fast rotary motion of the wash tub during the wring cycle. The new design using only 40 pieces is more reliable. The reduction in parts means a substantial reduction in cost with fewer designs and purchases, as well as less inventory and manufacturing expense.

3. improvement of functional aspects of the products
4. improved job design and job safety
5. improved maintainability (serviceability) of the product
6. quality robust design

Quality robust design

Quality robust design means that the product is designed so that small variations in production or assembly do not adversely affect the product. For instance, AT&T developed an integrated circuit that could be used in many products to amplify voice signals. As originally designed, the circuit had to be manufactured very precisely to avoid variations in the strength of the signal. Such a circuit would have been costly to make because of stringent quality controls needed during the manufacturing process. But AT&T's engineers, after testing and analyzing the design, realized that if the resistance of the circuit were reduced—a minor change with no associated costs—the circuit would be far less sensitive to manufacturing variations. The result was a 40% improvement in quality.[6]

Product development teams, design for manufacturability teams, and value engineering teams may be the best cost-avoidance technique available to operations management. They yield value improvement by defining the essential function(s) of the item and by achieving that function without lowering quality. Value engineering programs, when effectively managed, typically reduce cost between 15% and 70% without reducing quality. Some studies have indicated that for every dollar spent on value engineering, $10 to $25 in savings can be realized!

[6]John Mayo, "Process Design as Important as Product Design," *Wall Street Journal* (October 29, 1984): 32.

Product design has impact on virtually all aspects of operating expense. Consequently, development teams, regardless of their makeup, need to ensure a thorough evaluation of the product's design prior to a commitment to produce. The cost reduction achieved for a specific bracket via value engineering is shown in Figure 6.6.

Value Analysis

Value analysis

Whereas value engineering focusses on preproduction design improvement, value analysis, a related technique, takes place during the production process when it is clear that a new product is a success. **Value analysis** teams are charged with improvements that lead to either a better product or a product made more economically. The techniques and advantages for value analysis are the same as for value engineering, although minor changes in implementation may be necessary because analysis is taking place while the product is being produced.

Time-Based Competition

A firm may make a substantial investment to place a new product to market. With many products, the first company into production may have its product adopted for use in a variety of applications that will generate sales for years. It may become the "standard." Consequently, there is often more concern with getting the product to market than with optimum product design or process efficiency. Rapid introduction to the market may be good management because until competition begins to introduce copies or improved versions, the product can sometimes be priced high enough to earn a profit even using somewhat inefficient production design and methods. For example, when Kodak first introduced its Ektar film, the film sold for 10% to 15% more than conventional film. Motorola's pocket-sized cellular telephone was 50% smaller than any Japanese competitor's and sold for twice the price.[7]

The technology and affluence of modern society is also shortening product life. This increases the importance of product development because faster developers of new products continually gain a competitive advantage over slower developers.[8] Those who develop products faster are learning faster. Faster product introduction has a cumulative and positive effect not only in the marketplace, but also on innovative design, quality improvements, and cost reduction. **Time-based competition** is the concept that faster product development has a competitive advantage. As an example, see the *POM in Action* box "Orenda's New Line of V8 Piston Engines." Products must be developed fast, but they must also be developed well, and economically. Doing so is difficult.

Time-based competition

Product by Value

Product-by-value analysis

The effective operations manager directs efforts toward those items that show the greatest promise. This is the Pareto principle applied to product mix. Resources are invested in the critical few and not the trivial many. **Product-by-value analysis** lists products in descending order of their *individual dollar contribution* to the firm. It also

[7]J. Dean and J. Evans, *Total Quality* (St. Paul, West Publishing, 1994), p. 251.

[8]See related discussion in George Stalk, Jr., "Time—The Next Source of Competitive Advantage," *Harvard Business Review* (July/August 1988): 41–51; Joseph Blackburn, *Time-Based Competition: The Next Battleground in American Manufacturing* (Homewood, IL: Business One/Irwin, 1990); "Manufacturing: About Time," *Economist* (April 11, 1990): 72.

POM IN ACTION

Orenda's New Line of V8 Piston Engines

Orenda, a Canadian general aviation engine manufacturer, has decided to delay its new engine program to make changes to the powerplant design. Orenda, an operating company of Toronto-based Magellan Aerospace Corporation, said it decided to incorporate "additional powerplant enhancement prior to certification, in response to customer demands." Certification by the Canadian Ministry of Transport and the FAA had been initially scheduled for December 1995, but after a number of design delays certification was scheduled for the second quarter of 1997.

Orenda said the basic engine has been run in the Toronto, Ontario, test centre for extended periods at up to 750 horsepower, about 25% higher than its rating of 600 horsepower. The testing has verified that both performance and durability objectives are readily achievable, but it also revealed opportunities for optimization that will benefit the combined engine/aircraft installation in terms of weight, complexity, and maintenance costs. Orenda is now developing several improvements, including the replacement of the twin turbochargers with a single, more powerful unit and the modification of the oil system to reduce complexity and improve maintainability.

The company detailed its plans to develop a 500-horsepower engine, a turbocharged 600 horsepower engine, and a 750-horsepower powerplant. Target price for the engines is approximately $100,000, which should give aircraft manufacturers an incentive to use Orenda engines rather than turboprops, which can cost more than twice as much and have a similar power output. Larry Shiembob, vice-president and general manager of business development for Orenda, said initial market response was overwhelming. "We knew the marketplace would be excited about this engine, but we really didn't imagine just how strong and widespread the response would be. By responding early, we are increasing the level of confidence in our engine program."

Source: Adapted from "Orenda Delaying Certification Schedule for Aircraft Engines," *The Weekly of Business Aviation*, 61, no. 4 (July 24, 1995): 37.

FIGURE 6.6 ■ Cost Reduction of a Bracket via Value Engineering. Each time the bracket is redesigned and simplified, we are able to produce it for less.

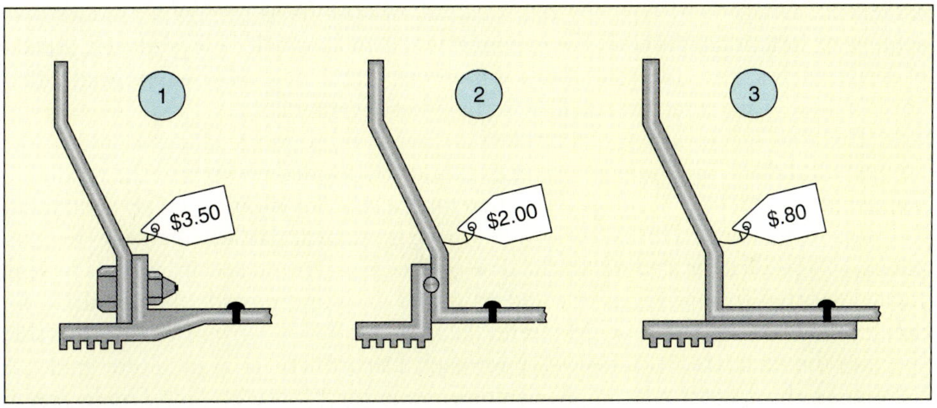

(*Source:* Adapted from Robert Goodell Brown, *Management Decisions for Production Operations*, Hinsdale, IL: Dryden Press, Inc., 1971, p. 353.)

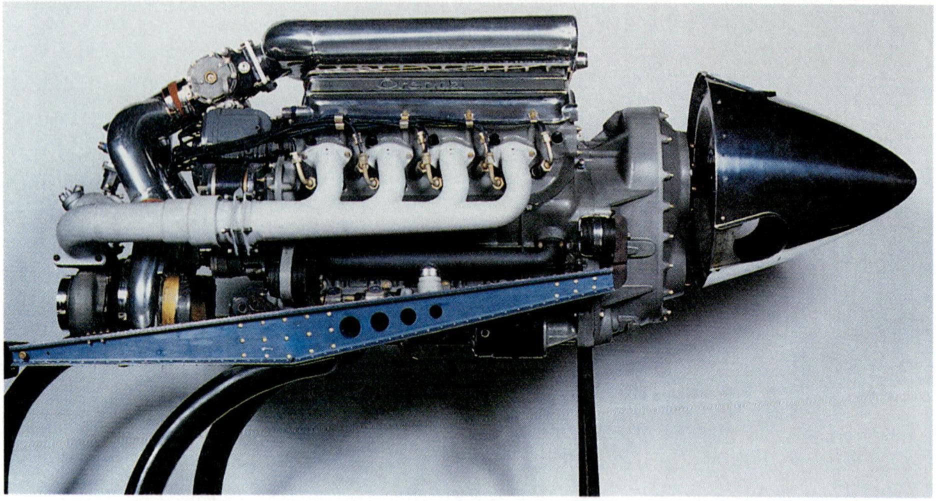

By concentrating their efforts on redesigning the traditional horizontally-opposed piston engine, Orenda has developed a product that is in high demand. Typically such engines could not supply more than 350 hp; Orenda has managed to increase output to up to 750 hp. This performance allows the new powerplant to compete against more expensive turboprop engines.

lists the *total annual dollar contribution* of the product. Low contribution on a per-unit basis by a particular product may look substantially different if it represents a large portion of the company's sales.

A product-by-value report allows management to evaluate possible strategies for each product. These might include increasing cash flow (for example, increasing contribution by raising selling price or lowering cost), increasing market penetration (for example, improving quality and/or reducing cost or price), or reducing costs (for example, improving the production process). The report may also tell management which product offerings should be eliminated and which fail to justify further investment in research and development or capital equipment. The report focuses management's attention on the strategic direction for each product.

DEFINING AND DOCUMENTING THE PRODUCT

Once new products or services are selected for introduction, they must be defined. First, a product or service is defined in terms of its functions, that is, what it is to do. The product is then designed, that is, it is determined how the functions are to be achieved. Management typically has a variety of options as to how a product is to achieve its functional purpose. For instance, when an alarm clock is produced, aspects of design such as the colour, size, or location of buttons may make substantial differences in ease of manufacture, quality, and market acceptance.

Rigorous specifications of a product are necessary to assure efficient production. Equipment, layout, and human resources cannot be decided upon until the product is defined, designed, and documented. Therefore, every organization needs documents to define its products. This is true of everything from meat patties, to cheese, to computers, to a medical procedure. In the case of cheese, a written specification is typical. Indeed, written specifications or standard grades exist and provide the definition for many products. For instance, Monterey Jack cheese has a written description that specifies the characteristics necessary for each Department of Agriculture grade. A portion of the Department of Agriculture grade for Monterey Jack Grade AA is shown in Figure 6.7. Similarly, Small Fry Snack Foods Inc. specifies P.E.I. potatoes, considered to be the best in Canada, for their products (see the photo on page 225).

FIGURE 6.7 ■ Monterey Jack. A portion of the general requirements for the U.S. grades of Monterey cheese is shown here.

§ 58.2469 Specifications for U.S. grades of Monterey (Monterey Jack) cheese

(a) *U.S. grade AA.* Monterey cheese shall conform to the following requirements:

(1) *Flavor.* Is fine and highly pleasing, free from undesirable flavors and odors. May possess a very slight acid or feed flavor.

(2) *Body and texture.* A plug drawn from the cheese shall be reasonably firm. It shall have numerous small mechanical openings evenly distributed throughout the plug. It shall not possess sweet holes, yeast holes, or other gas holes.

(3) *Color.* Shall have a natural, uniform, bright attractive appearance.

(4) *Finish and appearance—bandaged and paraffin-dipped.* The rind shall be sound, firm, and smooth providing a good protection to the cheese.

Source: Code of Federal Regulation, Parts 53 to 109, Revised as of Jan. 1, 1985, General Service Administration.

Most manufactured items as well as their components are typically defined by a drawing, usually referred to as an engineering drawing. An **engineering drawing** shows the dimensions, tolerances, materials, and finishes of a component. The engineering drawing will be an item on a bill of material. An engineering drawing is shown in Figure 6.8. The **bill of material** lists the components, their description, and the quantity of each required to make one unit of a product. A bill of material for a manufactured item is shown in Figure 6.9(a). A bill of material is often referred to as a BOM. An engineering drawing shows how to make one item on the bill of material.

Engineering drawing

Bill of material (BOM)

In the food-service industry, bills of material manifest themselves in portion-control standards. The portion-control standard for a "Juicy Burger" is shown in Figure 6.9(b). In a more complex product, a bill of material is referenced on other bills of material of which they are a part. In this manner, subunits (subassemblies) are part of the next higher unit (their parent bill of material), which ultimately make a final product. Products, in addition to being defined by a written specification, a portion-control document, or bill of material, can be defined in other ways. For example,

GE Motors has completely redesigned its washing machine motors, reducing individual parts from 87 to 23, manufacturing processes from 61 to 20 and the production cycle from 5 days to 12 hours. Here, Sheri Nemeth, who is leader of the site team responsible for getting manufacturing systems on line and employees trained, inspects one of the new Form W motors.

FIGURE 6.8 ■ Engineering Drawings Such as This One Show Dimensions, Tolerances, Materials, and Finishes

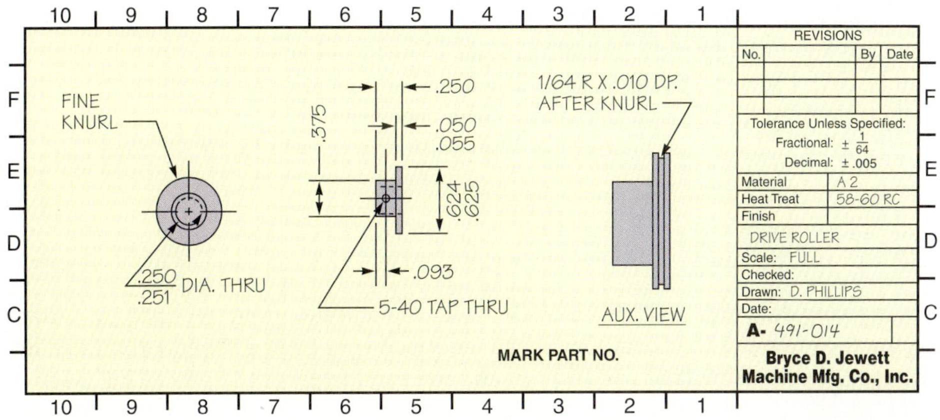

FIGURE 6.9 ■ Bills of Material Take Different Forms in a Manufacturing Plant (a) and a Fast-Food Restaurant (b), but in Both Cases, the Product Must Be Defined

Bill of Material for a Panel Weldment

NUMBER	DESCRIPTION	QTY
A 60-71	PANEL WELDM'T	1
A 60-7	LOWER ROLLER ASSM.	1
R 60-17	ROLLER	1
R 60-428	PIN	1
P 60-2	LOCKNUT	1
A 60-72	GUIDE ASSM. REAR	1
R 60-57-1	SUPPORT ANGLE	1
A 60-4	ROLLER ASSEM.	1
02-50-1150	BOLT	1
A 60-73	GUIDE ASSM. FRONT	1
A 60-74	SUPPORT WELDM'T	1
R 60-99	WEAR PLATE	1
02-50-1150	BOLT	1

(a)

Portion Control Standard for a Hamburger

PRODUCT: Juicy Burger

DESCRIPTION	QTY
Buns	1
Cheese	1 slice
Meat patties	2
Pickle slice	2
Dehydrated onions	1/250 pkg.
Sauce	1/137.5
Lettuce	1/26 head

(b)

products such as chemicals, paints, and petroleums may be defined by formulas or proportions that describe how they are to be made.

Make or Buy

Make-or-buy decision

For many components of products, firms have the option of producing the component themselves or purchasing it from an outside source. Choosing between these options is known as the make-or-buy decision. The **make-or-buy decision** distinguishes between what the firm wants to produce and what it wants to purchase. Because of variations in quality, cost, and delivery schedules, the make-or-buy decision is critical to product definition. Many items can be purchased as a "standard item" produced by someone else—an item that does not require its own bill of material or engineering drawing because its specification as a standard item is adequate. Examples are the standard bolts listed on the bill of material shown in Figure 6.9(a), for which there will be SAE (Society of Automotive Engineers) specifications. Therefore, there typically is no need for the firm to duplicate this specification in another document. We discuss what is known as the make-or-buy decision in more detail in Chapter 12.

Group Technology

Group technology

Engineering drawings may also include codes to facilitate group technology. **Group technology** requires that components be identified by a coding scheme that specifies the type of processing (such as drilling) and the parameters of the processing (such as size). Machines can then process families of parts as a group, minimizing setups, routings, and material handling. An example of how families of parts may be grouped is shown in Figure 6.10. Group technology provides a systematic way to review a family of components to see if an existing component might suffice on a new project. Using an existing component eliminates all the costs connected with the design and development of the new part, which is a major cost reduction. For these reasons, successful implementation of group technology leads to

1. improved design because more design time can be devoted to fewer products
2. reduced raw material and purchases
3. simplified production planning and control
4. improved routing and machine loading
5. reduced tooling setup time, and work-in-process and production time

The application of group technology helps the entire organization, as many costs are reduced.

Computer-Aided Design (CAD)

Computer-aided design (CAD)

Product design is greatly enhanced through the use of **computer-aided design (CAD)**. Increasingly, manufactured products are designed and documented on CAD.

Where CAD is used, a design engineer starts by developing a rough sketch or, conceivably, just an idea. The designer then utilizes a graphic display as a drafting

The facility of Small Fry Snack Foods Inc. in Prince Edward Island was estimated to produce more than $20 million worth of snack food products per year, create 80 new jobs, and employ 100 in total.

Catherine Callbeck, former Premier of Prince Edward Island, referred to the project as "a vote of confidence in the future of our economy. It [was] a vote of confidence in the skills and dedication of our workers and … a vote of confidence in the quality of our potatoes and our potato farmers."

The chairperson and CEO of Small Fry, Gerald Schmalz, echoed the praise: "Establishing a major production facility in P.E.I. … allow[ed] us to capitalize on the excellent quality of P.E.I. potatoes. Our new P.E.I. plant make[s] it possible to produce a superior quality of chips."

(*Source:* Adapted from Canada NewsWire Ltd., "Small Fry Plans new Production Plant for PEI," January 23, 1995.)

board to construct the geometry of a design. As a geometric definition is completed, a sophisticated CAD system will allow the designer to determine various kinds of engineering data, such as strength or heat transfer. CAD will also allow the designer to ensure that parts fit together so there will be no interferences when parts are subsequently assembled. Thus, if the designer is sketching the fender for an automobile, the brackets and related panels are changed as the fender is changed. Analysis of existing, as well as new, designs can be done expediently and economically. These advances in CAD systems are discussed further in the *POM in Action* box "Realism Comes to Computer Images" and in Chapter 8.

Once the designer is satisfied with the design, it becomes part of a drawing data base on electronic media. The CAD system, through a library of symbols and details, also helps to ensure adherence to the drafting standards. Additionally, because CAD data are available for subsequent use by others, tool design personnel and programmers of numerically controlled machines are aided. They can now proceed to design tooling and programs with confidence that they have the latest accurate engineering data and engineering drawings.

Once again, we see how decisions made when a product is designed have ramifications in many other P/OM decisions.

PREPARING FOR PRODUCTION

Once a product is selected and designed, a number of issues remain. Among these are (a) documentation to aid the production process, (b) configuration management, and (c) determining the exact time to stop design and move the product to production.

FIGURE 6.10 ■ A Variety of Coding Schemes Move Manufactured Components from (a) Ungrouped to (b) Grouped

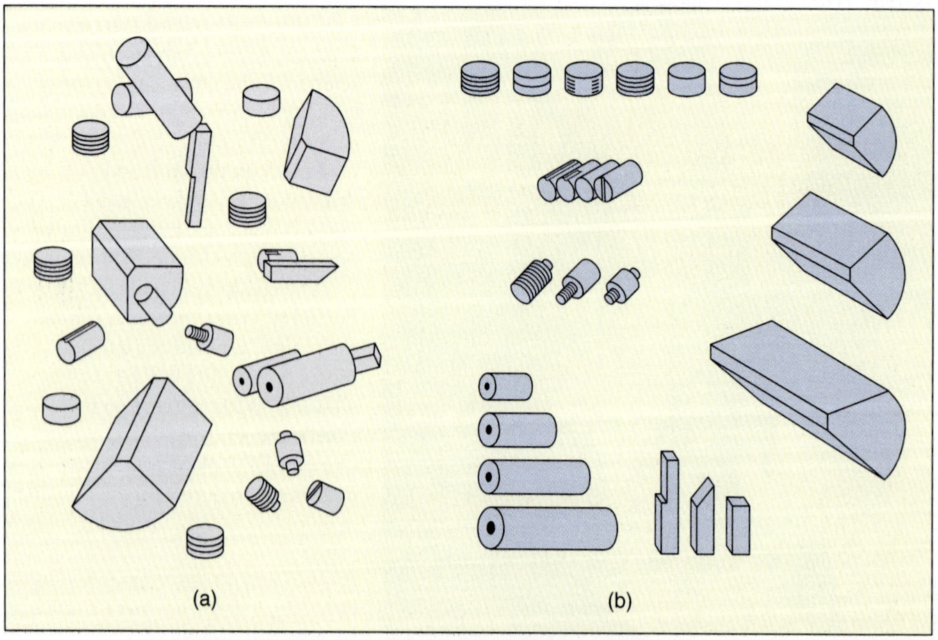

POM IN ACTION

Realism Comes to Computer Images

In 1994 Mental Images, a small German company, developed a software program that allows Boeing to design and create "photorealistic" images of interior layouts of their new 777 aircraft without needing to build expensive mockups. Boeing was able to visualize how different parts of the aircraft can be reached so that maintenance could be carried out.

In Europe, BMW and Mercedes used the software, which allowed them to see their cars on screen as though in a showroom, as a design aid. And it allowed Chrysler engineers to create the new Neon model in 29 months from concept to finished product.

Financial support from the European Community's Esprit program allowed Mental Images to upgrade the software to the point where designers with access to fast, parallel computers could make changes and see the results immediately.

The company was able to have its Mental Ray software added to a CAD/CAM program called Catia, produced by the French company Dassault Systems. Catia is used by many of the world's leading manufacturers. Mental Ray gave Catia the ability to "render" raw images, a technical term for creating a realistic picture from a computer design.

The Canadian firm Softimage, which created the dinosaurs used in *Jurassic Park*, signed up to use Mental Images products. Eventually Softimage was acquired by Microsoft—so Mental Images became a major supplier of software to the American giant.

Source: Adapted from "Realism Comes to Computer Images," *Sunday Times*, July 17, 1994.

Documentation

Assembly drawing

An **assembly drawing** simply shows an exploded view of the product. An assembly drawing is usually a three-dimensional drawing, known as an isometric drawing. The relative locations of the components are shown in relation to each other to show how to assemble the unit (see Figure 6.11(a)).

Computer aided design: B. F. Goodrich engineers and managers use software from Structural Dynamics Research Corporation (SDRC) to model wheel and brake assemblies. By analysis of stress and heat, they can often avoid costly design and production mistakes. Errors that are found at the design stage on a CRT screen can often be fixed for a nominal cost, but the cost is substantial once production has begun.

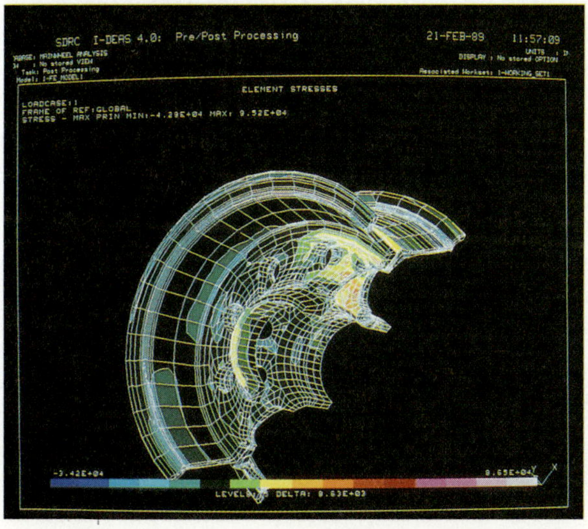

Assembly chart

The **assembly chart** shows in schematic form how a product is assembled. Manufactured components, purchased components, or a combination of both may be shown on an assembly chart. The assembly chart identifies the point of production where components flow into subassemblies and ultimately into a final product. An example of an assembly chart is shown in Figure 6.11(b).

Route sheet

The **route sheet** lists the operations (including assembly and inspection) necessary to produce the component with the material specified in the bill of material. The route sheet for an item will have one entry for each operation to be performed on the item. When route sheets include specific methods of operation and labour standards, they are often known as *process sheets*.

Job instructions

Standards manuals

Organizations also often find it necessary to develop **job instructions**, which provide detailed instructions about how to perform the task. Where there are a large variety of jobs, job instructions change often. Instruction manuals are used where the jobs seldom change. Various **standards manuals** provide standard times for setup and information about speed, capacity, and tolerances, and perhaps other pertinent data for each operation in a process. Standards manuals are found not only in manufacturing environments, but also in most operating areas, such as a well-organized institutional kitchen or a computer centre.

Work order

The **work order** is an instruction to make a given quantity of a particular item, usually to a given schedule. The ticket that a waiter writes in your favourite restaurant is a work order. In a hospital or factory, the work order is a more formal order that provides authorization to draw various pharmaceuticals or items from inventory, to perform various functions, and to assign personnel to perform those functions. Increasingly, job instructions, standards manuals, and work orders are maintained on computer.

Configuration Management

Engineering change notices (ECN)

Configuration management

Engineering change notices (ECN) change some aspect of the product's definition or documentation, such as an engineering drawing or a bill of material. For a complex product that has a long manufacturing cycle, such as a Boeing 747 jumbo jet, the changes may be so numerous that no two 747s are built exactly alike—which is indeed the case. Such dynamic design change has fostered the development of a discipline known as configuration management, which is concerned with product identification, control, and documentation. **Configuration management** is the system by which a product's planned and changing configurations are accurately identified and for which control and accountability of change are maintained.

SERVICE PRODUCTS ARE DIFFERENT

Much of our discussion so far has focussed on what we can call tangible products, that is, goods. On the other side of the product coin are, of course, services. Service industries include intangibles such as banking, finance, insurance, transportation, and communications.[9] They also include those medical procedures that leave only the tiniest scar after an appendectomy, as well as the shampoo and cut at a hair salon.

[9]The *Statistical Abstract of the United States* considers services as wholesale and retail trade, finance, insurance, real estate, and government. Most definitions also include education, health care, and the legal and lodging industries.

FIGURE 6.11 ■ Assembly Drawing and Assembly Chart

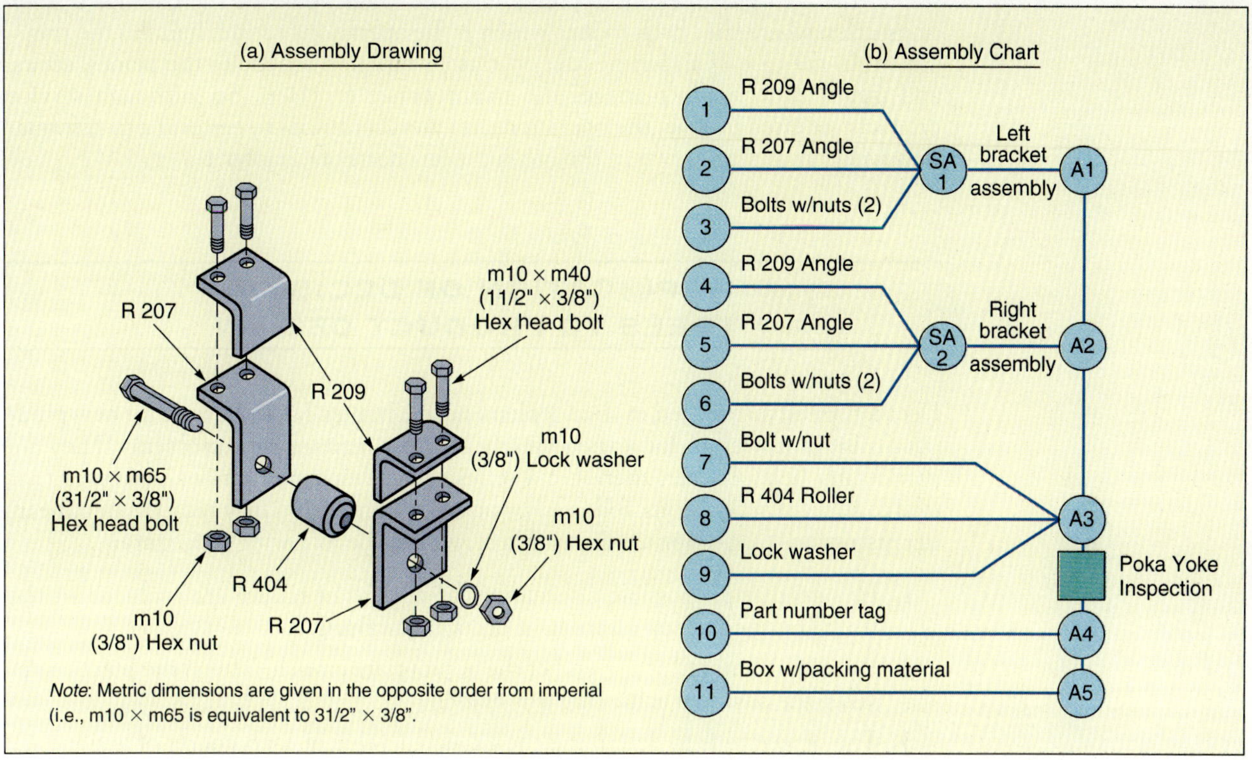

Thus, the first thing that is different about service is that it is *usually intangible* (your purchase of a ride in an empty airline seat between two cities) as opposed to a tangible product. Note, however, that the service may still be precisely defined. The airline seat may be defined by row, flight number, date, and class.

The second thing is that services are often *produced and consumed simultaneously*; there is no stored inventory. For instance, the beauty salon produces a haircut that is consumed simultaneously, or the doctor produces an operation that is consumed as it is produced.

The third item that makes services different is that although many goods are standardized or have standardized components, *many services are unique*. Your mix of financial coverage, which manifests itself in investments and insurance policies, may not be the same as anyone else's.

The fourth thing that makes the service product unique is *high customer interaction*. It is often difficult to standardize, automate, and be as efficient as we would like because customer interaction demands a uniqueness. This uniqueness in many cases is what the customer is paying for; therefore, the operations manager must ensure that the product is designed so that it can be delivered in the required unique manner.

The fifth item that makes service unique is *inconsistent product definition*. Product definition may be rigorous, as in the case of an insurance policy, or casual, as in the case of a haircut. Moreover, the haircut definition not only varies with each customer, but often with each haircut, even for the same customer.

In spite of these differences between products and services, there is still an operations function to be performed. This occurs when the insurance company defines the product (say, an insurance policy), processes the purchase transaction, issues premium statements, and processes those premiums. The same would be the case for a stock transaction where the "back room," which is the operations centre, handles the transaction. In the case of an airline, the operations function schedules the planes, crews, and meals, and usually manages the maintenance function. So, although service products are often unique, the operations function continues to perform a transformation function, as was shown in the organization charts of Chapter 1.

APPLICATION OF DECISION TREES TO PRODUCT DESIGN

Decision trees, introduced in the supplement to Chapter 2, can be used for new product decisions as well as for a wide variety of other management problems. They are particularly helpful when there are a series of decisions and various outcomes that lead to *subsequent* decisions, followed by other outcomes. You may recall from our earlier discussions that to form a decision tree, we use the following procedure:

1. Be sure that all possible alternatives and states of nature are included in the tree. This includes an alternative of "doing nothing."
2. Payoffs are entered at the end of the appropriate branch. This is the place to develop the payoff of achieving this branch.
3. The objective is to determine the expected value of each course of action. We accomplish this by starting at the end of the tree (the right-hand side) and working toward the beginning of the tree (the left), calculating values at each step and "pruning" alternatives that are not as good as others from the same node.

Example 1 shows the use of a decision tree applied to product design.

EXAMPLE 1

Silicon, Inc., a semiconductor manufacturer, is investigating the possibility of producing and marketing a microprocessor. Undertaking this project will require either purchasing a sophisticated CAD system or hiring and training several additional engineers. The market for the product could be either favourable or unfavourable. Silicon, Inc., of course, has the option of not developing the new product at all.

With favourable acceptance by the market, sales would be 25,000 processors selling for $100 each, and with unfavourable acceptance, sales would be only 8,000 processors selling for $100 each. The cost of the CAD equipment is $500,000, but that of hiring and training three new engineers is only $375,000. However, manufacturing cost should drop from $50 each when manufacturing without CAD to $40 each when manufacturing with CAD.

The probability of favourable acceptance of the new microprocessor is .40; the probability of unfavourable acceptance is .60. See Figure 6.12.

FIGURE 6.12 ■ Decision Tree for Development of a New Product

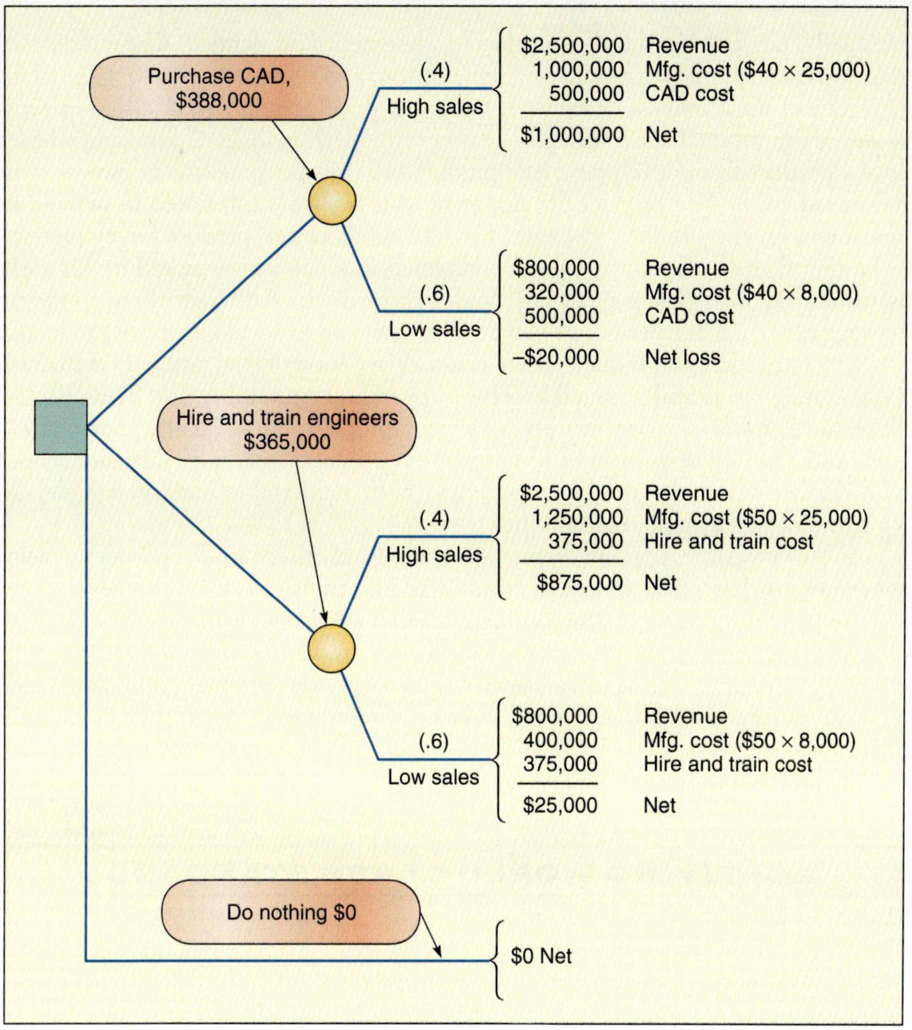

The expected monetary values (EMVs) have been circled at each step of the decision tree. For the top branch:

$$\text{EMV (purchase CAD system)} = (.4)(\$1{,}000{,}000) + (.6)(-\$20{,}000) = \$388{,}000$$

This represents the results that will occur if Silicon, Inc., purchases CAD.

The expected value of hiring and training engineers is the second series of branches:

$$\text{EMV (hire/train engineers)} = (.4)(\$875{,}000) + (.6)(\$25{,}000) = \$365{,}000$$

The EMV of doing nothing is $0.

Because the top branch has the highest expected monetary value (an EMV of $388,000 vs. $365,000 vs. $0), it represents the best decision. Management should purchase the CAD system.

TRANSITION TO PRODUCTION

Eventually, our product has been selected, designed, and defined. The product has progressed from an idea, to a functional definition, and then perhaps to a design. Now, management must make a decision as to further development, production, or termination of the product idea. One of the arts of modern manage is knowing when to move a product from development to production; this movement is known as *transition to production*. The product development staff is always interested in making improvements in the product. Because this staff tends to see product development as evolutionary, they may never have a completed product, but as noted in our earlier discussion, the cost of late product introduction is high. Although these conflicting pressures exist, management must make a decision—more development or production.

Once this decision is made, there is usually a period of trial production to ensure that the design is indeed producible. This is the manufacturability test. This also gives the production staff the opportunity to develop proper tooling, quality control procedures, and training of personnel to ensure that production can be initiated successfully. Finally, when the product is deemed both marketable and producible, line management will assume responsibility.

Some companies appoint a project manager and others use the product development teams we discussed earlier to ensure that the transition from the development phase to production is successful. Both approaches allow a wide range of resources and talents to be brought to bear to ensure satisfactory production of a product that is still in flux. A third approach is integration of the product development and manufacturing organizations. This allows for easy shifting of resources between the two organizations as needs change. The production manager's job is to make the transition from R&D to production smooth and without gaps.

ACHIEVING WORLD-CLASS STANDARDS

World-class firms recognize that anything less than an excellent product strategy can be devastating. Consequently, these firms focus on only a few businesses or technologies. For instance Honda's focus is engines. Virtually all of Honda's sales (for example, autos, motorcycles, generators, lawn mowers, etc.) are based on its outstanding engine technology. The same is true of Intel (microcomputer components) and Microsoft (PC software products). World-class firms design these products to be "quality robust" while continually improving them. Managers of world-class firms insist upon strong communication between customer, product, processes, and suppliers that results in a high success rate for their new products. Benchmarks, of course, vary by industry, but Rubbermaid introduces a new product each day!

World-class firms often allow customization around existing products or services. This approach allows the customer to choose product variations while reinforcing the organization's strength. This is the way Dell Computers has built a huge market. Dell delivers computers with the exact hardware and software desired by the end user. And they do it fast—which brings us to the next attribute of world-class companies. They understand that speed to market is important. They provide quick response. Motorola built its pager business on the basis of quick response. The firm reduced the time from order to delivery from over a month to less than 3 hours, providing a benchmark for others. Finally, a world-class product strategy links product strategy to investment, market share, product life cycles, and breadth of the product line. Product development and design are key to a successful business strategy.

SUMMARY

Selecting, designing, and defining a product has implications for all subsequent operations decisions. The operations manager must be imaginative and resourceful in the product development process. Products are defined by written specification, bills of material, and engineering drawings. Group technology, computer-aided design, and value engineering are helpful product design techniques. Assembly drawings, assembly charts, route sheets, job instruction, work orders, and standards manuals assist the manager in defining a product for production.

Once a product is in production, value analysis is appropriate for quality and production review. Configuration management allows the manager to track and document the product that has been produced.

How products move through their life cycle of introduction, growth, maturity, and decline influences the strategy the operations manager should pursue. And decision trees are particularly useful techniques in many product strategy decisions.

KEY TERMS

Product strategy (p. 212)
Product development teams (p. 218)
Design for manufacturability and value engineering teams (p. 218)
Quality robust design (p. 219)
Value analysis (p. 220)
Time-based competition (p. 220)
Product-by-value analysis (p. 220)
Engineering drawing (p. 223)
Bill of material (BOM) (p. 223)
Make-or-buy decision (p. 224)
Group technology (p. 224)
Computer-aided design (CAD) (p. 225)
Assembly drawing (p. 227)
Assembly chart (p. 228)
Route sheet (p. 228)
Job instructions (p. 228)
Standards manuals (p. 228)
Work order (p. 228)
Engineering change notice (ECN) (p. 228)
Configuration management (p. 228)

SOLVED PROBLEM

Solved Problem 6.1

Kris King, president of King Electronics, Inc., has two design options for her new line of high-resolution cathode-ray tubes (CRTs) for computer-aided design workstations. The life cycle sales forecast for the CRT is 100,000 units.

Design option A has a .90 probability of yielding 59 good CRTs per 100 and a .10 probability of yielding 64 good CRTs per 100. This design will cost $1,000,000.

Design option B has a .80 probability of yielding 64 good units per 100 and a .20 probability of yielding 59 good units per 100. This design will cost $1,350,000.

Good or bad, each CRT will cost $75. Each good CRT will sell for $150. Bad CRTs are destroyed and have no salvage value. There is little disposal cost as they break up when thrown in the trash. Therefore, we ignore any disposal costs in this problem.

Solution

We draw the decision tree to reflect the two decisions and the probabilities associated with each decision. We then determine the payoff associated with each branch. This is shown in Figure 6.13.

FIGURE 6.13 ■ Decision Tree for Solved Problem 6.1

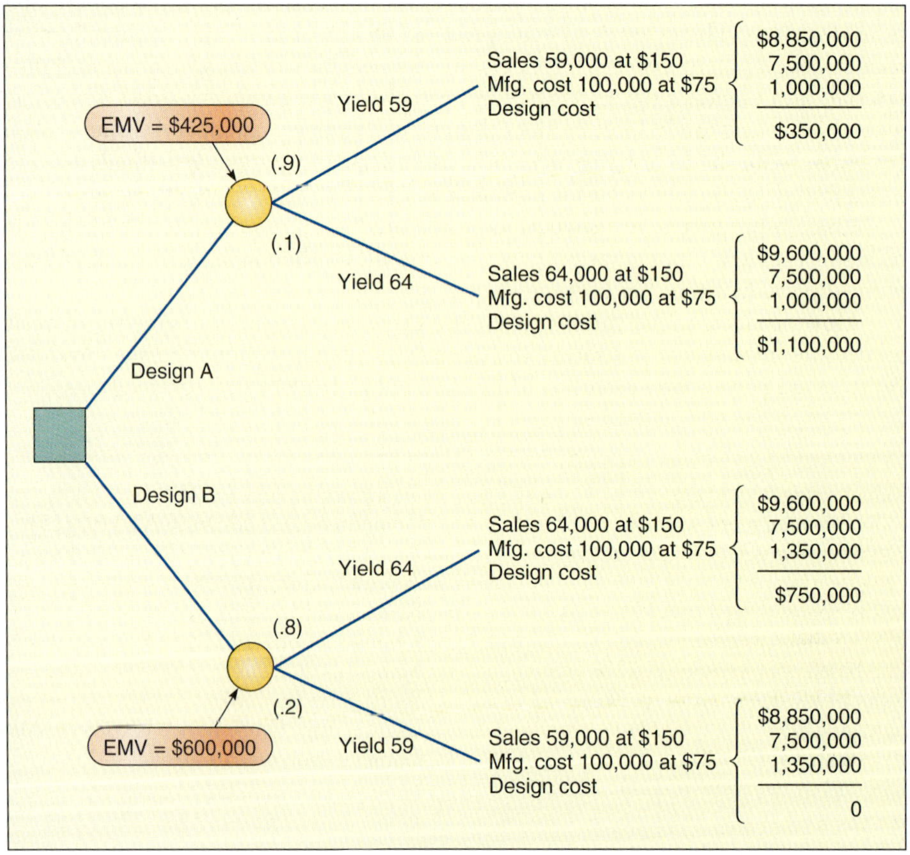

For design A,

$$\begin{aligned}\text{EMV (design A)} &= (.9)(\$350{,}000) + (.1)(\$1{,}100{,}000)\\ &= \$425{,}000\end{aligned}$$

For design B,

$$\begin{aligned}\text{EMV (design B)} &= (.8)(\$750{,}000) + (.2)(\$0)\\ &= \$600{,}000\end{aligned}$$

The highest payoff is design option B at $600,000.

DISCUSSION QUESTIONS

1. What management techniques may prove helpful in making the transition from design to production?
2. Why is it necessary to document a product explicitly?
3. What techniques do we use to document a product?
4. Configuration management has proved particularly useful in what industries? Why?
5. How does computer-aided design help other departments?
6. What is group technology and why is it proving helpful in our quest for productivity improvement?
7. What savings can be expected by computer-aided design?
8. How does computer-aided design help computer-aided manufacture?
9. What are the four phases of the product life cycle?
10. How does product selection (and design) affect quality?
11. Once a product is defined, what documents are used to assist production personnel in the manufacture of that product?
12. How does configuration management manifest itself when you ask for service on your automobile?
13. What are the similarities and dissimilarities between a manufactured product and a new type of life insurance policy referred to by the salespersons as their new "product."

CRITICAL THINKING EXERCISE

Rubbermaid's record of new product innovation is remarkable. With almost five thousand products, the firm continues to crank out a new one almost every day—and with great success. Rubbermaid has divided its product line into four dozen categories. Then it creates entrepreneurial teams of five to seven members in each category. Each team includes a product manager, research and manufacturing engineers, and financial sales and marketing executives. The teams conceive their own products, shepherding them from design stage to the marketplace.

Compare Rubbermaid's product approach to the Canadian and the Japanese approach discussed in this chapter.

PROBLEMS

• **6.1** Prepare a bill of material for a ballpoint pen.

• **6.2** Draw an assembly chart for a ballpoint pen.

• **6.3** Prepare a bill of material for a simple table lamp. Identify the items that you, as manufacturer of the body and related components, are likely to make and that you are likely to purchase. Justify your decision for each.

• **6.4** Prepare an assembly chart for the table lamp in Problem 6.3.

• **6.5** As a library project, find a series of group technology codes.

: **6.6** Given the contribution made on each of the three products in the table and their position in the life cycle, identify a reasonable operations strategy for each.

TABLE FOR PROBLEM 6.6

PRODUCT	PRODUCT CONTRIBUTION (PERCENT OF SELLING PRICE)	COMPANY CONTRIBUTION (PERCENT OF TOTAL ANNUAL CONTRIBUTION DIVIDED BY TOTAL ANNUAL SALES)	POSITION IN LIFE CYCLE
Portable computer	30	40	Growth
Laptop computer	30	50	Introduction
Hand calculator	50	10	Decline

6.7 The product planning group of Hawkes Electric Supplies, Inc., has determined that it needs to design a new series of switches. They must decide upon one of three design strategies. The market forecast is for 200,000 units. The better and more sophisticated the design strategy and the more time spent on value engineering, the less will be the variable cost. The chief of engineering design, Dr. Gerry Johnson has decided that the following costs are a good estimate of the initial and variable costs connected with each approach. These are

a) Low-tech: a low-technology, low-cost process consisting of hiring several new junior engineers. This has a cost of \$45,000 and variable cost probabilities of .2 for \$.55 each, .5 for \$.50, and .3 for \$.45.

b) Subcontract: a medium-cost approach utilizing a good outside design staff. This approach would have an initial cost of \$65,000 and variable cost probabilities of .7 of \$.45, .2 of \$.40 and .1 of \$.35.

c) High-tech: a high-technology approach utilizing the very best of the inside staff and the latest computer-aided design technology. This approach has a fixed cost of \$75,000 and variable cost probabilities of .9 of \$.40 and .1 of \$.35.

What is the best decision, using an expected monetary value (EMV) criterion? (*Note:* We want the lowest EMV as we are dealing with costs in this problem.)

6.8 Faber Manufacturing, Inc., of Montreal, Quebec, has the option of (a) proceeding immediately with production of a new top-of-the-line stereo TV, which has just completed prototype testing or (b) having the value analysis team complete a study. If Karita France, VP for Operations, proceeds with the existing prototype (option A), the firm can expect sales to be 100,000 units at \$550 each with a probability of .6, and a .4 probability of 75,000 at \$550. If, however, she uses the value analysis team (option B), the firm expects sales of 75,000 units at \$750 with a probability of .7, and a .3 probability of 70,000 units at \$750. Cost of the value analysis is \$100,000. Which option has the highest expected monetary value (EMV)?

6.9 Ritz Products' materials manager, Houston Griffin, must make a determination to make or buy a new semiconductor for the wrist TV it is about to produce. One million units are expected to be produced over the life cycle. If the product is made, the start-up and production cost of the make decision is \$1,000,000, with a probability of .4 that the product will be satisfactory and .6 probability that it will not. If the product is not satisfactory, the firm will have to reevaluate the decision. If the decision is reevaluated, the choice will be to spend another \$1,000,000 to redesign the semiconductor or to purchase. Likelihood of success the second time the make decision is made is .9. If the second make decision also fails, the firm must purchase. Regardless of when the purchase takes place, the best judgement Houston Griffin has of cost is that Ritz Products will pay \$.50 for each purchased semiconductor plus \$1,000,000 in vendor development cost.

a) Assuming that Ritz Products must have the semiconductor (stopping or doing without is not a viable option), what is their best decision?

b) What criteria did you use to make this decision?

c) What is the worst that can happen to Ritz Products on this particular decision? What is the best that can happen?

6.10 Use the data in Solved Problem 6.1 to examine what happens to the decision if Ms. King can increase the yield when the yield is 59 out of each 100. If the yield is 59 per 100, a special expensive phosphorus for the screen can be used at an added cost of $50 per CRT. This procedure will be good for only 5 units per 100 (that is, this procedure can bring the yield up to only 64 per 100). Prepare the modified decision tree. What are the payoffs and which branch has the greatest EMV?

CASE STUDY

GE's Rotary Compressor

In 1981, market share and profits in General Electric's appliance division were falling. The company's technology was antiquated compared to foreign competitors. For example, making refrigerator compressors required 65 minutes of labour in comparison to 25 minutes for competitors in Japan and Italy. Moreover, GE's labour costs were higher. The alternatives were obvious: Either purchase compressors from Japan or Italy or design and build a better model.

By 1983, the decision to build a new rotary compressor in house was made, along with a commitment for a new $120 million factory. GE was not a novice in rotary compressor technology; it had invented the technology and had been using it in air conditioners for many years. A rotary compressor weighed less, had one-third fewer parts, and was more energy-efficient than the current reciprocating compressors. The rotary compressor took up less space, thus providing more room inside the refrigerator and better meeting customer requirements.

Some engineers argued to the contrary, citing the fact that rotary compressors run hotter. This is not a problem in most air conditioners, because the coolant cools the compressor. In a refrigerator, however, the coolant flows only one-tenth as fast, and the unit runs about four times longer in 1 year than an air conditioner. GE had problems with the early rotary compressors in air conditioners. Although the bugs had been eliminated in smaller units, GE quit using rotaries in larger units due to frequent breakdowns in hot climates.

GE managers and design engineers were concerned about other issues. Rotary compressors make a high-pitched whine, and managers were afraid that this would adversely affect consumer acceptance. Many hours were spent on this issue by managers and consumer test panels. The new design also required key parts to work together with a tolerance of only 50 millionths of an inch. Nothing had been mass-produced with such precision before, but manufacturing engineers felt sure they could do it.

The compressor they finally designed was nearly identical to that used in air conditioners, with one change. Two small parts inside the compressor were made out of powdered metal, rather than the hardened steel and cast iron used in air conditioners. This material was chosen because it could be machined to much closer tolerances, and reduced machining costs. Powdered metal had been tried a decade earlier on air conditioners but did not work. The design engineers who were new to designing compressors did not consider the earlier failure important.

A consultant suggested that GE consider a joint venture with a Japanese company that had a rotary refrigerator compressor already on the market. The idea was rejected by management. The original designer of the air conditioner rotary compressor, who had left GE, offered his services as a consultant. GE declined his offer, writing him that they had sufficient technical expertise.

About 600 compressors were tested in 1983 without a single failure. They were run continuously for 2 months under elevated temperatures and pressures that were supposed to simulate 5 years' operation. GE normally conducts extensive field testing of new products; its original plan to test models in the

(Continued)

field for 2 years was reduced to 9 months due to time pressure to complete the project.

The technician who disassembled and inspected the parts thought they did not look right. Parts of the motor were discolored, a sign of excessive heat. Bearings were worn, and it appeared that high heat was breaking down the lubricating oil. The technician's supervisors discounted these findings and did not relay them to upper levels of management. Another consultant who evaluated the test results believed that something was wrong because only one failure was found in 2 years and recommended that test conditions be intensified. This suggestion was also rejected by management.

By 1986, only 2.5 years after board approval, the new factory was producing compressors at a rate of 10 per minute. By the end of the year, more than 1 million had been produced. Market share rose and the new refrigerator appeared to be a success. But in July 1987, the first compressor failed. Soon after, reports of other failures in Puerto Rico arrived. By September, the appliance division knew it had a major problem. In December, the plant stopped making the compressor. Not until 1988 was the problem diagnosed as excessive wear in the two powdered-metal parts that burned up the oil. The cost in 1989 alone was $450 million. By mid-1990, GE had voluntarily replaced nearly 1.1 million compressors with ones purchased from six suppliers, five of them foreign.

DISCUSSION QUESTIONS

1. What factors in the product development process caused this disaster? What individuals were responsible?
2. How might this disaster have been prevented? What lessons do you think GE learned for the future?
3. On what basis was GE attempting to achieve a competitive advantage? How did they fail?

Source: James Dean and James Evans, *Total Quality* (St. Paul: West Publishing, 1994) pp. 256–257. Modified for the Canadian edition.

BIBLIOGRAPHY

Akao, Y., ed. *Quality Function Deployment: Integrating Customer Requirements into Product Design*. Cambridge, MA: Productivity Press, 1990.

Ali, A., M. U. Kalwani, and D. Kovenock. "Selecting Product Development Projects: Pioneering Versus Incremental Innovation Strategies." *Management Science*, 39, no. 3 (March 1993): 255–274.

Berliner, C., and J. A. Brimson. *Cost Management for Today's Advanced Manufacturing*. Boston: Harvard Business School Press, 1988.

Bower, J. L., and T. M. Hout. "Fast Cycle Capacity for Competitive Power." *Harvard Business Review* (November/December 1988): 110–118.

Burbidge, J. L. "Production Flow Analysis for Planning Group Technology." *Journal of Operations Management*, 10, no. 1 (January 1991): 5–27.

Canada NewsWire Ltd. "Small Fry Plans New Production Plant for P.E.I." January 23, 1995.

Capon, N., J. U. Farley, D. R. Lehmann, and J. M. Hulbert. "Profiles of Product Innovators Among Large U.S. Manufacturers." *Management Science*, 38, no. 2 (February 1992): 157.

Choi, M. and W. E. Riggs. "GT Coding and Classification Systems for Manufacturing Cell Design." *Production and Inventory Management Journal*, 32 (First Quarter 1991): 28.

Clark, K., and S. Wheelwright. "Organizing and Leading 'Heavyweight' Development Teams." *The California Management Review*, (Spring 1992)

Eppen, G. D., W. A. Hanson, and R. K. Martin. "Bundling-New Products, New Markets, Low Risk." *Sloan Management Review*, 32 (Summer 1991): 7.

Fitzsimmons, J. A., P. Kouvelis, and D. N. Mallick. "Design Strategy and Its Interface with Manufacturing and Marketing: A Conceptual Framework." *Journal of Operations Management*, 10, no. 3 (August 1991): 398.

Garza, O., and T. L. Smunt. "Countering the Negative Impact of Intercell Flow in Cellular Manufacturing." *Journal of Operations Management*, 10, no. 1 (January 1991): 92–118.

Hastings, N. A., and C. Yeh. "Bill of Manufacture." *Production and Inventory Management Journal*, 33, no. 4 (Fourth Quarter 1992): 27–31.

Iansiti, M. "Real-World R&D: Jumping the Product Generation Gap." *Harvard Business Review*, 71, no. 3 (May/June 1993): 131–147.

Miltenburg, J., and W. Zhang. "A Comparative Evaluation of Nine Well-Known Algorithms for Solving the Cell Formation Problem in Group Technology." *Journal of Operations Management*, 10, no. 1 (January 1991): 44–72.

"Orenda Delaying Certification Schedule for Aircraft Engines." *The Weekly of Business Aviation*, 61, no. 4 (July 24, 1995): 37.

Otis, I., "Designing for Manufacture and Assembly to Improve Efficiency and Quality." *Industrial Engineering*, 24, no. 8 (August 1992): 60.

"Realism Comes to Comuter Images." *Sunday Times*, July 17, 1994.

Samoras, T. T., and F. L. Czerwinski. *Fundamentals of Configuration Management*. New York: John Wiley, 1971.

Smith, P. G., and D. G. Reinertsen. *Developing Products in Half the Time*. New York: Van Nostrand Reinhold, 1991.

Stalk, G., Jr., and T. M. Hout. *Competing Against Time*. New York: Free Press 1990.

Suri, R., and S. de Treville. "Full Speed Ahead: A Timely Look at Rapid Modeling and Operations Management." *OR/MS Today* (June 1991): 34–42.

Ulrich, K., D. Sartorius, S. Pearson, and M. Jakiela. "Including the Value of Time in Design-for-Manufacturing Decision Making." *Management Science*, 39, no. 4 (April 1993): 429–447.

"Vendors Respond to Pressure: Client/Server Processing Power Increases." *Computing Canada*, 21, no. 18 (September 1, 1995): 47.

6 SUPPLEMENT

LINEAR PROGRAMMING

SUPPLEMENT OUTLINE

The storm front closed in quickly on Chicago's O'Hare Airport, shutting it without warning. The heavy thunderstorms, lightning, and poor visibility sent American Airlines passengers and ground crew scurrying. Because American Airlines uses linear programming (LP) to schedule flights, hotels, crews, and refuelling, LP has a direct impact on profitability. As Thomas Cook, president of AA's Decision Technology Group, says, "Finding fast solutions to LP problems is essential. If we get a major weather disruption at one of the hubs, such as Dallas or Chicago, then a lot of flights may get cancelled, which means we have a lot of crews and airplanes in the wrong places. What we need is a way to put that whole operation back together again." LP is the tool that helps airlines such as American unsnarl and cope with this weather mess.[1] ♦

[1]Adapted from *Introduction to Contemporary Mathematics*, 2nd ed. (New York: W. H. Freeman, 1990), p. 82–83.

Many operations management decisions involve trying to make the most effective use of an organization's resources. Resources typically include machinery (such as planes), labor (such as pilots), money, time, and raw materials (such as jet fuel). These resources may be used to produce products (such as machines, furniture, food, or clothing) or services (such as airline schedules, advertising policies, or investment decisions). **Linear programming (LP)** is a widely used mathematical technique designed to help production and operations managers plan and make the decisions necessary to allocate resources.

Linear programming (LP)

A few examples of problems in which LP has been successfully applied in operations management are

1. selecting the product mix in a factory to make best use of machine- and labour-hours available while *maximizing* the firm's profit;
2. picking blends of raw materials in feed mills to produce finished feed combinations at *minimum* cost;
3. determining the distribution system that will *minimize* total shipping cost from several warehouses to various market locations;
4. developing a production schedule that will satisfy future demands for a firm's product and at the same time *minimize* total production and inventory costs.

As the *POM in Action* box "Using LP to Select Tenants in a Shopping Mall" suggests, LP can be used in a very broad range of applications.

REQUIREMENTS OF A LINEAR PROGRAMMING PROBLEM

All LP problems have four properties in common.

1. LP problems seek to *maximize* or *minimize* some quantity (usually profit or cost). We refer to this property as the **objective function** of an LP problem. The major objective of a typical firm is to maximize dollar profits in the long run. In the case of a trucking or airline distribution system, the objective might be to minimize shipping costs.

Objective function

2. The presence of restrictions, or **constraints**, limits the degree to which we can pursue our objective. For example, deciding how many units of each product in a firm's product line to manufacture is restricted by available labour and machinery. We want, therefore, to maximize or minimize a quantity (the objective function) subject to limited resources (the constraints).

Constraints

3. There must be *alternative courses of action* to choose from. For example, if a company produces three different products, management may use LP to decide how to allocate among them its limited production resources (of labour, machinery, and so on). If there were no alternatives to select from, we would not need LP.
4. The objective and constraints in linear programming problems must be expressed in terms of *linear equations* or inequalities.

POM IN ACTION

Using LP to Select Tenants in a Shopping Mall

CanMallCo Development Company is one of the largest shopping-centre developers in Canada. When developing a new centre, CanMallCo produces a tentative floor plan, or footprint, for the mall. This plan outlines sizes, shapes, and spaces for large department stores. Leasing agreements are reached with the two or three major department stores that will become anchor stores in the mall. The anchor stores are able to negotiate highly favourable occupancy agreements. Typically, they either pay low rent or receive other concessions. CanMallCo's profits come primarily from the rent paid by the nonanchor tenants—the smaller stores that lease space along the aisles of the mall. The decisions allocating space to potential tenants and establishing the tenant mix are therefore crucial to the success of the investment.

The tenant mix describes the desired stores in the mall by their size, general location, and type of merchandise or service provided. For example, the tenant mix might specify two small jewelry stores in a central section of the mall and a medium-sized shoe store and a large restaurant in one of the side aisles. In the past, CanMallCo developed a plan for tenant mix using "rules of thumb" developed over years of experience in mall development.

Now, to improve its bottom line in an increasingly competitive marketplace, CanMallCo treats the tenant-mix problem as a *linear programming* model. First, the model assumes that tenants can be classified into categories according to the type of merchandise or service they provide. Second, the model assumes that for each store type, store sizes can be made into distinct categories. For example, a small jewelry store is said to contain about 65 square metres and a large one about 204 square metres. The tenant-mix model is a powerful tool for enhancing CanMallCo's mall planning and leasing activities.

(*Source:* Adapted from James Bean et al., "Selecting Tenants in a Shopping Mall," *Interfaces* (March/April 1988): 1–9.)

Linear programming helps production and operations managers choose the most efficient allocation of resources. Here LP is used to decide a shopping mall's tenant-mix.

FORMULATING LINEAR PROGRAMMING PROBLEMS

One of the most common linear programming applications is the *product mix problem*. Two or more products are usually produced using limited resources. The company would like to determine how many units of each product it should produce in order to maximize overall profit given its limited resources. Let us look at an example.

Alpha Electronics Example

The Alpha Electronics Company produces two products: (1) the Alpha Beltmusic, a portable AM/FM cassette player, and (2) the Alpha Wristman, a wristwatch-sized black-and-white television. The production process for each product is similar in that both require a certain number of hours of electronic work and a certain number of labour-hours in the assembly department. Each Beltmusic takes 4 hours of electronic work and 2 hours in the assembly shop. Each Wristman requires 3 hours in electronics and 1 hour in assembly. During the current production period, 240 hours of electronic time are available and 100 hours of assembly department time are available. Each Beltmusic sold yields a profit of \$7; each Wristman produced may be sold for a \$5 profit.

Alpha's problem is to determine the best possible combination of Beltmusics and Wristmans to manufacture in order to reach the maximum profit. This production-mix situation can be formulated as a linear programming problem.

We begin by summarizing the information needed to formulate and solve this problem (see Table S6.1). Further, let us introduce some simple notation for use in the objective function and constraints. Let

$$X_1 = \text{number of Beltmusics to be produced}$$
$$X_2 = \text{number of Wristmans to be produced}$$

Now we can create the LP *objective function* in terms of X_1 and X_2:

$$\text{Maximize profit} = \$7X_1 + \$5X_2$$

Our next step is to develop mathematical relationships to describe the two constraints in this problem. One general relationship is that the amount of a resource *used* is to be less than or equal to (≤) the amount of resource *available*.

First Constraint: Electronic time used is ≤ electronic time available.

$$4X_1 + 3X_2 \leq 240 \text{ (hours of electronic time)}$$

Second Constraint: Assembly time used is ≤ assembly time available.

$$2X_1 + 1X_2 \leq 100 \text{ (hours of assembly time)}$$

Both of these constraints represent production capacity restrictions and, of course, affect the total profit. For example, Alpha Electronics cannot produce 70 Beltmusics during the production period because if $X_1 = 70$, both constraints will be violated. It also cannot make $X_1 = 50$ Beltmusics and $X_2 = 10$ Wristmans. This constraint brings out another important aspect of linear programming. That is, certain interactions will exist between variables. The more units of one product that a firm produces, the fewer it can make of other products.

New England Apple Products, the manufacturing of the Very Fine beverage line, has 16 different juice beverages, ranging from apple-cherry to cranapple to grapefruit. A large number of combinations of fruit juices are possible, but New England Apple has only limited supplies of each juice as ingredients. The firm has used linear programming to decide which combinations to market and how much of each to make. The bottom-line question is: "What product mix will yield the best profit?" Although there are many listed ingredients on the side of each bottle of fruit juice blend, LP is one *hidden ingredient*.

GRAPHICAL SOLUTION TO A LINEAR PROGRAMMING PROBLEM

The easiest way to solve a small LP problem such as that of the Alpha Electronics Company is the graphical solution approach. The graphical procedure can be used

TABLE S6.1 ■ **ALPHA ELECTRONICS COMPANY PROBLEM DATA**

	Hours Required to Produce 1 Unit		
Department	(X_1) Beltmusics	(X_2) Wristmans	Available Hours This Week
Electronic	4	3	240
Assembly	2	1	100
Profit/unit	$7	$5	

only when there are two decision variables (such as number of Beltmusics to produce, X_1, and number of Wristmans to produce, X_2). When there are more than two variables, it is *not* possible to plot the solution on a two-dimensional graph; we then must turn to more complex approaches described later in this supplement.

Graphical Representation of Constraints

In order to find the optimal solution to a linear programming problem, we must first identify a set, or region, of feasible solutions. The first step in doing so is to plot the problem's constraints on a graph.

The variable X_1 (Beltmusics, in our example) is usually plotted as the horizontal axis of the graph, and the variable X_2 (Wristmans) is plotted as the vertical axis. The complete problem may be restated as:

$$\text{Maximize profit} = \$7X_1 + \$5X_2$$

Subject to the constraints:

$$4X_1 + 3X_2 \leq 240 \quad \textit{(electronics constraint)}$$
$$2X_1 + 1X_2 \leq 100 \quad \textit{(assembly constraint)}$$
$$X_1 \geq 0 \quad \textit{(Number of Beltmusics produced is greater than or equal to 0.)}$$
$$X_2 \geq 0 \quad \textit{(Number of Wristmans produced is greater than or equal to 0.)}$$

The first step in graphing the constraints of the problem is to convert the constraint *inequalities* into *equalities* (or equations).

$$\text{Constraint A:} \quad 4X_1 + 3X_2 = 240$$
$$\text{Constraint B:} \quad 2X_1 + 1X_2 = 100$$

The equation for constraint A is plotted in Figure S6.1 and for constraint B in Figure S6.2.

FIGURE S6.1 ■ Constraint A

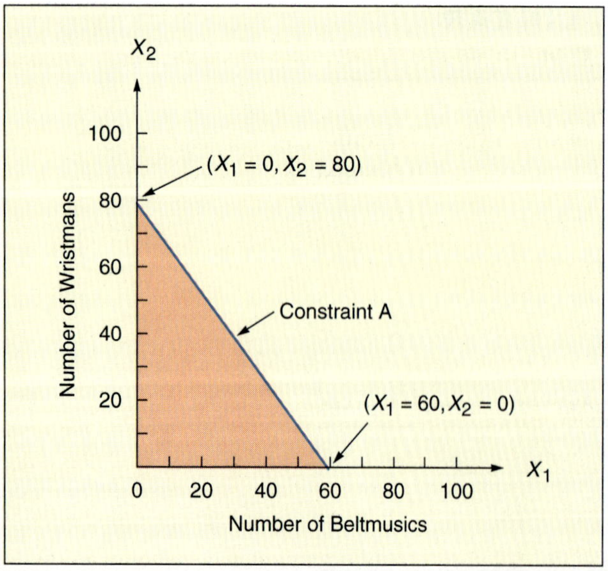

FIGURE S6.2 ■ Constraint B

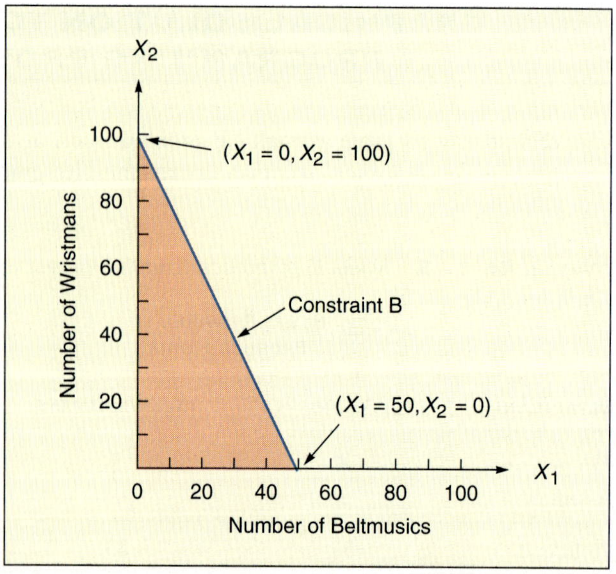

To plot the line in Figure S6.1, all we need to do is to find the points at which the line $4X_1 + 3X_2 = 240$ intersects the X_1 and X_2 axes. When $X_1 = 0$ (the location where the line touches the X_2 axis), it implies that $3X_2 = 240$ or that $X_2 = 80$. Likewise, when $X_2 = 0$, we see that $4X_1 = 240$ and that $X_1 = 60$. Thus, constraint A is bounded by the line running from ($X_1 = 0, X_2 = 80$) to ($X_1 = 60, X_2 = 0$). The shaded area represents all points that satisfy the original *inequality*.

Constraint B is illustrated similarly in Figure S6.2. When $X_1 = 0$, then $X_2 = 100$; and when $X_2 = 0$, then $X_1 = 50$. Constraint B then is bounded by the line between ($X_1 = 0, X_2 = 100$) and ($X_1 = 50, X_2 = 0$). The shaded area represents the original inequality.

Figure S6.3 shows both constraints together. The shaded region is the part that satisfies both restrictions. The shaded region in Figure S6.3 is called the *area of feasible solutions*, or simply the *feasible region*. This region must satisfy *all* conditions specified by the program's constraints and thus is the region where all constraints overlap. Any point in the region would be a *feasible solution* to the Alpha Electronics Company problem. Any point outside the shaded area would represent an *infeasible solution*. Hence, it would be feasible to manufacture 30 Beltmusics and 20 Wristmans ($X_1 = 30, X_2 = 20$), but it would violate the constraints to produce 70 Beltmusics and 40 Wristmans. This can be seen by plotting these points on the graph of Figure S6.3.

Iso-Profit Line Solution Method

Now that the feasible region has been graphed, we can proceed to find the optimal solution to the problem. The optimal solution is the point lying in the feasible region that produces the highest profit.

FIGURE S6.3 ■ Feasible Solution Region for the Alpha Electronics Company Problem

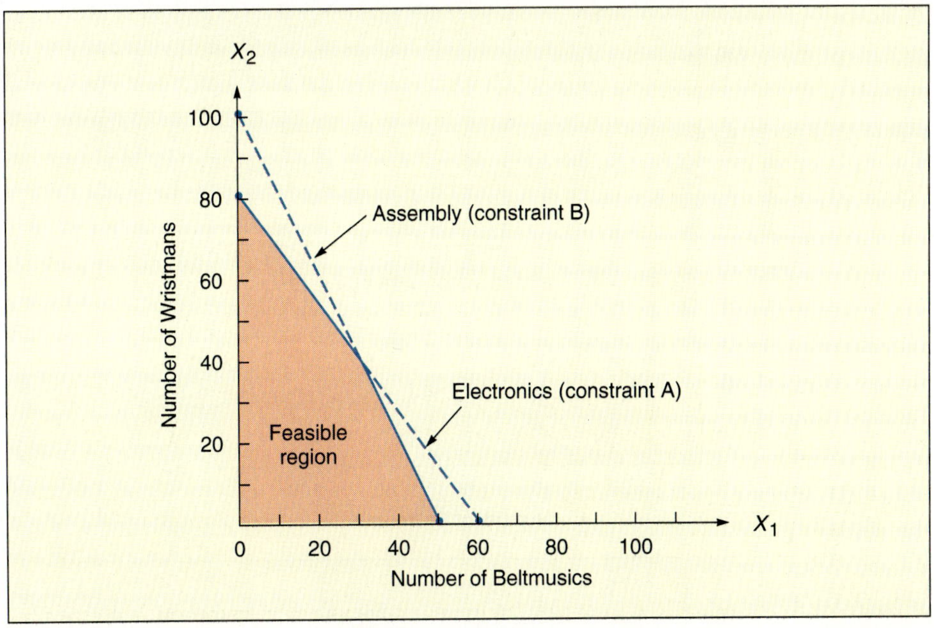

Iso-profit line method

Once the feasible region has been established, several approaches can be taken in solving for the optimal solution. The speediest one to apply is called the **iso-profit line method.**[2]

We start by letting profits equal some arbitrary but small dollar amount. For the Alpha Electronics problem, we may choose a profit of \$210. This is a profit level that can easily be obtained without violating either of the two constraints. The objective function can be written as $\$210 = 7X_1 + 5X_2$.

This expression is just the equation of a line; we call it an *iso-profit line*. It represents all combinations (of X_1, X_2) that would yield a total profit of \$210. To plot the profit line, we proceed exactly as we did to plot a constraint line. First, let $X_1 = 0$ and solve for the point at which the line crosses the X_2 axis.

$$\$210 = \$7(0) + \$5X_2$$
$$X_2 = 42 \text{ Wristmans}$$

Then let $X_2 = 0$ and solve for X_1.

$$\$210 = \$7X_1 + \$5(0)$$
$$X_1 = 30 \text{ Beltmusics}$$

We can now connect these two points with a straight line. This profit line is illustrated in Figure S6.4. All points on the line represent feasible solutions that produce a profit of \$210.

We see that the iso-profit line for \$210 does not produce the highest possible profit to the firm. In Figure S6.5, we try graphing two more lines, each yielding a higher profit. The middle equation, $\$280 = \$7X_1 + \$5X_2$, was plotted in the same fashion as the lower line. When $X_1 = 0$,

$$\$280 = \$7(0) + \$5X_2$$
$$X_2 = 56$$

FIGURE S6.4 ■ A Profit Line of \$210 Plotted for the Alpha Electronics Company

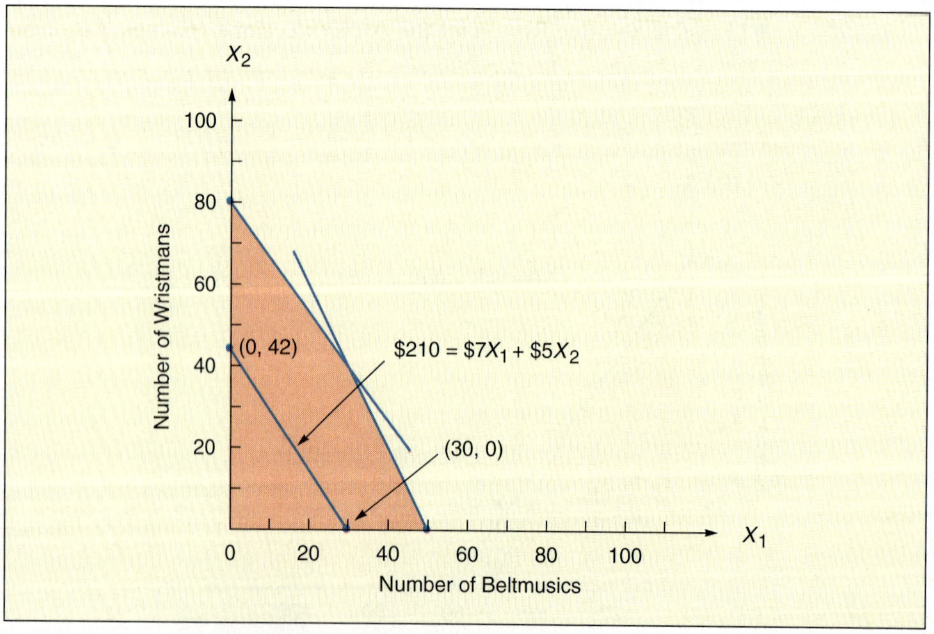

[2]*Iso* means "equal" or "similar." Thus, an iso-profit line represents a line with all profits the same, in this case \$210.

FIGURE S6.5 ■ Four Iso-Profit Lines Plotted for the Alpha Electronics Company

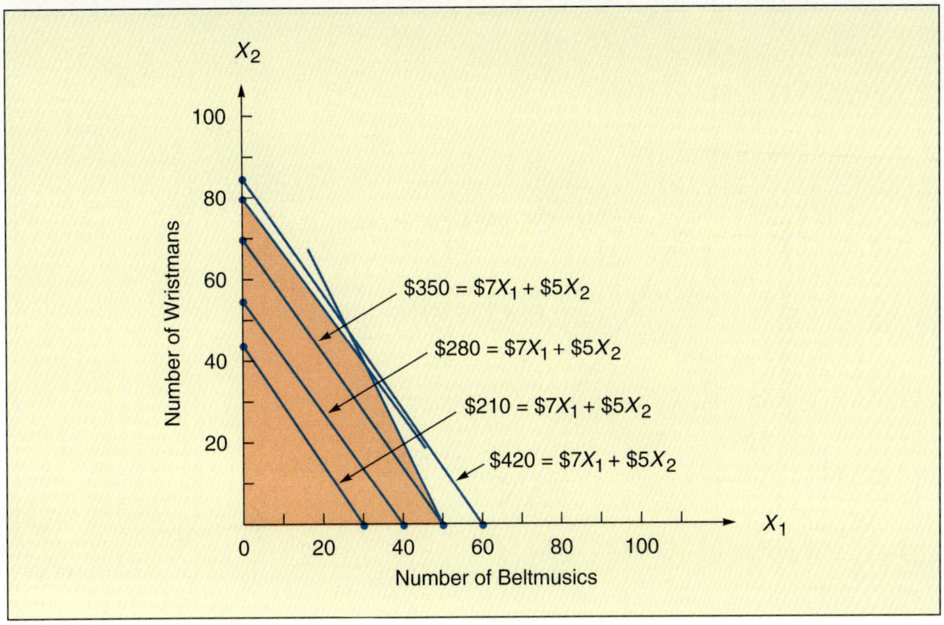

When $X_2 = 0$,

$$\$280 = \$7X_1 + \$5(0)$$
$$X_1 = 40$$

Again, any combination of Beltmusics (X_1) and Wristmans (X_2) on this iso-profit line will produce a total profit of $280.

Note that the third line generates a profit of $350, even more of an improvement. The farther we move from the 0 origin, the higher our profit will be. Another important point to note is that these iso-profit lines are parallel. We now have two clues as to how to find the optimal solution to the original problem. We can draw a series of parallel profit lines (by carefully moving our ruler in a plane parallel to the first profit line). The highest profit line that still touches some point of the feasible region will pinpoint the optimal solution. Notice that the fourth line ($420) is too high to count because it does not touch the feasible region.

The highest possible iso-profit line is illustrated in Figure S6.6. It touches the tip of the feasible region at the corner point ($X_1 = 30$, $X_2 = 40$) and yields a profit of $410.

Corner Point Solution Method

Corner point method

A second approach to solving linear programming problems employs the **corner point method**. This technique is simpler in concept than is the iso-profit line approach, but it involves looking at the profit at every corner point of the feasible region.

The mathematical theory behind linear programming states that an optimal solution to any problem (that is, the values of X_1, X_2 that yield the maximum profit) will lie at a *corner point*, or *extreme point*, of the feasible region. Hence, it is necessary

FIGURE S6.6 ■ Optimal Solution for the Alpha Electronics Problem

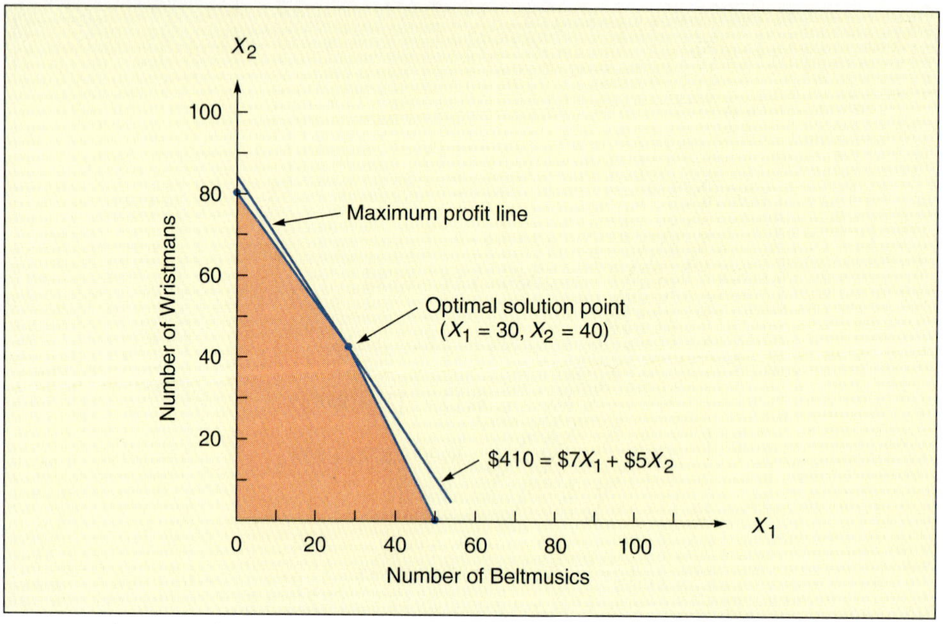

to find only the values of the variables at each corner; the maximum profit or optimal solution will lie at one (or more) of them.

Once again we can see (in Figure S6.7) that the feasible region for the Alpha Electronics Company problem is a four-sided polygon with four corner, or extreme, points. These points are labelled ①, ②, ③, and ④ on the graph. To find the (X_1, X_2) values producing the maximum profit, we find out what the coordinates of each corner point are and test their profit levels.

Point ①: $(X_1 = 0, X_2 = 0)$ Profit $\$7(0) + \$5(0) = \$0$
Point ②: $(X_1 = 0, X_2 = 80)$ Profit $\$7(0) + \$5(80) = \$400$
Point ④: $(X_1 = 50, X_2 = 0)$ Profit $\$7(50) + \$5(0) = \$350$

We skipped corner point ③ momentarily because in order to find *accurately* its coordinates, we will have to solve for the intersection of the two constraint lines. As you may recall from algebra, we can apply the method of *simultaneous equations* to the two constraint equations.

$$4X_1 + 3X_2 = 240 \quad \textit{(electronics line)}$$
$$2X_1 + 1X_2 = 100 \quad \textit{(assembly line)}$$

To solve these equations simultaneously, we multiply the second equation by –2:

$$-2(2X_1 + 1X_2 = 100) = -4X_1 - 2X_2 = -200$$

and then add it to the first equation:

$$\begin{array}{r} +4X_1 + 3X_2 = \ \ 240 \\ \underline{-4X_1 - 2X_2 = -200} \\ +1X_2 = \ \ \ 40 \end{array}$$

FIGURE S6.7 ■ The Four Corner Points of the Feasible Region

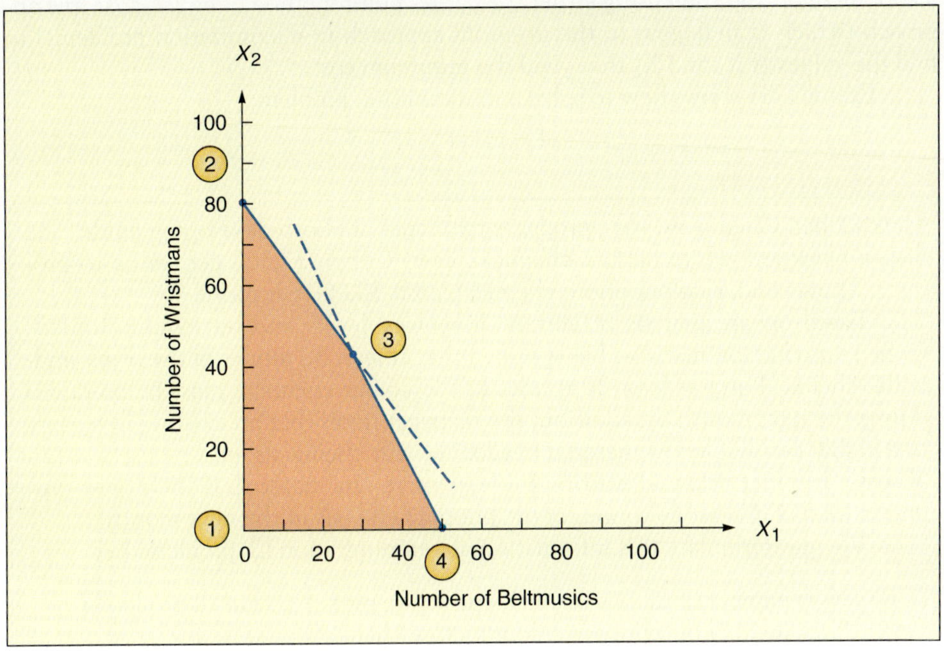

One of the early applications of LP is called the *diet problem*, which was originally used by hospitals to determine the most nutritious but economical diet for patients. Known in agricultural circles as the *feed mix problem*, the diet problem involves specifying a feed ingredient combination that will keep cows healthy. Dairy farmers find that they can use LP to minimize total feed cost, yet still provide a high protein diet that increases the efficiency of milk production in their cows.

or

$$X_2 = 40$$

Doing this has enabled us to eliminate one variable, X_1, and to solve for X_2. We can now substitute 40 for X_2 in either of the original equations and solve for X_1. Let us use the first equation. When $X_2 = 40$, then

$$4X_1 + 3(40) = 240$$
$$4X_1 + 120 = 240$$

or

$$4X_1 = 120$$
$$X_1 = 30$$

Thus, point ③ has the coordinates ($X_1 = 30$, $X_2 = 40$). We can compute its profit level to complete the analysis.

Point ③: $(X_1 = 30, X_2 = 40)$ Profit $= \$7(30) + \$5(40) = \$410$

Because point ③ produces the highest profit of any corner point, the product mix of $X_1 = 30$ Beltmusics and $X_2 = 40$ Wristmans is the optimal solution to Alpha Electronics' problem. This solution will yield a profit of \$410 per production period; it is the same solution we obtained using the iso-profit line method.

Solving Minimization Problems

Many linear programming problems involve *minimizing* an objective such as cost, instead of maximizing a profit function. A restaurant, for example, may wish to develop a work schedule to meet staffing needs while minimizing the total number of employees. Also, a manufacturer may seek to distribute its products from several factories to its many regional warehouses in such a way as to minimize total shipping costs.

Iso-cost

Minimization problems can be solved graphically by first setting up the feasible solution region and then using either the corner point method or an **iso-cost** line approach (which is analogous to the iso-profit approach in maximization problems) to find the values of X_1 and X_2 that yield the minimum cost.

Example S1 shows how to solve a minimization problem.

EXAMPLE S1

Mark Cohen Chemicals, Inc., produces two types of photo-developing fluids. The first, a black-and-white picture chemical, costs Cohen $2,500 per tonne to produce. The second, a colour photo chemical, costs $3,000 per tonne.

Based on an analysis of current inventory levels and outstanding orders, Cohen's production manager has specified that at least 30 tonnes of the black-and-white chemical and at least 20 tonnes of the colour chemical must be produced during the next month. In addition, the manager notes that an existing inventory of a highly perishable raw material needed in both chemicals must be used within 30 days. In order to avoid wasting the expensive raw material, Cohen must produce a total of at least 60 tonnes of the photo chemicals in the next month.

We may formulate this information as a minimization LP problem. Let

X_1 = number of tonnes of black-and-white picture chemical produced
X_2 = number of tonnes of colour picture chemical produced

Subject to:

$$X_1 \geq 30 \text{ tonnes of black-and-white chemical}$$
$$X_2 \geq 20 \text{ tonnes of colour chemical}$$
$$X_1 + X_2 \geq 60 \text{ tonnes total}$$
$$X_1, X_2 \geq 0 \text{ nonnegativity requirements}$$

To solve the Cohen Chemicals' problem graphically, we construct the problem's feasible region, shown in Figure S6.8.

FIGURE S6.8 ■ Cohen Chemical's Feasible Region

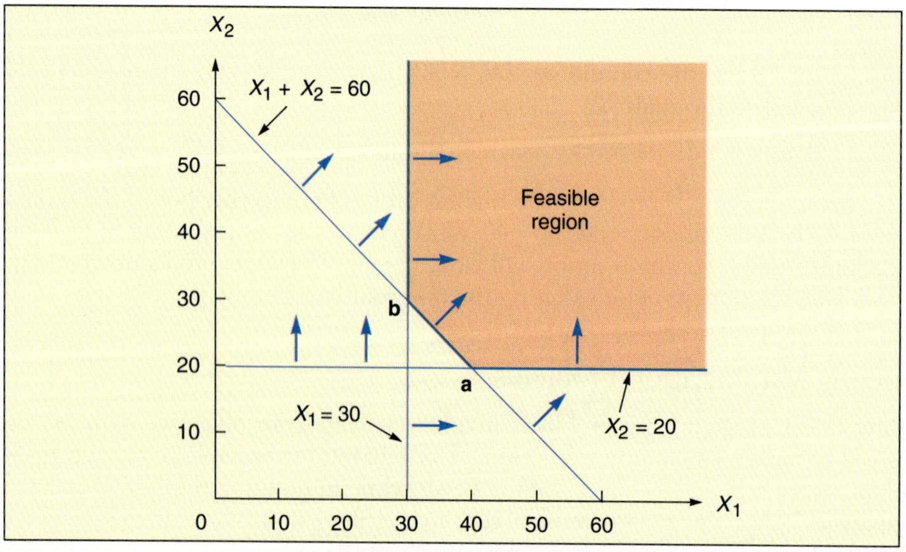

Minimization problems are often unbounded outward (that is, on the right side and on the top), but this characteristic causes no problem in solving them. As long as they are bounded inward (on the left side and the bottom), we can establish corner points. The optimal solution will lie at one of the corners.

In this case, there are only two corner points, **a** and **b** in Figure S6.8. It is easy to determine that at point **a**, $X_1 = 40$ and $X_2 = 20$ and that at point **b**, $X_1 = 30$ and $X_2 = 30$. The optimal solution is found at the point yielding the lowest total cost. Thus

$$\begin{aligned}\text{Total cost at } \mathbf{a} &= 2{,}500X_1 + 3{,}000X_2 \\ &= 2{,}500(40) + 3{,}000(20) \\ &= \$160{,}000 \\ \text{Total cost at } \mathbf{b} &= 2{,}500X_1 + 3{,}000X_2 \\ &= 2{,}500(30) + 3{,}000(30) \\ &= \$165{,}000\end{aligned}$$

The lowest cost to Mark Cohen Chemicals is at point **a**. Hence the production manager should produce 40 tonnes of the black-and-white chemical and 20 tonnes of the colour chemical.

THE SIMPLEX METHOD OF LP

Most real-world linear programming problems have more than two variables and thus are too complex for graphical solution. A procedure called the **simplex method** may be used to find the optimal solution to multivariable problems. The simplex method is actually an algorithm (or a set of instructions) with which we examine corner points in a methodical fashion until we arrive at the best solution—highest profit or lowest cost. Computer programs and spreadsheets (both described at the end of this supplement) are available to handle the simplex calculations for you. But you need to know what is involved behind the scenes in order to best understand their valuable outputs.

Simplex method

Converting the Constraints to Equations

The first step of the simplex method requires that we convert each inequality constraint in an LP formulation into an equation. Less-than-or-equal-to constraints (≤) can be converted to equations by adding *slack variables*, which represent the amount of an unused resource.

Earlier, we formulated the Alpha Electronics Company's product mix problem as follows, using linear programming:

$$\text{Maximize profit} = \$7X_1 + \$5X_2$$

Subject to LP constraints:

$$2X_1 + 1X_2 \leq 100$$
$$4X_1 + 3X_2 \leq 240$$

where X_1 equals the number of Beltmusics produced and X_2 equals the number of Wristmans produced.

To convert these inequality constraints to equalities, we add slack variables S_1 and S_2 to the left side of the inequality. The first constraint becomes

$$2X_1 + 1X_2 + S_1 = 100$$

and the second becomes

$$4X_1 + 3X_2 + S_2 = 240$$

To include all variables in each equation (a requirement of the next simplex step), we add slack variables not appearing in each equation with a coefficient of zero. The equations then appear as

$$2X_1 + 1X_2 + 1S_1 + 0S_2 = 100$$
$$4X_1 + 3X_2 + 0S_1 + 1S_2 = 240$$

Because slack variables represent unused resources (such as time on a machine or labour-hours available), they yield no profit, but we must add them to the objective function with zero profit coefficients. Thus, the objective function becomes

$$\text{Maximize profit} = \$7X_1 + \$5X_2 + \$0S_1 + \$0S_2$$

Setting Up the First Simplex Tableau

To simplify handling the equations and objective function in an LP problem, we put all of the coefficients into tabular form. We can express the preceding two constraint equations as:

SOLUTION MIX	X_1	X_2	S_1	S_2	QUANTITY (RHS)
S_1	2	1	1	0	100
S_2	4	3	0	1	240

The numbers (2, 1, 1, 0) and (4, 3, 0, 1) represent the coefficients of the first equation and second equation, respectively.

As in the earlier graphical approach, we begin the solution at the origin, where $X_1 = 0$, $X_2 = 0$, and profit = 0. The values of the two other variables, S_1 and S_2, then, must be nonzero. Because $2X_1 + 1X_2 + 1S_1 = 100$, we see that $S_1 = 100$. Likewise, $S_2 = 240$. These two slack variables make up the initial solution mix—as a matter of fact, their values are found in the quantity column across from each variable. Because X_1 and X_2 are not in the solution mix, their initial values are automatically equal to zero.

Some production-operations management books call this initial solution a *basic feasible solution* and describe it in vector, or column, form as

$$\begin{bmatrix} X_1 \\ X_2 \\ S_1 \\ S_2 \end{bmatrix} = \begin{bmatrix} 0 \\ 0 \\ 100 \\ 240 \end{bmatrix}$$

Variables in the solution mix, which is often called the *basis* in LP terminology, are referred to as *basic variables*. In this example, the basic variables are S_1 and S_2. Variables not in the solution mix—or basis—(X_1 and X_2, in this case) are called *nonbasic variables*.

Table S6.2 shows the complete initial simplex tableau for Alpha Electronics. The terms and rows that you have not seen before are as follows:

C_j: Profit contribution per unit of each variable. C_j applies to both the top row and first column. In the row, it indicates the unit profit for all variables in the LP objective function. In the column, C_j indicates the unit profit for each variable *currently* in the solution mix.

Z_j: In the quantity column, Z_j provides the total contribution (gross profit in this case) of the given solution. In the other columns (under the variables) it represents the gross profit *given up* by adding one unit of this variable into the current solution. The Z_j value for each column is found by multiplying the C_j of the row by the number in that row and *j*th column and summing.

The calculations for the values of Z_j in Table S6.2 are as follows:

$$Z_j \text{ (for column } X_1) = 0(2) + 0(4) = 0$$
$$Z_j \text{ (for column } X_2) = 0(1) + 0(3) = 0$$
$$Z_j \text{ (for column } S_1) = 0(1) + 0(0) = 0$$
$$Z_j \text{ (for column } S_2) = 0(0) + 0(1) = 0$$
$$Z_j \text{ (for total profit)} = 0(100) + 0(240) = 0$$

$C_j - Z_j$: This number represents the net profit (that is, the profit gained minus the profit given up), which will result from introducing one unit of each product (variable) into the solution. It is not calculated for the quantity column. To compute these numbers, we simply subtract the Z_j total from the C_j value at the very top of each variable's column.

The calculations for the net profit per unit ($C_j - Z_j$) row in this example are as follows:

	COLUMN			
	X_1	X_2	S_1	S_2
Cj for column	\$7	\$5	\$0	\$0
Zj for column	0	0	0	0
Cj – Zj for column	\$7	\$5	\$0	\$0

It was obvious to us when we computed a profit of \$0, that this initial solution was not optimal. Examining numbers in the $C_j - Z_j$ row of Table S6.2, we see that total profit can be increased by \$7 for each unit of X_1 (Beltmusics) and by \$5 for each unit of X_2 (Wristmans) added to the solution mix. A negative number in the $C_j - Z_j$ row would tell us that profits would *decrease* if the corresponding variable were added to the solution mix. An optimal solution is reached in the simplex method when the $C_j - Z_j$ row contains no positive numbers. Such is not the case in our initial tableau.

TABLE S6.2 ■ COMPLETED INITIAL SIMPLEX TABLEAU

$C_j \rightarrow$		\$7	\$5	\$0	\$0	
$\downarrow$	SOLUTION MIX	X_1	X_2	S_1	S_2	QUANTITY (RHS)
\$0	S_1	2	1	1	0	100
\$0	S_2	4	3	0	1	240
	Z_j	\$0	\$0	\$0	\$0	\$0
	$C_j - Z_j$	\$7	\$5	\$0	\$0	(total profit)

Simplex Solution Procedures

Once we have completed an initial tableau, we proceed through a series of five steps to compute all of the numbers we need for the next tableau. The calculations are not difficult, but they are sufficiently complex that the smallest arithmetic error can produce a very wrong answer.

We first list the five steps and then apply them in determining the second and third tableau for the data in the Alpha Electronics example.

1. Determine which variable to enter into the solution mix next. Identify the column—hence the variable—with the largest positive number in the $C_j - Z_j$ row of the previous tableau. This step means that we will now be producing some of the product contributing the greatest additional profit per unit.
2. Determine which variable to replace. Because we have just chosen a new variable to enter into the solution mix, we must decide which variable currently in the solution to remove to make room for it. To do so, we divide each amount in the quantity column by the corresponding number in the column selected in step 1. The row with the *smallest nonnegative number* calculated in this fashion will be replaced in the next tableau (this smallest number, by the way, gives the maximum number of units of the variable that we may place in the solution). This row is often referred to as the **pivot row**, and the column identified in step 1 is called the **pivot column**. The number at the intersection of the pivot row and pivot column is the **pivot number**.

Pivot row
Pivot column
Pivot number

3. Compute new values for the pivot row. To find them, we simply divide every number in the row by the *pivot number*.
4. Compute new values for each remaining row. (In our sample problems there have been only two rows in the LP tableau, but most larger problems have many more rows.) All remaining row(s) are calculated as follows:

$$\begin{pmatrix}\text{New row}\\\text{numbers}\end{pmatrix} = \begin{pmatrix}\text{numbers}\\\text{in old row}\end{pmatrix} - \left[\begin{pmatrix}\text{number in old row}\\\text{above or below}\\\text{pivot number}\end{pmatrix} \times \begin{pmatrix}\text{corresponding number in}\\\text{the new row, i.e., the row}\\\text{replaced in step 3}\end{pmatrix}\right]$$

5. Compute the Z_j and $C_j - Z_j$ rows, as demonstrated in the initial tableau. If all numbers in the $C_j - Z_j$ row are zero or negative, we have found an optimal solution. If this is not the case, we must return to step 1.

All of these computations are best illustrated by using an example. The initial simplex tableau computed in Table S6.2 is repeated below. We can follow the five steps just described to reach an optimal solution to the LP problem.

1st tableau

$C_j \rightarrow$ ↓		$7	$5	$0	$0		
	Solution Mix	**X_1**	**X_2**	**S_1**	**S_2**	**Quantity**	
$0	S_1	② (pivot number)	1	1	0	100	← pivot row
$0	S_2	4	3	0	1	240	
	Z_j	$0	$0	$0	$0	$0	
	$C_j - Z_j$	$7	$5	$0	$0	$0	
		↑ pivot column (maximum $C_j - Z_j$ values)					

Step 1. Variable X_1 enters the solution next because it has the highest contribution to profit value, $C_j - Z_j$. Its column becomes the pivot column.

Step 2. Divide each number in the quantity column by the corresponding number in the X_1 column: $100/2 = 50$ for the first row and $240/4 = 60$ for the second row. The smaller of these numbers—50—identifies the pivot row, the pivot number, and the variable to be replaced. The pivot row is identified above by an arrow, and the pivot number is circled. Variable X_1 replaces variable S_1 in the solution mix column, as shown in the second tableau.

Step 3. Replace the pivot row by dividing every number in it by the pivot number ($2/2 = 1$, $1/2 = 1/2$, $1/2 = 1/2$, $0/2 = 0$, $100/2 = 50$). This new version of the entire pivot row appears below.

C_j	**Solution Mix**	**X_1**	**X_2**	**S_1**	**S_2**	**Quantity**
$7	X_1	1	1/2	1/2	0	50

Step 4. Calculate the new values for the S_2 row.

$$\begin{pmatrix}\text{Number in}\\ \text{new } S_2 \text{ row}\end{pmatrix} = \begin{pmatrix}\text{number in}\\ \text{old } S_2 \text{ row}\end{pmatrix} - \left[\begin{pmatrix}\text{number below}\\ \text{pivot number}\\ \text{in old row}\end{pmatrix} \times \begin{pmatrix}\text{corresponding}\\ \text{number in the}\\ \text{new } X_1 \text{ row}\end{pmatrix}\right]$$

$$\begin{aligned}
0 &= 4 - [(4) \times (1)]\\
1 &= 3 - [(4) \times (1/2)]\\
-2 &= 0 - [(4) \times (1/2)]\\
1 &= 1 - [(4) \times (0)]\\
40 &= 240 - [(4) \times (50)]
\end{aligned}$$

C_j	SOLUTION MIX	X_1	X_2	S_1	S_2	QUANTITY
\$7	X_1	1	1/2	1/2	0	50
0	S_2	0	1	−2	1	40

Step 5. Calculate the Z_j and $C_j - Z_j$ rows.

Z_j (for X_1 column) $= \$7(1) + 0(0) = \$7$ $\quad C_j - Z_j = \$7 - \$7 = 0$
Z_j (for X_2 column) $= \$7(1/2) + 0(1) = \$7/2$ $\quad C_j - Z_j = \$5 - \$7/2 = \$3/2$
Z_j (for S_1 column) $= \$7(1/2) + 0(-2) = \$7/2$ $\quad C_j - Z_j = 0 - \$7/2 = -\$7/2$
Z_j (for S_2 column) $= \$7(0) + 0(1) = 0$ $\quad C_j - Z_j = 0 - 0 = 0$
Z_j (for total profit) $= \$7(50) + 0(40) = \$350$

2nd tableau

$C_j \rightarrow$ ↓		\$7	\$5	\$0	\$0		
	SOLUTION MIX	X_1	X_2	S_1	S_2	QUANTITY	
\$7	X_1	1	1/2	1/2	0	50	
\$0	S_2	0	① ↖ pivot number	−2	1	40	← pivot row
	Z_j	\$7	\$7/2	\$7/2	\$0	\$350 (total profit)	
	$C_j - Z_j$	\$0	\$3/2	−\$7/2	\$0		
			↑ pivot column				

Because not all numbers in the $C_j - Z_j$ row of this latest tableau are zero or negative, the solution (that is, $X_1 = 50$, $S_2 = 40$, $X_2 = 0$, $S_1 = 0$; profit = \$350) is not optimal; we then proceed to a third tableau and repeat the five steps.

Step 1. Variable X_2 enters the solution next because its $C_j - Z_j = 3/2$ is the largest (and only) positive number in the row. Thus, for every unit of X_2 that we start to produce, the objective function will increase in value by \$3/2, or \$1.50.

Step 2. The pivot row becomes the S_2 row because the ratio $40/1 = 40$ is smaller than the ratio $50/(\frac{1}{2}) = 100$.

Step 3. Replace the pivot row by dividing every number in it by the (circled) pivot number. Because every number is divided by one, there is no change.

Step 4. Compute the new values for the X_1 row.

$$\begin{pmatrix}\text{Number in}\\ \text{new } X_1 \text{ row}\end{pmatrix} = \begin{pmatrix}\text{number in}\\ \text{old } X_1 \text{ row}\end{pmatrix} - \left[\begin{pmatrix}\text{number above}\\ \text{pivot number}\end{pmatrix} \times \begin{pmatrix}\text{corresponding}\\ \text{number in the}\\ \text{new } X_2 \text{ row}\end{pmatrix}\right]$$

$$\begin{array}{ccccccc}
1 & = & 1 & - & [(1/2) & \times & (0)] \\
0 & = & 1/2 & - & [(1/2) & \times & (1)] \\
3/2 & = & 1/2 & - & [(1/2) & \times & (-2)] \\
-1/2 & = & 0 & - & [(1/2) & \times & (1)]
\end{array}$$

Step 5. Calculate the Z_j and $C_j - Z_j$ rows.

Z_j (for X_1 column) $= \$7(1) + \$5(0) = \$7$	$C_j - Z_j = \$7 - 7 = \$0$
Z_j (for X_2 column) $= \$7(0) + \$5(1) = \$5$	$C_j - Z_j = \$5 - 5 = \$0$
Z_j (for S_1 column) $= \$7(3/2) + \$5(-2) = \$1/2$	$C_j - Z_j = \$0 - 1/2 = -\$1/2$
Z_j (for S_2 column) $= \$7(-1/2) + \$5(1) = \$3/2$	$C_j - Z_j = \$0 - 3/2 = -\$3/2$
Z_j (for total profit) $= \$7(30) + \$5(40) = \$410$	

The results for the third and final tableau are seen in Table S6.3.

Because every number in the third tableau's $C_j - Z_j$ row is zero or negative, we have reached an optimal solution. That solution is: $X_1 = 30$ (Beltmusics), and $X_2 = 40$ (Wristmans), $S_1 = 0$ (slack in first resource), $S_2 = 0$ (slack in second resource), and profit = \$410.

Summary of Simplex Steps for Maximization Problems

The steps involved in using the simplex method to help solve an LP problem in which the objective function is to be maximized can be summarized as follows:

1. Choose the variable with the greatest positive $C_j - Z_j$ to enter the solution.
2. Determine the row to be replaced by selecting the one with the smallest (non-negative) ratio of quantity to pivot column.
3. Calculate the new values for the pivot row.
4. Calculate the new values for the other row(s).
5. Calculate the C_j and $C_j - Z_j$ values for this tableau. If there are any $C_j - Z_j$ numbers greater than zero, return to step 1.

Shadow Prices

A **shadow price** is the value of one additional unit of a resource in the form of one more hour of machine time, labour time, or other scarce resource. Exactly how much should a firm be willing to pay to make additional resources available? Is it worthwhile to pay workers an overtime rate to stay one extra hour each night in order to increase production output? Fortunately, such valuable management information is available to us in the final simplex tableau of an LP problem. An important property of the $C_j - Z_j$ row is that the *negatives of the numbers in its slack variable* (S_i) columns provide *shadow prices*.

Shadow price

TABLE S6.3 ■ THIRD AND FINAL TABLEAU

$C_j \rightarrow$ ↓		\$7	\$5	\$0	\$0	
	SOLUTION MIX	X_1	X_2	S_1	S_2	QUANTITY
\$7	X_1	1	0	3/2	--1/2	30
\$5	X_2	0	1	−2	1	40
	Z_j	\$7	\$5	\$1/2	\$3/2	\$410
	$C_j - Z_j$	\$0	\$0	−\$1/2	−\$3/2	

Table S6.3 indicates that the optimal solution to Alpha's problem is $X_1 = 30$ Beltmusics, $X_2 = 40$ Wristmans, $S_1 = 0$, $S_2 = 0$, and profit = \$410, where S_1 represents slack hours in the electronics department and S_2 represents slack or unused assembly department time.

Suppose Alpha is considering adding an extra assembler at a salary of \$5.00 per hour. Should the firm do so? The answer is *no*—the shadow price of the assembly department resource is only 50¢. Thus, the firm will lose \$4.50 for every hour the new assembler works.

Sensitivity Analysis

Sensitivity analysis

Shadow pricing is actually one form of **sensitivity analysis**, that is, the study of how sensitive the optimal solution would be to errors or changes in inputs to the LP problem. For example, if the manager at Alpha Electronics had been off by 100% in setting the net profit per Beltmusic at \$7, would that error drastically alter the decision to produce 30 Beltmusics and 40 Wristmans? What would be the impact of 265 electronic hours being available instead of 240?

Program S6.1 is part of the AB:POM computer-generated output available to help a decision maker know whether or not a solution is relatively insensitive to reasonable changes in one or more of the parameters of the problem. (The complete computer run for these data, including input and full output, is illustrated in Program S6.2 later in this supplement.)

First, let us consider changes to the right-hand side of a constraint. In Program S6.1, we assume changes are made in only one constraint at a time, while the other one remains fixed at its original values. *Right-hand side ranging* tells us over what range of right-hand side values the shadow prices for that constraint will remain valid. In the Alpha example, the \$1.50 shadow price for the electronic constraint will apply even if the current allowance of 240 hours drops as low as 200 or increases as high as 300.

This concept that the right-hand side range limits the shadow price is important in sensitivity analysis. Suppose Alpha Electronics could obtain additional electronic hours at a cost less than the shadow price. The question of how much to obtain is answered by the upper limit in Program S6.1, that is, secure 60 hours more than the current 240 hours.

PROGRAM S6.1 ■ Sensitivity Analysis for Alpha Electronics Using AB:POM

ALPHA ELECTRONICS EXAMPLE

Solution value = 410

Constraint	Shadow Prices		Original RHS	Lower Limit	Upper Limit
ASSEMBLY	0.50		100.00	80.00	120.00
ELECTRONIC	1.50		240.00	200.00	300.00

Variable	Optimal Value	Reduced Cost	Original Coef	Lower Limit	Upper Limit
BELTMUSICS	30.00	0.00	7.00	6.666667	10.00
WRISTMANS	40.00	0.00	5.00	3.50	5.25

Now let us look at changes in one of the objective function coefficients. Sensitivity analysis provides, for each decision variable in the solution, the range of profit values over which the answer will be the same. For example, the net profit of \$7 per Beltmusic (X_1) in the objective function could range from \$6.67 to \$10.00 without the final solution of $X_1 = 30$, $X_2 = 40$ changing. Of course, if a profit coefficient changed at all, the total profit of \$410 would change, even if the optimal quantities of X_1 and X_2 did not.

Artificial and Surplus Variables

Constraints in linear programming problems are seldom all of the "less-than-or-equal-to" (≤) variety seen in the examples thus far in this supplement. Just as common are "greater-than-or-equal-to" (≥) constraints and equalities. To use the simplex method, each of these also must be converted to a special form. If they are not, the simplex technique is unable to set an initial feasible solution in the first tableau. Example S2 shows how to convert such constraints.

EXAMPLE S2

The following constraints were formulated for an LP problem for the Claire Burns Publishing Company. We shall convert each constraint for use in the simplex algorithm.

Constraint 1. $25X_1 + 30X_2 = 900$. To convert an *equality*, we simply add an "artificial" variable (A_1) to the equation:

$$25X_1 + 30X_2 + A_1 = 900$$

An *artificial variable* is a variable that has no physical meaning in terms of a real-world LP problem. It simply allows us to create a basic feasible solution to start the simplex algorithm. An artificial variable is not allowed to appear in the final solution to the problem.

Constraint 2. $5X_1 + 13X_2 + 8X_3 \geq 2{,}100$. To handle ≥ constraints, a "surplus" variable (S_1) is first subtracted and then an artificial variable (A_2) is added to form a new equation:

$$5X_1 + 13X_2 + 8X_3 - S_1 + A_2 = 2{,}100$$

A **surplus variable** *does* have a physical meaning—it is the amount over and above a required minimum level set on the right-hand side of a greater-than-or-equal-to constraint. **Surplus variable**

Whenever an artificial or surplus variable is added to one of the constraints, it must also be included in the other equations and in the problem's objective function, just as was done for slack variables. Each artificial variable is assigned an extremely high cost to ensure that it does not appear in the final solution. Rather than set an actual dollar figure of \$10,000 or \$1 million, however, we simply use the symbol \$M to represent a very large number. Surplus variables, like slack variables, carry a zero cost. Example S3 shows how to figure in such variables.

EXAMPLE S3

The Montreal Chemical Corp. must produce 450 kilograms of a special mixture of phosphate and potassium for a customer. Phosphate costs $11 per kilogram and potassium costs $13 per kilogram. No more than 136 kilograms of phosphate can be used, and at least 68 kilograms of potassium must be used.

We wish to formulate this as a linear programming problem and to convert the constraints and objective function into the form needed for the simplex algorithm. Let

X_1 = number of kilograms of phosphate in the mixture
X_2 = number of kilograms of potassium in the mixture

Objective function: minimize cost = $\$11X_1 + \$13X_2$.
Objective function in simplex form:

$$\text{Minimize costs} = \$11X_1 + \$13X_2 + \$0S_1 + \$0S_2 + \$MA_1 + \$MA_2$$

Regular Form	Simplex Form
1st constraint: $1X_1 + 1X_2 = 450$	$1X_1 + 1X_2 \qquad +1A_1 = 450$
2nd constraint: $1X_1 \leq 136$	$1X_1 + 1S_1 = 136$
3rd constraint: $1X_2 \geq 68$	$1X_2 - 1S_2 + 1A_2 = 68$

Solving Minimization Problems

Now that you have worked a few examples of LP problems with the three different types of constraints, you are ready to solve a minimization problem using the simplex algorithm. Minimization problems are quite similar to the maximization problems tackled earlier in this supplement. The one significant difference involves the $C_j - Z_j$ row. Because our objective is now to minimize costs, the new variable to enter the solution in each tableau (the pivot column) will be the one with the *largest negative* number in the $C_j - Z_j$ row. Thus, we will be choosing the variable that decreases costs the most. In minimization problems, an optimal solution is reached when all numbers in the $C_j - Z_j$ row are *zero* or *positive*—just the opposite from the maximization case. All other simplex steps, as shown, remain the same.

1. Choose the variable with the largest negative $C_j - Z_j$ to enter the solution.
2. Determine the row to be replaced by selecting the one with the smallest (non-negative) quantity-to-pivot-column ratio.
3. Calculate new values for the pivot row.
4. Calculate new values for the other rows.
5. Calculate the $C_j - Z_j$ values for this tableau. If there are any $C_j - Z_j$ numbers less than zero, return to step 1.

SOLVING LP PROBLEMS BY COMPUTER

Large-scale LP problems, which you may be called on to formulate some day, could, with some long and careful computations, be solved by hand by following the steps of the simplex algorithm. It is, indeed, important to understand how that algorithm works. The only good way to master the algorithm is to solve several problems by hand. Once you comprehend the mechanics of the simplex technique, however, it should not be necessary to struggle with the manual method again.

All universities and most business and government organizations have access to programs that are capable of solving fairly large linear programming problems. Popular microcomputer software capable of handling these problems include such products as LINDO, STORM, QSB, and AB:POM.

KARMARKAR'S ALGORITHM

The biggest change in the field of linear programming solution techniques in four decades was the arrival in 1984 of an alternative to the simplex algorithm. Developed by Narendra Karmarkar, the new method, called Karmarkar's algorithm, often takes significantly less computer time to solve very-large-scale LP problems.[3]

As we saw, the simplex algorithm finds a solution by moving from one adjacent corner point to the next, following the outside edges of the feasible region. The major difference is that Karmarkar's method follows a path of points on the *inside* of the feasible region. Its uniqueness is its ability to handle an *extremely* large number of constraints and variables, giving LP users the capability to solve previously unsolvable problems. Although the simplex method will likely continue to be used for many LP problems, a new generation of LP software built around Karmarkar's algorithm is already being used.

SUMMARY

This chapter introduces a special kind of model, linear programming. LP has proven to be especially useful when trying to make the most effective use of an organization's resources.

The first step in dealing with LP models is problem formulation, which involves identifying and creating an objective function and constraints. The second step is to solve the problem. If there are only two decision variables, the problem can be solved graphically, using the corner point method or the iso-profit/iso-cost line method. With either approach, we first identify the feasible region, then find the corner point yielding the greatest profit or least cost.

All LP problems can also be solved with the simplex method, either by computer or by hand. This method is more complex mathematically than graphical LP, but it also produces such valuable economic information as shadow prices. LP is used in a wide variety of business applications, as the examples and homework problems in this chapter reveal.

[3]For details, see Narendra Karmarkar, "A New Polynomial Time Algorithm for Linear Programming," *Combinatorica*, 4, no. 4 (1984): 373–395; or J. N. Hooker, "Karmarkar's Linear Programming Algorithm," *Interfaces*, 16, no. 4 (July/August 1986): 75–90.

KEY TERMS

Linear programming (LP) (p. 241)
Objective function (p. 241)
Constraints (p. 241)
Iso-profit line method (p. 246)
Corner point method (p. 247)
Iso-cost (p. 250)
Simplex method (p. 251)
Pivot row (p. 254)
Pivot column (p. 254)
Pivot number (p. 254)
Shadow price (p. 257)
Sensitivity analysis (p. 258)
Surplus variable (p. 259)

USING AB:POM AND SPREADSHEETS TO SOLVE LP PROBLEMS

Using AB:POM's LP Module

AB:POM can handle linear programming problems with up to 99 constraints and 99 variables. Data entry and output for the Alpha Electronics example used earlier in this chapter are provided in Program S6.2. A nice feature of the program is that it allows us to give names to the variables (instead of just calling them X_1 and X_2) and to give names to the constraints.

As output, AB:POM provides optimal values for the variables, optimal cost/profit, shadow prices (duals), and sensitivity analysis. A further option on the LP module is the ability to "step through" the simplex tableau one at a time. This procedure allows us to observe changes in the solution from one iteration to the next. In addition, AB:POM provides graphical output for problems with only two variables, as shown in Program S6.3.

PROGRAM S6.2 ■ AB:POM's Computer Analysis of Alpha Electronics Data Including Optional Output of Tableaux

```
Data file: ALPHA                    Linear Programming                    Solution

Number of constraints (2-99) 2                    Number of variables (2-99) 2
maximize
--------------------------------------------------------------------------------

                           ALPHA ELECTRONICS EXAMPLE

Options ->           Step       Cmputr     PrtOFF

                BELTMUSICS  WRISTMANS            RHS
Objective                7          5                      Shadow
Electronics              4          3     ≤     240.00      1.50
Assembly                 2          1     ≤     100.00      0.50
Values ->            30.00      40.00          $410.00

                                  Phase 2    Iteration 3    0.38 seconds
--------------------------------------------------------------------------------
```

(continued)

PROGRAM S6.2 ■ AB:POM's Computer Analysis of Alpha Electronics Data Including Optional Output of Tableaux *(continued)*

F1 = Display solution table   F3 = Graph   F9 = Print   Esc

Press <Esc> key to continue or highlight key or function key for options

Iteration 1

	BELTMUSIC	WRISTMAN	slk 1	slk 2	RHS
maximize	− 7.00	− 5.00	0.00	0.00	0.00
slk 1	2.00	1.00	1.00	0.00	100.00
slk 2	4.00	3.00	0.00	1.00	240.00

Iteration 2

	BELTMUSIC	WRISTMAN	slk 1	slk 2	RHS
maximize	0.00	− 1.50	3.50	0.00	350.00
BELTMUSIC	1.00	0.50	0.50	0.00	50.00
slk 2	0.00	1.00	− 2.00	1.00	40.00

Iteration 3

	BELTMUSIC	WRISTMAN	slk 1	slk 2	RHS
maximize	0.00	0.00	0.50	1.50	410.00
BELTMUSIC	1.00	0.00	1.50	− 0.50	30.00
WRISTMAN	0.00	1.00	− 2.00	1.00	40.00

PROGRAM S6.3 ■ Alpha Electronics Optional Graphic Output

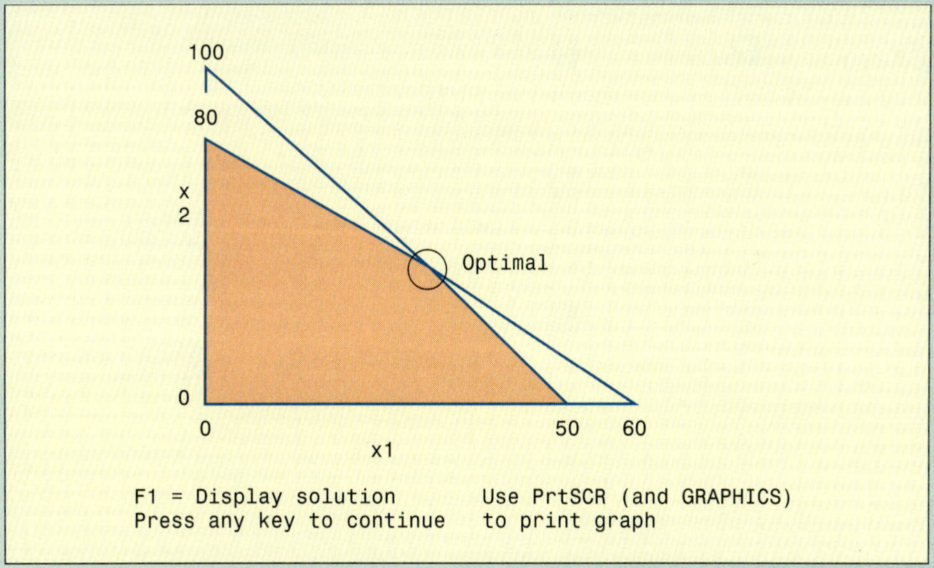

Using Spreadsheet Software

Program S6.4 shows a "symbolic spreadsheet" with each of the formulas needed to solve the Alpha Electronics LP problem. Known user-supplied numbers and labels are shown in appropriate cells. We see the profit contributions per Beltmusic ($7) and Wristman ($5) in cells B5 and C5, respectively.

The empty boxes in cells B4 and C4 are highlighted to draw your attention to them. In a what-if analysis (which is a major strength of the spreadsheet approach to LP) the user supplies values to these cells. The user can then see what effect different numbers of Beltmusics and Wristmans have on total profit (cell D6), total resource use (cells D9 and D12), and slack or unused resources (cells F9 and F12). Alternately, with a spreadsheet optimizing program such as What's Best!, the software finds the optimal values and places the answers in cells B4 and C4. Even if you do not have What's Best! available, you can still perform the what-if analysis in the spreadsheet by simply entering a series of values, using a trial-and-error approach, into cells B4 and C4.

PROGRAM S6.4 ■ Symbolic Spreadsheet (with Formulas) for Alpha Electronics Beltmusics and Wristmans

Value for number of Beltmusics to be supplied by user

Value for number of Wristmans to be supplied by user

	A	B	C	D	E	F
1	Alpha Company					
2						
3		Beltmusics	Wristmans	Total	Available	Slack
4	Quantity	[ ]	[ ]			
5	Unit Profit	7	5			
6	Profit Contrib	+B5*B4	+C5*C4	@SUM(B6..C6)		
7						
8	Unit Electronics	4	3			
9	Electronics Time	+B8*B4	+C8*C4	@SUM(B9..C9)	240	+E9–D9
10						
11	Unit Assembly	2	1			
12	Assembly Time	+B11*B4	+C11*C4	@SUM(B12..C12)	100	+E9–D9
13						
14						

SOLVED PROBLEMS

Solved Problem S6.1

Smitty's, a clothing manufacturer that produces men's shirts and pajamas, has two primary resources available: sewing-machine time (in the sewing department) and cutting-machine time (in the cutting department). Over the next month, Smitty can schedule up to 280 hours of work on sewing machines and up to 450 hours of work on cutting machines. Each shirt produced requires 1 hour of sewing time and 1.5 hours of cutting time. Outputting each pair of pajamas requires .75 hour of sewing time and 2 hours of cutting time.

To express the LP constraints for this problem mathematically, we let

X_1 = number of shirts produced
X_2 = number of pajamas produced

Solution

First Constraint: $1X_1 + .75X_2 \leq 280$ hours of sewing-machine time available—our first scarce resource

Second Constraint: $1.5X_1 + (2)X_2 \leq 450$ hours of cutting-machine time available—our second scarce resource

Note: This means that each pair of pajamas takes 2 hours of the cutting resource.

Smitty's accounting department analyzes cost and sales figures and states that each shirt produced will yield a \$4 contribution to profit and that each pair of pajamas will yield a \$3 contribution to profit.

This information can be used to create the LP *objective function* for this problem:

Objective function: maximize total contribution to profit = $\$4X_1 + \$3X_2$

Solved Problem S6.2

We want to solve the following LP problem for Failsafe Computers using the corner point method.

$$\text{Maximize profit} = \$9X_1 + \$7X_2$$
$$2X_1 + 1X_2 \leq 40$$
$$X_1 + 3X_2 \leq 30$$

Solution

Figure S6.9 illustrates these constraints.

Corner point **a**: $(X_1 = 0, X_2 = 0)$ Profit = 0

Corner point **b**: $(X_1 = 0, X_2 = 10)$ Profit $= 9(0) + 7(10) = \$70$

Corner point **d**: $(X_1 = 20, X_2 = 0)$ Profit $= 9(20) + 7(0) = \$180$

FIGURE S6.9 ■ Failsafe Computer Corp.'s Feasible Region

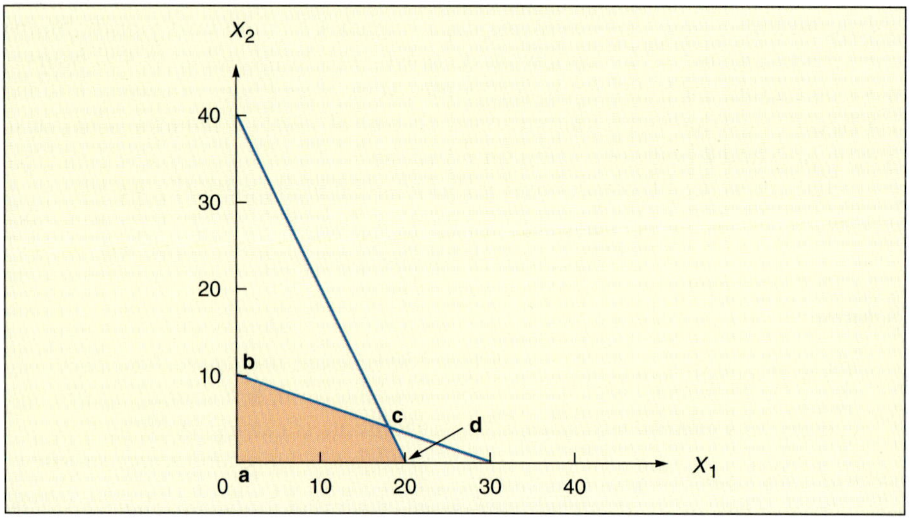

Corner point **c** is obtained by solving equations $2X_1 + 1X_2 = 40$ and $X_1 + 3X_2 = 30$ simultaneously. Multiply the second equation by –2 and add it to the first.

$$\begin{array}{r} 2X_1 + 1X_2 = 40 \\ \underline{-2X_1 - 6X_2 = -60} \\ -5X_2 = -20 \end{array}$$

Thus $X_2 = 4$.

$$X_1 + 3(X_2 = 4) = 30 \quad \text{or} \quad X_1 + 12 = 30 \quad \text{or} \quad X_1 = 18$$

Corner point **c**: $(X_1 = 18, X_2 = 4)$ Profit $= 9(18) + 7(4) = \$190$

Hence the optimal solution is

$$(X_1 = 18, X_2 = 4) \qquad \text{Profit} = \$190$$

Solved Problem S6.3

The Holiday Meal Turkey Ranch is considering buying two different types of turkey feed. Each feed contains, in varying proportions, some or all of the three nutritional ingredients essential for fattening turkeys. Brand Y feed costs the ranch \$.02 per pound. Brand Z costs \$.03 per pound. The rancher would like to determine the lowest-cost diet that meets the minimum monthly intake requirement for each nutritional ingredient.

The following table contains relevant information about the composition of Brand Y and Brand Z feeds, as well as the minimum monthly requirement for each nutritional ingredient per turkey.

	Composition of Each Pound of Feed		
Ingredient	Brand Y Feed	Brand Z Feed	Minimum Monthly Requirement
A	5 oz	10 oz	90 oz
B	4 oz	3 oz	48 oz
C	.5 oz	0	1.5 oz
Cost/lb.	$.02	$.03	

Solution

If we let

X_1 = number of pounds of Brand Y feed purchased
X_2 = number of pounds of Brand Z feed purchased

then we may proceed to formulate this linear programming problem as follows:

$$\text{Minimize cost (in cents)} = 2X_1 + 3X_2$$

subject to these constraints:

$$5X_1 + 10X_2 \geq 90 \text{ ounces} \quad \textit{(ingredient A constraint)}$$
$$4X_1 + 3X_2 \geq 48 \text{ ounces} \quad \textit{(ingredient B constraint)}$$
$$\tfrac{1}{2}X_1 \geq 1\tfrac{1}{2} \text{ ounces} \quad \textit{(ingredient C constraint)}$$

Figure S6.10 illustrates these constraints.

FIGURE S6.10 ■ Feasible Region for the Holiday Meal Turkey Ranch Problem

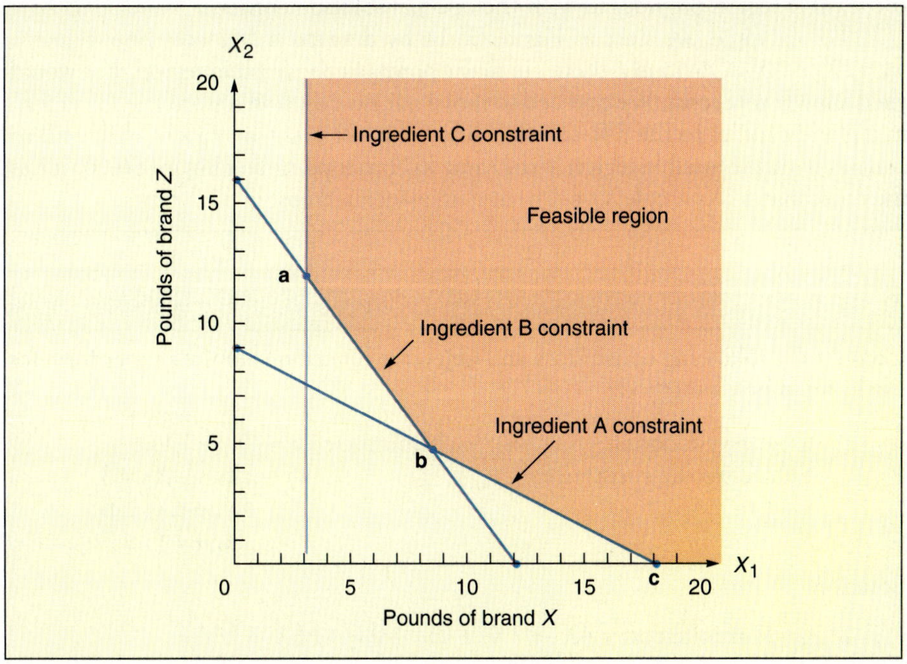

FIGURE S6.11 ■ Graphical Solution to the Holiday Meal Turkey Ranch Problem Using the Iso-Cost Line. Note that the last line parallel to the 54¢ iso-cost line that touches the feasible region indicates the optimal corner point.

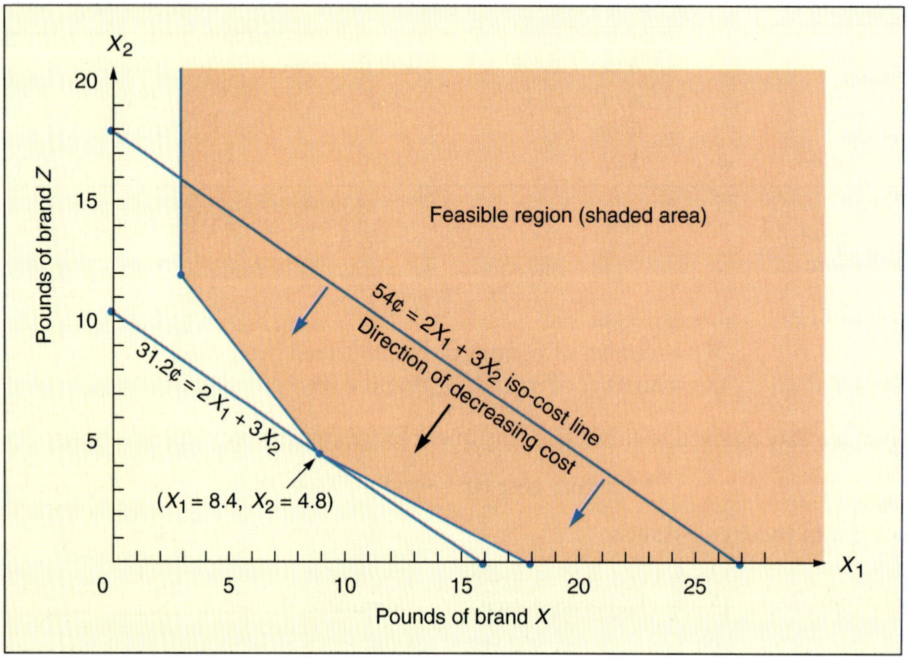

The iso-cost line approach may be used to solve LP minimization problems such as that of the Holiday Meal Turkey Ranch. As with iso-profit lines, we need not compute the cost at each corner point, but instead draw a series of parallel cost lines. The lowest cost line (that is, the one closest in toward the origin) to touch the feasible region provides us with the optimal solution corner.

For example, we start in Figure S6.11 by drawing a 54¢ cost line, namely, $54 = 2X_1 + 3X_2$. Obviously, there are many points in the feasible region that would yield a lower total cost. We proceed to move our iso-cost line toward the lower left, in a plane parallel to the 54¢ solution line. The last point we touch while still in contact with the feasible region is the same as corner point **b** of Figure S6.10. It has the coordinates ($X_1 = 8.4, X_2 = 4.8$) and an associated cost of 31.2 cents.

Solved Problem S6.4

Convert the following constraints and objective function into the proper form for use in the simplex method.

Objective function:	Minimize cost $= 4X_1 + 1X_2$
Subject to the constraints:	$3X_1 + X_2 = 3$
	$4X_1 + 3X_2 \geq 6$
	$X_1 + 2X_2 \leq 3$

Solution

$$\text{Minimize cost} = 4X_1 + 1X_2 + 0S_1 + 0S_2 + MA_1 + MA_2$$

$$\begin{aligned} \text{Subject to:} \quad & 3X_1 + 1X_2 \quad\quad\quad\quad + 1A_1 \quad\quad\quad = 3 \\ & 4X_1 + 3X_2 - 1S_1 \quad\quad\quad\quad + 1A_2 = 6 \\ & 1X_1 + 2X_2 \quad\quad + 1S_2 \quad\quad\quad\quad = 3 \end{aligned}$$

DISCUSSION QUESTIONS

1. Discuss the similarities and differences between minimization and maximization problems, using the graphical solution approach of linear programming.
2. It has been said that each linear programming problem that has a feasible region has an infinite number of solutions. Explain.
3. The production manager of a large manufacturing firm once made this statement: "I should like to use linear programming, but it's a technique that operates under conditions of certainty. My plant doesn't have that certainty; it's a world of uncertainty. So LP can't be used here." Do you think this statement has any merit? Explain why the manager may have made it.
4. Should people who will be using the results of a new quantitative model such as linear programming become involved in the technical aspects of the problem-solving procedure?
5. C. W. Churchman once said "mathematics . . . tends to lull the unsuspecting into believing that he who thinks elabourately thinks well." Do you think that the best models are the ones that are the most elabourate and complex mathematically? Why?
6. Explain the purpose and procedures of the simplex method.
7. How do the graphic and simplex methods of solving linear programming problems differ? In what ways are they the same? Under what circumstances would you prefer to use the graphic approach?
8. What are the simplex rules for selecting the pivot column? The pivot row? The pivot number?
9. A particular linear programming problem has the following objective function:

   $$\text{Maximize profit} = \$8X_1 + \$6X_2 + \$12X_3 - \$2X_4$$

   Which variable should enter at the second simplex tableau? If the objective function was

   $$\text{Minimize cost} = \$2.5X_1 + \$2.9X_2 + \$4.0X_3 + \$7.9X_4$$

   which variable would be the best candidate to enter the second tableau?
10. To solve a problem by the simplex method, when are slack variables added?
11. What is a shadow price?
12. Explain how to use the iso-profit line in a graphical maximization problem.
13. Explain how to use the iso-cost line in a graphical minimization problem.
14. Compare how the corner point and iso-profit line methods work for solving graphical problems.
15. Define the feasible region of a graphical LP problem. What is a feasible solution?
16. What are the properties of all LP problems?
17. List the steps in a simplex maximization problem.
18. What is a surplus variable? What is an artificial variable?

CRITICAL THINKING EXERCISE

One of the many areas of LP application is called the diet problem. Because many people who eat at McDonald's are concerned about how nutritionally complete their diet is, your assignment is to construct a daily diet that (1) meets the nutritional standards shown in the next paragraph, (2) is made up entirely of foods from McDonald's, and (3) is provided at the least cost. To complete this project, you will also need a copy of "McDonald's Food: the Facts," available at your local store or by calling the restaurant's Nutritional Information Centre at 416-443-1000.

Your diet should provide at least 100% of the U.S. RDA of vitamins A, C, B_1, B_2, niacin, calcium, and iron; supply at least 55 grams of protein; contain at most 3 grams of sodium; and obtain at most 30% of its calories from fat (each gram of fat contains 9 calories). Choose at least 10 foods from the McDonald's menu in formulating your LP problem.

PROBLEMS

• **S6.1** Ray Christiansen is trying to determine how many units of two cordless telephones to produce each day. One of these is the standard model; the other is the deluxe model. The profit per unit on the standard model is $40; the profit per unit on the deluxe model is $60. Each unit requires 30 minutes of assembly time. The standard requires 10 minutes of inspection time; the deluxe model requires 15 minutes of inspection time. The company must fill an order for six standard phones. There are 450 minutes of assembly time and 180 minutes of inspection time available each day. How many units of each product should be manufactured to maximize profits?

• **S6.2** Solve the following linear programming problem, using the corner point method.

$$\begin{aligned} \text{Maximize} \quad & X + 10Y \\ \text{subject to:} \quad & 4X + 3Y \leq 36 \\ & 2X + 4Y \leq 40 \\ & Y \geq 3 \\ & X, Y \geq 0 \end{aligned}$$

• **S6.3** Solve the following linear programming problem, using the corner point method.

$$\begin{aligned} \text{Maximize} \quad & 3X + 5Y \\ \text{subject to:} \quad & 4X + 4Y \leq 48 \\ & 1X + 2Y \leq 20 \\ & Y \geq 2 \\ & X, Y \geq 0 \end{aligned}$$

: **S6.4** Consider the following linear programming problem:

$$\begin{aligned} \text{Maximize} \quad & Z = 30X_1 + 10X_2 \\ \text{subject to:} \quad & 3X_1 + X_2 \leq 300 \\ & X_1 + X_2 \leq 200 \\ & X_1 \leq 100 \\ & X_2 \geq 50 \\ & X_1 - X_2 \leq 0 \\ & X_1, X_2 \geq 0 \end{aligned}$$

a) Solve the problem graphically.

b) Is there more than one optimal solution? Explain.

• **S6.5** Suppose a linear programming (maximization) problem has been solved and the optimal value of the objective function is $300. Suppose an additional constraint is added to this problem. Explain how this might affect each of the following:

a) the feasible region

b) the optimal value of the objective function

: **S6.6** John Bragg's Dog Food Company wishes to introduce a new brand of dog biscuits composed of chicken- and liver-flavoured biscuits that meet certain nutritional requirements. The liver-flavoured biscuits contain 1 unit of nutrient A and 2 units of nutrient B; the chicken-flavoured ones contain 1 unit of nutrient A and 4 units of nutrient B. According to federal requirements there must be at least 40 units of nutrient A and 60 units of nutrient B in a package of the new mix. In addition, the company has decided that there can be no more than 15 liver-flavoured biscuits in a package. If it costs 1 cent to make a liver-flavoured biscuit and 2 cents to make a chicken-flavoured one, what is the optimal product mix for a package of the biscuits in order to minimize the firm's cost?

a) Formulate this as a linear programming problem.

b) Solve this problem graphically, giving the optimal values of all variables.

c) What is the total cost of a package of dog biscuits using the optimal mix?

• **S6.7** The Electrocomp Corporation manufactures two electrical products: air conditioners and large fans. The assembly process for each is similar in that both require a certain amount of wiring and drilling. Each air conditioner takes 3 hours of wiring and 2 hours of drilling. Each fan must go through 2 hours of wiring and 1 hour of drilling. During the next production period, 240 hours of wiring time are available and up to 140 hours of drilling time may be used. Each air conditioner sold yields a profit of $25. Each fan assembled may be sold for a $15 profit.

Formulate and solve this LP production-mix situation and find the best combination of air conditioners and fans that yields the highest profit. Use the corner point graphical approach.

• **S6.8** The Greg Duncan Tub Company manufactures two lines of bathtubs, called Model A and Model B. Every tub requires blending a certain amount of steel and zinc; the company has available a total of 25,000 kilograms of steel and 6,000 kilograms of zinc. Each Model A bathtub requires a mixture of 125 kilograms of steel and 20 kilograms of zinc, and each yields a profit to the firm of $90. Each Model B tub produced can be sold for a profit of $70; it in turn requires 100 kilograms of steel and 30 kilograms of zinc.

Find by graphical linear programming the best production mix of bathtubs.

• **S6.9** The Outdoor Furniture Corporation manufactures two products, benches and picnic tables, for use in yards and parks. The firm has two main resources: its carpenters (labour force) and a supply of redwood for use in the furniture. During the next production cycle, 1,200 hours of labour are available under a union agreement. The firm also has a stock of 3,500 board feet of quality redwood. Each bench that Outdoor Furniture produces requires 4 labour-hours and 10 board feet of redwood; each picnic table takes 6 labour-hours and 35 board feet of redwood. Completed benches will yield a profit of $9 each, and tables will result in a profit of $20 each. How many benches and tables should Outdoor Furniture produce in order to obtain the largest possible profit? Use the graphical linear programming approach.

• **S6.10** MSA Computer Corporation manufactures two models of minicomputers, the Alpha 4 and the Beta 5. The firm employs five technicians, working 160 hours each per month, on its assembly line. Management insists that full employment (that is, *all* 160 hours of time) be maintained for each worker during next month's operations. It requires 20 labour-hours to assemble each Alpha 4 computer and 25 labour-hours to assemble each Beta 5 model. MSA wants to see at least 10 Alpha 4's and at least 15 Beta 5's produced during the production period. Alpha 4's generate a $1,200 profit per unit, and Beta's yield $1,800 each.

Determine the most profitable number of each model of minicomputer to produce during the coming month.

• **S6.11** Solve the following linear programming problem, using the corner point graphic method:

$$\begin{aligned} \text{Maximize profit} &= 4X_1 + 4X_2 \\ \text{Subject to: } 3X_1 + 5X_2 &\le 150 \\ X_1 - 2X_2 &\le 10 \\ 5X_1 + 3X_2 &\le 150 \\ X_1, X_2 &\ge 0 \end{aligned}$$

• **S6.12** Consider this linear programming formulation:

$$\begin{aligned} \text{Minimize cost} &= \$1X_1 + \$2X_2 \\ \text{Subject to: } X_1 + 3X_2 &\ge 90 \\ 8X_1 + 2X_2 &\ge 160 \\ 3X_1 + 2X_2 &\ge 120 \\ X_2 &\le 70 \end{aligned}$$

a) Graphically illustrate the feasible region and apply the iso-cost line procedure to indicate which corner point produces the optimal solution.

b) What is the cost of this solution?

• S6.13 Develop your own individual set of constraint equations and inequalities and use them to illustrate graphically each of the following conditions:

a) An "unbounded" problem. That is, a problem that has no constraints forcing profit limitation.

b) An "infeasible" problem. That is, a problem that has no solution, but satisfies all of the constraints.

c) A problem containing redundant constraints. That is, a problem that has one or more constraints that do not affect the solution.

• S6.14 The mathematical relationships that follow were formulated by an operations research analyst at the Jennifer Black Chemical Company. Which ones are invalid for use in a linear programming problem, and why?

$$
\begin{aligned}
\text{Maximize profit} &= 4X_1 + 3X_1X_2 + 5X_3 \\
\text{Subject to:} \quad 2X_1X_2 + 2X_3 &\leq 50 \\
8X_1 - 4X_2 &\geq 6 \\
1.5X_1 + 6X_2 + 3X_3 &\geq 21 \\
19X_2 - \tfrac{1}{3}X_3 &= 17 \\
5X_1 + 4X_2 + 3\sqrt{X_3} &\leq 80 \\
-X_1 - X_2 + X_3 &= 5
\end{aligned}
$$

: S6.15 Paul Feyen Corp. makes three products, and it has three machines available as resources as given in the following LP problem.

$$
\begin{aligned}
\text{Maximize profit} &= 4X_1 + 4X_2 + 7X_3 \\
\text{Subject to:} \quad 1X_1 + 7X_2 + 4X_3 &\leq 100 \text{ (hours on machine 1)} \\
2X_1 + 1X_2 + 7X_3 &\leq 110 \text{ (hours on machine 2)} \\
8X_1 + 4X_2 + 1X_3 &\leq 100 \text{ (hours on machine 3)}
\end{aligned}
$$

a) Determine the optimal solution.

b) Is there unused time available on any of the machines with the optimal solution?

: S6.16 Using the data from Paul Feyen Corp. in Problem S6.15, determine:

a) What would it be worth to the firm to make an additional hour of time available on the third machine?

b) How much would the firm's profit increase if an extra ten hours of time were made available on the second machine at no extra cost?

: S6.17 The Denise Davis Mfg. Corp. has $250,000 available to invest for 12 months prior to its plant expansion. The money can be placed in treasury bills yielding an 8% return or in municipal bonds at an average rate of 9%. Management requires that at least 50% of the investment be placed in treasury bills. Because of defaults in municipal bonds, it is decided that no more than 40% of the investment be placed in bonds.

How much should be invested in each security to maximize return on investment?

: S6.18 Malek Furniture manufactures two different types of china cabinets, a French provincial model and a Danish modern model. Each cabinet produced must go through three departments: carpentry, painting, and finishing. The accompanying table contains all relevant information concerning production times per cabinet produced and production capacities for each operation per day, along with net revenue per unit produced. The firm has a contract with a distributor to produce a minimum of 300 of each cabinet per week (or 60 cabinets per day). Owner Tom Malek would like to determine a product mix to maximize his daily revenue.

Cabinet Style	Carpentry (hr/cabinet)	Painting (hr/cabinet)	Finishing (hr/cabinet)	Net Revenue/ Cabinet
French provincial	3	1½	¾	$28
Danish modern	2	1	¾	$25
Department capacity (hours)	360	200	125	

Formulate this as a linear programming problem and solve.

:S6.19 The famous Sylvia Bonadio Restaurant is open 24 hours a day. Servers report for duty at 3 A.M., 7 A.M., 11 A.M., 3 P.M., 7 P.M., or 11 P.M., and each works an 8-hour shift. The following table shows the minimum number of workers needed during the six periods into which the day is divided.

Period	Time	Number of Servers Required
1	3 A.M.– 7 A.M.	3
2	7 A.M.–11 A.M.	12
3	11 A.M.– 3 P.M.	16
4	3 P.M.– 7 P.M.	9
5	7 P.M.–11 P.M.	11
6	11 P.M.– 3 A.M.	4

Bonadio's scheduling problem is to determine how many servers should report for work at the start of each time period in order to minimize the total staff required for 1 day's operation. (*Hint:* Let X_i equal the number of servers beginning work in time period i, where $i = 1, 2, 3, 4, 5, 6$.)

:S6.20 This is the slack time of year at JES, Inc. JES, Inc., would actually like to shut down the plant, but if the company laid off its core employees, they would probably go to work for a competitor. JES, Inc., could keep its core (full-time, year-round) employees busy by making 10,000 round tables per month, or by making 20,000 square tables per month (or some ratio thereof). JES, Inc., does, however, have a contract with a supplier to buy precut table tops for a minimum of 5,000 square tables per month. Handling and storage costs per round table will be $10; these costs would be $8 per square table.

Draw a graph, algebraically describe the constraint inequalities and the objective function, identify the points bounding the feasible solution area, and find the cost at each point and the optimum solution. Let X_1 equal the thousands of round tables per month and X_2 equal the thousands of square tables per month.

:S6.21 Each coffee table produced by John Alessi Designers nets the firm a profit of $9. Each bookcase yields a $12 profit. Alessi's firm is small and its resources limited. During any given production period (of one week), 38 litres of varnish and 12 lengths of high-quality redwood are available. Each coffee table requires approximately 3.8 litres of varnish and 1 length of redwood. Each bookcase takes 3.8 litres of varnish and 2 lengths of wood.

Formulate Alessi's production mix decision as a linear programming problem, and solve, using the simplex method. How many tables and bookcases should be produced each week? What will the maximum profit be?

:S6.22 **a)** Set up an initial simplex tableau, given the following two constraints and objective function:

$$1X_1 + 4X_2 \leq 24$$
$$1X_1 + 2X_2 \leq 16$$
$$\text{Maximize profit} = \$3X_1 + \$9X_2$$

You will have to add slack variables.

b) Briefly list the iterative steps necessary to solve the problem in part (a).

c) Determine the next tableau from the one you developed in part (a). Determine whether or not it is an optimum solution.

d) If necessary, develop another tableau and determine whether or not it is an optimum solution. Interpret this tableau.

e) Start with the same initial tableau from part (a) but use X_1 as the first pivot column. Continue to iterate it (a total of twice) until you reach an optimum solution.

:S6.23 Solve the following linear programming problem graphically. Then set up a simplex tableau and solve the problem, using the simplex method. Indicate the corner points generated at each iteration by the simplex on your graph.

$$\begin{aligned} \text{Maximize profit} &= \$3X_1 + \$5X_2 \\ \text{Subject to:} \quad X_2 &\le 6 \\ 3X_1 + 2X_2 &\le 18 \\ X_1, X_2 &\ge 0 \end{aligned}$$

:S6.24 Solve the following linear programming problem, first graphically and then by the simplex algorithm.

$$\begin{aligned} \text{Minimize cost} &= 4X_1 + 5X_2 \\ \text{Subject to:} \quad X_1 + 2X_2 &\ge 80 \\ 3X_1 + X_2 &\ge 75 \\ X_1, X_2 &\ge 0 \end{aligned}$$

What are the values of the basic variables at each iteration? Which are the nonbasic variables at each iteration?

:S6.25 Barrow Distributors packages and distributes industrial supplies. A standard shipment can be packaged in a Class A container, a Class K container, or a Class T container. A single Class A container yields a profit of \$8; a Class K container, a profit of \$6; and a Class T container, a profit of \$14. Each shipment prepared requires a certain amount of packing material and a certain amount of time.

RESOURCES NEEDED PER STANDARD SHIPMENT

CLASS OF CONTAINER	PACKING MATERIAL (KILOGRAMS)	PACKING TIME (HOURS)
A	2	2
K	1	6
T	3	4
Total amount of resource available each week	120 kilograms	240 hours

Joe Barrow, head of the firm, must decide the optimal number of each class of container to pack each week. He is bound by the previously mentioned resource restrictions but also decides that he must keep his six full-time packers employed all 240 hours (6 workers × 40 hours) each week.

Formulate and solve this problem, using the simplex method.

:S6.26 Set up a complete initial tableau for the data (repeated below) that were first presented in Solved Problem S6.4.

$$\text{Minimize cost} = 4X_1 + 1X_2 + 0S_1 + 0S_1 + MA_1 + MA_2$$

Subject to:

$$\begin{array}{llll} 3X_1 + 1X_2 & & + 1A_1 & & = 3 \\ 4X_1 + 3X_2 - 1S_2 & & & + 1A_2 & = 6 \\ 1X_1 + 2X_2 & + 1S_2 & & & = 3 \end{array}$$

a) Which variable will enter the solution next?

b) Which variable will leave the solution?

:S6.27 Solve Problem S6.26 for the optimal solution, using the simplex method.

:S6.28 Using the data from Problem S6.7 and LP software:

a) Determine the range within which the unit profit contribution of an air conditioner must fall for the current solution to remain optimal.

b) Determine the shadow price for the wiring constraint and range within which that value holds.

:S6.29 Using the data from Problem S6.8 and LP software:

a) Determine the range within which the unit profit contribution of a Model A tub must fall for the current solution to remain optimal.

b) Determine by how much the unit profit contribution of a Model B tub must increase before it would be desirable to produce any of them.

c) Determine the shadow price for the steel constraint and the range within which that value holds.

d) Determine the shadow price for the zinc constraint and the range within which that value holds.

:S6.30 Using the data from Problem S6.20 and LP software:

a) Determine the range within which the unit cost of a square table must fall for the current solution to remain optimal.

b) Determine the shadow price for the labour constraint and the range within which that value holds.

c) Determine the shadow price for the contract constraint and the range within which that value holds.

:S6.31 John DeBruzzi, the advertising director for Diversey Paint and Supply, a chain of four retail stores, is considering two media possibilities. One plan is for a series of half-page ads in the Sunday newspaper, and the other is for advertising time on TV. The stores are expanding their lines of do-it-yourself tools, and the advertising director is interested in an exposure level of at least 40% within the city's neighbourhoods and 60% in northwest suburban areas.

The TV viewing time under consideration has an exposure rating per spot of 5% in city homes and 3% in the northwest suburbs. The Sunday newspaper has corresponding exposure rates of 4% and 3% per ad. The cost of a half-page newspaper advertisement is $925; a television spot costs $2000.

Diversey Paint would like to select the least costly advertising strategy that would meet desired exposure levels. Formulate and solve this LP problem.

:S6.32 Bill Bilderback Manufacturing has three factories (1, 2, and 3) and three warehouses (A, B, and C). The diagram below shows the shipping costs between each factory and warehouse, the factory manufacturing capabilities (in 1000's) and the warehouse capacities (in 1000's). Write the objective function and the constraint inequations. Let X1A = 1000's of units shipped from factory 1 to warehouse A, et cetera.

FROM \ TO	A	B	C	PRODUCTION CAPABILITY
Factory 1	$ 6	$ 5	$ 3	6
Factory 2	$ 8	$10	$ 8	8
Factory 3	$11	$14	$18	10
Capacity	7	12	5	

S6.33 Andy's Bicycle Company (ABC) has the hottest new product on the upscale toy market—boys' and girls' bikes in bright fashion colours, with oversized hubs and axles, shell design safety tires, a strong padded frame, chrome-plated chains, brackets, and valves, and a nonslip handlebar. Due to the seller's market for high-quality toys for the newest baby boomers, ABC can sell all the bicycles it manufactures at the following prices: boys' bikes—$220, girls' bikes—$175. This is the price payable to ABC at its Fredericton plant.

The firm's accountant has determined that direct labour costs will be 45% of the price ABC receives for the boys' model and 40% of the price received for the girls' model. Production costs other than labour, but excluding painting and packaging, are $44 per boys' bicycle and $30 per girls' bicycle. Painting and packaging are $20 per bike, regardless of model.

The Fredericton plant's overall production capacity is 390 bicycles per day. Each boys' bike requires 2.5 labour-hours, each girls' model takes 2.4 hours to complete. ABC currently employs 120 workers, who each puts in an 8-hour day. The firm has no desire to hire or fire to affect labour availability for it believes its stable work force is one of its biggest assets.

Using a graphic approach, determine the best product mix for ABC.

S6.34 Red Deer's Mt. Sinai Hospital is a large, private, 600-bed facility complete with labouratories, operating rooms, and X-ray equipment. In seeking to increase revenues, Mt. Sinai's administration has decided to make a 90-bed addition on a portion of adjacent land currently used for staff parking. The administrators feel that the labs, operating rooms, and X-ray department are not being fully utilized at present and do not need to be expanded to handle additional patients. The addition of 90 beds, however, involves deciding how many beds should be allocated to the medical staff (for medical patients) and how many to the surgical staff (for surgical patients).

The hospital's accounting and medical records departments have provided the following pertinent information. The average hospital stay for a medical patient is 8 days, and the average medical patient generates $2,280 in revenues. The average surgical patient is in the hospital 5 days and receives a $1,515 bill. The labouratory is capable of handling 15,000 tests per year more than it *was* handling. The average medical patient requires 3.1 lab tests, and the average surgical patient takes 2.6 lab tests. Furthermore, the average medical patient uses one X-ray; the average surgical patient requires two X-rays. If the hospital were expanded by 90 beds, the X-ray department could handle up to 7,000 X-rays without significant additional cost. Finally, the administration estimates that up to 2,800 additional operations could be performed in existing operating room facilities. Medical patients, of course, require no surgery, while each surgical patient generally has one surgery performed.

Formulate this problem so as to determine how many medical beds and how many surgical beds should be added in order to maximize revenues. Assume that the hospital is open 365 days per year.

DATA BASE APPLICATION

S6.35 Bucyk Enterprises is a Winnipeg manufacturer of tables and accessories for personal computers. The company is caught in a vicious crossfire between rapidly dropping market prices from competitors worldwide for its products and stable domestic costs for its materials. The 15 different products noted below must be scheduled to maximize profits or there will be no jobs and no firm in another three months. Your job as the new P/OM graduate is to address the issues raised this morning by Laura Bucyk, the president, in an emergency meeting in her office. Without being told so explicitly, you concluded that if you didn't get the schedule done accurately and in a timely manner you would be history. To your relief the industrial engineers and accountants have provided the data shown below. The issues, as recorded in your notes, are shown in **a)** through **f)** below.

a) How many of each of the 15 products should be produced each month?

b) Clearly explain the meaning of each shadow price.

c) A number of workers interested in saving money for the holidays have offered to work overtime next month at a rate of $12.50 per hour. What should the response of management be?

d) Two tonnes of steel alloy are available from an overstocked supplier at a total cost of $8,000. Should the steel be purchased? All or part of the supply?

e) The accountants have just discovered that an error was made in the contribution to profit for product N150. The correct value is actually $8.88. What are the implications of this error?

f) Management is considering the abandonment of five product lines (those beginning with letters A through E). If no minimum monthly demand is established, what are the implications? Note that there already is no minimum for two of these products. Use the corrected value for N150.

PRODUCT	STEEL ALLOY REQUIRED (LB.)	PLASTIC REQUIRED (SQ. FT.)	WOOD REQUIRED (BD. FT.)	ALUMINUM REQUIRED (LB.)	FORMICA REQUIRED (BD. FT.)	LABOUR REQUIRED (HR.)	MINIMUM MONTHLY DEMAND (UNITS)	CONTRIBUTION TO PROFIT
A158	—	.4	.7	5.8	10.9	3.1	—	$18.79
B179	4	.5	1.8	10.3	2.0	1.0	20	6.31
C023	6	—	1.5	1.1	2.3	1.2	10	8.19
D045	10	.4	2.0	—	—	4.8	10	45.88
E388	12	1.2	1.2	8.1	4.9	5.5	—	63.00
F422	—	1.4	1.5	7.1	10.0	.8	20	4.10
G366	10	1.4	7.0	6.2	11.1	9.1	10	81.15
H600	5	1.0	5.0	7.3	12.4	4.8	20	50.06
I701	1	.4	—	10.0	5.2	1.9	50	12.79
J802	1	.3	—	11.0	6.1	1.4	20	15.88
K900	—	.2	—	12.5	7.7	1.0	20	17.91
L901	2	1.8	1.5	13.1	5.0	5.1	10	49.99
M050	—	2.7	5.0	—	2.1	3.1	20	24.00
N150	10	1.1	5.8	—	—	7.7	10	88.88
P259	10	—	6.2	15.0	1.0	6.6	10	77.01
Availability per month	980	400	600	2,500	1,800	1,000		

CASE STUDY

Golding Landscaping and Plants, Inc.

Kenneth and Patricia Golding spent a career as a husband-and-wife real estate investment partnership in Penticton, B.C. When they finally retired to a 10-hectare farm in northern Annapolis Valley, they became ardent amateur gardeners. When the volume of their shrubs and plants increased significantly, they built a greenhouse adjacent to their home and installed heating and watering systems in it.

By 1984, the Goldings realized their retirement from real estate had really only led to a second career—in the plant and shrub business—and they filed for a B.C. business licence. Within a matter of months, they had asked their attorney to file incorporation documents and formed the firm Golding Landscaping and Plants, Inc.

Early in the new business's existence, Kenneth Golding recognized the need for a high-quality commercial fertilizer that he could blend himself, both for sale and for his own nursery. His goal was to keep

(Continued)

his costs to a minimum while producing a top-notch product that was especially suited to the northern Annapolis Valley climate.

Working with chemists at Simon Fraser University and Capilano College, Golding blended "Golding-Grow." It consists of four chemical compounds, C-30, C-92, D-21, and E-11. The cost per kilogram for each compound is indicated in Table 1.

TABLE 1

CHEMICAL COMPOUND	COST PER KILOGRAM
C-30	$.12
C-92	.09
D-21	.11
E-11	.04

The specifications for Golding-Grow are established as:

a) Chemical E-11 must constitute at least 15% of the blend.

b) C-92 and C-30 must together constitute at least 45% of the blend.

c) D-21 and C-92 can together constitute no more than 30% of the blend.

d) Golding-Grow is packaged and sold in 50-kilogram bags.

DISCUSSION QUESTIONS

1. Formulate an LP problem to determine what blend of the four chemicals will allow Golding to minimize the cost of a 50-kilogram bag of the fertilizer.
2. Solve to find the best solution.

Source: Barry Render and Ralph Stair, *Introduction to Management Science* (Boston: Allyn and Bacon, 1992), p. 84. Modified for the Canadian edition.

CASE STUDY

Quebec Wire Winding

Gerard Bélanger felt good about his first week as management trainee at Quebec Wire Winding, Inc. He had not yet developed any technical knowledge about the manufacturing process, but he had toured the entire facility, located in the suburbs of Quebec City, and had met many people in various areas of the operation.

Quebec, a subsidiary of Montreal Wire Winding, is a medium-sized producer of wire windings used in making electrical transformers. Jules Cousineau, the production control manager, described the windings to Bélanger as being of standardized design. Bélanger's tour of the plant, laid out by process type (see Figure S6.12), followed the manufacturing sequence for the windings: drawing, extrusion, winding, inspection, and packaging. After inspection, good product is packaged and sent to finished product storage; defective product is stored separately until it can be reworked.

On March 8, Miriam Leblanc, Quebec's general manager, stopped by Bélanger's office and asked him to attend a staff meeting at 1:00 P.M.

"Let's get started with the business at hand," Miriam said, opening the meeting. "You all have met Gerard Bélanger, our new management trainee. Gerard studied operations management in his MBA program at H.E.C., Université de Montréal, so I think he is competent to help us with a problem we have been discussing for a long time without resolution. I'm sure that each of you on my staff will give Gerard your full cooperation."

Miriam turned to Giovanni DeTomaso, production control manager. "Giovanni, why don't you describe the problem we are facing?"

"Well," Giovanni said, "business is very good right now. We are booking more orders than we can fill. We will have some new equipment on line within the next several months, which will take care of our capacity problems, but that won't help us in April. I have located some retired employees who used to work in the drawing department, and I am planning to bring them in as temporary employees in April to increase capacity there. Because we are planning to refinance some of our long-term debt, Miriam wants our profits to look as good as possible in April. I'm having a hard time figuring out which orders to run and which to back-order so that I can make the bottom line look as good as possible. Can you help me with this?"

Bélanger was surprised and apprehensive to receive such a high-profile, important assignment so early in his career. Recovering quickly, he said,

(Continued)

FIGURE S6.12 ■ Quebec Wire Winding, Inc.

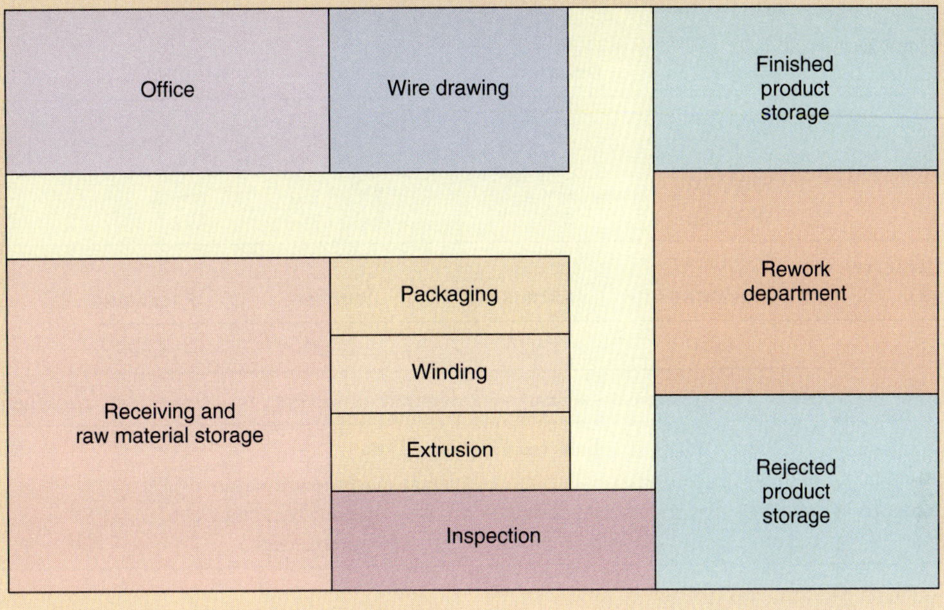

"Give me your data [Table 2] and let me work with it for a day or two."

DISCUSSION QUESTIONS

1. What recommendations should Gerard Bélanger make, with what justification? Provide a detailed analysis with charts, graphs, and computer printouts included.
2. Discuss the need for temporary workers in the drawing department.
3. Discuss the plant layout.

Source: Professor Victor E. Sower, Sam Houston State University. This case material is based on an actual situation, with names and data altered for confidentiality, and further modified for the Canadian edition.

TABLE 2

APRIL ORDERS

Product No. W0075C	1,400 units
Product No. W0033C	250 units
Product No. W0005X	1,510 units
Product No. W0007X	1,116 units

Note: Miriam Leblanc has given her word to a key customer that we will manufacture 600 units of Product No. W0007X and 150 units of Product No. W0075C for him during April.

STANDARD COST	PRODUCT	MATERIAL	LABOUR	O/H	SELLING PRICE
	W0075C	$33.00	$9.90	$23.10	$100.00
	W0033C	$25.00	$7.50	$17.50	$80.00
	W0005X	$35.00	$10.50	$24.50	$130.00
	W0007X	$75.00	$11.25	$63.75	$175.00

(Continued)

TABLE 2

BILL OF LABOUR (HOURS/UNIT)	PRODUCT	DRAWING	EXTRUSION	WINDING	PACKAGING
	W0075C	1.0	1.0	1.0	1.0
	W0033C	2.0	1.0	3.0	0.0
	W0005X	0.0	4.0	0.0	3.0
	W0007X	1.0	1.0	0.0	2.0

PLANT CAPACITY: (HOURS)	DRAWING	EXTRUSION	WINDING	PACKAGING
	4,000	4,200	2,000	2,300

Note: Inspection capacity is not a problem—we can work overtime as necessary to accommodate any schedule.

Selected Operating Data

Average output per month = 2,400 units   Average machine utilization = 63%
Average percentage of production sent to rework dept. = 5% (mostly from Winding Dept.)
Average no. of rejected units awaiting rework = 850 (mostly from Winding Dept.)

BIBLIOGRAPHY

Bodington, C. E., and T. E. Baker. "A History of Mathematical Programming in the Petroleum Industry." *Interfaces*, 20, no. 4 (July/August 1990): 117–132.

Farley, A. A. "Planning the Cutting of Photographic Color Paper Rolls for Kodak (Australasia) Pty. Ltd." *Interfaces*, 21, no. 1 (January/February 1991): 92–106.

Ferris, M. C., and A. B. Philpott. "On the Performance of Karmarkar's Algorithm." *Journal of the Operational Research Society*, 39 (March 1988): 257–270.

Gass, S. I. *An Illustrated Guide to Linear Programming*. New York: Dover, 1990.

Greenberg, H. J. "How to Analyze the Results of Linear Programs—Part 1: Preliminaries." *Interfaces*, 23, no. 4 (July/August 1993): 56–68.

———. "How to Analyze the Results of Linear Programs—Part 3: Infeasibility Diagnosis." *Interfaces*, 23, no. 6 (November/December 1993): 120–139.

Hirshfeld, D. S. "Some Thoughts on Math Programming Practice in the '90s." *Interfaces*, 20, no. 4 (July/August 1990): 158–165.

Oliff, M., and E. Burch. "Multiproduct Production Scheduling at Owens-Corning Fiberglass." *Interfaces*, 15 (September/October 1985): 25–34.

Orden, A. "LP from the '40s to the '90s." *Interfaces*, 23, no. 5 (September/October 1993): 2.

Quinn, P., B. Andrews, and H. Parsons. "Allocating Telecommunications Resources at L.L. Bean, Inc." *Interfaces*, 21, no. 1 (January/February 1991): 75–91.

Render, B., and R. M. Stair. *Introduction to Management Science*. Boston: Allyn and Bacon, 1992.

———. *Quantitative Analysis for Management*, 5th ed. Boston: Allyn & Bacon, 1994.

Rubin, D. S., and H. M. Wagner. "Shadow Prices: Tips and Traps for Managers and Instructors." *Interfaces*, 20, no. 4 (July/August 1990): 150–157.

Saltzman, M. J. "Survey: Mixed Integer Programming." *OR/MS Today*, 21, no. 2 (April 1994): 42–51.

Schindler, S., and T. Semmel. "Station Staffing at Pan American World Airways." *Interfaces*, 23, no. 3 (May/June 1993): 91.

Sexton, T. R., S. Sleeper, and R. E. Taggart, Jr. "Improving Pupil Transportation in North Carolina." *Interfaces*, 24, no. 1 (January/February 1994): 87–104.

Zangwill, W. I. *Lightning Strategies for Innovation: How the World's Best Firms Create New Products*. New York: Lexington Books, 1993.

Zappe, C., W. Webster, and I. Horowitz. "Using Linear Programming to Determine Post-Facto Consistency in Performance Evaluations of Major League Baseball Players." *Interfaces*, 23, no. 6 (November/December 1993): 107–119.

7

PROCESS STRATEGY AND CAPACITY PLANNING

CHAPTER OUTLINE

LEARNING OBJECTIVES

When you complete this chapter you should be able to:

Identify or define:
- Process focus
- Product focus
- Repetitive focus

Explain:
- Lean production
- The capacity issue
- Break-even analysis
- Financial considerations
- Strategy-driven investments

WORLD-CLASS PROFILE: HIBERNIA MANAGEMENT AND DEVELOPMENT COMPANY (HMDC)

An artist's impression of what the GBS would look like when completed. It contains two lifeboat stations and a helideck.

The completed GBS, showing the four shafts. The full height of the GBS is 111 metres, of which approximately 2/3 is presently under water. The track around the outside will be used during the offshore ballast installation operations.

In December 1996, Hibernia's offshore oil drilling platform, designed to withstand the impact of icebergs, was essentially completed and awaiting the second leg of its journey from dry-dock to the Hibernia oil field located 315 km east of St. John's.

The platform consists of two main elements, the gravity base structure (GBS) and the Topsides structure. The GBS is the concrete edifice that, positioned on the ocean floor and rising to the surface, will both support the Topsides drilling and production facilities and provide storage for 1.3 million barrels of crude oil.

Initial construction occurred in dry-dock at Bull Arm, Newfoundland, before five tugs towed the 18.8-metre-high GBS 1.5 nautical miles to its interim deep-water construction location in 200 metres of water. There it and the Topsides structure were worked on for three years and scheduled to be joined together in March of 1997 before being towed to the offshore production location in June. Drilling was scheduled to begin in August, and the first oil production was anticipated by the end of 1997.

The completed platform is more than 200 metres high (to the tip of the flareboom), and its towing (floating) weight was 600,000 tonnes. Once in position, 450,000 tonnes of ballast will be added, bringing the platform's total weight to over a million tonnes. (For purposes of comparison, the largest passenger liner in the world, the Norway, weighs in at 83, 829 tonnes and the U.S. aircraft carrier George Washington at 111, 163 tonnes.)

The successful use of slipforming technique (a continuous process of placing rebar and pouring concrete), the productivity rate of the rebar process (installing steel reinforcing rods), and using sheet piling to keep water out of the drydock all kept construction operations on or ahead of schedule.

Another notable feature in the GBS construction was the use of lightweight, high-performance concrete in the making of the icewall. The strength of the material is approximately twice that of the concrete used to build a bridge or tunnel. The icewall can absorb the impact of a multi-million-tonne iceberg.

Approximately $5 billion has been spent on the Hibernia project, of which more than $3.5 billion was spent in Canada, and approximately $2.3 billion of that figure was spent in Newfoundland. The contractors for the work indicated that the quality of the work carried out by skilled Newfoundlanders was comparable to that of their workers on projects in other parts of the world. During the construction period, 90% of the 5,800 employees in Bull Arm were Newfoundlanders, and this was scheduled to continue into the production phase. Production is scheduled to last for approximately 20 years.

Source: Adapted from Canada NewsWire Ltd., "Hibernia's GBS Successfully Towed to Deep Water Construction Site Early," (November 14, 1994); and *Hibernia Frontier*, vol. 1, issue 1 (December 1996).

The construction of the GBS continues at the deep water site.

The Topsides facilities, sitting on the assembly pier at Bull Arm.

Building compressors for air conditioners, Carrier Corporation faced severe worldwide competition. To fight back, Carrier recently decided to change its strategy to building compressors only to customer order. This means that the firm's big plants, built in the 1970s and 1980s, with their high fixed cost and inflexible production lines, are no good. It also means that Carrier has to build manufacturing processes that are flexible enough to respond to customer orders—and have no finished goods inventory. To be a world-class organization, Carrier has no choice but to change its process strategy.[1] ♦

In Chapter 6, we examined the need for the selection, definition, and design of products. We now turn to selection of the processes to be used in making these products and examine the advantages and disadvantages of process changes, such as the ones made by Carrier and Hibernia. A major decision for the operations manager is finding the best way to produce a product. This chapter looks at ways to help managers develop what is called a process strategy.

Process strategy

A **process** (or transformation) **strategy** is the approach that an organization takes to transform resources into goods and services. The *objective of a process strategy* is to find a way to produce goods that meet customer requirements and product specifications within cost and other managerial constraints.

The process selected will have a long-term effect on an organization's performance, efficiency, and production, as well as the flexibility, cost, and quality of the goods produced. Therefore, much of a firm's strategy is determined at the time of the process decision. The payoff from effective process selection prior to initial production is much more fruitful than the same effort expended later trying to improve the wrong process.

THREE PROCESS STRATEGIES

Virtually everything in the world is made by using some variation of one of three process strategies: process, repetitive, and product.

Process Focus

Process focus

Intermittent processes

Perhaps as much as 75% of Canadian production is devoted to making *low-volume, high-variety* products—in places called "job shops." The facilities are organized to perform a *process*. In a factory, these processes might be welding or painting departments, and in an office environment, they might be accounts payable, sales, and payroll departments. Such facilities have a **process focus** in terms of equipment, layout, and supervision. They provide a high degree of product flexibility because they are designed to process a wide variety of requirements and handle frequent changes. Consequently, they are also known as **intermittent processes**.

[1]Erle Norton, "Future Factories," *Wall Street Journal* (January 13, 1993): A1.

In 1947, like most restaurants, McDonald's paid out between 35% and 40% of gross income as wages. In 1948, Richard and Mac McDonald switched their process to a limited and rigidly standardized menu. The brothers developed specific portions to be served with each menu item. This included such things as dispensers that put an exact amount of catsup or mustard on each bun and paper goods to replace glassware and china. By 1952, it took 20 seconds for McDonald's to serve a customer a hamburger, a drink, french fries, and ice cream; labour costs had dropped to 17% of gross income and McDonald's was on its way to becoming the world-class fast-food restaurant.

Product Focus

High-volume, low-variety production is **product-focussed**. The equipment, layout, and supervision are organized to make a *product*. Because product-focussed facilities have very long continuous production runs, they are also called **continuous processes**. A continuous process is used to make products such as glass, paper, tin sheets, light bulbs, and nuts and bolts. Some products, such as light bulbs, are discrete, that is, distinct, separate units. Others, such as rolls of paper, are not discrete. An organization producing the same light bulb or hot dog bun day after day can invest in, and organize around, a product. Such an organization with a continuous process has an inherent ability to set standards and maintain a given quality, as opposed to an organization that is producing unique products every day. Note in the *POM in Action* box "Ontario Farmers to Receive Improved Farm Weather Bulletins" the agricultural industry's effort to improve the agricultural management system and protect the environment.

Product focus

Continuous processes

Repetitive Process

Production need not be either process- or product-focussed, as other possibilities exist. A third approach is a repetitive process. **Repetitive processes** use modules. **Modules** are parts or components previously prepared, often in a continuous process. An example of the repetitive process is the classic assembly line. The repetitive process is widely used, including the assembly of virtually all automobile and household appliances. The repetitive strategy has less flexibility than a process-focussed facility, but more flexibility than a product-focussed facility.

Repetitive processes

Modules

Fast-food firms provide another example of a repetitive process using modules. This type of production allows more customizing than a continuous process; so modules (for example, meat, cheese, sauce, tomato, onion) are assembled to get a quasi-custom product, a cheeseburger. In this manner, the firm obtains both the low-unit-cost advantages of the continuous model (where many of the modules are prepared) and the custom advantage of the low-volume, high-variety model.

Table 7.1 compares the major characteristics of process-focus, repetitive, and product-focussed strategies.

TABLE 7.1 ■ COMPARISON OF THE CHARACTERISTICS OF THREE TYPES OF PROCESSES

LOW-VOLUME, HIGH-VARIETY PROCESS (PROCESS FOCUS) (E.G., HOSPITALS)	MODULAR PROCESS (REPETITIVE FOCUS) (E.G., BURGER KING)	HIGH-VOLUME, LOW-VARIETY PROCESS (PRODUCT FOCUS) (E.G., NUCOR STEEL)
1. Small quantity and large variety of products are produced.	1. Long runs, usually a standardized product with options, are produced from modules.	1. Large quantity and small variety of products are produced.
2. Equipment used is general-purpose.	2. Special equipment aids in use of an assembly line.	2. Equipment used is special-purpose.
3. Operators are broadly skilled.	3. Employees are modestly trained.	3. Operators are less broadly skilled.
4. There are many job instructions because each job changes.	4. Repetitive operations reduce training and changes in job instructions.	4. Work orders and job instructions are few, because they are standardized.
5. Raw material inventories are high relative to the value of the product.	5. Just-in-time procurement techniques are used.	5. Raw materials inventories are low relative to the value of the product.
6. Work-in-process is high compared to output.	6. Just-in-time inventory techniques are used.	6. Inventory of work-in-process is low compared to output.
7. Units move slowly through the plant.	7. Movement is measured in hours and days.	7. Swift movement of units through the facility is typical.
8. Materials are moved via small flexible equipment.	8. Materials move by conveyor, transfer machines, AGVs, etc.	8. Materials move by connected pipes, material guides, etc.
9. Wide aisles and ample storage are typical.	9. Medium or narrow aisles, little storage space.	9. The facility is built around equipment, machinery, and product flows.
10. Finished goods are usually made to order and not stored.	10. Finished goods are made to frequent forecasts.	10. Finished goods are usually made to a forecast and stored.
11. Scheduling to orders is complex and concerned with the trade-off between inventory availability, capacity, and customer service.	11. Scheduling is based on building various models from a variety of modules to forecasts.	11. Scheduling is relatively simple and concerned with establishing a rate of output sufficient to meet sales forecasts.
12. Fixed costs tend to be low and variable costs high.	12. Fixed costs are dependent on flexibility of the facility.	12. Fixed costs tend to be high and variable costs low.
13. Costing, often done by the job, is estimated prior to doing the job, but known only after the job.	13. Costs are usually known, because of extensive prior experience.	13. Because fixed costs are high, costs are highly dependent on utilization of capacity.

POM IN ACTION

Ontario Farmers to Receive Improved Farm Weather Bulletins

"Knowing the weather conditions leading up to, during, and immediately after spraying pesticides will allow farmers to better time their application and ensure maximum protection of the environment. Linking either information to crop-efficient management practices will open up new opportunities for farmers to be better stewards of our natural resources," said Jim McWilliam, OSCIA president.

The Ontario Soil and Crop Improvement Association (OSCIA) in cooperation with Environment Canada provides farmers with weather forecasts which enable the farmer to better determine his or her crop needs.

The types of information available are: dewpoint indicators, drying index, heat units, growing degree days, evaporation estimates, pest management indices, wind velocity, temperature, and humidity levels. This information can be accessed by calling a 1-900 user pay line.

INDICATOR	USED TO INDICATE (EXAMPLES):
The dewpoint indicator	Leaf wetness: disease management
Drying index	Hay crop management
Heat units	Crop progress; hybrid selection
Growing degree days	Harvest timing; insect control
Evaporation estimates	Irrigation scheduling
Pest management indices	Timing of sprays
Wind velocity	Supports spraying; fertilizer spread
Temperature	Transporting livestock
Humidity	Maximising artificial and natural crop drying techniques
Specialized products	Customed-designed for client

On the basis of the forecasts, decisions are made within the hour, ensuring that Ontario agriculture remains competitive and environmentally responsible.

Source: Adapted from Canada NewsWire Ltd., "Ontario Farmers to Receive Improved Farm Weather Bulletins," April 29, 1996. Further information can be obtained from Environmental Services Branch, Environment Canada—Ontario, or from the Ontario Soil and Crop Improvement Association.

Moving Toward World-Class Performance with Lean Production

Lean producers

Lean producers is the term used to describe repetitive producers who are world-class.[2] The lean producer's mission is to achieve perfection. Lean production also means reducing staff positions so that those responsible are doing the entire job, from housekeeping chores, to execution, to planning. Lean production calls for continuous learning, creativity, and teamwork. It requires the full commitment and application of everyone's capabilities.

Lean producers understand what the customer wants and they rapidly design quality products to meet those requirements. The advantages held by lean producers are spectacular (see Table 7.2). The documented attributes of lean producers include the following:

- They remove waste by focussing on *inventory reduction*. They eliminate virtually all inventory. The removal of inventory removes the safety nets that allow a poor product to make its way through the product process.
- They use *just-in-time* techniques to reduce inventory and the waste caused by inventory. They drive down the time and cost of switching production from one product to another.
- They *build systems that help employees* produce a perfect part every time.

[2] *Synchronous manufacturing* is another term currently in vogue to describe efficient repetitive processes. General Motors has gone so far as to add the title Synchronous Manufacturing Manager to its lexicon.

TABLE 7.2 ■ SUMMARY OF AUTOMOTIVE ASSEMBLY PLANT PERFORMANCE

	LEAN PRODUCERS	OTHERS		
	JAPANESE IN JAPAN	JAPANESE IN NORTH AMERICA	AMERICAN IN NORTH AMERICA	ALL EUROPE
Inventories (days for 8 sample parts)	.2	1.6	2.9	2.0
Quality (assembly defects/100 vehicles)	60.0	65.0	82.3	97.0
Space (square metres/vehicle/year)	0.53	0.86	0.72	0.72
Supplier share of engineering	51%	14%	37%	32%
Work force:				
Productivity (hours/vehicle)	16.8	21.2	25.1	36.2
% of work force in teams	69.3	71.3	17.3	.6
Number of job classes	11.9	8.7	67.1	14.8
Training of new production workers (hours)	380.3	370.0	46.4	173.3
Suggestions/employee	61.6	1.4	.4	.4
Absenteeism	5.0	4.8	11.7	12.1

Source: Adapted from James P. Womack, Daniel T. Jones, and Daniel Roos, *The Machine That Changed the World* (New York: Macmillan, 1990), pp. 92, 118.

- They *reduce space requirements*. The technique is to minimize the distance a part travels.
- They *develop close relationships with suppliers;* suppliers understand their needs and their customers' needs.
- They *educate suppliers* to accept responsibility for helping meet customer needs.
- They strive for continually declining costs by *eliminating all but value-added activities*. They eliminate material handling, inspection, inventory, and rework jobs because they do not add value to the product. They retain only those activities that add value. Waste is eliminated.
- They *develop the work force*. They constantly improve job design, training, employee participation and commitment, and work teams.
- They *make jobs more challenging*, pushing responsibility to the lowest level possible. They reduce the number of job classes.

Viewed in this context, we see that traditional production techniques have set *limited* goals. For instance, traditionally, managers have accepted the production of a limited number of defective parts and have accepted safety stock as a limit on inventory reduction. Lean producers, on the other hand, set their sights on perfection; no bad parts and no inventory. The results are continually declining costs that are obtained via quality workmanship, zero inventory, a focus on teamwork and communications, and continuous self-improvement as employees broaden their skills. Lean producers are constantly building a better production system. A better system allows ever-more-challenging work for the employee and more rapid response to the market.

Lean production requires a commitment to remove continuously those activities that do not add value to the product. Thus, we can think of lean production as a waste-reduction philosophy. Lean producers enter a neverending battle to reduce idle time, changeover time, inventory, poor quality, poor suppliers, poor product design, and poor performance. Only when this is done is the organization lean and world-class.

We note successful lean production in the *POM in Action* box "Lean Production Methods Are a Success at Westinghouse."

Comparison of Process Strategies

Figure 7.1 further compares the three process strategies we have described. Advantages exist across the continuum. Unit costs will be less in the continuous process case if high volume exists because of specialized equipment and facilities. However, low-volume, unique service or product is more economical when produced under process focus. The bottom row of Figure 7.1 indicates that equipment utilization in a process-focussed facility is often in the range of 5% to 25%. Utilization above 15% suggests moving to the right on the process strategy continuum. McDonald's started a whole new industry by moving from the left toward the right of the continuum.

Pharmaceutical and petrochemicals are examples of "process industries." Process industries typically deal with liquids and bulk raw materials. Here, chemical operator John Walsh monitors a continuous reaction step in the chemical process for the active ingredient of Fosaxmax, Merck's new medicine for postmenopausal osteoporosis. This plant in Baloydine, Ireland, will be the worldwide source for the active ingredient.

FIGURE 7.1 ■ Process Continuum

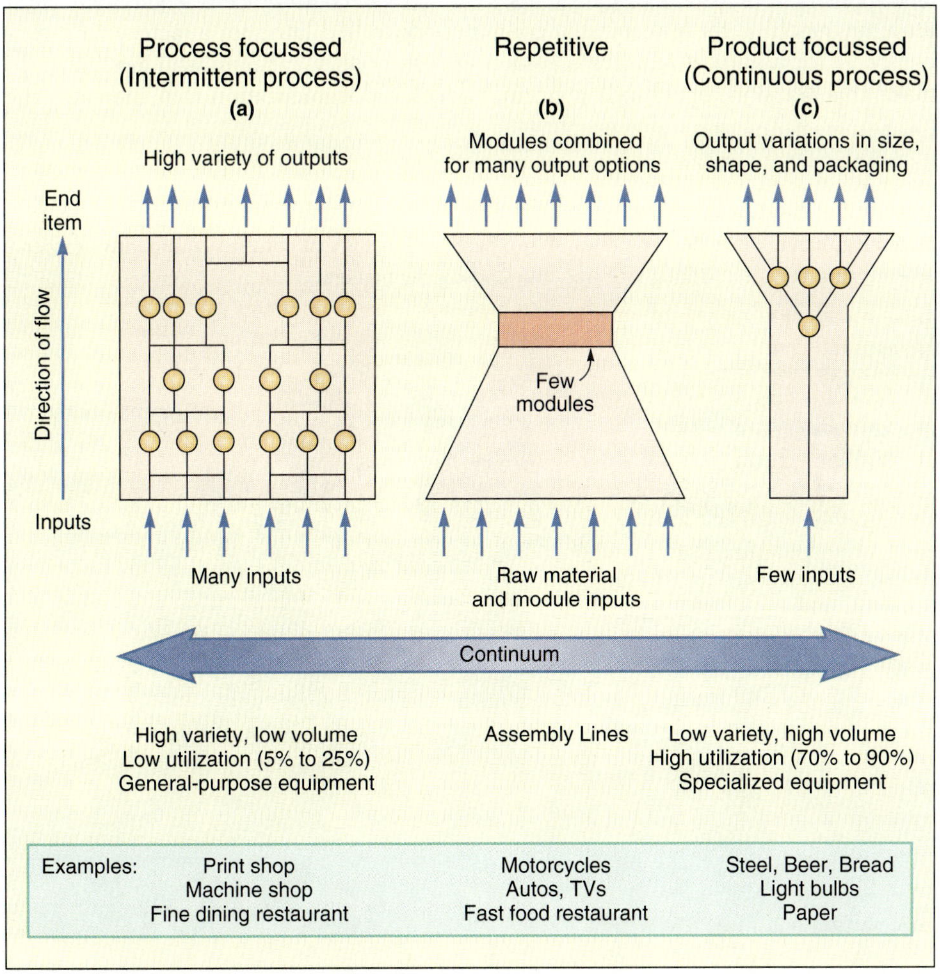

However, changing a production system from the process-focussed model to the product-focussed model is usually expensive. In some cases, this switch may necessitate starting over. Consequently, choosing where to operate on the process strategy continuum may determine the transformation strategy for an extended period.

Movement to the right of the continuum is desirable if the

1. *cash flows* to pay the fixed cost are adequate, and
2. risk of *lower demand* is insignificant, and
3. necessary *product variety* can be maintained.

The idea is to move to the right as far as possible to increase utilization without fixed costs becoming intolerable or the necessary product variety being destroyed.

Selection of Machinery and Equipment

Ultimately, the decisions about a particular process require decisions about machinery and equipment. Those decisions can be complex because alternative methods of production are present in virtually all operations functions, be they hospitals, restaurants, or manufacturing facilities. Picking the best equipment means understanding the specific industry, established processes, and technology. That choice of equipment, be it an X-ray machine for a hospital, a computer-controlled lathe for a factory, or a new computer for an office, requires considering cost, quality, capacity, and flexibility. To make this decision, operations personnel develop documentation that indicates the

Technology can result in new processes. shown here is a process that converts plastic into weather-resistant park benches, parking lot curbs, and landscaping timbers.

POM IN ACTION

Lean Production Methods Are a Success at Westinghouse

To Westinghouse, the problems were clear: Worldwide competition was increasing; the company was pressed to lower prices, yet cost of materials, employees, and overhead kept increasing; and higher customer expectations demanded shorter cycle times, superior quality, and customer satisfaction.

Lean production (known as reengineering at Westinghouse) was the answer. The phrase embraces such techniques as work teams—training employees in multiple skills so that they can do more than one job—and "empowerment," which means pushing decision-making authority as far down in the organization as possible. It also entails reorganizing assembly lines and offices to simplify and speed the flow of work.

The company's solution focussed on 12 years of experience to develop WESTIP (Westinghouse Technology to Improve Process), a method to radically reengineer or improve business processes. Cross-functional employee teams used WESTIP to perform process analysis, redesign, and implementation quickly and simply.

The result was a Baldrige National Quality Award and these benefits: $22 million in savings in 1 year, two-thirds reduction in material costs, reduced drawing time from 90 down to 10 days, 30% lower manufacturing costs through improved cellular layout, a drop in the time it takes to handle purchase orders from 14 days to 6 hours, and reduced order cost from $86 to $12. Finally, a factory that used to take 9,290 square metres to build Westinghouse components now only needs 3,716 square metres.

Sources: Westinghouse Productivity and Quality Center Workshop, Pittsburgh, December 1–3, 1993; and *Wall Street Journal* (March 16, 1993): A-1.

capacity, size, and tolerances of each option, and its maintenance requirements. Any one of these attributes may be the deciding factor regarding the use of a process.

The selection of machinery and equipment for a particular type of process can also provide competitive advantage. Many firms, for instance, develop a unique machine or technique within the established processes that provides an advantage. This advantage may result in added flexibility in meeting customer requirements, lower cost, or higher quality. Innovations and modification of equipment might also allow for a more stable production process that takes less adjustment, maintenance, and training of operators. In any case, specialized unique equipment often provides a way to win orders.

The study of specific industries and their technology is outside the scope of this book. However, the technological advances that influence P/OM process strategy, and the selection of machinery and equipment are substantial and are discussed in Chapter 8.

SERVICE PROCESS STRATEGY

Figure 7.1 can be applied to services as well as manufacturing. For instance, much of the service industry produces in very small lots. This is true for legal services, medical services, dental services, and many restaurants. They are often producing in lot sizes as small as one. Such organizations would be on the left of Figure 7.1.

Restaurants, such as General Mills' Red Lobster, are part of the service industry, but they are also the end of a long production line. At the beginning of the line, raw material goes in—at Red Lobster that means 27,000 tonnes of seafood a year. The seafood is purchased from all over the world. The shrimp arrives in frozen boxes from Ecuador and Thailand at a General Mills processing plant in St. Petersburg, Florida. There the shrimp is loaded onto a conveyor belt to be peeled, deveined, cooked, quick frozen, sorted, and repacked for ultimate delivery to individual restaurants.

Service Sector Considerations

As Figure 7.1 indicates, equipment utilization is extremely low in process-focussed facilities—perhaps as low as 5%. This is true not only for manufacturing, but also for services. An X-ray machine in a dentist's office and much of the equipment in a fine dining restaurant have low utilization. Hospitals, too, can be expected to be in that range, which would suggest why their costs are considered high. Why such low utilization? In part because excess capacity for peak loads is desirable. Hospital administrators, as well as managers of other service facilities and their patients and customers, expect equipment to be available as needed. Another reason utilization is low is poor scheduling (although substantial efforts have been made to forecast demand in the service industry) and the resulting imbalance in the use of facilities.

The service industry moves to the right of Figure 7.1 by establishing fast-food restaurants, legal clinics, auto lubrication shops, auto tune-up shops, and so forth. Notice how the pizza business moved to the right on our process continuum, as indicated in the *POM in Action* box earlier in this chapter. As the variety of services is reduced, we would expect per unit cost to drop also. This is typically what happens.

Customer Contact and Process Strategy

Customer contact is an important variable in a transformation system. In a process that directly interfaces with the customer, one expects the customer to affect process performance adversely. In a restaurant, a medical facility, a law office, or a retail store, interaction between the customer and the process keeps the process from operating as smoothly as it otherwise might. Individual attention and customizing of the product or service for the customer can play havoc with a process. The more the process can be insulated from the customer's unique requirements, the lower will be the cost. Improving productivity can be accomplished in a variety of ways, as shown in Table 7.3.

CAPACITY

After considering the process options, a number of issues remain. In the rest of this chapter, we deal with three issues that are important for good process decisions. These issues are capacity, break-even analysis, and the investment itself.

Capacity

Capacity is defined as the maximum output of a system in a given period under ideal conditions. In a process-focussed facility, capacity is often determined by some measure of size such as the number of beds in a hospital or seating capacity in a restaurant. In a repetitive process the number of units assembled each shift, such as number of refrigerators, may be the criterion for capacity. And in a product-focussed facility, such as Nucor, tons of steel processed per shift may be the measure of capacity. Whatever the measure, the capacity decision is critical to an organization because everything from cost to customer service depends upon the capacity of the process.

Many organizations operate their facilities at a rate less than capacity. They do so because they have found that they can operate more efficiently when their re-

TABLE 7.3 ■ CUSTOMER CONTACT AND PROCESS STRATEGY. THESE TECHNIQUES ARE USED TO IMPROVE PRODUCTIVITY.

TECHNIQUE	EXAMPLE
Restrict the offerings	Limited-menu restaurant
Structure service so customers must go where the service is offered	Banks where customers go to a service representative to open a new account, to loan officers for loans, or to tellers for deposits and withdrawals
Provide self-service so customers examine, compare, and evaluate at their own pace	Supermarkets and department stores
Separate services that may lend themselves to some type of automation	Automatic teller machines
Customize at delivery	Customize vans at delivery rather than at production

sources are not stretched to the limit. Instead, they operate at perhaps 92% of capacity. This concept is called effective capacity, or utilization. **Effective capacity**, or **utilization**, is simply the percent capacity *expected*. It can be computed from the following formula:

Effective capacity, or utilization

$$\text{Effective capacity, or utilization} = \frac{\text{expected capacity}}{\text{capacity}}$$

Effective capacity, or utilization, is the capacity a firm can *expect* to achieve given its product mix, methods of scheduling, maintenance, and standards of quality.

Another capacity consideration is efficiency. Depending on how facilities are used and managed, it may be difficult or impossible to reach 100% efficiency. Typically, **efficiency** is expressed as a percentage of the effective capacity. Efficiency is a measure of actual output over effective capacity:

Efficiency

$$\text{Efficiency} = \frac{\text{actual output}}{\text{effective capacity}}$$

The **rated capacity** is a measure of the maximum usable capacity of a particular facility. Rated capacity will always be less than or equal to the capacity. The equation used to compute rated capacity is

Rated capacity

$$\text{Rated capacity} = (\text{capacity})(\text{utilization})(\text{efficiency})$$

We determine rated capacity in the following example.

Forecasting Capacity Requirements

Determining future capacity requirements can be a complicated procedure, one based in large part on future demand. When demand for goods and services can be forecasted with a reasonable degree of precision, determining capacity requirements can be straightforward. It normally requires two phases. During the first phase, future demand is forecasted with traditional methods such as regression analysis. During the second phase, this forecast is used to determine capacity requirements.

EXAMPLE 1

The Sara James Bakery has a plant for processing breakfast rolls. The facility has an efficiency of 90%, and the utilization is 80%. Three process lines are used to produce the rolls. The lines operate 7 days a week and three 8-hour shifts per day. Each line was designed to process 120 standard (that is, plain) rolls per hour. What is the rated capacity?

In order to compute the rated capacity, we multiply the capacity (which is equal to the number of lines times the number of hours times the number of rolls per hour) times the utilization times the efficiency. Each facility is used 7 days a week, three shifts a day. Therefore, each process line is utilized for 168 hours per week (168 = 7 days × 3 shifts per day × 8 hours per shift). With this information, the rated capacity can be determined as follows:

$$\begin{aligned}\text{Rated capacity} &= (\text{capacity})(\text{utilization})(\text{efficiency})\\ &= [(120)(3)(168)](.8)(.9) = 43{,}546 \text{ rolls/week}\end{aligned}$$

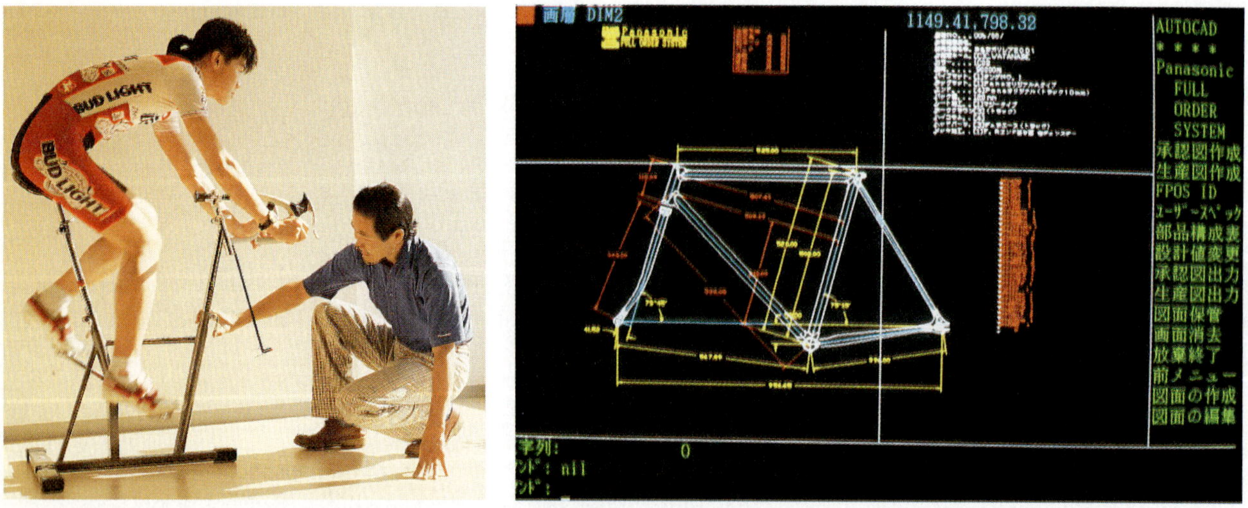

Flexible manufacturing can improve customer service and provide a competitive advantage. National Bicycle's customized Panasonic bicycle production process begins by defining individual customer needs. The customer mounts the special frame in a Panasonic bicycle store from which measurements are taken. These custom measurements are sent to the factory where CAD software produces a blueprint in about 3 minutes. At the same time, a bar-code label is prepared that will identify bicycle components as they move through production. Time—from beginning to end—is only 3 hours.

Once the rated capacity has been forecasted, managers must decide the size of each addition to capacity. The assumption here is that management knows the technology and the *type* of facilities to be employed to satisfy these future demands.

Figure 7.2 shows two ways new capacity can be planned for growth of future demand. In Figure 7.2(a), new capacity is acquired at the beginning of year 1. This capacity will be sufficient to handle increased demand until the beginning of year 2. At the beginning of year 2, new capacity is again acquired, which will allow the organization to meet demand until the beginning of year 3. This process can be continued indefinitely into the future.

An alternative is presented in Figure 7.2(b). In the figure, a large increase in capacity is acquired at the beginning of year 1, which will satisfy future demand until the beginning of year 3.

Figures 7.2(a) and 7.2(b) reveal only two of many possible alternatives. In some cases, determining capacity requirements and deciding between alternatives can be relatively easy. Managers determine the total cost of each alternative and select the alternative with the least total cost. In most cases, however, determining the capacity of future facilities can be much more complicated. Many factors are difficult to quantify and measure. A major factor is market acceptance for the goods and services being produced. However, other factors include changing technology, actions by competitors, building restrictions, future cost of capital, availability of human resource, and laws and regulations.

When the future is subject to significant unknowns, the direct approach suggested in Figure 7.2 may not be adequate. In these cases, "probabilistic" models may be more appropriate. One technique for making successful capacity planning decisions with an uncertain demand is decision theory, including the use of decision trees.

Decision Trees Applied to Capacity Decisions

Decision trees, as we saw in Chapter 2's supplement, require specifying alternatives and various states of nature. For capacity planning situations, the state of nature usually is future demand or market favorability. By assigning probability values to the various states of nature, it is possible to make decisions that maximize the expected value of the alternatives. Example 2 shows how to apply decision trees to a capacity decision.

Rather than strategically manage capacity, P/OM managers may tactically manage demand. We now discuss some techniques for managing demand.

EXAMPLE 2

Southern Hospital Supplies, a company that makes hospital gowns, is considering capacity expansion. Its major alternatives are to do nothing, build a small plant, build a medium plant, or build a large plant. The new facility would produce a new type of gown, and currently the potential or marketability for this product is unknown. If a large plant is built and a favourable market exists, a profit of $100,000 could be realized. An unfavourable market would yield a $90,000 loss. However, a medium plant would earn a $60,000 profit with a favourable market. A $10,000 loss would result from an unfavourable market. A small plant, on the other hand, would return $40,000 with favourable market conditions and lose only $5,000 in an unfavourable market. Of course, there is always the option of doing nothing.

Recent market research indicates that there is a .4 probability of a favourable market, which means that there is also a .6 probability of an unfavourable market. With this information, the alternative that will result in the highest expected monetary value (*EMV*) can be selected:

$$\begin{aligned}\text{EMV (large plant)} &= (.4)(\$100{,}000) + (.6)(-\$90{,}000) = -\$14{,}000\\ \text{EMV (medium plant)} &= (.4)(\$60{,}000) + (.6)(-\$10{,}000) = +\$18{,}000\\ \text{EMV (small plant)} &= (.4)(\$40{,}000) + (.6)(-\$5{,}000) = +\$13{,}000\\ \text{EMV (do nothing)} &= \$0\end{aligned}$$

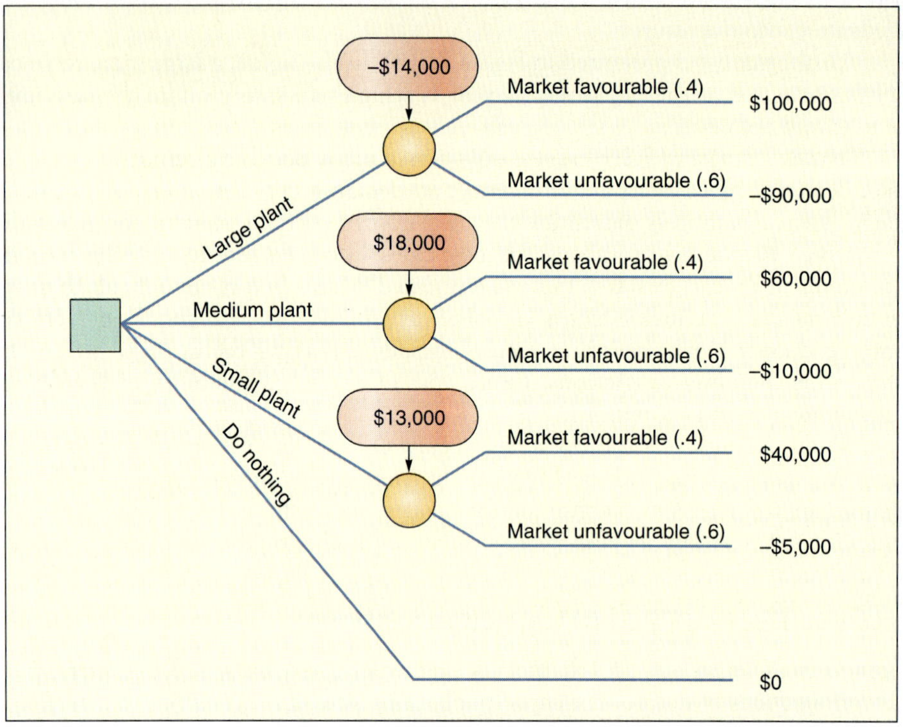

According to EMV criteria, Southern should build a medium plant.

FIGURE 7.2 ■ Adding Capacity

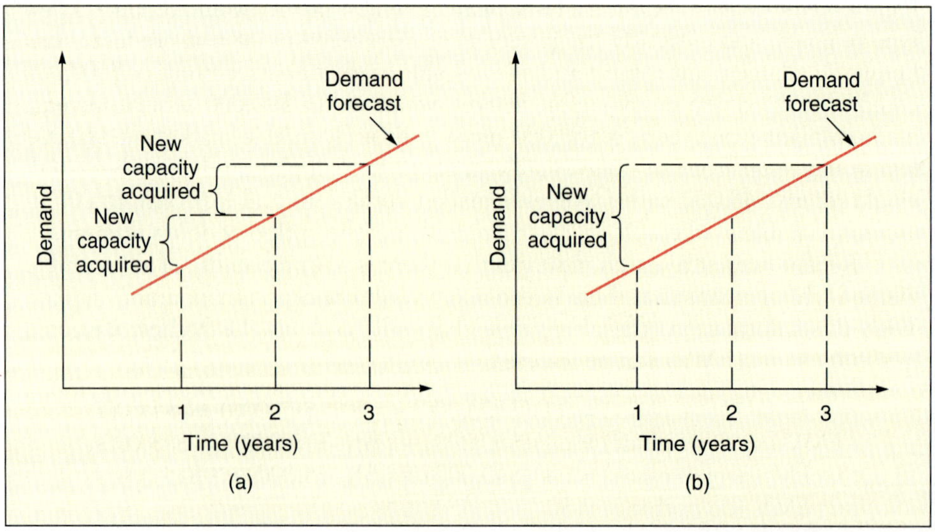

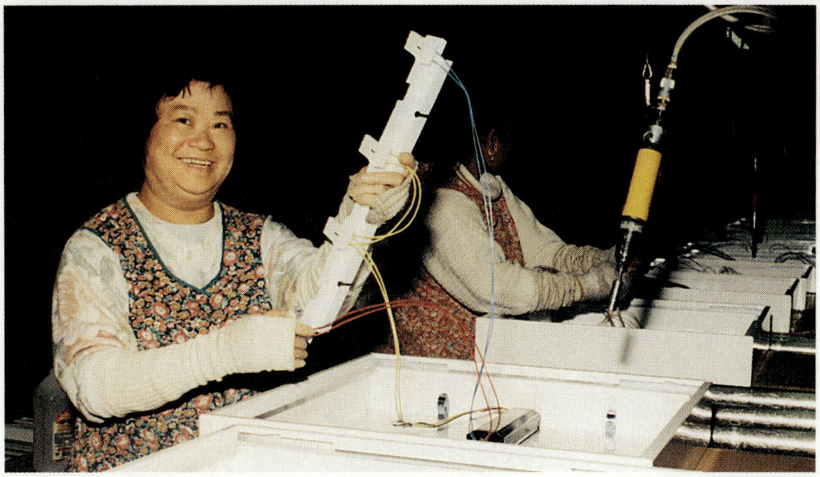

The capital expenditures for a capacity change can be tremendous. Many companies address this by making incremental changes when possible or by establishing joint ventures such as the one established between Vision Unlimited Equipment Inc. (Vision) — a division of Alex Ventures Inc. (Alexa)— and the Mexican corporation Transcom. The venture was undertaken to manufacture cost-efficient, energy-efficient electronic ballasts used in fluorescent lighting. It expands Vision's product lines and other energy-saving products directed to the Canadian, U.S., and Mexican markets.

Pemex, Mexico's national oil company, which performs all functions in Mexico's oil industry, chose the Transcom/Vision Joint venture to install and supply all the products in its "Save Energy" program. This installation is estimated to be worth $10 million Canadian. (Alexa is traded on the Vancouver Stock Exchange.)

Managing Demand

Even with good forecasting and facilities built to that forecast, there may be a poor match between the actual demand that occurs and capacity available. A poor match may mean demand exceeds capacity or capacity exceeds demand. However, in both cases firms have options.

DEMAND EXCEEDS CAPACITY. When *demand exceeds capacity*, the firm may be able to curtail demand simply by raising prices, scheduling long lead times (which may be inevitable), and discouraging marginally profitable business. Because inadequate facilities reduce revenue below what is possible, the long-term solution is usually to increase capacity.

CAPACITY EXCEEDS DEMAND. When *capacity exceeds demand*, the firm may want to stimulate demand through price reductions or aggressive marketing, or accommodate the market through product changes.

ADJUSTING TO SEASONAL DEMANDS. Another capacity issue with which management may be confronted is a seasonal or cyclical pattern of demand. In such cases, management may find it helpful to offer products with complementing demand patterns, that is, products for which the demand is the opposite. For example, in Figure 7.3 the firm is adding a line of snowmobile engines to its line of lawn mower engines to smooth demand. With appropriate complementing products, perhaps the utilization of facility, equipment, and personnel can be smoothed.

TACTICS FOR MATCHING CAPACITY TO DEMAND. Various tactics for matching capacity to demand exist. Internal changes include adjusting the process to a given volume through:

1. staffing changes;
2. adjusting equipment and processes, which might include purchasing additional machinery or selling or leasing existing equipment;
3. improving methods to increase throughput; and/or
4. redesigning the product to facilitate more throughput.

Forecasting capacity can be difficult, especially in the electronics industry, because of the fast changes taking place in the entertainment, consumer electronics, and multimedia computing markets. To try to respond quickly to changes, management may use the licensing agreement approach.

Here is a typical view of an electronic retail outlet, showing the various pieces of equipment offered by Sony only. Add to that all the other manufacturers' offerings and one can see the difficulty in forecasting sales.

The foregoing tactics can be used to adjust demand to existing facilities. The strategic issue is, of course, how to have a facility of the correct size. Break-even analysis may help with that decision.

BREAK-EVEN ANALYSIS

Break-even analysis

The objective of **break-even analysis** is to find the point, in dollars and units, at which costs equal revenues. This point is the break-even point. Break-even analysis requires an estimation of fixed costs, variable cost, and revenue.

Fixed costs
Variable costs

Fixed costs are costs that continue even if no units are produced. Examples include depreciation, taxes, debt, and mortgage payments. **Variable costs** are those that vary with the volume of units produced. The major components of variable costs are labour and materials. However, other costs, such as the portion of the utilities that varies with volume, are also variable costs.

Revenue function

Another element in break-even analysis is the **revenue function**. It begins at the origin and proceeds upward to the right, increasing by the selling price of each unit. This revenue line is shown in Figure 7.4. Where the revenue function crosses the total cost line is the break-even point, with a profit corridor to the right and a loss corridor to the left.

FIGURE 7.3 ■ By Combining Products That Have Complementary Seasonal Patterns, Capacity Can Be Better Utilized. A smoother demand for sales also contributes to improved scheduling and better human resource strategies.

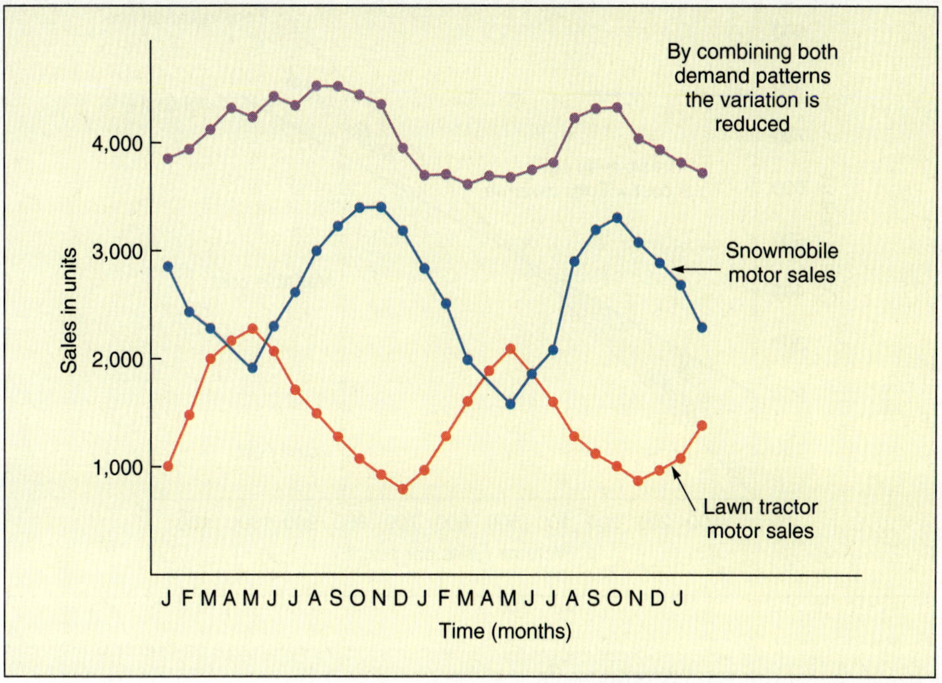

Break-even analysis assumes that within the relevant range, fixed costs will not change, and that variable costs will not vary in direct proportion to the volume of units produced. Since the relevant range can change, neither fixed nor variable costs need be straight-line. For example, fixed costs change as more capital equipment or warehouse space is used; labour costs change with overtime or as marginally skilled workers are employed; and the revenue function may change with such factors as volume discounts.

The first step in break-even analysis is to define those costs that are fixed and sum them. The variable costs are then estimated by an analysis of labour, materials, and other costs connected with the production of each unit. The fixed costs are drawn as a horizontal line beginning at that dollar amount on the vertical axis, as we see in Figure 7.4. The variable costs are then shown as an incrementally increasing cost, originating at the intersection of the fixed cost on the vertical axis and increasing with each change in volume as we move to the right on the volume (or horizontal) axis. Both fixed and variable cost information is usually available from a firm's cost accounting department, although an industrial engineering department may also maintain cost information.

The respective formulas for the break-even point in units and dollars are developed as follows:

$BEP(x)$ = break-even point in units
$BEP(\$)$ = break-even point in dollars
P = price per unit (dollars received per unit after all discounts)
x = number of units produced

FIGURE 7.4 ■ Basic Break-Even Point

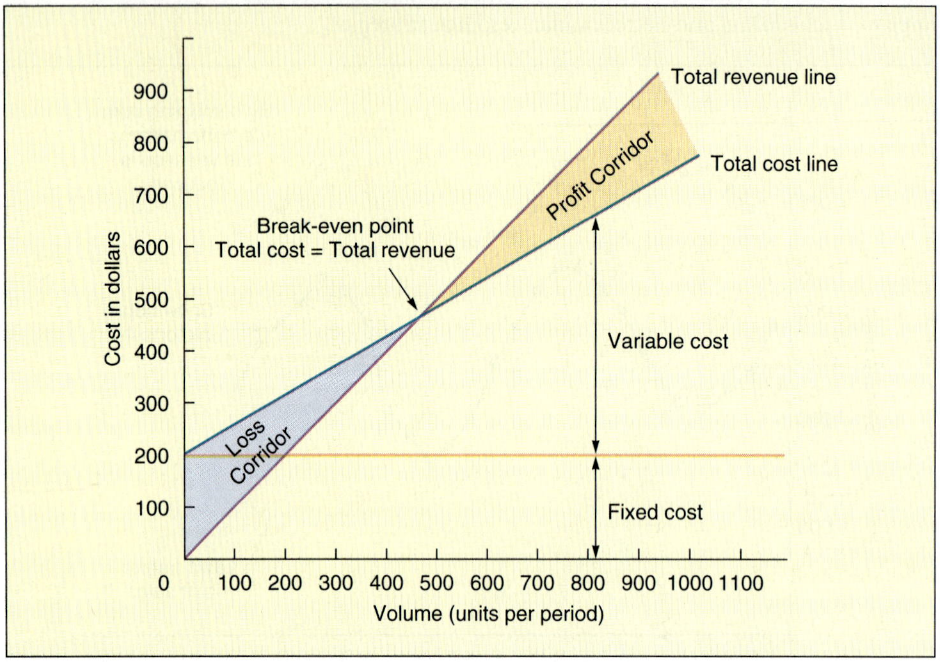

TR = total revenue = Px
F = fixed costs
V = variable costs per unit
TC = total costs = $F + Vx$

Setting total revenue equal to total costs, we get

$$TR = TC$$

or

$$Px = F + Vx$$

Solving for x, we get

$$BEP(x) = \frac{F}{P - V}$$

and

$$BEP(\$) = BEP(x)P$$
$$= \frac{F}{P - V}P = \frac{F}{(P - V)/P}$$
$$= \frac{F}{1 - V/P}$$

Using these equations, we can solve directly for break-even point and general profitability. The two formulas that are of particular interest are

$$\text{BEP}(x) = \text{Break-even in units} = \frac{\text{total fixed cost}}{\text{price} - \text{variable cost}} \qquad (7.1)$$

$$\text{BEP}(\$) = \text{Break-even in dollars} = \frac{\text{total fixed cost}}{1 - \dfrac{\text{variable cost}}{\text{selling price}}} \tag{7.2}$$

CROSSOVER CHARTS. Break-even analysis aids process selection by identifying the processes with the lowest total cost for the volume expected. Such a point will, of course, also indicate the largest profit corridor. We are, therefore, able to address two issues: the low-cost process and the absolute amount of profit. Only by directly addressing both issues can the process decision be successful. Figure 7.5 shows three alternative processes compared on a single chart. Such a chart is sometimes called a **crossover chart**. Process A has the lowest total cost for volumes below V_1. Process B has the lowest cost between V_1 and V_2. Process C has the lowest cost at volumes above V_2.

Crossover chart

Single-Product Case

In Example 3 we determine the break-even point in dollars and units for one product.

EXAMPLE 3

Jimmy Stephens, Inc., has fixed costs of $10,000 this period. Direct labour is $1.50 per unit, and material is $.75 per unit. The selling price is $4.00 per unit.

The break-even point in dollars is computed as follows:

$$BEP(\$) = \frac{F}{(1 - V/P)} = \frac{\$10{,}000}{1 - [(1.50 + .75)/(4.00)]} = \frac{\$10{,}000}{.4375} = \$22{,}857.14$$

and the break-even point in units is

$$BEP(x) = \frac{F}{P - V} = \frac{\$10{,}000}{4.00 - (1.50 + .75)} = 5714$$

Note that in this example, we must use the *total* variable costs (that is, both labour and material).

Multiproduct Case

Most firms, from manufacturers to restaurants (even fast-food restaurants), have a variety of offerings. Each offering may have a different selling price and variable cost. Utilizing break-even analysis, we modify Equation (7.2) to reflect the proportion of sales for each product. We do this by "weighting" each product's contribution by its proportion of sales. The formula is then

$$BEP(\$) = \frac{F}{\sum\left[\left(1 - \frac{V_i}{P_i}\right) \times (W_i)\right]} \tag{7.3}$$

where V = variable cost per unit
P = price per unit
F = fixed cost
W = percent each product is of total dollar sales
i = each product

Example 4 shows how to determine the break-even point for the multiproduct case.

EXAMPLE 4

The costs from Le Bistro, a French-style deli, follow. Fixed costs are \$3,500 per month.

ITEM	PRICE	COST	FORECASTED UNIT SALES
Sandwich	\$2.95	\$1.25	7,000
Soft drink	.80	.30	7,000
Baked potato	1.55	.47	5,000
Tea	.75	.25	5,000
Salad bar	2.85	1.00	3,000

With a variety of offerings, we proceed with break-even analysis just as in a single-product case, except that we weight each of the products by its proportion of total sales here.

MULTIPRODUCT BREAK-EVEN—DETERMINING CONTRIBUTION

1 ITEM (i)	2 SELLING PRICE (P)	3 VARIABLE COST (V)	4 (V/P)	5 1 − (V/P)	6 FORECASTED SALES	7 % OF SALES	8 WEIGHTED CONTRIBUTION (= COL. 5 × COL. 7)
Sandwich	\$2.95	\$1.25	.42	.58	\$20,650	.446	.259
Soft drink	.80	.30	.38	.62	5,600	.121	.075
Baked potato	1.55	.47	.30	.70	7,750	.167	.117
Tea	.75	.25	.33	.67	3,750	.081	.054
Salad bar	2.85	1.00	.35	.65	8,550	.185	.120
					\$46,300	1.000	.625

For instance, revenue for sandwiches is \$20,650, which is 44.6% of the total revenue of \$46,300. Therefore, the contribution for sandwiches is "weighted" by .446. The weighted contribution is .446 × .58 = .259. In this manner, its relative contribution would be properly reflected.

Using this approach for each product, we find that the total weighted contribution is .625 for each dollar sales, and the break-even point in dollars is \$67,200:

$$BEP(\$) = \frac{F}{\Sigma\left[\left(1-\frac{V_i}{P_i}\right)\times\left(W_i\right)\right]}$$

$$= \frac{\$3{,}500 \times 12}{.625} = \frac{\$42{,}000}{.625}$$

$$= \$67{,}200$$

The information given in this example implies total daily sales (52 weeks at 6 days each) of

$$\frac{\$67,200}{312 \text{ days}} = \$215.38$$

Break-even figures by product provide the manager with added insight as to the realism of his or her sales forecast. They indicate exactly what must be sold each day, as we have done in Example 5.

EXAMPLE 5

Using the data in Example 4, we take the forecast sandwich sales of 44.6% times the daily break-even of \$215.38 divided by the selling price of each sandwich (\$2.95). Then the sandwich sales must be

$$\frac{.446 \times \$215.38}{\$2.95} = \text{number of sandwiches} = 32.5 \approx 33 \text{ sandwiches each day}$$

Once break-even analysis of this type has been prepared, analyzed, and judged to be reasonable, decisions can be made about the types of equipment needed. Indeed, a better judgement of the likelihood of success of the enterprise can now be made.

STRATEGY-DRIVEN INVESTMENTS

Let us now address the integration of strategy and investment with our process decision. Increasingly, managers realize that sustained profits come from building competitive advantage, not from a good financial return on a specific process.[3] We recommend that the traditional approach to investment analysis (just looking at financial returns) be enhanced by strategic considerations. Specifically, the strategic considerations we suggest are

1. that investments be made as *part of a coordinated strategic plan*. Where are these investments taking the organization? Investments should not be made as isolated expenditures, but as part of a coordinated strategic plan that will place the firm in an advantageous position. The question to be asked is, "Will these investments eventually win customers?"
2. that investments *yield a competitive advantage* (process flexibility, speed of delivery, quality, and so on);
3. that investments *consider product life cycles;*
4. that a *variety of operating factors be included in the financial return analysis* (for instance, reductions in scrap, rework, floor space, and inventory increase returns);
5. that investments be *tested in light of several revenue projections* to ensure that upside potential and down-side risk are considered.

[3]For an excellent discussion on investments that support competitive advantage, see Terry Hill, *Manufacturing Strategy: Text and Cases* (Homewood, IL: Irwin, 1989). Also see "Selling Rockwell on Automation," *Business Week* (June 6, 1988): 104.

FIGURE 7.5 ■ Crossover Charts. Three different processes can be expected to have three different costs. However, at any given volume, only one will have the lowest cost.

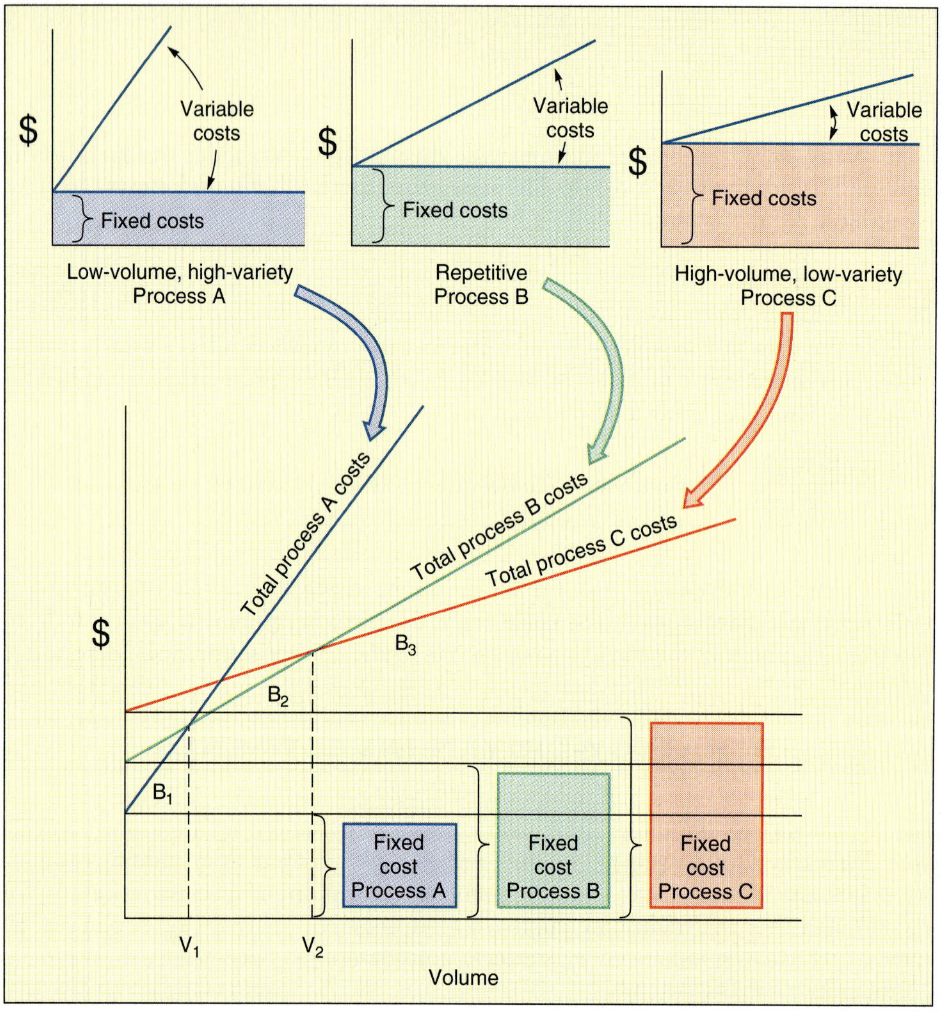

Once the strategy implications of potential investments have been considered, traditional investment analysis is appropriate. We introduce the investment aspects of process selection next.

Investment, Variable Cost, and Cash Flow

Because process alternatives exist, so do options with regard to capital investment and variable cost. Managers must choose from among different financial options as well as process alternatives. The number of initial alternatives may be large, but analysis of six major factors (cost, volume, human resource constraints, technology, quality, and reliability) typically reduces the number of alternatives to a few. Analysis should show the capital investment, variable cost, and cash flows as well as net present value for each alternative.

Net Present Value

Net present value

Determining the discount value of a series of future cash receipts is known as the **net present value** technique. By way of introduction, let us consider the time value of money. Say you invest \$100.00 in a bank at 5% for 1 year. Your investment will be worth \$100.00 + (\$100.00)(.05) = \$105.00. If you invest the \$105.00 for a second year, it will be worth \$105.00 + (\$105.00)(.05) = \$110.25 at the end of the second year. Of course, we could calculate the future value of \$100.00 at 5% for as many years as we wanted by simply extending this analysis. But there is an easier way to express this relationship mathematically. For the first year:

$$\$105 = \$100(1 + .05)$$

For the second year:

$$\$110.25 = \$105(1 + .05) = \$100(1 + .05)^2$$

In general,

$$F = P(1 + i)^N \tag{7.4}$$

where F = future value (such as \$110.25 or \$105)
P = present value (such as \$100.00)
i = interest rate (such as .05)
N = number of years (such as 1 year or 2 years)

In most investment decisions, however, we are interested in calculating the present value of a series of future cash receipts. Solving for P, we get

$$P = \frac{F}{(1 + i)^N} \tag{7.5}$$

When the number of years is not too large, the preceding equation is effective. When the number of years, N, is large, the formula is cumbersome. For 20 years, you would have to compute $(1 + i)^{20}$. Without a sophisticated calculator, this computation would be difficult indeed. Interest-rate tables, such as Table 7.4, alleviate this situation. First, let us rearrange the present value equation:

$$P = \frac{F}{(1 + i)^N} = FX$$

where

$$X = \text{a factor defined as}$$

$$= 1/(1 + i)^N \tag{7.7}$$

and

$$F = \text{future value}$$

Thus, all we have to do is find the factor X and multiply it by F to calculate the present value P. The factors, of course, are a function of the interest rate, i, and the number of years, N. Table 7.4 lists some of these factors.

Equations (7.4), (7.5), and (7.6) are used to determine the present value of one future cash amount, but there are situations in which an investment generates a series of uniform and equal cash amounts. This type of investment is called an *annuity*. For example, an investment might yield $300 per year for 3 years. Of course, you could use Equation 7.4 three times, for 1, 2, and 3 years, but there is a shorter method. Although there is a formula that can be used to solve for the present value of an annual series of uniform and equal cash flows (an annuity), an easy-to-use table has been developed for this purpose. Like the customary present value computations, this calculation involves a factor. The factors for annuities are in Table 7.5. The basic relationship is

$$S = RX$$

where X = factor from Table 7.5
S = present value of a series of uniform annual receipts
R = receipts that are received every year for the life of the investment (the annuity)

TABLE 7.4 ■ PRESENT VALUE OF $1

YEAR	5%	6%	7%	8%	9%	10%	12%	14%
1	.952	.943	.935	.926	.917	.909	.893	.877
2	.907	.890	.873	.857	.842	.826	.797	.769
3	.864	.840	.816	.794	.772	.751	.712	.675
4	.823	.792	.763	.735	.708	.683	.636	.592
5	.784	.747	.713	.681	.650	.621	.567	.519
6	.746	.705	.666	.630	.596	.564	.507	.456
7	.711	.665	.623	.583	.547	.513	.452	.400
8	.677	.627	.582	.540	.502	.467	.404	.351
9	.645	.592	.544	.500	.460	.424	.361	.308
10	.614	.558	.508	.463	.422	.386	.322	.270
15	.481	.417	.362	.315	.275	.239	.183	.140
20	.377	.312	.258	.215	.178	.149	.104	.073

TABLE 7.5 ■ PRESENT VALUE OF AN ANNUITY OF $1

YEAR	5%	6%	7%	8%	9%	10%	12%	14%
1	.952	.943	.935	.926	.917	.90	.893	.877
2	1.859	1.833	1.808	1.783	1.759	1.73	1.690	1.647
3	2.723	2.673	2.624	2.577	2.531	2.48	2.402	2.322
4	3.546	3.465	3.387	3.312	3.240	3.17	3.037	2.914
5	4.329	4.212	4.100	3.993	3.890	3.79	3.605	3.433
6	5.076	4.917	4.766	4.623	4.486	4.35	4.111	3.889
7	5.786	5.582	5.389	5.206	5.033	4.86	4.564	4.288
8	6.463	6.210	5.971	5.747	5.535	5.33	4.968	4.639
9	7.108	6.802	6.515	6.247	5.985	5.75	5.328	4.946
10	7.722	7.360	7.024	6.710	6.418	6.14	5.650	5.216
15	10.380	9.712	9.108	8.559	8.060	7.60	6.811	6.142
20	12.462	11.470	10.594	9.818	9.128	8.51	7.469	6.623

The present value of a uniform annual series of amounts is an extension of the present value of a single amount, and thus Table 7.5 can be directly developed from Table 7.4. The factors for any given interest rate in Table 7.5 are nothing more than the cumulative sum of the values in Table 7.4. In Table 7.4, for example, .952, .907, and .864 are the factors for years 1, 2, and 3 when the interest rate is 5%. The cumulative sum of these factors is 2.723 = .952 + .907 + .864. Now look in Table 7.5 to where the interest rate is 5% and the number of years is 3. The factor for the present value of an annuity is 2.723, as you would expect. Table 7.5 can be very helpful in reducing the computations necessary to make financial decisions.

Example 6 shows how to determine the present value of an annuity.

EXAMPLE 6

River Road Medical Clinic is thinking of investing in a sophisticated new piece of medical equipment. It will generate $7,000 per year in receipts for 5 years. What is the present value of this cash flow? Assume an interest rate of 6%.

$$S = RX = \$7{,}000(4.212) = \$29{,}484$$

The factor from Table 7.5 (4.212) was obtained by finding that value when the interest rate is 6% and the number of years is 5. There is another way of looking at this example. If you went to a bank and took a loan for $29,484 today, your payments would be $7,000 per year for 5 years if the bank used an interest rate of 6% compounded yearly. Thus, $29,484 is the *true* present value of the investment.

The net-present-value method is considered to be one of the best methods of ranking investment alternatives. The procedure is straightforward; you simply compute the present value of all cash flows for each investment alternative. When deciding among investment alternatives, you pick the investment that has the highest net present value. Similarly, when making several investments, those with higher net present values are preferable to investments with lower net present values.

Example 7 shows how to use the net present value to choose between investment alternatives.

EXAMPLE 7

Quality Plastics, Inc., is considering two different investment alternatives. Investment A has an initial cost of $25,000, and investment B has an initial cost of $26,000. Both investments have a useful life of 4 years. The cash flows for these investments follow. The cost of capital or the interest rate (i) is 8%.

Investment A's Cash Flow	Investment B's Cash Flow	Year	Present Value Factor at 8%
$10,000	$9,000	1	.926
9,000	9,000	2	.857
8,000	9,000	3	.794
7,000	9,000	4	.735

To find the present value of the cash flows for each investment, we multiply the present value factor by the cash flow for each investment for each year. The sum of these present-value calculations minus the initial investment is the net present value of each investment. The computations appear in the following table.

YEAR	INVESTMENT A'S PRESENT VALUES	INVESTMENT B'S PRESENT VALUES
1	$ 9,260 = (.926)($10,000)	$ 8,334 = (.926)($9,000)
2	7,713 = (.857)($9,000)	7,713 = (.857)($9,000)
3	6,352 = (.794)($8,000)	7,146 = (.794)($9,000)
4	5,145 = (.735)($7,000)	6,615 = (.735)($9,000)
Totals:	$28,470	$29,808
Minus initial investment	– 25,000	– 26,000
Net present value	$3,470	$3,808

The net present value criterion shows investment B to be more attractive than investment A because it has a higher present value.

In Example 7, it was not necessary to make all of those present-value computations for investment B. Because the cash flows are uniform, Table 7.5, the annuity table, gives the present value factor. Of course, we would expect to get the same answer. As you recall, Table 7.5 gives factors for the present value of an annuity. In this example, for payments of $9,000, cost of capital is 8% and the number of years is 4. Looking at Table 7.5 under 8% and 4 years, we find a factor of 3.312. Thus, the present value of this annuity is (3.312)($9,000) = $29,808, the same value as in Example 7.

Although net present value is one of the best approaches to evaluating investment alternatives, it does have its faults. Limitations of the net present value approach include the following:

1. Investments with the same present value may have significantly different project lives and different salvage values.
2. Investments with the same net present value may have different cash flows. Different cash flows may make substantial differences in the company's ability to pay its bills.
3. The assumption is that we know future interest rates, which we do not.
4. Payments are always made at the end of the period (week, month, or year).

ACHIEVING WORLD-CLASS STANDARDS

World-class producers use their process strategy as a competitive weapon. Operations managers select a production process with the necessary quality, flexibility, and cost structure to meet product and volume requirements. Increasingly, world-class competitors find ways to combine the low unit cost of high-volume, low-variety manufacturing with the customization available through low-volume, high-variety facilities. We began this chapter with a discussion of how Carrier Corporation is making such a change. Additionally, managers find ways to use the techniques of lean production and employee participation to build quality products as demanded by the customer.

World-class firms encourage the development of uniquely efficient proprietary equipment and processes. They design their equipment and processes to have capabilities beyond the tolerance required by their customers, while ensuring the flexibility needed for adjustments in technology and volumes.

Additionally, world-class firms make process investments that are efficient by ensuring that the investments support a long-term strategy. The criteria for investment decisions are contribution to the overall strategic plan and winning profitable orders, not just return on investment. World-class firms select the correct process and the correct capacity that contributes to their long-term strategy.

SUMMARY

The processes that operations managers use to perform transformations can be as important as the products themselves. Transformation processes determine much of the fixed and variable cost, as well as quantity and quality of the product. The process decision can result in selection of a transformation technology that is process-focussed or product-focussed or someplace in between. However, it must be of a capacity and technology that will provide a competitive advantage.

Good forecasting, break-even analysis, crossover charts, decision trees, cash flow, and net present value (NPV) techniques are particularly useful to operations managers when making the process decision.

KEY TERMS

Process strategy (p. 284)
Process focus (p. 284)
Intermittent processes (p. 284)
Product focus (p. 285)
Continuous processes (p. 285)
Repetitive processes (p. 285)
Modules (p. 285)
Lean producers (p. 287)
Capacity (p. 292)
Effective capacity, or utilization (p. 293)
Efficiency (p. 293)
Rated capacity (p. 293)
Break-even analysis (p. 298)
Fixed costs (p. 298)
Variable costs (p. 298)
Revenue function (p. 298)
Crossover chart (p. 301)
Net present value (p. 305)

SOLVED PROBLEMS

Solved Problem 7.1

Sara James Bakery, described earlier in Example 1, has decided to increase its facilities by adding one additional process line. The firm will have four process lines, each working 7 days a week, three shifts per day, 8 hours per shift. Utilization is 90%. This addition, however, will reduce its overall system efficiency to 85%. Compute the new rated capacity with this change in facilities.

Solution

$$\begin{aligned}\text{Rated capacity} &= \text{capacity} \times \text{utilization} \times \text{efficiency}\\ &= [(120)(4 \times 7 \times 3 \times 8)] \times (.9) \times (.85)\\ &= (80{,}640) \times (.9) \times (.85)\\ &= 61{,}689.6 \text{ per week}\\ &\quad\text{or}\\ &= 120 \times 4 \times .9 \times .85\\ &= 367.2 \text{ per hour}\end{aligned}$$

Solved Problem 7.2

Marty McDonald works part-time making canoe paddles in British Columbia. His annual fixed cost is $10,000, direct labour is $3.50 per paddle, and material is $4.50 per paddle. The selling price will be $12.50 per paddle. What is break-even in dollars? What is break-even in units?

Solution

$$BEP(\$) = \frac{F}{1 - V/P} = \frac{\$10{,}000}{1 - (\$8.00/\$12.50)} = \frac{\$10{,}000}{.36} = \$27{,}777$$

$$BEP(x) = \frac{F}{P - V} = \frac{\$10{,}000}{\$12.50 - \$8.00} = \frac{\$10{,}000}{\$4.50} = 2{,}222 \text{ units}$$

DISCUSSION QUESTIONS

1. What are the advantages of standardization? How do we obtain variety while maintaining standardization?
2. What type of process is used for each of the following?
   (a) beer
   (b) business cards
   (c) automobiles
   (d) telephone
   (e) "Big Macs"
   (f) custom homes
3. In an affluent society, how do we produce a wide number of options for products at low cost?
4. What products would you expect to have made by a repetitive process?
5. Where does the manager obtain data for break-even analysis?
6. What keeps plotted variable and fixed-cost data from falling on a straight line?
7. What keeps plotted revenue data from falling on a straight line?
8. What are the assumptions of break-even analysis?
9. How might we isolate the production/operations process from the customer?
10. What are assumptions of the net-present-value technique?
11. Identify two services located at the process-focussed side of the process strategy continuum (Figure 7.1).
12. Identify two services located at the product-focussed side of the process strategy continuum (Figure 7.1).
13. Identify two services that are organized as repetitive.
14. Distinguish between designed capacity, effective capacity, and efficiency.
15. Refer to the discussion of Carrier's manufacturing process that opened this chapter. How is its process strategy changing?

CRITICAL THINKING EXERCISE

As described in the *POM in Action* box "Ontario Farmers to Receive Improved Farm Weather Bulletins," Environment Canada is trying to turn the agricultural industry into a more efficient producer of food. However, the new service is not without cost to the farmer.

Now that the new service is paid for, what is the responsibility of Environment Canada and OSCIA when the forecast is wrong and leads to crop damage? Discuss the business/ethical issues for the agricultural industry.

PROBLEMS

• **7.1** River Road Medical Clinic, which runs an optometrist lab, has been blessed with substantial growth over the past decade. Additionally, it was able to buy additional increments of lens-grinding equipment in relatively small units. Prior analysis of its data (since its growth has been steady and constant) suggests that regression analysis (as described in Chapter 5) is adequate to determine its capacity demands. Data for the past decade follow:

	YEAR									
	1984	**1985**	**1986**	**1987**	**1988**	**1989**	**1990**	**1991**	**1992**	**1993**
Units Produced (in thousands)	15.0	15.5	16.25	16.75	16.9	17.24	17.5	17.3	17.75	18.1

a) Determine its capacity needs in units for 1994, 1996, and 2000.

b) If each machine is capable of producing 2,500 lenses, how many machines should it expect to have in 1996?

• **7.2** Assume River Road Medical Clinic (Problem 7.1) in 1994 has eight machines, each capable of producing 2,500 lenses per year. However, the new and best machine then on the market has the capability of producing 5,000 per year.

a) What is the status of capacity at the firm in the year 2000 if it buys the new and best machine in 1994?

b) What is the status of capacity at the firm in the year 2000 if it buys the standard machine with a capacity of 2,500?

• **7.3** A work centre operates two shifts per day 5 days per week (8 hours per shift) and has four machines of equal capability. If the machines are utilized 80% of the time at a system efficiency of 95%, what is the rated output in standard hours per week?

• **7.4** The minutes available for the next quarter of 1996 at MMU Mfg. in Halifax, Nova Scotia, for each of three departments is shown. Recent data on utilization and efficiency are also shown.

DEPARTMENT	MINUTES AVAILABLE	EFFECTIVE UTILIZATION	RECENT EFFICIENCY
Design	93,600	.92	.95
Fabrication	156,000	.95	1.03
Finishing	62,400	.96	1.05

Compute the expected capacity for next quarter for each department.

• **7.5** Butch Porter Manufacturing intends to increase capacity by overcoming a bottleneck operation through addition of new equipment. Two vendors have presented proposals. The fixed costs for Proposal A are $50,000 and for Proposal B, $70,000. The variable cost for A is $12.00 and for B, $10.00. The revenue generated by each of these units is $20.00.

a) What is the break-even point in units for Proposal A?

b) What is the break-even point in units for Proposal B?

• **7.6** You are given the data in Problem 7.5:

a) What is the break-even point in dollars for Proposal A?

b) What is the break-even point in dollars for Proposal B?

• **7.7** Given the data in Problem 7.5, at what volume (units) of output would the two alternatives yield the same profit?

• **7.8** Use the same data in Problem 7.5:

a) If the expected volume is 8,500 units, which alternative should be chosen?

b) If the expected volume is 15,000 units, which alternative should be chosen?

: **7.9** What is the net present value of an investment that costs $123,545, and has a salvage value of $44,560? The annual profit from the investment is $14,667 each year for 5 years. The cost of capital at this risk level is 12%.

• **7.10** The initial cost of an investment is $65,000 and the cost of capital is 10%. The return is $16,000 per year for 8 years. What is the net present value?

• **7.11** An investment will produce $1,000 2 years from now. What is the amount worth today? That is, what is the present value if the interest rate is 9%?

• **7.12** What is the present value of $5,600 when the interest rate is 8% and the return of $5,600 will not be received for 15 years?

: **7.13** Mr. Kulonda, VP Operations at McClain Manufacturing, has to make a decision between two investment alternatives. Investment A has an initial cost of $61,000, and investment B has an initial cost of $74,000. The useful life of investment A is 6 years; the useful life of investment B is 7 years. Given a cost of capital of 9% and the following cash flows for each alternative, determine the most desirable investment alternative according to the net present value criterion.

Investment A's Cash Flow	Investment B's Cash Flow	Year
$19,000	$19,000	1
19,000	20,000	2
19,000	21,000	3
19,000	22,000	4
19,000	21,000	5
19,000	20,000	6
19,000	11,000	7

: **7.14** An electronics firm is currently manufacturing an item that has a variable cost of $.50 per unit and a selling price of $1.00 per unit. Fixed costs are $14,000. Current volume is 30,000 units. The firm can substantially improve the product quality by adding a new piece of equipment at an additional fixed cost of $6,000. Variable cost would increase to $.60, but volume should jump to 50,000 units due to a higher-quality product. Should the company buy the new equipment?

: **7.15** The electronics firm in Problem 7.14 is now considering the new equipment with a price increase to $1.10 per unit. With the higher-quality product, the new volume is expected to be 45,000 units. Under these circumstances, should the company purchase the new equipment and increase the selling price?

· **7.16** Given the following data, calculate $BEP(x)$, $BEP(\$)$, and the profit at 100,000 units:

$$P = \$8/\text{unit} \qquad V = \$4/\text{unit} \qquad F = \$50{,}000$$

: **7.17** Kathleen Bentley has been asked to evaluate two machines. After some investigation, she determines that they have the following costs. She is told to assume that

a) the life of each machine is 3 years

b) the company thinks it knows how to make 12% on investments no more risky than this one.

	MACHINE A	MACHINE B
Original cost	$10,000	$20,000
Labour per year	2,000	4,000
Maintenance per year	4,000	1,000
Salvage value	2,000	7,000

Determine, via the present value method, which machine Kathleen should recommend.

: **7.18** Your boss has told you to evaluate two ovens for Tink-the-Tinkers, a gourmet sandwich shop. After some questioning of vendors and receipt of specifications, you are assured the ovens have the following attributes and costs. The following two assumptions are appropriate:

1. the life of each machine is 5 years
2. the company thinks it knows how to make 14% on investments no more risky than this one.

	THREE SMALL OVENS AT $1,250 EACH	TWO LARGE HIGH-QUALITY OVENS AT $2,500 EACH
Original cost	$3,750	$5,000
Labour per year in excess of larger models	$750 (total)	
Cleaning/maintenance	$750 ($250 each)	$400 ($200 each)
Salvage value	$750 ($250 each)	$1,000 ($500 each)

a) Determine via the present value method which machine to tell your boss to purchase.

b) What assumption are you making about the ovens?

c) What assumptions are you making in your methodology?

: **7.19** Tom Miller and Jeff Vollman have opened a copy service on Commonwealth Avenue. They estimate their fixed cost at $12,000 and their variable cost of each copy sold at $.01. They expect their selling price to average $.05.

a) What is their break-even point in dollars?

b) What is their break-even point in units?

7.20 Dr. Aleda Roth, a prolific author, is considering starting her own publishing company. She will call it DSI Publishing, Inc. DSI's estimated costs are

Fixed	$250,000.00
Variable cost per book	$20.00
Selling price per book	$30.00

How many books must DSI sell to break even?

7.21 In addition to the costs in Problem 7.20, Dr. Roth wants to pay herself a salary of $50,000 per year.

a) Now what is her break-even point in units?

b) What is her break-even point in dollars?

7.22 As a prospective owner of a club known as the Red Rose, you are interested in determining the volume of sales dollars necessary for the coming year to reach the break-even point. You have decided to break down the sales for the club into four categories, the first category being liquor and beer. Your estimate of the beer sales is that 30,000 drinks will be served. The selling price for each unit will average $1.50; the cost is $.75. The second major category is meals, which you expect to be 10,000 units with an average price of $10.00 and a cost of $5.00. The third major category is desserts and wine, of which you also expect to sell 10,000 units, but with an average price of $2.50 per unit sold and a cost of $1.00 per unit. The final category is lunches and inexpensive sandwiches, which you expect to total 20,000 units at an average price of $6.25 with a food cost of $3.25. Your fixed cost (that is, rent, utilities, and so on) is $1,800 per month plus $2,000 per month for entertainment.

a) What is your break-even point in dollars?

b) What is the expected number of meals each day if you are open 360 days a year?

7.23 Using the data in Problem 7.22, make the problem more realistic by adding labor cost at one-third of meals and sandwiches cost. Also add variable expenses (kitchen supplies, tablecloths, napkins, and so on) at 10% of cost for all categories.

a) What is your break-even point?

b) If you expect to make a profit of $35,000 (before taxes) for your 12-hour days, what must your total sales be?

7.24 As operations manager of Baby Furniture, Inc., you must make a decision about expanding your line of nursery furniture (that is, cribs, toy chests, dressers, and so on). In discussing the possibilities with your sales manager, Betsy Waugh-McCollum, you decide that there definitely will be a market and that your firm should enter that market. However, because nursery furniture is often painted rather than stained, you decide you need another process line. There is no doubt in your mind about the decision, and you are sure that you should have a second process. But you do question how large to make it. A large process line is going to cost $300,000; a small process line will cost $200,000. The question, therefore, is the demand for nursery furniture. After expensive discussion with Mrs. Waugh-McCollum and Mr. Utecht of Utecht Market Research, Inc., you determine that the best estimate you can make is that there is a two-out-of-three chance of profit from sales as large as $600,000 and a one-out-of-three chance as low as $300,000.

With a large process line, you could handle the high figure of $600,000. However, with a small process line you could not and would be forced to expand (at a cost of $150,000), after which time your profit from sales would be $500,000 rather than the $600,000 because of the lost time in expanding the process. If you do not expand the small process, your profit from sales would be held to $400,000. If you build a small process and the demand is low, you can handle all of the demand.

Should you open a large or small process line?

7.25 You are the new manager of the university basketball concession booths. You have been told in no uncertain terms that concession sales will support themselves. The following table provides the information you have been able to put together thus far.

ITEM	SELLING PRICE	VARIABLE COST	% OF REVENUE
Soft drink			
Large	$1.10	$ .65	10
Medium	.75	.45	10
Small	.60	.40	20
Hot dog	.75	.45	10
Coffee	.50	.25	20
Miscellaneous snacks	.40	.30	30

Last year's manager, La Tonya Thompson, has advised you to be sure to add 10% of variable cost as a waste allowance for all categories.

You estimate labor cost to be (five booths with three people each) $250.00. Even if nothing is sold, your cost will be $250.00, so you decide to consider this a fixed cost. Booth rental, which is a contractual cost at $50 *each* per game, is also a fixed cost.

a) What is break-even volume for all booths per game?

b) How many hot dogs would you expect to sell at the break-even point?

: **7.26** Rank the following investments according to net present value. Each alternative requires an initial investment of $20,000. Assume a 10% cost of capital.

YEAR	CASH FLOWS FROM INVESTMENT 1	CASH FLOWS FROM INVESTMENT 2	CASH FLOWS FROM INVESTMENT 3
1	$ 1,000	$ 7,000	$10,000
2	1,000	6,000	5,000
3	3,000	5,000	3,000
4	15,000	4,000	2,000
5	3,000	4,000	1,000
6	1,000	4,000	1,000
7	—	4,000	1,000
8	1,000	2,000	—
9	—	—	1,000

CASE STUDY

Matthew Yachts, Inc.

Matthew Yachts, located in Montauk, Long Island, manufactured sailing yachts of all descriptions. The company had begun by building custom-designed yachts for a largely New York–based clientele, and over the years, as Matthew Yachts' reputation for quality design and workmanship spread, sales broadened to cover all of the Eastern Seaboard.

In an effort to capitalize on this increased recognition and to secure a piece of the fastest growing market in sailing, Matthew Yachts began manufacturing a new standard, fixed-design craft. Matthew attacked only the high end of this market, as the boat measured 37 feet long. Nevertheless, even this end of the market was more price-sensitive and less conscious of performance than Matthew Yachts' custom-design customers were.

All of the company's yachts were manufactured at the Montauk plant and shared the same equipment and skilled labour force. Custom designs were given priority in scheduling, and the new boat was rotated into the schedule only when demand slackened. As sales of the fixed-design boat increased, however, scheduling the new boat on a regular basis became necessary.

The company's yachts were built basically from the bottom up. Fabricating hulls was the first step.

(Continued)

Afterward came the below-decks woodworking, followed by the fibreglass and woodworking on the deck itself. The masts were turned and drilled separately. Masts and hull were then joined and the work completed.

As the fixed-design craft continued its steady increase in sales, costs and deliveries began to slide, especially on the fixed-design yachts. During this period, construction of the fixed-design craft always yielded time and resources to the higher-profit-margin custom designs. As a result, many fixed-design yachts were strewn around the yard in various stages of construction. Moreover, space in the existing shipyard was becoming scarce, and a plant expansion of one sort or another appeared inevitable.

DISCUSSION QUESTIONS

1. Should Matthew Yachts, Inc., stay in the business of building standard, fixed-design yachts?
2. If Matthew does so, how should it continue?

Source: Roger W. Schmenner, *Production/Operations Management*, 5th ed., New York: Macmillan, 1993, p. 517. Modified for the Canadian edition.

BIBLIOGRAPHY

Berry, W. L., C. C. Bozarth, T. J. Hill, and J. E. Klompmaker. "Factory Focus: Segmenting Markets from an Operations Perspective." *Journal of Operations Management*, 10, no. 3 (August 1991): 363.

Burbidge, J. L. "Production Flow Analysis for Planning Group Technology." *Journal of Operations Management*, 10, no. 1 (January 1991): 5–27.

Canada NewsWire Ltd., "Hibernia's GBC Successfully Towed to Deep Water Construction Site Early," November 14, 1994.

Ettlie, J. E. "What Makes a Manufacturing Firm Innovative." *The Executive* (November 1990): 10.

Ettlie, J. E., and E. M. Reza. "Organizational Integration and Process Innovation." *The Academy of Management Journal* (October 1992): 795.

Ferguson, J. T., and J. H. Heizer. *Real Estate Investment Analysis*. Boston: Allyn and Bacon, 1990.

Grant, R. M., R. Krishnan, A. B. Shani, and R. Baer. "Appropriate Manufacturing Technology: A Strategic Approach." *Sloan Management Review*, 33, no. 1 (Fall 1991): 43–54.

Heizer, J. H. "Manufacturing Productivity: Japanese Techniques Not Enough." *Industrial Management* (September/October 1986): 21–23.

Hounshell, D. A. *From the American System to Mass Production, 1800–1932*. Baltimore: Johns Hopkins University Press, 1984.

Kim, D., V. A. Mabert, and P. A. Pinto. "Integrative Cycle Scheduling Approach for a Capacitated Flexible Assembly System." *Decision Sciences*, 24, no. 1 (January/February 1993): 126–147.

Kwan, C. C. Y., and Y. Yuan. "The Present Value Issue in a Sequential Selection Problem." *Decision Sciences*, 24, no. 5 (September/October 1993): 1057.

Leachman, R. C., and T. F. Carmon. "On Capacity Modeling for Production Planning with Alternative Machine Types." *Industrial Engineering Research & Development*, 24, no. 4 (September 1992): 62.

Mansfield, E. "The Diffusion of Flexible Manufacturing Systems in Japan, Europe, and the United States." *Management Science*, 39, no. 2 (February 1993): 149–159.

McCutcheon, D. M., A. S. Raturi, and J. R. Meredith. "The Customization-Responsiveness Squeeze." *Sloan Management Review*, 35, no. 2 (Winter 1994): 89–100.

Morris, J. S., and R. J. Tersine. "A Simulation Analysis of Factors Influencing the Attractiveness of Group Technology Cellular Layout." *Management Science*, 36 (December 1990): 1567–1578.

Parsaei, H. R., and A. Mital. *Economic Aspects of Advanced Production and Manufacturing Systems*. New York: Van Nostrand Reinhold, 1991.

Pine, B. J., II. *Mass Customization: The New Frontier in Business Competition*. Boston: Harvard Business School Press, 1993.

Pulp and Paper, 19, no. 2: 47.

Quinn, J. B., and J. A. Mueller. "Transferring Research Results to Operations." *Harvard Business Review* (January/February 1991): 39–40.

Sekine, K. *One-Piece Flow*. Cambridge, MA: Productivity Press, 1992.

"Veteran Recycler Has Big Plans," *Northern Ontario Business*, 15, no. 6, sec. 1: 17.

Womack, J. P., and D. T. Jones. "From Lean Production to the Lean Enterprise." *Harvard Business Review*, 72, no. 2 (March/April 1992): 93–103.

Young, S. M. "A Framework for Successful Adoption and Performance of Japanese Manufacturing Practices in the United States." *The Academy of Management Review*, 17, no. 4 (October 1992): 677.

8

STATE-OF-THE-ART TECHNOLOGY IN P/OM

CHAPTER OUTLINE

LEARNING OBJECTIVES

When you complete this chapter you should be able to:

Identify or define:

- Computer-aided design (CAD)
- Computer-aided manufacturing (CAM)
- Numerical control
- Process control
- Fuzzy logic
- Neural networks

Explain:

- Flexible manufacturing systems (FMS)
- Computer-integrated manufacturing (CIM)
- Expert systems
- Manufacturing uses of MIS

WORLD-CLASS PROFILE: AT&T MICROELECTRONICS

TECHNOLOGY PROVIDES THE COMPETITIVE ADVANTAGE AT AT&T

AT&T Microelectronics, a winner of the Shingo quality prize for manufacturing, is truly a global producer of computer chips. With fabrication plants in Allentown and Reading, Pennsylvania, Orlando, Florida, and Madrid, Spain, and with manufacturing facilities in Malmsbury, England, Matamoros, Mexico, Bangkok, Thailand, and Singapore, AT&T is one of the world's largest producer of chips that go into disk drives, cellular phones, and network switches.

Touring a fabrication plant is like entering a vacuum-sealed bag. It is not a place made for people, who by nature are "dirty," with flaking skin that creates showers of dust. Today's chips can be contaminated by a single particle of dust 1/100 the width of a human hair. The chips themselves are less than one-millionth of a metre (called a micron) in size.

What goes on in a fabrication or "fab" plant? Blank silicon wafers, valued at perhaps $200, are the starting product. The output is a wafer with complicated patterns transferred on it, now valued at $20,000 or more.

The real centre of a fab is the photolithography bays. Here a photosensitive gel is sprayed onto the wafers; they then go into a machine that projects the circuit elements onto the wafer. The projector is called a "stepper" because it projects the same image about 100 times onto each wafer, moving the wafer in steps to receive each successive image. The

Workers in "bunny suits" complete one step in the photolithographic process of developing a wafer full of chips. The process of producing thousands of chips onto a silicon wafer is like printing a silk-screen reproduction with 20 different colors of ink. At each step a fresh layer of silicon dioxide is baked on, parts of the new layer are etched away, and chemical elements are added to the exposed areas.

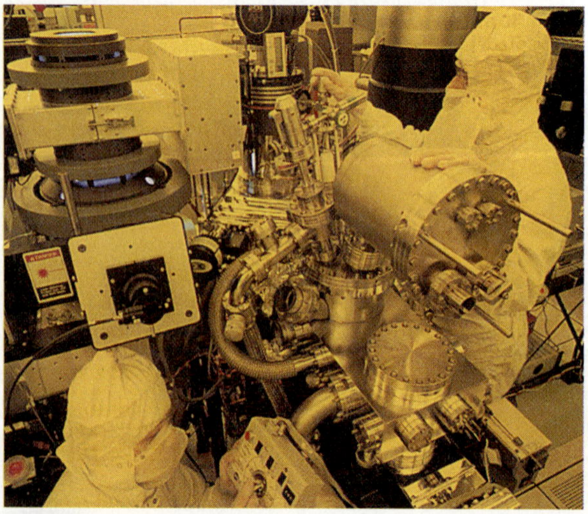

A designer of integrated circuits adjusts the tiny electro-optic crystal probe to try to tell what's going on within the circuits without taking them apart. Pointing the optic tip and micron-sized spot of laser light provides an electrical "window" into the world of the integrated circuit. The photo shows the microscope, crystal, laser, circuit board and computer used to measure the electrical currents.

photolithography equipment needed to print the circuit patterns is cutting-edge technology and can cost over $2 million per machine. It is not unusual for one production "clean room" to cost over half a billion dollars to build.

A magnified view of AT&T's new technique to make internal measurements of integrated circuits.

The fab room's cleanliness is specified in terms of the number of particles larger than one-half of one micron found in a cubic foot of air. A typical college classroom might have a few hundred thousand particles per cubic foot. A surgical operating room brings the level down to about 20,000. In AT&T's wafer-handling areas of the fab, the level is brought down to one!

To maximize the use of the capital equipment, AT&T's fab plant operates 24 hours a day, seven days a week. Workers pull 12-hour shifts, working 3 shifts one week and four the next.

These three researchers are examining a wafer in a "cleanroom." Their cleanroom "suits" consist of coats, gloves, and hoods, which are donned after the workers themselves are brushed and vacuumed. In some cleanroom environments, only non-smokers are permitted, as even a particulate of smoke residual in a man's mustache may contaminate the chip process.

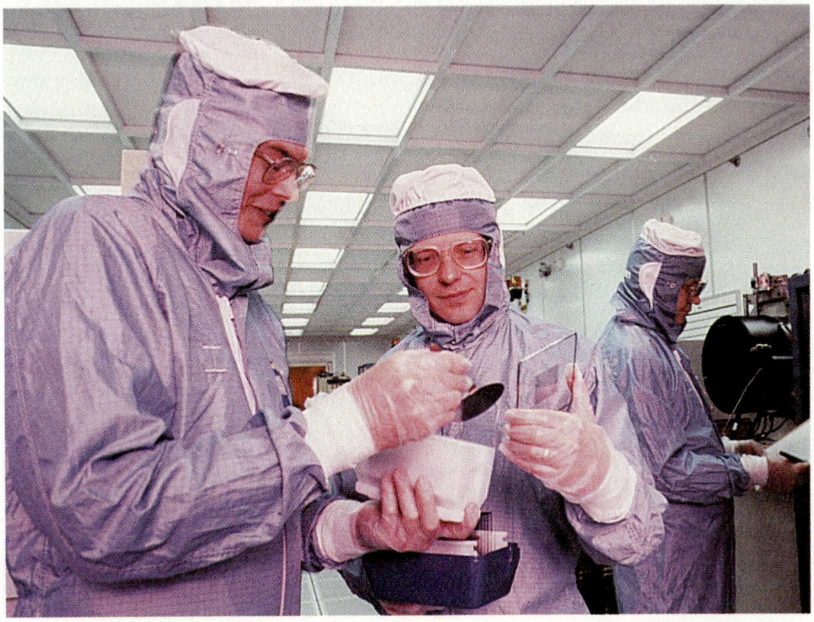

The process of completing a wafer's worth of chips takes as long as 12 weeks. It's not so much a linear assembly line as it is a loop. Over and over, the wafers are heat-treated, printed, etched, and doped with chemicals.

When the fab finishes a wafer, the wafer is sent to an overseas plant where it is sawed into chips. The chips are then put onto the familiar-looking plastic cases with wires coming out and are shipped to customers throughout the world.

In an industry where the life of a new product is measured in months, not years, AT&T must use its technology to maintain a global competitive edge.

Gillette is in the business of making razors and blades—and lots of other things that sell for very little. It has honed the art of using technology to cut fractions of a cent off production costs year after year. In just over 2 years, Gillette cut unit costs of its Sensor razor by 30%. How? By using advanced technology such as computers for tracking parts inventory and custom-designed laser welders for making the twin-blade Sensor cartridges. The company also uses specialized "vision" cameras to monitor and ensure product quality. Thanks to its use of technology, Gillette has become both a low-cost *and* a high-quality manufacturer. The company is a world-class leader, not just with its Sensor razor, but with its other brands as well.[1] ♦

In this chapter, we introduce the use of technology in P/OM. As Gillette and AT&T can testify, technology can be a powerful tool in developing a competitive advantage.[2] Firms that achieve competitive advantage through technology

- plan for a more distant time horizon;
- have a narrow product line and know their product and customer exceedingly well;
- have strong internal technical capabilities that are tied to their strategic analysis;
- have consistent and stable strategic management;
- have effective ways to implement the changes necessary for the constructive use of technology.

Opportunities for innovative uses of technology exist throughout P/OM—from product development to maintenance.[3] Because information technology is so pervasive, most of this chapter focusses on its application to P/OM.

One of the great advantages of robots is that they can be reprogrammed for different movements by merely changing the electronic signals that control them. However, one of the limitations of robots has been their inability to "sense" their strength or position or the pressure that is being exerted when they "grab" or "bump" something. Consequently, substantial effort has been made in recent years in this area. This picture indicates the tremendous strides being made in this area as robotic "fingers" pick up and hold a semiconductor chip.

TECHNOLOGY IN MANUFACTURING

Information sciences are the driving technology for both manufacturing and services. Among the tools provided by the information sciences are computer-aided design (CAD), computer-aided manufacturing (CAM), flexible manufacturing systems (FMSs), computer-integrated manufacturing (CIM), vision systems, automated storage and retrieval systems (ASRs), and automated guided vehicles (AGVs).

The electronic flow of data that ultimately becomes information is the communication that ties ever-improving equipment together. This electronic flow of

[1]*Wall Street Journal* (April 6, 1992): A1; and *AME News*, 7, no. 4 (July/August 1994): 3.

[2]See, for example, S. C. Fleming, "Using Technology for Competitive Advantage," *Research Technology Management*, 11, no. 5 (September/October 1994): 34–41; P. H. Biranbaum-Moore, A. R. Weiss, and R. W. Wright, "How Do Rivals Compete: Strategy, Technology, and Tactics," *Research Policy*, 23, no. 3 (May 1994): 249–265; Andrew Bartmess and Keith Cerny, "Building Competitive Advantage Through a Global Network of Capabilities," *California Management Review*, 35, no. 2 (Winter 1993): 78–103; and M. E. Porter, "The Technological Dimension of Competitive Strategy," in R. S. Rosenbloom, ed., *Research on Technology Innovation, Management and Policy* (Greenwich, CT: JAI Press), p. 3.

[3]For instance, see an excellent discussion on the strategic uses of technology in product innovation by Joseph Morone, "Strategic Use of Technology," *California Management Review* (Summer 1989): 81–110.

information allows the replacement of manual operations with automatic operations. The impact of information runs across the entire manufacturing spectrum, from design to manufacturing and from purchasing to shipping.

Computer-Aided Design (CAD) and Computer-Aided Manufacturing (CAM)

Computer-aided design (CAD) is the use of computers to interactively prepare engineering drawings. Although the variety of CAD software is extensive, most of it is used for drafting and three-dimensional drawings. Specialized CAD software exists for applications from electronic circuits to printed-circuit-board design. Still other CAD software is suited for mechanical applications including analysis of heat or stress. Additionally, some software focusses on how design affects processes.

Computer-aided design (CAD)

As we saw in Chapter 6, most of the manufacturing costs are determined at the design stage.[4] CAD software allows designers to save time and money by shortening development cycles for virtually all products. The speed and ease with which sophisticated designs can be manipulated, analyzed, and modified with CAD makes review of numerous options possible before final commitments are made. Faster development, better products, accurate flow of information to other departments, all contribute to a tremendous payoff for CAD.

The electronic transfer of product design information has proven so important that a standard for its exchange has been developed. That standard is known as the **Standard for the Exchange of Product Data (STEP)**. This standard allows manufacturers to express three-dimensional product information in a standard format so it can be exchanged internationally. STEP allows geographically dispersed manufacturers to integrate design, manufacture, and support processes. It also results in a reduction in design lead time and development costs. The *POM in Action* box "Electronic Design Speeds Development of Ford's Next 'World Car'" suggests the efficiencies that can be obtained with this technology.

Standard for the Exchange of Product Data (STEP)

Computer-aided manufacturing (CAM) refers to the use of specialized computer programs to direct and control manufacturing equipment. When computer-aided design (CAD) information is translated into instructions for computer-aided manufacturing (CAM), the result of these two technologies is CAD/CAM.

Computer-aided manufacturing (CAM)

The benefits of CAD and CAM include

1. *Product quality*. CAD provides an opportunity for the designer to investigate more alternatives, potential problems, and dangers.
2. *Shorter design time*. Because time is money, the shorter the design phase, the lower the cost.
3. *Production cost reductions*. Reduced inventory, more efficient use of personnel through improved scheduling, and faster implementation of design changes lower costs.
4. *Database availability*. Consolidating accurate product data so everyone is operating from the same information results in dramatic cost reductions.
5. *New range of capabilities*. For instance, the ability to rotate and depict objects in three-dimensional form, to check clearances, to relate parts and attachments,

[4]See Mohan V. Tatikunda, "Design for Assembly: A Critical Methodology for Product Reengineering and New Product Development," *Production and Inventory Management Journal* (First Quarter 1994): 31–38.

POM IN ACTION

Electronic Design Speeds Development of Ford's Next "World Car"

The key to its future, as Ford sees it, is a "world car" approach—the global manufacturing of a family of cars that share identical components produced in plants throughout the world. Its new series of common-component cars—the Ford Contour, the Mercury Mystique, and the Mondeo (their European version)—cost a whopping $6 billion to develop.

To dramatically cut costs of the 1999 rollout of its next new sedan, Ford is turning to an interactive process of design intended to cut lead time to 24 months. This compares positively to the 35 months it took to design the 1994 Mustang and the 54 months to design the average U.S. auto.

Here is how it works: A Ford engineer in England transmits a massive computer file of 3-D detailed drawings of the car to designers in Dearborn, Michigan, which takes only 15 minutes. The information is scrambled for satellite transmission. With revisions on hand, the Dearborn designers call England and coordinate final changes with their European counterpart. Each sees the latest images as they are made. The revised drawings are transmitted to Ford's design studio in Turin, Italy, where a computerized milling machine can turn out a clay or plastic-foam model in a matter of hours.

This interactive computer-aided design structure lets engineers, manufacturers, and suppliers worldwide get involved early in the automotive design stage. Not only does this technology reduce costs and speed development, but designers hope it will also mean that prototypes will not require substantial alteration once they hit the road.

Sources: New York Times (August 29, 1993); and *Forbes* (March 15, 1993): 54.

to improve use of numerically controlled machine tools—all provide new capability for manufacturing. CAD/CAM removes substantial detail work, allowing designers to concentrate on the conceptual and imaginative aspects of their task.

Numerical Control

CAD/CAM works because much of the machinery in the world can now be controlled electronically. Machinery can be designed for electronic control rather than manual and mechanical control. Electronic control increases both speed and flexibility. Machinery that can be controlled electronically, usually with magnetic tape, is called **numerical control (NC)** machinery. When machines have their own microcomputer *and* memory to store computer programs, they are called **computer numerical control (CNC)** machinery. Electronic control is accomplished by writing computer programs that are stored on the magnetic tape in the case of NC machines and in computer memory in the case of CNC machines. The computer program is written much as one might write a BASIC or COBOL program to produce a paycheque. The languages used include APT (Automatically Programmed Tool) and Compact II.

Numerical control (NC)

Computer numerical control (CNC)

The third phase of numerical control is **direct numerical control (DNC)**. DNC machines are wired to a central computer that can send (download) the necessary code to the memory in DNC machines.

Direct numerical control (DNC)

Process Control

Process control

Process control is the use of information technology to monitor and control a physical process. These processes usually meet our definition of a *continuous process*. For instance, process control is used to measure the moisture content and thickness of paper as it travels over a paper machine at hundreds of metres per minute. Process control is also used to determine and control temperatures, pressures, and quantities in petroleum refineries, petrochemical processes, cement plants, steel mills, nuclear reactors, and other continuous processes.

Process control systems operate in a number of ways, but the following is typical:

- They have sensors—often analog devices collecting data.
- The analog devices read data on some periodic basis, perhaps once a minute, or once every second.
- The measurements are translated into digital signals, which are transmitted to a digital computer.
- Computer programs read the file (the digital data) and analyze the data.
- The resulting output may take numerous forms. These include a message on a computer console or printer, a signal to a motor to change a valve setting, a warning light or horn, or a statistical process control chart.

Vision Systems

Vision systems combine video cameras and computer technology. These systems are primarily used in inspection roles. Visual inspection is an important task in most food-processing and manufacturing organizations. Moreover, in many applications, visual inspection performed by humans is tedious, mind-numbing, and error-prone. This is why vision systems are widely used when the items being inspected are very similar. For instance, vision systems are used to inspect french fries so that imperfections can be identified as the fries proceed down the production line. Vision systems are used to ensure that sealant is present and in the proper amount on Whirlpool's washing-machine transmissions. Such systems are also used to inspect switch assemblies at the Foster Plant in Des Plaines, Illinois. Vision systems are consistently accurate, do not become bored, and are of modest cost. Consequently, these systems are vastly superior to individuals trying to perform these tasks.

Vision systems

Robots

When a machine is flexible and has the ability to hold, move, and perhaps "grab" items, we tend to use the word **robot**. However, in spite of movies, cartoons, and stories about robots, they are not mechanical people. They are mechanical devices that may have a few electronic impulses stored on semiconductor chips that will activate motors or switches. When robots are part of a production process, they usually provide the movement of material between machines. They may also be used effectively to perform tasks that are especially monotonous, or dangerous, or when the task can be improved by the substitution of mechanical for human effort. This would be the case where consistency, accuracy, speed, or the necessary strength or power can be enhanced by the substitution of machines for people.

Robot

Robots and programmable machines are now cost-competitive for a wide range of applications from small-batch jobs through long, continuous jobs. Less flexible and, consequently, less expensive robots may substitute for specialized equipment even in continuous processes. Robot control and instructions are similar to those used for numerically controlled machine tools. These instructions provide complete task control providing position, orientation, velocity, and acceleration. Communication between the operator and the robot is typically provided by a computer terminal, although robots can also be instructed via a "lead-through" method. Once instructions are entered, they are stored in computer memory and modified or edited as changes are made in the product or processing. However, robots are not a panacea for every company and every task.

Automated Storage and Retrieval Systems (ASRSs)

Automated storage and retrieval systems (ASRSs)

Because of the tremendous labour involved in error-prone warehousing, computer-controlled warehouses have been developed. These systems, known as **automated storage and retrieval systems (ASRSs)**, provide for the automatic placement and withdrawal of parts into and from designated places in a warehouse. The systems are commonly used in distribution facilities of retailers such as Wal-Mart, Tupperware, and Benetton. (See the *POM in Action* box "Benetton: The World's Fastest Clothing Manufacturer.") These systems are also found in inventory and test areas of manufacturing firms.

Automated Guided Vehicles (AGVs)

Automated guided vehicles (AGVs)

Automated material handling can take the form of monorails, conveyors, robots, or automated guided vehicles (AGVs). **Automated guided vehicles (AGVs)** are electronically guided and controlled carts used in manufacturing to move parts and equipment. They are also used in offices to move mail and in hospitals and in jails to deliver meals.

Flexible Manufacturing Systems (FMSs)

In the sophisticated case, material handling equipment is used to complement direct numerical control (DNC) machines. The material handling equipment can be robots, transfer machines, or automated guided vehicles; it moves materials from one workstation to another. The material handling equipment and the workstation may be connected to a common centralized computer facility, which provides the instructions for routing jobs to the appropriate workstation and the instructions for each workstation. Such an arrangement is an automated work cell or, as it is more commonly known, a **flexible manufacturing system (FMS)**. (See Figure 8.1.)

Flexible manufacturing system (FMS)

While technological challenging, computer-aided scheduling and the improved utilization possible with FMS are making these systems ever more popular.

Computer-Integrated Manufacturing (CIM)

A flexible manufacturing system can be extended backward electronically into the engineering (computer-aided design), production, and inventory control departments. In this way, computer-aided drafting can ultimately generate the necessary electronic code (instructions) to control a direct numerically controlled (DNC)

FIGURE 8.1 ■ Flexible Manufacturing Systems (FMS) place machines and various computer-controlled material handling devices under computer control. Machines and material handling devices can be of different types. Setups and tool changing for each job are handled automatically.

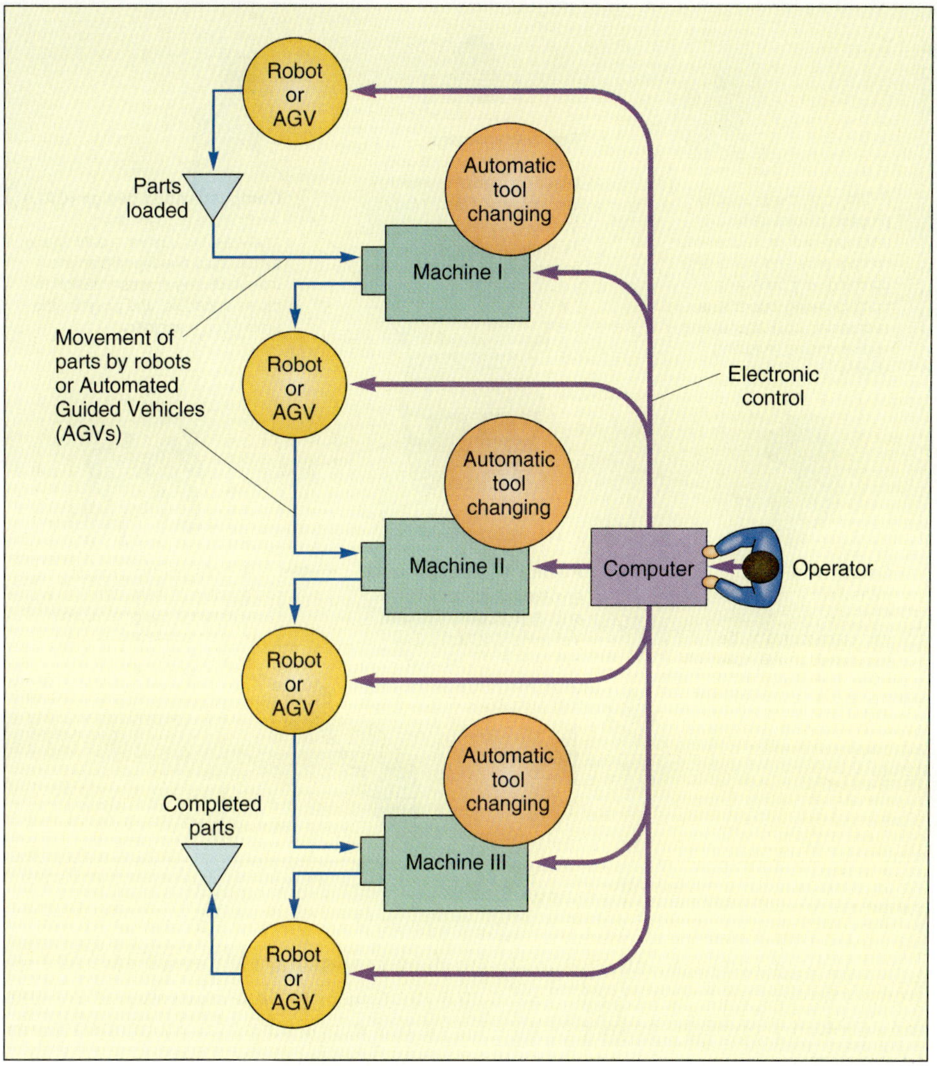

Spar Aerospace Limited, Brampton, Ontario, was awarded a $30 million contract to provide robotic workstations for the International Space Station program. Spar will design and build two-flight robotic workstations that include display and control functions enabling astronauts to operate the space station's robotics, known as the Mobile Servicing System (MSS). Spar currently is developing the Space Station Remote Manipulator System and Special-Purpose Dextrous Manipulator, which will be used to assist in the assembly and maintenance of the space station. A view of the U.S. space station with the Canadarm shown to the left (artist's rendering). This has been a successful venture for Spar and for Canada.

machine. If this machine is connected to others and to material handling equipment as a part of a flexible manufacturing system, then the entire system would be **computer-integrated manufacturing (CIM)** (Figure 8.2).

Computer-integrated manufacturing (CIM)

In a computer-integrated manufacturing environment, a design change initiated at a computer-aided design (CAD) terminal can result in that change being made in the part produced in a matter of minutes.

Expansion of FMS and CIM

Flexible manufacturing systems (FMS) and computer-integrated manufacturing (CIM) are reducing the distinction between low-volume, high-variety and high-volume,

Robots can do a variety of dangerous and monotonous tasks for which they are much better suited than people. However, even robots have to be taught to perform those tasks. Here a General Electric engineer, after analysis using motion studies, is using a "teaching" box to train an industrial robot to perform those tasks.

FIGURE 8.2 ■ **Computer-Integrated Manufacturing (CIM).** Computer-aided design (CAD), computer-aided manufacturing (CAM), flexible manufacturing systems (FMSs), brought together with automated storage and retrieval systems (ASRSs) and automated guided vehicles (AGVs).

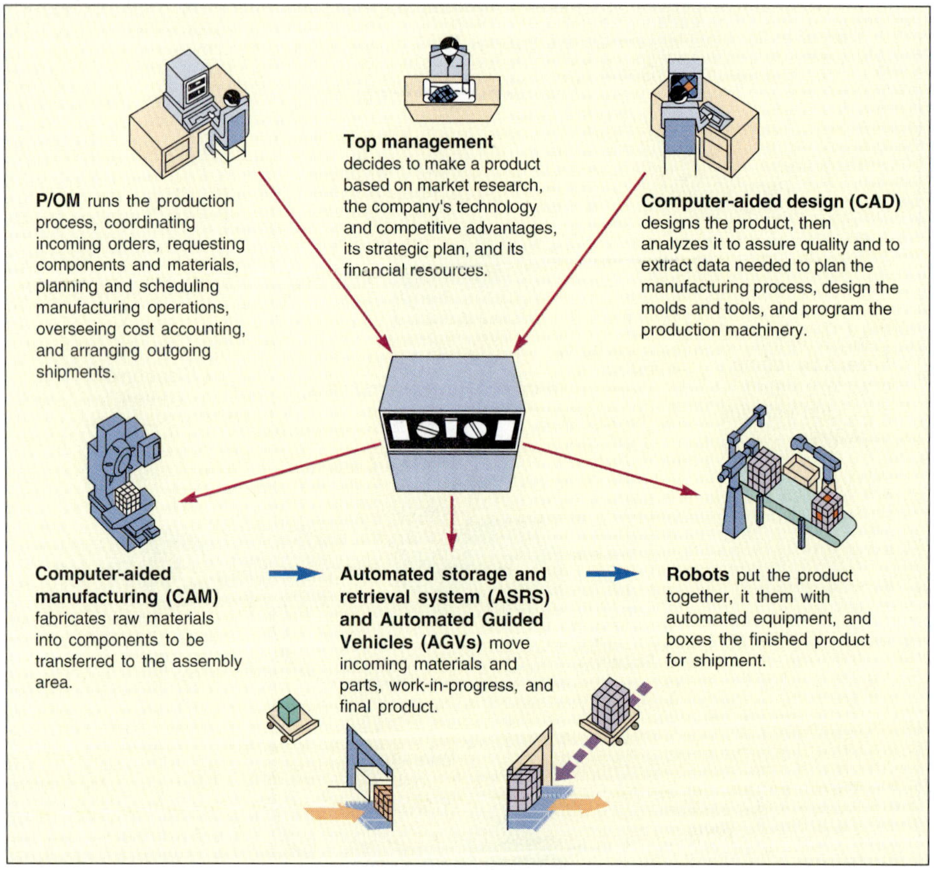

Firms often link several types of automated equipment together into a single, integrated system. Here an AGV feeds an ASRS.

low-variety production. Information technology is allowing FMS and CIM to be extremely flexible and expand to include a growing range of volumes, as shown in Figure 8.3. Table 8.1 provides a synopsis of some of the major advances in manufacturing technology.

TECHNOLOGY IN SERVICES

The use of technology extends beyond manufacturing. Technology also has a wide range of applications in the services industry. These include everything from diagnostic equipment at an auto repair shop, to blood and urine testing equipment at a hospital, to improved materials for a knee replacement. The lodging industry provides a good example of the many ways technology can be used in the service industry. As you may have experienced, you can now authorize payment of your bill from your hotel room via a channel on the room's television set. The labour savings at the

POM IN ACTION

Benetton: The World's Fastest Clothing Manufacturer

Benetton, the Italian sportswear company, can probably claim to have the world's fastest factory *and* the most efficient distributor in the garment industry. Located in Ponzano, Italy, Benetton makes and ships 50 million pieces of clothing—mostly slacks, dresses, and sweaters worldwide each year. Its one and only warehouse serves Benetton's 5,000 stores in 60 countries around the world. It cost $60 million, but this distribution centre, run by only eight people, ships 230,000 pieces of clothing each day.

Here is how efficient Benetton is in meeting market demands: Let us say a salesperson in a Boston shop finds she is running out of a best-selling blue sweater. She calls a Benetton sales agent, who enters the order in a PC, which electronically forwards the order to the mainframe computer in Italy. Because the blue sweater was originally created by computer-aided design (CAD), the mainframe retains all the proper measurements, which it passes on to a knitting machine. The machine makes the sweaters, which are boxed with a bar code addressed to the Boston store, and the box goes to the Italian warehouse.

Once the blue sweaters are snugly sitting in one of the 300,000 slots in the warehouse, a robot flies by, reading bar codes. It picks out the right box and any other boxes ready for the Boston store and loads them for shipment.

Including manufacturing time, Benetton gets the order to Boston in 4 weeks if none is in stock, 1 week if a supply is already in the warehouse. In the notoriously slow garment industry, Benetton responded to the customer by using electronic communication, a CAD/CAM, robots, and bar codes and became a world-class leader.

Sources: Fortune (February 13, 1989): 54–59; and *Distribution* (October 1993): 62–66.

registration desk and enhanced service for the customer are currently providing a competitive advantage to Sheraton Hotels.

Table 8.2 provides a glimpse of the impact of technology on services. Operations managers in services, as in manufacturing, must be able to evaluate the impact of technology on their firm. This requires particular skill when evaluating reliability, investment analysis, human resource requirements, and maintenance/service.

Robots are used not only for labour savings, but more importantly, for those jobs that are dangerous, or monotonous, or require consistency, as in the even spraying of paint on an automobile.

In an effort to manage the time and paperwork associated with insurance claims, State Farm Mutual Automobile Insurance is testing "notepad" computers. A "notepad" computer uses an electric pen that claims adjusters use to fill out insurance forms and mark damage on a schematic of a car. The computer then uses stored parts and price lists to calculate damage. The information, along with digitized versions of signatures, is then transferred to the central computer at the end of the day. The hope is that the system will improve accuracy and reduce time and costs associated with automobile insurance claims.

FIGURE 8.3 ■ Different Production Processes Provide Different Combinations of Volume and Variety. As FMS and CIM expand, more overlap among options will occur.

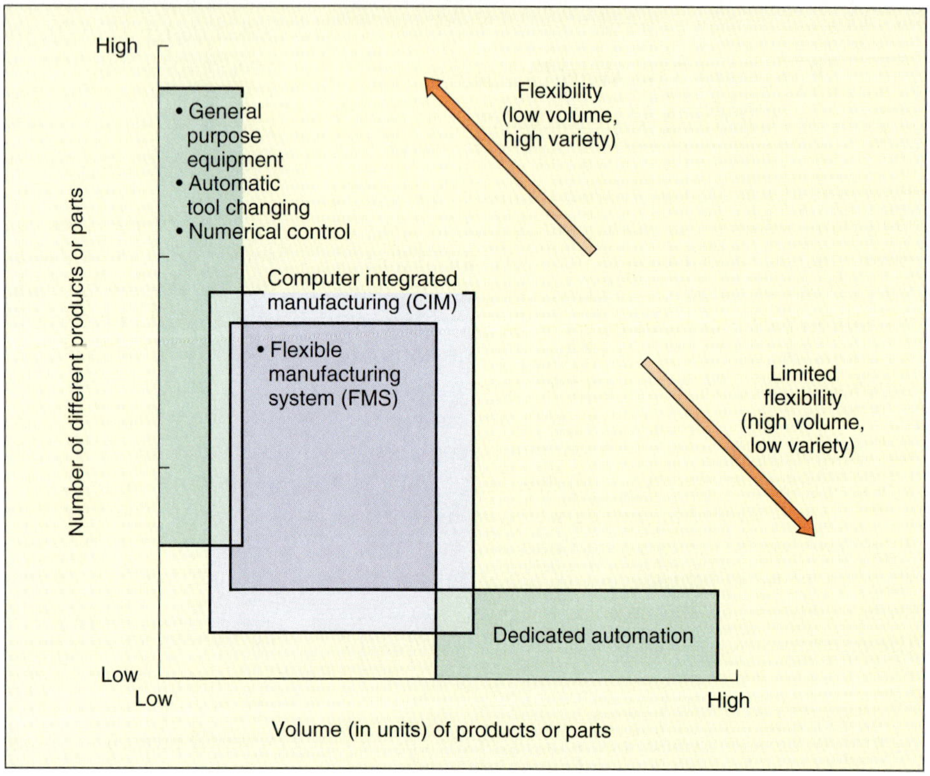

INFORMATION SCIENCES IN OPERATIONS

The information sciences are making a major impact in additional areas that have applications in operations. These areas are transaction processing, management information systems, and decision support systems. Figure 8.4 shows these information systems.

TABLE 8.1 ■ MAJOR INNOVATIONS IN MANUFACTURING TECHNOLOGY

MACHINERY	TECHNOLOGICAL INNOVATION
Numerical control (NC)	Electronic instructions read from a tape.
Computer numerical control (CNC)	Computer memory resident at machine.
Direct numerical control (DNC)	Computer memory resident at machine and machine wired to a central computer.
Flexible machining centre (FMC)	Electronic control of several DNC machines and the equipment (such as robots and AGVs) necessary to move material between those machines.
Computer-integrated manufacturing (CIM)	An FMS expanded to include design (CAD), inventory control, warehousing, and shipping.

Transaction Processing

A **transaction processing system** is a system that addresses the many transactions that occur within and between firms. These transactions have traditionally been paper transactions and include payroll, order entry, invoicing, receipt of checks, inventory, personnel, and so on. When these transactions are moved from paper to computerized processing and storage, we have a computer-based transaction system. The paperwork transactions at General Motors were so horrendous that GM bought Electronic Data Systems, Inc. (EDS) so that these transactions could be computerized and the cost reduced. To the extent that such systems can be automated beyond those of competitors, a competitive advantage in speed, accuracy, or cost reduction may be obtained. If General Motors has one billion paper transactions a year and is able to reduce the cost of each transaction by $5, the savings is tremendous.

Transaction processing system

Modern transaction processing systems rely on electronic signals, which are a great vehicle for transmitting information, but they have a major limitation—most P/OM data do not start out in bits and bytes. Therefore, we must get the data into an electronic form; **automatic identification systems (AISs)** are the technologies that provide the translation of data into electronic bits and bytes. Bar codes, radio frequencies, and those optical characters on bank cheques are automatic identification systems that help us move data to electronic media. Bar codes are used by Litton Industries for checking inventory and by nurses in hospitals to match bar codes on medication to ID bracelets on patients. For another application, see the *POM in Action* box "TRW and Ford Learn the Importance of Tracking in Airbag Production."

Automatic identification systems (AISs)

Management Information System (MIS)

The second form of information system is the **management information system (MIS)**. MIS systems are dedicated to obtaining, formatting, manipulating, and

Management information system (MIS)

TABLE 8.2 ■ EXAMPLES OF TECHNOLOGY'S IMPACT ON SERVICES

SERVICE INDUSTRY	EXAMPLE
Financial services	Debit cards, electronic funds transfer, automatic teller machines.
Education	Multimedia presentations, electronic bulletin boards, library cataloguing systems.
Utilities and government	Automated one-man garbage trucks, optical mail scanners, airborne warning and control systems.
Restaurant and foods	Optical check-out scanners, coupons based on specific purchases issued at check-out counters, wireless orders from waiters to the kitchen, robot butchering.
Communications	Electronic publishing, interactive TV, voice mail, "notepad" computers, cellular phones.
Hotels	Electronic check-in and check-out systems, electronic key/lock systems.
Wholesale/retail trade	Point-of-sale electronic terminals, dry cleaner's conveyors, bar-coded data, automated security systems.
Transportation	Automatic toll booths, space shuttle, satellite-directed navigation systems.
Health care	MRI scanners, sonograms, patient-monitoring systems, on-line medical information systems.

FIGURE 8.4 ■ DSS, MIS, and Transaction Processing in Production/Operations Management

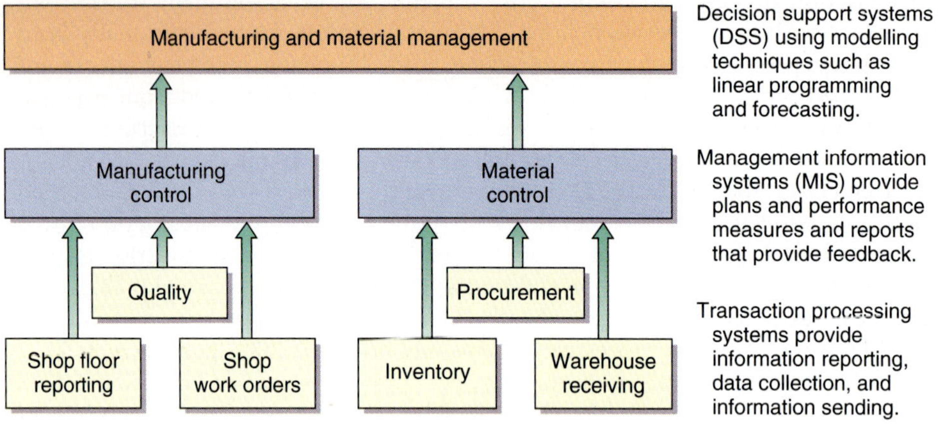

presenting data in the form of information to managers when needed. Much of the control information for a firm is provided by the MIS system. Information systems make their presence known in P/OM in a variety of ways, from scheduling to material requirements planning (MRP).

Decision Support System (DSS)

Decision support system (DSS)

Another area where information science is helping operations in service as well as in manufacturing is through the use of a decision support system. A **decision support system (DSS)** is a logical extension of MIS that aids managers in *modelling* and decision making. Rather than simply providing information, a DSS allows a manager to perform "what-if" analysis given certain financial or operating parameters. A DSS also can incorporate a wide variety of management science models and graphical outputs. A spreadsheet model that is used to examine various alternatives is one form of a DSS.

Artificial Intelligence

MIS and DSS are supported by recent advances in artificial intelligence. Three tools, *expert systems*, *fuzzy logic*, and *neural networks*, can be thought of as part of a general discipline known as artificial intelligence. We will now introduce each of these tools.

Expert systems (ESs)

Expert systems (ESs) are computer programs that mimic human logic and "solve" problems much as a human expert would. The idea behind the use of an expert system is to capture in a computer program the knowledge and skills of a person who is an expert in a given field. Indeed, five advantages of ESs are that they

1. make decisions faster than the expert;
2. derive the benefits of having an expert at its disposal without having the expert present;
3. equal and surpass, at least in terms of consistency, the human expert;
4. free the human expert for other work;
5. can be disseminated to numerous nonexperts for education and training.

POM IN ACTION

TRW and Ford Learn the Importance of Tracking in Airbag Production

Airbags are supposed to allay fears of injury, but the one in Audrey Baker's 1990 Ford had just the opposite effect. Ms. Baker's car was part of a 165,000-car, multimillion dollar recall by Ford, which feared that defective bags could leak burning gases on occupants. The 1991 experience was an expensive lesson to Ford in the value of bar codes.

The airbags, supplied by TRW, Inc., show the hazards of converting an experimental technology into a mass-produced good. An airbag is a complex system made up of sensors that detect an impact and then explode a small canister of gas, which temporarily inflates a parachutelike balloon to cushion the auto occupant's impact. To meet demand, TRW accelerated production by using robots to automate previously manual tasks. But an out-of-tolerance machine damaged a joint in the airbag module, which *might* have allowed a few bags to spill their gases. No injuries occurred because of the defect, and TRW stressed that only 3,133 airbags had the problem.

The only problem was that no one knew *which* airbags had the defect, for neither TRW nor Ford had used bar coding or any other system to identify individual airbags or their production lot. What should Ford do? The legal and moral implications caused the company to play it safe with a total recall. Ford also announced that it expected TRW to share in the expense. At the same time, it cancelled its exclusive contract with TRW and began plans to buy from multiple sources by 1996. This major blow to TRW left executives shaking their heads over the hidden expense of not tracking products, which can be done economically with bar codes.

Sources: Wall Street Journal (March 12, 1991): A4; and J.A.F. Stoner and R.E. Freeman, *Management*, 5th ed. (Englewood Cliffs, NJ: 653. Prentice-Hall, 1992)

Although the idea is quite simple, the mechanics of making an expert system work are difficult. To make the system function there must be a knowledge base that is supplied by an expert. Every step of the process must be programmed meticulously, including any and all options to decisions made throughout the process. This computerized knowledge base is designed to be updated periodically to include new rules and facts. An electronic representation of the expert's thought process is called the "inference engine"—this fuels the knowledge base.

Table 8.3 provides an indication of the areas in which expert systems have been developed. Their names and a brief explanation are also included. The *POM in Action* box "MasterCard Prepares for a Makeover" discusses a specific example of an expert system. A number of expert systems are discussed in more detail in the appropriate chapters of this text.

Although the use of expert systems is widespread and rapidly expanding, limitations do exist. Among these are determining the relevance of data and recognizing the lack of data—these abilities have yet to be incorporated into expert systems. However, these limitations are being addressed by fuzzy logic and neural networks.

Many decisions are not clear-cut enough for the use of expert systems. A yes or no may not be sufficient. Consequently, another tool, *fuzzy logic*, has been developed for the operations manager's tool kit. **Fuzzy logic** can deal with approximate values, influences, and incomplete or ambiguous data to make decisions. For example, when making concrete or steel, the expertise of years of training is often the critical ingredient for a good batch. Knowing when to add material, heat, or a minor ingredient may be critical. Adding fuzzy rules—such as "if too hot, cut back on fuel" or "if mix is not consistent or if mix is too moist, mix longer"—deals with such ambiguities. Fuzzy logic is now written into computer programs to make both concrete and steel. It is

Fuzzy logic

TABLE 8.3 ■ EXPERT SYSTEMS IN P/OM

NAME	USE	EXPLANATION
XCON (eXpert CONfigurer), Digital Equipment Corp.	Configuration	Checks sales orders and specifies components needed to configure the system
Authorizer's Assistant, American Express	Credit	Helps determine the appropriate level of credit, using a variety of criteria
CONSULTANT, IBM	Bids	Helps field representatives prepare bids by analyzing the request for quotation
PROPLAN	Scheduling	Schedules parts on the basis of their features and of machine capability and availability
SPC (Statistical Process Control), Automatix, Inc.	Process control	Data are analyzed to help the manufacturing process anticipate malfunctions
DELTA (Diesel Electric Locomotive Troubleshooting), General Electric	Maintenance	Assists maintenance staff isolate and repair various faults in locomotives
FADES (Facilities Design Expert System)	Layout	Develops a good facility design mixing quantitative tools and human judgement

Sources: Adapted from H. Raghav Rao and B. P. Lingaraj, "Expert Systems in Production and Operations Management: Classification and Prospects," *Interfaces*, 18 (November/December 1988): 80–91; and Dorothy Leonard-Barton and John J. Sviokla, "Putting Expert Systems to Work," *Harvard Business Review*, 66 (March/April 1988): 92.

also being used to add new features to consumer products, as we see in the *POM in Action* box "Matsushita's 'Fuzzy Logic' Microwaves and Washing Machines."

Neural networks

Neural networks, modelled on the brain's meshlike network of interconnected cells, recognize patterns and program themselves to solve related problems on their own. The advantage to the operations manager is that they are programmed to learn.

POM IN ACTION

MasterCard Prepares for a Makeover

MasterCard launched new product lines and a new image in 1995. Chief executive H. Euhgine Lockhart expected 1996 to start showing dividends from this repositioning with more visible media presence, new products, and more customers for MasterCard. His plan:

- Push more decision making to the regional level
- Reexamine the company's advertising, stressing security and reliability
- Provide Internet security protocol for on-line transactions
- Reverse the company's decline in membership direct mail solicitation

MasterCard explored offline debit cards, smart cards, and cobranding, which VISA won most of MasterCard's members in. MasterCard responded with the BJ's/Beneficial National Bank USA/MasterCard and 147 other cobranding deals. Industry speculation focussed on possible MasterCard involvement also with Modex, the British smart card electronic money system.

The changes seemed to have paid off for MasterCard, with year-over-year increases of 20% in global charge volume and 21.5% in global credit card circulation. A key indicator for MasterCard was that charge volume, card circulation, commercial cards, and gold cards all showed marked increases within all global regions (Asia, Europe, Latin America, and North America).

Source: Adapted from *Credit Card Management*, 9, no. 2 (May 1996): 60–61.

POM IN ACTION

Matsushita's "Fuzzy Logic" Microwaves and Washing Machines

Matsushita Electric Industries (MEI), Japan's giant appliance manufacturer, is building machines that mimic human logic. The cornerstone of its technology is neuro–fuzzy logic controllers. Instead of responding to yes-no, on-off digital commands, the fuzzy system can answer with "sort of" and "maybe, but let's see" actions based on if-then logic programming.

MEI's fuzzy logic microwave ovens, for example, simulate a cook's judgement, setting temperatures according to feedback from the cooking process. It monitors air temperature, food texture, and moisture content to trigger electronic controls with minute adjustments in timing and heat levels.

The firm also uses fuzzy logic to control washing machines so that wash cycles, water heat, and spinning speeds are adjusted in predetermined ways to match types of clothing. MEI claims its washers and dryers do a much better job at selecting settings than humans, who guess which is best and then walk away.

MEI's technology is also embedded in 2,000 other experimental home and office mechanisms, including camera processors. These processors improve automatic focussing features, trigger light-sensitive, flash-photo equipment, and operate shutter speed and aperture controls. Fuzzy logic technology is now using "neuro-networks" that can "learn" from preprogrammed expert data and from their own accumulation of process data.

Sources: Business Week (September 26, 1994): 144; and *Wall Street Journal* (October 21, 1991): R18.

They can, for instance, recognize unnatural patterns, such as cycles and trends in control charts. Because of this unique ability to learn and recognize patterns, they can provide valuable information for real-time process control.[5]

These three tools, and indeed the discipline of artificial intelligence, have developed to the point where they are now making a major impact on operations management.

MasterCard's new line of products and new image has resulted in significant payoffs.

ACHIEVING WORLD-CLASS STANDARDS

World-class firms distinguish themselves not just by using the latest technology, but by the way they *strategically* use technology. The objective is not to just grab hold of the latest technological gimmick, but to use technology to achieve the long-term strategic objectives of the firm. For world-class firms, return on investment is only one criterion for technological investment. Such companies also ask, "Does the technology win orders?" Moreover, these firms ensure that they have the financial and human resources to make the technology work. That was obviously not the case for many companies in the earlier *POM in Action* box "The Robot's Role Is Not in Every Factory."

SUMMARY

Technology is a major source of competitive advantage. Advances are being made in a number of areas, but particularly in the information sciences. Information sciences

[5]H. Brian Hwarng and Norma Faris Habele, "X Control Chart Pattern Identification Through Efficient Off-Line Neural Network Training," *IIE Transactions*, 25, no. 3 (May 1993): 27–40.

are improving management information systems, transaction processing systems, and decision support systems. Information technology is also enhancing machine controls, from numerical controls to computer-integrated manufacturing. These advances are, with proper management, providing improved flexibility in meeting customer requirements, higher quality, and greater utilization of resources.

KEY TERMS

Computer-aided design (CAD) (p. 321)
Standard for the Exchange of Product Data (STEP) (p. 321)
Computer-aided manufacturing (CAM) (p. 321)
Numerical control (NC) (p. 322)
Computer numerical control (CNC) (p. 322)
Direct numerical control (DNC) (p. 322)
Process control (p. 322)
Vision systems (p. 323)
Robot (p. 323)
Automated storage and retrieval systems (ASRSs) (p. 324)
Automated guided vehicles (AGVs) (p. 324)
Flexible manufacturing system (FMS) (p. 324)
Computer-integrated manufacturing (CIM) (p. 325)
Transaction processing system (p. 329)
Automatic identification systems (AISs) (p. 329)
Management information system (MIS) (p. 329)
Decision support system (DSS) (p. 330)
Expert systems (ESs) (p. 330)
Fuzzy logic (p. 331)
Neural networks (p. 332)

DISCUSSION QUESTIONS

1. What are possible applications of an expert system?
2. In what kind of situations are expert systems being used?
3. What is the difference between a management information system (MIS) and a decision support system (DSS)?
4. Give some recent examples of information technology successfully applied to new products and new processes in (a) manufacturing and (b) services.
5. Distinguish between flexible manufacturing systems (FMSs) and computer-integrated manufacturing (CIM).
6. What kinds of enhancements are being made to computer-aided design (CAD) systems?
7. Distinguish between expert systems, fuzzy logic, and neural networks.
8. How do "vision systems" work and where might they be used?
9. What are the advantages of a system like the Standard for the Exchange of Product Data (STEP)?
10. Explain the difference between NC, CNC, and DNC machines.
11. What are the different types of computer-aided design systems?

CRITICAL THINKING EXERCISE

1. Do you see any problems for the consumer with the concept of pushing more decision-making to the regional level as described in *POM in Action* box "MasterCard Prepares for a Makeover"?
2. What in your opinion are the ethical issues needed to be discussed with regard to the promoting and advertising of "consumer debt"?

PROBLEMS

8.1 Heyl Machine Shop, Inc., has a 1-year contract for the production of 200,000 gear housings for a new off-road vehicle. The owner, Jeff Heyl hopes the contract will be extended and the volume increased next year. Mr. Heyl has developed costs for three alternatives (see Figure 8.3). They are general-purpose equipment (GPE), flexible manufacturing system (FMS), and dedicated automation (DA). The cost data follow:

	General-Purpose Equipment (GPE)	Flexible Manufacturing System (FMS)	Dedicated Automation (DA)
Annual contracted units	200,000	200,000	200,000
Annual fixed cost	$100,000	$200,000	$500,000
Per-unit variable cost	$15.00	$14.00	$13.00

What process is best for this contract?

8.2 Using the data in Problem 8.1, determine the economical volume for each process.

8.3 Using the data in Problem 8.1, determine the best process for each of the following volumes: (1) 50,000, (2) 250,000, and (3) 350,000.

8.4 Refer to Problem 8.1. If a contract for the second and third years is pending, what are the implications for process selection?

CASE STUDY

Rochester Manufacturing Corporation

Rochester Manufacturing Corporation (RMC) was considering moving some of its production from traditional numerically controlled machines to a flexible machining system (FMS). Its traditional numerical control machines have been operating in a high-variety, low-volume, intermittent manner. Machine utilization, as near as it can determine, is hovering around 10%. The machine tool sales people and a consulting firm want to put the machines together in an FMS. They believe that a $3,000,000 expenditure on machinery and the transfer machines will handle about 30% of RMC's work. The firm has not yet entered all its parts into a comprehensive group technology system, but believes that the 30% is a good estimate. This 30% fits very nicely into a "family." A reduction, because of higher utilization, should take place in the number of pieces of machinery. The firm should be able to go from fifteen to about four machines and personnel should go from fifteen to perhaps as low as three. Similarly, floor space reduction will go from 20,000 feet to about 6,000. Throughput of orders should also improve with this family of parts being processed in 1 to 2 days rather than 7 to 10. Inventory reduction is estimated to yield a one-time $750,000 savings, and annual labour savings should be in the neighbourhood of $300,000.

Although the projections all look very positive, an analysis of the project's return on investment showed it to be between 10% and 15% per year. The company has traditionally had an expectation that projects should yield well over 15% and have payback periods of substantially less than 5 years.

DISCUSSION QUESTIONS

1. As a production manager for RMC, what do you recommend? Why?
2. Prepare a case by a conservative plant manager for maintaining the status quo until the returns are more obvious.
3. Prepare the case for an optimistic sales manager that you should move ahead with the FMS now.

BIBLIOGRAPHY

Beatty, C. A. "Implementing Advanced Manufacturing Technologies: Rules of the Road." *Sloan Management Review*, 33, no. 4 (Summer 1992): 49.

Byrd, T. A. "Expert Systems in Production and Operations Management: Results of a Survey." *Interfaces*, 23, no. 2 (March/April 1993): 118–129.

Davenport, T. H. *Process Innovation*, Cambridge, MA: Harvard Business School Press, 1993.

Grant, R. M., R. Krishnan, A. B. Shani, and R. Baer. "Appropriate Manufacturing Technology: A Strategic Approach." *Sloan Management Review*, 33 (Fall 1991): 43.

"MasterCard Prepares for a Makeover," *Credit Card Management*, 9, no. 2 (May 1996): 60–61.

Roberts, E. B. "The Success of High-Technology Firms: Early Technological and Marketing Influences." *Interfaces*, 22, no. 4 (July/August 1992): 3.

Robotics World, 14, no. 2: 10–14.

Rodriquiz, A. A., and O. R. Mitchell. "A Vision System for Manufacturing Applications Under Moderately Unconstrained Conditions." *Industrial Engineering Research & Development*, 25, no. 4 (July 1993): 15–25.

Roth, A. V., C. Gaimon, and L. Krajewski. "Optimal Acquisition of FMS Technology Subject to Technological Progress." *Decision Sciences*, 22 (Spring 1991): 308.

Stefik, M., J. Aikins, R. Balzer, J. Benoit, L. Birnbaum, F. Hayes-Roth, and E. Sacerdoti. "The Organization of Expert Systems: A Tutorial." *Artificial Intelligence*, 13 (March 1986): 135–173.

Turban, E. *Decision Support and Expert Systems: Managerial Perspectives*. New York: Macmillan, 1988.

Van Weelderen, J. A., and H. G. Sol. "MEDESS: A Methodology for Designing Expert Support Systems." *Interfaces*, 23, no. 3 (May/June 1993): 51–61.

Wu, B. *Fundamentals of Manufacturing Systems Design and Analysis*. New York: Van Nostrand Reinhold, 1991.

9

LOCATION STRATEGIES

CHAPTER OUTLINE

LEARNING OBJECTIVES

When you complete this chapter you should be able to:

Identify or define:

- Objective of location strategy
- International location issues

Explain:

- Three methods of solving the location problem:
  - Factor-rating method
  - Locational break-even analysis
  - Centre-of-gravity method

Location Provides Competitive Advantage for Federal Express

Fred Smith, founder and president of Federal Express, received a C on a college paper in which he proposed the "hub concept" (that Delta Airlines uses at Atlanta Airport), but for small packages. Since then, he has proven that the hub concept provides a radial distribution system that is unique and effective. He selected Memphis, Tennessee, as the central hub.

Memphis provides Federal Express with an uncongested airport, centrally located in the United States, with very few hours of closure because of weather. Competing carriers fly out of airports with substantially more weather problems. Location may be a contributor to the firm's safety record. In its 25 years of existence, Federal Express has never had an aircraft crash.

Each night, except Sunday, Federal Express brings to Memphis packages from throughout the world that are going to cities for which Federal Express does not have direct flights. The central hub permits service to a far greater number of points with fewer aircraft than the traditional city A to city B system. It also allows Federal Express to match aircraft flights with package loads each night and to reroute flights when load volume requires it, a major cost savings. Moreover, Federal Express also believes that the central hub system helps reduce mishandling and delay in transit because there is total control over the packages from pickup point through delivery.

At the Federal Express hub in Memphis, Tennessee, approximately 100 Federal Express aircraft converge each night around midnight with more than 700,000 documents and packages.

At the preliminary sorting area, packages and documents are sorted and sent to a secondary sorting area. The Memphis facility covers about 140,000 square metres; it is big enough to hold 33 football fields. Packages are sorted and exchanged until 4 A.M.

At the outbound slide/load area, the packages and documents that have already gone through the primary and secondary sorts are checked by city, state, and zip code. They are then placed in containers that will be loaded onto aircraft for delivery to their final destinations in 170 countries.

Containers carrying documents and packages are loaded onto a Federal Express aircraft. A series of rollers moves the containers into position on the aircraft; a system of locking mechanisms secures the containers in place on the floor.

At a Federal Express station, employees are picking the items for a particular route and are loading them into a Federal Express van for delivery to their final destination.

Epic Express, a subsidiary of Canadian Freightways Ltd., a new shipping company servicing central Canada, has taken a proactive stance when it comes to putting the customer first. Epic has achieved unparallelled levels of customer satisfaction and delivery completion by using precise logistics and advanced communications technology. It is the only regional carrier to guarantee next-business-day delivery by 10:30 A.M. Epic's service guarantee includes on-time pickup and delivery, damage-free delivery, and accurate invoicing.

Epic has targeted 1-to-30,000 pound deliveries in the Ontario/Quebec corridor. If Epic does not meet the delivery guarantee, a 50% reduction in net freight charges will be given; there are also a 50% reduction on missed same-day pickup, 100% on inaccurate invoicing, and 50% on damaged goods, with a voucher for replacement. "Epic Express represents a new level of delivery service quality," says Peter Colaccic, vice-president and general manager. He further says, "We are truly able to deliver what customers want: on-time, damage-free service at a competitive price, with a comprehensive service guarantee that makes our customer commitment clear from the outset."[1] ♦

One of the most important long-term decisions companies like Federal Express and Epic Express make is where to locate their operation. Location greatly affects costs, both fixed and variable. It can even have a large impact on the overall profit of the company. For instance, depending on the product and type of production or service taking place, transportation costs alone can total as much as 25% of the product's selling price. That is, one-fourth of the total revenue of a firm may be needed just to cover freight expenses of the raw materials coming in and the finished product going out. Other costs that may be influenced by location include taxes, wages, raw material costs, and, as we see in the quote above, rents.

Once management has committed an organization to a specific location, many costs are firmly in place and difficult to reduce. For instance, if a new factory location is in a region with high energy costs, even good management with an outstanding energy strategy is starting at a disadvantage. Management is in a similar bind with its human resource strategy if labour in the selected location is expensive, or ill-trained, or has a poor work ethic. Consequently, hard work to determine an optimal facility location is a good investment.

THE OBJECTIVE OF LOCATION STRATEGY

The best location for a given firm depends on its type of business. Industrial location decisions focus on minimizing costs, whereas retail and professional service organizations typically have a focus of maximizing revenue. Warehouse location, however, may be determined by a combination of cost and speed of delivery. In general though, the *objective of location strategy* is to maximize the benefit of location to the firm.

[1]Adapted from PR Newswire Association Inc., "Epic Brings Guaranteed Time-Definite Delivery to Central Canadian Market," October 2, 1995.

FIGURE 9.1 ■ Some Considerations and Factors That Affect Location Decisions

Country Decision

1. Government rules, attitudes, stability, incentives
2. Cultural and economic issues
3. Location of markets
4. Labour availability, attitudes, productivity, costs
5. Availability of supplies, communications, energy
6. Exchange rate

Region/Community Decision

1. Corporate desires
2. Attractiveness of region (culture, taxes, climate, etc.)
3. Labour availability, costs, attitudes toward unions
4. Cost and availability of utilities
5. Environmental regulations of province and town
6. Government incentives
7. Proximity to raw materials and customers
8. Land/construction costs

Site Decision

1. Site size and cost
2. Air, rail, highway, waterway systems
3. Zoning restrictions
4. Nearness of services/supplies needed
5. Environmental impact issues

Masaki Kaneho, plant manager of Motorola's integrated semiconductor plant in Aizu, Japan, with author Jay Heizer. As a world-class manufacturer, Motorola has located facilities throughout the world. Where labour costs are a significant part of product cost, S.E. Asia may be appropriate. For other countries, such as Japan, exchange rates or a local presence may be critical. While a S.E. Asian worker can wire 120 integrated circuits to metal frames each hour, an automated machine can do 640. And one worker can monitor eight machines for a total hourly production of 5,120. Clearly, in integrated circuit production direct labour costs have become less and other considerations more important.

FACTORS THAT AFFECT LOCATION DECISIONS

Selecting a facility location is becoming much more difficult with the globalization of the workplace. Globalization has taken place because of the push to find new markets for products and because of several major changes. These changes include (1) better international communications, (2) more rapid, reliable travel and shipping, (3) ease of capital flow between countries, and (4) high differences in labor costs. Whereas only a decade ago few firms considered opening new offices, factories, retail stores, or banks outside their own country, location decisions now transcend national borders. In fact, as Figure 9.1 shows, the sequence of location decisions often begins with choosing a country in which to operate. Before Germany's Mercedes-Benz chose Alabama as the location of its first major overseas plant, it first considered Mexico. In the end, the fear of marketing a $50,000 Mercedes that was "Made in Mexico" drove the firm back to the United States. The *POM in Action* box "Canada Set for Bigger Share of Japanese Auto Investment" illustrates similar Japanese behaviour towards Canada.

Once a firm decides which country is best for its location, it focuses on a region of the chosen country and a community. In the United States, the South has become a popular destination for a variety of reasons, including the hospitality so often found in smaller towns. It is easy to see why Canada's Norbord Industries found a home in Tupelo, Mississippi, when you read the *POM in Action* box telling that firm's story.

POM IN ACTION

Canada Set for Bigger Share of Japanese Auto Investment

Toyota and Honda have plants in Canada but the parts suppliers and assemblers are not following as quickly. This may be due to the political gains made by the Japanese firms to locate out of the U.S. auto market. In 1994 the Auto Parts Manufacturers Association (APMA) sold approximately $1 billion in parts to Japanese assembly plants: Honda $340 million, Toyota $320 million, and Suzuki $395 million. This figure was expected to double in 1995 and the APMA pressured Nissan to buy more from Canada. Canada is often overlooked as an independent auto industry because of its various trade agreements with the United States, which essentially eliminate the border in automotive trade. Global producers see a North American auto market rather than separate Canadian and U.S. auto markets. In 1995 Canada produced 18% of all light vehicles in North America and 12% of the auto parts. Seventy-five percent of the production in auto parts and vehicles was destined for the U.S. marketplace.

NAFTA increased the attractiveness of transplant businesses due to the North American content restrictions to qualify for duty-free movement of goods into the North American market. The fear was that political clout would force Japanese auto producers to buy parts from the United States and ship them to Canada for assembly. In 1992 the U.S. customs ruled that close to 100,000 Honda Civics produced in Canada between 1989 and 1992 did not meet the "50% North American content" rule. This was eventually overruled, but it proved the Americans' willingness to use political might if necessary, leaving Canadian firms the potentially daunting task of increasing the small, $70 million export market to Japan. The risk of political interference by the United States is compensated for in Canada by low inflation, high labour productivity, and low wage increases.

Source: Adapted from *Tokyo Business Today* (February, 1995): 38.

The final step in the location decision process is choosing a specific site within a community. The company must pick the one location that is best suited for shipping and receiving, zoning, utilities, size, and cost. Again, Figure 9.1 summarizes this series of decisions and the factors that affect them.

Besides globalization, a number of other factors affect the location decision. Among these are labour productivity, foreign exchange, and changing attitudes toward the industry, unions, employment, zoning, pollution, taxes, and so forth.

To continue to attract Japanese investment such as Honda, Canada must increase its political clout and overcome the foreign perception that its auto industry is a sub-sector of the U.S. industry.

Labour Productivity

When deciding on a location, management may be tempted by an area's low wage rates (see Figure 9.2 for a comparison of hourly manufacturing costs in 17 countries). However, wage rates cannot be considered by themselves, as Quality Coils discovered (see the *POM in Action* box in this chapter). Management must also consider productivity.

As discussed in Chapter 1, differences exist in productivity in various countries. What management is really interested in is the combination of productivity and the wage rate. For example, a firm paying $12.00 per hour with 1.25 units produced per hour will spend less on labour than one paying $10.00 per hour with productivity of 1.0 units per hour.

$$\frac{\text{Labour cost per hour}}{\text{Productivity (that is, units per hour)}} = \text{cost per unit}$$

Case 1: $$\frac{\text{\$12 Wages per hour}}{\text{1.25 units produced per hour}} = \frac{\$12}{1.25} = \$9.60$$

POM IN ACTION

Why Norbord Industries Headed to Mississippi

Why would Canadian wood-products manufacturer Norbord Industries select Tupelo, Mississippi, as the site for a new $83 million factory? It turns out that Tupelo, although a poor, low-wage town of 30,000, is the envy of economic development recruiters all across the United States. It has a proven track record of drawing the likes of Norbord, Sara Lee, Philip Morris, and Cooper Tire and Rubber—as well as a large number of furniture makers from as far away as Switzerland, Brazil, and Australia. And it does not give away the keys to the city.

What makes Tupelo so seductive is its good old-fashioned Southern hospitality, like answering phone calls. One Canadian CEO stated, "In New York, just to get someone to talk to me, I had to make three phone calls. With Tupelo, six guys met me at the airport. They had five different sites ready for me to look at." For another, Tupelo is smart in investing its small marketing budget.

Knowing that Norbord needed to be near its raw material, pine trees, Tupelo spent $15,000 to buy 300,000 pine seedlings even before Norbord scouts arrived. It then gave the seedlings to farmers, to other landowners, and even to 600 kids to plant in their yards. Because pines grow three times faster in Mississippi than in Canada, Norbord was impressed. The result: Norbord chose Tupelo over competitors.

The payoff to Tupelo: 1,000 new jobs/year on average over the past decade, second highest per capita income in the state, its own symphony orchestra, and the nation's largest rural hospital.

Sources: Wall Street Journal (March 4, 1994): A-1; *Economic Development Review*, 12 (Fall 1994): 78–82.

Case 2: $$\frac{\$10 \text{ Wages per hour}}{1.00 \text{ units produced per hour}} = \frac{\$10}{1.00} = \$10.00$$

Employees with poor training, poor education, or poor work habits may not be a good buy even at low wages. By the same token, employees who cannot or will not

FIGURE 9.2 ■ Manufacturing Labour Costs of 17 Nations, 1993. These average hourly costs, in U.S. dollars, include benefits.

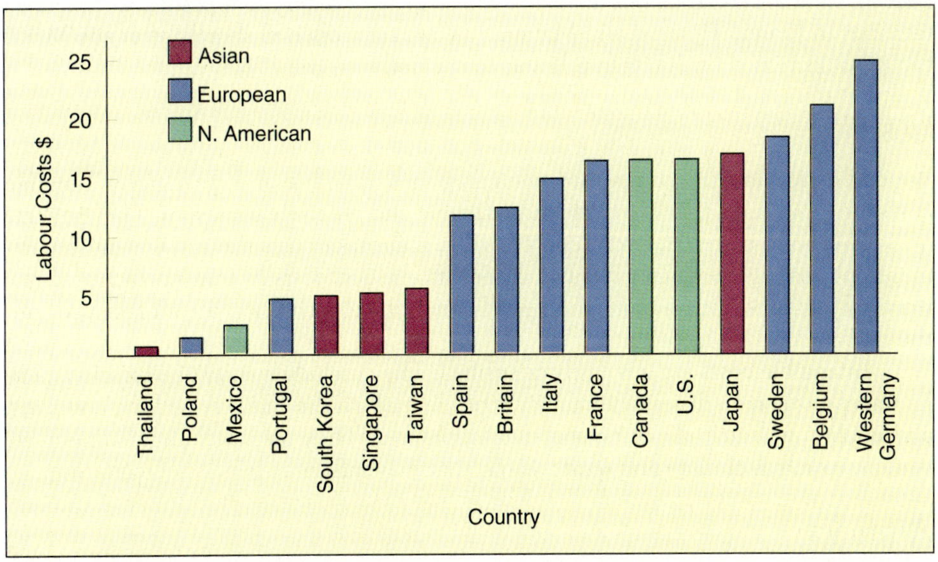

(*Sources: Wall Street Journal*, September 30, 1994: R-4; Morgan Stanley Research; DRI McGraw-Hill; and Alliance for Manufacturers and Exporters Canada.)

POM IN ACTION

Quality Coils Pulls the Plug on Mexico

Keith Gibson, President of Quality Coils Inc., saw the savings of low Mexican wages and headed South. He shut down a factory in Connecticut and opened one in Juarez, where he could pay Mexicans one-third the wage rates he was paying Americans. "All the figures pointed out we should make a killing," says Gibson.

Instead, his company was nearly destroyed. The electromagnetic coil maker regularly lost money during 4 years in Mexico. High absenteeism, low productivity, and problems of long-distance management wore Gibson down until he finally pulled the plug on Juarez.

Moving back to the United States and rehiring some of his original workers, Gibson learned, "I can hire one person in Connecticut for what three were doing in Juarez."

When American unions complain that they cannot compete against the low wages in other countries and when Teamster rallies chant "$4 a day/No way!," they overlook several factors. First, productivity in low-wage countries often erases a wage advantage, one that is not nearly as great as people believe. Second, a host of problems, from poor roads to corrupt governments, run up operating costs. And most importantly, the cost of labour for most U.S. manufacturers is less important than such factors as the skill of the work force, the quality of transportation, and access to technology.

Sources: Wall Street Journal (September 15, 1993): A-1; *CFO*, 10 (March 1994): 63–65.

"May I have my allowance in Deutsche Marks, Dad?"

always reach their place of work are not much good to the organization even at low wages. Labour cost per unit is sometimes called the *labour content* of the product.

Exchange Rates

Although wage rates and productivity may make different countries seem economical, unfavourable exchange rates might negate any savings. Sometimes, though, companies can take advantage of a particularly favourable exchange rate by relocating or exporting to a foreign country. However, the values of foreign currencies continually rise and fall in most countries. Such changes could well make what was a good location in 1995 a disastrous one in 1999. Many of the *maquiladora* plants, U.S.-owned factories in Juarez, Tijuana, and Matamoros, Mexico, opened shortly after the Mexican peso decreased by 200% in relation to the dollar in the 1980s.

Costs

Tangible costs

We can divide location costs into two categories, tangible and intangible. **Tangible costs** are those costs that are readily identifiable and precisely measured. They include utilities, labour, material, taxes, depreciation, and other costs the accounting department and management can identify. In addition, such costs as transportation of raw materials, transportation of finished goods, and site construction are all factored into the overall cost of a location.

Intangible costs

Intangible costs are less easily quantified. They include quality of education, public transportation facilities, community attitudes toward the industry and the company, and quality and attitude of prospective employees. They also include quality-of-life variables, such as climate and sports teams, that may influence personnel recruiting.

Attitudes

Attitudes of national, state, and local governments toward private property, zoning, pollution, and employment stability may be in flux. Governmental attitudes at the time a location decision is made may not be lasting ones. Moreover, management may find that these attitudes can be influenced by leadership.

METHODS OF EVALUATING LOCATION ALTERNATIVES

There are four major methods for solving location problems: the factor-rating method, locational break-even analysis, the centre-of-gravity method, and the transportation model.

The Factor-Rating Method

There are many factors, both qualitative and quantitative, to consider in choosing a location. Some of these factors are more important than others, so managers can use weightings to make the decision process more objective. The **factor-rating method** is popular, because a wide variety of factors from education to recreation to labour skills can be included.

Factor-rating method

To give you an idea what a set of typical location factors and their relative weights are in manufacturing, we present Table 9.1. This table was developed by Grant Thornton, a consulting firm headquartered in Chicago, on the basis of a survey of state manufacturing associations.

Assembly plants operating along the Mexican side of the border, from Texas to California, are called *maquiladoras*. Some 1,400 firms such as RCA, General Motors, Zenith, Hitachi, and GE operate these plants, which were designed to help both sides of the impoverished border region. After the 1982 devaluation of the peso, the number of *maquiladoras* nearly tripled, and it is believed that by the year 2000 as many as three million workers will be employed in these cross-border plants. Mexican wages are low, and at current exchange rates, companies don't look to the Far East as they once did.

TABLE 9.1 ■ LOCATIONAL FACTORS AND WEIGHTS

THE FOLLOWING 19 FACTORS HAVE BEEN IDENTIFIED AS IMPORTANT TO MANUFACTURING FIRMS:

FACTOR	WEIGHT (%)	FACTOR	WEIGHT (%)
Labour costs		**Government fiscal policies**	
Wages	8	Personal income growth	9
Unionization	6	Tax effort	4
Changes in wages	5	Changes in taxes	4
Changes in unionization	5	State business incentives	4
	24		21
Resource availability and productivity		**State-regulated employment costs**	
Available work force	7	Workers' compensation insurance	6
Energy costs	5	Unemployment compensation benefits	9
Value added	5	Average insurance cost per case	5
Labour-hours lost	4		20
	21	**Selected quality-of-life issues**	
		Education	5
		Cost of living	3
		Transportation	3
		Health care	3
			14

Sources: A series of annual Grant Thornton Manufacturing Climates studies. The factors were developed in discussion with state manufacturing associations, state economic development directors, and state Chambers of Commerce.

The factor-rating method has six steps:

1. Develop a list of relevant factors (such as those in Table 9.1).
2. Assign a weight to each factor to reflect its relative importance in the company's objectives.
3. Develop a scale for each factor (for example, 1–10 or 1–100 points).
4. Have management score each location for each factor, using the scale in step 3.
5. Multiply the score by the weights for each factor, and total the score for each location.
6. Make a recommendation based on the maximum point score, considering the results of quantitative approaches as well.

Example 1 shows how to use the factor-rating method.

EXAMPLE 1

Mademoiselle Linda Cosmetics of Quebec has decided to expand its production of Musk Cologne by opening a new factory location. The expansion is due to limited capacity at its existing plant. The rating sheet in Table 9.2 provides a list of qualitative factors that management has decided are important. Their weightings and their rating for two possible sites—Edmonton, Alberta, and Oshawa, Ontario, are shown.

TABLE 9.2 ■ WEIGHTS, SCORES, AND SOLUTION

		Scores (out of 100)		Weighted Scores	
Factor	Weight	Edmonton	Oshawa	Edmonton	Oshawa
Labour costs and attitude	.25	70	60	(.25)(70) = 17.5	(.25)(60) = 15.0
Transportation system	.05	50	60	(.05)(50) = 2.5	(.05)(60) = 3.0
Education and health	.10	85	80	(.10)(85) = 8.5	(.10)(80) = 8.0
Tax structure	.39	75	70	(.39)(75) = 29.3	(.39)(70) = 27.3
Resources and productivity	.21	60	70	(.21)(60) = 12.6	(.21)(70) = 14.7
Totals	1.00			70.4	68.0

Table 9.2 also shows the weights used to evaluate alternative site locations. Given the option of 100 points assigned to each factor, the Edmonton location is preferable. By changing the points or weights slightly for some factors, we can analyze the sensitivity of the decision. For instance, we can see that changing the scores for labour costs and attitudes by 10 points can change the decision.

When a decision is sensitive to minor changes, further analysis of either the weighting or the points assigned may be appropriate. Alternatively, management may conclude that these intangible factors are not the proper criteria on which to base a location decision and may therefore place primary weight on the more quantitative aspects of the decision.

Locational Break-Even Analysis

Locational break-even analysis is the use of cost-volume analysis to make an economic comparison of location alternatives. By identifying fixed and variable costs and graphing them for each location, we can determine which one provides the lowest cost. This graphic approach also provides the range of volume over which each location is preferable.

Locational break-even analysis

The three steps to locational break-even analysis are:

1. Determine the fixed and variable cost for each location.
2. Plot the costs for each location, with costs on the vertical axis of the graph and annual volume on the horizontal axis.
3. Select the location that has the lowest total cost for the expected production volume.

Example 2 shows how to use locational break-even analysis.

EXAMPLE 2

A manufacturer of automobile carburetors is considering three locations—Regina, Dartmouth, and Allison—for a new plant. Cost studies indicate that fixed costs per year at the sites are \$30,000, \$60,000, and \$110,000, respectively. Variable costs are \$75 per unit, \$45 per unit, and \$25 per unit, respectively. The expected selling price of the carburetors produced is \$120. The company wishes to find the most economical location for an expected volume of 2,000 units per year.

For each of the three, we can plot the fixed costs (those at a volume of zero units) and the total cost (fixed costs + variable costs) at the expected volume of output. These lines have been plotted in Figure 9.3.

For Regina,

$$\text{Total cost} = \$30{,}000 + \$75(2{,}000) = \$180{,}000$$

For Dartmouth,

$$\text{Total cost} = \$60{,}000 + \$45(2{,}000) = \$150{,}000$$

For Allison,

$$\text{Total cost} = \$110{,}000 + \$25(2{,}000) = \$160{,}000$$

With an expected volume of 2,000 units per year, Dartmouth provides the lowest-cost location. The expected profit is

$$\text{Total revenue} - \text{total cost} = \$120(2{,}000) - \$150{,}000 = \$90{,}000/\text{year}$$

FIGURE 9.3 ■ Crossover Chart for Locational Break-Even Analysis

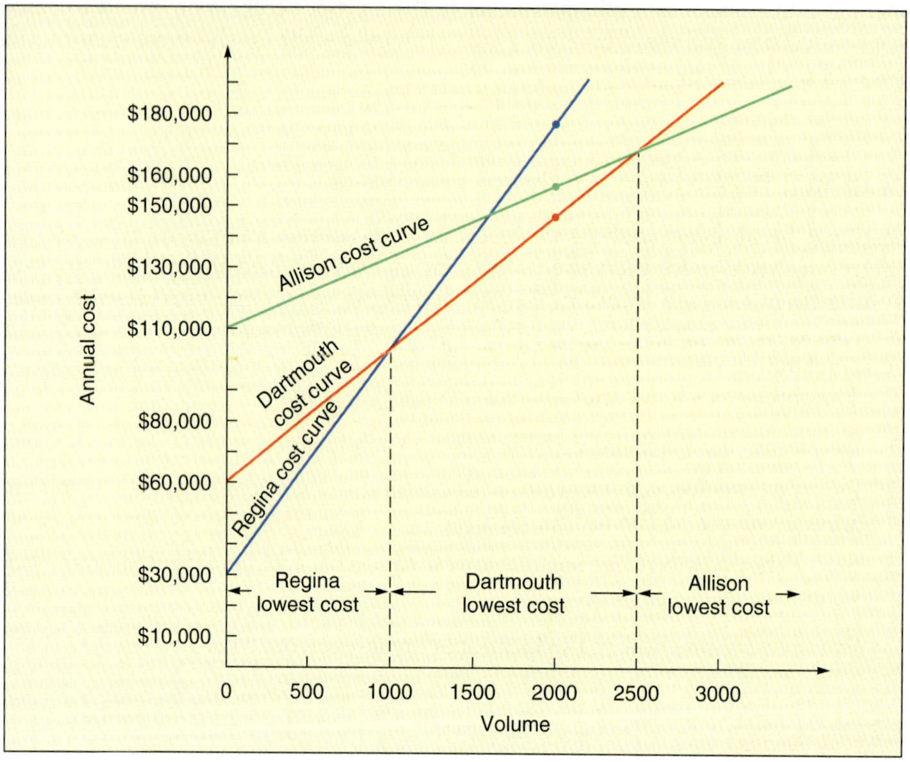

The chart also tells us that for a volume of less than 1,000, Regina would be preferred, and for a volume greater than 2,500, Allison would yield the greatest profit. The crossover points are 1,000 and 2,500.

The Centre-of-Gravity Method

Centre-of-gravity method

The **centre-of-gravity method** is a mathematical technique used for finding the location of a distribution centre that will minimize distribution costs. The method takes into account the location of markets, the volume of goods shipped to those markets, and shipping costs in finding a best location for a distribution centre.

The first step in the centre-of-gravity method is to place the locations on a coordinate system. The origin of the coordinate system and the scale used are arbitrary, just as long as the relative distances are correctly represented. This can be done easily by placing a grid over an ordinary map. The centre of gravity is determined by Equations (9.1) and (9.2):

$$C_x = \frac{\sum_i d_{ix} W_i}{\sum W_i} \qquad (9.1)$$

$$C_y = \frac{\sum_i d_{iy} W_i}{\sum W_i} \quad (9.2)$$

where C_x = x-coordinate of the centre of gravity
C_y = y-coordinate of the centre of gravity
d_{ix} = x-coordinate of location i
d_{iy} = y-coordinate of location i
W_i = volume of goods moved to or from location i

Note that Equations (9.1) and (9.2) include the term W_i, the volume of supplies transferred to or from location i.

Because the number of containers shipped each month affects cost, volume must be considered in the location decision. The centre-of-gravity method assumes that cost is directly proportional to both distance and volume shipped. The ideal location is that which minimizes the weighted distance between the warehouse and its retail outlets, where the distance is weighted by the number of containers shipped.

Example 3 shows how to use the centre-of-gravity method to choose a warehouse location.

EXAMPLE 3

Consider the case of Quain's Discount Department Stores, a chain of four large K-Mart-type outlets. The firm's store locations are in Winnipeg, North Bay, Fredericton, and Windsor; they are currently being supplied out of an old and inadequate warehouse in North Bay, the site of the chain's first store. Data on demand rates at each outlet are shown in Table 9.3.

TABLE 9.3 ■ DEMAND FOR QUAIN'S DISCOUNT STORES

STORE LOCATION	NUMBER OF CONTAINERS SHIPPED PER MONTH
Winnipeg	2,000
North Bay	1,000
Fredericton	1,000
Windsor	2,000

The firm has decided to find some "central" location in which to build a new warehouse. Its current store locations are shown in Figure 9.4. For example, location 1 is Winnipeg, and from Table 9.3 and Figure 9.4, we have

$$d_{1x} = 30$$
$$d_{1y} = 120$$
$$W_1 = 2{,}000$$

Using the data in Table 9.3 and Figure 9.4 for each of the other cities, in Equations (9.1) and (9.2), we find

$$C_x = \frac{(30)(2000) + (90)(1000) + (130)(1000) + (60)(2000)}{2000 + 1000 + 1000 + 2000} = \frac{400{,}000}{6{,}000}$$

$$= 66.7$$

$$C_y = \frac{(120)(2000) + (110)(1000) + (130)(1000) + (40)(2000)}{2000 + 1000 + 1000 + 2000} = \frac{560{,}000}{6{,}000}$$

$$= 93.3$$

This location (66.7, 93.3) is shown by the crosshair in Figure 9.4. By overlaying a Canadian map on this exhibit, we find that this location is near western Quebec. The firm may well wish to consider Hull, Quebec, or a nearby city as an appropriate location.

FIGURE 9.4 ■ Coordinate Locations of Four Quain's Department Stores

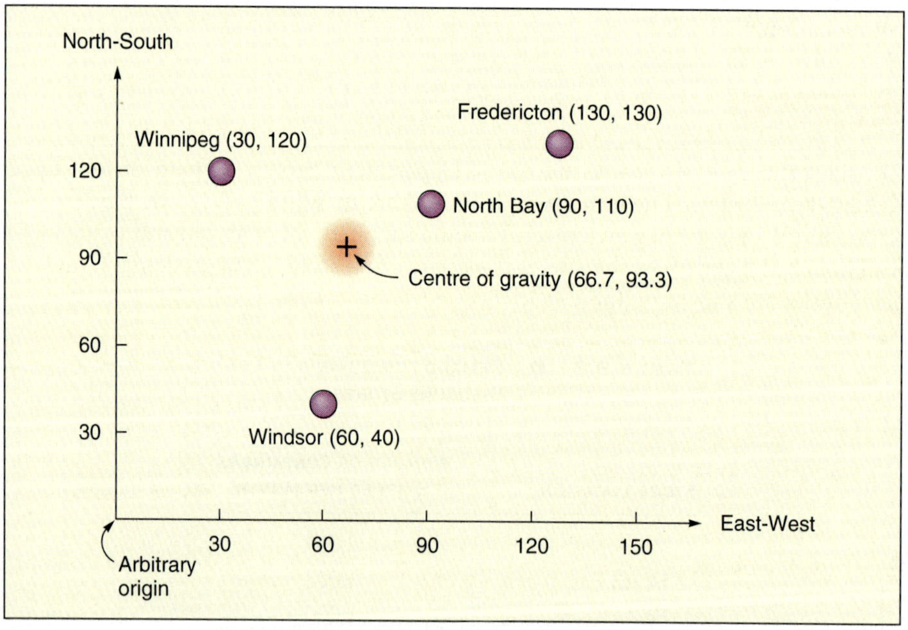

The Transportation Model

Transportation model

The objective of the **transportation model** is to determine the best pattern of shipments from several points of supply (sources) to several points of demand (destinations) so as to minimize total production and transportation costs. Every firm with a network of supply and demand points faces such a problem. The complex Volkswagen supply network (shown in Figure 9.5) provides one such illustration.

Although the linear programming (LP) technique introduced in the supplement to Chapter 6 can be used to solve this type of problem, more efficient, special-purpose algorithms have been developed for the transportation application. As in the LP approach, the transportation model finds an initial feasible solution and then makes step-by-step improvement until reaching an optimal solution. Unlike the LP simplex method, the transportation method is fairly simple to use.

A description of how the transportation model works and examples of its use in location decisions are found in detail in the supplement to this chapter.

SERVICE/RETAIL/PROFESSIONAL SECTOR

Whereas the focus in industrial sector location analysis is on minimizing cost, the focus in the service sector is on maximizing revenue. This is because manufacturing costs tend to vary substantially between locations, but in service firms, costs vary little within a market area. Therefore, for the service firm, a specific location influences revenue more than it does cost. This means that the location focus for service firms should be on determining the volume of business and revenue. There are eight major components of volume and revenue for the service firm. These are

1. purchasing power of the customer drawing area;
2. service and image compatibility with demographics of the customer drawing area;
3. competition in the area;
4. quality of the competition;
5. uniqueness of the firm's and competitor's locations;
6. physical qualities of facilities and neighbouring businesses;
7. operating policies of the firm;
8. quality of management.

Realistic analysis of these factors can provide a reasonable picture of the revenue expected. Table 9.4 provides a summary of location strategies for both service and industrial organizations.

FIGURE 9.5 ■ Worldwide Distribution of Volkswagens and Parts

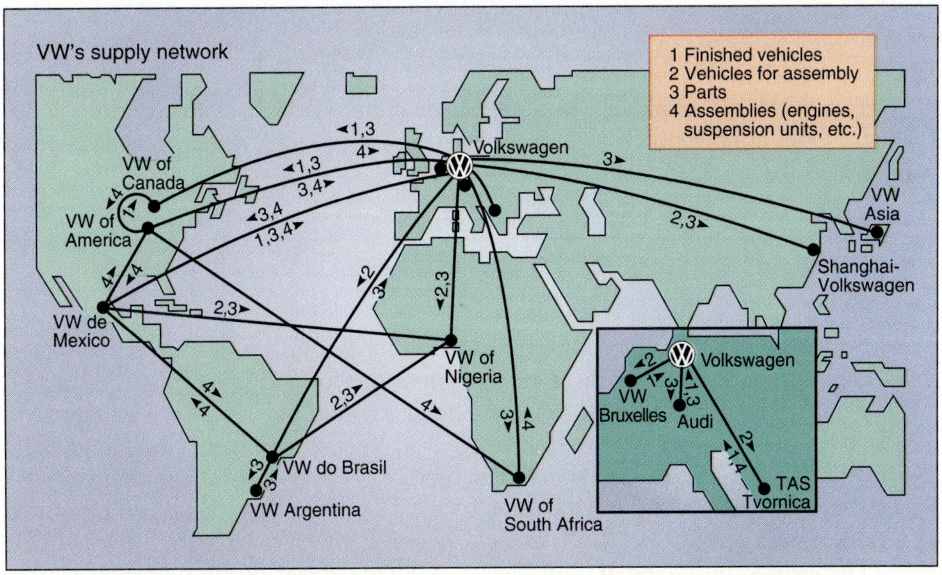

(*Source*: Copyright 1985, *The Economist Ltd.* Distributed by The New York Times/Special Features.)

TABLE 9.4 ■ LOCATION STRATEGIES—SERVICE VS. INDUSTRIAL ORGANIZATIONS

SERVICE/RETAIL/PROFESSIONAL	INDUSTRIAL LOCATION
REVENUE FOCUS	**COST FOCUS**
Volume/revenue Drawing area; purchasing power Competition; advertising/pricing **Physical quality** Parking/access; security/lighting; appearance/image **Cost determinants** Management calibre Operation policies	**Tangible costs** Transportation cost of raw material Shipment cost of finished goods Energy and utility cost; labour; raw material; taxes, etc. **Intangible and future costs** Attitude toward union Quality of life Education expenditures by province Quality of provincial and local government
TECHNIQUES	**TECHNIQUES**
Regression models to determine importance of various factors Traffic counts Demographic analysis of drawing area Purchasing power analysis of area	Transportation method Weighted approach to intangibles Break-even analysis Crossover charts
ASSUMPTIONS	**ASSUMPTIONS**
Location is a major determinant of revenue High customer contact issues are critical Costs are relatively constant for a given area; therefore, the revenue function is critical	Location is a major determinant of cost Most major costs can be identified explicitly for each site Low customer contact allows focus on the identifiable costs Intangible costs can be evaluated

The *POM in Action box* "Look West for Hotel Growth in Recession-Riddled Canada" looks at hour hotels are examining various locations with a view to improving their prospects.

ACHIEVING WORLD-CLASS STANDARDS

World-class organizations recognize that facility location decisions are critical long-term commitments. Because these firms want to be located optimally, they search globally for their new sites and are not bound by national borders. Mercedes and BMW have opened plants in the United States, Volkswagen is now in Mexico and Brazil, and, as we saw in the *POM in Action* box, Norbord Industries has found a home in Tupelo, Mississippi. At the same time, Quality Coils has left Mexico and returned to Connecticut.

The factors considered in these decisions differ, depending on the type of facility and the type of operation. However, all world-class firms take the time to gather the

POM IN ACTION

Look West for Hotel Growth in Recession-Riddled Canada

Even though in 1993 Canadian hotels were feeling the pinch of an economic downturn and an oversupply in the marketplace, according to many the following were hopeful geographic areas:

- *British Columbia.* Vancouver was a great deal healthier than all other Canadian cities, with occupancy in the the high 60% range. Victoria and Vancouver had opportunities for hotels to service their five-star clientele, and the secondary cities and towns along the B.C. coast had an undersupply of two- and three-star hotels to service those smaller communities that draw tourism.
- *Alberta.* Banff and other nearby resorts in the Rockies had ample luxury hotels in and around Canada's most famous ski resorts, but more moderately priced accommodations were definitely in short supply.
- *Ontario.* The northern Ontario communities of Thunder Bay, North Bay, and Sault Ste. Marie actively advertised themselves as fishing and hunting resort areas. If this niche took hold, there would be definite opportunities for three-star hotels there.
- *Maritime Provinces.* Newfoundland, Nova Scotia, and Prince Edward Island with its soon-to-be-completed bridge had opportunities, not in building new hotels, but in fully renovating existing ones. Most industry analysts were saying renovation was the major growth sector of the region.

Canadian hotels and resorts had been attractive to investors over the past few years, as could be seen in the merging of Canadian-owned Journey's End and Relax Inns with Choice Hotel's Comfort Inn and Forte Hotel's Travelodge, respectively, as well as the major entrance of Delta Hotels across Canada.

Western Canada was still considered to have stronger potential for development in the future, in part due to its being closer to the Pacific Rim travel and tourism market. Hotel Association of Canada president Anthony Pollard cautioned that there was still an oversupply in Canada.

Source: Adapted from *Hotel & Motel Management*, 208, no. 19 (November 1, 1993): 49.

Volkswagen has found substantial markets in many nations outside of Germany. The market in Mexico or Brazil may not now be big enough to support a major investment, but VW moved in and invested heavily because the market tomorrow is going to be 100 million people. Global location strategy demands bases that can reach the world's markets.

data needed for the analytic techniques we have just described. They also watch their competition closely and fight hard for the economic incentives that each country, region, and local government will offer. Clearly, location is one of the most important strategic choices an organization can make.

SUMMARY

Location may determine up to 10% of the total cost of an industrial firm. Location is also a critical element in determining revenue for the service/retail/professional firm. Industrial firms need to consider both tangible and intangible costs. We typically address industrial location problems via the factor-rating method, locational break-even analysis, the centre-of-gravity method, and the transportation method of linear programming.

For service/retail/professional organizations, analysis is typically made of a variety of variables including purchasing power of a drawing area, competition, advertising and promotion, physical qualities of the location, and operating policies of the organization.

KEY TERMS

Tangible costs (p. 344)
Intangible costs (p. 344)
Factor-rating method (p. 345)
Locational break-even analysis (p. 347)
Centre-of-gravity method (p. 348)
Transportation model (p. 350)

USING AB:POM AND SPREADSHEETS TO SOLVE LOCATION PROBLEMS

Solving Examples 1 and 3 with AB:POM's Facility Location Module

The facility location module in AB:POM includes two different models. The first, the Qualitative Weighting Model (also known as the factor-rating method), is used to solve Example 1. The second, Two-Dimensional Siting, is applied to the centre-of-gravity problem described in Example 3.

PROGRAM 9.1 ■ AB:POM's Factor-Rating Model Applied to Example 1. When running this module, we first enter the number of factors (up to 99) and locations (up to 6) to consider. In Example 1, we rated two cities over five factors. The program's particular strength is in demonstrating the sensitivity of one or more weights or scores on the final selection.

Plant Location — Solution

Number of factors (1–99) 5 Number of locations (1–6) 2

COSMETIC COMPANY, EXAMPLE 1

FACTORS	Weight	Edmonton	Oshawa
LABOUR	0.25	70.00	60.00
TRANSPORT	0.05	50.00	60.00
EDUCATION	0.10	85.00	80.00
TAXES	0.39	75.00	70.00
POWER	0.21	60.00	70.00
Weighted score		70.35	68.00

The location with the best (highest) score is city 1

PROGRAM 9.2 ■ AB:POM's Plant Location Program, Centre-of-Gravity Method for Example 3. This screen shows both the input and the output for Quain's Department Store.

Plant Location — Solution

Number of sites (1–99) 4

QUAIN'S DEPARTMENT STORES

SITES	Weight/trips	x coord	y coord	WEIGHTED COORDINATES X-coord	Y-coord
WINNIPEG	2000.00	30.00	120.00	60000	240000
NORTH BAY	1000.00	90.00	110.00	90000	110000
FREDERICTON	1000.00	130.00	130.00	130000	130000
WINDSOR	2000.00	60.00	40.00	120000	80000
TOTAL	6000.00	310.00	400.00	400000	560000
AVERAGE		77.50	100.00	66.6667	93.3333

The unweighted centre of gravity is x = 77.5 y = 100

The weighted centre of gravity is x = 66.66666 y = 93.33334

Solving Example 1 with Spreadsheet Software

Program 9.3 provides a spreadsheet alternative to Program 9.1. Program 9.3 illustrates how straightforward it is to solve a factor-rating problem with spreadsheet formulas.

PROGRAM 9.3 ■ Spreadsheet Solution to Example 1.

	A	B	C	D	E	F
1						
2			SCORES			
3			(OUT OF 100)		WEIGHTED SCORES	
4						
5	FACTOR	WEIGHT	Edmonton	Oshawa	Edmonton	Oshawa
6						
7	Labour costs	0.25	70	60	+B7*C7	+B7*D7
8	Transportation	0.05	50	60	+B8*C8	+B8*D8
9	Education	0.1	85	80	+B9*C9	+B9*D9
10	Tax structure	0.39	75	70	+B10*C10	+B10*D10
11	Resources	0.21	60	70	+B11*C11	+B11*D11
12						
13	Totals	@sum(B7..B11)			@sum(E7..E11)	@sum(F7..F11)

SOLVED PROBLEMS

Solved Problem 9.1

Just as cities and communities can be compared for location selection by the weighted approach model, as we saw earlier in this chapter, so can actual site decisions within those cities be helped. Table 9.5 illustrates four factors of importance to Ottawa health officials charged with opening that city's first public AIDS clinic. Of primary concern (and given a weight of 5) was location of the clinic so it would be as accessible as possible to the largest number of patients. The annual lease cost also was of some concern due to a tight budget. A suite in the new City Hall was highly rated because its rent would be free. An old office building near the downtown bus station received a much lower rating because of its cost. Equally important as lease cost was the need for confidentiality of patients and, therefore, for a relatively inconspicuous clinic. Finally, because so many of the staff at the AIDS clinic would be donating their time, the safety, parking, and accessibility of each site were of concern as well.

TABLE 9.5 ■ POTENTIAL AIDS CLINIC SITES IN OTTAWA

		Potential Locations*			Weighted Scores		
Factor	Importance Weight	Homeless Shelter	City Hall	Bus Terminal Area	Homeless Shelter	City Hall	Bus Terminal Area
Accessibility for infectives	5	9	7	7	45	35	35
Annual lease cost	3	6	10	3	18	30	9
Inconspicuous	3	5	2	7	15	6	21
Accessibility for health staff	2	3	6	2	6	12	4
				Total scores:	84	83	69

*All sites are rated on a 1 to 10 basis, with 10 as the highest score and 1 as the lowest.

Source: From R. Murdick, B. Render, and R. Russell, *Service Operations Management*. © 1990 by Allyn and Bacon. Reprinted by permission.

Solution

From the three rightmost columns in Table 9.5, the weighted scores are summed. It appears that the bus terminal area can be excluded from further consideration, but that the other two sites are virtually identical in total score. The city may now consider other factors, including political ones, in selecting between the two remaining sites.

Solved Problem 9.2

Chuck Bimmerle is considering opening a new foundry in Verdun, Quebec, St. John, New Brunswick, or Chicoutimi, Quebec, to produce high-quality rifle sights. He has assembled the following fixed- and variable-cost data:

		PER-UNIT COSTS		
LOCATION	FIXED COST PER YEAR	MATERIAL	LABOUR	VARIABLE OVERHEAD
Verdun	$200,000	$ .20	$ .40	$ .40
St. John	$180,000	$ .25	$ .75	$ .75
Chicoutimi	$170,000	$1.00	$1.00	$1.00

(a) Graph the total cost lines.

(b) Over what range of annual volume is each facility going to have a competitive advantage?

(c) What is the point volume at the intersection of St. John and Chicoutimi?

Solution

(a) A graph of the total cost lines is shown in Figure 9.6.

(b) Below 8,000 units, the Chicoutimi facility will have a competitive advantage (lowest cost); between 8,000 units and 26,666 units, St. John has an

FIGURE 9.6 ■ Graph of Total Cost Lines for Solved Problem 9.2

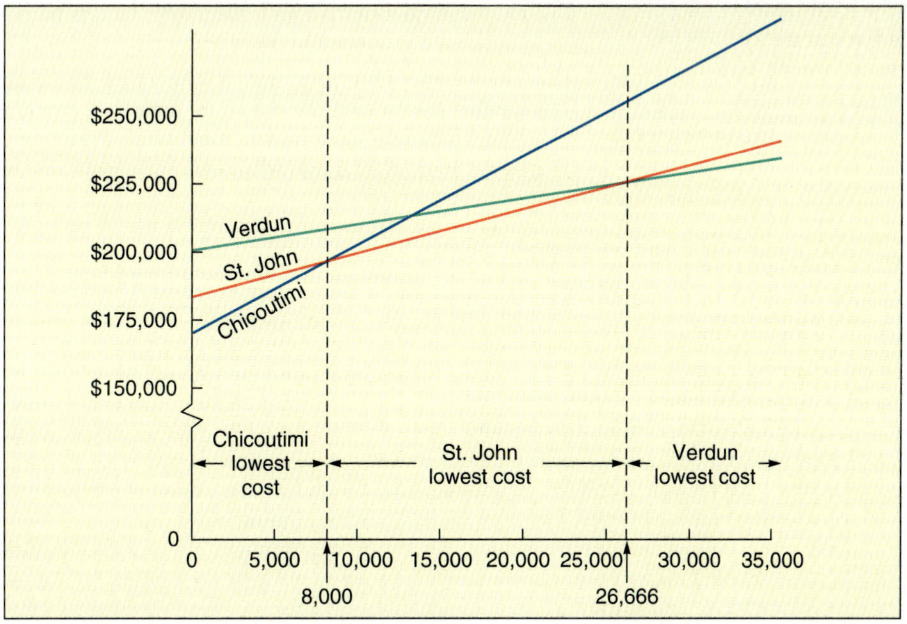

advantage; and above 26,666, Verdun has the advantage. (We have made the assumption in this problem that other costs, that is, delivery and intangible factors, are constant regardless of the decision.)

(c) From the chart, we can see that the cost line for Chicoutimi and the cost line for St. John cross at about 8,000. We can also determine this point with a little algebra:

$$\$180{,}000 + 1.75Q = \$170{,}000 + 3.00Q$$
$$\$10{,}000 = 1.25Q$$
$$8{,}000 = Q$$

DISCUSSION QUESTIONS

1. In terms of the strategic objective, how do industrial and service location decisions differ?
2. In recent years, the federal government has increased the latitude that railroads have in setting rates and deregulated much of the rate-setting structure of trucks and airlines. What will be the long-range impact of this deregulation on location strategies?
3. Beth Wood, city manager of a large eastern city, responding to a group of manufacturers who were complaining about the impact of increased taxes, said that taxes levied by a city were not an important consideration to a new business contemplating moving to that city. If you were president of the local chamber of commerce, how would you respond? If you are a person who is concerned about the unemployment rate in the inner city, how would you respond?
4. Explain the assumptions behind the centre-of-gravity method. How can the model be used in a service facility location?
5. How do service facility location decisions differ from industrial location decisions in terms of the techniques used to analyze them?
6. What is the objective of location strategy?
7. What are the three steps to locational break-even analysis?
8. What are the major factors firms consider when choosing a country in which to locate?
9. What factors affect region/community location decisions?
10. Name several factors that affect site location.
11. How can quantitative and qualitative factors both be considered in a location decision?
12. The Grant Thornton studies generated the factor weights similar to those shown in Table 9.1. Would all companies rate these factor weights of equal importance? If so, why? If not, why not?

CRITICAL THINKING EXERCISE

In this chapter, we have discussed a number of decisions, including Canada's Norbord Industries' choice to locate in Tupelo, Mississippi. In the Case Study at the end of the chapter, we see that Samuel Manu-Tech chose South Carolina for its new polyester strapping plant. The incentives offered to the company included tax advantages and an employee training program at a local technical college. Before selecting South Carolina, Samuel Manu-Tech had considered a number of other locations, as had Norbord Industries.

What in your opinion are the ethical/legal/economic implications of location wars such as these? Should taxpayers be allowed to vote on offers made by their cities, metropolitan areas, provinces, and the federal government? Should there be a limit on these incentives? Who pays for these incentives?

PROBLEMS

• **9.1** Esso Refineries, headquartered in Montreal, must decide between three sites for the construction of a new oil processing centre. The firm has selected the six factors listed as a basis for evaluation and has assigned rating weights from 1 to 5 on each factor.

FACTOR NO.	FACTOR NAME	RATING WEIGHT
1	Proximity to port facilities	5
2	Power source availability and cost	3
3	Workforce attitude and cost	4
4	Distance from Montreal	2
5	Community desirability	2
6	Equipment suppliers in area	3

Management has rated each location for each factor on a 1-to-100-point basis.

FACTOR NO.	LOCATION A	LOCATION B	LOCATION C
1	100	80	80
2	80	70	100
3	30	60	70
4	10	80	60
5	90	60	80
6	50	60	90

What site will be recommended?

• **9.2** The fixed and variable costs for four potential plant sites for a ski equipment manufacturer are shown.

SITE	FIXED COST PER YEAR	VARIABLE COST PER UNIT
Quebec City	$125,000	$ 6
Brampton	75,000	5
New Glasgow	100,000	4
Vancouver	50,000	12

a) Graph the total cost lines for the four potential sites.

b) Over what range of annual volume is each location the preferable one (which location has the lowest expected cost)?

c) If expected volume of the ski equipment is 5,000 units, which location would you recommend?

9.3 A Halifax seafood restaurant is considering opening a second facility in the suburb of Dartmouth. The table shows its ratings of five factors at each of four potential sites. Which site should be selected?

		Site			
Factor	Weight	1	2	3	4
Affluence of local population	10	70	60	85	90
Construction and land cost	10	85	90	80	60
Traffic flow	25	70	60	85	90
Parking availability	20	80	90	90	80
Growth potential	15	90	80	90	75

9.4 In placing a new medical clinic, county health offices wish to consider three sites. The pertinent data are given in the table. Which is the best site?

		Scores		
Location Factor	Weight	Downtown	Suburb A	Suburb B
Facility utilization	9	9	7	6
Average time per emergency trip	8	6	6	8
Employee preferences	5	2	5	6
Accessibility to major roadways	5	8	4	5
Land costs	4	2	9	6

9.5 The main post office in Corner Brook, Newfoundland, is due to be replaced with a much larger, more modern facility that can handle the tremendous flow of mail that has followed the city's growth since 1970. Because all mail, incoming or outgoing, travels from the seven regional post offices in Corner Brook through the main post office, its site selection can mean a big difference in overall delivery and movement efficiency. Using the data in the following table, calculate the centre of gravity for the proposed new facility.

Regional Post Office	Map Coordinates (x, y)	Truck Round-Trips per Day
Deer Lake	(10, 5)	3
Shearstown	(3, 8)	3
Turks Cove	(4, 7)	2
Westport	(15, 10)	6
Marys Harbour	(13, 3)	5
York Harbour	(1, 12)	3
Port-aux-Choix	(5, 5)	10

: **9.6** Gretchen Harris of Calgary owns two exclusive women's clothing stores in Miami. In her plan to expand to a third location, she has narrowed her decision down to three sites—one in a downtown office building, one in a shopping mall, and one in an old Victorian house in the suburban area of Coral Gables. She feels that rent is absolutely the most important factor to be considered, while walk-in traffic is 90% as important as rent. Further, the more distant the new store is from her two existing stores, the better, she thinks. She weights this factor to be 80% as important as walk-in traffic. Gretchen developed the following table, in which she graded each site on the same system used in her MBA program. Which site is preferable?

	DOWNTOWN	SHOPPING MALL	CORAL GABLES HOUSE
Rent	D	C	A
Walk-in traffic	B	A	D
Distance from existing stores	B	A	C

: **9.7** The following table gives the map coordinates and the shipping loads for a set of cities that we wish to connect through a central "hub." Near what map coordinates should the hub be located?

CITY	MAP COORDINATE (X, Y)	SHIPPING LOAD
A	(5, 10)	5
B	(6, 8)	10
C	(4, 9)	15
D	(9, 3)	5
E	(7, 9)	15
F	(3, 2)	10
G	(2, 6)	5

• **9.8** Nancy Hard Retailers is attempting to decide upon a location for a new retail outlet. At the moment, they have three alternatives—stay where they are, but enlarge the facility; locate along the main street in nearby Newbury; or locate in a new shopping mall in Hyde Park. They have selected the four factors listed in the following table as the basis for evaluation, and have assigned weights from 1 to 5 for each factor.

FACTOR	FACTOR DESCRIPTION	WEIGHT
1	Average community income	.30
2	Community growth potential	.15
3	Availability of public transportation	.20
4	Labour availability, attitude, and cost	.35

Ms. Hard has rated each location for each factor, on a 100-point basis. These ratings follow:

	LOCATION		
FACTOR	PRESENT LOCATION	NEWBURY	HYDE PARK
1	40	60	50
2	20	20	80
3	30	60	50
4	80	50	50

Which site should be recommended?

: **9.9** The fixed and variable costs for three potential manufacturing plant sites for Marty McDonald's firm follow:

SITE	FIXED COST PER YEAR	VARIABLE COST PER UNIT
Site 1	$ 500	$11
Site 2	1000	7
Site 3	1700	4

a) Over what range of production is each location optimal?

b) For a production of 200 units, which site is best?

DATA BASE APPLICATION

: **9.10** The unification of Europe has brought about changes in airline regulation that dramatically affect major European carriers such as British International Air, SAS, KLM, Air France, Alitalia, and Sabena. With ambitious expansion plans, British International Air (BIA) has decided it needs a second service hub on the continent, to complement its large Heathrow (London) repair facility. The location selection is critical, and with the potential for 4,000 new skilled blue-collar jobs on the line, virtually every city in western Europe is actively bidding for BIA's business.

After initial investigations by Harry Zipper, head of the Operations Department, BIA has narrowed the list to 16 cities. Each is then rated on 12 factors, with the following table resulting.

a) Help Zipper rank the top three cities that BIA should consider as its new site for servicing aircraft.

b) After further investigation, Harry Zipper decides that an existing set of hangar facilities for repairs is not nearly as important as earlier thought. In lowering the weight of that factor to 30, does the ranking change?

c) After Zipper makes the change in part (b), Germany announces it has reconsidered its offer of financial incentives, with an additional 200 million Deutsche mark package to entice BIA. Accordingly, BIA has raised Germany's rating to 10 on that factor. Is there any change in top rankings in part (b)?

Table for Data Base Application 9.10

		Location															
		Italy			France			Germany			Spain	Switzerland		Holland		Denmark	Portugal
Factor	Importance Weight	Milan	Rome	Genoa	Paris	Lyon	Nice	Munich	Bonn	Berlin	Madrid	Bern	Zurich	Amsterdam	The Hague	Copenhagen	Lisbon
Financial incentives	85	8	8	8	7	7	7	7	7	7	9	8	8	9	9	8	10
Skilled labour pool	80	4	6	5	9	9	7	10	8	9	4	9	10	9	8	7	3
Existing facility	70	5	3	2	9	6	5	9	9	2	5	7	8	8	2	8	6
Wage rates	70	9	8	9	4	6	6	4	5	5	10	3	3	5	9	5	10
Competition for jobs	70	7	3	8	2	8	7	4	8	9	6	5	4	3	7	6	6
Ease of air traffic access	65	5	4	6	2	8	8	4	8	9	5	5	5	3	9	4	6
Real estate cost	40	6	4	7	4	6	6	3	4	5	8	2	1	3	5	4	7
Communication links	25	6	7	6	9	9	9	10	9	8	2	8	8	8	6	9	2
Attractiveness to relocating executives	15	4	8	3	9	6	6	2	3	3	4	9	8	9	6	7	3
Political considerations	10	6	6	6	8	8	8	8	8	8	5	9	9	8	8	8	2
Expansion possibilities	10	10	2	8	1	5	4	4	5	6	5	3	2	3	8	4	6
Union strength	10	1	1	1	5	5	5	6	6	6	9	8	8	7	7	5	9

CASE STUDY

Samuel Manu-Tech Inc.

In May of 1996 Canadian-based Samuel Manu-Tech announced plans to bring 50 jobs and a $20 million investment to Lakemount Industrial Park in York County, South Carolina. The company would move into a 9,300-square-metre section of a building, said Don Eckhart, vice-president of operations. There, Samuel Manu-Tech would make polyester strapping—narrow strips used to bundle products ranging from lumber to cotton.

Samuel Manu-Tech wasn't new to York County. The company bought Brainard Strapping at 640 Celriver Road about 18 months previously.

The new plant would be the first polyester strapping centre for Samuel Manu-Tech. The company had been buying raw polyester materials to be converted into strapping. Other Samuel Manu-Tech plants made metal strapping and strapping from other plastics.

Incentives, location, and the interstate highway were what convinced the company to pick the site, Eckhart said. The location would qualify for tax incentives and an employee training program at York Technical College.

"We narrowed it down to North Carolina and South Carolina because of the proximity to [polyester] resin suppliers," he said. Samuel Manu-Tech had also considered sites in Georgia, Tennessee, and Virginia before culling the sites.

Most of the employees would come from the local area. The company would be looking for production workers for the plastic-extruding line and for quality assurance and production control.

Based in Etobicoke, Ontario, Samuel Manu-Tech has annual sales of about $400 million. Its stock is traded on the Toronto Stock Exchange.

DISCUSSION QUESTIONS

1. Evaluate the inducements offered Samuel Manu-Tech by community leaders in North and South Carolina.
2. Evaluate the reasons given by Mr. Eckhart for the relocation. Are they justifiable?
3. What effect will this new plant have on the attitude of present Canadian employees towards the security of Canadian operations?

Source: Adapted from "Industrial Area Draws Canadian Company," *The Herald (Rock Hill, S.C.)* (May 10, 1996, 1st Edition.)

BIBLIOGRAPHY

"Canada Set for Bigger Share of Japanese Auto Investment," *Tokyo Business Today* (February 1995): 38.

Craig, C. S., et al., "Models of the Retail Location Process." *Journal of Retailing*, 60 (April 1984): 5–36.

DeForest, M. E. "Thinking of a Plant in Mexico?" *The Academy of Management Executive*, 8, no. 1 (February 1994): 33–40.

Domich, P. D., K. L. Hoffman, R. H. F. Jackson, and M. A. McClain. "Locating Tax Facilities: A Graphics-Based Microcomputer Optimization Model." *Management Science*, 37 (August 1991): 960.

Fitzsimmons, J. A. "A Warehouse Location Model Helps Texas Comptroller Select Out-of-State Audit Officers." *Interfaces*, 13 (October 1983): 40–45.

"Industrial Area Draws Canadian Comapny," *The Herald (Rock Hill, S.C.)* (May 10, 1996, 1st Edition).

Kimes, S. E., and J. A. Fitzsimmons. "Selecting Profitable Hotel Sites at La Quinta Motor Inns." *Interfaces*, 20 (March/April 1990): 12–20.

"Look West for Hotel Growth in Recession-Riddled Canada," *Hotel & Motel Management*, 208, no. 19 (November 1, 1993): 49.

Murdick, R., B. Render, and R. Russell. *Service Operations Management*. Boston: Allyn and Bacon, 1990.

PR Newswire Association Inc., "Epic Brings Guaranteed Time-Definite Delivery to Central Canadian Market," October 2, 1995.

Price, W. L., and M. Turcotte. "Locating a Blood Bank." *Interfaces*, 16 (September/October 1986): 17–26.

Render, B., and R. M. Stair. *Introduction to Management Science*. Boston: Allyn and Bacon, 1992.

———. *Quantitative Analysis for Management*, 5th ed. Boston: Allyn and Bacon, 1994.

"The Checklist of Site Selection Factors." In *Site Selection Handbook*. Atlanta, GA: Conway, 1978.

Vargas, G. A., and T. W. Johnson. "An Analysis of Operational Experience in the US/Mexico Production Sharing (Maquiladora) Program." *Journal of Operations Management*, 11, no. 1 (March 1993): 17–34.

9 SUPPLEMENT

TRANSPORTATION MODELLING

SUPPLEMENT OUTLINE

The problem facing this Avis car rental company last year was cross-country travel. Lots of it. Cars rented in New York ended up in Chicago, cars from L.A. came to Philadelphia, and cars from Boston came to Miami. The scene was repeated in over 100 cities around the United States. As a result, there were many too many cars in some cities and way too few in others. Avis operations managers had to decide how many of these rentals should be trucked (by costly auto carriers) from each city with excess capacity to each city that needed more rentals. The process required quick action at the most economical routing. What did Avis do? It turned to the transportation method of linear programming for an optimal solution. ♦

The purpose of transportation modelling is to find the least cost means of shipping supplies from several origins to several destinations. Origin points (or sources) can be factories, warehouses, car rental agencies like Avis, or any other points from which goods are shipped. Destinations are any points that receive goods. To use the transportation model, we need to have the following:

1. The origin points and the capacity or supply per period at each.
2. The destination points and the demand per period at each.
3. The cost of shipping one unit from each origin to each destination.

The transportation model is actually a class of the linear programming model discussed in the Supplement to Chapter 6. As it is for linear programming, software is available to solve transportation problems. To fully use such programs, though, you need to understand the assumptions that underlie the model. To illustrate one transportation problem, we will look in this supplement at a company called Manitoba Plumbing, which makes, among other products, a full line of bathtubs. Data for Manitoba Plumbing's bathtubs are presented in Figure S9.1 and Table S9.1. The firm needs to decide which factories should supply which warehouses.

TABLE S9.1 ■ TRANSPORTATION COSTS PER BATHTUB FOR MANITOBA PLUMBING

From \ To	Sault Ste. Marie	Goose Bay	Sydney
Toronto	$5	$4	$3
Winnipeg	$8	$4	$3
Regina	$9	$7	$5

FIGURE S9.1 ■ Transportation Problem

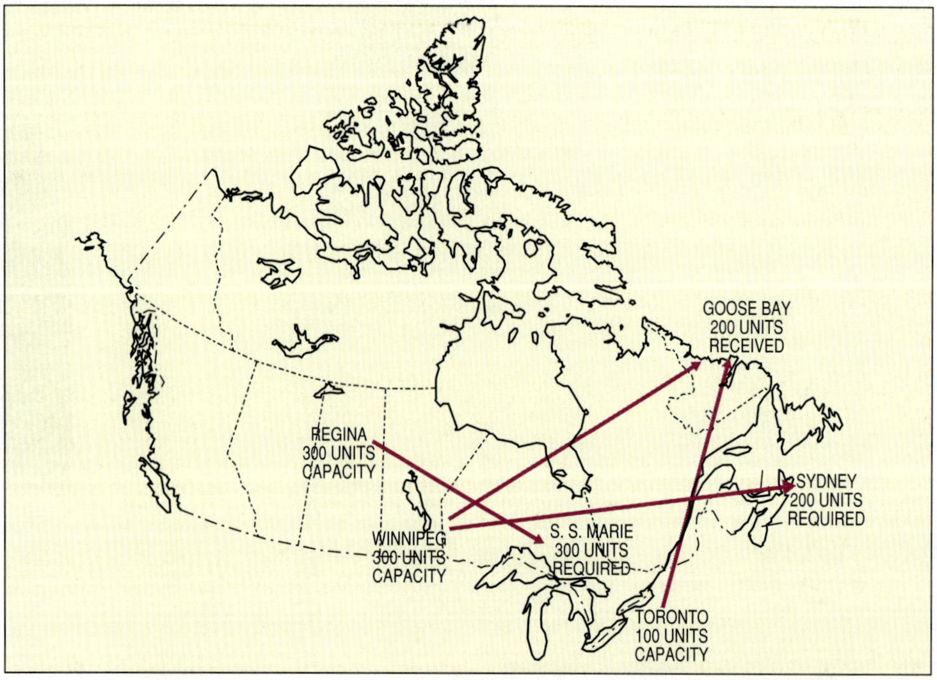

FIGURE S9.2 ■ Transportation Matrix for Manitoba Plumbing

From \ To	Sault Ste. Marie	Goose Bay	Sydney	Factory capacity
Toronto	$5	$4	$3	100
Winnipeg	$8	$4	$3	300
Regina	$9	$7	$5	300
Warehouse requirements	300	200	200	700

Toronto capacity constraint

Cell representing a possible source-to-destination shipping assignment (Winnipeg to Sydney)

Cost of shipping 1 unit from Regina factory to Goose Bay warehouse

Sydney warehouse demand

Total demand and total supply

The first step in the modelling process is to set up a transportation matrix. Its purpose is to summarize conveniently and concisely all relevant data and to keep track of algorithm computations. Using the information from Manitoba Plumbing displayed in Figure S9.1 and Table S9.1, we can construct a transportation matrix as shown in Figure S9.2.

DEVELOPING AN INITIAL SOLUTION—THE NORTHWEST-CORNER RULE

Once the data are arranged in tabular form, we must establish an initial feasible solution to the problem. One systematic procedure, known as the **northwest-corner rule**, requires that we start in the upper left-hand cell (or northwest corner) of the table and allocate units to shipping routes as follows:

Northwest-corner rule

1. Exhaust the supply (factory capacity) of each row before moving down to the next row.
2. Exhaust the (warehouse) requirements of each column before moving to the next column on the right.
3. Check that all supplies and demands are met.

Example S1 applies the northwest corner rule to the Manitoba Plumbing problem.

EXAMPLE S1

In Figure S9.3 we use the northwest-corner rule to find an initial feasible solution to the Manitoba Plumbing problem. Five steps are required in this example to make the initial shipping assignments:

1. Assign 100 tubs from Toronto to Sault Ste. Marie (exhausting Toronto's supply).
2. Assign 200 tubs from Winnipeg to Sault Ste. Marie (exhausting Sault Ste. Marie's demand).

3. Assign 100 tubs from Winnipeg to Goose Bay (exhausting Winnipeg's supply).
4. Assign 100 tubs from Regina to Goose Bay (exhausting Goose Bay's demand).
5. Assign 200 tubs from Regina to Sydney (exhausting Sydney's demand and Regina's supply).

FIGURE S9.3 ■ Northwest-Corner Solution to Manitoba Plumbing Problem

From \ To	(A) Sault Ste. Marie	(B) Goose Bay	(C) Sydney	Factory capacity
(D) Toronto	$5 — 100	$4	$3	100
(E) Winnipeg	$8 — 200	$4 — 100	$3	300
(F) Regina	$9	$7 — (100)	$5 — 200	300
Warehouse requirements	300	200	200	700

Means that the firm is shipping 100 bathtubs from Regina to Goose Bay

The total cost of this shipping assignment is $4,200 (see Table S9.2).

TABLE S9.2 ■ COMPUTED SHIPPING COST

ROUTE				
FROM	TO	TUBS SHIPPED	COST PER UNIT	TOTAL COST
D	A	100	$5	$ 500
E	A	200	8	1,600
E	B	100	4	400
F	B	100	7	700
F	C	200	5	1,000
				Total: $4,200

The solution given is feasible because it satisfies all demand and supply constraints. However, we would be very lucky if this solution yielded the minimum transportation cost for the problem. It is more likely we will have to employ an additional procedure to reach an optimal solution because the northwest-corner method is only meant to provide us with a starting point.

THE STEPPING-STONE METHOD

Stepping-stone method

The stepping-stone method helps to move from an initial feasible solution to an optimal solution. It is used to evaluate the cost-effectiveness of shipping goods via transportation routes not currently in the solution. We test each unused cell, or square, in the transportation table by asking: "What would happen to total shipping costs if one unit of the product (for example, one bathtub) were tentatively shipped on an unused route?" We conduct the test as follows:

1. Select any unused square to evaluate.
2. Beginning at this square, trace a closed path back to the original square via squares that are currently being used (only horizontal and vertical moves are permissible). You may, however, step over either an empty or an occupied square.
3. Beginning with a plus (+) sign at the unused square, place alternate minus signs and plus signs on each corner square of the closed path just traced.
4. Calculate an improvement index by first adding the unit cost figures found in each square containing a plus sign, and then by subtracting the unit costs in each square containing a minus sign.
5. Repeat steps 1 through 4 until you have calculated an improvement index for all unused squares. If all indices computed are greater than or equal to zero, you have reached an optimal solution. If not, it is possible to improve the current solution and decrease total shipping costs.

Example S2 illustrates how to use the stepping-stone method to move toward an optimal solution.

Moving sand to help expand Australia's Brisbane International Airport became a classic transportation problem. It involved the shipment of almost 2 million cubic metres of sand from 26 source sites to 35 final fill destinations. Using the transportation approach saved over $800,000, or about 27% of total hauling costs.

EXAMPLE S2

We can apply the stepping-stone method to the Manitoba Plumbing data in Figure S9.3 to evaluate unused shipping routes. The four currently unassigned routes are Toronto to Goose Bay, Toronto to Sydney, Winnipeg to Sydney, and Regina to Sault Ste. Marie.

Steps 1 and 2. Beginning with the Toronto–Goose Bay route, first trace a closed path using only currently occupied squares (see Figure S9.4). Place alternate plus signs and minus signs in the corners of this path. Note that we can use only squares currently used for shipping to turn the corners of the route we are tracing. Hence, the path Toronto–Goose Bay to Toronto–Sault Ste. Marie to Regina–Sault Ste. Marie to Regina–Goose Bay to Toronto–Goose Bay would not be acceptable, because the Regina–Sault Ste. Marie square is empty. It turns out that *only one closed route exists for each empty square.* Once this one closed path is identified, we can begin assigning plus and minus signs to these squares in the path.

Step 3. How do we decide which squares get plus signs and which squares get minus signs? The answer is simple. Because we are testing the cost-effectiveness of the Toronto–Goose Bay shipping route, we try shipping one bathtub from Toronto to Goose Bay. This is one more unit than we *were* sending between the two cities, so place a plus sign in the box. But if we ship one more unit than before from Toronto to Goose Bay, we end up sending 101 bathtubs out of the Toronto factory. Because the Toronto factory's capacity is only 100 units, we must ship one bathtub less from Toronto to Sault Ste. Marie. This change prevents us from violating the limit constraint.

To indicate that we have reduced the Toronto–Sault Ste. Marie shipment, place a minus sign in its box. Continuing along the closed path, notice that we are no longer meeting the warehouse requirement for 300 units. In fact, if we reduce the Toronto–Sault Ste. Marie shipment to 99 units, we must increase the Winnipeg–Sault Ste. Marie load by one unit, to 201 bathtubs. Therefore, place a plus sign in that box to indicate the increase. You may also observe that those squares where we turn (and only those squares) will have plus or minus signs.

Finally, note that if we assign 201 bathtubs to the Winnipeg–Sault Ste. Marie route, then we must reduce the Winnipeg–Goose Bay route by one unit, to 99 bathtubs, in order to maintain the Winnipeg factory's capacity constraint of 300 units. Thus, we insert a minus sign in the Winnipeg–Goose Bay box. As a result, we have balanced supply limitations among all four routes on the closed path.

FIGURE S9.4 ■ Stepping-Stone Evaluation of Alternative Routes for Manitoba Plumbing

Evaluation of Toronto to Goose Bay square

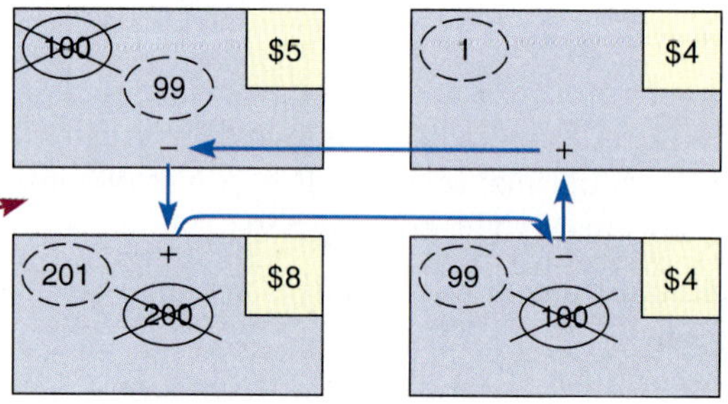

Result of proposed shift in allocation = 1 × $4 − 1 × $5 + 1 × $8 − 1 × $4 = +$3

From \ To	(A) Sault Ste. Marie	(B) Goose Bay	(C) Sydney	Factory capacity
(D) Toronto	$5 100 −	$4 Start +	$3	100
(E) Winnipeg	$8 200 +	$4 100 −	$3	300
(F) Regina	$9	$7 100	$5 200	300
Warehouse requirements	300	200	200	700

Step 4. Compute an improvement index for the Toronto–Goose Bay route by adding unit costs in squares with plus signs and subtracting costs in squares with minus signs.

$$\text{Toronto–Goose Bay index} = \$4 - \$5 + \$8 - \$4 = +\$3$$

This means that for every bathtub shipped via the Toronto–Goose Bay route, total transportation costs will increase by $3 over their current level.

Let us now examine the Toronto–Sydney unused route, one slightly more difficult to trace with a closed path. Again, notice that we turn each corner along the path only at squares on the existing route. The path can go through the Winnipeg–Sydney box but cannot turn a corner, and we cannot place a plus or minus sign there. We may use only an occupied square as a stepping stone (see Figure S9.5):

FIGURE S9.5 ■ Testing Toronto to Sydney

From \ To	(A) Sault Ste. Marie	(B) Goose Bay	(C) Sydney	Factory
(D) Toronto	$5 100 −	$4	Start $3 +	100
(E) Winnipeg	$8 200+	$4 − 100	$3	300
(F) Regina	$9	$7 + 100	$5 − 200	300
Warehouse requirements	300	200	200	700

$$\text{Toronto–Sydney index} = \$3 - \$5 + \$8 - \$4 + \$7 - \$5 = +\$4$$

Thus, opening this route will also not lower total shipping costs.

The other two routes can be evaluated in a similar fashion:

$$\text{Winnipeg–Sydney index} = \$3 - \$4 + \$7 - \$5 = +\$1$$
$$(\text{Closed path} = EC - EB + FB - FC)$$

$$\text{Regina–Sault Ste. Marie index} = \$9 - \$7 + \$4 - \$8 = -\$2$$
$$(\text{Closed path} = FA - FB + EB - EA)$$

Because this last index is negative, a cost savings can be attained by making use of the (currently unused) Regina–Sault Ste. Marie route.

In Example S2, we saw that a better solution is possible due to the presence of a negative improvement index on one of the unused routes. Each negative index represents the amount by which total transportation costs could be decreased if one unit or product were shipped by the source-destination combination. The next step, then, is to choose that route (unused square) with the largest negative improvement index. We can then ship the maximum allowable number of units on that route and reduce the total cost accordingly.

What is the maximum quantity that can be shipped on the new money-saving route? That quantity is found by referring to the closed path of plus signs and minus signs drawn for the route and selecting the smallest number found in the squares containing minus signs.

To obtain a new solution, we add that number to all squares on the closed path with plus signs and subtract it from all squares on the path assigned minus signs.

One iteration of the stepping-stone method is now complete. Again, we must test to see if the solution is optimal or whether we can make any further improvements. This is done by evaluating each unused square, as previously described. Example S3 continues Manitoba Plumbing's move toward a final solution.

EXAMPLE S3

To improve Manitoba Plumbing's solution, we can use the improvement indices calculated in Example S2. The largest (and only) negative index is the Regina–Sault Ste. Marie route, as shown in Figure S9.6.

The maximum quantity that may be shipped on the newly opened route (FA) is the smallest number found in squares containing minus signs—in this case, 100 units. Why 100 units? Because the total cost decreases by $2 per unit shipped, we know we would like to ship the maximum possible number of units. Previous stepping-stone calculations indicate that each unit shipped over the FA route results in an increase of one unit shipped from E to B and a decrease of one unit in both amounts shipped from F to B (now 100 units) and from E to A (now 200 units). Hence, the maximum we can ship over the FA route is 100 units. This solution results in zero units being shipped from F to B. Now we add 100 units (to the zero now being shipped) on route FA; then proceed to subtract 100 from route FB, leaving zero in that square (but still balancing the row total for F); then add 100 to route EB, yielding 200; and, finally, subtract 100 from route EA, leaving 100 units shipped. Note that the new numbers still produce the correct row and column totals as required. The new solution is shown in Figure S9.7.

FIGURE S9.6 ■ Transportation Table: Route FA

From \ To	(A) Sault Ste. Marie	(B) Goose Bay	(C) Sydney	Factory
(D) Toronto	$5 100	$4	$3	100
(E) Winnipeg	$8 200 −	$4 + 100	$3	300
(F) Regina	$9 +	$7 − 100	$5 200	300
Warehouse	300	200	200	700

FIGURE S9.7 ■ Solution at Next Iteration (Still Not Optimal)

From \ To	(A) Sault Ste. Marie	(B) Goose Bay	(C) Sydney	Factory
(D) Toronto	$5 100	$4	$3	100
(E) Winnipeg	$8 100	$4 200	$3	300
(F) Regina	$9 100	$7	$5 200	300
Warehouse	300	200	200	700

Total shipping cost has been reduced by (100 units) × ($2 saved per unit) = $200 and is now $4,000. This cost figure, of course, can also be derived by multiplying each unit shipping cost by the number of units transported on its route, namely:

$$100(\$5) + 100(\$8) + 200(\$4) + 100(\$9) + 200(\$5) = \$4{,}000$$

Looking carefully at Figure S9.7, you can see that it, too, is not yet optimal. Route EC (Winnipeg–Sydney) has a negative cost improvement index. See if you can find the final solution on your own. Programs S9.1 and S9.2, at the end of this supplement, provide the AB:POM solution.

DEMAND NOT EQUAL TO SUPPLY

A common situation in real-world problems is the case in which total demand is not equal to total supply. We can handle these "unbalanced" problems easily with the solution procedures discussed before if we first introduce **dummy sources** or **dummy destinations**. In the event that total supply is greater than total demand, we create a dummy destination, so the demand exactly equals the surplus. If total demand is greater than total supply, we introduce a dummy source (factory) with a supply equal to the excess of demand over supply. In each case, we assign cost coefficients of zero to each square on the dummy location because in fact these units will not be shipped. Hence, the cost is zero.

Dummy sources
Dummy destinations

Example S4 demonstrates the use of a dummy destination.

EXAMPLE S4

Manitoba Plumbing increases the rate of production of bathtubs in its Toronto factory to 250. To reformulate this unbalanced problem, we refer back to the data presented in Example S1 and present the new matrix in Figure S9.8. We use the northwest-corner rule to find the initial feasible solution. Once the problem is balanced, solution can proceed in the normal way.

FIGURE S9.8 ■ Northwest-Corner Rule with Dummy

From \ To	(A) Sault Ste. Marie	(B) Goose Bay	(C) Sydney	Dummy	Factory capacity
(D) Toronto	\$5 250	\$4	\$3	0	250
(E) Winnipeg	\$8 50	\$4 200	\$3 50	0	300
(F) Regina	\$9	\$7	\$5 150	0 150	300
Warehouse requirements	300	200	200	150	850

New Toronto capacity

Total cost = 250(\$5) + 50(\$8) + 200(\$4) + 50(\$3) + 150(\$5) + 150(0) = \$3,350

When the navy in Thailand drafts a young man, he first reports to the drafting centre closest to his home. From the country's 36 drafting centres, he is transported by truck to one of the four Thai naval bases. Deciding how many men should be assigned and transported from each centre to each base is solved using the transportation model. This way each base gets the number of recruits it needs and costly extra trips are avoided.

DEGENERACY

To apply the stepping-stone method to a transportation problem, we must observe a rule about the number of shipping routes being used: *The number of occupied squares in any solution (initial or later) must be equal to the number of rows in the table plus the number of columns minus 1.* Solutions that do not meet this rule are called degenerate.

Degeneracy

Degeneracy occurs when there are too few squares or shipping routes being used. As a result, it becomes impossible to trace a closed path for one or more unused squares. No problem discussed in this chapter so far has been degenerate. The original Manitoba Plumbing problem, for example, had five assigned routes (three rows or factories + 3 columns or warehouses − 1). Example S4, employing a dummy warehouse, had six assigned routes (3 rows + 4 columns − 1) and was not degenerate either.

To handle degenerate problems, we artificially create an occupied cell. That is, we place a zero or *very* small amount (representing a fake shipment) in one of the unused squares and *then treat that square as if it were occupied.* The square chosen, it should be noted, must be in such a position as to allow all stepping-stone paths to be closed or traced. We illustrate this in Example S5.

EXAMPLE S5

Martin Shipping Company has three warehouses from which it supplies its three major retail customers in San Jose. Martin's shipping costs, warehouse supplies, and customer demands are presented in the transportation table below. To make the initial shipping assignments in the table, we apply the northwest-corner rule (see Figure S9.9).

FIGURE S9.9 ■ Martin's Northwest-Corner Rule

From \ To	Customer 1	Customer 2	Customer 3	Warehouse supply
Warehouse 1	$8 100	$2	$6	100
Warehouse 2	$10 0	$9 100	$9 20	120
Warehouse 3	$7	$10	$7 80	80
Customer demand	100	100	100	300

The initial solution is degenerate because it violates the rule that the number of used squares must equal the number of rows plus the number of columns minus one. To correct the problem, we may place a zero in the unused square that permits evaluation of all empty cells. Some experimenting may be needed because not every cell will allow tracing a closed path for the remaining cells. Also, we want to avoid placing the 0 in a cell that has the negative sign in a closed path. No reallocation will be possible if we do this.

For this example, we try the empty square that represents the shipping route from warehouse 2 to customer 1. Now we can close all stepping-stone paths and compute improvement indices.

THE MODI METHOD

The **MODI (modified distribution) method** allows us to compute improvement indices for each unused square without drawing all of the closed paths. Thus, it can often save considerable time over the stepping-stone method for solving transportation problems.

Modified distribution (MODI) method

In applying the MODI method, we begin with an initial solution obtained by using the northwest-corner rule. We must compute a value for each row (call the values R_1, R_2, R_3, if there are three rows) and for each column (K_1, K_2, K_3, if there are three columns) in the transportation table. In general, we let

R_i = value assigned to row i
K_j = value assigned to column j
C_{ij} = cost in square ij (cost of shipping from source i to destination j)

The MODI method consists of five steps:

1. To compute the values for each row and column, set $R_i + K_j = C_{ij}$ but only for those squares that are currently used or occupied. For example, if the square at the intersection of row 2 and column 1 is occupied, we set $R_2 + K_1 = C_{21}$.
2. After you have written all equations, set $R_1 = 0$.
3. Solve the system of equations for all R and K values.
4. Compute the improvement index for each unused square by the formula

$$\text{Index} = C_{ij} - R_i - K_j$$

5. Select the largest negative index and proceed to solve the problem as you did using the stepping-stone method.

Example S6 uses the MODI method for the Manitoba Plumbing problem.

EXAMPLE S6

Given the initial solution to the Manitoba Plumbing problem (Example S1), we can use the MODI method to calculate an improvement index for each unused square. The initial transportation table is repeated in Figure S9.10.

First, set up an equation for each occupied square:

1. $R_1 + K_1 = 5$
2. $R_2 + K_1 = 8$
3. $R_2 + K_2 = 4$
4. $R_3 + K_2 = 7$
5. $R_3 + K_3 = 5$

Letting $R_1 = 0$, we can easily solve, step by step, for K_1, R_2, K_2, R_3, and K_3.

1. $0 + K_1 = 5 \Rightarrow K_1 = 5$
2. $R_2 + 5 = 8 \Rightarrow R_2 = 3$
3. $3 + K_2 = 4 \Rightarrow K_2 = 1$
4. $R_3 + 1 = 7 \Rightarrow R_3 = 6$
5. $6 + K_3 = 5 \Rightarrow K_3 = -1$

FIGURE S9.10 ■ Transportation Table

R_i	K_j / From \ To	K_1 Sault Ste. Marie	K_2 Goose Bay	K_3 Sydney	Factory capacity
R_1	Toronto	\$5 100	\$4	\$3	100
R_2	Winnipeg	\$8 200	\$4 100	\$3	300
R_3	Regina	\$9	\$7 100	\$5 200	300
	Warehouse requirements	300	200	200	700

The improvement index for each unused cell is $C_{ij} - R_i - K_j$:

$$\text{Toronto–Goose Bay} = C_{12} - R_1 - K_2 = 4 - 0 - 1 = \$3$$
$$\text{Toronto–Sydney} = C_{13} - R_1 - K_3 = 3 - 0 - (-1) = \$4$$
$$\text{Winnipeg–Sydney} = C_{23} - R_2 - K_3 = 3 - 3 - (-1) = \$1$$
$$\text{Regina–Sault Ste. Marie} = C_{31} - R_3 - K_1 = 9 - 6 - 5 = -\$2$$

Note that these indices are exactly the same as the ones calculated in Example S2. Now only one closed path, from Regina–Sault Ste. Marie, is necessary in order to proceed with the stepping-stone solution procedures.

FACILITY LOCATION ANALYSIS

As noted earlier, the location of a new factory or warehouse is an issue of major financial importance to a firm. Ordinarily, several alternative locations must be considered and evaluated. Even though a wide variety of subjective factors must be considered, rational decisions are needed to minimize costs.

The transportation methods just studied prove useful when considering alternative facility locations within the framework of an existing production-distribution system. Each new potential plant or warehouse will produce a different allocation of shipments, depending on its own production and shipping costs and the costs of each existing facility. The choice of a new location depends on which will yield the minimum cost for the entire system. This concept is illustrated in Example S7.

EXAMPLE S7

Williams Auto Top Carriers currently maintains plants in Oshawa and Cambridge to supply major distribution centres in Toronto and Vancouver. Because of an expanding demand, Williams has decided to open a third plant and has narrowed the choice to one of two cities—Windsor and Sarnia. Table S9.3 gives the pertinent production and distribution costs as well as the plant capacities and distribution demands.

TABLE S9.3 ■ PRODUCTION COSTS, DISTRIBUTION COSTS, PLANT CAPABILITIES, AND MARKET DEMANDS FOR WILLIAMS AUTO TOP CARRIERS

	From Plants	To Distribution Centres: Toronto	Vancouver	Normal Production	Unit Production Cost
Existing plants	Oshawa	$8	$5	600	$6
	Cambridge	$4	$7	900	$5
Proposed locations	Windsor	$5	$6	500	$4 (anticipated)
	Sarnia	$4	$6*	500	$3 (anticipated)
Forecast demand		800	1,200	2,000	

*Indicates distribution cost (shipping, handling, storage) will be $6 per carrier between Sarnia and Vancouver.

The important question that Williams faces is: "Which of the new locations will yield a lower cost for the firm in combination with the existing plants and distribution centres?" To determine the answer, we need to solve two transportation problems, one for each possible combination. The location that shows a lower total cost of distribution and production to the existing system will be recommended.

We begin by setting up a transportation table that represents the opening of a third plant in Windsor (see Figure S9.11). Use the northwest-corner method to find an initial solution. The total cost of this first solution is $23,600. Note that the cost of each individual "plant-to-distribution-centre" route is found by adding the distribution costs (in the body of Table S9.3) to the respective unit production costs (in the right-hand column of Table S9.3). Thus, the total production-plus-shipping cost of one auto top carrier from Oshawa to Toronto is $14 ($8 for shipping plus $6 for production).

FIGURE S9.11 ■ Williams Transportation Table for Windsor Plant

From \ To	Toronto	Vancouver	Production capacity
Oshawa	$14 600	$11	600
Cambridge	$9 200	$12 700	900
Windsor	$9	$10 500	500
Demand	800	1,200	2,000

$$\begin{aligned}\text{Total cost} &= (600 \text{ units} \times \$14) + (200 \text{ units} \times \$9) \\ &\quad + (700 \text{ units} \times \$12) + (500 \text{ units} \times \$10) \\ &= \$8{,}400 + \$1{,}800 + \$8{,}400 + \$5{,}000 \\ &= \$23{,}600\end{aligned}$$

Is this initial solution optimal? The stepping-stone method can be employed to test it and to compute improvement indices for unused routes.

Improvement index for Oshawa–Vancouver route = + \$11 (Oshawa–Vancouver) – \$14 (Oshawa–Toronto) + \$9 (Cambridge–Toronto) – \$12 (Cambridge–Vancouver)
= – \$6

Improvement index for Windsor–Toronto route = + \$9 (Windsor–Toronto)
– \$10 (Windsor–Vancouver)
+ \$12 (Cambridge–Vancouver)
– \$9 (Cambridge–Toronto)
= \$2

Because the firm can save \$6 for every unit it ships from Oshawa to Vancover, it will want to improve the initial solution and send as many as possible (600, in this case) on this currently unused route (see Figure S9.12).

FIGURE S9.12 ■ Improved Transportation Table for Williams

From \ To	Toronto	Vancouver	Production capacity
Oshawa	\$14	\$11 600	600
Cambridge	\$9 800	\$12 100	900
Windsor	\$9	\$10 500	500
Demand	800	1,200	2,000

You may want to confirm that the total cost is now \$20,000, a saving of \$3,600 over the initial solution.

Now, we must test the two unused routes to see if their improvement indices are negative numbers.

Index for Oshawa–Toronto = \$14 – \$11 + \$12 – \$9 = \$6

Index for Windsor–Toronto = \$9 – \$10 + \$12 – \$9 = \$2

Because both indices are greater than zero, we have reached an optimal solution using the Windsor plant. If Williams elects to open the Windsor plant, the firm's total production and distribution cost will be \$20,000.

Example S7, however, provides only half the answer to Williams' problem. The same procedure would be followed to determine the minimum cost with the new plant in Sarnia. Determining this cost is left as an exercise. You can help provide complete information and recommend a solution by solving Problem S9.4.

SUMMARY

This supplement introduced the transportation model, a form of linear programming used to help find the least-cost solutions to systemwide shipping problems. The northwest-corner method, which begins in the upper-left corner of the transportation table, is used for finding an initial feasible solution. The stepping-stone and MODI algorithm methods are then used for finding optimal solutions. We introduced degeneracy (that is, the case in which the number of rows + the number of columns – 1 is not equal to the number of occupied squares). We also illustrated unbalanced problems—problems in which the total demand is not equal to the total supply. Finally, we showed how to use the transportation model to help solve facility location problems. This approach is one of the four location models described earlier in Chapter 9.

KEY TERMS

Northwest-corner rule (p. 367)
Stepping-stone method (p. 368)
Dummy sources (p. 373)
Dummy destinations (p. 373)
Degeneracy (p. 373)
Modified distribution (MODI) method (p. 375)

USING AB:POM TO SOLVE TRANSPORTATION PROBLEMS

In this transportation modelling example, we use the data from Manitoba Plumbing. After entering the number of origins and destinations, we are prompted in Program S9.1 to provide demand data, supply data, and unit shipping costs. Program S9.2 displays the output screen computed by AB:POM.

PROGRAM S9.1 ■ Data Entry Screen for Transportation Problem in Examples S1, S2, and S3. AB:POM adds dummy rows and columns automatically, if needed. The program can handle up to 99 rows or columns. We *do* need to instruct AB:POM as to whether we want to *maximize* or *minimize*. Origin and destination names are entered below as an option.

```
———————————— Transportation ——————————— Data Screen ———
Number of sources (1-99) 3          Number of Destinations (1-99) 3
minimize
———————————————————————————————————————————————————————
———————— MANITOBA PLUMBING, EXAMPLES S1-S3 ————————
Options -> NO steps   Comptr   PrntOFF
```

	S.S. MARIE	GOOSE BAY	SYDNEY	Supply
TORONTO	5	4	3	100
WINNIPEG	8	4	3	300
REGINA	9	7	5	300
Demand	300	200	200	

Esc

PROGRAM S9.2 ■ AB:POM Solution to Transportation Problem in Examples S1, S2, and S3. Part (b) illustrates cell improvement indices.

(a) MANITOBA PLUMBING, EXAMPLES S1–S3

SHIPMENTS	S.S. MARIE	GOOSE BAY	SYDNEY	Supply
TORONTO	100			100
WINNIPEG		200	100	300
REGINA	200		100	300
Demand	300	200	200	

The minimum total cost = $3,900

(b) MANITOBA PLUMBING, EXAMPLES S1–S3

IMPROV IND	S.S. MARIE	GOOSE BAY	SYDNEY	Supply
TORONTO		+2	+2	100
WINNIPEG	+1			300
REGINA		+1		300
Demand	300	200	200	

The minimum total cost = $3,900

SOLVED PROBLEM

Solved Problem S9.1

Marion Sobol, president of Sobol Concrete Company, has plants in three locations and is currently working on three major construction projects, located at different sites. The shipping cost per truckload of concrete, plant capacities, and project requirements are provided below:

(a) Formulate an initial feasible solution to Sobol's transportation problem, using the northwest-corner rule.

(b) Then evaluate each unused shipping route (each empty cell) by applying the stepping-stone method and computing all improvement indices. Remember to

1. check that supply and demand are equal
2. load the table via the northwest-corner method
3. check that there is the proper number of occupied cells for a "normal" solution (number of rows + number of columns − 1 = number of occupied cells)
4. find a closed path to each empty cell
5. determine the index for each unused cell
6. move as many units as possible to the cell that provides the most improvement (if there is one)
7. repeat steps 3 through 6 until no further improvement can be found

	To			
From	**Project A**	**Project B**	**Project C**	**Plant Capacity**
Plant 1	$10	$ 4	$11	70
Plant 2	$12	$ 5	$ 8	50
Plant 3	$ 9	$ 7	$ 6	30
Project requirements	40	50	60	150

Solution

(a) Northwest-corner solution:

$$\text{Initial cost} = 40(\$10) + 30(\$4) + 20(\$5) + 30(\$8) + 30(\$6) = \$1,040$$

From \ To	Project A	Project B	Project C	Plant capacities
Plant 1	$10 / 40	$4 / 30	$11	70
Plant 2	$12	$5 / 20	$8 / 30	50
Plant 3	$9	$7	$6 / 30	30
Project requirements	40	50	60	150

(b) By using the stepping-stone method, the following improvement indices are computed:

Path: plant 1 to project C = $11 – $4 + $5 – $8 = +$4
(Closed path = 1C to 1B to 2B to 2C)

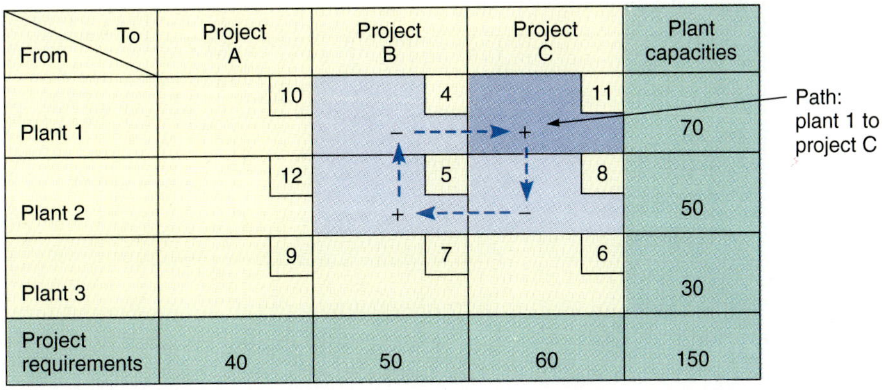

Path: plant 2 to project A = $12 – $5 + $4 – $10 = +$1
(Closed path = 2A to 2B to 1B to 1A)

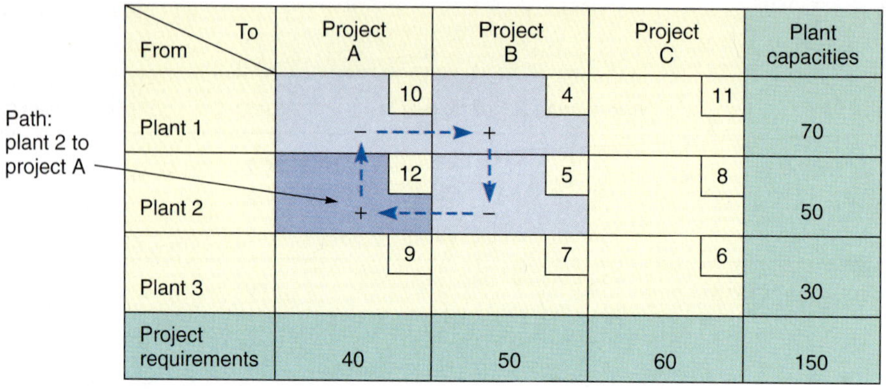

Path: plant 3 to project A = $9 – $6 + $8 – $5 + $4 – 10 = $0
(Closed path = 3A to 3C to 2C to 2B to 1B to 1A)

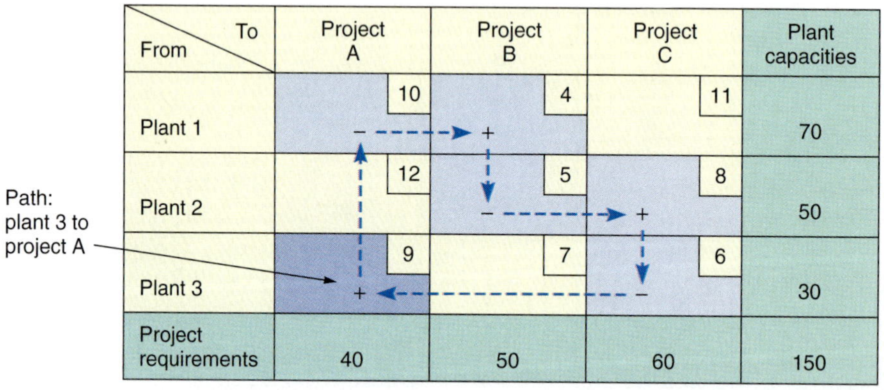

Path: plant 3 to project B = $7 – $6 + $8 – $5 – $4
(Closed path = 3B to 3C to 2C to 2B)

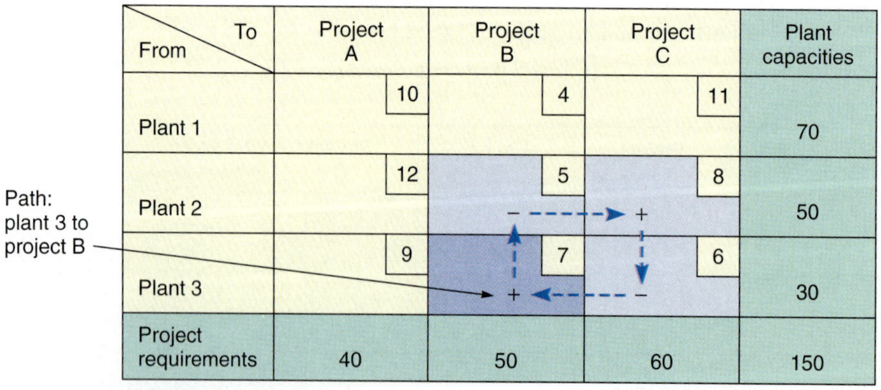

Because all indices are greater than or equal to zero (all are positive or zero), this initial solution provides the optimal transportation schedule, namely, 40 units from 1 to A, 30 units from 1 to B, 20 units from 2 to B, 30 units from 2 to C, and 30 units from 3 to C.

Had we found a path that allowed improvement, we would move all units possible to that cell and then check every empty cell again.

DISCUSSION QUESTIONS

1. What is a *balanced* transportation problem? Describe the approach you would use to solve an *unbalanced* problem.
2. How do the MODI and stepping-stone methods differ?
3. Develop a *northeast* corner rule and explain how it would work. Set up an initial solution for the Manitoba Plumbing problem in Example S1.
4. Explain what happens when the solution to a transportation problem does not have M + N –1 occupied squares.
5. When, in solving a transportation problem:
   a) is a northwest corner solution optimal?
   b) is a MODI solution optimal?
6. How can the transportation method address production costs in addition to transportation costs?
7. What is the difference between a feasible solution and an optimal one?
8. What is the purpose of the stepping stone method?
9. What is the solution to the problem of degeneracy?
10. What are the purposes of *dummy sources* or *dummy destinations* in a transportation problem?
11. Identify the three "steps" in the northwest corner rule.

CRITICAL THINKING EXERCISE

Cahill May Roberts (CMR) is Ireland's largest wholesale drug distributor. Its head office and three warehouses are in Dublin, with five more warehouses scattered around Ireland. CMR supplies about 400 retail druggists in Dublin and over 800 customers in 300 outlying villages. Customers are reached by a fleet of delivery vans, with drop-off frequency varying from twice a day to once per week. It is common for customers to receive supplies from more than one warehouse. Make specific recommendations to improve CMR's efficiency and to satisfy druggists' demands.

PROBLEMS

: **S9.1** The following table presents data for a transportation problem in Judeth Hall's furniture company. Set up the appropriate transportation table and find the initial solution, using northwest-corner data.

From \ To	1	2	3	Capacity
A	30	10	5	20
B	10	10	10	30
C	20	10	25	75
Supply	40	60	55	

: S9.2 The following table is the result of one or more iterations:

From \ To	1	2	3	Capacity
A	(30) 40	(10)	(5) 10	50
B	(10)	(10) 30	(10)	30
C	(20)	(10) 30	(25) 45	75
Demands	40	60	55	155

a) Complete the next iteration using the stepping-stone method.

b) Calculate the "total cost" incurred if your results were to be accepted as the final solution.

: S9.3 Determine whether the new solution table presented in Example S3 contains the optimal transportation allocation for Manitoba Plumbing. If not, compute an improved solution and test it for optimality.

: S9.4 In Example S7, Williams Auto Top Carrier proposed opening a new plant in either Windsor or Sarnia. The firm's management found that the total system cost (of production plus distribution) would be $20,000 if they chose the Windsor site.

What would be the total cost if Williams opened a plant in Sarnia? At which of the two proposed locations (Windsor or Sarnia) should Williams open the new facility?

: S9.5 After one iteration of the stepping-stone method, G. W. Willis Paint Company produced the transportation table below.

Complete the analysis, determining an optimal shipping solution.

G. W. Willis Paint Company

From \ To	Warehouse 1	Warehouse 2	Warehouse 3	Factory capacity
Factory A	($8) 120	($5)	($6)	120
Factory B	($15)	($10) 80	($14)	80
Factory C	($3) 30	($9)	($10) 50	80
Warehouse requirements	150	80	50	280

Cost = $2350

: **S9.6** The initial solution for the Hardrock Concrete Company's shipping problem, derived by using the northwest-corner rule, is presented below. Apply the MODI method in order to determine whether this allocation is optimal.

Hardrock Concrete Company

From \ To	Project A	Project B	Project C	Plant capacity
Plant 1	$10 40	$4 30	$11	70
Plant 2	$12	$5 20	$8 30	50
Plant 3	$9	$7	$6 30	30
Project requirements	40	50	60	150

: **S9.7** The JC Clothing Group owns factories in three towns (W, Y, and Z), which distribute to three JC retail dress shops in three other cities (in A, B, and C). The table below summarizes factory availabilities, projected store demands, and unit shipping costs.

JC Clothing Group

From \ To	Dress shop A	Dress shop B	Dress shop C	Factory availability
Factory W	$4	$3	$3	35
Factory Y	$6	$7	$6	50
Factory Z	$8	$2	$5	50
Store demand	30	65	40	135

a) Complete the analysis, determining the optimal solution for shipping at the JC Clothing Group.

b) How do you know if it is optimal or not?

: **S9.8** Sound Track Stereos assembles its high-fidelity stereophonic systems at three plants and distributes systems from three regional warehouses. The production capacities at each plant, demand at each warehouse, and unit shipping costs are presented below.

a) Set up this transportation problem by adding a dummy plant. Then use the northwest-corner rule to find an initial basic feasible solution.

b) What is the optimal solution?

Sound Track Stereos

From \ To	Warehouse A	Warehouse B	Warehouse C	Plant supply
Plant W	$6	$4	$9	200
Plant Y	$10	$5	$6	175
Plant Z	$12	$7	$8	75
Warehouse demand	250	100	150	500 \ 450

: **S9.9** Whybark Mill Works (WMW) ships French doors to three building supply houses from its mills in Mountpelier, Nixon, and Oak Ridge. Determine the best shipment schedule for WMW from the data provided by Tad Hixon, the traffic manager at WMW. Use the northwest-corner starting procedure and the stepping-stone method. Refer to the table below.

Whybark Mill Works

From \ To	Supply house 1	Supply house 2	Supply house 3	Mill capacity (in tonnes)
Mountpelier	$3	$3	$2	25
Nixon	$4	$2	$3	40
Oak Ridge	$3	$2	$3	30
Supply house demand (in tonnes)	30	30	35	95

:**S9.10** Using the data in Problem S9.8, resolve via the MODI method.

:**S9.11** Using the data in Problem S9.9, resolve via the MODI method.

:**S9.12** Jim Lloyd, vice president for operations of HHN, Inc., a manufacturer of cabinets for telephone switches, is constrained from meeting the 5-year forecast by limited capacity at the existing three plants. These three plants are Waterloo, Pusan, and Bogota. You, as his able assistant, have been told that because of existing capacity constraints and the expanding world market for HHN cabinets, a new plant is to be added to the existing three plants. The real estate department has advised Mr. Lloyd that two sites seem particularly good because of a stable political situation and tolerable exchange rate. These two acceptable locations are Dublin, Ireland, and Fontainebleau, France. Mr. Lloyd suggests that you should be able to take the data below and determine where the fourth plant should be located on the basis of production costs and transportation costs. *Note*: This problem is degenerate with the data for both locations.

Market Area	Plant Location: Waterloo	Pusan	Bogota	Fontainebleau	Dublin
Canada: Demand 4,000					
Production cost	50	30	40	50	45
Transportation cost	10	25	20	25	25
South America: Demand 5,000					
Production cost	50	30	40	50	45
Transportation cost	20	25	10	30	30
Pacific Rim: Demand 10,000					
Production cost	50	30	40	50	45
Transportation cost	25	10	25	40	40
Europe: Demand 5,000					
Production cost	50	30	40	50	45
Transportation cost	25	40	30	10	20
Capacity	8,000	2,000	5,000	9,000	9,000

:S9.13 Susan Helms Manufacturing Company has hired you to evaluate its shipping costs. The table that follows shows its present demand, capacity, and freight costs between each factory and each warehouse. Find the shipping pattern with the lowest cost.

Susan Helms Manufacturing Data

From \ To	Warehouse 1	Warehouse 2	Warehouse 3	Warehouse 4	Plant capacity
Factory 1	4	7	10	12	2000
Factory 2	7	5	8	11	2500
Factory 3	9	8	6	9	2200
Warehouse demand	1000	2000	2000	1200	

:S9.14 Cerveny Corporation is considering adding an additional plant to its three existing facilities in Barrie, Moncton, and Edmonton. Both Corner Brook and Campbell River are being considered. Evaluating only the transportation costs per unit as shown in the table, which site is best?

	From Existing Plants			
To	**Barrie**	**Moncton**	**Edmonton**	**Demand**
Blue Earth	$20	$17	$21	250
Ciro	25	27	20	200
Peterborough	22	25	22	350
Capacity	300	200	150	

	From Proposed Plants	
To	**Campbell River**	**Corner Brook**
Blue Earth	$29	$27
Ciro	30	28
Peterborough	30	31
Capacity	150	150

:S9.15 Using the data from Problem S9.14 and the unit production costs shown below, which locations yield the lowest cost?

Location	Production Costs
Barrie	$50
Moncton	60
Edmonton	70
Campbell River	40
Corner Brook	50

:S9.16 Find the result for the next iteration of the following transportation table for David Chou's chain of clothing stores.

David Chou's Store Data

To \ From	1	2	3	Demand
A	[1] 9	[6]	[7]	9
B	[2]	[5]	[3] 8	8
C	[3] 10	[2]	[4]	10
D	[6]	[3] 24	[9] 7	31
Capacity	19	24	15	

DATA BASE APPLICATION

S9.17 Duffy Pharmaceuticals holds a dominant position in the southeast United States, with over 800 discount retail outlets. These stores are served with twice-weekly deliveries from Duffy's 13 warehouses, which in turn are supplied daily by seven factories that manufacture about 70% of all of the chain's products.

It is clear to Jo Ann Duffy, VP Operations, that an additional warehouse is desperately needed to handle growth and backlogs. Three cities, Mobile, Tampa, and Huntsville, are under final consideration. The following table illustrates the current and proposed factory/warehouse capacities/demands and shipping costs per average box of supplies.

a) On the basis of shipping costs only, which city should be selected for the new warehouse?

b) Ocala's capacity, a study shows, can increase to 500 boxes per day. Would this affect your decision in part (a)?

c) Because of a new intrastate shipping agreement, rates for shipping from each factory in Florida to each warehouse in Florida drop by $1 per carton. How does this affect your answer to parts (a) and (b)?

TABLE FOR DATA BASE APPLICATION S9.17

Factory \ Warehouse	Atlanta, GA	New Orleans, LA	Jackson, MS	Birmingham, AL	Montgomery, AL	Raleigh, NC	Ashville, NC	Columbia, SC	Capacity (cartons per day)
Valdosta, GA	$3	$5	$4	$3	$4	$6	$8	$8	500
Ocala, FL	4	6	5	5	6	7	6	7	300
Augusta, GA	1	4	3	2	2	6	7	8	400
Stuart, FL	3	5	2	6	6	5	5	6	200
Biloxi, MS	4	1	4	3	3	8	9	10	600
Starkville, MS	3	3	1	2	2	6	5	6	400
Durham, NC	4	8	8	7	7	2	2	2	500
Requirements (cartons/day)	150	250	50	150	100	200	150	300	

TABLE FOR DATA BASE APPLICATION S9.17 (CONTINUED)

Factory \ Warehouse	Orlando, FL	Miami, FL	Jacksonville, FL	Wilmington, NC	Charlotte, NC	Mobile, AL	Tampa, FL	Huntsville, AL	Capacity (cartons per day)
Valdosta, GA	$9	$10	$8	$8	$11	$4	$6	$3	500
Ocala, FL	2	3	2	6	7	5	2	5	300
Augusta, GA	7	9	6	8	9	3	5	2	400
Stuart, FL	2	2	3	5	5	6	3	5	200
Biloxi, MS	7	13	9	8	8	2	6	3	600
Starkville, MS	6	8	7	7	8	3	6	2	400
Durham, NC	6	8	5	1	2	8	7	8	500
Requirements (cartons/day)	250	300	300	100	150	300	300	300	

CASE STUDY

Shuttle Craft

Shuttle Craft, formed in 1993, has rocked the four corners of the world with a totally new product, and in 1995 had to triple its manufacturing to over 3,000 square metres just to meet demand.

Shuttle Craft is the creation of three University of Saskatchewan commerce graduates. Their dream: a product that is unique in the world, and a strong position in the marketplace to help ward off copycats. The product, not unlike all other great inventions, is simple and brilliant. While boats and personal water craft aggressively competed with one another for the wet market, Dan Beaulac, Wayne Washington, and Trevor Hewison created the third competitor in a water craft accessory which effectively turns a personal water craft (PWC) into a five-seater jet boat. It's better than a boat and better than a PWC—it's both!

The operative word is *connection*, in that the Shuttle Craft is a U-shaped hull for a jet boat in which a PWC fits securely. The PWC is the power and the Shuttle is the boat. The Shuttle Craft's uniquely designed and patented hull allows the stability to pull a water skier and its top speed is limited only by the power of the PWC attached. The simplicity of the design allows for ease in setup from PWC to boat. The Shuttle Craft is designed to fit all two- and three-seater water craft, including Yamaha, Polaris, Kawasaki, Tiger Shark, and Wet Jet.

A variety of designs are available, with features including running lights for night use, a marine stereo, a sun deck, three large and insulated storage compartments, non-skid decking, a very sporty graphics package, grab rails, stainless steel hardware, and a fishing rod holder.

The three graduates worked for a year and a half on the project in Beaulac's dad's garage. They have said that they were very fortunate in that they all lived for free at home, which enabled them to have the time needed for the project. When Prince Albert reached temperatures of −40°C they put more wood in the garage woodburning stove and continued. "We kept each other going," Beaulac says.

They knew the first rule of invention: make it perfect the first time and get it to market as fast as possible. After the creation of a design that was functional and feasible, they had the challenge of raising financing for a factory. The boat used in their first trade show had never been in water; however, Beaulac says, "Wayne was right on track with marketing and when we were ready to build Shuttle Crafts the sales were there." When the time came to expand manufacturing to a larger scale, the province's "Future Skills" program came up with $126,548 towards training 25 new workers. The formal business plan was put together, and it gave Saskatchewan Opportunities Corporation (SOCO) and Business Development Bank of Canada (BDC) enough confidence in the project to offer financing. The trio also had help from the Industrial Research Program, Product Export Marketing Development, and Aboriginal Businesses of Canada.

The manufacturing plant recently moved from its beginnings in Prince Albert's SIAST Woodland Instate, where the job training took place, to the north end of Saskatoon, with quadruple the space—and there were plans to grow to over 5,500 square metres.

"We knew without a doubt, right from day one, that this would be a big hit if it was done properly," says Beaulac. "Being the best is being first in the world with the best product at the best price."

The three entrepreneurs had little or no knowledge of how to build a boat or work with fibreglass, so they bought back issues of *Boat Builder* and rented how-to videos. They all learned and grew together. Beaulac says there is no hierarchy with the three, even though he holds the title President and the other two Vice-President. Each knows exactly what has to be done and goes out and does it. The three have a profit-sharing plan in place to reward their efforts individually and as a group every three months.

The attitude on the shop floor is geared not so much to speed as to quality. The only competition is in how to produce the product more cost-effectively while maintaining this quality. Production is manned by young and enthusiastic employees who see their job as fun and exciting; they also have the

(Continued)

opportunity to move within the production process and learn it all, from R&D to production, fabric, and grinding.

The sales team has the same enthusiasm as the production staff. In fact, Kirk Holinaty, who has been involved from the garage days, and is the North American sales manager, says, "I've done everything—I can build a boat and then sell it." The overseas manager, Keven Jefferies, has made sales from Peru to Saudi Arabia.

Ninety percent of Shuttle Craft's business comes from the U.S. dealers. Wayne, however, keeps a world map in his office and has it impressively dotted with sales. He says, "Companies everywhere in the world know about us now—'You're up in Canada, aren't you?'" "We have contact with Americans all day long every day and they don't have a clue where we are," says Washington.

For Washington, the most important aspect is the channel through which you sell. "It's important to establish a strong dealer base," he says. "Direct sales are a one-shot deal, whereas dealers have the return business." The majority of Shuttle Craft dealers are in the southern United States, where most of the PWC owners are—mainly California, Florida, and Texas.

Washington feels that Shuttle Craft is an aftermarket accessory to the PWC, and that the push-through strategy is the best way to get the product and dealers together. He also knows that the second phase of his marketing plan, the "pull-through," which entails getting customers and dealers together, is soon approaching.

At startup, the three had assumed that the summer would be their busiest time for making and shipping Shuttle Craft. Never assume! Dealers buy in fall and winter—summer is for promotion.

For 1996 they had $1.3 million in funding behind them to cover the cost of moving to Saskatoon and for increased production and purchasing of new tools and equipment. The three see themselves as truly an international company. Yet they have never lost any control along the way, retaining 100% ownership.

Wayne and Trevor prepared for the upcoming summer with over 200 trade shows, including Los Angeles, New Orleans, Chicago, Cincinnati, and Miami. Sales for Shuttle Craft went from $200,000 in the first year to $2,000,000 in the second year and an estimated $6 to $8 million in 1996 and $15 million in the year after that.

The entrepreneurs say there isn't much difficulty in working ten hours per day, because they love what they do. And since they are all best friends, they still want to go out for a beer together after work. They've had a lot of laughs over the past few years, which may be the biggest asset of all. It's more than entrepreneurial achievement, more than friends—it's all about government and industry working in a partnership that fits together as successfully as the PWC and Shuttle Craft themselves.

DISCUSSION QUESTION

1. Do you feel the production facility for Shuttle Craft is in the right location? Explain why you feel the way you do.

Source: "The Perfect Connection," *Saskatchewan Business*, 16, no. 6 (November 1995): 12.

BIBLIOGRAPHY

See references at the end of Chapter 9.

10

OPERATIONS LAYOUT STRATEGY

CHAPTER OUTLINE

LEARNING OBJECTIVES

When you complete this chapter you should be able to:

Identify or define:

- Fixed-position layout
- Process-oriented layout
- Work cells
- Focussed work centre
- Retail/service layout
- Warehouse layout
- Product-oriented layout
- Assembly line factory

Explain:

- How to achieve a good layout for the process facility
- How to balance production flow in a repetitive or product-oriented facility

WORLD-CLASS PROFILE: PITTSBURGH AIRPORT

Layout Provides a Competitive Advantage for Airlines at Pittsburgh Airport

Pittsburgh International's X-shaped terminal reduces taxi time and improves gate access, thereby reducing airline fuel cost substantially. These dual taxiways contribute to reduced taxiing time for aircraft at the Pittsburgh airport as well as higher takeoff speeds.

Just as operations techniques can assist in layouts for factories, stores, and hospitals, they can also aid in airport layout. Important layout criteria include reducing congestion, distance, and delays. These criteria have been successfully applied to the new Pittsburgh airport. The Pittsburgh airport layout also had to accommodate passenger convenience, cost, and expandability as well as the traditional P/OM criterion of operational efficiency.

The terminal layout provides a mall-like environment for travellers.

A variety of people movers—from shuttle trains to escalators to these moving walkways—improve passenger convenience.

To address passenger convenience, designers created a revolutionary X-shaped airport. The airport includes a central shopping mall, a variety of people movers, and a $34 million baggage-handling system. The X shape positively influences the movement of passengers and aircraft. Combinations of escalators, moving sidewalks, and shuttle trains move passengers to any of the 75 gates in about 11 minutes.

The X-shaped terminal also proved to be an excellent vehicle for operational efficiency. Elaborate simulations were done to evaluate flight activity and its impact on runways, taxiways, and gates early in the design stage.

The layout also provides dual apron taxilanes around the jet gates to allow efficient aircraft access in and out of all positions. These are coupled with complementary dual taxiways running in opposite directions to and from existing runways. The combination is contributing to reduced delays and allowing faster takeoffs. The resultant efficiencies mean airlines using the Pittsburgh airport can expect to save as much as $15 million per year in operating expenses.

Pittsburgh airport, through the use of P/OM techniques, is setting a new standard for efficiency.

This $34 million dollar automated baggage handling system uses a 10-digit tag to sort bags. The system uses computer-directed laser scanners to route bags along more than 9 kilometres of conveyor belts.

Wal-Mart Canada "Greeter" welcomes customers too her store.

Wal-Mart's entry into the Canadian retail sector in the early 1990s has caused some of Canada's major retailers such as Eaton's of Canada, the Hudson Bay Company, and Canadian Tire Corporation to completely reconsider store layout and examine the lines of merchandise they stock. Traditional merchandise lines such as hardware no longer generate sufficient returns for many of Canada's major department stores. It would seem that more and more Canadians are self-serve individuals who prefer to browse through a large selection of merchandise and make their own choices. ♦

Layout is one of the strategic areas that determines the long-run efficiency of operations. Layout issues apply to Wal-Mart, to Toronto International Airport, and, in fact, to every organization in the world. Regular air travellers to and from Toronto have observed the layout design progression from Terminals 1 to 3 in terms of handling increasing volumes of traffic and improving efficiency. The *objective of the layout strategy* is to develop an economic layout that will meet the requirements of

1. product design and volume,
2. process equipment and capacity,
3. quality of work life,
4. building and site constraints.

A layout specifies the arrangement of processes (such as welding, milling, and painting), the related equipment, and work areas, including customer service and storage areas. An effective layout also facilitates the flow of materials and people within and between areas. Management's layout decisions must be made with this effectiveness and efficiency in mind. Layout decisions include the best placement of machines (in a production setting), offices and desks (in an office setting), or service centres (in settings such as hospitals or department stores).

TYPES OF LAYOUT

To achieve these layout objectives, a variety of classes have been developed. Among them are six that we discuss in this chapter:

Fixed-position layout

Process-oriented layout

Office layout

Retail/service layout

Warehouse layout

Product-oriented layout

1. **Fixed-position layout**—addresses the layout requirements of large, bulky projects such as ships and buildings.
2. **Process-oriented layout**—deals with low-volume, high-variety production (also called "job shop" or intermittent production).
3. **Office layout**—positions workers, their equipment, and spaces/offices to provide for movement of information.
4. **Retail/service layout**—allocates shelf space and responds to customer behaviour.
5. **Warehouse layout**—addresses trade-offs between space and material handling.
6. **Product-oriented layout**—seeks the best personnel and machine utilization in repetitive or continuous production.

TABLE 10.1 ■ LAYOUT STRATEGIES

PROJECT (FIXED-POSITION)	JOB SHOP (PROCESS-ORIENTED)	OFFICE	RETAIL (SERVICE/RETAIL)	WAREHOUSE (STORAGE)	REPETITIVE/CONTINUOUS (PRODUCT-ORIENTED)
Example:					
Ingall Ship Building Corp.	Royal Victoria Hospital (Barrie, Ont.)	Price Waterhouse	Canada Safeway Supermarket	Canadian Tire Distribution Centre (Brampton, Ont.)	Sony's TV assembly line
Saddledome (Calgary, Alta.)	Red Lobster Restaurants	Microsoft Corp.	Shoppers Drug Mart Eaton's of Canada		Ford of Canada (Oakville, Ont.)
Problem:					
Move material to the limited storage areas around the site.	Manage varied material flow for each product.	Locate workers requiring frequent contact close to one another.	Expose customer to high-margin items.	Balance low-cost storage with low-cost material handling.	Arrange product flow from one workstation to the next.

Examples for each of these classes of layout problems are noted in Table 10.1.

Only a few of these six classes can be modelled mathematically, so the layout and design of physical facilities are still something of an art. However, we do know that a good layout requires determining:

1. *Material handling equipment*. Managers must decide about the equipment to be used, including conveyors, cranes, lift trucks, pallet trucks, and automated storage and retrieval systems to deliver material or the mail.
2. *Capacity and space requirements*. Only when we know the personnel, machines, and equipment required can we proceed with the layout and provide space for each component. In the case of office work, operations managers must make judgements about the space requirements for each employee. It may be a 2 × 2-metre cubicle plus allowance for hallways, aisles, rest rooms, cafeterias, stairwells, elevators, and so forth, or it may be spacious executive offices and conference rooms. Management must also consider allowances for safety requirements that address noise, dust, fumes, temperature, and space around equipment and machines.
3. *Environment and aesthetics*. Layout concerns often require decisions about windows, planters, and height of partitions to facilitate air flow, to reduce noise, to provide privacy, and so forth.
4. *Flows of information*. Communication is important to any company and must be facilitated by the layout. This may require decisions about proximity as well as open spaces versus half-height dividers versus private offices.
5. *Cost of moving between the various work areas*. There may be unique considerations related to moving materials or the importance of certain areas being next to each other. For example, the movement of molten steel is more difficult than the movement of cold steel.
6. *Storage space height*. It may be cheaper to stack inventory higher using less floor space. There are still some costs: heavier-gauge "bedstead racks" may be required to bear the increased weight on the bottom racks and extra-high telescoping mast stacker trucks may be required at higher costs than standard stackers.

FIXED-POSITION LAYOUT

In a *fixed-position layout*, the project remains in one place and workers and equipment come to that one work area. Examples of this type of project are a ship, a highway, a bridge, a house, and an oil well.

The techniques for addressing the fixed-position layout are not well developed and are complicated by four factors.

First, there is limited space at virtually all sites. Second, at different stages in the construction process, different materials are needed; therefore, different items become critical as the project develops. Third, the volume of materials needed is dynamic. For example, the rate of use of steel panels for the hull of a ship changes as the project progresses. (Here a JIT inventory system which is constantly updated for such changing circumstances may be used to advantage.)

Fourth, because of the problem of theft from construction sites, a firm must balance this cost against the cost of security. The firm must also confront the problem of losses due to vandalism. Industrial plants are normally fenced in and secured; residential home sites are difficult to secure.

Different industries handle these problems in different ways. The construction industry usually has a "meeting of the trades" to assign space for various time periods. As you would suspect, this often yields less than an optimum solution, as the discussion may be more political than analytical. Shipyards, however, have loading areas called "platens" adjacent to the ship, which are loaded by a scheduling department.

Because the fixed-position layout is so difficult to solve well at the site, an alternative strategy is to complete as much of the project as possible off-site. This approach is used in the shipbuilding industry when standard units, say, pipe-holding brackets, are assembled in a nearby assembly line process (a product-oriented facility). Ingall Ship Building Corporation has built similar sections of a ship (modules) or the same section of several similar ships in a product-oriented line in an attempt to add efficiency to shipbuilding.[1] Similarly, other shipbuilding firms are experimenting with group technology to produce components.[2]

PROCESS-ORIENTED LAYOUT

The *process-oriented layout* can handle a wide variety of products or services at the same time. In fact, it is most efficient when making products that have different requirements or when handling customers who have different needs. A process-oriented layout is typically the low-volume, high-variety strategy discussed in Chapter 7. In this job shop environment, each product or each small group of products has a different sequence of operations. A product or small order is produced by moving it from one department to another in the sequence required for that product. Machines are arranged according to the type of process being performed.

[1] "Ingall's 130 Million Dollar Ship Factory," *Shipbuilding and Shipping Record*, 115, no. 22 (London: Transport and Technical Publications Ltd.): 25–26.

[2] Naboru Yamamoto, Kiyohi Terai, and Tatsumi Kurioka, "The Continuous Flow Production System Which Has Applied to Hull Works in Shipbuilding Industry," *Selected Journal of the Society of Naval Architects of Japan*, No. 35, Society of Naval Architects of Japan, Shiba-Kotohiracho, Minato-Ku, Tokyo, Japan, 5, no. 70: 153–174.

Figure 10.1 illustrates this process for two products, electric saws and electric drills. Another example of the process-oriented layout is a hospital or clinic. A continuous inflow of patients, each with his or her own processing needs, requires routing through records areas, admissions, laboratories, operating rooms, intensive care units, pharmacies, nursing stations, and so on.

A big advantage of process-oriented layout is its flexibility in equipment and labour assignments. The breakdown of one machine, for example, need not halt an entire process, because work can be transferred to other machines in the department. Process-oriented layout is also especially good for handling the manufacture of parts in small batches, or **job lots**, and for the production of a wide variety of parts in different sizes or forms. **Job lots**

The greatest problem for process-oriented layout is the lack of flexibility in the plant layout. A change in products which would normally dictate a new layout more in line with the processes required to produce the new products is impractical to consider in most cases. Many large, high-production machines must be installed "in place" on specially constructed, thick steel–reinforced floors necessary to carry their massive weight. In addition, special 220, 440, or 550 volt electrical service must be run to these machines. Should the process require welding machines, such as the massive underbody press welders used by the automotive industry, it is necessary to provide a large coolant circulation system for them. Moving such machines to a new layout may be prohibitively expensive, negating the potential advantages.

More disadvantages of process-oriented layout come from the general-purpose use of the equipment. Orders take more time and money to move through the system because of difficult scheduling, setups, and material handling. In addition, labour skill requirements and work-in-process inventories are higher because of larger imbalances in the production process. High labour skill needs increase the required level of training and experience; high work-in-process increases capital investment.

FIGURE 10.1 ■ A Process Layout Showing the Routing of Two Families of Parts

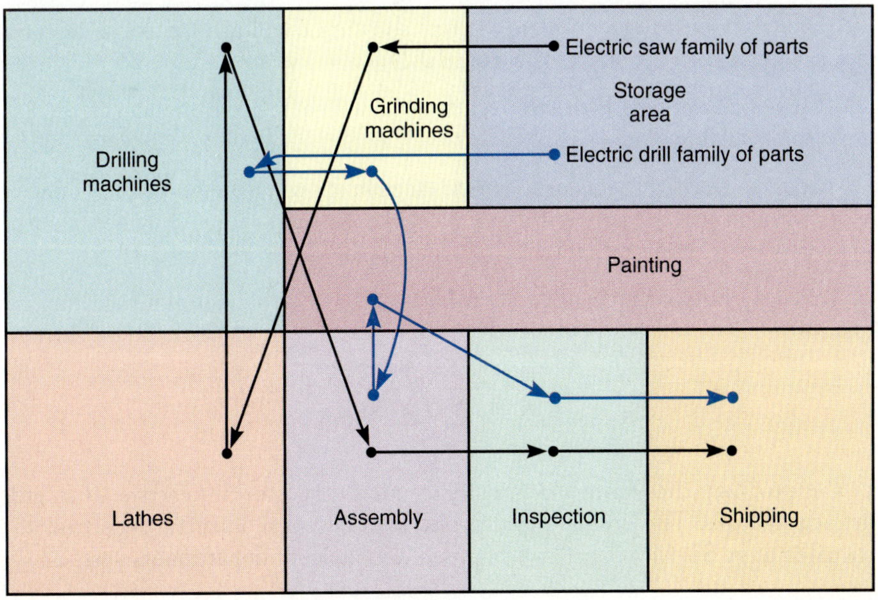

In process-layout planning, the most common tactic is to arrange departments or work centres so as to minimize the costs of material handling. In other words, departments with large flows of parts or people between them should be placed next to one another. Material handling cost in this approach depends on: (1) the number of loads (or people) to be moved during some period of time between two departments (i or j) and (2) the distance-related costs between departments. Cost can be a function of distance between departments. The objective can be expressed as follows:

$$\text{Minimize cost} = \sum_{i=1}^{n} \sum_{j=1}^{n} X_{ij} C_{ij} \qquad (10.1)$$

where n = total number of work centres or departments
i, j = individual departments
X_{ij} = number of loads moved from department i to department j
C_{ij} = cost to move a load between department i and department j

Process-oriented facilities (and fixed-position layouts as well) try to minimize the loads or trips times distance-related costs. The term C_{ij} combines distance and other costs into one factor. We thereby assume not only that the difficulty of movement is equal but also that the pickup and setdown costs are constant. Although they are not always constant, for simplicity's sake we summarize these data (that is, cost, difficulty, and pickup and setdown cost) into this one variable. The best way to understand the steps of process layout is to look at an example.

EXAMPLE 1

The Walters Company's management wants to arrange the six departments of its factory in a way that will minimize interdepartmental material handling costs. They make an initial assumption (to simplify the problem) that each department is 10 × 10 metres and that the building is 30 metres long and 20 metres wide. The process layout procedure that they follow involves six steps.

Step 1. *Construct a "from-to matrix"* showing the flow of parts or materials from department to department (Figure 10.2).

Step 2. *Determine the space requirements* for each department. (Figure 10.3 shows the available plant space.)

Step 3. *Develop an initial schematic diagram* showing the sequence of departments through which parts will have to move. Try to place departments with a heavy flow of materials or parts next to one another. (See Figure 10.4.)

Step 4. *Determine the cost* of this layout by using the material-handling cost equation:

$$\text{Cost} = \sum_{i=1}^{n} \sum_{j=1}^{n} X_{ij} C_{ij}$$

For this problem, the Walters Company assumes that a forklift carries all interdepartmental loads. The cost of moving one load between adjacent departments is estimated to be \$1. Moving a load between nonadjacent departments costs \$2.

Hence, the handling cost between departments 1 and 2 is \$50 (\$1 × 50 loads), \$200 between departments 1 and 3 (\$2 × 100 loads), \$40 between departments 1 and 6 (\$2 × 20 loads), and so on. The total cost for the layout shown in Figure 10.4 then is

$$\begin{aligned}\text{Cost} = {} & \underset{(1\text{ and }2)}{\$50} + \underset{(1\text{ and }3)}{\$200} + \underset{(1\text{ and }6)}{\$40} + \underset{(2\text{ and }3)}{\$30} + \underset{(2\text{ and }4)}{\$50} \\ & + \underset{(2\text{ and }5)}{\$10} + \underset{(3\text{ and }4)}{\$40} + \underset{(3\text{ and }6)}{\$100} + \underset{(4\text{ and }5)}{\$50} \\ = {} & \$570\end{aligned}$$

Step 5. By trial and error (or by a more sophisticated computer program approach that we discuss shortly), *try to improve this layout* to establish a reasonably good arrangement of departments.

FIGURE 10.2 ■ Interdepartmental Flow of Parts. The high flows between 1 and 3, and 3 and 6 are immediately apparent. Departments 1, 3, and 6, therefore, should be close together.

Number of loads per week

Department	1	2	3	4	5	6
1		50	100	0	0	20
2			30	50	10	0
3				20	0	100
4					50	0
5						0
6						

FIGURE 10.3 ■ Building Dimensions and a Possible Department Layout

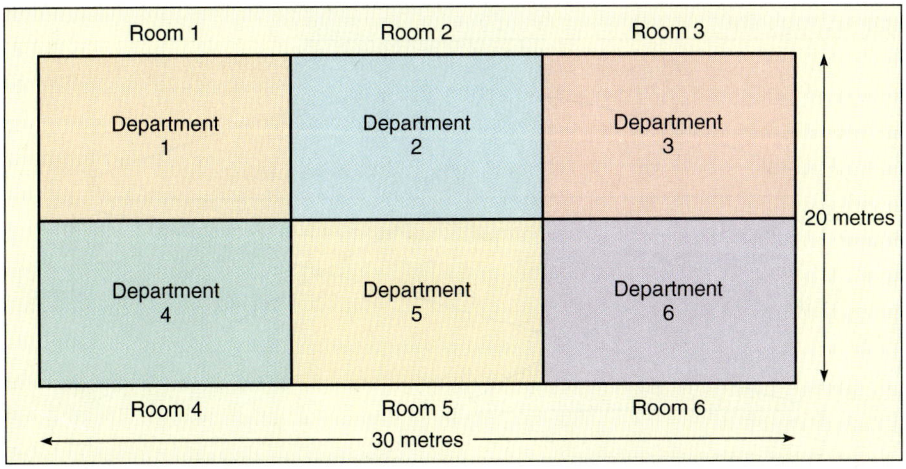

FIGURE 10.4 ■ Interdepartmental Flow Graph Showing Number of Weekly Loads

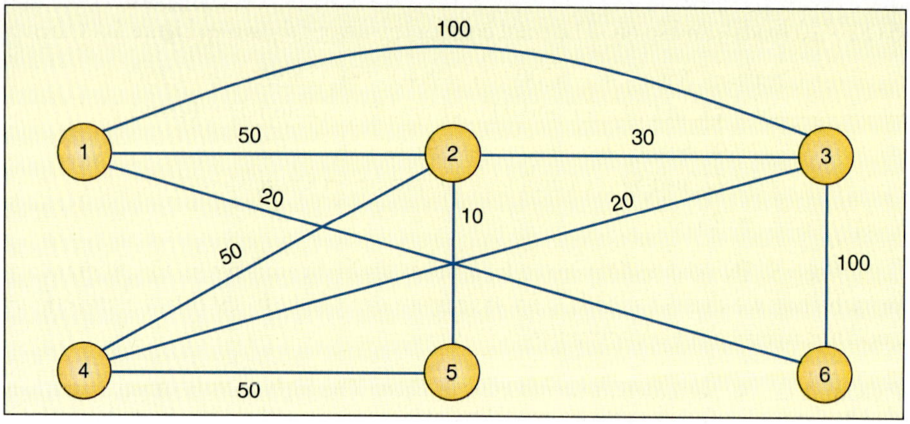

By looking at both the flow graph and the cost calculations, it appears desirable to place departments 1 and 3 closer together. They currently are nonadjacent, and the high volume of flow between them causes a large handling expense. Looking the situation over, we need to check the effect of shifting departments and possibly raising, instead of lowering, overall costs.

One possibility is to switch departments 1 and 2. This exchange produces the second departmental flow graph (Figure 10.5), which shows that it is possible to reduce the cost to $480, a savings in material handling of $90.

Cost = $50 (1 and 2) + $100 (1 and 3) + $20 (1 and 6) + $60 (2 and 3) + $50 (2 and 4)
+ $10 (2 and 5) + $40 (3 and 4) + $100 (3 and 6) + $50 (4 and 5)
= $480

FIGURE 10.5 ■ Second Interdepartmental Flow Graph

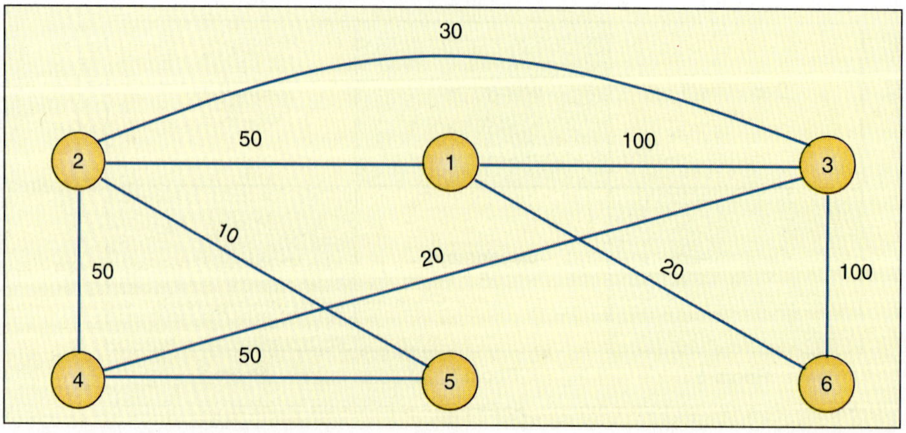

This switch, of course, is only one of a large number of possible changes. For a six-department problem there are actually 720 (or $6! = 6 \times 5 \times 4 \times 3 \times 2 \times 1$) potential arrangements! In layout problems, we seldom find the optimal solution and may have to be satisfied with a "reasonable" one reached after a few trials. Suppose the Walters Company is satisfied with the cost figure of $480 and the flow graph of Figure 10.5. The problem may not be solved yet. Often a sixth step is necessary.

Step 6. *Prepare a detailed plan* arranging the departments to fit the shape of the building and its nonmovable areas (such as the loading dock, washrooms, and stairways). Often this step involves making certain that the final plan can be accommodated by the electrical system, floor loads, aesthetics, and other factors.

In the case of the Walters Company, space requirements are a simple matter (see Figure 10.6).

FIGURE 10.6 ■ A Feasible Layout for the Walters Company

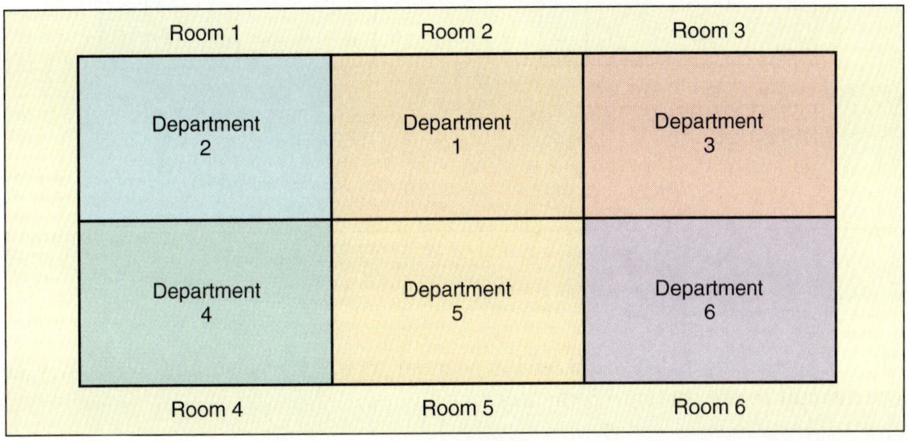

The graphic approach in Example 1 is fine for small problems.[3] However, this method does not suffice for larger problems. When 20 departments are involved in a layout problem, more than 600 *trillion* different department configurations are possible. Fortunately, computer programs have been written to handle layouts of up to 40 departments. The best-known of these is **CRAFT** (Computerized Relative Allocation of Facilities Technique),[4] a program that produces "good" but not always "optimal" solutions. CRAFT is a search technique that systematically examines alternative departmental rearrangements to reduce the total material handling cost (see Figure 10.7). CRAFT has the added advantage of allowing not only load and distance to be examined, but also a third factor, a difficulty rating.

CRAFT

Computerized techniques have been developed for both the two-dimensional and three-dimensional cases—the two-dimensional case is a one-story facility successfully addressed by CRAFT. The three-dimensional case is a multi-story facility

[3]See also Richard Muther, *Systematic Layout Planning*, 2nd ed. (Boston: Cahners, 1976), for a similar approach to what the author calls simplified layout planning.

[4]E. S. Buffa, G. S. Armor, and T. E. Vollman, "Allocating Facilities with CRAFT," *Harvard Business Review*, 42, no. 2 (March–April 1964): 136–159.

FIGURE 10.7 ■ In This Six-Department Example, CRAFT Has Rearranged the Initial Layout (a) with a Cost of $201.00, to the New Layout with a Lower Cost of $143.90 as Shown in (b).

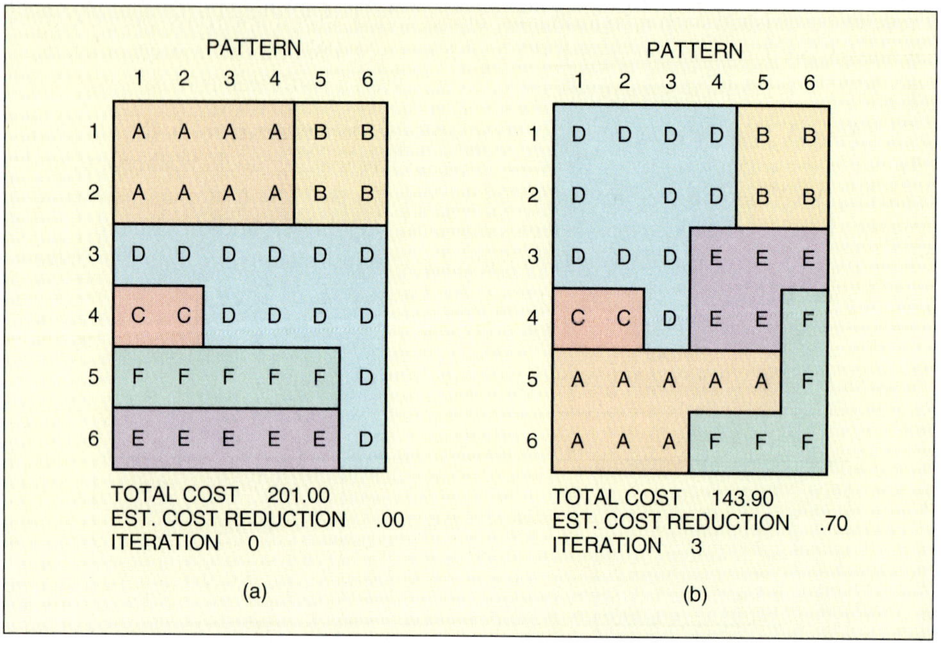

SPACECRAFT

and is addressed by **SPACECRAFT**.[5] Manual techniques also exist, but they are more difficult to use than are computer techniques.

Historically, 3-dimensional physical models were often built to address the layout problem. We now use 3-dimensional computer models to achieve the same purpose, but at greatly reduced cost. Here a transmission assembly line using AutoMod II, a computer simulation program, is shown.

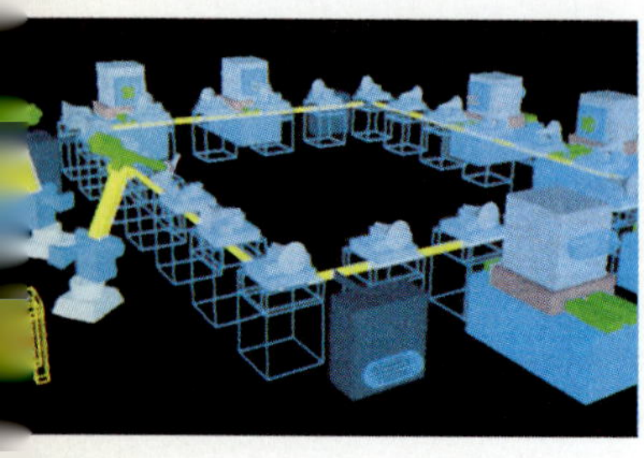

Expert Systems in Layout

CRAFT and SPACECRAFT are just two of the computerized techniques to aid in the design and layout of facilities. But these and the other popular programs, such as CORELAP, ALDEP, and COFAD, do not consider expert knowledge in ranking alternative plans. They do not have built-in rules to consider the creative aspects that a human designer would.

FADES (Facilities Design Expert System) is an *expert system*, that is a program that combines judgemental rules of human experts with the mathematical tools we have introduced earlier in this section.[6] It develops good facility designs for unstructured situations. FADES reflects the new breed of artificial intelligence decision-making aids described in detail in Chapter 8.

[5]R. V. Johnson, "SPACECRAFT for Multi-Floor Layout Planning," *Management Science*, 28, no. 4 (1982): 407–417. A discussion of CRAFT, COFAD, PLANET, CORELAP, and AIDED is available in James M. Moore and James A. Tompkins, *Computer Aided Layout: A User's Guide*, Publication Number 1 in the monograph series *Facilities Planning and Design Division* (American Institute of Industrial Engineers), p. 77–1. Norcross, GA.

[6]See E. L. Fisher, "An AI Based Methodology for Factory Design," *AI Magazine*, 3, no. 4 (Fall 1986): 72–85, and E. L. Fisher and S. F. Nof, "FADES," *Proceedings of the Annual IIE Meeting* (1984): 74–82.

Work Cells

A special case of process-oriented layout is the work cell. Although the idea of work cells was first presented by R. E. Flanders in 1925,[7] it is only with the increasing use of group technology (see Chapter 6) that the technique has reasserted itself. Cellular work arrangements are used where volume warrants a special arrangement of machinery and equipment. In a manufacturing environment, group technology identifies products that have similar characteristics and allows not just a particular batch (for example, several units of the same product), but also a family of batches, to be processed in a particular work cell.[8] The **work cell** idea is to take people and machines that would ordinarily be dispersed in various process departments and temporarily arrange them in a small group so that they can focus on making a single product or a group of related products (Figure 10.8). The work cell is built around the product. The advantages of work cells are:[9]

Work cell

1. *Reduced work-in-process inventory* because the work cell is set up to provide a balanced flow from machine to machine.
2. *Less floor space* required because less space is needed between the machines to accommodate the work-in-process inventory.
3. *Reduced raw material and finished goods inventories* because less work-in-process allows more rapid movement of materials through the work cell.
4. *Reduced direct labour cost* because of better flow of material and improved scheduling.
5. *Heightened sense of employee participation* in the organization and the product because employees accept the added responsibility of product quality being directly associated with them and the work cell.
6. *Increased use of equipment and machinery* because of better scheduling and faster material flow.
7. *Reduced investment in machinery and equipment* because good facility utilization reduces the number of machines and the amount of equipment and tooling.[10]

The requirements of cellular production include:

1. group technology codes or their equivalent
2. a high level of training and flexibility on the part of employees
3. either staff support or flexible, imaginative employees to establish the work cells initially.

Work cells are sometimes organized in a U-shape. U-shaped work cells, as shown in Figure 10.8, have several advantages over the straight ones. They help in five ways: (1) tasks can be grouped so inspection is immediate; (2) fewer workers are needed; (3) workers can reach more linear feet of the line; (4) the line can be more efficiently balanced; and (5) communication is enhanced.

[7]R. E. Flanders, "Design Manufacture and Production Control of a Standard Machine," *Transactions of ASME*, 46 (1925).

[8]Small batches in a process-oriented facility (e.g., a job shop) are called *job lots*.

[9]Burton I. Zisk, "Flexibility Is Key to Automated Material Transport System for Manufacturing Cells," *Industrial Engineering* (November 1983): 58–64 and Williams J. Dumoliem and William P. Santen, "Cellular Manufacturing Becomes Philosophy of Management at Components Facility," *Industrial Engineering* (November 1983): 72–76.

[10]In conflict with advantages 6 and 7, two researchers have reported an increase in capital investment and lower machine use when work cells are utilized. Perhaps different firms achieve different utilization depending on their ability to switch cell configuration and move personnel, as well as on the initial cost of their particular machinery and equipment. See Timothy J. Greene and Randall P. Sadowski, "A Review of Cellular Manufacturing Assumptions, Advantages and Design Techniques," *Journal of Operations Management*, 4, no. 2 (February 1984): 85–97.

FIGURE 10.8 ■ Improving Layouts by Moving to the Work Cell Concept

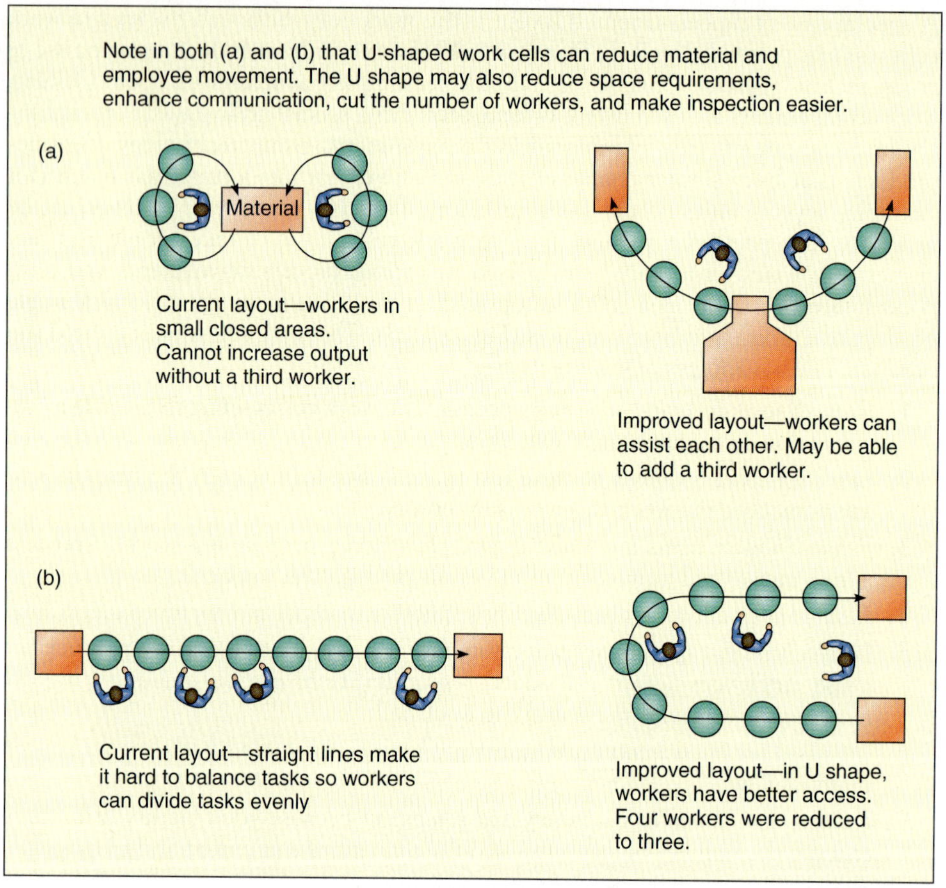

Focussed Work Centre and the Focussed Factory

Focussed work centre

Focussed factory

When a firm has *identified a large family of similar products that have a large and stable demand*, it may organize a focussed work centre. A **focussed work centre** moves production from a general-purpose, process-oriented facility to a large work cell. The large work cell may be a part of the present plant, in which case it may be called a focussed work centre. Or it may be separated and called a **focussed factory**. A fast-food restaurant is a focussed factory. Burger King, for example, changes the number of personnel and task assignments rather than moving machines and equipment. In this manner, the company balances the assembly line to meet changing production demands. In effect, the "layout" changes numerous times each day.

The term *focussed factories* may also refer to facilities that are focussed in ways other than by product line or layout. For instance, facility may be focussed in regard to meeting quality, new product introduction, or flexibility requirements.[11]

Focussed facilities in manufacturing and in services appear to be better able to stay in tune with their customers, to produce quality products, and to operate at higher margins. This is true whether they are steel mills such as SMI, Nucor, or Chaparral, or restaurants such as McDonald's and Burger King.

[11]See, for example, Wickham Skinner, "The Focussed Factory," *Harvard Business Review*, 52, no. 3 (May–June 1974): 113–121.

POM IN ACTION

The Factory of the Future at Square D

Square D, a division of Schneider Inc, the $1.6 billion Illinois-based manufacturer of electrical products, has revolutionized the way its employees think about work. At its Lexington, Kentucky, plant of the future, 800 workers are divided into teams of 20 to 30. Each team op-erates like a small business run by the workers themselves.

To accomplish this feat, Square D's plant layout has been redesigned into small factories within a factory. Each team is responsible for its product from start to finish. Now, without consulting management, a decision to change the order in which parts are assembled is made on the spot.

The transformation of Square D began in 1988, when chairman and CEO Jerre Stead discovered that more money was being spent on painting buildings than on training employees. Just 5 years later the company was spending 4% of its payroll on worker development, versus 1% at most other firms.

With today's shift almost over, employee Gloria Henry says, "I'm proud of my job. I really think I'm somebody now." Her team, Team 440, has finished its fifty-seventh day without a rejected part. Overall, the plant's rejection rate is down 75%. And whereas it used to take 6 weeks to process the average order, Team 440 now does it in 3 days. Schneider Canada's Square D division is in Mississauga, Ontario.

Source: Adapted from "American Agenda" ABC News (February 24, 1993).

Table 10.2 summarizes our discussion of work cells, focussed work centres, and focussed factories.

OFFICE LAYOUT

The main difference in the layout of offices and factories is the importance placed on information. In a manufacturing environment, work relies on the flow of parts and material, but office work relies on the movement of information.

Figure 10.9 shows a relationship chart. It is an extremely effective way to plan office activities. This chart, prepared for an office of consulting engineers, indicates that Ms. Payne must be (1) near the engineers' area, (2) less near the secretary and central files, and (3) not at all near the photocopy or storage room.

General office area guidelines allot an average of about 9.3 square metres per person (including corridors). A major executive is allotted about 37.2 square metres, and a conference room area is based on 2.3 square metres per person, up to 30 people.

TABLE 10.2 ■ WORK CELLS, FOCUSSED WORK CENTRES, AND THE FOCUSSED FACTORY

WORK CELL	FOCUSSED WORK CENTRE	FOCUSSED FACTORY
A work cell is a temporary product-oriented arrangement of machines and personnel in what is ordinarily a process-oriented facility. *Example:* A job shop with machinery and personnel rearranged to produce 30 unique control panels.	A focussed work centre is a permanent product-oriented arrangement of machines and personnel in what is ordinarily a process-oriented facility. *Example:* Pipe bracket manufacturing at a shipyard.	A focussed factory is a permanent facility to produce a product or component in a product-oriented facility. Many of the focussed factories currently being built in the United States were originally part of a process-oriented facility. *Example:* A plant to produce car radios.

Once the material and information flows of any layout provide a general arrangement, the layout details must be added. This has traditionally been done on a drafting board, cardboard cutouts, or a 3-dimensional model. However, AutoDesk of Sausalito, California, has a new program, Office Layout, that has many of the features of a CAD (Computer-Aided Design) product that allows dimensions, walls, dividers, and furniture, as well as people and even plants to be included and then printed.

FIGURE 10.9 ■ Office Relationship Chart

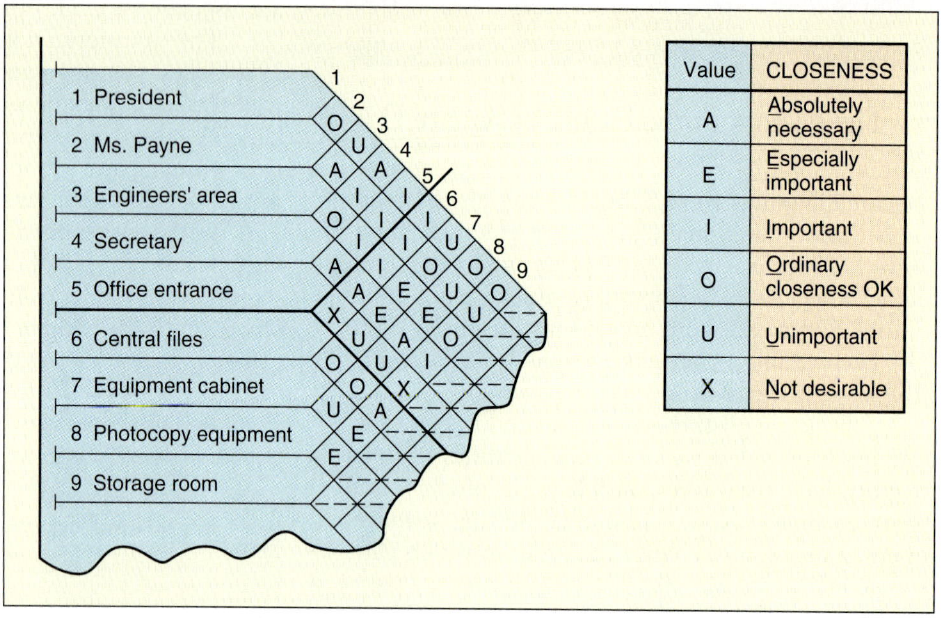

(*Source:* Adapted from Richard Muther, *Systematic Layout Planning,* 2nd ed., Boston: Cahners Publishing Company, 1973. Used by permission of the publisher.)

In contrast, restaurants provide from 1.5 to 4.6 square metres per customer (total kitchen and dining area divided by capacity). By making effective use of the vertical dimension in a workstation, some office designers expand upward instead of outward. This keeps each workstation unit (what designers call the "footprint") as small as possible.

These American concepts of space are not universal, however. In the Tokyo office of Toyota, for example, about 110 people work in one large room.[12] As is typical of Japanese offices, they work out in the open, with desks crammed together in clusters called islands. The islands are arranged in long rows; managers sit at the ends of the rows, with their subordinates in full view. (When important visitors arrive for meetings, they are ushered into special rooms and do not see these cramped offices.)

There are additional layout considerations that are universal (some of which apply to a factory as well as to an office). They have to do with teamwork, authority, and status. Should all or only part of the work area be air conditioned? Should all employees use the same entrance, rest rooms, lockers, and cafeteria? As mentioned earlier, layout decisions are part art and part science. Only the science part, flow of paper in an office, can be analyzed in the same manner as the flow of parts in a process layout.

Office layouts are far easier to manage than factory layouts. Most offices are temporary enclosures whose dimensions and shapes can be altered very quickly and at will. Office walls are made of modular units that can be released and moved quickly and without damage. Even older office walls are simply wood skeletons and drywall, which are easily demolished and rebuilt. More and more of today's employees find themselves working in free-standing cubicles—a collection of modular units not permanently affixed. Moreover, today's desktop and laptop computers require no special

[12] "Think Japan Inc. Is Lean and Mean? Step into This Office," the *New York Times* (March 20, 1994).

environments in which to function; more and more desktops are put on carts rather than desks. Thus, a large office complex with hundreds of employees can be altered dramatically and at low cost within days, while a factory layout change may require months, and costs will be high.

RETAIL STORE LAYOUT

Retail store layouts are based on the idea that sales vary directly with customer exposure to products. Thus, most retail store operations managers try to expose customers to as many products as possible. Studies do show that the greater the rate of exposure, the greater the sales and the higher return on investment. The operations manager can alter *both* with the overall arrangement of the store and the allocation of space within that arrangement to various products.

Although the *POM in Action* box "Lettuce in Aisle 4, Loans in Aisle 10 at Kroger" suggests that there is no longer any set pattern for store layouts, we can still note five ideas that are helpful for determining the overall arrangement of retail stores such as supermarkets and drug stores.

1. Locate the high-draw items around the periphery of the store. Thus, we tend to find dairy products on one side of a supermarket and bread and bakery products on another. An example of this is shown in Figure 10.10.
2. Use prominent locations for high-impulse and high-margin items such as housewares, beauty aids, and shampoos.
3. Distribute what are known in the trade as "power items"—items that may dominate a shopping trip—to both sides of an aisle, and disperse them to increase the viewing of other items.

POM IN ACTION

Lettuce in Aisle 4, Loans in Aisle 10 at Kroger

One reason supermarkets look much as they did 40 years ago is that they have all been using the same layout. But demographics and shopping patterns are changing. More and more, food is being purchased in restaurants, from fine dining to fast-food and carry-out. This is partly because both parents work in more families, and also because we have become more of a grazing, or nibbling, society. The bottom line is that the number of home-prepared meals, and the related purchase of groceries, is declining. Consequently, supermarkets are rethinking their layouts.

The modern supermarket may now include a fast-food restaurant, a deli, a photo lab, a video store, and a place to pay your bills. The high-draw items, such as meats, dairy, bakery, and produce items, are still at the far ends of the store, but high-margin items like deli, gourmet foods, pharmacy, beer and wine, and cosmetics are positioned for maximum exposure. And a variety of other services have been added to draw customers.

One of them is banking. NCB, for example, has added fourteen branches in Kroger's Memphis supermarkets. Enthusiastic young NCB bankers stop people in the aisles and use the public address system to push loans and promote the consumer banking services available from the NCB office in the store. The bright, verbal, and attractive (BVAer's, they're called) supermarket bankers do triple duty as tellers, loan officers, and salespeople who even know where to find the Cheez Whiz.

Sources: Adapted from *Forbes* (August 3, 1992): 39–40; *Forbes*, (February 17, 1992): 58–63; and the *Wall Street Journal* (May 20, 1994): B1.

Sharply declining retail sales have seen a major change in leading Canadian retail stores, principally Eaton's of Canada and the Hudson Bay Company: the transformation of men's and women's "fashion floors" into a boutiques approach featuring big names such as Tommy Hilfiger, Ralph Lauren, Levi Strauss, Nautica, Donna Karan New York, and others. This approach involves the introduction of very large, high, eyecatching signs featuring the designer's logo and name which help lead customers directly to those fashions. Customers, especially the late teens/early twenties market segment, seem to favour a particular designer, and wish to have a complete wardrobe of that designer's fashions. The new layout allows customers to locate the boutique of choice immediately.

4. Use end aisle locations because they have a very high exposure rate.
5. Convey the image of the store by careful selection in the positioning of the lead-off department. Some stores position the bakery and deli up front to appeal to convenience-oriented customers who want prepared foods.

Once the overall layout of a retail store has been decided, the products need to be arranged for sale. Many considerations go into this arrangement. However, the main *objective of retail layout is to maximize profitability per square metre of shelf space* (some stores may base this profitability on linear metre of shelf space in lieu of square metre of shelf space). Big-ticket, or expensive, items may yield greater dollar sales, but the profit per square metre may be lower. A number of computerized programs exist that can assist managers in evaluating the profitability of various merchandise. One, SLIM (Store Labour and Inventory Management), can help store managers determine when shelf space is adequate to accommodate another full case. Another software package is COSMOS (Computerized Optimization and Simulation Modelling for Operating Supermarkets), which matches shelf space with delivery schedules, allocating sufficient space to minimize out-of-stock between receipts.

WAREHOUSING AND STORAGE LAYOUTS

The objective of *warehouse layout* is to find the optimum trade-off between handling cost and warehouse space. Thus, management must maximize the use of the total "cube" of the warehouse—that is, use its full volume while maintaining low material handling costs. We define material handling costs as all the costs related to the incoming transport, storage, and outgoing transport of the material. These costs include equipment, people, material, supervision, insurance, and depreciation. Effective warehouse layout must, of course, also minimize the damage and spoilage of material within the warehouse. Management minimizes the sum of the resources spent on retrieving material plus the deterioration and damage to the material itself. The variety

FIGURE 10.10 ■ Store Layout with Dairy and Bread, High-Draw Items, in Different Corners of the Store

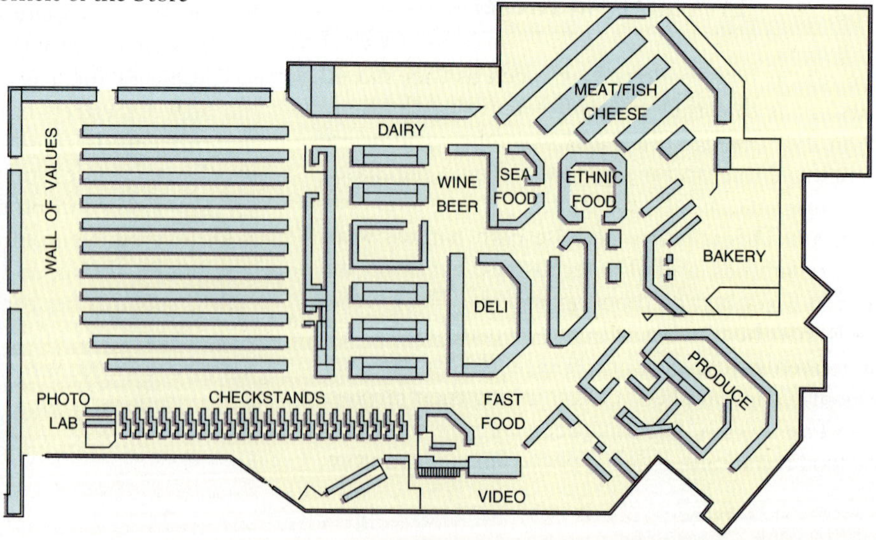

of items stored and the number of items "picked" have direct bearing on the optimum layout. A warehouse storing a few items lends itself to higher density more than does a warehouse storing a variety of items. Modern warehouse management is, in many instances, an automated procedure utilizing automatic stacking cranes, conveyors, and sophisticated controls that manage the flow of materials. Examples of firms that use the latest technology include Federal-Mogul, The Gap (illustrated in photo), and the new Canadian Tire fully automated warehouse in Brampton, Ontario, which has computerized handling, storage and retrieval.

PRODUCT-ORIENTED LAYOUT

Product-oriented layouts are organized around a product or a family of similar high-volume, low-variety products. Repetitive production and continuous production, discussed in Chapter 7, use product layouts. The assumptions are:

1. Volume is adequate for high equipment utilization.
2. Product demand is stable enough to justify high investment in specialized equipment.
3. Product is standardized or approaching a phase of its life cycle that justifies investment in specialized equipment. For example, Ford, General Motors, and Chrysler now produce convertible models on the same assembly line as regular sedan versions of the same vehicle. A cautious rebirth of convertible models in the early 1980s had convertible production contracted out to a specialty firm in suburban Detroit. The growing popularity of convertible models justified the expensive relayout of the plant to permit in-plant production.
4. Supplies of raw material and components are adequate and of uniform quality (adequately standardized) to ensure that they will work with the specialized equipment.

Two types of a product-oriented layout are a fabrication line and an assembly line. The **fabrication line** builds components, such as automobile tires or metal parts for a refrigerator, on a series of machines. An **assembly line** puts the fabricated parts together at a series of workstations. Both are repetitive processes, and in both cases, the line must be "balanced." That is, the work performed on one machine must balance with the work performed on the next machine in the fabrication line, just as the work done at one workstation by an employee on an assembly line must match up in time with the work done at the next workstation by the next employee.

Fabrication line

Assembly line

Fabrication lines tend to be machine-paced and require mechanical and engineering changes to facilitate balancing. Assembly lines, on the other hand, tend to be paced by work tasks assigned to individuals or to workstations. Assembly lines, therefore, can be balanced by moving tasks from one individual to another. In this manner, the amount of *time* required by each individual or station is equalized. The Boeing photo shows that the final assembly of even some huge products, such as a Boeing 747 airplane, is done in a product layout.

The central problem in product-oriented layout planning is to balance the output at each workstation on the production line so that it is nearly the same, while obtaining the desired amount of output. Management's goal is to create a smooth, continuous flow along the assembly line with a minimum of idle time at each person's workstation. A well-balanced assembly line has the advantage of high personnel and facility utilization *and* equity between employees' work loads. Some union contracts include a requirement that work loads must be nearly equal among those on the same assembly line. The term most often used to describe this process is **assembly line balancing**. Indeed, the *objective of the product-oriented layout is to minimize imbalance in the fabrication or assembly line.*

Assembly line balancing

The main advantage of product-oriented layout is the low variable cost per unit usually associated with high-volume, standardized products. The product-oriented layout also keeps material handling costs low, reduces work-in-process inventories, and makes training and supervision easier. These advantages often outweigh the disadvantages of product layout. These disadvantages are as follows:

1. High volume is required because of the large investment needed to set up the process.
2. Work stoppage at any one point ties up the whole operation.
3. There is a lack of flexibility in handling a variety of products or production rates.

Because the problems of fabrication lines and assembly lines are similar, we phrase our discussion in terms of an assembly line. On an assembly line, the product typically moves via automated means, such as a conveyor, through a series of workstations until completed (Figure 10.11). This is the way automobiles are assembled, television sets and ovens are produced, and fast-food hamburgers are made. Product-oriented layout uses more automated and specially designed equipment than is found in a process layout.

Assembly Line Balancing

Line balancing is usually done to minimize imbalance between machines or personnel while meeting a required output from the line. To balance a line, management must

FIGURE 10.11 ■ An Assembly Line Layout

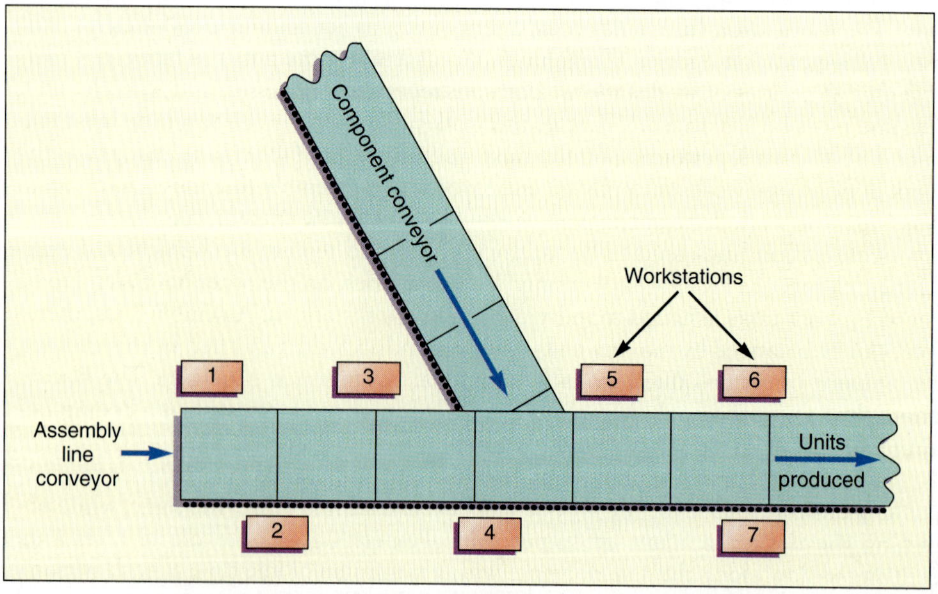

know the tools, equipment, and work methods used. Then the time requirements for each assembly task (such as drilling a hole, tightening a nut, or spray painting a part) must be determined. Management also needs to know the precedence relationship among the activities, that is, the order in which various tasks need to be performed. Example 2 shows how to turn these task data into a precedence diagram.

The Gap, Inc., strives for both high quality and low costs. It does this by (1) designing its own clothes, (2) quality control at the vendors, and (3) maintaining downward pressure on distribution costs. A new automatic distribution centre near Baltimore, Maryland, is designed to allow The Gap to stock East Coast stores daily, rather than three times a week. Gap Canada is a strong presence in major Canadian shopping malls coast to coast.

EXAMPLE 2

We want to develop a precedence diagram for an electrostatic copier that requires a total assembly time of 66 minutes. Table 10.3 and Figure 10.12 give the tasks, assembly times, and sequence requirements for the copier.

TABLE 10.3 ■ PRECEDENCE DATA

TASK	PERFORMANCE TIME (MINUTES)	TASK MUST FOLLOW TASK LISTED BELOW
A	10	—
B	11	A
C	5	B
D	4	B
E	12	A
F	3	C, D
G	7	F
H	11	E
I	3	G, H
Total time	66	

(Annotation pointing to tasks B and E: This means that tasks B and E cannot be done until task A has been completed.)

FIGURE 10.12 ■ Precedence Diagram

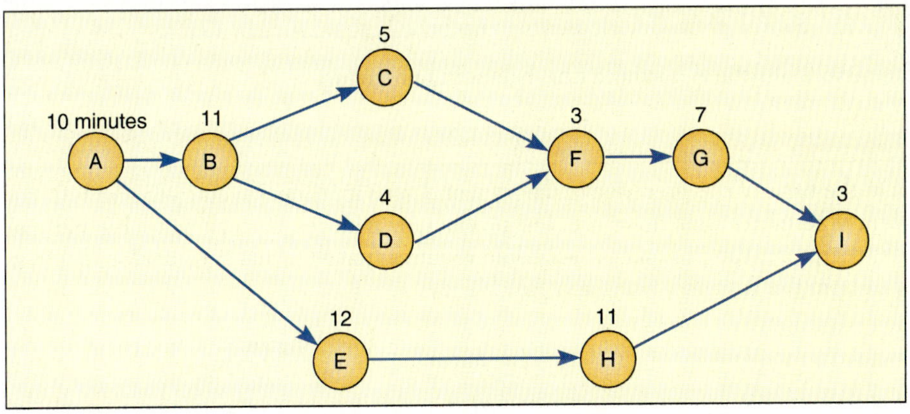

Once we have constructed a precedence chart summarizing the sequences and performance times, we turn to the job of grouping tasks into job stations to meet the specified production rate. This process involves three steps:

Cycle time

1. Take the demand (or production rate) per day and divide it into the productive time available per day (in minutes or seconds). This operation gives us the **cycle time**, namely, the time the product is available at each workstation:

$$\text{Cycle time} = \frac{\text{production time available per day}}{\text{demand per day or production per day}} \quad (10.2)$$

2. Calculate the theoretical minimum number of workstations. This is the total task-duration time divided by the cycle time. Fractions are rounded to the next higher whole number:

$$\text{Minimum number of workstations} = \frac{\sum_{i=1}^{m} \text{time for task } i}{\text{cycle time}} \quad (10.3)$$

where m is the number of assembly tasks.

3. Perform the line balance by assigning specific assembly tasks to each workstation. An efficient balance is one that will complete the required assembly, follow the specified sequence, and keep the idle time at each workstation to a minimum. A formal procedure for doing this is:
   a) Identify a master list of work elements and separate the available work elements from the unavailable work elements.
   b) Eliminate those work elements that have been assigned.
   c) Eliminate those work elements whose precedence relationship has not been satisfied.
   d) Eliminate those elements for which there is inadequate time available at the workstation.
   e) Identify a unit of work that can be assigned, such as the first unit of work in the list, the last unit of work in the list, the unit of work with the shortest time, the unit of work with the longest time, a randomly selected unit of work, or some other criterion.
   f) Switch the work elements to find the best balance available.

Example 3 illustrates a simple line-balancing procedure.

EXAMPLE 3

On the basis of the precedence diagram and activity times given in Example 2, the firm determines that there are 480 productive minutes of work available per day. Furthermore, the production schedule requires that 40 units be completed as output from the assembly line each day. Hence,

$$\text{Cycle time (in minutes)} = \frac{480 \text{ minutes}}{40 \text{ units}}$$

$$= 12 \text{ minutes/unit}$$

$$\text{Minimum number of workstations} = \frac{\text{total task time}}{\text{cycle time}} = \frac{66}{12}$$

$$= 5.5 \text{ or } 6 \text{ stations}$$

FIGURE 10.13 ■ A Six-Station Solution to the Line-Balancing Problem

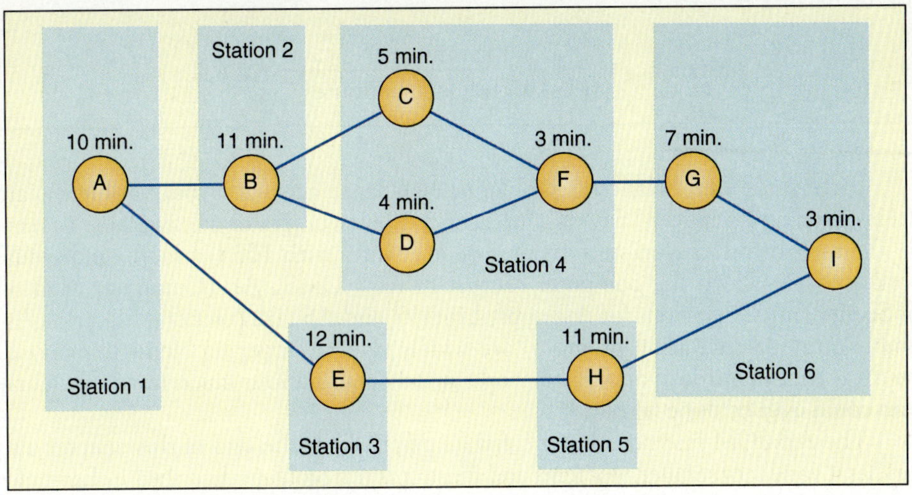

Figure 10.13 shows one solution that does not violate the sequence requirements and in which the tasks are grouped into six stations. To obtain this solution, appropriate activities were moved into workstations that use as much of the available cycle time of 12 minutes as possible. The first workstation consumes 10 minutes and has an idle time of 2 minutes.

The second workstation uses 11 minutes, and the third consumes the full 12 minutes. The fourth workstation groups three small tasks and balances perfectly at 12 minutes. The fifth has 1 minute of idle time, and the sixth (consisting of tasks G and I) has 2 minutes of idle time per cycle. Total idle time for this solution is 6 minutes per cycle.

Boeing, the world's largest manufacturer of commercial jetliners, employs a modular construction to assemble its "parts." These "parts" of tail, aft body section, centre body section, wings, front body, and nose are joined above. Workers "inch" the body sections together, measuring and levelling them for a perfect fit. Landing gear is installed and the airplane is ready for its final five assembly line operations.

We can compute the efficiency of a line balance by dividing the total task time by the product of the number of workstations times the assigned cycle time:

$$\text{Efficiency} = \frac{\sum \text{task times}}{(\text{number of workstations}) \times (\text{assigned cycle time})} \qquad (10.4)$$

Management often compares different levels of efficiency for various numbers of workstations. In this way, the firm can determine the sensitivity of the line to changes in the production rate and workstation assignments.

EXAMPLE 4

We can calculate the balance efficiency for Example 3 as follows:

$$\text{Efficiency} = \frac{66 \text{ minutes}}{(6 \text{ stations}) \times (12 \text{ minutes})} = \frac{66}{72} = 91.7\%$$

In the case of slaughtering operations, the assembly line is actually a disassembly line. The line balancing procedures described in this chapter are the same as for an assembly line. The chicken processing plant shown here must balance the work of several hundred employees. Division of labour produces efficiency. Because one's skills develop with repetition, there is less time lost in changing tools, and specialized tools are developed. The total labour content in each of the chickens processed is a few minutes. How long would it take you to process a chicken by yourself?

Opening a seventh workstation, for whatever reason, would decrease the efficiency of the balance to 78.6%:

$$\text{Efficiency} = \frac{66 \text{ minutes}}{(7 \text{ stations}) \times (12 \text{ minutes})} = 78.6\%$$

Large-scale line-balancing problems, like large process-layout problems, are often solved by computers. Several different computer programs are available to handle the assignment of workstations on assembly lines with 100 (or more) individual work activities. Both the computer routine called COMSOAL (Computer Method for Sequencing Operations for Assembly Lines)[13] and ASYBL (General Electric's Assembly Line Configuration program) are widely used in larger problems to evaluate the thousands or millions of possible workstation combinations much more efficiently than could ever be done by hand.

The AB:POM microcomputer software described at the end of this chapter also handles a variety of smaller problems and illustrates the problem described in Examples 2, 3, and 4. It offers five different heuristics (or "rules of thumb") for balancing the line.

ACHIEVING WORLD-CLASS STANDARDS

World-class organizations pay a great deal of attention to facility layouts because layout affects the whole company's performance. As service-oriented firms compete for customers, they focus on strategies that keep the customers' needs in mind. The opening quotation in this chapter refers to Wal-Mart's drive to make shopping more comfortable and organized. World-class retailers increase their sales by optimizing shelf layout with computer programs such as COSMOS and SLIM.

World-class manufacturers look for flexibility in layouts, so that changes in product models and in production rates are easy and quick. To obtain flexibility in layout, they cross-train their workers, maintain equipment in top condition, keep their inventories low, place workstations close together, and use small, flexible equipment. By following the Japanese model, layouts are close and compact, with more U-shaped production lines that permit worker interaction and job rotation. World-class companies also use more cellular manufacturing layouts.

In terms of material handling and warehousing, world-class firms keep costs low with automation. "Dark warehouses," run by a handful of employees and their fleet of automated guided vehicles (AGVs), use sophisticated computer-driven systems. At Tupperware International's South Carolina facility, for example, human hands need not touch an order as it is plucked from its shelf and boxed.

Other New Approaches

There is an approach to plant layout that uses a model factory, a calculator, and a drafting board. See:

http://www.mghr.com/./webdeck/011043-3.html

[13] A. L. Arcus, "COMSOAL: A Computer Method of Sequencing Operations for Assembly Line," *International Journal of Production Research*, 4, no. 4 (1966).

POM IN ACTION

Automobile Disassembly Lines: The Wave of the Ecologically Correct Future

Visionaries like Walter Chrysler and Louis Chevrolet could not have imagined the sprawling graveyards of rusting cars and trucks that bear testimony to the automotive culture they helped invent. These days, the graveyards are shrinking slightly, however. "By the end of the century we think people will be buying cars based on how 'green' they are," says David Millerick, Ford's manager of vehicle recycling. Millerick's counterpart at BMW, Horst Wolf, agrees: "In the long term, all new vehicles will have to be designed in such a way that their materials can be easily reused in the next generation of cars."

BMW, sensitive to the political power of Germany's Green movement, has already built a pilot "auto disassembly" plant. In the United States, the company offers $500 toward the purchase of a new-model BMW to anyone bringing a junked BMW to its salvage centres in New York, Los Angeles, or Orlando.

The disassembly line involves removing most of a car's plastic parts and sorting them for recycling. But this is not easy. Disassembly alone might take five people an hour. BMW also had to invent tools to safely puncture and drain fuel tanks with gas in them. Various plastics are recycled differently, so each must be labelled or colour-coded. Some types of plastics can be remelted and turned into new parts, such as intake manifolds. Nissan Motor, with disassembly plants in Germany and Japan, now turns 2,000 bumpers a month into air ducts, foot rests, bumper parts, and shipping pallets.

The scrap metal part of the disassembly line is easier. With shredders and magnets, baseball-sized chunks of metal are sorted after the engines, transmissions, radio, batteries, and exhausts have been removed. Steel makers have helped over the past 20 years by building minimills that use scrap metal.

The ironic twist for an industry pushed to improve the crashworthiness of its vehicles is that automakers now also need to design cars and trucks that will come apart more easily.

In the 1920s, Ford Motor Company was the largest motor vehicle firm in the world and was twice the size of General Motors. At the heady height of Ford's dominance, the gigantic Rouge operations of Ford were built at Allen Park, Michigan. Included in the complex was a Ford steel mill. Ford were able to completely recycle cars back into the production of new vehicles. At the time, it was said that a steel strike would shut down the entire auto industry with the exception of Ford; they owned their own steel mill and processed scrap vehicles as well as iron ore.

Sources: Adapted from *The New York Times* (September 8, 1992): and *Machine Design* (February 12, 1993): 56–57. Further adapted for the Canadian edition.

for details of Jay Cedarleaf's book *Plant Layout and Flow Improvement*, which describes this system.

Another system that can aid in plant layout is VIRART's Virtual Environments, which enables the designer to move around in a virtual environment. The system has applicability to product design as well. See:

http://quoll.maneng.nott.ac.uk/Research/virart/industry/factplan.html

WEB LINKS

for more details on this system.

SUMMARY

Good layout strategies make a substantial difference in operating efficiency. The six classic layout situations are (1) fixed position, (2) process-oriented, (3) office, (4) retail, (5) warehouse, and (6) product-oriented. A variety of techniques have been developed in attempts to solve these layout problems. Industrial firms focus on reducing material movement and assembly line balancing. Retail firms focus on product exposure. Storage layouts focus on the optimum trade-offs between storage costs and material handling costs.

Often the variables in the layout problem are so wide-ranging and numerous as to preclude finding an optimal solution. For this reason, layout decisions, although having received substantial research effort, remain something of an art.

KEY TERMS

Fixed-position layout (p. 396)
Process-oriented layout (p. 396)
Office layout (p. 396)
Retail/service layout (p. 396)
Warehouse layout (p. 396
Product-oriented layout (p. 396)
Job lots (p. 399)
CRAFT (p. 403)
SPACECRAFT (p. 404)
Work cell (p. 405)
Focussed work centre (p. 406)
Focussed factory (p. 406)
Fabrication line (p. 411)
Assembly line (p. 411)
Assembly line balancing (p. 412)
Cycle time (p. 414)

USING AB:POM TO SOLVE LAYOUT PROBLEMS

Solving Example 1 Using AB:POM's Operations Layout Module

AB:POM's facility layout module can be used to place up to ten departments in ten rooms in order to minimize the total distance travelled as a function of the distances between the rooms and the flow between departments. The program performs pairwise comparisons, exchanging departments until no exchange will reduce the total amount of movement.

After the number of departments is entered (which is 6 in the case of Example 1), then the data screen will be generated and appear as in Program 10.1. The data essentially consist of two tables of numbers—one for the flows and one for the distances.

PROGRAM 10.1 ■ AB:POM's Operations Layout Program Applied to Example 1's Walter's Company Data. Departments may be named in their columns. Typically, the distance matrix will be symmetric. If not, all entries must be made. The solution appears on the right-hand side of the printout.

Data file: WALTERS ——— Operations Layout ——— Solution ———

Number of departments (3–10) 6 Symmetric distances

WALTERS COMPANY, EXAMPLE 1

Flow matrix

	Dept 1	Dept 2	Dept 3	Dept 4	Dept 5	Dept 6	Department in Room	
Dept 1	0	50	100	0	0	20	Dept 1 in	Room 3
Dept 2	0	0	30	50	10	0	Dept 2 in	Room 5
Dept 3	0	0	0	20	0	100	Dept 3 in	Room 2
Dept 4	0	0	0	0	50	0	Dept 4 in	Room 4
Dept 5	0	0	0	0	0	0	Dept 5 in	Room 1
Dept 6	0	0	0	0	0	0	Dept 6 in	Room 6

(cont'd)

(Program 10.1 cont'd)

Distance Matrix

	Room 1	Room 2	Room 3	Room 4	Room 5	Room 6
Room 1	0	1	2	1	1	2
Room 2	1	0	1	1	1	1
Room 3	2	1	0	2	1	1
Room 4	1	1	2	0	1	2
Room 5	1	1	1	1	0	1
Room 6	2	1	1	2	1	0

The total movement is 430

Solving Examples 2, 3, and 4 Using AB:POM's Assembly Line Balancing Module

AB:POM's module for line balancing can handle a line with up to 99 tasks, each with up to six immediate predecessors. Programs 10.2 and 10.3 illustrate the input and output computer screens for this module applied to Examples 2, 3, and 4.

PROGRAM 10.2 ■ AB:POM's Assembly Line Balancing Program Data Entry Screen. Cycle time can be entered in two ways: (1) either directly to the right of "cycle time" if known or (2) demand rate can be entered with time available as shown below. Five "heuristic rules" may be used: (1) longest operation time, (2) most following tasks, (3) ranked positional weight, (4) shortest operation time, and (5) least number of following tasks. No one rule can guarantee an optimal solution. The default rule is the longest operation time.

Balancing, Assembly line — Data Screen

Number of tasks (1–99) 9

ASSEMBLY LINE BALANCING, EXAMPLES 2–4

Rule: Longest operation time

Demand rate: 40 units per 480.00 minutes

Cycle Time: 0.00

Task	minutes	Predecessors					
a	10.00	– –	– –	– –	– –	– –	– –
b	11.00	A	– –	– –	– –	– –	– –
c	5.00	B	– –	– –	– –	– –	– –
d	4.00	B	– –	– –	– –	– –	– –
e	12.00	A	– –	– –	– –	– –	– –
f	3.00	C	D	– –	– –	– –	– –
g	7.00	F	– –	– –	– –	– –	– –
h	11.00	E	– –	– –	– –	– –	– –
i	3.00	G	H	– –	– –	– –	– –

PROGRAM 10.3 ■ AB:POM's Assembly Line Balancing Output for Examples 2 to 4 and Program 10.2. Note that longest operation time heuristic provides a different solution than the one we found in Figure 10.13.

```
-------------- ASSEMBLY LINE BALANCING, EXAMPLES 2-4 --------------
Longest operation time                    cycle time = 12 minutes
Station     Task      Time       Time left ready tasks
                                          a
   1          a       10.00        2.00 b,  e
   2          e       12.00        0.00 b,  h
   3          b       11.00        1.00 h,  c,  d
   4          h       11.00        1.00 c,  d
   5          c        5.00        7.00 d
              d        4.00        3.00 f
              f        3.00        0.00 g
   6          g        7.00        5.00 i
              i        3.00        2.00
Time allocated (cyc*sta) =   72.00; Min (theoretical) # of stations = 6
Time needed (sum task) =     66.00; EFFICIENCY = 91.67%;
Idle time (alloc-needed) =    6.00 minutes per cycle
```

SOLVED PROBLEMS

Solved Problem 10.1

The Snow-Bird Hospital is a small emergency-oriented facility located in a popular ski resort area in northern Manitoba. Its new administrator, Mary Lord, decides to reorganize the hospital, using the process-layout method she studied in business school. The current layout of Snow-Bird's eight emergency departments is shown in Figure 10.14.

FIGURE 10.14 ■ Snow-Bird Hospital Layout

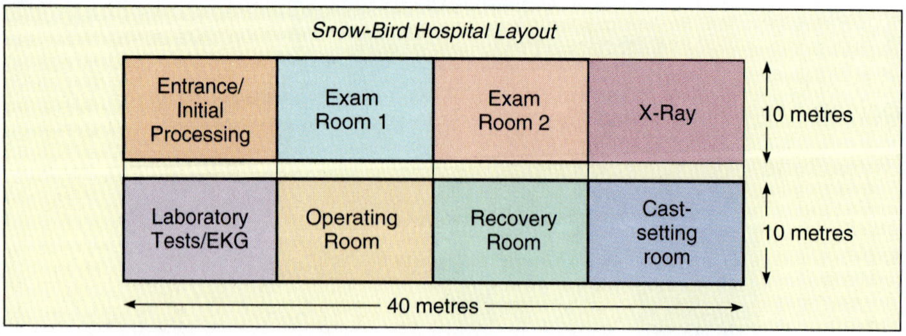

The only physical restriction Lord perceives is the need to keep the entrance and initial processing room in its current location. All other departments or rooms (each 10 metres square) can be moved if the layout analysis indicates this would be beneficial.

Mary's first step is to analyze records in order to determine the number of trips made by patients between departments in an average month. The data are shown in Figure 10.15. The objective, Lord decides, is to lay out the rooms so as to minimize the total distance walked by patients who enter for treatment. She writes her objective as:

$$\text{Minimize patient movement} = \sum_{i=1}^{8} \sum_{j=1}^{8} X_{ij}\, C_{ij}$$

where X_{ij} = number of patients per month (loads or trips) moving from department i to department j

C_{ij} = distance in metres between departments i and j (which, in this case, is the equivalent of cost per load to move between departments)

Note that this is only a slight modification of the cost-objective equation shown earlier in the chapter.

FIGURE 10.15 ■ Number of Patients Moving Between Departments in One Month

1	2	3	4	5	6	7	8	Department
	100	100	0	0	0	0	0	1. Entrance and initial processing room
		0	50	20	0	0	0	2. Examination room 1
			30	30	0	0	0	3. Examination room 2
				20	0	0	20	4. X-ray room
					20	0	10	5. Laboratory tests and EKG room
						30	0	6. Operating room
							0	7. Recovery room
								8. Cast-setting room

Departments next to one another, such as the entrance and examination room 1, are assumed to carry a walking distance of 10 metres. Diagonal departments are also considered adjacent and assigned a distance of 10 metres. Nonadjacent departments such as the entrance and examination room 2 or the entrance and recovery room are 20 metres apart, and nonadjacent rooms such as entrance and X-ray are 30 metres apart. (Hence, 10 metres is considered 10 units of cost, 20 metres is 20 units of cost, and 30 metres is 30 units of cost.)

Given the above information, redo the layout of Snow-Bird Hospital to improve its efficiency in terms of patient flow.

Solution

First, establish Snow-Bird's current layout, as shown in Figure 10.16. By using Snow-Bird's current layout, the patient movement may be computed.

$$\text{Total movement} = \underset{1\text{ to }2}{(100 \times 10)} + \underset{1\text{ to }3}{(100 \times 20)} + \underset{2\text{ to }4}{(50 \times 20)} + \underset{2\text{ to }5}{(20 \times 10)}$$

$$+ \underset{3\text{ to }4}{(30 \times 10)} + \underset{3\text{ to }5}{(30 \times 20)} + \underset{4\text{ to }5}{(20 \times 30)} + \underset{4\text{ to }8}{(20 \times 10)}$$

$$+ \underset{5\text{ to }6}{(20 \times 10)} + \underset{5\text{ to }8}{(10 \times 30)} + \underset{6\text{ to }7}{(30 \times 10)}$$

$$= 1{,}000 + 2{,}000 + 1{,}000 + 200 + 300 + 600 + 600 + 200 + 200 + 300 + 300$$

$$= 6{,}700 \text{ metres}$$

FIGURE 10.16 ■ Current Snow-Bird Patient Flow

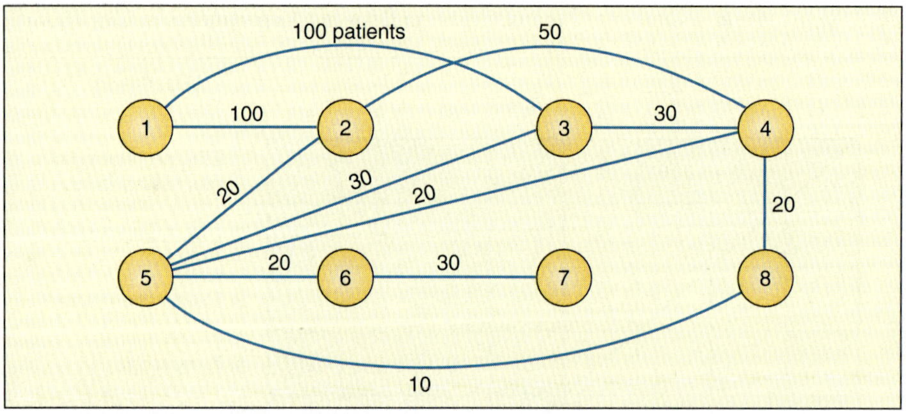

It is not possible to prove a mathematically "optimal" solution, but you should be able to propose a new layout that will reduce the current figure of 6,700 metres. Two useful changes, for example, are to switch rooms 3 and 5 and to interchange rooms 4 and 6. This change would result in the schematic shown in Figure 10.17.

$$\text{Total movement} = \underset{1\text{ to }2}{(100 \times 10)} + \underset{1\text{ to }3}{(100 \times 10)} + \underset{2\text{ to }4}{(50 \times 10)} + \underset{2\text{ to }5}{(20 \times 10)}$$

$$+ \underset{3\text{ to }4}{(30 \times 10)} + \underset{3\text{ to }5}{(30 \times 20)} + \underset{4\text{ to }5}{(20 \times 10)} + \underset{4\text{ to }8}{(20 \times 20)}$$

$$+ \underset{5\text{ to }6}{(20 \times 10)} + \underset{5\text{ to }8}{(10 \times 10)} + \underset{6\text{ to }7}{(30 \times 10)}$$

$$= 1{,}000 + 1{,}000 + 500 + 200 + 300 + 600 + 200 + 400 + 200 + 100 + 300$$

$$= 4{,}800 \text{ metres}$$

FIGURE 10.17 ■ Improved Layout

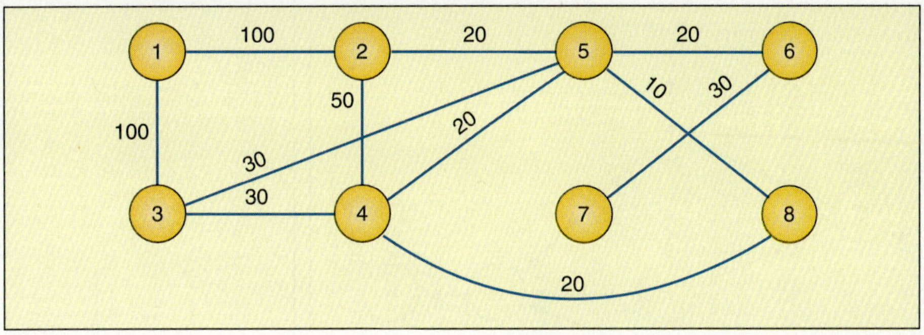

Do you see any room for further improvement? (See Homework Problem 10.2.)

Solved Problem 10.2

An assembly line, whose activities are shown in Figure 10.18, has an 8-minute cycle time. Draw the precedence graph and find the minimum possible number of workstations. Then arrange the work activities into workstations so as to balance the line. What is the efficiency of this line balance?

Task	Performance Time (Minutes)	Task Must Follow This Task
A	5	—
B	3	A
C	4	B
D	3	B
E	6	C
F	1	C
G	4	D, E, F
H	2	G
	28	

Solution

The theoretical minimum number of workstations is

$$\frac{\sum t_i}{\text{Cycle time}} = \frac{28 \text{ minutes}}{8 \text{ minutes}} = 3.5 \text{ or } 4 \text{ stations}$$

The precedence graph and one good layout are shown in Figure 10.18.

$$\text{Efficiency} = \frac{\text{total task time}}{(\text{number of workstations}) \times (\text{cycle time})} = \frac{28}{(4)(8)} = 87.5\%$$

FIGURE 10.18 ■ A Four-Station Solution to the Line Balancing Problem

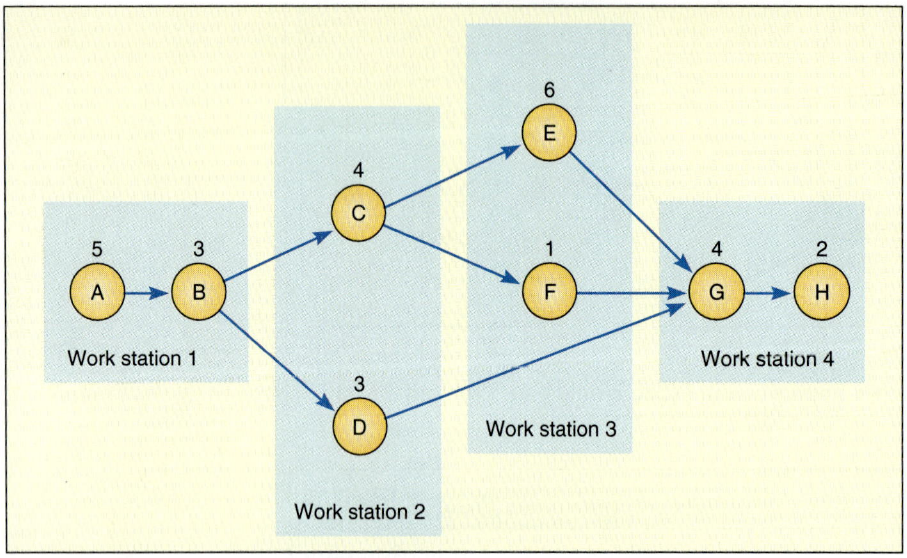

DISCUSSION QUESTIONS

1. What is the layout strategy of your local print shop?
2. How would you go about collecting data to help a small business, like a print shop, improve its layout?
3. What are the six layout strategies presented in this chapter?
4. What are the advantages and disadvantages of product layout?
5. What are the advantages and disadvantages of process layout?
6. What are the advantages and disadvantages of work cells?
7. What layout innovations have you noticed recently in retail establishments?
8. What techniques can be used to overcome the inherent problems of fixed-position layout?
9. What layout variables might you want to consider as particularly important in an office layout where computer programs are written?
10. What is required for a focussed work centre or focussed factory to be appropriate?
11. Which of the layout types described in this chapter assume that demand is stable?
12. What are the variables that a manager can manipulate in a retail store layout?
13. Visit a local supermarket and sketch its layout. What are your major observations regarding departments and their locations?
14. Given that most engineering students in Canada are male, and that most nursing students are female, should colleges build classroom buildings to accommodate the actual ratio of the sexes?

CRITICAL THINKING EXERCISE

Our discussion of office layout included a note about the difference between North American and Japanese firms. Offices are more cramped and less automated in Japan; it also is not uncommon for two workers to share a telephone. No one at Tokyo's Toyota office has his or her own PC; rather, there is an alcove of machines to share.

Discuss your perceptions of the importance of the North American and Japanese styles of office layout. Which yields greater productivity?

PROBLEMS

10.1 Given the following flow and distance matrices in Roy Martin's job shop, what is the appropriate layout?

FLOW MATRIX

	DEPT. A	DEPT. B	DEPT. C	DEPT. D	DEPT. E	DEPT. F
Dept. A	0	100	50	0	0	50
Dept. B	25	0	0	50	0	0
Dept. C	25	0	0	0	50	0
Dept. D	0	25	0	0	20	0
Dept. E	50	0	100	0	0	0
Dept. F	10	0	20	0	0	0

DISTANCE MATRIX

	DEPT. A	DEPT. B	DEPT. C	DEPT. D	DEPT. E	DEPT. F
Dept. A	0	1	2	3	4	5
Dept. B	1	0	5	4	3	2
Dept. C	2	5	0	6	7	6
Dept. D	3	4	6	0	4	3
Dept. E	4	3	7	4	0	5
Dept. F	5	2	6	3	5	0

10.2 In Solved Problem 10.1 we improved Snow-Bird's layout to 4,800 metres of movement. Is an improved layout possible? What is it?

10.3 Registration period at most universities and and community colleges in Canada has always been a time of emotion, commotion, and lines. Students must move among four stations to complete the trying semiannual process. Last semester's registration, held in the fieldhouse, is described in Figure 10.19. You can see, for example, that 450 students moved from the paperwork station (A) to advising (B), and 550 went directly from A to picking up their class cards (C). Graduate students, who for the most part had preregistered, proceeded directly from A to the station where the registration was verified and payment collected (D). The layout used last semester is also shown in Figure 10.19. The registrar is preparing to set up this semester's stations and is anticipating similar numbers.

a) What is the "load × distance," or cost, of the layout shown?

b) Provide an improved layout and compute its cost.

10.4 You have just been hired as the Director of Operations for Fournier Chocolates, in Quebec City, a purveyor of exceptionally fine chocolates. Fournier Chocolates has two kitchen layouts under consideration for its recipe-making and testing department. The strategy is to provide the best kitchen layout possible so the food scientists can devote

FIGURE 10.19 ■ Registration Flow of Students

Interstation Activity Mix

	Pick up paperwork and forms (A)	Advising station (B)	Pick up class cards (C)	Verification of status and payment (D)
Paperwork/forms (A)	—	450	550	50
Advising (B)	200	—	200	0
Class cards (C)	0	0	—	750
Verification/payment (D)	0	0	0	—

Existing Layout

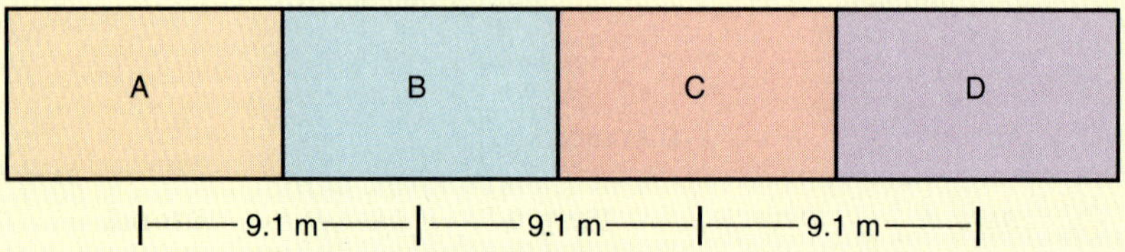

their time and energy toward product improvement, not wasted effort in the kitchen. You have been asked to evaluate these two kitchen layouts and to prepare a recommendation for your boss, Mr. Fournier, so that he can proceed with placing the contract for building the testing kitchens. (See Figure 10.20.)

FIGURE 10.20 ■ Layout Options

Number of trips between work centres:

From: \ To:		Refrigerator 1	Counter 2	Sink 3	Storage 4	Stove 5
Refrig.	1	0	8	13	0	0
Counter	2	5	0	3	3	8
Sink	3	3	12	0	4	0
Storage	4	3	0	0	0	5
Stove	5	0	8	4	10	0

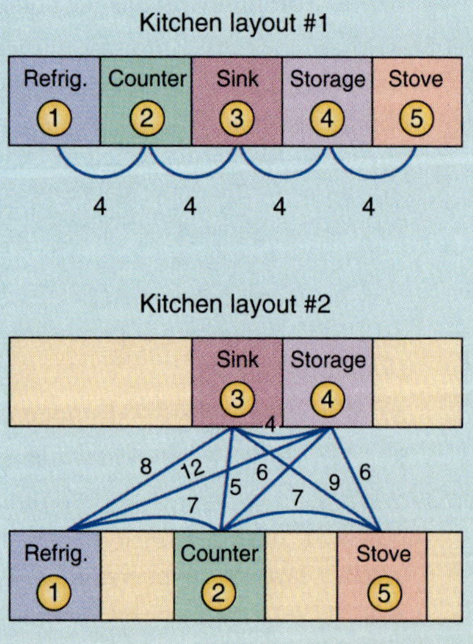

: **10.5** Fournier Chocolates (see Problem 10.4) is considering a third layout, as shown below. Evaluate its effectiveness in trip-distance feet.

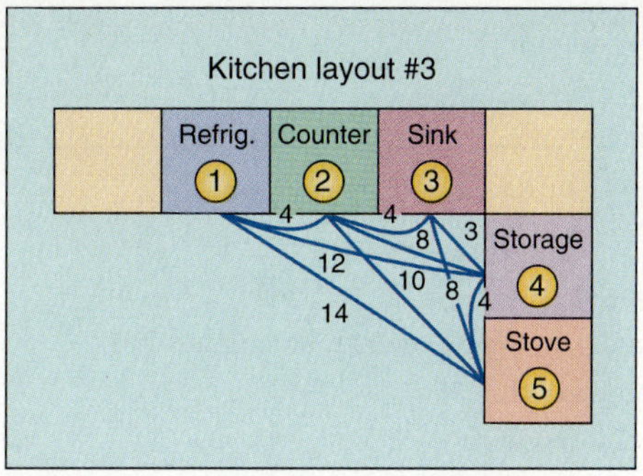

: **10.6** Fournier Chocolates (see Problems 10.4 and 10.5) has yet two more layouts to consider.

a) Layout #4 is shown below. What is the total trip distance?

b) Layout #5, also below, has what total trip distance?

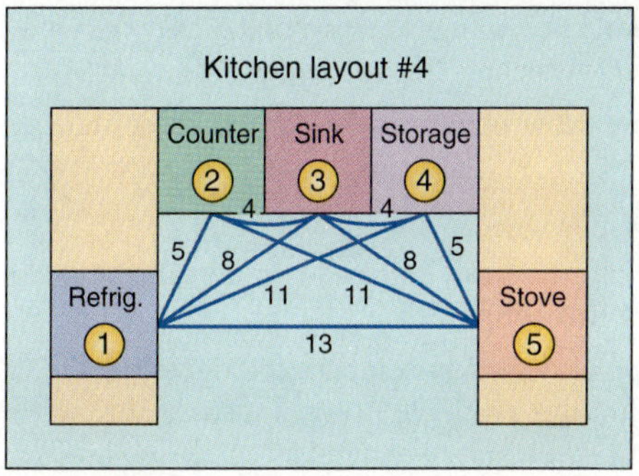

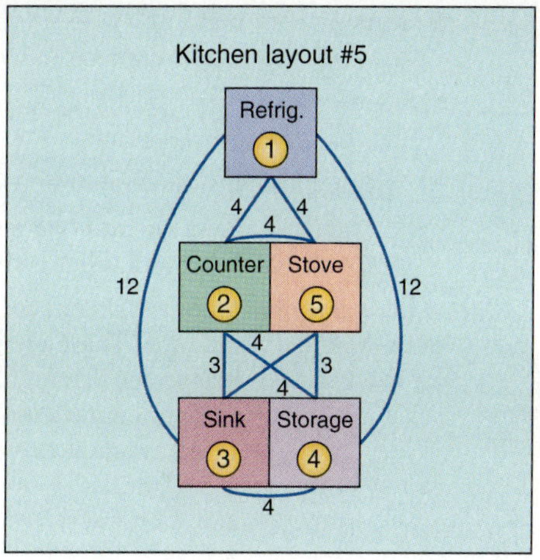

• **10.7** Given the following task, times, and sequence, develop a balanced line capable of operating with a 10-minute cycle time at Paul Reed's company. What is the efficiency of that line?

TASK ELEMENT	TIME (MINUTES)	ELEMENT PREDECESSOR
A	3	—
B	5	A
C	7	B
D	5	—
E	3	C
F	3	B, D
G	5	D
H	6	G

: **10.8** The preinduction physical examination given by the Canadian Armed Forces involves the following seven activities:

ACTIVITY	AVERAGE TIME (MINUTES)
Medical history	10
Blood tests	8
Eye examination	5
Measurements (i.e., weight, height, blood pressure)	7
Medical examination	16
Psychological interview	12
Exit medical evaluation	10

These activities can be performed in any order, with two exceptions: The medical history must be taken first and the exit medical evaluation is the final step. At present, there are three paramedics and two physicians on duty during each shift. Only a physician can perform the exit evaluation or conduct the psychological interview. Other activities can be carried out by either physicians or paramedics.

a) Develop a layout and balance the line. How many people can be processed per hour?

b) What activity is the current bottleneck?

c) If one more physician and one more paramedic can be placed on duty, how would you redraw the layout? What is the new throughput?

: **10.9** A final assembly plant for Dictatape, a popular dictation company, produces the DT, a hand-held dictation unit. There are 400 minutes available in the final assembly plant for the DT, and the average demand is 80 units per day. The final assembly requires six separate tasks. Information concerning these tasks is given in the following table. What tasks should be assigned to various workstations, and what is the overall efficiency of the assembly line?

TASK	PERFORMANCE TIME (MINUTES)	TASK MUST FOLLOW TASK LISTED BELOW
1	1	—
2	1	1
3	4	1, 2
4	1	2, 3
5	2	4
6	4	5

: **10.10** FFI, Fredericton Furniture, Inc., produces all types of office furniture. The Executive Secretary is a chair that has been designed using ergonomics to provide comfort during long work hours. The chair sells for $130. There are 480 minutes available during the day, and the average daily demand has been 50 chairs. There are eight tasks. Given the information below, solve this assembly line-balancing problem.

Task	Performance Time (minutes)	Task Must Follow Task Listed Below
1	4	—
2	7	1
3	6	1, 2
4	5	2, 3
5	6	4
6	7	5
7	8	5
8	6	6, 7

: **10.11** Tailwind, Inc., produces high-quality but expensive training shoes for runners. The Tailwind shoe, which sells for $110, contains both gas- and liquid-filled compartments to provide more stability and better protection against knee, foot, and back injuries. Manufacturing the shoes requires 10 separate tasks. How should these tasks be grouped into workstations? There are 400 minutes available for manufacturing the shoes in the plant each day. Daily demand is 60. The information for the tasks is as follows:

Task	Performance Time (minutes)	Task Must Follow Task Listed Below
1	1	—
2	3	1
3	2	2
4	4	2
5	1	3, 4
6	3	1
7	2	6
8	5	7
9	1	5, 8
10	3	9

: **10.12** The Mach 10 is a one-person sailboat designed to be used in the ocean. Manufactured by Creative Leisure, the Mach 10 can handle 65-kilometre-per-hour winds and over 3-metre seas. The final assembly plant for Creative Leisure is in Oakville, Ontario. At this time, 200 minutes are available each day to manufacture a Mach 10. The daily demand is 60 boats. Given the following information, how many workstations would you recommend?

Task	Performance Time (Minutes)	Task Must Follow Task Listed Below
1	1	—
2	1	1
3	2	1
4	1	3
5	3	3
6	1	3
7	1	4, 5, 6
8	2	2
9	1	7, 8

:10.13 Because of the expected high demand for the Mach 10, Creative Leisure has decided to increase the manufacturing time available to produce the Mach 10 (see Problem 10.12). What impact would 300 available minutes per day have on the assembly line? What impact would 400 minutes have?

:10.14 Nearbeer Products, Inc., manufactures drinks that taste the same as a good draft beer but do not contain any alcohol. With changes in drinking laws and demographics, there has been an increased interest in Nearbeer Lite. Nearbeer Lite has fewer calories than the regular beer, is less filling, and tastes great. The final packing operation for Nearbeer Lite requires 13 tasks. Nearbeer bottles Nearbeer Lite 5 hours a day, 5 days a week. Each week there is a demand for 3,000 bottles of Nearbeer Lite. Given the following information, solve this assembly line-balancing problem.

Data for Problems 10.14 and 10.15

Task	Performance Time (Minutes)	Task Must Follow Task Listed Below
1	0.1	—
2	0.1	1
3	0.1	2
4	0.2	2
5	0.1	2
6	0.2	3, 4, 5
7	0.1	1
8	0.1	7
9	0.2	7, 8
10	0.1	9
11	0.2	6
12	0.2	10, 11
13	0.1	12

:10.15 Nearbeer's president, Reed Doke, believes that weekly demand for Nearbeer Lite could explode (see Problem 10.14). What would happen if demand doubled?

:10.16 Suppose production requirements in Solved Problem 10.2 increase and necessitate a reduction in cycle time from 8 minutes to 7 minutes. Balance the line once again using the new cycle time. Note that it is not possible to combine task times so as to group tasks into the minimum number of workstations. This condition occurs in actual balancing problems fairly often.

:10.17 Marilyn Hart, operations manager at Nesa Electronics, prides herself on excellent assembly line balancing. She has been told that the firm needs 1,400 electronic relays completed per day. There are 420 minutes of productive time in each working day (which is equivalent to 25,200 seconds). Group the assembly line activities below into appropriate workstations and calculate the efficiency of the balance.

Task	Time (seconds)	Must Follow Task:	Task	Time (seconds)	Must Follow Task:
A	13	—	G	5	E
B	4	A	H	6	F, G
C	10	B	I	7	H
D	10	—	J	5	H
E	6	D	K	4	I, J
F	12	E	L	15	C, K

:10.18 Given the following data describing a line-balancing problem at Sung Woo's company, develop a solution allowing a cycle time of 3 minutes. What is the efficiency of that line?

Task Element	Time (minutes)	Element Predecessor
A	1	—
B	1	A
C	2	B
D	1	B
E	3	C, D
F	1	A
G	1	F
H	2	G
I	1	E, H

DATA BASE APPLICATION

:10.19 As the Williams Bicycle Co., in Oshawa, Ontario, completes plans for its new assembly line, it identifies 25 different tasks in the production process. R. Don Williams, the VP-Operations, now faces the job of balancing the line. He lists precedences and provides time estimates for each step based on work-sampling techniques. Williams's goal is to produce 1,000 bicycles per standard 40-hour work week.

Task	Time (seconds)	Predecessor Tasks	Task	Time (seconds)	Predecessor Tasks
K3	60	—	E3	109	F3
K4	24	K3	D6	53	F4
K9	27	K3	D7	72	F9, E2, E3
J1	66	K3	D8	78	E3, D6
J2	22	K3	D9	37	D6
J3	3	—	C1	78	F7
G4	79	K4, K9	B3	72	D7, D8, D9, C1
G5	29	K9, J1	B5	108	C1
F3	32	J2	B7	18	B3
F4	92	J2	A1	52	B5
F7	21	J3	A2	72	B5
F9	126	G4	A3	114	B7, A1, A2
E2	18	G5, F3			

a) Balance this operation, using various "heuristics." Which is best?

b) What happens if the firm can change to a 41-hour work week?

CASE STUDY

Winnipeg National Bank

Winnipeg National Bank (WNB) recently finished construction on a new building in the downtown business district. Moving into a new building provides an opportunity to arrange the various departments to optimize the efficiency and effectiveness of the operations.

One primary operation of WNB is its cheque-processing division. This division acts as a clearinghouse for commercial and personal cheques. These cheques are received from the tellers downstairs as well as from other, smaller financial institutions that WNB has contracted for cheque processing. Cheques are sorted to be sent to the bank from which they are drawn, using the magnetic-ink characters located at the bottom of the cheque. The reconcilement area ensures that the incoming and outgoing totals balance, and the crediting area makes the entries to complete the transaction. Finally, the sorted cheques are bundled and shipped from the distribution area.

The personnel in this division are also responsible for processing government cheques and for handling any returned cheques coming back through the system. Because these cheques require very different processing operations, they are placed in departments separate from the commercial cheque operations but are located on the same floor.

The service elevator only travels from the basement to the second floor, so it has been decided that the cheque-processing division will be located on the second floor of the new WNB building. The second floor is divided into eight equal-sized rooms, as shown in Figure 10.21. (We call them rooms even though they are not separated by walls.) Each room is 23 metres square. Fortunately, this will not be a concern to bank management, as each of the eight departments to be located on this floor require roughly 464.5 square metres; these rooms will allow for some additional storage space and for future expansion.

The physical flow of materials—such as the cheques being processed and computer printouts for the reconcilement and crediting areas—will be on aisles that run between the centres of the rooms, as shown in Figure 10.21. The cheques will arrive and be

(Continued)

distributed from the service elevator, so it is necessary to put the distribution department in the room with the elevator. There are no other physical restrictions that require any department to be placed in a given room.

FIGURE 10.21 ■ Floor Plan of the Second Floor of the WNB Building

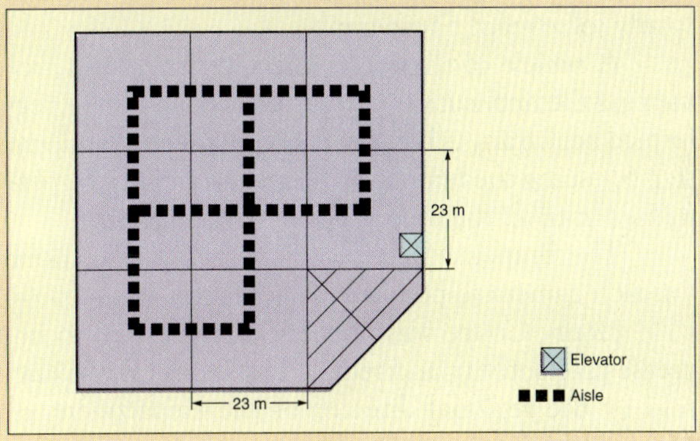

For the first step in this analysis, it was necessary to determine the amount of workflow that travels between the departments. Data collected for several weeks determined the average daily traffic—measured in the number of trips between departments. Although there is some fluctuation in the number of cheques processed during the different days of the week, these average figures provide a good estimate of the relative workflow between each pair of departments.

A review of the workflow data revealed that several important relationships were not being considered. For example, although no material flows directly between the commercial cheque-sorting area and the government cheque area, they use the same type of equipment This equipment is very noisy and requires a "soundproof" wall to control the noise, so it is necessary to keep all of this equipment together to minimize the construction cost. Also, due to this noise, it is desirable to keep this department removed from areas that require concentration, such as the reconcilement area and the offices. To account for these types of concerns, closeness ratings were identified for each pair of departments using the following rating scheme:

A—Absolutely necessary
E—*E*specially important
I—*I*mportant
O—Ordinary closeness OK
U—*U*nimportant
X—*Not* desirable

Table 10.4 provides the average daily workflow between departments in the upper-right portion and the closeness ratings in the lower-left portion. For example, the workflow between the cheque-sorting and reconcilement departments is 50 units per day, and there is a closeness rating of "X."

DISCUSSION QUESTIONS

1. Develop a layout that minimizes the total workflow.
2. Develop a layout using the relationships defined by the closeness ratings.
3. Develop a layout that considers both the workflow and closeness relationships between departments.
4. Comment on the various layouts developed.
5. Discuss any other factors that should be considered when developing a layout of the cheque-processing division.

Source: Professor Timothy L. Urban, The University of Tulsa. Modified for the Canadian edition.

TABLE 10.4 ■ WORKFLOW AND CLOSENESS RELATIONSHIPS BETWEEN DEPARTMENTS

DEPARTMENT	1	2	3	4	5	6	7	8
1. Cheque sorting	—	50	0	250	0	0	0	0
2. Cheque reconcilement	X	—	50	0	0	0	0	0
3. Cheque crediting	X	A	—	0	0	0	0	10
4. Cheque distribution	U	U	U	—	40	60	0	0
5. Government cheques	A	U	U	E	—	0	0	0
6. Returned cheques	U	U	U	E	U	—	12	0
7. Credit adjustment	X	A	A	U	U	E	—	10
8. Offices	X	I	I	U	O	O	I	—

CASE STUDY

B.C. Automobile Licence Renewals

Henry Coupe, the manager of a metropolitan branch office of the B.C. Department of Motor Vehicles, attempted to perform an analysis of the driver's licence renewal operations. Several steps were to be performed in the process. After examining the licence renewal process, he identified the steps and associated times required to perform each step, as shown in the following table:

B.C. AUTOMOBILE LICENCE RENEWALS PROCESS TIMES

STEP	AVERAGE TIME TO PERFORM (SECONDS)
1. Review renewal application for correctness	15
2. Process and record payment	30
3. Check file for violations and restrictions	60
4. Conduct eye test	40
5. Photograph applicant	20
6. Issue temporary licence	30

Coupe found that each step was assigned to a different person. Each application was a separate process in the sequence shown above. Coupe determined that his office should be prepared to accommodate the maximum demand of processing 120 renewal applicants per hour.

He observed that the work was unevenly divided among the clerks, and the clerk who was responsible for checking violations tended to shortcut her task to keep up with the other clerks. Long lines built up during the maximum demand periods.

Coupe also found that steps 1 to 4 were handled by general clerks who were each paid \$6.00 per hour. Step 5 was performed by a photographer paid \$8 per hour. Step 6, the issuing of a temporary licence, was required by provincial policy to be handled by a uniformed motor vehicle officer. Officers were paid \$9.00 per hour, but they could be assigned to any job except photography.

A review of the jobs indicated that step 1, reviewing the application for correctness, had to be performed before any other step could be taken. Similarly, step 6, issuing the temporary licence, could not be performed until all the other steps were completed.

The branch offices were charged \$5 per hour for each camera to perform photography.

Henry Coupe was under severe pressure to increase productivity and reduce costs, but he was also told by the regional director of the Department of Motor Vehicles that he had better accommodate the demand for renewals. Otherwise, "heads would roll."

DISCUSSION QUESTIONS

1. What is the maximum number of applications per hour that can be handled by the present configuration of the process?
2. How many applications can be processed per hour if a second clerk is added to check for violations?
3. Assuming the addition of one more clerk, what is the maximum number of applications the process can handle?
4. How would you suggest modifying the process in order to accommodate 120 applications per hour?

Source: W. Earl Sasser, Paul R. Olson, and D. Daryl Wyckoff, *Management of Services Operations: Text, Cases, and Readings* (Boston: Allyn and Bacon, 1978). Modified for the Canadian edition.

BIBLIOGRAPHY

Balakrishnan, J. "Notes: The Dynamics of Plant Layout." *Management Science*, 39, no. 5 (May 1993): 654–655.

Cedarleaf, Jay. *Plant Layout and Flow Improvement* (Homewood, IL: Richard D. Irwin Inc.).

Ding, F., and L. Cheng. "An Effective Mixed-Model Assembly Line Sequencing Heuristic for Just-In-Time Production Systems." *Journal of Operations Management*, 11, no. 1 (March 1993): 45–50.

Faaland, B. H., T. D. Klastorin, T. G. Schmitt, and A. Shtub. "Assembly Line Balancing with Resource Dependent Task Times." *Decision Sciences*, 23, no. 2 (March–April 1992): 343.

Francis, R. L., L. F. McGinnis, and J. A. White. *Facility Layout and Location*, 2nd ed. Englewood Cliffs, NJ: Prentice Hall, 1992.

Huang, P. Y., and B. L. W. Houck. "Cellular Manufacturing: An Overview and Bibliography." *Production and Inventory Management*, 26 (Fourth Quarter 1985): 83–92.

Joshi, S., and M. Sudit. "Procedures for Solving Single-Pass Strip Layout Problems." *IIE Transactions*, 26, no. 1 (January 1994): 27–37.

Leung, J. "A New Graph-Theoretic Heuristic for Facility Layout." *Management Science*, 38, no. 4 (April 1992): 594.

Makens, P. K., D. F. Rossin, and M. C. Springer. "A Multivariate Approach for Assessing Facility Layout Complexity." *Journal of Operations Management*, 9, no. 2 (April 1990): 185.

Montreuil, B., U. Venkatadri, and H. D. Ratliff. "Generating a Layout from a Design Skeleton." *Industrial Engineering Research & Development*, 25, no. 1 (January 1993): 3–15.

Morris, J. S., and R. J. Tersine. "A Comparison of Cell Loading Practices in Group Technology." *Journal of Manufacturing and Operations Management*, 2, no. 4 (Winter 1989): 299.

Vakharia, A. J., and B. K. Kaku. "Redesigning a Cellular Manufacturing System to Handle Long-Term Demand Changes: A Methodology and Investigation." *Decision Sciences*, 24, no. 5 (September–October 1993): 909.

10 SUPPLEMENT

WAITING-LINE MODELS

SUPPLEMENT OUTLINE

The situation at Zayres had taken a turn for the worse. Once the leading discount department store chain in the United States, Zayres was losing market share, and sales were dropping dramatically. K-Mart, Wal-Mart, J. C. Penney, and others had closed the gap, and one reason was clear. A customer could enter a huge Zayres store at almost any time of day or night, pick up 30 items or just one, and then be stuck in a check-out line for what seemed like an eternity. It was time for decisive action and Zayres took it. An extensive and costly national ad campaign touted "If there are 3 or more people in a line, we'll open another cash register." But it was too late. Zayres folded. No one likes a long queue.

Until the adoption of "fast teller" service approximately 25 years ago, the typical customer of a Canadian bank had to play "line roulette" and guess which queue to join in the typical bank branch. Join the line with the fewest in line? Join the one which seemed to be moving most quickly? Avoid any lines which contained newspaper carriers who seemed to have taken their entire route collection in pennies, nickels, and dimes and they would have to stand there while everything was counted out or the teller showed them how to roll the coins? Whichever queue one joined seemed to stop moving at all once you had joined it.

Was there a better way? The "fast teller" service introduced by one, then all, of the major Canadian banks was a direct application of operations management. "Fast teller" was simply a change from multiple lines/multiple servers queue discipline to a single queue/multiple servers model. This approach has worked well. A customer may not always be served any faster this way, but each feels that he or she is being served in correct sequence—something that was not necessarily happening under the old system.

The body of knowledge about waiting lines, often called **queuing theory**, is an important part of P/OM and a valuable tool for the operations manager. **Waiting lines** are a common situation—they may, for example, take the form of cars waiting for repair at a Midas Muffler Shop, jobs waiting to be completed at a Kinkos print shop, or unhappy customers waiting to check out at a Zayres type of store. Table S10.1 lists just a few P/OM uses of waiting-line models.

Queuing theory
Waiting line

TABLE S10.1 ■ COMMON QUEUING SITUATIONS

SITUATION	ARRIVALS IN QUEUE	SERVICE PROCESS
Supermarket	Grocery shoppers	Check-out clerks at cash register
Highway toll booth	Automobiles	Collection of tolls at booth
Doctor's office	Patients	Treatment by doctors and nurses
Computer system	Programs to be run	Computer processes jobs
Telephone company	Callers	Switching equipment to forward calls
Bank	Customers	Transactions handled by teller
Machine maintenance	Broken machines	Repair people fix machines
Harbour	Ships and barges	Dock workers load and unload

Waiting-line models are useful in both manufacturing and service areas. Analysis of queues in terms of waiting-line length, average waiting time, and other factors helps us to understand service systems (such as bank teller stations), maintenance activities (that might repair broken machinery), and shop-floor control activities. As a matter of fact, patients waiting in a doctor's office and broken drill presses waiting in a repair facility have a lot in common from a P/OM perspective. Both use human resources and equipment resources to restore valuable production assets (people and machines) to good condition.

QUEUING COSTS

Operations managers recognize the trade-off that must take place between the cost of providing good service and the cost of customer or machine waiting time. Managers want queues that are short enough so that customers do not become unhappy and either leave without buying or buy but never return. However, managers are willing to allow some waiting if it is balanced by a significant savings in service costs.

One means of evaluating a service facility is to look at total expected cost (Figure S10.1). Total cost is the sum of expected service costs plus expected waiting costs.

Service costs increase as a firm attempts to raise its level of service. Managers in *some* service centres can vary their capacity by having standby personnel and machines that can be assigned to specific service stations to prevent or shorten excessively long lines. In grocery stores, managers and stock clerks can operate extra check-out counters when needed. In banks and airport check-in points, part-time workers may be called in to help. As service improves (that is, speeds up), however, the cost of time spent waiting in lines decreases. Waiting cost may reflect lost productivity of workers while their tools or machines are awaiting repairs, or may simply be an estimate of the cost of customers lost because of poor service and long queues. In some service systems (for example, an emergency ambulance service), the cost of long waiting lines may be intolerably high.

CHARACTERISTICS OF A WAITING-LINE SYSTEM

In this section, we take a look at the three parts of a waiting-line, or queuing, system:

1. arrivals or inputs to the system;
2. queue discipline, or the waiting line itself;
3. the service facility.

FIGURE S10.1 ■ The Trade-Off between Waiting Costs and Service Costs

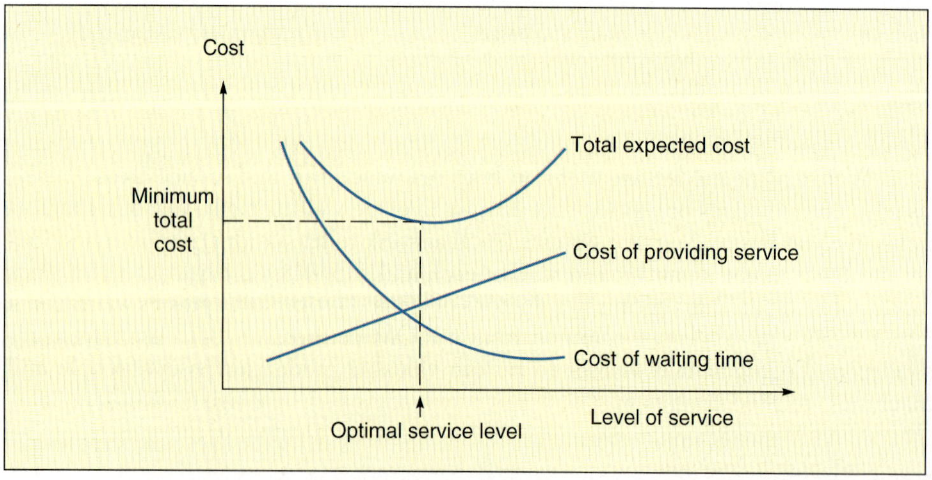

Arrival Characteristics

The input source that generates arrivals or customers for a service system has three major characteristics: the *size* of the arrival population, the *pattern* of arrivals at the queuing system, and the *behaviour* of the arrivals.

SIZE OF THE SOURCE POPULATION. Population sizes are considered to be either unlimited (essentially infinite) or limited (finite). When the number of customers or arrivals on hand at any given moment is just a small portion of potential arrivals, the arrival population is considered **unlimited**, or **infinite**. Examples of unlimited populations include cars arriving at a highway toll booth, shoppers arriving at a supermarket, and students arriving to register for classes at a large university. Most queuing models assume such an infinite arrival population. An example of a **limited**, or **finite**, population is a copying shop with only eight copying machines, which might break down and require service. The eight machines are the limited population. Arriving customers are an infinite source.

Unlimited, or infinite, population

Limited, or finite, population

PATTERN OF ARRIVALS AT THE SYSTEM. Customers either arrive at a service facility according to some known schedule (for example, one patient every 15 minutes or one student every half-hour because they have been prescheduled by booking an appointment) or else they arrive *randomly*. Arrivals are considered random when they are independent of one another and their occurrence cannot be predicted exactly. Frequently in queuing problems, the number of arrivals per unit of time can be estimated by a probability distribution known as the **Poisson distribution**. For any given arrival time (such as two customers per hour, or four trucks per minute), a discrete Poisson distribution can be established by using the formula

Poisson distribution

$$P(x) = \frac{e^{-\lambda}\lambda^x}{x!} \quad \text{for } x = 0, 1, 2, 3, 4, \ldots \tag{S10.1}$$

FIGURE S10.2 ■ Two Examples of the Poisson Distribution for Arrival Times

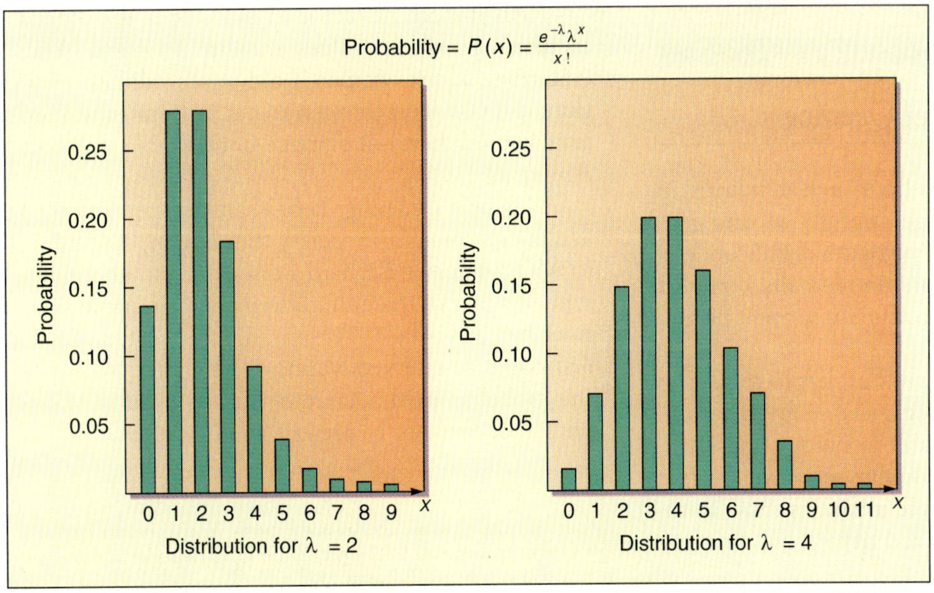

where $P(x)$ = probability of x arrivals
x = number of arrivals per unit of time
λ = average arrival rate
e = 2.7183 (which is the base of the natural logarithms)

With the help of the table in Appendix C, these values are easy to compute. Figure S10.2 illustrates the Poisson distribution for $\lambda = 2$ and $\lambda = 4$. This means that if the average arrival rate is $\lambda = 2$ customers per hour, the probability of 0 customers arriving in any random hour is about 13%, probability of 1 customer is about 27%, 2 customers about 27%, 3 customers about 18%, 4 customers about 9%, and so on. The chances that 9 or more will arrive are virtually nil. Arrivals, of course, are not always Poisson-distributed (they may follow some other distribution) and should be examined to make certain that they are well approximated by Poisson before that distribution is applied.

BEHAVIOUR OF THE ARRIVALS. Most queuing models assume that an arriving customer is a patient customer. Patient customers are people or machines that wait in the queue until they are served and do not switch between lines. Unfortunately, life is complicated by the fact that people have been known to balk or to renege. Customers who *balk* refuse to join the waiting line because it is too long to suit their needs or interests. *Reneging* customers are those who enter the queue but then become impatient and leave without completing their transaction. Actually, both of these situations just serve to accentuate the need for queuing theory and waiting line analysis (see the *POM in Action* box "The Culture of Queuing").

Waiting-Line Characteristics

The waiting line itself is the second component of a queuing system. The length of a line can be either limited or unlimited. A queue is *limited* when it cannot, by law or

POM IN ACTION

The Culture of Queuing

Americans spend 37 billion hours a year waiting in lines, during which they fidget, fret, scowl, and generally miss the larger anthropological significance of what they are doing. Queues are actually complex social systems, embodying culturally specific principles of fairness and justice.

Sociologists have shown that, left to their own devices, homo sapiens do not queue. And in certain parts of the world, particularly in Europe and Latin America, the practice is virtually unknown—a fact that Disney found out when it first opened Euro-Disney in France and expected ticket buyers to line up in an orderly fashion.

An important factor in queuing is the extent to which a culture values equality. In many Arab countries, where women hold a subordinate position, it is common for men to cut in front of women at ticket windows—a practice unthinkable in North America.

"People's queuing behaviour can be explained as a microcosm of the society they live in," according to MIT professor Richard Larson. "In southern Europe, it's part of the culture to jockey for queue position, but in Canada, Britain and the United States, first-come, first-served is almost a religion." Note that the problems in this chapter assume a queue discipline that may not be present in all cultures.

Sources: Adapted from *San Antonio Express-News* (February 7, 1993): 3-G; *Orlando Sentinel* (December 18, 1992): E7; and *Cornell Hotel and Restaurant Quarterly* (February 1991): 94–99.

physical restrictions, increase to an infinite length. This may be the case in a small barbershop that has only a limited number of waiting chairs. Analytic queuing models are treated in this supplement under an assumption of *unlimited* queue length. A queue is *unlimited* when its size is unrestricted, as in the case of the toll booth serving arriving automobiles.

A second waiting-line characteristic deals with *queue discipline*. This refers to the rule by which customers in the line are to receive service. Most systems use a queue discipline known as the **first-in, first-out (FIFO) rule**. In a hospital emergency room or an express check-out line at a supermarket, however, various assigned priorities may preempt FIFO. Patients who are critically injured will move ahead in treatment priority over patients with broken fingers or noses. Shoppers with fewer than 10 items may be allowed to enter the express check-out queue (but are *then* treated as first-come, first-served). Computer programming runs are another example of queuing systems that operate under priority scheduling. In most large companies, when computer-produced paycheques are due out on a specific date, the payroll program has highest priority over other runs.[1]

First-in, first-out (FIFO) rule

Service Facility Characteristics

The third part of any queuing system is the service facility. Two basic properties are important: (1) the configuration of the service system and (2) the pattern of service times.

BASIC QUEUING SYSTEM CONFIGURATIONS. Service systems are usually classified in terms of their number of channels (for example, number of servers) and number of phases (for example, number of service stops that must be made). A **single-channel queuing system**, with one server, is typified by the drive-in bank that has only one open teller, or by a drive-through fast-food restaurant. If, on the other hand, the bank had several tellers on duty, and each customer waited in one common line for the first available teller, then we would have a **multiple-channel queuing system** at work. Most banks today are multichannel service systems, as are most large barber shops, airline ticket counters, and post offices.

Single-channel queuing system

Multiple-channel queuing system

A **single-phase system** is one in which the customer receives service from only one station and then exits the system. A fast-food restaurant in which the person who takes your order also brings you the food and takes your money is a single-phase system. So is a driver's licence agency in which the person taking your application also grades your test and collects the licence fee. But if the restaurant requires you to place your order at one station, pay at a second, and pick up the food at a third service stop, it becomes a **multiphase system**. Likewise, if the driver's licence agency is large or busy, you will probably have to wait in a line to complete the application (the first service stop), then queue again to have the test graded (the second service stop), and finally go to a third service counter to pay the fee. To help you relate the concepts of channels and phases, Figure S10.3 presents four possible configurations.

Single-phase system

Multiphase system

[1]The term *FIFS* (first in, first served) is often used in place of FIFO. Another discipline, LIFS (last in, first served) also called last in, first out (LIFO), is common when material is stacked or piled and the items on top are used first. In inventory control, FIFO and "random draw from the bin" are the usual approach. FIFO is used only for items with limited shelf life—food items in a supermarket or restaurant being the most common example. Other items, such as most tools used in a manufacturing plant, have effectively infinite lives before use. A new order of standard tools is simply dropped into the bin and mixes indistinguishably with the existing tools. Cost accounting uses a blended average price when charging costs to various departments if the cost of the item has changed.

SERVICE TIME DISTRIBUTION. Service patterns are like arrival patterns in that they may be either constant or random. If service time is constant, it takes the same amount of time to take care of each customer. This is the case in a machine-performed service operation such as an automatic car wash. More often, service times are randomly distributed. In many cases, we can assume that random service times are described by the **negative exponential probability distribution**.

Negative exponential probability distribution

Figure S10.4 illustrates that if *service times* follow a negative exponential distribution, the probability of any very long service time is low. For example, when an average service time is 20 minutes, seldom if ever will a customer require more than 90 minutes in the service facility. If the mean service time is 1 hour, the probability of spending more than 180 minutes in service is virtually zero.

Measuring the Queue's Performance

Years of listening to howling customers have taught the airlines some baggage-retrieval lessons. One airline put its baggage-claim area close to the gates, so disembarking passengers would not have to trudge too far. But even though passengers reach the area quickly, they still have to wait for their luggage. At another airport, passengers have to walk quite some distance to the claim area but when they arrive their suitcases are usually there. Even though the travellers spend more total time picking up their baggage, the second airline found that they do not grouse as much about baggage delays as do the passengers of the first airline.

Queuing models help managers make decisions that balance desirable service costs with waiting-line costs. Some of the many measures of a waiting-line system's performance that are commonly obtained in a queuing analysis are as follows:

1. average time each customer or object spends in the queue;
2. average queue length;
3. average time each customer spends in the system (waiting time plus service time);
4. average number of customers in the system;
5. probability that the service facility will be idle;
6. utilization factor for the system;
7. probability of a specific number of customers in the system.

THE VARIETY OF QUEUING MODELS

A wide variety of queuing models may be applied in operations management. We will introduce you to four of the most widely used models. These are outlined in Table S10.2, and examples of each follow in the next few sections. More complex models are described in queuing theory textbooks[2] or can be developed through the use of simulation (which is the topic of the supplement to Chapter 13). Note that the four queuing models listed in Table S10.2 have three characteristics in common. They all assume

1. Poisson-distribution arrivals;
2. FIFO discipline;
3. a single-service phase.

In addition, they describe service systems that operate under steady, ongoing conditions. This means that arrival and service rates remain stable during the analysis.

Model A: Single-Channel Queuing Model with Poisson Arrivals and Exponential Service Times

The most common case of queuing problems involves the *single-channel*, or single-server, waiting line. In this situation, arrivals form a single line to be serviced by a single

[2]See, for example, W. Griffin, *Queuing: Basic Theories and Applications* (Columbus: Grid Publishing, 1978); or R. B. Cooper, *Introduction to Queuing Theory*, 2nd ed. (New York: Elsevier-North Holland, 1980).

FIGURE S10.3 ■ Basic Queuing System Configurations

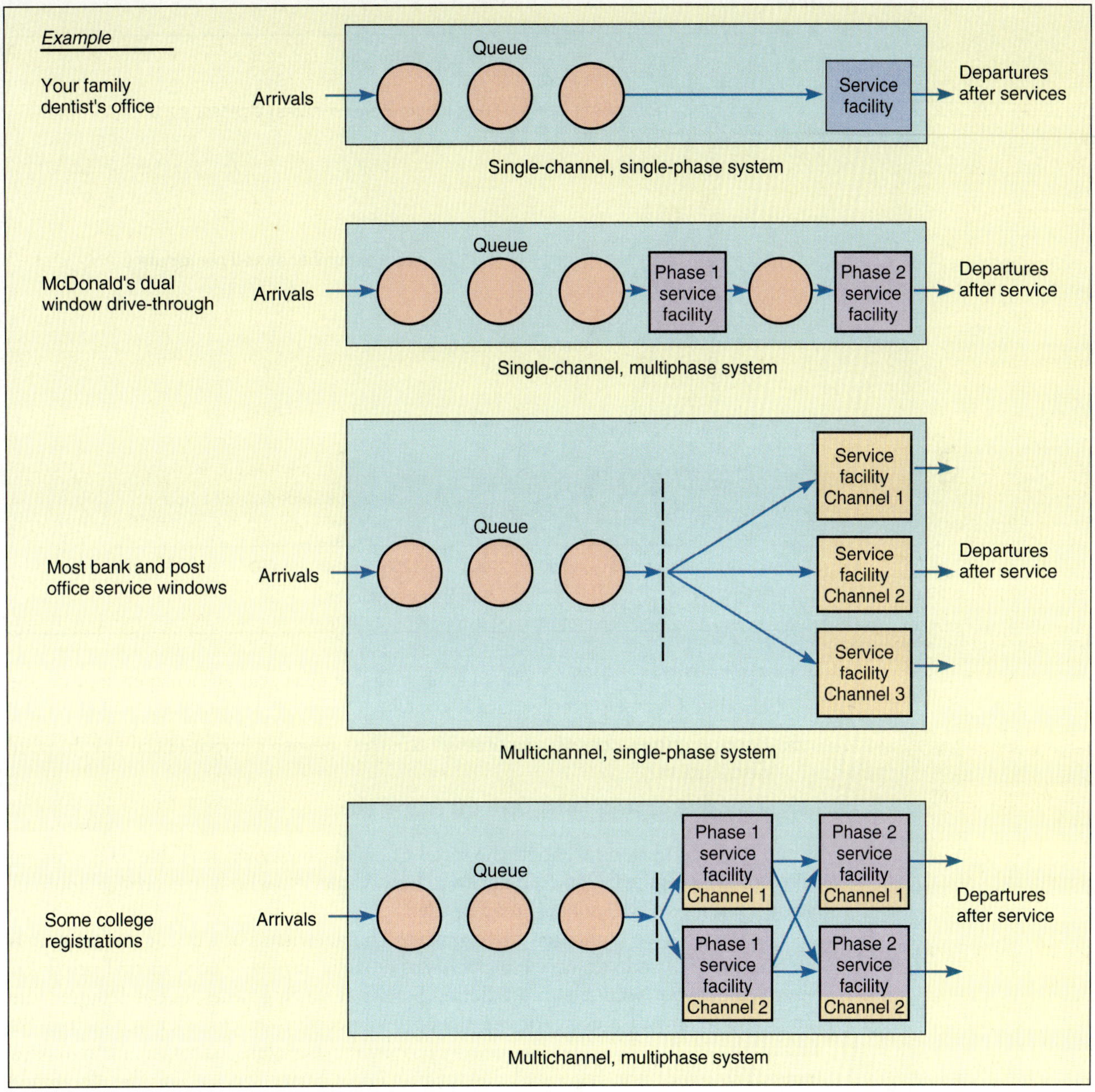

station (Figure S10.3). We assume that the following conditions exist in this type of system:

1. Arrivals are served on a first-in, first-out (FIFO) basis, and every arrival waits to be served, regardless of the length of the line or queue.
2. Arrivals are independent of preceding arrivals, but the average number of arrivals (arrival rate) does not change over time.
3. Arrivals are described by a Poisson probability distribution and come from an infinite (or very, very large) population.

FIGURE S10.4 ■ Two Examples of the Negative Exponential Distribution for Service Times

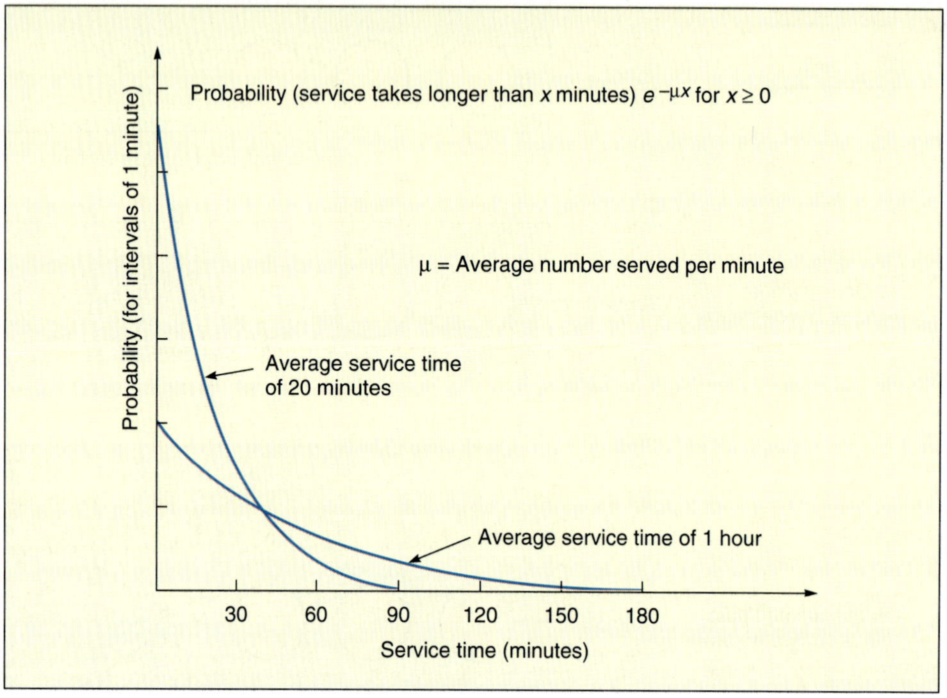

4. Service times vary from one customer to the next and are independent of one another, but their average rate is known.
5. Service times occur according to the negative-exponential probability distribution.
6. The service rate is faster than the arrival rate.

When these conditions are met, the series of equations shown in Table S10.3 can be developed. Examples S1 and S2 illustrate how Model A (which in technical journals is known as the M/M/1 model) may be used.

Once we have computed the operating characteristics of a queuing system, it is often important to do an economic analysis of their impact. The waiting-line model described above is valuable in predicting potential waiting times, queue lengths, idle times, and so on, but it does not identify optimal decisions or consider cost factors. As we saw earlier, the solution to a queuing problem may require management to make a trade-off between the increased cost of providing better service and the decreased waiting costs derived from providing that service.

Example S2 examines the costs involved in Example S1.

EXAMPLE S1

Jones, the mechanic at Golden Muffler Shop, is able to install new mufflers at an average rate of three per hour (or about one every 20 minutes), according to a negative exponential distribution. Customers seeking this service arrive at the shop on the average of two per hour, following a Poisson distribution. The customers are served on a first-in, first-out basis and come from a very large (almost infinite) population of possible buyers.

From this description, we are able to obtain the operating characteristics of Golden Muffler's queuing system:

$$\lambda = 2 \text{ cars arriving per hour}$$

$$\mu = 3 \text{ cars serviced per hour}$$

$$L_s = \frac{\lambda}{\mu - \lambda} = \frac{2}{3-2} = \frac{2}{1}$$

$$= 2 \text{ cars in the system, on average}$$

$$W_s = \frac{1}{\mu - \lambda} = \frac{1}{3-2} = 1$$

$$= \text{1-hour average waiting time in the system}$$

$$L_q = \frac{\lambda^2}{\mu(\mu - \lambda)} = \frac{2^2}{3(3-2)} = \frac{4}{3(1)} = \frac{4}{3}$$

$$= 1.33 \text{ cars waiting in line, on average}$$

$$W_q = \frac{\lambda}{\mu(\mu - \lambda)} = \frac{2}{3(3-2)} = \frac{2}{3} \text{ hour}$$

$$= \text{40-minute average waiting time per car}$$

$$\rho = \frac{\lambda}{\mu} = \frac{2}{3}$$

$$= 66.6\% \text{ of time mechanic is busy}$$

$$P_0 = 1 - \frac{\lambda}{\mu} = 1 - \frac{2}{3}$$

$$= .33 \text{ probability there are 0 cars in the system}$$

PROBABILITY OF MORE THAN K CARS IN THE SYSTEM

K	$P_{N>K} = (2/3)^{K+1}$
0	.667 ← Note that this is equal to $1 - P_0 = 1 - .33 = .667$.
1	.444
2	.296
3	.198 ← Implies that there is a 19.8% chance that more than 3 cars are in the system.
4	.132
5	.088
6	.058
7	.039

EXAMPLE S2

The owner of the Golden Muffler Shop estimates that the cost of customer waiting time, in terms of customer dissatisfaction and lost goodwill, is $10 per hour of time spent *waiting* in the line. Since the average car has a 2/3-hour wait (W_q) and there are approximately sixteen cars serviced per day (two per hour times eight working hours per day), the total number of hours that customers spend waiting for mufflers to be installed each day is

$$\frac{2}{3}(16) = \frac{32}{3} = 10\frac{2}{3} \text{ hour}$$

Hence, in this case,

$$\text{Customer waiting-time cost} = \$10\left(10\frac{2}{3}\right) = \$107 \text{ per day}$$

The only other major cost that Golden's owner can identify in the queuing situation is the salary of Jones, the mechanic, who earns $7 per hour, or $56 per day. Thus,

$$\begin{aligned}\text{Total expected costs} &= \$107 + \$56\\ &= \$163 \text{ per day}\end{aligned}$$

This approach will be useful in Solved Problem S10.2.

TABLE S10.2 ■ QUEUING MODELS DESCRIBED IN THIS CHAPTER

Model	Name (Technical Name in Parentheses)	Example	Number of Channels	Number of Phases	Arrival Rate Pattern	Service Time Pattern	Population Size	Queue Discipline
A	Simple system (M/M/1)	Information counter at department store	Single	Single	Poisson	Exponential	Unlimited	FIFO
B	Multichannel (M/M/S)	Airline ticket counter	Multi-channel	Single	Poisson	Exponential	Unlimited	FIFO
C	Constant service (M/D/1)	Automated car wash	Single	Single	Poisson	Constant	Unlimited	FIFO
D	Limited population (finite population)	Shop with only a dozen machines that might break	Single	Single	Poisson	Exponential	Limited	FIFO

Model B: Multiple-Channel Queuing Model

Now let us turn to a multiple-channel queuing system in which two or more servers or channels are available to handle arriving customers. Let us still assume that customers awaiting service form one single line and then proceed to the first available server. An

TABLE S10.3 ■ QUEUING FORMULAS FOR MODEL A: SIMPLE SYSTEM, ALSO CALLED M/M/1

λ = Mean number of arrivals per time period

μ = Mean number of people or items served per time period

L_s = Average number of units (customers) in the system

$$= \frac{\lambda}{\mu - \lambda}$$

W_s = Average time a unit spends in the system (waiting time plus service time)

$$= \frac{1}{\mu - \lambda}$$

L_q = Average number of units in the queue

$$= \frac{\lambda^2}{\mu(\mu - \lambda)}$$

W_q = Average time a unit spends waiting in the queue

$$= \frac{\lambda}{\mu(\mu - \lambda)}$$

ρ = Utilization factor for the system

$$= \frac{\lambda}{\mu}$$

P_0 = Probability of 0 units in the system (that is, the service unit is idle)

$$= 1 - \frac{\lambda}{\mu}$$

$P_{n>k}$ = Probability of more than k units in the system, where n is the number of units in the system

$$= \left(\frac{\lambda}{\mu}\right)^{k+1}$$

The Epcot Center and Disney World in Orlando, Disneyland in California, EuroDisney near Paris, and Disney Japan near Tokyo have one feature in common—long lines and seemingly endless waits. But Disney is one of the world's leading companies in the scientific analysis of queuing theory. It analyzes queuing behaviours and can predict which rides will draw what length crowds. To keep visitors happy, Disney does three things: (1) it makes lines appear to be constantly moving forward; (2) it entertains people while they wait; and (3) it posts signs telling visitors how many minutes in line they are away from each ride. That way parents can decide whether a 20-minute wait for Small World is worth more than a 30-minute wait for Mr. Frog's Wild Ride.

example of such a multichannel, single-phase waiting line is found in many banks today. A common line is formed, and the customer at the head of the line proceeds to the first free teller. (Refer back to Figure S10.3 for a typical multichannel configuration.)

The multiple-channel system presented in Example S3 again assumes that arrivals follow a Poisson probability distribution and that service times are exponentially distributed. Service is first-come, first-served, and all servers are assumed to perform at the same rate. Other assumptions listed earlier for the single-channel model apply as well.

EXAMPLE S3

The Golden Muffler Shop has decided to open a second garage bay and to hire a second mechanic to handle muffler installations. Customers, who arrive at the rate of about $\lambda = 2$ per hour, will wait in a single line until one of the two mechanics is free. Each mechanic installs mufflers at the rate of about $\mu = 3$ per hour.

To find out how this system compares to the old single-channel waiting-line system, we will compute several operating characteristics for the M = 2 channel system and compare the results with those found in Example S1.

$$P_0 = \frac{1}{\left[\sum_{n=0}^{1} \frac{1}{n!}\left(\frac{2}{3}\right)^n\right] + \frac{1}{2!}\left(\frac{2}{3}\right)^2 \frac{2(3)}{2(3)-2}}$$

$$= \frac{1}{1 + \frac{2}{3} + \frac{1}{2}\left(\frac{4}{9}\right)\left(\frac{6}{6-2}\right)} = \frac{1}{1 + \frac{2}{3} + \frac{1}{3}} = \frac{1}{2}$$

$= .5$ probability of zero cars in the system

Then,

$$L_s = \frac{(2)(3)(2/3)^2}{1![2(3)-2]^2}\left(\frac{1}{2}\right) + \frac{2}{3} = \frac{8/3}{16}\left(\frac{1}{2}\right) + \frac{2}{3} = \frac{3}{4}$$

$= .75$ average number of cars in the system

$$W_s = \frac{L_s}{\lambda} = \frac{3/4}{2} = \frac{3}{8} \text{ hour}$$

$= 22.5$ minutes average time a car spends in the system

$$L_q = L_s - \frac{\lambda}{\mu} = \frac{3}{4} - \frac{2}{3} = \frac{1}{12}$$

$= .083$ average number of cars in the queue

$$W_q = \frac{L_q}{\lambda} = \frac{.083}{2} = .0415 \text{ hour}$$

$= 2.5$ minutes average time a car spends in the queue

We can summarize these characteristics and compare them to those of the single-channel model as follows:

	SINGLE CHANNEL	TWO CHANNELS
P_0	.33	.5
L_s	2 cars	.75 car
W_s	60 minutes	22.5 minutes
L_q	1.33 cars	.083 car
W_q	40 minutes	2.5 minutes

The increased service has a dramatic effect on almost all characteristics. In particular, time spent waiting in line drops from 40 minutes to only 2.5 minutes.

The queuing equations for Model B (which also has the technical name of M/M/S) are shown in Table S10.4. These equations are obviously more complex than the ones used in the single-channel model; yet they are used in exactly the same fashion and provide the same type of information as the simpler model. The AB:POM microcomputer software described later in this chapter proves very useful in solving multiple-channel, as well as other, queuing problems.

Model C: Constant Service Time Model

Some service systems have constant, instead of exponentially distributed service times. When customers or equipment are processed according to a fixed cycle, as in the case of an automatic car wash or an amusement park ride, constant service times are appropriate. Because constant rates are certain, the values for L_q, W_q, L_s, and W_s are always less than they would be in Model A, which has variable service rates. As a matter of fact, both the average queue length and the average waiting time in the queue are halved with Model C. Constant service model formulas are given in Table S10.5. Model C also has the technical name of M/D/1 in the literature of queuing theory. Example S4 gives a constant service time analysis.

EXAMPLE S4

Solway-Leblanc Recycling, Inc., collects and compacts aluminum cans and glass bottles in Montreal. Its truck drivers, who arrive to unload these materials for recycling, currently wait an average of 15 minutes before emptying their loads. The cost of the driver and truck time while in queue is valued at \$60 per hour. A new automated compactor can be purchased that will process truckloads at a constant rate of 12 trucks per hour (that is, 5 minutes per truck). Trucks arrive according to a Poisson distribution at an average rate of 8 per hour. If the new compactor is put in use, its cost will be amortized at a rate of \$3 per truck unloaded. The firm hires a summer college intern, who conducts the following analysis to evaluate the costs vs. benefits of the purchase:

Current waiting cost/trip = (1/4 hr. waiting now) (\$60/hr. cost) = \$15/trip

New system: $\lambda = 8$ trucks/hr. arriving $\mu = 12$ trucks/hr. served

$$\text{Average waiting time in queue} = W_q = \frac{\lambda}{2\mu(\mu-\lambda)} = \frac{8}{2(12)(12-8)} = \frac{1}{12}\text{ hr.}$$

Waiting cost/trip with new compactor = (1/12 hr. wait) (\$60/hr. cost) = \$ 5/trip

Savings with new equipment = \$15 (current system) – \$5 (new system) = \$10/trip

Cost of new equipment amortized = \$ 3/trip

Net savings \$ 7/trip

Model D: Limited Population Model

When there is a limited population of potential customers for a service facility, we need to consider a different queuing model. This model would be used, for example, if you were considering equipment repairs in a factory that has five machines, if you were in charge of maintenance for a fleet of 10 commuter airplanes, or if you ran a hospital ward that has 20 beds. The limited population model permits any number of repair people (servers) to be considered.

The reason this model differs from the three earlier queuing models is that there is now a *dependent* relationship between the length of the queue and the arrival rate.

TABLE S10.4 ■ QUEUING FORMULAS FOR MODEL B: MULTICHANNEL SYSTEM, ALSO CALLED M/M/S

M = number of channels open

λ = average arrival rate

μ = average service rate at each channel

The probability that there are zero people or units in the system is

$$P_0 = \frac{1}{\left[\sum_{n=0}^{M-1} \frac{1}{n!}\left(\frac{\lambda}{\mu}\right)^n\right] + \frac{1}{M!}\left(\frac{\lambda}{\mu}\right)^M \frac{M\mu}{M\mu - \lambda}} \quad \text{for } M\mu > \lambda$$

The average number of people or units in the system is

$$L_s = \frac{\lambda\mu(\lambda/\mu)^M}{(M-1)!(M\mu - \lambda)^2} P_0 + \frac{\lambda}{\mu}$$

The average time a unit spends in the waiting line or being serviced (namely, in the system) is

$$W_s = \frac{\mu(\lambda/\mu)^M}{(M-1)!(M\mu - \lambda)^2} P_0 + \frac{1}{\mu} = \frac{L_s}{\lambda}$$

The average number of people or units in line waiting for service is

$$L_q = L_s - \frac{\lambda}{\mu}$$

The average time a person or unit spends in the queue waiting for service is

$$W_q = W_s - \frac{1}{\mu} = \frac{L_q}{\lambda}$$

To illustrate the extreme situation, if your factory had five machines and all were broken and awaiting repair, the arrival rate would drop to zero. In general, as the waiting line becomes longer in the limited population model, the arrival rate of customers or machines drops lower.

Table S10.6 displays the queuing formulas for the limited population model. Note that they employ a different notation than seen in Models A, B, and C. To simplify what can become very time-consuming calculations, finite queuing tables have been developed that determine *D* and *F*. *D* represents the probability a machine needing repair will have to wait in line. *F* is a waiting-time efficiency factor. *D* and *F* are needed to compute most of the other finite model formulas.

A small part of the published finite queuing tables is illustrated in this section. Table S10.7 provides for a population of $N = 5$.[3]

[3]Limited, or finite, queuing tables are available to handle arrival populations of up to 250. Although there is no definite number that we can use to divide limited from unlimited populations, the general rule of thumb is this: If the number in the queue is a significant proportion of the arrival population, use a limited population queuing model. For a complete set of *N* values, see L. G. Peck and R. N. Hazelwood, *Finite Queuing Tables* (New York: John Wiley, 1958).

To use Table S10.7, we follow four steps:

1. Compute X (the service factor, where $X = T(T + U)$).
2. Find the value of X in the table and then find the line for M (where M is the number of service channels).
3. Note the corresponding values for D and F.
4. Compute L, W, J, H, or whichever are needed to measure the service system's performance.

Example S5 illustrates these steps.

In office buildings and hotels, mirrors next to elevators or on elevator doors seem to make people happier to wait. People comb their hair; they check their clothes. One study showed that guests in hotels with mirrors thought elevators were faster in arriving than guests in hotels where there were no mirrors near the elevators. The *reality* was that elevator delays were exactly the same—the only difference was *perception*.

EXAMPLE S5

Past records indicate that each of the five laser computer printers at Revenue Canada needs repair after about 20 hours of use. Breakdowns have been determined to be Poisson-distributed. The one technician on duty can service a printer in an average of 2 hours, following an exponential distribution. Printer downtime costs $120 per hour. Technicians are paid $25 per hour. Should Revenue Canada hire a second technician?

Assuming the second technician can repair a printer in an average of 2 hours, we can use Table S10.7 (because there are $N = 5$ machines in this limited population) to compare the costs of one vs. two technicians.

1. First, we note that $T = 2$ hours and $U = 20$ hours.
2. Then, $X = \frac{T}{T+U} = \frac{2}{2+20} = \frac{2}{22} = .091$ (close to .090).
3. For M = 1 server, $D = .350$ and $F = .960$.
4. For M = 2 servers, $D = .044$ and $F = .998$.
5. The average number of printers *working* is $J = NF(1 - X)$.
   For M = 1, this is $J = (5)(.960)(1 - .091) = 4.36$.
   For M = 2, it is $J = (5)(.998)(1 - .091) = 4.54$.
6. The cost analysis follows:

Number of Technicians	Average Number Printers Down (N – J)	Average Cost/Hr. for Downtime (N – J)($120/hr.)	Cost/Hr. for Technicians (at $25/hr.)	Total Cost/Hr.
1	.64	$76.80	$25.00	$101.80
2	.46	$55.20	$50.00	$105.20

This analysis suggests that having only one technician on duty will save a few dollars per hour ($105.20 – $101.80 = $3.40).

Queues exist throughout industry and around the world. Here, the Moscow McDonald's on Puskin Square, four blocks from the Kremlin, boasts 700 indoor and 200 outdoor seats, employs 800 Russian citizens, and generates annual revenues of 80 million dollars. In spite of its size and volume, it still has queues and had to develop a strategy for dealing with them.

TABLE S10.5 ■ QUEUING FORMULAS FOR MODEL C: CONSTANT SERVICE, ALSO CALLED THE M/D/1 MODEL

Average length of queue: $L_q = \dfrac{\lambda^2}{2\mu(\mu - \lambda)}$

Average waiting time in queue: $W_q = \dfrac{\lambda}{2\mu(\mu - \lambda)}$

Average number of customers in system: $L_s = L_q + \dfrac{\lambda}{\mu}$

Average waiting time in system: $W_s = W_q + \dfrac{1}{\mu}$

OTHER QUEUING APPROACHES

Many practical waiting-line problems that occur in production and operations service systems have characteristics like the four mathematical models described before. Often, however, *variations* of these specific cases are present in an analysis. Service times in an automobile repair shop, for example, tend to follow the normal probability distribution instead of the exponential. A college registration system in which seniors have first choice of courses and hours over all other students is an example of a first-come, first-served model with a preemptive priority queue discipline. A physical examination for military recruits is an example of a multiphase system, one that differs from the single-phase models discussed in this supplement. A recruit first lines up to

TABLE S10.6 ■ QUEUING FORMULAS AND NOTATION FOR MODEL D: LIMITED POPULATION

FORMULAS

Service factor: $X = \dfrac{T}{T + U}$

Average number running: $J = NF(1 - X)$

Average number waiting: $L = N(1 - F)$

Average number being serviced: $H = FNX$

Average waiting time: $W = \dfrac{L(T + U)}{N - L} = \dfrac{T(1 - F)}{XF}$

Number of population: $N = J + L + H$

NOTATION

D = probability that a unit will have to wait in queue
F = efficiency factor
H = average number of units being served
J = average number of units not in queue or in service bay
L = average number of units waiting for service
M = number of service channels
N = number of potential customers
T = average service time
U = average time between unit service requirements
W = average time a unit waits in line
X = service factor

Source: L. G. Peck and R. N. Hazelwood, *Finite Queuing Tables* (New York: John Wiley, 1958).

TABLE S10.7 ■ FINITE QUEUING TABLES FOR A POPULATION OF N = 5

X	M	D	F	X	M	D	F	X	M	D	F	X	M	D	F	X	M	D	F
.012	1	.048	.999		1	.404	.945		1	.689	.801	.330	4	.012	.999		3	.359	.927
.019	1	.076	.998	.110	2	.065	.996	.210	3	.032	.998		3	.112	.986	.520	2	.779	.728
.025	1	.100	.997		1	.421	.939		2	.211	.973		2	.442	.904		1	.988	.384
.030	1	.120	.996	.115	2	.071	.995		1	.713	.783		1	.902	.583	.540	4	.085	.989
.034	1	.135	.995		1	.439	.933	.220	3	.036	.997	.340	4	.013	.999		3	.392	.917
.036	1	.143	.994	.120	2	.076	.995		2	.229	.969		3	.121	.985		2	.806	.708
.040	1	.159	.993		1	.456	.927		1	.735	.765		2	.462	.896		1	.991	.370
.042	1	.167	.992	.125	2	.082	.994	.230	3	.041	.997		1	.911	.569	.560	4	.098	.986
.044	1	.175	.991		1	.473	.920		2	.247	.965	.360	4	.017	.998		3	.426	.906
.046	1	.183	.990	.130	2	.089	.933		1	.756	.747		3	.141	.981		2	.831	.689
.050	1	.198	.989		1	.489	.914	.240	3	.046	.996		2	.501	.880		1	.993	.357
.052	1	.206	.988	.135	2	.095	.993		2	.265	.960		1	.927	.542	.580	4	.113	.984
.054	1	.214	.987		1	.505	.907		1	.775	.730	.380	4	.021	.998		3	.461	.895
.056	2	.018	.999	.140	2	.102	.992	.250	3	.052	.995		3	.163	.976		2	.854	.670
	1	.222	.985		1	.521	.900		2	.284	.955		2	.540	.863		1	.994	.345
.058	2	.019	.999	.145	3	.011	.999		1	.794	.712		1	.941	.516	.600	4	.130	.981
	1	.229	.984		2	.109	.991	.260	3	.058	.944	.400	4	.026	.977		3	.497	.883
.060	2	.020	.999		1	.537	.892		2	.303	.950		3	.186	.972		2	.875	.652
	1	.237	.983	.150	3	.012	.999		1	.811	.695		2	.579	.845		1	.996	.333
.062	2	.022	.999		2	.115	.990	.270	3	.064	.994		1	.952	.493	.650	4	.179	.972
	1	.245	.982		1	.553	.885		2	.323	.944	.420	4	.031	.997		3	.588	.850
.064	2	.023	.999	.155	3	.013	.999		1	.827	.677		3	.211	.966		2	.918	.608
	1	.253	.981		2	.123	.989	.280	3	.071	.993		2	.616	.826		1	.998	.308
.066	2	.024	.999		1	.568	.877		2	.342	.938		1	.961	.471	.700	4	.240	.960
	1	.260	.979	.160	3	.015	.999		1	.842	.661	.440	4	.037	.996		3	.678	.815
.068	2	.026	.999		2	.130	.988	.290	4	.007	.999		3	.238	.960		2	.950	.568
	1	.268	.978		1	.582	.869		3	.079	.992		2	.652	.807		1	.999	.286
.070	2	.027	.999	.165	3	.016	.999		2	.362	.932		1	.969	.451	.750	4	.316	.944
	1	.275	.977		2	.137	.987		1	.856	.644	.460	4	.045	.995		3	.763	.777
.075	2	.031	.999		1	.597	.861	.300	4	.008	.999		3	.266	.953		2	.972	.532
	1	.294	.973	.170	3	.017	.999		3	.086	.990		2	.686	.787	.800	4	.410	.924
.080	2	.035	.998		2	.145	.985		2	.382	.926		1	.975	.432		3	.841	.739
	1	.313	.969		1	.611	.853		1	.869	.628	.480	4	.053	.994		2	.987	.500
.085	2	.040	.998	.180	3	.021	.999	.310	4	.009	.999		3	.296	.945	.850	4	.522	.900
	1	.332	.965		2	.161	.983		3	.094	.989		2	.719	.767		3	.907	.702
.090	2	.044	.998		1	.638	.836		2	.402	.919		1	.980	.415		2	.995	.470
	1	.350	.960	.190	3	.024	.998		1	.881	.613	.500	4	.063	.992	.900	4	.656	.871
.095	2	.049	.997		2	.117	.980	.320	4	.010	.999		3	.327	.936		3	.957	.666
	1	.368	.955		1	.665	.819		3	.103	.988		2	.750	.748		2	.998	.444
.100	2	.054	.997	.200	3	.028	.998		2	.422	.912		1	.985	.399	.950	4	.815	.838
.100	1	.386	.950	.200	2	.194	.976		1	.892	.597	.520	4	.073	.991		3	.989	.631
.105	2	.059	.997																

Source: From L. G. Peck and R. N. Hazelwood, *Finite Queuing Tables* (New York: John Wiley, 1958, p. 4). © 1985, John Wiley & Sons, Inc.

POM IN ACTION

Using Queuing Theory in Finland to Implement Time-Based Competition

The Finnish company Helkama Bica Oy faced two severe economic blows in 1990: a rapid increase in competition due to European integration into one market bloc and the loss of the Soviet Union as a customer. With sales of $50 million, the bicycle and cable manufacturer had been able, until then, to compete based on short delivery times and high quality. In 1988, Helkama was ranked first in Finland in profitability and fifth in growth.

Helkama's response to the pressure has been to increase its focus on time-based competition, yet invest as frugally as possible. Queuing theory is now used throughout the firm to calculate and reduce lead times, aid in capacity planning, and reduce lot sizes. Even more importantly, the queuing models built to describe the factory operation serve as a control against traditional ways of tackling efficiency problems, such as increasing lot sizes.

Using computer software produced by a Massachusetts firm, Helkama's attempts to reduce production lead times have been rapid and successful. Reductions of as much as 40% have reinforced the company's ability to use time-based competition as a strategic weapon. The result has been increased sales and profits.

Sources: OR/MS Today (October 1992): 30–34; and *OR/MS Today* (June 1991): 34–42.

have blood drawn at one station, then waits to take an eye exam at the next station, talks to a psychiatrist at the third, and is examined by a doctor for medical problems at the fourth. At each phase, the recruit must enter another queue and wait his or her turn. Many models, some very complex, have been developed to deal with situations such as these.

SUMMARY

Queues are an important part of the world of operations management. In this supplement, we describe several common queuing systems and present mathematical models for analyzing them.

The models we illustrate are Model A, the basic single-channel, single-phase system with Poisson arrivals and exponential service times; Model B, the multichannel equivalent of Model A; Model C, a constant service rate model; and Model D, a limited population system. All four of these allow for Poisson arrivals, first-in, first-out service, and a single-service phase. Typical operating characteristics we examine include average time spent waiting in queue and in the system, average number of customers in the queue and system, idle time, and utilization rate.

A variety of queuing models exist for which all of the assumptions of the traditional models need not be met. In these cases, we use more complex mathematical models or turn to a technique called simulation. The application of simulation to problems of queuing systems is addressed in the Supplement to Chapter 13.

The reader might wish to visit the "Queueing Theory Page" on the Internet, created by Dr. Myron Hlynka of the University of Windsor, Windsor, Ontario:

http://supernova.uwindsor.ca/people/hlynka/queue.html

KEY TERMS

Queuing theory (p. 437)
Waiting line (p. 437)
Unlimited, or infinite, population (p. 439)
Limited, or finite, population (p. 439)
Poisson distribution (p. 439)
First-in, first-out (FIFO) rule (p. 441)
Single-channel queuing system (p. 441)
Multiple-channel queuing system (p. 441)
Single-phase system (p. 441)
Multiphase system (p. 441)
Negative exponential probability distribution (p. 442)

USING AB:POM AND SPREADSHEETS TO SOLVE QUEUING PROBLEMS

Solving Example S3 With AB:POM's Queuing Module

As in this chapter, there are four AB:POM queuing models from which to select, each with or without cost analysis (see Program S10.1): The programs that include cost can compute waiting costs charged against either the time a customer spends in the system or the time spent waiting in the queue.

PROGRAM S10.1 ■ AB:POM's Queuing Options

```
Model
Single Channel
Multiple Channel
Constant Service Time
Limited Population
```

The left-hand side of Program S10.2 shows the input data for Example S3, the Golden Muffler Shop with two mechanics. The right-hand side illustrates the program's outputs.

PROGRAM S10.2 ■ AB:POM's Queuing Program Using Example S3's Data with Optional Conversion of Times into Minutes. AB:POM can also handle the other three queuing models in this supplement, and is capable of conducting economic cost analysis on each model. As a further option, the F3 function key was used to display probabilities of various numbers of people/items in the system.

Waiting Line Models — Solution

Multiple Channel

GOLDEN MUFFLER SHOP, EXAMPLE S3

arrival rate (lambda)	2.00	Average server utilization	.3333333
service rate (mu)	3.00	Average number in the queue (Lq)	0.083333
number of servers	2	Average number in the system (Ls)	0.7500
		Average time in the queue (Wq)	0.041667
		Answer * 60	2.50
		Average time in the system (Ws)	0.3750
		Answer * 60	22.50

F1 = Help   F2 = Multiply times by 60   F3 = Display Probabilities   F9 = Print   Esc

Number in system, k	Probability P (n=k)	Cumulative P (n<k)	Decum P (n>k)
0	.5000	0.5000	0.5000
1	.3333	0.8333	0.1667
2	.1111	0.9444	0.0556
3	.0370	0.9815	0.0185
4	.0123	0.9938	0.0062
5	.0041	0.9979	0.0021
6	.0014	0.9993	0.0007
7	.0005	0.9998	0.0002
8	.0002	0.9999	0.0001
9	.0001	1.0000	0.0000

Queuing Analysis with Spreadsheets

The four queuing models developed in this supplement can be analyzed by spreadsheet as well as with software such as AB:POM. Program S10.3 provides an example of a *single* channel analysis using the data from the Golden Muffler Shop in Example S1.

This "symbolic" spreadsheet shows the formulas and the input data for an arrival rate of 2 (in cell B4) and service rate of 3 (in cell B5). Cells D4 through D9 contain the output parameters such as average time and average number of people or items in the system, average number and time in the queue, utilization, and idle percent. Cells D12 through D20 provide the probabilities of more than 0 through 8 customers in the system.

PROGRAM S10.3 ■ Using Spreadsheets to Develop Queuing Parameters. The symbolic spreadsheet, showing formulas in cells, is provided.

	A	B	C	D
1	Golden Muffler Shop Queuing With M/M/1			Single Channel Model
2				
3	Inputs			Outputs
4	Arrival rate (lambda)	2	Av.#system (L)	+B4/(B5-B4)
5	Service rate (mu)	3	Av. time sys (W)	1/(B5-B4)
6			Av.#queue (Lq)	+B4^2/B5*(B5-B4)
7			Av. time queue (Wq)	+B4/B5*(B5-B4)
8			Util. factor (rho)	+B4/B5
9			Percent idle (Po)	1-B4/B5
10				
11			K	P(n>k) cust in system
12			0	($B$4/$B$5) ^ (C12+1)
13			1	($B$4/$B$5) ^ (C13+1)
14			2	($B$4/$B$5) ^ (C14+1)
15			3	($B$4/$B$5) ^ (C15+1)
16			4	($B$4/$B$5) ^ (C16+1)
17			5	($B$4/$B$5) ^ (C17+1)
18			6	($B$4/$B$5) ^ (C18+1)
19			7	($B$4/$B$5) ^ (C19+1)
20			8	($B$4/$B$5) ^ (C20+1)

SOLVED PROBLEMS

Solved Problem S10.1

Giovanni Di Prata and Sons Brick Distributors currently employ one worker, whose job is to load bricks on outgoing company trucks. An average of 24 trucks per day, or three per hour, arrive at the loading gate, according to a Poisson distribution. The worker loads them at a rate of four per hour, following approximately the exponential distribution in his service times.

Di Prata believes that adding a second brick loader will substantially improve the firm's productivity. He estimates that a two-person crew at the loading gate will double the loading rate from four trucks per hour to eight trucks per hour. Analyze the effect on the queue of such a change and compare the results to those found with one worker. What is the probability that there will be more than three trucks either being loaded or waiting?

Solution

	Number of Brick Loaders	
	1	2
Truck arrival rate (λ)	3/hr.	3/hr.
Loading rate (μ)	4/hr.	8/hr.
Average number in system (L_s)	3 trucks	.6 truck
Average time in system (W_s)	1 hr.	.2 hr.
Average number in queue (L_q)	2.25 trucks	.225 truck
Average time in queue (W_q)	.75 hr.	.075 hr.
Utilization rate (ρ)	.75	.375
Probability system empty (P_0)	.25	.625

Probability of More Than k Trucks in System

	Probability N > K	
K	One Loader	Two Loaders
0	.75	.375
1	.56	.141
2	.42	.053
3	.32	.020

These results indicate that when only one loader is employed, the average truck must wait three-quarters of an hour before it is loaded. Furthermore, there are an average of 2.25 trucks waiting in line to be loaded. This situation may be unacceptable to management. Note the decline in queue size after the addition of a second loader.

Solved Problem S10.2

Truck drivers working for Giovanni Di Prata and Sons (see Solved Problem S10.1) earn $10 per hour on the average. Brick loaders receive about $6 per hour. Truck drivers waiting *in the queue or at the loading gate* are drawing a salary but are productively idle and unable to generate revenue during that time. What would be the *hourly* cost savings to the firm associated with employing two loaders instead of one?

Referring to the data in Solved Problem S10.1, we note that the average number of trucks *in the system* is 3 when there is only one loader and .6 when there are two loaders.

Solution

	NUMBER OF LOADERS	
	1	2
Truck driver idle time costs [(average number of trucks) × (hourly rate)] = (3)($10) =	$30	$ 6 = (.6)($10)
Loading costs	6	12 = (2)($6)
Total expected cost per hour	$36	$18

The firm will save $18 per hour by adding the second loader.

Solved Problem S10.3

Giovanni Di Prata and Sons Brick Distributors are considering building a second platform or gate to speed the process of loading their brick trucks. This system, they think, will be even more efficient than simply hiring another loader to help out on the first platform (as in Solved Problem S10.1).

Assume that workers at each platform will be able to load four trucks per hour each and that trucks will continue to arrive at the rate of three per hour. Then apply the appropriate equations to find the waiting line's new operating conditions. Is this new approach indeed more speedy than the other two considered?

Solution

$$P_0 = \frac{1}{\left[\sum_{n=0}^{1} \frac{1}{n!}\left(\frac{3}{4}\right)^n\right] + \frac{1}{2!}\left(\frac{3}{4}\right)^2 \frac{2(4)}{2(4)-3}}$$

$$= \frac{1}{1 + \frac{3}{4} + \frac{1}{2}\left(\frac{3}{4}\right)^2\left(\frac{8}{8-3}\right)} = .454$$

$$L_s = \frac{3(4)(3/4)^2}{(1)!(8-3)^2}(.4545) + \frac{3}{4} = .873$$

$$W_s = \frac{.873}{3} = .291 \text{ hr.}$$

$$L_q = .873 - 3/4 = .123$$

$$W_q = \frac{.123}{3} = .041 \text{ hr.}$$

Looking back at Solved Problem S10.1, we see that although length of the *queue* and average time in the queue are lowest when a second platform is open, the average number of trucks in the *system* and average time spent waiting in the system are smallest when two workers are employed loading at a *single* platform. Hence, we would probably recommend not building a second gate.

Solved Problem S10.4

Hotêl Dieu Hospital's Cardiac Care Unit (CCU) has five beds, which are virtually always occupied by patients who have just undergone major heart surgery. Two registered nurses are on duty in the CCU in each of the three 8-hour shifts. About every 2 hours (following a Poisson distribution), one of the patients requires a nurse's attention. The nurse will then spend an average of 30 minutes (exponentially distributed) assisting the patient and updating medical records regarding the problem and care provided.

Because immediate service is critical to the five patients, two important questions are: What is the average number of patients being attended by the nurses? What is the average time a patient spends waiting for one of the nurses to arrive at bedside?

Solution

$$N = 5 \text{ patients}$$
$$M = 2 \text{ nurses}$$
$$T = 30 \text{ minutes}$$
$$U = 120 \text{ minutes}$$
$$X = \frac{T}{T+U} = \frac{30}{30+120} = .20$$

From Table S10.7, with $X = .20$ and $M = 2$, we see that

$$F = .976$$
$$H = \text{average number being attended to} = FNX$$
$$= (.976)(5)(.20) = .98 \approx \text{one patient at any given time}$$
$$W = \text{average waiting time for a nurse} = \frac{T(1-F)}{XF}$$
$$= \frac{30(1-.976)}{(.20)(.976)} = 3.69 \text{ minutes}$$

DISCUSSION QUESTIONS

1. What is the waiting-line problem? What are the components in a waiting-line system?
2. What are the assumptions underlying the queuing models described in this chapter?
3. Describe the important operating characteristics of a queuing system.
4. Why must the service rate be greater than the arrival rate in a single-channel queuing system?
5. Briefly describe three situations in which the first-in, first-out (FIFO) discipline rule is not applicable in queuing analysis.
6. Provide examples of four situations in which there is a limited, or finite, waiting line.
7. What are the components of the following queuing systems? Draw and explain the configuration of each.
   (a) Barber shop
   (b) Car wash
   (c) Laundromat
   (d) Small grocery store
8. Do doctors' offices generally have random arrival rates for patients? Are service times random? Under what circumstances might service times be constant?

9. Do you think the Poisson distribution, which assumes independent arrivals, is a good estimation of arrival rates in the following queuing systems? Defend your position in each case.
   (a) School cafeteria
   (b) Barber shop
   (c) Hardware store
   (d) Dentist's office
   (e) College class
   (f) Movie theater
10. What is the utilization factor for a system?
11. What happens if two single-channel systems have the same mean arrival and service rates, but the service time is constant in one and exponential in the other?
12. What dollar value do you place on yourself per hour that you spend waiting in lines? What value do your classmates assess? Why do they differ?
13. Provide an example of a situation where a manager actually wants to have a queue. Why would the manager do so?
14. Most banks have changed from having a line in front of each teller to a system whereby one line feeds all tellers. Which system is better, and why?
15. Justify the queuing system used in most supermarkets today (i.e., a line for each register, with those customers having 10 items or less going to special registers).
16. What cost trade-offs need to be considered in queuing analysis?

CRITICAL THINKING EXERCISE

Queues are a critical component in the operation of service organizations. Yet most managers understand very little about this important subject. Visit two service organizations in your community and observe the use of waiting lines. (Examples might be airline check-ins, fast-food restaurants, muffler or oil-change shops, movie theatres, sports arenas, or banks.) What approaches are taken? Diagram the service areas that involve queuing. Do you have any suggestions for improvement in service?

PROBLEMS

• **S10.1** Due to a recent increase in business, a secretary in a certain law firm is now having to word-process 20 letters a day on the average (assume a Poisson distribution). It takes him approximately 20 minutes to type each letter (assume an exponential distribution). Assuming the secretary works eight hours a day:

a) What is his utilization rate?

b) What is the average waiting time before he word-processes a letter?

c) What is the average number of letters waiting to be done?

d) What is the probability that the secretary has more than five letters to do?

• **S10.2** Sam the Vet is running a rabies vaccination clinic for dogs at the local grade school. Sam can "shoot" a dog every 3 minutes. It is estimated that the dogs will arrive independently and randomly throughout the day at a rate of one dog every 6 minutes according to a Poisson distribution. Also assume that Sam's shooting times are exponentially distributed. Find the following:

a) the probability that Sam is idle

b) the proportion of the time that Sam is busy

c) the average number of dogs being shot and waiting to be shot

d) the average number of dogs waiting to be shot

e) the average time a dog waits before getting shot

f) the average amount (mean) of time a dog spends between waiting in line and being shot

• **S10.3** Refer to Problem S10.2. It turns out that dogs arrive at the rate of one dog every 4 minutes (*not* every 6 minutes). Recompute your answers to parts (a) through (f) in Problem S10.2.

• **S10.4** Calls arrive at Timothy Cronan's hotel switchboard at a rate of two per minute. The average time to handle each of these is 20 seconds. There is only one switchboard operator at the current time. The Poisson and exponential distributions appear to be relevant in this situation.

a) What is the probability that the operator is busy?

b) What is the average time that a call must wait before reaching the operator?

c) What is the average number of calls waiting to be answered?

• **S10.5** At the start of football season, the ticket office gets very busy the day before the first game. Customers arrive at the rate of four every 10 minutes, and the average time to transact business is 2 minutes.

a) What is the average number of people in line?

b) What is the average time that a person would spend in the ticket office?

c) What proportion of time is the server busy?

• **S10.6** The Charles Leitle Electronics Corporation retains a service crew to repair machine breakdowns that occur on an average of $\lambda = 3$ per day (approximately Poisson in nature). The crew can service an average of $\mu = 8$ machines per day, with a repair time distribution that resembles the exponential distribution.

a) What is the utilization rate of this service system?

b) What is the average down time for a machine that is broken?

c) How many machines are waiting to be serviced at any given time?

d) What is the probability that more than one machine is in the system? The probability that more than two are broken and waiting to be repaired or being serviced? More than three? More than four?

: **S10.7** Dan Bower's Car Wash is open 6 days a week, but its heaviest day of business is always Saturday. From historical data, Dan estimates that dirty cars arrive at the rate of 20 per hour all day Saturday. With a full crew working the hand wash line, he figures that cars can be cleaned at the rate of one every 2 minutes. One car at a time is cleaned in this example of a single-channel waiting line.

Assuming Poisson arrivals and exponential service times, find the following:

a) The average number of cars in line.

b) The average time a car waits before it is washed.

c) The average time a car spends in the service system.

d) The utilization rate of the car wash.

e) The probability no cars are in the system.

f) Dan is thinking of switching to an all-automated car wash that uses no crew. The equipment under study washes one car every minute at a constant rate. How will your answers to parts (a) and (b) change with the new system?

: **S10.8** Lisa Kennally manages a large Mississauga, Ontario, movie theatre complex with four auditoriums called Cinema I, II, III, and IV. Each of the auditoriums plays a different film; the schedule is set so that starting times are staggered to avoid the large crowds that would occur if all four movies started at the same time. The theatre has a single ticket booth and a cashier who can maintain an average service rate of 280 movie patrons per hour. Service times are assumed to follow an exponential distribution. Arrivals on a normally active day are Poisson-distributed and average 210 per hour.

In order to determine the efficiency of the current ticket operation, Lisa wishes to examine several queue operating characteristics.

a) Find the average number of moviegoers waiting in line to purchase a ticket.

b) What percentage of the time is the cashier busy?

c) What is the average time a customer spends in the system?

d) What is the average time spent waiting in line to get to the ticket window?

e) What is the probability that there are more than two people in the system? More than three people? More than four?

: **S10.9** A university cafeteria line in the student centre is a self-serve facility in which students select the food items they want and then form a single line to pay the cashier. Students arrive at a rate of about four per minute according to a Poisson distribution. The single cashier takes about 12 seconds per customer, following an exponential distribution.

a) What is the probability there are more than two students in the system? More than three students? More than four?

b) What is the probability that the system is empty?

c) How long will the average student have to wait before reaching the cashier?

d) What is the expected number of students in the queue?

e) What is the average number in the system?

f) If a second cashier is added (who works at the same pace), how will the operating characteristics computed in parts (b), (c), (d), and (e) change? Assume customers wait in a single line and go to the first available cashier.

:**S10.10** The wheat harvesting season in the Canadian west is short, and farmers deliver their truckloads of wheat to a giant central storage bin within a 2-week span. Because of this, wheat-filled trucks waiting to unload and return to the fields have been known to back up for a block at the receiving bin. The central bin is owned cooperatively, and it is to every farmer's benefit to make the unloading/storage process as efficient as possible. The cost of grain deterioration caused by unloading delays and the cost of truck rental and idle driver time are significant concerns to the cooperative members. Although farmers have difficulty quantifying crop damage, it is easy to assign a waiting and unloading cost for truck and driver of $18 per hour. The storage bin is open and operated 16 hours per day and 7 days per week during the 2-week harvest season and is capable of unloading 35 trucks per hour according to an exponential distribution. Full trucks arrive all day long (during the hours the bin is open) at a rate of about 30 per hour, following a Poisson pattern.

To help the cooperative get a handle on the problem of lost time while trucks are waiting in line or unloading at the bin, find the following:

a) The average number of trucks in the unloading system.

b) The average time per truck in the system.

c) The utilization rate for the bin area.

d) The probability that there are more than three trucks in the system at any given time.

e) The total daily cost to the farmers of having their trucks tied up in the unloading process.

f) The cooperative, as mentioned, uses the storage bin heavily only 2 weeks per year. Farmers estimate that enlarging the bin would cut unloading costs by 50% next year. It will cost $9,000 to do so during the off-season. Would it be worth the cooperative's while to enlarge the storage area?

:S10.11 Michael Hanna's Department Store in Portage la Prairie, Manitoba, maintains a successful catalogue sales department in which a clerk takes orders by telephone. If the clerk is occupied on one line, incoming phone calls to the catalogue department are answered automatically by a recording machine and asked to wait. As soon as the clerk is free, the party that has waited the longest is transferred and answered first. Calls come in at a rate of about 12 per hour. The clerk is capable of taking an order in an average of 4 minutes. Calls tend to follow a Poisson distribution, and service times tend to be exponential.

The clerk is paid $5 per hour, but because of lost goodwill and sales, Hanna's loses about $25 per hour of customer time spent waiting for the clerk to take an order.

a) What is the average time that catalogue customers must wait before their calls are transferred to the order clerk?

b) What is the average number of callers waiting to place an order?

c) Hanna's is considering adding a second clerk to take calls. The store would pay that person the same $5 per hour. Should it hire another clerk? Explain.

•S10.12 Customers arrive at an automated coffee-vending machine at a rate of four per minute, following a Poisson distribution. The coffee machine dispenses a cup of coffee at a constant rate of 10 seconds.

a) What is the average number of people waiting in line?

b) What is the average number in the system?

c) How long does the average person wait in line before receiving service?

:S10.13 Robert Olney's Barber Shop is a popular haircutting and styling salon near the campus of Ryerson Polytechnic University in downtown Toronto. Four barbers work full-time and spend an average of 15 minutes on each customer. Customers arrive all day long at an average rate of 12 per hour. Arrivals tend to follow the Poisson distribution, and service times are exponentially distributed. The software described in this supplement may be used to answer these questions.

a) What is the probability that the shop is empty?

b) What is the average number of customers in the barber shop?

c) What is the average time spent in the shop?

d) What is the average time that a customer waits to be called to the barber chair?

e) What is the average number waiting to be served?

f) What is the shop's utilization factor?

g) Robert is thinking of adding a fifth barber. How will this affect the utilization rate?

:S10.14 The administrator at a large hospital emergency room faces a problem of providing treatment for patients who arrive at different rates during the day. There are four doctors available to treat patients when needed. If not needed, they can be assigned to other responsibilities (for example, lab tests, reports, X-ray diagnoses) or else rescheduled to work at other hours.

It is important to provide quick and responsive treatment, and the administrator feels that, on average, patients should not have to sit in the waiting area for more than 5 minutes before being seen by a doctor. Patients are treated on a first-come, first-served basis and see the first available doctor after waiting in the queue. The arrival pattern for a typical day is as follows:

TIME	ARRIVAL RATE
9 A.M.–3 P.M.	6 patients/hour
3 P.M.–8 P.M.	4 patients/hour
8 P.M.–midnight	12 patients/hour

These arrivals follow a Poisson distribution, and treatment times, 12 minutes on the average, follow the exponential pattern.

How many doctors should be on duty during each period in order to maintain the level of patient care expected?

:S10.15 One mechanic services five drilling machines for a steel plate manufacturer. Machines break down on an average of once every 6 working days, and breakdowns tend to follow a Poisson distribution. The mechanic can handle an average of one repair job per day. Repairs follow an exponential distribution.

a) How many machines are waiting for service, on average?

b) How many drills are in running order, on average?

c) How much would the waiting time be reduced if a second mechanic were hired?

:S10.16 Two technicians monitor a group of five computers that run an automated manufacturing facility. It takes an average of 15 minutes (exponentially distributed) to adjust a computer that develops a problem. The computers run for an average of 85 minutes (Poisson-distributed) without requiring adjustments. Determine the following:

a) The average number of computers waiting for adjustment.

b) The average number being adjusted.

c) The average number of computers not in working order.

:S10.17 The Duffy Department Store has approximately 300 customers shopping in its store between 9 A.M. and 5 P.M. on Saturdays. In deciding how many cash registers to keep open each Saturday, Jo Ann Duffy, the owner, considers two factors: customer waiting time (and the associated waiting cost) and the service costs of employing additional check-out clerks. Check-out clerks are paid an average of $4 per hour. When only one is on duty, the waiting time per customer is about 10 minutes (or 1/6 of an hour); when two clerks are on duty, the average check-out time is 6 minutes per person; 4 minutes when three clerks are working; and 3 minutes when four clerks are on duty.

Ms. Duffy has conducted customer satisfaction surveys and has been able to estimate that the store suffers approximately $5 in lost sales and goodwill for every *hour* of customer time spent waiting in check-out lines. Using the information provided, determine the optimal number of clerks to have on duty each Saturday in order to minimize the store's total expected cost.

CASE STUDY

New Liskeard Castings

For over 75 years, New Liskeard Castings, Inc. (NLCI), has manufactured wood stoves for home use. In recent years, with increasing energy prices, George Mathison, president, has seen sales triple. This dramatic increase in sales has made it difficult for George to maintain quality in all of the wood stoves and related products.

Unlike other companies manufacturing wood stoves, NLCI is *only* in the business of making stoves and stove-related products. Their major products are the Warmglo I, the Warmglo II, the Warmglo III, and the Warmglo IV. The Warmglo I is the smallest wood stove, with a heat output of 30,000 BTUs, and the Warmglo IV is the largest, with a heat output of 60,000 BTUs.

The Warmglo III outsold all of the other stoves by a wide margin. The heat output and available accessories were ideal for the typical home. The Warmglo III also had a number of outstanding features that made it one of the most attractive and heat-efficient stoves on the market. These features, along with the accessories, resulted in expanding sales and prompted George to build a new factory to manufacture Warmglo III stoves. An overview diagram of the factory is shown in Figure S10.5.

FIGURE S10.5 ■ Overview of Factory

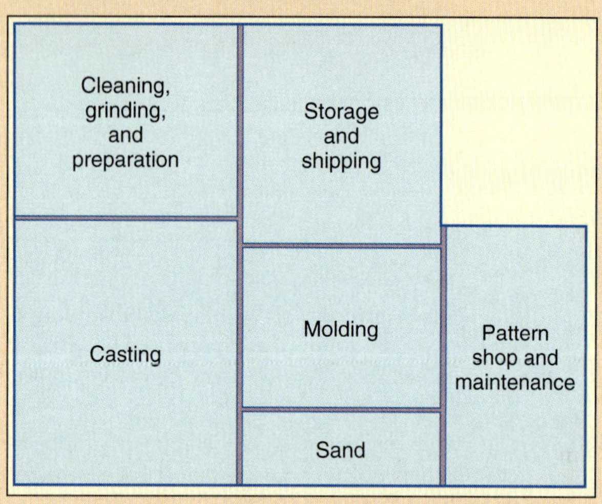

The new foundry used the latest equipment, including a new Disamatic that helped in manufacturing stove parts. Regardless of new equipment or procedures, casting operations have remained basically unchanged for hundreds of years. To begin with, a wooden pattern is made for every cast-iron piece in the stove. The wooden pattern is an exact duplication of the cast-iron piece that is to be manufactured. NLCI has all of its patterns made by Precision Patterns, Inc., and these patterns are stored in the pattern shop and maintenance room. Then, a specially formulated sand is molded around the wooden pattern. There can be two or more sand molds for each pattern. Mixing the sand and making the molds is done in the molding room. When the wooden pattern is removed, the resulting sand molds form a negative image of the desired casting. Next, the molds are transported to the casting room, where molten iron is poured into the molds and allowed to cool. When the iron has solidified, the molds are moved into the cleaning, grinding, and preparation room. The molds are dumped into large vibrators that shake most of the sand from the casting. The rough castings are then subjected to both sandblasting to remove the rest of the sand and grinding to finish some of the surfaces of the castings. The castings are then painted with a special heat-resistant paint, assembled into workable stoves, and inspected for manufacturing defects that may have gone undetected thus far. Finally, the finished stoves are moved to storage and shipping, where they are packaged and shipped to the appropriate locations.

At present, the pattern shop and the maintenance department are located in the same room. One large counter is used by maintenance personnel to get tools and parts, and by sand molders who need various patterns for the molding operation. Pete Nawler and Bob Dillman, who work behind the counter, are able to service a total of 10 people per hour (about 5 per hour each). On the average, four people from maintenance and three people from the molding department arrive at the counter per hour. People from the molding department and from maintenance arrive randomly, and to be served, they form a single line.

Pete and Bob have always had a policy of first come, first served. Because of the location of the

(Continued)

pattern shop and maintenance department, it takes about 3 minutes for an individual from the maintenance department to walk to the pattern and maintenance room, and it takes about 1 minute for an individual to walk from the molding department to the pattern and maintenance room.

After observing the operation of the pattern shop and maintenance room for several weeks, George decided to make some changes to the layout of the factory. An overview of these changes appears in Figure S10.6.

Separating the maintenance shop from the pattern shop had a number of advantages. It would take people from the maintenance department only 1 minute instead of 3 to get to the new maintenance department. Using motion and time studies, George was also able to determine that improving the layout of the maintenance department would allow Bob to serve six people from the maintenance department per hour, and improving the layout of the pattern department would allow Pete to serve seven people from the molding shop per hour.

FIGURE S10.6 ■ Overview of Factory After Changes

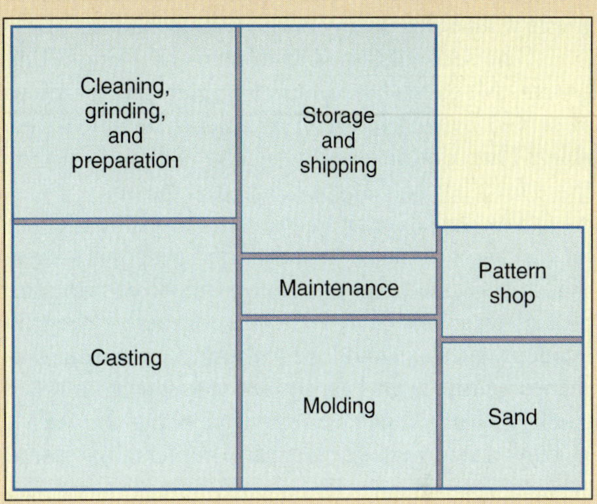

DISCUSSION QUESTIONS

1. How much time would the new layout save?
2. If maintenance personnel were paid \$9.50 per hour and molding personnel were paid \$11.75 per hour, how much could be saved per hour with the new factory layout?
3. Should George have made the change in layout?

Source: B. Render and R. M. Stair, Jr., *Quantitative Analysis for Management*, 5th ed. (Boston: Allyn and Bacon, 1994): p. 673–4. Modified for the Canadian edition.

CASE STUDY

The Winter Park Hotel

Donna Shader, manager of the Winter Park Hotel, is considering how to restructure the front desk to reach an optimum level of staff efficiency and guest service. At present, the hotel has five clerks on duty, each with a separate waiting line, during peak check-in time of 3:00 P.M. to 5:00 P.M. Observation of arrivals during this time show that an average of 90 guests arrive each hour (although there is no upward limit on the number that could arrive at any given time). It takes an average of 3 minutes for the front-desk clerk to register each guest.

Ms. Shader is considering three plans for improving guest service by reducing the length of time guests spend waiting in line. The first proposal would designate one employee as a quick-service clerk for guests registering under corporate accounts, a market segment that fills about 30% of all occupied rooms. Because corporate guests are preregistered, their registration takes just 2 minutes. With these guests separated from the rest of the clientele, the

(Continued)

average time for registering a typical guest would climb to 3.4 minutes. Under plan one, noncorporate guests would choose any of the remaining four lines.

The second plan is to implement a single-line system. All guests could form a single waiting line to be served by whichever of five clerks became available. This option would require sufficient lobby space for what could be a substantial queue.

The use of an automatic teller machine (ATM) for check-ins is the basis of the third proposal. Given that initial use of this technology might be minimal, Shader estimated that 20% of customers, primarily frequent guests, would be willing to use the machines. (This might be a conservative estimate if the guests perceive direct benefits from using the ATM, as bank customers do. Citibank reports that some 80% of its Vancouver, British Columbia, customers use its ATMs.) Ms. Shader would set up a single queue for customers who prefer human check-in clerks. This would be served by the five clerks, although Shader is hopeful that the machine will allow a reduction to four.

DISCUSSION QUESTIONS

1. Determine the average amount of time that a guest spends checking in. How would this change under each of the state options?
2. Which option do you recommend?

Source: B. Render and R. M. Stair, Jr., *Quantitative Analysis for Management*, 5th ed. (Boston: Allyn and Bacon, 1994): p. 672. Modified for the Canadian edition.

BIBLIOGRAPHY

Becker, L. C., and E. G. Landauer. "Reducing Waiting Time at Security Checkpoints." *Interfaces*, 19, no. 5 (September/October 1989): 57–65.

Byrd, J. "The Value of Queuing Theory." *Interfaces*, 8, no. 3 (May 1978): 22–26.

Cooper, R. B. *Introduction to Queuing Theory*, 2nd ed. New York: Elsevier-North Holland, 1980.

Foote, B. L. "Queuing Case Study of Drive-In Banking." *Interfaces*, 6, no. 4 (August 1976): 31.

Grassmann, W. K. "Finding the Right Number of Servers in Real-World Queuing Systems." *Interfaces*, 18, no. 2 (March/April 1988): 94–104.

Ho, C., and H. Lau. "Minimizing Total Cost in Scheduling Outpatient Appointments." *Management Science*, 38, no. 12 (December 1992): 1750.

Katz, K., B. Larson, and R. Larson. "Prescription for the Waiting-in-Line Blues: Entertain, Enlighten, and Engage." *Sloan Management Review* (Winter 1991): 44–53.

Morse, P. M. *Queues, Inventories and Maintenance*. New York: John Wiley, 1958.

Render, B., and R. M. Stair. *Introduction to Management Science*. Boston: Allyn and Bacon, 1992.

———. *Quantitative Analysis for Management*. 5th ed. Boston: Allyn and Bacon, 1994.

Solomon, S. *Simulation of Waiting Lines*. Englewood Cliffs, NJ: Prentice Hall, 1983.

Sze, D. Y. "A Queuing Model for Telephone Operator Staffing." *Operations Research*, 3, no. 2 (March/April 1984): 229–249.

Worthington, D. J. "Queuing Models for Hospital Waiting Lists." *Journal of the Operational Research Society*, 38, no. 5 (May 1987): 413–422.

11

Human Resource Strategy

CHAPTER OUTLINE

LEARNING OBJECTIVES

When you complete this chapter you should be able to:

Identify or define:
- Job specialization
- Job expansion
- Tools of methods analysis
- Ergonomics
- Job design
- Lean production
- Labour standards

Explain:
- Requirements of good job design

WORLD-CLASS PROFILE: THE LEARNING ORGANIZATION TREND

Left to right: James Chestnutt and Tony Lamantia, Eaton's executives; Marilyn Booth, Dean of Continuing Education, Ryerson Polytechnic University; John Crag Eaton, Eaton's of Canada.

A personal bank representative talking to her "coach," assistant manager personal banking. Illustrates the type of training now standard practice in many organizations.

Employees today are encouraged to look at the "big picture" with regard to their jobs. That means they are encouraged to think outside their particular job and concern themselves with the company's larger objectives.

The continuous learning approach has developed a strong following over the past three years, believes Connie Martin, Ottawa-based partner with Andersen Consulting. Andersen Consulting are in the change management practice field. Ms. Martin's clients realize the "only way to achieve competitive advantage is to have the work force well trained and developed." The phrase "training and development" is being reworked to just "development," according to Robert Sterling, Business Effectiveness Consultant with DuPont Canada Inc. In contrast to schooling the staff in specific tasks, development "is always in relationship to business issues we're trying to advance."

The Bank of Montreal has spent $40 million to open its Institute for Learning, the key goal being "to increase the level of conversion," a phrase used by Dr. James Rush. Dr. Rush has the view that "training" implies someone is in control, while "learning" allows independence and creativity. Given continuing opportunities to learn, he believes, people will be "committed" as opposed to "loyal".

Peter Senge, in his latest book, *Fifth Discipline: The Art and Prac-*

tice of the Learning Organization, articulates the theory clearly and in some detail.

Mr. Hubert Saint-Onge, head of the Canadian Imperial Bank of Commerce's leadership centre, criticizes the rhetoric but uses the concept: "In fact, all organizations are learning organizations ... it's a matter of speed at which they're seizing the capabilities." He distinguishes between explicit knowledge, which can be readily explained and consists of concrete elements such as numbers, and tacit knowledge, which is deeply integrated—that is, it is there but not expressed. According to Saint-Onge, "There is a close relationship between strategies and culture" and "The element of organizational learning that is most important is the culture of the organization."

"It's perfect for busy people, because we can learn at our own pace," says one of the employees. CD-ROM technology permits them to manage their own training time.

Math made easy. Intensive classroom sessions are still the most common way employees learn. Algebra is the subject under discussion.

How widespread are the new learning approaches? Things may not be operating everywhere at a high level of sophistication, but in the retailing business some giant strides have been made.

James Chestnutt, General Manager of Strategic Alliances and the Eaton's School of Retailing, (ESR), says, "We're talking about education versus training," and he hopes to see individuals who will take responsibility for their own upgrading through continuous learning.

ESR, affiliated with Ryerson Polytechnic University in Toronto, will eventually offer the country's first business degree with a retailing specialty. Eight hundred fifty attended courses in the past year. Mr. Chestnutt notes that you see people that you didn't think were leaders become real leaders and that a third of the Eaton's students are university graduates. Eaton's suppliers, such as Levi Strauss & Co. (Canada) and Canada Post, are sitting in on the classes, which in the future will be offered to the general public.

Meanwhile, Hudson's Bay Co. has entered into an agreement with the University of British Columbia to provide management training for their managers. The company sends about 40 managers a year to Vancouver for the three-week interdisciplinary program.

David Crisp, Hudson's Bay Vice-President of Human Resources, has remarked that this was a huge change for the company. "There was some initial resistance, but that's changed.... A year later, probably half have been promoted. So the message gets out that this does not hurt your career any."

Source: Adapted from Salem Alaton, "The Learning Organization Trends," *The Globe and Mail* (December 19, 1995).

At 9 A.M. the assembly line has been moving for only 1 hour, but already the day is dragging. In position five on line four, Michel Jones catches the next circuit board crawling down the line. At the current pace, one board passes his workstation every minute and a half. Forty down, 280 left to go today. Over in quality control, Ismael Hernandez puts his soldering gun back in its holster, fidgets with his left shirt sleeve and steals a quick glance at his watch. Thirty more minutes before coffee break. Two and a half hours to lunch. Seven and a half more until quitting time. ♦

Assembly line scenes such as these are repeated a thousand times over every day all over the world. Why are Michel's and Ismael's jobs like this? Is it a good human resource strategy for firms to have such jobs? In this chapter, we will examine these and related questions.

HUMAN RESOURCE STRATEGY

Human performance is crucial to an organization's performance. An organization does not function without people. It does not function well without competent people. It does not excel without competent, motivated people. Consequently, how the production operations manager formulates a human resource strategy determines the talents available to operations. Moreover, people are expensive; in many organizations, about a third of total cost is in wages and salaries. Therefore, this chapter considers human resource strategy options.

Objective of the Human Resource Strategy

The *objective of a human resource strategy* is to manage labour and design jobs and processes so people are *efficiently utilized*. This must be done within the constraints of other P/OM decisions, while maintaining a *reasonable quality of work life* in an atmosphere of *mutual commitment and trust*.

Quality of work life

Mutual commitment

Mutual trust

By reasonable **quality of work life**, we mean a job that not only is reasonably safe and for which the pay is equitable, but also that achieves an appropriate level of both physical and psychological requirements. By **mutual commitment**, we mean both management and employee strive to meet common objectives. By **mutual trust**, we mean reasonable, documented employment policies that are honestly and equitably implemented to the satisfaction of both management and employee.[1] When management has a genuine respect for its employees and their contribution to the firm, establishing a reasonable quality of work life and mutual trust is not particularly difficult.

Constraints on Human Resource Strategy

Human resource strategies are constrained by other strategic decisions. First, the product mix may determine seasonality and stability of employment. Second,

[1]With increasing frequency, we find companies calling their employees *associates*, *individual contributors*, or members of a particular *team*.

FIGURE 11.1 ■ Constraints on Human Resource Strategy. The effective operations manager understands how decisions blend together to constrain the human resource strategy.

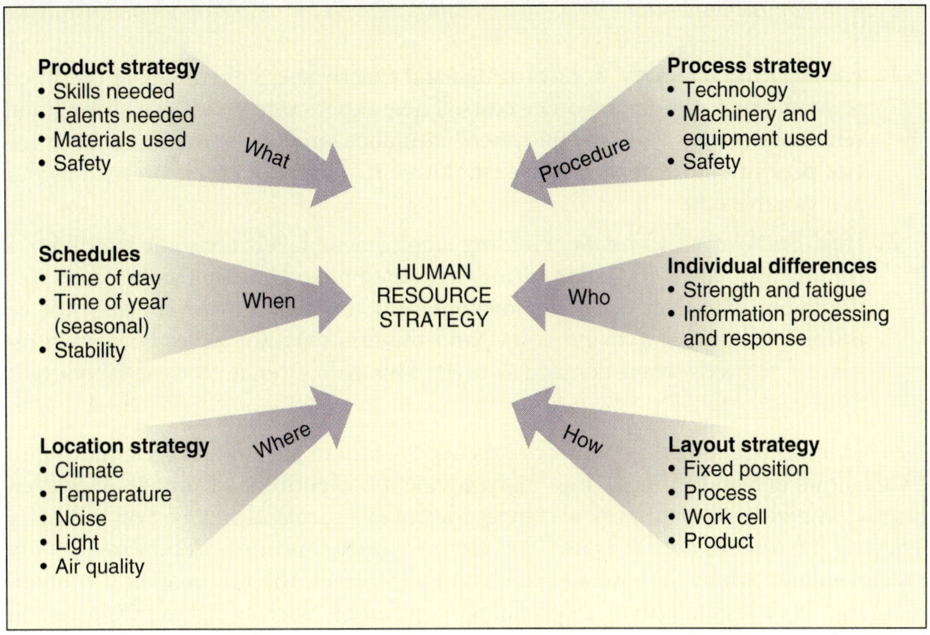

technology, equipment, and processes may affect safety and job content. Third, location may have an impact on the ambient environment in which the employees work. Finally, decisions regarding layout influence job content.

The technology decision imposes substantial constraints. For instance, some of the jobs in steel mills are dirty, noisy, and dangerous; slaughterhouse jobs may be stressful and include a stomach-turning stench; and assembly line jobs are often boring and mind-numbing.

We are not going to change these jobs without making changes in our other strategic decisions. So, the trade-offs necessary to reach a tolerable quality of work life are difficult.

Much of our human resource strategy is a result of other operation design decisions (Figure 11.1). It behooves a prudent manager to ensure that such decisions are considered simultaneously. The manager blends ingredients so that the result is an effective, efficient system where individuals have optimum job design.

Acknowledging the constraints imposed on human resource strategy, we now look at three distinct decision areas of human resource strategy. These three areas are labour planning, job design, and labour standards. The supplement to this chapter expands on the discussion of labour standards and introduces work measurement.

LABOUR PLANNING

Labour planning is determining staffing policies that deal with (1) employment stability and (2) work schedules.

Labour planning

Employment Stability Policies

Employment stability deals with the number of employees that are maintained by an organization at any given time. There are two very basic policies for dealing with stability.

1. *Follow Demand Exactly.* Following demand exactly keeps direct labour costs tied to production, but incurs other costs. These other costs include (a) hiring and termination costs, (b) unemployment insurance, and (c) premium wages to entice personnel to accept unstable employment. This policy tends to treat labour as a variable cost.
2. *Hold Employment Constant.* Holding employment levels constant maintains a trained work force and keeps hiring, termination, and unemployment costs to a minimum. However, with employment held constant, employees may not be utilized fully when demand is low, and the firm may not have the human resources it needs when demand is high. This policy tends to treat labour as a fixed cost.

Maintaining a stable work force may allow a firm to pay lower wages than a firm that follows demand. This savings may provide a competitive advantage. However, firms with highly seasonal work and little control over demand may be best served by a fluctuating work force. For example, a salmon cannery in British Columbia can only process salmon when the salmon are running. However, the firm may find complementary labour demands in other products or operations, such as making the cans and labels or repairing and maintaining facilities.

Firms must determine policies about employment stability. The above policies are only two of many that can be efficient *and* provide a reasonable quality of work life.

Work Schedules

Standard work schedule
Flextime

Although the **standard work schedule** in Canada is five $7^1/_2$-hour days, variations do exist. A currently popular variation is a work schedule called flextime. **Flextime** allows employees, within limits, to determine their own schedules. A flextime policy might allow an employee (with proper notification) to be at work at 8 A.M. plus or minus 2 hours. This allows more autonomy and independence on the part of the employee. Some firms have found flextime a low-cost fringe benefit that enhances job satisfaction. The problem from the P/OM perspective is that much production work requires full staffing for efficient operations. A machine that requires three people cannot run at all if only two show up. Having a waiter show up to serve lunch at 1:30 P.M. rather than 11:30 A.M. is not much help either.

Some industries find that their process strategy has severely constrained their human resource scheduling option. For instance, paper manufacturing, petroleum refining, and power stations must be staffed around the clock except for maintenance and repair shutdown. Firms in these industries are severely constrained when implementing variable-time policies.

Flexible work week

Another work schedule is a **flexible work week**. This often manifests itself in fewer but longer days, such as four 10-hour days. These schedules are viable for many operations functions, provided suppliers and customers can be accommodated. Firms that have high process startup times (say, to get a boiler up to operating temperature) find longer workday options particularly appealing. A 1994 Gallup survey in the United States showed that two-thirds of working adults would prefer toiling four 10-hour days to the standard 5-day schedule. Duke Power Co., Los Angeles county, AT&T, and General Motors are just a few organizations to offer the 4-day week.

Another option is to have shorter days rather than longer days. This often moves employees to **part-time status**. Such an option is particularly attractive in service industries, where staffing for peak loads is necessary. Banks and restaurants often hire part-time workers. Also, many firms reduce labour costs by reducing fringe benefits for part-time employees.

Part-time status

Job Classifications and Work Rules

Many organizations have strict job classifications and work rules that specify who can do what, when they can do it, and under what conditions they can do it. These job classifications and work rules restrict employee flexibility on the job, which in turn reduces the flexibility of the production/operations function. But part of an operations manager's task is to manage the unexpected. Therefore, the more flexibility a firm has when staffing and establishing work schedules, the more efficient it can be. Building morale and meeting staffing requirements that result in an efficient production function are easier if managers have fewer job classifications and work-rule constraints.

JOB DESIGN

Job design is specifying the tasks that constitute a job for an individual or a group. We examine six components of job design: (1) job specialization, (2) job expansion, (3) psychological components, (4) self-directed teams, (5) motivation and incentive systems, and (6) ergonomics and work methods.

Job design

Job Specialization

Job design's importance as a management variable is credited to Adam Smith.[2] Smith suggested that a division of labour, also known as **labour specialization** and job specialization, would assist in reducing labour costs in several ways.

Labour specialization

1. *development of dexterity* and faster learning by the employee because of repetition,
2. *less loss of time* because the employee would not be changing jobs or tools,
3. *development of specialized tools* and the reduction of investment because each employee has only a few tools needed for a particular task.

Charles Babbage determined that a fourth consideration was also important for labour efficiency.[3] Because pay tends to follow skill with a rather high correlation, Babbage suggested *paying exactly the wage needed for the particular skill required*. If the entire job consists of only one skill, then we would pay for only that skill. Otherwise,

[2]Adam Smith, *On the Creation of the Wealth of Nations* (London, 1876).

[3]Charles Babbage, *On the Economy of Machinery and Manufacturers* (London, 1832), Chapter 18.

we would tend to pay for the highest skill contributed by the employee. These four advantages of labour specialization are still valid today.

A classic example of labour specialization is the assembly line, as described in the opening paragraph of this chapter. Such systems are often very efficient, although they may require employees to do repetitive, mind-numbing jobs. The wage rate for many of these jobs, however, is very good. Given the relatively high wage rate for the modest skills required in many of these jobs, there is often a large pool of employees from which to choose. This is not an incidental consideration for the manager with responsibility for staffing the operations function. It is estimated that 2% to 3% of the work force in industrialized nations perform highly specialized, repetitive, assembly-line jobs. The traditional way of developing and maintaining worker commitment under labour specialization has been good selection (matching people to the job), good wages, and incentive systems.

Job Expansion

In recent years, there has been an effort to improve the quality of work life by moving from the labour specialization toward a more varied job design. The theory is that variety makes the job "better" and the employee therefore finds a higher quality of work life. This in turn benefits the employee and the organization. We modify jobs in a variety of ways. The first approach is **job enlargement**, which occurs when we add tasks of similar skill to the existing job. **Job rotation** is a version of job enlargement that occurs when the job per se is not enlarged, but rather the employee is allowed to move from one specialized job to another. Variety has been added to the employee's perspective of the job. Another approach is **job enrichment**, which adds planning and control to the job. Job enrichment can be thought of as *vertical expansion*, as opposed to job enlargement, which is *horizontal*. These ideas and others are shown in Figure 11.2.

Job enlargement

Job rotation

Job enrichment

Employee empowerment

Employee empowerment is the practice of enriching jobs so employees accept responsibility for a variety of decisions normally associated with staff specialists.[4] Employee empowerment is a popular extension of job enrichment. Empowering employees helps them take ownership of their jobs so they have a personal interest in improving performance. (See the *POM in Action* box "Markham Stouffville Hospital.")

Psychological Components of Job Design

An effective human resources strategy also requires consideration of the psychological components of job design. Psychological components of job design focus on how to design jobs that meet some minimum psychological requirements.

HAWTHORNE STUDIES. The Hawthorne studies introduced psychology to the workplace. They were conducted in the late 1920s at GE's Hawthorne Plant near Chicago. Publication of the findings in 1939[5] showed conclusively that there is a dynamic social system at the workplace. Ironically, these studies were initiated to determine the impact of lighting on productivity. Instead they found the social system and distinct roles played by employees to be more important than the intensity of the

[4]See W. C. Byham, *Zapp! The Lightning of Empowerment* (New York: Ballantine, 1992).

[5]F. J. Roethlisberger and William J. Dickinson, *Management and the Workers* (New York: John Wiley, 1964, copyright 1939, by the President & Fellows of Harvard College).

POM IN ACTION

Markham Stouffville Hospital

Markham Stouffville Hospital, a full-service community health care facility, offers services such as surgery, emergency and intensive care, obstetrical and paediatric care, long-term care, mental health care, palliative, telemetry and a variety of other diagnostic and patient support services. MSH opened in March of 1990 as a 245-bed hospital. Due to MSH's attention to high-quality outpatient services, the hospital has achieved recognition for a unique approach to care, and has better integrated itself with the community, with only 214 operating beds.

In 1993 MSH's senior management team moved from the traditional "hierarchical structure" management style to a much more effective, efficient, and flexible "program management" system. This system gave the health care providers and professionals from many different departments the chance to work in multidisciplinary "patient care teams" that served common patient needs (e.g., obstetrics and pediatrics were linked under a new Maternal/ Child Program). The key innovation was to empower each team to develop and monitor the budgets in their area. Further evolution of program management to a systems approach has provided seamless, responsive service.

All levels of staff are consistently given responsibility and accountability for decision making. With a systems approach and the empowerment of staff, traditional reporting styles have been eliminated. Directors now report to a senior management team rather than to individual vice-presidents. The role of senior management is that of executive resource and coach. This has led to decisions based on patient needs and outcomes rather than on hospital policies. The front-line staff are able to make continuous improvements in cost-efficient, high-quality patient care.

Source: Adapted from "Markham Stouffvile Hospital" (The National Quality Institute, 1995).

lighting. They also found that individual differences may be dominant in what an employee expects from the job and what the employee thinks her or his contribution to the job should be.

Core Job Characteristics. In the six decades since the Hawthorne studies, substantial research regarding the psychological components of job design has

FIGURE 11.2 ■ Job Design Continuum

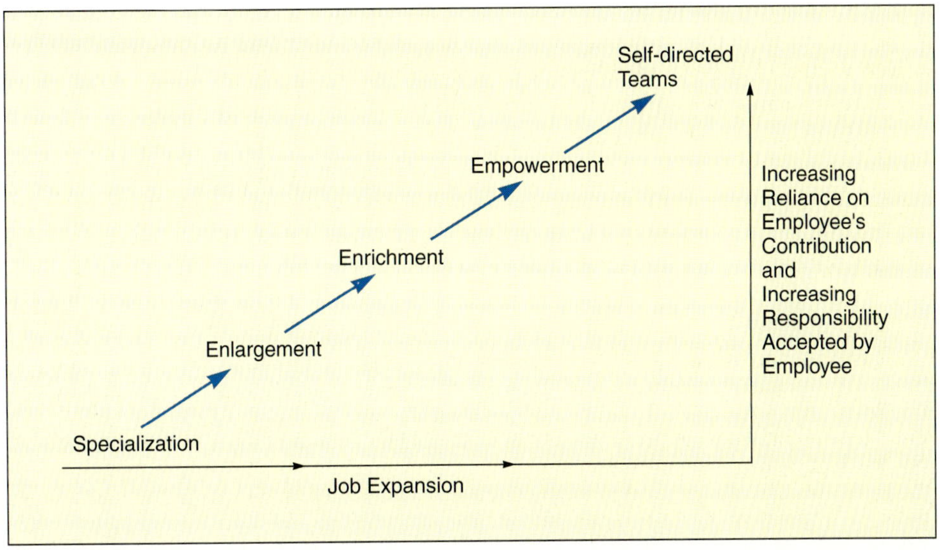

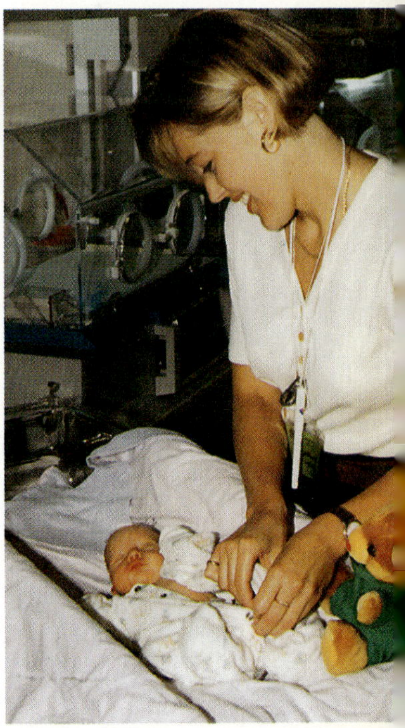

A company volunteer working with premature babies.

taken place.[6] Hackman and Oldham have incorporated much of that work into five desirable characteristics of job design.[7] Their summary suggests that jobs should include:

1. *Skill Variety*. The job should require the worker to use a variety of skills and talents.
2. *Job Identity*. The job should allow the worker to perceive the job as a whole and recognize a start and a finish.
3. *Job Significance*. The job should provide a sense that the job has impact on the organization and society.
4. *Autonomy*. The job should permit freedom, independence, and discretion.
5. *Feedback*. The job should provide clear, timely information about performance.

Including these five ingredients in job design is consistent with job enlargement, job enrichment, and employee empowerment. We now want to look at teams to expand jobs and achieve these five job characteristics.

Self-Directed Teams

Many world-class organizations have adopted teams to foster mutual trust and commitment, and provide the core job characteristics. This is illustrated in the *POM in Action* box dealing with Mazda's worker selection. One team concept of particular note is the self-directed team. A **self-directed team** is a group of empowered individuals working together to reach a common goal. These teams may be organized for long-term or short-term objectives. The major reasons teams are effective are because they can easily provide employee empowerment, core job characteristics, and many of the psychological needs of team members.[8]

Self-directed team

Of course, many good job designs *can* provide these psychological needs. Therefore, to maximize team effectiveness, managers do more than just form "teams." For instance, they (1) ensure that those who have a legitimate contribution are on the team, (2) provide management support, (3) ensure the necessary training, and (4) endorse a clear objective for the team. Successful teams should also receive rewards and recognition. (A good example would be the Achievers Award at Honeywell, Canada.) Finally, managers must recognize that teams have a life cycle and that achieving an objective may suggest disbanding the team. However, teams may be renewed with a change in members or new assignments. Empowered employees working in teams can make a powerful contribution to world-class performance.

Teams and other approaches to job expansion should not only improve the quality of work life and job satisfaction, but also motivate employees to achieve organizational objectives. Both managers *and* employees need to be committed to achieving organizational objectives. However, employee contribution is fostered in a variety of ways, including organizational climate, supervisory action, *and* job/process design.

[6]See, for instance, the work of Abraham H. Maslow, "A Theory of Human Motivation," *Psychological Review*, 50 (1943): 370–396; and Frederick Herzberg, B. Mausner, and B. B. Snyderman, *The Motivation to Work* (New York: John Wiley, 1965).

[7]See "Motivation Through the Design of Work," in Jay Richard Hackman and Greg R. Oldham, *Work Redesign* (Reading, MA: Addison-Wesley, 1980).

[8]Per H. Engelstad, "Sociotechnical Approach to Problems of Process Control," in Louis E. Davis and James C. Taylor, eds., *Design of Jobs* (Santa Monica: Goodyear Publishing, 1979), pp. 184–205.

POM IN ACTION

How Does Mazda Pick Workers for Its U.S. Plants? Very Carefully.

It was not long ago that the auto industry did not want educated people in its factories. As former United Auto Worker's President Douglas Fraser said, "You don't need to be a rocket scientist to assemble a car." But a new breed of auto worker is emerging. Over a quarter of the workers just hired for a new shift at a Chrysler plant in Ontario, Canada, have college degrees.

Mazda Motors' assembly plant in Flat Rock, Michigan, is even pickier, hiring only 1,300 of nearly 10,000 applicants who passed its five-step screening process. It spent about $40 million—roughly $13,000 per employee—to staff the plant. The Japanese firm believes the key to success is picking the best employees and training them well.

A clear goal emerges. Interpersonal skills and team participation are mandatory. The basic philosophy: reward flows not so much from your personal performance as from your impact on team and company.

In Mazda training rooms, employees learn to chart quality by building paper airplanes and checking their flight performance. "If a part doesn't meet specifications," they are told, "you reject it. That's your job." Mazda devotes 3 training days just to the philosophy of *Kaizen,* or continual improvement. After 3 weeks of this "basic training," each new hire spends 5 to 7 weeks on specific technical training and then 3 to 4 weeks being supervised on the assembly line.

Overkill? Maybe, but Mazda is not taking any chances. The company believes that teams are the key to its success and wants to build its plant around that concept from scratch.

Sources: Wall Street Journal (March 11, 1994): A-1; and *Business Week* (October 3, 1988): 84–85.

Expanded job designs allow the employee to accept more responsibility. For employees who accept this responsibility, we may well expect some enhancement in productivity and product quality. Among the other positive aspects of job expansion are reduced turnover, tardiness, and absenteeism. Managers who expand jobs and build communication systems that elicit suggestions from employees have an added potential for efficiency. But as the *POM in Action* box "World-Class Standards Are Tough" suggests, there is no guarantee that productivity or quality will improve with the use of job expansion. These job designs have a number of limitations.

LIMITATIONS OF JOB EXPANSION. If job designs that enlarge, enrich, empower, and use teams are so good, why are they not universally used? Let us identify some limitations of these expanded job designs:

1. *Higher Capital Cost.* Job expansion requires facilities that cost more than a conventional layout. This extra expenditure must be generated through savings (greater efficiency) or through higher prices.
2. *Many Individuals Prefer Simple Jobs.* Some studies indicate that many employees opt for the less complex jobs.[9] In a discussion about improving the quality of work life, we cannot forget the importance of individual differences. Differences in individuals provide latitude for the resourceful operations manager when designing jobs.

[9]Michell Fein, "Job Enrichment Does Not Work," *Atlanta Economic Review* (November/December 1975): 50–54.

POM IN ACTION

World-Class Standards Are Tough

In 1988, Volvo opened its car-assembly factory in Uddevalla, Sweden, and claimed leadership in a bold experiment in job design. Volvo's chairperson wanted to prove that the craftsman approach of having a small team of highly skilled workers build an entire car, when linked with advanced materials handling, could compete after all.

The Uddevalla approach of cutting out layers of management and removing all forepersons aimed to give workers more control over their jobs, reduce the tedium of the assembly line, and encourage workers to broaden their skills. In doing so, Volvo hoped also to tackle the special Swedish problems of absenteeism and turnover, which are among the highest in the developed world.

But as the chart shows, it took 50 hours of labour to assemble a car at Uddevalla, compared with 37 hours at Volvo's 17-year-old plant at Kalmar, and 25 hours at its conventional assembly line in Ghent, Belgium. Finally, Volvo conceded that the Uddevalla plant could not achieve world-class productivity levels, and it closed the plant. The Kalmar plant may be the next victim of world-class standards.

COMPANY	LOCATION	HOURS	REGIONAL AVERAGES	
Volvo	Ghent, Belgium	25	Japan—domestic	17
Volvo	Kalmar, Sweden	37	Japan—United States	22
Volvo	Uddevalla, Sweden	50	United States—domestic	25
			Europe	36

Sources: Sloan Management Review (Winter 1994): 32–39, and (Spring 1993): 85–94; and *Personnel Management* (June 1993): 34–38.

3. *Higher Wage Rates Are Required.* People often receive wages for their highest skills, not their lowest.[10] So, expanded jobs may well require a higher average wage than jobs that are not.
4. *Smaller Labour Pool Exists.* Because expanded jobs require more skill and acceptance of more responsibility, the job requirements have increased. Depending upon the availability of labour, this may be a constraint.
5. *Increased Accident Rates May Occur.* Expanded jobs may contribute to a higher accident rate.[11] This indirectly increases wages, insurance costs, and worker's compensation.
6. *Current Technology May Not Lend Itself to Job Expansion.* The disassembly jobs at a slaughterhouse and computer assembly jobs are that way because alternative technologies (if any) are thought to be unacceptable.

These six points provide the constraints on job expansion. These practices increase costs. Therefore, for the firm to have a competitive advantage, its savings must be greater than its cost. It is not always obvious that such is the case. The strategic decision is not an easy one.

Motivation and Incentive Systems

Our discussion of psychology provides insight into the factors that may contribute to job satisfaction and motivation. In addition to these psychological factors, there are

[10]Charles Babbage, *On the Economy of Machinery and Manufacturers* (London, 1832), Chapter 18.

[11]J. Tsaari and J. Lahtella, "Job Enrichment: Cause of Increased Accidents?" *Industrial Engineering* (October 1978): 41–45.

monetary factors. Money often serves as a psychological, as well as a financial motivator. Monetary rewards take the form of bonuses, profit and gain sharing, and incentive systems.

Bonuses, typically in cash or stock options, are often used at the executive level to reward management. **Profit-sharing** systems provide some part of the profit for distribution to employees. A variation of profit sharing is gain sharing. **Gain-sharing** techniques reward employees for improvements made in an organization's performance. **Incentive systems** based on individual or group productivity are used in close to half of the manufacturing firms in Canada. These systems are often based on the employee or crew achieving production above a predetermined standard. The standard can be based on a standard time per task or number of pieces made. Standard time systems are sometimes called **measured daywork**, where employees are paid based on the amount of standard time accomplished. A **piece-rate** system assigns a standard time for each piece, and the employee is paid based on the number of pieces made. Both measured daywork and piece-rate systems typically guarantee the employee at least a base rate for the shift.

Bonus
Profit sharing
Gain sharing
Incentive system
Measured daywork
Piece rate

Lean Production

When mutual trust and commitment are combined with good job designs/processes, lean production may be possible. Under **lean production**, highly trained employees are committed to removing waste and doing only those activities where value is added. Empowered employees analyze every detail of serving the customer and are increasingly successful in squeezing out waste. The concept of lean production varies substantially from a more traditional effort to make jobs ever more simple and require ever less training. Indeed, when effectively implemented, lean production utilizes the employee's *mental* as well as physical attributes to continually improve the production system. Because of a reasonable quality of work life and mutual trust, the employee buys into mutual commitment. In this way, the production process is constantly improving and ever higher levels of efficiency are achieved. Under lean production, the employee is not a robot; he or she is an empowered member of the organization who uses both mental and physical abilities to help serve the customer through ever higher levels of productivity.

Lean production

Ergonomics and Work Methods

As mentioned in Chapter 1, Frederick W. Taylor began the era of scientific management in the late 1800s.[12] He and his contemporaries began to examine personnel selection, work methods, labour standards, and motivation.

With the foundation provided by Taylor, we have developed a body of knowledge about people's capabilities and limitations. This knowledge is necessary because humans are a hand/eye animal possessing exceptional capabilities and some limitations. Because managers must design jobs that can be done, we now introduce a few of the issues related to people's capabilities and limitations.

Ergonomics has a place in sports as well as in the workplace. Here, a stationary swimmer in a 50,000 gallon tank swims against a pump-generated current while her oxygen intake is measured and evaluated.

[12]Frederick W. Taylor, *Scientific Management* (New York: Harper & Row, 1911), p. 204.

Ergonomics

ERGONOMICS. The operations manager is interested in building a good interface between human and machine. Studies of this interface are known as **ergonomics**. Ergonomics means "the study of work." (*Ergo* is from the Greek word for *work.*) In Canada, the term *human factors* is sometimes substituted for the word *ergonomics*.

Male and female adults come in limited configurations.[13] Therefore, design of tools and the workplace depends on the study of people to determine what they can and cannot do. Substantial data have been collected that provide basic strength and measurement data needed to design tools and the workplace. The design of the workplace can make the job easier or impossible. Additionally, we now have the ability, through the use of computer modelling, to analyze human motions and efforts.

Let us look briefly at one instance of human measurements, to determine the proper height for a writing desk. The desk has an optimum height depending on the size of the individual and the task to be performed. The common height for a writing desk is 29 inches. For typing or data entry at a CRT, the surface should be lower. The preferred chair and desk height should result in a very slight angle between the body and arm when the individual is viewed from the front and when the back is straight.[14] This is the critical measurement; it can be achieved via adjustment in either table or chair height.

OPERATOR INPUT TO MACHINES. Operator response to machines, be they hand tools, pedals, levers, or buttons, needs to be evaluated. Operations managers need to be sure that operators have the strength, reflexes, perception, and mental capacity to provide the necessary control. The discussion of carpal tunnel syndrome in the photo shows what can happen when a tool as simple as a keyboard is poorly designed. Figure 11.3 indicates recent innovations designed to improve this common tool.

FEEDBACK TO OPERATORS. Feedback to operators is provided by sight, sound, and feel; it should not be left to chance. The mishap at the Three Mile Island nuclear facility, America's worst nuclear experience, was in large part the result of poor feedback to the operators about reactor performance. Nonfunctional groups of large, unclear instruments and inaccessible controls, combined with hundreds of confusing warning lights, contributed to that nuclear failure. Such relatively simple issues make a difference in operator response and therefore performance.

THE WORK ENVIRONMENT. The physical environment in which employees work affects their performance, safety, and quality of work life. Illumination, noise and vibration, temperature, humidity, and air quality are work environment factors under the control of the organization and the operations manager. The manager must approach them as controllable.

Illumination is necessary, but the proper level depends upon the work being performed. Figure 11.4 provides some guidelines. However, other factors of lighting are important. These other factors include reflective ability, contrast of the work surface with surroundings, glare, and shadows.

Noise of some form is usually present in the work area, and many employees seem to adjust well. However, high levels of sound will damage hearing. Figure 11.5 provides indications of the sound generated by various activities. Extended periods of

[13]Henry Dreyfuss, *The Measure of Man* (New York: Whitney Library of Design, 1960).

[14]Edwin R. Tichauer, "Biomechanics Sustains Occupational Safety and Health," *Industrial Engineering* (February 1976): 46–55.

FIGURE 11.3 ■ Job Design and the Keyboard

Apple Computers' new adjustable keyboard is divided into two hinged sections that can be customized. (Apple Computers, Cupertino, California)

Most of the usual QWERTY letter layout is retained, but tests indicate that the keyboard is less physically demanding and more comfortable to use than a traditional computer keyboard. The keyboard is a closer fit to the natural shape of the hand. (Kinesis Corp., Bellevue, Washington)

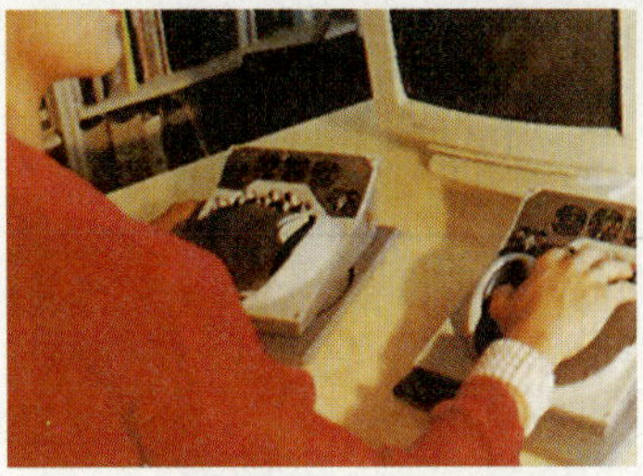

The "DataHand" keyboard allows each hand to rest on its own ergonomically shaped and padded palm support. Five keys surround each fingertip and thumb. (Industrial Innovations, Inc., Scottsdale, Arizona)

exposure to levels above 85 decibels are permanently damaging to hearing. The Occupational Safety and Health Administration (OSHA) requires ear protection above this level if exposure equals or exceeds 8 hours. Even at low levels, noise and vibration can be distracting. Therefore, most managers make substantial effort to reduce noise and vibration through good machine design, enclosures, or segregation of sources of noise and vibration.

Temperature and humidity parameters have been well established. Managers with activities operating outside of the established comfort zone should expect some adverse effect on performance.

FIGURE 11.4 ■ Levels of Illumination Recommended for Various Task Conditions.

Task Condition	Type of Task or Area	Illumination Level (luces)*	Type of Illumination
Small detail, extreme accuracy	Sewing, inspecting dark materials	1000	Overhead ceiling lights and desk lamp
Normal detail, prolonged periods	Reading, parts assembly, general office work	200–500	Overhead ceiling lights
Good contrast, fairly large objects	Recreational facilities	50–100	Overhead ceiling lights
Large objects	Restaurants, stairways, warehouses	20–50	Overhead ceiling lights

*The source states the data in foot-candles. The foot-candle is a measure of illumination equal to 10.76 luces (sing. *lux*).

(*Sources:* C. T. Morgan, J. S. Cook III, A. Chapanis, and M. W. Lund, eds., *Human Engineering Guide to Equipment Design*, New York: McGraw-Hill, 1963; Illuminating Engineering Society of North America, New York, NY).

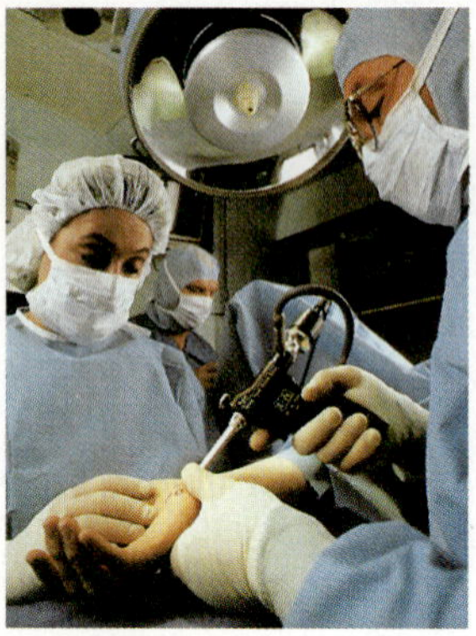

Carpal tunnel syndrome is a wrist disorder that afflicts 23,000 workers annually and costs employers and insurers an average of $30,000 per affected worker. Many of the tools, handles, and typewriter keyboards now in use put the wrists in an unnatural position. An unnatural position, combined with extended repetition, can cause this syndrome. One of the medical procedures for carpal tunnel syndrome is the operation shown here that reduces the symptoms; but the cure is in the ergonomics of work place and tool design.

FIGURE 11.5 ■ Decibel (dB) Levels for Various Sounds. Decibel levels are A-weighted sound levels measured with a sound-level meter.

Environment Noises	Common Noise Sources	Decibels	
	Jet takeoff (61 m)	120	
Casting shakeout area	Riveting machine*	110	
Electric furnace area	Pneumatic peen hammer*	100	Very annoying
	Textile weaving plant*		
Printing press plant	Subway train (6.1 m)	90	
	Pneumatic drill (15.2 m)	80	Ear protection required if exposed for 8 or more hours
Inside sports car (80.5 km/h)	Freight train (30.5 m)		
	Vacuum cleaner (3 m)	70	
Near freeway (auto traffic)	Speech (0.3 m)		Intrusive
Large store		60	
Private business office			
Light traffic (30.5 m)	Large transformer (61 m)	50	Quiet
Minimum levels, residential areas in large city at night		40	
	Soft whisper (1.5 m)		
Studio (speech)		30	Very quiet
		20	
		10	Threshold of hearing

*At operator's position

(*Source:* Adapted from A.P.G. Peterson and E. E. Gross, Jr., *Handbook of Noise Measurement*, 7th ed. (New Concord, MA: General Radio Co.)).

METHODS ANALYSIS. Methods analysis focusses on *how* a task is accomplished. Whether controlling a machine or making or assembling components, how a task is done makes a difference in performance, safety, and quality. Using knowledge from ergonomics and methods analysis, methods engineers are charged with ensuring that quality and quantity standards are achieved efficiently and safely. Methods analysis and related techniques are useful in office environments as well as in the factory. The techniques include flow diagrams, process charts, activity charts, and operations charts.

Flow diagrams

Process charts

Flow diagrams are schematics (drawings) used to investigate movement of people or material. They provide a systematic procedure for looking at long-cycle repetitive tasks (Figure 11.6). **Process charts** use symbols (Figure 11.7) to help us understand the movement of people or material. In this way, movement and delays can be reduced and operations made more efficient. Figure 11.7 shows an actual process chart used to supplement the flow diagram shown in Figure 11.6.

Activity charts

Activity charts are used to study and improve utilization of an operator and a machine or some combination of operators (a "crew") and machines. Through observation, the analyst records the present method (see Figure 11.8) and then on a second chart the proposed improvement.

FIGURE 11.6 ■ Flow Diagram of Axle-Stand Production Line at Paddy Hopkirk Factory: (a) old method; (b) new method.

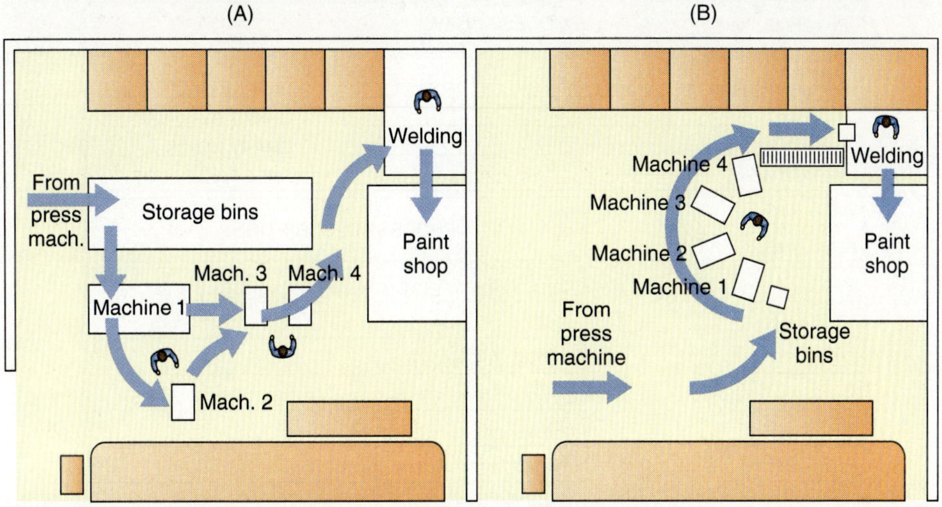

(*Source: Financial Times* [January 4, 1994].)

Body movement is analyzed by an **operations chart**. It is designed to show economy of motion by pointing out wasted motion and idle time (delay). The operations chart (also known as left-hand, right-hand chart) is shown in Figure 11.9.

Operations charts

LABOUR STANDARDS

So far in this chapter, we have discussed labour planning and job design. The third requirement of an effective human resource strategy is the establishment of labour standards. Effective manpower planning is dependent upon a knowledge of the labour required.

Labour standards are the amount of time required to perform a job or part of a job. Every firm has labour standards, although they may vary from those established via informal methods to those established by professionals. Only when accurate labour standards exist can management know what its labour requirements are, what its costs should be, and what constitutes a fair day's work. Techniques for setting labour standards are presented in the supplement to this chapter.

Labour standards

ACHIEVING WORLD-CLASS STANDARDS

World-class producers realize the importance of an effective human resource strategy. Good job design, manpower planning, and an environment of mutual commitment and trust are recognized by all members of the organization as critical to world-class performance. World-class firms have high training budgets, most well in excess of 40 hours per year per employee, and some as high as 200 hours. Employees are trained in problem solving and teamwork, and teams are encouraged and supported. Training

Disasters at nuclear power plants in the United States (Three Mile Island) and in the Ukraine (Chernobyl) have frightened federal and local regulators into increasingly stricter maintenance and reliability standards. At Pickering, Ontario, the AECB has given the plant until early 1997 to meet certain standards or lose their licence to operate. Some experts believe that there is still insufficient attention given to the human side of reactor control systems. Designers, they believe, do not appreciate the fact that plants are man-machine systems.

FIGURE 11.7 ■ Process Chart of Axle-Stand Production Using Paddy Hopkirk's New Method Shown in the Flow Diagram (Figure 11.6b)

Present Method ☐ PROCESS CHART
Proposed Method ☒
SUBJECT CHARTED Axle-stand Production DATE 1/1/96
CHART BY JH
CHART NO. 1
DEPARTMENT Work cell for axle stand SHEET NO. 1 OF 1

DIST. IN FEET	TIME IN MINS.	CHART SYMBOLS	PROCESS DESCRIPTION
50		○ ⇨ □ D ▽	From press machine to storage bins at work cell
	3	○ ⇨ □ D ▽	Storage bins
5		○ ⇨ □ D ▽	Move to machine 1
	4	○ ⇨ □ D ▽	Operation at machine 1
4		○ ⇨ □ D ▽	Move to machine 2
	2.5	○ ⇨ □ D ▽	Operation at machine 2
4		○ ⇨ □ D ▽	Move to machine 3
	3.5	○ ⇨ □ D ▽	Operation at machine 3
4		○ ⇨ □ D ▽	Move to machine 4
	4	○ ⇨ □ D ▽	Operation at machine 4
20		○ ⇨ □ D ▽	Move to welding
	Poka-yoke	○ ⇨ □ D ▽	Poka-yoke inspection at welding
	4	○ ⇨ □ D ▽	Weld
10		○ ⇨ □ D ▽	Move to painting
	4	○ ⇨ □ D ▽	Paint
		○ ⇨ □ D ▽	
97	30		Total

○ = operation; ⇨ = transportation; □ = inspection; D = delay; ▽ = storage.

also includes tools such as flow process diagrams and charts, activity charts, and micromotion charts. These organizations have designed jobs that use both the mental and physical capabilities of their employees. Most world-class organizations have a human resource strategy that has many of the attributes of lean production and provides a competitive advantage.

SUMMARY

How well a firm manages its human resource strategy ultimately determines its success. The P/OM activity usually has a large role to play in achieving human resource objectives. The first objective is to achieve efficient use of human resources within the operations function. This is often a major goal of a firm because operations is usually the function with the highest labour cost, and labour is often a large part of the total cost of the product. The second objective is the design of jobs that are effective, safe, and provide a reasonable quality of work life for the employee in an atmosphere of mutual respect.

FIGURE 11.8 ■ Activity Chart

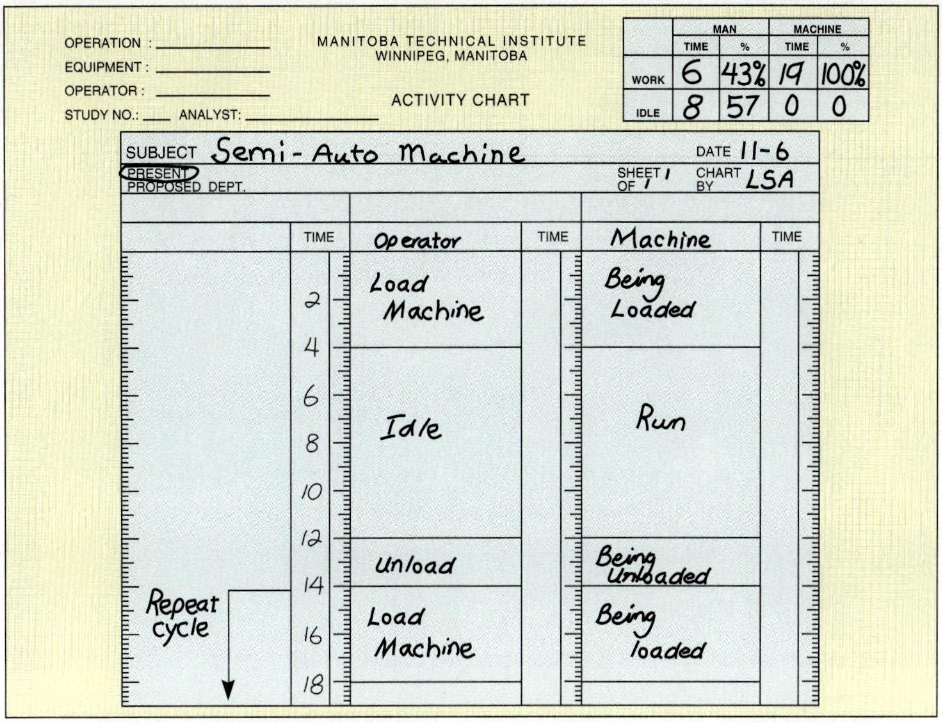

(*Source:* Adapted from L. S. Aft, *Productivity Measurement and Improvement,* © 1983, p. 67. Reprinted by permission of Prentice Hall, Inc., Englewood Cliffs, NJ.)

FIGURE 11.9 ■ Operations Chart (Left-Hand/Right-Hand Chart) for Bolt-Washer Assembly.

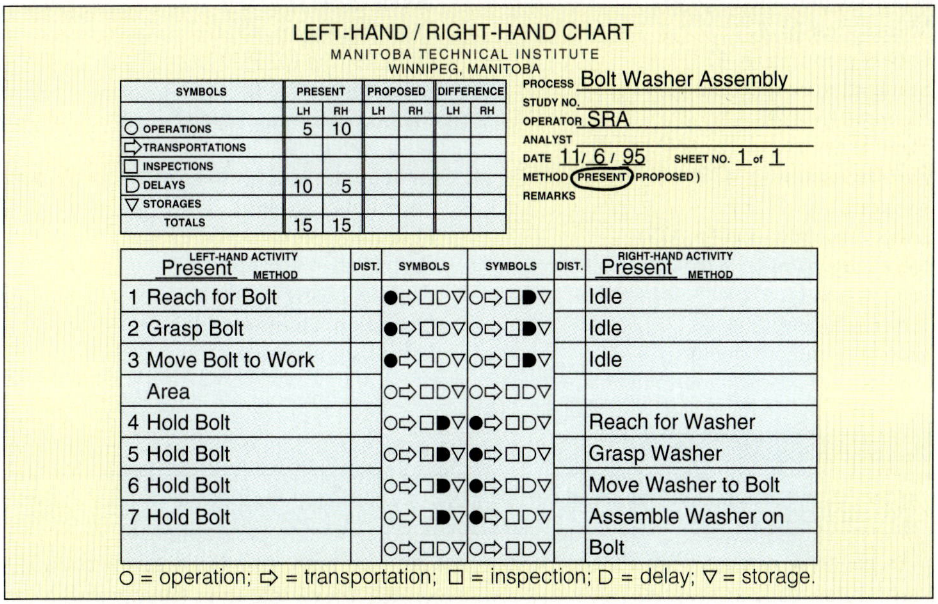

LEFT-HAND / RIGHT-HAND CHART
MANITOBA TECHNICAL INSTITUTE
WINNIPEG, MANITOBA

SYMBOLS	PRESENT LH	PRESENT RH	PROPOSED LH	PROPOSED RH	DIFFERENCE LH	DIFFERENCE RH
○ OPERATIONS	5	10				
⇨ TRANSPORTATIONS						
□ INSPECTIONS						
D DELAYS	10	5				
▽ STORAGES						
TOTALS	15	15				

PROCESS Bolt Washer Assembly
STUDY NO.
OPERATOR SRA
ANALYST
DATE 11/6/95 SHEET NO. 1 of 1
METHOD (PRESENT) PROPOSED
REMARKS

LEFT-HAND ACTIVITY Present METHOD	DIST.	SYMBOLS	SYMBOLS	DIST.	RIGHT-HAND ACTIVITY Present METHOD
1 Reach for Bolt		●⇨□D▽	○⇨□◗▽		Idle
2 Grasp Bolt		●⇨□D▽	○⇨□◗▽		Idle
3 Move Bolt to Work		●⇨□D▽	○⇨□◗▽		Idle
Area		○⇨□D▽	○⇨□D▽		
4 Hold Bolt		○⇨□◗▽	●⇨□D▽		Reach for Washer
5 Hold Bolt		○⇨□◗▽	●⇨□D▽		Grasp Washer
6 Hold Bolt		○⇨□◗▽	●⇨□D▽		Move Washer to Bolt
7 Hold Bolt		○⇨□◗▽	●⇨□D▽		Assemble Washer on
		○⇨□D▽	○⇨□D▽		Bolt

○ = operation; ⇨ = transportation; □ = inspection; D = delay; ▽ = storage.

(*Source:* Adapted from L. S. Aft, *Productivity Measurement and Improvement,* 1983, p. 75. Reprinted by permission of Prentice Hall, Inc., Englewood Cliffs, NJ.)

Performance during a pit stop makes a difference between winning and losing a race. Activity charts are used to orchestrate the movement of members of a pit crew, an operating room staff, or machine operators in a factory. Solved Problem 11.1 shows an activity chart applied to a pit crew.

KEY TERMS

Quality of work life (p. 472)
Mutual commitment (p. 472)
Mutual trust (p. 472)
Labour planning (p. 473)
Standard work schedule (p. 474)
Flextime (p. 474)
Flexible work week (p. 474)
Part-time status (p. 475)
Job design (p. 475)
Labour specialization (p. 475)
Job enlargement (p. 476)
Job rotation (p. 476)
Job enrichment (p. 476)
Employee empowerment (p. 476)
Self-directed team (p. 478)
Bonus (p. 481)
Profit sharing (p. 481)
Gain sharing (p. 481)
Incentive system (p. 481)
Measured daywork (p. 481)
Piece rate (p. 481)
Lean production (p. 481)
Ergonomics (p. 482)
Flow diagrams (p. 484)
Process charts (p. 484)
Activity charts (p. 484)
Operations charts (p. 485)
Labour standards (p. 485)

SOLVED PROBLEM

Solved Problem 11.1

As pit crew manager for Prototype Sports Car, you have just been given the pit stop rules for next season. You will be allowed only six people over the pit wall at any one time and one of these must be a designated *fire extinguisher/safety* crew member. This person must carry a fire extinguisher and may not service the car. However, the fire extinguisher/safety person may also signal the driver where to stop the car in the pit lane and when to leave the pit.

You expect to have air jacks on this year's car. These built-in jacks require the use of only an air hose to make them work. Fuel will also be supplied via a hose, with a second hose used for venting air from the fuel cells. The rate of flow for the fuel hose will be 4.4 litres per second. The tank will hold 110 litres. You expect to have to change all four tires on most pit stops. The length of the races will vary this year, but you expect that the longer races will also require the changing of drivers. Recent stopwatch studies have verified the following times for your experienced crew. These times are as follows:

Activity	Time in Minutes
Install air hose	.075
Remove tire	.125
Mount new tire	.125
Move to air jack hose	.050
Move to rear of car	.050
Help driver	.175
Wipe windshield	.175
Load fuel (per litre)	.016

Your job is to develop the initial plan for the best way to utilize your six-person pit crew. The six crew are identified with letters, as shown in Figure 11.10. You decide to use an activity chart similar to the one shown in Figure 11.8 to aid you.

FIGURE 11.10 ■ Position of Car and Six Crewmen (see chart on next page)

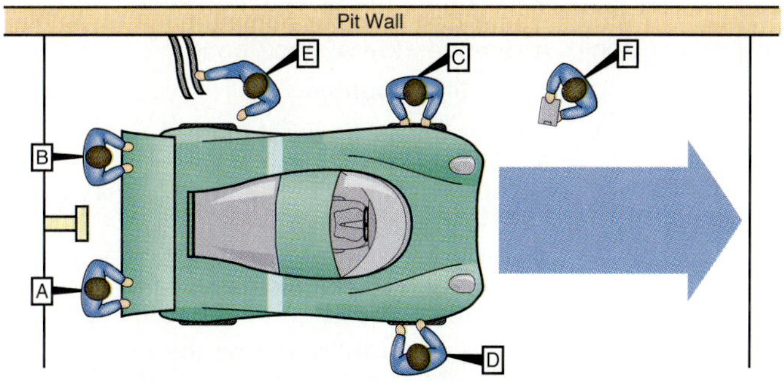

Solution

Your activity chart showing each member of the crew what they are to do during each second of the pit stop is shown in the chart.

FIGURE 11.10 ■ *(Continued)*

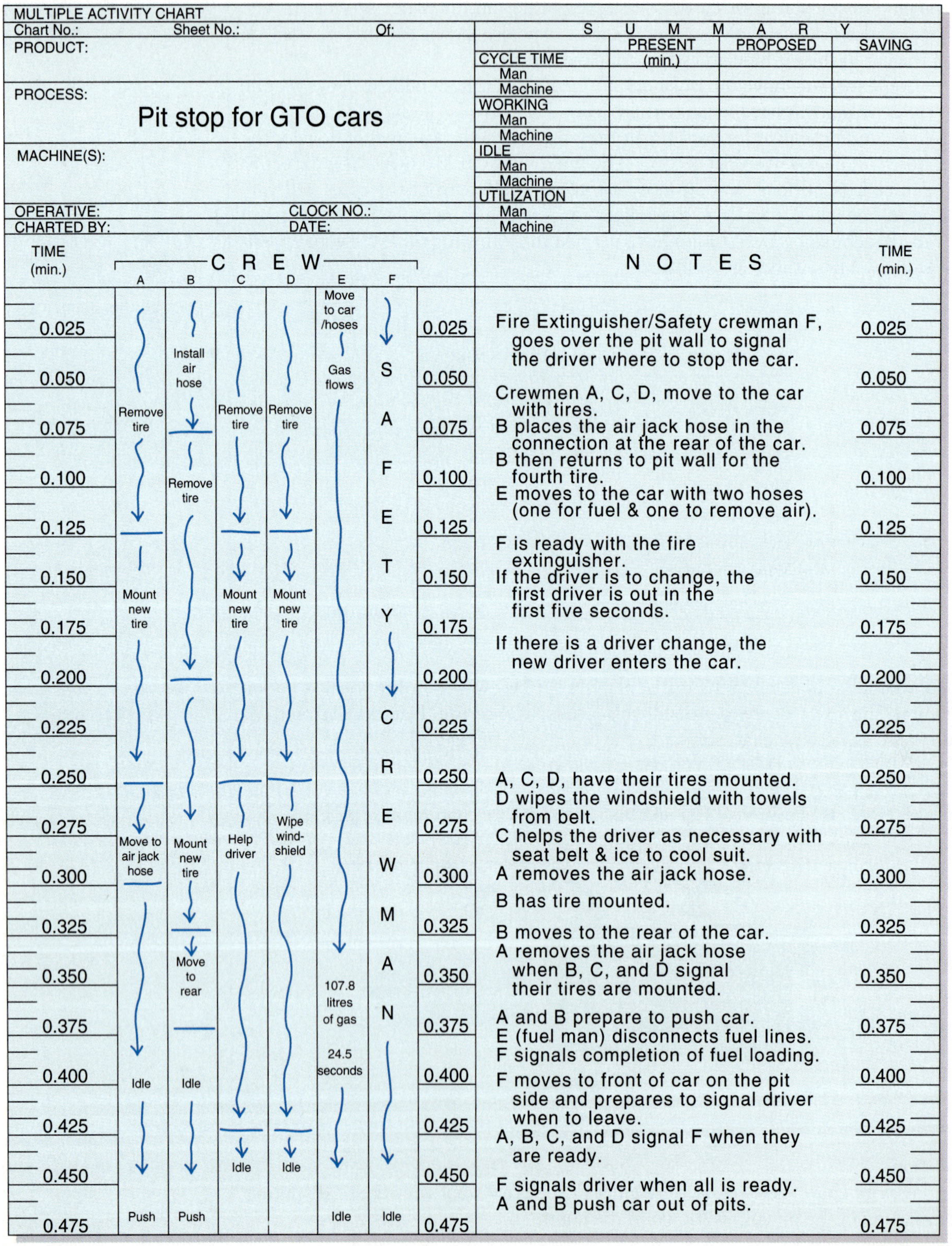

DISCUSSION QUESTIONS

1. What are some of the worst jobs you know about? Why are they bad jobs? Why do people want these jobs?
2. What factor would you add to, or delete from, the psychological factors given in the chapter?
3. If you were redesigning the job described in Question 1, what changes would you make? Are your changes realistic? Would they improve productivity (not just production, but productivity)?
4. How would you define a good quality of work life?
5. What is the difference between job enrichment, job enlargement, job rotation, job specialization, and employee empowerment?
6. Do you know of any jobs that push the man-machine interface to the limits of human capabilities?
7. Why prepare flow diagrams and process charts for tasks that are poorly done?
8. What are the six core characteristics of a good job design?

CRITICAL THINKING EXERCISE

In October 1992 two employees of Canron Inc. were working on the erection of a flash furnace when a 4.4 tonne beam being hoisted by a crane slipped out of its clamp and fell on them, killing them. Canron was fined $300,000 for failing to ensure that a beam clamp was suitable for its intended use and $200,000 for failing to warn workers that steel was being hoisted overhead. Canron was in violation of two counts of the Occupational Health and Safety Act.

The company appealed the conviction and the fines, the highest ever imposed in a contested health and safety trial in Canada. Counsel for the company argued that the fines were excessive. In other cases of this nature, certain considerations were taken into account, such as the size of the company, the scope of economic activity at issue, the extent of the actual and potential harm to the public, and the maximum penalty prescribed by statute. Also, they argued that the behaviour of the company in complying with Labour Ministry guidelines on health and safety, the safety training given by the company, the financial position of the company, and the expense already incurred by the company as a result of the accident had not been considered. In the past Canron had always cooperated with the Ministry. Canron had already had three previous convictions.

What decision would you make with regard to the size of the fines?

Do you feel that the company was in fact negligent in its duties toward the employees?

What should the Labour Ministry propose to the company so that this type of accident does not happen again?

PROBLEMS

- **11.1** Make a process chart for going from the living room to the kitchen for a glass, to the refrigerator for milk, and to a kitchen cabinet for cookies. Use a layout of your choosing. How can you make the task more efficient (that is, less time or fewer steps)?
- **11.2** Draw an activity chart for a machine operator with the following operation. The relevant times are as follows:

Prepare mill for loading (cleaning, oiling, and so on)	.50 min.
Load mill	1.75 min.
Mill operating (cutting material)	2.25 min.
Unload mill	.75 min.

: **11.3** Draw an activity chart (a multiactivity chart) for a concert (for example, Phil Collins, Neil Diamond, The Grateful Dead, Bruce Springsteen) and determine how to put the concert together so the star has reasonable breaks. For instance, at what point is there an instrumental number, a visual effect, a duet, a dance moment, that allows the star to pause and rest physically or at least rest his voice? Do other members of the show have moments of pause or rest?

• **11.4** Make an operations chart of one of the following:

a) Putting a new eraser in (or on) a pencil.

b) Putting a paper clip on two pieces of paper.

c) Putting paper in a typewriter.

• **11.5** Having made the operations chart in Problem 11.4 and now being told that you were going to do the task 10,000 times, how would you improve the procedure? Prepare an operations chart of the improved task. What motion, time, and effort have you saved over the life of the task by redesigning it?

• **11.6** For a job you have had, rate each of Hackman and Oldham's core job characteristics on a scale from 1 to 10. What is your total score? What about the job could have been changed so you would be inclined to give it a higher score?

: **11.7** Using the data provided in Solved Problem 11.1, prepare an activity chart (a crew chart) similar to the one in the solved problem, but based on having a total of only five crew members.

: **11.8** Using the data provided in Solved Problem 11.1, prepare an activity chart similar to the one in the solved problem. However, fuel will now be delivered at the rate of 5½ litres per second.

CASE STUDY

The Lanark Anthropological Society

1995 marked the 125th anniversary of the Lanark Anthropological Society. Judging from the public patronage and support, the following exhibits had been resounding successes: The Golden People—Aztecs; Tutankhamen—Egyptian Sun God; Finding the Titanic; Treasures of the Bible; and The Lost Civilization of Mu.

However, of major concern to the Board of Trustees was the lack of "team spirit" among the three major factions at the Society: senior management, curators, and the administration—a lack that had resulted in the low pace of development of new exhibits and fear that higher costs for new exhibits would need to be faced. A further matter of concern was the poor communication between the various sections of the Society and between the Society and the public.

The CEO of the Society, Dr. Finlay Currie, in his 1995 report, said: "There is a particular challenge facing the Society which I describe as the need to forge from the several parts of the institution a unified Society that has developed common goals and at the same time time encouraged diversity of effort, emphasis, and responsibility."

To attract additional funding from the public, the Society needed to promote a high profile in public programs and projects. Anything that did not enhance this high profile would have a lower prioroty in the public's eyes.

DISCUSSION QUESTIONS

1. Since you have been introduced to human resource strategy, what action should the Society take to develop the "team spirit"?
2. How can poor communications between the three factions of the society, and between the society and the public, be eliminated?

BIBLIOGRAPHY

Alexander, D. C. *Industrial Ergonomics: A Practitioner's Guide*. Norcross, GA: IE & MP Publishers, 1985.

Barnes, R. M. *Motion and Time Study, Design and Measurement of Work*. New York: John Wiley, 1968.

Berggren, C. *Alternatives to Lean Production: Work Organization in the Swedish Auto Industry*. Ithaca, NY: ILR Press, 1993.

———. "Point/Counterpoint: Nummi vs. Uddevalla." *Sloan Management Review*, 35, no. 2 (Winter 1994): 37–50.

Bowen, D. E., G. E. Ledford, Jr., and B. R. Nathan. "Hiring for the Organization, Not the Job." *The Executive*, 5, no. 4 (November 1991): 35.

Carson, R. "Ergonomically Designed Tools: Selecting the Right Tool for the Job." *Industrial Engineering*, 25, no. 7 (July 1993): 27–29.

Chapman, A. *Man-Machine Engineering*. Belmont, CA: Wadsworth, 1965.

Corlett, N., J. Wilson, F. Manencia, eds. *Ergonomics of Working Posture*. New York: Taylor and Francis, 1986.

Denton, D. K. "Redesigning A Job by Simplifying Every Task and Responsibility." *Industrial Engineering*, 24, no. 8 (August 1992): 46.

Dreyfuss, H. *The Measure of Man*. New York: Whitney Library of Design, 1970.

Franke, R. H. "The Ultimate Advantage: Creating the High-Involvement Organization." *The Executive*, 7, no. 1 (February 1993): 105–106.

Hall, G., J. Rosenthal, and J. Wade. "How to Make Reengineering Really Work." *Harvard Business Review*, 71, no. 6 (November/December 1993): 119–131.

Konz, S. *Work Design*. Columbia, OH: Grid, 1979.

McCormick, E. J. *Human Factors in Engineering and Design*, 4th ed. New York: McGraw-Hill, 1976.

Mesch, D. J., and D. R. Dalton. "Unexpected Consequences of Improving Workplace Justice: A Six-Year Time Series Assessment." *The Academy of Management Journal*, 35, no. 5 (December 1992): 1,099.

Meyer, C. "How the Right Measures Help Teams Excel." *Harvard Business Review* (May/June 1994): 95.

Snell, S., and J. Dean. "Integrated Manufacturing and Human Resource Management: A Human Capital Perspective." *The Academy of Management Journal*, 35, 3 (August 1992): 467–497.

Staughton, R. V. W., N. J. Kinnie, E. H. Davies, and R. L. C. Smith. "Modelling the Manufacturing Strategy Process: An Analysis of the Role Played by Human Resources Issues." *OM Review*, 9, no. 2 (April 1992): 48–68.

Stepkin, R. L., and R. E. Mosely, eds. *Noise Control: A Guide for Workers and Employers*. American Society of Safety Engineers, 1984.

Zammuto, R. F., and E. J. O'Connor. "Gaining Advanced Manufacturing Technologies' Benefits: The Roles of Organization Design and Culture." *The Academy of Management Review*, 17, no. 4 (October 1992): 701.

11 SUPPLEMENT

WORK MEASUREMENT

SUPPLEMENT OUTLINE

It was 2:36 P.M. and the 132 workers on the American Plastics Inc. factory floor were busy manning their noisy machines. When Bob Markland, a newly hired engineer, entered this production area through an office door, he was dressed in a white shirt and tie and carried a clipboard. He strode purposefully to his destination, the lathe area where he was to time three workers whose labour standards had not been updated in a decade. One pair of eyes after another followed his movement, almost like a wave building as it approaches the shore. Before Markland was within 15 metres of his target, a loud whistle blew. The shop's union steward, Roscoe Davis, had just called a work stoppage. A "suit" was on the floor to time workers without union authorization. American Plastics was silent. ♦

LABOUR STANDARDS AND WORK MEASUREMENT

Effective management of people requires knowledge of labour standards. Even though employees and unions may be opposed to jobs being observed and timed, as in the preceding quotation, labour standards are necessary. They help a firm determine the

1. labour content of items produced (the labour cost);
2. staffing needs of organizations (how many people it will take to make the required production);
3. cost and time estimates prior to production (to assist in a variety of decisions from developing cost estimates for customers, to the make-or-buy decision);
4. crew size and work balance (who does what on a group activity or assembly line);
5. production expected (both manager and worker should know what constitutes a fair day's work);
6. basis of wage-incentive plans (what provides a reasonable incentive);
7. efficiency of employees and supervision (a standard is necessary against which to determine efficiency).

Properly set labour standards represent the amount of time it should take an average employee to perform specific job activities under normal working conditions. The *POM in Action* box "Glegg Water Conditioning, Inc." indicates an incentive system application of effective labour standards.

How are labour, or production, standards set? Labour standards are set five ways:

1. historical experience;
2. time studies;
3. predetermined time standards;
4. time standard team approach;
5. work sampling.

This supplement covers each of these techniques.

HISTORICAL EXPERIENCE

Labour standards can be estimated on the basis of *historical experience*, that is, how many labour-hours were required to do a task the last time it was performed. Historical standards do have the distinct advantage of being relatively easy and inexpensive to obtain. They are usually available from employee time cards or production records. But they are not objective, and we do not know their accuracy, whether they represent a reasonable or a poor work pace, and if unusual occurrences are included. Because these variables are unknown, their use is not recommended. Instead time studies, predetermined time standards, and work sampling are preferred to set production standards.

TIME STUDIES

The classical stopwatch study, or time study, originally proposed by Frederick W. Taylor in 1881, is still the most widely used time-study method. A **time-study** procedure

Time study

POM IN ACTION

Glegg Water Conditioning, Inc.

Robert Glegg started Glegg Water Conditioning (GWC) at the age of 26 and with only $10,000 to invest. GWC manufactures large industrial water purification systems that can deliver up to 20,000 litres of purified water a minute. These systems are used for everything from rinsing computer chips to generating steam in large industrial boilers. When GWC entered the market in 1978, it faced stiff competition from large, well-established players. Glegg didn't want to make the strategic error of overextending himself early in the game, so he focussed business development efforts to a limited number of industries within specific geographical areas. High-quality products, impeccable customer service, and competitive prices have been Glegg's priorities from day one. He pays particular attention to recruiting good people and motivating staff to excel. Glegg also initiated the company's Innovation Program, whereby staff, customers, and suppliers provide input on how to make continuous product and process improvements. These improvements have led to:

- An annual growth in sales of 22% since 1990
- Capturing a 20% market share in the United States
- Sales per employee exceeding $400,000

Robert Glegg's innovative entrepreneurial techniques have earned him a Certificate of Merit in the 1995 Canada Awards for Excellence for entrepreneurship.

Source: Adapted from "Robert Glegg—Glegg Water Conditioning, Inc." (The National Quality Institute, 1995).

involves timing a sample of a worker's performance and using it to set a standard. A trained and experienced person can establish a standard by following these eight steps:

1. Define the task to be studied (after methods analysis has been conducted).
2. Divide the task into precise elements (parts of a task that often take no more than a few seconds).
3. Decide how many times to measure the task (the number of cycles or samples needed).
4. Time and record the elemental times and ratings of performance.
5. **Average actual cycle time** Compute the average actual cycle time. The **average actual cycle time** is the arithmetic mean of the times for *each* element measured, adjusted for unusual influence for each element:

$$\text{Average actual cycle time} = \frac{\begin{pmatrix}\text{sum of the times recorded}\\ \text{to perform each element}\end{pmatrix}}{\text{number of cycles observed}} \qquad \text{(S11.1)}$$

6. **Normal time** Compute the **normal time** for each element. This measure is a "performance rating" for the particular worker pace observed:

$$\text{Normal time} = (\text{average actual cycle time}) \times (\text{rating factor}) \qquad \text{(S11.2)}$$

The performance rating adjusts the observed time to what a normal worker could expect to accomplish. For example, a normal worker should be able to walk 4.5 kilometres per hour. He or she should also be able to deal a deck of 52 cards into four equal piles in 30 seconds. There are numerous films specifying work pace on which professionals agree; and activity benchmarks have been

FIGURE S11.1 ■ Rest Allowances (in percentage) for Various Classes of Work.

1. Constant allowances:
   - (A) Personal allowance 5
   - (B) Basic fatigue allowance 4
2. Variable allowances:
   - (A) Standing allowance 2
   - (B) Abnormal position allowance:
     - (i) Awkward (bending) 2
     - (ii) Very awkward (lying, stretching) 7
   - (C) Use of force or muscular energy in lifting, pulling, pushing
     - Weight lifted (pounds):
     - 20 3
     - 40 9
     - 60 17
   - (D) Bad light:
     - (i) Well below recommended 2
     - (ii) Quite inadequate 5
   - (E) Atmospheric conditions (heat and humidity):
     - Variable 0–10
   - (F) Close attention:
     - (i) Fine or exacting 2
     - (ii) Very fine or very exacting 5
   - (G) Noise level:
     - (i) Intermittent—loud 2
     - (ii) Intermittent—very loud or high-pitched . . . 5
   - (H) Mental strain:
     - (i) Complex or wide span of attention 4
     - (ii) Very complex 8
   - (I) Tediousness:
     - (i) Tedious 2
     - (ii) Very tedious 5

Source: Excerpted from B. W. Niebel, *Motion and Time Study*, 7th ed. (Homewood, IL: Richard D. Irwin, 1982) p. 393. © 1982 by Richard D. Irwin, Inc.

established by the Society for the Advancement of Management. However, performance rating is still something of an art.

7. Add the normal times for each element to develop a total normal time for the task.
8. Compute the **standard time**. This adjustment to the total normal time provides for allowances such as *personal* needs, unavoidable work *delays*, and worker *fatigue*:

Standard time

$$\text{Standard time} = \frac{\text{total normal time}}{1 - \text{allowance factor}} \tag{S11.3}$$

Personal time allowances are often established in the range of 4% to 7% of total time, depending upon nearness to rest rooms, water fountains, and other facilities. Delay standards are often set as a result of the actual studies of the delay that occurs. Fatigue standards are based on our growing knowledge of human energy expenditure under various physical and environmental conditions. A sample set of personal and fatigue allowances is shown in Figure S11.1. Example S1 illustrates the computation of standard time.

EXAMPLE

The time study of a work operation yielded an average actual cycle time of 4.0 minutes. The analyst rated the observed worker at 85%. This means the worker performed at 85% of normal when the study was made. The firm uses a 13% allowance factor. We want to compute the standard time.

Average actual time = 4.0 min.

$$\text{Normal time} = (\text{average actual cycle time}) \times (\text{rating factor})$$
$$= (4.0)(.85)$$
$$= 3.4 \text{ min.}$$

$$\text{Standard time} = \frac{\text{normal time}}{1 - \text{allowance factor}} = \frac{3.4}{1 - .13} = \frac{3.4}{.87}$$
$$= 3.9 \text{ min.}$$

Example S2 works from a series of actual stopwatch times for each element.

EXAMPLE

Management Science Associates promotes its management development seminars by mailing thousands of individually typed letters to various firms. A time study has been done on the task of preparing letters for mailing. On the basis of the observations below, Management Science Associates wants to develop a time standard for the task. The firm's personal, delay, and fatigue allowance factor is 15%.

	Cycle Observed (in minutes)					
Job Element	**1**	**2**	**3**	**4**	**5**	**Performance Rating**
(A) Type letter	8	10	9	21*	11	120%
(B) Type envelope address	2	3	2	1	3	105%
(C) Stuff, stamp, seal, and sort envelopes	2	1	5*	2	1	110%

The procedure after the data have been collected is as follows:

1. Delete all unusual or nonrecurring observations such as those marked with an asterisk (*). (They might be due to an unscheduled business interruption, a conference with the boss, or a mistake of an unusual nature; these are not part of the job.)
2. Compute the average cycle time for each job element:

$$\text{Average time for A} = \frac{8 + 10 + 9 + 11}{4}$$
$$= 9.5 \text{ min.}$$

$$\text{Average time for B} = \frac{2 + 3 + 2 + 1 + 3}{5}$$
$$= 2.2 \text{ min.}$$

$$\text{Average time for C} = \frac{2 + 1 + 2 + 1}{4}$$
$$= 1.5 \text{ min.}$$

3. Compute the normal time for each job element:

$$\text{Normal time for A} = (\text{Average actual time}) \times (\text{Rating}) = (9.5)(1.2) = 11.4 \text{ min.}$$

$$\text{Normal time for B} = (2.2)(1.05) = 2.31 \text{ min.}$$

$$\text{Normal time for C} = (1.5)(1.10) = 1.65 \text{ min.}$$

Normal times are computed for each element because the rating factor may vary for each element, which it did in this case.

4. Add the normal times for each element to find the total normal time (the normal time for the whole job):

$$\text{Total normal time} = 11.40 + 2.31 + 1.65 = 15.36 \text{ min.}$$

5. Compute the standard time for the job:

$$\text{Standard time} = \frac{\text{total normal time}}{1 - \text{allowance factor}} = \frac{15.36}{1 - .15} = 18.07 \text{ min.}$$

Thus, 18.07 minutes is the time standard for this job.

Time study is a sampling process, and the question of sampling error in the average actual cycle time naturally arises. Error, according to statistics, varies inversely with sample size. In order to determine just how many cycles we should time, we must consider the variability of each element in the study.

To determine an adequate sample size, three items must be considered. They are as follows:

1. How accurate we want to be (for example, is ±5% of actual close enough?).
2. The desired level of confidence (for example, the z value; is 95% adequate or is 99% required?).
3. How much variation exists within the job elements (for example, if the variation is large, a larger sample will be required).

The formula for finding the appropriate sample size given these three variables is

$$n = \left(\frac{zs}{h\bar{x}}\right)^2 \qquad \text{(S11.4)}$$

where h = accuracy level desired in percent of the job element, expressed as a decimal (5% = .05)

z = number of standard deviations required for desired level of confidence (90% confidence = 1.65; see Table S11.1 for the more common z values)[1]

[1]The values of z for any desired confidence level can be found in Appendix A, "Normal Curve Areas."

Sleep Inn is showing the world that big gains in productivity can be made not only by manufacturers, but in the service industry as well. Designed with labour efficiency in mind, Sleep Inn is staffed with 13% fewer employees than similar budget hotels. Its features include a laundry room that is almost completely automated, round shower stalls that eliminate dirty corners, and closets that have no doors for maids to open and shut.

TABLE S11.1

DESIRED CONFIDENCE (%)	Z VALUE (STANDARD DEVIATION REQUIRED FOR DESIRED LEVEL OF CONFIDENCE)
90.0	1.65
95.0	1.96
95.4	2.00
99.0	2.58
99.7	3.00

s = standard deviation of the initial sample
$\bar{x}$ = mean of the initial sample.

We demonstrate with Example S3.

EXAMPLE

Thomas W. Jones Mfg. has asked you to check a labour standard prepared by a recently terminated analyst. Your first task is to determine the correct sample size. Your accuracy is to be within 5% and your confidence level to be 95%. The standard deviation of the sample is 1.0 and the mean is 3.00.

Solution:

$$h = .05 \qquad \bar{x} = 3.00 \qquad s = 1.0$$

$$z = 1.96 \text{ (from Table S11.1 or Appendix A)}$$

$$n = \left(\frac{zs}{h\bar{x}}\right)^2$$

$$n = \left(\frac{(1.96 \times 1.0)}{(.05 \times 3)}\right)^2 = 170.74 \approx 171$$

Therefore, you recommend a sample size of 171.

Let us look at two variations of Example S3.

First, if h, the desired accuracy, is expressed as an absolute amount of error (say, 1 minute of error is acceptable), then substitute e for $h\bar{x}$, and the appropriate formula is

$$n = \left(\frac{zs}{e}\right)^2 \qquad \text{(S11.5)}$$

where e is the absolute amount of acceptable error.

Second, for those cases when s, the standard deviation of the sample, is not provided (which is typically the case outside the classroom), it must be computed. The formula for doing so is

$$s = \sqrt{\frac{\Sigma(x_i - \bar{x})^2}{n-1}} = \sqrt{\frac{\Sigma(\text{each sample observation} - \bar{x})^2}{\text{number in sample} - 1}} \qquad \text{(S11.6)}$$

where x_i = value of each observation
$\bar{x}$ = mean of the observations
n = number of observations

An example of this computation is provided in Solved Problem S11.3.

Time studies provide accuracy in setting labour standards (see the *POM in Action* box on UPS), but they have two disadvantages. First, they require a trained staff of analysts. Second, labour standards cannot be set before the task is actually performed. This leads us to two alternative work measurement techniques.

PREDETERMINED TIME STANDARDS

A third way to set production standards is to use predetermined time standards. **Predetermined time standards** divide manual work into small basic elements that already have established times (based on very large samples of workers). To estimate the time for a particular task, the time factors for each basic element of that task are added together. For any given firm to develop a comprehensive system of predetermined time standards would be prohibitively expensive. Consequently, a number of systems are commercially available. Among these are MTM and CSD. The most common predetermined time standard is *methods time measurement* (MTM), which is a product of the MTM Association.[2] CSD (computerized standard data) is a product of Rath and Strong, a management consulting firm.

Predetermined time standards

Predetermined time standards are an outgrowth of basic motions called therbligs. The term *therblig* was coined by Frank Gilbreth (*Gilbreth* spelled backwards with the *t* and *h* reversed). Therbligs include activities such as select, grasp, position, assemble, reach, hold, rest, and inspect. These activities are stated in terms of time measurement units (TMUs), which are each equal to only .00001 hour, or .0006 minute. MTM values for various therbligs are specified in very detailed tables. Figure S11.2 provides, as an example, the set of time standards for the motion REACH. Note that reaching 10 centimetres for a part will have a TMU very different from reaching 30 centimetres.

Example S4 shows the use of predetermined time standards.

EXAMPLE

Riveting a transistor board in an assembly process is assigned an MTM value of 70.0 TMU, on the basis of industry data standards. Before riveting, a worker must reach 40 centimetres for a small part (17.0 TMU), grasp the part (9.1 TMU), move the part to the assembly (27.0 TMU), and position the transistor (32.3 TMU).

This very small task, which consists of five elements, takes a total of 155.4 TMU (17.0 + 9.1 + 27.0 + 32.3 + 70.0). Translating into minutes involves multiplying 155.4 TMU × .0006 minute = .0932 minute = 5.6 seconds.

[2]MTM is really a family of products available from the Methods Time Measure Association. For example, MTM-HC deals with the health care industry, MTM-C handles clerical activities, MTM-M involves microscope activities, MTM-V deals with machine shop tasks, and so on.

FIGURE S11.2 ■ Methods Time Measurement Data for REACH Motion.

Distance Moved (centimetres)	Time (TMU)				Hand in Motion	
	A	B	C or D	E	A	B
2 or less	2.0	2.0	2.0	2.0	1.6	1.6
2.5	2.5	2.5	3.6	2.4	2.3	2.3
5	4.0	4.0	5.9	3.8	3.5	2.7
10	6.1	6.4	8.4	6.8	4.9	4.3
15	7.0	8.6	10.1	8.0	5.7	5.7
20	7.9	10.1	11.5	9.3	6.5	7.2
25	8.7	11.5	12.9	10.5	7.3	8.6
30.5	9.6	12.9	14.2	11.8	8.1	10.1
35.5	10.5	14.4	15.6	13.0	8.9	11.5
40	11.4	15.8	17.0	14.2	9.7	12.9
46	12.3	17.2	18.4	15.5	10.5	14.4
50	13.1	18.6	19.8	16.7	11.3	15.8

Case and Description

A: Reach to object in fixed location, or to object in other hand or on which other hand rests.

B: Reach to single object in location that may vary slightly from cycle to cycle.

C: Reach to object jumbled with other objects in a group so that search and select occur.

D: Reach to a very small object or where accurate grasp is required.

E: Reach to indefinite location to get hand in position for body balance or next motion or out of way.

Predetermined time standards have several advantages over direct time studies. They may be established in a labouratory environment, which will not upset production activities (which time studies tend to do). The standard can be set before a task is done and can be used for planning. No performance ratings are necessary. Unions tend to accept this method as a fair means of setting standards. Predetermined time standards are particularly effective in firms that do substantial numbers of studies in which the tasks are similar. Some firms use both time studies and predetermined time standards to ensure accurate labour standards.

Examples from the Service Sector

MTM's health care and clerical (MTM-HC and MTM-C) standards have extended the use of predetermined time standards to help set *service* labour standards. Figure S11.3 provides the set of time standards for the motion GET and PLACE. To use GET and PLACE (the most complex motion in the MTM system), one needs to know what is "gotten," its approximate weight, and where and how far it is placed. Example S5 helps clarify this concept.

POM IN ACTION

UPS: The Tightest Ship in the Shipping Business

United Parcel Service (UPS) employs 150,000 people and delivers an average of nine million packages a day to locations throughout the United States and 180 other countries. To achieve its claim of "running the tightest ship in the shipping business," UPS methodically trains its delivery drivers in how to do their jobs as efficiently as possible.

Industrial engineers at UPS have time-studied each driver's route and set standards for each delivery, stop, and pickup. These engineers have recorded every second taken up by stoplights, traffic volume, detours, doorbells, walkways, stairways, and coffee breaks. Even bathroom stops are put into the standards. All of this information is then fed into company computers to provide detailed time standards for every driver, every day.

To meet their objective of 200 deliveries and pickups each day (versus only 80 stops a day at Federal Express), drivers must follow the engineers' procedures exactly. As they approach a delivery stop, drivers unbuckle their seat belts, honk their horns, and cut their engines. In one seamless motion, they are required to yank up their emergency brakes and push their gearshifts into first. The drivers slide to the ground with their clipboards under their right arms and their packages in their left hands. Their keys, teeth up, are in their right hands. They walk to the customer's door at the prescribed 0.9 metres per second and knock first to avoid lost seconds searching for the doorbell. After making the delivery, they do the paperwork on the way back to the truck.

Productivity experts describe UPS as one of the most efficient companies anywhere in applying the principles of scientific management.

Sources: Wall Street Journal (May 24, 1995): B1, B4; and S. P. Robbins, *Management*, 4th ed. (Englewood Cliffs, NJ: Prentice Hall, 1994), p. 28.

FIGURE S11.3 ■ Sample MTM Table for GET Motion. Time values are in TMUs.

GET AND PLACE			DISTANCE RANGE IN IN.	<8	>8 <20	>20 <32
WEIGHT	CONDITIONS OF GET	PLACE ACCURACY	CODE	1	2	3
<2 LBS	EASY	APPROXIMATE	AA	20	35	50
		LOOSE	AB	30	45	60
		TIGHT	AC	40	55	70
	DIFFICULT	APPROXIMATE	AD	20	45	60
		LOOSE	AE	30	55	70
		TIGHT	AF	40	65	80
	HANDFUL	APPROXIMATE	AG	40	65	80
>2 LBS <18 LBS		APPROXIMATE	AH	25	45	55
		LOOSE	AJ	40	65	75
		TIGHT	AK	50	75	85
>18 LBS <45 LBS		APPROXIMATE	AL	90	106	115
		LOOSE	AM	95	120	130
		TIGHT	AN	120	145	160

EXAMPLE

Pouring a tube specimen in a hospital lab is a repetitive task for which the MTM data in Figure S11.3 may be used to develop standard times. The sample tube is in a rack and the centrifuge tubes are in a nearby box. A technician removes the sample tube from the rack, uncaps it, gets the centrifuge tube, pours, and places both tubes in the rack.

The first work element involves getting the tube from the rack. Suppose the conditions for GETTING the tube and PLACING it in front of the technician are

- weight (less than 2 pounds)
- conditions of GET (easy)
- place accuracy (approximate)
- distance range (8 to 20 inches)

Then the MTM element for this activity is AA2 (as seen from Figure S11.3). The rest of Table 11.2 is developed from similar MTM tables.

TABLE S11.2 ■ MTM-HC ANALYSIS: POURING TUBE SPECIMEN.

ELEMENT DESCRIPTION	ELEMENT	TIME	FREQUENCY	TOTAL
Get tube from rack	AA2	35	1	35
Get stopper, place on counter	AA2	35	1	35
Get centrifuge tube, place at sample tube	AD2	45	1	45
Pour (3 sec.)	PT	83	1	83
Place tubes in rack (simo)	PC2	40	1	40
			Total TMU	238

$.0006 \times 238$ = Total Standard minutes = .14

Source: A. S. Helms, B. W. Shaw, and C. A. Lindner, "The Development of Laboratory Workload Standards Through Computer-Based Work Measurement Technique, Part I," *Journal of Methods-Time Measurement*, 12, p. 43. Used with permission of MTM Association for Standards and Research.

Most MTM calculations, by the way, are computerized, so the user need only key in the appropriate MTM codes, such as AA2 in Example S5.

TIME STANDARD TEAM APPROACH

Time standard team approach

A fourth approach which has gained favour in recent years in the setting of labour standards and labour rates is "agreeing to" by the union and management—the **time standard team approach.** For example, if a new process, procedure, or product is to be

Plus Fine Papers uses an employee stock purchase plan to encourage productivity and loyalty among workers.

installed, the line employee is asked to determine the time required. The time determined by the line employee is accepted on a trial basis and is monitored over the next six months. After six months adjustments/concessions are made. The time is then "set," and this becomes the standard for the new process, procedure, or product. The approach has been very successful with production companies in Ontario.

WORK SAMPLING

The fifth method of developing labour or production standards, work sampling, was developed in England by L. Tippet in the 1930s. **Work sampling** estimates the percent of the time that a worker spends on various tasks. The method involves random observations to record the activity that the worker is performing.

Work sampling

Work sampling is used in the following:

1. *Ratio Delay Studies*. These estimate the percentage of time employees spend in unavoidable delays. The results are used to investigate work methods, to estimate activity costs, and to set allowances in labour standards.
2. *Setting Labour Standards*. For setting standard task times, the observer must be experienced enough to rate the worker's performance.
3. *Measuring Worker Performance*. Sampling can develop a performance index for workers for periodic evaluations.

The work-sampling procedure can be summarized in seven steps:

1. Take a preliminary sample to obtain an estimate of the parameter value (such as percent of time a worker is busy).
2. Compute the sample size required.
3. Prepare a schedule for observing the worker at appropriate times. The concept of random numbers (discussed in the supplement to Chapter 13) is used to provide for random observation.
4. Observe and record worker activities; rate the worker's performance.
5. Record the number of units produced during the applicable portion of the study.
6. Compute the normal time per part.
7. Compute the standard time per part.

To determine the number of observations required, management must decide the desired confidence level and accuracy. But, first, the work analyst must select a preliminary value of the parameter under study (step 1 above). The choice is usually based on a small sample of perhaps 50 observations. The following formula then gives the sample size for a desired confidence and accuracy:

$$n = \frac{z^2\, p(1-p)}{h^2} \qquad \text{(S11.7)}$$

where n = required sample size

z = standard normal deviate for the desired confidence level ($z = 1$ for 68% confidence, $z = 2$ for 95.45% confidence, and $z = 3$ for 99.7% confidence—these values are obtained from Table S11.1 or the normal table in Appendix A)

p = estimated value of sample proportion (of time worker is observed busy or idle)

h = accuracy level desired, in percent

Example S6 shows how to apply the formula.

Optical scanners at IGA supermarkets are used to read the codes on each item at the check-out counters. This procedure provides information for inventory control, quicker check-out, and monitoring of the cashier's speed. The food items and dollars rung by each cashier and the number of customers served are recorded on the printout, which IGA posts in the workplace.

EXAMPLE

The head of one western province's welfare office estimates that the assistants are idle 25% of the time. The supervisor would like to take a work sample that would be accurate within 3% and wants to have 95.45% confidence in the results.

In order to determine how many observations should be taken, the supervisor applies the equation:

$$n = \frac{z^2 p(1-p)}{h^2}$$

where n = sample size required
z = 2 for 95.45% confidence level
p = estimate of idle proportion = 25% = .25
h = accuracy desired of 3% = .03

It is found that

$$n = \frac{(2)^2(.25)(.75)}{(.03)^2} = 833 \text{ observations}$$

Thus, 833 observations should be taken. If the percent idle time noted is not close to 25% as the study progresses, then the number of observations may have to be recalculated and increased or decreased as appropriate.

Work sampling is used to set labour standards in a fashion similar to that used in time studies. The analyst, however, simply records whether a worker is busy or idle during the observation. After all the observations have been recorded, the worker rated, and the units produced counted (steps 4 and 5), we can determine the normal time by the formula

$$\text{Normal time} = \frac{\begin{pmatrix}\text{total study}\\ \text{time}\end{pmatrix} \times \begin{pmatrix}\text{percent of time employee}\\ \text{observed working}\end{pmatrix} \times \begin{pmatrix}\text{performance}\\ \text{rating factor}\end{pmatrix}}{\text{number of pieces produced}}$$

The standard time is the normal time adjusted by the allowance factor, computed as

$$\text{Standard time} = \frac{\text{normal time}}{1 - \text{allowance factor}}$$

Example S7 demonstrates the calculation of normal and standard times.

EXAMPLE

A work-sample study conducted over the 80 hours (or 4,800 minutes) of a 2-week period yielded the following data. The number of parts produced was 225 by an operator who was performance rated at 100%. The operator's idle time was 20%, and the total allowance given by the company for this task is 25%.

$$\text{Normal time} = \frac{\begin{pmatrix}\text{total}\\\text{time}\end{pmatrix} \times \begin{pmatrix}\text{percent of time}\\\text{working}\end{pmatrix} \times \begin{pmatrix}\text{rating}\\\text{factor}\end{pmatrix}}{\text{number of units completed}}$$

$$= \frac{(4{,}800 \text{ min.})(.80)(1.00)}{225} = 17.07 \text{ min./part}$$

$$\text{Standard time} = \frac{\text{normal time}}{1 - \text{allowance factor}}$$

$$= \frac{17.07}{1 - .25} = 22.76 \text{ min./part}$$

Work sampling offers several advantages over time-study methods. First, it is less expensive, because a single observer can observe several workers simultaneously. Second, observers usually do not require much training, and no timing devices are needed. Third, the study can be delayed temporarily at any time with little impact on the results. And fourth, because work sampling uses instantaneous observations over a long period, the worker has little chance of affecting the study's outcome.

The disadvantages of work sampling are that it does not divide work elements as completely as time studies, it can yield biased or incorrect results if the observer does not follow random routes of travel and observation, and it is less effective than time studies when cycle times are short.

SUMMARY

Labour standards are required for an efficient operations system. They are needed for production planning, labour planning, costing, and evaluating performance. They can also be used as a basis for incentive systems. They are used in both the factory and the office. Standards may be established via historical data, time studies, predetermined time standards, and work sampling.

KEY TERMS

Time study (p. 495)
Average actual cycle time (p. 496)
Normal time (p. 496)
Standard time (p. 497)
Predetermined time standards (p. 501)
Time standard team approach (p. 504)
Work sampling (p. 505)

USING SPREADSHEETS TO SOLVE WORK MEASUREMENT PROBLEMS

To illustrate spreadsheet software in solving for normal and standard times in a time study, we present Program S11.1. This "symbolic" spreadsheet shows all the formulas needed to solve Example S2.

PROGRAM S11.1 ■ Using Spreadsheets to Solve a Time-Study Problem. Example S2 is illustrated with the formulas shown.

	A	B	C	D	E	F	G	H	I
1	EXAMPLE S2 SOLVED BY SPREADSHEET—MANAGEMENT SCIENCE ASSOCIATES								
2									
3		PERFORM-	CYCLE OBSERVED						
4		ANCE	(IN MINUTES)					AVERAGE	NORMAL
5	JOB ELEMENT	RATING	1	2	3	4	5	TIME	TIME
6	(A) Type Letter	1.20	8	10	9		11	(C6+D6+E6+G6)/4	B6*H6
7	(B) Type envelope	1.05	2	3	2	1	3	(C7+D7+E7+F7+G7)/5	B6*H7
8	(C) Stuff, stamp, seal	1.10	2	1		2	1	(C8+D8+F8+G8)/4	B8*H8
9									
10									
11	Allowance factor	.15						Total normal time	@sum(I6..I8)
12								Standard time	I10/(1-B11)
13									
14									
15									

SOLVED PROBLEMS

Solved Problem S11.1

A work operation consisting of three elements has been subjected to a stopwatch time study. The observations recorded are shown. By union contract, the allowance time for the operation is personal time 5%, delay 5%, and fatigue 10%. Determine the standard time for the work operation.

Job Element	Cycle Observations (in minutes) 1	2	3	4	5	6	Performance Rating (%)
A	.1	.3	.2	.9	.2	.1	90
B	.8	.6	.8	.5	3.2	.7	110
C	.5	.5	.4	.5	.6	.5	80

Solution

First, delete the two observations that appear to be very unusual (.9 minute for job element A and 3.2 minutes for job element B). Then,

$$\text{A's average cycle time} = \frac{.1 + .3 + .2 + .2 + .1}{5} = .18 \text{ min.}$$

$$\text{B's average cycle time} = \frac{.8 + .6 + .8 + .5 + .7}{5} = .68 \text{ min.}$$

$$\text{C's average cycle time} = \frac{.5 + .5 + .4 + .5 + .6 + .5}{6} = .50 \text{ min.}$$

$$\text{A's normal time} = (.18)(.90) = .16 \text{ min.}$$
$$\text{B's normal time} = (.68)(1.10) = .75 \text{ min.}$$
$$\text{C's normal time} = (.50)(.80) = .40 \text{ min.}$$
$$\text{Normal time for job} = .16 + .75 + .40 = 1.31 \text{ min.}$$
$$\text{Standard time} = \frac{1.31}{1 - .20} = 1.64 \text{ min.}$$

Solved Problem S11.2

A preliminary work sample of an operation indicates the following:

Number of times operator working	60
Number of times operator idle	40
Total number of preliminary observations	100

What is the required sample size for a 99.7% confidence level with ±4% precision?

Solution

$$n = \frac{z^2 p(1-p)}{h^2} = \frac{(3)^2(.6)(.4)}{(.04)^2} = 1{,}350 \text{ sample size}$$

Solved Problem S11.3

Amor Manufacturing Co. of Geneva, Switzerland, has just studied a job in its labouratory in anticipation of releasing the job to the factory. It wants rather good accuracy for costing and labour forecasting. Specifically, it wants you to provide a 99% confidence level and a cycle time that is within 3% of the true value. How many observations should it make? The data collected so far are as follows:

OBSERVATION	CYCLE TIME
1	1.7
2	1.6
3	1.4
4	1.4
5	1.4

Solution

First, solve for the mean, $\bar{x}$, and the sample standard deviation, s.

$$s = \sqrt{\frac{\Sigma(\text{each sample observation} - \bar{x})^2}{\text{number in sample} - 1}}$$

OBSERVATION	$\bar{x}_i$	$\bar{x}$	$x_i - \bar{x}$	$(x_i - \bar{x})^2$
1	1.7	1.5	.2	0.04
2	1.6	1.5	.1	0.01
3	1.4	1.5	–.1	0.01
4	1.4	1.5	–.1	0.01
5	1.4	1.5	–.1	0.01
	$\bar{x} = 1.5$	7.5		$0.08 = \Sigma(x_i - \bar{x})^2$

$$s = \sqrt{\frac{.08}{n-1}} = \sqrt{\frac{.08}{4}} = .141$$

Then, solve for $n = \left(\frac{zs}{h\bar{x}}\right)^2 = \left[\frac{(2.58)(.141)}{(.03)(1.5)}\right]^2 = 65.3$

where $\bar{x} = 1.5$

$s = .141$

$z = 2.58$

$h = .03$

Therefore, you recommend 65 observations.

Solved Problem S11.4

Each printed-circuit board at Maggard Micro Manufacturing, Inc., has a semiconductor pressed into predrilled slots. The elemental motions for normal time used by the company are as follows:

Reach 15 centimetres for semiconductors	10.5 TMU
Grasp the semiconductor	8.0 TMU
Move semiconductor to printed-circuit board	9.5 TMU
Position semiconductor	20.1 TMU
Press semiconductor into slots	20.3 TMU
Move board aside	15.8 TMU

(Each time measurement unit is equal to .0006 min.) Determine the normal time for this operation in minutes and in seconds.

Solution

Add the time measurement units:

$$10.5 + 8.0 + 9.5 + 20.1 + 20.3 + 15.8 = 84.2$$

$$\text{Time in minutes} = (84.2)(.0006 \text{ min.}) = .05052 \text{ min.}$$

$$\text{Time in seconds} = (.05052)(60 \text{ sec.}) = 3.0312 \text{ sec}$$

Solved Problem S11.5

To obtain the random sample needed for work sampling, a manager divides a typical workday into 480 minutes. Using a random-number table to decide what time to go to an area to sample work occurrences, the manager records observations on a tally sheet such as the following:

STATUS	TALLY	FREQUENCY
Productively working	卌 卌 卌 I	16
Idle	IIII	4

Solution

In this case, the supervisor made 20 observations and found that employees were working 80% of the time. So, out of 480 minutes in an office workday, 20%, or 96 minutes, was idle time, and 384 minutes was productive. Note that this procedure describes what a worker *is* doing, not necessarily what he or she *should* be doing.

DISCUSSION QUESTIONS

1. Why do operations managers require labour standards?
2. How do we establish a fair day's work?
3. Is a "normal" pace the same thing as a 100% pace?
4. What is the difference between "normal" and "standard" times?
5. What kind of work pace would you expect from an employee during a time study? Why?
6. As a new time-study engineer in your plant, you are engaged in studying an employee operating a drill press. Somewhat to your surprise, one of the first things you notice is that the drill press operator is doing a lot of operations besides just drilling holes. Your problem is what to include in your time study. From the following examples, indicate how, as the individual responsible for labour standards in your plant, you would handle them.
   a) Every so often, perhaps every 50th unit or so, the drill press operator takes an extra-long look at the piece, which apparently is misshaped, and then typically throws it in the scrap barrel.
   b) Approximately 1 out of 100 units has a rough edge and will not fit in the jig properly; therefore, the drill press operator picks up the piece, hits the lower right-hand edge with a file a few times, puts the file down, and returns to normal operation.
   c) About every hour or so, the drill press operator stops to change the drill in the machine, even if he or she is in the middle of a job. (We can assume that the drill has become dull.)
   d) Between every job and sometimes in the middle of jobs, the drill press operator turns off the machine and goes for stock.
   e) The drill press operator is idle for a few minutes at the beginning of every job waiting for the setup man to complete the setup. Some of the setup time is used in going for stock, but the drill press operator typically returns with stock before the setup person is finished with the setup.
   f) The operator stops to talk to you.
   g) The operator lights up a cigarette.
   h) The operator opens his lunch pail (it is not lunch time), removes an apple, and takes an occasional bite.
   i) The operator drops a part, and you pick it up and hand it to him. Does this make any difference in the time study? How?
7. Describe Gilbreth's approach to setting work standards.

CRITICAL THINKING EXERCISE 1

McNeil Consumer Products of Guelph, Ontario, produces Tylenol's acetaminophen products for the Canadian market. Formerly, label inspection at McNeil was performed by a human inspector. Now, they use Machine Vision, a cost-effective system based on blending image acquisition with computer processing, providing speed, accuracy, and user-friendliness. "We wanted a solution which would accurately tell you if the correct lot and expiration had been printed," says David Jones, a senior project engineer. He also wanted a proven and stable supplier who would provide long-term support.

Vision tracks more than 75,000 bottles per day, giving an up-to-date view of the status of production and the system. Current reject rates are less than half of 1%. And only a safe product reaches the store shelves.

1. Make a case for maintaining human involvement in the labelling process.
2. Make a case for changing the labelling process to an automated system.
3. Decide what should be done and explain how your decision affects the outcome mentioned in the final sentence.

Source: Adapted from "Taking the Headache out of Container Inspections," *Canadian Packaging* (September 1995): 2.

CRITICAL THINKING EXERCISE 2

At Northwest Airlines, data-entry workers are expected to type between 9,000 and 16,000 keystrokes per hour as they feed payroll and ticketing information into company computers. The computer keeps track of speed, and whereas slower typists can be penalized by losing pay, fast workers are rewarded with flexibility in arranging their schedules. A speed at least 75% as fast as the three fastest workers must be maintained by all workers or they can be dismissed.

Evaluate and critique Northwest's approach.

PROBLEMS

• **S11.1** The cycle time for performing a certain task was clocked at 10 minutes. The performance rating of the worker timed was estimated at 110%. Common practice in this department is to allow 5 minutes of personal time and 3 minutes of fatigue time per hour. In addition, it is estimated that there should be an extra allowance of 2 minutes per hour.

a) Find the normal time for the operation.

b) Compute the allowance factor and the standard time for the operation.

: **S11.2** A time study revealed an average cycle time of 5 minutes, with a standard deviation of 1.25 minutes. These figures were based on a sample of 75 cycles. Is this sample large enough that one can be 99% confident that the standard time is within 5% of the true value?

: **S11.3** The data in the following table represent time-study observations for an assembly process. On the basis of these observations, find the standard time for the process. Assume a 10% allowance factor.

Element	Performance Rating (%)	Observation (Minutes per Cycle)				
		1	2	3	4	5
1	100	1.5	1.6	1.4	1.5	1.5
2	90	2.3	2.5	2.1	2.2	2.4
3	120	1.7	1.9	1.9	1.4	1.6
4	100	3.5	3.6	3.6	3.6	3.2

: **S11.4** The following data represent observations for the cycle time of an assembly process. How many observations would be necessary for the observer to be 99% confident that the average cycle time is within 5% of the true value?

OBSERVATION (IN MINUTES)				
1	2	3	4	5
1.5	1.6	1.4	1.5	1.5

(*Hint:* Compute the sample standard deviation as shown in Solved Problem S11.3.)

: **S11.5** A work sample taken over a 100-hour work month produced the following results:

Units produced	200
Idle time	25%
Performance rating	110%
Allowance time	15%

What is the standard time for the job?

• **S11.6** Rebecca Page clocked the cycle time for welding a part onto truck doors at 5.3 minutes. The performance rating of the worker timed was estimated at 105%. Find the normal time for this operation.

According to a local union contract, each welder is allowed 3 minutes of personal time per hour and 2 minutes of fatigue time per hour. Further, it is estimated that there should be an average delay allowance of 1 minute per hour. Compute the allowance factor, and then find the standard time for this welding activity.

: **S11.7** A time study of a factory worker revealed an average cycle time of 3.20 minutes, with a standard deviation of 1.28 minutes. These figures were based on a sample of 45 cycles observed.

Is this sample adequate in size for the firm to be 99% confident that the standard time is within 5% of the true value? If not, what should be the proper number of observations?

: **S11.8** The data in the following table represent time-study observations for a metalworking process. On the basis of these observations, find the standard time for the process, assuming a 25% allowance factor.

		OBSERVATIONS (MINUTES PER CYCLE)						
ELEMENT	PERFORMANCE RATING (%)	1	2	3	4	5	6	7
1	90	1.80	1.70	1.66	1.91	1.85	1.77	1.60
2	100	6.9	7.3	6.8	7.1	15.3*	7.0	6.4
3	115	3.0	9.0*	9.5*	3.8	2.9	3.1	3.2
4	90	10.1	11.1	12.3	9.9	12.0	11.9	12.0

*Disregard—unusual observation.

: S11.9 In a careful work study in the Honornell Sandling Company, the results shown in the table are observed:

Element	Cycle (in minutes) 1	2	3	4	5	Performance Rating (%)
Prepare daily reports	35	40	33	42	39	120
Photocopy results	12	10	36*	15	13	110
Label and package reports	3	3	5	5	4	90
Distribute reports	15	18	21	17	45†	85

*Photocopying machine broken.
†Power outage.

a) Compute the normal time for each work element.

b) If the allowance for this type of work is 15%, what is the standard time?

c) How many observations are needed for a 95% confidence level within 5% accuracy? (*Hint:* Calculate the sample size of each element.)

:S11.10 The Division of Continuing Education at John's College promotes a wide variety of executive training courses for its audience of firms in the Edmonton, Alberta, region. The division's director, Christine Adams, believes that individually typed letters add a personal touch to marketing. To prepare letters for mailing, she conducts a time study of her secretaries. On the basis of the observations shown in the table, she wishes to develop a time standard for the whole job.

The college has an allowance factor of 12%. Adams decides to delete all unusual observations from the time study.

Element	Cycle Observed (in minutes) 1	2	3	4	5	6	Performance Rating (%)
Typing letter	2.5	3.5	2.8	2.1	2.6	3.3	85
Typing envelope	.8	.8	.6	.8	3.1	.7	100
Stuffing envelope	.4	.5	1.9	.3	.6	.5	95
Sealing, sorting	1.0	2.9	.9	1.0	4.4	.9	125

:S11.11 A time study at the phone company observed a job that contained three elements. The times and ratings for 10 cycles are shown in the table.

Element	Performance Rating (%)	Observations (minutes per cycle) 1	2	3	4	5	6	7	8	9	10
1	85	.40	.45	.39	.48	.41	.50	.45	.39	.50	.40
2	88	1.5	1.7	1.9	1.7	1.8	1.6	1.8	1.8	2.0	2.1
3	90	3.8	3.4	3.0	4.8	4.0	4.2	3.5	3.6	3.7	4.3

a) Find the average cycle time for each element.

b) Find the normal time for each element.

c) Assuming an allowance factor for 20% of job time, determine the standard time for this job.

:S11.12 The St. Hyacinthe Cement Company packs 36 kilogram bags of concrete mix. Time-study data for the filling activity are shown in the table.

The company's policy is a 20% allowance for workers. Compute the standard time for this work task. How many cycles are necessary for 99% confidence, within 5% accuracy?

	Cycle Time (Seconds per Cycle)					
Element	1	2	3	4	5	Performance Rating (%)
Grasp and place bag	8	9	8	11	7	110
Fill bag	36	41	39	35	112*	85
Seal bag	15	17	13	20	18	105
Place bag on conveyor	8	6	9	30†	35†	90

*Bag breaks open.
†Conveyor jams.

:S11.13 An office worker is clocked performing three work elements, with the results shown in the following table. The allowance for tasks such as this is 15%.

	Minutes per Cycle						
Element	1	2	3	4	5	6	Performance Rating (%)
1	13	11	14	16	51	15	100
2	68	21	25	73	26	23	110
3	3.0	3.3	3.1	2.9	3.4	2.8	100

a) Find the normal time.

b) Find the standard time.

:S11.14 Installing mufflers at the McElroy Garage in Morden, Manitoba, involves five work elements. Judy McElroy times workers performing these tasks seven times with the results shown in the table.

	Cycle Observations (Minutes)							
Job Element	1	2	3	4	5	6	7	Performance Rating (%)
1. Select correct mufflers	4	5	4	6	4	15	4	110
2. Remove old muffler	6	8	7	6	7	6	7	90
3. Weld/install new muffler	15	14	14	12	15	16	13	105
4. Check/inspect work	3	4	24	5	4	3	18	100
5. Complete paperwork	5	6	8	—	7	6	7	130

By agreement with her workers, McElroy allows a 10% fatigue factor and a 10% personal-time factor. To compute standard time for the work operation, McElroy excludes all observations that appear to be unusual or nonrecurring. She does not want an error of more than 5%.

a) What is the standard time for the task?

b) How many cycles are needed to assure a 95% confidence level?

:S11.15 Sample observations of an assembly-line worker made over a 40-hour work week revealed that the worker produced a total of 320 completed parts. The performance rating was 125%. The sample also showed that the worker was busy assembling the parts 80% of the time. Allowances for work on the assembly line total 10%. Find the normal time and standard time for this task.

•S11.16 Bank manager Carrie Mattanini wants to determine the percent of time her tellers are working and idle. She decides to use work sampling, and its initial estimate is that the tellers are idle 30% of the time. How many observations should be taken to be 95.45% confident that the results will not be more than 5% away from the true result?

:S11.17 A work sample taken over a 160-hour work month produced the following results. What is the standard time for the job?

Units manufactured	220
Idle time	20%
Performance rating	90%
Allowance time	10%

•S11.18 Sharpening your pencil is an operation that may be divided into eight small elemental motions. In MTM terms, each element may be assigned a certain number of TMUs.

Reach 10 centimetres for the pencil	6 TMU
Grasp the pencil	2 TMU
Move the pencil 15 centimetres	10 TMU
Position the pencil	20 TMU
Insert the pencil into the sharpener	4 TMU
Sharpen the pencil	120 TMU
Disengage the pencil	10 TMU
Move the pencil 15 centimetres	10 TMU

What is the total normal time for sharpening one pencil? Convert this time to minutes and seconds.

CASE STUDY

Plus Fine Papers Corporation

Halifax's Plus Fine Papers Corporation was started in 1956 on Duke Street to provide the business enterprises of Nova Scotia with the whitest and finest writing paper in Canada.

Plus Fine's factory workers are paid the minimum wage to start, with a review after six months of satisfactory work. On the recommendation of the supervisor the employee is then placed on the company's "regular payroll," which means that in addition to a substantial increase in salary the employee is entitled to participate in the company's stock purchase

(Continued)

plan. Though the stock purchase plan does not come into effect until the employee has been regularly employed for tow years, the employee is meanwhile entitled to share in the bonus distribution. The stock purchase plan is based on merit rating, as are the bonus scheme and pay.

Since early 1995, the company began having difficulties it had not had since 1956. Absenteeism was becoming a problem, tardiness was beginning to draw management's attention, and a sloppy, "couldn't care less" attitude permeated the plant operations. In short, the operations had lost sharpness and yet the return on investment each year continued to increase. The only change to the company's operations over the years had been the introduction of some Japanese-style management techniques in 1995.

In 1994 the average salary in the plant was $48,000, and with bonuses that increased to $55,000. When the market value of the stock plan was also considered, most of the employees' compensation on average was in the range of $74,000 to $85,000.

As soon as their two years' regular employment was reached, employees subscribed to the stock plan immediately. They could buy one share for every $100 they earned. Thus, an employee earning $48,000 could buy 480 shares.

The cost to the employee was the book value of the shares, which in 1996 was $32. The market value in 1996 was $65. The result over the years is that the long-term employees each own between 8,000 and 11,000 shares. The only stipulations the company makes are that the shares cannot be sold on the the market for three years after buying them and that the market value per share must be above $56.

Since early 1995, the new system made each employee responsible for his or her output before passing the output to the next employee. Employees must correct any imperfections on their own time. Each is responsible for his or her own quality of work and if anything slips by and is caught by the quality control department the employee gets demerit points, which reduces bonuses, pay, and the ability to buy shares. If the employee responsible for the defective part cannot be determined, the department is assigned the demerit points—i.e., all employees in the department receive demerit points.

DISCUSSION QUESTIONS

1. How would you establish output standards for an incentive scheme such as this?
2. What corrections if any would you make to the scheme?
3. List the problems that management might face in the future with this scheme.
4. Identify the characteristics that employees might possess to be satisfied working at Plus Fine Papers.

BIBLIOGRAPHY

Barnes, R. M. *Motion and Time Study*. New York: John Wiley, 1980.

Flynn, B. B., C. Blair, and M. Walters. "Flexible Compensation for World Class Manufacturers: Creating a Labor Skill Inventory Using Skill-Based Pay." *OM Review*, 9, no. 3: 22–36.

Jacobs, L. W., and S. E. Bechtold. "Labor Utilization Effects of Labor Scheduling Flexibility Alternatives in a Tour Scheduling Environment." *Decision Sciences*, 24, no. 1 (January/February 1993): 148–166.

Karger, D. W. *Advanced Work Measurement*. New York: Industrial Press, 1982.

Konz, S. *Work Design*. Columbia, OH: Grid, 1975.

Neibel, B. W. *Motion and Time Study*, 7th ed. Homewood, IL: Irvin, 1982.

12

PURCHASING MANAGEMENT AND JUST-IN-TIME

CHAPTER OUTLINE

LEARNING OBJECTIVES

When you complete this chapter you should be able to:

Identify or define:
- Purchasing
- Vertical integration
- Materials management
- Virtual companies

Explain:
- Just-in-time purchasing
- Make-or-buy decisions

WORLD-CLASS PROFILE: BOEING

BOEING FINDS COMPETITIVE ADVANTAGE WITH INTERNATIONAL PURCHASING

The relationship with suppliers in the aircraft business is complex. Aircraft system design and tremendous financial risk require that suppliers be a part of the concept from the very beginning.

The new Boeing 777 took an investment of about $4 billion. Boeing's out-of-pocket costs were about $2.5 billion, with suppliers investing the remaining $1.5 billion. With investments of this magnitude, Boeing designers and purchasing personnel work with suppliers early and in earnest. Engines, landing gear, and thousands of other parts and components procured from others are an integral part of plane design. Therefore, suppliers get on board in the early phases of design. Unless sales of the 777 reach 6 or 7 planes per month with total sales of 300 aircraft, Boeing may lose money on the plane. When the risks are this high, supplying "partners" must make a commitment, too.

Effective purchasing not only finds exceptional suppliers wherever they may be, but must also find suppliers who are willing to step up to the risk associated with new products. Those suppliers are diverse. Boeing finds such "partners" throughout the world, in over a dozen countries from next-door neighbour Canada to the Middle East to the Pacific Rim.

International procurement of components spreads Boeing's risk and has the added advantage of including local content in the plane. Countries that have a manufacturing stake in Boeing's 777 are more likely to buy from Boeing than from competing McDonnell Douglas or Airbus.

Boeing 777 International Purchasing. *This figure shows the worldwide purchasing effort for Boeing's new 777, with 20% of the plane's structure contracted to a Japanese consortium.*

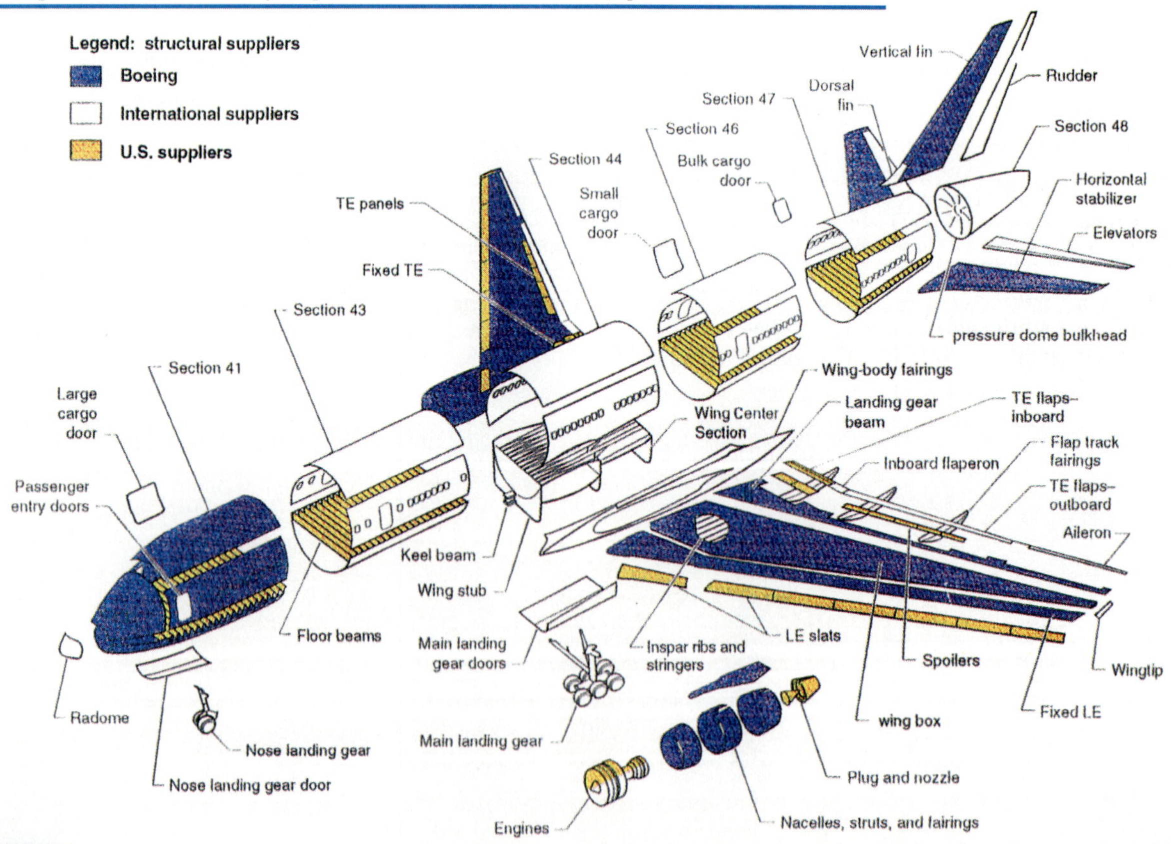

Boeing 777 Fuselage Rotated in Fixture. *The Boeing 777 aircraft fuselage section, or belly of the aircraft, is shown rotated upright after it was assembled in an inverted position. This 6.4-tonne section housed the aft lower cargo hold and the economy section for the interior passenger cabin. Inverted sections give Boeing employees better access to all parts during assembly.*

Computer-Aided Design Helps Boeing 777 Designers. *The Boeing 777 was designed entirely on computer screens and assembled without mockups. Designers created and manipulated full-colour, 3-D solid images representing aircraft sections and systems. The Boeing 777 design was "paperless."*

Boeing 777 Being Assembled at Everett, Washington. *Purchasing personnel work with suppliers to develop contracts. These contracts ensure that quality components are delivered on time and within cost to Boeing's final assembly line in Everett, Washington.*

"There is nothing in this world that some man cannot make a little less well and sell a bit cheaper. Those who buy on price alone are this man's lawful prey."
—John Ruskin, Scottish economist and social commentator

Suppliers for Chrysler Corporation's new Dodge Stratus were chosen before the parts were even designed. Chrysler evaluated suppliers on a number of criteria, but virtually eliminated traditional supplier bidding. As a part of this new and unique process, Chrysler has adopted contracts that extend for at least the life of the model. Additionally, the contracts call for periodic price reductions as the auto manufacturer helps suppliers eliminate the forces that push up costs. By working with Chrysler in these "partnerships," suppliers are to become more efficient, reducing prices as they move down the learning curve. ♦

As both Boeing and Chrysler have shown, no organization finds it economical to make all the material it uses. The advantages of specialization are too pervasive. Consequently, many items are purchased from others. The purchasing function often spends more money than any other function in the business, so purchasing provides a major opportunity to reduce costs and increase profit margins.

Purchasing

This leads to the creation of a purchasing (sometimes called procurement) department and the role of a purchasing agent. **Purchasing** is the acquisition of goods and services. The purchasing activity

1. Ensures continuity of supply to maintain production, as the cost of lost production greatly exceeds the cost of premium transportation;
2. Examines requirements for goods and services to determine which their firms should make or buy;
3. Determines which suppliers will provide the buyer's firm with the best value for the purchasing dollar.

PURCHASING

Operations Environments

Purchasing agent

In operations environments, the purchasing function is usually managed by a **purchasing agent** who has legal authority to execute contracts on behalf of the firm. In a large firm, the purchasing agent may also have a staff that includes buyers and expediters. Buyers represent the company, performing all activities of the purchasing department except that the buyers who are delegated authority to sign purchase orders and other contracts will normally be restricted to a lower dollar amount than the purchasing agent. Expediters assist buyers in following up on purchases to ensure timely delivery. In *manufacturing* firms, the purchasing function is supported by product engineering drawings and specifications, quality control documents, and testing activities that evaluate the purchased items.

Inspection of incoming items is normally restricted to "blue print" items bought to the firm's own design. Standard items such as commercial hand tools from recognized suppliers are not normally inspected.

Service Environments

In many service environments, purchasing's role may be difficult to define. Services such as lawn care, office cleaning, and maintenance of photocopy equipment have the main difficulty that they are produced and delivered simultaneously and problems

TABLE 12.1 ■ CONSIDERATIONS FOR THE MAKE-OR-BUY DECISION

REASONS FOR MAKING	REASONS FOR BUYING:
1. Lower unit cost	1. Lower unit cost
2. Unused productive capacity	2. Small quantity required
3. Stable work force in a period of low sales	3. Stable work force in a period of high sales
4. Suppliers lack expertise	4. Standard commercial item
5. Control of delivery/quality	5. Obtain supplier expertise
6. Policy of vertical integration	6. Patented item
7. Reduce supplier dependence	7. Lack productive capacity
8. Product secrecy	8. Lower inventories
9. Emergency requirements	9. Allow firm to concentrate on its core competencies

become evident *after* the service has been delivered. Some service firms suffer from the problem of high employee turnover and thus the service delivery may vary in quality. Purchasing must monitor service contracts carefully and regularly to ensure that the service provider is delivering as specified in the contract.

Buyers for retailers, normally called **merchandisers**, have quite a different job description than industrial buyers, as they are buying for resale and are responsible for buying goods and services that can be resold for a profit. While a few items or services may be bought to the retailer's specifications (e.g., Eaton's and the Hudson's Bay Company have "house brands" made to their specifications), most items are bought from manufacturers on the basis of past performance or industry standard grades (e.g., Agriculture Canada Grade "A" eggs, or Lumber Association "Construction Grade Lumber"). Some items may have to be resold at a discount or even a loss. Thus the retail merchandiser is simultaneously a buyer and a seller.

Merchandiser

Make or Buy

Wholesalers or retailers buy virtually everything they sell. Manufacturers make some items and buy others for the creation of their products. Well-equipped firms such as automotive assembly plants have the necessary equipment, materials, and expertise to manufacture almost any item purchased from outside suppliers, and in the case of plant shutdowns may well make rather than buy if the item cannot be obtained immediately. The **make or buy decision** may vary according to a periodic evaluation of the factors listed in Table 12.1. It is normally a joint decision involving purchasing, engineering, and cost accounting. However, the evaluation of outside suppliers in a "buy" decision remain the responsibility of purchasing.

Make-or-buy decision

THE PURCHASING OPPORTUNITY

With increasing specialization, our industrialized society spends an increasing proportion of revenue on purchases. This occurs because some part of a firm's product is very likely made more efficiently by someone else. The percent of revenue spent on purchases in a variety of industries is shown in Table 12.2. As the table suggests, many firms spend over half of their revenue on purchases. Consequently, improvements in

Each company in each industry makes its own judgement about the appropriate degree of vertical integration. Jaguar is changing its approach to vertical integration. In the past, Jaguar made virtually every part it could, even where it made little sense. It even manufactured some simple items such as washers. However, Jaguar is now focussing on those items that make a car unique: the body, engine, and suspension. Outside suppliers with their capabilities, expertise, and efficiencies provide most other components.

Jaguar, now a subsidiary of the Ford Motor Company, has benefited from Ford's purchasing and worldwide supply chain.

TABLE 12.2 ■ TOTAL OPERATING REVENUE BY TRADE GROUP

TRADE GROUP	TOTAL OPERATING REVENUE (MILLIONS OF DOLLARS)
Machinery, equipment, and supplies	46,441
Other products	34,687
Petroleum products	32,048
Motor vehicles—parts and accessories	22,368
Lumber and building materials	19,717
Metals, hardware, plumbing, and heating equipment	14,929
Household goods	7,530
Farm machinery, equipment, supplies	5,104
Total	182,824

Source: Statistics Canada, *Wholesaling and Retailing in Canada, 1993*, cat. no. 63-236, p. 24.

purchasing provide a tremendous opportunity for cost reduction. As the *POM in Action* box "The Dr. José Ignacio Lopez de Arriotua Escapade" suggests, both GM and Volkswagen understand the purchasing opportunity.

Table 12.3 illustrates the amount of leverage available to the operations manager through purchasing. Firms spending 50% of their sales dollar on purchases and having a net profit of 6% would require $3.57 worth of sales in order to equal the savings that accrues the company from a $1 savings in procurement. These numbers indicate the strong role that procurement can play in profitability. This is true in both manufacturing and service organizations.

EXAMPLE 1

The Goodwin Company spends 50% of its sales dollar on purchased goods. The firm has a net profit of 4%. Of the remaining 46%, 23% is fixed and the remaining 23% is variable. From Table 12.3, we see that the dollar value of sales needed to generate the same profit as results from $1 of purchase savings would be $3.70.

VERTICAL INTEGRATION

Vertical integration

Purchasing can be extended to take the form of vertical integration. By **vertical integration**, we mean developing the ability to produce goods or services previously purchased, or actually buying a supplier or a distributor. Vertical integration can take the form of forward or backward integration, as shown in Figure 12.1

Backward integration suggests a firm purchase its suppliers, as in the case of Ford Motor Company and General Motors Corporation deciding to gain control of the manufacturing of their own car radios by the acquisition of leading stereo electronics manufacturers (Ford bought JBL and GM bought Bose). Another example is Texas Instruments, a manufacturer of integrated circuits that also manufactures calculators and computers.

Vertical integration can offer a strategic opportunity for the operations manager. For firms whose internal analysis suggests that they have the necessary capital,

TABLE 12.3 ■ DOLLARS OF ADDITIONAL SALES NEEDED TO EQUAL $1 SAVED THROUGH PURCHASING*

PERCENT NET PROFIT OF FIRM	PERCENT OF SALES SPENT FOR PURCHASES 20%	30%	40%	50%	60%	70%	80%	90%
2	$2.44	$2.78	$3.23	$3.85	$4.76	$6.25	$9.09	$16.67
4	$2.38	$2.70	$3.13	$3.70	$4.55	$5.88	$8.33	$14.29
6	$2.33	$2.63	$3.03	$3.57	$4.35	$5.56	$7.69	$12.50
8	$2.27	$2.56	$2.94	$3.45	$4.17	$5.26	$7.14	$11.11
10	$2.22	$2.50	$2.86	$3.33	$4.00	$5.00	$6.67	$10.00

*The required increase in sales assumes that 50% of the costs other than purchases are variable and that 1/2 of the remaining (less profit) are fixed. Therefore, at sales of $100 (50% purchases and 2% margin), $50 are purchases, $24 are other variable costs, $24 are fixed costs, and $2 profit. Increasing sales by $3.85 yields the following:

Purchases at 50%	$51.93
Other variable costs	24.92
Fixed cost	24.00
Profit	3.00
	$103.85

Through $3.85 of additional sales, we have increased the profit by $1, from $2 to $3. The same increase in margin could have been obtained by reducing purchasing costs by $1.

managerial talent, and required demand, vertical integration may provide substantial opportunities for cost reduction. Other advantages in inventory reduction and scheduling can accrue to the company that effectively manages vertical integration or close, mutually beneficial relationships with suppliers.

Because purchased items represent such a large part of the costs of sales, it is obvious why so many organizations find interest in vertical integration. Vertical integration can yield cost reduction, quality adherence, and timely delivery. Additionally, vertical integration appears to work best when the organization has large market share or has the management talent to operate an acquired vendor successfully.[1]

FIGURE 12.1 ■ Vertical Integration Can Be Forward or Backward

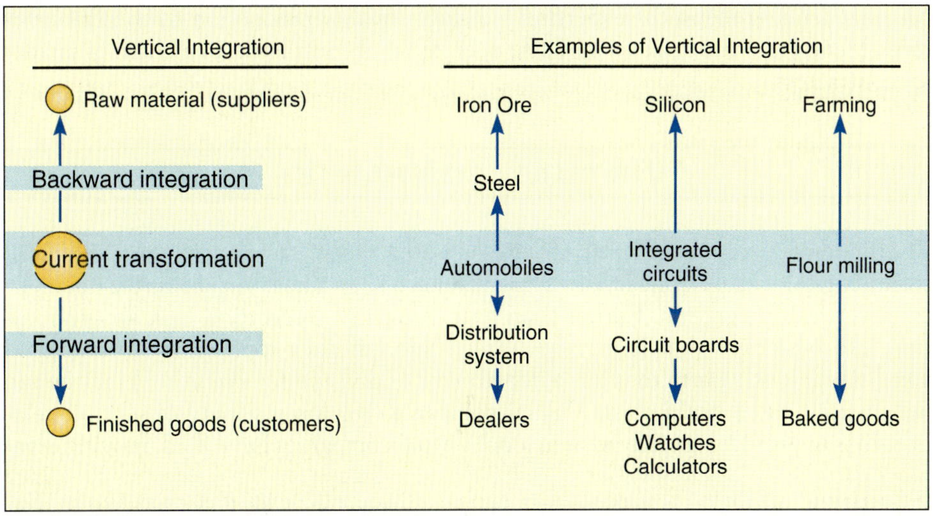

[1]Robert D. Buzzell, "Is Vertical Integration Profitable?" *Harvard Business Review*, 61, no. 1 (January/February 1983): 92–102.

POM IN ACTION

The Dr. José Ignacio Lopez de Arriotua Escapade

When General Motors brought José Ignacio Lopez from Europe to improve its purchasing and performance, he proceeded to challenge suppliers on cost, quality, and delivery. His methodology, called PICOS (Purchasing Input Concept Optimizing Systems), was to drive waste out of the procurement process while improving quality and responsiveness.

As the company's worldwide purchasing director, Lopez threatened both internal and outside suppliers. To GM divisions that make parts for the final product, he vowed to go to the "outside option" if costs were not slashed. To outside suppliers, who account for 30% of GM's parts needs, Lopez ordered price cuts of 20% immediately and 50% over the next few years. The result was turmoil and rebellion among General Motors' suppliers. Nonetheless, most responded with improvements. By some estimates, supplier productivity improved 55% with similar reductions in lead time.

Watching GM's improvements, Volkswagen wanted Lopez to do the same for them. They made him an offer to return to Europe; GM counteroffered. Volkswagen made another offer. As GM held a news conference to announce that Lopez was staying with GM, he was instead boarding a plane to Germany. A number of key General Motors' purchasing personnel and several boxes of documents also ended up in Germany. The result was that Dr. Lopez, Volkswagen, General Motors, and a number of associates ended up in the German court system.

This escapade points up just how important purchasing has become in today's organizations—the idea that two huge corporations would engage in a bidding war for the services of a purchasing executive.

Sources: Wall Street Journal (May 18, 1994): A11, (April 4, 1994): B-3, and (December 1, 1993): A10.

However, backward integration may be particularly dangerous for firms in industries undergoing technological change if management cannot keep abreast of those changes or invest the financial resources necessary for the next technological evolution.[2]

Many large Japanese manufacturers have found a middle ground between purchasing from a subcontractor and vertical integration. These manufacturers are often financial supporters through ownership or loans to subcontractors. The subcontractors then become part of a company coalition known as a **keiretsu**. Members of the keiretsu are assured long-term relationships and are therefore expected to function as partners, lending technical expertise and stable quality production to the manufacturer. Members of the keiretsu may also operate as subcontractors to a chain of smaller subcontractors.

Keiretsu

VIRTUAL COMPANIES

The limitations to vertical integration, as noted before, are severe. Moreover, our technological society continually demands more specialization that further complicates vertical integration. Rather than letting vertical integration lock an organization into businesses that it may not understand, another approach is to find good flexible suppliers. A firm that has a department or division for everything may be too bureaucratic to be world-class. **Virtual companies** rely on a variety of supplier relationships to provide services on demand.[3] Virtual companies have fluid, moving orga-

Virtual companies

[2]See, for instance, Robert H. Hayes and William J. Abernathy, "Managing Our Way to Economic Decline," *Harvard Business Review*, 58, no. 4 (July/August 1980): 72–73.

[3]Virtual companies are also known as *hollow corporations* or *network companies*. See *Business Week* (October 17, 1994): 86.

nizational boundaries that allow them to create a unique enterprise to meet changing market demands. These relationships may provide a variety of services that include doing the payroll, hiring personnel, designing products, providing consulting services, manufacturing components, conducting tests, or distributing products. The relationships may be short-term or long-term, true partners or only collaborators, or simply able suppliers and subcontractors. But whatever the formal relationship, the result can be lean world-class performance. The advantages of virtual companies include specialized management expertise, low capital investment, flexibility, and speed. The result is efficiency.

Silicon Valley provides a contemporary example of a virtual company. The apparel business provides a *traditional* example of virtual organizations. The designers of clothes seldom manufacture their designs; they license the manufacture. The manufacturer may then rent a loft, lease sewing machines, and contract for the labour. The result is an organization that has low overhead, is flexible, and can respond rapidly to the market. In the virtual company, the purchasing function is demanding and dynamic.

Sanford Corporation is one of Canada's largest suppliers of highlighters and markers. Sanford is vertically integrated, making its own inks, which gives it a research, development, quality, and product flexibility advantage.

PURCHASING MANAGEMENT

A firm that decides to buy material rather than make it must manage a purchasing function. **Purchasing management** considers numerous factors, such as inventory and transportation costs, availability of supply, delivery performance, and quality of suppliers. A firm may have some competence in all areas of purchasing management, but exceptional competence may require a more narrow focus.

Purchasing management

The Purchasing Focus

A further demonstration of the critical importance of the purchasing function in the 1990s and beyond was the announcement in 1995 by the Purchasing Management Association of Canada (PMAC) that all persons wishing to enter PMAC's "CPP" (Certified Professional Purchaser) certification program must hold a bachelor's degree in business or engineering prior to acceptance. CPP is the official recognition of a qualified professional purchaser in Canada and has been approved by the legislature of each province. Similar legislation in the United States was passed in regard to the National Association of Purchasing Management (NAPM) headquartered in Tempe, Arizona.

PMAC and NAPM work together to provide portability of qualifications between Canada and the United States for professional purchasers. An increasing number of universities now offer degrees at the master's and doctoral levels in purchasing and materials management. In the past, many universities had not offered even a single course in this field.

Source management

One focus of purchasing is *source management*. **Source management** is concerned with developing new reliable suppliers. The product may be a high-technology, custom-made, or specialty item for which there are few, if any, suppliers. Management must be able to seek out likely suppliers, develop their ability to produce, and negotiate acceptable relationships.

Supply management

Alternatively, purchasing may focus on *supply management*.[4] A **supply management** focus suggests a concern with long-term availability of high-dollar or critical

[4]Peter Kraljic, "Purchasing Must Become Supply Management," *Harvard Business Review*, 61, no. 5 (September/October 1983): 109–117.

POM IN ACTION

Outsourcing Paces Growth of IT Services

In 1995, the rate of growth in outsourcing was highest for desktop services, platform operations, and business operations—approximately 25%, leading the overall growth rate of IT services and software, which is expected to grow at a compound rate of 15% over the next five years according to INPUT, an IT consulting firm.

The main driving force behind the IT industry's growth rate is the North American Free Trade Agreement and the businesses directly affected by it, such as banking, finance, and telecommunications.

Source: Adapted from Business Wire Inc., "Steep Jump in Outsourcing Paces Sharp Growth of Information Services in Canada," June 24, 1996. For further information contact Erika Meir at (415) 528-6329 or **media@input.com**.

purchases; future reliable supplies are critical to success of the enterprise. An example is General Motors' development of palladium and platinum suppliers so it would have reliable and reasonably priced raw materials for catalytic converters. The evaluation was global and development of the supplier was expensive. A supply management focus is also necessary if the dollar value of the purchases or fluctuations in cost are substantial. The extreme of this focus is for the firm to pursue backward integration to assure future supplies.

Materials management

Purchasing may be combined with various warehousing and inventory activities to form a materials management system. The purpose of **materials management** is to obtain efficiency of operations through the integration of all material acquisition, movement, and storage activities in the firm. When transportation and inventory costs are substantial on both the input and output side of the production process, an emphasis of materials management may be appropriate. The potential for competitive advantage is found via both reduced costs and improved customer service. Many manufacturing companies have moved to some form of material management structure.[5]

Vendor Relations

The competitive advantage that can be obtained through purchasing can only be achieved with outstanding vendor relations. Viewing the supplier as an adversary is counterproductive. Long-term, close relationships with a few suppliers is a better way (see the *POM in Action* box "Firms Slash Vendor Rolls"). A healthy vendor relationship is one in which the supplier is committed to helping the purchaser improve its product and win orders. Suppliers can also be a source of ideas about new technology, materials, and processes, as Chrysler discovered with its SCORE program (see Table 12.4). Purchasing is a way to convey such information to the proper people in the organization.

Likewise, healthy relationships also include those in which the purchaser is committed to keeping the supplier informed of possible changes in product and production schedule. The purchasing function and suppliers must develop mutually advantageous relationships. Because an outstanding operations function requires excellent vendor relations, purchasing conducts a three-stage process.

VENDOR EVALUATION. The first stage, *vendor evaluation,* involves finding potential vendors and determining the likelihood of their becoming good suppliers.

[5]Jeffrey G. Miller and Peter Gilman, "Materials Managers: Who Needs Them?" *Harvard Business Review,* 57, no. 4 (July/August 1979): 143.

TABLE 12.4 ■ CHRYSLER'S SUPPLIER COST REDUCTION EFFORT (SCORE) HAS PRODUCED $161,000,000 IN SAVINGS IN 2 YEARS

SUPPLIER	SUGGESTION	MODEL	ANNUAL SAVINGS
Rockwell	Use passenger car door locks on 1991 Dodge trucks	Dodge trucks	$280,000
Rockwell	Simplify design and substitute materials on manual window-regulator systems	Various	$300,000
3M	Change tooling for wood-grain panels to allow three parts to be made in one die instead of two	Caravan, Voyager	$1,500,000
Trico	Change wiper-blade formulations to eliminate the disposable plastic shield used during assembly and shipping	Various	$140,000
Leslie Metal Arts	Exterior lighting suggestions	Various	$1,500,000

Source: James Welch, Laddie Cook, and Joseph Blackburn, "The Bridge to Competitiveness, Building Supplier-Customer Linkages," *Target* (November/December 1992): 17–29. Reprinted from *Target* with permission of the Association for Manufacturing Excellence.

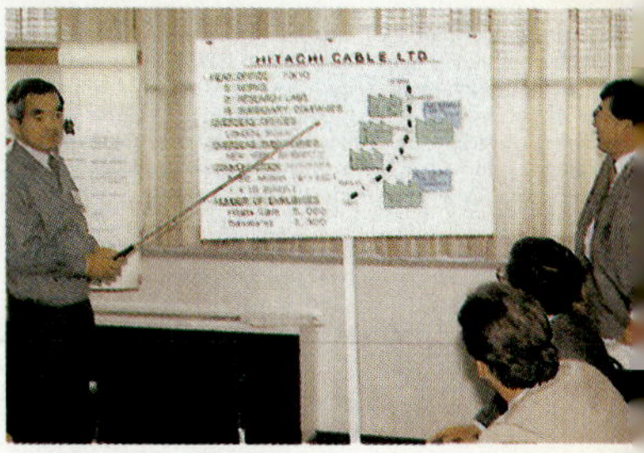

As a world-class telecommunications company, AT&T has an aggressive supplier evaluation and quality improvement program. Part of this program requires that vendors provide company profile and capability information. Providing this information is often done in formal presentations, as Hitachi Cable Ltd. is doing above. Once vendors are approved and orders placed, AT&T tracks key supplier variables, such as order cycle time and quality yield to determine effectiveness of the program.

Many firms such as Ford Motor Company, General Motors, and Chrysler Corporation have "manufacturing standards" that detail their requirements and provide a basis for suppliers to become certified. After a review of the appropriate standards, the would-be supplier submits product samples for evaluation at engineering headquarters. A successful manufacturer is then listed as an "approved source" in purchasing department bulletins.

The vendor evaluation phase requires the development of evaluation criteria such as those in Figure 12.2. Both the criteria and the weights are dependent upon the needs of the organization. The selection of competent suppliers is critical. If good suppliers are not selected, then all other purchasing efforts are wasted. As firms move toward fewer longer-term suppliers, the issues of financial strength, quality, management, research, and technical ability play an increasingly important role. These attributes should be noted in the evaluation process.

VENDOR DEVELOPMENT. The second stage is *vendor development.* Assuming a firm wants to proceed with a particular vendor, how does it integrate this supplier into its system? Purchasing makes sure the vendor has an appreciation of quality requirements, engineering changes, schedules and delivery, the payment system, and procurement policies. Vendor development may include everything from training, to engineering and production help, to formats for electronic information transfer. Purchasing policies might include issues such as percent of business done with any one supplier or the development of suppliers throughout Canada.

Negotiation strategies

NEGOTIATIONS. The third stage is *negotiations.*[6] **Negotiation strategies** are of two classic types. First is the *cost-based price model.* This model requires that the supplier open its books to the purchaser. The contract price is then based on time and materials or on a fixed cost with an escalation clause to accommodate changes in the vendor's labour and materials cost. This type of negotiation is common when parts or components are bought to the buyer firm's own design or when there is only a single supplier, known as a "captive source."

[6]Gary J. Zenz, *Purchasing and the Management of Materials,* 7th ed. (New York: John Wiley, 1994).

FIGURE 12.2 ■ Vendor Rating Form Used by J. M. Huber Corporation. Evaluation categories are weighted according to importance (for example, "Product" category is weighted 1.25; "Service" is next at 0.69). Individual factors (for example, quality, delivery, and so on) have descending values, from 4 points for excellent to 1 point for poor. Total of points in each category is multiplied by the weight for that category.

VENDOR RATING REPORT J. M. HUBER CORPORATION

COMPANY TOTAL RATING

Company:	Excellent (4)	Good (3)	Fair (2)	Poor (1)
Size and/or Capacity	4			
Financial Strength		3		
Operational Profit		3		
Manufacturing Range	4			
Research Facilities			2	
Technical Service		3		
Geographical Locations	4			
Management		3		
Labour Relations		3		
Trade Relations		3		
Total 32	12	18	2	
.63 x Total = 20.16				

Service	Excellent (4)	Good (3)	Fair (2)	Poor (1)
Deliveries on Time	4			
Condition on Arrival		3		
Follow Instructions		3		
Number of Rejections	4			
Handling of Complaints		3		
Technical Assistance			2	
Emergency Aid		3		
Supply Up-to-Date Catalogues, Etc.				1
Supply Price Changes Promptly	4			
Total 27	12	12	2	1
.69 x Total = 18.63				

Products:	Excellent (4)	Good (3)	Fair (2)	Poor (1)
Quality	4			
Price		3		
Packaging	4			
Uniformity		3		
Warranty	4			
Total 18	12	6		
1.25 x Total = 22.50				

Sales Personnel	Excellent (4)	Good (3)	Fair (2)	Poor (1)
1. Knowledge				
His company		3		
His product	4			
Our industry		3		
Our Company		3		
2. Sales Calls				
Properly Spaced	4			
By Appointment		3		
Planned and Prepared		3		
Mutually Productive	4			
3. Sales-Service				
Obtain Information		3		
Furnish Quotations Promptly	4			
Follow Orders		3		
Expedite Delivery		3		
Handle Complaints		3		
Total 43	16	27		
.48 x Total = 20.64				

(*Source:* Stuart F. Heinritz, Paul V. Farrell, Larry Giunipero, and Michael Kolchin, *Purchasing: Principles and Applications*, 8th ed., Englewood Cliffs, NJ: Prentice Hall, 1992, p. 180.)

Both Levi Strauss as the purchaser and Milliken as the supplier have found advantages in a closer relationship. Milliken developed a *partners for profit* program so its customers could concentrate on their business rather than on the management of raw materials inventory. Shown here is a Levi Strauss factory that is benefiting from this program.

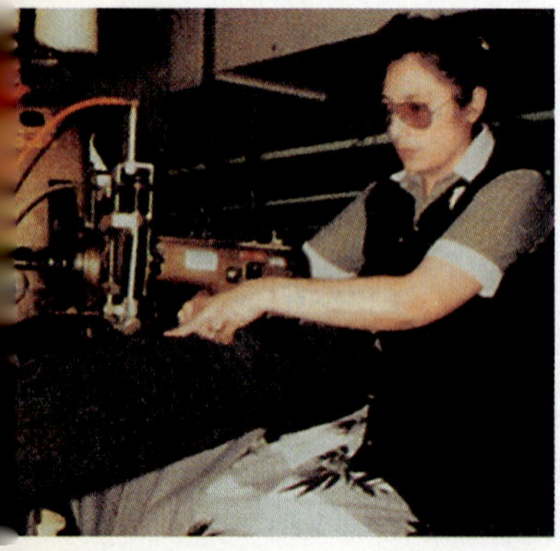

Second is the *market-based price model*. In this model, price is based on a published price or index. Paperboard prices, for instance, are published weekly in the "yellow sheet,"[7] and nonferrous metal prices in *Metals Week*.[8] An example is "silver solder," used in the electronics and automotive industries, whose price is subject to the bid prices on the commodity futures market.

The third method is *competitive bidding*. In cases where suppliers are not willing to discuss costs or where near-perfect markets do not exist, competitive bidding is often appropriate. Competitive bidding is the typical policy in many firms for the majority of their purchases. The policy usually requires that the purchasing agent have several potential suppliers of the product (or its equivalent) and quotations from each. The major disadvantage of this method is that the development of long-term

[7]The "yellow sheet" is the commonly used name of the *Official Board Markets*, published by Magazines for Industry, Chicago. It contains announced paperboard prices for containerboard and boxboard.

[8]*Metals Week*, A. Patrick Ryan, editor and publisher, New York.

POM IN ACTION

Firms Slash Vendor Rolls

Corporate America's drive for quality is squeezing thousands of suppliers. The pressure on suppliers results from American industry's struggle to slim down and tone up to meet global competition. Companies around the country are cutting back the number of suppliers they use by as much as 90%. They are demanding higher levels of service and product quality from the survivors. And they are willing to pay a premium on the theory that getting things right initially is cheaper in the long run.

"A revolution is going on in the relationships between suppliers and customers," says quality expert J. M. Juran.

In the change, many suppliers will eventually "fade away," says Richard Buetow, senior vice-president of Motorola. In the current climate of worldwide competition, he adds, no one can "accept just sweat; you have to show results." Over the past several years, Motorola has cut its 10,000-company supplier base by 70% and is still slashing.

	Number of Suppliers		
	Current	Previous*	% Change
Xerox	500	5,000	–90
Motorola	3,000	10,000	–70
General Motors	5,500	10,000	–45
Ford Motor	1,000	1,800	–44
Texas Instruments	14,000	22,000	–36

*The number of suppliers firm had prior to starting reduction programs.

Sources: Wall Street Journal (August 16, 1991): B1; and *Production & Inventory Management Journal* (Third Quarter 1991): 22–25.

relations between the buyer and seller are hindered. Competitive bidding may effectively determine cost. But it may also make difficult the communication and performance that are vital for engineering changes, quality, and delivery.

Yet a fourth approach is to *combine one or more* of the preceding negotiation techniques. The supplier and purchaser may agree on review of certain cost data, accept some form of market data for raw material costs, or agree that the supplier will "remain competitive."

A good supplier relationship is one in which the partners have established a degree of mutual trust and a belief in the competence of each other.

Purchasing Techniques

Blanket Purchase Orders. For an order complete in a single shipment, "regular" purchase orders are used. Repetitive items may be covered by a blanket order. A *blanket order* is an order based on a stated time period, usually one year, for one or more items or services. The items or services are standard commercial items or are to the buyer firm's design.

Blanket order quantities are usually stated as the buyer's estimated requirements for the specified period and the quotation basis is historic usage data from the buyer's records. Quantities are normally not guaranteed unless the items are bought according to the buyer firm's design. Supplier pricing normally contains an "escalation clause" that permits the supplier to apply for price increases if advance notice is given to the buyer. The buyer may ask all suppliers to requote the affected items to validate the requested price increase. If the increase is unacceptable, the buyer will amend the order to delete the item(s).

Actual ordering against the blanket order is accomplished using a *release authorization* cross-referenced to the order number. As the buyer has selected the source and pricing, release authorization may be delegated to the department using the items.

The advantages of the blanket order include:

1. Better prices, as the supplier is bidding on a larger-quantity contract.
2. Delegation of releasing authority, permitting the buyer to concentrate on high-dollar-value, "one time" buys where the potential for substantial savings exists.

SYSTEMS CONTRACTING. This is a purchasing technique that can be used to advantage for certain standard items where small quantities may be needed of a large number of different items. The most common such items are office supplies. The basis of such a *systems contract* would be a special blanket order based on a supplier catalogue and price list with a discount based on annual dollar volume.

One person per department is delegated direct release authority and delivery is normally in one to two days. The "stock room" and its attendant costs are eliminated altogether, and each person is responsible for his or her own supplies inventory. The supplier, of course, has these standard items in stock for supply to many customers. The buyer firm gets fresher supplies at lower cost, and more choices.

ELECTRONIC ORDERING AND FUNDS TRANSFER. Electronic ordering and funds transfer reduce paper transactions. Paper transactions consist of a purchase order, a purchase release, a receiving document, authorization to pay an invoice (which is matched with the approved receiving report), and finally the issuance of a cheque. Purchasing departments can reduce this barrage of paperwork by electronic ordering, acceptance of all parts as 100% good, and electronic funds transfer to pay for units received. Not only can electronic ordering reduce paperwork, but it also speeds up the traditionally long procurement cycle. General Motors has saved billions of dollars over the past few years through exactly this kind of electronic transfer.[9]

Electronic data interchange (EDI)

Transactions between firms are increasingly done via electronic data interchange. **Electronic data interchange (EDI)** is a standardized data transmittal format for computerized communications between organizations. EDI provides data transfer for virtually any business application, including purchasing. Data are transmitted directly from electronic media of the sender via a third party (usually, the phone company) to electronic media of the receiver. For instance, under EDI, data for a purchase order, such as order date, due date, quantity, part number, purchase order number, address, and so forth, are fitted into the standard EDI format. The data are then sent, usually from one computer to another, by phone line. The receiving organization knows where the data are on the standardized format; a computer program is used to read those data into the receiving company's files. (For more information on EDI, contact the Electronic Data Interchange Council of Canada, Toronto, Ontario.)

STOCKLESS PURCHASING. The term *stockless purchasing* has come to mean that the supplier maintains the inventory for the purchaser. If the supplier can maintain the stock of inventory for a variety of customers who use the same product or whose differences are very minor, say, perhaps at the packaging stage, then there may be a net savings. Consignment inventories, discussed shortly, are a related option.

[9]See J. Carbonne, "G.M. After Lopez," *Electronic Business Buyer* (October 1993): 56–60.

STANDARDIZATION. The purchasing department should make special efforts toward increased levels of standardization. That is, rather than obtaining a variety of very similar components with labelling, colouring, packaging, or perhaps even slightly different engineering specifications, the purchasing agent should endeavour to have those components standardized.

JUST-IN-TIME (JIT) PURCHASING

In the traditional flow of material through the transformation process, there are many potential delays. Incoming material is delayed at receiving and incoming inspection; work-in-process is delayed at numerous workstations; and finished goods held at finished goods storage. **Just-in-time (JIT) purchasing** reduces the waste that is present at receiving and incoming inspection. It also reduces excess inventory, poor quality, and delay. This waste is present in virtually all production processes—and purchasing is a critical function in removing the waste and making JIT work. Every moment material is held should add value. And every movement of material should add value.

Just-in-time purchasing

Table 12.5 shows the characteristics of JIT purchasing. The *POM in Action* box "Hempz USA Inc." mentions one company's use of JIT delivery systems.

Goals of Just-in-Time Purchasing

The goals of JIT purchasing are:

1. *Elimination of Unnecessary Activities*. For instance, receiving activity and incoming inspection activity are unnecessary under just-in-time. If purchasing personnel have been effective in selecting and developing vendors, the purchased items can be received without formal counting, inspection, and testing procedures. To do its job well, the purchasing staff requires support from other sections of the operations function. Production can contribute by providing accurate, stable schedules, adequate lead time for engineering changes to be implemented, and time to develop ethical suppliers.
2. *Elimination of In-Plant Inventory*. Virtually no raw material inventory is necessary if materials that meet quality standards are delivered where and when they are needed. Raw material inventory is necessary only if there is reason to believe that supplies are undependable. Likewise, parts or components for processing at some intermediate stage should be delivered in small lots directly to the using department as needed. Reduction or elimination of inventory allows problems with other aspects of the production process to be observed and corrected. Inventory tends to hide problems.
3. *Elimination of In-Transit Inventory*. At any given time, over one-half of General Motors' inventory is moving between plants; it is in transit. For global manufacturers such as General Motors and Toyota, the problem is severe, but it also provides substantial opportunity for improvement.[10] Modern purchasing departments address in-transit inventory reduction by encouraging suppliers to locate near the plant and support rapid transportation of purchases. The shorter the flow of material and money in the resource "pipeline," the less inventory (see

[10]See Joseph Bonney, "Toyota's Global Conveyorbelts," *American Shipper*, 36, no. 9 (September 1994): 50.

Automobile seats made 2 hours earlier are being delivered to Chryslers Brampton, Ontario, factory. The seats are then quickly transferred in proper sequence to the assembly line for JIT installations.

TABLE 12.5 ■ CHARACTERISTICS OF JIT PURCHASING

SUPPLIERS
Few suppliers
Nearby suppliers or clusters of remote suppliers
Repeat business with same suppliers
Active use of analysis to enable desirable suppliers to become/stay price-competitive
Competitive bidding mostly limited to new purchases
Buyer resists vertical integration and subsequent wipeout of supplier business
Suppliers encouraged to extend JIT buying to *their* suppliers
QUANTITIES
Steady output rate (a desirable prerequisite)
Frequent deliveries in small lot quantities
Long-term contract agreements
Minimal paperwork to release orders
Delivery quantities variable from release to release but fixed for whole contract term
Little or no permissible overage or underage of receipts
Suppliers encouraged to package in exact quantities
Suppliers encouraged to reduce their production lot sizes (or store unreleased material)
QUALITY
Minimal product specifications imposed on supplier
Help suppliers to meet quality requirements
Close relationships between buyers' and suppliers' quality assurance people
Suppliers encouraged to use process control charts instead of lot sampling inspection
SHIPPING
Scheduling of inbound freight
Gain control by use of company-owned or contract shipping and warehousing

Source: Richard J. Schonberger and James P. Gilbert, "Just-in-Time Purchasing: A Challenge for U.S. Industry." Copyright 1983 by The Regents of the University of California. Reprinted from the *California Management Review,* 26, no. 1. By permission of The Regents.

Consignment

Figure 12.3). Another way to reduce in-transit inventory is to have inventory on **consignment**. Under a consignment arrangement, the supplier maintains title to the inventory. For instance, an assembly plant may find a hardware supplier that is willing to locate its warehouse where the user currently has its stockroom. In this manner, when hardware is needed, it is no farther than the stockroom. And the supplier can ship to other, perhaps smaller, purchasers from the "stockroom." The supplier bills the user on the basis of the signed pickup receipt or number of units shipped.

4. *Quality and Reliability Improvement.* Reducing the number of suppliers and increasing long-term commitments to suppliers tends to improve supplier quality and reliability. Vendors and purchasers must have mutual understanding and trust. To achieve deliveries only when needed, in the exact quantities needed,

FIGURE 12.3 ■ Shorter Processing Time Also Lowers Costs.

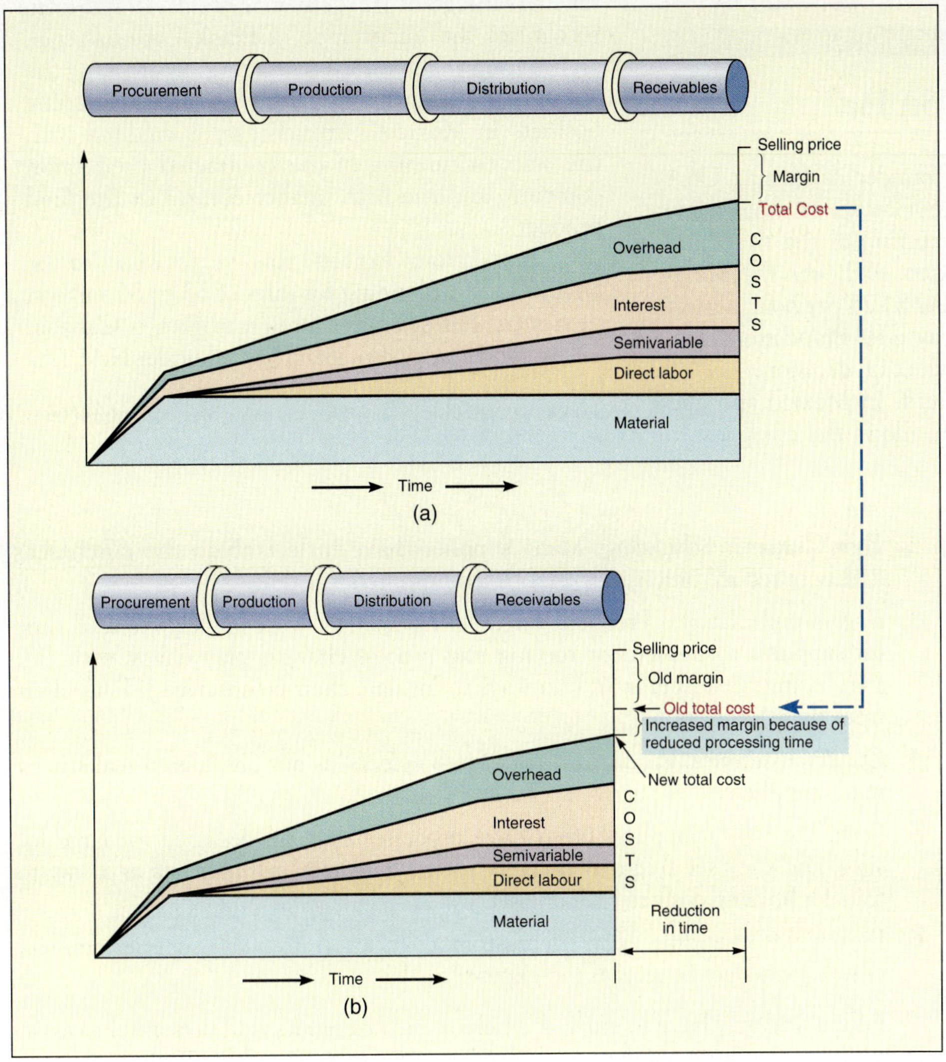

also requires perfect quality—or as it is also known, zero defects. And, of course, both the supplier and the delivery system must be excellent.

Supplier Concerns

To implement JIT purchasing successfully, purchasing personnel must work closely with suppliers to overcome supplier concerns. These supplier concerns include:[11]

1. *Desire for Diversification*. Many suppliers do not want to tie themselves to long-term contracts with one customer. The suppliers' perception is that their risk is reduced if they have a variety of customers.

[11]This summary is based on a study by Tom Schmitt and Mary Connors, "A Survey of Suppliers' Attitudes Toward the Establishment of JIT," *Operations Management Review*, 3, no. 4 (Summer 1985): 36.

POM IN ACTION

Hempz USA Inc.

Baron Brandstrom is the founder of Hempz USA Inc., an Arizona-based manufacturer of shoes made from hemp fibres. Manufacturing of the shoes has been located in Leon, Mexico. Although the Mexican operation pays employees $1.25 per hour, almost double that of the Asian pay rate, Brandstrom does not regret the Mexican production decision.

Hempz pays less in tariffs in Mexico and gets the product quicker, which allows the company to take advantage of JIT delivery systems. Brandstrom recognizes the importance of Frank Urtuzuastegui, an international business consultant, to breaking the cultural and language barriers associated with doing business in Mexico. Urtuzuastegui is credited with the smooth running of the contracted production company and the high quality control of the final product.

Brandstrom expects this year's sales to be $400,000 and is aiming for sales of $3 to $5 million next year. His strongest foreign market is Canada, where tariffs have also been reduced under NAFTA.

Source: Adapted from "Shoemakers Leap into Mexico," *Arizona Business Gazette* (July 4, 1996).

2. *Poor Customer Scheduling*. Many suppliers have little faith in the purchaser's ability to reduce orders to a smooth, coordinated schedule.
3. *Engineering Changes*. Frequent engineering changes with inadequate lead time for suppliers to implement tooling and process changes play havoc with JIT. Purchasing personnel must find ways to insulate their prospective JIT suppliers from these changes.
4. *Quality Assurance*. Production with "zero defects" is not considered realistic by many suppliers.
5. *Small Lot Sizes*. Suppliers often have processes that are designed for large lot sizes, and they see frequent delivery to the customer in small lots as a way to transfer holding costs to the supplier.
6. *Proximity*. Depending upon the customer's location, frequent supplier delivery of small lots may be seen as too expensive.

Purchasing may have to enlist the help of its own production personnel to assist suppliers in overcoming many of the preceding objections, but there is no doubt that those firms that have not developed JIT suppliers are at a distinct disadvantage. For those who remain skeptical of the use of JIT, we would point out that virtually every restaurant in the world practices JIT, and with minimal staff support.

BREAK-EVEN ANALYSIS APPLIED TO PURCHASING

When a purchaser understands the cost structure of suppliers, more intelligent negotiations and purchases can take place. Cost data may be obtained from the supplier, from financial statements, or from analysis of the supplier's sales or purchases, labour, and overhead costs. The objective is to determine both the fixed and variable portions of the supplier's cost. Once this is done, the purchaser is in a much better position to work with the supplier. If we know the approximate cost structure and related break-even of the supplier, then we know the impact of our purchases on the supplier. Under some conditions, an astute buyer can purchase more during the next buying cycle (say, a year) at lower cost and leave the supplier better off financially. Example 2 shows how this is done.

Example 2 shows one avenue a resourceful purchasing department can pursue to reduce costs *and* improve the strength of a supplier. There are, of course, some issues that the supplier, Laurier Tires, must address. Among these issues is the concern that Laurier may have if it devotes 50% of its capacity to one customer. Such a move may limit its flexibility in the marketplace. Second, if Laurier thinks it can sell that capacity at a higher price, then the WARS offer may not be of interest.

EXAMPLE 2

Using the data in Figure 12.4, Waterloo Auto Repair Stations (WARS) knows that Laurier Tires makes a combination of units for various customers that moves them out on the (horizontal) percent capacity axis to point A. WARS also knows that it purchases about half of the tires made by Laurier. Analysis in the WARS purchasing department suggests that Laurier is not operating at capacity, but at about 70% of capacity. Laurier's realistic capacity and top efficiency is point B on the capacity axis (about 85%). WARS can move some purchases from another supplier (with whom it has had quality problems) to Laurier. It is therefore very interested in the impact of such a move on Laurier. If Laurier maintains its existing sales and adds 15% from WARS to its volume, Laurier's profit corridor increases (the vertical distance *X* is larger than the vertical distance *Y*) even if the slope of the revenue line is slightly less. (With WARS paying less per tire, the revenue line drops to the proposed level.) But because volume has increased with an attendant increase in the profit corridor, Laurier has more profit and WARS pays less for its tires.

FIGURE 12.4 ■ Purchasing Break-Even Analysis. WARS reduces costs whereas Laurier Tire increases profit.

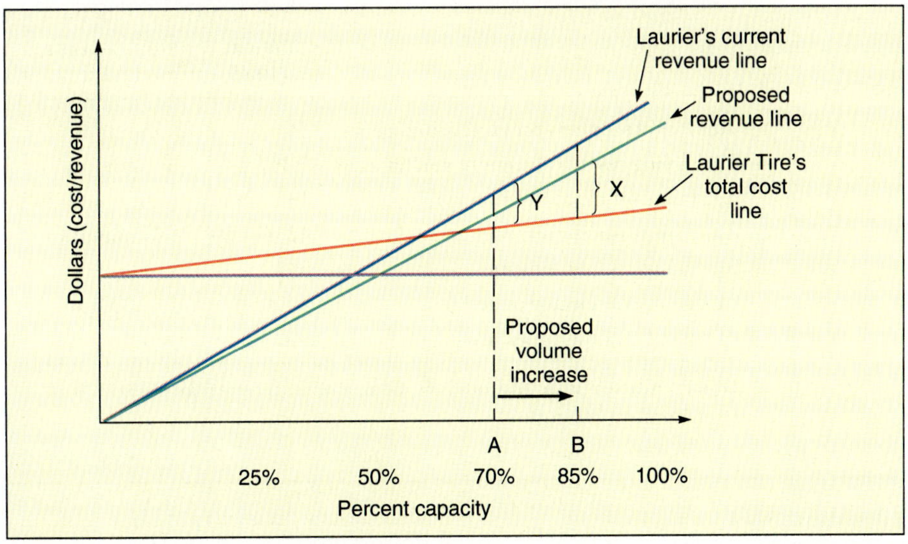

ACHIEVING WORLD-CLASS STANDARDS

World-class firms understand that a huge part of revenue is spent on purchases and that a dollar saved in purchasing flows directly to profit. These firms find the right mix of vertical integration, traditional purchasing, and "virtual" organization techniques. Evaluation, selection, and development of suppliers ensure that suppliers warrant being partners in long-term relationships seeking to satisfy the same customers. JIT is the norm in world-class firms and JIT techniques are expected of suppliers as well.

World-class firms practice supply chain management. These firms see themselves in customer-supplier relationships where 100% good quality is always expected. As Table 12.6 shows, world-class firms do indeed set world-class benchmarks in purchasing.

Examples of world-class firms are: Ford Motor Company, General Motors, Motorola, and Intel. Ford, for example, sells its products in virtually every country in the world and has a policy of worldwide sourcing.

SUMMARY

Purchasing is responsible for a substantial portion of the cost of many firms, including most manufacturing, restaurant, wholesale, and retail firms. Consequently, procurement provides a great opportunity for such firms to develop a competitive advantage. The purchasing function may focus on traditional purchasing activities, source development, supply management, or materials management; but at some time, purchasing may have to engage in all of these activities regardless of the focus. Developing close, long-term relationships with suppliers of integrity is, for many organizations, a prerequisite to efficient operations. For many firms, just-in-time purchasing is another opportunity to obtain competitive advantage.

TABLE 12.6 ■ PURCHASING PERFORMANCE IN WORLD-CLASS FIRMS

	TYPICAL FIRMS	WORLD-CLASS FIRMS
Number of suppliers per purchasing agent	34	5
Purchasing costs as percent of purchases	3.3%	.8%
Lead time for purchases (weeks)	15	8
Time spent placing an order	42 minutes	15 minutes
Percentage of late deliveries	33%	2%
Percentage of rejected material	1.5%	.0001%
Number of shortages per year	400	4

Source: Adapted from McKinsey & Company, as reported in *Business Week* (November 30, 1992): 72.

KEY TERMS

Purchasing (p. 522)
Purchasing agent (p. 522)
Merchandiser (p. 523)
Make-or-buy decision (p. 523)
Vertical integration (p. 524)
Keiretsu (p. 526)

Virtual companies (p. 526)
Purchasing management (p. 527)
Source management (p. 527)
Supply management (p. 527)
Materials management (p. 528)
Negotiation strategies (p. 529)
Electronic data interchange (EDI) (p. 532)
Just-in-time (JIT) purchasing (p. 533)
Consignment (p. 534)

SOLVED PROBLEM

Solved Problem 12.1

Super Discount knows that Plastics, Inc., of St. Jerome, Quebec, makes a great plastic cabinet for small items for home and shop. Through its research, Super Discount suspects that Plastics is operating at only 75% of capacity. Super Discount wants to do a major promotion of the plastic cabinet and would like all of Plastics' remaining capacity. Super Discount judges that the maximum effective capacity of Plastics is 88%. (See the horizontal axis of Figure 12.5.)

Super Discount is interested in the impact of such a move on Plastics and thinks Plastics' profit corridor will increase. Super Discount's purchasing agent explains to the management of Plastics that the profit corridor (Z) is larger even if the slope of the Plastics, Inc., revenue line is slightly less. (The Plastics' revenue line moves from Plastics(a) to Plastics(b).) This means Super Discount is paying less per cabinet, but because volume has increased, with an attendant increase in the profit corridor (that is, Z is greater than X), Plastics has more profit and Super Discount pays less for its cabinets.

FIGURE 12.5 ■ Purchasing Break-Even Analysis

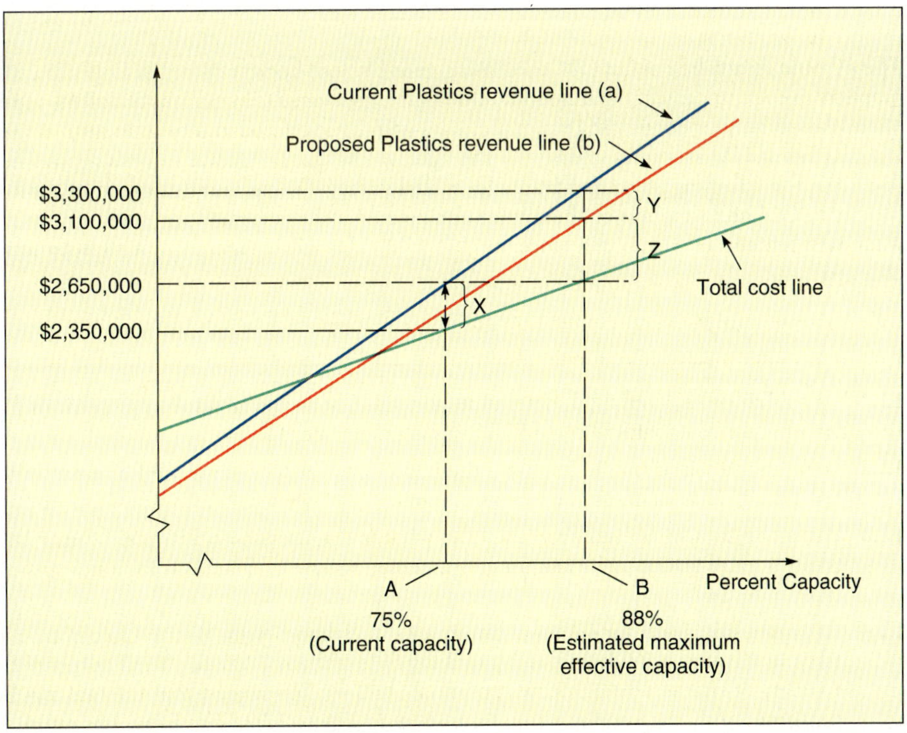

How much less can Super Discount expect to pay for cabinets? What is Plastics' increase in profit?

Solution
The dollar value of X is $300,000 ($2,650,000 – $2,350,000). This is Plastics' current profit. The dollar value of Y is $200,000 ($3,300,000 – $3,100,000), and this represents the savings to Super Discount. The dollar value of Z minus X is the increase in profit to Plastics if it accepts the contract, approximately $150,000 (Z – X = $450,000 – $300,000 = $150,000).

DISCUSSION QUESTIONS

1. Under what conditions might a firm decide to organize its purchasing function as a materials management function? As a supply management function? As a source management function?
2. What can the purchasing function do to implement just-in-time techniques with suppliers?
3. What information does purchasing receive from other functional areas of the firm?
4. How does an adversarial relationship with suppliers change when a firm makes a decision to move to just-in-time deliveries?
5. What are the three basic approaches to negotiations?
6. What are the characteristics of JIT purchasing?
7. What reservations do suppliers have about JIT purchasing?
8. How do restaurants implement JIT purchasing?
9. How does the apparel business have the characteristics of a "virtual" company?

CRITICAL THINKING EXERCISE

The *POM in Action* box about GM purchasing guru Dr. José Lopez noted that Lopez forced suppliers to cut costs quickly and sharply. Although Lopez saved GM billions of dollars, suppliers blamed him for demanding major sacrifices with little offered in return. Industry analysts wonder if GM sacrificed quality for the sake of low costs. Analyze Lopez's approach, discussing the advantages and disadvantages of that strategy. What are the long-term implications to GM and suppliers of these price cuts? Find out from newspapers and magazines what has become of Dr. Lopez since he left GM. Has GM's approach with suppliers changed?

PROBLEMS

• **12.1** Using Tables 12.2 and 12.3, determine how much a food firm with a net profit of 8% has to increase its sales to equal $1 of procurement savings.

: **12.2** Using the data in Example 2, what is the impact on WARS' costs if WARS wants Tarleton Tires to have additional funds for research?

: **12.3** Using the data in Solved Problem 12.1, what is the impact on Plastics if Super Discount wants Plastics to increase its engineering budget by $200,000 for a new plastic cabinet design?

: **12.4** As purchasing agent for Woolsey Enterprises in Salmon Arm, British Columbia, you ask your buyer to provide you with a ranking of "excellent," "good," "fair," or "poor" for a variety of characteristics for two potential vendors. You suggest that the rankings be consistent with the vendor rating form show in Figure 12.2. The buyer has returned the ranking shown on the next page.

How do you rank these potential vendors? (*Hint:* Figure 12.2 provides an excellent approach.)

: **12.5** As a library assignment, identify organizations that are

a) engaged in vertical integration

b) engaged in reducing their vertical integration

c) moving toward "virtual" companies

DONNA INC. = D VENDOR RATING:
KAY CORP. = K

Company	Excellent (4)	Good (3)	Fair (2)	Poor (1)
Size and/or capacity		K	D	
Financial strength			K	D
Operational profit			K	D
Manufacturing range			KD	
Research facilities	K		D	
Technical service		K	D	
Geographical locations		K	D	
Management		K	D	
Labour relations			K	D
Trade relations			KD	
Service				
Deliveries on time		KD		
Condition on arrival		KD		
Follow instructions			D	K
Number of rejections				KD
Handling of complaints		KD		
Technical assistance		K	D	
Emergency aid				KD
Supply up-to-date catalogues, etc.				KD
Supply price changes promptly				KD

Products	Excellent (4)	Good (3)	Fair (2)	Poor (1)
Quality	KD			
Price			KD	
Packaging			KD	
Uniformity			KD	
Warranty			KD	
Sales Personnel				
1. Knowledge				
Of his or her company			D	K
Of his or her products			K	D
Of our industry			KD	
Of our company			K	D
2. Sales calls				
Properly spaced			D	K
By appointment				KD
Planned and prepared			K	D
Mutually productive			K	D
3. Sales service				
Obtain information			D	K
Furnish quotations promptly		K		D
Follow orders			D	K
Expedite delivery			K	D
Handle complaints		KD		

CASE STUDY

Hahn and Pinto Manufacturing

As purchasing manager of the consolidated purchasing department of Hahn and Pinto, you have decided to use decision-tree techniques to evaluate the cost of (1) a blanket contract from the home office, (2) individual large contracts from the home office, and (3) orders placed directly by the three company plants. Regardless of how the orders are placed, you expect the total quantity purchased to be 30.5 kilometres of multistrand wire. You estimate the cost and related probability for each of the three alternatives as follows:

ALTERNATIVES	PROBABILITY	COST
Individual orders placed by the home office	.50	$.71
	.25	.68
	.25	.74
Individual orders placed by each plant	.40	.82
	.50	.65
	.10	.70
Blanket order	1.0	.70

(Continued)

DISCUSSION QUESTIONS

1. Use a decision tree to analyze the alternatives, using highest expected monetary value as a decision criteria. (*Hint:* Review the supplement to Chapter 2 for examples and explanations of decision trees.)
2. As purchasing agent, what is your recommendation for the purchase?
3. What will be the expected total cost to the firm next year if your recommendation is followed?

CASE STUDY

Thomas Manufacturing Company

Mr. Thomas, president of Thomas Manufacturing Company, and Mr. McDonnell, the vice president, were discussing how future economic conditions would affect their product, home air purifiers. They were particularly concerned about cost increases. They increased selling prices last year, and thought another price increase would have an adverse affect on sales. They wondered if there was some way to reduce costs in order to maintain the existing price structure.

Mr. McDonnell had attended a purchasing association meeting the previous night and heard a presentation by the president of a tool company on how they were approaching cost reduction. The tool company had just hired a purchasing agent with a business degree who was reducing costs by 15%. Mr. McDonnell thought some of the ideas might be applicable to Thomas Manufacturing. The present purchasing agent, Mr. Older, had been with the company for 25 years and they had no complaints. Production never stopped for lack of material. Yet a 15% cost reduction was something that could not be ignored. Mr. Thomas suggested that Mr. McDonnell look into this area and come up with a recommendation.

Mr. McDonnell contacted several business schools in the area. He said he would be interested in hiring a new graduate. One of the requirements for applicants was a paper on how to improve the company's purchasing function. Several applicants visited the plant and analyzed the purchasing department before they wrote their papers. The most dynamic paper was submitted by Tim Younger. He recommended:

1. Lower stock reorder levels (from 60 days to 45 days) for many items, thus reducing inventory.
2. Analyze specifications on many parts.
3. Standardize many of the parts to reduce the variety of items.
4. Analyze items to see whether more products can be purchased by blanket purchase orders, with the ultimate goal of reducing the purchasing staff.
5. Look for new and lower cost sources of supply.
6. Increase the number of requests for bids, to get still lower prices.
7. Be more aggressive in negotiations. Make fewer concessions.
8. Make sure all trade, quantity, and cash discounts are taken.
9. Buy from the lowest price source, disregarding local public relations.
10. Stop showing favouritism to customers who also buy from the company. Reciprocity comes second to price.
11. Purchase to current requirements rather than to market conditions. Too much money is tied up in inventory.

After reading all the papers Mr. McDonnell was debating with himself what he should recommend to Mr. Thomas. Just the previous week at the department meeting, Mr. Older was recommending

(Continued)

many of the opposite actions. In particular, he recommended an increase in inventory levels anticipating future rising prices. Mr. Older also stressed the good relations the company had with all their suppliers and how they can be relied upon for good service and a possible extension of credit, if the situation warrants it. Most of their suppliers bought their home air purifiers from Thomas Manufacturing. Yet Mr. Younger said the practice of favouring them was wrong and should be eliminated. Mr. McDonnell was hesitant about what action he should recommend; Mr. Thomas wanted a decision in the morning.

DISCUSSION QUESTIONS

1. What recommendation would you make if you were Mr. McDonnell? Why?
2. Analyze each of Mr. Younger's recommendations. Do you agree or disagree with them? Why?

Source: Professor Richard J. Tersine, University of Oklahoma.

CASE STUDY

Caninco Buys a Printer

Caninco (Canadian Insurance Company of Halifax, Nova Scotia) decided in 1996 to replace with state-of-the art technology the Troy brand of cheque printers that were being used in two of its operations sites. These sites printed cheques for Payroll, Accounts Payable, Employee Reimbursements, and Billing Customer Refunds. Total annual print volume was estimated to be 15 million cheques for 1995 and growing.

Treasury Operation's management thought that serving Caninco cheque printing needs in the future would require a major reengineering of the cheque issuance process and that replacement of the printers was a first step. The current systems and equipment, for example, could not meet requirements for printing cheques as part of Caninco's marketing promotions. The marketing team, therefore, was forced to use outside services to print these cheques. While the outside services met most of the requirements, the accounting transactions that were associated with these cheques were often incorrect, and cheque reconciliation for these cheques was almost impossible. Treasury Operations believed that they could eliminate the use of outside services and improve the quality and costs of their current service if they purchased print equipment that was computer-controlled. In addition, it was important that the magnetic ink character recognition (MICR) line that was printed at the bottom of the cheque be of high quality, because banks charge extra for processing cheques with unreadable MICR lines.

The team looking into new printers had identified Siemens, Delphax, Xerox, IBM, and NCR as the vendors that had printers that should be considered. Team members then decided on the following six criteria:

1. Features: Documented the technical features of each printer, maintenance availability, and requirements.
2. User rating: Documented results of a survey of users of each of the printers.
3. Pros/cons: Documented overall team observations.
4. Cost: Cost analysis included purchase of printers, maintenance, supplies, and software.
5. MICR quality: Conformance to MICR standards.
6. Print quality: Conformance to print quality standards.

The team then assigned a point value (10 being the highest score), for each printer for each situation. Their final tabulation is shown on the next page.

(Continued)

CRITERIA	SIEMENS	DELPHAX	XEROX	IBM	NCR
Features	9.9	6.6	5.2	7.7	8.2
User ratings	8.0	8.3	6.7	8.6	8.6
Pros/cons	10.0	1.0	5.0	8.0	8.0
Cost	10.0	6.0	4.0	2.0	8.0
MICR quality	9.7	5.4	6.0	9.4	9.4
Print quality	9.7	5.7	8.0	8.4	8.6
Total	57.3	33.0	34.9	44.1	50.8
Ranking	1	5	4	3	2

DISCUSSION QUESTIONS

1. Is it appropriate that in the final analysis MICR Quality was given the same weight as Cost?
2. Recompute the comparisons, using the following weight factors: Features 15%, User Ratings 15%, Pros/Cons 15%, Cost 30%, MICR Quality 12.5%, Print Quality 12.5%. Does this change the end result?

Source: Written by Paula Beavers, under the supervision of Prof. B. Render, Rollins College. Modified for the Canadian edition.

BIBLIOGRAPHY

Akinc, U. "Selecting a Set of Vendors in a Manufacturing Environment." *Journal of Operations Management*, 11, no. 2 (June 1993): 107–122.

Billington, C. "Supply Chain Management." *OR/MS Today*, 21, no. 2 (April 1994): 20–29.

Blumenfeld, D. E., L. D. Burns, C. F. Daganzo, M. D. Frick, and R. W. Hall. "Reducing Logistics Costs at General Motors." *Interfaces*, 17 (January/February 1987): 26–47.

Chapman, S. N., and P. L. Carter. "Supplier/Customer Inventory Relationships Under JIT." *Decision Sciences* (Winter 1990): 35–51.

Davis, T. "Effective Supply Chain Management." *Sloan Management Review*, 34, no. 4 (Summer 1993): 35–46.

Datar, S., K. Sunder, T. Mukhopadyay, and E. Svaan. "Overloaded Overheads: Activity-Based Cost Analysis of Material Handling in Cell Manufacturing." *Journal of Operations Management*, 10, no. 1 (January 1993): 119–137.

Drtina, R. "The Outsourcing Decision." *Management Accounting*, 75, no. 9 (March 1994): 56–62.

Dyer, J. H., and W. G. Ouchi. "Japanese-Style Partnerships: Giving Companies a Competitive Edge." *Sloan Management Review*, 35, no. 1 (Fall 1993): 51–64.

Freeland, J. R. "A Survey of Just-in-Time Purchasing Practices in the United States." *Production and Inventory Management Journal*, 32 (Second Quarter 1991): 43.

Frey, S. C., Jr., and M. M. Schlosser. "ABB and Ford: Creating Value Through Cooperation." *Sloan Management Review*, 35, no. 1 (Fall 1993): 65–72.

Fuller, J. B., J. O'Conor, and R. Rawlinson. "Tailored Logistics: The Next Advantage." *Harvard Business Review*, 71, no. 3 (May/June 1993): 87–98.

Golhar, D. Y. "JIT Purchasing Practices in Manufacturing Firms." *Production and Inventory Management Journal*, 34, no. 3 (Third Quarter 1993): 75–79.

Helper, S. "How Much Has Really Changed Between U.S. Automakers and Their Suppliers?" *Sloan Management Review*, 32 (Summer 1991): 15.

Inman, A. R., and S. Mehra. "Determining the Critical Elements of Just-in-Time Implementation." *Decision Sciences*, 23 (January/February 1992): 160–174.

Tersine, R. J., and J. H. Campbell. *Modern Materials Management*. New York: North-Holland, 1977.

Venkatesan, R. "Strategic Sourcing: To Make or Not to Make." *Harvard Business Review*, 70, no. 6 (November/December 1992): 98.

Zenz, G. J. *Purchasing and the Management of Materials*. New York: John Wiley, 1994.

12 SUPPLEMENT

LEARNING CURVES

SUPPLEMENT OUTLINE

Korean electronics giant Samsung entered the microwave oven market in 1978. On a makeshift assembly line, its production team began making one oven a day, then two, and then five, as employees began to learn the assembly process. With long hours spent redesigning the line at night, Samsung engineers worked out the bugs discovered by day. Production improved to 10 ovens a day, then 15, and soon to 50. By the end of 1981, the learning process allowed workers to produce 300 ovens a day, and by 1982, that number doubled again. By 1983, Samsung was making 2,500 microwaves a day, and continuing to improve.[1] ♦

[1]Ira C. Magaziner and Mark Patinkin, "Fast Heat: How Korea Won the Microwave War," *Harvard Business Review*, 89, 10 (January/February 1989): 83–92.

Learning curve

In 1936, T. P. Wright of Curtis-Wright Corporation published the first report of **learning curves** applied to industry.[2] Learning curves, or as they are sometimes called, experience curves, are based on the premise that organizations, like people, become better at their tasks as the tasks are repeated. A learning curve graph, of labour-hours per unit versus the number of units produced, normally has the negative exponential distribution shape illustrated in Figure S12.1.

The learning curve is based on a doubling of productivity. That is, when production doubles, the decrease in time per unit effects the rate of the learning curve. So, if the learning curve is an 80% rate, the second unit takes 80% of the time of the first unit, the fourth unit takes 80% of the time of the second unit, the eighth unit takes 80% of the time of the fourth unit, and so forth. This is shown as

$$T \times L^n = \text{time required for the } N\text{th unit} \qquad \text{(S12.1)}$$

where T = unit cost or unit time
L = learning curve rate
n = number of times Y is doubled

If the first unit of a particular product took 10 labour-hours, and if a 70% learning curve is present, the hours the fourth unit will take require doubling twice—from 1 to 2 to 4. Therefore, the formula is

Hours required for unit 2 = $10(.7)^1$ (one doubling from unit 1 to unit 2) = 7 hours

Hours required for unit 4 = $10(.7)^2$ (two doublings from unit 1 to unit 2 to unit 4) = 4.9 hours

FIGURE S12.1 ■ The Learning Curve Effect States that Time per Repetition Decreases as the Number of Repetitions Increases. This means *it takes less time to complete each additional unit a firm produces*. But the time savings in completing each unit decreases with each additional unit. These are the major implications of the learning curve effect.

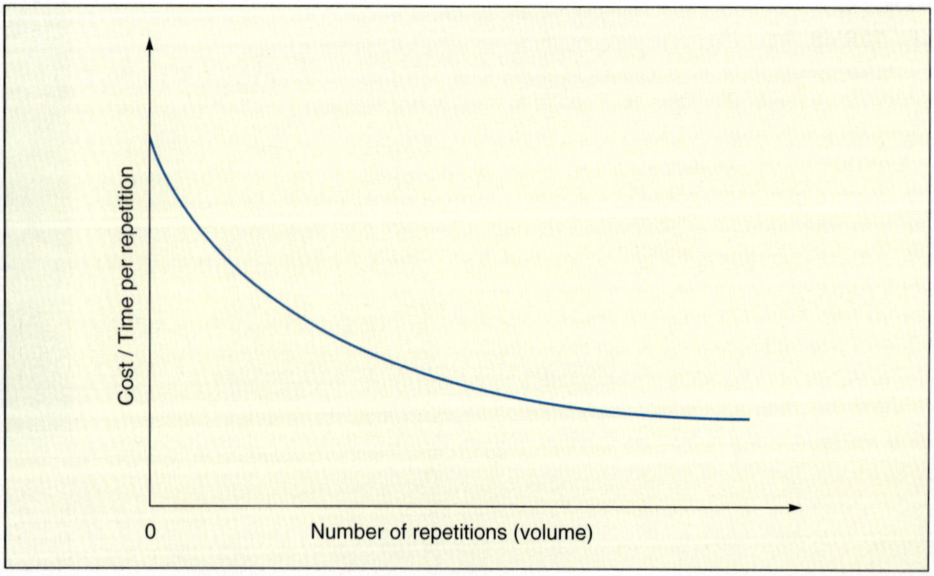

[2]T. P. Wright, "Factors Affecting the Cost of Airplanes," *Journal of the Aeronautical Sciences* (February 1936).

Hours required for unit 8 = $10(.7)^3$ (three doublings from 1 to 2 to 4 to 8)
= 3.43 hours, and so on.

Different organizations, and different products, have different learning curves. The rate of learning varies depending upon the quality of management and the potential of the process and product. *Any change in process, product, or personnel disrupts the learning curve.* Caution should be exercised in assuming that a learning curve is continuing and permanent.

Industry learning curves vary widely, as shown in Table S12.1. The lower the number, such as 70% compared to 90%, the steeper the slope and the faster the drop in costs. By tradition, learning curves are defined in terms of the *complements* of their improvement rates. For example, a 70% learning curve implies a 30% decrease in time each time the number of repetitions is doubled. A 90% curve means there is a corresponding 10% rate of improvement.

Stable, standardized, labour-intensive products and processes tend to have costs that decline more steeply than others. Between 1929 and 1955, for instance, the steel industry was able to reduce labour-hours per unit to 79% each time cumulative production doubled. The *POM in Action* box, coincidentally, finds that doctors follow the same 79% learning curve in performing heart transplants.

Learning curves are useful for a variety of applications. These include

1. internal labour forecasting, production scheduling, establishing costs and budgets;
2. external purchasing and subcontracting of items (see the SMT case study at the end of this supplement);
3. strategic evaluation of company and industry performance.

APPLYING THE LEARNING CURVE

A mathematical relationship enables us to express the time it takes to produce a certain unit. This relationship is a function of how many units have been produced

TABLE S12.1 ■ EXAMPLES OF LEARNING CURVE EFFECTS IN U.S. INDUSTRY

Example	Improving Parameter	Cumulative Parameter	Learning Curve Slope (%)	Time Frame
1. Model T Ford production	Price	Units produced	86	1910–1926
2. Aircraft assembly	Direct labour-hours per unit	Units produced	80	1925–1957
3. Equipment maintenance at GE	Average time to replace a group of parts	Number of replacements	76	Around 1957
4. Steel production	Production worker labour-hours per unit produced	Units produced	79	1920–1955
5. Integrated circuits	Average price per unit	Units produced	72*	1964–1972
6. Hand-held calculator	Average factory selling price	Units produced	74	1975–1978
7. Disk memory drives	Average price per bit	Number of bits	76	1975–1978

*Constant dollars.

Source: James A. Cunningham, "Using the Learning Curve as a Management Tool," *IEEE Spectrum* (June 1980): 45. © 1980 IEEE.

POM IN ACTION

The Impact of Learning Curves on Heart Transplants

The concept of the learning curve has long been documented in the production of goods and services. Studies now indicate that even the medical profession can look to learning curves to predict the success of surgeries. And today, as more hospitals face pressure from insurance companies and the government to enter fixed-priced negotiations for their services, their ability to learn from experience will become critical.

Temple University Hospital researchers evaluated learning effects for heart transplants. An expensive operation, averaging $60,000 in actual cost to a hospital, a transplant requires complex, precise coordination of a large team. In addition, hospitals doing heart transplants rarely recover the full costs of these procedures and therefore have a strong incentive to reduce these costs whenever possible.

The results of a 3-year study of 62 patients receiving transplants revealed a 79% learning curve, as measured by 1-year death rates (that is, the number of patients dying within the first year of surgery). In this case, every three operations resulted in a halving of the death rate. This ultimate measure of improvement estimates not just the lives lost, but the loss of a scarce and valued medical resource—the donor heart.

This Temple University Hospital experience places learning curves for heart transplants on a par with what has been found almost universally in industrial production.

Source: David B. Smith and Jan L. Larsson, "The Impact of Learning on Cost: The Case of Heart Transplantation," *Hospital and Health Services Administration* (Spring 1989): 85–97.

before it and how long it took to produce them. Although this procedure determines how long it takes to produce a given unit, the consequences of this analysis are more far-reaching. Costs drop and efficiency goes up for individual firms and the industry. Therefore, severe problems in scheduling occur if operations are not adjusted for implications of the learning curve. Learning curve improvement may result in labour and productive facilities being idle a portion of the time. Furthermore, firms may refuse additional work because they do not consider the improvement that results from learning. The foregoing are only a few of the ramifications of not considering the effect of learning. Learning curve effects occur in marketing and financial planning. From a purchasing perspective, our interest is in judging what a supplier's cost should be for further production.

Let us look at three approaches to learning curves: arithmetic analysis, logarithmic analysis, and learning curve coefficients.

Arithmetic Approach

The arithmetic approach is the simplest approach to learning curve problems. As we noted at the beginning of this supplement, each time production doubles, the labour per unit declines by a constant factor, known as the learning rate. So, if we know that the learning rate is 80% and that the first unit produced took 100 hours, the hours required to produce the second, fourth, eighth, and sixteenth units are:

NTH UNIT PRODUCED	HOURS FOR NTH UNIT
1	100.0
2	80.0 = (.8 × 100)
4	64.0 = (.8 × 80)
8	51.2 = (.8 × 64)
16	41.0 = (.8 × 51.2)

As long as we wish to find the hours required to produce *n* units and *n* is one of the doubled values, then this approach works. Arithmetic analysis does not answer the question for other units. However, the logarithmic approach does give us this flexibility.

Logarithmic Approach

The logarithmic approach allows the determination of *any* unit of production using the formula:

$$Y_N = Y_1(N)^{\log L/\log 2} \qquad \text{(S12.2)}$$

where Y_1 = time required for the first unit of production
Y_N = time required for the Nth unit of production
L = the "learning" rate
and log2 accounts for the "doubling" of production basis for learning curves.

EXAMPLE S1

The learning rate for a particular operation is 80% and the first unit of production took 100 hours. The hours required to produce the third unit may be computed as follows:

$$Y_N = Y_1(N)^{\log L/\log 2}$$
$$Y_3 = (100)(3)^{\log .8/\log 2}$$
$$= 70.2$$

The logarithmic approach allows us to determine the hours required for *any* unit produced, but there *is* a simpler method.

Learning Curve Coefficient Approach

The learning curve coefficient technique is embodied in Appendix D and the following equation:

$$Y_N = Y_1 C \qquad \text{(S12.3)}$$

where Y_N = number of labour-hours required to produce the Nth unit
Y_1 = number of labour-hours required to produce the first unit
C = learning curve coefficient

The learning curve coefficient, C, depends on the learning rate (70%, 75%, 80%, and so on) and the unit of interest.

Example S2 uses the preceding equation and Appendix D to calculate learning curve effects.

EXAMPLE S2

It took 125,000 labour-hours to produce the first of several tugboats you expect to purchase for your shipping company, Great Lakes Services, Inc. Boats 2 and 3 have been produced with a learning factor of 85%. At $40 per hour, what should you, as purchasing agent, expect to pay for the fourth unit?

First, search Appendix D for the fourth unit and a learning factor of 85%. The learning curve coefficient, C, is .723. To produce the fourth unit, then, takes

$$Y_N = Y_1 C$$
$$Y_4 = (125{,}000 \text{ hours})(.723)$$
$$= 90{,}375 \text{ hours}$$

To find the cost, multiply by $40:

$$90{,}375 \text{ hours} \times \$40/\text{hour} = \$3{,}615{,}000$$

Appendix D also shows cumulative values. These allow us to compute the total number of hours needed to complete a specified number of units. Again, the computation is straightforward. Just multiply the table value times the time required for the first unit. Example S3 illustrates this concept.

EXAMPLE S3

Example S2 computed the time to complete the fourth tugboat Great Lakes Services plans to buy. How long will *all four* boats require?

Looking this time at the total column in Appendix D, we find the cumulative coefficient is 3.345. Thus, the time required is

$$Y_N = Y_1 C$$
$$Y_4 = (125{,}000)(3.345) = 418{,}125 \text{ hours in total for all four boats}$$

For an illustration of how AB:POM can be used to solve Examples S2 and S3, see Program S12.1 at the end of this supplement.

Using Appendix D requires that we know how long it takes to complete the first unit. But what happens if our most recent or most reliable information available pertains to some other unit? The answer is that we must use this data to find a revised estimate for the first unit, and then apply the table to that number. Example S4 illustrates this concept.

EXAMPLE S4

Great Lakes Services believes that unusual circumstances in producing the first boat (see Example S2) imply that the time estimate of 125,000 hours is not as valid a base as the time of the third boat. Boat number 3 was completed in 100,000 hours.

To solve for the revised estimate for boat number 1, we turn to Appendix D with a unit value of $N = 3$ and a learning curve coefficient of $C = .773$ in the 85% column. We divide the actual time for boat three, 100,000 hours, by $C = .773$ to find the revised estimate:

$$\frac{100{,}000}{.773} = 129{,}366 \text{ hours}$$

STRATEGIC IMPLICATIONS OF LEARNING CURVES

So far, we have shown how operations managers can forecast labour-hour requirements for a product. We have also shown how purchasing agents can determine a supplier's cost, which can help in price negotiations. An important additional application of learning curves concerns strategic planning.

An example of a steep semiconductor industry price line is so labelled in Figure S12.2. These learning curves are straight because the scales are both log scales. When the *rate* of change is constant, a log-log graph yields a straight line. If a particular company believes its cost line to be the "company cost" line and the industry price is indicated by the dashed horizontal line, then the company must have costs at the points below the dotted line (for example, points *a* or *b*) or else operate at a loss (point *c*). When a firm's strategy is to pursue the company curve, a curve steeper than the industry average, it does this by

FIGURE S12.2 ■ Industry Learning Curve for Price Compared with Company Learning Curve for Cost. *Note*: Both the vertical and the horizontal axis of this figure are log scales. This is known as a log-log chart.

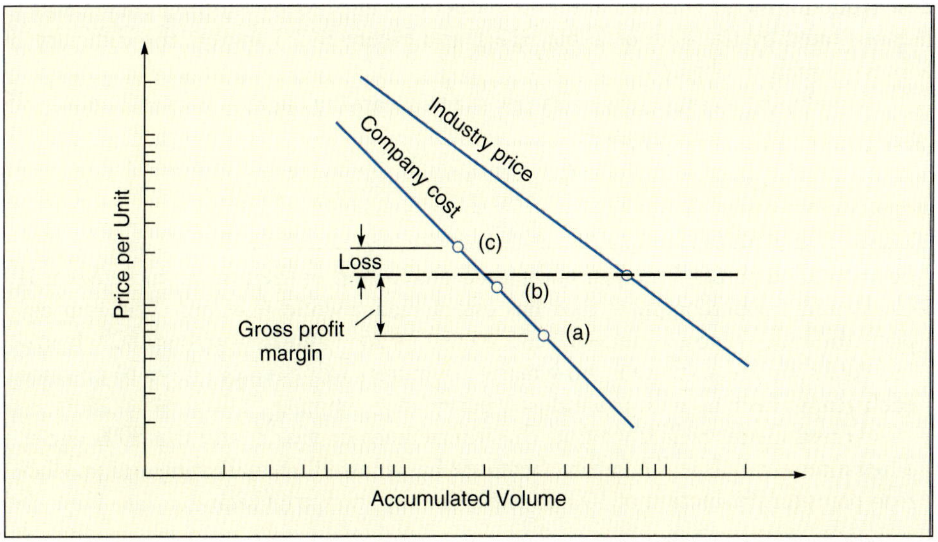

POM IN ACTION

Gallatin Focusses on Learning Curve

For the first time since its IPO in 1986, Co-Steel, which manufactures a variety of steel products in Canada, the United States, and Europe, has announced a quarterly loss. The loss is due to poor performance of its subsidiary, newly formed Gallatin Steel, whose overall company performance decreased by 14% in revenue and 5% in shipping.

These reductions were traceable to weak steel prices on the international market and very severe weather conditions, but there were two other identifiable factors: the increased production cost during the learning curve for Gallatin in the startup process and the high scrap cost. Gallatin has moved to resolve these issues by focussing primarily on internal performance which continues to improve while maintaining very-high-quality production. Co-Steel has also made an offer to increase its ownership of Mayer Parry Recycling from 60% to 75% in the hope that the capital investment will show returns from the incurred cost of its primary business.

Prices of steel have since stabilized and are forcasted to increase in the upcoming quarter. The extent of vertical integration is a source of security for Co-Steel's investment and the effect of Gallatin's progression along its learning curve is the source of production cost reductions.

Source: Adapted from Canada NewsWire Ltd., "Co-Steel Announces First Quarter Results," April 18, 1996.

1. following an aggressive price reduction policy as a barrier to market entry by competitors, or following the example of leading firms such as Maytag and Sony, whose clearly demonstrated superior quality allows them to charge a price premium for their products.
2. focussing on continuing cost reduction and productivity improvement;
3. building on shared experience;
4. keeping capacity growing ahead of demand.

Costs may drop as a firm pursues the learning curve, but volume must increase for the learning curve to exist. For instance, Figure S12.3 shows the units that have to be produced per year for a reduction of 25% when operating with a 60% or 80% learning curve. In recent years, much of the computer industry has operated at a 25% cost reduction. The volumes and cost reductions implied by learning curves and as demonstrated by the data of Table S12.1 and Figure S12.3 suggest the difficulty of achieving such an objective.

Developing a competitive strategy via the learning curve is not, as Example S5 suggests, a solution for everyone.

EXAMPLE S5

Seymore Computers, Inc., just completed production of the first Seymore Mark II Computer, a supercomputer that has established a world standard. The firm expects the industry to continue to reduce costs by 25% annually with an 80% learning curve. By the sixth year, how many computers will Seymore have to produce each year to keep up with the industry curve?

From Figure S12.3, we find the intersection of year 6 and the 80% curve. They intersect at 100. Therefore, Seymore has to establish marketing and production plans for production of 100 units per year by the sixth year.

Because the total worldwide demand for supercomputers is less than 20 per year, it seems unlikely that this is a reasonable strategy. Perhaps maintaining low levels of production with state-of-the-art technology is preferable to a standardized product for Seymore.

FIGURE S12.3 ■ The 80% and 60% Curves Show the Number of Units That Must Be Produced to Reduce Costs 25% Annually If the Firm Is Operating on One of Those Curves.

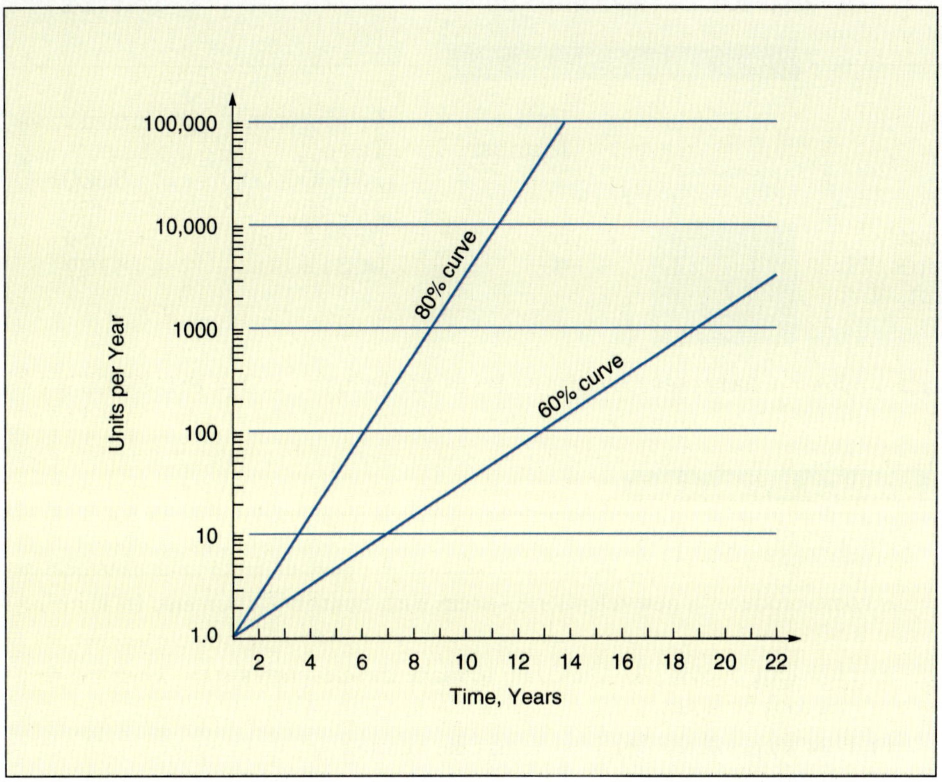

(*Source*: James A. Cunningham, "Using the Learning Curve as a Management Tool," *IEEE Spectrum* (June 1980): 47. © 1980 IEEE.)

SUMMARY

The learning curve is a powerful tool for the operations manager. This tool can assist operations managers in determining future cost standards for items produced as well as purchased. Additionally, the learning curve can provide understanding about company and industry performance. We saw three approaches to learning curves: arithmetic analysis, logarithmic analysis, and learning curve coefficients found in tables. AB:POM software can also help analyze learning curves.

KEY TERMS

Learning curve (p. 546)

USING AB:POM FOR LEARNING CURVES

AB:POM's Learning Curve Module computes the length of time that future units will take, given the time required for the base unit and the learning rate (expressed as a number between 0 and 1). As an option, if the time required for the first and Nth units are already known, the learning *rate* can be computed.

PROGRAM S12.1 ■ AB:POM's Learning Curve Module Applied to Examples S2 and S3. The program also has graphics capability.

Experience (learning) Curves — Solution

Great Lakes Services, Inc.

		Unit Number	Production Time	Cumulative Time
		1	125000.00	125000
		2	106250.00	231250
Unit number of base unit	1	3	96614.48	327864
Labour time for base unit, T1	125000.0	4	90312.50	418177
Unit number of last unit, N	4			
Learning coefficient	0.850			

F1 = Help F3 = Graph F4 = Character Graph F8 = All Print F9 = Print ESC

SOLVED PROBLEMS

Solved Problem S12.1

Digicomp produces a new telephone system with built-in TV screens. Its learning rate is 80%.

a) How long does it take Digicomp to make the eleventh system when the first one took 56 hours?

b) How long will the first 11 systems take in total?

c) As a purchasing agent, you expect to buy units 12 through 15 of the new phone system. What would be your expected cost for the units if Digicomp charges $30 for each labour-hour?

Solution

a) $T_N = T_1C$ (from Appendix D—80% unit time)
$T_{11} = (56 \text{ hours})(.462) = 25{,}872 \text{ hours}$

b) Total time for the first 11 units = (56 hours)(6.771) = 379.5 hours
(from Appendix D—80% unit time)

c) To find the time for units 12 through 15, we take the total cumulative time for units 1 to 15 and subtract the total time for units 1 to 11, which was computed in part (b). Total time for the first 15 units = (56 hours)(8.511) = 476.6 hours. So the time for units 12 through 15 is 476.6 − 379.5 = 97.1 hours. (This could also be confirmed by computing the times for units 12, 13, 14, and 15 separately using the unit time column and then adding them.) Expected cost for units 12 through 15 = (97.1 hours)($30/hour) = $2,913.

Solved Problem S12.2

If the first time you perform a job takes 60 minutes, how long will the eighth job take if you are on an 80% learning curve?

Solution

Three doublings from 1 to 2 to 4 to 8 implies 8^3. Therefore, we have

$$60 \times (.8)^3 = 60 \times .512 = 30.72 \text{ minutes}$$

or, using Appendix D, we have C = .512. Therefore:

$$60 \times .512 = 30.72 \text{ minutes}$$

DISCUSSION QUESTIONS

1. What are some of the limitations to the use of learning curves?
2. What techniques can a firm use to move to a steeper learning curve?
3. What are the approaches to solving learning curve problems?
4. What are the implications for Great Lakes Services, Inc., of Example S1 if the engineering department wants to change the engine in the third and subsequent tugboats Great Lakes Services purchases?
5. Under what conditions should a firm avoid "pricing on the learning curve"?
6. Why isn't the learning curve concept as applicable in a high-volume assembly line as it is in most other human activities?
7. What can cause a learning curve to vary from a smooth downward slope?
8. Explain the concept of the "doubling" effect in learning curves.

CRITICAL THINKING EXERCISE

A *POM in Action* box in this chapter discusses how the learning effect was found to take place in predicting the decline in death rates for heart transplant operations. Yet the same researchers at Temple University Hospital found that the learning curve did not seem to be valid in predicting length of hospital stay for transplant survivors or in the average unit cost of a transplant. Explain why these two factors do not seem to follow the traditional learning curve concept whereas the death rates do. If necessary, visit a hospital administrator to discuss whether this issue has been addressed locally. Have learning curves been applied in any other areas of the hospital? Why?

PROBLEMS

: **S12.1** Beth Zion Hospital has received initial certification from the Government of Ontario to become a centre for kidney transplants. The hospital, however, must complete the first 18 transplants under great scrutiny and at no cost to the patients. The very first transplant, just completed, required 30 hours. Beth Zion estimates it will have an 82% learning curve. Estimate the time it will take to complete the following:

a) The fifth kidney transplant.

b) All of the first five transplants.

c) The eighteenth transplant.

d) All eighteen transplants.

: **S12.2** Beth Zion Hospital (see Problem S12.1) has just been informed that only the first 10 transplants must be performed at the hospital's expense. The cost per hour of surgery is estimated to be $5,000. Again, the learning rate is 82% and the first surgery took 30 hours.

a) How long will the tenth surgery take?

b) How much will the tenth surgery cost?

c) How much will all ten cost the hospital?

: **S12.3** If the fourth oil change/lube job at Trendo-Lube took 18 minutes and the second took 20 minutes, estimate how long:

a) The first job took.

b) The third job took.

c) The eighth job will take.

d) The actual learning rate.

• **S12.4** A student at St. Francis Xavier University bought six bookcases for her dorm room. Each required unpacking of parts and assembly, which included some nailing and bolting. She completed the first bookcase in 2½ hours and the second in 2 hours.

a) What is her learning rate?

b) Assuming the same rate continues, how long will the third bookcase take?

c) The fourth, fifth, and sixth cases?

d) All six cases?

• **S12.5** Cleaning a toxic landfill took one Environment-Canada-certified contractor 300 worker-days. If the contractor follows an 85% learning rate, how long will it take in total to clean the next five, that is, landfills 2 through 6?

• **S12.6** The first vending machine that Smith Inc. assembled took 80 labour-hours. Estimate how long the fourth machine will require for each of the following learning rates:

a) 92% using Appendix D.

b) 87% using Appendix D.

c) 72% using Appendix D.

d) 95% using a calculator.

e) 86% using a calculator.

f) 65% using a calculator.

• **S12.7** Fraser-MacTavish Ltd. of Vernon, British Columbia, builds special-purpose, large industrial electric motors rated at 440 volts. Each unit is built by a new specialist team. The first motor required 97 worker-hours to complete. Similar jobs in the past showed a learning rate of 87%. Using 87% as the learning rate:

a) Calculate the time required to produce unit 2, i.e., Y_2.

b) Calculate the time required to produce unit 16, i.e., Y_{16}.

c) Calculate the time required to produce unit 47, i.e., Y_{47}.

d) Calculate the *total* time required to produce the *first* 24 units (i.e., units 1 to 24).

e) Calculate the *total* time required to produce the *second* 24 units (i.e., units 25 to 48).

f) Calculate the *average* time per unit required for the *first* 50 units.

: **S12.8** As the purchasing agent for Northeast Airlines, you are interested in determining what you can expect to pay for airplane number 4 if the third plane took 20,000 hours to produce. What would you expect to pay for plane number 5? Number 6? Use an 85% learning curve and a $40 per hr. labour charge.

: **S12.9** Using the data from Problem S12.8, how long will it take to complete the twelfth plane? How long will it take to complete the fifteenth plane? How long will it take to complete planes 12 through 15 inclusive? At $40 per hour, what can you, as purchasing agent, expect to pay for the four planes?

:S12.10 Dynamic RAM Corporation produces semiconductors and has a learning curve of .7. The price per bit is 100 millcents when the volume is $.7 \times 10^{12}$ bits. What is the expected price at 1.4×10^{12} bits? What is the expected price at 89.6×10^{12} bits?

·S12.11 If it takes 80,000 hours to produce the first jet engine at T.R.'s aerospace division and the learning factor is 90%, how long does it take to produce the eighth engine?

:S12.12 It takes 28,718 hours to produce the eighth locomotive at a large Quebec-based manufacturing firm. If the learning factor is 80%, how long does it take to produce the tenth locomotive?

:S12.13 If the first unit of a production run takes 1 hour and the firm is on an 80% learning curve, what will unit 100 take? (*Hint*: Apply the coefficient in Appendix D twice.)

:S12.14 As the estimator for Umble Enterprises, your job is to prepare an estimate for a potential service contract from a customer. The potential contract is for the service of diesel locomotive cylinder heads. The shop has done some of these in the past on a sporadic basis. The time for each cylinder head has been exactly 4 hours and similar work has been accomplished at an 85% learning curve. The customer wants you to quote in batches of 12 and 20.

a) Prepare the quote.

b) After preparing the quote, you find a labour ticket for this customer for five locomotive cylinder heads. From the sundry notations on the labour ticket, you conclude that the fifth unit took 2.5 hours. What do you conclude about the learning curve and your quote?

⁝S12.15 Goodwin & Goodwin Manufacturing is producing new sophisticated hip-joint replacements. Goodwin & Goodwin knows that the industry is on a 80% learning curve that reduces costs by 25% per year for similar products. To maintain the industry average, how many units must be produced in the first 3 years?

CASE STUDY

SMT's Negotiation with IBM

SMT and one other, much larger company were asked by IBM to bid on 85 more units of a particular computer product. The RFQ asked that the overall bid be broken down to show the hourly rate, the parts and materials component in the price, and any charges for subcontracted services. SMT quoted $1.62 million and supplied the cost breakdown as requested. The second company submitted only one total figure, $5.0 million, with no cost breakdown. The decision was made to negotiate with SMT.

The IBM negotiating team included two purchasing managers and two cost engineers. One cost engineer had developed manufacturing cost estimates for every component, working from engineering drawings and cost-data books that he had built up from previous experience and that contained time factors, both setup and run times, for a large variety of operations. He estimated materials costs by working both from data supplied by the IBM Corporate Purchasing Staff and from purchasing journals. He visited SMT facilities to see the tooling available so that he would know what processes were being used. He assumed that there would be perfect conditions and trained operators, and he developed cost estimates for the 158th unit (previous orders were for 25, 15, and 38 units). He added 5% for scrap-and-flow loss; 2% for the use of temporary tools, jigs, and fixtures; 5% for quality control; and 9% for purchasing burden. Then, using an 85% learning curve, he backed up his costs to get an estimate for the first

(Continued)

unit. He next checked the data on hours and materials for the 25, 15, and 38 units already made and found that his estimate for the first unit was within 4% of actual cost. His check, however, had indicated a 90% learning curve effect on hours per unit.

In the negotiations, SMT was represented by one of the two owners of the business, two engineers, and one cost estimator. The sessions opened with a discussion of learning curves. The IBM cost estimator demonstrated that SMT had in fact been operating on a 90% learning curve. But, he argued, it should be possible to move to an 85% curve, given the longer runs, reduced setup time, and increased continuity of workers on the job that would be possible with an order for 80 units. The owner agreed with this analysis and was willing to reduce his price by 4%.

However, as each operation in the manufacturing process was discussed, it became clear that some IBM cost estimates were too low because certain crating and shipping expenses had been overlooked. These oversights were minor, however, and in the following discussions, the two parties arrived at a common understanding of specifications and reached agreements on the costs of each manufacturing operation.

At this point, SMT representatives expressed great concern about the possibility of inflation in materials costs. The IBM negotiators volunteered to include a form of price escalation in the contract, as previously agreed among themselves. IBM representatives suggested that if overall materials costs changed by more than 10%, the price could be adjusted accordingly. However, if one party took the initiative to have the price revised, the other could require an analysis of *all* parts and materials invoices in arriving at the new price.

Another concern of the SMT representatives was that a large amount of overtime and subcontracting would be required to meet IBM's specified delivery schedule. IBM negotiators thought that a relaxation in the delivery schedule might be possible if a price concession could be obtained. In response, the SMT team offered a 5% discount, and this was accepted. As a result of these negotiations, the SMT price was reduced almost 20% below its original bid price.

In a subsequent meeting called to negotiate the prices of certain pipes to be used in the system, it became apparent to an IBM cost estimator that SMT representatives had seriously underestimated their costs. He pointed out this apparent error because he could not understand why SMT had quoted such a low figure. He wanted to be sure that SMT was using the correct manufacturing process. In any case, if SMT estimators had made a mistake, it should be noted. It was IBM's policy to seek a fair price both for itself and for its suppliers. IBM procurement managers believed that if a vendor was losing money on a job, there would be a tendency to cut corners. In addition, the IBM negotiator felt that by pointing out the error, he generated some goodwill that would help in future sessions.

DISCUSSION QUESTIONS

1. What are the advantages and disadvantages to IBM and SMT from this approach?
2. How does SMT's proposed learning rate compare with that of other companies?

Source: Adapted from E. Raymond Corey, *Procurement Management: Strategy, Organization, and Decision Making* (New York: Van Nostrand Reinhold).

BIBLIOGRAPHY

Abernathy, W. J., and K. Wayne. "Limits of the Learning Curve." *Harvard Business Review*, 52 (September/October 1974): 109–119.

Camm, J. "A Note on Learning Curve Parameters." *Decision Sciences* (Summer 1985): 325–327.

Hall, G., and S. Howell. "The Experience Curve from the Economist's Perspective." *Strategic Management Journal* (July/September 1985): 197–210.

Hart, C. W., G. Spizizen, and D. D. Wyckoff. "Scale Economies and the Experience Curve." *The Cornell H.R.A. Quarterly*, 25 (May 1984): 91–103.

Smith, D. B., and J. L. Larsson. "The Impact of Learning on Cost: The Case of Heart Transplantation." *Hospital & Health Services Administration*, 34 (Spring 1989): 85–97.

Smith, J. *Learning Curve for Cost Control.* Industrial Engineering & Management Press, 1989.

Taylor, M. L. "The Learning Curve—A Basic Cost Projection Tool." *N.A.A. Bulletin* (February 1961): 21–26.

13

INVENTORY MANAGEMENT AND JUST-IN-TIME TACTICS

CHAPTER OUTLINE

LEARNING OBJECTIVES

When you complete this chapter you should be able to:

Identify or define:
- ABC analysis
- Cycle counting
- Kanban
- Holding, ordering, and setup Costs
- Independent and dependent demand
- JIT inventory
- Record accuracy

Explain:
- The functions of inventory and basic inventory models

WORLD-CLASS PROFILE: HARLEY-DAVIDSON

JIT BRINGS A COMPETITIVE ADVANTAGE TO HARLEY-DAVIDSON

Harley-Davidson is a repetitive manufacturer. This means that they assemble modules. Like most repetitive manufacturers, Harley produces on an assembly line and the end product takes a variety of forms depending on the mix of modules. In Harley's case, the modules are motorcycle components in the form of two engine types in three displacement sizes for 20 street bike models, which are available in 13 colours and two wheel options. This adds up to 95 combinations. In addition, Harley produces 4 police, 2 Shrine, and 19 custom paint options. This requires that no fewer than 20,000 different pieces be assembled on one product line. The use of modules reduces some of the management tasks associated with an inventory of 20,000 parts.

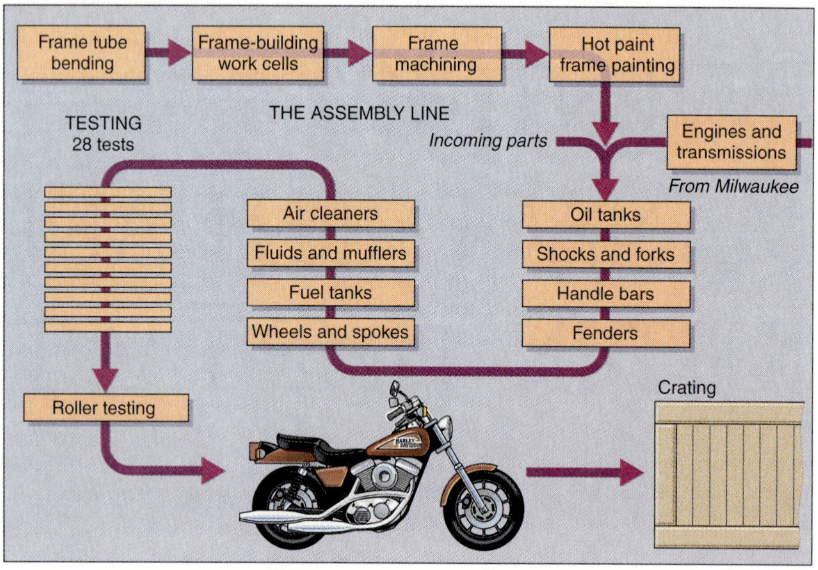

This is a flowchart of Harley-Davidson's York, Pennsylvania, assembly plant.

Most containers are specially made for individual parts, and many feature padding to protect the finish. Containers serve an important role in inventory reduction: the containers are the only place inventory is stored on the assembly line, so they serve as a signal to supply new parts to the line. After all the pieces have been removed, the container is returned to its originating cell, to signal the worker there to build more.

The Harley-Davidson engines are produced in Milwaukee and shipped to York, Pennsylvania. At the production facilities in York, both suppliers and the production departments deliver to the assembly line on a just-in-time (JIT) basis.

Harley-Davidson was founded in Milwaukee in 1903. Since that time, it has competed with hundreds of manufacturers, foreign and domestic. The competition has been tough, especially with the Japanese. Indeed, after almost nine decades, Harley is the only motorcycle company still producing in the United States.

Laser trimming fenders at a fixture setup. Harley workers have standardized die and fixture setups and located them near the machine where they will be used. An operator simply rolls up the next fixture or die and sets up for the next job in an average of 12 minutes, saving an average of 30 minutes over Harley's earlier processes. With more than 500 operations requiring such setups, the saving is substantial enough to give Harley a competitive edge.

a total quality control program driven by JIT.

By using JIT, large parts inventories with their inherent problems and high costs were eliminated. Now, management insists on delivery of small quantities of parts with no defects to the assembly line. The concept applies to suppliers as well as workers within Harley-Davidson. Indeed, Harley is so good at supplier development that they now do consulting in this area.

The Japanese motorcycle invasion of the 1970s caught Harley in the crossfire between Honda and Yamaha. The competition was so intense that Honda introduced 81 new models and Yamaha 34 in only 18 months. To meet the challenge, Harley-Davidson management emphasized quality improvement.

An emphasis on quality is a marvelous tonic for any management. And just-in-time tactics force operations managers to address improvements in virtually every area. At Harley-Davidson, this meant product and process improvement, JIT inventory, and a host of other modern manufacturing methods. But mostly it meant

Completed Harleys coming from the assembly line in preparation for a series of 28 tests and inspections.

Fansteel California supplies a critical steel part to Beckman Instruments, a medical instrument producer in Palo Alto, California. Beckman is a practitioner of Kanban, the famous Japanese system of inventory control. For Kanban to work, Beckman production personnel order parts directly by fax from Fansteel. There are no purchase orders and no bureaucratic go-between. The parts are shipped straight to the production line, so a high degree of trust in Fansteel's quality and reliability must exist. There is no excess inventory of parts to soften the blow of rejected pieces. A long-term commitment of both partners is required to achieve the economics of production inherent in Kanban. Results? Lead times are cut from 2 months to 5 days. Inventory and warehousing costs are slashed. Production schedules are coordinated. It works . . . if you have a partner you can trust. ♦

As Beckman and Fansteel both know, inventory is one of the most expensive assets of many companies, representing as much as 40% of total invested capital. Operations managers at these firms, at Harley-Davidson, and around the globe have long recognized that good inventory control is crucial. On one hand, a firm can try to reduce costs by reducing on-hand inventory levels. On the other hand, customers become dissatisfied when an item is frequently out of stock. Thus, companies must strike a balance between inventory investment and customer service levels. As you would expect, cost minimization is a major factor in obtaining this delicate balance.

All organizations have some type of inventory planning and control system. A bank has methods to control its inventory of cash. A hospital has methods used to control blood supplies and pharmaceuticals. Government agencies, schools, and, of course, virtually every manufacturing and production organization are concerned with inventory planning and control.

In cases of physical products, the organization must determine whether to produce goods or to purchase them. Once this has been determined, the next step is to forecast demand, as discussed in Chapter 5. Then operations managers determine the inventory necessary to service that demand. In this chapter, we discuss the functions, types, and management of inventory. We then address two basic inventory issues: how much to order and when to order.

FUNCTIONS AND TYPES OF INVENTORY

Inventory

Inventory is a stored resource that is used to satisfy a current or future need. In this section, we discuss the main functions of inventory and the four types of inventory.

Functions of Inventory

Inventory can serve several important functions that add flexibility to the operation of a firm. Six uses of inventory are

1. To provide a stock of goods to *meet anticipated demand* by customers.
2. To *separate production and distribution* processes. For example, if product demand is high only during summer, a firm may build up stock during the winter and thus avoid the costs of shortages and stockouts in summer. Similarly, if a firm's

supplies fluctuate, extra raw materials of inventory may be needed to separate (or "decouple") production processes.

3. To take advantage of *quantity discounts* because purchases in larger quantities can substantially reduce the cost of goods.
4. To *hedge against inflation* and price changes.
5. To *protect against stockouts* that can occur due to bad weather, supplier shortages, quality problems, or improper deliveries. "Safety stocks," namely, extra goods on hand, can reduce the risk of stockouts.
6. To *permit operations to continue smoothly* with the use of "work-in-process" inventory. This inventory exists because it takes time to make goods and because a pipeline of inventories is stocked throughout the process.

Litton Industries uses bar code readers to automate inventory control at its production and distribution facilities. The scanning device shown is linked to the central computer by wireless data transmission. Litton Canada is located in Rexdale, Ontario.

Types of Inventory

Firms maintain four types of inventories: raw material inventory, work-in-process inventory, maintenance/repair/operating supply (MRO) inventory, and finished goods inventory.

Raw material inventory
Work-in-process inventory

Raw material inventory has been purchased, but not processed. The items can be used to separate suppliers from the production process. However, the preferred approach is to eliminate supplier variability in quality, quantity, or delivery time so that separating is not needed. **Work-in-process (WIP) inventory** has undergone some change, but is not completed. WIP exists because of the time it takes for a product to be made (called cycle time). Reducing the cycle time reduces inventory. Often this is not difficult. As Figure 13.1 shows, most of the time a product is "being made," it is in fact sitting idle. Actual work time or "run" time is a small portion of the material flow time, perhaps as low as 5%.

MRO

Finished goods inventory

MROs are inventories devoted to **maintenance/repair/operating** supplies. Some firms use the term *facilities and operating supplies*. They exist because the need and timing for maintenance and repair of some equipment are unknown. Although the demand for MRO inventories is often a function of maintenance schedules, other MRO demands must be anticipated. Similarly, **finished goods inventory** is completed and awaiting shipment. Finished goods may be inventoried because customer demands for a given time period may be unknown.

INVENTORY MANAGEMENT

Operations managers establish systems for managing inventory. In this section, we briefly examine two ingredients of such systems: (1) how inventory items can be classified (called ABC analysis) and (2) how accurate inventory records can be maintained.

ABC Analysis

ABC analysis

This is an older system, but it is easily understood and can provide a quick look at the state of an inventory. **ABC analysis** divides on-hand inventory into three classifications on the basis of annual dollar volume.[1] ABC analysis is an inventory application

[1]H. Ford Dickie, *Modern Manufacturing* (formerly *Factory Management and Maintenance*) (July 1951).

FIGURE 13.1 ■ The Material Flow Cycle

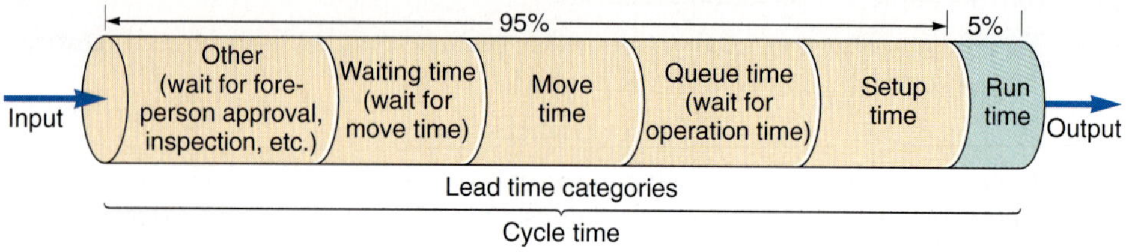

of what is known as the Pareto principle. The Pareto principle states that there are a critical few and trivial many.[2] The idea is to focus resources on the critical few and not the trivial many.

To determine annual dollar volume for ABC analysis, we measure the *annual demand* of each inventory item times the *cost per unit*. Class A items are those on which the annual dollar volume is high. Such items may represent only about 15% of the total inventory items, but they represent 70 to 80% of the total inventory cost. Class B items are those inventory items of medium annual dollar volume. These items may represent about 30% of the items and 15 to 25% of the value. Those with low annual dollar volume are class C, which may represent only 5% of the annual dollar volume, but about 55% of the total items.

An example is powered tools in manufacturing plants, especially in the automotive industry. Power screwdrivers, multispindle nut runners, and other high-volume-usage power tools, are used 16 to 18 hours per day at the rate of more than one vehicle per minute. Thus, quick repair is essential. Such tools comprise hundreds of parts, many in the $.10 to $10 price range. These parts are typical class C items. Spray-painting and lift truck repair parts are similar types of items where hundreds or even thousands of low-dollar-value items must be inventoried.

Graphically, the inventory of many organizations would appear as presented in Figure 13.2. An example of the use of ABC analysis is shown in Example 1.

FIGURE 13.2 ■ Graphic Representation of ABC Analysis

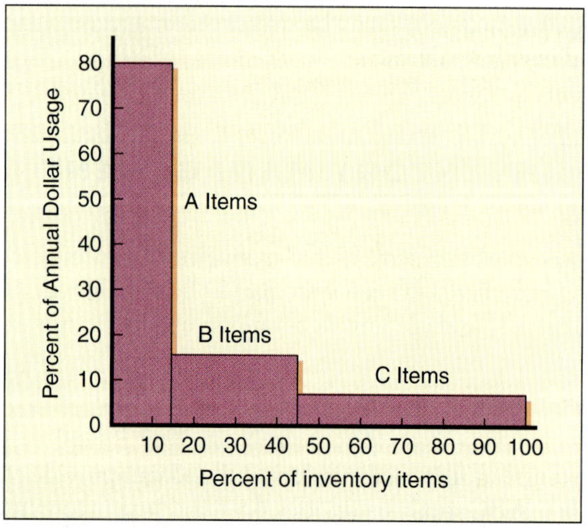

[2]Vilfredo Pareto, nineteenth-century Italian economist.

EXAMPLE 1

Silicon Chips, Inc., maker of super-fast 4-meg chips, has organized its 10 inventory items on an annual dollar volume basis. Shown below are the items, their annual demand, unit cost, annual dollar volume, and the percent each item represents of the total. In the last column on the right of the table below, we show these items grouped into ABC classifications.

ABC CALCULATION

ITEM STOCK NUMBER	PERCENT OF NUMBER OF ITEMS STOCKED	ANNUAL VOLUME (UNITS)	UNIT COST	ANNUAL DOLLAR VOLUME	PERCENT OF ANNUAL DOLLAR VOLUME		CLASS
#10286	20%	1,000	$ 90.00	$ 90,000	38.8%	72%	A
#11526		500	154.00	77,000	33.2%		A
#12760		1,550	17.00	26,350	11.4%		B
#10867	30%	350	42.86	15,001	6.5%	23%	B
#10500		1,000	12.50	12,500	5.4%		B
#12572		600	$ 14.17	8,502	3.7%		C
#14075		2,000	.60	1,200	.5%		C
#01036	50%	100	8.50	850	.4%	5%	C
#01307		1,200	.42	504	.2%		C
#10572		250	.60	150	.1%		C
		8,550		$232,057	100.0%		

Inventory items can be classified by criteria other than annual dollar volume. For instance, anticipated engineering changes or high unit cost may dictate upgrading items to a higher classification. By dividing inventory items into classes, operations managers can set different policies and controls for each class.

Policies that may be based on ABC classification include the following:

1. Purchasing resources expended should be much higher for A items than for C items.
2. Physical inventory control should be tighter for A items; perhaps they belong in a more secure area, with the accuracy of their records being verified more frequently.
3. Forecasting A items may warrant more care than forecasting other items.

Better forecasting, physical control, supplier reliability, and an ultimate reduction in safety stock and inventory investment can all result from ABC analysis.

An ABC analysis example can easily be worked through using an electronic spreadsheet such as Lotus 1-2-3, Excel, or QuattroPro. A standard database computer program can also provide practice.

These Levis are being scanned as part of the retailer's inventory control information system. Use of bar codes allows faster, more accurate data entry, better tracking of sales items, and reduced inventory costs. Bar-coding systems frequently pay for themselves within the first year of use.

POM IN ACTION

The Body Shop

The Body Shop has grown over the past nine years from one store in Toronto to 115 across Canada, and from one IBM XT to a network environment of six Compaq servers with remote access, fax gateways, e-mail, and a point-of-sale statistics system complete with sales and inventory databases.

Peter Chu, Body Shop's system manager, chose to use multiple servers instead of one super server because it made more sense for the Body Shop: "If you have one single server and it crashes, then everything is down ... with six separate servers only the applications on that particular server are affected." Of the Body Shop's server computers, three poll sales stats from the three Canadian regions and six more poll point-of-sale information from all retail stores. The point-of-sale computer software also inventories twice a day.

Chu has found Windows NT faster and better at multitasking than Windows 95, but warns any company looking into IS equipment to find out what support services warranties will be in place for after-sale questions and problems. He also suggests that they find out what computer know-how their in-house employees have.

The next step for the Body Shop is a virtual store on the Internet and multimedia kiosks in every retail outlet. Neither is intended to replace the store or the salesperson, merely to enhance the staff's sales abilities. Paul Rosenberg, manager of operations for the Body Shop, believes that people will always want face-to-face interaction in this business.

Source: Adapted from "The Body Shop: From One XT to Windows NT," *Computing Canada* (July 4, 1996).

Record Accuracy

Inventory systems require accurate records. Without them, managers cannot make precise decisions about ordering, scheduling, and shipping. Record accuracy allows organizations to move away from being sure that "some of everything" is in inventory to focussing on only those items that are required.

An example of the problems caused by inaccurate records was seen in the automotive industry especially in the area of MRO (maintenance, repair, and operating) supplies. New inventory items were established using a setup form created by Plant or Process Engineering. The form included a field for delivery lead time, where most originators routinely filled in "Two Weeks" for all items. As the originators did not deal with suppliers, they were not aware of the correct delivery lead time. Even though accurate lead time data were available in the computer system, it was not used to update the inventory files, so that items which were shown as having two weeks' lead time when set up 20 years earlier, were still indicated that way. Consequently, easily obtained items tended to be greatly overstocked and long-lead-time items were chronically out of stock. For example, standard hand tools such as wrenches, pliers, and screwdrivers would typically arrive in one or two days while items such as seam welding wheels required 14 weeks' delivery, as they were made to the automotive company's drawings and specifications. As a result, service provided to the production lines was poor in the midst of high inventories.

The solution to such a situation is to provide accurate lead times based on previous actual deliveries and to constantly update the lead time of each item on the basis of each receipt. The example cited demonstrates the problems caused by having no mechanism in place to update inaccurate rercords. It should be borne in mind that data can become quickly outdated.

To ensure accuracy, incoming and outgoing record keeping must be good, as must be stockroom security. A well-organized stockroom will have limited access, good housekeeping, and storage areas that hold fixed amounts of inventory. Bins, shelf space, and parts will be labelled accurately.

Automated storage and retrieval systems like those in use in the new Canadian Tire Distribution Centre in Brampton, Ontario, promise not only quicker storage and retrieval but greatly increased security as well. There are no "open bins" that goods can be stolen from, which means less theft and damage.

Cycle Counting

Even though an organization may have made substantial efforts to maintain accurate inventory records, these records must be verified through continuing audits. Such audits are known as **cycle counting**. Historically, many firms take annual physical inventories. This procedure often involves shutting down the facility and having inexperienced people counting parts and material. Inventory records instead should be verified via cycle counting. Cycle counting uses inventory classifications developed through ABC analysis. With cycle counting procedure, items are counted, records are verified, and inaccuracies are periodically documented. The cause of inaccuracies is then traced, and appropriate action is taken. Most cycle counting procedures are established so that some of each classification are counted each day. "A" items will be counted frequently, perhaps once a month. "B" items will be counted less frequently, perhaps once a quarter. "C" items will be counted even less frequently, perhaps once every 6 months.

Cycle counting

In addition, some firms will make use of their computer systems to generate a random list of 50 or 100 items which must by cycle-checked that day. Every day will see the generation of a new list. As well, from time-to-time, an outside accounting firm may be hired to do an independent check. This may be carried out during regular production times for MRO items in the stock room and in the middle of the night or on weekends for production items.

Example 2 illustrates how many items of each classification to count.

EXAMPLE 2

Cole's Trucks, Inc., a builder of high-quality refuse trucks, has about 5,000 items in its inventory. After hiring Matt Clark, a bright young P/OM student, for the summer, the firm determined that it has 500 A items, 1,750 B items, and 2,750 C items. The policy is to count all A items every month (every 20 working days), all B items every quarter (every 60 working days), and all C items every 6 months (every 120 working days). How many items should be counted each day?

Item Class	Quantity	Cycle Counting Policy	Number of Items Counted per Day
A	500	Each month (20 working days)	500/20 = 25/day
B	1,750	Each quarter (60 working days)	1,750/60 = 29/day
C	2,750	Every 6 months (120 working days)	2,750/120 = 23/day
			77/day

77 items are counted each day.

In Example 2, the particular items to be cycle counted are randomly selected each day. Another option is only to cycle count items when they are reordered.

Cycle counting also has the following advantages:

1. eliminating the shutdown and interruption of production necessary for annual physical inventories
2. eliminating annual inventory adjustments
3. providing professional personnel to audit the accuracy of inventory
4. allowing the cause of the errors to be identified and remedial action to be taken
5. maintaining accurate inventory records.

JUST-IN-TIME INVENTORY

Just-in-time inventory

Inventories in production and distribution systems often exist "just in case" something goes wrong, that is, just in case some variation from the production plan occurs. The "extra" inventory is then used to cover the variations or problems. We suggest that good inventory tactics require not "just-in-case," but "just-in-time" (JIT). **Just-in-time inventory** is the minimum inventory necessary to keep a perfect system running. With just-in-time inventory, the exact amount of good items arrive at the moment they are needed, not a minute before or a minute after the units are required.

JIT is an essential inventory approach for an automotive plant when dealing with a bulky component such as tires. The typical assembly line runs at approximately 60 cars per hour. This is equivalent to 300 tires per hour or 4,800 tiers for a two-shift, 16-hour day. Tires must arrive "just-in-time," or huge storage facilities would have to be built. JIT will frequently work hand-in-hand with the concept of "transit" inventories whereby items such as tires are delivered continuously throughout the production day. The variety of tire makes and sizes makes a highly organized technique such as JIT an absolute essential to smooth and cost-effective inventory management.

Variability

To achieve just-in-time inventory, managers *reduce variability caused by both internal and external factors*. Inventory hides variability—a polite word for problems. The less variability in the system, the less inventory is required.

Most variability is caused by tolerating waste or by poor management. Some of the reasons variability occurs are

1. employees, machines, and suppliers produce units that do not conform to standards, are late, or are not the proper quantity; or
2. engineering drawings or specifications are inaccurate; or
3. production personnel try to produce before drawings or specifications are complete; or
4. customer demands are unknown.

The idea is to eliminate variability and problems, as illustrated in Figure 13.3, which shows a stream full of rocks. The water in the stream represents inventory flow, and the rocks represent problems such as late deliveries, machine breakdown, and poor personnel performance. The water level in the stream hides variability and problems.

POM IN ACTION

Systems Maintenance at Canada Post

We may think that faxes and e-mail accounts have sounded the death knell for Canada Post, but that is far from the truth. The first place people go when sending a package overseas or to friends and family at Christmas, birthdays, anniversaries, etc., is the post office.

One thing we may not realize is that if the computer systems used by Canada Post ever go down, the physical movement of mail stops.

Canada Post spends considerable time and money ensuring their software and systems are running, not just sometimes but all the time. Systems maintenance is still seen as a cost of doing business, not a revenue generator. Even though the maintenance costs of a system within a typical network setup are approximately 50% of the IS budget, the cost associated with downtime of a system is extraordinarily higher.

That's the niche for Paul Salfi, associate director of the DMR Group in Saint John, New Brunswick, who maintain 90% of Canada Post's systems. They have a multiple task: analyze the problem, find a way to fix it, take the repaired system for a test drive, and finally—and most importantly—make sure the owner is satisfied.

Source: Adapted from "It's the Test Drive That's Critical," *Computing Canada* (June 20, 1996).

Because problems are hidden by inventory, they are sometimes hard to find. Perhaps the manager who said, "Inventory is the root of operations management evil" was not far from the truth. Inventory may not be evil, but it tends to hide the evil at great cost.

Therefore, to achieve just-in-time inventory, management must begin by reducing inventory. Reducing inventory uncovers the rocks that represent the variability and problems currently being tolerated. With reduced inventory, management chips away at the exposed problems until the stream is clear, and then makes additional cuts in inventory, chipping away at the next level of exposed problems. Ultimately, there will be virtually no inventory and no problems (variability).

One of the main external factors in variability is inconsistent delivery times. Working with the Traffic Department may assist in reducing the delivery time variability.

FIGURE 13.3 ■ Inventory Hides Problems, Just as Water in a Stream Hides the Rocks. (a) Reduce inventory so the problems can be found; (b) solve those problems, then reduce inventory again. Eventually the material should flow smoothly.

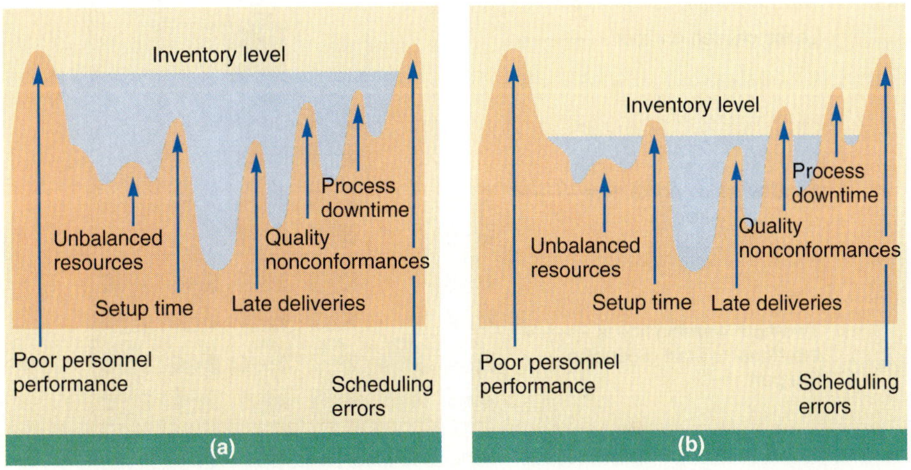

Just-in-time has come to mean elimination of waste, synchronized manufacture, and little inventory. The key to JIT is producing small lot sizes to standards. Reducing the size of batches can be a major help in reducing inventory and inventory costs. When inventory usage is constant, the average inventory level is the sum of the maximum inventory plus the minimum inventory divided by 2.

The average inventory drops as the inventory reorder quantity drops because the maximum inventory level drops. Moreover, the smaller the lot size (batch), the fewer problems are hidden. One way to achieve small lot sizes is to move inventory through the shop only as needed rather than *pushing* it on to the next workstation, whether the personnel there are ready for it or not. When inventory is moved only as needed, it is referred to as a *pull* system and the ideal lot size is one. The Japanese call this system *Kanban*.

Kanban

Kanban

Kanban is a Japanese word for "card." In their effort to reduce inventory, the Japanese use systems that "pull" inventory through the shop. They often use a "card" to signal the need for more material, hence the name Kanban. The card is the authorization for the next batch of material to be produced. The Kanban *"pulls"* the material through the plant. The system has been modified in many facilities so that, even though it is called a Kanban, the card does not exist. In some cases, an empty position on the floor is indication that the next lot is needed (Figure 13.4). In other cases, some sort of signal, such as a flag or rag (Figure 13.5) is used to signify that it is time for the next batch.

The batches are typically very small, usually a matter of a few hours' worth of production. Such a system requires tight schedules and frequent setups of machines. Small quantities of everything must be produced several times a day. Such a system

FIGURE 13.4 ■ Diagram of Stockpoint Lanes at Tachikawa Spring Co. Press Shop. From the status shown in the diagram, the lane has just been filled with part G82; they may be working on part H31 and getting ready for part G30, but that depends on the pull signals.

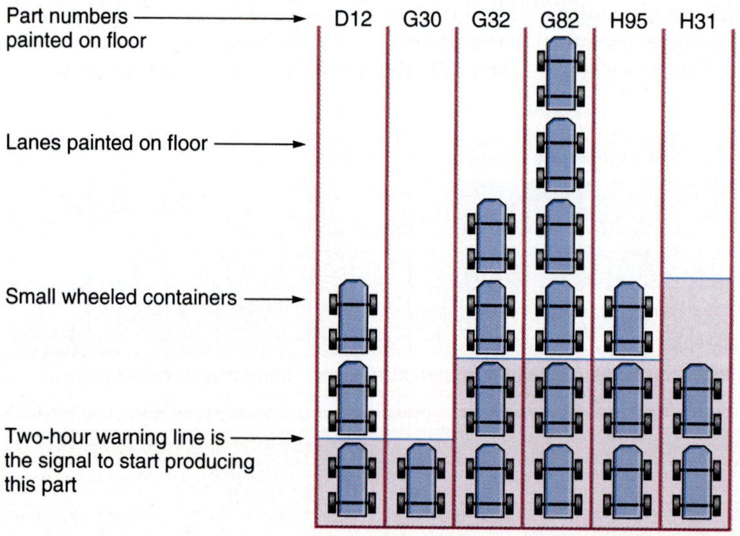

(*Source:* Robert W. Hall, *Zero Inventories*, Homewood, IL: Dow Jones-Irwin, 1983, p. 51.)

POM IN ACTION

SAAB Gets Handle on Inventory

Burlington Air Express has been chosen by SAAB to manage all their spare parts shipments from Canada, the United States, and Japan to the Swedish spare parts distribution centre in Nykøping, Sweden. Burlington understands cost-effective, multi-modal shipping and has extensive experience with the complexities of shipping and transportation within the automotive business. Burlington's automotive logistics expertise has been proven through a long-standing shipping relationship with General Motors, a 50% owner of SAAB.

Burlington's Argus+® worldwide shipment tracking system was a key advantage in winning the SAAB contract. This system gives SAAB a much better handle on inventory throughout the shipping and manufacturing cycle. Burlington offers international air freight, ocean forwarding, and worldwide customs brokerage through 500 offices in 118 countries.

Source: Adapted from PR Newswire Association Inc., "SAAB Picks Burlington Air Express," May 29, 1996.

must run smoothly because any shortage has an almost immediate impact on the entire system. Kanban places added emphasis on meeting schedules and reducing the time and cost required by setups.

Whether it is called Kanban or not, the advantages of small inventory and *pulling* material through the plant only when needed are significant. For instance, small batches allow a very limited amount of faulty material. Numerous aspects of inventory are bad, and only one aspect, availability, is good. Among the bad aspects are poor quality, obsolescence, damage, occupied space, committed assets, increased insurance, increased material handling, and increased accidents. All of these negative aspects add to the costs associated with holding (carrying) inventory.

INVENTORY MODELS

We now examine a variety of inventory models and the costs associated with them.

FIGURE 13.5 ■ Diagram of Outbound Stockpoint with Warning Signal Marker

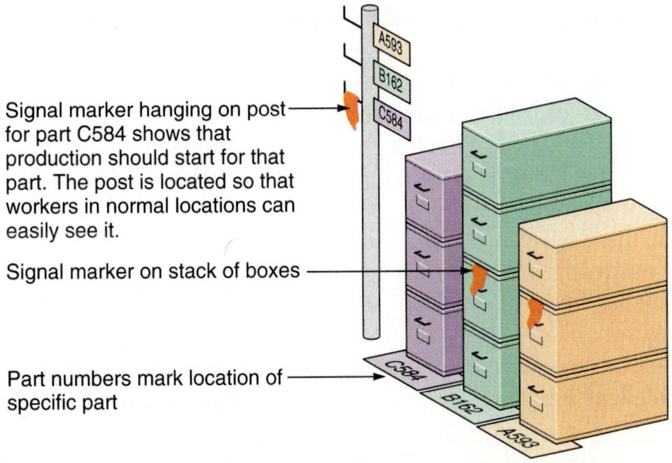

(*Source:* Robert W. Hall, *Zero Inventories*, Homewood, IL: Dow Jones-Irwin, 1983, p. 51.)

TABLE 13.1 ■ DETERMINING INVENTORY HOLDING COSTS

CATEGORY	COST AS A PERCENT OF INVENTORY VALUE*
Housing costs, such as building rent, depreciation, operating cost, taxes, insurance, heating or cooling	6% (3 to 10%)
Material handling costs, including equipment, lease, or depreciation, power, operating cost	3% (1 to 3.5%)
Labour cost from extra handling	3% (3 to 5%)
Investment costs, such as borrowing costs, taxes, and insurance on inventory	11% (6 to 24%)
Pilferage, scrap, and obsolescence	3% (2 to 5%)
Overall carrying cost	26%

*All figures are approximate, as they vary substantially depending on the nature of the business, location, and current interest rates. Any inventory cost of less than 15% is suspect, but annual inventory costs often approach 40% of the value of inventory.

Independent versus Dependent Demand

Inventory control models assume that demand for an item is either independent of or dependent on the demand for other items. For example, the demand for refrigerators is *independent* of the demand for toaster ovens. However, the demand for toaster oven components is *dependent* on the production requirements of toaster ovens.

This chapter focusses on managing *independent* demand items. Chapter 14 presents the topic of *dependent* demand.

Holding, Ordering, and Setup Costs

Holding costs

Holding costs are the costs associated with holding or "carrying" inventory over time. Therefore, holding costs also include costs related to storage, such as insurance, extra staffing, and interest payments. Table 13.1 shows the kinds of costs that need to be evaluated to determine holding costs. Many firms fail to include all of the inventory holding costs. Consequently, inventory holding costs are often understated.[3]

Ordering cost

Setup cost

Ordering cost includes costs of supplies, forms, order processing, clerical support, and so forth. When orders are being manufactured, ordering costs also exist, but they are known as setup costs. **Setup cost** is the cost to prepare a machine or process for manufacturing an order. Operations managers can lower ordering costs by reducing setup costs and by using such efficient procedures as electronic ordering and payment.

Setup time

In many environments setup cost is highly correlated with **setup time**. Setups usually require a substantial amount of work prior to an operation actually being accomplished at the work centre. Much of the preparation required by a setup can be done prior to shutting down the machine or process. Setup times can be reduced substantially, as shown in Figure 13.6. Machines and processes that traditionally have taken hours to set up are now being set up in less than a minute by the more imaginative world-class manufacturers. As we shall see later in this chapter, reducing setup times is an excellent way to reduce inventory investment and to improve productivity.

[3]Jack G. Wacker, "Can Holding Costs Be Overstated for 'Just-in-Time' Manufacturing System?" *Production and Inventory Management*, 27 (Third Quarter, 1986): 11–14.

FIGURE 13.6 ■ Steps to Reduce Setup Times. Reduced setup times are a major JIT component.

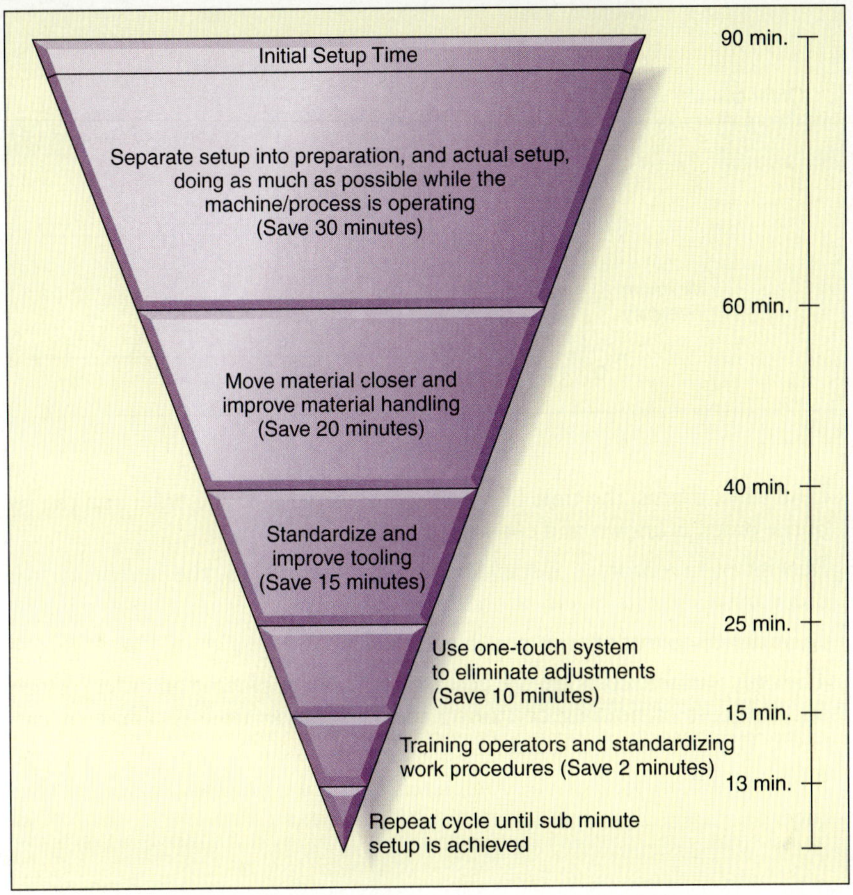

Inventory Models for Independent Demand

In this section, we introduce three inventory models that address two important questions: *when to order* and *how much to order*. These *independent* demand models are

1. the basic economic order quantity (EOQ) model
2. production order quantity model
3. quantity discount model

The Basic Economic Order Quantity (EOQ) Model

The economic order quantity (EOQ) is one of the oldest and most commonly known inventory control techniques.[4] This technique is relatively easy to use but is based on several assumptions:

1. Demand is known and constant.

[4]The research on EOQ dates back to 1915; see Ford W. Harris, *Operations and Cost* (Chicago: A. W. Shaw, 1915).

FIGURE 13.7 ■ Inventory Usage Over Time

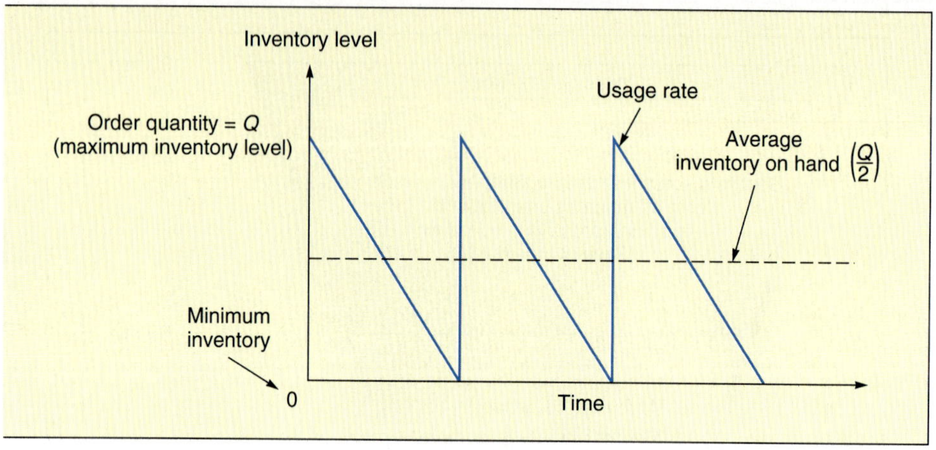

2. Lead time, that is, the time between the placement of the order and the receipt of the order, is known and constant.
3. Receipt of inventory is instantaneous. In other words, the inventory from an order arrives in one batch, at one time.
4. Quantity discounts are not possible.
5. The only variable costs are the cost of setting up or placing an order (setup cost) and the cost of holding or storing inventory over time (holding or carrying cost). These costs are discussed in the previous section.
6. Stockouts (shortages) can be completely avoided if orders are placed at the right time.

FIGURE 13.8 ■ Total Cost as a Function of Order Quantity

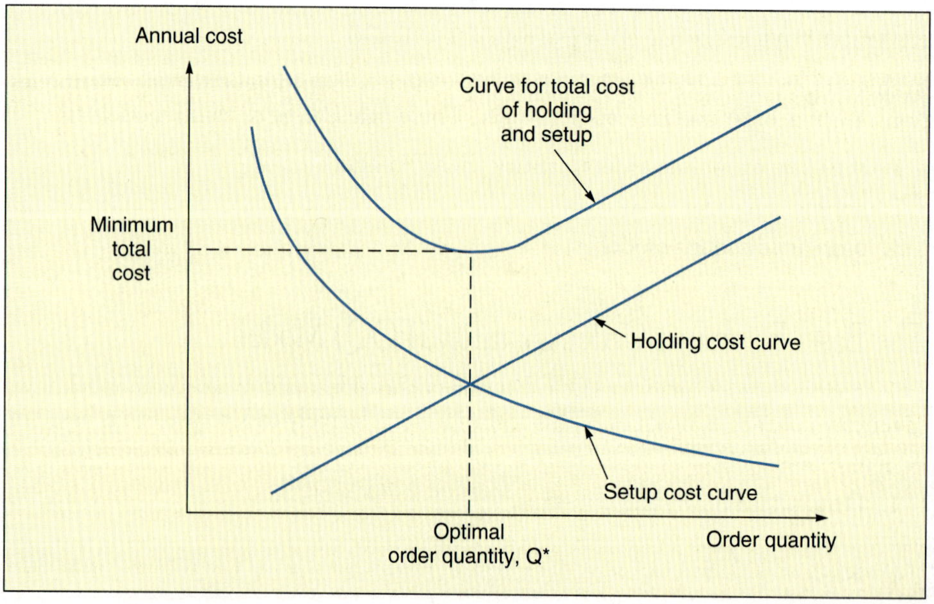

Under these assumptions, the graph of inventory usage over time has a sawtooth shape as in Figure 13.7. In Figure 13.7, Q represents the amount that is ordered. Let us say this amount is 500 dresses of a certain design at a Montreal retail store. Then all 500 dresses arrive at one time when an order is received. Thus, the inventory level jumps from 0 to 500 dresses. In general, an inventory level increases from 0 to Q units when an order arrives.

Because demand is constant over time, inventory drops at a uniform rate over time. (Refer to the sloped line in Figure 13.7.) When the inventory level reaches 0, the new order is placed and received, and the inventory level again jumps to Q units (represented by the vertical lines). This process continues indefinitely over time.

MINIMIZE COSTS. The objective of most inventory models is to minimize total costs. For the EOQ model, the significant costs are the setup (or ordering) cost and the holding (or carrying) cost. All other costs, such as the cost of the inventory itself, are constant. Therefore, if we minimize the sum of the setup and holding costs, we will also be minimizing the total costs. To help you visualize this situation, in Figure 13.8 we graph total costs as a function of the order quantity, Q. The optimal order size, Q^*, will be the quantity that minimizes the total costs. As the quantity ordered increases, the total number of orders placed per year will decrease. Thus, as the quantity ordered increases, the annual setup or ordering cost will decrease. But as the order quantity increases, the holding cost will increase due to larger average inventories that are maintained.

As we can see in Figure 13.8, a reduction in either the holding cost or the setup cost will reduce the total cost curve. A reduction in the total cost curve also reduces the optimal order quantity (lot size). And smaller lot sizes have a positive impact on quality[5] and production flexibility.

You should note that in Figure 13.8, the optimal order quantity occurred at the point where the ordering cost curve and the carrying cost curve intersected. This was not by chance. With the EOQ model, the optimal order quantity will occur at a point where the total setup cost is equal to the total holding cost.[6] We can use this fact to develop equations that solve directly for Q^*. We must

1. develop an expression for setup or ordering cost
2. develop an expression for holding cost
3. set setup cost equal to holding cost
4. solve the equation for the best order quantity.

Using the following variables, we can determine setup and holding costs and solve for Q^*:

$$\begin{aligned} Q &= \text{number of pieces per order} \\ Q^* &= \text{optimum number of pieces per order (EOQ)} \\ D &= \text{annual demand in units for the inventory item} \\ S &= \text{setup or ordering cost for each order} \\ H &= \text{holding or carrying cost per unit per year} \end{aligned}$$

[5]R. Anthony Inman, "The Impact of Lot-Size Reduction on Quality," *Production and Inventory Management Journal*, 35, no. 1 (First Quarter 1994): 5–8.

[6]This is the case where holding costs are linear and begin at the origin—that is, when inventory costs do not decline (or increase) as inventory volume increases and all holding costs are in small increments. Additionally, there is probably some learning each time a setup (or order) is executed, which lowers subsequent setup costs. Consequently, the EOQ model is probably a special case. However, we abide by the conventional wisdom that this model is a reasonable approximation.

1. Annual setup cost = (no. of orders placed/yr.)(setup or order cost/order)

$$= \left(\frac{\text{annual demand}}{\text{no. units in each order}}\right)(\text{setup or order cost/order})$$

$$= \frac{D}{Q}S$$

2. Annual holding cost = (average inventory level)(holding cost/unit/yr.)

$$= \left(\frac{\text{order quantity}}{2}\right)(\text{holding cost/unit/yr.})$$

$$= \frac{Q}{2}H$$

3. Optimal order quantity is found when annual setup cost = annual holding cost, namely,

$$\frac{D}{Q}S = \frac{Q}{2}H$$

4. To solve for Q^*, simply cross-multiply terms and isolate Q on the left of the equals sign.

$$2DS = Q^2H$$

$$Q^2 = \frac{2DS}{H}$$

$$Q^* = \sqrt{\frac{2DS}{H}} \qquad (13.1)$$

Now that we have derived equations for the optimal order quantity, Q^*, it is possible to solve inventory problems directly, as is done in Example 3.

EXAMPLE 3

Squirt, Inc., a company that markets hypodermic needles to hospitals, would like to reduce its inventory cost by determining the optimal number of hypodermic needles to obtain per order. The annual demand is 1,000 units, the setup or ordering cost is $10 per order, and the holding cost per unit per year is $0.50. Using these figures, we can calculate the optimal number of units per order:

1. $Q^* = \sqrt{\frac{2DS}{H}}$
2. $Q^* = \sqrt{\frac{2(1{,}000)(10)}{0.50}}$
3. $Q^* = \sqrt{40{,}000}$
4. $Q^* = 200$ units

5. It should be noted that the EOQ is a guide to ordering only, affected by other considerations:
   (a) For example, an EOQ calculation may indicate that one should order 98 $\frac{1}{8}$ inch drill bits. Such items are normally boxed in packages of 100. As the usage rate is not usually constant for most low-value items, one should order the 100, not 98. Standard packages are preferred as a major assistance in cycle checking. It is far easier to count three full unopened packages of 25 screwdrivers and six loose ones than to have to physically count 81. Also, as the supplier stocks items in standard packages, a "broken package" premium may be charged.
   (b) The EOQ is a mathematical optimization, and usually calculation results have a decimal portion. With the exception of items bought by weight, the decimal portion is inappropriate. One cannot call a supplier and order 27.03 screwdrivers. Therefore the EOQ answer should be rounded to the nearest integer and perhaps to the nearest standard package.

We can also determine the expected number of orders placed during the year (N) and the expected time between orders (T) as follows:

$$\text{Expected number of orders} = N = \frac{\text{demand}}{\text{order quantity}} = \frac{D}{Q^*} \quad (13.2)$$

$$\text{Expected time between orders} = T = \frac{\text{number of working days in a year}}{\text{order quantity}} \quad (13.3)$$

Example 4 illustrates this concept.

EXAMPLE 4

Using the data from Squirt, Inc., in Example 3, and a 250-day working year, we find the number of orders (N) and the expected time between orders (T) as:

$$N = \frac{\text{demand}}{\text{order quantity}} = \frac{1{,}000}{200} = 5 \text{ orders per year}$$

$$T = \frac{\text{number of working days /year}}{\text{expected number of orders}}$$

$$= \frac{250 \text{ working days/year}}{5 \text{ orders}} = 50 \text{ days between orders}$$

As mentioned earlier in this section, the total annual inventory cost is the sum of the setup and holding costs:

$$\text{Total annual cost} = \text{setup cost} + \text{holding cost} \quad (13.4)$$

In terms of the variables in the model, we can express the total cost as

$$\text{Total cost} = \frac{D}{Q}S + \frac{Q}{2}H \quad (13.5)$$

Example 5 shows how to use this formula.

EXAMPLE 5

Again using the Squirt, Inc., data (Examples 3 and 4), we determine that the total annual inventory costs are

$$\text{Total Cost} = \frac{D}{Q}S + \frac{Q}{2}H$$

$$= \frac{1{,}000}{200}(\$10) + \frac{200}{2}(\$0.50)$$

$$= (5)(\$10) + (100)(\$0.50)$$

$$= \$50 + \$50 = \$100$$

Often, the total inventory cost expression is written to include the actual cost of the material purchased. If we assume that the annual demand and the price per hypodermic are known values (for example, 1,000 hypodermics per year at P = $10), total annual cost should include purchase cost. Material cost does not depend on the particular order policy found to be optimal, because regardless of how many units are ordered each time, we still incur an annual material cost of $D \times P$ = (1,000)($10) = $10,000. (Shortly, we discuss the case in which this may not be true, namely, when a quantity discount is available to the customer who orders a certain amount each time.)

Robust

ROBUST MODELS. A benefit of the EOQ model is that it is robust. By **robust** we mean that it gives satisfactory answers even with substantial variation in the parameters. As we have observed, determining accurate ordering costs and holding costs for inventory is often difficult. Consequently, a robust model is advantageous. Total cost of the EOQ changes little in the neighbourhood of the minimum. The curve is very shallow. This means that variations in setup costs, holding costs, demand, or even EOQ make relatively modest differences in total cost. Example 6 shows how EOQ can be robust.

EXAMPLE 6

If management in the Squirt, Inc., example underestimated total annual demand by 50% (say it is actually 1,500 needles rather than 1,000 needles) while using the same Q, the annual inventory cost increases only $25.00 ($100 versus $125), or 25%. Similarly, if management cuts its order size by 50% from 200 to 100, cost increases by $25 ($100 versus $125), or 25%.

(a) If demand in Example 5 is actually 1,500 needles rather than 1,000, but management uses an EOQ of Q = 200 (when it should be Q = 244.9 based on D = 1,500), total costs increase 25%:

$$\text{Annual cost} = \frac{D}{Q}S + \frac{Q}{2}H$$

$$= \frac{1{,}500}{200}(\$10) + \frac{200}{2}(\$0.50)$$

$$= \$75.00 + \$50.00 = \$125.00$$

(b) If the order size is reduced from 200 to 100 needles, but other parameters remain the same, cost also increases 25%:

$$\text{Annual cost} = \frac{1{,}000}{100}(10) + \frac{100}{2}(\$0.50)$$

$$= \$100.00 + \$25.00 = \$125.00$$

REORDER POINTS. Now that we have decided how much to order, we must determine when to order. Simple inventory models assume that receipt of an order is instantaneous. In other words, they assume that a firm will wait until its inventory level for a particular item reaches zero before placing an order, and that all of the order is received at once. However, the time between the placement and receipt of an order, called the **lead time** or delivery time, can be as short as a few hours to as long as months. Thus, the when-to-order decision is usually expressed in terms of a reorder point, the inventory level at which an order should be placed. See Figure 13.9.

Lead time

The **reorder point (ROP)** is given as:

Reorder point (ROP)

$$\text{ROP} = (\text{demand per day})(\text{lead time for a new order in days}) \quad (13.6)$$

$$= d \times L$$

FIGURE 13.9 ■ The Reorder Point (ROP) Curve

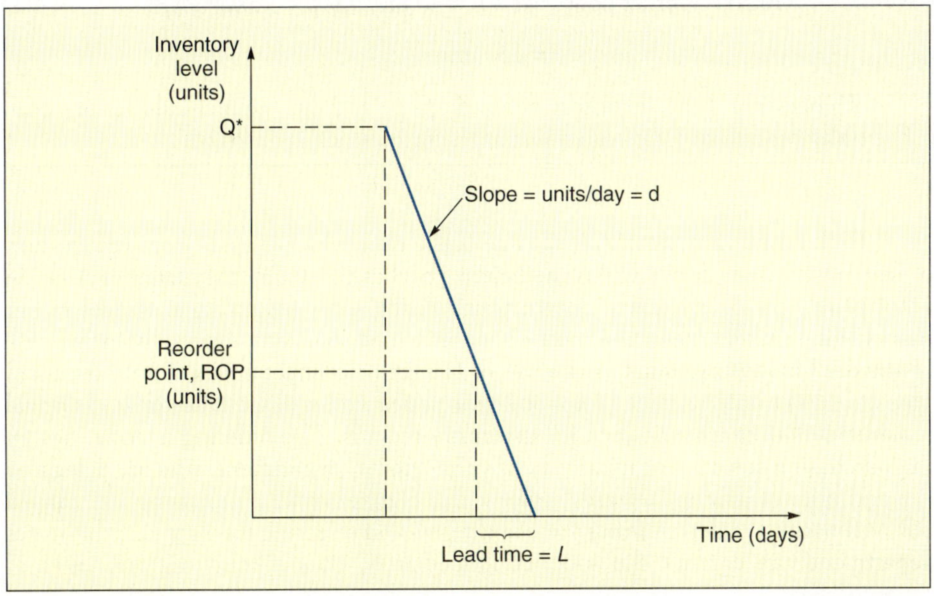

Safety stock

This equation for ROP *assumes that demand is uniform and constant.* When this is not the case, extra stock, often called **safety stock**, should be added.

The purpose of safety stock is to protect against variances in lead time and/or usage rate. If there were no variance in either factor, no safety stock would be needed. Conversely, the greater the variance in either or both factors, the higher the safety stock level must be. It should be noted that safety stock is costed out at full value, i.e., it is a measure that one hopes one will never have to use. As safety stock is used only occasionally in a smoothly functioning inventory, its carrying cost is at its full amount. Unlike regular inventory, no "sawtooth" graph applies to such stock.

Some firms will keep the safety stock in a second bin, which may be inside the main bin, and give instructions to the stockkeeper *not to draw* from the second bin until the main bin has been depleted. As a further backup, stockkeepers are asked to contact the inventory controller when they begin drawing from the safety stock.

The demand per day, d, is found by dividing the annual demand, D, by the number of working days in a year:

$$d = \frac{D}{\text{number of working days in a year}}$$

Computing the reorder point is demonstrated in Example 7.

EXAMPLE 7

Electronic Assembler, Inc., has a demand for TX512 VCRs of 8,000 per year. The firm operates a 200-day working year. On the average, delivery of an order takes 3 working days. We calculate the reorder point as follows:

$$d = \text{daily demand} = \frac{D}{\text{number of working days}} = \frac{8{,}000}{200}$$

$$= 40$$

$$\text{ROP} = \text{reorder point} = d \times L = 40 \text{ units/day} \times 3 \text{ days}$$

$$= 120 \text{ units}$$

Hence, when the inventory stock drops to 120, an order should be placed. The order will arrive 3 days later, just as the firm's stock is depleted.

To the using department, lead time is the time which elapses from recognition of lead until actual delivery. An inefficient purchasing system may cause a delay in order placement of unknown length, thus causing some inventory shortages rather than solving them. One of the most commonly used solutions, especially in the case of standard inventory items, is the use of *blanket* or *contract orders*. The most usual type of blanket order is issued for a one-year period and is based on estimated annual requirements from historic data for inventory records. The ordering is done, not by the purchasing department usually, but by the "stores" department, who are delegated the authority of issuing "releases" against the blanket order. Purchasing has carried out its functions of determining price and terms and selecting the supplier; the stores department can contact the supplier immediately, thus eliminating any internal causes of delay.

Production Order Quantity Model

In the previous inventory model, we assumed that the entire inventory order was received at one time. There are times, however, when the firm may receive its inventory over a period of time. Such cases require a different model. This model applies when inventory continuously flows or builds up over a period of time after an order has been placed or when units are produced and sold simultaneously. Under these circumstances, we take into account the daily production (or inventory flow) rate and the daily demand rate. Figure 13.10 shows inventory levels as a function of time.

Because this model is especially suitable for the production environment, it is commonly called the **production order quantity model**. (The terms ELS [economic lot size] and EPQ (economic production quantity) are also commonly used.) This model is useful when inventory continuously builds up over time, but the other economic order quantity assumptions are valid. We derive this model by setting ordering or setup costs equal to holding costs and solving for Q^*. Using the following symbols, we can determine the expression for annual inventory holding cost for the production run model:

Production order quantity model

Q = number of pieces per order
H = holding cost per unit per year
p = daily production rate
d = daily demand rate, or usage rate
t = length of the production run in days

1. $$\begin{pmatrix}\text{Annual inventory}\\ \text{holding cost}\end{pmatrix} = (\text{average inventory level}) \times \begin{pmatrix}\text{holding cost}\\ \text{per unit per year}\end{pmatrix}$$
$$= (\text{average inventory level}) \times H$$

2. $$\begin{pmatrix}\text{Average inventory}\\ \text{level}\end{pmatrix} = (\text{maximum inventory level})/2$$

3. $$\begin{pmatrix}\text{Maximum}\\ \text{inventory level}\end{pmatrix} = \begin{pmatrix}\text{total produced during}\\ \text{the production run}\end{pmatrix} - \begin{pmatrix}\text{total used during}\\ \text{the production run}\end{pmatrix}$$
$$= pt - dt$$

FIGURE 13.10 ■ Change in Inventory Levels over Time for the Production Model

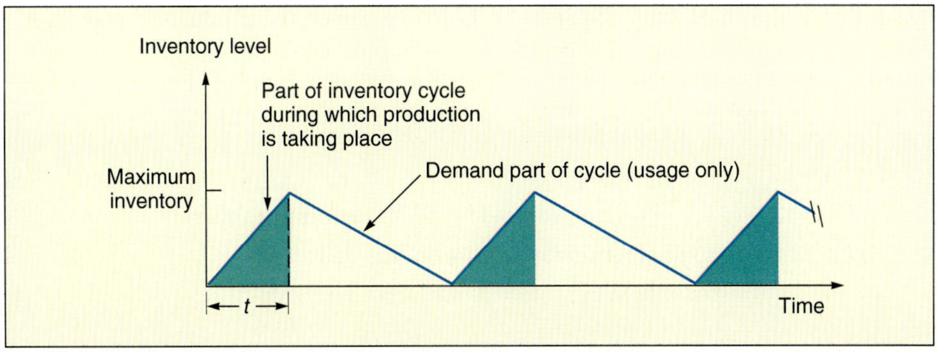

But Q = total produced = pt, and thus $t = Q/p$. Therefore,

$$\text{Maximum inventory level} = p\left(\frac{Q}{p}\right) - d\left(\frac{Q}{p}\right)$$

$$= Q - \frac{d}{p}Q$$

$$= Q\left(1 - \frac{d}{p}\right)$$

4. Annual inventory holding cost (or simply holding cost)

$$= \frac{\text{maximum inventory level}}{2}(H) = \frac{Q}{2}\left[1 - \left(\frac{d}{p}\right)\right]H$$

Using the expression for holding cost above and the expression for setup cost developed in the basic EOQ model, we solve for the optimal number of pieces per order by equating setup cost and holding cost:

$$\text{Setup cost} = (D/Q)S$$

$$\text{Holding cost} = \tfrac{1}{2}HQ\,[1 - (d/p)]$$

Set ordering cost equal to holding cost to obtain Q^*:

$$\frac{D}{Q}S = \tfrac{1}{2}HQ\,[1 - (d/p)]$$

$$Q^2 = \frac{2DS}{H[1 - (d/p)]}$$

$$Q_p^* = \sqrt{\frac{2DS}{H[1 - (d/p)]}} \qquad (13.7)$$

Example 8 shows how to use the above equation, Q_p^*, to solve for the optimum order or production quantity when inventory is consumed as it is produced.

EXAMPLE 8

Nathan Manufacturing, Inc., makes and sells specialty hubcaps for the retail automobile aftermarket. Nathan's forecast for its wire-wheel hubcap is 1,000 units next year, with an average daily demand of 6 units. However, the production process is most efficient at 8 units per day. So the company produces 8 per day but uses only 6 per day. Given the following values, solve for the optimum number of units per order.

Annual demand = D = 1,000 units
Setup cost = S = \$10
Holding cost = H = \$0.50 per unit per year
Daily production rate = p = 8 units daily
Daily demand rate = d = 6 units daily

1. $$Q_p^* = \sqrt{\frac{2DS}{H[1-(d/p)]}}$$

2. $$Q_p^* = \sqrt{\frac{2(1{,}000)(10)}{0.50[1-(6/8)]}}$$

$$= \sqrt{\frac{20{,}000}{0.50(1/4)}} = \sqrt{160{,}000}$$

$$= 400 \text{ hubcaps}$$

Also note that we can compute daily demand:

$$d = \frac{D}{\text{number of days the plant is open}}$$

and

$$\text{Number of days the plant is open} = \frac{D}{d}$$

Therefore, Nathan Manufacturing, Inc., in Example 8, is open only 167 days each year because

$$\text{Number of days the plant is open} = \frac{1{,}000}{6} = 167$$

You may want to compare the solution in Example 8 with the answer in Example 3. Eliminating the instantaneous receipt assumption, where $p = 8$ and $d = 6$, has resulted in an increase in Q^* from 200 in Example 3 to 400 in Example 8.

We can also calculate Q_p^* when annual data are available. When annual data are used, we can express Q_p^* *as*

$$Q_p^* = \sqrt{\frac{2DS}{H[1-(d/p)]}} \qquad (13.8)$$

where D = annual demand rate
P = annual production rate

Quantity Discount Models

To increase sales, many companies offer quantity discounts to their customers. A **quantity discount** is simply a reduced price (P) for the item when it is purchased in larger quantities. It is not uncommon to have a discount schedule with several discounts for large orders.

Quantity discount

(It should be noted here that, in practice, the quantity discount model is not used frequently in major industrial firms, who tend to use blanket purchase orders where pricing tends to be based on the annual quantity bought rather than individual order quantities. Many large firms use blanket order pricing for cost accounting for departmental budget charges. Changing prices would mean frequent accounting adjustments. A notable exception is suppliers selling unique items of their own design which, by virtue of patents or for similar reasons, may make them the sole supplier.)

A typical quantity discount schedule appears in Table 13.2. As can be seen, the normal price of the item is \$5. When 1,000 to 1,999 units are ordered at one time, then the price per unit drops to \$4.80; and when the quantity ordered at one time is 2,000 units or more, the price is \$4.75 per unit. As always, management must decide when and how much to order. But with quantity discounts, how does the operations manager make these decisions?

As with other inventory models discussed so far, the overall objective will be to minimize the total cost. Because the unit cost for the third discount in Table 13.2 is the lowest, you might be tempted to order 2,000 units or more to take advantage of the lower product cost. Placing an order for that quantity with the greatest discount price, however, might not minimize the total inventory cost. As the discount quantity goes up, the product cost goes down, but the holding cost increases because the orders are large. Thus, the major trade-off when considering quantity discounts is between the reduced product cost and the increased holding cost. When we include the cost of the product, the equation for the total annual inventory cost becomes

$$\text{Total cost} = \text{setup cost} + \text{holding cost} + \text{product cost}$$

or

$$\text{Total Cost} = \frac{D}{Q}S + \frac{QH}{2} + PD \tag{13.9}$$

where D = annual demand in units
S = ordering or setup cost per order or per setup
P = price per unit
H = holding cost per unit per year

TABLE 13.2 ■ A QUANTITY DISCOUNT SCHEDULE

DISCOUNT NUMBER	DISCOUNT QUANTITY	DISCOUNT (%)	DISCOUNT PRICE (P)
1	0 to 999	0	\$5.00
2	1,000 to 1,999	4	\$4.80
3	2,000 and over	5	\$4.75

Now, we have to determine the quantity that will minimize the total annual inventory cost. Because there are several discounts, this process involves four steps:

1. For each discount, calculate a value for Q^*, using the following equation:

$$Q^* = \sqrt{\frac{2DS}{IP}} \tag{13.10}$$

   You should note that the holding cost is IP instead of H. Because the price of the item is a factor in annual holding cost, we cannot assume that the holding cost is a constant when the price per unit changes for each quantity discount. Thus, it is common to express the holding cost (I) as a percentage of unit price (P) instead of as a constant cost per unit per year (H).

2. For any discount, if the order quantity is too low to qualify for the discount, adjust the order quantity upward to the lowest quantity that will qualify for the

discount. For example, if Q^* for discount 2 in Table 13.2 were 500 units, you would adjust this value up to 1,000 units. Order quantities between 1,000 and 1,999 will qualify for the 4% discount.

The reasoning for step 2 may not be obvious. If the order quantity is below the quantity range that will qualify for a discount, a quantity within this range may still result in the lowest total cost.

As shown in Figure 13.11, the total cost curve is broken into three different total cost curves. There is a total cost curve for the first ($0 \leq Q \leq 999$), second ($1{,}000 \leq Q \leq 1{,}999$), and third ($2{,}000 \leq Q$) discount. Look at the total cost curve for discount 2. Q^* for discount 2 is less than the allowable discount range, which is from 1,000 to 1,999 units. As the figure shows, the lowest allowable quantity in this range, which is 1,000 units, is the quantity that minimizes the total cost. Thus, the second step is needed to ensure that we do not discard an order quantity that may indeed produce the minimum cost. Note that an order quantity computed in step 1 that is greater than the range that would qualify it for a discount may be discarded.

3. Using the previous total cost equation, compute a total cost for every Q^* determined in steps 1 and 2. If you had to adjust Q^* upward because it was below the allowable quantity range, make sure to use the adjusted value for Q^*.
4. Select that Q^* that has the lowest total cost as computed in step 3. It will be the quantity that will minimize the total inventory cost.

Example 9 shows how to apply this model.

EXAMPLE 9

Wohl's Discount Store stocks Cool Wheels cars. Recently, they have been given a quantity discount schedule for the cars. This quantity schedule was shown in Table 13.2. Thus, the normal cost for the Cool Wheels cars is \$5. For orders between 1,000 and 1,999 units, the unit cost is \$4.80; and for orders of 2,000 or more units, the unit cost is \$4.75. Furthermore, the ordering cost is \$49 per order, the annual demand is 5,000 Cool Wheels cars, and the inventory carrying charge as a percentage of cost, I, is 20% or .2. What order quantity will minimize the total inventory cost?

The first step is to compute Q^* for every discount in Table 13.2. This is done as follows:

$$Q_1^* = \sqrt{\frac{2(5{,}000)(49)}{(.2)(5.00)}} = 700 \text{ cars/order}$$

$$Q_2^* = \sqrt{\frac{2(5{,}000)(49)}{(.2)(4.80)}} = 714 \text{ cars/order}$$

$$Q_3^* = \sqrt{\frac{2(5{,}000)(49)}{(.2)(4.75)}} = 718 \text{ cars/order}$$

The second step is to adjust upward those values of Q^* that are below the allowable discount range. Because Q_1^* is between 0 and 999, it does not have to be adjusted. Q_2^* is below the allowable range of 1,000 to 1,999, and therefore, it must be adjusted to 1,000 units. The same is true for Q_3^*. It must be adjusted to 2,000 units. After this step, the following order quantities must be tested in the total cost equation:

$$Q_1^* = 700$$

$$Q_2^* = 1{,}000 - \text{adjusted}$$

$$Q_3^* = 2{,}000 - \text{adjusted}$$

The third step is to use the total cost equation and compute a total cost for each of the order quantities. This is accomplished with the aid of Table 13.3.

The fourth step is to select that order quantity with the lowest total cost. Looking at Table 13.3, you can see that an order quantity of 1,000 Cool Wheels cars will minimize the total cost. It should be recognized, however, that the total cost for ordering 2,000 cars is only slightly greater than the total cost for ordering 1,000 cars. Thus, if the third discount cost is lowered to $4.65, for example, then this order quantity might be the one that minimizes the total inventory cost.

TABLE 13.3 ■ TOTAL COST COMPUTATIONS FOR WOHL'S DISCOUNT STORE

DISCOUNT NUMBER	UNIT PRICE	ORDER QUANTITY	ANNUAL PRODUCT COST	ANNUAL ORDERING COST	ANNUAL HOLDING COST	TOTAL
1	$5.00	700	$25,000	$350	$350	$25,700
2	$4.80	1,000	$24,000	$245	$480	$24,725
3	$4.75	2,000	$23,750	$122.5	$950	$24,822.5

FIGURE 13.11 ■ Total Cost Curve for the Quantity Discount Model

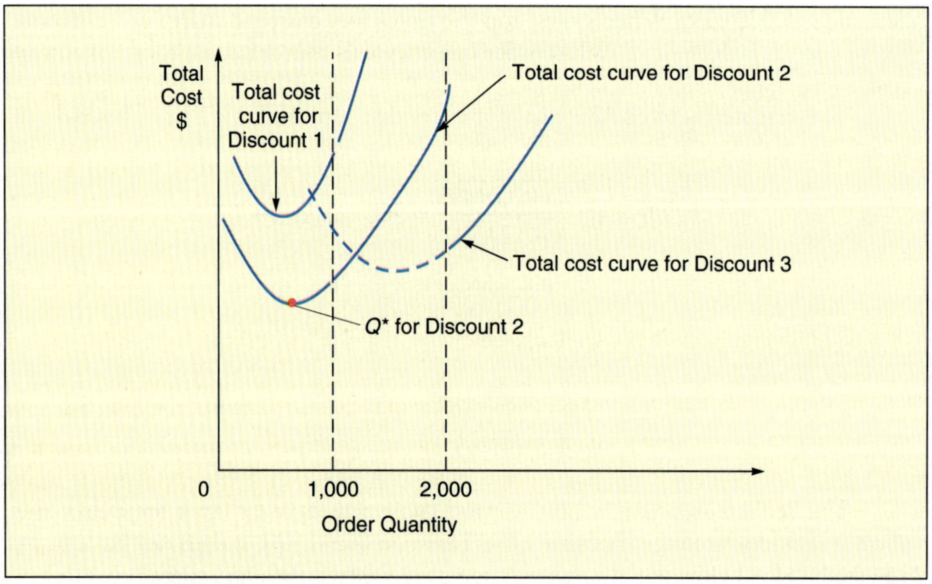

Calculations will verify that the most advantageous quantity to buy is just at the start of the price break, and the least advantageous quantity is just before the price break. Examination of Figure 13.11 will demonstrate this.

PROBABILISTIC MODELS WITH CONSTANT LEAD TIME

All of the inventory models we have discussed so far make the assumption that the demand for a product is constant and uniform. We now relax this assumption. The following inventory models, known as **probabilistic models**, apply *when product demand is not constant* but can be specified by a probability distribution.

Probabilistic models

An important concern of management is maintaining an adequate service level in the face of uncertain demand. The **service level** is the complement of the probability of a stockout. For instance, if the probability of a stockout is .05, then the service level is .95. Uncertain demand raises the possibility of a stockout. One method of reducing stockouts is to hold extra units in inventory to avoid this possibility—i.e., safety stock. As you recall from our previous discussion:

Service level

$$\text{Reorder point} = \text{ROP} = d \times L$$

d = daily demand

L = order lead time, or number of working days it takes to deliver an order

The inclusion of safety stock changes the expression to

$$\text{ROP} = d \times L + \text{safety stock} \tag{13.11}$$

The amount of safety stock depends on the cost of incurring a stockout and the cost of holding the extra inventory. Example 10 shows how this is done for David Rivera Optical.

EXAMPLE 10

David Rivera Optical has determined that its reorder point for eyeglass frames is 50 ($d \times L$) units. Its carrying cost per frame per year is \$5, and stockout cost is \$40 per frame. The optical store has experienced the following probability distribution for inventory demand during the reorder period. The optimum number of orders per year is six.

	NUMBER OF UNITS	PROBABILITY
	30	.2
	40	.2
ROP→	50	.3
	60	.2
	70	.1
		1.0

How much safety stock should David Rivera Optical keep on hand?

The objective is to find the safety stock that minimizes the total additional inventory holding costs and stockout costs on an annual basis. The annual holding cost is simply the holding cost multiplied by the units added to the ROP. For example, a safety stock of 20 frames, which implies that the new ROP, with safety stock, is 70 (= 50 + 20) raises the annual carrying cost by $5(20) = $100.

The stockout cost is more difficult to compute. For any level of safety stock, the stockout cost is the expected cost of stocking out. We can compute it by multiplying the number of frames short by the probability by the stockout cost by the number of times per year the stockout can occur (or the number of orders per year). Then we add stockout costs for each possible stockout level for a given ROP. For zero safety stock, a shortage of 10 frames will occur if demand is 60, and a shortage of 20 frames will occur if the demand is 70. Thus the stockout costs for zero safety stock are

(10 frames short)(.2)($40/stockout)(6 possible stockouts per year)
+ (20 frames short)(.1)($40)(6) = $960

The following table summarizes the total costs for each alternative.

Safety Stock	Additional Holding Cost	Stockout Cost		Total Cost
20	(20)($5) = $100	$0		$100
10	(10)($5) = $50	(10)(.1)($40)(6)	= $240	$290
0	$0	(10)(.2)($40)(6) + (20)(.1)($40)(6)	= $960	$960

The safety stock with the lowest total cost is 20 frames. This safety stock changes the reorder point to 50 + 20 = 70 units.

When it is difficult or impossible to determine the cost of being out of stock, a manager may decide to follow a policy of keeping enough safety stock on hand to meet a prescribed customer service level. For instance, Figure 13.12 shows the use of safety stock when demand is probabilistic. We see that the safety stock in Figure 13.12 is 16.5, and the reorder point is also increased by 16.5.

The manager may want to define the service level as meeting 95% of the demand (or conversely having stockouts only 5% of the time). Assuming that demand during lead time (the reorder period) follows a normal curve, only the mean and standard deviation are needed to define the inventory requirements for any given service level. Sales data are usually adequate for computing the mean and standard deviation. In the following example we use a normal curve with a known mean (μ) and standard deviation (σ) to determine the safety stock necessary for a 95% service level.

FIXED-PERIOD SYSTEMS

The inventory models we have considered so far in this chapter all fall into a class called *fixed-quantity systems*. That is to say, the same fixed amount is added to inventory every time an order for an item is placed. We saw that orders are event-triggered with the event triggering a reorder point occurring any time.

EXAMPLE 11

Charlottetown Regional Hospital in Prince Edward Island stocks a "code blue" resuscitation kit that has a normally distributed demand during the reorder period. The mean (average) demand during the reorder period is 350 kits, and the standard deviation is 10 kits. Regional Hospital wants to follow a policy that results in stockouts occurring only 5% of the time. How much safety stock should the hospital maintain? The following figure may help you visualize the example:

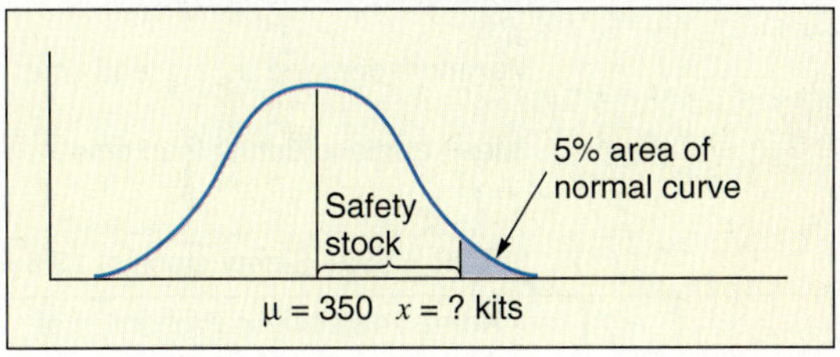

$$\mu = \text{mean demand} = 350 \text{ kits}$$
$$\sigma = \text{standard deviation} = 10 \text{ kits}$$

or

$$\text{Safety stock} = x - \mu$$

Since

$$Z = \frac{x - \mu}{\sigma}$$

Then

$$\text{Safety stock} = Z\sigma \tag{13.12}$$

We use the properties of a standardized normal curve to get a Z value for an area under the normal curve of .95 (or 1 – .05). Using a normal table (see Appendix A), we find a Z value of 1.65 standard deviations from the mean. Also:

$$Z = \frac{x - \mu}{\sigma} = \frac{\text{safety stock}}{\sigma}$$

$$= 1.65 = \frac{\text{safety stock}}{\sigma}$$

Solving for safety stock, as in Equation 13.12, gives

$$\text{Safety stock} = 1.65(10) = 16.5 \text{ kits}$$

This is the situation illustrated in Figure 13.12. The reorder point becomes (350 kits + 16.5 kits of safety stock =) 366.5, or 367 kits.

It typically takes this store 4 weeks to get an order for Levis 501 jeans filled by the manufacturer. If the store sells 10 pairs of size 30–32 Levis a week, the store manager could set up two containers, keep 40 pairs of jeans in the second container, and place an order whenever the first container is empty. This would be a fixed-point reordering system. It is also called a "two-bin" system and is an example of a very elementary, but effective, inventory approach.

Fixed-period system

In a **fixed-period system**, however, inventory is ordered at the end of a given period. Then, and only then, on-hand inventory is counted. Only the amount necessary to bring total inventory up to a prespecified target level is ordered. Figure 13.13 illustrates this concept.

The advantage of the fixed-period system is that there is no physical count of inventory items after an item is withdrawn—this occurs only when the time for the

FIGURE 13.12 ■ Probabilistic Demand

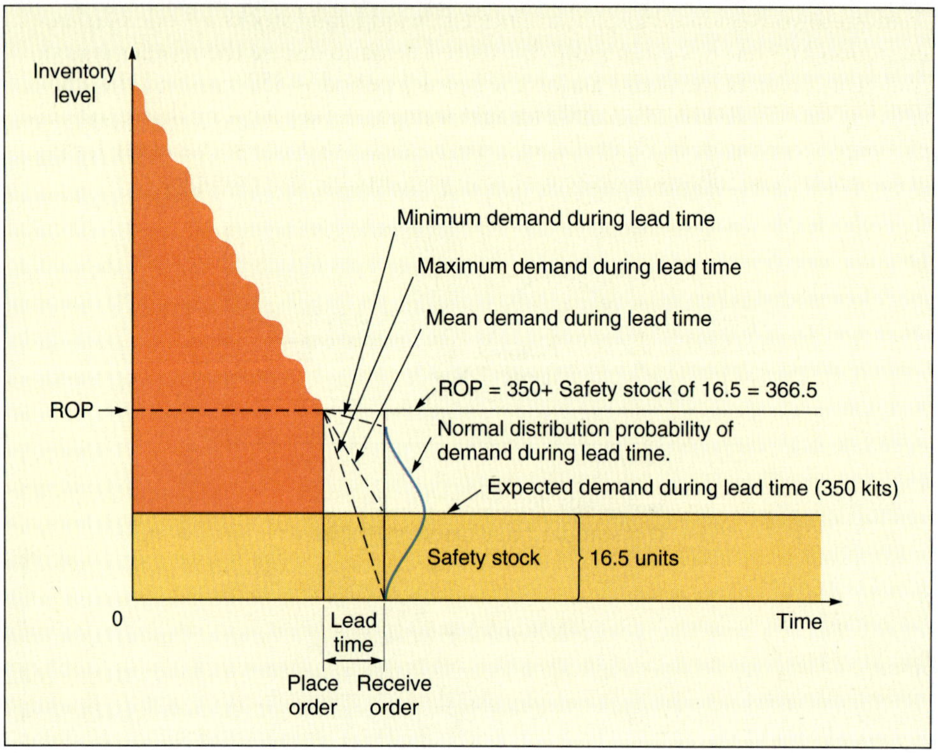

FIGURE 13.13 ■ Inventory Level in a Fixed-Period System. Various amounts are ordered based on the quantity necessary to bring inventory up to the target maximum.

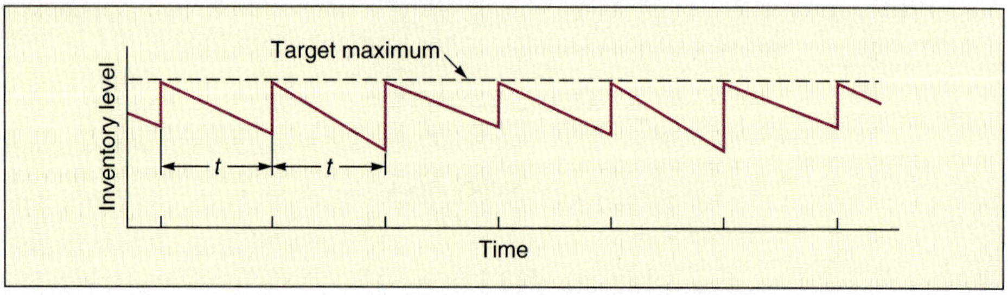

next review comes up. This procedure is also convenient administratively, especially if inventory control is only one of several duties of an employee.

A fixed-period system is appropriate when vendors make routine (that is, at a fixed time interval) visits to customers to take fresh orders or when purchasers want to combine orders to save ordering and transportation costs (therefore, they will have the same review period for similar inventory items).

The disadvantage of this system is that since there is no tally of inventory during the time between reviews, there is the possibility of a stockout during this time. This scenario is possible if a large purchase draws the inventory level down to zero right after an order is placed. Therefore, a higher level of safety stock (as compared to a fixed-quantity system) needs to be maintained to provide protection against stockout both during the time between reviews and the lead time.

MARGINAL ANALYSIS

For many inventory models, the optimal stocking policy can be determined through **marginal analysis**, which takes into account marginal profit (MP) and marginal loss (ML). Given any inventory level, we would add an additional unit to the inventory level only if its expected marginal profit equals or exceeds its expected marginal loss. This relationship is expressed symbolically in what follows: First, we let

Marginal analysis

$\hat{p}$ = probability that demand will be greater than or equal to a given supply (or the probability of selling at *least* one additional unit)

$1 - \hat{p}$ = probability that demand will be less than supply

The expected marginal profit is then found by multiplying the probability that a given unit will be sold by the marginal profit, $\hat{p}(\text{MP})$. Likewise, the expected marginal loss is the probability of not selling the unit multiplied by the marginal loss, or $(1 - \hat{p})(\text{ML})$. The decision rule is

$$\hat{p}(\text{MP}) \geqslant (1 - \hat{p})(\text{ML})$$

With some basic mathematical manipulations, we can determine the level of p that will help solve inventory problems:

$$\hat{p}(\text{MP}) \geqslant \text{ML} - \hat{p}(\text{ML})$$

or

$$\hat{p}(\text{MP}) + \hat{p}(\text{ML}) \geqslant \text{ML}$$

or

$$\hat{p}(\text{MP} + \text{ML}) \geqslant \text{ML}$$

or

$$\hat{p} \geqslant \frac{\text{ML}}{\text{MP} + \text{ML}} \qquad (13.13)$$

We can use this relationship to solve inventory problems directly. This type of analysis is especially good for one-time inventory decisions when reordering and back-ordering are not possible. We present the use of marginal analysis in Example 12. Note that we have added three possible demands (5, 6, and 7 units, with probabilities of .2, .3, and .5, respectively). As long as the cumulative probability exceeds p, we keep stocking additional units.

EXAMPLE 12

Cases of paper towel rolls sell at Price-Mart for \$6 each. The cost per case is \$3, and unsold cases may be returned to the supplier, who will refund the cost for each case returned minus \$1 per case for handling and storage. The probability distribution of demand is as follows:

DEMAND	PROBABILITY THAT DEMAND WILL BE AT THIS LEVEL
5	.2
6	.3
7	.5

1. From the previously developed relationship (Equation 13.13), we know that:

$$\hat{p} \geqslant \frac{ML}{MP + ML} \tag{13.13}$$

2. The next step is to determine $\hat{p}$. As you recall, $\hat{p}$ is the probability that demand will be at this level or greater. We can compute this *cumulative* probability as follows:

DEMAND	PROBABILITY THAT DEMAND WILL BE AT THIS LEVEL	(CUMULATIVE) PROBABILITY THAT DEMAND WILL BE AT THIS LEVEL OR GREATER
5	.2	$1.0 \geqslant 0.25$
6	.3	$.8 \geqslant 0.25$
7	.5	$.5 \geqslant 0.25$

$$ML = \text{marginal loss} = \$1$$
$$MP = \text{marginal profit} = \$6 - \$3 = \$3$$

Thus,

$$\hat{p} \geq \frac{1}{3+1} \geq .25$$

3. We keep adding additional cases as long as the $\hat{p} \geqslant ML/(MP + ML)$ relationship holds. If we stock 7 cases, our marginal profit will be greater than our marginal loss:

$$\hat{p} \text{ at 7 cases} \geq \frac{ML}{MP + ML}$$

Thus, the optimal policy is to stock 7 cases of paper towels.

ACHIEVING WORLD-CLASS STANDARDS

World-class firms *manage* their inventory. These firms know how much to order and when to place the order. They reduce inventory by driving down lot sizes. Inventories are not sitting and gathering dust. *Just-in-case* inventory does not exist. Material is moving or being worked on. JIT systems are commonplace, as are Kanban systems that pull material through the plant.

World-class organizations are also reducing inventory by developing computer information systems with increasingly accurate forecasts, or they have moved to short order cycles that allow them to produce to order. Incoming inventory is driven down, quality goes up, and cycle counting yields record accuracy. Orders can be filled faster so work-in-progress inventories are also reduced. The result of reduced inventory is less money tied up, increased quality, and, at the same time, increased responsiveness to customers. In world-class firms, "lean inventory" becomes a competitive advantage.

SUMMARY

Inventory represents a major investment for most firms. This investment is often larger than it should be because firms find it easier to have "just-in-case" inventory rather than "just-in-time" inventory. Inventories are of four types:

1. raw material and purchased components;
2. work-in-process;
3. maintenance, repair, and operating (MRO); and
4. finished goods.

In this chapter, we discussed independent inventory, ABC analysis, record accuracy, JIT, inventory costs, and inventory models used to control independent inventories. We presented the EOQ model, the production run model, the quantity discount model, the probabilistic model, the fixed-period system, and marginal analysis. The formulas for the inventory models presented in this chapter are summarized in Table 13.4.

KEY TERMS

Inventory (p. 562)
Raw material inventory (p. 563)
Work-in-process (WIP) inventory (p. 563)
MRO (p. 563)
Finished goods inventory (p. 563)
ABC analysis (p. 0563)
Cycle counting (p. 567)
Just-in-time inventory (p. 568)
Kanban (p. 570)
Holding costs (p. 572)
Ordering cost (p. 572)
Setup cost (p. 572)
Setup time (p. 572)
Robust (p. 578)
Lead time (p. 579)
Reorder point (ROP) (p. 579)
Safety stock (p. 580)
Production order quantity model (p. 581)
Quantity discount (p. 583)
Probabilistic models (p. 587)
Service level (p. 587)
Fixed-period system (p. 589)
Marginal analysis (p. 591)

TABLE 13.4 ■ STATISTICAL MODELS FOR INDEPENDENT DEMAND SUMMARIZED

Q = number of pieces per order
Q^* = EOQ = optimal order quantity
ROP = reorder point
D = annual demand in units
S = setup or ordering cost for each order
H = holding or carrying cost per unit per year in dollars
p = daily production rate
d = daily demand rate
t = length of production run in days
P = price
I = annual inventory carrying cost as a percentage of price
$\hat{p}$ = probability
MP = marginal profit
ML = marginal loss
μ = mean demand
σ = standard deviation
x = mean demand + safety stock
Z = standardized value under the normal curve

EOQ basic model

$$Q^* = \sqrt{\frac{2DS}{H}} \qquad (13.1)$$

Production run EOQ model

$$Q^* = \sqrt{\frac{2DS}{H[1-(d/p)]}} \qquad (13.7)$$

Total cost

$$\text{total cost} = \text{setup cost} + \text{holding cost} + \text{product cost} = \frac{D}{Q}S + \frac{QH}{2} + PD \qquad (13.9)$$

Quantity discount EOQ model

$$Q^* = \sqrt{\frac{2DS}{IP}} \qquad (13.10)$$

Probability model

$$\text{Safety stock} = Z\sigma \qquad (13.12)$$

Marginal analysis

$$\hat{p} \geq \frac{\text{ML}}{\text{MP} + \text{ML}} \qquad (13.13)$$

USING AB:POM AND SPREADSHEETS TO SOLVE INVENTORY PROBLEMS

Solving Examples 8 and 9 with AB:POM

All three of the EOQ family of models presented in this chapter can be solved by AB:POM. We illustrate the production run model using the data from Example 8 in Program 13.1. The data we entered are on the left-hand side, and the computed output on the right.

Program 13.2 provides a second illustration of AB:POM, this time on the quantity discount data for Example 9.

PROGRAM 13.1 ■ AB:POM's Production Run Module. Note that Holding Cost (H) may be entered in dollars or as a percentage of the price of the item (by typing the percentage with the % sign). *Holding cost* (H) and *demand rate* (D) must both be in the same time unit, that is, either daily, annual, etc.

Days per year will vary depending on the *daily demand rate* (d). If the *production rate* (p) and *daily demand rate* (d) are entered, then the *days per year* entry will be automatically computed and default to the appropriate value. If the *production rate* (p) is in days, but the *demand rate* (D) entry is annual, *days per year* must be entered.

Example 8

Model	Production order quantity model		
Demand Rate (D)	1000.00	Optimal order quantity (Q*)	400.00
Setup costs (S)	10.00	Maximum inventory level (Imax)	100.00
Holding costs (H)	0.50		
Production Rate (p)	8.00	Inventory $$ (Hold, Setup, Short)	$50.00
Days per year	166.6667	Unit costs (pD)	$1,000.00
or			
Daily demand rate (d)	6.00	Total cost	$1,050.00
Unit cost	1.00		

PROGRAM 13.2 ■ AB:POM's Quantity Discount Module. Starting and ending values for each price range must be input. The input is shown on the left of Program 13.2 and the answers on the right.

Wohl's Discount Store

Model		EOQ with quantity discount		
Demand Rate (D)		5000.00	Optimal order quantity (Q*)	1000.00
Setup cost (S)		49.00	Maximum inventory level (Imax)	1000.00
Holding cost (H)		20.00%		
Price Ranges			Inventory $$ (Hold, Setup, Short)	$725.00
From	To	Price	Unit costs (PD)	$24,000.00
1	999	5.00	Total cost	$24,725.00
1000	1999	4.80		
2000	999999	4.75		

Using a Spreadsheet to Solve Examples 3 and 4

EOQ calculations can be easily determined using a spreadsheet, as seen in Program 13.3. The input data, from Examples 3 and 4, appear in cells B5 through B7 of this "symbolic" spreadsheet. The formulas representing output are in cells B11 through B13. The formula in B11, @SQRT (2 * B7 * B5/B6), for example, represents the economic order quantity.

PROGRAM 13.3 ■ Using a Spreadsheet to Solve the EOQ Model in Examples 3 and 4.

	A	B
1	Squirt Inc. Example-EOQ	
2		
3	Inventory Input Data	
4		
5	Ordering Cost	10
6	Carrying Cost	0.5
7	Annual Demand	1000
8		
9	Inventory Output Results	
10		
11	EOQ in Units (Q*)	@SQRT (2*B7*B5/B6)
12	Optimal Number of Orders/Year (N)	+B7/B11
13	Expected Time between Orders (T)	250/B12

SOLVED PROBLEMS

Solved Problem 13.1

Eric Severson's FAX manufacturing firm purchases 8,000 modems each year for use in the faxes it produces. The unit cost of each modem is $10, and the cost of carrying 1 modem in inventory for a year is $3. Ordering cost is $30 per order.

What are the optimal order quantity, the expected number of orders placed each year, and the expected time between orders? Assume that Severson operates a 200-day working year.

Solution

$$Q^* = \sqrt{\frac{2DS}{H}} = \sqrt{\frac{2(8{,}000)(30)}{3}} = 400 \text{ modems}$$

$$N = \frac{D}{Q^*} = \frac{8{,}000}{400} = 20 \text{ orders}$$

$$\text{Time between orders} = T = \frac{\text{no. working days}}{N} = \frac{200}{20} = 10 \text{ working days}$$

Hence, an order for 400 modems is placed every 10 days. Presumably, then, 20 orders are placed each year.

Solved Problem 13.2

Annual demand for the notebook binders at McClellan's Stationery Shop is 10,000 units. Jill McClellan operates her business 300 days per year and finds that deliveries from her supplier generally take 5 working days. Calculate the reorder point for the notebook binders that she stocks.

Solution

$$d = \frac{10{,}000}{300} = 33.3 \text{ units/day}$$

$$\text{ROP} = d \times L = (33.3 \text{ units/day})(5 \text{ days}) = 166.7 \text{ units}$$

Thus, Jill should reorder when her stock of notebook binders reaches 167.

Solved Problem 13.3

Joe Murray, Inc., a supplier to schools, has an annual demand rate of 1,000 blackboards but can produce at an average annual production rate of 2,000 blackboards. Setup cost is $10 and carrying cost is $1.00. What is the optimal number of blackboards to be produced each time?

Solution

$$Q^* = \sqrt{\frac{2DS}{H[1 - (d/p)]}}$$

$$= \sqrt{\frac{2(1{,}000)(10)}{1[1 - (1{,}000/2{,}000)]}} = \sqrt{\frac{20{,}000}{1/2}} = \sqrt{40{,}000}$$

Solved Problem 13.4

What safety stock should Leslie Oliver Corporation maintain if mean sales are 80 during the reorder period, the standard deviation is 7, and Oliver can tolerate stockouts 10% of the time?

Solution

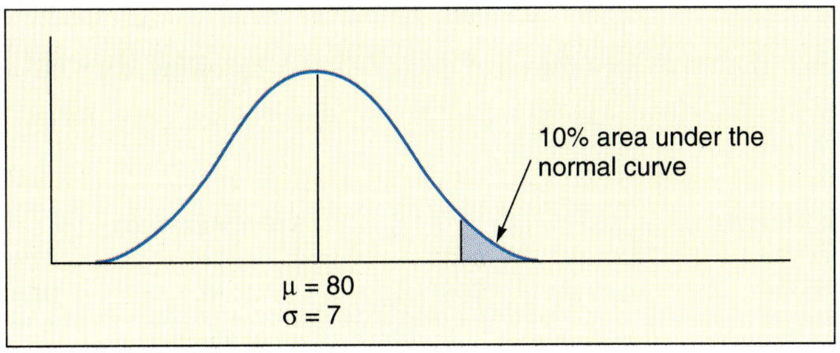

From Appendix A, Z at an area of .9 (or 1 – .10) = 1.28

$$Z = 1.28 = \frac{x - \mu}{\sigma} = \frac{\text{safety stock}}{\sigma}$$

$$\text{Safety stock} = 1.28\sigma$$

DISCUSSION QUESTIONS

1. What are the main reasons that an organization has inventory?
2. Describe each of the four types of inventory.
3. Describe the costs that are associated with ordering and maintaining inventory.
4. With the advent of low-cost computing, do you see alternatives to the popular ABC classifications?
5. What is cycle counting and what are its benefits?
6. What is a Kanban?
7. How is a Kanban used?
8. What is the difference between the standard EOQ model and the production inventory model?
9. What are the assumptions of the EOQ model?
10. How sensitive is EOQ to variations in demand or costs?
11. Does the production model or the standard EOQ model yield a higher EOQ if setup costs and holding costs are the same? Why?
12. When is a good time for cycle counting personnel to proceed with auditing a particular item?
13. What impact does a decrease in setup time have on EOQ?
14. What is meant by service level?
15. How would a firm go about determining a service level?
16. What happens to total inventory costs (and EOQ) if inventory holding costs per unit increase (that is, increase at an increasing rate) as inventory increases?
17. What happens to total inventory costs (and EOQ) if there is a fixed cost associated with inventory holding costs (for example, leasing the warehouse)?
18. Describe the difference between a fixed-quantity and a fixed-period inventory system.

CRITICAL THINKING EXERCISE

Espanola Hospital, in tiny Espanola, Ontario, faces a problem common to large, urban hospitals as well as small, remote ones like itself: deciding how much of each type of whole blood to keep in stock. Because blood is expensive and has a limited shelf life (up to 5 weeks under 1–6°C refrigeration), Espanola naturally wants to keep its stock as low as possible. Unfortunately, disasters such as a major tornado in 1986 and a train wreck in 1991 illustrated that lives would be lost because not enough blood was available to handle massive needs. The hospital administrator wants to set an 85% service level based on demand over the past decade. Discuss the implications of this decision. What is the hospital's responsibility with regard to stocking lifesaving medicines that have short shelf lives? How would you set the inventory level for a commodity such as blood?

PROBLEMS

• **13.1** Ramona Sherman's company has compiled the following data on a small set of products:

Stock Keeping Unit (SKU)	Annual Demand	Unit Cost	Stock Keeping Unit (SKU)	Annual Demand	Unit Cost
A	100	$250	D	200	$150
B	75	$100	E	150	$75
C	50	$50			

Use her data to illustrate an ABC analysis.

• 13.2 Fernandes Enterprise has 10 items in inventory. Dennis Fernandes asks you, the recent P/OM graduate, to divide these items into three ABC classifications. What do you report back to Mr. Fernandes?

ITEM	ANNUAL DEMAND	COST/UNIT	ITEM	ANNUAL DEMAND	COST/UNIT
A2	3000	$50	F3	500	$ 500
B8	4000	12	G2	300	1,500
C7	1500	45	H2	600	20
D1	6000	10	I5	1750	10
E9	1000	20	J8	2500	5

• 13.3 Angelo Corio opened a new beauty products retail store. There are numerous items in inventory, and Angelo knows that there are costs associated with inventory. However, her time is limited, so she cannot carefully evaluate the inventory policy for all products. Angelo wants to classify the items according to the dollars invested in them. The following table provides information about the 10 items that she carries:

ITEM NUMBER	UNIT COST	DEMAND (UNITS)
E102	$4.00	800
D23	8.00	1200
D27	3.00	700
R02	2.00	1000
R19	8.00	200
S107	6.00	500
S123	1.00	1200
U11	7.00	800
U23	1.00	1500
V75	4.00	1500

Use ABC analysis to classify these items into categories A, B, and C.

• 13.4 It takes approximately 2 weeks (14 days) for an order of steel bolts to arrive once the order has been placed. The demand for the bolts is fairly constant; on the average, the manager has observed that the hardware store sells 500 of these bolts each day. Because the demand is fairly constant, she believes she can avoid stockouts completely if she orders the bolts at the correct time. What is the reorder point?

• 13.5 Lead time for one of your fastest-moving products is 21 days. Demand during this period averages 100 units per day. What would be an appropriate reorder point?

: 13.6 Sande Johnson is attempting to perform an inventory analysis on one of her most popular products. Annual demand for this product is 5,000 units; unit cost is $200; carrying cost is considered to be approximately 25% of the unit price. Order costs for her company typically run nearly $30.00 per order and lead time averages 10 days. (Assume a 50-week year.)

a) What is the economic order quantity?

b) What is the reorder point?

c) What is the total inventory + ordering cost?

d) What is the optimal number of orders per year?

e) What is the optimal number of days between orders (assume 200 working days per year)?

• **13.7** Clarissa Seager is the purchasing agent for Central Valve Company, which sells industrial valves and fluid-control devices. One of its most popular valves is the Western, which has an annual demand of 4,000 units. The cost of each valve is $90.00, and the inventory carrying cost is estimated to be 10% of the cost of each valve. Clarissa has made a study of the costs involved in placing an order for any of the valves that Central Valve stocks, and she has concluded that the average ordering cost is $25.00 per order. Furthermore, it takes about 8 days for an order to arrive from the supplier. During this time, the demand per week for Central's valves is approximately 80.

a) What is the economic order quantity?

b) What is the reorder point?

c) What is the total annual inventory cost (carrying cost + ordering cost)?

d) What is the optimal number of orders per year?

e) What is the optimal number of days between any two orders assuming there are 200 working days per year?

: **13.8** Happy Pet, Inc., is a large pet store located in West Edmonton Mall. Although the store specializes in dogs, it also sells fish, turtle, and bird supplies. Everlast Leader, a leather lead for dogs, costs Happy Pet $7.00 each. There is an annual demand for 6,000 Everlast Leaders. The manager of Happy Pet has determined that the ordering cost is $20 per order, and the carrying cost as a percentage of the unit cost is 15%. Happy Pet is now considering a new supplier of Everlast Leaders. Each lead would cost only $6.65; but in order to get this discount, Happy Pet would have to buy shipments of 3,000 Everlast Leaders at a time. Should Happy Pet use the new supplier and take this discount for quantity buying?

• **13.9** Paul Misselwitz uses 1,500 per year of a certain subassembly that has an annual holding cost of $45 per unit. Each order placed costs Paul $150. Paul operates 300 days per year and has found that an order must be placed with his supplier 6 working days before he can expect to receive that order. For this subassembly, find:

a) the economic order quantity

b) the annual holding cost

c) the annual ordering cost

d) the reorder point

: **13.10** Christine Adams, of Adams Plumbing, uses 1,200 of a certain spare part that costs $25 for each order and $24 annual holding cost. Calculate the total cost for order sizes of 25, 40, 50, 60, and 100. Identify the economic order quantity and consider the implications for making an error in calculating the economic order quantity.

• **13.11** Teresa Ryu's Dream Store sells waterbeds and assorted supplies. The best-selling bed in the store has an annual demand of 400 units. The ordering cost is $40; the holding cost is $5 per unit per year. There are 250 working days per year, and the lead time is 6 days.

a) To minimize the total cost, how many units should be ordered each time an order is placed?

b) If the holding cost per unit were $6 instead of $5, what would the optimal order quantity be?

: **13.12** Jim Spivey's Computer Store in North Bay, Ontario, sells a printer for $200. Demand for this is constant during the year, and annual demand is forecasted to be 600 units.

The holding cost is $20 per unit per year, and the cost of ordering is $60 per order. Currently, the company is ordering 12 times per year (50 units each time). There are 250 working days per year, and the lead time is 10 days.

a) Given the current policy of ordering 50 units at a time, what is the total of the annual ordering cost and the annual holding cost?

b) If the company used the absolute best inventory policy, what would the total of the ordering and holding costs be?

c) What is the reorder point?

: 13.13 Jim Walsh is the owner of a small company that produces electric knives used to cut fabric. The annual demand is for 8,000 knives, and Jim produces them in batches. On average, Jim can produce 150 per day; during the production process, demand has been about 40 per day. The cost to set up production is $100.00, and it costs Jim $0.80 to carry a knife for 1 year. How many knives should Jim produce in each batch?

Draw an inventory diagram showing the production of one lot. Show the production and the usage only after production has stopped. How many days does Jim's firm both produce and use? How many days of usage only does the lot provide for?

: 13.14 John Mayleben, inventory control manager for Cal-Tex, receives wheel bearings from Wheel-Rite, a small producer of metal parts. Wheel-Rite can produce only 500 wheel bearings per day. Cal-Tex receives 10,000 wheel bearings from Wheel-Rite each year. Because Cal-Tex operates 200 working days each year, the average daily demand of wheel bearings by Cal-Tex is 50. The ordering cost for Cal-Tex is $40 per order, and the carrying cost is $0.60 per wheel bearing per year. How many wheel bearings should Cal-Tex order at one time? Wheel-Rite has agreed to ship the maximum number of wheel bearings that it produces each day to Cal-Tex once an order has been received.

: 13.15 McLeavey Manufacturing has a demand for 1,000 pumps each year. The cost of a pump is $50. It costs McLeavey Manufacturing $40 to place an order, and the carrying cost is 25% of the unit cost. If pumps are ordered in quantities of 200, McLeavey Manufacturing can get a 3% discount on the cost of the pumps. Should McLeavey Manufacturing order 200 pumps at a time and take the 3% discount?

: 13.16 Froelich Products offers the following discount schedule for 4′ × 8′ sheets of plywood:

ORDER	UNIT COST
9 sheets or less	$18.00
10 to 50 sheets	$17.50
More than 50 sheets	$17.25

Home Sweet Home Company orders plywood from Froelich Products. Home Sweet Home has an ordering cost of $45. The carrying cost is 20%, and the annual demand is 100 sheets. What ordering policy do you recommend?

: 13.17 Should the quantity discount be taken, given the following data on a hardware item stocked by the Steven Hazelwood and Sons Paint Store?

$$D = 2{,}000 \text{ units}$$
$$S = \$10$$
$$H = \$1$$
$$P = \$1$$
$$\text{Discount price} = \$.75$$
$$\begin{pmatrix}\text{Quantity needed to}\\ \text{qualify for discount}\end{pmatrix} = 2{,}000 \text{ units}$$

: 13.18 The regular price of a tape deck component is \$20. On orders of 75 units or more, the price is discounted to \$18.50. On orders of 100 units or more, the discount price is \$15.75. At present, Sound Business, Inc., a manufacturer of stereo components, has an inventory carrying cost of 5% per unit per year, and its ordering cost is \$10. Annual demand is 45 components. What should Sound Business do?

⁝ 13.19 A product is ordered once each year, and the reorder point without safety stock ($d \times L$) is 100 units. Inventory carrying cost is \$10 per unit per year, and the cost of a stockout is \$50 per unit per year. Given the following demand probabilities during the reorder period, how much safety stock should be carried?

	Demand During Reorder Period	Probability
	0	.1
	50	.2
ROP→	100	.4
	150	.2
	200	.1
		1.0

: 13.20 For a given product, ML = \$4 and MP = \$1. What stocking policy would you recommend in regard to the following demand distribution?

Demand (in units)	Probability That Demand Will Be at This Level	Demand (in units)	Probability That Demand Will Be at This Level
0	.05	7	.10
1	.05	8	.05
2	.05	9	.05
3	.1	10	.03
4	.15	11	.02
5	.15		1.00
6	.20		

⁝ 13.21 Carole Horton, Inc., an organization that sells children's art sets, has an ordering cost of \$40 for the BB-1 set. The carrying cost for BB-1 is \$5 per set per year. In order to meet demand, Carole orders large quantities of BB-1 seven times a year. The stockout cost for BB-1 is estimated to be \$50 per set. Over the last several years, Carole has observed the following demand during the lead time for BB-1:

Demand During Lead Time	Probability	Demand During Lead Time	Probability
40	.1	70	.2
50	.2	80	.2
60	.2	90	.1
			1.0

The reorder point for BB-1 is 60 units. What level of safety stock should be maintained for BB-1?

: 13.22 Jon Ahlbrand's company produces a product for which the annual demand is 10,000. Production averages 200 per day, and demand is about 50 per day. Holding costs are $1.00 per unit per year; setup costs $200.00. If you wish to produce this product in batches, what size batch should be used?

: 13.23 For a given product, ML = $5 and MP = $2. What stocking policy would you recommend in regard to the following demand distribution?

DEMAND (IN UNITS)	PROBABILITY THAT DEMAND WILL BE AT THIS LEVEL (P)	PROBABILITY THAT DEMAND WILL BE AT THIS LEVEL OR GREATER (P)
0	.1	1.0
1	.1	.9
2	.2	.8
3	.2	.6
4	.3	.4
5	.1	.1

: 13.24 A product is delivered to Neil Marquardt's company once a year. The reorder point, without safety stock, is 200 units. Carrying cost is $15 per unit per year, and the cost of a stockout is $70 per unit per year. Given the following demand probabilities during the reorder period, how much safety stock should be carried?

DEMAND DURING REORDER PERIOD	PROBABILITY
0	.1
100	.1
200	.2
300	.2
400	.2

: 13.25 Demand during lead time for one brand of TV is normally distributed with a mean of 36 TVs and a standard deviation of 15 TVs. What safety stock should be carried for a 90% service level? What is the appropriate reorder point?

CASE STUDY

Sturdivant Sound Systems

Sturdivant Sound Systems manufactures and sells sound systems for both home and auto. All parts of the sound systems, with the exception of CD players, are produced in the North York, Ontario, plant. CD players used in the assembly of Sturdivant's systems are purchased from Morris Electronics of Markham, Ontario.

Mary Kim, purchasing agent for Sturdivant Sound Systems, submits a purchase requisition for the CD players once every 4 weeks. The company's annual requirements total 5,000 units (20 per working day), and the cost per unit is $60. (Sturdivant does not purchase in greater quantities because Morris Electronics, the supplier, does not offer quantity discounts.) Rarely does a shortage of CD players occur because Morris promises delivery within 1 week following receipt of a purchase requisition. (Total time between date of order and date of receipt is 10 days.)

Associated with the purchase of each shipment are procurement costs. These costs, which amount to $20 per order, include the costs of preparing the requisition, inspecting and storing the delivered goods, updating inventory records, and issuing a voucher and a cheque for payment. In addition to procurement costs, Sturdivant Sound Systems incurs inventory carrying costs that include insurance, storage, handling, taxes, and so forth. These costs equal $6 per unit per year.

Beginning in August of this year, management of Sturdivant Sound Systems will embark on a companywide cost control program in an attempt to improve its profits. One area to be closely scrutinized for possible cost savings is inventory procurement.

DISCUSSION QUESTIONS

1. Compute the optimal order quantity of CD players.
2. Determine the appropriate reorder point (in units).
3. Compute the cost savings that the company will realize if it implements the optimal inventory procurement decision.
4. Should procurement costs be considered a linear function of the number of orders?

Source: Professor Jerry Kinard, Western Carolina University. Modified for the Canadian edition.

CASE STUDY

Martin-Pullin Bicycle Corporation

Martin-Pullin Bicycle Corp. (MPBC), located in Barrie, is a wholesale distributor of bicycles and bicycle parts. Formed in 1981 by cousins Ray Martin and Jim Pullin, the firm's primary retail outlets are located within a 400-mile radius of the distribution centre. These retail outlets receive the order from Martin-Pullin within 2 days after notifying the distribution centre, provided the stock is available. However, if an order is not fulfilled by the company, then no back order is placed; the retailers arrange to get their shipment from other distributors, and MPBC loses that amount of business.

The company distributes a wide variety of bicycles. The most popular model, and the major source of revenue to the company, is the AirWing. MPBC receives all the models from a single manufacturer overseas, and shipment takes as long as 4 weeks from the time an order is placed. With the cost of communication, paperwork, and customs clearance included, MPBC estimates that each time an order is placed, it incurs a cost of $65. The purchase price paid by MPBC, per bicycle, is roughly 60% of the suggested retail price for all the styles available, and the inventory carrying cost is 1% per

(Continued)

month (12% per year) of the purchase price paid by MPBC. The retail price (paid by the customers) for the AirWing is $170 per bicycle.

MPBC is interested in making the inventory plan for 1996. The firm wants to maintain a 95% service level with its customers to minimize the losses on the lost orders. The data collected for the last 2 years are summarized in Table 13.5. A forecast for AirWing model sales in the upcoming year of 1996 has been developed and will be used to make an inventory plan for MPBC.

DISCUSSION QUESTIONS

1. Develop an inventory plan to help MPBC.
2. Discuss reorder points and total costs.
3. How can you address the demand that is not level of the planning horizon?

Source: Professor Kala Chand Seal, Loyola Marymount University. Modified for the Canadian edition.

TABLE 13.5 ■ DEMANDS FOR AIRWING MODEL

	Year		
Months	1994	1995	Forecast for 1996
January	6	7	8
February	12	14	15
March	24	27	31
April	46	53	59
May	75	86	97
June	47	54	60
July	30	34	39
August	18	21	24
September	13	15	16
October	12	13	15
November	22	25	28
December	38	42	47
Totals	343	391	439

BIBLIOGRAPHY

Berkley, B. J. "Simulation Tests of FCFS and SPT Sequencing in Kanban Systems." *Decision Sciences*, 24, no. 1 (January–February 1993): 218.

Brown, R. G. *Decision Rules for Inventory Management*. New York: Holt, Rinehart and Winston, 1967.

Freeland, J. R., J. P. Leschke, and E. N. Weiss. "Guidelines for Setup-Cost Reduction Programs to Achieve Zero Inventory." *Journal of Operations Management*, 9 (January 1990): 85.

Groenevelt, H., L. Pintelon, and A. Seidmann. "Production Lot Sizing with Machine Breakdowns." *Management Science*, 38, no. 1 (January 1992): 104.

Hall, R. *Zero Inventories*. Homewood, IL: Dow Jones-Irwin, 1983.

Inman, R. A., and S. Mehra. "JIT Applications for Service Environments." *Production and Inventory Management Journal*, 32, no. 3 (Third Quarter 1991): 16.

Jinchiro, N., and R. Hall. "Management Specs for Stockless Production." *Harvard Business Review*, 63 (May–June 1983): 89–91.

Landvater, D. V. *World Class Production and Inventory Management*. Newburg, NH: Oliver Wight Publications, 1993.

Louis, R. S. *How to Implement Kanban for American Industry*. Cambridge, MA: Productivity Press, 1992.

Schniederjans, M. *Topics in Just-in-Time Management*. Boston: Allyn & Bacon, 1993.

Shingo, S. *A Revolution in Manufacturing: The SMED System*. Cambridge, MA: Productivity Press, 1986.

Vollmann, T. E., W. L. Berry, and D. C. Whybark. *Manufacturing Planning and Control Systems*. Homewood, IL: Irwin, 1988.

Wight, O. W. *Production and Inventory Management in the Computer Age*. Boston: Cahners, 1974.

13 SUPPLEMENT

Simulation models abound in our world. The city of Toronto looks to them to control traffic. Boeing Aircraft uses them to test the aerodynamics of proposed jets. The U.S. Army simulates war games on computers. Business students use management gaming to simulate realistic business competition. And thousands of organizations develop simulation models to help make operations decisions.

SIMULATION

SUPPLEMENT OUTLINE

Over half of the large manufacturing companies in North America are estimated to use simulation models. Table S13.1 lists just a few areas in which simulation is now being applied.

TABLE S13.1 ■ SOME APPLICATIONS OF SIMULATION

Ambulance location and dispatching	Bus scheduling
Assembly line balancing	Design of library operations
Parking lot and harbour design	Taxi, truck, and railroad dispatching
Distribution system design	Production facility scheduling
Scheduling aircraft	Plant layout
Labour-hiring decisions	Capital investments
Personnel scheduling	Production scheduling
Traffic-light timing	Sales forecasting
Voting pattern prediction	Inventory planning and control

SIMULATION DEFINED

Simulation is the attempt to duplicate the features, appearance, and characteristics of a real system. In this supplement, we will show how to simulate part of an operations management system by building a mathematical model that comes as close as possible to representing the reality of the system. The model will then be used to estimate the effects of various actions. The idea behind simulation is (1) to imitate a real-world process mathematically, (2) then to study its properties and operating characteristics, and (3) finally to draw conclusions and make action decisions based on the results of the simulation. In this way, a real-life system need not be touched until the advantages and disadvantages of a major policy decision are first measured on the model.

Simulation

To use simulation, a P/OM manager should:

1. define the problem;
2. introduce the important variables associated with the problem;
3. construct a numerical model;
4. set up possible courses of action for testing;
5. run the experiment;
6. consider the results (possibly modify the model or change data inputs);
7. decide what course of action to take.

These steps are illustrated in Figure S13.1.

The problems tackled by simulation may range from very simple to extremely complex, from bank teller lines to an analysis of the Canadian economy. Although small simulations could be conducted by hand, effective use of this technique requires a computer. Even large-scale models, simulating perhaps years of business decisions, can be handled by computer.

In this supplement, we examine the basic principles of simulation and then tackle some problems in the areas of waiting-line analysis and inventory control. Why do we use simulation in these areas when mathematical models described in other chapters can solve the problems? The answer is that simulation provides an

FIGURE 13.1 ■ The Process of Simulation

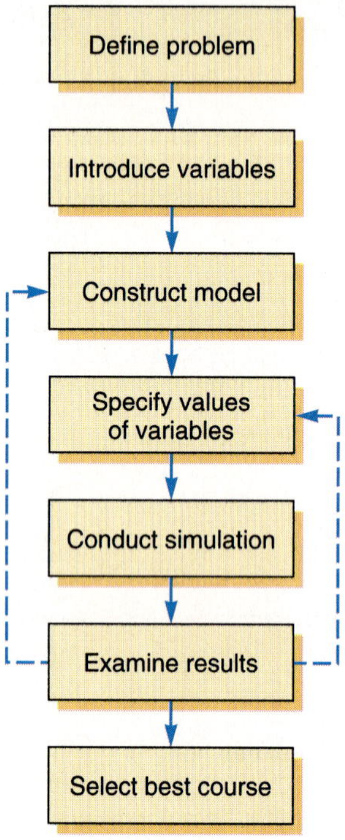

alternative approach for problems that are very complex mathematically. It can handle, for example, inventory problems in which demand or lead time is not constant.

ADVANTAGES AND DISADVANTAGES OF SIMULATION

Simulation is a tool that has become widely accepted by managers for several reasons. The main *advantages* of simulation are as follows:

1. Simulation is relatively straightforward and flexible.
2. It can be used to analyze large and complex real-world situations that cannot be solved by conventional operations management models.
3. Real-world complications can be included that most P/OM models cannot permit. Simulation can use *any* probability distribution the user defines. It does not require standard distributions.
4. "Time compression" is possible with simulation. The effects of P/OM policies over many months or years can be obtained by computer simulation in a short time.
5. Simulation allows "what-if" types of questions. Managers like to know in advance what options will be most attractive. With a computerized model, a manager can try out several policy decisions within a matter of minutes.
6. Simulations do not interfere with the real-world system. It may be too disruptive, for example, actually to experiment with new policies or ideas in a hospital, manufacturing plant, or Canada Post.
7. With simulation, we can study the interactive effect of individual components or variables in order to determine which ones are important.

The main *disadvantages* of simulation are as follows:

1. Good simulation models can be very expensive. They may take years to develop.
2. Simulation does not generate optimal solutions to problems as does linear programming. It is a trial-and-error approach that may produce different solutions in repeated runs.
3. Managers must generate all of the conditions and constraints for solutions that they want to examine. The simulation model does not produce answers without adequate, realistic input.
4. Each simulation model is unique. Its solutions and inferences are not usually transferable to other problems.

MONTE CARLO SIMULATION

Monte Carlo method

When a system contains elements that exhibit chance in their behaviour, the **Monte Carlo method** of simulation may be applied.

POM IN ACTION

U.S. Postal Service Plants Its Automation Through Simulation

No public agency, perhaps with the exception of the IRS, touches the lives of the American public as closely as the U.S. Postal Service (USPS). For two centuries, the post office has played a key role in the lives of all citizens.

Today, the USPS delivers over 500 million pieces of mail each day, or 166 billion pieces a year, to over 100 million delivery locations. It handles 40% of the world's volume at a unit cost that is the lowest in the world. With approximately 750,000 career employees, it is the nation's largest civilian employer. Faced with both rising mail volumes and escalating costs, USPS is always looking for ways to improve its mail-processing methods.

A major decision facing the Postal Service is automation—how much, what approach, and when. To keep up with increasing demands without adding more highly paid employees, capital investments of $12 billion have been proposed. Before spending that kind of money, USPS developed a huge simulation model called META.

META's job is to examine the impacts of changes in mail processing and delivery operations. Managers input the type and quantity of mail to be processed, the methods (equipment and people) used to sort mail, the flow of mail through the postal network of sorting operations, and unit costs. META models how the entire nationwide mail processing system would function given these inputs, and it produces figures for capacity utilization, total pieces handled, and the work hours and costs required.

Results achieved to date show total annual savings of one million work years of mail carrier labour, which will allow the USPS to maintain its lowest-cost status and to continue to keep postage rate increases in the United States lower than inflation.

Sources: Interfaces (January/February 1992): 110–130; and B. Render and R. Stair, *Quantitative Analysis for Management*, 5th ed. (Boston: Allyn and Bacon, 1994): 700.

The popularity and wide-ranging uses of Monte Carlo simulations can be shown with a search on "Monte Carlo simulations" on the World Wide Web. Such a search in October 1996 yielded 25,272 hits, from business applications to atomic physics.

One of the first publications on this topic appeared in the 1950s in *Scientific American*, in an article by Daniel D. McCracken. McCracken details the origin of Monte Carlo simulations in the work of mathematicians John von Neumann and Stanislas Ulam in Los Alamos Scientific Laboratories during World War II.

The basis of Monte Carlo simulation is experimentation on chance (or *probabilistic*) elements through random sampling.

The technique breaks down into five simple steps:

1. Setting up a probability distribution for important variables.
2. Building a cumulative probability distribution for each variable.
3. Establishing an interval of random numbers for each variable.
4. Generating random numbers.
5. Actually simulating a series of trials.

Let us examine these steps in turn.

Step 1. Establishing Probability Distributions. The basic idea in the Monte Carlo simulation is to generate values for the variables making up the model being studied. There are a lot of variables in real-world systems that are probabilistic in nature and that we might want to simulate. To name just a few:

Computer simulation models have been developed to address a variety of productivity issues at Burger King. In one, the ideal distance between the drive-through order station and the pickup window was simulated. A longer distance reduced waiting time, and consequently 12 to 13 additional customers could be served per hour, a benefit of over $10,000 in extra sales per restaurant per year. In a second simulation, a second drive-through window was considered. This second window was to be placed in series to the first, rather than in a two-lane configuration. The simulation model predicted a sales increase of 15% during the busiest lunch hours or a sales increase of $13,000 per year per restaurant.

1. inventory demand on a daily or weekly basis;
2. lead time for inventory orders to arrive;
3. times between machine breakdowns;
4. times between arrivals at a service facility;
5. service times;
6. times to complete project activities;
7. number of employees absent from work each day.

One common way to establish a *probability distribution* for a given variable is to examine historical outcomes. The probability, or relative frequency, for each possible outcome of a variable is found by dividing the frequency of observation by the total number of observations. Let us consider an example.

The daily demand for radial tires at Barry's Auto Tire over the past 200 days is shown in columns 1 and 2 of Table S13.2. We can convert this demand to a probability distribution (if we assume that past arrival rates will hold in the future) by dividing each demand frequency by the total demand, 200. The result is shown in column 3.

Cumulative probability distribution

Step 2. Building a Cumulative Probability Distribution for Each Variable. The conversion from a regular probability distribution, such as in column 3 of Table S13.2, to a **cumulative probability distribution** is an easy job. In column 4, we see that the cumulative probability for each level of demand is the sum of the number in the probability column (column 3) added to the previous cumulative probability.

TABLE S13.2 ■ DEMAND FOR BARRY'S AUTO TIRE

(1) DEMAND FOR TIRES	(2) FREQUENCY	(3) PROBABILITY OF OCCURRENCE	(4) CUMULATIVE PROBABILITY
0	10	$^{10}/_{200}$ = .05	.05
1	20	$^{20}/_{200}$ = .10	.15
2	40	$^{40}/_{200}$ = .20	.35
3	60	$^{60}/_{200}$ = .30	.65
4	40	$^{40}/_{200}$ = .20	.85
5	30	$^{30}/_{200}$ = .15	1.00
	200 days	$^{200}/_{200}$ =1.00	

Step 3. Setting Random-Number Intervals. Once we have established a cumulative probability distribution for each variable included in the simulation, we must assign a set of numbers to represent each possible value or outcome. These are referred to as **random-number intervals**. Basically, a **random number** is one or more digits (say, two digits from 01, 02, . . ., 98, 99, 00) that have been selected by a totally random process.

Random-number intervals
Random number

Random numbers are often obtained by consulting a random number table. The nature of these tables is such that one can start at any place and proceed in any direction so long as once your pattern of motion has commenced it is not changed. Any change will tend to destroy the truly random nature of the numbers. While random number tables appear to be printed as 2-, 3-, or 4-digit numbers, such spacing is simply provided for easier reading. For example, three-digit numbers may be obtained from a table that appears to be a series of 2-digit numbers. The user simply takes the desired number of digits in sequence. The intervals are set up according to the number of digits the user prefers for random numbers.

If there is a 5% chance that demand for a product (such as Barry's radial tires) will be 0 units per day, then we will want 5% of the random numbers available to correspond to a demand of 0 units. If a total of 100 two-digit numbers is used in the simulation, we could assign a demand of 0 units to the first five random numbers: 01, 02, 03, 04, and 05.[2] Then a simulated demand for 0 units would be created every time one of the numbers 01 to 05 was drawn. If there is also a 10% chance that demand for the same product will be one unit per day, we could let the next 10 random numbers (06, 07, 08, 09, 10, 11, 12, 13, 14, and 15) represent that demand—and so on for other demand levels.

Similarly, we can see in Table S13.3 that the length of each interval on the right corresponds to the probability of one of each of the possible daily demands. Hence, in assigning random numbers to the daily demand for three radial tires, the range of the random-number interval (36 to 65) corresponds *exactly* to the probability (or proportion) of that outcome. A daily demand for three radial tires occurs 30% of the time. Any of the 30 random numbers greater than 35 up to and including 65 are assigned to that event.

[2]Alternatively, we could have assigned the random numbers 00, 01, 02, 03, and 04 to represent a demand of 0 units. The two digits 00 can be thought of as either 0 or 100. As long as five numbers out of one hundred are assigned to the 0 demand, it does not make any difference which five they are.

In the past, most simulations were done by mathematical experts, who developed long, complex computer printouts. But with graphical displays, simulation can be played out on the screen, step by step, for users to watch. "Animation give managers confidence in the results," says simulation pioneer and creator of SLAM, Alan B. Pritsker. Such software can make a major contribution to productivity.

TABLE S13.3 ■ THE ASSIGNMENT OF RANDOM-NUMBER INTERVALS FOR BARRY'S AUTO

DAILY DEMAND	PROBABILITY	CUMULATIVE PROBABILITY	INTERVAL OF RANDOM NUMBERS
0	.05	.05	01 through 05
1	.10	.15	06 through 15
2	.20	.35	16 through 35
3	.30	.65	36 through 65
4	.20	.85	66 through 85
5	.15	1.00	86 through 00

Step 4. Generating Random Numbers. Random numbers may be generated for simulation problems in two ways. If the problem is large and the process being studied involves many simulation trials, computer programs are available to generate the random numbers needed. If the simulation is being done by hand, the numbers may be selected from a table of random digits.

Step 5. Simulating the Experiment. We may simulate outcomes of an experiment by simply selecting random numbers from Table S13.4. Beginning anywhere in the table, we note the interval in Table S13.3 into which each number falls. For example, if the random number chosen is 81 and the interval 66 to 85 represents a daily demand for four tires, then we select a demand of four tires. Example S1 carries the simulation further.

EXAMPLE S1

Let us illustrate the concept further by simulating 10 days of demand of radial tires at Barry's Auto Tire (see Table S13.3). We select the random numbers needed from Table S13.4, starting in the upper left-hand corner and continuing down the first column.

DAY NUMBER	RANDOM NUMBER	SIMULATED DAILY DEMAND	
1	52	3	
2	37	3	
3	82	4	
4	69	4	
5	98	5	
6	96	5	
7	33	2	
8	50	3	
9	88	5	
10	90	5	
		39	Total 10-day demand
		39/10 = 3.9 =	Tires average daily demand

It is interesting to note that the average demand of 3.9 tires in this 10-day simulation differs significantly from the *expected* daily demand, which we may calculate from the data in Table S13.3:

$$\text{Expected demand} = \sum_{i=1}^{5} (\text{probability of } i \text{ units}) \times (\text{demand of } i \text{ units})$$
$$= (.05)(0) + (.10)(1) + (.20)(2) + (.30)(3) + (.20)(4) + (.15)(5)$$
$$= 0 + .1 + .4 + .9 + .8 + .75$$
$$= 2.95 \text{ tires}$$

However, if this simulation were repeated hundreds or thousands of times, the average *simulated* demand would be nearly the same as the expected demand.

Naturally, it would be risky to draw any hard and fast conclusions regarding the operation of a firm from only a short simulation. It is also unlikely that anyone would actually want to go to the effort of simulating such a simple model containing only one variable. Simulating by hand does, however, demonstrate the important principles involved and may be useful in small-scale studies.

TABLE 13.4 ■ TABLE OF RANDOM NUMBERS

52	06	50	88	53	30	10	47	99	37	66	91	35	32	00	84	57	07
37	63	28	02	74	35	24	03	29	60	74	85	90	73	59	55	17	60
82	57	68	28	05	94	03	11	27	79	90	87	92	41	09	25	36	77
69	02	36	49	71	99	32	10	75	21	95	90	94	38	97	71	72	49
98	94	90	36	06	78	23	67	89	85	29	21	25	73	69	34	85	76
96	52	62	87	49	56	59	23	78	71	72	90	57	01	98	57	31	95
33	69	27	21	11	60	95	89	68	48	17	89	34	09	93	50	44	51
50	33	50	95	13	44	34	62	64	39	55	29	30	64	49	44	30	16
88	32	18	50	62	57	34	56	62	31	15	40	90	34	51	95	26	14
90	30	36	24	69	82	51	74	30	35	36	85	01	55	92	64	09	85
50	48	61	18	85	23	08	54	17	12	80	69	24	84	92	16	49	59
27	88	21	62	69	64	48	31	12	73	02	68	00	16	16	46	13	85
45	14	46	32	13	49	66	62	74	41	86	98	92	98	84	54	33	40
81	02	01	78	82	74	97	37	45	31	94	99	42	49	27	64	89	42
66	83	14	74	27	76	03	33	11	97	59	81	72	00	64	61	13	52
74	05	81	82	93	09	96	33	52	78	13	06	28	30	94	23	37	39
30	34	87	01	74	11	46	82	59	94	25	34	32	23	17	01	58	73
59	55	72	33	62	13	74	68	22	44	42	09	32	46	71	79	45	89
67	09	80	98	99	25	77	50	03	32	36	63	65	75	94	19	95	88
60	77	46	63	71	69	44	22	03	85	14	48	69	13	30	50	33	24
60	08	19	29	36	72	30	27	50	64	85	72	75	29	87	05	75	01
80	45	86	99	02	34	87	08	86	84	49	76	24	08	01	86	29	11
53	84	49	63	26	65	72	84	85	63	26	02	75	26	92	62	40	67
69	84	12	94	51	36	17	02	15	29	16	52	56	43	26	22	08	62
37	77	13	10	02	18	31	19	32	85	31	94	81	43	31	58	33	51

Source: Reprinted from *A Million Random Digits with 100,000 Normal Deviates*, Rand (New York: Free Press, 1995). Used by permission.

SIMULATION OF A QUEUING PROBLEM

An important use of simulation is in the analysis of waiting-line problems. As mentioned in Chapter 10's supplement, the assumptions required for solving queuing problems are quite restrictive. For most realistic queuing systems, simulation may be the only approach available.

Example S2 illustrates the use of simulation for a large unloading dock and its associated queue. Arrivals of barges at the dock are not Poisson-distributed, and unloading rates (service times) are not exponential or constant. This being the case, the mathematical waiting-line models of the Chapter 10 Supplement cannot be used.

EXAMPLE S2

Fully loaded barges arrive at night in Kingston, Ontario, following their long trips down the St. Lawrence Seaway from industrial eastern Canadian cities. The number of barges docking on any given night ranges from 0 to 5. The probability of 0, 1, 2, 3, 4, and 5 arrivals is displayed in Table S13.5. In the same table, we establish cumulative probabilities and corresponding random-number intervals for each possible value.

TABLE S13.5 ■ OVERNIGHT BARGE ARRIVAL RATES AND RANDOM-NUMBER INTERVALS

NUMBER OF ARRIVALS	PROBABILITY	CUMULATIVE PROBABILITY	RANDOM-NUMBER INTERVAL
0	.13	.13	01 through 13
1	.17	.30	14 through 30
2	.15	.45	31 through 45
3	.25	.70	46 through 70
4	.20	.90	71 through 90
5	.10	1.00	91 through 00
	1.00		

A study by the dock superintendent reveals that the number of barges unloaded also tends to vary from day to day. The superintendent provides information from which we can create a probability distribution for the variable *daily unloading rate* (see Table S13.6). As we just did for the arrival variable, we can set up an internal of random numbers for the unloading rates.

TABLE S13.6 ■ UNLOADING RATES AND RANDOM NUMBER INTERVALS

DAILY UNLOADING RATES	PROBABILITY	CUMULATIVE PROBABILITY	RANDOM-NUMBER INTERVAL
1	.05	.05	01 through 05
2	.15	.20	06 through 20
3	.50	.70	21 through 70
4	.20	.90	71 through 90
5	.10	1.00	91 through 00
	1.00		

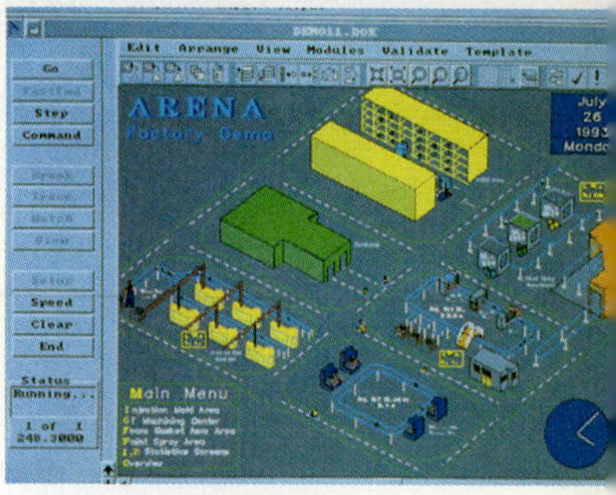

ARENA, a graphical simulation program developed by Systems Modeling Corporation of Sewickley, PA, takes advantage of new object-oriented technology. Virtually any process, from customer service banking to manufacturing assembly lines to material handling systems, can be simulated.

Barges are unloaded on a first-in, first-out basis. Any barges that are not unloaded the day of arrival must wait until the following day. Tying up a barge in dock is an expensive proposition, and the superintendent cannot ignore the angry phone calls from barge line owners reminding him that "time is money!" He decides that, before going to the Port of Kingston's controller to request additional unloading crews, a simulation study of arrivals, unloadings, and delays should be conducted. A 100-day simulation would be ideal, but for purposes of illustration, the superintendent begins with a shorter 15-day analysis. Random numbers are drawn from the top row of Table S13.4 to generate daily arrival rates. They are drawn from the second row of Table S13.4 to create daily unloading rates. Table S13.7 shows the day-to-day port simulation.

TABLE S13.7 ■ QUEUING SIMULATION OF PORT OF KINGSTON BARGE UNLOADINGS

(1) DAY	(2) NUMBER DELAYED FROM PREVIOUS DAY	(3) RANDOM NUMBER	(4) NUMBER OF NIGHTLY ARRIVALS	(5) TOTAL TO BE UNLOADED	(6) RANDOM NUMBER	(7) NUMBER UNLOADED
1	⊖[1]	52	3	3	37	3
2	0	06	0	0	63	0[2]
3	0	50	3	3	28	3
4	0	88	4	4	02	1
5	3	53	3	6	74	4
6	2	30	1	3	35	3
7	0	10	0	0	24	0[3]
8	0	47	3	3	03	1
9	2	99	5	7	29	3
10	4	37	2	6	60	3
11	3	66	3	6	74	4
12	2	91	5	7	85	4
13	3	35	2	5	90	4
14	1	32	2	3	73	3[4]
15	0	00	5	5	59	3
	20 Total delays		41 Total arrivals			39 Total unloadings

1. We can begin with no delays from the previous day. In a long simulation, even if we started with five overnight delays, that initial condition would be averaged out.
2. Three barges *could* have been unloaded on day 2. But because there were no arrivals and no backlog existed, zero unloadings took place.
3. The same situation as noted in footnote 2 takes place.
4. This time four barges could have been unloaded, but since only three were in queue, the number unloaded is recorded as 3.

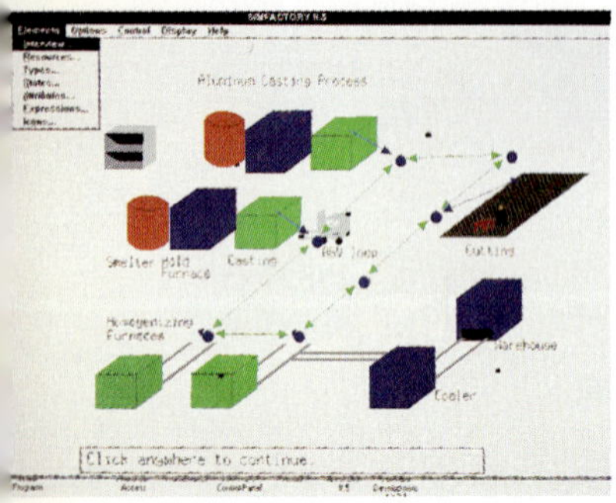

SIMSCRIPT, one of the most widely used special-purpose simulation languages, has graphic capabilities that include animation of the system being simulated. The software permits specialized simulations of such diverse applications as telecommunications systems, factories, and weather movement.

The superintendent will likely be interested in at least three useful and important pieces of information:

$$\left(\text{Average number of barges}\right) = \frac{20 \text{ delays}}{15 \text{ days}} = 1.33 \text{ barges delayed per day}$$

$$\text{Average number of nightly arrivals} = \frac{41 \text{ arrivals}}{15 \text{ days}} = 2.73 \text{ arrivals per night}$$

$$\text{Average number of barges unloaded each day} = \frac{39 \text{ unloadings}}{15 \text{ days}} = 2.60 \text{ unloadings per day}$$

When data from Example S2 are analyzed in the context of delay costs, idle labour costs, and the cost of hiring extra unloading crew, it will be possible for the dock superintendent and port controller to make a better staffing decision. They may even elect to resimulate the process assuming different unloading rates that would correspond to increased crew sizes. Although simulation cannot guarantee an optimal solution to problems such as this, it can be helpful in recreating a process and identifying good decision alternatives.

SIMULATION AND INVENTORY ANALYSIS

In Chapter 13, we introduced inventory models. The commonly used EOQ models are based on the assumption that both product demand and reorder lead time are known, constant values. In most real-world inventory situations, though, demand and lead time are variables, and accurate analysis becomes extremely difficult to handle by any means other than simulation.

In this section, we present an inventory problem with two decision variables and two probabilistic components. The owner of the hardware store in Example S3 would like to establish *order quantity* and *reorder point* decisions for a particular product that has probabilistic (uncertain) daily demand and reorder lead time. He wants to make a series of simulation runs, trying out various order quantities and reorder points, in order to minimize his total inventory cost for the item. Inventory costs in this case will include ordering, holding, and stockout costs.

EXAMPLE S3

Simkin's Hardware sells the Ace model electric drill. Daily demand for the drill is relatively low but subject to some variability. Over the past 300 days, Simkin has observed the sales shown in column 2 of Table S13.8. He converts this historical frequency into a probability distribution for the variable daily demand (column 3). A cumulative probability distribution is formed in column 4 of Table S13.8. Finally, Simkin establishes an interval of random numbers to represent each possible daily demand (column 5).

TABLE S13.8 ■ PROBABILITIES AND RANDOM-NUMBER INTERVALS FOR DAILY ACE DRILL DEMAND

(1) Demand for Ace Drill	(2) Frequency	(3) Probability	(4) Cumulative Probability	(5) Interval of Random Numbers
0	15	.05	.05	01 through 05
1	30	.10	.15	06 through 15
2	60	.20	.35	16 through 35
3	120	.40	.75	36 through 75
4	45	.15	.90	76 through 90
5	30	.10	1.00	91 through 00
	300 days	1.00		

When Simkin places an order to replenish his inventory of Ace electric drills, there is a delivery lag of from 1 to 3 days. This means that lead time may also be considered a probabilistic variable. The number of days it took to receive the past 50 orders is presented in Table S13.9. In a fashion similar to that for the demand variable, Simkin establishes a probability distribution for the lead time variable (column 3 of Table S13.9), computes the cumulative distribution (column 4), and assigns random-number intervals for each possible time (column 5).

TABLE S13.9 ■ PROBABILITIES AND RANDOM-NUMBER INTERVALS FOR REORDER LEAD TIME

(1) Lead Time (Days)	(2) Frequency	(3) Probability	(4) Cumulative Probability	(5) Random-Number Interval
1	10	.20	.20	01 through 20
2	25	.50	.70	21 through 70
3	15	.30	1.00	71 through 00
	50 orders	1.00		

The first inventory policy that Simkin's Hardware wants to simulate is an order quantity of 10 with a reorder point of 5. That is, every time the on-hand inventory level at the end of the day is 5 or less, Simkin will call his supplier and place an order for 10 more drills. If the lead time is 1 day, by the way, the order will not arrive the next morning, but rather at the beginning of the following work day.

The entire process is simulated in Table S13.10 for a 10-day period. We assume that beginning inventory is 10 units on day 1. We took the random numbers from column 2 of Table S13.4.

Table S13.10 was filled in by proceeding 1 day (or line) at a time, working from left to right. It was a four-step process:

1. Begin each simulated day by checking whether any ordered inventory has just arrived. If it has, increase the current inventory by the quantity ordered (10 units, in this case).
2. Generate a daily demand from the demand probability distribution by selecting a random number.
3. Compute ending inventory = beginning inventory minus demand. If on-hand inventory is insufficient to meet the day's demand, satisfy as much as possible and note the number of lost sales.
4. Determine whether the day's ending inventory has reached the reorder point (five units). If it has, and if there are no outstanding orders, place an order. Lead time for a new order is simulated by choosing a random number and using the distribution in Table S13.9.

Simkin's first inventory simulation yields some interesting results. The average daily ending inventory is

$$\text{Average ending inventory} = \frac{41 \text{ total units}}{10 \text{ days}} = 4.1 \text{ units/day}$$

We also note the average lost sales and number of orders placed per day:

$$\text{Average lost sales} = \frac{2 \text{ sales lost}}{10 \text{ days}} = .2 \text{ unit/day}$$

$$\text{Average number of orders placed} = \frac{3 \text{ orders}}{10 \text{ days}} = .3 \text{ order/day}$$

TABLE S13.10 ■ SIMKIN HARDWARE'S FIRST INVENTORY SIMULATION. ORDER QUANTITY = 10 UNITS; REORDER POINT = 5 UNITS

(1) Day	(2) Units Received	(3) Beginning Inventory	(4) Random Number	(5) Demand	(6) Ending Inventory	(7) Lost Sales	(8) Order?	(9) Random Number	(10) Lead Time
1		10	06	1	9	0	No		
2	0	9	63	3	6	0	No		
3	0	6	57	3	(3)[1]	0	Yes	(02)[2]	1
4	0	3	(94)[3]	5	0	2	No[4]		
5	(10)[5]	10	52	3	7	0	No		
6	0	7	69	3	4	0	Yes	33	2
7	0	4	32	2	2	0	No		
8	0	2	30	2	0	0	No		
9	(10)[6]	10	48	3	7	0	No		
10	0	7	88	4	3	0	Yes	14	
				Totals:	41	2			

1. This is the first time inventory dropped to the reorder point of five drills. Because no prior order was outstanding, an order is placed.
2. The random number 02 is generated to represent the first lead time. It was drawn from column 2 of Table S13.4 as the next number in the list being used. A separate column could have been used from which to draw lead time random numbers if we had wanted to do so, but in this example, we did not do so.
3. Again, notice that the random digits 02 were used for lead time (see footnote 2). So the next number in the column is 94.
4. No order is placed on day 4 because there is one outstanding from the previous day that has not yet arrived.
5. The lead time for the first order placed is one day, but as noted in the text, an order does not arrive the next morning, but rather the beginning of the following day. Thus, the first order arrives at the start of day 5.
6. This is the arrival of the order placed at the close of business on day 6. Fortunately for Simkin, no lost sales occurred during the two-day lead time until the order arrived.

Example S4 shows how these data can be useful in studying the inventory costs of the policy being simulated.

EXAMPLE S4

Simkin estimates that the cost of placing each order for Ace drills is \$10, the holding cost per drill held at the end of each day is \$.50, and the cost of each lost sale is \$8. This information enables us to compute the total daily inventory cost for the simulated policy in Example S3. Let us examine the three cost components:

$$
\begin{aligned}
\text{Daily order cost} &= (\text{cost of placing one order}) \\
&\times (\text{number of orders placed per day}) \\
&= \$10 \text{ per order} \times .3 \text{ order per day} = \$3 \\
\text{Daily holding cost} &= (\text{cost of holding one unit for 1 day}) \\
&\times (\text{average ending inventory}) \\
&= 50¢ \text{ per unit per day} \times 4.1 \text{ units per day} = \$2.05 \\
\text{Daily stockout cost} &= (\text{cost per lost sale}) \\
&\times (\text{average number of lost sales per day}) \\
&= \$8 \text{ per lost sale} \times .2 \text{ post sales per day} = \$1.60 \\
\text{Total daily inventory cost} &= \text{daily order cost} + \text{daily holding cost} \\
&+ \text{daily stockout cost} = \$6.65
\end{aligned}
$$

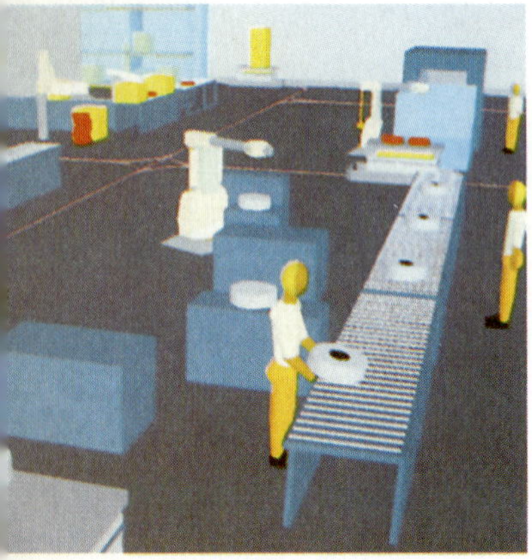

AutoMod simulation software, designed by AutoSimulations Inc., is a graphical system that allows users to model and analyze a variety of manufacturing problems with minimal programming knowledge. AutoMod features include three-dimensional computer-aided design (CAD)-like drawings and interactive, animated graphics. Here we see a 3D model of a transmission assembly line.

After working through Example S3, we want to emphasize something very important. This simulation should be extended many more days before we draw any conclusions as to the cost of the order policy being tested. If a hand simulation is being conducted, 100 days would provide a better representation. If a computer is doing the calculations, 1,000 days would be helpful in reaching accurate cost estimates.[3]

Let us say that Simkin *does* complete a 1,000-day simulation of the policy from Example S3 (order quantity = 10 drills, reorder point = 5 drills). Does this complete his analysis? The answer is no—this is just the beginning! Simkin must now compare *this* potential strategy to other possibilities. For example, what about order quantity = 10, reorder point = 4; or order quantity = 12, reorder point = 6; or order quantity = 14, reorder point = 5? Perhaps every combination of values of order quantity from 6 to 20 drills, and reorder points from 3 to 10 should be simulated. After simulating all reasonable combinations of order quantities and reorder points, Simkin would likely select the pair yielding the lowest total inventory cost. Problem S13.12 gives you a chance to help Simkin begin this series of comparisons.

THE ROLE OF COMPUTERS IN SIMULATION

Computers are critical in simulating complex tasks. They can generate random numbers, simulate thousands of time periods in a matter of seconds or minutes, and provide management with reports that make decision making easier. A computer approach is almost a necessity in order to draw valid conclusions from a simulation.

Computer programming languages can help the simulation process. *General purpose languages* such as FORTRAN, BASIC, COBOL, PL/1, or PASCAL are one approach. *Special-purpose simulation languages*, such as GPSS, SIMSCRIPT, and DYNAMO have a few advantages: (1) they require less programming time for large simulations, (2) they are usually more efficient and easier to check for errors, and (3) they have random-number generators already built in as subroutines.

Commercial, easy-to-use prewritten simulation programs are also available. Some are generalized to handle a wide variety of situations ranging from queuing to inventory. The names of a few such programs are: Witness, Xcell, MAP/1, Slam II, SIMFACTORY, ARENA, Micro Saint, and Taylor II. Some of the newest software available for Monte Carlo simulations includes DynRisk, C++Sim, Casino, and DecisionPro. The program @RISK by Palisade is a risk analysis and simulation add-in that provides Monte Carlo simulation capabilities for Windows (Excel and Lotus), DOS (Lotus), and MacOS (Excel).

Spreadsheet software can also be used to develop simulations quickly and easily. Such packages have built-in random-number generators (through the @ RAND command) and develop outputs through "data-fill" table commands.

The reader may wish to visit the "Random Numbers and Monte Carlo Methods" World Wide Web site at:

http://random.mat.sbg.ac.at/others/

[3]Moreover, even with a 1,000-day simulation, the generated distribution should be compared with the desired distribution to ensure valid results.

Taylor II is an example of a commercial, prewritten simulation program that contains simulations, animations (such as the airport luggage-sorting system one shown here), management reports, and graphs. The business version of this software costs about $50,000.

SUMMARY

Simulation involves attempting to build mathematical models that behave like real operations. In this way, a real-world situation can be studied without imposing on the actual system. Simulation models can be developed manually, but simulation by computer is generally more desirable. The Monte Carlo approach uses random numbers to represent variables, such as inventory demand or people waiting in line, which are then simulated in a series of trials. The advantages of simulation usually outweigh the disadvantages, leading to its wide use as an operations tool.

KEY TERMS

Simulation (p. 607)
Monte Carlo method (p. 608)
Cumulative probability distribution (p. 610)
Random-number intervals (p. 611)
Random number (p. 611)

USING AB:POM AND SPREADSHEETS TO SOLVE SIMULATION PROBLEMS

Using AB:POM's Simulation Module

AB:POM's simulation module allows us to simulate one variable that has up to 10 possible outcomes. Program S13.1 takes the data for Barry's Auto Tire seen in Table S13.2 and conducts a simulation similar to Example S1.

PROGRAM S13.1 ■ AB:POM's Simulation Module. Users may select any number of trials and may choose their own seed number as the first random number. Users may also select random numbers from any row or column of Table S13.4.

Simulation —— Solution

Number of categories (2–10) 6

Barry's Auto Tire

Options -> NOStep Computer

Trials -> 100 0 <– Seed or row or column

	Frequency	Probability	Cumulative	Occurrences	Percentage
Demand = 0	10.00	0.05	0.05	7	0.0769
1	20.00	0.10	0.15	10	0.1219
2	40.00	0.20	0.35	27	0.2700
3	60.00	0.30	0.65	23	0.2421
4	40.00	0.20	0.85	19	0.1938
5	30.00	0.15	1.00	14	0.1505
Total	200.00			100	

Conducting a Simulation with Spreadsheets

Spreadsheet software has two features that make it a useful tool for conducting simulation analysis: (1) built-in random-number functions and generators (through the @ RAND command), and (2) lookup tables that easily permit us to match a simulated random number to a specific event (through the @ VLOOKUP command).

Program S13.2 illustrates these concepts on the Barry's Auto Tire example shown at the beginning of this supplement. The @ RAND function (in C15 through C24) returns a random number between 0 and 1, all values being equally likely. This is an example of a "continuous uniform distribution" in which each random number may take on any fractional value. The actual simulated demand is in cells D15 through D24 and employs the @ VLOOKUP function.

To simulate the first day's demand for tires, the @ VLOOKUP in cell D15 looks first to the random number just generated in C15. It then takes that number and moves to the small table of probabilities for demand just above it. Cells B5 through C10 comprise the "value lookup" table. These random variables for demand have one

PROGRAM 13.2 ■ A Spreadsheet Simulation for Barry's Auto Tire Seen in Table S13.3 and Example S1. A symbolic spreadsheet, using formulas, is shown here.

	A	B	C	D
1	[*Note:* This table is slightly different in structure from Table S13.3			
2	in order to accommodate the @ VLOOKUP command.]			
3		Cumulative	Demand	
4	Probability	Probability	for Tires	
5	0.05	0	0	
6	0.1	0.05	1	
7	0.2	0.15	2	
8	0.3	0.35	3	
9	0.2	0.65	4	
10	0.15	0.85	5	
11				
12	Ten-day simulation of demand for radial tires [as in Example S1]			
13		Day	Random	Simulated Daily
14		Number	Number	Demand
15		1	@RAND	@VLOOKUP (C15, $B$5 . . $C$10, 1)
16		2	@RAND	@VLOOKUP (C16, $B$5 . . $C$10, 1)
17		3	@RAND	@VLOOKUP (C17, $B$5 . . $C$10, 1)
18		4	@RAND	@VLOOKUP (C18, $B$5 . . $C$10, 1)
19		5	@RAND	@VLOOKUP (C19, $B$5 . . $C$10, 1)
20		6	@RAND	@VLOOKUP (C20, $B$5 . . $C$10, 1)
21		7	@RAND	@VLOOKUP (C21, $B$5 . . $C$10, 1)
22		8	@RAND	@VLOOKUP (C22, $B$5 . . $C$10, 1)
23		9	@RAND	@VLOOKUP (C23, $B$5 . . $C$10, 1)
24		10	@RAND	@VLOOKUP (C24, $B$5 . . $C$10, 1)
25			Total	@SUM (D15 . . D24)
26			Aver.	+D25/10
27				
28	Press F9 to recalculate the numbers.			

of several discrete values (0–5 in our case). Cumulative probabilities always start at zero. If the random number generated is between 0 and .05, a demand of 0 tires results. If the random number falls between .05 and .15, the lookup table indicates a demand for one tire, and so on. The "1" in the @ VLOOKUP command, by the way, means that demand is "looked up" in the first column to the right of the cumulative probability.

The F9 function key permits the entire simulation to be redone, with all new random numbers, each time it is pressed.

SOLVED PROBLEMS

Solved Problem S13.1

Higgins Plumbing and Heating maintains a stock of 100-litre hot-water heaters that it sells to homeowners and installs for them. Owner Jerry Higgins likes the idea of having a large supply on hand to meet any customer demand. But he also recognizes that it is expensive to do so. He examines hot-water heater sales over the past 50 weeks and notes the following:

Hot-Water Heater Sales per Week	Number of Weeks This Number Was Sold
4	6
5	5
6	9
7	12
8	8
9	7
10	3
	50 weeks total data

(a) If Higgins maintains a constant supply of eight hot-water heaters in any given week, how many times will he stock out during a 20-week simulation? We use random numbers from the seventh column of Table S13.4, beginning with the random digit 10.

(b) What is the average number of sales per week over the 20-week period?

(c) Using an analytic nonsimulation technique, what is the expected number of sales per week? How does this compare to the answer in part (b)?

Solution

Heater Sales	Probability	Random-Number Intervals
4	.12	01 through 12
5	.10	13 through 22
6	.18	23 through 40
7	.24	41 through 64
8	.16	65 through 80
9	.14	81 through 94
10	.06	95 through 100
	1.00	

(a)

Week	Random Number	Simulated Sales	Week	Random Number	Simulated Sales
1	10	4	11	08	4
2	24	6	12	48	7
3	03	4	13	66	8
4	32	6	14	97	10
5	23	6	15	03	4
6	59	7	16	96	10
7	95	10	17	46	7
8	34	6	18	74	8
9	34	6	19	77	8
10	51	7	20	44	7

With a supply of eight heaters, Higgins will stock out three times during the 20-week period (in weeks 7, 14, and 16).

(b) Average sales by simulation = total sales/20 weeks = 135/20 = 6.75 per week

(c) Using expected values,

$$E\text{ (sales)} = .12(4\text{ heaters}) + .10(5) + .18(6) + .24(7) + .16(8) + .14(9) + .06(10) = 6.88\text{ heaters}$$

With a longer simulation, these two approaches will lead to even closer values.

Solved Problem S13.2

Random numbers may be used to simulate continuous distributions. As a simple example, assume that fixed cost equals \$300, profit contribution equals \$10 per item sold, and you expect an equally likely chance of 0 to 99 units to be sold. That is, profit equals − \$300 + \$10X, where X is the number sold. The mean amount you would expect to sell is 49.5 units.

(a) Calculate the expected value.

(b) Simulate the sale of 5 items, using the following double-digit random numbers: 37 77 13 10 85

(c) Calculate the expected value of part (b) and compare with the results of part (a).

Solution

(a) Expected value = −300 + 10(49.5) = \$195

(b) −300 + \$10(37) = \$70
−300 + \$10(77) = \$470
−300 + \$10(13) = −\$170
−300 + \$10(10) = −\$200
−300 + \$10(85) = \$550

(c) The mean of these simulated sales is $144. If the sample size were larger, we would expect the two values to be closer.

DISCUSSION QUESTIONS

1. What are the advantages and limitations of simulation models?
2. Why might a manager be forced to use simulation instead of an analytical model in dealing with a problem of:
   (a) inventory order policy?
   (b) ships docking in a port to unload?
   (c) bank teller service windows?
   (d) the Canadian economy?
3. What types of management problems can be solved more easily by techniques other than simulation?
4. What are the major steps in the simulation process?
5. What is Monte Carlo simulation? What principles underlie its use, and what steps are followed in applying it?
6. What are the origins of Monte Carlo simulation?
7. In the simulation of an order policy for drills at Simkin's Hardware, would the results (of Table S13.10) change significantly if a longer period were simulated? Why is the 10-day simulation valid or invalid?
8. Why is a computer necessary in conducting a real-world simulation?
9. Do you think the application of simulation will increase strongly in the next 10 years? Why?
10. Why would an analyst ever prefer a general-purpose language such as FORTRAN or BASIC in a simulation when there are advantages to using special-purpose languages such as GPSS or SIMSCRIPT?
11. What is the role of random numbers in a Monte Carlo simulation?
12. Why do the results of a simulation differ each time you make a run?
13. List six ways that simulation can be used in business.
14. Why is simulation such a widely used technique?

CRITICAL THINKING EXERCISE

The caption to the photo of cars waiting in line at a Burger King drive-through that you saw earlier in this supplement described two uses of simulation at Burger King. One application dealt with the distance between the drive-through order station and the pickup window. Saving $10,000 per restaurant translated into $15 million annual systemwide sale capacity. The second application hoped to expand sales capacity during peak drive-through hours by adding a second window. This small change added close to $20 million per year in sales to the corporation.

Examine any fast-food chain operation very carefully, and propose two more changes that could be tested by simulation before their actual implementations.

PROBLEMS

The problems that follow involve simulations that are to be done by hand. However, to obtain accurate and meaningful results, long periods must be simulated. This is usually handled by a computer. If you are able to program some of the problems by computer, we suggest you try to do so. If not, the hand simulations will still help you in understanding the simulation process.

• **S13.1** The daily demand for newspapers at a particular machine is either 20, 21, 22, or 23 with probabilities 0.4, 0.3, 0.2, or 0.1, respectively. Assume the following random numbers have been generated: 08, 54, 74, 66, 52, 58, 03, 22, 89, and 85. Using these numbers, generate the daily sales of newspaper for 10 days.

• **S13.2** The number of machine breakdowns in a day at Katie Park's factory is either 0, 1 or 2, with probabilities 0.5, 0.3, or 0.2, respectively. The following random numbers have been generated: 13, 14, 02, 18, 31, 19, 32, 85, 31, and 94. Use these numbers to generate the number of breakdowns for 10 consecutive days. What proportion of these days had at least 1 breakdown?

• **S13.3** The number of cars arriving at Dave Cole's self-service gasoline station during the last 50 hours of operation are as follows:

NUMBER OF CARS ARRIVING	FREQUENCY
6	10
7	12
8	20
9	8

The following random numbers have been generated: 44, 30, 26, 09, 49, 13, 33, 89, 13, and 37. Simulate 10 hours of arrivals at this station. What is the average number of arrivals during this period?

• **S13.4** Kate Moore has a newspaper stand where she sells papers for $.35. The papers cost her $.25, giving her a 10-cent profit on each one she sells. From past experience Kate knows that

20% of the time she sells 100 papers
20% of the time she sells 150 papers
30% of the time she sells 200 papers
30% of the time she sells 250 papers

Assuming that Kate believes that the cost of a lost sale is $.05 and any unsold papers cost her $.25, simulate her profit outlook over 5 days if she orders 200 papers for each of the 5 days. Use the following random numbers: 52, 06, 50, 88, and 53.

• **S13.5** Refer to Problem S13.4. Kate's new strategy is to order 175 papers for each of the 5 days. Use the same random numbers and simulate Kate's profits. What is the average daily profit?

: **S13.6** Stacey Strah's grocery store has noted the following figures with regard to the number of people who arrive at the store's three check-out stands ready to check out and the time it takes to check out the individuals.

ARRIVALS/MIN.	FREQUENCY
0	.3
1	.5
2	.2

SERVICE TIME IN MIN.	FREQUENCY
1	.1
2	.3
3	.4
4	.2

Simulate the utilization of the three check-out stands over 5 minutes, using the following random numbers: 07, 60, 77, 49, 76, 95, 51, and 16. Note the results at the end of the 5-minute period.

:S13.7 Average daily sales of a product in Pam Lancaster's store are 8 units. The actual number of sales each day is either 7, 8, or 9 with probabilities 0.3, 0.4, or 0.3, respectively. The lead time for delivery averages 4 days, although the time may be 3, 4, or 5 days with probabilities .2, .6, and .2. The company plans to place an order when the inventory level drops to 32 units (based on the average demand and average lead time). The following random numbers have been generated:

60, 87, 46, 63 (set 1)

52, 78, 13, 06, 99, 98, 80, 09, 67, 89, 45 (set 2)

Use set 1 to generate lead times and use set 2 to simulate daily demand. Simulate two ordering periods and determine how often the company runs out of stock before the shipment arrives.

:S13.8 The time between arrivals at a drive-through window of Jackie Senich's fast-food restaurant follows the distribution given below. The service time distribution is also given in the table. Use the random numbers provided to simulate the activity of the first five arrivals. Assume that the window opens at 11:00 A.M. and the first arrival is after this, based on the first interarrival time generated.

Time Between Arrivals	Probability	Service Time	Probability
1	.2	1	.3
2	.3	2	.5
3	.3	3	.2
4	.2		

Random numbers for arrivals: 14, 74, 27, 03
Random numbers for service times: 88, 32, 36, 24

What time does the fourth customer leave the system?

• S13.9 Ventra Property Management is responsible for the maintenance, rental, and day-to-day operation of a large apartment complex on the east side of New Brunswick. Mark Ventra is especially concerned about the cost projections for replacing air conditioner compressors. He would like to simulate the number of compressor failures each year over the next 20 years. Using data from a similar apartment building he manages in a New Brunswick suburb, Ventras establishes a table of relative frequency of failures during a year as follows:

Number of A.C. Compressor Failures	Probability (Relative Frequency)
0	.06
1	.13
2	.25
3	.28
4	.20
5	.07
6	.01

He decides to simulate the 20-year period by selecting two-digit random numbers from column 3 of Table S13.4 (starting with the random number 50).

Conduct the simulation for Ventra. Is it common to have three or more consecutive years of operation with two or less compressor failures per year?

•**S13.10** The number of cars arriving at Marcus Chapman's Car Wash during the last 200 hours of operation is observed to be the following:

NUMBER OF CARS ARRIVING	FREQUENCY
3 or less	0
4	20
5	30
6	50
7	60
8	40
9 or more	0
	200

a) Set up a probability and cumulative probability distribution for the variable of car arrivals.

b) Establish random-number intervals for the variable.

c) Simulate 15 hours of car arrivals and compute the average number of arrivals per hour. Select the random numbers needed from column 1, Table S13.4, beginning with the digits 52.

:**S13.11** An increase in the size of the barge-unloading crew at the Port of Kingston (see Example S2) has resulted in a new probability distribution for daily unloading rates. In particular, Table S13.6 may be revised as shown here.

DAILY UNLOADING RATE	PROBABILITY
1	.03
2	.12
3	.40
4	.28
5	.12
6	.05

a) Resimulate 15 days of barge unloading and compute the average number of barges delayed, average number of nightly arrivals, and average number of barges unloaded each day. Draw random numbers from the bottom row of Table S13.4 to generate daily arrivals and from the second-from-the-bottom row to generate daily unloading rates.

b) How do these simulated results compare to those in the supplement?

:**S13.12** Simkin's Hardware Store simulated an inventory ordering policy for Ace electric drills that involved an order quantity of 10 drills with a reorder point of 5. This first attempt to develop a cost-effective ordering strategy was illustrated in Table S13.10 of Example S3. The brief simulation resulted in a total daily inventory cost of $6.65.

Simkin would now like to compare this strategy to one in which he orders 12 drills, with a reorder point of 6. Conduct a 10-day simulation for him and discuss the cost implications.

:S13.13 Carol Pharo, a Ph.D. student at the University of Toronto, has been having problems balancing her chequebook. Her monthly income is derived from a graduate research assistantship; however, she also makes extra money in most months by tutoring undergraduates in their quantitative analysis course. Her chances of various income levels are shown here (on the left).

Pharo's expenditures also vary from month to month, and she estimates that they will follow the distribution on the right.

MONTHLY INCOME*	PROBABILITY	MONTHLY EXPENSES	PROBABILITY
$350	.40	$300	.10
$400	.20	$400	.45
$450	.30	$500	.30
$500	.10	$600	.15

*Assume this income is received at the beginning of each month.

She begins her final year with $600 in her chequing account. Simulate the entire year (12 months) and discuss Pharo's financial picture.

·S13.14 Refer to the data in Solved Problem S13.1, which deals with Higgins Plumbing and Heating. Higgins has now collected 100 weeks of data and finds the following distribution for sales.

HOT WATER HEATER SALES PER WEEK	NUMBER OF WEEKS THIS NUMBER WAS SOLD	HOT WATER HEATER SALES PER WEEK	NUMBER OF WEEKS THIS NUMBER WAS SOLD
3	2	8	21
4	9	9	12
5	10	10	10
6	15	11	5
7	25		100

a) Resimulate the number of stockouts incurred over a 20-week period (assuming Higgins maintains a constant supply of 8 heaters).

b) Conduct this 20-week simulation two more times and compare your answers with those in part (a). Did they change significantly? Why or why not?

c) What is the new expected number of sales per week?

:S13.15 Helms Aircraft Co. operates a large number of computerized plotting machines. The plotting machines are highly reliable, with the exception of the four sophisticated built-in ink pens. The pens constantly clog and jam in a raised or lowered position. When this occurs, the plotter is unusable.

Currently, Helms Aircraft replaces every pen as it fails. The service manager has, however, proposed replacing all four pens every time one fails. This should cut down the frequency of plotter failures. At present, it takes 1 hour to replace one pen. All four pens could be replaced in 2 hours. The total cost of a plotter being unusable is $50 per hour. Each pen costs $8.

If only one pen is replaced each time a clog or jam occurs, the following breakdown data are thought to be valid:

HOURS BETWEEN PLOTTER FAILURES IF ONE PEN IS REPLACED DURING A REPAIR	PROBABILITY
10	.05
20	.15
30	.15
40	.20
50	.20
60	.15
70	.10

According to the service manager's estimates, if all four pens are replaced each time one pen fails, the probability distribution between failures is

HOURS BETWEEN PLOTTER FAILURES IF ALL FOUR PENS ARE REPLACED DURING A REPAIR	PROBABILITY
100	.15
110	.25
120	.35
130	.20
140	.05

a) Simulate Helms Aircraft's problem and determine the best policy. Should the firm replace one pen or all four pens on a plotter each time a failure occurs?

b) Develop a second approach to solving this problem (this time without simulation). Compare the results. How does it affect Helms' policy decision using simulation?

:S13.16 Tia Thompson owns and operates one of the largest Mercedes-Benz auto dealerships in Vancouver, British Columbia. In the past 36 months, her sales of this luxury car have ranged from a low of 6 new cars to a high of 12 new cars, as reflected in the following table:

SALES OF NEW CARS/MONTH	FREQUENCY
6	3
7	4
8	6
9	12
10	9
11	1
12	1
	36 months

She believes that sales will continue during the next 24 months at about the same historical rates, and that delivery times will also continue to follow this pace (stated in probability form):

DELIVERY TIME (IN MONTHS)	PROBABILITY
1	.44
2	.33
3	.16
4	.07
	1.00

Thompson's current policy is to order 14 cars at a time (two full truckloads), with 7 autos on each truck), and to place a new order whenever the stock on hand reaches 12 autos. What are the results of this policy when simulated over the next 2 years?

:S13.17 Refer to Problem S13.16. Tia Thompson establishes the following relevant costs: (1) the carrying cost per Mercedes per month is $600; (2) the cost of a lost sale averages $4,350; and (3) the cost of placing an order is $570. What is the total inventory cost of the policy simulated in Problem S13.16?

:S13.18 Tia Thompson (see Problems S13.16 and S13.17) wishes to try a new simulated policy, ordering 21 cars per order, with a reorder point of 10 autos. Which policy is better, this one or the one formulated in Problems S13.16 and S13.17?

:S13.19 The Eichler Corporation is the nation's largest manufacturer of industrial-size washing machines. A main ingredient in the production process is 8-by-10-foot sheets of stainless steel. The steel is used for both interior washer drums and outer casings.

Steel is purchased weekly on a contractual basis from the RTT Foundry, which, because of limited availability and lot-sizing, can ship either 8,000 or 11,000 square fee of stainless steel each week. When Eichler's weekly order is placed, there is a 45% chance that 8,000 square feet will arrive and a 55% chance of receiving the larger-size order.

Eichler uses the stainless steel on a stochastic (nonconstant) basis. The probabilities of demand each week are

STEEL NEEDED PER WEEK (SQ. FT.)	PROBABILITY
6,000	.05
7,000	.15
8,000	.20
9,000	.30
10,000	.20
11,000	.10

Eichler has a capacity to store no more than 25,000 square feet of steel at any time. Because of the contract, orders must be placed each week regardless of the on-hand supply.

a) Simulate stainless steel order arrivals and use for 20 weeks. (Begin the first week with a starting inventory of 0 stainless steel.) If an end-of-week inventory is ever negative, assume that "back orders" are permitted and fill the demand from the next arriving order.

b) Should Eichler add more storage area? If so, how much? If not, comment on the system.

:S13.20 The general hospital in Berthierville, Quebec, has an emergency room that is divided into six departments: (1) the initial exam station to treat minor problems or make diagnoses; (2) an X-ray department; (3) an operating room; (4) a cast-fitting room; (5) an observation room (for recovery and general observation before final diagnosis or release); (6) an out-processing department (where clerks check out patients and arrange for payment or insurance forms).

The probabilities that a patient will go from one department to another are presented in the table show below.

FROM:	TO:	PROBABILITY
Initial exam at emergency room entrance	X-ray department	.45
	Operating room	.15
	Observation room	.10
	Out-processing clerk	.30
X-ray department	Operating room	.10
	Cast-fitting room	.25
	Observation room	.35
	Out-processing clerk	.30
Operating room	Cast-fitting room	.25
	Observation room	.70
	Out-processing clerk	.05
Cast-fitting room	Observation room	.55
	X-ray department	.05
	Out-processing clerk	.40
Observation room	Operating room	.15
	X-ray department	.15
	Out-processing clerk	.70

a) Simulate the trail followed by 10 emergency room patients. Proceed, one patient at a time, from each one's entry at the initial exam station until he or she leaves through out-processing. You should be aware that a patient can enter the same department more than once.

b) Using your simulation data, what are the chances that a patient enters the X-ray department twice?

:S13.21 Management of Alberta Trust is concerned over a loss of customers at its main office downtown. One solution that has been proposed is to add one or more drive-through teller stations to make it easier for customers in cars to obtain quick service without parking. Steve Shoff, the bank president, thinks the bank should risk only the cost of installing one drive-through. He is informed by his staff that the cost (amortized over a 20-year period) of building a drive-through is $12,000 per year. It also costs $16,000 per year in wages and benefits to staff each new teller window.

The director of Management Analysis, Jennifer Jaenicke, believes that the following two factors encourage the immediate construction of two drive-through stations, however. According to a recent article in *Banking Research* magazine, customers who wait in long lines for drive-through teller service will cost banks an average of $1.00 per minute, in loss of goodwill. Also, adding a second drive-through will cost an additional $16,000 in staffing, but amortized construction costs can be cut to a total of

$20,000 per year if two drive-throughs are installed together, instead of one at a time. To complete her analysis, Mrs. Jaenicke collected 1 month's worth of arrival and service rates at a competing downtown bank's drive-through stations. These data follow:

Interarrival Times for 1,000 Observations

Time Between Arrivals (in minutes)	Number of Occurrences
1	200
2	250
3	300
4	150
5	100

Customer Service Time for 1,000 Customers

Service Time (in minutes)	Number of Occurrences
1	100
2	150
3	350
4	150
5	150
6	100

a) Simulate a 1-hour time period, from 1 to 2 P.M., for a single-teller drive-through.

b) Simulate a 1-hour time period, from 1 to 2 P.M., for a two-teller system.

c) Conduct a cost analysis of the two options. Assume the bank is open 7 hours per day and 200 days per year.

CASE STUDY

Noront Airlines

Noront Airlines opened its doors in June 1995 as a commuter service with its headquarters and only hub located in North Bay, Ontario. A product of airline deregulation, Noront joined the growing number of successful short-haul, point-to-point airlines.

Noront Air was started and managed by two former pilots, David Douglas (who had been with the now-defunct Wardair) and Michael Hanna (formerly with Air Canada). It acquired a fleet of 12 used propjet planes and the airport gates vacated by Wardair.

With business growing quickly, Douglas turned his attention to Noront Air's "800" reservations system. Between midnight and 6:00 A.M., only one telephone reservations agent had been on duty. The time between incoming calls during this period is distributed as shown in Table 1. Douglas carefully observed and timed the agent and estimated that the time taken to process passenger inquiries is distributed as shown in Table 2.

All customers calling Noront Air go "on hold" and are served in the order of the calls unless the reservations agent is available for immediate service. Douglas is deciding whether a second agent should be on duty to cope with customer demand. To maintain customer satisfaction, Noront Air does not want a customer "on hold" for more than 3 to 4 minutes and also wants to maintain a "high" operator utilization.

Further, the airline is planning a new TV advertising campaign. As a result, it expects an increase in "800" line phone inquiries. On the basis of similar campaigns in the past, the incoming call distribution from midnight to 6 A.M. is expected to be as shown in Table 3. (The same service time distribution will apply.)

(Continued)

TABLE 1 ■ INCOMING CALL DISTRIBUTION

TIME BETWEEN CALLS (IN MINUTES)	PROBABILITY
1	.11
2	.21
3	.22
4	.20
5	.16
6	.10

TABLE 2 ■ SERVICE TIME DISTRIBUTION

TIME TO PROCESS CUSTOMER ENQUIRIES (IN MINUTES)	PROBABILITY
1	.20
2	.19
3	.18
4	.17
5	.13
6	.10
7	.03

TABLE 3 ■ INCOMING CALL DISTRIBUTION

TIME BETWEEN CALLS (IN MINUTES)	PROBABILITY
1	.22
2	.25
3	.19
4	.15
5	.12
6	.07

DISCUSSION QUESTIONS

1. What would you advise Noront Air to do for the current reservation system based on the original call distribution? Create a simulation model to investigate the scenario. Describe the model carefully and justify the duration of the simulation, assumptions, and measures of performance.
2. What are your recommendations regarding operator utilization and customer satisfaction if the airline proceeds with the advertising campaign?

Source: Professor Zbigniew H. Przasnyski, Loyola Marymount University. Modified for the Canadian edition.

BIBLIOGRAPHY

Abdou, G. and S. P. Dutta. "A Systematic Simulation Approach for the Design of JIT Manufacturing Systems." *Journal of Operations Management*, 11, no. 3 (September 1993): 25–38.

Brennan, J. E., B. L. Golden, and H. K. Rappoport. "Go with the Flow: Improving Red Cross Bloodmobiles Using Simulation Analysis." *Interfaces*, 22, no. 5 (September/October 1992): 1.

Buchanan, E., and R. Keeler. "Simulating Health Expenditures Under Alternative Insurance Plans." *Management Science* (September 1991): 1069–1088.

Evans, J. R. "A Little Knowledge Can Be Dangerous: Handle Simulation with Care." *Production and Inventory Management Journal*, 33, no. 2 (Second Quarter 1992): 51.

Fishman, G. S., and V. G. Kulkarni. "Improving Monte Carlo Efficiency by Increasing Variance." *Management Science*, 38, no. 10 (October 1992): 1432.

Flowers, A. D., and J. R. Cole. "An Application of Computer Simulation to Quality Control in Manufacturing." *IIE Transactions*, 17, no. 3 (September 1985): 277–283.

Greenwood, A. G., L. P. Rees, and I. W. M. Crouch, "Separating the Art and Science of Simulation Optimization: A Knowledge-Based Architecture Providing for Machine Learning." *IIE Transactions*, 25, no. 6 (November 1993): 70.

Heizer, J. H., and A. P. de la Garza. "Using Simulation to Evaluate Airplane Dealership Operations." *Airport Services Management*, 16, no. 6 (June 1976): 30–32.

Hendricks, K. B., and J. O. McClain. "The Output Processes of Serial Production Lines of General Machines with Finite Buffers." *Management Services*, 39, no. 10 (October 1993): 1194.

Hutchinson, J., G. K. Leong, and P. T. Ward. "Improving Delivery Performance in Gear Manufacturing at Jeffrey Division of Dresser Industries." *Interfaces*, 23, no. 2 (March/April 1993): 69–79.

Lev, B. "Simulation of Manufacturing Systems." *Interfaces*, 20, no. 3 (May/June 1990): 99.

Render, B., and R. M. Stair. *Introduction to Management Science*. Boston: Allyn and Bacon, 1992.

———. *Quantitative Analysis for Management*, 5th ed. Boston: Allyn and Bacon, 1994.

14

MATERIAL REQUIREMENTS PLANNING (MRP)

CHAPTER OUTLINE

LEARNING OBJECTIVES

When you complete this chapter you should be able to:

Identify or define:
- Lot-sizing
- Low-level coding
- Planning bills, pseudo bills, and kits
- Phantom bills

Explain:
- Material requirements planning
- Distribution requirements planning

WORLD-CLASS PROFILE: COLLINS INDUSTRIES

MRP PROVIDES A COMPETITIVE ADVANTAGE FOR COLLINS INDUSTRIES

On the six parallel assembly lines, ambulances move forward each day to the next workstation. The MRP system makes certain that just the materials needed at each station arrive overnight for assembly the next day.

Collins Industries, headquartered in Hutchinson, Kansas, is the largest manufacturer of ambulances in the world. The $150 million firm is an international competitor that sells more than 20% of its vehicles to markets outside the United States. In its largest ambulance plant, located in Winter Park, Florida, vehicles are produced on assembly lines (i.e., a repetitive process). There are 12 major ambulance designs assembled at the Florida plant, and they use 18,000 different inventory items, including 6,000 manufactured parts and 12,000 purchased parts.

This variety of products and the nature of the process demand good material requirements planning. The system at Collins Industries has daily updates. The firm uses the MAPICS DB software on an IBM AS400 minicomputer. Effective use of MAPICS forces Collins to maintain accurate bills of material and inventory records. The system has reduced inventory by over 30% in just 2 years.

Collins insists that four key tasks be performed properly. First, the material plan must meet both the requirements of the master schedule and the capabilities of the production facility. Second, the plan must be executed as designed. Third, effective "time-phased" material deliveries, consignment inventories, and a constant review of purchase methods reduce inventory invest

This cutaway of one ambulance interior indicates the complexity of the product, which for some rural locations may be the equivalent of a hospital emergency room in miniature. To complicate production, virtually every ambulance is custom-ordered, with 7,000 different options available. This necessitates precise orders and good bills of materials.

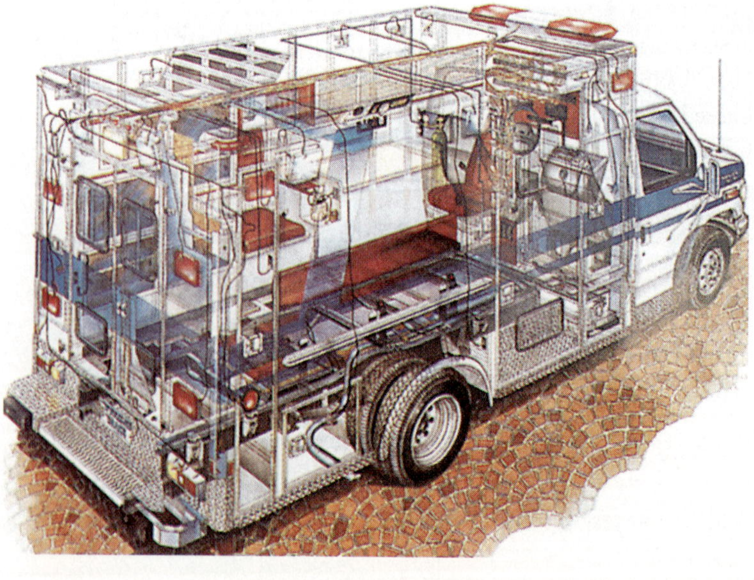

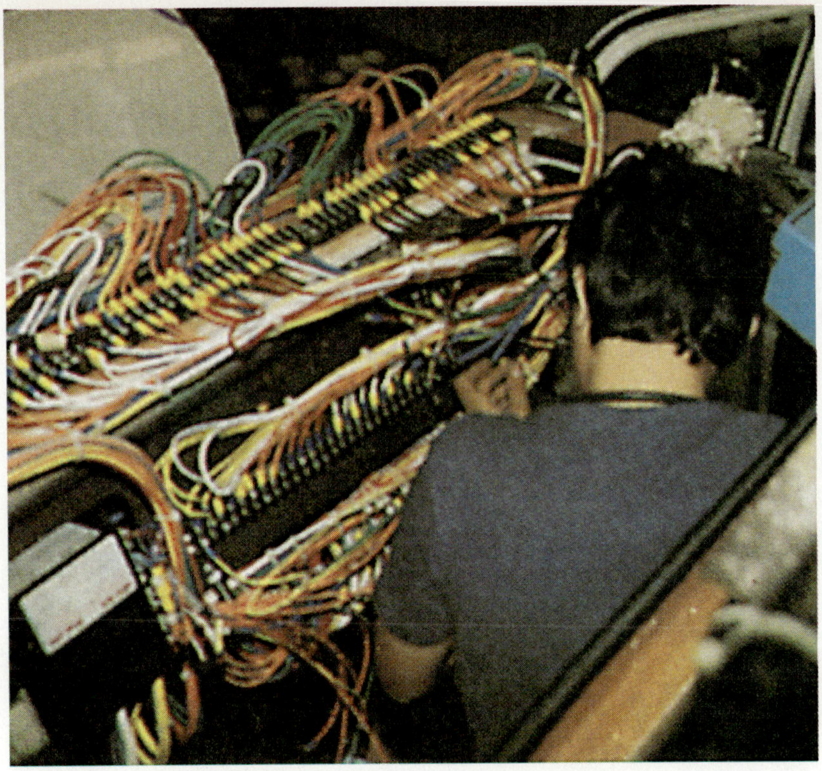

This photo shows a worker wiring an electronic board. Ambulance wiring is so complex that there is an average of more than 24 kilometres of wire in a Collins vehicle. Compare this to the 26 kilometres in a sophisticated F-16 fighter jet.

ment. Finally, Collins maintains record integrity. Record accuracy is recognized as a fundamental ingredient of its successful MRP program. Collins' cycle counters are charged with material audits that not only correct errors, but also investigate and correct problems.

Collins Industries has used MRP as the catalyst for low inventory, high quality, tight schedules, and accurate records. Collins has found competitive advantage via MRP.

The company uses a job shop environment to feed assembly-line needs. It maintains a complete carpentry shop (to provide interior cabinetry), a metal fabrication shop (to construct the shell of the ambulance), a paint shop (to prepare, paint, and detail each vehicle), an electrical shop (to provide for the complex electronics in a modern ambulance), and as shown here, an upholstery shop (to make interior seats and benches).

Nancy Mueller turns quiche into cash. Her firm, Nancy's Specialty Foods, is designed for today's busy lifestyle, producing 750,000 prepackaged, frozen quiche hors d'ouevres each month. Material requirements planning (MRP) software has been key to her growing success. MRP is the primary management tool that keeps the ingredients and labour coming at the proper times and the schedule firm. Once Nancy's Specialty Foods knows the demand for her crab meat quiche, she knows the demand for all of the ingredients from dough, to cheese, to crab meat because *all of the ingredients are dependent.*[1] ♦

As we see at Collins Industries and Nancy's Specialty Foods, the demand for many items is dependent. By *dependent,* we mean the demand for one item is related to the demand for another item. Consider the Ford Explorer. Ford's demand for auto tires and radiators depends on the production of Explorers. Five tires and one radiator go into each finished Explorer. Demand for items is *dependent* when the relationship between the items can be determined. Therefore, once management can make a forecast of the demand for the final product, quantities required for all components can be computed, because all components are *dependent* items. The Boeing Aircraft operations manager scheduling production of one plane per week, for example, knows the requirements down to the last rivet. For any product, all components of that product are *dependent* demand items. *More generally, for any item where a schedule can be established, dependent techniques should be used.*

Dependent models, when they can be used, are preferable to the models of Chapter 13.[2] Dependency exists for all component parts, subassemblies, and supplies when a schedule is known. Dependent models are better not only for manufacturers and distributors, but also for a wide variety of firms from restaurants[3] to hospitals.[4] When dependent techniques are used in a production environment, they are called **material requirements planning (MRP)** (sometimes referred to as *manufacturing resources planning,* with the same acronym).

Material requirements planning (MRP)

DEPENDENT INVENTORY MODEL REQUIREMENTS

Effective use of dependent inventory models requires that the operations manager know the:

1. master production schedule (what is to be made and when);
2. specifications or bill of material (how to make the product);
3. inventory availability (what is in stock);
4. purchase orders outstanding (what is on order);
5. lead times (how long it takes to get various components).

[1]*Source:* Bob Sperber. "Computers Turn Quiche To Cash." *Food Processing,* 53 (October 1992): 91–92.

[2]The inventory models discussed in Chapter 13 assumed that the demand for one item was independent of the demand for another item. For example, the demand for refrigerators may be *independent* of the demand for dishwashers. Moreover, the demand today may have little, if anything, to do with the demand tomorrow.

[3]John G. Wacker, "Effective Planning and Cost Control for Restaurants: Making Resource Requirements Planning Work," *Production and Inventory Management,* 26 (First Quarter 1985): 55–70.

[4]David W. Pentico, "Material Requirements Planning: A New Tool for Controlling Hospital Inventories," *Hospital Topics,* 57 (May/June 1979): 40–43.

In this chapter, we discuss each of these requirements in the context of material requirements planning (MRP). We then introduce a variation of MRP known as distribution resource planning (DRP).

Master Production Schedule

Master production schedule

A **master production schedule** specifies what is to be made and when. The schedule must be in accordance with a production plan. The production plan sets the overall level of output in broad terms (for example, product families, standard hours, or dollar volume). Such plans include a variety of inputs, including financial plans, customer demand, engineering capabilities, labour availability, inventory fluctuations, supplier performance, and other considerations. Each contributes in its own way to the production plan, as shown in Figure 14.1, which shows the planning process from the production plan to execution. Each of the lower-level plans must be feasible. When it is not, feedback to the next higher level is used to make the necessary adjustment. One of the major strengths of MRP is its ability to determine precisely the feasibility of a schedule within capacity constraints. This planning process can yield excellent results. The production plan sets the upper and lower bounds on the master production schedule. From this production planning process, the master production schedule is developed.

The master production schedule tells us what is required to satisfy demand and meet the production plan. This schedule establishes what items to make and when. Managers must adhere to the schedule for a reasonable length of time (usually a major portion of the production cycle). Many organizations establish a master production schedule and then "fix" the near-term portion of the plan. The fixed portion of the schedule is then referred to as the "fixed," "firm," or "frozen" schedule. Only changes beyond the fixed schedule are permitted. The schedule then becomes a rolling production schedule. For example, a fixed 7-week plan has an additional week added to it as each week is completed, so a 7-week fixed schedule is maintained. Note that the master production schedule is a statement of what is to be produced, not a forecast of demand. The master schedule can be expressed in terms of

1. an *end item in a continuous* (make-to-stock) company;
2. *modules in a repetitive* (assemble-to-stock) company;
3. a *customer order in a job shop* (make-to-order) company.

A master production schedule for two of Nancy's Specialty Foods' products, crab meat quiche and spinach quiche, might look like Table 14.1.

TABLE 14.1 ■ MASTER PRODUCTION SCHEDULE FOR PRODUCTS CRAB MEAT QUICHE AND SPINACH QUICHE

GROSS REQUIREMENTS FOR PRODUCT CRAB MEAT QUICHE

Day	6	7	8	9	10	11	12	13	14	and so on
Amount	50		100	47	60		110	75		

GROSS REQUIREMENTS FOR PRODUCT SPINACH QUICHE

Day	7	8	9	10	11	12	13	14	15	16	and so on
Amount	100	200	150			60	75		100		

FIGURE 14.1 ■ The Planning Process

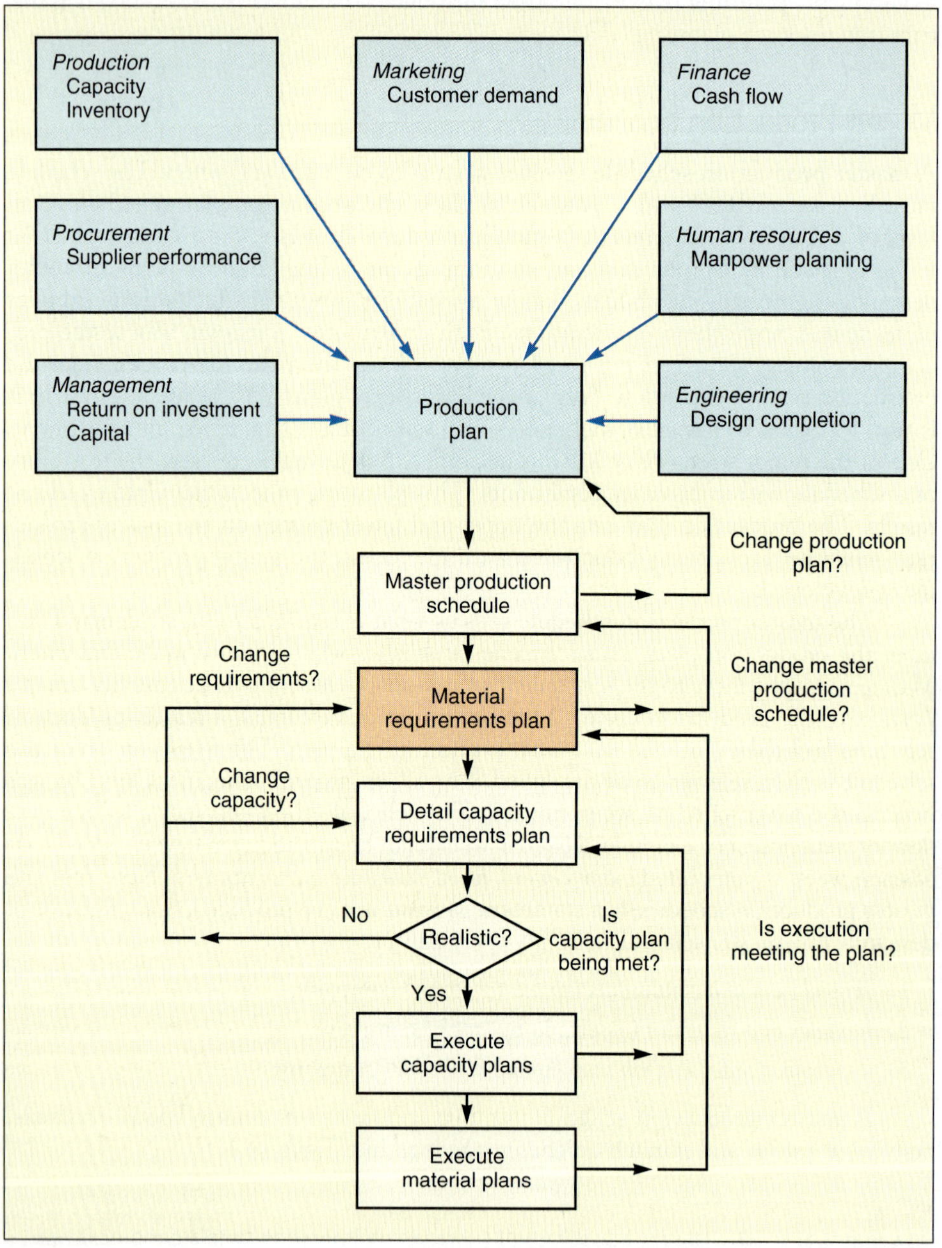

Specifications or Bills of Material

Determining what goes in a product may seem simple, but it can be difficult in practice. As we saw in Chapter 6, there is usually a rush to get a new product to market. Therefore, the drawings and specifications may be incomplete or even nonexistent. Moreover, complete drawings and specifications often contain errors in dimensions, quantities, or countless other areas. Then, engineering change notices (ECNs) are created, further complicating the process. An **engineering change notice (ECN)** is a change or correction to an engineering drawing or specification.

Engineering change notice (ECN)

Units to be produced are often specified via a bill of material, which we introduced in Chapter 6. A **bill of material (BOM)** is a list of quantities of components, ingredients, and materials required to make a product. The individual drawings describe not only physical dimensions, but also any special processing as well as the raw material from which each part is made. Nancy's Specialty Foods' recipe for quiche, specifying ingredients and quantities, and a full set of drawings for a Collins ambulance are both bills of material (although they do vary somewhat in scope).

Bill of material (BOM)

A bill of material provides the product structure. Example 1 shows how to develop the product structure and "explode" it to reveal the requirements for each component. A bill of material for item A in Example 1 consists of items B and C. Items above any level are called *parents;* items below any level are called *components*, or *children*.

EXAMPLE 1

Speaker Kits, Inc., packages high-fidelity components for mail order. The components for their top-of-the-line speaker kit, Awesome (A), includes two standard 12-inch speaker kits (B's) and three speaker kits with amp-boosters (C's).

Each B consists of two speakers (D's) and two shipping boxes with an installation kit (E's). Each of the three 300-watt stereo kits (C's) has two speaker boosters (F's) and two installation kits (E's). Each speaker booster (F) includes two speakers (D's), and one amp-booster (G). The total for each Awesome is four standard 12-inch speakers and twelve 12-inch speakers with the amp-booster. (Most purchasers require hearing aids within 2 years; and at least one court case is pending because of structural damage to a men's dormitory.) The demand for B, C, D, E, F, and G, as we can see, is completely dependent on the demand for A, actual orders for the Awesome speaker kits. Given this information, we can construct the product structure that follows.

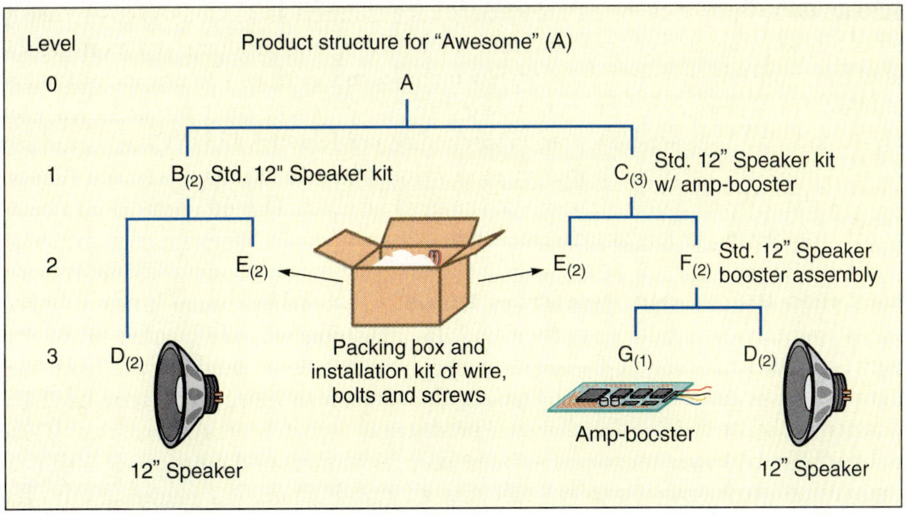

The structure has four levels: 0, 1, 2, and 3. There are four parents: A, B, C, and F. Each parent item has at least one level below it. Items B, C, D, E, F, and G

For manufacturers like Harley-Davidson who produce a large number of end products from a relatively small number of options, modular bills of material provide an effective solution.

are components because each item has at least one level above it. In this structure, B, C, and F are parents and components. The number of parentheses indicates how many units of that particular item are needed to make the item immediately above it. Thus, $B_{(2)}$ means that it takes two units of B for every unit of A, and $F_{(2)}$ means that it takes two units of F for every unit of C.

Once we have developed the product structure, we can determine the number of units of each item required to satisfy demand for a new order of 50 Awesome speaker kits. This information is displayed in the following table:

Part B:	2 × number of A's =	(2)(50) =	100
Part C:	3 × number of A's =	(3)(50) =	150
Part D:	2 × number of B's + 2 × number of F's =	(2)(100) + (2)(300) =	800
Part E:	2 × number of B's + 2 × number of C's =	(2)(100) + (2)(150) =	500
Part F:	2 × number of C's =	(2)(150) =	300
Part G:	1 × number of F's =	(1)(300) =	300

Thus, for 50 units of A, we will need 100 units of B, 150 units of C, 800 units of D, 500 units of E, 300 units of F, and 300 units of G.

Bills of material not only specify requirements, but are also useful for costing, and they can serve as a list of items to be issued to production or assembly personnel. When bills of material (BOM) are used in this way, they are usually called *pick lists*.

Modular bills

MODULAR BILLS. Bills of material may be organized around product modules (see Chapter 6). Modules are not final products to be sold, but are components that can be produced and assembled into units. They may be major components of the final product or product options. The bills of material for these modules are called **modular bills**. Bills of material are sometimes organized as modules (rather than as part of a final product) because production scheduling and production are often facilitated by organizing around relatively few modules rather than a multitude of final assemblies. For instance, a firm may make 138,000 different final products but have only 40 modules that are mixed and matched to produce the 138,000 final products. The firm forecasts, prepares its master production schedule, and builds to the 40 modules, not the 138,000 configurations of the final product. The 40 modules can be assembled for specific orders at final assembly.

Planning bills

Pseudo bills

Kit number

Phantom bills of material

PLANNING BILLS AND PHANTOM BILLS. Two other special kinds of bills of material are planning bills and phantom bills. **Planning bills** are created in order to assign an artificial parent to the bill of material. Such bills are used (1) when we want to group subassemblies together to reduce the number of items to be scheduled and (2) when we want to issue "kits" to the production department. For instance, it may not be efficient to issue inexpensive items such as washers and cotter pins with each of numerous subassemblies, so we call this a *kit* and generate a planning bill. The planning bill specifies the *kit* to be issued. A planning bill may also be known as **pseudo bill** or **kit number**. **Phantom bills of material** are bills of material for components, usually subassemblies that exist only temporarily. These components go directly into another assembly and are never inventoried. Therefore, components of phantom bills of material are coded to receive special treatment; lead times are zero, and they are handled as an integral part of their parent item.

LOW-LEVEL CODING. Low-level coding of an item in a BOM is necessary when identical items exist at various levels in the BOM. **Low-level coding** means the item is coded at the lowest level at which it occurs. For example, item D in Example 1 is coded at the lowest level at which it is used. Item D could be coded as part of B and occur at level 2. But because D is also part of F, and F is level 2, item D becomes a level 3 item. Low-level coding is a convention to allow easy computing of the requirements of an item. When the BOM has thousands of items and when requirements are frequently recomputed, the ease and speed of computation become a major concern.

Low-level coding

Accurate Inventory Records

Knowledge of what is in stock is the result of good inventory management, as discussed in Chapter 13. Good inventory management is an absolute necessity for an MRP system to work. If the firm has not yet achieved at least 99% record accuracy, then material requirements planning will not work.

Purchase Orders Outstanding

Knowledge of outstanding orders should exist as a by-product of well-managed purchasing and inventory control departments. When purchase orders are executed, records of those orders and their scheduled delivery date must be available to production personnel. Only with good purchasing data can managers prepare good production plans and effectively execute an MRP system.

Lead Times for Each Component

Once managers determine when products are needed, they determine when to acquire them. The time required to acquire (that is, purchase, produce, or assemble) an item is known as **lead time**. Lead time for a manufactured item consists of move, setup, and assembly or run times for each component. For a purchased item, the lead time includes the time between when a part is ordered and when it is available for production.

Lead time

When the bill of material for Awesome speaker kits (A's), in Example 1, is turned on its side and lead times for each component are added (see Table 14.2), we then have a *time-phased product structure*. Time in this structure is shown on the horizontal axis (see Figure 14.2).

TABLE 14.2 ■ LEAD TIMES FOR AWESOME SPEAKER KITS (A'S)

COMPONENT	LEAD TIME
A	1 week
B	2 weeks
C	1 week
D	1 week
E	2 weeks
F	3 weeks
G	2 weeks

MRP STRUCTURE

Although most MRP systems are computerized, the MRP procedure is straightforward and can be done by hand. A master production schedule, a bill of material, inventory and purchase records, and lead times for each item are ingredients of a material requirements planning system (see Figure 14.3).

FIGURE 14.2 ■ Time-Phased Product Structure

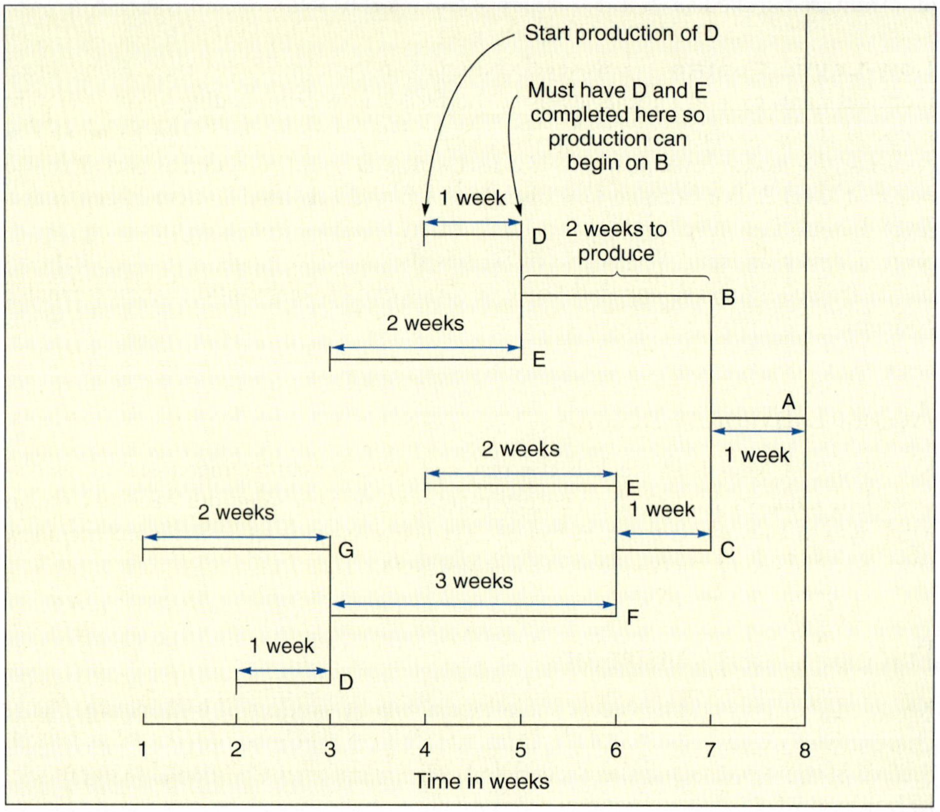

Gross material requirements plan

Once these ingredients are available and accurate, the next step is to construct a gross material requirements plan. The **gross material requirements plan** is a schedule. It combines a master production schedule (that requires a unit of A in week 8) and the time-phased schedule (Figure 14.2). It shows when an item must be ordered from suppliers if there is no inventory on hand or when the production of an item must be started in order to satisfy the demand for the finished product by a particular date.

EXAMPLE 2

Each Awesome speaker kit (item A of Example 1) requires all of the items in the product structure for A. The lead times were shown in Table 14.2. Using this information, we construct the gross material requirements plan and draw up a production schedule that will satisfy the demand of 50 units of A by week 8. This is shown in Table 14.3.

The interpretation of the gross material requirements is as follows: If you want 50 units of A at week 8, you must start assembling A in week 7. Thus, in week 7, you will need 100 units of B and 150 units of C. These two items take 2 weeks and 1 week, respectively, to produce. Production of B should start in week 5, and production of C should start in week 6 (lead time subtracted from the required date for these items). Working backward, we can perform the same computations for all of the other items. The material requirements plan shows when production of each item should begin and end in order to have 50 units of A at week 8.

TABLE 14.3 ■ GROSS MATERIAL REQUIREMENTS PLAN FOR 50 AWESOME SPEAKER KITS (A)

	Week 1	2	3	4	5	6	7	8	Lead Time
A. Required date								50	1 week
Order release date							50		
B. Required date							100		2 weeks
Order release date					100				
C. Required date							150		1 week
Order release date						150			
D. Required date					200				1 week
Order release date				200					
E. Required date					200	300			2 weeks
Order release date			200	300					
F. Required date						300			3 weeks
Order release date			300						
D. Required date			600						1 week
Order release date		600							
G. Required date			300						2 weeks
Order release date	300								

So far, we have considered *gross material requirements*, which assumes that there is no inventory on hand. When there is inventory on hand, we prepare a net requirements plan. When considering on-hand inventory, we must realize that many items in inventory contain subassemblies or parts. If the gross requirement for Awesome speaker kits (A's) is 100 and there are 20 of those speakers on hand, the net requirement for Awesome speaker kits (A's) is 80 (that is, 100 – 20). But each Awesome speaker kit on hand contains 2 B's. As a result, the requirement for B's drops by 40 B's (20 A kits on hand × 2 B's per A). Therefore, if inventory is on hand for a parent item, the requirements for the parent item and all its components decrease because each Awesome kit contains the components for lower-level items. Example 3 shows how to create a net requirements plan.

EXAMPLE 3

In Example 1, we developed a product structure from a bill of material (BOM), and in Example 2, we developed a gross requirements plan. Given the following on-hand inventory, we now construct a net requirements plan.

Item	On Hand	Item	On Hand
A	10	E	10
B	15	F	5
C	20	G	0
D	10		

FIGURE 14.3 ■ Structure of the MRP System

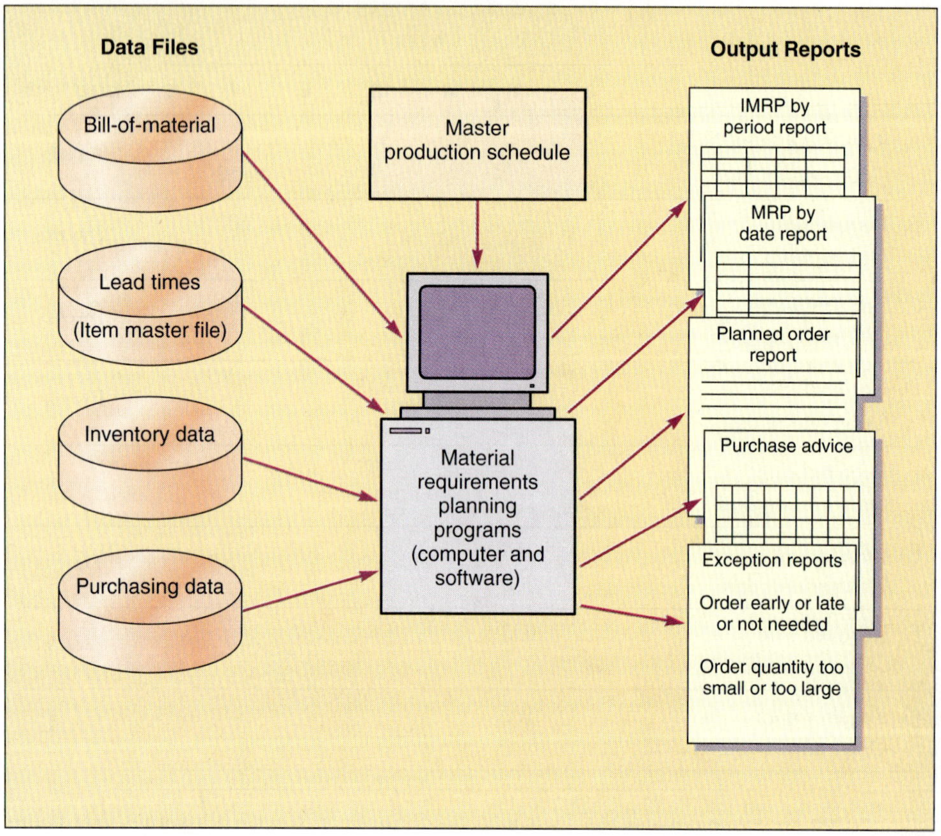

A net material requirements plan includes gross requirements, on-hand inventory, net requirements, planned order receipt, and planned order release for each item. We begin with A and work backward through the components. Shown in the chart is the net material requirements plan for product A.

Constructing a net requirements plan is similar to constructing the gross requirements plan. Starting with item A, we work backward to determine net requirements for all items. To do these computations, we refer to the product structure, on-hand inventory, and lead times. The gross requirement for A is 50 units in week 8. Ten items are on hand; therefore, the net requirements and planned order receipt both are 40 items in week 8. Because of the 1-week lead time, the planned order release is 40 items in week 7 (see the arrow connecting the order receipt and order release). Referring to week 7 and the product structure in Example 1, we can see 80 (2 × 40) items of B and 120 (3 × 40) items of C are required in week 7 in order to have a total for 50 items of A in week 8. The letter A to the right of the gross figure for items B and C was generated as a result of the demand for the parent, A. Performing the same type of analysis for B and C yields the net requirements for D, E, F, and G. Note the on-hand inventory in row E in week 6. It is zero because the on-hand inventory (10 units) was used to make B in week 5. By the same token, the inventory for D was used to make F.

Net Material Requirements Plan for Product A. Note that the superscript is the source of the demand.

Lot Size	Lead Time (weeks)	On Hand	Safety Stock	Allo-cated	Low Level Code	Item Identi-fication			Week 1	2	3	4	5	6	7	8
Lot-for-Lot	1	10	—	—	0	A	Gross Requirements									50
							Scheduled Receipts									
							Projected on Hand	10	10	10	10	10	10	10	10	10
							Net Requirements									40
							Planned Order Receipts									40
							Planned Order Releases								40	
Lot-for-Lot	2	15	—	—	1	B	Gross Requirements								80^{A}	
							Scheduled Receipts									
							Projected on Hand	15	15	15	15	15	15	15	15	
							Net Requirements								65	
							Planned Order Receipts								65	
							Planned Order Releases						65			
Lot-for-Lot	1	20	—	—	1	C	Gross Requirements								120^{A}	
							Scheduled Receipts									
							Projected on Hand	20	20	20	20	20	20	20	20	
							Net Requirements								100	
							Planned Order Receipts								100	
							Planned Order Releases							100		
Lot-for-Lot	2	10	—	—	2	E	Gross Requirements						130^{B}	200^{C}		
							Scheduled Receipts									
							Projected on Hand	10	10	10	10	10	10			
							Net Requirements						120	200		
							Planned Order Receipts						120	200		
							Planned Order Releases				120	200				
Lot-for-Lot	3	5	—	—	2	F	Gross Requirements							200^{C}		
							Scheduled Receipts									
							Projected on Hand	5	5	5	5	5	5	5		
							Net Requirements							195		
							Planned Order Receipts							195		
							Planned Order Releases				195					
Lot-for-Lot	1	10	—	—	3	D	Gross Requirements				390^{F}		130^{B}			
							Scheduled Receipts									
							Projected on Hand	10	10	10	10					
							Net Requirements				380		130			
							Planned Order Receipts				380		130			
							Planned Order Releases			380		130				
Lot-for-Lot	2	0	—	—	3	G	Gross Requirements				195^{F}					
							Scheduled Receipts									
							Projected on Hand				0					
							Net Requirements				195					
							Planned Order Receipts				195					
							Planned Order Releases		195							

Examples 2 and 3 considered only product A, the Awesome speaker kit, and its completion only in week 8. Fifty units of A were required in week 8. Normally, there is a demand for many products over time. For each product, management must prepare a master production schedule (as we saw earlier in Table 14.1). Scheduled

3COM Corporation, headquartered in Santa Clara, CA, is a manufacturer of local and wide-area computer network systems. 3COM uses MRP to manage its production of printed-circuit boards. Timely and accurate information obtained from the system is forwarded to suppliers that deliver parts and material directly to the line on a JIT basis. 3COM's MRP system allows them to keep inventory levels low and track vendor performance.

production of each product contributes to the master schedule and ultimately to the net material requirements plan. Figure 14.4 shows how several product schedules can contribute to one gross material requirements plan.

Most inventory systems also note the number of units in inventory that have been assigned to specific future production but not yet used. Such items are often referred to as *allocated* items. Allocated items may then be included in an MRP planning sheet, as shown in Figure 14.5.

The allocated quantity has the effect of increasing the requirements (or, alternatively, reducing the quantity on hand). The logic, then, of a net requirements MRP is

$$\underbrace{\left[\begin{pmatrix}\text{gross}\\\text{requirements}\end{pmatrix} + \begin{pmatrix}\text{allocations}\end{pmatrix}\right]}_{\text{total requirements}} - \underbrace{\left[\begin{pmatrix}\text{on}\\\text{hand}\end{pmatrix} + \begin{pmatrix}\text{scheduled}\\\text{receipts}\end{pmatrix}\right]}_{\text{available inventory}} = \begin{matrix}\text{net}\\\text{requirements}\end{matrix}$$

MRP DYNAMICS

A material requirements plan is not static. Even though a bill of material and material requirements plan are established, changes in design, schedules, and production processes continue to occur. For example, if one of the production time estimates was 1 week less than it should have been, that week must be added to the material

FIGURE 14.4 ■ Several Schedules Contributing to a Gross Requirements Schedule for B. One *B* is in each A and one *B* in each S, and 10 *B*'s are sold directly in week 1 and 10 more are sold directly in week 2.

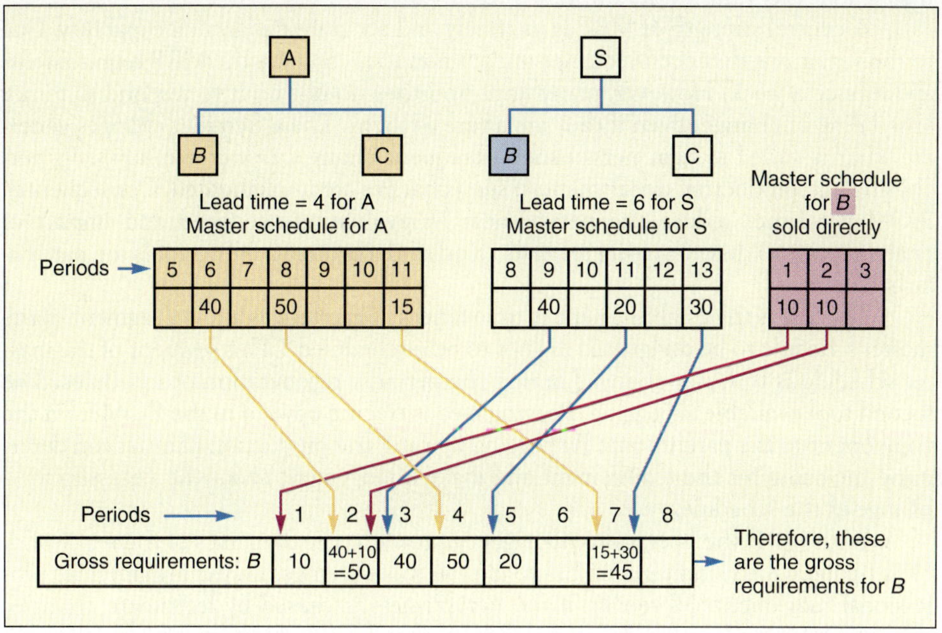

requirements plan. Likewise, if a design improvement allows construction of one of the intermediate inventory items with fewer parts, then the bill of material and the material requirements plan must be altered. Scrapped components, missed receiving dates, and machine breakdowns contribute to such alterations in the material requirements plan. Similarly, alterations occur in an MRP system when changes are made to the master production schedule. Regardless of the cause of any changes, the MRP model can be manipulated to reflect them. In this manner, an up-to-date schedule is possible. Such schedule changes reflect the most recent data so the production schedule can be satisfied.

Modifying the MRP schedule in response to changes is cumbersome if done by hand, and errors are likely when the plan is complex. Therefore, most MRP systems

FIGURE 14.5 ■ Sample MRP Planning Sheet for Item A

Lot Size	Lead Time	On Hand	Safety Stock	Allocated	Low Level Code	Item Id
Lot For Lot	1	0	0	10	0	B

		Period 1	2	3	4	5	6	7	8
Gross Requirements									~~80~~ 90
Scheduled Receipts									0
Projected on Hand	0	0	0	0	0	0	0	0	0
Net Requirements									90
Planned Order Receipts									90
Planned Order Releases								90	

are computerized. Indeed, only because they are computerized are they the popular and practical tool they have become.[5] Computerized programs perform the same types of calculations that we have demonstrated in this chapter and are widely used throughout the industrialized world.

A central strength of MRP is its timely and accurate replanning capability. Due to the variations that occur, it is not uncommon to recompute the MRP requirements about once a week. However, many firms find they do not want to respond to minor scheduling or changes even if they are aware of them. These frequent changes generate what is called **system nervousness**. Frequent changes can create havoc in purchasing and production departments if such changes are implemented. Consequently, P/OM personnel reduce the nervousness by evaluating the need and impact of changes prior to disseminating requests to other departments.[6] Two tools are particularly helpful.

System nervousness

The first is the establishment of time fences. **Time fences** allow a segment of the master schedule to be designated as "not to be rescheduled." This segment of the master schedule is thus not changed during the periodic regeneration of schedules. The second tool available is pegging. **Pegging** means tracing upward in the BOM from the component to the parent item. By pegging upward, the production planner can determine the cause for the requirement and make a judgement about the necessity for a change in the schedule.

Time fences

Pegging

With MRP, the operations manager *can* react to the dynamics of the real world. How frequently the manager wishes to impose those changes on the firm requires professional judgement. Moreover, if the nervousness is caused by legitimate changes, then the proper response of operations management may be to investigate the production environment—not adjust via MRP.

LOT-SIZING TECHNIQUES

An MRP system is an excellent way to determine production schedules and net requirements. However, whenever we have a net requirement, a decision must be made about how much to order. These decisions are called **lot-sizing decisions**. There are a variety of ways to determine lot sizes in an MRP system; commercial MRP software usually includes the choice of several lot-sizing techniques. We will now review a few of them.

Lot-sizing decisions

LOT-FOR-LOT. In Example 3, we used a lot-sizing technique known as **lot-for-lot**, which produced exactly what was required. This is consistent with the objective of an MRP system, which is to meet the requirements of *dependent* demand. Thus, an MRP system should produce units only as needed with no safety stock and no anticipation of further orders. When frequent orders are economical and just-in-time inventory techniques implemented, lot-for-lot can be very efficient. However, in cases where setup costs are significant or where management has been unable to implement JIT, lot-for-lot can be expensive. Example 4 uses the lot-for-lot criteria and determines its cost for 10 weeks of demand.

Lot-for-lot

[5] As early as 1920, Al Sloan, president of GM, understood the basic ingredients of MRP. See Alfred P. Sloan, Jr., *My Years with General Motors* (Garden City, NY: Anchor Books, 1972), p. 145.

[6] Jay H. Heizer, "The Production Manager Can Be a Good Guy in the Factory with a Future," *APICS—The Performance Advantage* (July 1994): 30–34.

EXAMPLE 4

Speaker Kits, Inc., wishes to compute its ordering and carrying cost of inventory on lot-for-lot criteria. Speaker Kits has determined that, for the 12-inch speaker/booster assembly, setup cost is $100 and holding cost is $1 per period. The production schedule as reflected in net requirements for assemblies is as follows:

MRP LOT-SIZING PROBLEM: LOT-FOR-LOT TECHNIQUE

		1	2	3	4	5	6	7	8	9	10
Gross Requirements		35	30	40	0	10	40	30	0	30	55
Scheduled Receipts											
Projected on Hand	35	0	0	0	0	0	0	0	0	0	0
Net Requirements		0	30	40	0	10	40	30	0	30	55
Planned Order Receipts			30	40		10	40	30		30	55
Planned Order Releases		30	40		10	40	30		30	55	

Holding costs = $1/unit/week; setup cost = $100; gross requirements average per week = 27; lead time = 1 week.

Shown is the lot-sizing solution using the lot-for-lot technique and its cost. The holding cost is zero, but seven separate setups yield a total cost of $700.

ECONOMIC ORDER QUANTITY. As discussed in Chapter 13, EOQ can be used as a lot-sizing technique. But as we indicated there, EOQ is preferable where relatively constant independent demand exists, not where we know the demand. EOQ is a statistical technique using averages, typically average demand for a year, whereas our MRP procedure assumes known (dependent) demand. Operations managers should take advantage of this information, rather than assuming a constant demand. EOQ is examined in Example 5.

This Nissan pickup truck assembly line has little inventory, because Nissan schedules to a razor's edge. At Nissan Motor Company plants, MRP helps to reduce inventory to world-class standards. World-class automobile assembly requires that purchased parts have a turnover of slightly more than once a day and that overall turnover approaches 150 times per year.

EXAMPLE 5

Speaker Kits, Inc., with a setup cost of $100 and a holding cost per week of $1, examines its cost with lot sizes based on an EOQ criteria. The net requirements and lot sizes using the same requirements as in Example 4 follow:

MRP LOT-SIZING PROBLEM: EOQ TECHNIQUE

		1	2	3	4	5	6	7	8	9	10
Gross Requirements		35	30	40	0	10	40	30	0	30	55
Scheduled Receipts											
Projected on Hand	35	35	0	43	3	3	66	26	69	69	39
Net Requirements		0	30	0	0	7	26	4	0	0	16
Planned Order Receipts			73			73		73			73
Planned Order Releases		73			73		73			73	

Holding costs = $1/unit/week; setup cost = $100; gross requirements average per week = 27; lead time = 1 week.

Ten-week usage equals 270 units; therefore, weekly usage equals 27, and 52 weeks (annual usage) equals 1,404 units. From Chapter 13, the EOQ model is

$$Q^* = \sqrt{\frac{2DS}{H}}$$

where D = annual usage = 1,404
S = setup cost = $100
H = holding (carrying) cost, on an annual basis per unit = $1 × 52 weeks = $52

$$Q^* = 73 \text{ units}$$

$$\text{Setups} = 1{,}404/73 = 19 \text{ per year}$$

$$\text{Setup cost} = 19 \times \$100 = \$1{,}900$$

$$\text{Holding cost} = \frac{73}{2} \times (\$1 \times 52 \text{ weeks}) = \$1{,}898$$

$$\text{Setup cost} + \text{holding cost} = \$1{,}900 + 1{,}898 = \$3{,}798$$

The EOQ solution yields a computed 10-week cost of $730 [$3,798 × (10 weeks/52 weeks) = $730].

Notice that actual holding cost will vary from the computed $730, depending upon the rate of actual usage. From the preceding table, we can see that in our 10-week example costs really are $400 for four setups, plus a holding cost of 375 units at $1 per week for a total of $775. Because usage was not constant, the actual computed cost was in fact more than the theoretical EOQ ($730) and more than the lot-for-lot rule ($700). If any stockouts had occurred, these costs too would need to be added to our actual EOQ of $775.

PART PERIOD BALANCING. **Part period balancing (PPB)** is a more dynamic approach to balance setup and holding cost.[7] PPB uses additional information by changing the lot size to reflect requirements of the next lot size in the future. PPB attempts to balance setup and holding cost for known demands. Part period balancing develops an **economic part period (EPP)**, which is the ratio of setup cost to holding cost. For our Speaker Kits example, EPP = \$100/\$1 = 100 units. Therefore, holding 100 units for one period would cost \$100, exactly the cost of one setup. Similarly, holding 50 units for two periods also costs \$100 (2 periods × \$1 × 50 units). PPB merely adds requirements until the number of part periods approximates the EPP, in this case 100. Example 6 shows the application of part period balancing.

Part period balancing (PPB)

Economic part period (EPP)

EXAMPLE 6

Once again, Speaker Kits, Inc., computes the costs associated with a lot size by using a \$100 setup cost and a \$1 holding cost, only this time part period balancing is used. The data are shown in the following table:

PPB CALCULATIONS

Periods Combined	Trial Lot Size (Cumulative Net Requirements)	Part Periods	Costs: Setup	Holding	Total
2	30	0			
2, 3	70	40 = 40 × 1			
2, 3, 4	70	40			
2, 3, 4, 5	80	70 = 40 × 1 + 10 × 3	100 +	70 =	170
2, 3, 4, 5, 6	120	230 = 40 × 1 + 10 × 3 + 40 × 4			
(Therefore, combine periods 2 through 5; 70 is as close to our EPP of 100 as we are going to get.)					
6	40	0			
6, 7	70	30			
6, 7, 8	70	30			
6, 7, 8, 9	100	120 = 30 × 1 + 30 × 3	100 +	120 =	220
(Therefore, combine periods 6 through 9; 120 is as close to our EPP of 100 as we are going to get.)					
10	55	0	100 +	0 =	100
			300 +	190 =	490

(Annotations: 40 units held for 1 period = \$40; 10 units held for 3 periods = \$30; total holding 70.)

MRP LOT-SIZING PROBLEM: PPB TECHNIQUE

		1	2	3	4	5	6	7	8	9	10
Gross Requirements		35	30	40	0	10	40	30	0	30	55
Scheduled Receipts											
Projected on Hand	35	35	0	50	10	10	0	60	30	30	0
Net Requirements		0	30	0	0	0	40	0	0	0	55
Planned Order Receipts			80				100				55
Planned Order Releases		80				100				55	

Holding costs = \$1/unit/week; setup cost = \$100; gross requirements average per week = 27; lead time = 1 week.

[7] J. J. DeMatteis, "An Economic Lot-Sizing Technique: The Part-Period Algorithms," *IBM Systems Journal*, 7 (1968): 30–38.

EPP is 100 (setup cost divided by holding cost = \$100/\$1). The first lot is to cover periods one, two, three, four, and five and is 80.

The total costs are \$490, with setup costs totalling \$300 and holding costs totalling \$190.

Wagner-Whitin procedure

WAGNER-WHITIN ALGORITHM. The **Wagner-Whitin procedure** is a dynamic programming model that adds some complexity to the lot-size computation. It assumes a finite time horizon beyond which there are no additional net requirements. It does, however, provide good results.[8] The technique is seldom used in practice, but this may change with increasing understanding and software sophistication.

LOT-SIZING SUMMARY. In the three Speaker Kits lot-sizing examples, we found the following costs:

Lot-for-lot	\$700
EOQ	\$775
Part period balancing	\$490

These examples should not, however, lead operations personnel to hasty conclusions about the preferred lot-sizing technique. In theory, new lot sizes should be computed whenever there is a schedule or lot-size change anywhere in the MRP hierarchy. But in practice such changes cause the instability and system nervousness referred to earlier in this chapter. Consequently, such frequent changes are not made. This means that all lot sizes are wrong because the production system can not respond to frequent changes.

In general, the lot-for-lot approach should be used wherever economical. Lot-for-lot is the goal. Lots can be modified as necessary for scrap allowances, process constraints (for example, a heat-treating process may require a lot of a given size), or raw material purchase lots (for example, a truckload of chemicals may be available in only one lot size). However, caution should be exercised prior to any modification of lot size because the modification can cause substantial distortion of actual requirements at lower levels in the MRP hierarchy. Where setup costs are significant and the demand is reasonably smooth, part period balancing (PPB), Wagner-Whitin, or even EOQ should provide satisfactory results. Too much concern with lot sizing yields false accuracy because of MRP dynamics. A correct lot size can be determined only after the fact, based on what actually happened in terms of requirements.[9]

[8]See James M. Fordyce and Francis M. Webster, "The Wagner-Whitin Algorithm Made Simple," *Production and Inventory Management* (Second Quarter 1984): 21–27. This article provides as straightforward an explanation of the Wagner-Whitin technique as we have found. The Wagner-Whitin Algorithm yields a cost of \$455 for the data in Examples 4, 5, and 6.

[9]See discussions by Joseph Orlicky, *Material Requirements Planning* (New York: McGraw-Hill, 1975), pp. 136–137, and G. Nandakumar, "Lot-Sizing Techniques in a Multiproduct Multilevel Environment," *Production and Inventory Management*, 26 (First Quarter 1985): 46–54.

EXTENSIONS OF MRP

Recent years have seen the development of a number of extensions of MRP. In this section, we review three of them.

Closed-Loop MRP

Closed-loop material requirements planning implies an MRP system that provides feedback to scheduling from the inventory control system. Specifically, a **closed-loop MRP system** provides feedback to the capacity plan, master production schedule, and ultimately to the production plan (as shown in Figure 14.6). Virtually all commercial MRP systems are closed-loop.

Closed-loop MRP system

FIGURE 14.6 ■ Closed-Loop Material Requirements Planning

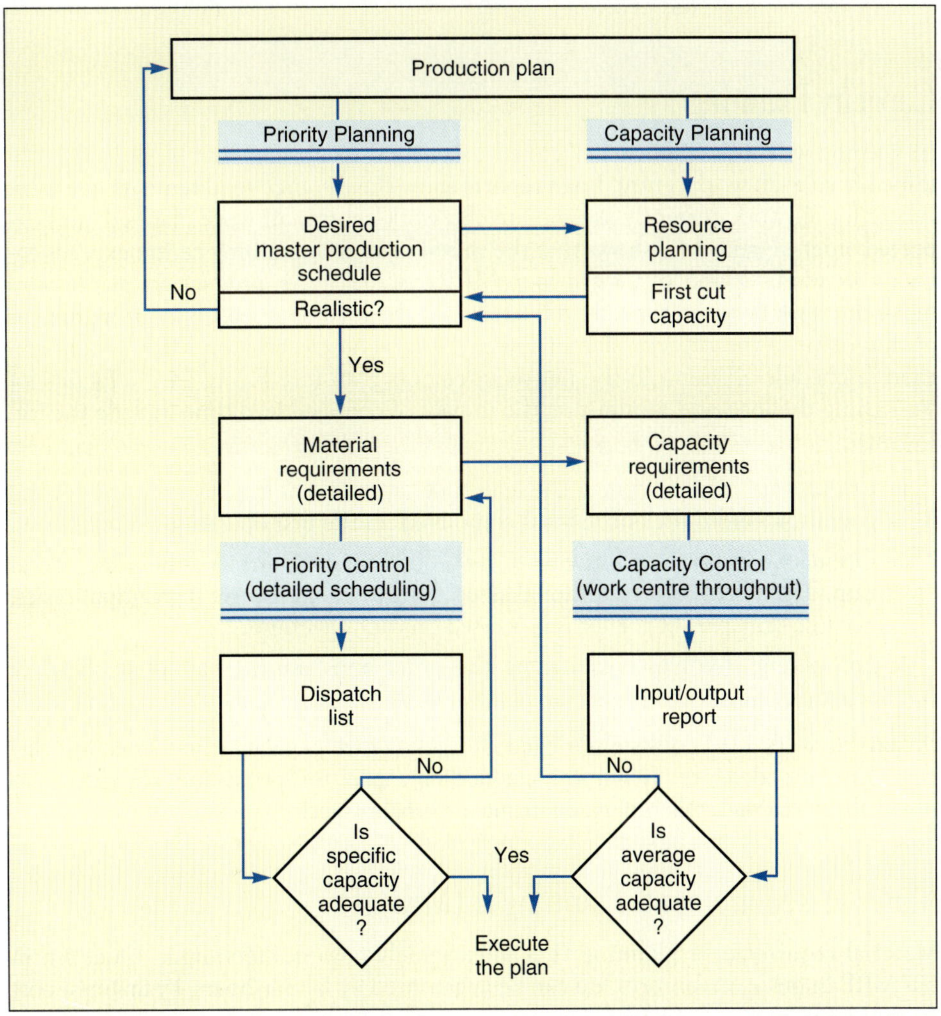

(*Source:* Adapted from *Capacity Planning and Control Study Guide*, Falls Church, VA: American Production and Inventory Control Society.)

FIGURE 14.7 ■ (a) Initial Resource Requirements Profile for a Milling Centre (b) Smoothed Resource Requirements Profile for a Milling Centre

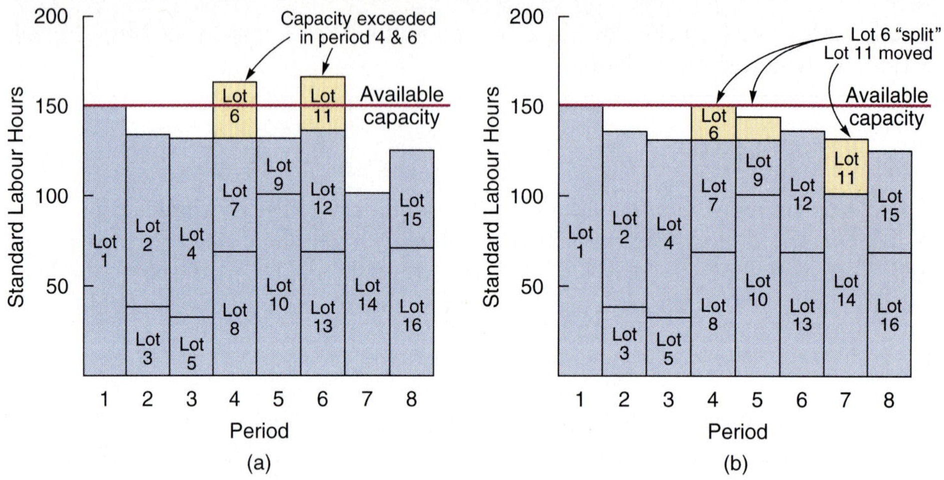

Capacity Planning

Load reports

In keeping with the definition of closed-loop MRP, feedback about work load is obtained from each work centre. **Load reports** show the resource requirements in a work centre for all work currently assigned to the work centre, all work planned, and expected orders. Figure 14.7 shows that the initial load in the milling centre exceeds capacity in weeks 4 and 6. Closed-loop MRP systems allow production planners to move the work between time periods to smooth the load or at least bring it within capacity. (This is the *capacity* side of Figure 14.6.) The closed-loop MRP system can then reschedule all items in the net requirements plan (see Figure 14.7). Tactics for smoothing the load and minimizing the impact of changed lead time include the following:

1. *Overlapping*, which reduces the lead time, entails sending pieces to the second operation before the entire lot is completed on the first operation.
2. *Operations splitting* sends the lot to two different machines for the same operation. This involves an additional setup, but results in shorter throughput times, because only part of the lot is processed on each machine.
3. *Lot splitting* involves breaking up the order and running part of it ahead of schedule.

When the work load consistently exceeds work centre capacity, the tactics just discussed are not adequate. This may mean adding capacity. Options include adding capacity via personnel, machinery, overtime, or subcontracting.

Material Requirements Planning II (MRP II)

Material requirements planning II (MRP II)

Material requirements planning II is an extremely powerful technique. Once a firm has MRP in place, inventory data can be augmented by labour-hours, by material cost (rather than material quantity), by capital cost, or by virtually any resource. When MRP is used this way, it is usually referred to as **MRP II**, and *resource* is usually substituted for *requirements*. MRP then stands for material *resource* planning.

For instance, so far in our discussion of MRP, we have scheduled units (quantities), but each of these units requires resources in addition to its components. Those additional resources include labour-hours, machine-hours, and accounts payable (cash). Each of these resources can be used in an MRP format just as we used quantities. Table 14.4 shows how to determine the labour-hours, machine-hours, and cash that a sample master production schedule will require in each period. These requirements are then compared with the respective capacity (that is, labour-hours, machine-hours, cash, and so forth), so operations managers can make schedules that will work. The potential of MRP II, combined with other information, is discussed further in the *POM in Action* box "Fourth Shift Corp."

Furthermore, most MRP II computer programs are tied into other computer programs that provide data to the MRP system or receive data from the MRP system. Order entry, invoicing, billing, purchasing, production scheduling, capacity planning, and warehouse management are a few examples. A schematic showing how these sources of data for a manufacturing organization tie together is shown in Figure 14.8.

MRP IN SERVICES

The demand for many services or service items is classified as dependent demand when it is directly related to or derived from the demand for other services. For example, in a restaurant where bread and vegetables are included in every meal ordered, the demand for bread and vegetables is dependent on the demand for meals. The meal is an end item and the bread and vegetables are component items.

Figure 14.9 shows a bill of materials and accompanying product structure tree for veal picante, a top-selling entree in a New Orleans restaurant. Note that the various components of veal picante (that is, veal, sauce, and linguini) are prepared by

TABLE 14.4 ■ **MATERIAL RESOURCE PLANNING (MRP II). BY UTILIZING THE LOGIC OF MRP, RESOURCES SUCH AS LABOUR, MACHINE-HOURS, AND COST CAN BE ACCURATELY DETERMINED AND SCHEDULED. WEEKLY DEMAND FOR LABOUR, MACHINE-HOURS, AND PAYABLES FOR 100 UNITS ARE SHOWN.**

	WEEK			
	5	6	7	8
A. (Lead time 1 week)				100
Labour: 10 hours each				1,000
Machine: 2 hours each				200
Payable: $0 each				0
B. (Lead time 2 weeks, 2 each required)			200	
Labour: 10 hours each			2,000	
Machine: 2 hours each			400	
Payable: Raw material at $5 each			1,000	
C. (Lead time 4 weeks, 3 each required)	300			
Labour: 2 hours each	600			
Machine: 1 hour each	300			
Payable: Raw material at $10 each	3,000			

POM IN ACTION

Fourth Shift Corp.

On July 11, 1996, Jim Kridel, vice-president of Fourth Shift Corp.'s worldwide channel distribution, announced that DES Informatiques Inc. of Montreal would be the Quebec distributor for its client server software.

DES Informatiques was selected from a number of manufacturers of software systems to play an essential role in Fourth Shift's worldwide growth objectives. DES's adherence to sound financial and manufacturing standards and their ability to provide service in English and French were of paramount importance.

Fourth Shift will be a powerful ally for DES, having won *Manufacturing Systems* magazine's Readers' Choice Award for best PC/LAN-based MRP II system for an unprecedented three consecutive years.

Fourth Shift's MSS has been licensed to more than 2,200 customers in 50 countries, including 120 U.S. and 52 global Fortune 500 companies.

Source: Adapted from Business Wire Inc., "Fourth Shift Corp. Names Quebec Distributor," July 11, 1996.

different kitchen personnel (see part (a) of Figure 14.9). These preparations also require different amounts of time to complete. Figure 14.9(c) shows a bill of labour for the veal dish. It lists the operations to be performed, the order of operations, and the labour requirements for each operation (types of labour and labour-hours).

MRP is also applied in hospitals, especially when dealing with surgeries that require equipment, materials, and supplies. The Park Plaza Hospital in Houston, Texas,

FIGURE 14.8 ■ MRP Information Flow Integrated with Other Information Systems. *Note:* Arrowheads indicate the flow of data.

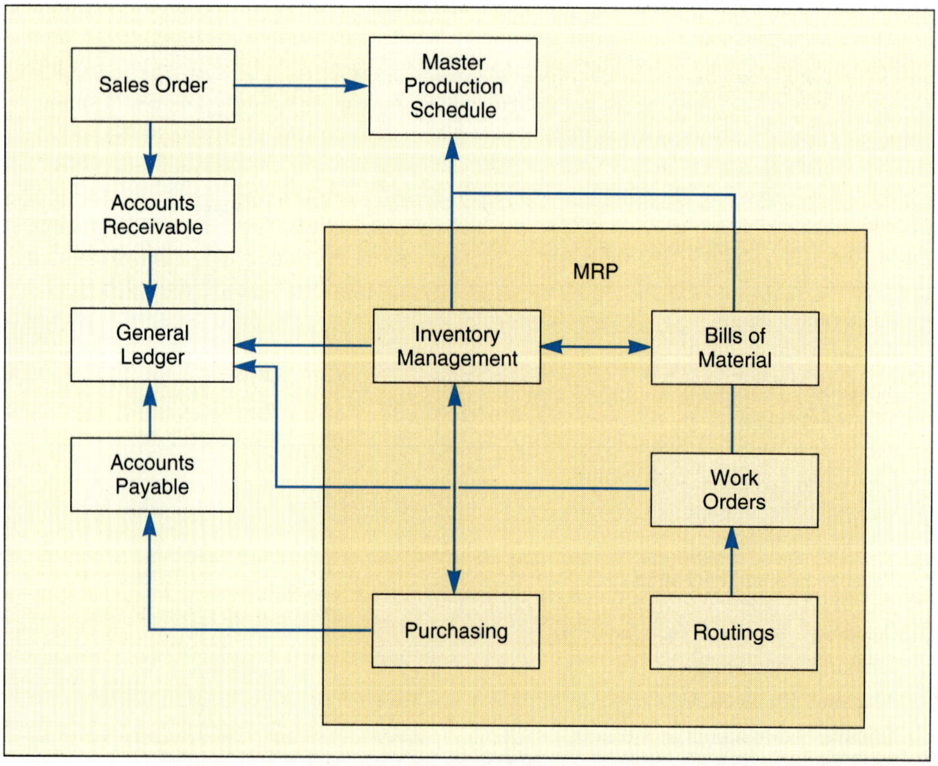

FIGURE 14.9 ■ Product Structure Tree, Bill of Material, and Bill of Labour for Veal Picante

(a) PRODUCT STRUCTURE TREE

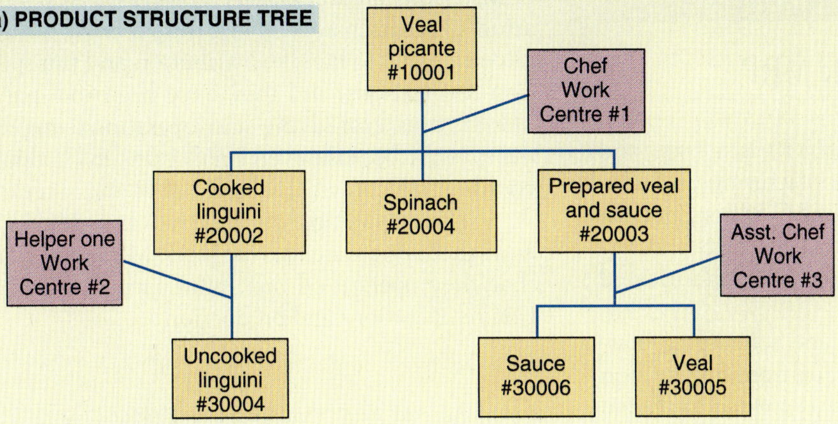

(b) BILL OF MATERIALS

Part Number	Description	Quantity	Unit of Measure	Unit Cost
10001	Veal picante	1	Serving	—
20002	Cooked linguini	1	Serving	—
20003	Prepared veal and sauce	1	Serving	—
20004	Spinach	0.1	Bag	0.94
30004	Uncooked linguini	0.5	Pound	—
30005	Veal	1	Serving	2.15
30006	Sauce	1	Serving	0.80

(c) BILL OF LABOUR FOR VEAL PICANTE

			Labour-Hours	
Work Centre	Operation	Labour Type	Setup Time	Run Time
1	Assemble dish	Chef	.0069	.0041
2	Cook linguini	Helper one	.0005	.0022
3	Cook veal and sauce	Assistant chef	.0125	.0500

Source: Adapted from John G. Wacker, "Effective Planning and Cost Control for Restaurants," *Production and Inventory Management* (First Quarter 1985): 60.

for example, uses the technique to improve the management of expensive surgical inventory.[10]

DISTRIBUTION RESOURCE PLANNING (DRP)

When dependent techniques are used in distribution environments, they are called distribution resource planning (DRP). See, for instance, the *POM in Action* box, "Moving the Pampers Faster Cuts Everyone's Costs."

[10]See E. Steinberg, B. Khumawala, and R. Scamell, "Requirements Planning in the Health Care Environment," *Journal of Operations Management*, 2, no. 4 (August 1982): 251–259.

POM IN ACTION

ERP with Rapid MRP

Enterprise resource planning (ERP) is a large and growing segment of the manufacturing industry. Growth was 40% this year, to $5.5 billion, not including the many complementary products and services associated with technologically sophisticated manufacturing.

The advanced planning and scheduling market was $125 million this year, up from $35 million two years ago. This segment was created by Rapid MRP, a Canadian company, which in 1986 developed an algorithm that compressed the running time of MRP software from hours to minutes. New-generation products based on the Rapid MRP program have emerged to handle distribution and transportation applications, and they have been indisputably identified as cost-saving and operational improvement tools, because even small gains in production coordination can yield substantial financial returns.

The advantage of these advanced planning and scheduling systems over MRP, MPS, and CRP is that they operate off-line, eliminating any disruption to operations and production.

Source: Adapted from "Plan for Success," *Manufacturing Systems* (May 1966).

Distribution resource planning (DRP)

Distribution resource planning (DRP) is a time-phased stock replenishment plan for all levels of a distribution network. Its procedures and logic are analogous to those of MRP. DRP requires

1. gross requirements, which are the same as expected demand or sales forecasts;
2. minimum levels of inventory to meet customer service levels;
3. accurate lead time;
4. definition of the distribution structure.

DRP Structure

When DRP is used, expected demand becomes gross requirements. Net requirements are determined by allocating available inventory to gross requirements. The DRP procedure starts with the forecast at the retail level (or the most distant point of the distribution network being supplied). All other levels are computed. As is the case with MRP, inventory is then reviewed with an aim to satisfying demand. So that stock will arrive when it is needed, net requirements are offset by the necessary lead time. A planned order release quantity becomes the gross requirement at the next level down the distribution chain.

Allocation

Pull system

The traditional DRP network, known as a **pull system**, is driven by the top or retail level ordering more stock. Allocations are made to the top level from available stock after being modified to obtain shipping economies. These modifications might include changing the shipping quantity to a truckload or a pallet load. The pull system has three notable problems. First, the pulls are often distorted (increased) at subsequent levels in the network.[11] Second, each ordering location ignores the replenishment requirements at other locations. Third, ordering locations also ignore the stock status at the supplying location.

Push system

The alternative system is the **push system**. In the push system, orders are received from upstream locations, but they are evaluated by the supplying location. The evaluation includes determining not only requirements at each requesting location but also total system requirements and stock availability at the supplying locations. Such a system is designed to combine information from both using and supplying locations. In theory, the combination yields an improved allocation of stock, because replenishment policies can be established based on both availability and system demand.

ACHIEVING WORLD-CLASS STANDARDS

Although MRP is complex, it improves scheduling and inventory management. World-class firms know this. They have found that MRP systems have a number of benefits. Among these benefits are (1) increased performance to schedules and improved customer service, (2) improved utilization of facilities and labour, (3) faster response to market changes, and (4) reduced inventory levels.

These benefits have allowed world-class organizations to build and achieve schedule performance. The result is improved customer service that wins orders and market share. World-class firms use MRP in a proactive way, not only to improve delivery to customers, but to gather materials from suppliers. Schedules are shared with suppliers to yield better coordination. The result is improved supplier relations that improve purchasing activities, from price and quality to delivery.

Utilization of facilities and labour yields higher productivity and return-on-investment, just as less inventory frees up capital and floor space for other uses. Inventory turnover in some world-class firms approaches 150 times per year. The improvement in utilization, supplier relations, and scheduling allows movement toward smaller lot sizes and shorter lead times. These improvements in turn allow better response to market.

Once the foregoing capabilities are demonstrated, world-class MRP users usually become innovative users of MRP II by scheduling resources such as product development and testing.

SUMMARY

Material requirements planning (MRP) is the preferred way to schedule production and inventory when demand is dependent. For MRP to work, management must have a master schedule, precise requirements for all components, accurate inventory and

[11]This is the same type of response recognized in Jay Forrester's *Industrial Dynamics*. Forrester noted that small changes in demand at the retail level stimulated wider variations at the wholesale level and even greater deviations at the factory level. J. Forrester, *Industrial Dynamics* (Cambridge, MA: MIT Press, 1964).

purchasing records, and accurate lead times. Distribution resource planning (DRP) is a time-phased stock replacement technique for distribution networks based on MRP procedures and logic.

Production should often be lot-for-lot in an MRP system, and replenishment orders in a DRP system should be small and frequent, given the constraints of ordering and transportation costs.

Both MRP and DRP, when properly implemented, can contribute in a major way to reduction in inventory while improving customer service levels. These techniques allow the operations manager to schedule and replenish stock on a "need-to-order" basis rather than simply a "time-to-order" basis.

KEY TERMS

Material requirements planning (MRP) (p. 640)
Master production schedule (p. 641)
Engineering change notice (ECN) (p. 642)
Bill of material (BOM) (p. 643)
Modular bills (p. 644)
Planning bills (p. 644)
Pseudo bills (p. 644)
Kit number (p. 644)
Phantom bills of material (p. 644)
Low-level coding (p. 645)
Lead time (p. 645)
Gross material requirements plan (p. 646)
System nervousness (p. 652)
Time fences (p. 652)
Pegging (p. 652)
Lot-sizing decisions (p. 652)
Lot-for-lot (p. 652)
Part period balancing (PPB) (p. 655)
Economic part period (EPP) (p. 655)
Wagner-Whitin procedure (p. 656)
Closed-loop MRP system (p. 657)
Load reports (p. 658)
Material requirements planning II (MRP II) (p. 658)
Distribution resource planning (DRP) (p. 662)
Pull system (p. 662)
Push system (p. 663)

USING AB:POM TO SOLVE MRP AND LOT-SIZING PROBLEMS

Solving Examples 1, 2, and 3 with AB:POM

Programs 14.1 and 14.2 show the detailed input and output respectively for solving Examples 1 to 3 using AB:POM. Here are the inputs used in Program 14.1:

1. *Item names*. The item names are entered in the left column. The same item name will appear in more than one row if the item is used by two parent items. Each item must follow its parents, as shown in Program 14.1.
2. *Item level* (Lvl). The level in the indented BOM must be given here. The item *cannot* be placed at a level more than one below the item immediately above.
3. *Lead time* (ldtm). The lead time for an item is entered here. The default is 1 week.
4. *Number* (#per). The number of units of this subassembly needed for its parent is entered here. The default is one.
5. *On-hand* (nhnd). List current inventory on hand once, even if the subassembly is listed twice.
6. *Lot size* (Lot). The lot size can be specified here. A 0 or 1 will perform lot-for-lot ordering. If another number is placed here, then all orders for that item will be in integer multiples of that number.
7. *Demands* (entered in the first row). The demands are entered in the end item row in the period in which the items are demanded.
8. *Scheduled receipts*. If units are scheduled to be received in the future, they should be listed in the appropriate time period (column) and item (row). (An entry here in level one is a demand; all other levels are receipts.)

PROGRAM 14.1 ■ AB:POM's MRP Module Applied to Examples 1, 2, and 3. AB:POM's material requirements planning (MRP) module can be used to perform an MRP analysis for up to 18 periods. The data screen shown is generated by indicating the number of lines in the bill of materials. In our sample problem, we created a BOM with 7 items, but 9 lines.

Data File:HREX3 ——— Material Requirements Planning ——— Data Screen —

Number of BOM lines (1–90) 9 Number of demand periods (1–18) 8

Item	Level	Lead time	#per	On-hand inv	Lot size	pd1	pd2	pd3	pd4	pd5	pd6	pd7	pd8
A	0	1	0	10	0	0	0	0	0	0	0	0	50
B	1	2	2	15	0	0	0	0	0	0	0	0	0
D	2	1	2	10	0	0	0	0	0	0	0	0	0
E	2	2	2	0	0	0	0	0	0	0	0	0	0
C	1	1	3	20	0	0	0	0	0	0	0	0	0
E	2	2	2	10	0	0	0	0	0	0	0	0	0
F	2	3	2	5	0	0	0	0	0	0	0	0	0
G	3	2	1	0	0	0	0	0	0	0	0	0	0
D	3	1	2	0	0	0	0	0	0	0	0	0	0

PROGRAM 14.2 ■ Printed Solution to MRP Run on Examples 1, 2, and 3 Data. The printed solution for items A, B, and D in Examples 1, 2, and 3 is shown in this output of Program 14.1. The meaning of each item on the left-hand column of the printed output is explained in items 1 through 5 below.

1. *Total required*. The total number of units required in each week is listed in the first row. For the end item, the first row contains the demand schedule that was input on the data screen (Program 14.1). Other requirements are computed.
2. *On-hand*. The number on-hand is listed here. The on-hand amount starts as given on the data screen and is reduced according to needs.
3. *Order receipt*. The amount that was scheduled in the original data screen is shown here.
4. *Net required*. The net amount required is the amount needed after the on-hand inventory is used.
5. *Order release*. Order release is the net amount required, offset by the lead time.

Item A	Week 1	Week 2	Week 3	Week 4	Week 5	Week 6	Week 7	Week 8
TOT. REQ.	0	0	0	0	0	0	0	50
ON HAND	10	10	10	10	10	10	10	10
ORD REC.	0	0	0	0	0	0	0	0
NET REQ.	0	0	0	0	0	0	0	40
ORD REL.	0	0	0	0	0	0	40	0

Item B	Week 1	Week 2	Week 3	Week 4	Week 5	Week 6	Week 7	Week 8
TOT. REQ.	0	0	0	0	0	0	80	0
ON HAND	15	15	15	15	15	15	15	0
ORD REC.	0	0	0	0	0	0	0	0
NET REQ.	0	0	0	0	0	0	65	0
ORD REL.	0	0	0	0	65	0	0	0

Item D	Week 1	Week 2	Week 3	Week 4	Week 5	Week 6	Week 7	Week 8
TOT. REQ.	0	0	390	0	130	0	0	0
ON HAND	10	10	10	0	0	0	0	0
ORD REC.	0	0	0	0	0	0	0	0
NET REQ.	0	0	380	0	130	0	0	0
ORD REL.	0	380	0	130	0	0	0	0

Solving Example 5 with AB:POM Lot-Sizing Module

Program 14.3 illustrates the use of AB:POM in solving lot-sizing problems.

PROGRAM 14.3 ■ Solving Example 5 with the AB:POM Lot-Sizing Module. The data screen for lot sizing is initialized by indicating the number of periods over which the lot sizing is to be performed. In this example we use 10 periods.

The lot-sizing module will perform lot sizing for minimizing total holding and setup costs when demands in each period are not equal. You may input your own ordering schedule, or use *economic order quantity (EOQ)*, *lot-for-lot*, *part period balancing*, or *Wagner-Whitin*. Use the toggle menu to select the desired option.

Data file:hrex5 —— Sizing, Lot —— Solution ——
Number of time periods (1–98) 10

METHOD -> Economic Order Quantity   Total cost = $775.00

Holding cost	1.00	EOQ = 73
Setup cost	100.00	
Initial inventory	35.00	
Lead time	1	

Period	Demand	Release	Receipt	Inventory	Holding $	Setup $
Period 1	35	73	0	0	0.00	
Period 2	30	0	73	43	43.00	100.00
Period 3	40	0	0	3	3.00	
Period 4	0	73	0	3	3.00	
Period 5	10	0	73	66	66.00	100.00
Period 6	40	73	0	26	26.00	
Period 7	30	0	73	69	69.00	100.00
Period 8	0	0	0	69	69.00	
Period 9	30	73	0	39	39.00	
Period 10	55	0	73	57	57.00	100.00
	------	------	------	------	------	------
Totals	270	292	292	375	$375.00	$400.00

SOLVED PROBLEMS

Solved Problem 14.1

Determine the low-level coding and the quantity of each component necessary to produce 10 units of an assembly we will call Alpha. The product structure and quantities of each component needed for each assembly are noted in parentheses.

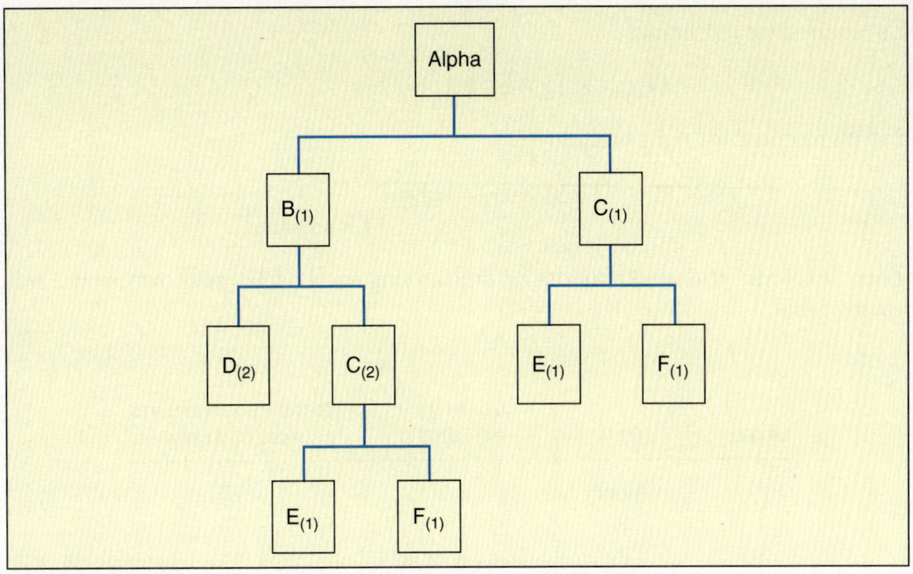

Solution

Redraw the product structure with low-level coding. Then multiply down the structure until the requirements of each branch are determined. Then add across the structure until the total for each is determined.

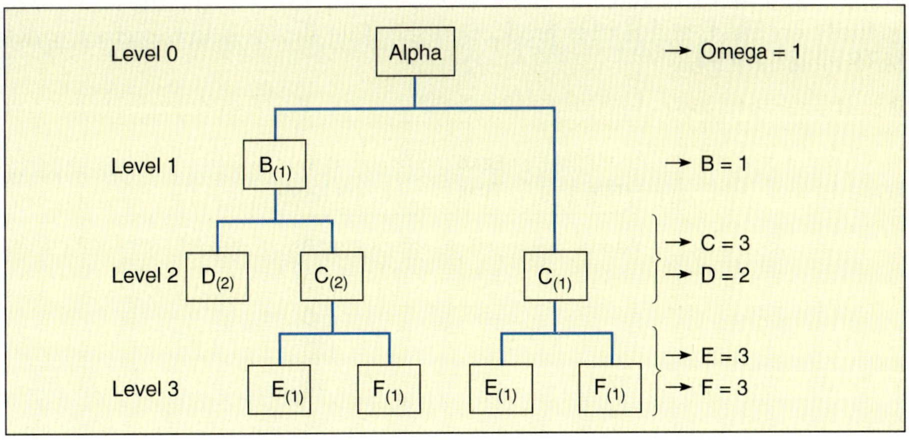

E's required for left branch:

$$(1_{\text{alpha}} \times 1_B \times 2_C \times 1_E) = 2$$

and E's required for right branch:

$$(1_{\text{alpha}} \times 1_C \times 1_E) = \underline{1}$$

3 E's required

Then "explode" the requirements by multiplying each by 10, as shown in the following table.

LEVEL	ITEM	QUANTITY PER UNIT	TOTAL REQUIREMENTS FOR 10 ALPHA
0	Alpha	1	10
1	B	1	10
2	C	3	30
2	D	2	20
3	E	3	30
3	F	3	30

Solved Problem 14.2

Using the product structure for Alpha in Solved Problem 14.1, and the lead times, quantity on hand, and master production schedule shown below, prepare a net MRP table for Alphas.

ITEM	LEAD TIME	QTY. ON HAND
Alpha	1	10
B	2	20
C	3	0
D	1	100
E	1	10
F	1	50

MASTER PRODUCTION SCHEDULE FOR ALPHA

PERIOD	6	7	8	9	10	11	12	13
Gross requirements			50			50		100

Solution

See the chart on the next page.

Net Material Requirements Planning Sheet for Alpha. *Note:* The letter in parentheses (A) is the source of the demand.

Lot Size	Lead Time (# of Periods)	On Hand	Safety Stock	Allo-cated	Low Level Code	Item ID			Period (week,day) 1	2	3	4	5	6	7	8	9	10	11	12	13
Lot-for-Lot	1	10	—	—	0	Alpha (A)	Gross Requirements									50			50		100
							Scheduled Receipts														
							Projected on Hand	10								10			—		—
							Net Requirements									40			50		100
							Planned Order Receipts														
							Planned Order Releases								40			50		100	
Lot-for-Lot	2	20	—	—	1	B	Gross Requirements								40(A)			50(A)		100(A)	
							Scheduled Receipts														
							Projected on Hand	20							20			—		—	
							Net Requirements								20			50		100	
							Planned Order Receipts								20			50		100	
							Planned Order Releases						20			50		100			
Lot-for-Lot	3	0	—	—	2	C	Gross Requirements						40(B)		40(A)	100(B)		200(B) + 50(A)		100(A)	
							Scheduled Receipts														
							Projected on Hand	0					—			—		—		—	
							Net Requirements						40		40	100		250		100	
							Planned Order Receipts						40		40	100		250		100	
							Planned Order Releases			40		40	100		250		100				
Lot-for-Lot	1	100	—	—	2	D	Gross Requirements						40(B)			100(B)		200(B)			
							Scheduled Receipts														
							Projected on Hand	100					100			60		—			
							Net Requirements						0			40		200			
							Planned Order Receipts						0			40		200			
							Planned Order Releases					0			40		200				
Lot-for-Lot	1	10	—	—	3	E	Gross Requirements			40(C)		40(C)	100(C)		250(C)		100(C)				
							Scheduled Receipts														
							Projected on Hand	10		10		—	—		—		—				
							Net Requirements			30		40	100		250		100				
							Planned Order Receipts			30		40	100		250		100				
							Planned Order Releases		30		40	100		250		100					
Lot-for-Lot	1	50	—	—	3	F	Gross Requirements			40(C)		40(C)	100(C)		250(C)		100(C)				
							Scheduled Receipts														
							Projected on Hand	50		50		10	—		—		—				
							Net Requirements			0		30	100		250		100				
							Planned Order Receipts					30	100		250		100				
							Planned Order Releases		—		30	100		250		100					

DISCUSSION QUESTIONS

1. What is the difference between a *gross* requirements plan and a *net* requirements plan?
2. Once a material requirements plan (MRP) has been established, what other managerial applications might be found for the technique?
3. What are the similarities between MRP and DRP?
4. How does MRP II differ from MRP?
5. Which is the best lot-sizing policy for manufacturing organizations?
6. What impact does ignoring carrying cost in the allocation of stock in a DRP system have on lot sizes?
7. What do we mean by *closed-loop* MRP?
8. What are the options for the production planner that has (a) scheduled more than capacity in a work centre next week and (b) a consistent lack of capacity in that work centre?
9. What types of resources might be scheduled via an MRP II?
10. What functions of the firm impact an MRP system? How?
11. What is the rationale for (a) a phantom bill of material, (b) a planning bill of material, and (c) a pseudo bill of material?
12. Identify five specific requirements of an effective MRP system.
13. What are some of the benefits of MRP?

CRITICAL THINKING EXERCISE

The very structure of MRP systems suggests fixed lead times. However, many firms are moving toward JIT and Kanban techniques. What are the issues and the impact of adding JIT inventory and purchasing techniques and Kanban to an organization that has MRP?

PROBLEMS

• **14.1** The product structure for a product we make, called Alpha, is shown below. We need 10 units of Alpha in week 6. Three units of D and two units of F are required for each Alpha. The lead time for Alpha is 1 week. We have no units of Alpha, D, or F on hand. Lead time for D is 1 week and lead time for F is 2 weeks. Using the format below, prepare a gross and net material requirements plan for Alpha. (*Hint:* For this and other problems in this chapter, a copy of the form on the page may be helpful.)

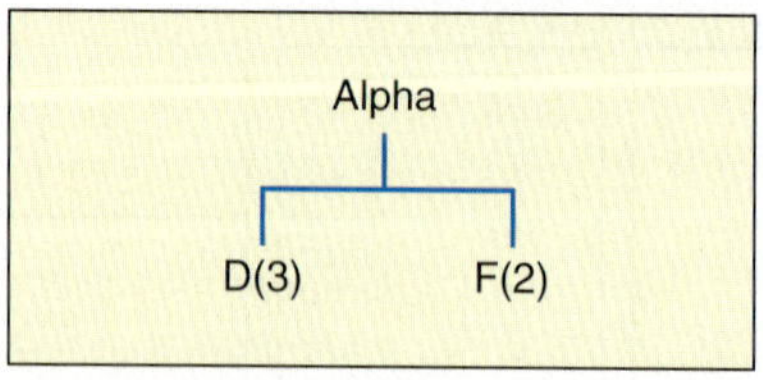

: **14.2** The demand for subassembly S is 100 units in week 7. Each unit of S requires one unit of T and .5 unit of U. Each unit of T requires one unit of V, two units of W, and one unit of X. Finally, each unit of U requires .5 units of Y and three units of Z. One firm manufactures all items. It takes 2 weeks to make S, 1 week to make T, 2 weeks to make U, 2 weeks to make V, 3 weeks to make W, 1 week to make X, 2 weeks to make Y, and 1 week to make Z.

Lot Size	Lead Time (# of periods)	On Hand	Safety Stock	Allo-cated	Low Level Code	Item ID		Period (week,day)							
								1	2	3	4	5	6	7	8
							Gross Requirements								
							Scheduled Receipts								
							Projected on Hand								
							Net Requirements								
							Planned Order Receipts								
							Planned Order Releases								
							Gross Requirements								
							Scheduled Receipts								
							Projected on Hand								
							Net Requirements								
							Planned Order Receipts								
							Planned Order Releases								
							Gross Requirements								
							Scheduled Receipts								
							Projected on Hand								
							Net Requirements								
							Planned Order Receipts								
							Planned Order Releases								
							Gross Requirements								
							Scheduled Receipts								
							Projected on Hand								
							Net Requirements								
							Planned Order Receipts								
							Planned Order Releases								
							Gross Requirements								
							Scheduled Receipts								
							Projected on Hand								
							Net Requirements								
							Planned Order Receipts								
							Planned Order Releases								

a) Construct a product structure and a gross material requirements plan for the dependent inventory items. Identify all levels, parents, and components.

b) Construct a net material requirements plan from the product structure and the following on-hand inventory.

ITEM	ON-HAND INVENTORY	ITEM	ON-HAND INVENTORY
S	20	W	30
T	20	X	25
U	10	Y	15
V	30	Z	10

: 14.3 In addition to 100 units of S (per Problem 14.2), there is also a demand for 20 units of U, which is a component of S. The 20 units of U are needed for maintenance purposes. These units are needed 1 week before S, in week 6. Modify the gross and net material requirements plan to reflect this change.

14.4 Given the following bill of material, master production schedule, and inventory status, develop: (a) a gross requirements plan for all items and (b) net materials requirements (planned order release) for all items.

MASTER PRODUCTION SCHEDULE: X1

PERIOD	7	8	9	10	11	12
Gross requirements		50		20		100

ITEM	LEAD TIME	ON HAND	ITEM	LEAD TIME	ON HAND
X1	1	50	C	3	10
B1	2	20	D	1	0
B2	2	20	E	1	0
A1	1	5			

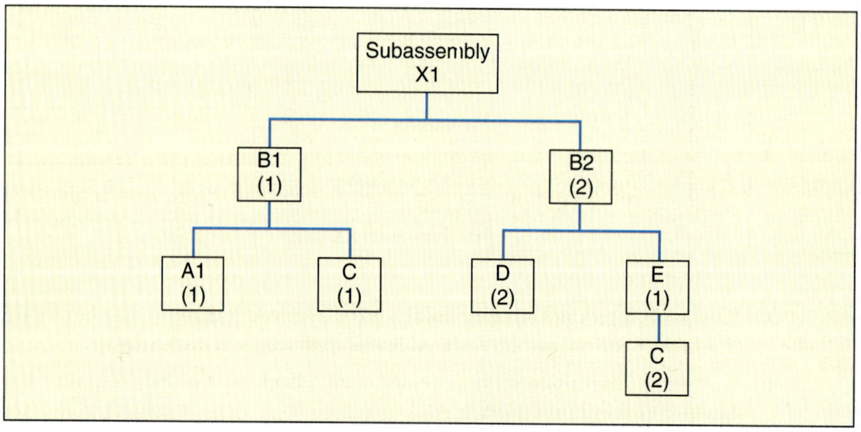

Problems 14.5 and 14.6 use the data shown below and at the top of the next page.

DATA FOR PROBLEMS 14.5 AND 14.6

PERIOD	8	9	10	11	12
Gross requirements: A	100		50		150
Gross requirements: H		100		50	

DATA FOR PROBLEMS 14.5 AND 14.6 (CONT'D)

ITEM	ON HAND	LEAD TIME	ITEM	ON HAND	LEAD TIME
A	0	1	F	75	2
B	100	2	G	75	1
C	50	2	H	0	1
D	50	1	J	100	2
E	75	2	K	100	2

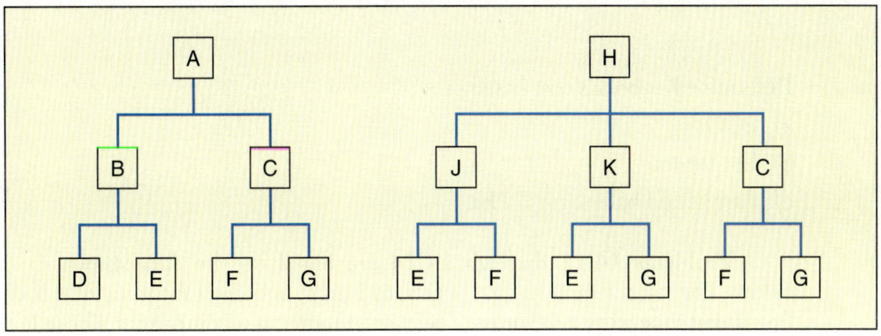

14.5 Given the bill of material, master production schedule, and inventory status shown above, develop (a) a gross requirements plan for C and (b) a planned order release for C.

14.6 On the basis of the preceding data, complete a net planned order release schedule for all items (10 schedules in all).

Problems 14.7 through 14.9 are based on an item that has the gross requirements shown in the following table and a beginning inventory of 40 units.

DATA FOR PROBLEMS 14.7–14.9

PERIOD	1	2	3	4	5	6	7	8	9	10	11	12
Gross requirements	30		40		30	70	20		10	80		50

Holding cost = $2.50/unit/week; setup cost = $150; lead time = 1 week.

14.7 Develop a lot-for-lot solution and calculate total relevant costs.

14.8 **a)** Develop an EOQ solution and calculate total relevant costs. Stockout costs equal $10 per unit.

b) Solve part (a) with lead time = 0.

14.9 a) Develop a PPB solution and calculate total relevant costs.

b) Solve part (a) with lead time = 0.

14.10 Keebock, a maker of outstanding running shoes, keeps the soles of its size 13 running shoes in inventory for one period at a cost of $.25 per unit. The setup costs are $50. Beginning inventory is zero and lead time is 1 week; stockout cost is $5 per unit. Shown in the following table are the net requirements per period.

DATA FOR PROBLEM 14.10

PERIOD	0	1	2	3	4	5	6	7	8	9	10
Net requirements		35	30	45	0	10	40	30	0	30	55

Determine Keebock's cost based on:

a) EOQ.

b) Lot-for-lot.

c) Part period balancing (PPB).

Problems 14.11 through 14.14 are based on the data shown in the table below. The parent item has a 1-week lead time, and the lot-for-lot rule is employed. Beginning inventory is 20 units. The parent item has a component whose lead time is also 1 week and whose starting inventory position is 30 units. At the component level, production occurs in lot sizes to cover three periods of net requirements.

DATA FOR PROBLEMS 14.11–14.14

PERIOD	1	2	3	4	5	6	7	8	9	10
Gross requirements	0	40	30	40	10	70	40	10	30	60

14.11 Develop the parent and component MRP tables to show the original planned positions.

14.12 At the parent level, gross requirements for period 2 are cancelled. Develop the parent and component net MRP tables to show the net effect of this cancellation.

14.13 With the parent level gross requirements cancelled for period 2, what is the effect on inventory quantity, setup costs, and holding costs?

14.14 At the component level, there is enough capacity to produce 75 units in period 1. Gross requirements at the parent level increase from 40 to 50 units in period 2. What problem arises? What solution would you recommend?

14.15 A part structure, lead time (weeks), and on-hand quantities for product A are shown on the next page.

From the information shown, generate:

a) An indented bill of material for product A (see Figure 6.9).

b) A bill of material showing the quantity of each part required to produce one A.

c) An exploded bill of material showing the quantity of each part required to produce ten A's.

DATA FOR PROBLEMS 14.15, 14.16, 14.17, AND THE DATA BASE APPLICATION 14.19

PART	INVENTORY ON HAND
A	0
B	2
C	10
D	5
E	4
F	5
G	1
H	10

PART STRUCTURE TREE

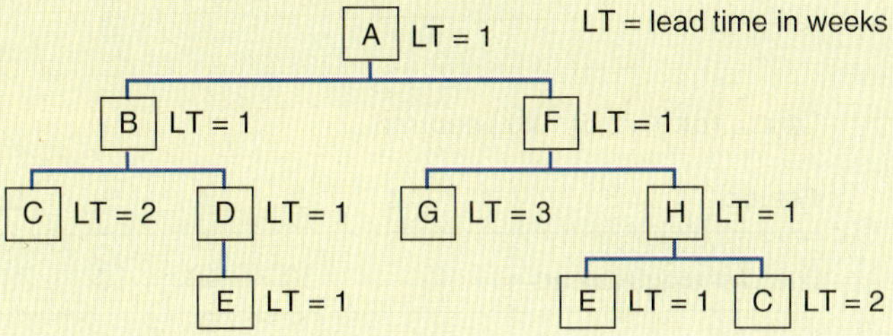

d) Net requirements for each part to produce ten A's in week 8 using lot-for-lot.

(*Hint:* The AB:POM can help with parts (b) and (c), but not produce an output other than in MRP format.)

:14.16 You are product planner for product A (in Problem 14.15). The field service manager, Al Trostel, has just called and told you that the requirements for B and F should each be increased by 10 units for his repair requirements in the field.

a) Prepare an exploded bill of material showing the quantity of each part required to produce the requirements for the service manager *and* the production request of 10.

b) What are the net requirements (i.e., exploded bill of materials less on-hand inventory)?

c) Prepare a net requirement plan by date for the new requirements (for both production and field service), assuming that the field service manager wants his 10 units in week 6 and the 10 production units are still due in week 8.

:14.17 You have just been notified by fax that the lead time for component G of product A (Problem 14.16) has just been increased to 4 weeks.

a) Which items have changed and why?

b) What are the implications for the production plan?

c) As production planner, what can you do?

:14.18 As director of operations, you have recently installed a distribution requirements planning (DRP) system. The company has an East Coast and a West Coast warehouse, as well as a main factory warehouse in Mississauga, Ontario. You have just received the orders for the next planning period from the managers at each of the three facilities. Their reports are shown below. The lead time to both the East Coast and the West Coast warehouse is 2 weeks, and there is a 1-week lead time to bring material to the factory warehouse. Shipments are in truckload quantities of 100 each. There is no initial inventory in the system. The factory is having trouble installing the level of material work schedule and still has a lot size in multiples of 100.

DATA FOR EAST COAST WAREHOUSE

PERIOD	1	2	3	4	5	6	7	8	9	10	11	12
Forecast requirements			40	100	80	70	20	25	70	80	30	50

Lead time = 2 weeks

DATA FOR WEST COAST WAREHOUSE

PERIOD	1	2	3	4	5	6	7	8	9	10
Forecast requirements		30	45	60	70	40	80	70	80	55

Lead time = 2 weeks

DATA FOR FACTORY WAREHOUSE

PERIOD	1	2	3	4	5	6	7	8	9	10
Forecast requirements			30	40	10	70	40	10	30	60

Lead time = 1 week

a) Show the plan for *receipt* of orders from the factory.

b) If the factory requires 2 weeks to produce the merchandise, when must the orders be *released* to the factory?

DATA BASE APPLICATION

:14.19 Your stockroom manager, Yamil Bermudez, arrived at your desk just after you had completed the net requirements plan for product A (use data in Problem 14.15), exclaiming that the cycle counter should be fired. It seems that the cycle counter was wrong; there are three A's available now, not zero as the original data showed; moreover, five E's are also available. About then, your boss, Sam Melnyk, who overheard the discussion, says, "You might as well extend the net requirements plan out to 16 weeks, because we just received an order for 10 more A's in week 12 and five more in week 15. Additionally, count on the field service department wanting three more B's in week 16, as well as those 10 units in week 8." You decide to use the lead times in Problem 14.15, but item G now has a lead time of 4 weeks.

Now you must prepare a new net requirements plan, based on the actual inventory (as reported) and the new schedule. Your assignment is to do so.

CASE STUDY

Service, Inc.

Service, Inc., is a distributor of automotive replacement parts. With no manufacturing capability, all products it sells are purchased, assembled, and repackaged. Service, Inc., does have extensive inventory and final assembly facilities. Among its products are private-label carburetor and ignition kits. The company has been experiencing difficulties for the last 2 years. First, profits have fallen considerably. Second, customer service levels have declined, with late deliveries now exceeding 25% of orders. Third, customer returns have been rising at a rate of 3% per month.

Bob Hass, vice-president of sales, claims that most of the problem lies with the assembly department. He says that they are not producing the proper mix of the product, they have poor quality control, their productivity has fallen, and their costs are too high.

Dick Houser, the treasurer, believes that problems have arisen due to investment in the wrong inventories. He thinks that marketing has too many options and products. Dick also thinks that the purchasing department buyers have been hedging their

(Continued)

inventories and requirements with excess purchasing commitments.

John Burnham, assembly manager, says, "The symptom is that we have a lot of parts in inventory, but no place to assemble them in the production schedule." An additional comment by John was, "When we have the right part, it is not very good, but we use it anyway to meet the schedule."

Freddy Fearon, manager of purchasing, has taken the stance that purchasing has not let Service, Inc., down. He has stuck by his old suppliers, used historical data to determine requirements, maintained what he views as excellent prices from suppliers, and evaluated new sources of supply with an aim of lowering cost. Where possible, Freddy reacted to the increased pressure for profitability by emphasizing low cost and early delivery.

You are the president of Service, Inc., and must get the firm back on a course toward improved profitability.

DISCUSSION QUESTIONS

1. Identify both the symptoms and the problems at Service, Inc.
2. What specific changes would you implement?

BIBLIOGRAPHY

Akinc, U. "A Practical Approach to Lot and Setup Scheduling at a Textile Firm." *Industrial Engineering Research & Development*, 25, no. 2 (March 1993): 54–64.

Bookbinder, J. H., and L. A. Koch. "Production Planning for Mixed Assembly/Arborescent Systems." *Journal of Operations Management*, 9, no. 1 (1990): 7–23.

Brown, R. G. *Advanced Service Parts Inventory Control*. Norwich, VT: Materials Management Systems, 1982.

Brucker, H. D., G. A. Flowers, and R. D. Peck. "MRP Shop-Floor Control in a Job Shop: Definitely Works." *Production and Inventory Management Journal*, 33, no. 2 (Second Quarter 1992): 43.

Campbell, G. M. "Master Production Scheduling Under Rolling Planning Horizons with Fixed Order Intervals." *Decision Sciences*, 23, no. 2 (March/April 1992): 312.

Davis, S. G. "Scheduling Economic Lot Size Production Runs." *Management Science*, 36, no. 8 (August 1990): 985–998.

Deleersnyder, J., T. J. Hodgson, R. E. King, P. J. O'Grady, and A. Savva. "Integrating Kanban Type Pull Systems and MRP Type Push Systems: Insights from a Markovian Model." *Industrial Engineering Research & Development*, 24, no. 3 (July 1992): 43.

Ding, F., and M. Yuen. "A Modified MRP for a Production System with the Coexistence of MRP and Kanbans." *Journal of Operations Management*, 10, no. 2 (April 1991): 267–277.

Dolinsky, L. R., T. E. Vollmann, and M. J. Maggard. "Adjusting Replenishment Orders to Reflect Learning in a Material Requirements Planning Environment." *Management Science*, 36 (December 1990): 1,532–1,547.

El-Najdawi, M. K., and P. R. Kleindorfer. "Common Cycle Lot-Size Scheduling for Multi-Product, Multi-Stage Production." *Management Science*, 39, no. 7 (July 1993): 872–885.

Freeland, J. R., J. P. Leschke, and E. N. Weiss. "Guidelines for Setup Cost Reduction Programs to Achieve Zero Inventory." *Journal of Operations Management*, 9 (January 1990): 85.

Gardiner, S. C., and J. H. Blackstone, Jr. "The Effects of Lot Sizing and Dispatching on Customer Service in an MRP Environment." *Journal of Operations Management*, 11, no. 2 (June 1993): 143–160.

Haddock, J., and D. E. Hubicki. "Which Lot-Sizing Techniques Are Used in Material Requirements Planning?" *Production and Inventory Management*, 30 (Third Quarter 1989): 57.

Hopp, W. J., M. L. Spearman, and I. Duenyas. "Economic Production Quotas for Pull Manufacturing Systems." *Industrial Engineering Research & Development*, 25, no. 2 (March 1993): 71–79.

Jacobs, F. R., and D. C. Whybark. "A Comparison of Reorder Point and Material Requirements Planning Inventory Control Logic." *Decision Sciences*, 23, no. 2 (March/April 1992): 332.

Ledbetter, M. E., C. A. Snyder, and S. C. Gardiner. "Work-in-Process Inventory Control for Repetitive Manufacturing in an MRP Environment: A Case Study." *Production and Inventory Management Journal*, 34, no. 2 (Second Quarter 1993): 48–52.

Martin, A. J. *DRP: Distribution Resource Planning*. Englewood Cliffs, NJ: Prentice Hall, 1983.

Meckler, V. A. "Setup Cost Reduction in the Dynamic Lot-Size Model." *Journal of Operations Management*, 11, no. 1 (March 1993): 35–44.

St. Johns, R. "The Evils of Lot Sizing in MRP." *Production and Inventory Management*, 25 (Fourth Quarter 1984): 75–85.

Sridharan, V., and R. Lawrence LaForge. "Freezing the Master Production Schedule: Implications for Customer Service." *Decision Sciences*, 25, no. 3 (May/June 1994): 461–469.

Sum, C., D. O. Png, and K. Yang. "Effects of Product Structure Complexity on Multi-level Lot Sizing." *Decision Sciences*, 24, no. 6 (November/December 1993): 1,135–1,156.

Wagner, H. M., and T. M. Whitin. "Dynamic Version of the Economic Lot Size Model." *Management Science*, 5, no. 1 (1958): 89–96.

Zhao, X., and T. S. Lee. "Freezing the Master Production Schedule for Material Requirements Planning Systems under Demand Uncertainty." *Journal of Operations Management*, 11, no. 2 (June 1993): 185–206.

WEB SITES OF INTEREST

1. pc/MRP: The Complete Business Software Program for MRP, Accounting, and Inventory Control: Modules include: Bills of Materials, General Ledger, Accounts Payable, Accounts Receivable, Purchasing, Inventory, Receiving, Sales, Invoicing, Stock Room, Address Book. Compatible with Excel, AutoCAD, Lotus, Access, dBase, FoxPro. Reviewed in *APICS Magazine* (June 1996).

http://www.pcmrp.com

2. ObviousMRP™ for Windows: A very interesting GUI-based software package.

http://www.obviousmrp.com

3. Caliach MRP: A computer modelling technique for analyzing and controlling complicated manufacturing operations.

http://www.caliach.com/whatMRP.html

4. APICS CPIM Study Materials: Details can be found at:

http://www.caliach.com/whatMRP.html

15

AGGREGATE PLANNING

CHAPTER OUTLINE

LEARNING OBJECTIVES

When you complete this chapter you should be able to:

Identify or define:
- Aggregate planning
- Tactical scheduling
- Graphical technique for aggregate planning
- Mathematical techniques for planning

Explain:
- How to do aggregate planning

WORLD-CLASS PROFILE: ANHEUSER-BUSCH

AGGREGATE PLANNING PROVIDES A COMPETITIVE ADVANTAGE AT ANHEUSER-BUSCH

In the starting cellar control room, process control uses computers to monitor the starting cellar process, where wort is in its final stage of preparation before being fermented into beer.

Anheuser-Busch is a major beer producer, producing close to 40% of the beer consumed in the United States. The company achieves efficiency at such volume by doing an excellent job of matching capacity to demand.

Matching capacity and demand in the intermediate term (3–18 months) is the heart of aggregate planning. Anheuser-Busch matches fluctuating demand by brand to specific plant, labour, and inventory capacity. Meticulous cleaning between batches, effective maintenance, and efficient employee and facility scheduling contribute to high facility utilization, a major factor in all high capital investment facilities.

Beer is produced in a product-focused facility, one that produces high volume and low variety. Product-focussed production processes usually require high fixed cost, but typically have the benefit of low variable costs. Maintaining high use of such facilities is critical because high capital costs require high use to be competitive. Performance above the break-even point requires high use—and downtime is disastrous.

Beer production can be divided into four stages. The first stage is the selection and assurance of raw material delivery and quality. The second stage is the actual

Shown are brew kettles where wort, later to become beer, is boiled and hops are added for the flavour and bitter character they impart.

Automated guided vehicles are used to transfer full kegs to storage prior to shipping.

brewing process from milling to aging. The third stage is packaging into the wide variety of containers desired by the market.

The fourth and final stage is distribution, which includes temperature-controlled delivery and storage. Each stage has its resource limitations. Developing the aggregate plan to make it all work is demanding.

Effective aggregate scheduling is a major ingredient in competitive advantage at Anheuser-Busch.

The canning line imprints on each can: a code that identifies the day, year, and 15-minute period of production; the plant at which the product was brewed and packaged; and the production line used. This allows any quality control problems to be tracked and corrected.

Unlike most other appliances, room air conditioners are heavily dependent on weather for sales. That makes decisions on aggregate planning schedules a tough call for manufacturers like Whirlpool, which produces air conditioners for Sears. If Whirlpool increases output and the summer is warmer than usual, it stands to increase sales and market share. But if the summer is cool, it may be stuck with expensive unsold machines. "You have to plan for the average year," says Whirlpool's director of merchandising. "If not, you are likely to go broke carrying over excessive inventory."[1] ♦

Aggregate planning

Planning for seasonal demands of air conditioners at Whirlpool is one aspect of aggregate planning. **Aggregate planning** is concerned with determining the quantity and scheduling of production for the intermediate future, usually from 3 to 18 months ahead. Operations managers try to determine the best way to meet forecasted demand by adjusting production rates, labour levels, inventory levels, overtime work, subcontracting rates, and other controllable variables. *The objective of the process usually is to minimize costs over the planning period.* Other objectives may be to minimize fluctuations in the work force or inventory levels, or to obtain a certain standard of service performance.

Four things are needed for aggregate planning. First, the firm needs a logical overall unit for measuring sales and output, such as air conditioning units in the case of Whirlpool or cases of beer at Anheuser-Busch. Second, managers must be able to forecast for a reasonable intermediate planning period in these aggregate terms. Third, they must be able to determine the relevant costs we discuss in this chapter. And fourth, operations managers need to develop a model that combines these forecasts and costs so that good scheduling decisions can be made for the planning period.

In this chapter, we describe the nature of the aggregate planning decisions in both manufacturing and service sector firms. To this end, we will show how the aggregate plan fits into the overall planning process, as well as describe several techniques that managers use in developing a plan.

THE PLANNING PROCESS

In Chapter 5, we saw that demand forecasting can address short-, medium-, and long-range plans. Long-range forecasts help managers deal with capacity and strategic issues and are the responsibility of top management (see Figure 15.1). Management formulates policy-related questions, such as facility location and expansion, new product development, research funding, and investment over a period of several years.

Tactical scheduling decisions

Once long-term capacity decisions are made, operations managers begin medium-range planning that meets the objectives of the firm. **Tactical scheduling decisions** include making monthly or quarterly plans, which address the problem of matching productivity to fluctuating demands. All of these plans need to be consistent with top management's long-range strategy and work within the resources allocated by earlier strategic decisions. The heart of the medium- (or "intermediate-") range plan is the aggregate production plan.

[1]*New York Times* (February 23, 1989): D1, D4.

FIGURE 15.1 ■ Planning Tasks and Responsibilities

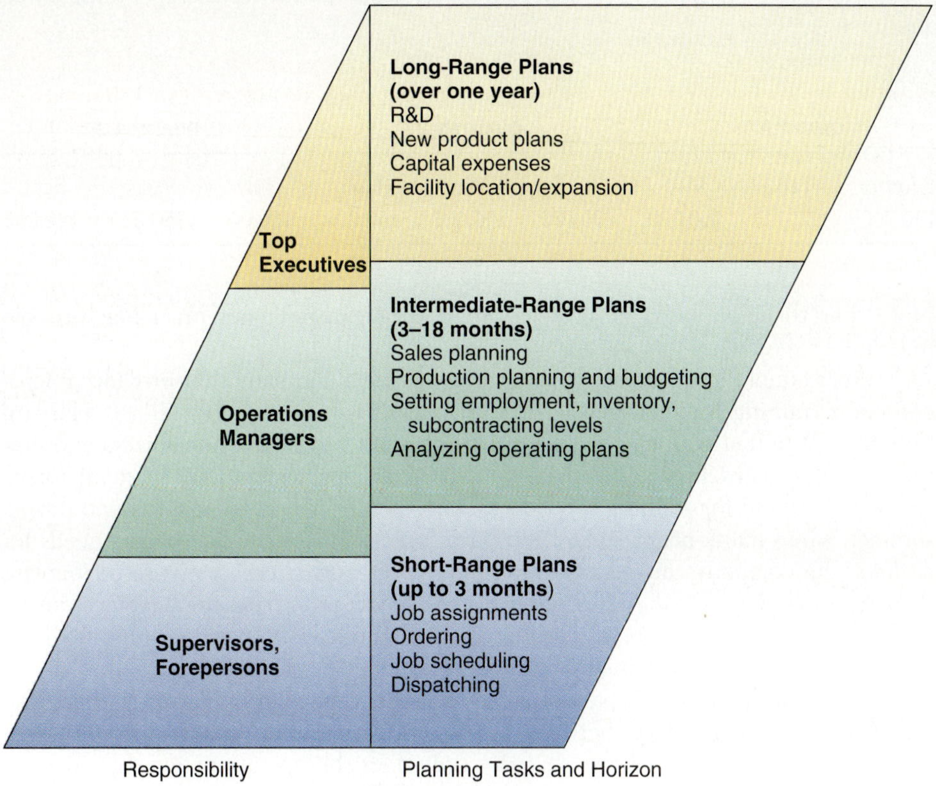

Short-range planning extends up to a year but is usually less than 3 months. Operations managers make these plans in conjunction with supervisors and forepersons, who "disaggregate" the intermediate plan into weekly, daily, and hourly schedules. Tactics for dealing with short-term planning involving loading, sequencing, expediting and dispatching, and other issues are discussed in Chapter 16.

Figure 15.1 illustrates the time horizons, features, and responsibilities for short-, intermediate-, and long-range planning.

THE NATURE OF AGGREGATE PLANNING

As the term *aggregate* implies, an aggregate plan means combining the appropriate resources into general, or overall, terms. Given the demand forecast, the facility capacity, overall inventory levels, the size of the work force, and related inputs, the operations manager has to select the rate of output for the facility over the next 3 to 18 months. The plan can be for manufacturing firms such as Whirlpool or Anheuser-Busch, for hospitals, for colleges, or for Prentice Hall, the company that published this textbook.

Take, for a manufacturing example, IBM or Compaq, each of which produces different models of microcomputers. They make: (1) laptops, (2) desktops, (3) notebook computers, and (4) advanced technology machines with high-speed chips. The aggregate plan for IBM or Compaq might have the following output (in units of production) for this "family" of microcomputers each month in the upcoming three quarters:

QUARTER 1			QUARTER 2			QUARTER 3		
Jan.	Feb.	Mar.	April	May	June	July	Aug.	Sept.
150,000	120,000	110,000	100,000	130,000	150,000	180,000	150,000	140,000

Note that the plan looks at production in the aggregate, not on a machine-by-machine breakdown.

An example from the service sector would be a company that provides microcomputer training for managers. The firm offers courses on Lotus, dBase, Harvard Graphics, WordPerfect, and a wide variety of other programs and subjects and employs several instructors to meet the demand from business and government for its services. Demand for training tends to be very low near holiday seasons and during summer, when many people take their vacations. To meet the fluctuating needs for courses, the company can perhaps hire and lay off instructors, advertise to increase demand in slow seasons, or subcontract its work to other training agencies during peak periods. Again, the operations planner will make decisions about intermediate-range capacity without getting into details of specific courses or instructors.

Aggregate planning is part of a larger production planning system; therefore, understanding the interfaces between the plan and several internal and external factors is useful. Figure 15.2 shows that not only does the operations manager receive input from the marketing department's demand forecast, but he or she has to deal with financial data, personnel, capacity, and availability of raw materials as well. In a manufacturing environment, the resulting master production schedule provides input to material requirements planning (MRP) systems, which address the procurement or production of parts or components needed to make the final product (see Chapter 14). Detailed work schedules for people and priority scheduling for products result as the final step of the production planning system (and are discussed in Chapter 16).

AGGREGATE PLANNING STRATEGIES

There are several questions the operations manager must answer when making an aggregate plan:

1. Should inventories be used to absorb changes in demand during the planning period?
2. Should changes in demand be accommodated by varying the size of the work force?
3. Should part-timers be used or should overtime and idle time absorb changing demand?
4. Should subcontractors be used during increased demand so that a stable work force can be maintained?
5. Should prices or other factors be changed to influence demand?

FIGURE 15.2 ■ Relationships of the Aggregate Plan

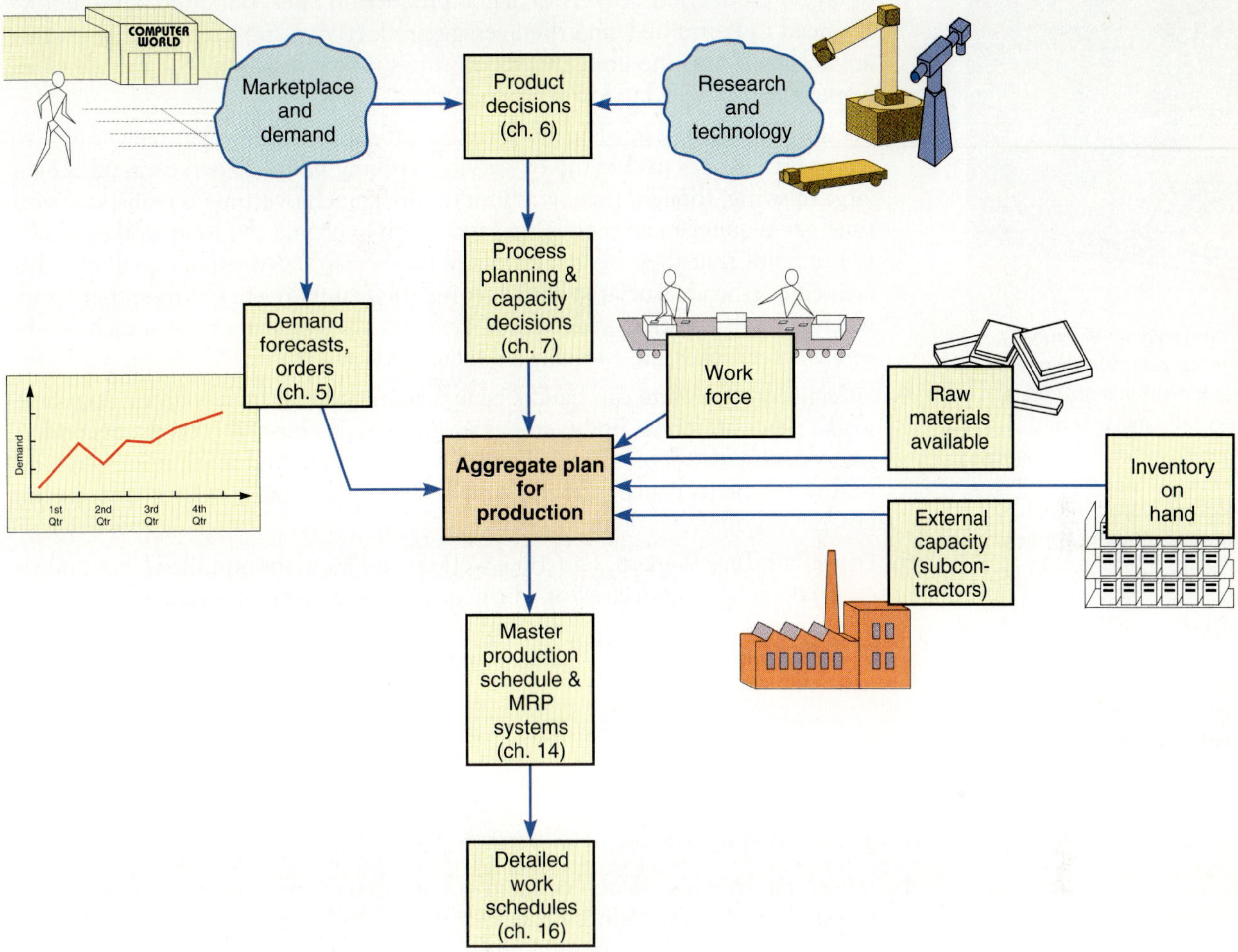

All of the foregoing are legitimate planning strategies available to management. They involve the manipulation of inventory, production rates, labour levels, capacity, and other controllable variables.

We will now examine eight options in more detail. The first five are called *capacity options* because they do not try to change demand but attempt to absorb the fluctuations in it. The last three are *demand options* through which firms try to influence the demand pattern to smooth out its changes over the planning period.

Capacity Options

The basic capacity (supply) options that a firm can choose are as follows:

1. *Changing Inventory Levels*. Managers can increase inventory during periods of low demand to meet high demand in future periods. Using this strategy increases costs associated with storage, insurance, handling, obsolescence, pilferage, and capital invested. (These costs typically range from 15 to 50% of the value of an item annually.) However, when the firm enters a period of increasing demand, shortages can result in lost sales due to potentially longer lead times and poorer customer service.

John Deere and Company, the "granddaddy" of farm equipment manufacturers, uses sales incentives to smooth demand. During the fall and winter off-seasons, sales are helped with price cuts and other incentives. About 70% of Deere's big machines are ordered in advance of seasonal use; this is about double the industry rate. The incentives hurt margins, but Deere keeps its market share and controls costs by producing more steadily all year long.

2. *Varying Work-Force Size by Hiring or Layoffs*. One way to meet demand is to hire or lay off production workers to match production rates. But often new employees need to be trained, and the average productivity drops temporarily as they are absorbed into the firm. Layoffs or firings, of course, lower the morale of all workers and can lead to lower productivity.
3. *Varying Production Rates Through Overtime or Idle Time*. Managers may be able to adjust for changes in demand by varying working hours. When demand is on a large upswing, though, there is a limit on how much overtime is realistic. Overtime pay requires more money, and too much overtime can wear workers down to the point that their overall productivity drops off. Overtime also implies increased overhead associated with keeping the facility open. On the other hand, when there is a period of decreased demand, the company must somehow absorb workers' idle time—usually a difficult process.
4. *Subcontracting*. A firm can handle peak demand periods by subcontracting some work. Subcontracting, however, has several pitfalls. First, it is costly. Second, it risks opening the door of your client to a competitor. And third, it is often hard to find the perfect subcontractor supplier, one who always delivers the quality product on time.
5. *Using Part-Time Workers*. Part-time workers can fill in for unskilled labour needs especially in the service sector. Hiring part-time workers is common practice at most supermarkets, retail stores, and restaurants like McDonald's and Wendy's. The *POM in Action* box "Teleworking" provides a new strategy in the use of part-time workers.

Demand Options

The basic demand options are as follows:

1. *Influencing Demand*. When demand is low, a company can try to increase demand through advertising, promotion, increased personal selling, and price cuts. For example, airlines and hotels have long offered weekend discounts and off-season rates; telephone companies charge less at night; and air conditioners are least expensive in winter. Special advertising, promotions, selling, and pricing are not always able, however, to balance the demand with the production capacity.
2. *Back Ordering During High Demand Periods*. Back orders are orders for goods or services that a firm accepts but is unable (either on purpose or by chance) to fill at the moment. Back ordering works only if customers are willing to wait without loss of their goodwill or cancelling their order. For instance, many auto dealers purposely back-order, but the approach is often unacceptable in the sale of many consumer goods.
3. *Counterseasonal Product Mixing*. Many manufacturing firms try to make several products that are sold in opposite seasons. Examples include companies that make both furnaces and air conditioners or lawn mowers and snowblowers. Service companies (and manufacturers also, for that matter) that follow this approach, however, may find themselves involved in services or products beyond their area of expertise or beyond their target market.[2]

[2]A good discussion of this subject in general is given by W. E. Sasser, "Match Supply and Demand in Service Industries," *Harvard Business Review*, 54, no. 6 (November/December 1976): 133–140.

These eight options, along with their advantages and disadvantages, are summarized in Table 15.1.

Mixing Options to Develop a Plan

Although each of the five capacity options and three demand options described above might produce a cost-effective aggregate plan, a combination of them—called a **mixed strategy**—often works best. Mixed strategies involve the combination of two or more controllable variables to set a feasible production plan. For example, a firm might use a combination of overtime, subcontracting, and inventory levelling as its strategy. Finding the one "optimal" aggregate plan is not always possible, though, because there are a huge number of combinations.

Mixed strategy

The mix of strategy options is different for service firms than for manufacturing firms. For instance, stocking inventory may not be an option and subcontracting may invite competition. Consequently, service firms often address aggregate scheduling via changes in personnel. They do this by changing labour requirements, cross-training, job rotation, and using part-time employees.

Level Scheduling

Level scheduling, or level capacity planning, is a strategy popularized by the Japanese and their desire for "lifetime employment." **Level scheduling** involves aggregate plans in which daily capacities from month to month are uniform. In effect, firms like Toyota and Nissan keep production systems at uniform levels and may let the finished

Level scheduling

TABLE 15.1 ■ AGGREGATE PLANNING OPTIONS: ADVANTAGES AND DISADVANTAGES

OPTION	ADVANTAGES	DISADVANTAGES	SOME COMMENTS
Changing inventory level.	Changes in human resources are gradual or none; no abrupt production changes.	Inventory holding costs. Shortages, resulting in lost sales, may occur if demand increases.	This applies mainly to production, not service, settings.
Varying work-force size by hiring or layoffs.	Avoids the costs of other alternatives.	Hiring, layoff, and training costs may be significant.	Used where many unskilled people seek extra income.
Varying production rates through overtime or idle time.	Matches seasonal fluctuations without hiring/training costs.	Overtime premiums; tired workers; may not meet demand.	Allows flexibility within the aggregate plan.
Subcontracting.	Permits flexibility and smoothing of the firm's output.	Loss of quality control; reduced profits; loss of future business.	Applies mainly in production settings.
Using part-time workers.	Is less costly and more flexible than full-time workers.	High turnover/training costs; quality suffers; scheduling difficult.	Good for unskilled jobs in areas with large temporary labour pools.
Influencing demand.	Tries to use excess capacity. Discounts draw new customers.	Uncertainty in demand. Hard to exactly match demand to supply.	Creates marketing ideas. Overbooking used in some businesses.
Back-ordering.	May avoid overtime. Keeps capacity constant.	Customer must be willing to wait, but goodwill is lost.	Many companies backlog.
Counterseasonal product and service mixing.	Fully utilizes resources; allows stable work force.	May require skills or equipment outside firm's areas of expertise.	Risky finding products or services with opposite demand patterns.

POM IN ACTION

Teleworking

The growing phenomenon of "teleworking"—working from home rather than commuting to an office—gives the employees a sense of freedom and excitement, and a burning desire to accomplish as much as they can, followed by burnout, skepticism, and a feeling of loneliness and isolation. But finally they adjust and learn to live with some equanimity—usually an 18-to-24-month process. According to Roberta Fox, these emotional stages determine whether this working style is right for you and for the firm.

Given the wide range of job descriptions, it is difficult to approximate how many Canadians are teleworkers (salespeople, field engineers, consultants, etc.). Some estimates suggest that by the end of 1997 at least 20% of Canadian employees will be teleworkers. This rapid change can be directly linked to the advancement in computing power technology, which allows employees to set up virtually anywhere and anytime.

Source: Adapted from "Home Is Where the Office Is," *CMA Magazine*, 70, no. 1 (February 1996): 19–22.

goods inventory of autos go up or down to buffer the difference between monthly demand and production level or find alternative work for production employees. Their philosophy is that stable employment leads to better-quality autos, less turnover, less absenteeism, and more employee commitment to corporate goals.

Level scheduling usually results in lower labour costs than other strategies. Workers tend to be more experienced, so supervision is easier, costs of hiring/firing and overtime are minimized, and the operation is smoother with less dramatic start-ups and shutdowns.

METHODS FOR AGGREGATE PLANNING

Some companies have no formal aggregate planning process. They use the same plan from year to year, making adjustments up or down just enough to fit the new demand. This method certainly does not provide much flexibility, and if the original plan was suboptimal, the entire production process will be locked into suboptimal performance.

In this section, we introduce several techniques operations managers use in developing more useful and appropriate aggregate plans. They range from the widely used charting (or graphical) method, to a series of more formal mathematical approaches, including the transportation method of linear programming.

Graphical and Charting Methods

Graphical and charting methods

Graphical and charting methods are popular because they are easy to understand and use. Basically, these plans work with a few variables at a time to allow planners to compare projected demand with existing capacity. Although they are only trial-

and-error approaches that do not guarantee an optimal production plan, they are popular because they require only limited computations and can be performed by clerical staff.

In general, graphical methods follow five steps:

1. Determine the demand in each period.
2. Determine what the capacity is for regular time, overtime, and subcontracting each period.
3. Find the labour costs, hiring and layoff costs, and inventory holding costs.
4. Consider company policy that may apply to the workers or to stock levels.
5. Develop alternative plans and examine their total costs.

Examples 1 to 4 illustrate these steps.

EXAMPLE 1

Spar Marathon Roofing, a Weston, Ontario, manufacturer of roofing supplies, has developed monthly forecasts for roofing tiles and presented the period January–June in Table 15.2. The demand per day is computed by simply dividing the expected demand by the number of working days each month.

TABLE 15.2

MONTH	EXPECTED DEMAND	PRODUCTION DAYS	DEMAND PER DAY (COMPUTED)
January	900	22	41
February	700	18	39
March	800	21	38
April	1,200	21	57
May	1,500	22	68
June	1,100	20	55
	6,200	124	

To represent the projected demand, Spar Marathon also draws a graph (Figure 15.3) that charts the daily demand each month. The dotted line across the chart represents the production rate required to meet average demand. It is computed by

$$\text{Average requirement} = \frac{\text{total expected demand}}{\text{number of production days}} = \frac{6{,}200}{124} = 50 \text{ units/day}$$

FIGURE 15.3 ■ Graph of Forecast and Average Forecast Demand

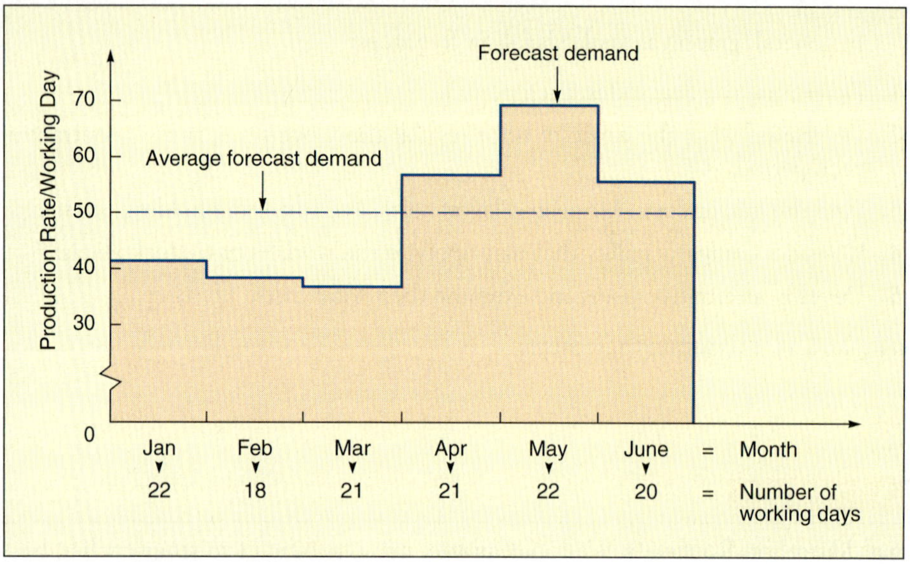

The graph in Figure 15.3 illustrates how the forecast differs from the average demand. Some strategies for meeting the forecast were listed earlier. The roofing firm, for example, might staff to yield a production rate that meets the average demand (as indicated by the dashed line). Or it might produce a steady rate of, say, 30 units and then subcontract excess demand to other roofing suppliers. A third plan might be to combine overtime work with some subcontracting to absorb demand. Examples 2 to 4 illustrate three possible strategies.

EXAMPLE 2

One possible strategy (call it Plan 1) for Spar Marathon, the manufacturer described in Example 1, is to maintain a constant work force throughout the 6-month period. A second (Plan 2) is to maintain a constant work force at a level necessary for the lowest demand month (March), and to meet all demand above this level by subcontracting. Yet a third plan is to hire and lay off workers as needed to produce to exact monthly requirements. Table 15.3 provides cost information needed to analyze these plans.

TABLE 15.3 ■ COST INFORMATION

Inventory carrying cost	\$5/unit/month
Subcontracting cost per unit	\$10/unit
Average pay rate	\$5/hour (\$40/day)
Overtime pay rate	\$7/hour (above 8 hours)
Labour-hours to produce a unit	1.6 hours/unit
Cost of increasing production rate (training and hiring)	\$10/unit
Cost of decreasing production rate (layoffs)	\$15/unit

ANALYSIS OF PLAN 1. When analyzing this approach, which assumes that 50 units are produced per day, we have a constant work force, no overtime or idle time, use no safety stock, and use no subcontractors. The firm accumulates inventory during the slack period of demand, which is January through March, and depletes it during the higher-demand warm season, April through June. We assume beginning inventory is 0, and planned ending inventory is 0.

Month	Production at 50 Units/Day	Demand Forecast	Monthly Inventory Change	Ending Inventory
January	1,100	900	+ 200	200
February	900	700	+ 200	400
March	1,050	800	+250	650
April	1,050	1,200	– 150	500
May	1,100	1,500	– 400	100
June	1,000	1,100	– 100	0
				1,850

$$\left(\begin{array}{c}\text{Total units of inventory carried over}\\ \text{from one month to the next month}\end{array}\right) = 1{,}850 \text{ units}$$

Work force required to produce 50 units/day = 10 workers

(Because each unit requires 1.6 labour-hours to produce, each worker can make 5 units in an 8-hour day. Hence to produce 50 units, 10 workers are needed.)

Plan 1's costs are computed as follows:

Costs	Calculations	
Inventory carrying	$ 9,250	(= 1,850 units carried × $5/unit)
Regular time labour	49,600	(= 10 workers × $40/day × 124 days)
Other costs (overtime, hiring, layoffs, subcontracting)	0	
Total cost	$58,850	

The graph for Example 2 was shown in Figure 15.3. Some planners prefer a *cumulative* graph to display visually how the forecast deviates from the average requirements. Such a graph is provided in Figure 15.4.

The final step in the graphical method is to compare the costs of each proposed plan and to select the approach with the least total cost. A summary analysis is provided in Table 15.5. We see there that Plan 2 has the lowest cost and is the best of the three options.

FIGURE 15.4 ■ Cumulative Graph for Plan 1

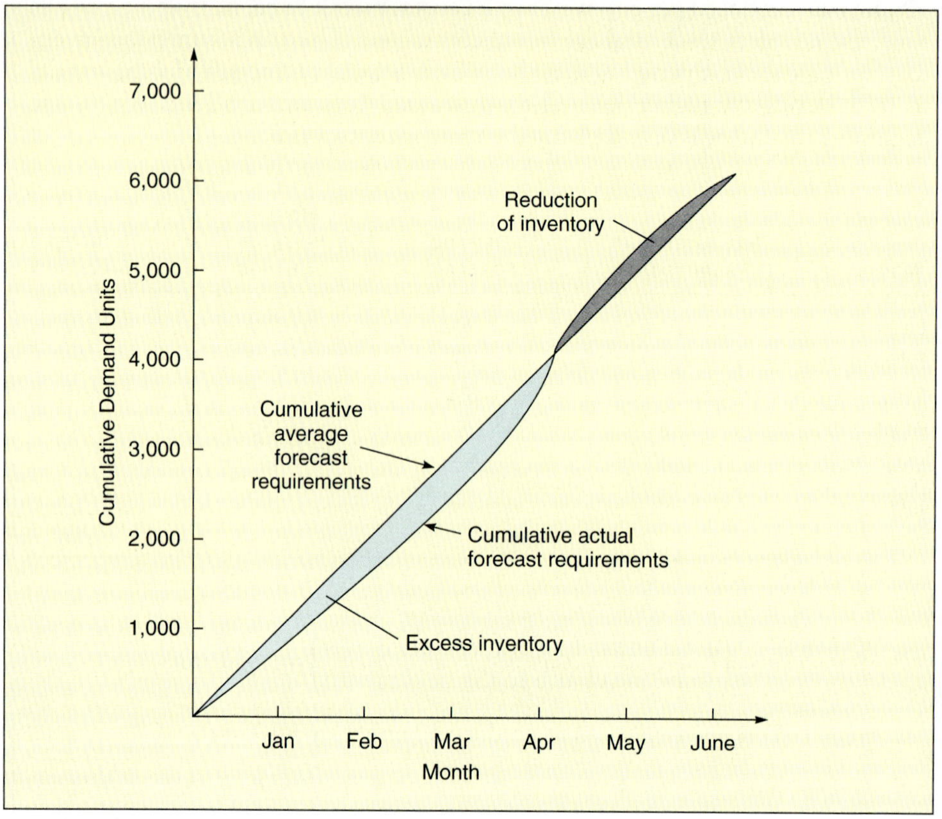

EXAMPLE 3

ANALYSIS OF PLAN 2. A constant work force is also maintained in Plan 2, but set low enough to meet demand in March, the lowest month. To produce 38 units/day in-house, 7.6 workers are needed. (You can think of this as 7 full-time workers and 1 part-timer.) All other demand is met by subcontracting, which is thus required in every month. No inventory holding costs are incurred in Plan 2.

Because 6,200 units are required during the aggregate plan period, we must compute how many can be made by the firm and how many subcontracted for:

$$\text{In-house production} = 38 \text{ units/day} \times 124 \text{ production days}$$
$$= 4{,}712 \text{ units}$$
$$\text{Subcontract units} = 6{,}200 - 4{,}712 = 1{,}488 \text{ units}$$

Plan 2's costs are:

COSTS		CALCULATIONS
Regular-time labour	$37,696	(= 7.6 workers × $40/day × 124 days)
Subcontracting	14,880	(= 1,488 units × $10/unit)
Total cost	$52,576	

EXAMPLE 4

ANALYSIS OF PLAN 3. The final strategy, Plan 3, involves varying the workforce size by hiring and firing as necessary. The production rate will equal the demand. Table 15.4 shows the calculations and the total cost of plan 3. Recall that it costs $15 per unit produced to reduce production from the previous month's level and $10 per unit change to increase production through hirings.

TABLE 15.4 ■ COST COMPUTATIONS FOR PLAN 3

MONTH	FORECAST (UNITS)	BASIC PRODUCTION COST (DEMAND × 1.6 HR./UNIT × $5/HR.)	EXTRA COST OF INCREASING PRODUCTION (HIRING COST)	EXTRA COST OF DECREASING PRODUCTION (LAYOFF COST)	TOTAL COST
January	900	$ 7,200	—	—	$ 7,200
February	700	5,600	—	$3,000 (= 200 × $15)	8,600
March	800	6,400	$1,000 (= 100 × $10)	—	7,400
April	1,200	9,600	4,000 (= 400 × $10)	—	13,600
May	1,500	12,000	3,000 (= 300 × $10)	—	15,000
June	1,100	8,800	—	$6,000 (= 400 × $15)	14,800
		$49,600	$8,000	$9,000	$66,600

Of course, many other feasible strategies can be considered in problems like this, including combinations that use some overtime. Although charting and graphing are popular management tools, their help is in evaluating strategies, not generating them. Managers need a systematic approach that considers all costs and produces an effective solution. Mathematical models provide one such approach.

Mathematical Methods for Planning

This section introduces some of the mathematical approaches to aggregate planning that have been developed over the past 40 years.

THE TRANSPORTATION METHOD OF LINEAR PROGRAMMING. Linear programming can be used in aggregate planning to allocate operating capacity to meet forecasted demand. The **transportation method of LP** (discussed in the supplement to Chapter 9) is not a trial-and-error approach like charting, but produces an optimal plan for minimizing costs. It is also flexible in that it can specify the regular and overtime production in each time period, the number of units to be subcontracted, extra shifts, and the inventory carryover from period to period.

Transportation method of LP

In Example 5, the supply consists of on-hand inventory and units produced by regular time, overtime, and subcontracting. Costs, in the upper right-hand corner of each cell of the matrix, relate to units produced in a given period or units carried in inventory from an earlier period.

TABLE 15.5 ■ COMPARISON OF THE THREE PLANS

COST	PLAN 1 (CONSTANT WORK FORCE OF 10 WORKERS)	PLAN 2 (WORK FORCE OF 7.6 WORKERS PLUS SUBCONTRACT)	PLAN 3 (HIRING AND LAYOFFS TO MEET DEMAND)
Inventory carrying	$ 9,250	$ 0	$ 0
Regular labour	49,600	37,696	49,600
Overtime labour	0	0	0
Hiring	0	0	8,000
Layoffs	0	0	9,000
Subcontracting	0	14,880	0
Total cost	$58,850	$52,576	$66,600

The optimal solution to the problem in Example 5 can be easily found using our AB:POM microcomputer software package described at the end of this chapter.

EXAMPLE 5

Kumar Radial Tire Company developed data that relate to production, demand, capacity, and costs at its Manitoba plant, as shown in Table 15.6. Table 15.7 illustrates the structure of the transportation table and an initial feasible solution.

TABLE 15.6 ■ KUMAR'S PRODUCTION, DEMAND, CAPACITY, AND COST DATA

	SALES PERIOD		
	MARCH	APRIL	MAY
Demand	800	1,000	750
Capacity			
Regular	700	700	700
Overtime	50	50	50
Subcontracting	150	150	130
Beginning inventory	100 tires		
	COSTS		
Regular time	$40/tire		
Overtime	$50/tire		
Subcontract	$70/tire		
Carrying cost	$2/tire/month		

TABLE 15.7 ■ KUMAR'S TRANSPORTATION TABLE

SUPPLY FROM		DEMAND FOR				TOTAL CAPACITY AVAILABLE (SUPPLY)
		Period 1 (March)	*Period 2 (April)*	*Period 3 (May)*	*Unused Capacity (Dummy)*	
Beginning inventory		[0] 100	[2]	[4]	[0]	100
Period 1	Regular time	[40] 700	[42]	[44]	[0]	700
	Overtime	[50]	[52] 50	[54]	[0]	50
	Subcontract	[70]	[72] 150	[74]	[0]	150
Period 2	Regular time	[ ]	[40] 700	[42]	[0]	700
	Overtime	[ ]	[50] 50	[52]	[0]	50
	Subcontract	[ ]	[70] 50	[72]	[0] 100	150
Period 3	Regular time	[ ]	[ ]	[40] 700	[0]	700
	Overtime	[ ]	[ ]	[50] 50	[0]	50
	Subcontract	[ ]	[ ]	[70]	[0] 130	130
TOTAL DEMAND		800	1,000	750	230	2,780

You should note the following:

1. Carrying costs are $2 per tire per month. Because holding cost is linear, 2 months' holdover costs $4.
2. Transportation problems require that supply equal demand. Hence, a dummy column called "unused capacity" has been added. Costs of not using capacity are zero.
3. The quantities in each column of Table 15.7 are levels of inventory needed to meet demand requirements. We see that demand of 800 tires in March is met by using 100 tires from beginning inventory and 700 tires from regular time.

Using the transportation LP approach to solve aggregate planning problems works well in analyzing the effects of holding inventories, using overtime, and subcontracting. But it does not work when more factors are introduced.[3] So, when hiring and layoffs are introduced, the more general method of simplex linear programming, seen in the supplement to Chapter 6, must be used.

[3]See R. DeMatta and T. Miller, "A Note on the Growth of a Production Planning System," *Interfaces*, 23 (April 1993): 27–31, for a description of how American Olean Tile Co. uses the transportation method. This large manufacturer of ceramic tiles generates plans that minimize total production and freight costs while meeting quarterly product demands.

Linear decision rule

LINEAR DECISION RULE. The **linear decision rule** (LDR) is an aggregate planning method that attempts to specify an optimum production rate and work-force level over a specific period. It minimizes the total costs of payroll, hiring, layoffs, overtime, and inventory through a series of quadratic cost curves.[4]

MANAGEMENT COEFFICIENT MODEL. A *heuristics decision rule* is a rule of thumb based on a manager's previous experiences in tackling a problem.

Management coefficient model

A classic heuristics application is E. H. Bowman's **management coefficient model.**[5] This unique approach builds a formal decision model around a manager's experience and performance. The theory is that the manager's past performance is fairly good, so it can be used as a basis for future decisions. This method uses a regression analysis of past production decisions made by managers. The regression line provides the relationship between variables (say, demand and labour) for future decisions. According to Bowman, managers' deficiencies were mostly inconsistencies in decision making.

Scheduling by simulation

SIMULATION. A computer model called **scheduling by simulation** was developed in 1966 by R. C. Vergin.[6] This simulation approach uses a search procedure to look for the minimum-cost combination of values for the size of the work force and the production rate.

Search decision rule

SEARCH DECISION RULE. The **search decision rule**, developed by W. H. Taubert, is a pattern search algorithm that tries to find the minimum-cost combination of various work-force and production levels.[7] A computer makes the thousands of systematic searches for points that produce a cost reduction. Search rules such as this do not yield optimal solutions, but are flexible enough to be used on any type of cost function.

Comparison of Aggregate Planning Methods

Although the search decision rule, linear programming, and other mathematical models have found some acceptance in industry, the fact is that most sophisticated planning models are not widely used.[8,9] Why? Perhaps it reflects the average manager's attitude about what he or she views as overly complex models. Planners, like all of us, like to understand how and why the models on which they are basing important decisions work. This may explain why the simpler charting and graphical approach is more generally accepted.

Table 15.8 highlights some of the main features of the planning methods we discussed in this chapter.

[4]Because LDR was developed by Charles C. Holt, Franco Modigliani, John F. Muth, and Nobel Prize–winner Herbert Simon, it is popularly known as the HMMS rule. For details, see C. C. Holt et al., *Production Planning, Inventories, and Work Force* (Englewood Cliffs, NJ: Prentice Hall, 1960).

[5]E. H. Bowman, "Consistency and Optimality in Managerial Decision Making," *Management Science*, 9, no. 2 (January 1963): 310–321.

[6]R. C. Vergin, "Production Scheduling Under Seasonal Demand," *Journal of Industrial Engineering*, 17, no. 5 (May 1966): 260–266.

[7]W. H. Taubert, "A Search Decision Rule for the Aggregate Scheduling Problem," *Management Science*, 14, no. 6 (February 1968): 343–359.

DISAGGREGATION

The output of the aggregate planning process is usually a production schedule for family groupings of products. It tells an auto manufacturer how many cars to make, but not how many should be two-door versus four-door or red versus green. It tells a steel manufacturer how many tonnes of steel to produce, but does not differentiate rolled steel from sheet steel. However, firms still need a plan dealing with specific products: What quantities should each one be produced in, and by what date? The process of breaking the aggregate plan down into greater detail is called **disaggregation**. Disaggregation results in a **master production schedule**, which, as we saw in Chapter 14, specifies:

Disaggregation
Master production schedule

1. the sizing and timing of specific item production quantities;
2. the sizing and timing of manufactured or purchased components;
3. the sequencing of individual orders or jobs;
4. the short-term allocation of resources to individual operations.

AGGREGATE PLANNING IN SERVICES

Some service organizations conduct aggregate planning in exactly the same way as we did in Examples 1 through 5 in this chapter. Most services pursue a number of the eight capacity and demand strategy options discussed earlier in Table 15.1 in combination,

TABLE 15.8 ■ SUMMARY OF AGGREGATE PLANNING METHODS

Technique	Solution Approaches	Important Aspects
Charting/graphical methods	Trial and error	Simple to understand and easy to use. Many solutions; one chosen may not be optimal.
Transportation method of linear programming	Optimization	LP software available; permits sensitivity analysis and new constraints; linear functions may not be realistic.
Linear decision rule	Optimization	Model takes 1 to 3 months to develop; complex cost functions not always valid; does not always produce a feasible solution.
Management coefficient model	Heuristic	Simple, easy to implement; tries to mimic manager's decision process; uses regression.
Simulation	Trial and error	Able to test many relationships among variables; can be costly; computerized; can handle any cost function.
Search decision rules	Heuristic	Widely used; permits any cost function; can test alternative decisions and do sensitivity analysis; 3 to 6 months to develop; expensive search cycle.

[8]W. B. Lee and B. M. Khumawala, "Simulation Testing of Aggregate Production Planning Models in an Implementation Methodology," *Management Science*, 20, no. 6 (February 1974): 903–911.

[9]W. N. Ledbetter and J. F. Cox, "Operations Research in Production Management," *Production and Inventory Management* (Third Quarter 1977): 84–91.

resulting in a *mixed* aggregate planning strategy for meeting demand. In actuality, in some firms, such as banking, trucking, and fast foods, aggregate planning may be even easier than in manufacturing.

Approaches to aggregate planning differ by the type of service provided. Here are five service scenarios.[10]

Restaurants

Aggregate planning in the case of a high-volume-product output business such as a restaurant is directed toward (1) smoothing the production rate, (2) finding the size of the work force to be employed, and (3) attempting to manage demand to keep equipment and employees working. The general approach usually requires building inventory during slack periods and depleting inventory during peak periods.

Because this is very similar to manufacturing, traditional aggregate planning methods may be applied to high-volume tangible services as well. One difference that should be noted is that in restaurants, inventory is perishable. In addition, the relevant units of time may be much smaller than in manufacturing. For example, in fast-food restaurants, peak and slack periods may be measured in hours and the "product" may be inventoried for only as long as 10 minutes.

Miscellaneous Services

Most "miscellaneous" services—financial services, hospitality services, transportation services, and many communication and recreation services—provide a high-volume, but intangible output. Aggregate planning for these services deals mainly with planning for human resource requirements and managing demand. The goal is to level the demand peak and to design methods for fully utilizing labour resources during forecasted low-demand periods.

Part-time workers are a proven planning resource tactic, especially in restaurants and supermarkets. McDonald's, for example, has found that hiring retired workers for part-time jobs pays off. Older workers are effective and loyal employees whose absentee rates are typically much lower than those of their teenage co-workers.

National Chains of Small Service Firms

With the advent of national chains of small service businesses such as funeral homes, fast-food outlets, photocopy/printing centres, and computer centres, the question of aggregate planning versus independent planning at each business establishment becomes an issue. One component of aggregate planning for a service chain is centralized purchasing, which has many advantages. Output also may be centrally planned when demand can be influenced through special promotions. This approach is advantageous because it reduces advertising costs and helps regulate cash flow at the independent sites.

Airline Industry

Another service example may be found in the airline industry. Consider an airline that has its headquarters in Montreal, two hub sites in cities such as Vancouver and

[10]The first four of these scenarios and their discussion are excerpted from R. Murdick, B. Render, and R. Russell, *Service Operations Management* (Boston: Allyn and Bacon, 1990), pp. 219–221.

Toronto, and 150 offices in airports throughout the country. Aggregate planning consists of tables or schedules of (1) number of flights in and out of each hub; (2) number of flights on all routes; (3) number of passengers to be serviced in all flights; and (4) number of air personnel and ground personnel required at each hub and airport.

This planning is considerably more complex than aggregate planning for a single site or a number of independent sites. Additional capacity decisions are focussed on determining the percentage of seats to be allocated to various fare classes in order to maximize profit or yield. This type of capacity allocation problem is called **yield management**.

Yield management

Hospitals

Hospitals face the aggregate planning problem by allocating money, staff, and supplies to meet the demands of patients for their medical services. Quebec's Hôtel Dieu Hospital, for example, plans for bed capacity and personnel needs in the light of a patient load forecast developed by moving averages. Its aggregate plan has led to the creation of a new floating staff pool serving each nursing pod.[11]

ACHIEVING WORLD-CLASS STANDARDS

Aggregate planning provides companies with a competitive weapon to help capture market shares in the global economy. By looking at an intermediate planning horizon, the aggregate plan provides the ability to respond to changing customer demands while still producing at low-cost and high-quality levels.

Managers at world-class firms schedule well because they know what to schedule, how to schedule, and why. While their world-class orientation is toward level schedules, they effectively balance capacity, inventory, personnel, and supplier/subcontractors. They prefer to invest in optimizing methods such as linear programming rather than trial-and-error approaches. The result is an effective and efficient use of resources to meet market demands.

SUMMARY

The aggregate plan sets levels of inventory, production, subcontracting, and employment over an intermediate time range, usually 3 to 18 months. This chapter describes several aggregate planning techniques, ranging from the popular charting approach to a variety of mathematical and computer-oriented models such as linear programming.

The aggregate plan is an important tactical responsibility of an operations manager and a key to smooth production. Output from the aggregate plan leads to a more detailed master production schedule, which is the basis for disaggregation, job scheduling, and MRP systems.

[11] G. Buxey, "Production Planning for Seasonal Demand," *International Journal of Operations and Production Management*, 13, no. 7 (1993): 4–21.

Although the discussion in the early part of this chapter dealt mostly with the manufacturing environment, we just saw that aggregate plans for service systems are similar. Banks, restaurants, airlines, and auto repair facilities are all service systems that can employ the concepts developed here. Regardless of the industry or planning method, though, the most important issue is the implementation of the plan. Managers appear to be more comfortable with less complex and less mathematical approaches to planning, often because they are untrained in using quantitative methods.

KEY TERMS

Aggregate planning (p. 682)
Tactical scheduling decisions (p. 682)
Mixed strategy (p. 687)
Level scheduling (p. 687)
Graphical and charting methods (p. 688)
Transportation method of LP (p. 693)
Linear decision rule (p. 696)
Management coefficient model (p. 696)
Scheduling by simulation (p. 696)
Search decision rule (p. 696)
Disaggregation (p. 697)
Master production schedule (p. 697)
Yield management (p. 699)

USING AB:POM TO SOLVE AGGREGATE PLANNING PROBLEMS

Solving Example 2 with AB:POM's Aggregate Planning Module

AB:POM's Aggregate Planning module performs aggregate or production planning for up to 12 time periods. Given a set of demands for future periods, you can try various plans to determine the lowest-cost plan based on holding, shortage, production, and changeover costs. The initial input is the number of periods in the planning horizon.

As shown in Program 15.1, four methods are available. More help is available on each of these methods *after* you choose the method.

In addition to the method, there is a *toggle* on the second row that lets you indicate whether excess demands should be handled first by overtime or by subcontracting. That is, if your *production amount* is larger than *regular-time* capacity—which option should be used next.

The table has two different sides. On the left side, capacities can be given, and on the right side, the costs can be given. Furthermore, the costs may be the same in each period or may vary from period to period. If they are the same, then the easiest way to enter the column is to go to the top of the column and place the cost.

Initial inventory is set at the top of the demand column.

Programs 15.1 and 15.2 illustrate the use of AB:POM for analyzing Plan 1 (the first strategy) for Example 2. That "user-defined" plan kept a constant work force throughout the 6-month planning period.

PROGRAM 15.1 ■ AB:POM's Aggregate Planning Program, with Options Menu and Data-Entry Screen for Plan 1 of Example 2. Note that on the left side of the table, capacities are input, and on the right-hand side, costs are input. "User-defined" method was chosen for this analysis.

Toggle Menu

- Smooth production (let inventory vary)
- Produce to demand (let work force vary)
- Constant Reg time, then OT and sub
- User defined

Data file: PLAN1 —— Aggregate Planning —— Data Screen

Number of time periods (1–99) 6

ANALYSIS OF PLAN1 OF EXAMPLE 2

METHOD -> User defined

PRIORITY Overtime precedes subcontracting

Pd	Demnd	Regtm	Ovrtm	Subcn	Regtim	Ovrtim	Subcon	Holdng	Shortg	Incres	Decres
		SCHEDULE					COSTS				
All Pds ->		0	0	0	$8.00	$11.20	$10.	$5.0	$0.0	$0.0	0.00
Init	0	0	0	0							
Pd1	900	1100	0	0	8.00	11.20	10.00	5.00	0.00	0.00	0.00
Pd2	700	900	0	0	8.00	11.20	10.00	5.00	0.00	0.00	0.00
Pd3	800	1050	0	0	8.00	11.20	10.00	5.00	0.00	0.00	0.00
Pd4	1200	1050	0	0	8.00	11.20	10.00	5.00	0.00	0.00	0.00
Pd5	1500	1100	0	0	8.00	11.20	10.00	5.00	0.00	0.00	0.00
Pd6	1100	1000	0	0	8.00	11.20	10.00	5.00	0.00	0.00	0.00

PROGRAM 15.2 ■ Output of AB:POM's Aggregate Planning Analysis of Plan 1

ANALYSIS OF PLAN1 OF EXAMPLE 2

METHOD -> User defined

PRIORITY Overtime precedes subcontracting

Pd	Demnd	Regtm	Ovrtm	Subcn	Regtim	Ovrtim	Subcon	Holdng	Shortg	Incres	Decres
		SCHEDULE					UNITS				
All Pds ->		0	0	0	8.00	11.20	10.00	5.00	$0.0	$0.0	0.00
Init	0	0	0	0							
Pd1	900	1100	0	0	1100	0	0	200	0	1100	0
Pd2	700	900	0	0	900	0	0	400	0	0	200
Pd3	800	1050	0	0	1050	0	0	650	0	150	0
Pd4	1200	1050	0	0	1050	0	0	500	0	0	0
Pd5	1500	1100	0	0	1100	0	0	100	0	50	0
Pd6	1100	1000	0	0	1000	0	0	0	0	0	100
TOTL	6200	6200	0	0	6200	0	0	1850	0	1300	300
	SUBTOTAL COSTS ->				49600	0	0	9250	0	0	0

TOTAL COSTS = 58850

Solving Aggregate Planning Problems with AB:POM's Transportation LP Module

AB:POM's Transportation Model module was first introduced as a tool for facility location in the Supplement to Chapter 9. In using the transportation linear programming program, we can also view the "origins" as supply sources and the "destinations" as periods, usually months or quarters. The program may then be used to solve Example 6 (Kumar Radial Tire Company) and other problems. Origin and destination names should be edited to reflect the aggregate plan. Cells that are clearly not feasible for the plan (namely, those that require back ordering) should be given *very* high costs. This will force the computer to avoid producing in those sources. For details as to the use of this approach, refer back to Programs S9.1 and S9.2.

SOLVED PROBLEMS

Solved Problem 15.1

Spar Marathon, the roofing manufacturer described in Examples 1 to 4, wishes to consider yet a fourth planning strategy (Plan 4). This one maintains a constant work force of eight people and uses overtime whenever necessary to meet demand. Cost information in Table 15.3 is to be used. Again, assume beginning and ending inventories are equal to zero.

Solution

Employ eight workers and use overtime when necessary. Carrying costs will be encountered now.

Month	Production at 40 Units/Day	Beginning of Month Inventory	Forecast Demand This Month	Overtime Production Needed	Ending Inventory
Jan.	880	—	900	20	0
Feb.	720	0	700	0	20
Mar.	840	20	800	0	60
Apr.	840	60	1,200	300	0
May	880	0	1,500	620	0
June	800	0	1,100	300	0
				1,240 units	80 units

$$\text{Carrying cost totals} = 80 \text{ units} \times \$5/\text{unit/month} = \$400$$

To produce 1,240 units at overtime rate (of $7/hour) requires 1,984 hours.

Overtime pay = $7/hour × 1,984 hours = $13,888

Regular pay = 8 workers × $40/day × 124 days = $39,680

Cost	Plan 4 (Work force of 8 plus overtime)	
Carrying cost	$ 400	(80 units carried × $5/unit)
Regular labour	39,680	(8 workers × $40/day × 124 days)
Overtime	13,888	(1,984 hours × $7/hour)
Hiring or firing	0	
Subcontracting	0	
Total costs	$53,968	

Solved Problem 15.2

Watson-McHale, a bicycle manufacturer in Charlottetown, Prince Edward Island, has developed the accompanying supply, demand, cost, and inventory data. The firm has a constant work force and meets all of its demand. Allocate the production capacity to satisfy demand at a minimum cost. What is the cost of this plan?

Supply Capacity Available (in units)

Period	Regular Time	Overtime	Subcontract
1	300	50	200
2	400	50	200
3	450	50	200

Demand Forecast

Period	Demand (units)
1	450
2	550
3	750

Other Data

Initial inventory: 50 units
Regular-time cost per unit: $50
Overtime cost per unit: $65
Subcontract cost per unit: $80
Carrying cost per unit per period: $1

Solution

SUPPLY FROM		DEMAND FOR *Period 1*	*Period 2*	*Period 3*	*Unused Capacity (Dummy)*	TOTAL CAPACITY AVAILABLE (SUPPLY)
Beginning inventory		0 50	1	2	0	50
Period 1	Regular time	50 300	51	52	0	300
	Overtime	65 50	66	67	0	50
	Subcontract	80 50	81	82	0 150	200
Period 2	Regular time		50 400	51	0	400
	Overtime		65 50	66	0	50
	Subcontract		80 100	81 50	0 50	200
Period 3	Regular time			50 450	0	450
	Overtime			65 50	0	50
	Subcontract			80 200	0	200
Total	DEMAND	450	550	750	200	1,950

Cost of plan:

Period 1: 50($0) + 300($50) + 50($65) + 50($80) = $22,250

Period 2: 400($50) + 50($65) + 100($80) = $31,250

Period 3: 50($81) + 450($50) + 50($65) + 200($80) = $45,800

Total cost $99,300

DISCUSSION QUESTIONS

1. What is the purpose of aggregate planning? Describe some demand and capacity options for implementing plans.
2. What is the difference between mixed production planning strategies and those eight demand and capacity options that are not mixed? Name four strategies that are not mixed.
3. Why are mathematical models not more widely used in aggregate planning?
4. What are the advantages and disadvantages of varying the size of the work force to meet demand requirements each period?
5. Why would some firms have longer planning horizons than others?

6. What is the relationship between the aggregate plan and the master production schedule?
7. Briefly describe four mathematical approaches to aggregate planning.
8. How does the aggregate planning differ for services versus manufacturing?
9. Why are graphical aggregate planning methods useful?
10. What are major limitations of using the transportation method for aggregate planning?
11. What impact on quality do you think each of eight production planning strategies might have?
12. What are the disadvantages that the following two strategies have in common: (1) varying inventory levels and (2) back ordering during periods of high demand?

CRITICAL THINKING EXERCISE

Many companies deal with aggregate planning by forcing overtime on their employees to adjust for the peaks of seasonal demand. For example, the *Wall Street Journal*'s report on long and irregular hours in the United States (July 14, 1994, p. B1) highlights Angie Clark, a J.C. Penney supervisor in Springfield, Virginia. Mrs. Clark works at least 44 hours a week, including evenings and frequent weekend shifts. Because of the recent recession, staffers are busier than 5 years earlier, when Mrs. Clark had 38 salespeople instead of the current 28. The result of this pressure is a 40% turnover. Because employee turnover is so large, training consists of the bare minimum—mostly how to operate the cash registers.

Discuss the implications of a strategy of heavy use of overtime in retailing, as well as in other fields such as manufacturing, hospitals, and airlines. How does this American approach compare with that in other countries?

PROBLEMS

: **15.1** Develop another plan for Spar Marathon, the roofing manufacturer described in Examples 1 to 4 and Solved Problem 15.1. For this plan, Plan 5, the firm wishes to maintain a constant work force of six and to pay overtime to meet demand. Is this plan preferable?

: **15.2** Spar Marathon, the roofing manufacturer in Examples 1 to 4 and Solved Problem 15.1, has yet a sixth plan. A constant work force of seven is selected and the remainder of demand is filled by subcontracting. Is this a better plan?

: **15.3** The president of King Enterprises, Kris King, projects the firm's aggregate demand requirements over the next 8 months as follows:

Jan.	1,400	May	2,200
Feb.	1,600	June	2,200
Mar.	1,800	July	1,800
Apr.	1,800	Aug.	1,400

Her operations manager is considering a new plan, which begins in January with 200 units on hand. Stockout cost of lost sales is $100 per unit. Inventory holding cost is $20 per unit per month. Ignore any idle time costs. The plan is called Plan A.

Plan A—Vary the work-force level to meet exactly the demand requirements. The December rate of production is 1,600 units per month. The cost of hiring additional workers is $5,000 per 100 units. The cost of laying off workers is $7,500 per 100 units.

Evaluate this plan.

15.4 Refer to Problem 15.3. King Enterprises is now looking at Plan B, below. Beginning inventory, stockout costs, and holding costs were provided in Problem 15.3.

> Plan B—Produce a constant rate of 1,400 units per month (which will meet minimum demands). Then subcontract additional units at a premium price of $75 per unit.

Evaluate this plan.

15.5 Refer to Problem 15.3. Plan C is shown below. Beginning inventory, stockout costs, and holding costs were provided in Problem 15.3.

> Plan C—Keep a stable work force by maintaining a constant production rate equal to the average requirements and by varying inventory levels. Plot the demand with a histogram that also shows average requirements.

Evaluate this plan.

15.6 King's operations manager (see Problems 15.3 to 15.5) is also considering these two mixed strategies:

> Plan D—Keep the current work force stable at 1,600 units per month. Permit a maximum of 20% overtime at an additional cost of $50 per unit. A warehouse now constrains the maximum allowable inventory on hand to 400 units or less.

> Plan E—Keep the current work force, which is producing 1,600 units per month, and subcontract to meet the rest of the demand.

15.7 Mark and Ventra is a VCR manufacturer in need of an aggregate plan for July–December. The company has gathered the following data:

Costs	
Holding cost	$8/VCR/month
Subcontracting	$80/VCR
Regular-time labour	$10/hour
Overtime labour	$16/hour above 8 hours/worker/day
Hiring cost	$40/worker
Layoff cost	$80/worker

Demand	
July	400
August	500
September	550
October	700
November	800
December	700

Other Data	
Current work force	8
Labour-hours/VCR	4
Workdays/month	20
Beginning VCR inventory	150

What will the two following strategies cost?

a) Vary the work force to have exact production to meet the forecast demand. Begin with eight workers on board at the end of June.

b) Vary overtime only, and use a constant work force of eight.

: **15.8** Develop your own aggregate plan for Mark and Ventra (see Problem 15.7). Justify your approach.

⁝ **15.9** Vanessa Juenger, the operations manager at The Brick Furniture, has received the following estimates of demand requirements.

APR.	MAY	JUNE	JULY	AUG.	SEPT.
1,000	1,200	1,400	1,800	1,800	1,600

Assuming stockout costs for lost sales are $100 and inventory carrying costs are $25/unit/month, evaluate these two plans on an *incremental* cost basis.

Plan A—Produce at a steady rate (equal to minimum requirements) of 1,000 units per month and subcontract the additional units at a $60 per unit premium cost.

Plan B—Vary the work force, which is at a current production level of 1,300 units per month. The cost of hiring additional workers is $3,000 per 100 units produced. The cost of layoffs is $6,000 per 100 units cut back.

⁝ **15.10** Vanessa Juenger (see Problem 15.9) is considering two more mixed strategies. Using the data of Problem 15.9, compare Plans C and D with the earlier ones and make a recommendation.

Plan C—Keep the current work force steady at a level producing 1,300 units per month. Subcontract the remainder to meet demand. Assume 300 units remain from March that are available in April.

Plan D—Keep the current work force at a level capable of producing 1,300 units per month. Permit a maximum of 20% overtime at a premium of $40 per unit. Assume warehouse limitations permit no more than 180 units carryover from month to month. This means that any time inventories reach 180, the plant is kept idle. Idle time per unit is $60. Any additional needs are subcontracted at a cost of $60 per incremental unit.

• **15.11** Consider the following aggregate problem for one quarter.

	REGULAR TIME	OVERTIME	SUBCONTRACTING
Production capacity/month	1,000	200	150
Production cost/unit	$5	$7	$8

Assume there is no initial inventory and a forecasted demand of 1,250 units in each of the 3 months. Carrying cost is $1 per unit per month. Solve this aggregate planning problem.

:15.12 Carrie Mattanini's firm had developed the accompanying supply, demand, cost, and inventory data. Allocate the production capacity to meet demand at a minimum cost. What is the cost?

SUPPLY AVAILABLE

PERIOD	REGULAR TIME	OVERTIME	SUBCONTRACT	DEMAND FORECAST
1	30	10	5	40
2	35	12	5	50
3	30	10	5	40

Initial inventory	20 units
Regular-time cost per unit	$100
Overtime cost per unit	$150
Subcontract cost per unit	$200
Carrying cost per unit per month	$4

:15.13 The production planning period of 10-megabyte RAM boards for CDM personal computers is 4 months. Cost data are as follows:

Regular-time cost per board	$70
Overtime cost per board	$110
Subcontract cost per board	$120
Carrying cost per board per month	$4

Capacity and demand for RAM boards for each of the next 4 months are as follows:

	PERIOD			
	MONTH 1	MONTH 2	MONTH 3*	MONTH 4
Demand	2,000	2,500	1,500	2,100
Capacity				
Regular time	1,500	1,600	750	1,600
Overtime	400	400	200	400
Subcontract	600	600	600	600

*Factory closes for 2 weeks of vacation.

CDM expects to enter the planning period with 500 RAM boards in stock. Back-ordering is not permitted (meaning, for example, that boards produced in the second month cannot be used in the first month). Set a production plan that minimizes costs.

:15.14 Haifa Instruments, an Israeli producer of portable kidney dialysis units and other medical products, develops a 4-month aggregate plan. Demand and capacity (in units) are forecast as follows:

CAPACITY SOURCE	MONTH 1	MONTH 2	MONTH 3	MONTH 4
Labour				
Regular time	235	255	290	300
Overtime	20	24	26	24
Subcontract	12	15	15	17
Demand	255	294	321	301

The cost of producing each dialysis unit is \$985 on regular time, \$1,310 on overtime, and \$1,500 on a subcontract. Inventory carrying cost is \$100 per unit per month. There is to be no beginning or ending inventory in stock. Set up a production plan that minimizes cost.

:15.15 A Moncton, New Brunswick, factory produces cast iron ingots according to a 3-month capacity plan. The cost of labour averages \$100 per regular shift-hour and \$140 per overtime (O.T.) hour. Inventory carrying cost is thought to be \$4 per labour-hour of inventory carried. There are 50 direct labour-hours of inventory left over from March. For the next 3 months, demand and capacity (in labour-hours) are as follows:

	CAPACITY		
MONTH	REGULAR LABOUR-HOURS	O.T. LABOUR-HOURS	DEMAND
April	2,880	355	3,000
May	2,780	315	2,750
June	2,760	305	2,950

Develop an aggregate plan for the 3-month period.

:15.16 A large Saskatchewan feed mill prepares its 6-month aggregate plan by forecasting demand for 25 kilogram bags of cattle feed as follows: January, 1,000 bags; February, 1,200; March, 1,250; April, 1,450; May 1,400; and June, 1,400. The feed mill plans to begin the new year with no inventory left over from the previous year. It projects that capacity (during regular hours) for producing bags of feed will remain constant at 800 until the end of April, and then increase to 1,100 bags per month when a planned expansion is completed on May 1. Overtime capacity is set at 300 bags per month until the expansion, at which time it will increase to 400 bags per month. A friendly competitor in Manitoba is also available as a backup source to meet demand—but it insists on a firm contract and can provide only 500 bags total during the 6-month period.

Cost data are as follows:

Regular-time cost per bag (until April 30)	$12
Regular-time cost per bag (after May 1)	$11
Overtime cost per bag (during entire period)	$16
Cost of outside purchase per bag	$18.50
Carrying cost per bag per month	$1

Develop a 6-month production plan for the feed mill.

:15.17 The Todd Corbin Chemical Supply Company manufactures and packages expensive vials of mercury. Given the accompanying demand, supply, cost, and inventory data, allocate production capacity to meet demand at minimum cost. A constant work force is expected and no back orders are permitted.

	SUPPLY CAPACITY (IN UNITS)			
PERIOD	REGULAR TIME	OVERTIME	SUBCONTRACT	DEMAND (IN UNITS)
1	25	5	6	32
2	28	4	6	32
3	30	8	6	40
4	29	6	7	40

OTHER DATA	
Initial inventory	4 units
Ending inventory desired	3 units
Regular-time cost per unit	$2,000
Overtime cost per unit	$2,475
Subcontract cost per unit	$3,200
Carrying cost per unit per period	$200

:15.18 Given the following information, solve for the minimum-cost plan:

	PERIOD					
	1	2	3	4	5	
Demand	150	160	130	200	210	Subcontracting: 100 units available over the 5-month period
Capacity						
Regular	150	150	150	150	150	Beginning inventory: 0 units
Overtime	20	20	10	10	10	Ending inventory required: 20 units

COST	
Regular-time cost per unit	$100
Overtime cost per unit	$125
Subcontract cost per unit	$135
Inventory cost per unit per period	$3

Assume that back orders are not permitted.

DATA BASE APPLICATION

15.19 Rich Rowe, owner of a dry-cleaning equipment manufacturer, develops an 8-month aggregate plan. Demand and capacity (in units) are forecast as follows:

CAPACITY SOURCE	JAN.	FEB.	MAR.	APR.	MAY	JUNE	JULY	AUG.
Labour								
Regular time	235	255	290	300	300	290	300	290
Overtime	20	24	26	24	30	28	30	30
Subcontract	12	16	15	17	17	19	19	20
Demand	255	294	321	301	330	320	345	340

The cost of producing each dry-cleaning unit is $1,000 on regular time, $1,300 on overtime, and $1,500 on a subcontract. Inventory carrying cost is $100 per unit per month. There is no beginning or ending inventory in stock and no back orders are permitted from period to period.

a) Set up a production plan that minimizes cost by producing exactly what the demand is each month and letting the work force vary. What is this plan's cost?

b) Through better planning, regular-time production can be set at exactly the same value, 275, per month. Does this alter the solution?

c) If overtime costs rise from $1,300 to $1,400, will your answer to part (a) change? What if they fall to $1,200?

CASE STUDY

Andrew-Carter, Inc.

Andrew-Carter, Inc. (A-C) is a major Canadian producer and distributor of outdoor lighting fixtures. Its fixture is distributed throughout North America and has been in high demand for several years. The company operates three plants that manufacture the fixture and distribute it to five distribution centres (warehouses).

During the present recession, A-C has seen a major drop in demand for its fixture as the housing market has declined. Based on the forecast of interest rates, the head of operations feels that demand for housing and thus for its product will remain depressed for the foreseeable future. A-C is considering closing one of its plants, as it is now operating with a forecasted excess capacity of 34,000 units per week. The forecasted weekly demands for the coming year are:

Warehouse 1	9,000 units
Warehouse 2	13,000 units
Warehouse 3	11,000 units
Warehouse 4	15,000 units
Warehouse 5	8,000 units

The plant capacities, in units per week, are

Plant 1, regular time	27,000 units
Plant 1, on overtime	7,000 units
Plant 2, regular time	20,000 units
Plant 2, on overtime	5,000 units
Plant 3, regular time	25,000 units
Plant 3, on overtime	6,000 units

If A-C shuts down any plants, its weekly costs will change, as fixed costs are lower for a nonoperating plant. Table 1 shows production costs at each plant, both variable at regular time and overtime, and fixed when operating and shut down. Table 2 shows distribution costs from each plant to each warehouse (distribution centre).

DISCUSSION QUESTIONS

1. Evaluate the various configurations of operating and closed plants that will meet weekly demand. Determine which configuration minimizes total costs.
2. Discuss the implications of closing a plant.

Source: Professor Michael Ballot, University of the Pacific.

TABLE 1 ■ ANDREW-CARTER, INC. VARIABLE COSTS AND FIXED PRODUCTION COSTS PER WEEK

		Fixed Cost per Week	
Plant	Variable Cost	Operating	Not Operating
No. 1, regular time	$2.80/unit	$14,000	$6,000
No. 1, overtime	3.52		
No. 2, regular time	2.78	12,000	5,000
No. 2, overtime	3.48		
No. 3, regular time	2.72	15,000	7,500
No. 3, overtime	3.42		

TABLE 2 ■ ANDREW-CARTER, INC. DISTRIBUTION COSTS PER UNIT

	To Distribution Centres				
From Plants	W1	W2	W3	W4	W5
No. 1	$0.50	$0.44	$0.49	$0.46	$0.56
No. 2	0.40	0.52	0.50	0.56	0.57
No. 3	0.56	0.53	0.51	0.54	0.35

BIBLIOGRAPHY

Armacost, R. L., R. J. Penlesky, and S. C. Ross. "Avoiding Problems Inherent in Spreadsheet-Based Simulation Models—An Aggregate Planning Application." *Production and Inventory Management,* 31 (Second Quarter 1990): 62–68.

Bowers, M. R., and J. P. Jarvis. "A Hierarchical Production Planning and Scheduling Model." *Decision Sciences,* 23 (January/February 1992): 144–157.

Buxey, G. "Production Planning and Scheduling for Seasonal Demand." *International Journal of Operations and Production Management,* 13, no. 7 (1993): 4–21.

Coker, J. L. "Analyzing Production Switching Heuristics for Aggregate Planning Models via an Application." *Production and Inventory Management* (Fourth Quarter 1985): 1–13.

DeMatta, R., and T. Miller. "A Note on the Growth of a Production Planning System." *Interfaces,* 23 (April 1993): 27–31.

Heskett, J., W. E. Sasser, and C. Hart. *Service Breakthroughs: Changing the Rules of the Game.* New York: Free Press, 1990.

"Home Is Where the Office Is," CMA *Magazine,* 70, no. 1 (February 1996): 19–22.

Krajewski, L. J., and L. B. Ritzman. "Disaggregation in Manufacturing and Service Organizations." *Decision Sciences,* 8 (January 1977): 1–18.

Leone, R. A., and J. R. Meyer. "Capacity Strategies for the 1980's." *Harvard Business Review* 58 (November/December 1980): 133.

McLeavey, D. W., and S. L. Narasimham. *Production Planning and Inventory Control.* Boston: Allyn and Bacon, 1985.

Murdick, R., B. Render, and R. Russell. *Service Operations Management.* Boston: Allyn and Bacon, 1990.

Sasser, W. E. "Match Supply and Demand in Service Industries." *Harvard Business Review,* 54 (November/December 1976): 133–140.

Schramm, W. R., and L. E. Freund. "Application of Economic Control Charts by a Nursing Modeling Team." *Industrial Engineering,* 25 (April 1993): 27–31.

Vollmann, T. E., W. L. Berry, and D. C. Whybark. *Manufacturing Planning and Control Systems,* Third Edition. Homewood, IL: Irwin, 1992.

16

SHORT-TERM SCHEDULING TACTICS

CHAPTER OUTLINE

LEARNING OBJECTIVES

When you complete this chapter you should be able to:

Identify or define:
- Gantt charts
- The assignment method
- Sequencing rules
- Johnson's rule

Explain:
- Shop loading
- Sequencing
- Scheduling

WORLD CLASS PROFILE: LTV

SCHEDULING AT LTV PROVIDES A COMPETITIVE ADVANTAGE

With the development of numerical control machines (machines controlled by computer software), companies now control (1) piece movement on the machine, (2) tool changing at the machine, and (3) the movement of materials between machines. When these capabilities are combined, we have a flexible machining system (FMS).

This FMS at LTV Aircraft Products Group in Dallas allows a number of good things to happen. Among these are rapid movement of pieces between machines, rapid tool setup, efficient waste handling, economical use of floor space, and high machine utilization. In a well-scheduled FMS, machine use can increase to 200% or 300% more than in a standard numerical control shop.

All machine and material movement instructions (computer code) are loaded into a mainframe computer. The mainframe computer downloads schedules to a computer at the FMS, where an on-site scheduler makes final determination about what job should be processed next. The on-site scheduler determines available tooling and risers (which hold the fixtures), as well as the final schedule.

The FMS makes possible the scheduling of parts in random order, handling similar or dissimilar parts and accommodating varying shapes and sizes without disrupting the production flow. This versatility results in parts being manufactured on a just-in-time (JIT) basis. Therefore, processing flexibility has improved.

Competitive advantage accrues to LTV in a variety of ways. First, machine utilization is about three times that of a normal machining centre. Second, less than three hours are required to produce a piece, so work-in-process is less. Third, because the time to set up for one piece is low and throughput is rapid, customer service is improved.

Using computer-generated job instructions, planning and scheduling personnel determine the tooling necessary for each job. Then the appropriate tools for that job are loaded into the proper position at the machine to which the job has been assigned.

A carousel is shown receiving and delivering each fixture holder, called risers, *which hold fixtures to the* automated guided vehicle (AGV). *The carousel has two workstations for mounting and dismounting pieces on the various risers. Here an operator on the far left is removing completed work and the operator in the red shirt determines the next order. Operators who do part loading and unloading also do a verification check prior to marking the part as complete and sending it on for inspection. The second floor control room in the background provides visual feedback to the scheduler.*

The AGV releases its tooling holder (riser 35) to the loading conveyer of the washing station. The automatic washing station allows for complete rotation of the piece while it is being washed with high-pressure coolant. As each piece is washed, the metal chips flow into drainways in the floor to the central chip-sorting station.

The problem of scheduling American League umpire crews from one series of games to the next is complicated by many restrictions on travel, ranging from coast-to-coast time changes, airline flight schedules, and night games running late.

The league strives to achieve two major objectives: (1) balance crew assignments relatively evenly among all teams over the course of a season and (2) minimize travel costs. These objectives are by nature conflicting, as attempting to balance crew assignments necessitates considerable airline travel and equipment moves, and hence increased travel costs. By using the assignment problem formulation described in this chapter, the time it takes the league to generate a schedule has been significantly decreased. And the quality of the schedule has improved.[1] ♦

Scheduling assigns resources, like equipment at LTV or umpires in baseball, over time to accomplish an organization's tasks. Table 16.1 illustrates scheduling decisions in four organizations, a hospital, a college, a factory, and an airline.

The process of scheduling (see Figure 16.1) begins with *capacity* planning, which involves facility and equipment acquisition. In the aggregate planning stage, decisions regarding the *use* of facilities, inventory, people, and outside contractors are made. Then the master schedule separates the aggregate plan and develops an *overall* schedule for outputs. Short-term schedules then translate capacity decisions, intermediate planning, and master schedules into job sequences, specific assignments of personnel, materials, and machinery. In this chapter, we describe the narrow issue of scheduling goods and services in the *short run* (that is, on a weekly, daily, or hourly basis).

SCHEDULING ISSUES

Scheduling involves assigning due dates to specific jobs, but many jobs compete simultaneously for the same resources. To help address the difficulties inherent in

TABLE 16.1 ■ SCHEDULING DECISIONS

ORGANIZATION	MANAGERS MUST SCHEDULE THE FOLLOWING:
Hospital	Operating room use Patient admissions Nursing, security, maintenance staffs Outpatient treatments
University	Classrooms and audiovisual equipment Student and instructor schedules Graduate and undergraduate courses
Factory	Production of goods Purchases of materials Workers
Airline	Maintenance of aircraft Departure timetables Flight crews, catering, gate, and ticketing personnel

[1]James Evans, "Scheduling American League Umpires," *Interfaces* (November/December 1988): 42–51.

FIGURE 16.1 ■ The Relationship Between Capacity Planning, Aggregate Planning, Master Schedule, and Short-Term Scheduling

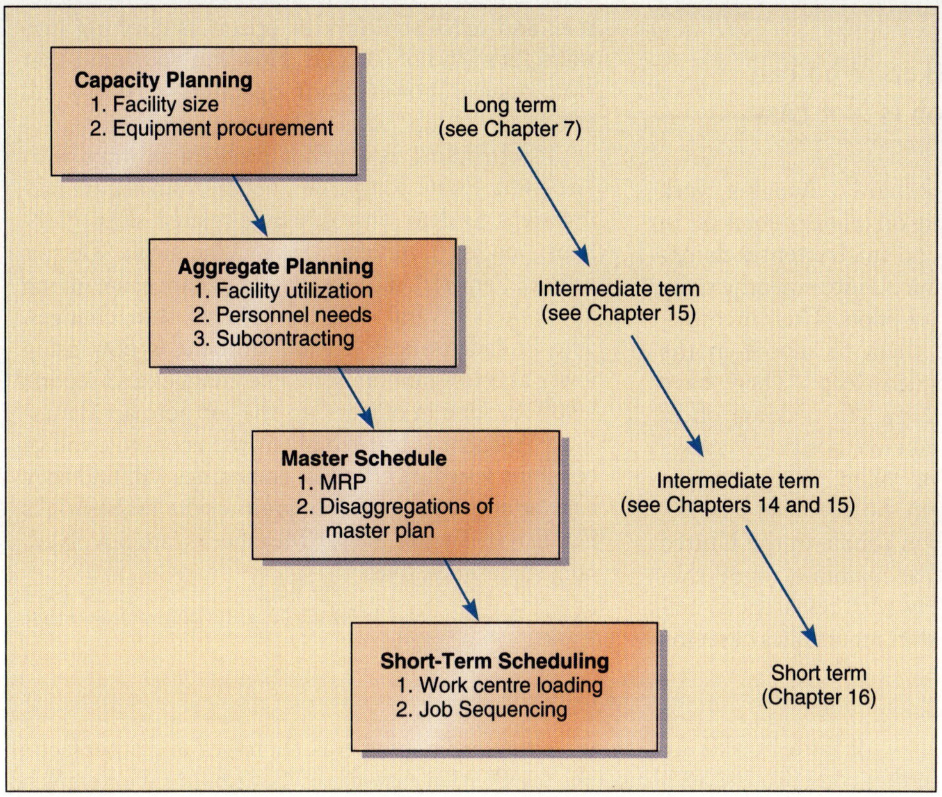

scheduling, we can categorize scheduling techniques as (1) forward scheduling and (2) backward scheduling.

Forward and Backward Scheduling

Forward scheduling starts the schedule as soon as the requirements are known. Forward scheduling is used in a variety of organizations such as hospitals, clinics, fine-dining restaurants, and machine tool manufacturers. In these facilities, jobs are performed to customer order and delivery is often requested as soon as possible. Forward scheduling is usually designed to produce a schedule that can be accomplished even if it means not meeting the due date. In many instances, forward scheduling causes a buildup of work-in-process inventory.

Forward scheduling

Backward scheduling begins with the due date, scheduling the final operation first. Steps in the job are then scheduled, one at a time, in reverse order. By subtracting the lead time for each item, the start time is obtained. However, the resources necessary to accomplish the schedule may not exist. Backward scheduling is used in many manufacturing environments, as well as service environments such as catering a banquet or scheduling surgery. In practice, a combination of forward and backward scheduling is often used to find a reasonable trade-off between what can be achieved and customer due dates.

Backward scheduling

POM IN ACTION

Scheduling Workers Who Fall Asleep on the Job Is Not Easy

Unable to cope with a constantly changing work schedule, an operator at a big oil refinery dozes off in the middle of the night—and inadvertently dumps thousands of gallons of chemicals into a nearby river.

A similar story holds for pilots. Their inconsistent schedules often force them to snooze in the cockpit in order to get enough sleep. "There have been times I've been so sleepy, I'm nodding off as we're taxiing to get into take-off position," says a Federal Express pilot. "I've fallen asleep reading checklists. I've fallen asleep in the middle of a word."

An estimated 20 million people in the United States work in industries that maintain round-the-clock schedules. In interviews with researchers, employees from the graveyard shift report tales of seeing sleeping assembly-line workers fall off their stools, batches of defective parts sliding past dozing inspectors, and exhausted forklift operators crashing into walls. "It's kind of too ugly. How can you admit that your nuclear power plant operators regularly fall asleep on the job?" says a Harvard researcher.

Scheduling is a major problem in firms with late shifts. Some companies, but far from all, are taking steps to deal with schedule-related sleep problems among workers. Dow Chemical, Detroit Edison, Pennzoil, and Exxon, for instance, are giving all workers several days off between shift changes. The Philadelphia Police Department is now using fewer and less random schedule changes and reports a 40% decline in officers' on-the-job auto accidents.

As more is learned about the economic toll of constant schedule changes, companies will find they cannot afford to continue ignoring the problem. As Dr. David Kupfer says, "Megabucks are involved, and, sometimes, lives."

Sources: Prevention (May 1994): 72–80; and *Wall Street Journal* (July 7, 1988): 1.

Machine breakdowns, absenteeism, quality problems, shortages, and other factors further complicate scheduling. (See the *POM in Action* box "Scheduling Workers Who Fall Asleep on the Job Is Not Easy.") Consequently, assignment of a date does not ensure that the work will be performed according to the schedule. Many specialized techniques, therefore, have been developed to aid us in preparing reliable schedules.

Scheduling Criteria

The correct scheduling technique depends on the volume of orders, the nature of operations, and the overall complexity of jobs, as well as importance placed on each of four criteria. Those four criteria are:

1. *Minimize Completion Time:* This is evaluated by determining the average completion time for each job.
2. *Maximize Utilization:* This is evaluated by determining the percent of the time the facility is utilized.
3. *Minimize Work-in-Process (WIP) Inventory:* This is evaluated by determining the average number of jobs in the system. The relationship between the number of jobs in the system and WIP inventory is high. Therefore, the fewer the number of jobs in the system, the lower the inventory.
4. *Minimize Customer Waiting Time:* This is evaluated by determining the average number of late days.

These four criteria are used in this chapter, as they are in industry, to evaluate scheduling performance. Additionally, good scheduling approaches should be simple, clear, easily understood, easy to carry out, flexible, and realistic. Given these considerations, *the objective of scheduling is to optimize the use of resources so the production objectives are met*. In this chapter, we examine scheduling in process-focussed (intermittent) production, repetitive production, and the service sector.

SCHEDULING PROCESS-FOCUSSED WORK CENTRES

Process-focussed facilities (also known as intermittent or job shop facilities)[2] are high-variety, low-volume systems commonly found in manufacturing and service organizations. It is a production system in which products are made to order. Items made under this system usually differ considerably in terms of materials used, order of processing, processing requirements, time of processing, and setup requirements. Because of these differences, scheduling can be complex. To run a facility in a balanced and efficient manner, the manager needs a production planning and control system. This system should:

1. Schedule incoming orders without violating capacity constraints of individual work centres.
2. Check the availability of tools and materials before releasing an order to a department.
3. Establish due dates for each job and check progress against need dates and order lead times.
4. Check work in progress as jobs move through the shop.
5. Provide feedback on plant and production activities.
6. Provide work efficiency statistics and monitor operator times for payroll and labour distribution analyses.

Whether the scheduling system is manual or automated, it must be accurate and relevant. This means it requires a production data base with both planning and control files.[3] Three types of **planning files** are (1) an *item master file*, which contains information about each component the firm produces or purchases; (2) a *routing file*, which indicates each component's flow through the shop; and (3) a *work centre master file*, which contains information about the work centre, such as capacity and efficiency. **Control files** track the actual progress made against the plan for each work order.

Planning files

Control files

LOADING JOBS IN WORK CENTRES

Loading means the assignment of jobs to work or processing centres. Operations managers assign jobs to work centres so that costs, idle time, or completion times are kept to a minimum. Loading work centres takes two forms.[4] One is oriented to capacity; the second is related to assigning specific jobs to work centres. First, we examine

Loading

[2]Much of the literature on scheduling is about manufacturing; therefore, the traditional term *job shop scheduling* is often used.

[3]For an expanded discussion, see *APICS Training Aid—Shop Floor Control* (Falls Church, VA: American Production and Inventory Control Society).

[4]Note that this discussion can apply to work centres that might be called a "shop" in a manufacturing firm, or a "ward" in a hospital, or a "department" in an office or large kitchen.

loading from the perspective of capacity via a technique known as input-output control. Then, we present two approaches used for loading: *Gantt charts* and the *assignment method* of linear programming.

Input-Output Control

Many firms have difficulty scheduling (that is, achieving effective throughput) because they overload the production processes. This often occurs because they do not know actual performance in the work centres. Effective scheduling depends on matching the schedule to performance. Lack of knowledge about capacity and performance causes reduced throughput.

Input-output control

Input-output control is a technique that allows operations personnel to manage facility work flows. If the work is arriving faster than it is being processed, we are overloading the facility and a backlog develops. Overloading causes crowding in the facility, leading to inefficiencies and quality problems. If the work is arriving at a slower rate than it is being performed, we are underloading the facility and the work centre may run out of work. Underloading the facility results in idle capacity and wasted resources. Example 1 shows the use of input-output controls.

EXAMPLE 1

Figure 16.2 shows the planned capacity for the DNC Milling work centre for 8 weeks (weeks 6/6 through 7/25). The planned input is 280 standard hours per week. The actual input is close to this figure, varying between 250 and 285. Output is

FIGURE 16.2 ■ Input-Output Control

Work Centre DNC Milling (In standard hours)

Week ending	6/6	6/13	6/20	6/27	7/4	7/11	7/18	7/25
Planned Input	280	280	280	280	280	280	280	280
Actual Input	270	250	280	285	280	285		
Cumulative Deviation	−10	−40	−40	−35	−35	−30		
Planned Output	320	320	320	320				
Actual Output	270	270	270	270				
Cumulative Deviation	−50	−100	−150	−200				
Cumulative Change in Backlog*	0	−20	−10	+5				

*Sum of actual inputs minus sum of actual outputs = cumulative change in backlog

scheduled at 320 standard hours, which is the assumed capacity. A backlog of 300 hours exists in the work centre. However, actual output (270 hours) is substantially less than planned. Therefore, neither the input plan nor the output plan is being achieved. Indeed, the backlog of work in this work centre has actually increased by 5 hours by week 4. This increases work-in-process inventory, complicating the scheduling task and indicating the need for manager action.

The options available to operations personnel to manage facility work flow include

1. correction of performances;
2. increasing facility size;
3. increasing or reducing input to the work centre by
   (a) routing work to or from other work centres,
   (b) increasing or decreasing subcontracting,
   (c) producing less (or producing more).

Producing less is not a popular solution for many managers, but the advantages can be substantial. First, the customer service level may improve because units may be produced on time. Second, efficiency may actually improve because of less work-in-process cluttering the work centre and adding to overhead costs. Third, quality may improve because less work-in-process hides fewer problems.

Gantt Charts

Gantt charts are visual aids that are useful in loading and scheduling. Their name is derived from Henry Gantt, who developed them in the late 1800s. The charts help describe the use of resources, such as work centres and overtime.

Gantt charts

When used in *loading*, Gantt charts show the loading and idle time of several departments, machines, or facilities. They display the relative workloads in the system so that the manager knows what adjustments are appropriate. For example, when one work centre becomes overloaded, employees from a low-load centre can be transferred temporarily to increase the work force. Or if waiting jobs can be processed at different work centres, some jobs at high-load centres can be transferred to low-load centres. Versatile equipment may also be transferred between centres. Example 2 illustrates a simple Gantt load chart.

EXAMPLE 2

A New Brunswick washing machine manufacturer accepts special orders for machines to be used in unique facilities such as submarines, hospitals, and large industrial laundries. The production of each machine requires varying tasks and durations. Figure 16.3 shows the load chart for the week of March 8.

The four work centres process several jobs during the week. This particular chart indicates that the Metal Works and Painting centres are completely loaded for the entire week. The Mechanical and Electronic centres have some idle time scattered during the week. We also note that the Metal Works centre is unavailable on Tuesday, perhaps for preventive maintenance.

FIGURE 16.3 ■ Gantt Load Chart for the Week of March 8

Work centre \ Day	Monday	Tuesday	Wednesday	Thursday	Friday
Metal works	Job 349	(Centre not available)		Job 350	
Mechanical			Job 349	Job 408	
Electronics	Job 408			Job 349	
Painting		Job 295	Job 408	(Centre not available)	Job 349

Processing

Centre not available (for example, maintenance time, repairs, shortages)

The Gantt *load chart* does have some major limitations. For one, it does not account for production variability such as unexpected breakdowns or human errors that require reworking a job. The chart must also be updated regularly to account for new jobs and revised time estimates.

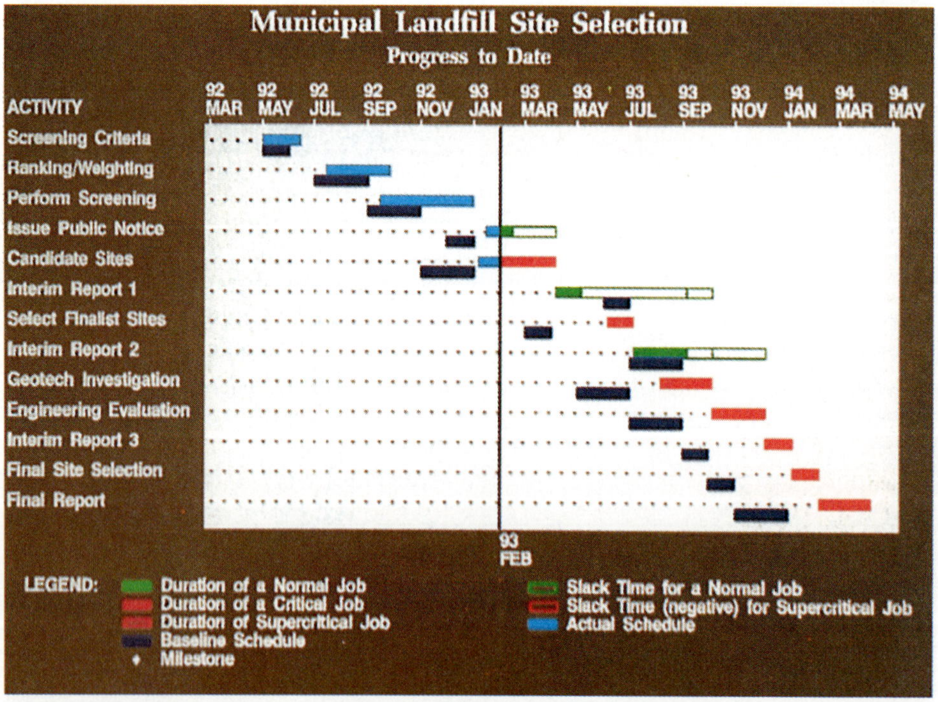

Gantt chart software, such as this one from the SAS Institute Inc. in Cary, N.C., helps managers schedule projects easily. Time, resource, and procedure constraints can be included to track project progress. Here the SAS Gantt chart monitors the selection process for a municipal landfill site.

A Gantt *schedule chart* is used to monitor jobs in progress.[5] It indicates which jobs are on schedule and which are ahead of or behind schedule. In practice, many versions of the chart are found. The schedule chart in Example 3 places jobs in progress on the vertical axis and time on the horizontal axis.

EXAMPLE 3

JH Products Corporation uses the Gantt chart in Figure 16.4 to show the scheduling of three orders, jobs A, B, and C. Each pair of brackets on the time axis denotes the estimated starting and finishing of a job enclosed within it. The solid bars reflect the actual status or progress of the job. Job A, for example, is about one-half day behind schedule at the end of day 5. Job B was completed after equipment maintenance. Job C is ahead of schedule.

FIGURE 16.4 ■ Gantt Scheduling Chart for Jobs A, B, and C

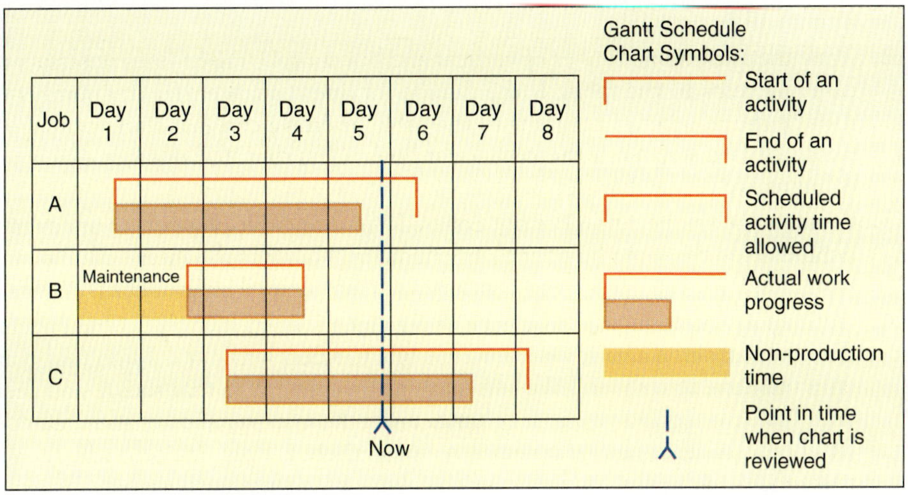

The Assignment Method

The **assignment method** is a special class of the linear programming model that involves assigning tasks or jobs to resources. Examples include assigning jobs to machines, contracts to bidders, people to projects, and salespeople to territories. The objective is most often to minimize total costs or time required to perform the tasks at hand. One important characteristic of assignment problems is that only one job (or worker) is assigned to one machine (or project).

Assignment method

Each assignment problem uses a table. The numbers in the table will be the costs or times associated with each particular assignment. For example, if a facility has three available machines (A, B, and C) and three new jobs to be completed, its table might appear as follows. The dollar entries represent the firm's estimate of what it will cost for each job to be completed on each machine.

[5]Gantt charts are also used for project scheduling and are again noted in Chapter 17, "Project Management."

Job \ Machine	A	B	C
R-34	$11	$14	$6
S-66	$8	$10	$11
T-50	$9	$12	$7

The assignment method involves adding and subtracting appropriate numbers in the table in order to find the lowest *opportunity cost*[6] for each assignment. There are four steps to follow:

1. Subtract the smallest number in each row from every number in that row and then subtract the smallest number in each column from every number in that column. This step has the effect of reducing the numbers in the table until a series of zeros, meaning *zero opportunity costs*, appear. Even though the numbers change, this reduced problem is equivalent to the original one, and the same solution will be optimal.
2. Draw the minimum number of vertical and horizontal straight lines necessary to cover all zeros in the table. If the number of lines equals either the number of rows or the number of columns in the table, then we can make an optimal assignment (see step 4). If the number of lines is less than the number of rows or columns, we proceed to step 3.
3. Subtract the smallest number not covered by a line from every other uncovered number. Add the same number to any number(s) lying at the intersection of any two lines. Return to step 2 and continue until an optimal assignment is possible.
4. Optimal assignments will always be at zero locations in the table. One systematic way of making a valid assignment is first to select a row or column that contains only one zero square. We can make an assignment to that square and then draw lines through its row and column. From the uncovered rows and columns, we choose another row or column in which there is only one zero square. We make that assignment and continue the above procedure until we have assigned each person or machine to one task.

Example 4 shows how to use the assignment method.

EXAMPLE 4

The cost table shown earlier in this section is repeated below. We find the minimum total cost assignment of jobs to machines by applying steps 1 through 4.

Job \ Machine	A	B	C
R-34	$11	$14	$6
S-66	$8	$10	$11
T-50	$9	$12	$7

[6]Opportunity costs are those profits forgone or not obtained.

Step 1a. Using the previous table, subtract the smallest number in each row from every number in the row. The result is shown below.

Job \ Machine	A	B	C
R-34	5	8	0
S-66	0	2	3
T-50	2	5	0

Step 1b. Using the previous table, subtract the smallest number in each column from every number in the column. The result is shown below.

Job \ Machine	A	B	C
R-34	5	6	0
S-66	0	0	3
T-50	2	3	0

Step 2. Draw the minimum number of straight lines needed to cover all zeroes. Because two lines suffice, the solution is not optimal.

Job \ Machine	A	B	C
R-34	5	6	0
S-66	0	0	3
T-50	2	3	0

Smallest uncovered number

Step 3. Subtract the smallest uncovered number (2 in this table) from every other uncovered number and add it to numbers at the intersection of two lines.

Job \ Machine	A	B	C
R-34	3	4	0
S-66	0	0	5
T-50	0	1	0

Return to step 2. Cover the zeroes with straight lines again.

Job \ Machine	A	B	C
R-34	3	4	0
S-66	0	0	5
T-50	0	1	0

Because three lines are necessary, an optimal assignment can be made (see step 4 on page 000). Assign R-34 to machine C, S-66 to machine B, and T-50 to machine A.

$$\text{Minimum cost} = \$6 + \$10 + \$9 = \$25$$

(*Note:* If we had S-66 assigned to machine A, we could not assign T-50 to a zero location.)

Some assignment problems entail *maximizing* the profit, effectiveness, or payoff of an assignment of people to tasks or of jobs to machines. It is easy to obtain an equivalent minimization problem by converting every number in the table to an *opportunity loss*. To convert a maximizing problem to an equivalent minimization problem, we subtract every number in the original payoff table from the largest single number in that table. We then proceed to step 1 of the four-step assignment method. It turns out that minimizing the opportunity loss produces the same assignment solution as the original maximization problem.

SEQUENCING JOBS IN WORK CENTRES

Sequencing

Scheduling provides a basis for assigning jobs to work centres. *Loading* is a capacity control technique that highlights overloads and underloads. **Sequencing** specifies the order in which jobs should be done at each centre. For example, suppose that 10 patients are assigned to a medical clinic for treatment. In what order should they be treated? Should the first patient to be served be the one who arrived first or the one who needs emergency treatment? Sequencing methods provide such detailed information. These methods are referred to as priority rules for dispatching jobs to work centres.

Priority Rules for Dispatching Jobs

Priority rules

Priority rules provide guidelines for the sequence in which jobs should be worked. The rules are especially applicable for process-focussed facilities such as clinics, print shops, and manufacturing job shops. We will examine a few of the most popular priority rules. Priority rules try to minimize completion time, number of jobs in the system, and job lateness, while maximizing facility utilization.

The most popular priority rules are:

FCFS: First-come, first-served. The first job to arrive at a work centre is processed first. **FCFS**

SPT: Shortest processing time. The shortest jobs are handled first and completed. **SPT**

EDD: Earliest due date. The job with the earliest due date is selected first. **EDD**

LPT: Longest processing time. The longer, bigger jobs are often very important and are selected first. **LPT**

Example 5 compares these rules.

EXAMPLE 5

Five sheet metal jobs are waiting to be assigned at Ajax Company's Long Beach work centre. Their work (processing) times and due dates are given below. We want to determine the sequence of processing according to (1) FCFS, (2) SPT, (3) EDD, and (4) LPT rules. Jobs were assigned a letter in the order they arrived.

Job	Job Work (Processing) Time (Days)	Job Due Date (Days)	Job	Job Work (Processing) Time (Days)	Job Due Date (Days)
A	6	8	D	3	15
B	2	6	E	9	23
C	8	18			

1. The *FCFS* sequence is simply A–B–C–D–E. The "flow time" in the system for this sequence measures the time each job spends waiting plus being processed. Job B, for example, waits 6 days while job A is being processed, then takes 2 more days of operation time itself; so it will be completed in 8 days—which is 2 days later than its due date.

Job Sequence	Job Work (Processing) Time	Flow Time	Job Due Date	Job Lateness
A	6	6	8	0
B	2	8	6	2
C	8	16	18	0
D	3	19	15	4
E	9	28	23	5
	28	77		11

The first-come, first-served rule results in the following measures of effectiveness:

(a) Average completion time $= \dfrac{\text{sum of total flow time}}{\text{no. of jobs}}$

$$= \frac{77 \text{ days}}{5} = 15.4 \text{ days}$$

Your doctor may use a first-come-first-served priority rule satisfactorily. However, such a rule may be less than optimal for this emergency room. What priority rule might be best, and why? What priority rule was often used on the TV program *M*A*S*H*?

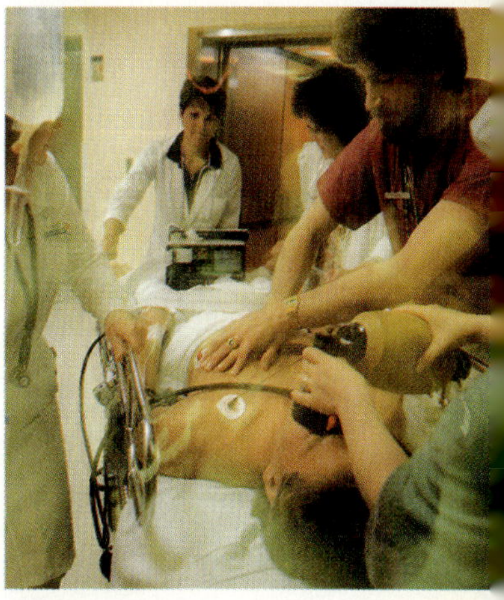

"We've been at it all night, J.B., and we've narrowed it down to 36,000 possibilities. We should have today's schedule firmed up by noon."
Source: CMCS News.

(b) Utilization $= \dfrac{\text{total job work (processing) time}}{\text{sum of total flow time}}$

$$= \frac{28}{77} = 36.4\%$$

(c) Average number of jobs in the system $= \dfrac{\text{sum of total flow time}}{\text{total job work (processing) time}}$

$$= \frac{77 \text{ days}}{28 \text{ days}} = 2.75 \text{ jobs}$$

(d) Average job lateness $= \dfrac{\text{total late days}}{\text{no. of jobs}} = \dfrac{11}{5} = 2.2$ days

2. The *SPT* rule results in the sequence B–D–A–C–E (see below). Orders are sequenced according to processing time, with the highest priority given to the shortest job.

Job Sequence	Job Work (Processing) Time	Flow Time	Job Due Date	Job Lateness
B	2	2	6	0
D	3	5	15	0
A	6	11	8	3
C	8	19	18	1
E	9	28	23	5
	28	65		9

Measurements of effectiveness for SPT are:

(a) Average completion time $= \dfrac{65}{5} = 13$ days

(b) Utilization $= \dfrac{28}{65} = 43.1\%$

(c) Average number of jobs in the system $= \dfrac{65}{28} = 2.32$

(d) Average job lateness $= \dfrac{9}{5} = 1.8$ days

3. The *EDD* rule gives the sequence B–A–D–C–E. Note that jobs are ordered by earliest due date first.

Job Sequence	Job Work (Processing) Time	Flow Time	Job Due Date	Job Lateness
B	2	2	6	0
A	6	8	8	0
D	3	11	15	0
C	8	19	18	1
E	9	28	23	5
	28	68		6

Measurements of effectiveness for EDD are:

(a) Average completion time $= \frac{68}{5} = 13.6$ days

(b) Utilization $= \frac{28}{68} = 41.2\%$

(c) Average number of jobs in the system $= \frac{68}{28} = 2.42$

(d) Average job lateness $= \frac{6}{5} = 1.2$ days

4. The *LPT* results in the order E–C–A–D–B.

Job Sequence	Job Work (Processing) Time	Flow Time	Job Due Date	Job Lateness
E	9	9	23	0
C	8	17	18	0
A	6	23	8	15
D	3	26	15	11
B	2	28	6	22
	28	103		48

Measures of effectiveness for LPT are:

(a) Average completion time $= \frac{103}{5} = 20.6$ days

(b) Utilization $= \frac{28}{103} = 28.2\%$

(c) Average number of jobs in the system $= \frac{103}{28} = 3.68$

(d) Average job lateness $= \frac{48}{5} = 9.6$ days

The results of these four rules are summarized below.

Rule	Average Completion Time (Days)	Utilization (%)	Average No. of Jobs in System	Average Lateness (Days)
FCFS	15.4	36.4	2.75	2.2
SPT	13.0	43.1	2.32	1.8
EDD	13.6	41.2	2.42	1.2
LPT	20.6	28.2	3.68	9.6

As we can see in Example 5, LPT is the least effective measurement of sequencing for the Ajax Company. SPT is superior in three measures and EDD in the fourth (average lateness). This is typically true in the real world also and has been supported by a number of simulation experiments.[7] We find that no one sequencing rule always excels on all criteria. Experience indicates the following:

1. Shortest processing time is generally the best technique for minimizing job flow and minimizing the average number of jobs in the system. Its chief disadvantage is that long-duration jobs may be continuously pushed back in priority in favour of short-duration jobs. Customers may view this dimly, and a periodic adjustment for longer jobs has to be made.
2. First-come, first-served does not score well on most criteria (but neither does it score particularly poorly). It has the advantage, however, of appearing fair to customers, which is important in service systems.

Critical Ratio

Critical ratio

Another type of sequencing rule is the **critical ratio**. The critical ratio (CR) is an index number computed by dividing the time remaining until due date by the work time remaining. As opposed to the priority rules, critical ratio is dynamic and easily updated. It tends to perform better than FCFS, SPT, EDD, or LPT on the average job lateness criterion.

The critical ratio gives priority to jobs that must be done to keep shipping on schedule. A job with a low critical ratio (less than 1.0) is one that is falling behind schedule. If CR is exactly 1.0, the job is on schedule. A CR greater than 1.0 means the job is ahead of schedule and has some slack.

The formula for critical ratio is

$$CR = \frac{\text{time remaining}}{\text{work days remaining}} = \frac{\text{due date} - \text{today's date}}{\text{work (lead) time remaining}}$$

Example 6 shows how to use the critical ratio.

EXAMPLE 6

Today is day 25 on S. Geraud Food's production schedule. Three jobs are on order, as indicated below:

Job	Due Date	Work Days Remaining
A	30	4
B	28	5
C	27	2

We compute the critical ratios, using the formula for CR.

Job	Critical Ratio	Priority Order
A	(30 – 25)/4 = 1.25	3
B	(28 – 25)/5 = .60	1
C	(27 – 25)/2 = 1.00	2

Job B has a critical ratio less than 1, meaning it will be late unless expedited. Thus, it has the highest priority. Job C is on time and job A has some slack.

[7] See R. W. Conway, W. L. Maxwell, and L. W. Miller, *Theory of Scheduling* (Reading, MA: Addison-Wesley, 1976).

The critical-ratio rule can help in most production scheduling systems to do the following:

1. Determine the status of a specific job.
2. Establish relative priority among jobs on a common basis.
3. Relate both stock and make-to-order jobs on a common basis.
4. Adjust priorities (and revise schedules) automatically for changes in both demand and job progress.
5. Dynamically track job progress and location.

Sequencing N Jobs on Two Machines: Johnson's Rule

The next step in complexity is the case where *N* jobs (where *N* is 2 or more) must go through two machines or work centres in the same order. This is called the *N*/2 problem.

Johnson's rule can be used to minimize the processing time for sequencing a group of jobs through two facilities.[8] It also minimizes total idle time on the machines. *Johnson's rule* involves four steps:

Johnson's rule

1. All jobs are to be listed, and the time each requires on a machine is to be shown.
2. We select the job with the shortest activity time. If the shortest time lies with the first machine, the job is scheduled first. If the shortest time lies with the second machine, schedule the job last. Ties in activity times can be broken arbitrarily.
3. Once a job is scheduled, eliminate it.
4. Apply steps 2 and 3 to the remaining jobs, working toward the centre of the sequence.

Example 7 shows how to apply Johnson's Rule.

EXAMPLE 7

Five specialty jobs at a Fredonia, New York, tool and die shop must be processed through two work centres (drill machine and lathe machine). The time for processing each job follows:

WORK (PROCESSING) TIME FOR JOBS (IN HOURS)

JOB	WORK CENTRE 1 (DRILL)	WORK CENTRE 2 (LATHE)
A	5	2
B	3	6
C	8	4
D	10	7
E	7	12

[8]S. M. Johnson, "Optimal Two and Three Stage Production Schedules with Set-Up Times Included," *Naval Research Logistics Quarterly*, 1, no. 1 (March 1954): 61–68.

Scheduling machines and people to provide the services on which we rely is an important part of P/OM. TV stations such as the one shown use algorithms to deal with the scheduling of tape editing machines. The news department's biggest job is taking several hours of video tape daily and editing it down to 7 or 8 one- to two-minute clips plus a four-minute feature and yet have everything in place by the evening news show deadline. Scheduling limited resources is a critical job. It is often tackled by operations personnel using the techniques of this chapter.

1. We wish to set the sequence that will minimize the total processing time for the five jobs. The job with the shortest processing time is A, in work centre 2 (with a time of 2 hours). Because it is at the second centre, schedule A last; eliminate it from consideration.

				A

2. Job B has the next shortest time (3). Because that time is at the first work centre, we schedule it first and eliminate it from consideration.

B				A

3. The next shortest time is job C (4) on the second machine. Therefore, it is placed as late as possible.

B			C	A

4. There is a tie (at 7 hours) for the shortest remaining job. We can place E, which was on the first work centre, first. Then D is placed in the last sequencing position.

B	E	D	C	A

The sequential times are:

Work Centre 1	3	7	10	8	5
Work Centre 2	6	12	7	4	2

The time-phased flow of this job sequence is best illustrated graphically:

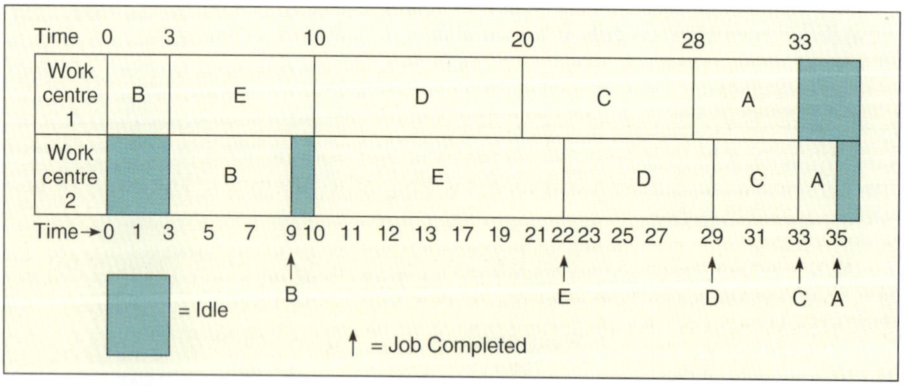

Thus, the five jobs are completed in 35 hours. The second work centre will wait 3 hours for its first job, and it will also wait 1 hour after completing job B.

Sequencing N Jobs on Three Machines

The optimal solution to sequencing N jobs on three machines is quite complicated. However, if either or both of the following conditions are met, the solution is possible by Johnson's rule:

1. The smallest duration on machine 1 is at least as great as the largest duration on machine 2.
2. The smallest duration on machine 3 is at least as great as the largest duration on machine 2.

Example 8 illustrates this concept.

EXAMPLE 8

Consider the following jobs and their processing times at corresponding machines:

	DURATION (HOURS)		
JOB	MACHINE 1, T_1	MACHINE 2, T_2	MACHINE 3, T_3
A	13	5	9
B	5	3	7
C	6	4	5
D	7	2	6

We want to use Johnson's rule to find the optimal sequence. Because both conditions of Johnson's rule are met, we can apply it. First, form a new table as follows:

JOB	$T_1 + T_2$	$T_2 + T_3$
A	18	14
B	8	10
C	10	9
D	9	8

Now, using Johnson's rule for the *N*/2 problem, we get the optimal sequence: B, A, C, D.

Essentially, Johnson's rule converts an *N*/3 problem into an *N*/2 problem, provided that certain conditions are met. Even if these conditions are not met, the rule still provides a near-optimal solution.

Sequencing N Jobs on M Machines

When *several* jobs have to be processed through many facilities, finding an optimal sequence requires a complex search procedure. An efficient heuristic procedure is known as the CDS algorithm.[9] The CDS algorithm extends the *N*/3 Johnson's rule to a general *N*/*M* problem and provides a near-optimal solution.

[9]H. G. Campbell, R. A. Dudek, and M. L. Smith, "A Heuristic Algorithm for the (*n*) Job, (*m*) Machine Sequencing Problem," *Management Science*, 16, no. 10 (June 1970): 630–637.

Bottleneck Work Centres

Bottleneck work centres limit the output of production. Bottlenecks have less capacity than the prior or following work centres. Bottlenecks are a common occurrence because even well-designed systems are seldom balanced for very long. Changing products, product mixes, and volumes often create multiple and shifting bottlenecks. Consequently, bottleneck work centres occur in virtually all production processes, from hospitals and restaurants to factories. Approaches used to address bottlenecks include increasing capacity of the bottleneck, rerouting work, changing lot size, changing work sequence, or accepting idleness at other workstations. Substantial research has been done on the bottleneck issue;[10] an easy-to-read analysis of the bottleneck issue is found in *The Goal: A Process of Ongoing Improvement*.[11]

Bottleneck

To manage her hundreds of retail cookie outlets, Debbi Fields decided to capture her experience in an "expert system" that every store could access at any time. Her Retail Operations Intelligence System (ROIS) takes advantage of headquarters expertise in scheduling minimum-wage employees, the predominant counter help. The software draws up a work schedule, including breaks, to best use hourly employees' time. ROIS also creates a full-day projection of the amount of dough to be processed and charts progress and sales on an hourly basis. It even tells staff when to cut back production and start offering free samples to passing customers.

Limitations of Rule-Based Systems

Traditional rule-based systems have a number of limitations. Among those are

1. Scheduling is dynamic, therefore, rules need to be revised to adjust to changes in process, equipment, product mix, and so forth.
2. Rules do not look upstream or downstream; idle resources and bottleneck resources in other departments may not be recognized.
3. Rules do not look beyond due dates. For instance, two orders may have the same due date. One order involves restocking a distributor and the other is a custom order that will shut down the customer's factory if not completed. Both may have the same due date, but clearly the custom order is more important.

As may be obvious from this list of limitations and from the preceding discussion of bottleneck resources, scheduling can be complex to perform and still yield poor results—not a very fruitful combination. For instance, an operations manager may pick a decision rule such as *critical ratio* and "start the order with the least slack time remaining," or "start the order that uses the same machine setup." Both examples might seem like reasonable decisions. The first focusses on meeting customer due dates and the second focusses on improving efficiency. But the "order with least slack time remaining" may be a very inefficient setup, and the order with the "same setup" may not be needed for a week. Or it may be that the schedule really should include a new order that is to be shipped with an order going out tonight. Our point is that even with sophisticated rules, good scheduling is very difficult.

So how do schedulers tackle the sequencing decisions that have to be made every day? The answer is that in spite of their limitations, they often use sequencing rules such as SPT, EDD, or critical ratio. They apply these methods periodically at each work centre and then the scheduler modifies the sequence to deal with a multitude of real-world variables.

[10]See, for instance, Thomas E. Morton and David W. Pentico, *Heuristic Scheduling Systems* (New York: John Wiley, 1993).

[11]Eliyahu, M. Goldratt, and Jeff Cox, *The Goal: A Process of Ongoing Improvement* (Croton-on-Hudson, NY: North River Press, 1986).

ADVANCES IN SCHEDULING AND SEQUENCING

Two recent advances are proving very beneficial to operations scheduling. They are *expert systems* and *finite scheduling*.

Expert Systems

As described in Chapter 8, an **expert system** is a computer program that makes decisions and solves problems much as a human expert would handle them. The idea in scheduling is to use the knowledge and skills of a person who is an expert at sequencing and scheduling. The firm can then derive the benefits of expert judgement without having the expert present.

Expert system

There is a growing number of scheduling expert systems, dating back to *Intelligent Scheduling and Information System (ISIS)* in 1984.[12] ISIS works by searching for solutions that satisfy the scheduling constraints. When it cannot find a feasible solution, it relaxes the constraints based on their relative importance. Texas Instruments is a company that uses an expert system at its manufacturing plant in Carrolton, Texas. The TI system coordinates the scheduling, dispatching, and tool loading on the plant floor.[13]

Finite Scheduling

The second recent advance is interactive finite scheduling. **Finite scheduling** overcomes the disadvantages of rule-based systems by providing the scheduler with graphical interactive computing. This system is characterized by the ability of the scheduler to make changes based on up-to-the-minute information. These schedules are often displayed in Gantt chart form (see Figure 16.5). The scheduler has the flexibility to handle any situation, including order, labour, or machine changes.

Finite scheduling

Finite scheduling allows delivery needs to be balanced against efficiency based on today's conditions and today's orders, not according to some predefined rule. Many of the current finite scheduling computer programs offer resource constraint features, a multitude of rules, and the ability of the scheduler to work interactively with the scheduling system to create a realistic schedule.[14] These systems may also combine an expert system[15] and simulation techniques[16] and allow the scheduler to assign costs to various options. Finite scheduling helps the scheduler, but leaves it up to the scheduler to determine what constitutes a "good" schedule.

[12]M. S. Fox and S. F. Smith, "ISIS: A Knowledge-Based System for Factory Scheduling." *Expert Systems*, 1, no. 1 (July 1984): 25–49.

[13]J. Lyman, "Manufacturing," *Electronics* (October 16, 1986): 105–106.

[14]Andrew Gilman, "Interest in Finite Scheduling Is Growing ... Why?" *APICS: The Performance Advantage*, 4, no. 8 (August 1994): 45–48.

[15]Factrol, Inc., West Lafayette, Indiana 47906.

[16]AutoSimulations, Bountiful, Utah 84010.

FIGURE 16.5 ■ Most Finite Scheduling Systems Generate a Gantt Chart That Can Be Manipulated by the User on a Computer Screen

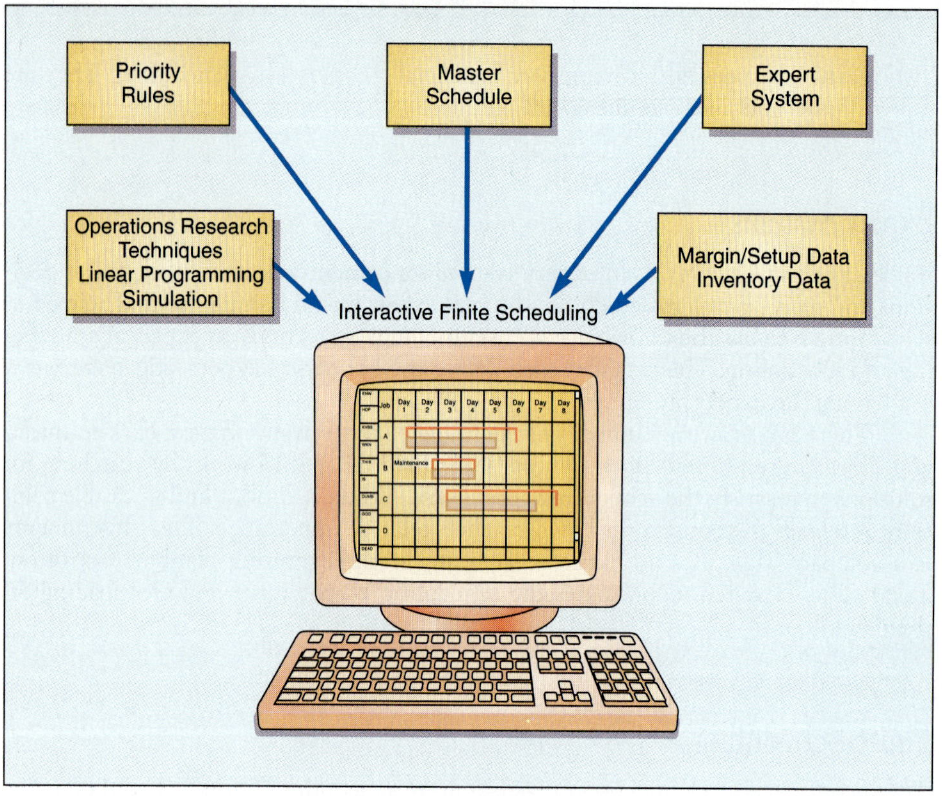

REPETITIVE MANUFACTURING

The scheduling goals as defined at the beginning of this chapter are also appropriate for repetitive production. You may recall from Chapter 7 that repetitive producers make standard products from modules. Repetitive producers want to satisfy customer demands, lower inventory investment, reduce the batch (or lot) size, and utilize equipment and processes. The way to move toward these goals is to move to a level material use schedule. **Level material use** means frequent, high-quality, small lot sizes that contribute to just-in-time production. This is exactly what world-class producers such as Harley-Davidson and John Deere do. The advantages of level material use are:

Level material use

1. Lower inventory levels, which release capital for other uses.
2. Faster product throughput (that is, shorter lead times).
3. Improved component quality and hence improved product quality.
4. Reduced floor-space requirements.
5. Improved communication among employees because they are closer together (which can result in improved teamwork and *esprit de corps*).
6. Smoother production process because large lots have not "hidden" the problems.

TABLE 16.2 ■ L SERIES TRACTOR AT A U.S. TRACTOR MANUFACTURER

MODEL	TRADITIONAL BATCH SIZE (MONTHLY REQUIREMENT; 20-DAY MONTH)	LEVEL MATERIAL USE SCHEDULE (DAILY REQUIREMENT TO MEET DEMAND)
LA30	120	6
LB38	220	11
LB46	180	9
LC38	240	12
LC46	240	12
LD38	500	25
LE38	1,160	58
	2,660	133

Suppose a repetitive producer runs large monthly batches. With a level material use schedule, management would move toward shortening this monthly cycle. Management might run this cycle every week, day, or hour.

Table 16.2 shows a *traditional batch* and a new *level material use* schedule for an actual Midwestern repetitive manufacturer of small tractors. Their daily level material use schedule meets daily demand with substantial savings over the costs of the batch system, which met a monthly demand. All direct costs except material handling have been reduced substantially.

One way to develop a level material use schedule is to determine first the minimum lot size that will keep the production process moving. Ideally, this is the one unit that is being moved from one adjacent process to the next. More realistically, analysis of the process, transportation time, and containers used for transport are considered when determining lot size. Such analysis typically results in a small lot size but a lot size larger than one. Once a lot size has been determined, the EOQ production-run model can be modified to determine the desired setup time. We saw in Chapter 13 that the production-run model takes the form

$$Q^* = \sqrt{\frac{2DS}{H[1-(d/p)]}}$$

where D = annual demand
S = setup cost
H = holding cost
d = daily demand
p = daily production

Example 9 shows how Crate Furniture, Inc., a firm that produces rustic furniture, moves toward a level material use schedule.

EXAMPLE 9

Crate Furniture's production analyst, Aleda Roth, determined that a 2-hour production cycle would be acceptable between two departments. Further, she concluded that a setup time that would accommodate the 2-hour cycle time could be achieved. Aleda developed the following data and procedure to determine analytically that optimum setup time:

D = annual demand = 400,000 units
d = daily demand = 400,000/250 days = 1,600 units per day
p = daily production rate = 4,000 units per day
Q = EOQ desired = 400 (which is the 2-hour demand, that is, 1,600 per day/4 2-hour periods)
H = holding cost = \$20 per unit per year
S = setup cost (to be determined)

Aleda determines that the cost, on an hourly basis, of setting up equipment is \$30. Further, she computes that the setup cost per setup should be

$$Q = \sqrt{\frac{2DS}{H(1 - d/p)}}$$

$$Q^2 = \frac{2DS}{H(1 - d/p)}$$

$$S = \frac{(Q^2)(H)(1 - d/p)}{2D}$$

$$S = \frac{(400)^2(20)(1 - 1{,}600/4{,}000)}{2(400{,}000)}$$

$$= \frac{(3{,}200{,}000)(0.6)}{800{,}000} = \$2.40$$

Setup time = \$2.40/(hourly labour rate)
= \$2.40/(\$30 per hour)
= 0.08 hour, or 4.8 minutes

Now, rather than producing components in large lots, Crate Furniture can produce in a 2-hour cycle with the advantage of an inventory turnover of four *per day*.

Only two changes need to be made for this type of level material flow to work. First is the radical reduction in setup times, which is usually not difficult from a technical point of view. Second, changes may need to be made to improve material handling. With short production cycles, there can be very little wait time.

SCHEDULING FOR SERVICES

Scheduling service systems differs from scheduling manufacturing systems in several ways. First, in manufacturing, the scheduling emphasis of the operations manager is on materials, but in services, it is on staffing levels. Second, service systems do not store inventories of services. Third, services are labour-intensive, and the demand for this labour can be highly variable.

A hospital is an example of a service facility that may use a scheduling system every bit as complex as one found in a job shop. Hospitals seldom use a machine shop priority system such as first-come, first-served (FCFS) for treating emergency case patients. But they do schedule products (such as surgeries) just like a factory, even though finished goods inventories cannot be kept and capacities must meet wide variations in demand.

This section discusses scheduling in four typical service organizations: banks, hospitals, airlines, and restaurants.

Scheduling Bank Personnel with Linear Programming

Linear programming, as we saw in the Supplement to Chapter 6, can be a useful tool for scheduling service employees. Chase Manhattan Bank used this technique to deal with the work-load curve illustrated in Figure 16.6.[17] Employing part-time personnel effectively provided a variable capacity. Part-timers at Chase work at least 4 hours/day, take no lunch, and are not entitled to all of the bank's fringe benefits, making them less expensive than full-timers. But corporate considerations limited the extent to which part-timers could be hired in other departments. So Chase's problem was to find an optimal work-force schedule that would meet labour requirements (in the upper half of Table 16.3), and also be economical. A linear programming model with 18 variables and 21 constraints yielded the schedule seen in the lower half of Table 16.3.

A much larger LP application is discussed in the *POM in Action* box "Scheduling Crews with LP at American Airlines."

Scheduling Nurses with Cyclical Scheduling

Head nurses in large hospitals often spend more than 20 hours a month establishing schedules for their departments. They consider a fairly long planning period (say, 6 weeks) and then need to set timely and efficient schedules so that adequate health care can be delivered to patients while keeping personnel happy with their hours. Although there are several ways of tackling this problem, including linear programming, one approach that is both workable yet simple is *cyclical scheduling*.[18]

Cyclical scheduling has seven steps:

1. Plan a schedule equal in length to the number of people being scheduled.
2. Determine how many of each of the least desirable off-shifts must be covered each week.

[17]S. L. Moondra, "An L.P. Model for Workforce Scheduling for Banks," *Journal of Bank Research* (Winter 1976).

[18]For more details, see R. Murdick, B. Render, and R. Russell, *Service Operations Management* (Boston: Allyn and Bacon, 1990), pp. 336–340, or J. D. Megeath, "Successful Hospital Personnel Scheduling," *Interfaces*, 8, no. 6 (February 1978): 55–59.

TABLE 16.3 ■ RESULTS OF CHASE MANHATTAN LINEAR PROGRAMMING ANALYSIS FOR PERSONNEL SCHEDULING

WORK-FORCE SCHEDULE

TIME PERIOD	NUMBER OF PERSONS REQUIRED	NUMBER OF PERSONS AVAILABLE: FULL-TIME	PART-TIME	TOTAL
9–10 A.M.	14	29	—	29
10–11	25	29	—	29
11–12	26	15	11	26
12–1 P.M.	38	14	26	40
1–2	55	29	26	55
2–3	60	29	31	60
3–4	51	29	22	51
4–5	29	29	5	34
5–6	14	9	5	14
6–7	9	9	0	9

RESULTS USING LP: TIME SCHEDULES

FULL-TIME EMPLOYEES

NUMBER OF EMPLOYEES	STARTING TIME	NUMBER OF EMPLOYEES	LUNCH PERIOD	NUMBER OF EMPLOYEES	LEAVING TIME
29	9 A.M.	14	11–12	20	5 P.M.
		15	12–1	9	7 P.M.

PART-TIME EMPLOYEES

NUMBER OF EMPLOYEES	STARTING TIME	NUMBER OF EMPLOYEES	LEAVING TIME
11	11 A.M.	9	3 P.M.
		2	4 P.M.
15	12 noon	15	4 P.M.
5	2 P.M.	5	6 P.M.

FIGURE 16.6 ■ Work-Load Curve at Chase Manhattan Bank

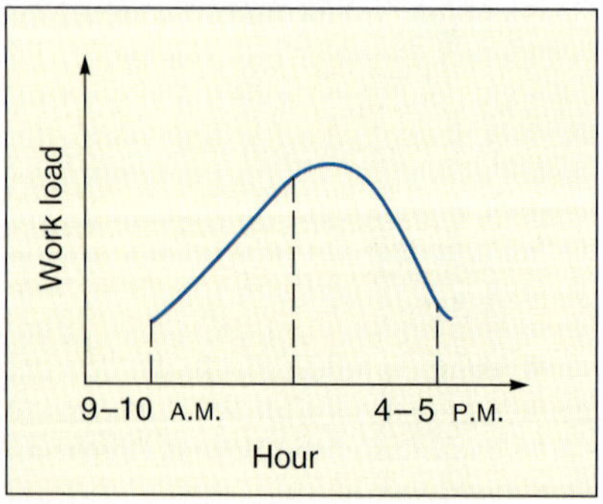

POM IN ACTION

Scheduling Crews with LP at American Airlines

American Airlines employs more than 8,300 pilots and 16,200 flight attendants to fly more than 500 aircraft. Total crew cost exceeds $1.4 billion every year and is second only to fuel cost. But unlike fuel costs, a large part of crew costs is controllable. To develop crew assignment plans that achieve a high level of crew utilization, American relies heavily on linear programming.

Clearly, every airline flight needs a full crew of pilots and flight attendants, but because crew members are people and not machines, scheduling their deployment is considerably more complicated than scheduling the use of aircraft, gates, or other equipment. The FAA has established a complex set of work-time limitations designed to ensure that crew members can safely fulfill their duties.

In addition, financial issues affect scheduling practices. Union contracts specify that flight crews will be guaranteed pay for some number of hours each day or each trip. Therefore, airline planners must try to build crew schedules that meet or exceed the crews' pay guarantees to the maximum extent possible. A trip containing one or more days with small amounts of flying time might be very expensive, because the crews would receive extra pay over and above the assigned flying time.

The LP model, 15 labour-years in the making, assigns crews in 12 cities. It takes about 500 hours of mainframe computer time per month, but generates annual savings of over $20 million. Considered the best scheduling approach for problems of its type, the LP model has been sold by American to 10 other airlines and one railroad.

Sources: Interfaces (January/February 1991): 62–74; and *Management Science* (June 1993): 657–682.

3. Begin the schedule for one nurse by scheduling the days off during the planning cycle (at a rate of 2 days per week on the average).
4. Assign off-shifts for that first nurse using step 2. Here is an example of one nurse's 42-day schedule, where X is the day off, D is the day shift, and E is the evening shift:

S	M	T	W	T	F	S
E	E	E	E	E	X	X

S	M	T	W	T	F	S
X	X	E	E	E	E	E

S	M	T	W	T	F	S
E	D	X	D	D	D	D

S	M	T	W	T	F	S
D	D	X	X	D	E	X

S	M	T	W	T	F	S
X	E	E	E	E	E	X

S	M	T	W	T	F	S
D	E	D	D	X	X	E

5. Repeat this pattern for each of the other nurses, but offsetting each one by 1 week from the previous one.
6. Allow each nurse to pick his or her "slot" or "line" in order of seniority.
7. Mandate that any changes from a chosen schedule are strictly between the personnel wanting to switch.

When this approach was applied at Foothills General Hospital, the head nurse saved an average of 10 to 15 hours a month and found these advantages: (1) no computer was needed, (2) the nurses were happy with the schedule, (3) the cycles could be changed during different seasons (to accommodate avid skiers), and (4) recruiting was easier because of predictability and flexibility.

Large savings of time can also be found in scheduling at small businesses, such as restaurants. As the *POM in Action* box "Scheduling Employees at McDonald's Becomes a Lot Easier" notes, PC-based scheduling systems can be a great boon to managers.

POM IN ACTION

Scheduling Employees at McDonald's Becomes a Lot Easier

Al Boxley, the progressive owner of four McDonald's restaurants in the Cumberland, Maryland, area, faced an operations problem that still haunts most small businesses. Every week, the manager in each of Boxley's restaurants was spending more than 8 hours to prepare manually the work schedules for 150 employees. This weekly routine involved forecasting sales by hour; translating these sales to hourly staff needs in the grill, counter, and drive-through work areas; and then matching the mostly part-time employee availabilities and work skills with McDonald's hourly needs. This time-consuming activity was further complicated by high turnover, movement of employees among restaurants, and constant change in the availability of student workers.

Boxley decided he needed a cheap, simple-to-use, PC-based scheduling system that could seriously cut the manager's time loss. Turning to linear programming, he found that for a restaurant with 3 work areas, 150 employees, and 30 possible work shifts, formulating a scheduling problem results in 100,000 decision variables and 3,000 constraints. Clearly, such a large problem could not be solved very quickly on a PC. But by dividing the LP problem into a number of simpler subproblems (in a process called "decomposition into network flows"), the schedule could actually be developed in only 15 minutes.

The results were impressive: Managers reported an 80–90% reduction in the time it took to generate employee schedules. Costs were kept down by eliminating overstaffing, and employee morale and efficiency were improved. Also, managers now had a valuable "what-if" tool to measure the sensitivity of employee schedules to a variety of operating conditions.

Source: Robert Love and James Hoey, *Interfaces* (March/April 1990): 21–29.

ACHIEVING WORLD-CLASS STANDARDS

Because customers expect deliveries on schedule, world-class firms perform scheduling correctly. Scheduling plays a very large role in employee morale, plant utilization, and winning orders. Consequently, world-class firms are moving toward scheduling systems that use a combination of both computers and people. Increasingly, this means using systems that include dispatching rules, expert systems, simulation, and finite scheduling systems. Computer-generated schedules, adjusted by humans, are proving to yield exceptionally good scheduling. World-class firms such as Pratt & Whitney, LTV, Texas Instruments, and NUCOR have verified this trend. All of these firms are now using one or more of these techniques.

SUMMARY

Scheduling involves the timing of operations to achieve the efficient movement of units through a system. This chapter addressed the issues of short-term scheduling in process-focussed, repetitive, and service environments. We saw that process-focussed facilities are production systems in which products are made to order, and that scheduling tasks in them can become complex. Several aspects and approaches to scheduling, loading, and sequencing of jobs were introduced. These ranged from Gantt charts and the assignment methods of scheduling to a series of priority rules, the critical-ratio rule, and Johnson's rule for sequencing. We also examined the use of level material flow in repetitive manufacturing environments.

Service systems generally differ from manufacturing systems. This leads to the use of appointment systems, first-come, first-served systems, and reservation systems, as well as to heuristics and mathematical programming approaches to servicing customers.

KEY TERMS

Forward scheduling (p. 719)
Backward scheduling (p. 719)
Planning files (p. 721)
Control files (p. 721)
Loading (p. 721)
Input-output control (p. 722)
Gantt charts (p. 723)
Assignment method (p. 725)
Sequencing (p. 728)
Priority rules (p. 728)
FCFS (p. 729)
SPT (p. 729)
EDD (p. 729)
LPT (p. 729)
Critical ratio (p. 732)
Johnson's rule (p. 733)
Bottleneck (p. 736)
Expert system (p. 737)
Finite scheduling (p. 737)
Level material use (p. 738)

USING AB:POM TO SOLVE SCHEDULING PROBLEMS

AB:POM's assignment module is used to solve the traditional one-to-one assignment problem of people to tasks, machines to jobs, and such. Program 16.1 shows the input screen for a three-job, three-machine problem using Example 4's data. The very straightforward output and solution are seen in Program 16.2.

PROGRAM 16.1 ■ AB:POM's Assignment Model Program Using Example 4 Data as Input

Assignment — Data Screen

Number of jobs (2–99) 3 Number of machines (2–99) 3

minimize

EXAMPLE 4 ASSIGNMENT

	MACH A	MACH B	MACH C
R–34	11	14	6
S–66	8	10	11
T–50	9	12	7

PROGRAM 16.2 ■ Output from Assignment Program on Example 4 Data

EXAMPLE 4 ASSIGNMENT

SHIPMENTS	MACH A	MACH B	MACH C
R–34			1
S–66		1	
T–50	1		

The minimum total cost = $25

Note: Alternate optimal solutions exist.

Program 16.3 illustrates AB:POM's job shop scheduling module, which can solve a one- or two-machine job shop problem. Example 5's data are used as input. Outputs appear on the same screen.

PROGRAM 16.3 ■ AB:POM's Job Shop Scheduling Program Using Example 5 Data. Available priority rules include SPT, FCFS, EDD, and LPT. Each can be examined in turn once the data are all entered.

Job Shop Sequencing — Solution

Number of jobs (1–14) 5 Number of machines (1–2) 1

AJAX COMPANY, EXAMPLE 5

SPT	mach. 1	Due Dat	EXTRA	Order	Flow tm	Tardy
JOB A	6	8	0	third	11	3
JOB B	2	6	0	first	2	0
JOB C	8	18	0	fourth	19	1
JOB D	3	15	0	second	5	0
JOB E	9	23	0	fifth	28	5
Average # of jobs in system = 2.32				TOTAL	65	9
SEQUENCE				AVERAGE	13.00	1.80

JOB B, JOB D, JOB A, JOB C, JOB E

SOLVED PROBLEMS

Solved Problem 16.1

Prairie Finance Corporation, headquartered in Edmonton, Alberta, wants to assign three recently hired university graduates, Julie Jones, Al Smith, and Pat Wilson, to regional offices. But the firm also has an opening in Edmonton and would send one of the three there if it were more economical than a move to Calgary, Winnipeg, or Saskatoon. It will cost $1,000 to relocate Jones in Edmonton, $800 to relocate Smith there, and $1,500 to move Wilson. What is the optimal assignment of personnel to offices?

HIREE \ OFFICE	CALGARY	SASKATOON	WINNIPEG
Jones	$800	$1,100	$1,200
Smith	$500	$1,600	$1,300
Wilson	$500	$1,000	$2,300

Solution

(a) The cost table has a fourth column to represent Edmonton. To "balance" the problem, we add a "dummy" row (person) with a zero relocation cost to each city.

HIREE \ OFFICE	CALGARY	SASKATOON	WINNIPEG	EDMONTON
Jones	$800	$1,100	$1,200	$1,000
Smith	$500	$1,600	$1,300	$ 800
Wilson	$500	$1,000	$2,300	$1,500
Dummy	0	0	0	0

(b) Subtract the smallest number in each row and cover all zeroes (column subtraction will give the same numbers and therefore is not necessary).

HIREE \ OFFICE	CALGARY	SASKATOON	WINNIPEG	EDMONTON
Jones	0	300	400	200
Smith	0	1,100	800	300
Wilson	0	500	1,800	1,000
Dummy	0	0	0	0

(c) Subtract the smallest uncovered number (200), add it to each square where two lines intersect, and cover all zeroes.

HIREE \ OFFICE	CALGARY	SASKATOON	WINNIPEG	EDMONTON
Jones	0	100	200	0
Smith	0	900	600	100
Wilson	0	300	1,600	800
Dummy	200	0	0	0

(d) Subtract the smallest uncovered number (100), add it to each square where two lines intersect, and cover all zeroes.

HIREE \ OFFICE	CALGARY	SASKATOON	WINNIPEG	EDMONTON
Jones	0	0	100	0
Smith	0	800	500	100
Wilson	0	200	1,500	800
Dummy	300	0	0	100

(e) Subtract the smallest uncovered number (100), add it to squares where two lines intersect, and cover all zeroes.

HIREE \ OFFICE	CALGARY	SASKATOON	WINNIPEG	EDMONTON
Jones	100	0	100	0
Smith	0	700	400	0
Wilson	0	100	1,400	700
Dummy	400	0	0	100

(f) Because it takes four lines to cover all zeroes, an optimal assignment can be made at zero squares. We assign

Dummy (no one) to Winnipeg
Wilson to Calgary
Smith to Edmonton
Jones to Saskatoon

$$\text{Cost} = \$0 + \$500 + \$800 + \$1{,}100 = \$2{,}400$$

Solved Problem 16.2

A defense contractor in Ottawa has six jobs awaiting processing. Processing time and due dates are given below. Assume jobs arrive in the order shown. Set the processing sequence according to FCFS and evaluate.

Job	Job Processing Time (days)	Job Due Date (days)
A	6	22
B	12	14
C	14	30
D	2	18
E	10	25
F	4	34

Solution

FCFS has the sequence A–B–C–D–E–F.

Job Sequence	Job Processing Time	Flow Time	Due Date	Job Lateness
A	6	6	22	0
B	12	18	14	4
C	14	32	30	2
D	2	34	18	16
E	10	44	25	19
F	4	48	34	14
	48	182		55

1. Average completion time = 182/6 = 30.33.
2. Average no. jobs in system = 182/48 = 3.79.
3. Average job lateness = 55/6 = 9.16 days.
4. Utilization = 48/182 = 26.4%.

Solved Problem 16.3

The Ottawa firm noted in Solved Problem 16.2 wants also to consider job sequencing by the SPT priority rule. Apply SPT to the same data and provide a recommendation.

Solution

SPT has the sequence D–F–A–E–B–C.

Job Sequence	Job Processing Time	Flow Time	Due Date	Job Lateness
D	2	2	18	0
F	4	6	34	0
A	6	12	22	0
E	10	22	25	0
B	12	34	14	20
C	14	48	30	18
	48	124		38

1. Average completion time = 124/6 = 20.67 days.
2. Average no. jobs in system = 124/48 = 2.58.
3. Average job lateness = 38/6 = 6.33 days.
4. Utilization = 48/124 = 38.7%.

SPT is superior to FCFS in this case on all four measures. If we were to also analyze EDD, we would, however, find its average job lateness to be lowest at 5.5 days. SPT is a good recommendation. SPT's major disadvantage is that it makes long jobs wait, sometimes for a long time.

Solved Problem 16.4

Use Johnson's rule to find the optimum sequence for processing the jobs below through two work centres. Times at each centre are in hours.

Job	Work Centre 1	Work Centre 2
A	6	12
B	3	7
C	18	9
D	15	14
E	16	8
F	10	15

Solution

B	A	F	D	C	E

The sequential times are

Work Centre 1	3	6	10	15	18	16
Work Centre 2	7	12	15	14	9	8

Solved Problem 16.5

Illustrate the throughput time and idle time at the two work centres in Solved Problem 16.4 by constructing a time-phased chart.

Solution

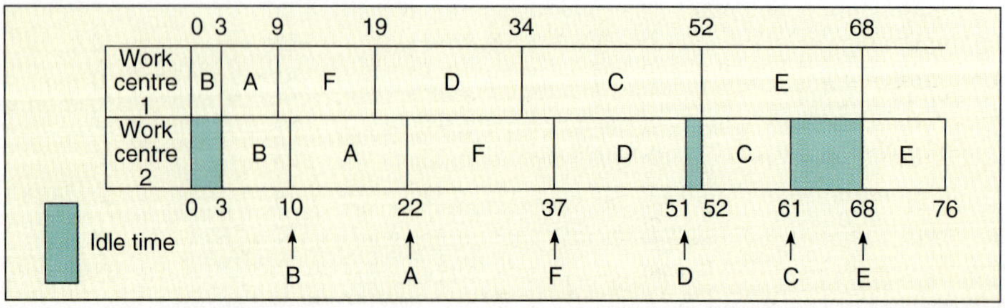

Solved Problem 16.6

Swearingen Products makes microwave ovens and desires to move to a level material use schedule for the various components used in those ovens. The firm has traditionally made both components and units in large batches and stored them in inventory until needed because the foreperson liked it that way. Because the foreperson retired last week, the president, John Swearingen, wants to move to a level material use schedule. When reviewing the flow of the first component, a control panel, the P/OM analyst found that the standard tote tray holds 2 hours of assembly-line work (100 units) and that move time is less than 1 hour even when allowing for the occasional delay that sometimes occurs. With these data, the analyst concludes that a 3-hour cycle would be a good place to begin. Swearingen's production data for control panels are:

Annual demand = 104,000
Daily demand rate = 400
Daily production rate = 1,000
Desired lot size (a 3-hour supply) = 300
Holding cost = $10 per unit per year
Setup labour cost per hour = $12

What should be the setup time?

Solution

$$Q = \sqrt{\frac{2DS}{H(1 - d/p)}}$$

$$Q^2 = \frac{2DS}{H(1 - d/p)}$$

$$S = \frac{Q^2H(1 - d/p)}{2D} = \text{setup cost per setup}$$

$$S = \frac{(300)^2(10)(1 - 400/1{,}000)}{2(104{,}000)} = (4.327)(.6) = \$2.59$$

Setup time = $2.59/(labour rate per hour)
= $2.59/($12) = 0.1295 hour = 7.77 minutes

DISCUSSION QUESTIONS

1. Name five priority sequencing rules. Explain how each works to assign jobs.
2. When is Johnson's rule best applied in scheduling?
3. Describe the differences between forward and backward scheduling.
4. What is the difference between a Gantt load chart and a Gantt schedule chart?
5. Briefly describe how the assignment method works.
6. What is the most popular priority rule and why?
7. Why is the scheduling of services a difficult problem?
8. What is input-output control? How does it help the operations manager?
9. What are the criteria by which we evaluate sequencing rules?
10. What are the advantages of level material flow?
11. How does a bottleneck work centre impact scheduling?

CRITICAL THINKING EXERCISE

Scheduling people to work the late, or "graveyard," shift is a problem in almost every 24-hour company. The *POM in Action* box "Scheduling Workers Who Fall Asleep on the Job Is Not Easy" describes night-shift dilemmas at an oil refinery and a police department. Scheduling is also difficult for airlines that fly long routes, such as El Al Airline's popular 11-hour nonstop Tel Aviv–to–New York flight.

Select five companies that require night shifts and discuss how each can deal with its staffing requirements. What are the major issues in each that impact on morale, productivity, alertness, and safety?

PROBLEMS

: **16.1** David Gillespie's company has scheduled five jobs. Today, which is day 7, David is reviewing the Gantt chart depicting these schedules.

- Job A was scheduled to begin on day 3 and to take 6 days. As of now, it is 1 day ahead of schedule.
- Job B was scheduled to begin on day 1 and take 4 days. It is currently on time.
- Job C was scheduled to start on day 7 and take 3 days. It actually got started on day 6 and is progressing according to plan.
- Job D was scheduled to begin on day 5, but missing equipment delayed it until day 6. It is progressing as expected and should take 3 days.
- Job E was scheduled to begin on day 4 and take 5 days. It got started on time, but has since fallen behind 2 days.

Draw the Gantt chart as it looks to David.

• **16.2** Alice Harra's company wishes to assign a set of jobs to a set of machines. The following table provides data as to the productivity of each machine when performing the specific job.

a) Determine the most appropriate assignments of jobs to machines so as to maximize total productivity.

b) What is the total cost of your assignments?

Job \ Machine	A	B	C	D
1	7	9	8	10
2	10	9	7	6
3	11	5	9	6
4	9	11	5	8

• **16.3** Bill Hendee's company wishes to assign a set of jobs to a set of machines. The following table provides data as to the cost of each job when performed on a specific machine.

a) Determine the most appropriate assignments of jobs to machines so as to minimize Bill's total cost.

b) What is the total cost of your assignments?

JOB \ MACHINE	A	B	C	D
1	7	9	8	10
2	10	9	7	6
3	11	5	9	6
4	9	11	5	8

: **16.4** JH Products Corporation has four more jobs to be scheduled, in addition to those shown in Example 3. JH production scheduling personnel are reviewing the Gantt chart at the end of day 4.

- Job D was scheduled to begin early on day 2 and to end on the middle of day 9. As of now (the review point after day 4), it is 2 days ahead of schedule.
- Job E should begin on day 1 and end on day 3. It was on time.
- Job F was to begin on day 3, but maintenance forced a delay of 1½ days. The job should now take 5 full days. It is now on schedule.
- Job G is a day behind schedule. It started at the beginning of day 2 and should require 6 days to complete.

Develop a Gantt schedule chart for JH Corporation.

· **16.5** The operations manager of King Manufacturing must assign three tasks to three machines. Cost data are presented below.

JOB \ MACHINE	#1	#2	#3
C-3	$800	$1,100	$1,200
C-5	$500	$1,600	$1,300
C-8	$500	$1,000	$2,300

Use the assignment algorithm to solve this problem.

: **16.6** The scheduler at a small midwestern Canadian plant has six jobs that can be processed on any of six machines, with respective times as shown (in hours) below. Determine the allocation of jobs to machines that will result in minimum time.

	MACHINE					
JOB	#1	#2	#3	#4	#5	#6
A-52	60	22	34	42	30	60
A-53	22	52	16	32	18	48
A-56	29	16	58	28	22	55
A-59	42	32	28	46	15	30
A-60	30	18	25	15	45	42
A-61	50	48	57	30	44	60

• **16.7** The hospital administrator at St. Charles General must appoint head nurses to four newly established departments: urology, cardiology, orthopedics, and obstetrics. In anticipation of this staffing problem, she had hired four nurses: Hawkins, Condriac, Bardot, and Hoolihan. Believing in the P/OM analysis approach to problem solving, the administrator has interviewed all the nurses; considered their backgrounds, personalities, and talents; and developed a cost scale ranging from 0 to 100 to be used in the assignment. A 0 for Nurse Hawkins being assigned to the cardiology unit implies that she would be perfectly suited to that task. A value close to 100, on the other hand, would imply that she is not at all suited to head that unit. The accompanying table gives the complete set of cost figures that the hospital administrator felt represented all possible assignments. Which nurse should be assigned to which unit?

	Department			
Nurse	**Urology**	**Cardiology**	**Orthopedics**	**Obstetrics**
Hawkins	28	18	15	75
Condriac	32	48	23	38
Bardot	51	36	24	36
Hoolihan	25	38	55	12

• **16.8** The Gleaming Company has just developed a new dishwashing liquid and is preparing for a national television promotional campaign. The firm has decided to schedule a series of 1-minute commercials during the peak housewife audience viewing hours of 1:00 to 5:00 P.M. To reach the widest possible audience, Gleaming wants to schedule one commercial on each of four networks and have one commercial appear during each of the four 1-hour time blocks. The exposure ratings for each hour, representing the number of viewers per $1,000 spent, are presented in the accompanying table. Which network should be scheduled each hour in order to provide the maximum audience exposure?

	Networks			
Time	**A**	**B**	**C**	**Independent**
1:00–2:00 P.M.	27.1	18.1	11.3	9.5
2:00–3:00 P.M.	18.9	15.5	17.1	10.6
3:00–4:00 P.M.	19.2	18.5	9.9	7.7
4:00–5:00 P.M.	11.5	21.4	16.8	12.8

: **16.9** The Kevin Johnson Manufacturing Company is putting out seven new electronic components. Each of Johnson's eight plants has the capacity to add one more product to its current line of electronic parts. The unit manufacturing costs for producing the different parts at the eight plants are shown in the accompanying table. How should Johnson assign the new products to the plants in order to minimize manufacturing costs?

Electronic Components	Plants 1	2	3	4	5	6	7	8
C53	10¢	12¢	13¢	11¢	10¢	6¢	16¢	12¢
C81	5	6	4	8	4	9	6	6
D5	32	40	31	30	42	35	36	49
D44	17	14	19	15	10	16	19	12
E2	6	7	10	5	8	10	11	5
E35	8	10	12	8	9	10	9	6
G99	55	62	61	70	62	63	65	59

:16.10 The following jobs are waiting to be processed at the same machine centre. Jobs are logged as they arrive:

Job	Due Date	Duration (Days)
A	313	8
B	312	16
C	325	40
D	314	5
E	314	3

In what sequence would the jobs be ranked according to the following decision rules: (a) FCFS, (b) EDD, (c) SPT, and (d) LPT? All dates are specified as manufacturing planning calendar days. Assume that all jobs arrive on day 275. Which decision is best and why?

•16.11 Suppose that today is day 300 on the planning calendar and that we have not started any of the jobs given in Problem 16.10. Using the critical-ratio technique, in what sequence would you schedule these jobs?

:16.12 A British Columbia lumberyard has four jobs on order, as shown below. Today is day 205 on the yard's schedule. Establish processing priorities.

Job	Due Date	Remaining Time in Days
A	212	6
B	209	3
C	208	3
D	210	8

:16.13 The following jobs are waiting to be processed at a small machine centre:

JOB	DUE DATE	DURATION (DAYS)
010	260	30
020	258	16
030	260	8
040	270	20
050	275	10

In what sequence would the jobs be ranked according to the following decision rules: (a) FCFS, (b) EDD, (c) SPT, and (d) LPT? All dates are specified as manufacturing planning calendar days. Assume that all jobs arrive on day 210. Which is the best decision rule?

:16.14 The following jobs are waiting to be processed at Bill Leonard's machine centre:

JOB	DATE ORDER RECEIVED	PRODUCTION DAYS NEEDED	DATE ORDER DUE
A	110	20	180
B	120	30	200
C	122	10	175
D	125	16	230
E	130	18	210

In what sequence would the jobs be ranked according to the following rules: (a) FCFS, (b) EDD, (c) SPT, and (d) LPT? All dates are according to shop calendar days. Today on the planning calendar is day 130. Which rule is best?

·16.15 Suppose that today is day 150 on the planning calendar and that we have not yet started any of the jobs in Problem 16.14. Using the critical-ratio technique, in what sequence would you schedule these jobs?

:16.16 Barry Automation Company estimates the data entry and verifying times for four jobs as follows:

JOB	DATA ENTRY (HOURS)	VERIFY (HOURS)
A	2.5	1.7
B	3.8	2.6
C	1.9	1.0
D	1.8	3.0

In what order should the jobs be done if the company has one operator for each job? Illustrate the time-phased flow of this job sequence graphically.

:16.17 Six jobs are to be processed through a two-step operation. The first operation involves sanding and the second involves painting. Processing times are as follows:

JOB	OPERATION 1 (HOURS)	OPERATION 2 (HOURS)
A	10	5
B	7	4
C	5	7
D	3	8
E	2	6
F	4	3

Determine a sequence that will minimize the total completion time for these jobs. Illustrate graphically.

:16.18 Consider the following jobs and their processing times at the three machines. No passing of jobs is allowed.

JOB	MACHINE 1 (HOURS)	MACHINE 2 (HOURS)	MACHINE 3 (HOURS)
A	6	4	7
B	5	2	4
C	9	3	10
D	7	4	5
E	11	5	2

Using Johnson's rule, find the sequence in which the jobs are to be processed.

:16.19 Bill Penny has a repetitive manufacturing plant producing trailer hitches in St. John's, Newfoundland. The plant has an average inventory of only 12 turns per year. He has, therefore, determined that he will reduce his component lot sizes. He has developed the following data for one component, the safety chain clip.

Annual demand = 31,200

Daily demand = 120

Daily production = 960

Desired lot size (1 hour of production) = 120 units

Holding cost per unit per year = $12

Setup labour cost per hour = $20

What setup time should he have his plant manager aim for regarding this component?

:16.20 Mark Davis is the manager of the body shop at Cumberland Ford. On Monday morning, he arrived at work at 7:30 A.M. and discovered that the firm's wrecker service had towed in five automobiles involved in weekend accidents. In all cases, the owners had authorized Cumberland Ford to make all necessary repairs. Mark carefully analyzed the extent of damage to each car and noted the amount of time (in hours) that each car would require at each station in the body shop. The following table shows these time estimates.

AUTOMOBILE	METAL WORK AND REPLACEMENT OF PARTS	SANDING AND MASKING	PAINTING AND BAKING
Crown Victoria	9 hours	8 hours	2 hours
Mustang	12	6	3
Escort	10	3	5
Tempo	8	7	4
T Bird	14	2	1

Mark wanted to minimize waiting time and total time consumed in repairing the five automobiles. However, he was uncertain about the priority to give each car to accomplish this objective. After rechecking his time estimates for accuracy, he pondered his decision.

a) Suggest a scheduling method that Mark could substitute for his "trial-and-error, hit-or-miss" sequencing decisions. Illustrate.

b) In what sequence should the cars be routed through the various operations to minimize waiting time and total time consumed?

DATA BASE APPLICATION

:16.21 NASA's astronaut crew currently includes 10 mission specialists who hold a Ph.D. in either astrophysics or astromedicine. One of these specialists will be assigned to each of the 10 flights scheduled for the upcoming 9 months. Mission specialists are responsible for carrying out scientific and medical experiments in space or for launching, retrieving, or repairing satellites. The chief of astronaut personnel, himself a former crew member with three missions under his belt, must decide who should be assigned and trained for each of the very different missions. Clearly, astronauts with medical educations are more suited to missions involving biological or medical experiments, whereas those with engineering- or physics-oriented degrees are best suited to other types of missions. The chief assigns each astronaut a rating on a scale of 1 to 10 for each possible mission, with a 10 being a perfect match for the task at hand and a 1 being a mismatch. Only one specialist is assigned to each flight, and none is reassigned until all others have flown at least once.

	MISSION									
ASTRONAUT	JAN. 12	JAN. 27	FEB. 5	FEB. 26	MAR. 26	APR. 12	MAY 1	JUN. 9	AUG. 20	SEP. 19
Vincze	9	7	2	1	10	9	8	9	2	6
Veit	8	8	3	4	7	9	7	7	4	4
Anderson	2	1	10	10	1	4	7	6	6	7
Herbert	4	4	10	9	9	9	1	2	3	4
Schatz	10	10	9	9	8	9	1	1	1	1
Plane	1	3	5	7	9	7	10	10	9	2
Certo	9	9	8	8	9	1	1	2	2	9
Moses	3	2	7	6	4	3	9	7	7	9
Brandon	5	4	5	9	10	10	5	4	9	8
Drtina	10	10	9	7	6	7	5	4	8	8

a) Who should be assigned to which flight?

b) We have just been notified that Anderson is getting married in February and he has been granted a highly sought publicity tour in Europe that month. (He intends to take his wife and let the trip double as a honeymoon.) How does this change the final schedule?

c) Certo has complained that he was misrated on his January mission. Both ratings should be 10's, he claims to the chief, who agrees and recomputes the schedule. Do any changes occur over the schedule set in part (b)?

d) What are the strengths and weaknesses of this approach to scheduling?

CASE STUDY

Old Ontario Wood Store

In 1995, George Brown started the Old Ontario Wood Store to manufacture Old Ontario tables. Each table is carefully constructed by hand, using the highest-quality oak.

The manufacturing process consists of four steps: preparation, assembly, finishing, and packaging. Each step is performed by one person. In addition to overseeing the entire operation, George does all of the finishing. Tom Surowski performs the preparation step, which involves cutting and forming the basic components of the tables. Leon Davis is in charge of the assembly, and Cathy Stark performs the packaging.

Although each person is responsible for only one step in the manufacturing process, everyone can perform any one of the steps. It is George's policy that occasionally everyone should complete several tables on his or her own without any help or assistance. A small competition is used to see who can complete an entire table in the least amount of time. George maintains average total and intermediate completion times. The data are shown in Figure 16.7.

FIGURE 16.7 ■ Manufacturing Time in Minutes

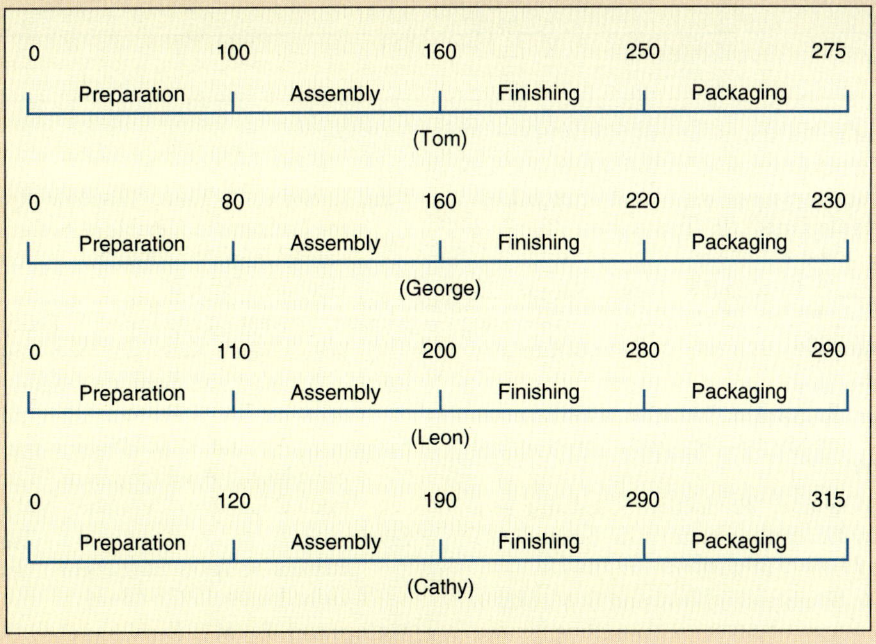

(Continued)

It takes Cathy longer than the other employees to construct an Old Ontario table. In addition to being slower than the other employees, Cathy is also unhappy about her current responsibility of packaging, which leaves her idle most of the day. Her first preference is finishing, and her second preference is preparation.

In addition to quality, George is concerned with costs and efficiency. When one of the employees misses a day, it causes major scheduling problems. Overtime is expensive, and waiting for the employee to return to work causes delay and sometimes stops the entire manufacturing process.

To overcome some of these problems, Randy Lane was hired. Randy's major duties are to perform miscellaneous jobs and to help out if one of the employees is absent. George has given Randy training in all phases of the manufacturing process, and he is pleased with the speed at which Randy has been able to learn how to completely assemble Old Ontario tables. Total and intermediate completion times for Randy are given in Figure 16.8.

DISCUSSION QUESTIONS

1. What is the fastest way to manufacture Old Ontario tables using the original crew? How many could be made per day?
2. Would production rates and quantities change significantly if George would allow Randy to perform one of the four functions and make one of the original crew the backup person?
3. What is the fastest time to manufacture a table with the original crew if Cathy is moved to either preparation or finishing?
4. Whoever performs the packaging function is severely underutilized. Can you find a better way of utilizing the 4- or 5-person crew than either giving each a single job or allowing each to manufacture an entire table? How many tables could be manufactured per day with this scheme?

Source: B. Render and R. M. Stair, *Quantitative Analysis for Management*, 5th ed. (Boston: Allyn and Bacon, 1994), p. 583. Modified for the Canadian edition.

FIGURE 16.8 ■ Manufacturing Time in Minutes for Randy Lane

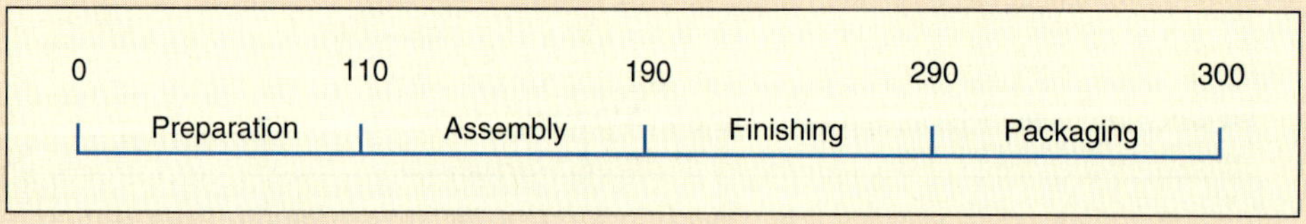

BIBLIOGRAPHY

Akinc, U. "A Practical Approach to Lot and Setup Scheduling at a Textile Firm." *IIE Transactions*, 25, no. 2 (March 1993): 54–64.

Anbil, R., E. Gelman, B. Patty, and R. Tanga. "Recent Advances in Crew-Pairing Optimization at American Airlines." *Interfaces*, 21, no. 1 (January/February 1991): 62–74.

Bauer, A., J. Browne, R. Bowden, J. Duggan, and G. Lyons. *Shop Floor Control Systems*. New York: Van Nostrand Reinhold, 1991.

Ghosh, S., and C. Gaimon. "Production Scheduling in a Flexible Manufacturing System with Setups." *IIE Transactions*, 25, no. 5 (September 1993): 21.

Gopalakrishnan, M., S. Gopalakrishnan, and D. M. Miller. "A Decision Support System for Scheduling Personnel in a Newspaper Publishing Environment." *Interfaces*, 23, no. 4 (July/August 1993): 104–115.

Kim, Y., and C. A. Yano. "Heuristic Approaches for Loading Problems in Flexible Manufacturing Systems." *Industrial Engineering Research & Development*, 25, no. 1 (January 1993): 26.

Morton, Thomas E., and David W. Pentico. *Heuristic Scheduling Systems*. New York: John Wiley, 1993.

Render, B., and R. M. Stair. *Quantitative Analysis for Management*, 5th ed. Boston: Allyn and Bacon, 1994.

Schartner, A., and J. M. Pruett. "Interactive Job Shop Scheduling: An Experiment." *Decision Sciences*, 22, no. 5 (November/December 1991).

Sivakumar, R. A., R. Batta, and K. Tehrani. "Scheduling Repairs at Texas Instruments." *Interfaces*, 23, no. 4 (July/August 1993): 68–74.

Vollmann, T. E., W. L. Berry, and D. C. Whybark. *Manufacturing Planning and Control Systems*, 3rd ed. Homewood, IL: Irwin, 1992.

17

PROJECT MANAGEMENT

CHAPTER OUTLINE

LEARNING OBJECTIVES

When you complete this chapter you should be able to:

Identify or define:

- Activity
- Event
- Critical path
- PERT/cost
- Dummy activity

Explain:

- Critical path method (CPM)
- Program evaluation and review technique (PERT)
- Crashing a project

WORLD-CLASS PROFILE: BECHTEL

PROJECT MANAGEMENT PROVIDES A COMPETITIVE ADVANTAGE FOR BECHTEL

Fire-fighting crews relied on explosives and heavy machinery to remove the hardened petroleum residue that had formed around many wells. Even a day after a fire is out, the surface is still hot enough to boil water.

More than 200 lagoons filled with more than 3,500 kilolitres of seawater were built. Pumps and hose lines to throw 23 kilolitres of water a minute were installed.

In the late fall of 1990, Iraq invaded Kuwait. In one final devastating act before Iraq's defeat in "Operation Desert Storm," Saddam Hussein torched the oil wells of Kuwait. To begin the rebuilding of its lands, the government of Kuwait called in one of the world's largest construction firms, Bechtel, which is headquartered in San Francisco. When the first three-member Bechtel advance team landed, within days of Desert Storm's end, the panorama of destruction was breathtaking.

Nearly 650 wells were ablaze, and others were gushing thousands of barrels of oil into dark lakes in the desert. Fire roared out of the ground from virtually every compass point.

Restoring the oil fields of Kuwait was a monumental project. There was no water, electricity, food, or facilities. Also, the country was littered with unexploded mines, bombs, grenades, and artillery shells. Finally, a good portion of the fires were inaccessible as lakes of oil-covered roads and fire spread to the ground surrounding many of the wells.

Even for Bechtel, whose competitive advantage is project management, this was a first-of-a-kind logistics problem. The number of specific project events that needed to be identified and accomplished was huge. Bechtel launched an on-site assessment effort, with a worldwide planning team to support the effort. A major global procurement program was needed. Bechtel equipment specialists in San Francisco, Houston, and London were called on to tap the company's computer network of buyers and suppliers worldwide.

Then the issue was how to feed, house, and equip a work force

The dense black clouds produced by burning oil wells turned day into night and added new meaning to "reading by firelight."

that would grow into thousands by the time the effort was fully mobilized.

About 550 miles to the southeast of Kuwait, at the port of Dubai, Bechtel established storage, docking, and warehousing facilities. As a central transshipment point into Kuwait, the port received and processed hundreds of shipments from chartered seacraft and aircraft.

The Bechtel project management team procured, shipped, and deployed more than 113,000 tonnes of equipment and supplies, including some 4,000 pieces of operating equipment, ranging from bulldozers to ambulances. The team also managed a work force that laid some 150 kilometres of pipeline, capable of delivering 75,700 kilolitres of water a day to the fire site.

The Bechtel project management team also mobilized:

- an international force of nearly 8,000 manual workers
- 1,000 project and construction professionals
- 6 full-service dining halls
- 27,000 meals a day
- 2 helicopter evacuation teams
- a 40-bed field hospital
- a team of 100 medical personnel for seven medical stations

The fires are out. Kuwait is once again shipping oil and Bechtel has demonstrated its competitive advantage—project management.

Source: Adapted from *Bechtel Briefs*, San Francisco: Bechtel.

The damage was extensive to facilities as well as oil fields and each item had to be included in the schedule that the project managers developed to tackle this huge problem.

The deadline problems Microsoft experienced with Windows NT in 1993 plagued their Windows 95 project also, but the delay did not cause a loss of market share for Microsoft, as its chief desktop operation system competitor, IBM's OS/2 Warp, had not been well received. Windows 95 has sold 40 million copies during the first year since its release.

The mid-1996 release of NT4.0, a higher-level operating system, appears to have been more on schedule. Now Microsoft plans to spend about $2 billion on R&D in 1997 on projects such as (1) Microsoft Exchange, a new competitor to IBM's Lotus Notes, (2) an Internet-based travel agency, and (3) a stock trading service.

More than 8,000 technical staff are employed by Microsoft on these and similar projects. Project teams are now in place for these high-profile ventures. ♦

At one point or another, almost every organization will take on a large and complex project like the one David Cutler managed for Microsoft Corp. A construction company like Bechtel, helping to restore Kuwait's oil wells, must complete thousands of costly activities. A government agency installing and debugging an expensive computer spends months preparing the details for smooth conversion to new equipment. An oil refinery about to shut down for a major maintenance project faces astronomical expenses if this difficult task is unduly delayed for any reason. The problem every time is how to manage such a complicated project effectively.

Large, often one-time, projects are difficult challenges to operations managers. The stakes are high. Millions of dollars in cost overruns can be wasted due to poor planning on projects. Unnecessary delays can occur due to poor scheduling. And companies can go bankrupt due to poor controls.

Special projects that take months or years to complete are usually developed outside the normal production system. Project organizations within the firm are set up to handle such jobs and are often disbanded when the project is complete. The management of large projects involves three phases (see Figure 17.1):

1. *Planning*. This includes goal setting, defining the project, and team organization. Note in Figure 17.1 that it is completed before the project even begins.
2. *Scheduling*. This relates people, money, and supplies to specific activities and relates activities to each other.
3. *Controlling*. Here the firm monitors resources, costs, quality, and budgets. It also revises/changes plans and shifts resources to meet time and cost demands.

PROJECT PLANNING

For the construction of family housing in a new subdivision, a large number of diverse tasks must be scheduled and completed. In order to compete successfully and generate a profit for their shareholders, construction firms must complete the projects on time and within cost parameters. Project control is the core of a construction firm's success.

Construction clearly involves myriad activities that must be carried out in proper sequence. For example, on day one of such a project, the arrival of a truckload of roofing materials would be inappropriate! Such materials are not needed for weeks, even months. Also, early arrival means storage costs, potential theft, and deterioria-

FIGURE 17.1 ■ Project Planning, Scheduling, and Controlling

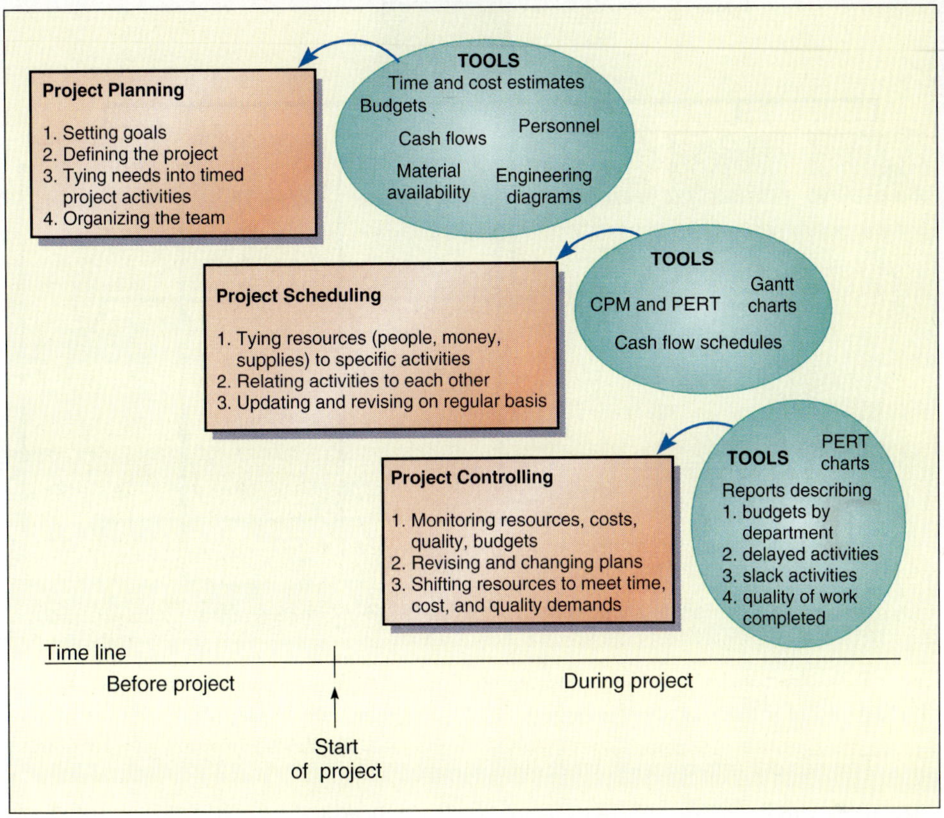

Toronto's SkyDome, home of the Toronto Blue Jays (American League) and the Toronto Argonauts (Canadian Football League), was built by Ellis-Don Construction. The SkyDome was a world-class project, managed by the techniques discussed in this chapter.

tion—not to mention financing problems, as the roofing supplier will be requesting payment. *The concept of "just-in-time" must be applied to projects as well as to manufacturing inventories.*

Projects can usually be defined as a series of related tasks or activities directed toward a major output. A **project organization** is developed to make sure existing programs continue to run smoothly on a day-to-day basis while new projects are successfully completed.

Project organization

A project organization is an effective way of pooling the people and physical resources needed for a limited time to complete a specific project. It is basically a temporary organization structure designed to achieve results by using specialists from throughout the firm.

For many years, NASA successfully used the project approach to reach its goals. You may recall Project Gemini and Project Apollo. These terms were used to describe teams NASA organized to reach space exploration objectives. Specialized project teams were also put together for such projects as Toronto's SkyDome and Vancouver's BC Place. A team may soon be formed to plan, locate, and build a new professional sports arena in Toronto to accommodate both the Toronto Maple Leafs and the Toronto Raptors. In the past decade, project teams have completed new sports arenas in Montreal, New York, Boston, Detroit, and Chicago.

FIGURE 17.2 ■ A Sample Project Organization

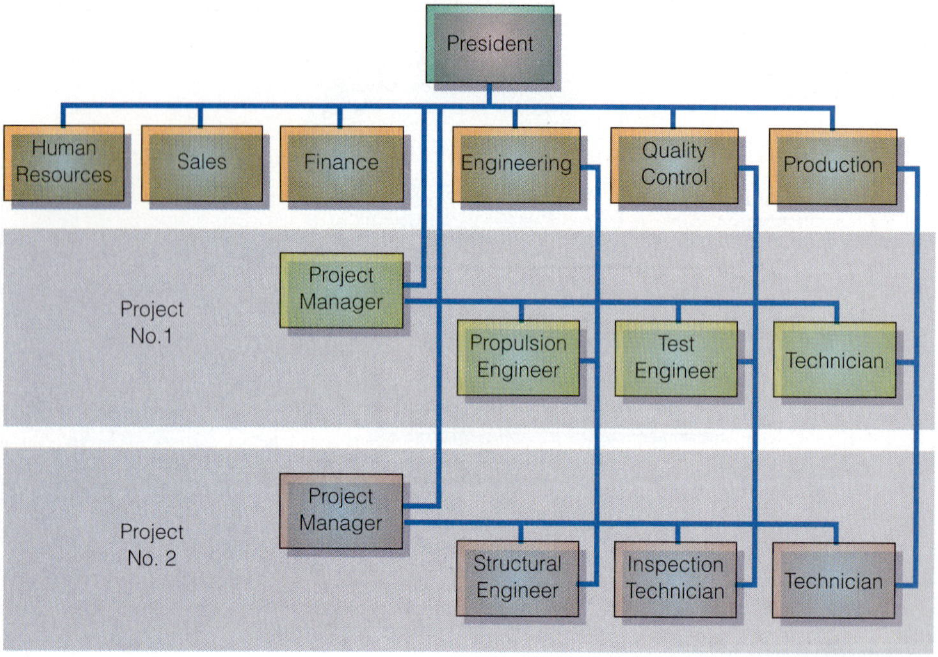

(*Source:* R. W. Mondy and S. R. Premeaux, *Management: Concepts, Practices and Skills*, 6th ed., Boston: Allyn and Bacon, 1993, p. 247.)

The project organization works best when

1. work can be defined with a specific goal and deadline;
2. the job is unique or somewhat unfamiliar to the existing organization;
3. the work contains complex interrelated tasks requiring specialized skills;
4. the project is temporary but critical to the organization.

An example of a simplified project organization that is part of an ongoing firm is shown in Figure 17.2. The project team members are temporarily assigned to the project and report to the project manager. The manager heading the project coordinates its activities with other departments and reports directly to top management, often the president, of the company. Project managers receive high visibility in a firm and are a key element in the planning and control of project activities.

The project management team begins its task well in advance of the project so that a plan can be developed. One of its first steps is to set the project's objectives carefully and then define the project and break it down into a set of activities and related costs. Gross requirements for people, supplies, and equipment are also estimated in the planning phase.

PROJECT SCHEDULING

Project scheduling involves sequencing and allotting time to all project activities. At this stage, managers decide how long each activity will take and compute how many people and materials will be needed at each stage of production. Managers also chart

FIGURE 17.3 ■ Sample Gantt Chart. Circled items represent precedence relationships (for example, activity *c*, construct collection stack, may not begin until activity *a*, which is circled, is completed).

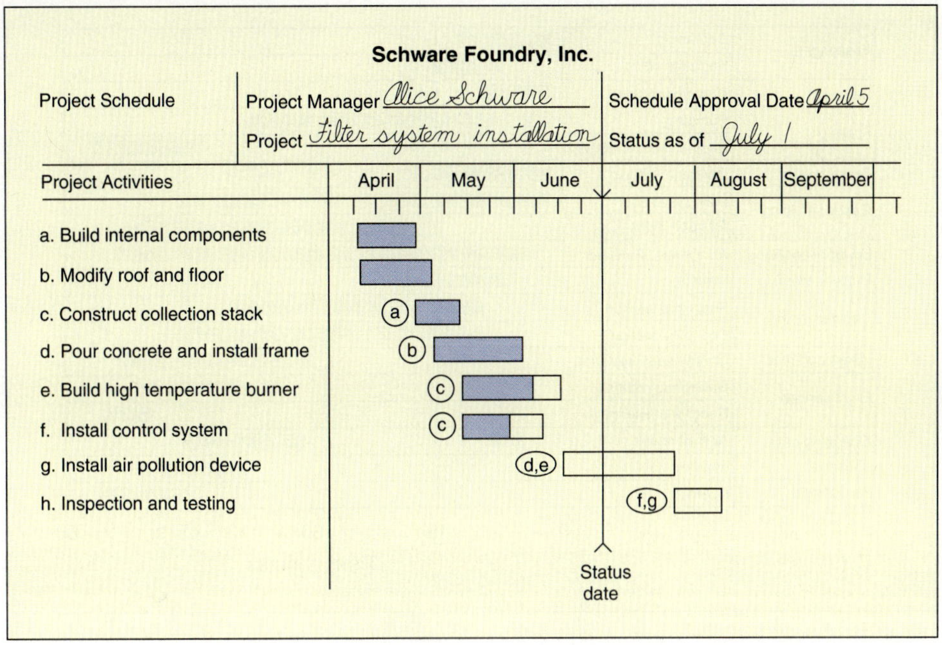

separate schedules for personnel needs by type of skill (management, engineering, or pouring concrete, for example). Charts also can be developed for scheduling materials.

Gantt charts

One popular project scheduling approach is the Gantt chart. **Gantt charts** are low-cost means of helping managers make sure that (1) all activities are planned for, (2) their order of performance is accounted for, (3) the activity time estimates are recorded, and (4) the overall project time is developed. As Figure 17.3 shows, Gantt charts are easy to understand. Horizontal bars are drawn for each project activity along a time line. The letters to the left of each bar tell the planner which other activities have to be completed before that one can begin.

Activity progress is noted, once the actual project is under way, by shading the horizontal bars as an activity is partially or fully completed. For example, we see in Figure 17.3 that activities a, b, c, and d are on schedule because their bars have been shaded up to the vertical status date line. The date line, July 1 in this case, is a status reporting period that lets participants see which tasks are on time, which are ahead of time, and which have fallen behind schedule. Activities e, f, and g are all behind schedule, because their bars are not shaded in their entirety or up to the status date line.

A second example of a Gantt chart is shown in Figure 17.4. This illustration of a routine servicing of a Delta jetliner during a 60-minute layover shows that Gantt charts also can be used for scheduling repetitive operations. In this case, the chart helps point out potential delays. The *POM in Action* box on Delta provides additional insights.

Scheduling charts such as these can be used alone on simple projects. They permit managers to observe the progress of each activity and to spot and tackle problem areas. Gantt charts are not easily updated, though. And more importantly, they do not adequately illustrate the interrelationships between the activities and the resources.

PERT and CPM, the two widely used network techniques that we shall discuss shortly, *do* have the ability to consider precedence relationships and interdependency

FIGURE 17.4 ■ Service Activities for a Commercial Jetliner During a 60-Minute Layover

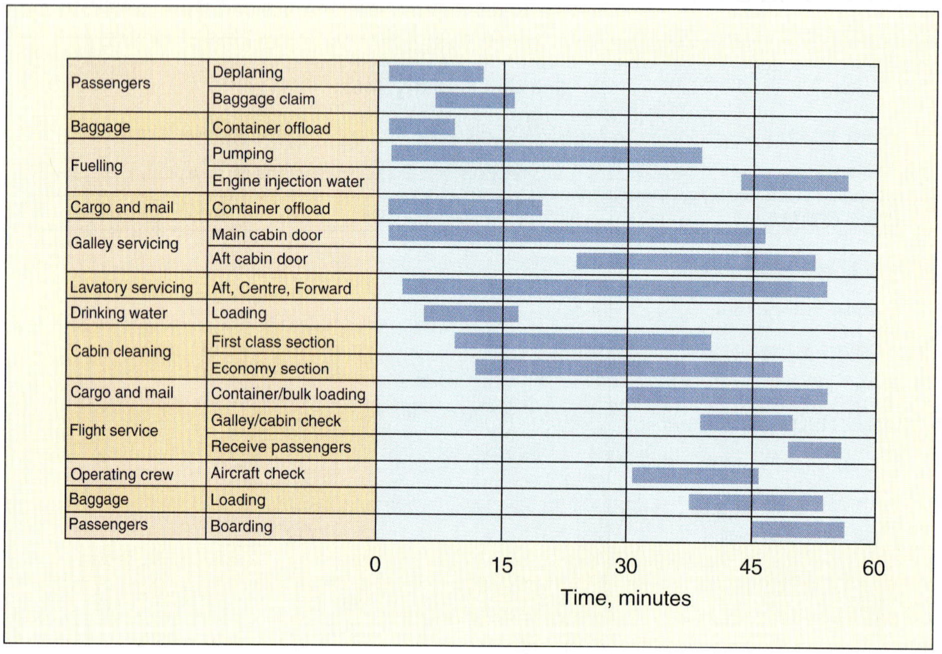

of activities. On complex projects, the scheduling of which is almost always computerized, PERT and CPM thus hold an edge on the simpler Gantt charts. Even on huge projects, though, Gantt charts can be used as a summary of project status and may complement the other network approaches.

To summarize, whatever the approach taken by a project manager, project scheduling serves several purposes:

1. It shows the relationship of each activity to others and to the whole project. To continue the home construction example cited earlier: the foundations of the home must be completed before the floors and walls can begin to be built.

Being able to use powerful project manager software packages such as Primavera (shown here) first requires an understanding of the principles of PERT and CPM. In a competitive job environment, a graduate who has experience with one of the popular programs will find himself or herself a valued member of any organization involved in project planning.

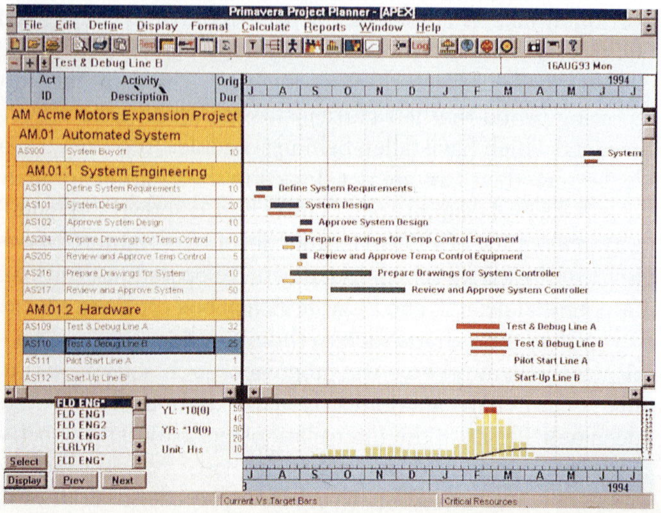

POM IN ACTION

Delta's Ground Crew Orchestrates a Smooth Takeoff

Flight 199's three engines screech its arrival as the wide-bodied L-1011 jet lumbers down Orlando's taxiway with 200 passengers arriving from San Juan. In an hour the plane is to be airborne again.

But before this jet can depart, there is business to attend to: hundreds of passengers and tonnes of luggage and cargo to unload and load; hundreds of meals, thousands of litres of jet fuel, countless soft drinks and bottles of liquor to restock; cabin and restrooms to clean; toilet holding tanks to drain; and engines, wings, and landing gear to inspect.

The 12-person ground crew knows that a miscue anywhere—a broken cargo loader, lost baggage, misdirected passengers—can mean a late departure and trigger a chain reaction of headaches from Orlando to Dallas to every destination of a connecting flight.

Dennis Dettro, the operations manager for Delta's Orlando International Airport, likes to call the turnaround operation "a well-orchestrated symphony." Like a pit crew awaiting a race car, trained crews are in place for Flight 199 with baggage carts and tractors, hydraulic cargo loaders, a truck to load food and drinks, another to lift the cleanup crew, another to put fuel on, and a fourth to take water off. The "orchestra" usually performs so smoothly that most passengers never suspect the proportions of the effort. Gantt charts, such as the one in Figure 17.4, aid Delta and other airlines with the staffing and scheduling that are necessary for this symphony to perform.

Sources: Orlando Sentinel (December 21, 1993): A-1; *Distribution* (October 1991): 38–40; and *Aviation Week* (November 23, 1992): 42–43.

2. It identifies the precedence relationships among activities. It is clear in home construction that plumbing and wiring must be substantially complete before plastering or drywalling can begin.
3. It encourages the setting of realistic time and cost estimates for each activity. In the home construction example, many homes are sold prior to construction for a legally-agreed-upon amount and the builder has no recourse but to be realistic. Unsold homes which come in over cost may not be able to ask for higher prices, as competition, not cost, will set the prices.
4. It helps make better use of people, money, and material resources by identifying critical bottlenecks in the project. A firm building homes in a major city would likely be building at two or three locations around the city. By using scheduling techniques such as those mentioned in this chapter, a firm can make much better use of resources. Wise scheduling would permit the use of one set of concrete forms for house foundations, one crew of electricians, one crew of plumbers, one crew of carpenters, roofers, drywallers, floor installers, etc. Coordinated planning of multiple projects of a similar nature will maximize the use of capital equipment and human resources.

PROJECT CONTROLLING

The control of large projects, like the control of any management system, involves close monitoring of resources, costs, quality, and budgets. Control also means using a feedback loop to revise the project plan and having the ability to shift resources to where they are needed most. Computerized PERT/CPM reports and charts are widely available today on personal computers. Some of the more popular of these programs

POM IN ACTION

Controlling Projects at M. W. Kellogg Company

Houston's M. W. Kellogg Company is one of the world's largest construction contractors, specializing in engineering and building petroleum and petrochemical complexes. Until 10 years ago, it used commercial project management software to control its numerous and wide-ranging projects. When Kellogg outgrew the software, it decided to write its own program to integrate time analysis, scheduling, networking, and charting of project schedules, materials, and costs. The huge new program, called Integrated Project Control System (IPCS), had to manage about 20 projects at a time. A typical Kellogg project would involve 1,500 engineering activities, 1,100 requisitions, and forecasts for 4,000 cost account lines.

IPCS now tracks each project's performance every 2 weeks by measuring the actual hours expended against planned base lines. IPCS has cut the time for updating from 24 hours under the old software to a matter of minutes today. It also makes project management at Kellogg more efficient than at competing companies. In the dynamic, visible, and safety-conscious environment of large-scale engineering projects, IPCS is able to reduce risks, control projects, and give Kellogg's management more exact and flexible information.

Sources: A. M. Hickman, "Refining the Process of Project Control," *Production and Inventory Management* (February 1992): 26–27; and P. W. Stonebraker and G. K. Leong, *Operations Strategy* (Boston: Allyn and Bacon, 1994), p. 505.

are Harvard Total Project Manager (by Software Publishing Corporation, Inc.), Primavera (by Primavera Systems, Inc.), Project (by Microsoft Corp.), MacProject (by Apple Computer Corp.), Pertmaster (by Westminster Software, Inc.), VisiSchedule (by Paladin Software Corp.), and Time Line (by Symantec Corp.).

These programs produce a broad variety of reports including (1) detailed cost breakdowns for each task, (2) total program labour curves, (3) cost distribution tables, (4) functional cost and hour summaries, (5) raw material and expenditure forecasts, (6) variance reports, (7) time analysis reports, and (8) work status reports. When commercially available software does not provide all of the features a company wants, the company may even develop its own project management programs, as we see in the M. W. Kellogg Company *POM in Action* box.

The size and complexity of many of today's construction projects make computerized management an absolute essential. There are too many complex and interrelated activities which are subject to ongoing changes involved to allow a manual system to effectively manage the project.

PROJECT MANAGEMENT TECHNIQUES: PERT AND CPM

Program evaluation and review technique (PERT)
Critical path method (CPM)

Program evaluation and review technique (PERT) and the **critical path method (CPM)** were both developed in the 1950s to help managers schedule, monitor, and control large and complex projects. CPM arrived first, in 1957, as a tool developed by J. E. Kelly of Remington Rand and M. R. Walker of Dupont to assist in the building and maintenance of chemical plants at Dupont. Independently, PERT was developed in 1958 by the U.S. Navy with Booz, Allen and Hamilton.

The Framework of PERT and CPM

PERT and CPM both follow six basic steps:

1. Define the project and all of its significant activities or tasks.
2. Develop the relationships among the activities. Decide which activities must precede and which must follow others.
3. Draw the network connecting all of the activities.
4. Assign time and/or cost estimates to each activity.
5. Compute the longest time path through the network. This is called the **critical path**. **Critical path**
6. Use the network to help plan, schedule, monitor, and control the project.

Step 5, finding the critical path, is a major part of controlling a project. The activities on the critical path represent tasks that will delay the entire project unless they are completed on time. Managers can gain the flexibility needed to complete critical tasks by identifying noncritical activities and replanning, rescheduling, and reallocating resources such as labour and finances.

Although PERT and CPM differ to some extent in terminology and in the construction of the network, their objectives are the same. Furthermore, the analysis used in both techniques is very similar. The major difference is that PERT employs three time estimates for each activity. Each estimate has an associated probability of occurrence, which, in turn, is used in computing expected values and standard deviations for the activity times. CPM makes the assumption that activity times are known with certainty, and hence requires only one time factor for each activity.

For purposes of illustration, the rest of this chapter concentrates on a discussion of PERT and PERT/Cost. PERT/Cost is a technique that combines the benefits of both PERT and CPM. Most of the comments and procedures described, however, apply just as well to CPM.

PERT, PERT/Cost, and CPM are important because they can help answer questions such as the following about projects with thousands of activities:

1. When will the entire project be completed?
2. What are the critical activities or tasks in the project, that is, the ones that will delay the entire project if they are late?
3. Which are the noncritical activities, that is, the ones that can run late without delaying the whole project's completion?
4. What is the probability that the project will be completed by a specific date?
5. At any particular date, is the project on schedule, behind schedule, or ahead of schedule?
6. On any given date, is the money spent equal to, less than, or greater than the budgeted amount?
7. Are there enough resources available to finish the project on time?
8. If the project is to be finished in a shorter amount of time, what is the best way to accomplish this at the least cost?

It was clear during the construction of Toronto's SkyDome that a strong possibility existed that one or more of the skilled trades (plumbers, electricians, carpenters, etc.) would call a strike. Revenue losses of several hundred thousand dollars per lost

TABLE 17.1 ■ EVENTS, ACTIVITIES, AND HOW THEY RELATE

Name and Symbol	Description
 Event (node)	A point in time, usually a completion date or a starting date
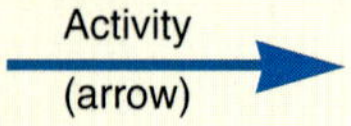 Activity (arrow)	A task or a certain amount of work required in the project
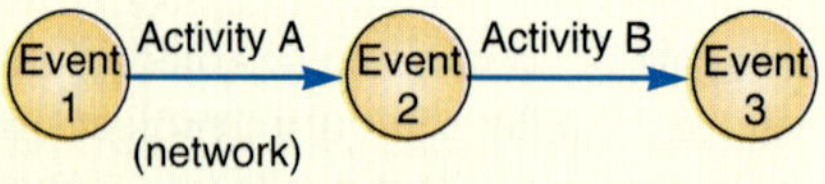 Event 1, Activity A, Event 2, Activity B, Event 3 (network)	A sequence of activities with beginning and ending events

game were forecast, should a strike delay the Toronto Blue Jays American League Baseball season. A PERT technique referred to as *project crashing*, wherein the costs involved in adding more equipment, workers, or overtime would be compared to the projected revenue losses and the most advantageous option selected, would be appropriate in this situation.

Activities, Events, and Networks

Event
Activity

The first step in PERT is to divide the entire project into significant events and activities. An **event** marks the start or completion of a particular task or activity. An **activity** is a task or a subproject that occurs between two events. Table 17.1 shows the symbols used to represent events and activities.

This approach is the most common one to drawing networks and is also referred to as the Activity-on-Arrow (AOA) convention. A less popular convention, called Activity-on-Node (AON), places activities on nodes. For simplicity, we will discuss only AOA.

Network

Any project that can be described by activities and events may be analyzed by a PERT **network**. A network, illustrated in Example 1, is a sequence of activities defined by starting and ending events.

EXAMPLE 1

Given the following information, develop a network.

ACTIVITY	IMMEDIATE PREDECESSOR(S)
A	—
B	—
C	A
D	B

In the network below, we assign each event a number. It is also possible to identify each activity with a beginning and an ending event or node. For example, activity A is the activity that starts with event 1 and ends at node, or event, 2. In general, we number nodes from left to right. The beginning node, or event, of the entire project is number 1, and the last node, or event, in the entire project bears the largest number. The last node below shows the number 4.

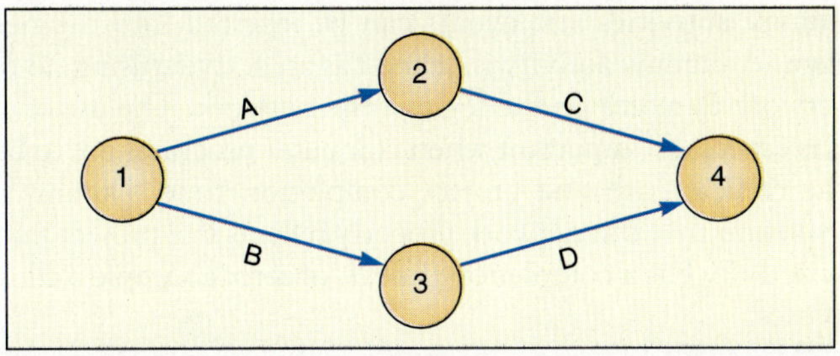

We can also specify networks by events and the activities that occur between events. Example 2 shows how to develop a network based on this type of specification scheme.

EXAMPLE 2

Given the following table, develop a network.

BEGINNING EVENT	ENDING EVENT	ACTIVITY
1	2	1–2
1	3	1–3
2	4	2–4
3	4	3–4
3	5	3–5
4	6	4–6
5	6	5–6

Instead of using a letter to signify activities and their predecessor activities, we can specify activities by their starting event and their ending event. Beginning with the activity that starts at event 1 and ends at event 2, we can construct the following network.

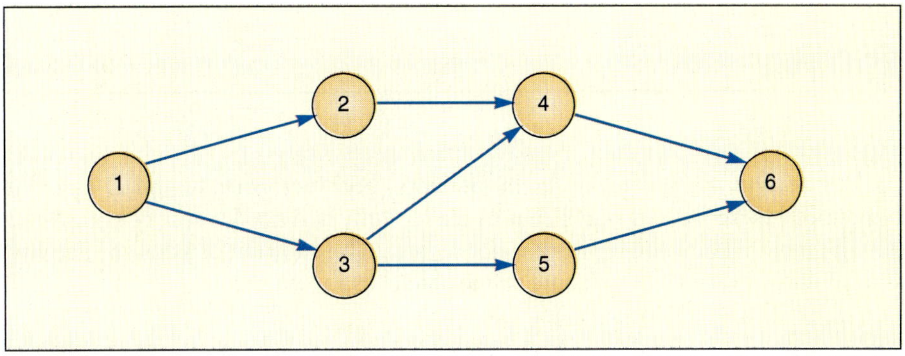

All that is required to construct a network is the starting and ending event for each activity.

Dummy Activities and Events

Dummy activities

You may encounter a network that has two activities with identical starting and ending events. **Dummy activities** and events can be inserted into the network to deal with this problem. A dummy activity is defined as an activity using no time, but is inserted into a network to maintain the logic of the network. The use of dummy activities and events is especially important when computer programs are to be employed in determining the critical path and project completion time. Dummy activities and events can also ensure that the network properly reflects the project under consideration. A dummy activity has a completion time, *t*, of zero. Example 3 illustrates the use of dummy activities.

EXAMPLE 3

Develop a network based on the following information:

Activity	Immediate Predecessor(s)	Activity	Immediate Predecessor(s)
A	—	E	C, D
B	—	F	D
C	A	G	E
D	B	H	F

Given these data, you might develop the following network.

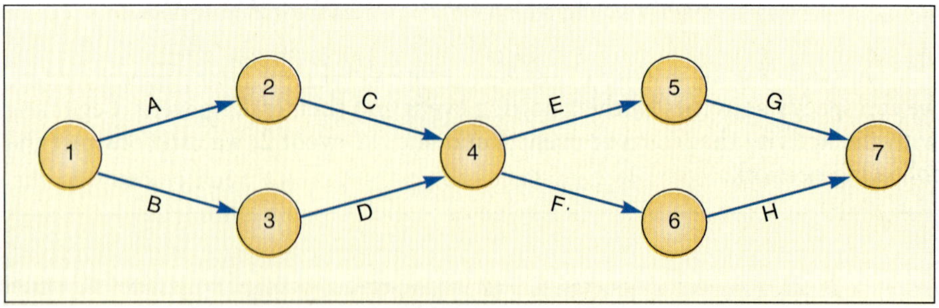

Look at activity F. According to the network, both activities C and D must be completed before we can start F, but in reality, only activity D must be completed (see the table). Thus, the network is not correct. The addition of a dummy activity and a dummy event can overcome this problem, as shown below.

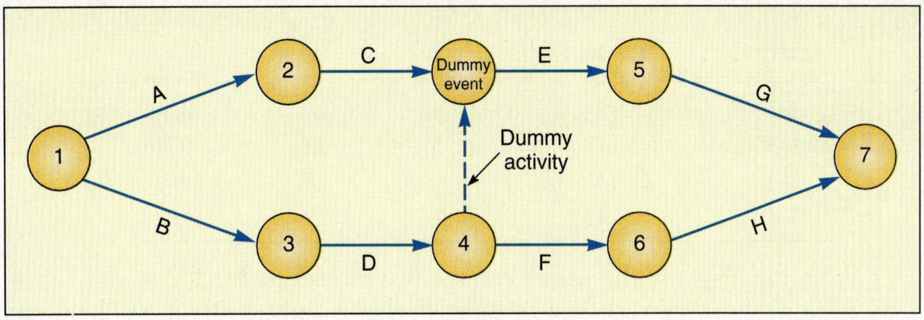

Now the network embodies all of the proper relationships and can be analyzed as usual.

PERT and Activity Time Estimates

As mentioned earlier, one distinguishing difference between PERT and CPM is the use of three **activity time estimates** for each activity in the PERT technique. Only one time factor is given for each activity in CPM.

Activity time estimates

For each activity in PERT, we must specify an **optimistic time**, a most **probable** (or most likely) **time**, and a **pessimistic time** estimate. We then use these three time estimates to calculate an expected completion time and variance for each activity. If we assume, as many researchers do, that activity times follow a **beta probability distribution**, we can use the formula:[1]

Optimistic time
Probable time
Pessimistic time
Beta probability distribution

$$t = \frac{a + 4m + b}{6} \quad \text{and} \quad v = \left(\frac{b - a}{6}\right)^2 \qquad (17.1)$$

where a = optimistic time for activity completion
b = pessimistic time for activity completion
m = most likely time for activity completion
t = expected time of activity completion
v = variance of activity completion time

In PERT, after we have developed the network, we compute expected times and variances for each activity. Example 4 shows these computations.

EXAMPLE 4

Compute expected times and variances of completion for each activity on the basis of the following time estimates (see Example 1 for diagram):

ACTIVITY	a	m	b
1–2	3	4	5
1–3	1	3	5
2–4	5	6	7
3–4	6	7	8

[1]Although the beta distribution has been widely used in PERT analysis for 40 years, its applicability has been called into question. See M. W. Sasieni, "A Note on PERT Times," *Management Science*, 32, no. 12 (December 1986): 1,662–1,663.

ACTIVITY	a + 4m + b	t	$\frac{b-a}{6}$	v
1–2	24	4	2/6	4/36
1–3	18	3	4/6	16/36
2–4	36	6	2/6	4/36
3–4	42	7	2/6	4/36

From the diagram, the reader can see two project paths: 1–2–4 and 1–3–4. Under PERT, three scenarios are considered: the optimistic, the most likely, and the pessimistic. The pathway length can be computed for all three scenarios.

All optimistic: 1–2–4: length 1–2 plus 2–4, i.e., 3 + 5 = 8
1–3–4: length 1–3 plus 3–4, i.e., 1 + 6 = 7

Thus 1–2–4 is the critical path for the "All Optimistic" scenario.

All expected (t): 1–2–4: length 1–2 plus 2–4, i.e., 4 + 6 = 10
1–3–4: length 1–3 plus 3–4, i.e., 3 + 7 = 10

Thus both are "co-critical" for the "All Expected" scenario.

All pessimistic: 1–2–4: length 1–2 plus 2–4, i.e., 5 + 7 = 12
1–3–4: length 1–3 plus 3–4, i.e., 5 + 8 = 13

Thus 1–3–4 is the critical path for the "All Pessimistic" scenario.

Calculating the critical path lengths for the "All Optimistic" and "All Pessimistic" scenarios will serve to provide "end points" for the project under discussion. The "All Optimistic" scenario is the scenario wherein everything is "perfect"; there are no delays or difficulties at all. Thus, the probability of project completion can have a theoretical minimum, and by considering the "All Pessimistic" scenario, a theoretical maximum.

In this example, one can conclude that 8 is the minimum possible completion time, while 13 is the maximum or "Disaster Scenario" completion time.

Critical Path Analysis

Critical path analysis

The objective of **critical path analysis** is to determine the following quantities for each activity:

ES: Earliest activity start time. *All predecessor activities* must be completed before an activity can be started. The ending time of the predecessor activities is the earliest time an activity can be started.

LS: Latest activity start time. *All following activities* must be completed without delaying the entire project. This is the latest time an activity can be started without delaying the entire project.

EF: Earliest activity finish time.

LF: Latest activity finish time.

Slack time

S: Activity **slack time**, which is equal to (LS – ES) or (LF – EF).

For any activity, if we can calculate ES and LS, we can find the other three quantities as follows:

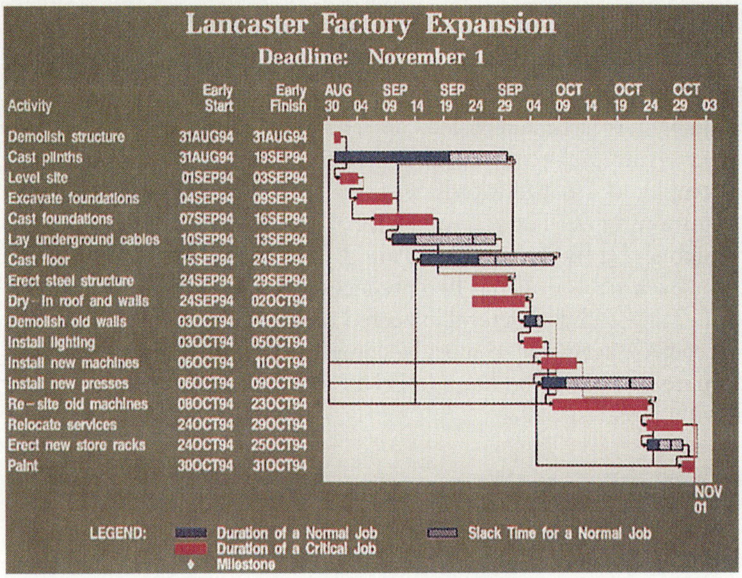

PERT software is also available from SAS Institute, Inc. Here early starts, early finishes, normal tasks, and slack times are indicated for a factory expansion project in Lancaster, PA.

$$EF = ES + t$$

$$LF = LS + t$$

$$S = LS - ES$$

or

$$S = LF - EF$$

Once we know these quantities for every activity, we can analyze the overall project. Typically, this analysis includes an examination of the following:

1. The critical path—the group of activities in the project that have a slack time of zero. This path is *critical* because a delay in any activity along this path would delay the entire project.
2. T—the total project completion time, which is calculated by adding the expected time (t) values of those activities on the critical path.
3. V—variance of the critical path, which is computed by adding the variance (v) of those individual activities on the critical path.

Critical path analysis normally starts with the determination of ES and EF. Example 5 illustrates the procedure.

EXAMPLE 5

Given the following information, determine ES and EF for each activity.

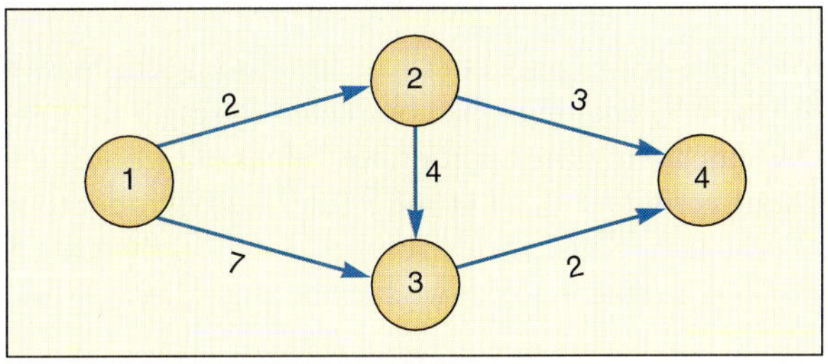

ACTIVITY	t
1–2	2
1–3	7
2–3	4
2–4	3
3–4	2

We find ES by moving from the starting activities of the project to the ending activities of the project. For the starting activities, ES is either zero or the actual starting date, say, August 1. For activities 1–2 and 1–3, ES is zero. (By convention, all projects start at time zero.)

There is one basic rule. Before an activity can be started, *all* of its predecessor activities must be completed. In other words, we search for the *longest* path leading to an activity in determining ES. For activity 2–3, ES is 2. Its only predecessor activity is 1–2, for which $t = 2$. By the same reasoning, ES for activity 2–4 also is 2. For activity 3–4, however, ES is 7. It has two predecessor paths: activity 1–3 with $t = 7$ and activities 1–2 and 2–3 with a total expected time of 6 (or 2 + 4). Thus, ES for activity 3–4 is 7 because activity 1–3 must be completed before activity 3–4 can be started. We compute EF next by adding t to ES for each activity.

See the following table.

ACTIVITY	ES	t	EF
1–2	0	2	2
1–3	0	7	7
2–3	2	4	6
2–4	2	3	5
3–4	7	2	9

The next step is to calculate LS, the latest starting time for each activity. We start with the last activities and work backward to the first activities to determine the latest possible starting time (LS) without increasing the earliest finishing time (EF). This task seems more difficult than it really is. Example 6 shows how to calculate LS.

EXAMPLE 6

Determine LS, LF, and S (the slack) for each activity based on the following data:

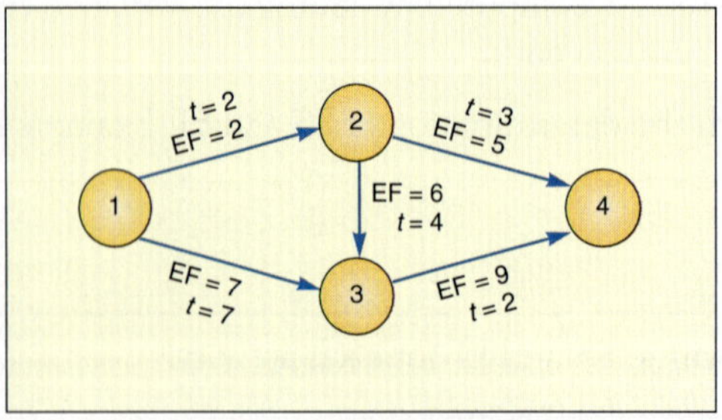

ACTIVITY	t	ES	EF
1–2	2	0	2
1–3	7	0	7
2–3	4	2	6
2–4	3	2	5
3–4	2	7	9

The earliest time by which the entire project can be finished is 9 because activities 2–4 (EF = 5) and 3–4 (EF = 9) *both* must be completed. Using 9 as a basis, we now will work backward by subtracting the appropriate values of t from 9.

The latest time we can start activity 3–4 is at time 7 (or 9 – 2) in order to still complete the project by time period 9. Thus, LS for activity 3–4 is 7. By using the same reasoning, LS for activity 2–4 is 6 (or 9 –3). If we start activity 2–4 at 6 and it takes 3 time units to complete the activity, we can still finish in 9 time units. The latest we can start activity 2–3 is 3 (or 9 – 2 – 4). If we start activity 2–3 at 3 and it takes 2 and 4 time units for activities 2–3 and 3–4, respectively, we can still finish on time. Thus, LS for activity 2–3 is 3. By using the same reasoning, LS for activity 1–3 is 0 (or 9 – 2 – 7). Analyzing activity 1–2 is more difficult because there are two paths. Both must be completed in 9 time units.

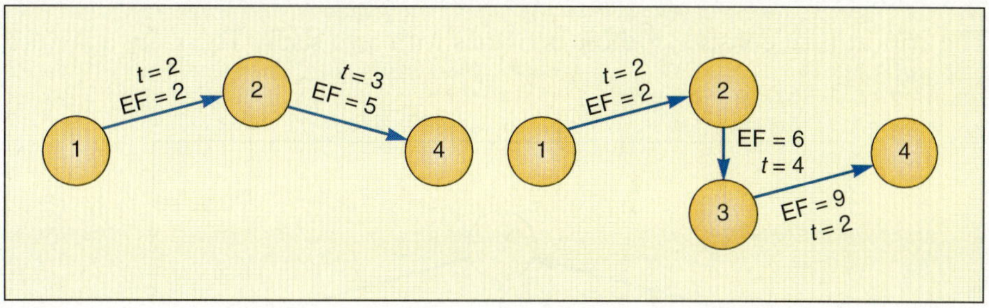

Because both of the above paths must be completed, LS for activity 1–2 is computed from the most binding, or slowest, path. Thus, LS for activity 1–2 *is* 1 (or 9 – 2 – 4 – 2) and *not* 4 (or 9 – 3 – 2). Noting the following relationships, we can construct a table summarizing the results.

$$\mathrm{LF} = \mathrm{LS} + t$$

$$\mathrm{S} = \mathrm{LF} - \mathrm{EF}$$

or

$$\mathrm{S} = \mathrm{LS} - \mathrm{ES}$$

ACTIVITY	ES	EF	LS	LF	S
1–2	0	2	1	3	1
1–3	0	7	0	7	0
2–3	2	6	3	7	1
2–4	2	5	6	9	4
3–4	7	9	7	9	0

Once we have computed ES, EF, LS, LF, and S, we can finish analyzing the entire project. Analysis includes determining the critical path, project completion time, and project variance. Example 7 shows this procedure.

EXAMPLE 7

We have computed times, activity variances, and other information for the following network. What is the critical path, total completion time *T*, and project variance *V* of this network?

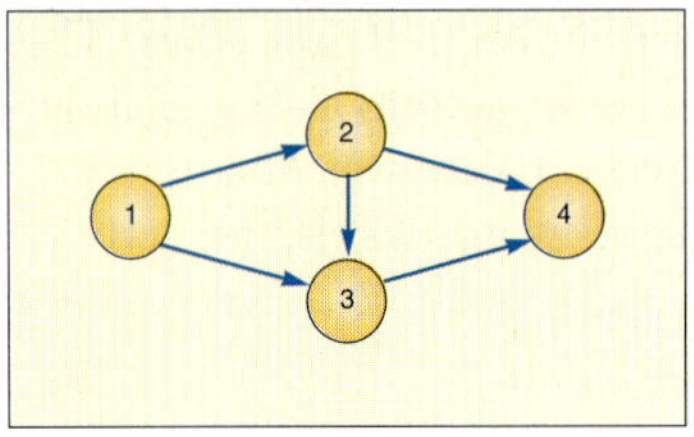

ACTIVITY	t	V	ES	EF	LS	LF	S
1–2	2	2/6	0	2	1	3	1
1–3	7	3/6	0	7	0	7	0
2–3	4	1/6	2	6	3	7	1
2–4	3	2/6	2	5	6	9	4
3–4	2	4/6	7	9	7	9	0

The critical path consists of those activities with zero slack. These are activities 1–3 and 3–4.

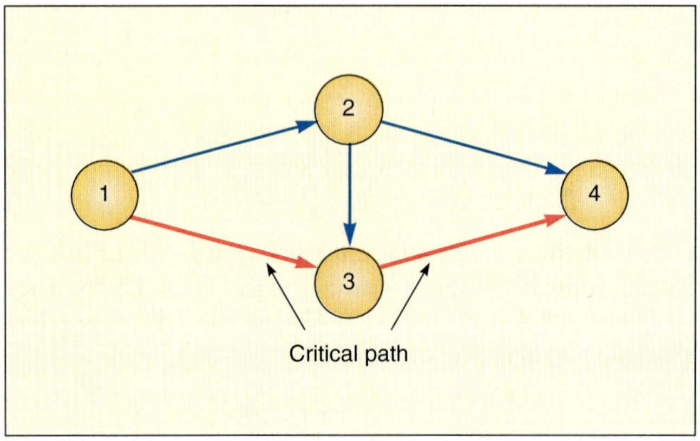

The total project completion time is 9 (or 7 + 2). The project variance is the sum of the *activity variances* along the *critical path*, which is 7/6 (or 3/6 + 4/6).

The Probability of Project Completion

Having computed the expected completion time T and completion variance V, we can determine the probability that the project will be completed at a specified date. If we make the assumption that the distribution of completion dates follows a normal curve, we can calculate the probability of completion as in Example 8.

EXAMPLE 8

If the expected project completion time T_e is 20 weeks and the project variance V is 100, what is the probability that the project will be finished on or before week 25?

$$T_e = 20$$
$$V = 100$$
$$\sigma = \text{standard deviation} = \sqrt{\text{project variance}} = \sqrt{V}$$
$$= \sqrt{100} = 10$$
$$T_s = \text{desired completion date}$$
$$= 25 \text{ weeks}$$

The normal curve would appear as follows:

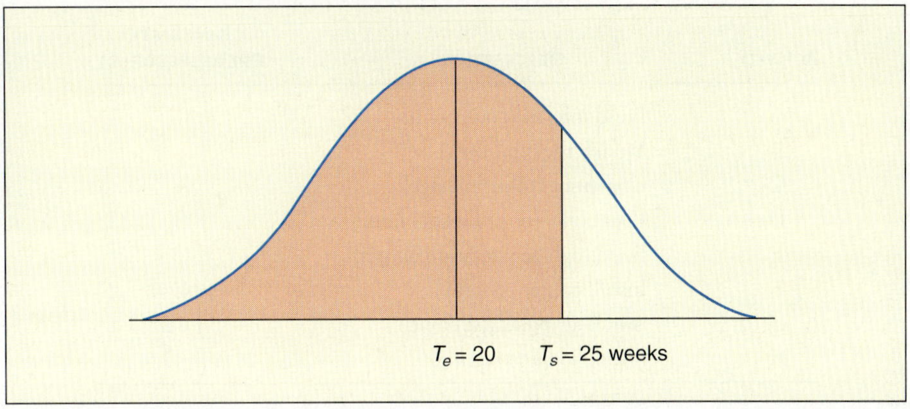

$$Z = \frac{T_s - T_e}{\sigma} = \frac{25 - 20}{10} = .5$$

where Z equals the number of standard deviations from the mean. The area under the curve for Z = .5 is .6915. (See the normal curve table in Appendix A.) Thus, the probability of completing the project in 25 weeks is approximately .69, or 69%.

We must point out that probability analysis should be used with caution. *For example, a noncritical path activity with a large variance could become a critical path activity. This occurrence would cause the analysis to be in error.* Consider the network pictured in Figure 17.5. The critical path is 1–3 and 3–4 with T_s = 12 and V = 4. If the desired completion date is 14, the value of Z is 1 [or $(14-12)/\sqrt{4}$]. The chance of completion is 84% from the normal distribution in the appendix. What would happen if activities 1–2 and 2–4 became the critical path? Because of the high variance, this event is not unlikely. With the same values for T_e and T_s, Z becomes 0.4 [or $(14-12)/\sqrt{25}$]. Looking at the normal distribution, we see that the chance of project completion is 66%. If activities 1–2 and 2–4 became the critical path, the chance of project completion would drop significantly due to the large total variance (25 = 16 + 9) of these activities. A simulation of the project could provide better data.

FIGURE 17.5 ■ Critical Path Analysis

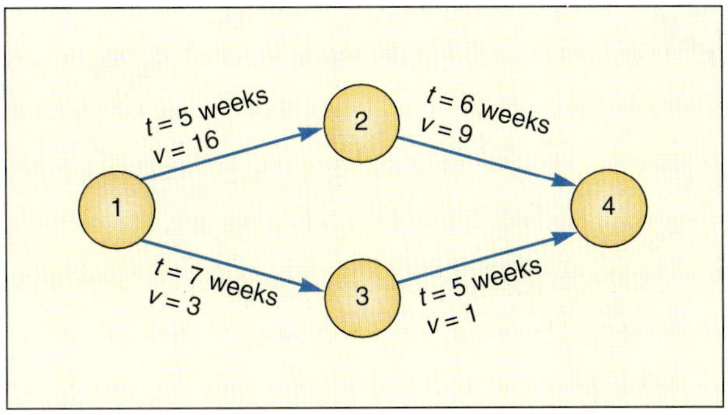

To transform the corporate image of an international airline is a huge task. Aircraft, check-in desks, lounges, shops, ground vehicles, printed materials—including company stationery, timetables, tickets, baggage tags, and, of course, uniforms—all need to be changed. To help British Airways (BA) plan the changes, a computerized project management package, PertMaster, was used. PertMaster uses the same concepts presented in this chapter. By understanding and using PERT, BA was able to make the project requirements fit together on schedule.

TABLE 17.2 ■ ACTIVITIES AND IMMEDIATE PREDECESSORS FOR SCHWARE FOUNDRY, INC.

ACTIVITY	DESCRIPTION	IMMEDIATE PREDECESSOR(S)
A	Build internal components	—
B	Modify roof and floor	—
C	Construct collection stack	A
D	Pour concrete and install frame	B
E	Build high-temperature burner	C
F	Install control system	C
G	Install air pollution device	D, E
H	Inspection and testing	F, G

Case Study of PERT: Schware Foundry

Schware Foundry, Inc., a metalworks plant in Longueuil, Quebec, has just decided to make a major investment in new air pollution control equipment. The plant, however, must be shut down during this installation process. Schware's board of directors estimates that the company can survive no more than 16 weeks without production in full swing. Alice Schware, the managing partner, wants to make sure the installation of the filtering system progresses smoothly and on time.

All activities involved in the foundry project are shown in Table 17.2. (You may recall seeing the same data earlier in the Gantt chart example of Figure 17.3.) We see in the table that before the collection stack can be constructed (activity C), the internal components must be built (activity A). Thus, activity A is the immediate predecessor to activity C. Likewise, both activities D and E must be performed just prior to installation of the air pollution device (activity G). The network for Schware Foundry is illustrated in Figure 17.6.

FIGURE 17.6 ■ Network for Schware Foundry, Inc.

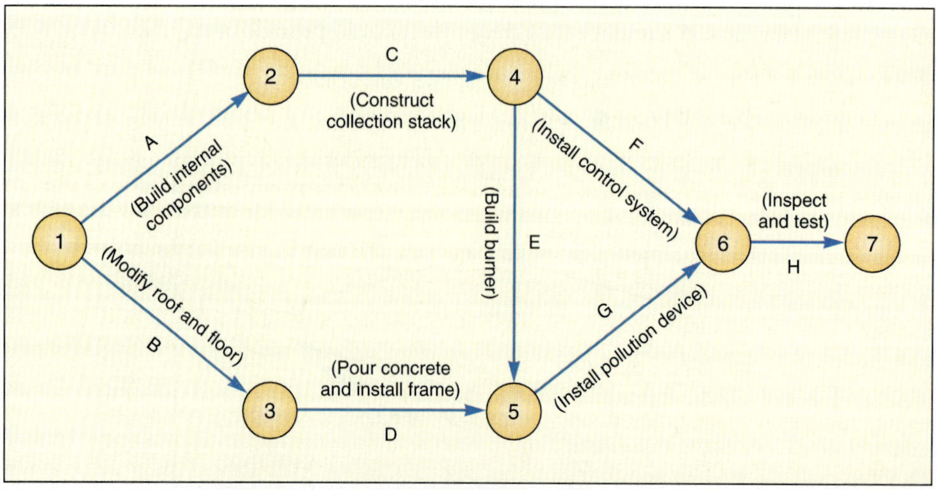

TABLE 17.3 ■ TIME ESTIMATES (IN WEEKS) FOR SCHWARE FOUNDRY, INC.

ACTIVITY	OPTIMISTIC a	MOST PROBABLE m	PESSIMISTIC b	EXPECTED TIME $t = (a + 4m + b)/6$	VARIANCE $[(b - a)/6]^2$
A	1	2	3	2	$\left(\frac{3-1}{6}\right)^2 = \frac{4}{36}$
B	2	3	4	3	$\left(\frac{4-2}{6}\right)^2 = \frac{4}{36}$
C	1	2	3	2	$\left(\frac{3-1}{6}\right)^2 = \frac{4}{36}$
D	2	4	6	4	$\left(\frac{6-2}{6}\right)^2 = \frac{16}{36}$
E	1	4	7	4	$\left(\frac{7-1}{6}\right)^2 = \frac{36}{36}$
F	1	2	9	3	$\left(\frac{9-1}{6}\right)^2 = \frac{64}{36}$
G	3	4	11	5	$\left(\frac{11-3}{6}\right)^2 = \frac{64}{36}$
H	1	2	3	2	$\left(\frac{3-1}{6}\right)^2 = \frac{4}{36}$
				Total: 25 weeks	

Table 17.3 shows Schware's optimistic, most probable, and pessimistic time estimates for each activity. It also reveals the expected time (t) and variance for each of the activities. Table 17.4 summarizes the critical path analysis for the activities and network. The total project completion time, 15 weeks, is seen as the largest number in the EF or LF columns of Table 17.4. Operations managers may refer to this as a boundary timetable.

TABLE 17.4 ■ SCHWARE FOUNDRY'S SCHEDULE AND SLACK TIMES

ACTIVITY	EARLIEST START (ES)	EARLIEST FINISH (EF)	LATEST START (LS)	LATEST FINISH (LF)	SLACK (LS – ES)	ON CRITICAL PATH?
A	0	2	0	2	0	Yes
B	0	3	1	4	1	No
C	2	4	2	4	0	Yes
D	3	7	4	8	1	No
E	4	8	4	8	0	Yes
F	4	7	10	13	6	No
G	8	13	8	13	0	Yes
H	13	15	13	15	0	Yes

FIGURE 17.7 ■ Probability of Schware Foundry's Meeting the 16-Week Deadline

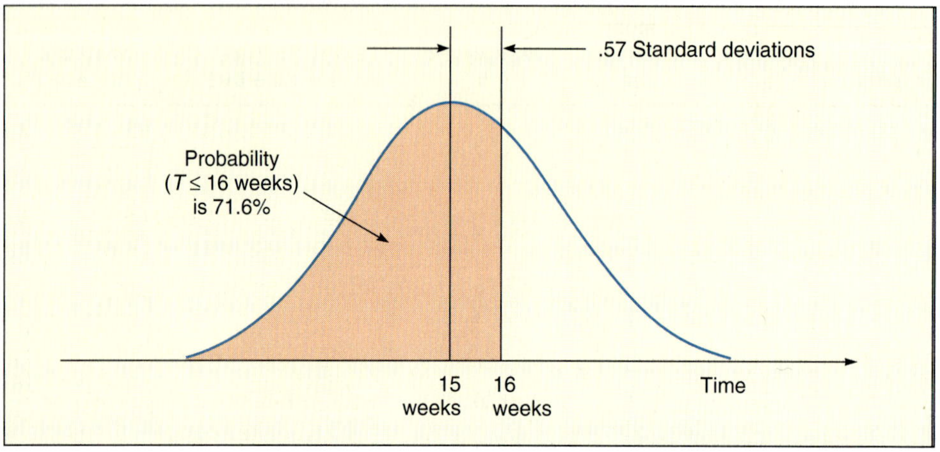

PROBABILITY OF PROJECT COMPLETION. The critical path analysis helped us determine that the foundry's expected project completion time is 15 weeks. Alice is aware, however, that there is significant variation in the time estimates for several activities. Variation in activities that are on the critical path can impact on overall project completion, possibly delaying it. This is one occurrence that worries Alice considerably.

PERT uses the variance of critical path activities to help determine the variance of the overall project. Project variance is computed by summing variances of critical activities.

From Table 17.3 and Equation (17.1), we know that

CRITICAL ACTIVITY	VARIANCE
A	4/36
C	4/36
E	36/36
G	64/36
H	4/36

Hence, the project variance = 4/36 + 4/36 + 36/36 + 64/36 + 4/36 = 3.111.

$$\text{Project standard deviation} = \sqrt{\text{project variance}}$$
$$= \sqrt{3.111} = 1.76 \text{ weeks}$$

In order for Alice to find the probability that her project will be finished on or before the 16-week deadline, she needs to determine the appropriate area under the normal curve in Figure 17.7. The standard normal equation can be applied as follows:

$$Z = \frac{\text{due date} - \text{expected date of completion}}{\text{standard deviation}} \tag{17.2}$$

$$= \frac{16 \text{ weeks} - 15 \text{ weeks}}{1.76 \text{ weeks}} = \frac{1}{1.76} = .57$$

where Z is the number of standard deviations the due date or target date lies from the mean or expected date.

Referring to the normal table in Appendix A, we find a probability of .71567. Thus, there is a 71.6% chance that the pollution control equipment can be put in place in 16 weeks or less.

What PERT Was Able to Provide Schware Foundry. PERT has thus far been able to provide Alice Schware with several valuable pieces of management information.

1. The project's expected completion date is 15 weeks.
2. There is a 71.6% chance the equipment will be in place within the 16-week deadline. And PERT can easily find the probability of finishing by any other date in which Alice is interested.
3. Five activities (A, C, E, G, H) are on the critical path. If any one of them is delayed for any reason, the whole project will be delayed.
4. Three activities (B, D, F) are not critical but have some slack time built in. This means Alice can borrow from their resources, and, if necessary, she may be able to speed up the whole project.
5. A detailed schedule of activity starting and ending dates has been made available (Table 17.4).

PERT/COST

Until now, we have assumed that it is not possible to reduce activity times. This is usually not the case, however. Perhaps additional resources can reduce activity times for certain activities within the project. These resources might be additional labour, more equipment, and so on. Although it can be expensive to shorten activity times, doing so might be worthwhile.

Suppose a homeowner purchases a prefabricated garage and must install a foundation for it. He or she has the option of (1) buying cement, sand, and gravel or premixed dry concrete in a bag and renting a cement mixer or (2) arranging for delivery of "ready-mixed" cement. The "ready-mixed" is more expensive, but it is properly mixed in a truck and delivered ready to pour, saving the homeowner time and energy. The garage itself is another example: you can buy the lumber etc. and build your own, or, for more money, a prefabricated garage can be delivered from the factory, and for still more money the factory will install the garage. One must weigh the costs against the benefits.

Similarly, if a company faces costly penalties for being late with a project, using additional resources to complete the project on time might be economical. There may be fixed costs every day the project is in process. Thus, it might be profitable to use additional resources to shorten the project time and save some of the daily fixed costs. But what activities should be shortened? How much will this action cost? Will a reduction in the activity time in turn reduce the time needed to complete the entire project? Ideally, we would like to find the least expensive method of shortening the entire project. This is the purpose of **PERT/Cost**.

PERT/Cost

Figure 17.8 shows cost-time curves for two activities. For activity 5–6, it costs $300 to complete the activity in 8 weeks, $400 for 7 weeks, and $600 for 6 weeks. Activity 2–4 requires $3,000 of additional resources for completion in 12 weeks and $1,000 for 14 weeks. Similar cost-time curves or relationships can usually be developed for all activities in the network.

FIGURE 17.8 ■ Cost-Time Curves Used in PERT/Cost Analysis

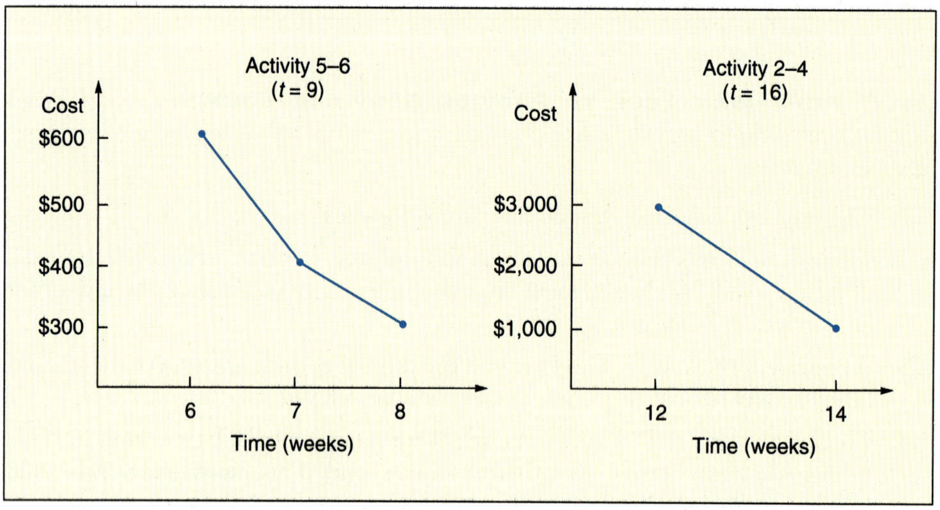

The objective of PERT/Cost is to reduce the entire project completion time by a certain amount at the least cost. To accomplish this objective, we must introduce a few more variables. For each activity, there will exist a reduction in activity time and the cost incurred for that time reduction. Let:

M_i = maximum reduction of time for activity i

C_i = additional cost associated with reducing activity time for activity i

K_i = cost of reducing activity time by one time unit for activity i

$$K_i = \frac{C_i}{M_i} \tag{17.3}$$

With this information, it is possible to determine the least cost of reducing the project completion date. Example 9 illustrates the procedure.

EXAMPLE 9

Given the following information, determine the least cost of reducing the project completion time by 1 week.

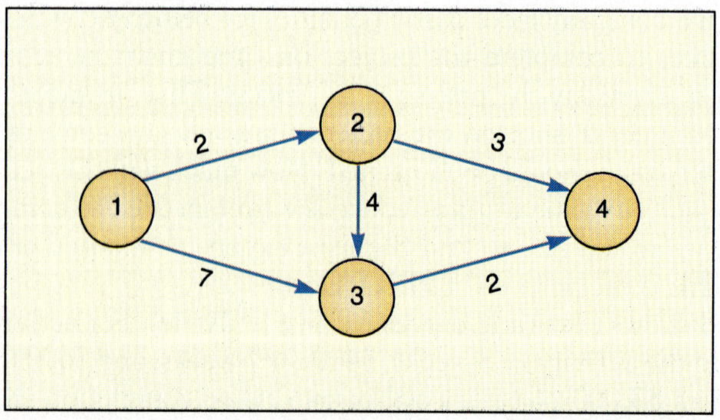

ACTIVITY	t (WEEKS)	M (WEEKS)	C
1–2	2	1	$ 300
1–3	7	4	2,000
2–3	4	2	2,000
2–4	3	2	4,000
3–4	2	1	2,000

ACTIVITY	ES	EF	LS	LF	S
1–2	0	2	1	3	1
1–3	0	7	0	7	0
2–3	2	6	3	7	1
2–4	2	5	6	9	4
3–4	7	9	7	9	0

The first step is to compute K for each activity:

ACTIVITY	M	C	K	CRITICAL PATH
1–2	1	$ 300	$ 300	No
1–3	4	2,000	500	Yes
2–3	2	2,000	1,000	No
2–4	2	4,000	2,000	No
3–4	1	2,000	2,000	Yes

The second step is to locate that activity on the critical path with the smallest value of K_i. The critical path consists of activities 1–3 and 3–4. Because activity 1–3 has a lower value of K_i, we can reduce the project completion time by 1 week, to 8 weeks, by incurring an additional cost of $500.

We must be very careful in using this procedure. Any further reduction in activity time along the critical path would cause the critical path also to include activities 1–2, 2–3, and 3–4. In other words, there would be two critical paths and activities on both would need to be "crashed" to reduce project completion time.

A CRITIQUE OF PERT AND CPM

As a critique of our discussions of PERT, here are some of its features of which operations managers need to be aware.

ADVANTAGES

1. Useful at several stages of project management, especially in the scheduling and control of large projects.
2. Straightforward in concept and not mathematically complex.
3. Graphical displays using networks help to perceive quickly relationships among project activities.
4. Critical path and slack time analyses help pinpoint activities that need to be closely watched.
5. Networks generated provide valuable project documentation and graphically point out who is responsible for various activities.

6. Applicable to a wide variety of projects and industries.
7. Useful in monitoring not only schedules, but costs as well.

LIMITATIONS

1. Project activities have to be clearly defined, independent, and stable in their relationships.
2. Precedence relationships must be specified and networked together.
3. Time estimates tend to be subjective and are subject to fudging by managers who fear the dangers of being overly optimistic or not pessimistic enough.
4. There is the inherent danger of too much emphasis being placed on the longest, or critical, path. Near-critical paths need to be monitored closely as well.

ACHIEVING WORLD-CLASS STANDARDS

World-class firms effectively manage projects and the resources required to accomplish those projects. Using project management tools, they manage numerous complex projects such as implementing computer systems, building factories, and automating warehouses. The tools used include computerized Gantt charts, PERT, CPM, and PERT/Cost. With these tools, managers understand the status of each activity and know which activities are critical and which have slack; in addition, they know where crashing makes the most sense. Projects are segmented into discrete activities and the specific resources are identified. This allows project managers in world-class organizations to respond aggressively to global competition. Moreover, effective project management also allows these firms to create products and services for global markets.

Such firms know the amount of human resources as well as capital resources necessary for each phase of a project. This knowledge allows managers to hire and train exactly the employees needed for each new challenge. The results are projects accomplished efficiently. This effective utilization of both labour and capital provides world-class firms, such as Bechtel (as we saw in the World-Class Profile that opened this chapter), a competitive advantage.

SUMMARY

PERT, CPM, and other scheduling techniques have proven to be valuable tools in controlling large and complex projects. A wide variety of software packages to help managers handle network modeling problems are also available.

PERT, CPM, and PERT/Cost will not, however, solve all the project scheduling and management problems of business and government. Good management practices, clear responsibilities for tasks, and straightforward and timely reporting systems are also needed. It is important to remember that the models we described in this chapter are only tools to aid managers make better decisions.

KEY TERMS

Project organization (p. 765)
Gantt charts (p. 767)
Program evaluation and review technique (PERT) (p. 770)
Critical path method (CPM) (p. 770)
Critical path (p. 771)
Event (p. 772)
Activity (p. 772)
Network (p. 772)
Dummy activities (p. 774)
Activity time estimates (p. 775)
Optimistic time (p. 775)
Probable time (p. 775)
Pessimistic time (p. 775)
Beta probability distribution (p. 775)
Critical path analysis (p. 776)
Slack time (p. 776)
PERT/Cost (p. 785)

USING AB:POM AND SPREADSHEETS TO SOLVE PROJECT MANAGEMENT PROBLEMS

Solving the Schware Foundry Example with AB:POM's CPM/PERT Module

The project scheduling module will find the expected project completion time for a PERT and CPM network with either one or three time estimates. Program 17.1 contains the input data for Schware Foundry. Program 17.2 provides Schware Foundry's completed input repeated, as well as the final output. The CPM/PERT *one-time estimate* program contains less output.

Using Spreadsheets for PERT/CPM

Spreadsheet formulas can easily be developed to compute expected values and variances for activities, as we did by hand for Schware Foundry in Table 17.3. Table 17.4 then summarized the PERT analysis for that firm. Program 17.3 performs that same analysis. ES for activity C is equal to EF for activity A (or + C13). EF for activity C is ES for activity C plus the activity time (or + B15 + B5). Note the use of the @MAX function to make sure that both activities leading into G and then both leading into H are completed before these activities are started. Computing ES and EF completes the "forward pass" through the network.

PROGRAM 17.1 ■ AB:POM's CPM/PERT Module, Data Entry Screen for Schware Foundry. The screen allows for naming of tasks and entry of times and predecessors for those activities that have predecessors.

CPM/PERT Project Scheduling — Data Screen

Number of activities (1–99) 8

SCHWARE FOUNDRY

Task	opt time	lik time	pes time	Predecessors			
a	1	2	3	—	—	—	—
b	2	3	4	—	—	—	—
c	1	2	3	a	—	—	—
d	2	4	6	b	—	—	—
e	1	4	7	c	—	—	—
f	1	2	9	c	—	—	—
g	3	4	11	d	e	—	—
h	1	2	3	f	g	—	—

PROGRAM 17.2 ■ Solution to Schware Foundry Example Using AB:POM. The critical path consists of those activities that have zero slack, namely, a, c, e, g, and h.

SCHWARE FOUNDRY

Project completion time = 15 Project standard deviation = 1.7638

Task	opt time	lik time	pes time	Time	ES	EF	LS	LF	slack	σ
a	1	2	3	2	0	2	0	2	0	.33
b	2	3	4	3	0	3	1	4	1	.33
c	1	2	3	2	2	4	2	4	0	.33
d	2	4	6	4	3	7	4	8	1	.67
e	1	4	7	4	4	8	4	8	0	1
f	1	2	9	3	4	7	10	13	6	1.33
g	3	4	11	5	8	13	8	13	0	1.33
h	1	2	3	2	13	15	13	15	0	.33

PROGRAM 17.3 ■ Using a Spreadsheet to Perform PERT Analysis. Input data (activity times, which are already calculated) appear in rows 3 through 10. Output appears in rows 13 through 20.

	A	B	C	D	E	F
1	Input Data					
2	Activity	Times				
3	A	2				
4	B	3				
5	C	2				
6	D	4				
7	E	4				
8	F	3				
9	G	5				
10	H	2				
11	Output Results					
12	Activity	ES	EF	LS	LF	Slack
13	A	0	+B3	+E13–B3	+D15	+E13–C13
14	B	0	+B4	+E14–B4	+D16	+E14–C14
15	C	+C13	+B15+B5	+E15–B5	@MIN(D17..D18)	+E15–C15
16	D	+C14	+B16+B6	+E16–B6	+D19	+E16–C16
17	E	+C15	+B17+B7	+E17–B7	+D19	+E17–C17
18	F	+C15	+B18+B8	+E18–B8	+D20	+E18–C18
19	G	@MAX(C16..C17)	+B19+B9	+E19–B9	+D20	+E19–C19
20	H	@MAX(C18..C19)	+B20+B10	+E20–B10	+C20	+E20–C20

The "backward pass" starts with the last activity—activity H. The LF value for activity H is the same as EF for this activity (15, or + C20). The LS value is computed by subtracting the activity time from the LF value. For activity H, this is + E20 – B10. The same calculations are then made for the other activities starting with activity G and proceeding to activity A. Note the use of @MIN for activity C. This is needed because there are two paths between activity C and the end of the network. After the backward pass has been completed, slack values are determined. This is done in column F. Slack is equal to LF minus EF.

SOLVED PROBLEMS

Solved Problem 17.1

Construct a network based on the following table.

ACTIVITY			
1–2	1–4	3–5	5–7
1–3	2–5	4–6	6–7

Solution

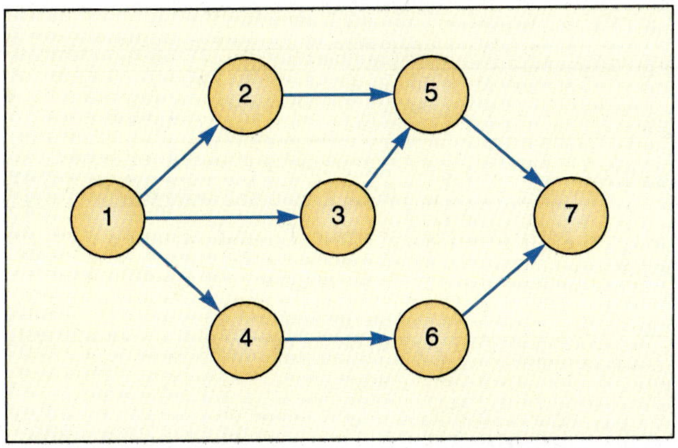

Solved Problem 17.2

Insert dummy activities and events to correct the following network:

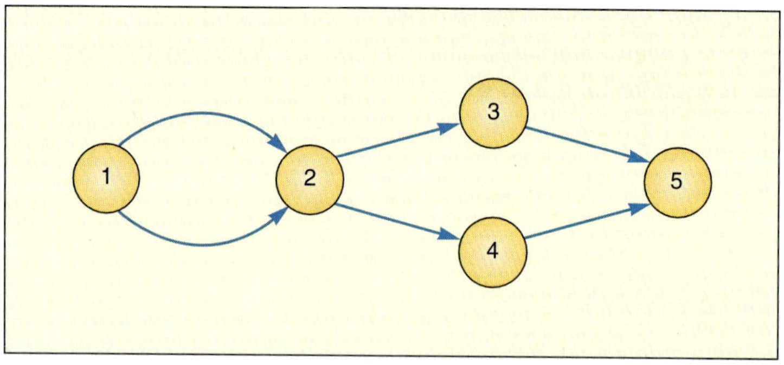

Solution

We can add the following dummy activity and dummy event to obtain the correct network:

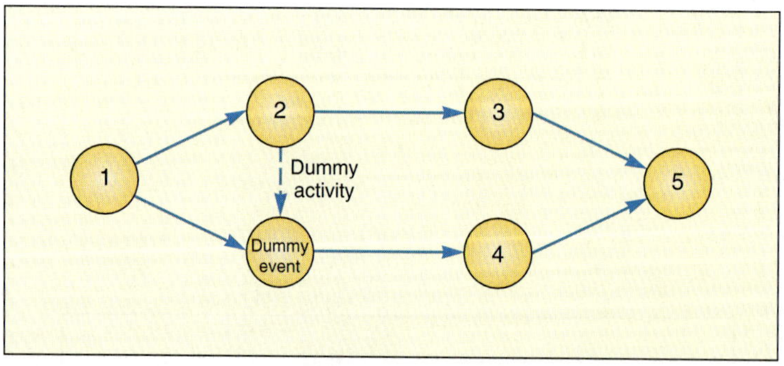

Solved Problem 17.3

Calculate the critical path, completion time T_e, and variance V on the basis of the following information.

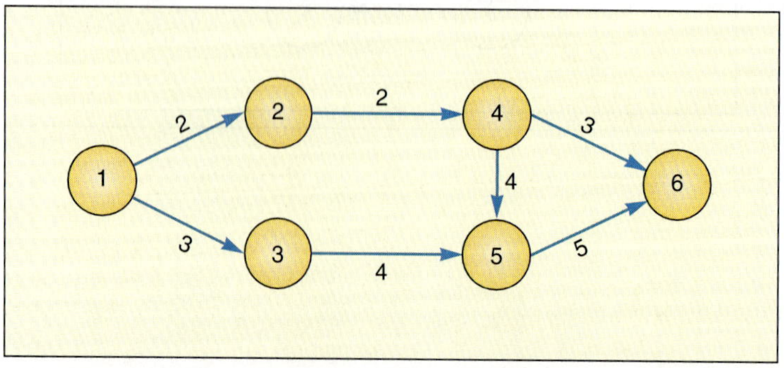

ACTIVITY	t	V	ES	EF	LS	LF	S
1–2	2	2/6	0	2	0	2	0
1–3	3	2/6	0	3	1	4	1
2–4	2	4/6	2	4	2	4	0
3–5	4	4/6	3	7	4	8	1
4–5	4	2/6	4	8	4	8	0
4–6	3	1/6	4	7	10	13	6
5–6	5	1/6	8	13	8	13	0

Solution

We conclude that the critical path is $1 \rightarrow 2 \rightarrow 4 \rightarrow 5 \rightarrow 6$.

$$T_e = 2 + 2 + 4 + 5 = 13$$

and

$$V = \frac{2}{6} + \frac{4}{6} + \frac{2}{6} + \frac{1}{6} = \frac{9}{6} = 1.5$$

Solved Problem 17.4

Given the following information, perform a critical path analysis.

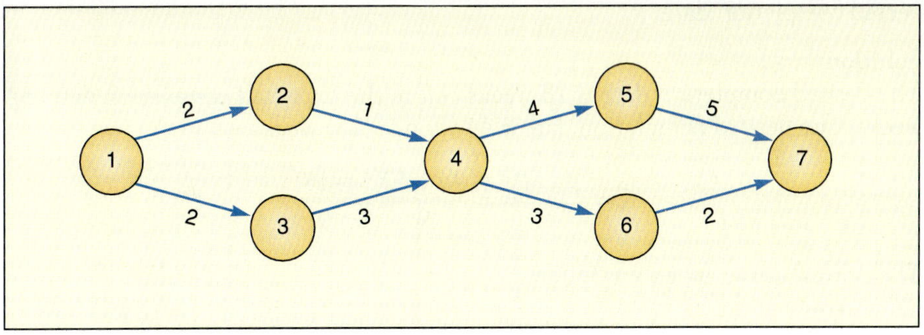

ACTIVITY	t	V	ACTIVITY	t	V
1–2	2	1/6	4–5	4	4/6
1–3	2	1/6	4–6	3	2/6
2–4	1	2/6	5–7	5	1/6
3–4	3	2/6	6–7	2	2/6

Solution

The solution begins with the determination of ES, EF, LS, LF, and S. We can find these values from the above information and then enter them into the following table:

ACTIVITY	t	V	ES	EF	LS	LF	S
1–2	2	1/6	0	2	2	4	2
1–3	2	1/6	0	2	0	2	0
2–4	1	2/6	2	3	4	5	2
3–4	3	2/6	2	5	2	5	0
4–5	4	4/6	5	9	5	9	0
4–6	3	2/6	5	8	9	12	4
5–7	5	1/6	9	14	9	14	0
6–7	2	2/6	8	10	12	14	4

Then we can find the critical path, T_e, and V. The critical path is 1–3, 3–4, 4–5, 5–7.

$$T_e = 2 + 3 + 4 + 5 = 14 \qquad \text{and} \qquad V = \frac{1}{6} + \frac{2}{6} + \frac{4}{6} + \frac{1}{6} = \frac{8}{6}$$

Solved Problem 17.5

The following information has been computed from a project:

$$T_e = 62 \text{ weeks}$$
$$V = 81$$

What is the probability that the project will be completed 18 weeks *before* its expected completion date?

Solution

The desired completion date is 18 weeks before the expected completion date, 62 weeks. The desired completion date is 44 (or 62 – 18) weeks.

$$Z = \frac{T_s - T_e}{\sigma} = \frac{44 - 62}{9} = \frac{-18}{9}$$

The normal curve appears as follows:

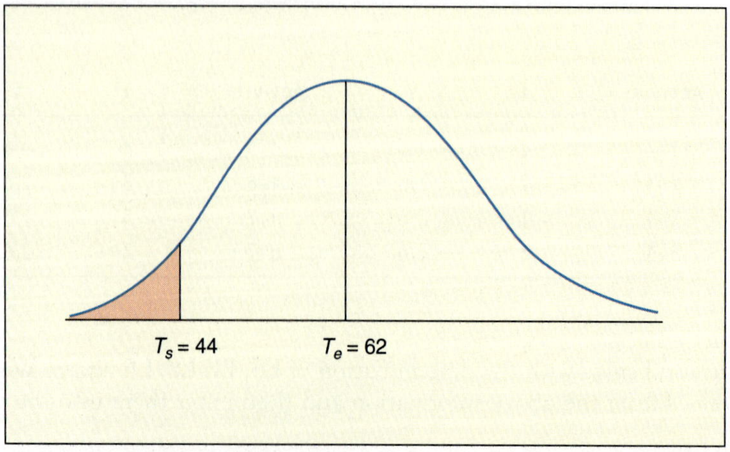

Because the normal curve is symmetrical and table values are calculated for positive values of Z, the area desired is equal to 1 – (table value). For $Z = +2.0$, the area from the table is .97725. Thus, the area corresponding to a Z value of –2.0 is .02275 (or 1 – 0.97725). Hence, the probability of completing the project 18 weeks before the expected completion date is approximately .02, or 2%.

Solved Problem 17.6

Determine the least cost of reducing the project completion date by 3 months based on the following information:

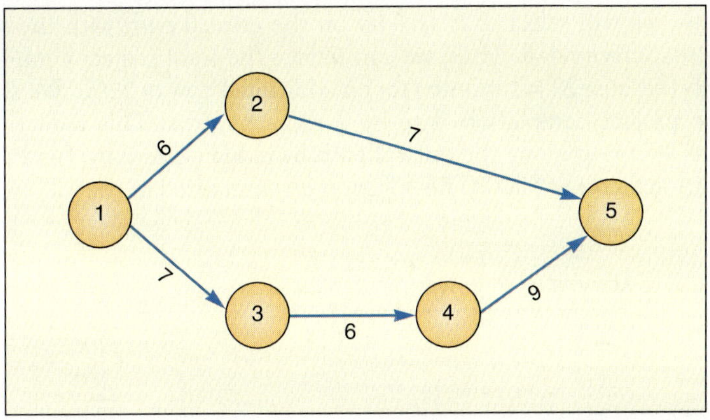

ACTIVITY	t (MONTHS)	M (MONTHS)	C
1–2	6	2	$400
1–3	7	2	500
2–5	7	1	300
3–4	6	2	600
4–5	9	1	200

Solution

The first step in this problem is to compute ES, EF, LS, LF, and S for each activity.

ACTIVITY	ES	EF	LS	LF	S
1–2	0	6	9	15	9
1–3	0	7	0	7	0
2–5	6	13	15	22	9
3–4	7	13	7	13	0
4–5	13	22	13	22	0

The critical path consists of activities 1–3, 3–4, and 4–5.

Next, K must be computed for each activity by dividing C by M for each activity.

ACTIVITY	M	C	K	CRITICAL PATH?
1–2	2	$400	$200/month	No
1–3	2	500	250/month	Yes
2–5	1	300	300/month	No
3–4	2	600	300/month	Yes
4–5	1	200	200/month	Yes

Finally, we will select that activity on the critical path with the smallest K_i value. This is activity 4–5. Thus, we can reduce the total project completion date by 1 month (because M = 1 month) for an additional cost of $200. We still need to reduce the project completion date by 2 more months. This reduction can be achieved at least cost along the critical path by reducing activity 1–3 by 2 months for an additional cost of $500. This solution is summarized in the following table:

ACTIVITY	MONTHS REDUCED	COST
4–5	1	$200
1–3	2	500
	Total:	$700

DISCUSSION QUESTIONS

1. What are some of the questions that can be answered with PERT and CPM?
2. What is an activity? What is an event? What is an immediate predecessor?
3. Describe how expected activity times and variances can be computed in a PERT network.
4. Briefly discuss what is meant by critical path analysis. What are critical path activities and why are they important?
5. What are the earliest activity start time and latest activity start time and how are they computed?
6. Describe the meaning of slack and discuss how it can be determined.
7. How can we determine the probability that a project will be completed by a certain date? What assumptions are made in this computation?
8. Briefly describe PERT/Cost and how it is used.
9. What is project crashing and how is it done by hand?
10. What are the three phases involved in the management of a large project?
11. What is a dummy activity and when is it required?
12. What is the basic difference between PERT and CPM?
13. How is the variance of the total project computed in PERT?
14. How is the expected completion time of a PERT project computed?
15. What is a project organization?
16. Describe the differences between a Gantt chart and a PERT/CPM network.
17. Name some of the widely used project management software programs.
18. What is the difference between an Activity-on-Arrow (AOA) network and an Activity-on-Node (AON) network? Which is used in this chapter?

CRITICAL THINKING EXERCISE

The *POM in Action* box in this chapter that describes Delta Airlines' "well-orchestrated" ground turnaround procedures deals with a serious issue for all airlines. As a matter of fact, the *Wall Street Journal*'s article "New Airline Fad: Faster Airport Turnarounds" (August 4, 1994, pp. B1–B2) describes similar scheduling improvements at USAir, Continental, and Southwest. For years, Southwest has turned its planes around in 15 minutes.

Provide detailed suggestions as to how airlines can speed up their turnaround times. What are Southwest's processes? What problems keep other airlines from emulating Southwest? Which is the preferable tool—Gantt charts or PERT/CPM—and why?

PROBLEMS

• **17.1** Draw the PERT network associated with the following activities for Bill Beville's next homework project.

Activity	Immediate Predecessor(s)	Activity	Immediate Predecessor(s)
A	—	E	B
B	A	F	C
C	A	G	D
D	B	H	E, F

• **17.2** Given the activities whose sequence is described by the following table:

Activity	Immediate Predecessor(s)	Activity	Immediate Predecessor(s)
A	—	F	C
B	A	G	E, F
C	A	H	D
D	B	I	G, H
E	B		

Draw the appropriate PERT diagram.

• **17.3** The following represent activities in Daniella Popoff's Construction Company project. Draw the network to represent this situation.

Activity	Immediate Predecessor(s)	Activity	Immediate Predecessor(s)
A	—	E	B
B	—	F	C, E
C	A	G	D
D	B	H	F, G

• **17.4** Sally McPherson is the personnel director of Babson and Willcount, a company that specializes in consulting and research. One of the training programs that Sally is considering for the middle-level managers of Babson and Willcount is leadership training. Sally has listed a number of activities that must be completed before a training program of this nature could be conducted. The activities and immediate predecessors appear in the accompanying table.

ACTIVITY	IMMEDIATE PREDECESSOR	ACTIVITY	IMMEDIATE PREDECESSOR
A	—	E	A, D
B	—	F	C
C	—	G	E, F
D	B		

Develop a network for this problem.

• **17.5** Sally McPherson was able to determine the activity times for the leadership training program. She would like to determine the total project completion time and the critical path. The activity times appear in the accompanying table. (See Problem 17.4).

ACTIVITY	TIME (DAYS)
A	2
B	5
C	1
D	10
E	3
F	6
G	8
Total:	35 days

• **17.6** The activities needed to build an experimental weed-harvesting machine at Timothy Urban Machinery Corp. are listed in the accompanying table. Construct a network for these activities.

ACTIVITY	IMMEDIATE PREDECESSORS	ACTIVITY	IMMEDIATE PREDECESSORS
A	—	E	B
B	—	F	B
C	A	G	C, E
D	A	H	D, F

• **17.7** Timothy Urban (see Problem 17.6) was able to determine the activity times for constructing his weed-harvesting machine. Urban would like to determine ES, EF, LS, LF, and slack for each activity. The total project completion time and the critical path should also be determined. Here are the activity times:

ACTIVITY	TIME (WEEKS)	ACTIVITY	TIME (WEEKS)
A	6	E	4
B	5	F	6
C	3	G	10
D	2	H	7

• **17.8** Riddick Wiring and Electric is a company that installs wiring and electrical fixtures in residential construction. Anne Riddick has been very concerned with the amount of time that it takes to complete wiring jobs. Some of her workers are very unreliable. A list of activities and their optimistic completion time, the pessimistic completion time, and the most likely completion time (all in days) is given in the table below.

Determine the expected completion time and variance for each activity.

ACTIVITY	a	m	b	IMMEDIATE PREDECESSORS
A	3	6	8	—
B	2	4	4	—
C	1	2	3	—
D	6	7	8	C
E	2	4	6	B, D
F	6	10	14	A, E
G	1	2	4	A, E
H	3	6	9	F
I	10	11	12	G
J	14	16	20	C
K	2	8	10	H, I

: **17.9** Anne Riddick would like to determine the total project completion time and the critical path for installing electrical wiring and equipment in residential houses. See Problem 17.8 for details. In addition, determine ES, EF, LS, LF, and slack for each activity.

: **17.10** What is the probability that Riddick will finish the project described in Problems 17.8 and 17.9 in 40 days or less?

• **17.11** The activities described by the following table are given for the Rivera Corporation:

ACTIVITY	IMMEDIATE PREDECESSOR(S)	TIME
A	—	9
B	A	7
C	A	3
D	B	6
E	B	9
F	C	4
G	E, F	6
H	D	5
I	G, H	3

a) Draw the appropriate PERT diagram for David Rivera's management team.

b) Find the critical path.

:17.12 A small software development project at Jack McGarrie's firm has four major activities. The times are estimated and provided in the table below. Find the expected time for completing McGarrie's project.

ACTIVITY	IMMEDIATE PREDECESSOR	a	m	b
A	—	2	5	8
B	—	3	6	9
C	A	4	7	10
D	B	2	5	14
E	C	3	3	3

a) What is the expected completion time for this project?

b) What variance would be used in finding probabilities of finishing by a certain time?

:17.13 Given the activities described by the following table:

ACTIVITY	EXPECTED TIME	STANDARD DEVIATION OF TIME ESTIMATE	IMMEDIATE PREDECESSOR(S)
A	7	2	—
B	3	1	A
C	9	3	A
D	4	1	B, C
E	5	1	B, C
F	8	2	E
G	8	1	D, F
H	6	2	G

a) Draw the appropriate PERT diagram.

b) Find the critical path and project completion time.

c) Find the probability that the project will take more than 49 time periods to complete.

17.14 Development of a new deluxe version of a particular software product is being considered by Joan Blasco-Paul's software house. The activities necessary for the completion of this are listed in the table below.

ACTIVITY	NORMAL TIME	CRASH TIME	NORMAL COST	CRASH COST	IMMEDIATE PREDECESSOR(S)
A	4	3	2,000	2,600	—
B	2	1	2,200	2,800	—
C	3	3	500	500	—
D	8	4	2,300	2,600	A
E	6	3	900	1,200	B
F	3	2	3,000	4,200	C
G	4	2	1,400	2,000	D, E

a) What is the project completion date?

b) What is the total cost required for completing this project on normal time?

c) If you wish to reduce the time required to complete this project by 1 week, which activity should be crashed, and how much will this increase the total cost?

17.15 A project in Janice Laughlin's company has an expected completion time of 40 weeks and a standard deviation of 5 weeks. It is assumed that the project completion time is normally distributed.

a) What is the probability of finishing the project in 50 weeks or less?

b) What is the probability of finishing the project in 38 weeks or less?

c) The due date for the project is set so that there is a 90% chance that the project will be finished by this date. What is the due date?

17.16 B&R Manufacturing produces custom-built pollution-control devices for medium-sized steel mills. The most recent project undertaken by B&R requires 14 different activities. B&R's managers would like to determine the total project completion time and those activities that lie along the critical path. The appropriate data are shown in the table below.

ACTIVITY	IMMEDIATE PREDECESSORS	OPTIMISTIC TIME	MOST LIKELY TIME	PESSIMISTIC TIME
A	—	4	6	7
B	—	1	2	3
C	A	6	6	6
D	A	5	8	11
E	B, C	1	9	18
F	D	2	3	6
G	D	1	7	8
H	E, F	4	4	6
I	G, H	1	6	8
J	I	2	5	7
K	I	8	9	11
L	J	2	4	6
M	K	1	2	3
N	L, M	6	8	10

17.17 Bill Trigiero, director of personnel of Trigiero Resources, Inc., is in the process of designing a program that his customers can use in the job-finding process. Some of the activities include preparing resumes, writing letters, making appointments to see prospective employers, researching companies and industries, and so on. Some of the information on the activities appears in the following table:

ACTIVITY	TIME (DAYS) a	m	b	IMMEDIATE PREDECESSORS
A	8	10	12	—
B	6	7	9	—
C	3	3	4	—
D	10	20	30	A
E	6	7	8	C
F	9	10	11	B, D, E
G	6	7	10	B, D, E
H	14	15	16	F
I	10	11	13	F
J	6	7	8	G, H
K	4	7	8	I, J
L	1	2	4	G, H

a) Construct a network for this problem.
b) Determine the expected times and variances for each activity.
c) Determine ES, EF, LS, LF, and slack for each activity.
d) Determine the critical path and project completion time.
e) Determine the probability that the project will be finished in 70 days.
f) Determine the probability that the project will be finished in 80 days.
g) Determine the probability that the project will be finished in 90 days.

17.18 Using PERT, Marcie Pleau-Watson was able to determine that the expected project completion time for the construction of a pleasure yacht is 21 months, and the project variance is 4.

a) What is the probability that the project will be completed in 17 months?
b) What is the probability that the project will be completed in 20 months?
c) What is the probability that the project will be completed in 23 months?
d) What is the probability that the project will be completed in 25 months?

17.19 Norris Builders manufactures steel storage sheds for commercial use. Clay Norris, president of Norris Builders, is contemplating producing sheds for home use. The activities necessary to build an experimental model and related data are given in the accompanying table.

ACTIVITY	NORMAL TIME	CRASH TIME	NORMAL COST ($)	CRASH COST ($)	IMMEDIATE PREDECESSORS
A	3	2	1,600	1,600	—
B	2	1	2,700	2,700	—
C	1	0	300	600	—
D	7	3	1,300	1,600	A
E	6	3	850	1,000	B
F	2	1	4,000	5,000	C
G	4	2	1,500	2,000	D, E

a) What is the project completion date?

b) Crash this project to 10 weeks at the least cost.

:17.20 The Maser is a new custom-designed sports car. An analysis of the task of building the Maser reveals the following list of relevant activities, their immediate predecessors, and their duration.[2]

Job Letter	Description	Immediate Predecessors	Normal Time (Days)
A	Start	—	0
B	Design	A	8
C	Order special accessories	B	0.1
D	Build frame	B	1
E	Build doors	B	1
F	Attach axles, wheels, gas tank	D	1
G	Build body shell	B	2
H	Build transmission and drivetrain	B	3
I	Fit doors to body shell	G, E	1
J	Build engine	B	4
K	Bench-test engine	J	2
L	Assemble chassis	F, H, K	1
M	Road-test chassis	L	0.5
N	Paint body	I	2
O	Install wiring	N	1
P	Install interior	N	1.5
Q	Accept delivery of special accessories	C	5
R	Mount body and accessories on chassis	M, O, P, Q	1
S	Road-test car	R	0.5
T	Attach exterior trim	S	1
U	Finish	T	0

a) Draw a network diagram for the project.

b) Mark the critical path and state its length.

c) If the Maser had to be completed 2 days earlier, would it help to:

i) Buy preassembled transmissions and drivetrains?

ii) Install robots to halve engine-building time?

iii) Speed delivery of special accessories by 3 days?

d) How might resources be borrowed from activities on the noncritical path to speed activities on the critical path?

[2]*Source:* James A. F. Stoner and Charles Wankel, *Management*, 3rd ed. (Englewood Cliffs, NJ: Prentice Hall, 1986), p. 195.

17.21 Getting a degree from a college or university is a long and difficult task. Certain courses must be completed before other courses may be taken. Develop a network diagram in which every activity is a particular course that must be taken for a given degree program. The immediate predecessors will be course prerequisites. Do not forget to include all university, college, and departmental course requirements. Then try to group these courses into semesters or quarters for your particular school. Which courses, if not taken in the proper sequence, could delay your graduation?

DATA BASE APPLICATION

17.22 The Van Voorhis Construction Company is involved with constructing municipal buildings and other structures that are used primarily by city and provincial municipalities. This requires developing legal documents, drafting feasibility studies, obtaining bond ratings, and so forth. Recently, Jamie Van Voorhis was given a request to submit a proposal for the construction of a municipal building. The first step is to develop legal documents and to perform all necessary steps before the construction contract is signed. This requires approximately 20 separate activities that must be completed. These activities, their immediate predecessors, and time requirements are given in the table shown below. As you can see, optimistic (a), most likely (m), and pessimistic (b) time estimates have been given for all of the activities described in the table. Using these data, determine the total project completion time for this preliminary step, the critical path, and slack time for all activities involved.

	Time Required (Weeks)				
Activity	a	m	b	Description	Immediate Predecessor(s)
1	1	4	5	Drafting legal documents	—
2	2	3	4	Preparation of financial statements	—
3	3	4	5	Draft of history	—
4	7	8	9	Draft demand portion of feasibility study	—
5	4	4	5	Review and approval of legal documents	1
6	1	2	4	Review and approval of history	3
7	4	5	6	Review feasibility study	4
8	1	2	4	Draft final financial portion of feasibility study	7
9	3	4	4	Draft facts relevant to the bond transaction	5
10	1	1	2	Review and approval of financial statements	2
11	18	20	26	Firm price received of project	—
12	1	2	3	Review and completion of financial portion of feasibility study	8
13	1	1	2	Draft statement completed	6, 9, 10, 11, 12
14	.10	.14	.16	All materials sent to bond rating services	13
15	.2	.3	.4	Statement printed and distributed to all interested parties	14
16	1	1	2	Presentation to bond rating services	14
17	1	2	3	Bond rating received	16
18	3	5	7	Marketing of bonds	15, 17
19	.1	.1	.2	Purchase contract executed	18
20	.1	.14	.16	Final statement authorized and completed	19
21	2	3	6	Purchase contract	19
22	.1	.1	.2	Bond proceeds available	20
23	.0	.2	.2	Sign construction contract	21, 22

CASE STUDY

The Family Planning Research Centre of Nigeria

Dr. Adinombe Watage, deputy director of the Family Planning Research Centre in Nigeria's Over-the-River Province, was assigned the task of organizing and training five teams of field workers to do education and outreach as part of a large project to demonstrate acceptance of a new method of birth control. These workers had already had training in family planning education, but must receive specific training regarding the new method of contraception. Two types of materials must also be prepared: (1) those for use in training the workers, and (2) those for distribution in the field. Training faculty must be brought in and arrangements made for transportation and accommodations for the participants.

Dr. Watage first called a meeting of his office staff. Together they identified the activities that must be carried out, their necessary sequences, and the time that they would require. Their results are displayed in Table 1.

Louis Odaga, the chief clerk, noted that the project had to be completed in 60 days. Whipping out his solar-powered calculator, he added up the time needed. It came to 94 days. "An impossible task then," he noted. "No," Dr. Watage replied, "some of these tasks can go forward in parallel." "Be careful though," warned Mr. Oglagadu, the chief nurse, "there aren't that many of us to go around. There are only 10 of us in this office."

"I can check whether we have enough heads and hands, once I have tentatively scheduled the activities," Dr. Watage responded. "If the schedule is too tight, I have permission from the Pathminder Fund to spend some funds to speed it up, just so long as I can prove that it can be done at the least cost necessary. Can you help me prove that? Here are the costs for the activities with the elapsed time that we planned and the costs and times, if we shorten them to an absolute minimum." Those data are in Table 2.

TABLE 1 ■ THE FAMILY PLANNING RESEARCH CENTRE

ACTIVITY	MUST FOLLOW	TIME (IN DAYS)	STAFFING NEEDED
A. Identify faculty and their schedules	—	5	2
B. Arrange transport to base	—	7	3
C. Identify and collect training materials	—	5	2
D. Arrange accommodations	A	3	1
E. Identify team	A	7	4
F. Bring in team	B, E	2	1
G. Transport faculty to base	A, B	3	2
H. Print program material	C	10	6
I. Have program materials delivered	H	7	3
J. Conduct training program	D, F, G, I	15	0
K. Perform fieldwork training	J	30	0

DISCUSSION QUESTIONS

1. Some of the tasks in this project can be done in parallel. Prepare a diagram showing the required network of tasks and define the critical path. What is the length of the project without crashing?
2. At this point, can the project be done given the personnel constraint of 10 persons?
3. If the critical path is longer than 60 days, what is the least amount that Dr. Watage can spend and still achieve this schedule objective? How can he prove to Pathminder Foundation that this is the minimum cost alternative?

Source: Professor Curtis P. McLaughlin, Kenan-Flagler Business School, University of North Carolina at Chapel Hill.

(Continued)

TABLE 2 ■ THE FAMILY PLANNING RESEARCH CENTRE

	Normal		Minimum		
Activity	Time	Cost ($)	Time	Cost ($)	Average Cost per Day Saved ($)
A. Identify faculty	5	400	2	700	100
B. Arrange transport	7	1,000	4	1,450	150
C. Identify materials	5	400	3	500	50
D. Make accommodations	3	2,500	1	3,000	250
E. Identify team	7	400	4	850	150
F. Bring team in	2	1,000	1	2,000	1,000
G. Transport faculty	3	1,500	2	2,000	500
H. Print materials	10	3,000	5	4,000	200
I. Deliver materials	7	200	2	600	80
J. Train team	15	5,000	10	7,000	400
K. Do fieldwork	30	10,000	20	14,000	400

CASE STUDY

Shale Oil Company

The Shale Oil Company contains several operating units that make up its Aston, Ohio, manufacturing complex. These units process the crude oil that is pumped through and transform it into a multitude of hydrocarbon products. The units run 24 hours a day, 7 days a week, and must be shut down for maintenance on a predetermined schedule. One such unit is Distillation Unit No. 5, or DU5. Studies have shown that DU5 can operate only 3½ years without major equipment breakdowns and excessive loss of efficiency. Therefore, DU5 is shut down every 3½ years for cleaning, inspection, and repairs.

DU5 is the only distillation unit for crude oil in the Aston complex, and its shutdown severely affects all other operating units. Some of the production can be compensated by Shale refineries in other locations, but the rest must be processed before the shutdown and stored. Without proper planning, a nationwide shortage of Shale gasoline could occur. The time of DU5's shutdown is critical, and the length of time the unit is down must be kept to a minimum to limit production loss. Shale uses PERT as a planning and controlling tool to minimize shutdown time.

The first phase of a shutdown is to open and clean the equipment. Inspectors can then enter the unit and examine the damage. Once damages are determined, the needed repairs can be carried out. Repair times can vary considerably depending on what damage the inspection reveals. On the basis of previous inspection records, some repair work is known ahead of time. Thorough cleaning of the equipment is also necessary to improve the unit's

(Continued)

operating efficiency. Table 3 lists the many maintenance activities and their estimated completion times.

DISCUSSION QUESTIONS

1. Determine the expected shutdown time and the probability the shutdown can be completed 1 week earlier.
2. What are the probabilities that Shale finishes the maintenance project 1, 2, 3, 4, 5, or 6 days earlier?
3. Shale Oil is considering increasing the budget to shorten the shutdown. How do you suggest the company proceed?

TABLE 3 ■ PREVENTIVE MAINTENANCE OF DU5

		TIME ESTIMATES (IN DAYS)		
	ACTIVITIES	OPTIMISTIC	MOST LIKELY	PESSIMISTIC
1–2	Circulate wash water throughout unit	1	2	2.5
2–3	Install blinds	1.5	2	2.5
3–4	Open and clean vessels and columns	2	3	4
3–5	Open and clean heat exchangers; remove tube bundles	1	2	3
3–6	Open and clean furnaces	1	2	4
3–7	Open and clean mechanical equipment	2	2.5	3
3–8	Inspect instrumentation	2	4	5
4–9	Inspect vessels and columns	1	2	3
5–10	Inspect heat-exchanger shells	1	1.5	2
5–11	Inspect tube bundles	1	1.5	2
6–12	Inspect furnaces	2	2.5	3
6–17	Retube furnaces	15	20	30
7–13	Inspect mechanical equipment	1	1.5	2
7–18	Install new pump mechanical seals	3	5	8
8–19	Repair instrumentation	3	8	15
9–14	Repair vessels and columns	14	21	28
10–16	Repair heat-exchanger shells	1	5	10
11–15	Repair tube bundles; retube	2	5	10
12–17	Repair furnaces	5	10	20
13–18	Repair mechanical equipment	10	15	25
14–20	Test and close vessels and columns	4	5	8
15–16	Install tube bundles into heat-exchanger shells	1	2	3
16–20	Test and close heat exchangers	1	2	2.5
17–20	Test and close furnaces	1	2	3
18–20	Test and close mechanical equipment	1	2	3
19–20	Test instrumentation	2	4	6
20–21	Pull blinds	1.5	2	2.5
21–22	Purge all equipment with steam	1	3	5
22–23	Start up unit	3	5	10

BIBLIOGRAPHY

Cleland, D. I., and W. R. King. *Project Management Handbook*. New York: Van Nostrand Reinhold, 1984.

Dean, B. V. "Getting the Job Done! Managing Project Teams and Task Forces for Success." *The Executive*, 6, no. 4 (November 1992): 94.

Dusenberry, W. "CPM for New Product Introductions." *Harvard Business Review* (July/August 1967): 124–139.

Hickman, Anita. "Refining the Process of Project Control." *Production and Inventory Management* (February 1992): 26–27.

Keefer, D. L., and W. A. Verdini. "Better Estimation of PERT Activity Time Parameters." *Management Science*, 39, no. 9 (September 1993): 1,086.

Kerzner, H., and H. Thamhain. *Project Management for Small and Medium Size Business*. New York: Van Nostrand Reinhold, 1984.

Kim, S., and R. C. Leachman. "Multi-Project Scheduling with Explicit Lateness Costs." *IIE Transactions*, 25, no. 2 (March 1993): 34–44.

Pinto, M. B., J. K. Pinto, and J. E. Prescott. "Antecedents and Consequences of Project Team Cross-functional Cooperation." *Management Science*, 39, no. 10 (October 1993): 1,281.

Render, B., and R. M. Stair. *Introduction to Management Science*. Boston: Allyn and Bacon, 1992.

———. *Quantitative Analysis for Management*, 5th ed. Boston: Allyn and Bacon, 1994.

18

MAINTENANCE AND RELIABILITY

CHAPTER OUTLINE

LEARNING OBJECTIVES

When you complete this chapter you should be able to:

Identify or define:

- Maintenance
- Redundancy
- Preventive maintenance
- Breakdown maintenance
- Mean time between failures
- Infant mortality

Explain:

- How to measure system reliability
- How to improve maintenance
- How to evaluate maintenance performance

WORLD-CLASS PROFILE: ORLANDO UTILITIES COMMISSION

Maintenance Provides a Competitive Advantage for Orlando Utilities Commission

The Orlando Utilities Commission (OUC) owns and operates power plants that supply power to 13 central Florida counties. Every year, OUC takes each one of its power-generating units off-line for 1 to 3 weeks to perform maintenance work.

Additionally, each unit is also taken off-line every 3 years for a complete overhaul and turbine generator inspection. Overhauls are scheduled for spring and fall, when the weather is mildest and demand for power is low. These overhauls last from 6 to 8 weeks.

Units at OUC's Stanton Energy Center require that maintenance personnel perform approximately 12,000 repair and preventive maintenance tasks a year. To accomplish these tasks efficiently, many of these jobs are scheduled daily via a computerized maintenance management program. The computer generates preventive maintenance work orders and lists of required materials.

Every day that a plant is down for maintenance costs OUC about $55,000 extra for the replacement cost of power that must be generated elsewhere. However, these costs pale beside the costs associated with a forced outage. An unexpected outage could cost OUC an additional $250,000 to $500,000 each day!

Scheduled overhauls are not easy; each one has 1,800 distinct tasks and requires 72,000 labour-hours. But the value of preventive maintenance was illustrated by the first overhaul of a new turbine generator. Workers discovered a cracked rotor blade, which could have destroyed a $27 million piece of equipment. To find such cracks, which are invisible to the naked eye, metals are examined by dye tests, X-rays, and ultrasound.

At OUC, preventive maintenance is worth its weight in gold. As a result, OUC's electric distribution system is ranked number 1 in Florida for reliability. Effective maintenance provides a competitive advantage for the Orlando Utilities Commission.

Maintenance of capital-intensive facilities requires good planning to minimize downtime. Here, turbine overhaul is under way. Organizing the thousands of parts and pieces necessary for a shutdown is a major effort.

The high pressure/low pressure section of turbine has been removed for overhaul. When steam first enters this 21-tonne high-pressure rotor, it bears hurricane-strength force.

Inspection is proceeding on low pressure section of turbine. The tips of these turbine blades will travel at supersonic speeds of about 2,100 kilometres per hour when the plant is in operation. And a crack in any one of these blades can cause a catastrophic failure.

When the United Airlines DC-10 left Denver, three engines and all three hydraulic systems were working. But at 3:17 P.M., an explosion shook the plane. Number 2 engine had torn itself apart. The three separate hydraulic lines ceased to work. Despite the work of dedicated designers and well-trained maintenance personnel, the engine failed. Despite having three separate hydraulic lines, the aircraft had no working hydraulic system. Despite eight million hours of no fatal United Airlines accidents, over one hundred people were about to die. ♦

Failure

This chapter is concerned with avoiding undesirable results of system failure. A **failure** is the change in a product or system from a satisfactory working condition to a condition that is below an acceptable standard. Even when the results are not catastrophic, the results of failure can be disruptive, inconvenient, wasteful, and expensive.

Consider a North American automotive manufacturing plant employing approximately 5,000 hourly-paid workers. (The North American automotive industry has more than 50 such plants in Canada, the United States, and Mexico.) Suppose such a plant is idled for just one day's production. Workers in such plants are paid more than \$20 per hour and are contractually guaranteed a minimum of four hours' pay in the event of a shutdown. Such a breakdown would cost $\$20 \times 4 \times 5{,}000$ or \$400,000 in wages, for which no products are produced. In addition, overtime hours at time-and-a-half would have to be paid to make up the lost production, at a cost of \$600,000. Thus the real breakdown loss is \$600,000 to the firm (the \$400,000 would have been paid in wages had the breakdown not occurred). Skimping on maintenance procedures is a false economy when the "savings" are compared to such a loss.

A study addressing the weaknesses in British productivity compared British and German firms.[1] The study found that although the machinery in the British plants was no older than that in the German plants, it was badly maintained. Breakdowns were found to be more frequent and lasted longer. Operators were found less able to do repairs themselves. Machine and product failures can have far-reaching effects on a firm's operation and profitability. In complex, highly mechanized plants, an out-of-tolerance process or a machine breakdown may result in idle employees and facilities, loss of customers and goodwill, and profits turning into losses. Likewise, in an office, the failure of a generator, an air-conditioning system, or a computer may halt operations.

Reliability is important to P/OM managers. Maintenance is important to P/OM managers. System failures cause undesirable results.

Good managers maintain a system while keeping maintenance and breakdown costs under control. Reliability and maintenance protect both a firm's performance and its investment. Systems must be designed and maintained to reach expected performance and quality standards. **Reliability** is the probability that a machine part or product will function properly for a given length of time. **Maintenance** includes all activities involved in keeping a system's equipment in working order. *The objective of reliability and maintenance is to maintain the capability of the system while controlling costs.*

Reliability
Maintenance

It should be noted that certain pieces of capital equipment do have relatively short useful lives (i.e., under 10 years), and it is essential that the P/OM manager not allow a piece of equipment to be retained beyond the point at which even a well-designed maintenance program cannot be economically justified. Detailed studies done

[1]National Institute of Economic and Social Research as reported in "Britain's Economy," *The Economist* (March 9, 1985): 62–63.

on material handling equipment such as forklift trucks have shown that the optimal value is received from them if after 5,000 operating hours they are given a complete overhaul and rebuilding, put back into service for an additional 3,000 operating hours, and then disposed of. The 8,000 hours represented the point of "diminishing marginal returns" and to continue beyond this lifetime was to incur costs well out of proportion to the value received.

In such equipment, working in various operations anywhere from 2 to 16 hours per day, the essential measure for maintenance service is not the actual age of the equipment, but the accumulated number of operating hours.

In this chapter, we examine four tactics for improving reliability and maintenance of products and equipment as well as the systems that produce them. The four tactics are organized around reliability and maintenance.

The reliability tactics are

1. improving individual components;
2. providing redundancy (redundancy in the context of reliability means duplicating certain companents to provide a backup).

The maintenance tactics are

1. implementing or improving preventive maintenance;
2. increasing repair capabilities or speed.

RELIABILITY

Systems are composed of a series of individual interrelated components, each performing a specific job. If any *one* component fails to perform, for whatever reason, the overall system (for example, an airplane or machine) can fail.

Improving Individual Components

As the story about United Airlines at the beginning of this chapter shows, failures do occur. That failures occur is an important reliability concept.

Figure 18.1 shows that as the number of components in a *series* increases, the reliability of the whole system declines very quickly. A system of $n = 50$ interacting parts, each of which has a 99.5% reliability, has an overall reliability of 78%. If the system or machine has 100 interacting parts, each with an individual reliability of 99.5%, the overall reliability will be only about 60%!

To measure system reliability in which each individual part or component may have its own unique rate of reliability, we cannot use the reliability curve in Figure 18.1. However, the method of computing system reliability (R_s) is simple. It consists of finding the product of individual reliabilities as follows:

$$R_s = R_1 \times R_2 \times R_3 \times \cdots \times R_n \qquad (18.1)$$

where R_1 = reliability of component 1
R_2 = reliability of component 2

and so on.

FIGURE 18.1 ■ Overall System Reliability as a Function of Number of Components and Component Reliability with Components in a Series

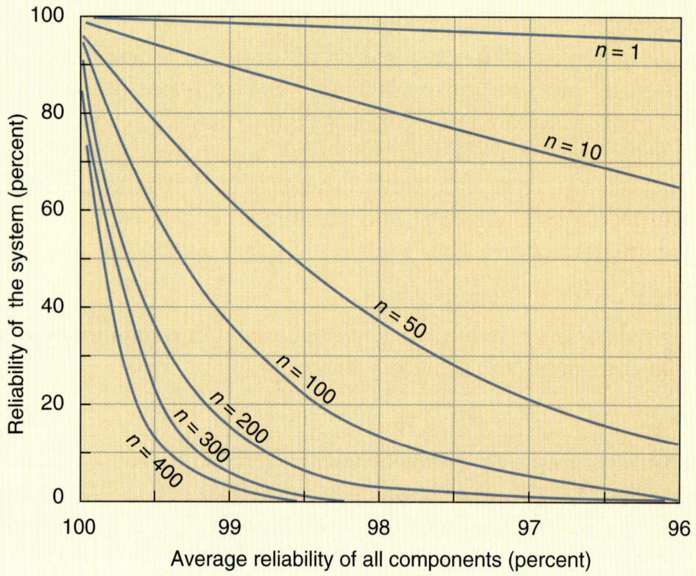

Equation (18.1) assumes that the reliability of an individual component does not depend on the reliability of other components (that is, each component is independent). Additionally, in this equation, as in most reliability discussions, reliabilities are presented as probabilities. A .90 reliability means that the unit will perform as intended 90% of the time. It also means that it will fail 1 – .90 = .1 = 10% of the time. We can use this method to evaluate the reliability of a product, such as the one we examine in Example 1.

EXAMPLE 1

Consider a system of 100 components, each with a reliability .9. If any component fails, the system will fail.

$$\text{Reliability} = R_1 \times R_2 \times R_3 \times \ldots \times R_{100}$$

In this example, since all components have a reliability of .9, then the system reliability is $R^{100} = .9^{100} = .000027$.

What would the resulting reliability be if each component was improved to .95? To .99? To .999?

$$.95^{100} = .005921 \text{ (works slightly more than } \tfrac{1}{2}\% \text{ of the time)}$$
$$.99^{100} = .366032$$
$$.999^{100} = .904792$$

Such dramatic increases in component reliability are likely to be very expensive and likely cannot be achieved.

EXAMPLE 2

Prairie Electric of Saskatoon, Saskatchewan, produces an electrical relay switch that has three components set up in series:

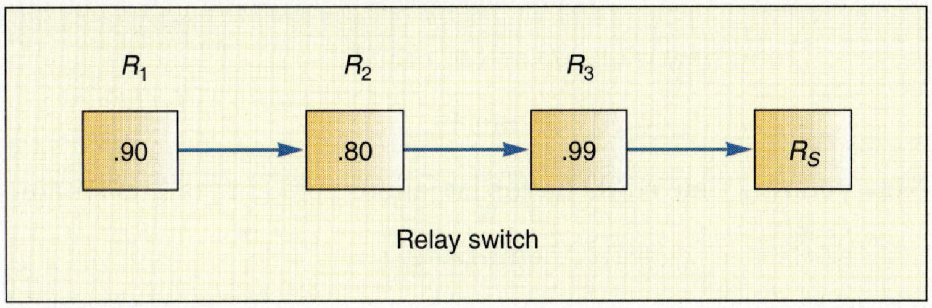

If the individual reliabilities are .90, .80, .99, then the reliability of the entire relay switch is

$$R_s = R_1 R_2 R_3 = (.90)(.80)(.99) = .713, \text{ or } 71.3\%$$

Component reliability is often a design or specification issue for which engineering design personnel may be responsible. However, purchasing personnel may be able to improve components of systems by staying abreast of suppliers' products and research efforts. Purchasing personnel can also directly contribute to evaluation of supplier performance.

The basic unit of measure for reliability is the product failure rate (FR). Firms producing high-technology equipment often provide failure rate data on their products. The failure rate measures the percentage of failures among the total number of products tested, FR(%), or a number of failures during a period of time, FR(N):

$$\text{FR}(\%) = \frac{\text{number of failures}}{\text{number of units tested}} \times 100\% \tag{18.2}$$

$$\text{FR}(N) = \frac{\text{number of failures}}{\text{number of unit-hours of operating time}} \tag{18.3}$$

Perhaps the most common term in reliability analysis is the **mean time between failures (MTBF)**, which is the reciprocal of FR(N):

Mean time between failures (MTBF)

$$\text{MTBF} = \frac{1}{\text{FR}(N)} \tag{18.4}$$

In Example 3, we compute the percentage of failure FR(%), number of failures FR(N), and mean time between failures (MTBF).

EXAMPLE 3

Twenty air-conditioning systems to be used by astronauts in NASA space shuttles were operated for 1,000 hours at NASA's Huntsville, Alabama, test facility. Two of the systems failed during the test—one after 200 hours and the other after 600 hours. To compute the percentage of failures,

$$\text{FR}(\%) = \frac{\text{number of failures}}{\text{number tested}} = \frac{2}{20}(100\%) = 10\%$$

Today's jetliners are expected to be designed so that one system's failure doesn't automatically cripple others. But the 1989 crash of this United Airlines DC-10 in Sioux City, Iowa, seems to indicate that the McDonnell Douglas plane's hydraulic systems aren't providing good enough protection. The DC-10 has three separate mazes of half-inch pipes running throughout the plane. Each pipe is designed to continuously pump fluid that operates control devices. But federal investigators think the pipes in the plane's tail were severed by flying tail parts. Hydraulic fluid then sprayed out, causing loss of control and, ultimately, the crash.

Next we compute the number of failures per operating hour:

$$\text{FR}(N) = \frac{\text{number of failures}}{\text{operating time}}$$

where

$$\text{Total time} = (1{,}000 \text{ hr})(20 \text{ units})$$
$$= 20{,}000 \text{ unit-hr.}$$
$$\text{Nonoperating time} = 800 \text{ hr. for 1st failure} + 400 \text{ hr. for 2nd failure}$$
$$= 1{,}200 \text{ unit-hr.}$$
$$\text{Operating time} = \text{total time} - \text{nonoperating time}$$
$$\text{FR}(N) = \frac{2}{20{,}000 - 1{,}200} = \frac{2}{18{,}800}$$
$$= .000106 \text{ failure/unit-hr.}$$

and because $\text{MTBF} = \dfrac{1}{\text{FR}(N)}$

$$\text{MTBF} = \frac{1}{.000106} = 9{,}434 \text{ hr.}$$

If the typical space shuttle trip lasts 60 days, NASA may be interested in the failure rate per trip:

$$\text{Failure rate} = (\text{failures/unit-hr.})(24 \text{ hr./day})(60 \text{ days/trip})$$
$$= (.000106)(24)(60)$$
$$= .152 \text{ failure/trip}$$

Because the failure rate of Example 3 is likely too high, NASA will have to either increase the reliability of individual components, and hence of the system, or install several backup air-conditioning units on each space shuttle. Backup units provide redundancy.

Providing Redundancy

To increase the reliability of systems, redundancy ("backing up" the components) is added. Redundancy is provided if one component fails, and the system has recourse to another.

The most common example of redundancy is a spare tire; redundancy's critical importance can be seen when you suffer a blowout in a remote area. Another example is the splitting of a car's hydraulic braking system into two separate systems, one for the front and another for the rear wheels. Should a hydraulic leak develop, only half of the braking system is rendered inoperative.

Say the reliability of a component is .80 and we back it up with another component with reliability of .80. Then the resulting reliability is the probability of the first component working plus the probability of the backup component working multiplied by the probability of needing the backup component (1 – .8 = .2). Therefore:

$$\begin{pmatrix}\text{Probability}\\\text{of first}\\\text{component}\\\text{working}\end{pmatrix} + \left[\begin{pmatrix}\text{Probability}\\\text{of second}\\\text{component}\\\text{working}\end{pmatrix} \times \begin{pmatrix}\text{Probability}\\\text{of needing}\\\text{second}\\\text{component}\end{pmatrix}\right] =$$

$$(.8) \quad + \quad [(.8) \quad \times \quad (1 - .8)] \quad = .8 + .16 = .96$$

Example 4 shows how redundancy can improve the reliability of the system presented in Example 2.

EXAMPLE 4

Prairie Electric is disturbed that its electrical relay has a reliability of only .713 (see Example 2). Therefore, Prairie decides to provide redundancy for the two least reliable components. This results in the system shown below:

$$\begin{array}{ccccc} R_1 & & R_2 & & R_3 \\ \boxed{0.90} & & \boxed{0.8} & & \\ \downarrow & & \downarrow & & \\ \boxed{0.90} & \rightarrow & \boxed{0.8} & \rightarrow & \boxed{0.99} \end{array} = [.9 + .9(1 - .9)] \times [.8 + .8(1 - .8)] \times .99$$

$$= [.9 + (.9)(.1)] \times [.8 + (.8)(.2)] \times .99$$

$$= .99 \times .96 \times .99 = .94$$

So by providing redundancy for two components, Nels has increased reliability of the switch from .713 to .94.

MAINTENANCE

There are two types of maintenance: preventive maintenance and breakdown maintenance. **Preventive maintenance** involves performing routine inspections and servicing and keeping facilities in good repair. These activities are intended to build a system that will find potential failures and make changes or repairs that will prevent failure. Preventive maintenance is much more than just keeping machinery and equipment running. It also involves designing technical and human systems that will keep the productive process working within tolerance; it allows the system to perform. The emphasis of preventive maintenance is on understanding the process and allowing it to work without interruption. **Breakdown maintenance** occurs when equipment fails and then must be repaired on an emergency or priority basis.

Preventive maintenance

Breakdown maintenance

Implementing Preventive Maintenance

Preventive maintenance implies that we can determine when a system needs service or will need repair. Figure 18.2 indicates that failure occurs at different rates during the life of a product. This failure rate may follow different statistical distributions. A high initial failure rate, known as **infant mortality**, exists initially for many products. This is the reason many electronic firms "burn in" their products prior to shipment. That is to say, many firms execute a variety of tests to detect "startup" problems prior to shipment. Other firms provide 90-day warranties.

Infant mortality

FIGURE 18.2 ■ Lifetime Failure Rates

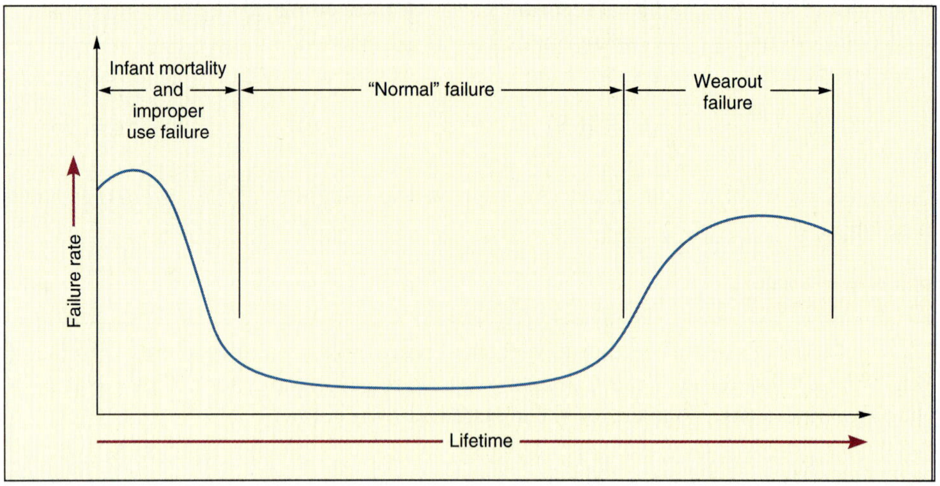

We should note that many infant mortality failures are not product failures per se, but failure due to improper use. A very common example of improper use occurs after installation of a new office photocopier when, even though employees are provided with training courses, few bother to attend in the belief that "If you've seen one photocopier, you've see them all." Of course, this is simply not true, and a large number of these breakdowns are attributable to the resulting improper use. This fact points up the importance of operations management's building a maintenance system that includes training and personnel selection.

Once the product, machine, or process "settles in," a study can be made of the MTBF (mean time between failure) distribution. When the distributions have a small standard deviation, then we know we have a candidate for preventive maintenance even if the maintenance is expensive.[2]

Once we have a candidate for preventive maintenance, we want to determine when preventive maintenance is economical. Typically, the more expensive the maintenance, the narrower must be the MTBF distribution. Additionally, if the process is no more expensive to repair when it breaks down than the cost of preventive maintenance, perhaps we should let the process break down and then do the repair. However, the consequence of the breakdown must be fully considered. Some relatively minor breakdowns have *catastrophic* and expensive consequences as noted in the previous automotive-industry example. At the other extreme, preventive maintenance costs may be so incidental that preventive maintenance is appropriate even if the distribution is rather flat (that is, it has a large standard deviation). In any event, all machine operators must be held responsible for preventive maintenance of their own equipment and tools.

A variety of sensing devices exist to help determine when a process should receive maintenance. For instance, many aircraft engines have a sensor that indicates the presence of metals in the lubricating oils. This sensor indicates unusual wear and the need for preventive maintenance prior to a breakdown (which is a nice idea, particularly on airplanes). An additional example: the disc brake pad wear indicator "fingers" provided by some manufacturers. When the pads are due for replacement, a

[2]See, for example, the work of P. M. Morse, *Queues, Inventories, and Maintenance* (New York: John Wiley, 1958), pp. 161–168; and "Using Statistical Thinking to Solve Maintenance Problems," *Quality Progress* (May 1989): 55–60.

FIGURE 18.3 ■ A Computerized Maintenance System

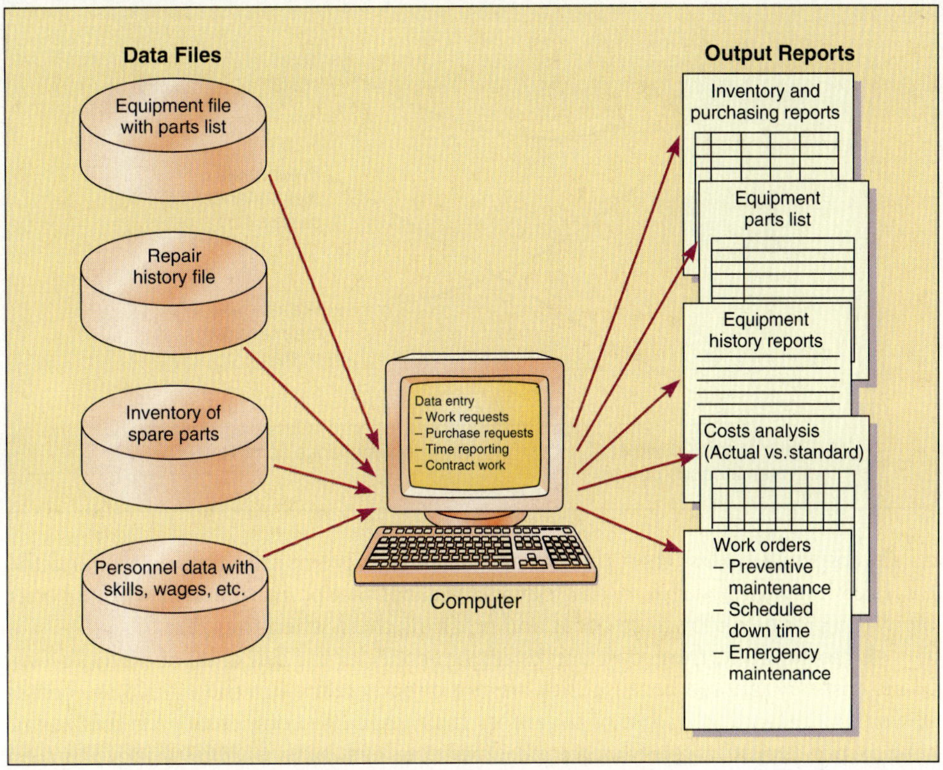

squealing sound is made by the "fingers," warning the motorist to replace the pads. Failure to do so means that the now-exposed brake pad rivets will begin to groove the brake rotors and a replacement that would have cost $100 is now a $400 job because the rotors must be replaced as well as the brake pads. Mechanics regularly tell stories of customers who bend the warning fingers out of the way to stop the squealing and later complain about the now $400 brake job.

A variety of other devices, from vibration sensors to infrared thermography, are available to help determine preventive maintenance requirements.[3] Additionally, with good reporting techniques, firms can maintain records of individual processes, machines, or equipment. Such records can provide a profile of both the kinds of maintenance required and timing of maintenance needed. Maintaining equipment history is an important part of a preventive maintenance system, as is a record of the time and cost to make the repair. Such records can also contribute to similar information about the family of equipment as well as suppliers.

Record keeping is of such importance that most good maintenance systems are now computerized. Figure 18.3 shows the major components of such a system with files to be maintained on the left and reports generated on the right.

Figure 18.4 shows the relationship between preventive maintenance and breakdown maintenance. Operations managers need to consider a balance between the two costs. Allocating more money and crew to preventive maintenance will reduce the number of breakdowns. But, at some point, the decrease in breakdown mainte-

[3]Ronald L. Stiemsma, "Vibration Monitoring Proves Itself at Clinton Power Station," *Electric Light and Power,* 70, no. 6 (June 1992): 2; and Bruce D. Nordwall, "Engine Monitoring System May Provide 100-Hr. Warning Before Jet Failure," *Aviation Week and Space Technology,* 136, no. 10 (March 9, 1992): 54–56.

FIGURE 18.4 ■ Maintenance Costs

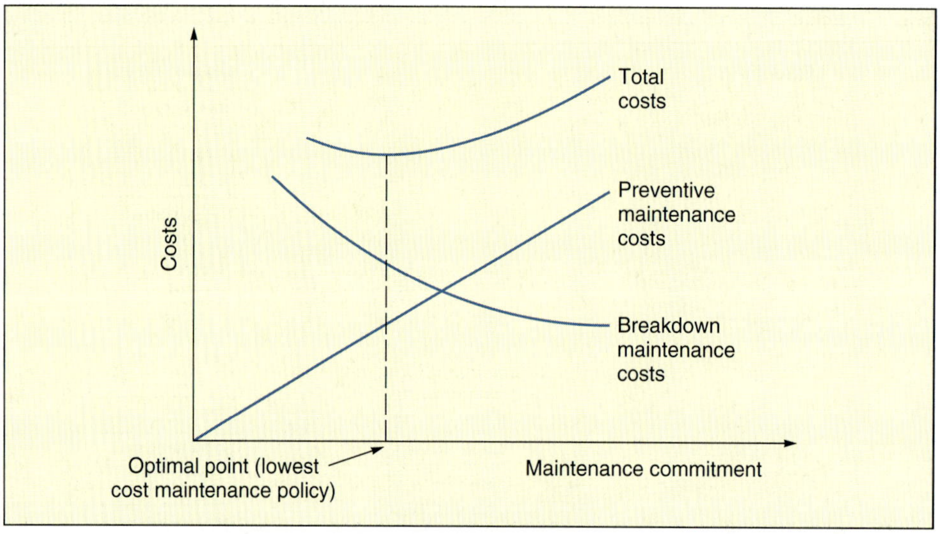

nance costs will be less than the increase in preventive maintenance costs, and the total cost curve will begin to rise. Beyond this optimal point, the firm will be better off waiting for breakdowns to occur and repairing them when they do.

Unfortunately, these cost curves seldom consider the full costs of a breakdown. Many costs are ignored because they are not directly related to the immediate breakdown. For instance, the cost of inventory maintained to compensate for this downtime is not typically considered; and downtime can have a devastating effect on morale. Employees may begin to believe that performance to standard and maintaining equipment are not important. In addition, downtime can adversely affect delivery schedules, destroying customer relations and future sales.

Assuming that all costs associated with downtime have been identified, the operations staff can compute the optimal level of maintenance activity on a theoretical basis. The analysis, of course, also requires accurate historical data on maintenance costs, breakdown probabilities, and repair times. Example 5 illustrates how to compare preventive and breakdown maintenance costs in order to select the least expensive maintenance policy.

EXAMPLE 5

Huntsman and Associates (H&A) is an accounting firm specializing in payroll preparation. The accountants have been successful in automating much of their work, using computers for processing and report preparation. The computerized approach has problems, however. Over the past 20 months, the computer system has broken down, as indicated below.

Number of Breakdowns	Number of Months That Breakdowns Occurred
0	4
1	8
2	6
3	2
Total:	20

Each time the computer breaks down, the partners estimate that the firm loses an average of $300 in time and service expenses. One alternative is for the firm to accept a service contract for preventive maintenance. If they accept preventive maintenance, they expect an *average* of only one computer breakdown per month. The price for this service is $220 per month. We will follow a four-step approach to answer the question of whether H&A should contract for preventive maintenance:

Step 1. Compute the *expected number* of breakdowns (based on past history) if the firm continues as is, without the service contract.

Step 2. Compute the expected breakdown cost per month with no preventive maintenance contract.

Step 3. Compute the cost of preventive maintenance.

Step 4. Compare the two options and select the one that will cost less.

1.

Number of Breakdowns	Frequency	Number of Breakdowns	Frequency
0	4/20 = .2	2	6/20 = 0.3
1	8/20 = .4	3	2/20 = 0.1

$$\begin{pmatrix}\text{Expected number}\\ \text{of breakdowns}\end{pmatrix} = \Sigma\left[\begin{pmatrix}\text{number of}\\ \text{breakdowns}\end{pmatrix} \times \begin{pmatrix}\text{corresponding}\\ \text{frequency}\end{pmatrix}\right]$$

$$= (0)(.2) + (1)(.4) + (2)(.3) + (3)(.1)$$

$$= 0 + .4 + .6 + .3$$

$$= 1.3 \text{ breakdowns/month}$$

2. $$\text{Expected breakdown cost} = \begin{pmatrix}\text{expected number}\\ \text{of breakdowns}\end{pmatrix} \times \begin{pmatrix}\text{cost per}\\ \text{breakdown}\end{pmatrix}$$

$$= (1.3)(\$300)$$

$$= \$390/\text{month}$$

3. $$\begin{pmatrix}\text{Preventive}\\ \text{maintenance cost}\end{pmatrix} = \begin{pmatrix}\text{cost of expected}\\ \text{breakdowns if service}\\ \text{contract signed}\end{pmatrix} + \begin{pmatrix}\text{cost of}\\ \text{service contract}\end{pmatrix}$$

$$= (1 \text{ breakdown/month})(\$300) + \$220/\text{month}$$

$$= \$520/\text{month}$$

4. Because it is less expensive to suffer the breakdowns *without* a maintenance service contract ($390) than with one ($520), the firm should continue its present policy.

Through variations of the technique shown in Example 5, operations managers can determine minimum-cost maintenance policies.

INCREASING REPAIR CAPABILITIES

When neither reliability nor preventive maintenance has been achieved, operations managers need good repair facilities. Enlarging or improving repair facilities can get the system back in operation faster. A good maintenance facility should have these six features:

1. well-trained personnel;
2. adequate resources;
3. ability to establish a repair plan and priorities;[4]
4. ability and authority to do material planning;
5. ability to identify the cause of breakdowns;
6. ability to design ways to extend MTBF.

However, not all repairs can be done in the firm's facility. Managers must therefore decide where repairs are to be performed. Figure 18.5 shows some of the options and how they rate in terms of speed, cost, and competence. Consistent with employee empowerment, a strong case can be made for employees' maintaining their own equipment, but this type of repair may also be the weakest link in the repair chain. Not every employee can be trained in all aspects of equipment repair.

Whichever preventive maintenance policies and techniques management chooses must include an emphasis on employees' accepting responsibility for the maintenance they are capable of doing. Employee maintenance may be only of the "clean, check, and observe" variety, but if each operator does those activities within his or her capability, the manager has made a step toward employee empowerment and toward maintaining system performance.

An example of extending the MTBF: In the past few years, the North American auto industry has received many complaints about the short lifetimes of brake system components to the extent that specialty automotive supply houses specializing in premium quality replacement brake components have appeared as new businesses. One such example is the Best Price Brake Warehouse in Ottawa, Ontario, which specializes in providing cross-drilled rotors and carbon-fibre disk brake pads (previously only available for competition cars). These not only have a longer lifetime and better braking distances than standard automotive replacement parts but also leave little of the residue on wheels that normal disk brake pads do. Surprisingly, a recent quotation showed these cross-drilled rotors to be more than 20% cheaper than automobile dealers' prices for standard rotors.

OTHER MAINTENANCE POLICY TECHNIQUES

Two other P/OM techniques have proven beneficial to maintenance systems: simulation and expert systems.

[4]You may recall from our discussion of network planning in Chapter 17 that Dupont developed the critical path method (CPM) to improve the scheduling of maintenance projects.

FIGURE 18.5 ■ The Operations Manager Must Determine How Maintenance Will Be Performed

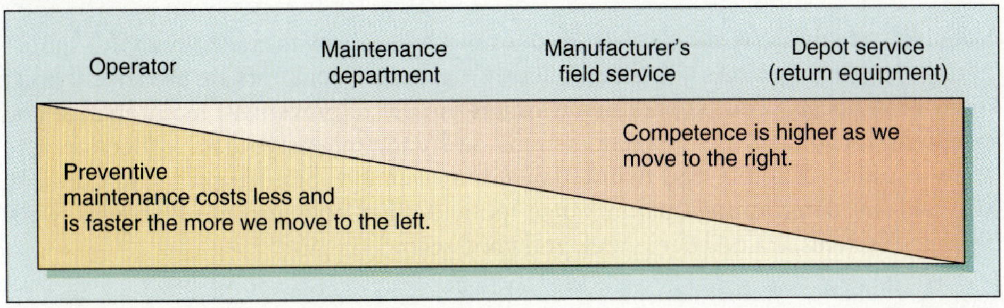

SIMULATION. Because of the complexity of some maintenance decisions, simulation is a good tool for evaluating the impact of various maintenance policies. For instance, operations personnel can decide whether to add more maintenance staff on the basis of the trade-offs between machine downtime costs and the costs of additional labor. Management can also simulate replacing parts that have not yet failed as a way of preventing future breakdowns. Simulation via physical models can also be useful. For example, a physical model can vibrate an airplane to simulate thousands of hours of flight time in order to evaluate maintenance needs. The Supplement to Chapter 13 covers the topic of simulation in more detail.

EXPERT SYSTEMS. P/OM managers use expert systems to assist staff in isolating and repairing various faults in machinery and equipment. For instance, General Electric's DELTA system asks a series of detailed questions leading and aiding the user in identifying the problem. Expert systems are discussed in Chapter 8.

ACHIEVING WORLD-CLASS STANDARDS

World-class firms have reliable systems. Such firms achieve reliability through systems design and effective maintenance. Companies like Orlando Utilities, featured earlier in this chapter, and Ontario Hydro use sophisticated computer software to schedule maintenance projects, control inventory of spare parts, and track the failure of parts.

Other firms use automated sensors and controls to warn when production machinery is about to fail or is becoming damaged by heat, vibration, or fluid leaks. General Motors, for example, has developed a computer system to sense unusual vibrations of machines while they are running. Dupont uses expert systems to monitor equipment and to train repair personnel. Paper mills such as that in Espanola, Ontario, have automatic oiling devices installed on some machinery. A main reservoir need only be filled several times a year. Such an approach allows necessary lubricants to be supplied automatically and is far easier to monitor. The key is to avoid failures and to perform preventive maintenance before machines are damaged.

Finally, world-class companies give their employees a sense of "ownership" in their equipment. When a worker repairs or does preventive maintenance on his or her own machine, breakdowns are often avoided. Well-trained and empowered employees ensure reliable systems through preventive maintenance. Reliable, well-maintained equipment not only provides higher utilization, but also improves quality and performance to schedule. World-class firms build and maintain systems so their customers can count on products produced to specifications on time.

SUMMARY

Reliable systems are a necessity. In spite of our best efforts to design reliable components, systems sometimes fail. Consequently, backup components are used. Reliability improvements also can be obtained through the use of preventive maintenance and excellent repair facilities. Expert systems and comprehensive data collection and analysis assist reliability and maintenance management. Simulation techniques can also aid in determining maintenance policies. Reliable processes require well-designed systems, trained personnel, and good record keeping.

KEY TERMS

Failure (p. 812)
Reliability (p. 812)
Maintenance (p. 812)
Mean time between failures (MTBF) (p. 815)
Preventive maintenance (p. 817)
Breakdown maintenance (p. 817)
Infant mortality (p. 817)

USING AB:POM TO SOLVE RELIABILITY PROBLEMS

Solving Example 3 Using AB:POM's Reliability Module

Program 18.1 illustrates the use of AB:POM in solving a reliability problem.

PROGRAM 18.1 ■ AB:POM's Reliability Module Example. The entries for reliability are: **1.** *number of systems* (components) in the series (1 through 10); **2.** *number of backup or parallel components* (1 through 10); **3.** *component reliability*. Enter the reliability of each component in the body of the table. Series data are entered across the table and backup or parallel data down the table. The program will disregard any zeroes in the table.

```
                                        Reliability                            Data Screen
Number of systems in series (1-10)  3         Max # of parallel components (1-10)
Parl l       Parl l       Parl l                                                        2
Sys 1        Sys 2        Sys 3
.9000        .8000        .0000
.9000        .8000        .9900
                                                                                      Esc
Output:                                  Reliability
Parl l             Parl l                 Parl l
Sys 1              Sys 2                  Sys 3
.9000              .8000
.9000              .8000                  .9900
.9900              .9600                  .9900
System reliability = .94090
```

Notice that the entries that were 0 have been eliminated. The products for each column show the combined parallel (backup) component reliability.

SOLVED PROBLEMS

Solved Problem 18.1

The semiconductor used in the Sullivan Wrist Calculator has five parts, each of which has its own reliability rate. Component 1 has a reliability of .90; component 2, .95; component 3, .98; component 4, .90; and component 5, .99. What is the reliability of one semiconductor?

Solution

$$\text{Semiconductor reliability, } R_s = R_1 R_2 R_3 R_4 R_5$$
$$= (.90)(.95)(.98)(.90)(.99)$$
$$= .7466$$

Solved Problem 18.2

A recent engineering change at Sullivan Wrist Calculator places a backup component in each of the two least reliable transistor circuits. The new circuit will look like the following:

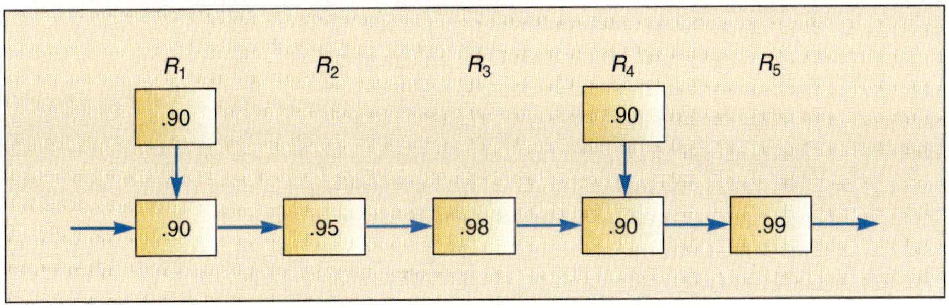

What is the reliability of the new system?

Solution

$$\text{Reliability} = [.9 + (1 - .9) \times .9] \times .95 \times .98 \times [.90 + (1 - .9) \times .9] \times .99$$
$$= [.9 + .09] \times .95 \times .98 \times [.90 + .09] \times .99$$
$$= .99 \times .95 \times .98 \times .99 \times .99$$
$$= .903$$

DISCUSSION QUESTIONS

1. What are the variables that contribute to infant mortality for new machinery? What can the P/OM manager do to reduce the incidence of infant mortality?
2. What techniques can management use to improve system reliability?
3. Under what conditions is preventive maintenance likely to be appropriate? Can preventive maintenance be overdone?
4. Why is simulation often an appropriate technique for maintenance problems?
5. What is the trade-off between operator-performed maintenance and supplier-performed maintenance?
6. How can the manager evaluate the effectiveness of the maintenance function?

7. What kind of records are helpful when developing a good maintenance system?
8. How do expert systems improve maintenance systems?
9. How can a firm improve or speed up its repair facilities?

CRITICAL THINKING EXERCISE

The 1989 crash of a McDonnell Douglas DC-10 suggests that the plane's hydraulic systems may not provide enough protection. The DC-10 has three separate hydraulic systems, all of which failed when an engine exploded. The engine threw off shreds of metal that severed two of the lines, and the third line required power from the demolished engine that was no longer available. The DC-10, unlike other commercial jets, has no shutoff valves that might have stemmed the flow of hydraulic fluid. Lockheed's similar L-1011 trijet has four hydraulic systems. A McDonnell Douglas VP says, "You can always be extreme and not have a practical airplane. You can be perfectly safe and never get off the ground." Discuss the pros and cons of McDonnell's position. How might you design a reliability experiment?

PROBLEMS

: **18.1** A system consists of 5 components with the following reliabilities: .85, .88, .89, .94, and .97.

a) Calculate the overall reliability of the existing system.

b) The chief engineer has proposed an improvement to system reliability by noting that the system has space available to provide a single redundant component with reliability equal to that of the component being backed up. Calculate the potential reliabilities of the new system by evaluating the backup of each component in turn. Which redundant component will provide the highest system reliability? Why?

c) Further miniaturization has provided enough space for a second redundant backup. Which component should be selected? What is the resultant reliability with both redundant backup components in place?

: **18.2** Nova Scotia Hospital Equipment Corp., a medical equipment manufacturer, has subjected 100 heart pacemakers to 5,000 hours of testing. Halfway through the testing, 5 of the pacemakers failed. What was the failure rate in terms of:

a) Percent of failures?

b) Number of failures per unit-hour?

c) Number of failures per unit-year?

d) If 1,100 people receive pacemaker implants, how many units can we expect to fail during the following 1 year?

• **18.3** Given the probabilities that follow for a machine shop, find the expected breakdown cost.

Number of Breakdowns	Daily Frequency
0	.3
1	.2
2	.2
3	.3
	1.0

The cost per breakdown is $10.

• **18.4** You have a system composed of four components in series. The reliability of each component is .95. What is the reliability of the system?

• **18.5** You have a system composed of a serial connection of four components with the following reliabilities:

COMPONENT	RELIABILITY
1	.90
2	.95
3	.80
4	.85

What is the reliability of the system?

: **18.6** You have a system composed of three components in parallel. The components have the following reliabilities:

$$R_1 = 0.90, \quad R_2 = 0.95, \quad R_3 = 0.85$$

What is the reliability of the system?

• **18.7** A hydraulic control system has three components in series with individual reliabilities (R_1, R_2, and R_3) as shown.

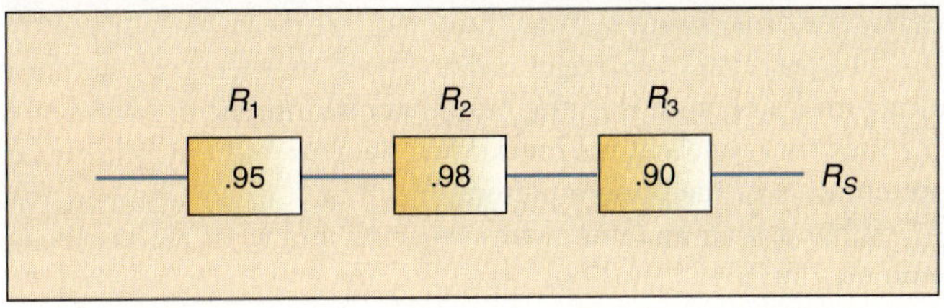

What is the reliability of the system?

: **18.8** What is the reliability of the system shown below?

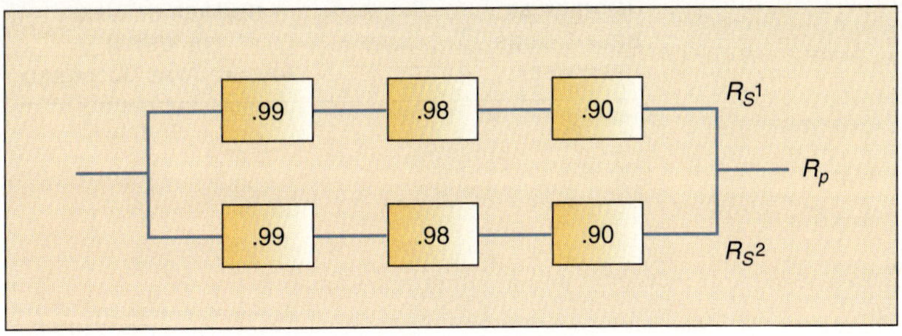

: **18.9** What is the impact on reliability if the hydraulic control system shown in Problem 18.7 is changed to the parallel system shown in Problem 18.8?

: **18.10** Your design team has proposed the following system with component reliabilities as indicated.

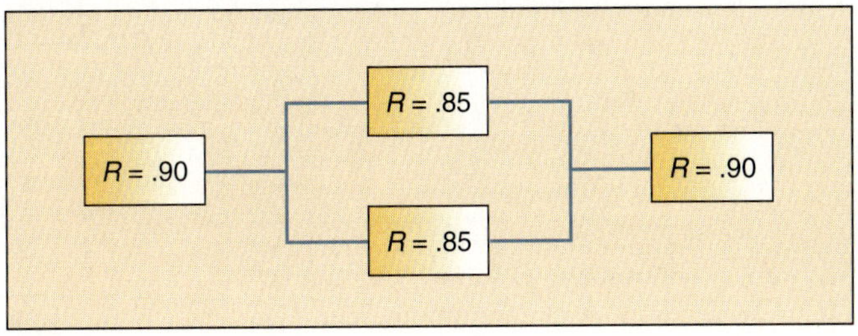

What is the reliability of the system?

:18.11 Randolph Manufacturing has tested 200 units of a product. After 2,000 hours, four units have failed; the remainder functioned for the full 4,000 hours of the testing.

a) What is the percent of failures?

b) What is the number of failures per unit hour?

c) What is the number of failures per unit year?

d) If you sell 500 units, how many are likely to fail within a 1-year time period?

:18.12 Montreal Manufacturing Company operates its 23 large and expensive grinding and lathe machines from 7 A.M. to 11 P.M., 7 days a week. For the past year, the firm has been under contract with Lajeunesse Service Corp. for daily preventive maintenance (lubrication, cleaning, inspection, and so on). Lajeunesse' crew works between 11 P.M. and 2 A.M. so as not to interfere with the daily manufacturing crew. Lajeunesse charges $645 per week for this service. Since signing the maintenance contract, Montreal Manufacturing has noted an average of only three breakdowns per week. When a grinding or lathe machine *does* break down during a working shift, it costs Montreal about $250 in lost production and repair costs.

After reviewing past breakdown records (for the period before signing a preventive maintenance contract with Lajeunesse), Montreal's production manager summarizes the patterns shown below.

The production manager is not certain that the contract for preventive maintenance with Lajeunesse is in the best financial interest of Montreal Manufacturing. He recognizes that much of his breakdown data are old but is fairly certain that they are representative of the present picture.

What is your analysis of this situation and what recommendations do you think the production manager should make?

Number of Breakdowns per Week	Number of Weeks in Which Breakdowns Occurred
0	1
1	1
2	3
3	5
4	9
5	11
6	7
7	8
8	5
Total weeks of historical data:	50

18.13 Alexander Kirk, salesman for Wave Soldering Systems, Inc. (WSSI), has provided you with a proposal for improving the temperature control on your present machine. The present machine uses a hot-air knife to remove cleanly excess solder from printed-circuit boards; this is a great concept, but the hot-air temperature control lacks reliability. The engineers at WSSI have, says Alexander, improved the reliability of the critical temperature controls. The new system still has the four sensitive integrated circuits controlling the temperature, but the new machine has a backup for each. The four integrated circuits have reliabilities of .90, .92, .94, and .96. The four backup circuits all have a reliability of .90.

a) What is the reliability of the new temperature controller?

b) If you pay a premium, Alexander says he can improve all four of the backup units to .93. What is the reliability of this option?

18.14 The Beta II computer's electronic processing unit contains 50 components in series. The average reliability of each component is 99.0%. Using Figure 18.1, determine the overall reliability of the processing unit.

CASE STUDY

Worldwide Chemical Company

Jack Smith wiped the perspiration from his face. It was another scorching-hot summer day and one of the four process refrigeration units was down. The units were critical to the operation of Worldwide Chemical Company's Fibres Plant, which produced synthetic fibres and polymer flake for a global market.

Before long Al Henson, the day-shift production superintendent, was on the intercom, shouting his familiar proclamation that "heads would roll" if the unit was not back online within the hour. But Jack Smith, the maintenance superintendent, had heard it all before—nothing ever happened as a result of those temper tantrums. "Serves him right," he thought, "Henson is uncooperative when we want to perform scheduled maintenance, so it doesn't get done and the equipment goes down."

At that moment, Henson, furious over the impact the equipment breakdown would have on his process yield figures, was meeting with Beth Conner, the plant manager, charging that all the maintenance department did was to "sit around" and play cards like firefighters waiting for an alarm to send them on their way to a three-alarm blaze across town. It was true that the "fix-it" approach to maintenance was costing the plant throughput that was vital to meeting standard costs and avoiding serious variances. Foreign competitors were delivering high-quality fibres in less time, at lower prices. Beth Conner had already been "on the carpet" at corporate headquarters over output levels that were significantly below the budgeted numbers. The business cycle contained seasonal variations that were predictable. That meant building inventories that would be carried for months, tying up scarce capital, a characteristic of most continuous processes. Monthly shipments would look bad. Year-to-date shipments would look even worse because of machine breakdowns and lost output to date. Conner knew that something had to be done to develop machine reliability. Capacity on demand was needed to respond to the growing foreign competition. Unreliable production equipment was jeopardizing the company's TQM effort by causing process variations that affected first-quality product yields and on-time deliveries, but no one seemed to have the answer to the problem of machine breakdowns.

The maintenance department operated much as a fire department, rushing to a breakdown with a swarm of mechanics, some who disassembled the machine, others who poured over wiring schematics, and others who hunted spare parts in the maintenance warehouse. Eventually, they would have the machine back up, sometimes only after working through the night to get the production line going again. Maintenance had always been done this way.

(Continued)

But, with new competitors, machine reliability had suddenly become a major barrier to competing successfully.

Rumours of a plant closing were beginning to circulate and morale was suffering, making good performance that much more difficult. Beth Conner knew she needed solutions if the plant had any chance of survival.

DISCUSSION QUESTIONS

1. Could Smith and Hensen do anything to improve performance?
2. Is there an alternative to the current operations approach of the maintenance department?
3. How would production make up for lost output resulting from scheduled maintenance?
4. How could maintenance mechanics be better utilized?
5. Is there any way to know when a machine breakdown is probable?

Source: Patrick Owings under the supervision of Professor Marilyn M. Helms, University of Tennessee at Chattanooga.

BIBLIOGRAPHY

Hayes, R. H., and K. B. Clark. "Why Some Factories Are More Productive Than Others." *Harvard Business Review*, 64, no. 5 (September/October 1986): 66–73.

Joshi, S., and R. Gupta. "Scheduling of Routine Maintenance Using Production Schedules and Equipment Failure History." *Computers and Industrial Engineering*, 10, no. 1 (1986): 11–20.

Laudon, K. C., and Laudon, J. P. "Expert Systems." *Management Information Systems*, 4th ed. (Englewood Cliffs, NJ: Prentice Hall, 1996).

Linder-Dutton, L., M. Jordan, and M. Karwan. "Beyond Mean Time to Failure." *OR/MS Today*, 21, no. 2 (April 1994): 30–33.

Maggard, B. N., and D. M. Rhyne. "Total Productive Maintenance: A Timely Integration of Production and Maintenance." *Production and Inventory Management Journal*, 33, no. 4 (Fourth Quarter 1992): 6–10.

Mann, L., Jr. *Maintenance Management*. Lexington, MA: Lexington Books, 1983.

Schneeweiss, C. A., and H. Schroder. "Planning and Scheduling the Repair Shops of the Deutsche Lufthansa AG: A Hierarchical Approach." *Production and Operations Management*, 1, no. 1 (Winter 1992): 22.

Sherwin, D. J. "Inspect or Monitor." *Engineering Costs and Production Economics*, 18 (January 1990): 223–231.

Vaziri, H. K. "Using Competitive Benchmarking to Set Goals." *Quality Progress*, 25, no. 10 (October 1992): 81.

APPENDICES

APPENDIX A AREAS UNDER THE STANDARD NORMAL CURVE

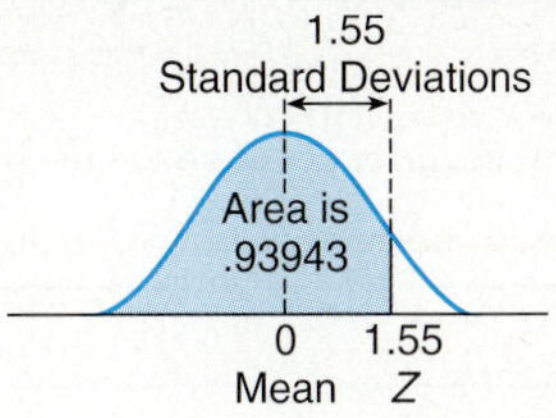

To find the area under the normal curve, you must know how many standard deviations that point is to the right of the mean. Then, the area under the normal curve can be read directly from the normal table. For example, the total area under the normal curve for a point that is 1.55 standard deviations to the right of the mean is .93943.

	.00	.01	.02	.03	.04	.05	.06	.07	.08	.09
.0	.50000	.50399	.50798	.51197	.51595	.51994	.52392	.52790	.53188	.53586
.1	.53983	.54380	.54776	.55172	.55567	.55962	.56356	.56749	.57142	.57535
.2	.57926	.58317	.58706	.59095	.59483	.59871	.60257	.60642	.61026	.61409
.3	.61791	.62172	.62552	.62930	.63307	.63683	.64058	.64431	.64803	.65173
.4	.65542	.65910	.66276	.66640	.67003	.67364	.67724	.68082	.68439	.68793
.5	.69146	.69497	.69847	.70194	.70540	.70884	.71226	.71566	.71904	.72240
.6	.72575	.72907	.73237	.73536	.73891	.74215	.74537	.74857	.75175	.75490
.7	.75804	.76115	.76424	.76730	.77035	.77337	.77637	.77935	.78230	.78524
.8	.78814	.79103	.79389	.79673	.79955	.80234	.80511	.80785	.81057	.81327
.9	.81594	.81859	.82121	.82381	.82639	.82894	.83147	.83398	.83646	.83891
1.0	.84134	.84375	.84614	.84849	.85083	.85314	.85543	.85769	.85993	.86214
1.1	.86433	.86650	.86864	.87076	.87286	.87493	.87698	.87900	.88100	.88298
1.2	.88493	.88686	.88877	.89065	.89251	.89435	.89617	.89796	.89973	.90147
1.3	.90320	.90490	.90658	.90824	.90988	.91149	.91309	.91466	.91621	.91774
1.4	.91924	.92073	.92220	.92364	.92507	.92647	.92785	.92922	.93056	.93189
1.5	.93319	.93448	.93574	.93699	.93822	.93943	.94062	.94179	.94295	.94408
1.6	.94520	.94630	.94738	.94845	.94950	.95053	.95154	.95254	.95352	.95449
1.7	.95543	.95637	.95728	.95818	.95907	.95994	.96080	.96164	.96246	.96327
1.8	.96407	.96485	.96562	.96638	.96712	.96784	.96856	.96926	.96995	.97062
1.9	.97128	.97193	.97257	.97320	.97381	.97441	.97500	.97558	.97615	.97670
2.0	.97725	.97784	.97831	.97882	.97932	.97982	.98030	.98077	.98124	.98169
2.1	.98214	.98257	.98300	.98341	.98382	.98422	.98461	.98500	.98537	.98574
2.2	.98610	.98645	.98679	.98713	.98745	.98778	.98809	.98840	.98870	.98899
2.3	.98928	.98956	.98983	.99010	.99036	.99061	.99086	.99111	.99134	.99158
2.4	.99180	.99202	.99224	.99245	.99266	.99286	.99305	.99324	.99343	.99361
2.5	.99379	.99396	.99413	.99430	.99446	.99461	.99477	.99492	.99506	.99520
2.6	.99534	.99547	.99560	.99573	.99585	.99598	.99609	.99621	.99632	.99643
2.7	.99653	.99664	.99674	.99683	.99693	.99702	.99711	.99720	.99728	.99736
2.8	.99744	.99752	.99760	.99767	.99774	.99781	.99788	.99795	.99801	.99807
2.9	.99813	.99819	.99825	.99831	.99836	.99841	.99846	.99851	.99856	.99861
3.0	.99865	.99869	.99874	.99878	.99882	.99886	.99899	.99893	.99896	.99900
3.1	.99903	.99906	.99910	.99913	.99916	.99918	.99921	.99924	.99926	.99929
3.2	.99931	.99934	.99936	.99938	.99940	.99942	.99944	.99946	.99948	.99950
3.3	.99952	.99953	.99955	.99957	.99958	.99960	.99961	.99962	.99964	.99965
3.4	.99966	.99968	.99969	.99970	.99971	.99972	.99973	.99974	.99975	.99976
3.5	.99977	.99978	.99978	.99979	.99980	.99981	.99981	.99982	.99983	.99983
3.6	.99984	.99985	.99985	.99986	.99986	.99987	.99987	.99988	.99988	.99989
3.7	.99989	.99990	.99990	.99990	.99991	.99991	.99992	.99992	.99992	.99992
3.8	.99993	.99993	.99993	.99994	.99994	.99994	.99994	.99995	.99995	.99995
3.9	.99995	.99995	.99996	.99996	.99996	.99996	.99996	.99996	.99997	.99997

Source: From *Quantitative Approaches to Management,* 4th ed., by Richard I. Levin and Charles A. Kirkpatrick.

APPENDIX B POISSON DISTRIBUTION VALUES

$$P(X \leq c; \lambda) = \sum_{0}^{c} \frac{\lambda^x e^{-\lambda}}{x!}$$

Table shows 1000 times the probability of c or less occurrences of an event that has an average number of occurrences of λ.

λ	Values of c										
	0	1	2	3	4	5	6	7	8	9	10
.02	980	1000									
.04	961	999	1000								
.06	942	998	1000								
.08	923	997	1000								
.10	905	995	1000								
.15	861	990	999	1000							
.20	819	982	999	1000							
.25	779	974	998	1000							
.30	741	963	996	1000							
.35	705	951	994	1000							
.40	670	938	992	999	1000						
.45	638	925	989	999	1000						
.50	607	910	986	998	1000						
.55	577	894	982	998	1000						
.60	549	878	977	997	1000						
.65	522	861	972	996	999	1000					
.70	497	844	966	994	999	1000					
.75	472	827	959	993	999	1000					
.80	449	809	953	991	999	1000					
.85	427	791	945	989	998	1000					
.90	407	772	937	987	998	1000					
.95	387	754	929	984	997	1000					
1.00	368	736	920	981	996	999	1000				
1.1	333	699	900	974	995	999	1000				
1.2	301	663	879	966	992	998	1000				
1.3	273	627	857	957	989	998	1000				
1.4	247	592	833	946	986	997	999	1000			
1.5	223	558	809	934	981	996	999	1000			
1.6	202	525	783	921	976	994	999	1000			
1.7	183	493	757	907	970	992	998	1000			
1.8	165	463	731	891	964	990	997	999	1000		
1.9	150	434	704	875	956	987	997	999	1000		
2.0	135	406	677	857	947	983	995	999	1000		

Source: Adapted from E. L. Grant, *Statistical Quality Control*, McGraw-Hill Book Company, New York, 1964. Reproduced by permission of the publisher.

APPENDIX B POISSON DISTRIBUTION VALUES (CONTINUED)

λ	Values of c																						
	0	1	2	3	4	5	6	7	8	9	10	11	12	13	14	15	16	17	18	19	20	21	22
2.2	111	359	623	819	928	975	993	998	1000														
2.4	091	308	570	779	904	964	988	997	999	1000													
2.6	074	267	518	736	877	951	983	995	999	1000													
2.8	061	231	469	692	848	935	976	992	998	999	1000												
3.0	050	199	423	647	815	916	966	988	996	999	1000												
3.2	041	171	380	603	781	895	955	983	994	998	1000												
3.4	033	147	340	558	744	871	942	977	992	997	999	1000											
3.6	027	126	303	515	706	844	927	969	988	996	999	1000											
3.8	022	107	269	473	668	816	909	960	984	994	998	999	1000										
4.0	018	092	238	433	629	785	889	949	979	992	997	999	1000										
4.2	015	078	210	395	590	753	867	936	972	989	996	999	1000										
4.4	012	066	185	359	551	720	844	921	964	985	994	998	999	1000									
4.6	010	056	163	326	513	686	818	905	955	980	992	997	999	1000									
4.8	008	048	143	294	476	651	791	887	944	975	990	996	999	1000									
5.0	007	040	125	265	440	616	762	867	932	968	986	995	998	999	1000								
5.2	006	034	109	238	406	581	732	845	918	960	982	993	997	999	1000								
5.4	005	029	095	213	373	546	702	822	903	951	977	990	996	999	1000								
5.6	004	024	082	191	342	512	670	797	886	941	972	988	995	998	999	1000							
5.8	003	021	072	170	313	478	638	771	867	929	965	984	993	997	999	1000							
6.0	002	017	062	151	285	446	606	744	847	916	957	980	991	996	999	999	1000						
6.2	002	015	054	134	259	414	574	716	826	902	949	975	989	995	998	999	1000						
6.4	002	012	046	119	235	384	542	687	803	886	939	969	986	994	997	999	1000						
6.6	001	010	040	105	213	355	511	658	780	869	927	963	982	992	997	999	999	1000					
6.8	001	009	034	093	192	327	480	628	755	850	915	955	978	990	996	998	999	1000					
7.0	001	007	030	082	173	301	450	599	729	830	901	947	973	987	994	998	999	1000					
7.2	001	006	025	072	156	276	420	569	703	810	887	937	967	984	993	997	999	999	1000				
7.4	001	005	022	063	140	253	392	539	676	788	871	926	961	980	991	996	998	999	1000				
7.6	001	004	019	055	125	231	365	510	648	765	854	915	954	976	989	995	998	999	1000				
7.8	000	004	016	048	112	210	338	481	620	741	835	902	945	971	986	993	997	999	1000				
8.0	000	003	014	042	100	191	313	453	593	717	816	888	936	966	983	992	996	998	999	1000			
8.5	000	002	009	030	074	150	256	386	523	653	763	849	909	949	973	986	993	997	999	999	1000		
9.0	000	001	006	021	055	116	207	324	456	587	706	803	876	926	959	978	989	995	998	999	1000		
9.5	000	001	004	015	040	089	165	269	392	522	645	752	836	898	940	967	982	991	996	998	999	1000	
10.0	000	000	003	010	029	067	130	220	333	458	583	697	792	864	917	951	973	986	993	997	998	999	1000

APPENDIX C VALUES OF $e^{-\lambda}$ FOR USE IN THE POISSON DISTRIBUTION

Values of $e^{-\lambda}$

λ	$e^{-\lambda}$	λ	$e^{-\lambda}$	λ	$e^{-\lambda}$	λ	$e^{-\lambda}$
.0	1.0000	1.6	.2019	3.1	.0450	4.6	.0101
.1	.9048	1.7	.1827	3.2	.0408	4.7	.0091
.2	.8187	1.8	.1653	3.3	.0369	4.8	.0082
.3	.7408	1.9	.1496	3.4	.0334	4.9	.0074
.4	.6703	2.0	.1353	3.5	.0302	5.0	.0067
.5	.6065	2.1	.1225	3.6	.0273	5.1	.0061
.6	.5488	2.2	.1108	3.7	.0247	5.2	.0055
.7	.4966	2.3	.1003	3.8	.0224	5.3	.0050
.8	.4493	2.4	.0907	3.9	.0202	5.4	.0045
.9	.4066	2.5	.0821	4.0	.0183	5.5	.0041
1.0	.3679	2.6	.0743	4.1	.0166	5.6	.0037
1.1	.3329	2.7	.0672	4.2	.0150	5.7	.0033
1.2	.3012	2.8	.0608	4.3	.0136	5.8	.0030
1.3	.2725	2.9	.0550	4.4	.0123	5.9	.0027
1.4	.2466	3.0	.0498	4.5	.0111	6.0	.0025
1.5	.2231						

APPENDIX D LEARNING CURVE COEFFICIENTS AND

N	70%	Total	72%	Total	74%	Total	75%	Total	78%	Total	80%	Total	82%	Total
1	1.000	1.000	1.000	1.000	1.000	1.000	1.000	1.000	1.000	1.000	1.000	1.000	1.000	1.000
2	0.700	1.700	0.720	1.720	0.740	1.740	0.750	1.750	0.780	1.780	0.800	1.800	0.820	1.820
3	0.568	2.268	0.594	2.314	0.620	2.360	0.634	2.384	0.674	2.454	0.702	2.502	0.730	2.550
4	0.490	2.758	0.518	2.833	0.548	2.908	0.563	2.946	0.608	3.063	0.640	3.142	0.672	3.223
5	0.437	3.195	0.466	3.299	0.497	3.405	0.513	3.459	0.562	3.625	0.596	3.738	0.631	3.853
6	0.398	3.593	0.428	3.727	0.459	3.864	0.475	3.934	0.526	4.151	0.562	4.299	0.599	4.452
7	0.367	3.960	0.398	4.124	0.429	4.294	0.446	4.380	0.498	4.648	0.534	4.834	0.573	5.025
8	0.343	4.303	0.373	4.498	0.405	4.699	0.422	4.802	0.475	5.123	0.512	5.346	0.551	5.576
9	0.323	4.626	0.353	4.851	0.385	5.084	0.402	5.204	0.455	5.578	0.493	5.839	0.533	6.109
10	0.306	4.932	0.336	5.186	0.368	5.452	0.385	5.589	0.438	6.016	0.477	6.315	0.517	6.627
11	0.291	5.223	0.321	5.507	0.353	5.805	0.370	5.958	0.423	6.439	0.462	6.777	0.503	7.130
12	0.278	5.501	0.308	5.815	0.340	6.144	0.357	6.315	0.410	6.850	0.449	7.227	0.491	7.621
13	0.267	5.769	0.297	6.112	0.328	6.473	0.345	6.660	0.399	7.248	0.438	7.665	0.480	8.101
14	0.257	6.026	0.286	6.398	0.318	6.790	0.334	6.994	0.388	7.637	0.428	8.092	0.470	8.570
15	0.248	6.274	0.277	6.675	0.308	7.099	0.325	7.319	0.379	8.016	0.418	8.511	0.461	9.031
16	0.240	6.514	0.269	6.944	0.300	7.399	0.316	7.635	0.370	8.386	0.410	8.920	0.452	9.483
17	0.233	6.747	0.261	7.205	0.292	7.691	0.309	7.944	0.362	8.748	0.402	9.322	0.444	9.927
18	0.226	6.973	0.254	7.459	0.285	7.976	0.301	8.245	0.355	9.103	0.394	9.716	0.437	10.365
19	0.220	7.192	0.248	7.707	0.278	8.254	0.295	8.540	0.348	9.451	0.388	10.104	0.430	10.795
20	0.214	7.407	0.242	7.949	0.272	8.526	0.288	8.828	0.342	9.793	0.381	10.485	0.424	11.219
21	0.209	7.615	0.236	8.185	0.266	8.792	0.283	9.111	0.336	10.128	0.375	10.860	0.418	11.637
22	0.204	7.819	0.231	8.416	0.261	9.054	0.277	9.388	0.330	10.458	0.370	11.230	0.413	12.050
23	0.199	8.018	0.226	8.642	0.256	9.310	0.272	9.660	0.325	10.783	0.364	11.594	0.408	12.458
24	0.195	8.213	0.222	8.864	0.251	9.561	0.267	9.928	0.320	11.104	0.359	11.954	0.403	12.860
25	0.191	8.404	0.218	9.082	0.247	9.808	0.263	10.191	0.315	11.419	0.355	12.309	0.398	13.258
26	0.187	8.591	0.214	9.295	0.243	10.051	0.259	10.449	0.311	11.730	0.350	12.659	0.393	13.651
27	0.183	8.774	0.210	9.505	0.239	10.290	0.255	10.704	0.307	12.037	0.346	13.005	0.389	14.041
28	0.180	8.954	0.206	9.711	0.235	10.525	0.251	10.955	0.303	12.340	0.342	13.347	0.385	14.426
29	0.177	9.131	0.203	9.914	0.232	10.757	0.247	11.202	0.299	12.639	0.338	13.685	0.381	14.807
30	0.174	9.305	0.200	10.113	0.228	10.985	0.244	11.446	0.295	12.934	0.335	14.020	0.378	15.185
31	0.171	9.476	0.196	10.310	0.225	11.210	0.240	11.686	0.292	13.226	0.331	14.351	0.374	15.559
32	0.168	9.644	0.193	10.503	0.222	11.432	0.237	11.924	0.289	13.515	0.328	14.679	0.371	15.930
33	0.165	9.809	0.191	10.694	0.219	11.651	0.234	12.158	0.286	13.801	0.324	15.003	0.367	16.297
34	0.163	9.972	0.188	10.882	0.216	11.867	0.231	12.389	0.283	14.083	0.321	15.324	0.364	16.662
35	0.160	10.133	0.185	11.067	0.213	12.080	0.229	12.618	0.280	14.363	0.318	15.643	0.361	17.023
36	0.158	10.291	0.183	11.250	0.211	12.291	0.226	12.844	0.277	14.639	0.315	15.958	0.358	17.381
37	0.156	10.447	0.181	11.431	0.208	12.499	0.223	13.067	0.274	14.914	0.313	16.271	0.356	17.737
38	0.154	10.601	0.178	11.609	0.206	12.705	0.221	13.288	0.271	15.185	0.310	16.581	0.353	18.090
39	0.152	10.753	0.176	11.785	0.204	12.909	0.219	13.507	0.269	15.454	0.307	16.888	0.350	18.440
40	0.150	10.902	0.174	11.959	0.201	13.110	0.216	13.723	0.267	15.721	0.305	17.193	0.348	18.788
41	0.148	11.050	0.172	12.131	0.199	13.310	0.214	13.937	0.264	15.985	0.303	17.496	0.345	19.133
42	0.146	11.196	0.170	12.302	0.197	13.507	0.212	14.149	0.262	16.247	0.300	17.796	0.343	19.476
43	0.144	11.341	0.168	12.470	0.195	13.702	0.210	14.359	0.260	16.506	0.298	18.094	0.341	19.817
44	0.143	11.484	0.166	12.636	0.193	13.895	0.208	14.567	0.258	16.764	0.296	18.390	0.338	20.156
45	0.141	11.625	0.165	12.801	0.191	14.087	0.206	14.773	0.256	17.019	0.294	18.684	0.336	20.492
46	0.139	11.764	0.163	12.964	0.190	14.276	0.204	14.977	0.253	17.273	0.292	18.975	0.334	20.826

CUMULATIVE TOTALS YN = Y1*(N)^(LOG L/ LOG 2)

84%	Total	85%	Total	87%	Total	89%	Total	90%	Total	92%	Total	N
1.000	1.000	1.000	1.000	1.000	1.000	1.000	1.000	1.000	1.000	1.000	1.000	1
0.840	1.840	0.850	1.850	0.870	1.870	0.890	1.890	0.900	1.900	0.920	1.920	2
0.759	2.599	0.773	2.623	0.802	2.672	0.831	2.721	0.846	2.746	0.876	2.796	3
0.706	3.304	0.723	3.345	0.757	3.429	0.792	3.513	0.810	3.556	0.846	3.643	4
0.667	3.971	0.686	4.031	0.724	4.153	0.763	4.276	0.783	4.339	0.824	4.467	5
0.637	4.608	0.657	4.688	0.698	4.850	0.740	5.016	0.762	5.101	0.806	5.273	6
0.613	5.221	0.634	5.322	0.676	5.527	0.721	5.737	0.744	5.845	0.791	6.064	7
0.593	5.814	0.614	5.936	0.659	6.185	0.705	6.442	0.729	6.574	0.779	6.843	8
0.575	6.389	0.597	6.533	0.643	6.828	0.691	7.133	0.716	7.290	0.768	7.610	9
0.560	6.950	0.583	7.116	0.630	7.458	0.679	7.812	0.705	7.994	0.758	8.368	10
0.547	7.497	0.570	7.686	0.618	8.076	0.668	8.481	0.695	8.689	0.749	9.118	11
0.535	8.032	0.558	8.244	0.607	8.683	0.659	9.139	0.685	9.374	0.742	9.860	12
0.525	8.557	0.548	8.792	0.597	9.280	0.650	9.789	0.677	10.052	0.735	10.594	13
0.515	9.072	0.539	9.331	0.588	9.868	0.642	10.431	0.670	10.721	0.728	11.322	14
0.506	9.578	0.530	9.861	0.580	10.449	0.634	11.065	0.663	11.384	0.722	12.044	15
0.498	10.075	0.522	10.383	0.573	11.022	0.627	11.692	0.656	12.040	0.716	12.760	16
0.490	10.566	0.515	10.898	0.566	11.588	0.621	12.313	0.650	12.690	0.711	13.472	17
0.483	11.049	0.508	11.405	0.559	12.147	0.615	12.928	0.644	13.334	0.706	14.178	18
0.477	11.526	0.501	11.907	0.553	12.701	0.610	13.538	0.639	13.974	0.702	14.880	19
0.471	11.997	0.495	12.402	0.548	13.248	0.604	14.142	0.634	14.608	0.697	15.577	20
0.465	12.462	0.490	12.892	0.542	13.791	0.599	14.742	0.630	15.237	0.693	16.270	21
0.460	12.921	0.484	13.376	0.537	14.328	0.595	15.336	0.625	15.862	0.689	16.960	22
0.454	13.376	0.479	13.856	0.533	14.861	0.590	15.927	0.621	16.483	0.686	17.646	23
0.450	13.825	0.475	14.331	0.528	15.389	0.586	16.513	0.617	17.100	0.682	18.328	24
0.445	14.270	0.470	14.801	0.524	15.913	0.582	17.095	0.613	17.713	0.679	19.007	25
0.441	14.711	0.466	15.267	0.520	16.432	0.578	17.673	0.609	18.323	0.676	19.683	26
0.436	15.147	0.462	15.728	0.516	16.948	0.575	18.248	0.606	18.929	0.673	20.355	27
0.432	15.580	0.458	16.186	0.512	17.460	0.571	18.819	0.603	19.531	0.670	21.025	28
0.429	16.008	0.454	16.640	0.508	17.968	0.568	19.386	0.599	20.131	0.667	21.692	29
0.425	16.434	0.450	17.091	0.505	18.473	0.564	19.951	0.596	20.727	0.664	22.356	30
0.422	16.855	0.447	17.538	0.502	18.975	0.561	20.512	0.593	21.320	0.662	23.018	31
0.418	17.273	0.444	17.981	0.498	19.473	0.558	21.071	0.590	21.911	0.659	23.677	32
0.415	17.688	0.441	18.422	0.495	19.969	0.556	21.626	0.588	22.498	0.657	24.334	33
0.412	18.100	0.437	18.859	0.492	20.461	0.553	22.179	0.585	23.084	0.654	24.988	34
0.409	18.509	0.434	19.294	0.490	20.951	0.550	22.729	0.583	23.666	0.652	25.640	35
0.406	18.915	0.432	19.725	0.487	21.437	0.547	23.276	0.580	24.246	0.650	26.290	36
0.403	19.318	0.429	20.154	0.484	21.921	0.545	23.821	0.578	24.824	0.648	26.937	37
0.401	19.719	0.426	20.580	0.482	22.403	0.543	24.364	0.575	25.399	0.646	27.583	38
0.398	20.117	0.424	21.004	0.479	22.882	0.540	24.904	0.573	25.972	0.644	28.227	39
0.395	20.512	0.421	21.425	0.477	23.358	0.538	25.442	0.571	26.543	0.642	28.868	40
0.393	20.905	0.419	21.844	0.474	23.833	0.536	25.978	0.569	27.111	0.640	29.508	41
0.391	21.296	0.416	22.260	0.472	24.305	0.533	26.511	0.567	27.678	0.638	30.146	42
0.388	21.684	0.414	22.674	0.470	24.774	0.531	27.042	0.565	28.243	0.636	30.782	43
0.386	22.070	0.412	23.086	0.468	25.242	0.529	27.572	0.563	28.805	0.634	31.416	44
0.384	22.454	0.410	23.496	0.465	25.707	0.527	28.099	0.561	29.366	0.633	32.049	45
0.382	22.835	0.408	23.903	0.463	26.171	0.525	28.624	0.559	29.925	0.631	32.680	46

(continued)

APPENDIX D LEARNING CURVE COEFFICIENTS AND

N	70%	Total	72%	Total	74%	Total	75%	Total	78%	Total	80%	Total	82%	Total
47	0.138	11.902	0.161	13.125	0.188	14.464	0.202	15.180	0.252	17.524	0.290	19.265	0.332	21.158
48	0.136	12.038	0.160	13.285	0.186	14.650	0.201	15.380	0.250	17.774	0.288	19.552	0.330	21.488
49	0.135	12.173	0.158	13.443	0.184	14.834	0.199	15.579	0.248	18.022	0.286	19.838	0.328	21.816
50	0.134	12.307	0.157	13.599	0.183	15.017	0.197	15.776	0.246	18.268	0.284	20.122	0.326	22.143
51	0.132	12.439	0.155	13.754	0.181	15.198	0.196	15.972	0.244	18.512	0.282	20.404	0.324	22.467
52	0.131	12.570	0.154	13.908	0.180	15.378	0.194	16.166	0.243	18.755	0.280	20.684	0.323	22.790
53	0.130	12.700	0.152	14.061	0.178	15.556	0.192	16.358	0.241	18.996	0.279	20.963	0.321	23.110
54	0.128	12.828	0.151	14.212	0.177	15.733	0.191	16.549	0.239	19.235	0.277	21.239	0.319	23.430
55	0.127	12.955	0.150	14.361	0.175	15.909	0.190	16.739	0.238	19.473	0.275	21.515	0.317	23.747
56	0.126	13.081	0.148	14.510	0.174	16.083	0.188	16.927	0.236	19.709	0.274	21.788	0.316	24.063
57	0.125	13.206	0.147	14.657	0.173	16.255	0.187	17.114	0.235	19.944	0.272	22.060	0.314	24.377
58	0.124	13.330	0.146	14.803	0.171	16.427	0.185	17.299	0.233	20.177	0.271	22.331	0.313	24.690
59	0.123	13.453	0.145	14.948	0.170	16.597	0.184	17.483	0.232	20.409	0.269	22.600	0.311	25.001
60	0.122	13.574	0.144	15.091	0.169	16.766	0.183	17.666	0.230	20.640	0.268	22.868	0.310	25.311
61	0.121	13.695	0.143	15.234	0.168	16.933	0.182	17.847	0.229	20.869	0.266	23.134	0.308	25.619
62	0.120	13.814	0.141	15.375	0.166	17.100	0.180	18.028	0.228	21.096	0.265	23.399	0.307	25.926
63	0.119	13.933	0.140	15.516	0.165	17.265	0.179	18.207	0.226	21.323	0.263	23.662	0.305	26.231
64	0.118	14.051	0.139	15.655	0.164	17.429	0.178	18.385	0.225	21.548	0.262	23.924	0.304	26.535
65	0.117	14.167	0.138	15.793	0.163	17.592	0.177	18.562	0.224	21.772	0.261	24.185	0.303	26.838
66	0.116	14.283	0.137	15.930	0.162	17.754	0.176	18.737	0.223	21.995	0.260	24.445	0.301	27.139
67	0.115	14.398	0.136	16.067	0.161	17.915	0.175	18.912	0.222	22.216	0.258	24.703	0.300	27.439
68	0.114	14.512	0.135	16.202	0.160	18.075	0.174	19.086	0.220	22.437	0.257	24.960	0.299	27.738
69	0.113	14.625	0.134	16.337	0.159	18.234	0.173	19.258	0.219	22.656	0.256	25.216	0.298	28.036
70	0.112	14.738	0.134	16.470	0.158	18.392	0.171	19.430	0.218	22.874	0.255	25.471	0.296	28.332
71	0.112	14.849	0.133	16.603	0.157	18.549	0.170	19.600	0.217	23.091	0.254	25.724	0.295	28.627
72	0.111	14.960	0.132	16.734	0.156	18.705	0.169	19.770	0.216	23.307	0.252	25.977	0.294	28.921
73	0.110	15.070	0.131	16.865	0.155	18.860	0.169	19.938	0.215	23.522	0.251	26.228	0.293	29.214
74	0.109	15.179	0.130	16.995	0.154	19.014	0.168	20.106	0.214	23.735	0.250	26.478	0.292	29.505
75	0.108	15.287	0.129	17.125	0.153	19.168	0.167	20.272	0.213	23.948	0.249	26.727	0.291	29.796
76	0.108	15.395	0.128	17.253	0.152	19.320	0.166	20.438	0.212	24.160	0.248	26.975	0.289	30.085
77	0.107	15.502	0.128	17.381	0.152	19.472	0.165	20.603	0.211	24.371	0.247	27.222	0.288	30.374
78	0.106	15.608	0.127	17.508	0.151	19.622	0.164	20.767	0.210	24.580	0.246	27.468	0.287	30.661
79	0.106	15.714	0.126	17.634	0.150	19.772	0.163	20.930	0.209	24.789	0.245	27.713	0.286	30.947
80	0.105	15.819	0.125	17.759	0.149	19.921	0.162	21.092	0.208	24.997	0.244	27.957	0.285	31.232
81	0.104	15.923	0.125	17.884	0.148	20.069	0.161	21.253	0.207	25.204	0.243	28.200	0.284	31.516
82	0.104	16.027	0.124	18.007	0.147	20.217	0.161	21.414	0.206	25.410	0.242	28.442	0.283	31.800
83	0.103	16.130	0.123	18.131	0.147	20.364	0.160	21.574	0.205	25.615	0.241	28.683	0.282	32.082
84	0.102	16.232	0.122	18.253	0.146	20.509	0.159	21.733	0.204	25.820	0.240	28.924	0.281	32.363
85	0.102	16.333	0.122	18.375	0.145	20.655	0.158	21.891	0.203	26.023	0.239	29.163	0.280	32.643
86	0.101	16.435	0.121	18.496	0.144	20.799	0.157	22.048	0.203	26.226	0.238	29.401	0.279	32.923
87	0.100	16.535	0.120	18.616	0.144	20.943	0.157	22.205	0.202	26.427	0.237	29.639	0.278	33.201
88	0.100	16.635	0.120	18.736	0.143	21.086	0.156	22.361	0.201	26.628	0.237	29.875	0.278	33.479
89	0.099	16.734	0.119	18.855	0.142	21.228	0.155	22.516	0.200	26.828	0.236	30.111	0.277	33.755
90	0.099	16.833	0.119	18.974	0.142	21.370	0.154	22.671	0.199	27.028	0.235	30.346	0.276	34.031
91	0.098	16.931	0.118	19.092	0.141	21.511	0.154	22.825	0.199	27.226	0.234	30.580	0.275	34.306
92	0.098	17.029	0.117	19.209	0.140	21.651	0.153	22.978	0.198	27.424	0.233	30.813	0.274	34.580
93	0.097	17.126	0.117	19.326	0.140	21.790	0.152	23.130	0.197	27.621	0.232	31.046	0.273	34.853

CUMULATIVE TOTALS   YN = Y1*(N)^(LOG L/ LOG 2)

84%	Total	85%	Total	87%	Total	89%	Total	90%	Total	92%	Total	N
0.380	23.215	0.405	24.309	0.461	26.632	0.523	29.148	0.557	30.482	0.629	33.309	**47**
0.378	23.593	0.403	24.712	0.459	27.091	0.522	29.669	0.555	31.037	0.628	33.937	**48**
0.376	23.969	0.402	25.113	0.458	27.549	0.520	30.189	0.553	31.590	0.626	34.563	**49**
0.374	24.342	0.400	25.513	0.456	28.005	0.518	30.707	0.552	32.142	0.625	35.187	**50**
0.372	24.714	0.398	25.911	0.454	28.459	0.516	31.224	0.550	32.692	0.623	35.811	**51**
0.370	25.084	0.396	26.307	0.452	28.911	0.515	31.738	0.548	33.241	0.622	36.432	**52**
0.368	25.453	0.394	26.701	0.450	29.361	0.513	32.251	0.547	33.787	0.620	37.053	**53**
0.367	25.819	0.392	27.094	0.449	29.810	0.511	32.763	0.545	34.333	0.619	37.671	**54**
0.365	26.184	0.391	27.484	0.447	30.257	0.510	33.272	0.544	34.877	0.618	38.289	**55**
0.363	26.548	0.389	27.873	0.445	30.702	0.508	33.781	0.542	35.419	0.616	38.905	**56**
0.362	26.909	0.388	28.261	0.444	31.146	0.507	34.287	0.541	35.960	0.615	39.520	**57**
0.360	$27.269	0.386	28.647	0.442	31.588	0.505	34.793	0.539	36.499	0.614	40.134	**58**
0.359	27.628	0.384	29.031	0.441	32.029	0.504	35.296	0.538	37.037	0.612	40.746	**59**
0.357	$27.985	0.383	29.414	0.439	32.468	0.502	35.799	0.537	37.574	0.611	41.357	**60**
0.356	28.341	0.381	29.796	0.438	32.906	0.501	36.300	0.535	38.109	0.610	41.967	**61**
0.354	28.695	0.380	30.176	0.436	33.343	0.500	36.800	0.534	38.643	0.609	42.575	**62**
0.353	29.047	0.379	30.554	0.435	33.778	0.498	37.298	0.533	39.176	0.608	43.183	**63**
0.351	29.399	0.377	30.931	0.434	34.211	0.497	37.795	0.531	39.708	0.606	43.789	**64**
0.350	29.749	0.376	31.307	0.432	34.643	0.496	38.290	0.530	40.238	0.605	44.395	**65**
0.349	30.097	0.374	31.682	0.431	35.074	0.494	38.785	0.529	40.767	0.604	44.999	**66**
0.347	30.444	0.373	32.055	0.430	35.504	0.493	39.278	0.528	41.294	0.603	45.602	**67**
0.346	30.790	0.372	32.427	0.428	35.932	0.492	39.770	0.527	41.821	0.602	46.204	**68**
0.345	31.135	0.371	32.797	0.427	36.360	0.491	40.261	0.525	42.346	0.601	46.805	**69**
0.343	31.479	0.369	33.166	0.426	36.785	0.490	40.750	0.524	42.871	0.600	47.404	**70**
0.342	31.821	0.368	33.534	0.425	37.210	0.488	41.239	0.523	43.394	0.599	48.003	**71**
0.341	32.162	0.367	33.901	0.423	37.634	0.487	41.726	0.522	43.916	0.598	48.601	**72**
0.340	32.502	0.366	34.267	0.422	38.056	0.486	42.212	0.521	44.437	0.597	49.198	**73**
0.339	32.841	0.365	34.632	0.421	38.477	0.485	42.697	0.520	44.957	0.596	49.794	**74**
0.338	33.178	0.363	34.995	0.420	38.897	0.484	43.181	0.519	45.475	0.595	50.389	**75**
0.336	33.514	0.362	35.357	0.419	39.316	0.483	43.664	0.518	45.993	0.594	50.983	**76**
0.335	33.850	0.361	35.718	0.418	39.734	0.482	44.146	0.517	46.510	0.593	51.576	**77**
0.334	34.184	0.360	36.078	0.417	40.151	0.481	44.626	0.516	47.025	0.592	52.168	**78**
0.333	34.517	0.359	36.437	0.416	40.566	0.480	45.106	0.515	47.540	0.591	52.759	**79**
0.332	34.849	0.358	36.795	0.415	40.981	0.479	45.585	0.514	48.054	0.590	53.349	**80**
0.331	35.180	0.357	37.152	0.414	41.394	0.478	46.062	0.513	48.567	0.589	53.939	**81**
0.330	35.511	0.356	37.508	0.413	41.807	0.477	46.539	0.512	49.078	0.589	54.527	**82**
0.329	35.840	0.355	37.863	0.412	42.219	0.476	47.015	0.511	49.589	0.588	55.115	**83**
0.328	36.168	0.354	38.217	0.411	42.629	0.475	47.489	0.510	50.099	0.587	55.702	**84**
0.327	36.495	0.353	38.570	0.410	43.039	0.474	47.963	0.509	50.608	0.586	56.288	**85**
0.326	36.821	0.352	38.922	0.409	43.447	0.473	48.436	0.508	51.116	0.585	56.873	**86**
0.325	37.146	0.351	39.272	0.408	43.855	0.472	48.908	0.507	51.624	0.584	57.457	**87**
0.324	37.470	0.350	39.622	0.407	44.262	0.471	49.379	0.506	52.130	0.584	58.041	**88**
0.323	37.794	0.349	39.972	0.406	44.668	0.470	49.849	0.505	52.635	0.583	58.624	**89**
0.322	38.116	0.348	40.320	0.405	45.072	0.469	50.319	0.505	53.140	0.582	59.206	**90**
0.322	38.438	0.347	40.667	0.404	45.477	0.468	50.787	0.504	53.644	0.581	59.787	**91**
0.321	38.758	0.346	41.013	0.403	45.880	0.468	51.255	0.503	54.147	0.580	60.367	**92**
0.320	39.078	0.346	41.359	0.402	46.282	0.467	51.721	0.502	54.649	0.580	60.947	**93**

(continued)

APPENDIX D LEARNING CURVE COEFFICIENTS AND

N	70%	Total	72%	Total	74%	Total	75%	Total	78%	Total	80%	Total	82%	Total
94	0.097	17.222	0.116	19.442	0.139	21.929	0.152	23.282	0.196	27.817	0.232	31.277	0.272	35.125
95	0.096	17.318	0.116	19.557	0.138	22.068	0.151	23.433	0.195	28.013	0.231	31.508	0.271	35.397
96	0.095	17.414	0.115	19.672	0.138	22.205	0.150	23.583	0.195	28.207	0.230	31.738	0.271	35.667
97	0.095	17.509	0.114	19.787	0.137	22.342	0.150	23.733	0.194	28.401	0.229	31.967	0.270	35.937
98	0.094	17.603	0.114	19.901	0.136	22.479	0.149	23.882	0.193	28.595	0.229	32.196	0.269	36.206
99	0.094	17.697	0.113	20.014	0.136	22.615	0.149	24.031	0.193	28.787	0.228	32.424	0.268	36.475
100	0.094	17.791	0.113	20.127	0.135	22.750	0.148	24.179	0.192	28.979	0.227	32.651	0.268	36.742
101	0.093	17.884	0.112	20.239	0.135	22.885	0.147	24.326	0.191	29.170	0.226	32.877	0.267	37.009
102	0.093	17.976	0.112	20.351	0.134	23.019	0.147	24.473	0.191	29.361	0.226	33.103	0.266	37.275
103	0.092	18.068	0.111	20.462	0.134	23.152	0.146	24.619	0.190	29.551	0.225	33.328	0.265	37.540
104	0.092	18.160	0.111	20.572	0.133	23.285	0.145	24.764	0.189	29.740	0.224	33.552	0.265	37.805
105	0.091	18.251	0.110	20.683	0.132	23.418	0.145	24.909	0.189	29.929	0.224	33.775	0.264	38.069
106	0.091	18.342	0.110	20.792	0.132	23.550	0.144	25.053	0.188	30.116	0.223	33.998	0.263	38.332
107	0.090	18.432	0.109	20.902	0.131	23.681	0.144	25.197	0.187	30.304	0.222	34.220	0.262	38.594
108	0.090	18.522	0.109	21.010	0.131	23.812	0.143	25.340	0.187	30.490	0.222	34.442	0.262	38.856
109	0.089	18.612	0.108	21.118	0.130	23.942	0.143	25.483	0.186	30.677	0.221	34.663	0.261	39.117
110	0.089	18.701	0.108	21.226	0.130	24.072	0.142	25.625	0.185	30.862	0.220	34.883	0.260	39.377
111	0.089	18.789	0.107	21.334	0.129	24.201	0.142	25.767	0.185	31.047	0.220	35.103	0.260	39.637
112	0.088	18.877	0.107	21.440	0.129	24.330	0.141	25.908	0.184	31.231	0.219	35.321	0.259	39.896
113	0.088	18.965	0.106	21.547	0.128	24.458	0.141	26.049	0.184	31.415	0.218	35.540	0.258	40.154
114	0.087	19.053	0.106	21.653	0.128	24.586	0.140	26.189	0.183	31.598	0.218	35.757	0.258	40.412
115	0.087	19.140	0.106	21.758	0.127	24.713	0.140	26.328	0.183	31.780	0.217	35.975	0.257	40.669
116	0.087	19.226	0.105	21.863	0.127	24.840	0.139	26.467	0.182	31.962	0.216	36.191	0.256	40.926
117	0.086	19.313	0.105	21.968	0.126	24.966	0.139	26.606	0.181	32.144	0.216	36.407	0.256	41.181
118	0.086	19.398	0.104	22.072	0.126	25.092	0.138	26.744	0.181	32.325	0.215	36.622	0.255	41.436
119	0.086	19.484	0.104	22.176	0.125	25.218	0.138	26.881	0.180	32.505	0.215	36.837	0.255	41.691
120	0.085	19.569	0.103	22.280	0.125	25.343	0.137	27.019	0.180	32.685	0.214	37.051	0.254	41.945
121	0.085	19.654	0.103	22.383	0.125	25.467	0.137	27.155	0.179	32.864	0.214	37.264	0.253	42.198
122	0.084	19.738	0.103	22.485	0.124	25.591	0.136	27.291	0.179	33.043	0.213	37.477	0.253	42.451
123	0.084	19.822	0.102	22.587	0.124	25.715	0.136	27.427	0.178	33.221	0.212	37.690	0.252	42.703
124	0.084	19.906	0.102	22.689	0.123	25.838	0.135	27.562	0.178	33.399	0.212	37.902	0.252	42.955
125	0.083	19.989	0.101	22.791	0.123	25.961	0.135	27.697	0.177	33.576	0.211	38.113	0.251	43.206
126	0.083	20.072	0.101	22.892	0.122	26.083	0.134	27.831	0.177	33.752	0.211	38.324	0.250	43.456
127	0.083	20.155	0.101	22.992	0.122	26.205	0.134	27.965	0.176	33.928	0.210	38.534	0.250	43.706
128	0.082	20.238	0.100	23.093	0.122	26.327	0.133	28.099	0.176	34.104	0.210	38.744	0.249	43.955
129	0.082	20.320	0.100	23.193	0.121	26.448	0.133	28.232	0.175	34.279	0.209	38.953	0.249	44.204
130	0.082	20.401	0.100	23.292	0.121	26.569	0.133	28.365	0.175	34.454	0.209	39.162	0.248	44.452
131	0.081	20.483	0.099	23.391	0.120	26.689	0.132	28.497	0.174	34.628	0.208	39.370	0.248	44.700
132	0.081	20.564	0.099	23.490	0.120	26.809	0.132	28.629	0.174	34.802	0.208	39.578	0.247	44.947
133	0.081	20.644	0.099	23.589	0.120	26.928	0.131	28.760	0.173	34.975	0.207	39.785	0.247	45.193
134	0.080	20.725	0.098	23.687	0.119	27.047	0.131	28.891	0.173	35.148	0.207	39.991	0.246	45.440
135	0.080	20.805	0.098	23.785	0.119	27.166	0.131	29.021	0.172	35.320	0.206	40.197	0.246	45.685
136	0.080	20.885	0.097	23.882	0.118	27.284	0.130	29.152	0.172	35.492	0.206	40.403	0.245	45.930
137	0.080	20.964	0.097	23.979	0.118	27.402	0.130	29.281	0.171	35.664	0.205	40.608	0.244	46.174
138	0.079	21.044	0.097	24.076	0.118	27.520	0.129	29.411	0.171	35.835	0.205	40.813	0.244	46.418
139	0.079	21.122	0.096	24.173	0.117	27.637	0.129	29.540	0.171	36.005	0.204	41.017	0.243	46.662
140	0.079	21.201	0.096	24.269	0.117	27.754	0.129	29.668	0.170	36.175	0.204	41.221	0.243	46.905

CUMULATIVE TOTALS YN = Y1*(N)^(LOG L/ LOG 2)

84%	Total	85%	Total	87%	Total	89%	Total	90%	Total	92%	Total	N
0.319	39.397	0.345	41.704	0.401	46.683	0.466	52.187	0.501	55.150	0.579	61.526	**94**
0.318	39.715	0.344	42.047	0.401	47.084	0.465	52.652	0.500	55.650	0.578	62.104	**95**
0.317	40.032	0.343	42.390	0.400	47.484	0.464	53.117	0.500	56.150	0.577	62.682	**96**
0.316	40.349	0.342	42.732	0.399	47.882	0.463	53.580	0.499	56.649	0.577	63.258	**97**
0.316	40.664	0.341	43.074	0.398	48.280	0.463	54.043	0.498	57.147	0.576	63.834	**98**
0.315	40.979	0.340	43.414	0.397	48.678	0.462	54.505	0.497	57.644	0.575	64.410	**99**
0.314	41.293	0.340	43.754	0.396	49.074	0.461	54.966	0.497	58.141	0.575	64.984	**100**
0.313	41.606	0.339	44.093	0.396	49.470	0.460	55.426	0.496	58.637	0.574	65.558	**101**
0.312	41.919	0.338	44.431	0.395	49.865	0.460	55.885	0.495	59.132	0.573	66.132	**102**
0.312	42.230	0.337	44.768	0.394	50.259	0.459	56.344	0.494	59.626	0.573	66.704	**103**
0.311	42.541	0.337	45.105	0.393	50.652	0.458	56.802	0.494	60.120	0.572	67.276	**104**
0.310	42.851	0.336	45.441	0.393	51.045	0.457	57.259	0.493	60.613	0.571	67.848	**105**
0.309	43.161	0.335	45.776	0.392	51.436	0.457	57.716	0.492	61.105	0.571	68.418	**106**
0.309	43.470	0.334	46.110	0.391	51.828	0.456	58.172	0.492	61.597	0.570	68.988	**107**
0.308	43.778	0.334	46.444	0.390	52.218	0.455	58.627	0.491	62.087	0.569	69.558	**108**
0.307	44.085	0.333	46.776	0.390	52.608	0.454	59.081	0.490	62.577	0.569	70.126	**109**
0.307	44.391	0.332	47.109	0.389	52.996	0.454	59.535	0.489	63.067	0.568	70.694	**110**
0.306	44.697	0.331	47.440	0.388	53.385	0.453	59.988	0.489	63.556	0.567	71.262	**111**
0.305	45.002	0.331	47.771	0.388	53.772	0.452	60.441	0.488	64.044	0.567	71.829	**112**
0.304	45.307	0.330	48.101	0.387	54.159	0.452	60.892	0.487	64.531	0.566	72.395	**113**
0.304	45.611	0.329	48.430	0.386	54.545	0.451	61.343	0.487	65.018	0.566	72.961	**114**
0.303	45.914	0.329	48.759	0.385	54.931	0.450	61.794	0.486	65.504	0.565	73.526	**115**
0.302	46.216	0.328	49.087	0.385	55.315	0.450	62.243	0.486	65.990	0.564	74.090	**116**
0.302	46.518	0.327	49.415	0.384	55.700	0.449	62.692	0.485	66.475	0.564	74.654	**117**
0.301	46.819	0.327	49.741	0.383	56.083	0.448	63.141	0.484	66.959	0.563	75.218	**118**
0.301	47.120	0.326	50.067	0.383	56.466	0.448	63.588	0.484	67.442	0.563	75.780	**119**
0.300	47.420	0.325	50.393	0.382	56.848	0.447	64.036	0.483	67.925	0.562	76.343	**120**
0.299	47.719	0.325	50.718	0.382	57.230	0.447	64.482	0.482	68.408	0.562	76.904	**121**
0.299	48.018	0.324	51.042	0.381	57.610	0.446	64.928	0.482	68.890	0.561	77.465	**122**
0.298	48.316	0.324	51.366	0.380	57.991	0.445	65.373	0.481	69.371	0.561	78.026	**123**
0.297	48.613	0.323	51.688	0.380	58.370	0.445	65.818	0.481	69.851	0.560	78.586	**124**
0.297	48.910	0.322	52.011	0.379	58.749	0.444	66.262	0.480	70.332	0.559	79.145	**125**
0.296	49.2206	0.322	52.333	0.378	59.128	0.443	66.706	0.479	70.811	0.559	79.704	**126**
0.296	49.502	0.321	52.654	0.378	59.506	0.443	67.148	0.479	71.290	0.558	80.262	**127**
0.295	49.797	0.321	52.974	0.377	59.883	0.442	67.591	0.478	71.768	0.558	80.820	**128**
0.295	50.092	0.320	53.294	0.377	60.260	0.442	68.033	0.478	72.246	0.557	81.378	**129**
0.294	50.386	0.319	53.614	0.376	60.636	0.441	68.474	0.477	72.723	0.557	81.934	**130**
0.293	50.679	0.319	53.933	0.376	61.011	0.441	68.914	0.477	73.200	0.556	82.491	**131**
0.293	50.972	0.318	54.251	0.375	61.386	0.440	69.354	0.476	73.676	0.556	83.047	**132**
0.292	51.264	0.318	54.569	0.374	61.761	0.439	69.794	0.476	74.151	0.555	83.602	**133**
0.292	51.556	0.317	54.886	0.374	62.134	0.439	70.233	0.475	74.626	0.555	84.157	**134**
0.291	51.847	0.317	55.202	0.373	62.508	0.438	70.671	0.474	75.101	0.554	84.711	**135**
0.291	52.138	0.316	55.518	0.373	62.880	0.438	71.109	0.474	75.575	0.554	85.265	**136**
0.290	52.428	0.316	55.834	0.372	63.252	0.437	71.546	0.473	76.048	0.553	85.818	**137**
0.290	52.717	0.315	56.149	0.372	63.624	0.437	71.983	0.473	76.521	0.553	86.371	**138**
0.289	53.006	0.314	56.463	0.371	63.995	0.436	72.419	0.472	76.993	0.552	86.923	**139**
0.289	53.295	0.314	56.777	0.371	64.366	0.436	72.855	0.472	77.465	0.552	87.475	**140**

(continued)

APPENDIX D LEARNING CURVE COEFFICIENTS AND

N	70%	Total	72%	Total	74%	Total	75%	Total	78%	Total	80%	Total	82%	Total
141	0.078	21.279	0.096	24.365	0.117	27.871	0.128	29.797	0.170	36.345	0.203	41.424	0.242	47.147
142	0.078	21.358	0.095	24.460	0.116	27.987	0.128	29.924	0.169	36.514	0.203	41.627	0.242	47.389
143	0.078	21.435	0.095	24.555	0.116	28.103	0.127	30.052	0.169	36.683	0.202	41.829	0.242	47.631
144	0.078	21.513	0.095	24.650	0.115	28.218	0.127	30.179	0.168	36.851	0.202	42.031	0.241	47.872
145	0.077	21.590	0.095	24.745	0.115	28.333	0.127	30.306	0.168	37.019	0.201	42.233	0.241	48.112
146	0.077	21.667	0.094	24.839	0.115	28.448	0.126	30.432	0.168	37.187	0.201	42.434	0.240	48.353
147	0.077	21.744	0.094	24.933	0.114	28.562	0.126	30.558	0.167	37.354	0.201	42.634	0.240	48.592
148	0.076	21.820	0.094	25.026	0.114	28.676	0.126	30.684	0.167	37.521	0.200	42.835	0.239	48.831
149	0.076	21.896	0.093	25.120	0.114	28.790	0.125	30.809	0.166	37.687	0.200	43.034	0.239	49.070
150	0.076	21.972	0.093	25.213	0.113	28.904	0.125	30.934	0.166	37.853	0.199	43.234	0.238	49.308
151	0.076	22.048	0.093	25.306	0.113	29.017	0.125	31.059	0.166	38.019	0.199	43.432	0.238	49.546
152	0.075	22.123	0.092	25.398	0.113	29.129	0.124	31.183	0.165	38.184	0.198	43.631	0.237	49.783
153	0.075	22.198	0.092	25.490	0.112	29.242	0.124	31.307	0.165	38.349	0.198	43.829	0.237	50.020
154	0.075	22.273	0.092	25.582	0.112	29.354	0.124	31.431	0.164	38.513	0.198	44.026	0.236	50.257
155	0.075	22.348	0.092	25.674	0.112	29.466	0.123	31.554	0.164	38.677	0.197	44.224	0.236	50.493
156	0.074	22.422	0.091	25.765	0.112	29.577	0.123	31.677	0.164	38.841	0.197	44.420	0.236	50.728
157	0.074	22.496	0.091	25.856	0.111	29.689	0.123	31.800	0.163	39.004	0.196	44.617	0.235	50.963
158	0.074	22.570	0.091	25.947	0.111	29.799	0.122	31.922	0.163	39.167	0.196	44.813	0.235	51.198
159	0.074	22.644	0.091	26.037	0.111	29.910	0.122	32.044	0.163	39.329	0.196	45.008	0.234	51.432
160	0.073	22.717	0.090	26.128	0.110	30.020	0.122	32.166	0.162	39.491	0.195	45.203	0.234	51.666
161	0.073	22.791	0.090	26.218	0.110	30.130	0.121	32.287	0.162	39.653	0.195	45.398	0.233	51.899
162	0.073	22.864	0.090	26.307	0.110	30.240	0.121	32.408	0.161	39.815	0.194	45.593	0.233	52.133
163	0.073	22.936	0.089	26.397	0.109	30.349	0.121	32.529	0.161	39.976	0.194	45.787	0.233	52.365
164	0.072	23.009	0.089	26.486	0.109	30.459	0.120	32.649	0.161	40.136	0.194	45.980	0.232	52.597
165	0.072	23.081	0.089	26.575	0.109	30.567	0.120	32.769	0.160	40.297	0.193	46.174	0.232	52.829
166	0.072	23.153	0.089	26.664	0.109	30.676	0.120	32.889	0.160	40.457	0.193	46.366	0.231	53.061
167	0.072	23.225	0.088	26.752	0.108	30.784	0.120	33.009	0.160	40.617	0.193	46.559	0.231	53.292
168	0.072	23.296	0.088	26.840	0.108	30.892	0.119	33.128	0.159	40.776	0.192	46.751	0.231	53.522
169	0.071	23.368	0.088	26.928	0.108	31.000	0.119	33.247	0.159	40.935	0.192	46.943	0.230	53.752
170	0.071	23.439	0.088	27.016	0.107	31.107	0.119	33.366	0.159	41.094	0.191	47.134	0.230	53.982
171	0.071	23.510	0.087	27.103	0.107	31.214	0.118	33.484	0.158	41.252	0.191	47.325	0.229	54.212
172	0.071	23.581	0.087	27.190	0.107	31.321	0.118	33.602	0.158	41.410	0.191	47.516	0.229	54.441
173	0.071	23.651	0.087	27.277	0.107	31.428	0.118	33.720	0.158	41.568	0.190	47.706	0.229	54.669
174	0.070	23.722	0.087	27.364	0.106	31.534	0.118	33.837	0.157	41.725	0.190	47.896	0.228	54.898
175	0.070	23.792	0.086	27.451	0.106	31.640	0.117	33.954	0.157	41.882	0.190	48.086	0.228	55.126
176	0.070	23.862	0.086	27.537	0.106	31.746	0.117	34.071	0.157	42.039	0.189	48.275	0.228	55.353
177	0.070	23.931	0.086	27.623	0.106	31.852	0.117	34.188	0.156	42.195	0.189	48.464	0.227	55.580
178	0.070	24.001	0.086	27.709	0.105	31.957	0.116	34.305	0.156	42.351	0.189	48.653	0.227	55.807
179	0.069	24.070	0.086	27.794	0.105	32.062	0.116	34.421	0.156	42.507	0.188	48.841	0.226	56.034
180	0.069	24.139	0.085	27.880	0.105	32.167	0.116	34.537	0.155	42.662	0.188	49.029	0.226	56.260
181	0.069	24.208	0.085	27.965	0.105	32.271	0.116	34.652	0.155	42.817	0.188	49.216	0.226	56.486
182	0.069	24.277	0.085	28.050	0.104	32.376	0.115	34.768	0.155	42.972	0.187	49.404	0.225	56.711
183	0.069	24.345	0.085	28.134	0.104	32.480	0.115	34.883	0.155	43.127	0.187	49.591	0.225	56.936
184	0.068	24.414	0.084	28.219	0.104	32.583	0.115	34.997	0.154	43.281	0.187	49.777	0.225	57.161
185	0.068	24.482	0.084	28.303	0.104	32.687	0.115	35.112	0.154	43.435	0.186	49.963	0.224	57.385
186	0.068	24.550	0.084	28.387	0.103	32.790	0.114	35.226	0.154	43.589	0.186	50.149	0.224	57.609
187	0.068	24.618	0.084	28.471	0.103	32.893	0.114	35.340	0.153	43.742	0.186	50.335	0.224	57.833

CUMULATIVE TOTALS YN = Y1*(N)^(LOG L/ LOG 2)

84%	Total	85%	Total	87%	Total	89%	Total	90%	Total	92%	Total	N
0.288	53.583	0.313	57.091	0.370	64.736	0.435	73.290	0.471	77.936	0.551	88.026	**141**
0.287	53.870	0.313	57.403	0.369	65.105	0.435	73.725	0.471	78.407	0.551	88.577	**142**
0.287	54.157	0.312	57.716	0.369	65.474	0.434	74.159	0.470	78.877	0.550	89.128	**143**
0.286	54.444	0.312	58.028	0.368	65.842	0.434	74.593	0.470	79.347	0.550	89.678	**144**
0.286	54.730	0.311	58.339	0.368	66.210	0.433	75.026	0.469	79.817	0.550	90.227	**145**
0.285	55.015	0.311	58.650	0.367	66.578	0.433	75.458	0.469	80.285	0.549	90.776	**146**
0.285	55.300	0.310	58.960	0.367	66.945	0.432	75.890	0.468	80.754	0.549	91.325	**147**
0.285	55.585	0.310	59.270	0.366	67.311	0.432	76.322	0.468	81.222	0.548	91.873	**148**
0.284	55.869	0.309	59.579	0.366	67.677	0.431	76.753	0.467	81.689	0.548	92.421	**149**
0.284	56.152	0.309	59.888	0.365	68.042	0.431	77.184	0.467	82.156	0.547	92.968	**150**
0.283	56.435	0.308	60.197	0.365	68.407	0.430	77.614	0.466	82.622	0.547	93.515	**151**
0.283	56.718	0.308	60.505	0.364	68.772	0.430	78.044	0.466	83.088	0.546	94.062	**152**
0.282	57.000	0.307	60.812	0.364	69.136	0.429	78.473	0.466	83.554	0.546	94.608	**153**
0.282	57.282	0.307	61.119	0.363	69.499	0.429	78.902	0.465	84.019	0.546	95.153	**154**
0.281	57.563	0.307	61.426	0.363	69.862	0.428	79.330	0.465	84.483	0.545	95.698	**155**
0.281	57.844	0.306	61.732	0.363	70.225	0.428	79.758	0.464	84.947	0.545	96.243	**156**
0.280	58.124	0.306	62.037	0.362	70.587	0.427	80.185	0.464	85.411	0.544	96.787	**157**
0.280	58.404	0.305	62.342	0.362	70.949	0.427	80.612	0.463	85.874	0.544	97.331	**158**
0.279	58.683	0.305	62.647	0.361	71.310	0.426	81.039	0.463	86.337	0.543	97.875	**159**
0.279	58.962	0.304	62.951	0.361	71.670	0.426	81.465	0.462	86.800	0.543	98.418	**160**
0.279	59.241	0.304	63.255	0.360	72.031	0.426	81.890	0.462	87.261	0.543	98.960	**161**
0.278	59.519	0.303	63.558	0.360	72.391	0.425	82.316	0.461	87.723	0.542	99.503	**162**
0.278	59.797	0.303	63.861	0.359	72.750	0.425	82.740	0.461	88.184	0.542	100.045	**163**
0.277	60.074	0.302	64.164	0.359	73.109	0.424	83.164	0.461	88.645	0.541	100.586	**164**
0.277	60.351	0.302	64.466	0.358	73.4672	0.424	83.588	0.460	89.105	0.541	101.127	**165**
0.276	60.627	0.302	64.767	0.358	73.825	0.423	84.012	0.460	89.565	0.541	101.668	**166**
0.276	60.903	0.301	65.069	0.358	74.183	0.423	84.435	0.459	90.024	0.540	102.208	**167**
0.276	61.179	0.301	65.369	0.357	74.540	0.423	84.857	0.459	90.483	0.540	102.748	**168**
0.275	61.454	0.300	65.670	0.357	74.897	0.422	85.279	0.459	90.941	0.540	103.287	**169**
0.275	61.729	0.300	65.970	0.356	75.253	0.422	85.701	0.458	91.399	0.539	103.827	**170**
0.274	62.003	0.300	66.269	0.356	75.609	0.421	86.122	0.458	91.857	0.539	104.365	**171**
0.274	62.277	0.299	66.568	0.356	75.965	0.421	86.543	0.457	92.314	0.538	104.904	**172**
0.274	62.551	0.299	66.867	0.355	76.320	0.420	86.964	0.457	92.771	0.538	105.442	**173**
0.273	62.824	0.298	67.165	0.355	76.675	0.420	87.384	0.456	93.228	0.538	105.979	**174**
0.273	63.097	0.298	67.463	0.354	77.029	0.420	87.803	0.456	93.684	0.537	106.517	**175**
0.272	63.369	0.298	67.761	0.354	77.383	0.419	88.223	0.456	94.140	0.537	107.053	**176**
0.272	63.641	0.297	68.058	0.353	77.736	0.419	88.642	0.455	94.595	0.537	107.590	**177**
0.272	63.912	0.297	68.355	0.353	78.089	0.418	89.060	0.455	95.050	0.536	108.126	**178**
0.271	64.184	0.296	68.651	0.353	78.442	0.418	89.478	0.455	95.504	0.536	108.662	**179**
0.271	64.455	0.296	68.947	0.352	78.794	0.418	89.896	0.454	95.958	0.535	109.197	**180**
0.270	64.725	0.296	69.242	0.352	79.146	0.417	90.313	0.454	96.412	0.535	109.732	**181**
0.270	64.995	0.295	69.538	0.351	79.498	0.417	90.730	0.453	96.866	0.535	110.267	**182**
0.270	65.265	0.295	69.832	0.351	79.849	0.417	91.146	0.453	97.319	0.534	110.801	**183**
0.269	65.534	0.294	70.127	0.351	80.199	0.416	91.563	0.453	97.771	0.534	111.335	**184**
0.269	65.803	0.294	70.421	0.350	80.550	0.416	91.978	0.452	98.223	0.534	111.869	**185**
0.269	66.072	0.294	70.715	0.350	80.900	0.415	92.394	0.452	98.675	0.533	112.402	**186**
0.268	66.340	0.293	71.008	0.350	81.249	0.415	92.809	0.452	99.127	0.533	112.935	**187**

(continued)

APPENDIX D LEARNING CURVE COEFFICIENTS AND

N	70%	Total	72%	Total	74%	Total	75%	Total	78%	Total	80%	Total	82%	Total
188	0.068	24.685	0.084	28.554	0.103	32.996	0.114	35.454	0.153	43.895	0.185	50.520	0.223	58.056
189	0.067	24.752	0.083	28.638	0.103	33.099	0.114	35.568	0.153	44.048	0.185	50.705	0.223	58.279
190	0.067	24.820	0.083	28.721	0.102	33.201	0.113	35.681	0.152	44.200	0.185	50.890	0.223	58.502
191	0.067	24.887	0.083	28.804	0.102	33.303	0.113	35.794	0.152	44.352	0.184	51.074	0.222	58.724
192	0.067	24.954	0.083	28.887	0.102	33.405	0.113	35.907	0.152	44.504	0.184	51.258	0.222	58.946
193	0.067	25.020	0.083	28.969	0.102	33.507	0.113	36.019	0.152	44.656	0.184	51.442	0.222	59.167
194	0.066	25.087	0.082	29.052	0.101	33.608	0.112	36.132	0.151	44.807	0.183	51.626	0.221	59.389
195	0.066	25.153	0.082	29.134	0.101	33.709	0.112	36.244	0.151	44.958	0.183	51.809	0.221	59.610
196	0.066	25.219	0.082	29.216	0.101	33.810	0.112	36.356	0.151	45.109	0.183	51.992	0.221	59.830
197	0.066	25.285	0.082	29.298	0.101	33.911	0.112	36.467	0.151	45.260	0.183	52.174	0.220	60.051
198	0.066	25.351	0.082	29.379	0.101	34.012	0.111	36.579	0.150	45.410	0.182	52.356	0.220	60.271
199	0.066	25.417	0.081	29.461	0.100	34.112	0.111	36.690	0.150	45.560	0.182	52.538	0.220	60.490
200	0.065	25.482	0.081	29.542	0.100	34.212	0.111	36.801	0.150	45.709	0.182	52.720	0.219	60.710
201	0.065	25.547	0.081	29.623	0.100	34.312	0.111	36.911	0.149	45.859	0.181	52.901	0.219	60.929
202	0.065	25.612	0.081	29.703	0.100	34.412	0.110	37.022	0.149	46.008	0.181	53.082	0.219	61.148
203	0.065	25.677	0.081	29.784	0.099	34.511	0.110	37.132	0.149	46.157	0.181	53.263	0.218	61.366
204	0.065	25.742	0.080	29.865	0.099	34.610	0.110	37.242	0.149	46.306	0.180	53.444	0.218	61.584
205	0.065	25.807	0.080	29.945	0.099	34.709	0.110	37.352	0.148	46.454	0.180	53.624	0.218	61.802
206	0.064	25.871	0.080	30.025	0.099	34.808	0.110	37.461	0.148	46.602	0.180	53.804	0.218	62.020
207	0.064	25.936	0.080	30.105	0.099	34.907	0.109	37.571	0.148	46.750	0.180	53.983	0.217	62.237
208	0.064	26.000	0.080	30.184	0.098	35.005	0.109	37.680	0.148	46.897	0.179	54.163	0.217	62.454
209	0.064	26.064	0.080	30.264	0.098	35.103	0.109	37.789	0.147	47.045	0.179	54.342	0.217	62.670
210	0.064	26.128	0.079	30.343	0.098	35.201	0.109	37.897	0.147	47.192	0.179	54.521	0.216	62.887
211	0.064	26.191	0.079	30.422	0.098	35.299	0.108	38.006	0.147	47.339	0.179	54.699	0.216	63.103
212	0.064	26.255	0.079	30.501	0.098	35.397	0.108	38.114	0.147	47.485	0.178	54.878	0.216	63.319
213	0.063	26.318	0.079	30.580	0.097	35.494	0.108	38.222	0.146	47.632	0.178	55.056	0.215	63.534
214	0.063	26.381	0.079	30.659	0.097	35.591	0.108	38.330	0.146	47.778	0.178	55.233	0.215	63.749
215	0.063	26.444	0.078	30.737	0.097	35.688	0.108	38.438	0.146	47.924	0.177	55.411	0.215	63.964
216	0.063	26.507	0.078	30.815	0.097	35.785	0.107	38.545	0.146	48.069	0.177	55.588	0.215	64.179
217	0.063	26.570	0.078	30.894	0.097	35.882	0.107	38.652	0.145	48.215	0.177	55.765	0.214	64.393
218	0.063	26.633	0.078	30.972	0.096	35.978	0.107	38.759	0.145	48.360	0.177	55.942	0.214	64.607
219	0.062	26.695	0.078	31.049	0.096	36.074	0.107	38.866	0.145	48.505	0.176	56.118	0.214	64.821
220	0.062	26.757	0.078	31.127	0.096	36.171	0.107	38.973	0.145	48.649	0.176	56.294	0.213	65.034
221	0.062	26.820	0.077	31.204	0.096	36.266	0.106	39.079	0.144	48.794	0.176	56.470	0.213	65.247
222	0.062	26.882	0.077	31.282	0.096	36.362	0.106	39.185	0.144	48.938	0.176	56.646	0.213	65.460
223	0.062	26.944	0.077	31.359	0.095	36.458	0.106	39.291	0.144	49.082	0.175	56.821	0.213	65.673
224	0.062	27.005	0.077	31.436	0.095	36.553	0.106	39.397	0.144	49.226	0.175	56.996	0.212	65.885
225	0.062	27.067	0.077	31.512	0.095	36.648	0.106	39.503	0.143	49.369	0.175	57.171	0.212	66.098
226	0.061	27.128	0.077	31.589	0.095	36.743	0.105	39.608	0.143	49.512	0.175	57.346	0.212	66.309
227	0.061	27.190	0.076	31.665	0.095	36.838	0.105	39.714	0.143	49.655	0.174	57.520	0.212	66.521
228	0.061	27.251	0.076	31.742	0.095	36.932	0.105	39.819	0.143	49.798	0.174	57.694	0.211	66.732
229	0.061	27.312	0.076	31.818	0.094	37.027	0.105	39.923	0.143	49.941	0.174	57.868	0.211	66.943
230	0.061	27.373	0.076	31.894	0.094	37.121	0.105	40.028	0.142	50.083	0.174	58.042	0.211	67.154
231	0.061	27.434	0.076	31.970	0.094	37.215	0.104	40.133	0.142	50.225	0.173	58.215	0.211	67.365
232	0.061	27.494	0.076	32.045	0.094	37.309	0.104	40.237	0.142	50.367	0.173	58.388	0.210	67.575
233	0.061	27.555	0.076	32.121	0.094	37.402	0.104	40.341	0.142	50.509	0.173	58.561	0.210	67.785
234	0.060	27.615	0.075	32.196	0.093	37.496	0.104	40.445	0.141	50.651	0.173	58.734	0.210	67.995

CUMULATIVE TOTALS $YN = Y1*(N)^{(LOG\ L/\ LOG\ 2)}$

84%	Total	85%	Total	87%	Total	89%	Total	90%	Total	92%	Total	N
0.268	66.608	0.293	71.301	0.349	81.599	0.415	93.223	0.451	99.578	0.533	113.468	**188**
0.268	66.875	0.293	71.593	0.349	81.947	0.414	93.638	0.451	100.029	0.532	114.000	**189**
0.267	67.143	0.292	71.886	0.348	82.296	0.414	94.051	0.450	100.479	0.532	114.532	**190**
0.267	67.409	0.292	72.178	0.348	82.644	0.414	94.465	0.450	100.929	0.532	115.064	**191**
0.266	67.676	0.292	72.469	0.348	82.992	0.413	94.878	0.450	101.379	0.531	115.595	**192**
0.266	67.942	0.291	72.760	0.347	83.339	0.413	95.291	0.449	101.828	0.531	116.126	**193**
0.266	68.208	0.291	73.051	0.347	83.686	0.412	95.703	0.449	102.277	0.531	116.657	**194**
0.265	68.473	0.290	73.341	0.347	84.033	0.412	96.116	0.449	102.726	0.530	117.187	**195**
0.265	68.738	0.290	73.632	0.346	84.379	0.412	96.527	0.448	103.174	0.530	117.717	**196**
0.265	69.003	0.290	73.921	0.346	84.725	0.411	96.939	0.448	103.622	0.530	118.247	**197**
0.264	69.268	0.289	74.211	0.346	85.071	0.411	97.350	0.448	104.070	0.529	118.776	**198**
0.264	69.532	0.289	74.500	0.345	85.416	0.411	97.760	0.447	104.517	0.529	119.305	**199**
0.264	69.795	0.289	74.789	0.345	85.761	0.410	98.171	0.447	104.964	0.529	119.834	**200**
0.263	70.059	0.288	75.077	0.345	86.105	0.410	98.581	0.447	105.411	0.528	120.362	**201**
0.263	70.322	0.288	75.365	0.344	86.450	0.410	98.990	0.446	105.857	0.528	120.890	**202**
0.263	70.585	0.288	75.653	0.344	86.793	0.409	99.400	0.446	106.303	0.528	121.418	**203**
0.262	70.847	0.287	75.940	0.344	87.137	0.409	99.809	0.446	106.748	0.527	121.945	**204**
0.262	71.109	0.287	76.227	0.343	87.480	0.409	100.217	0.445	107.194	0.527	122.473	**205**
0.262	71.371	0.287	76.514	0.343	87.823	0.408	100.626	0.445	107.639	0.527	122.999	**206**
0.261	71.633	0.286	76.800	0.343	88.166	0.408	101.034	0.445	108.083	0.527	123.526	**207**
0.261	71.894	0.286	77.086	0.342	88.508	0.408	101.441	0.444	108.527	0.526	124.052	**208**
0.261	72.155	0.286	77.372	0.342	88.850	0.407	101.849	0.444	108.971	0.526	124.578	**209**
0.261	72.415	0.285	77.658	0.342	89.191	0.407	102.256	0.444	109.415	0.526	125.104	**210**
0.260	72.675	0.285	77.943	0.341	89.532	0.407	102.662	0.443	109.858	0.525	125.629	**211**
0.260	72.935	0.285	78.227	0.341	89.873	0.406	103.069	0.443	110.301	0.525	126.154	**212**
0.260	73.195	0.284	78.512	0.341	90.214	0.406	103.475	0.443	110.744	0.525	126.679	**213**
0.259	73.454	0.284	78.796	0.340	90.554	0.406	103.880	0.442	111.186	0.524	127.203	**214**
0.259	73.713	0.284	79.080	0.340	90.894	0.405	104.286	0.442	111.628	0.524	127.727	**215**
0.259	73.972	0.284	79.364	0.340	91.234	0.405	104.691	0.442	112.070	0.524	128.251	**216**
0.258	74.230	0.283	79.647	0.339	91.573	0.405	105.095	0.441	112.512	0.524	128.774	**217**
0.258	74.488	0.283	79.930	0.339	91.912	0.404	105.500	0.441	112.953	0.523	129.298	**218**
0.258	74.746	0.283	80.212	0.339	92.250	0.404	105.904	0.441	113.393	0.523	129.821	**219**
0.258	75.004	0.282	80.495	0.338	92.589	0.404	106.308	0.440	113.834	0.523	130.343	**220**
0.257	75.261	0.282	80.777	0.338	92.927	0.404	106.711	0.440	114.274	0.522	130.866	**221**
0.257	75.518	0.282	81.059	0.338	93.265	0.403	107.115	0.440	114.714	0.522	131.388	**222**
0.257	75.774	0.281	81.340	0.337	93.602	0.403	107.517	0.440	115.154	0.522	131.909	**223**
0.256	76.031	0.281	81.621	0.337	93.939	0.403	107.920	0.439	115.593	0.522	132.431	**224**
0.256	76.287	0.281	81.902	0.337	94.276	0.402	108.322	0.439	116.032	0.521	132.952	**225**
0.256	76.543	0.281	82.183	0.337	94.613	0.402	108.724	0.439	116.471	0.521	133.473	**226**
0.255	76.798	0.280	82.463	0.336	94.949	0.402	109.126	0.438	116.909	0.521	133.994	**227**
0.255	77.053	0.280	82.743	0.336	95.285	0.401	109.527	0.438	117.347	0.520	134.514	**228**
0.255	77.308	0.280	83.023	0.336	95.620	0.401	109.929	0.438	117.785	0.520	135.035	**229**
0.255	77.563	0.279	83.302	0.335	95.956	0.401	110.329	0.438	118.222	0.520	135.554	**230**
0.254	77.817	0.279	83.581	0.335	96.291	0.401	110.730	0.437	118.660	0.520	136.074	**231**
0.254	78.071	0.279	83.860	0.335	96.626	0.400	111.130	0.437	119.097	0.519	136.593	**232**
0.254	78.325	0.279	84.139	0.334	96.960	0.400	111.530	0.437	119.533	0.519	137.112	**233**
0.2542	78.579	0.278	84.417	0.334	97.294	0.400	111.930	0.436	119.970	0.519	137.631	**234**

(continued)

APPENDIX D LEARNING CURVE COEFFICIENTS AND

N	70%	Total	72%	Total	74%	Total	75%	Total	78%	Total	80%	Total	82%	Total
235	0.060	27.675	0.075	32.271	0.093	37.589	0.104	40.549	0.141	50.792	0.172	58.907	0.209	68.204
236	0.060	27.736	0.075	32.347	0.093	37.682	0.104	40.652	0.141	50.933	0.172	59.079	0.209	68.413
237	0.060	27.796	0.075	32.421	0.093	37.775	0.103	40.756	0.141	51.074	0.172	59.251	0.209	68.622
238	0.060	27.855	0.075	32.496	0.093	37.868	0.103	40.859	0.141	51.214	0.172	59.423	0.209	68.831
239	0.060	27.915	0.075	32.571	0.093	37.961	0.103	40.962	0.140	51.355	0.172	59.594	0.208	69.040
240	0.060	27.975	0.074	32.645	0.092	38.053	0.103	41.065	0.140	51.495	0.171	59.765	0.208	69.248
241	0.059	28.034	0.074	32.720	0.092	38.145	0.103	41.167	0.140	51.635	0.171	59.936	0.208	69.456
242	0.059	28.094	0.074	32.794	0.092	38.238	0.102	41.270	0.140	51.775	0.171	60.107	0.208	69.663
243	0.059	28.153	0.074	32.868	0.092	38.330	0.102	41.372	0.140	51.914	0.171	60.278	0.207	69.871
244	0.059	28.212	0.074	32.942	0.092	38.421	0.102	41.474	0.139	52.054	0.170	60.448	0.207	70.078
245	0.059	28.271	0.074	33.015	0.092	38.513	0.102	41.576	0.139	52.193	0.170	60.618	0.207	70.285
246	0.059	28.330	0.074	33.089	0.091	38.605	0.102	41.678	0.139	52.332	0.170	60.788	0.207	70.492
247	0.059	28.388	0.073	33.162	0.091	38.696	0.102	41.780	0.139	52.471	0.170	60.958	0.207	70.698
248	0.059	28.447	0.073	33.236	0.091	38.787	0.101	41.881	0.139	52.609	0.169	61.128	0.206	70.905
249	0.058	28.505	0.073	33.309	0.091	38.878	0.101	41.982	0.138	52.748	0.169	61.297	0.206	71.111
250	0.058	28.564	0.073	33.382	0.091	38.969	0.101	42.083	0.138	52.886	0.169	61.466	0.206	71.317
251	0.058	28.622	0.073	33.455	0.091	39.060	0.101	42.184	0.138	53.024	0.169	61.635	0.206	71.522
252	0.058	28.680	0.073	33.528	0.091	39.150	0.101	42.285	0.138	53.162	0.169	61.803	0.205	71.727
253	0.058	28.738	0.073	33.600	0.090	39.240	0.101	42.386	0.138	53.299	0.168	61.972	0.205	71.933
254	0.058	28.796	0.072	33.673	0.090	39.331	0.100	42.486	0.137	53.437	0.168	62.140	0.205	72.137
255	0.058	28.854	0.072	33.745	0.090	39.421	0.100	42.586	0.137	53.574	0.168	62.308	0.205	72.342
256	0.058	28.911	0.072	33.817	0.090	39.511	0.100	42.686	0.137	53.711	0.168	62.476	0.204	72.547
257	0.058	28.969	0.072	33.889	0.090	39.600	0.100	42.786	0.137	53.848	0.168	62.643	0.204	72.751
258	0.057	29.026	0.072	33.961	0.090	39.690	0.100	42.886	0.137	53.984	0.167	62.811	0.204	72.955
259	0.057	29.084	0.072	34.033	0.089	39.780	0.100	42.986	0.136	54.121	0.167	62.978	0.204	73.158
260	0.057	29.141	0.072	34.105	0.089	39.869	0.099	43.085	0.136	54.257	0.167	63.145	0.204	73.362
261	0.057	29.198	0.072	34.176	0.089	39.958	0.099	43.185	0.136	54.393	0.167	63.311	0.203	73.565
262	0.057	29.255	0.071	34.248	0.089	40.047	0.099	43.284	0.136	54.529	0.167	63.478	0.203	73.768
263	0.057	29.312	0.071	34.319	0.089	40.136	0.099	43.383	0.136	54.665	0.166	63.644	0.203	73.971
264	0.057	29.369	0.071	34.390	0.089	40.225	0.099	43.482	0.136	54.800	0.166	63.810	0.203	74.174
265	0.057	29.425	0.071	34.461	0.089	40.313	0.099	43.580	0.135	54.935	0.166	63.976	0.202	74.376
266	0.057	29.482	0.071	34.532	0.088	40.402	0.099	43.679	0.135	55.071	0.166	64.142	0.202	74.578
267	0.056	29.538	0.071	34.603	0.088	40.490	0.098	43.777	0.135	55.206	0.166	64.308	0.202	74.780
268	0.056	29.594	0.071	34.674	0.088	40.578	0.098	43.875	0.135	55.340	0.165	64.473	0.202	74.982
269	0.056	29.651	0.071	34.744	0.088	40.666	0.098	43.974	0.135	55.475	0.165	64.638	0.202	75.184
270	0.056	29.707	0.070	34.815	0.088	40.754	0.098	44.071	0.134	55.609	0.165	64.803	0.201	75.385
271	0.056	29.763	0.070	34.885	0.088	40.842	0.098	44.169	0.134	55.744	0.165	64.968	0.201	75.586
272	0.056	29.819	0.070	34.955	0.088	40.929	0.098	44.267	0.134	55.878	0.165	65.132	0.201	75.787
273	0.056	29.874	0.070	35.025	0.087	41.017	0.097	44.364	0.134	56.012	0.164	65.297	0.201	75.988
274	0.056	29.930	0.070	35.095	0.087	41.104	0.097	44.462	0.134	56.145	0.164	65.461	0.200	76.188
275	0.056	29.986	0.070	35.165	0.087	41.191	0.097	44.559	0.134	56.279	0.164	65.625	0.200	76.388
276	0.055	30.041	0.070	35.235	0.087	41.278	0.097	44.656	0.133	56.412	0.164	65.788	0.200	76.588
277	0.055	30.096	0.070	35.304	0.087	41.365	0.097	44.753	0.133	56.545	0.164	65.952	0.200	76.788
278	0.055	30.152	0.069	35.374	0.087	41.452	0.097	44.850	0.133	56.678	0.163	66.115	0.200	76.988
279	0.055	30.207	0.069	35.443	0.087	41.539	0.097	44.946	0.133	56.811	0.163	66.278	0.199	77.187
280	0.055	30.262	0.069	35.512	0.086	41.625	0.096	45.043	0.133	56.944	0.163	66.441	0.199	77.387
281	0.055	30.317	0.069	35.581	0.086	41.711	0.096	45.139	0.133	57.076	0.163	66.604	0.199	77.586

CUMULATIVE TOTALS $YN = Y1*(N)^\wedge(LOG\ L/\ LOG\ 2)$

84%	Total	85%	Total	87%	Total	89%	Total	90%	Total	92%	Total	N
0.253	78.832	0.278	84.695	0.334	97.628	0.399	112.329	0.436	120.406	0.519	138.150	**235**
0.253	79.085	0.278	84.973	0.334	97.962	0.399	112.728	0.436	120.842	0.518	138.668	**236**
0.253	79.338	0.277	85.250	0.333	98.295	0.399	113.127	0.436	121.277	0.518	139.186	**237**
0.252	79.590	0.277	85.527	0.333	98.628	0.399	113.525	0.435	121.712	0.518	139.704	**238**
0.252	79.842	0.277	85.804	0.333	98.961	0.398	113.924	0.435	122.147	0.517	140.221	**239**
0.252	80.094	0.277	86.081	0.332	99.293	0.398	114.322	0.435	122.582	0.517	140.738	**240**
0.252	80.346	0.276	86.357	0.332	99.626	0.398	114.719	0.434	123.017	0.517	141.255	**241**
0.251	80.597	0.276	86.633	0.332	99.958	0.397	115.117	0.434	123.451	0.517	141.772	**242**
0.251	80.848	0.276	86.909	0.332	100.289	0.397	115.514	0.434	123.885	0.516	142.289	**243**
0.251	81.099	0.276	87.185	0.331	100.621	0.397	115.911	0.434	124.318	0.516	142.805	**244**
0.251	81.350	0.275	87.460	0.331	100.952	0.397	116.307	0.433	124.752	0.516	143.321	**245**
0.250	81.600	0.275	87.735	0.331	101.283	0.396	116.704	0.433	125.185	0.516	143.836	**246**
0.250	81.850	0.275	88.010	0.331	101.613	0.396	117.100	0.433	125.618	0.515	144.352	**247**
0.250	82.100	0.275	88.284	0.330	101.944	0.396	117.495	0.433	126.050	0.515	144.867	**248**
0.250	82.350	0.274	88.559	0.330	102.274	0.395	117.891	0.432	126.482	0.515	145.382	**249**
0.249	82.599	0.4274	88.833	0.330	102.603	0.395	118.286	0.432	126.914	0.515	145.897	**250**
0.249	82.848	0.274	89.106	0.330	102.933	0.395	118.681	0.432	127.346	0.514	146.411	**251**
0.249	83.097	0.273	89.380	0.329	103.262	0.395	119.076	0.431	127.778	0.514	146.925	**252**
0.249	83.346	0.273	89.653	0.329	103.591	0.394	119.470	0.431	128.209	0.514	147.439	**253**
0.248	83.594	0.273	89.926	0.329	103.920	0.394	119.864	0.431	128.640	0.514	147.953	**254**
0.248	83.842	0.273	90.199	0.328	104.248	0.394	120.258	0.431	129.071	0.513	148.466	**255**
0.248	84.090	0.272	90.471	0.328	104.577	0.394	120.652	0.430	129.501	0.513	148.980	**256**
0.248	84.338	0.272	90.744	0.328	104.904	0.393	121.045	0.430	129.931	0.513	149.492	**257**
0.247	84.585	0.272	91.016	0.328	105.232	0.393	121.438	0.430	130.361	0.513	150.005	**258**
0.247	84.832	0.272	91.287	0.327	105.560	0.393	121.831	0.430	130.791	0.513	150.518	**259**
0.247	85.079	0.272	91.559	0.327	105.887	0.393	122.224	0.429	131.220	0.512	151.030	**260**
0.247	85.326	0.271	91.830	0.327	106.214	0.392	122.616	0.429	131.650	0.512	151.542	**261**
0.246	85.572	0.271	92.101	0.327	106.540	0.392	123.009	0.429	132.079	0.512	152.054	**262**
0.246	85.819	0.271	92.372	0.326	106.867	0.392	123.400	0.429	132.507	0.512	152.565	**263**
0.246	86.065	0.271	92.643	0.326	107.193	0.392	123.792	0.428	132.936	0.511	153.077	**264**
0.246	86.310	0.270	92.913	0.326	107.519	0.391	124.183	0.428	133.364	0.511	153.588	**265**
0.245	86.556	0.270	93.183	0.326	107.845	0.391	124.575	0.428	133.792	0.511	154.099	**266**
0.245	86.801	0.270	93.453	0.325	108.170	0.391	124.965	0.428	134.220	0.511	154.609	**267**
0.245	87.046	0.270	93.722	0.325	108.495	0.391	125.356	0.427	134.647	0.510	155.120	**268**
0.245	87.291	0.269	93.992	0.325	108.820	0.390	125.746	0.427	135.074	0.510	155.630	**269**
0.245	87.536	0.269	94.261	0.325	109.145	0.390	126.137	0.427	135.501	0.510	156.140	**270**
0.244	87.780	0.269	94.530	0.324	109.469	0.390	126.526	0.427	135.928	0.510	156.649	**271**
0.244	88.024	0.269	94.798	0.324	109.794	0.390	126.916	0.427	136.355	0.509	157.159	**272**
0.244	88.268	0.268	95.067	0.324	110.118	0.389	127.306	0.426	136.781	0.509	157.668	**273**
0.244	88.512	0.268	95.335	0.324	110.441	0.389	127.695	0.426	137.207	0.509	158.177	**274**
0.243	88.755	0.268	95.603	0.324	110.765	0.389	128.084	0.426	137.633	0.509	158.686	**275**
0.243	88.998	0.268	95.870	0.323	111.088	0.389	128.472	0.426	138.058	0.509	159.195	**276**
0.243	89.241	0.267	96.138	0.323	111.411	0.388	128.861	0.425	138.484	0.508	159.703	**277**
0.243	89.484	0.267	96.405	0.323	111.734	0.388	129.249	0.425	138.909	0.508	160.211	**278**
0.243	89.727	0.267	96.672	0.323	112.057	0.388	129.637	0.425	139.334	0.508	160.719	**279**
0.242	89.969	0.267	96.939	0.322	112.379	0.388	130.025	0.425	139.758	0.508	161.227	**280**
0.242	90.211	0.267	97.206	0.322	112.701	0.388	130.412	0.424	140.183	0.507	161.734	**281**

(continued)

APPENDIX D LEARNING CURVE COEFFICIENTS AND

N	70%	Total	72%	Total	74%	Total	75%	Total	78%	Total	80%	Total	82%	Total
282	0.055	30.372	0.069	35.650	0.086	41.798	0.096	45.235	0.132	57.209	0.163	66.767	0.199	77.784
283	0.055	30.426	0.069	35.719	0.086	41.884	0.096	45.331	0.132	57.341	0.162	66.929	0.199	77.983
284	0.055	30.481	0.069	35.788	0.086	41.970	0.096	45.427	0.132	57.473	0.162	67.092	0.198	78.181
285	0.055	30.536	0.069	35.857	0.086	42.055	0.096	45.523	0.132	57.605	0.162	67.254	0.198	78.380
286	0.054	30.590	0.069	35.925	0.086	42.141	0.096	45.618	0.132	57.737	0.162	67.416	0.198	78.578
287	0.054	30.644	0.068	35.994	0.086	42.227	0.095	45.714	0.132	57.868	0.162	67.577	0.198	78.776
288	0.054	30.699	0.068	36.062	0.085	42.312	0.095	45.809	0.131	57.999	0.162	67.739	0.198	78.973
289	0.054	30.753	0.068	36.130	0.085	42.397	0.095	45.904	0.131	58.131	0.161	67.900	0.197	79.171
290	0.054	30.807	0.068	36.198	0.085	42.483	0.095	45.999	0.131	58.262	0.161	68.061	0.197	79.368
291	0.054	30.861	0.068	36.266	0.085	42.568	0.095	46.094	0.131	58.392	0.161	68.222	0.197	79.565
292	0.054	30.915	0.068	36.334	0.085	42.653	0.095	46.189	0.131	58.523	0.161	68.383	0.197	79.762
293	0.054	30.968	0.068	36.402	0.085	42.737	0.095	46.284	0.131	58.654	0.161	68.544	0.197	79.958
294	0.054	31.022	0.068	36.469	0.085	42.822	0.095	46.378	0.130	58.784	0.160	68.704	0.196	80.155
295	0.054	31.076	0.068	36.537	0.085	42.907	0.094	46.473	0.130	58.914	0.160	68.865	0.196	80.351
296	0.053	31.129	0.067	36.604	0.084	42.991	0.094	46.567	0.130	59.044	0.160	69.025	0.196	80.547
297	0.053	31.183	0.067	36.672	0.084	43.075	0.094	46.661	0.130	59.174	0.160	69.185	0.196	80.743
298	0.053	31.236	0.067	36.739	0.084	43.159	0.094	46.755	0.130	59.304	0.160	69.344	0.196	80.939
299	0.053	31.289	0.067	36.806	0.084	43.244	0.094	46.849	0.130	59.434	0.160	69.504	0.196	81.134
300	0.053	31.342	0.067	36.873	0.084	43.327	0.094	46.943	0.129	59.563	0.159	69.663	0.195	81.330
301	0.053	31.395	0.067	36.940	0.084	43.411	0.094	47.036	0.129	59.692	0.159	69.823	0.195	81.525
302	0.053	31.448	0.067	37.007	0.084	43.495	0.093	47.130	0.129	59.821	0.159	69.982	0.195	81.720
303	0.053	31.501	0.067	37.073	0.084	43.579	0.093	47.223	0.129	59.950	0.159	70.141	0.195	81.915
304	0.053	31.554	0.067	37.140	0.083	43.662	0.093	47.316	0.129	60.079	0.159	70.299	0.195	82.109
305	0.053	31.607	0.066	37.206	0.083	43.745	0.093	47.409	0.129	60.208	0.159	70.458	0.194	82.304
306	0.053	31.659	0.066	37.273	0.083	43.829	0.093	47.502	0.129	60.336	0.158	70.616	0.194	82.498
307	0.053	31.712	0.066	37.339	0.083	43.912	0.093	47.595	0.128	60.465	0.158	70.775	0.194	82.692
308	0.052	31.764	0.066	37.405	0.083	43.995	0.093	47.688	0.128	60.593	0.158	70.933	0.194	82.886
309	0.052	31.816	0.066	37.471	0.083	44.077	0.093	47.781	0.128	60.721	0.158	71.091	0.194	83.080
310	0.052	31.869	0.066	37.537	0.083	44.160	0.092	47.873	0.128	60.849	0.158	71.248	0.194	83.273
311	0.052	31.921	0.066	37.603	0.083	44.243	0.092	47.965	0.128	60.977	0.158	71.406	0.193	83.466
312	0.052	31.973	0.066	37.669	0.083	44.325	0.092	48.058	0.128	61.104	0.157	71.563	0.193	83.660
313	0.052	32.025	0.066	37.734	0.082	44.408	0.092	48.150	0.127	61.232	0.157	71.721	0.193	83.853
314	0.052	32.077	0.066	37.800	0.082	44.490	0.092	48.242	0.127	61.359	0.157	71.878	0.193	84.045
315	0.052	32.129	0.065	37.865	0.082	44.572	0.092	48.334	0.127	61.486	0.157	72.035	0.193	84.238
316	0.052	32.180	0.065	37.931	0.082	44.654	0.092	48.425	0.127	61.614	0.157	72.191	0.192	84.430
317	0.052	32.232	0.065	37.996	0.082	44.736	0.092	48.517	0.127	61.740	0.157	72.348	0.192	84.623
318	0.052	32.284	0.065	38.061	0.082	44.818	0.091	48.608	0.127	61.867	0.156	72.504	0.192	84.815
319	0.051	32.335	0.065	38.126	0.082	44.900	0.091	48.700	0.127	61.994	0.156	72.661	0.192	85.007
320	0.051	32.386	0.065	38.191	0.082	44.981	0.091	48.791	0.126	62.120	0.156	72.817	0.192	85.199
321	0.051	32.438	0.065	38.256	0.082	45.063	0.091	48.882	0.126	62.247	0.156	72.973	0.192	85.390
322	0.0521	32.489	0.065	38.321	0.081	45.144	0.091	48.973	0.126	62.373	0.156	73.129	0.191	85.582
323	0.051	32.540	0.065	38.386	0.081	45.226	0.091	49.064	0.126	62.499	0.156	73.284	0.191	85.773
324	0.051	32.591	0.065	38.450	0.081	45.307	0.091	49.155	0.126	62.625	0.156	73.440	0.191	85.964
325	0.051	32.642	0.064	38.515	0.081	45.388	0.091	49.246	0.126	62.751	0.155	73.595	0.191	86.155
326	0.051	32.693	0.064	38.579	0.081	45.469	0.091	49.336	0.126	62.876	0.155	73.750	0.191	86.346
327	0.051	32.744	0.064	38.643	0.081	45.550	0.090	49.427	0.126	63.002	0.155	73.906	0.191	86.536
328	0.051	32.795	0.064	38.708	0.081	45.630	0.090	49.517	0.125	63.127	0.155	74.060	0.190	86.727

CUMULATIVE TOTALS YN = Y1*(N)^(LOG L/ LOG 2)

84%	Total	85%	Total	87%	Total	89%	Total	90%	Total	92%	Total	N
0.242	90.453	0.266	97.472	0.322	113.023	0.387	130.800	0.424	140.607	0.507	162.242	282
0.242	90.695	0.266	97.738	0.322	113.345	0.387	131.187	0.424	141.031	0.507	162.749	283
0.241	90.936	0.266	98.004	0.321	113.666	0.387	131.574	0.424	141.455	0.507	163.256	284
0.241	91.178	0.266	98.270	0.321	113.987	0.387	131.960	0.424	141.878	0.507	163.762	285
0.241	91.419	0.266	98.535	0.321	114.308	0.386	132.347	0.423	142.301	0.506	164.269	286
0.241	91.659	0.265	98.801	0.321	114.629	0.386	132.733	0.423	142.724	0.506	164.775	287
0.241	91.900	0.265	99.066	0.321	114.950	0.386	133.119	0.423	143.147	0.506	165.281	288
0.240	92.140	0.265	99.331	0.320	115.270	0.386	133.505	0.423	143.570	0.506	165.787	289
0.240	92.381	0.265	99.595	0.320	115.590	0.385	133.890	0.422	143.992	0.506	166.292	290
0.240	92.621	0.264	99.860	0.320	115.910	0.385	134.275	0.422	144.414	0.505	166.798	291
0.240	92.861	0.264	100.124	0.320	116.230	0.385	134.660	0.422	144.836	0.505	167.303	292
0.240	93.100	0.264	100.388	0.319	116.549	0.385	135.045	0.422	145.258	0.505	167.808	293
0.239	93.340	0.264	100.652	0.319	116.868	0.385	135.430	0.422	145.680	0.505	168.312	294
0.239	93.579	0.264	100.915	0.319	117.187	0.384	135.814	0.421	146.101	0.505	168.817	295
0.239	93.818	0.263	101.179	0.319	117.506	0.384	136.198	0.421	146.522	0.504	169.321	296
0.239	94.056	0.263	101.442	0.319	117.825	0.384	136.582	0.421	146.943	0.504	169.825	297
0.239	94.295	0.263	101.705	0.318	118.143	0.384	136.966	0.421	147.363	0.504	170.329	298
0.238	94.533	0.263	101.968	0.318	118.461	0.384	137.350	0.420	147.784	0.504	170.833	299
0.238	94.772	0.263	102.230	0.318	118.779	0.383	137.733	0.420	148.204	0.504	171.337	300
0.238	95.010	0.262	102.492	0.318	119.097	0.383	138.116	0.420	148.624	0.503	171.840	301
0.238	95.247	0.262	102.755	0.317	119.414	0.383	138.499	0.420	149.044	0.503	172.343	302
0.238	95.485	0.262	103.016	0.317	119.732	0.383	138.881	0.420	149.463	0.503	172.846	303
0.237	95.722	0.262	103.278	0.317	120.049	0.382	139.264	0.419	149.883	0.503	173.349	304
0.237	95.960	0.262	103.540	0.317	120.365	0.382	139.646	0.419	150.302	0.503	173.851	305
0.237	96.197	0.261	103.801	0.317	120.682	0.382	140.028	0.419	150.721	0.502	174.354	306
0.237	96.433	0.261	104.062	0.316	120.999	0.382	140.410	0.419	151.140	0.502	174.856	307
0.237	96.670	0.261	104.323	0.316	121.315	0.382	140.792	0.419	151.558	0.502	175.358	308
0.236	96.906	0.261	104.584	0.316	121.631	0.381	141.173	0.418	151.976	0.502	175.859	309
0.236	97.143	0.261	104.844	0.316	121.947	0.381	141.554	0.418	152.395	0.502	176.361	310
0.236	97.379	0.260	105.105	0.316	122.262	0.381	141.935	0.418	152.813	0.501	176.862	311
0.236	97.615	0.260	105.365	0.315	122.578	0.381	142.316	0.418	153.230	0.501	177.363	312
0.236	97.850	0.260	105.625	0.315	122.893	0.381	142.697	0.418	153.648	0.501	177.864	313
0.235	98.086	0.260	105.885	0.315	123.208	0.380	143.077	0.417	154.065	0.501	178.365	314
0.235	98.321	0.260	106.144	0.315	123.523	0.380	143.457	0.417	154.482	0.501	178.866	315
0.235	98.556	0.259	106.403	0.315	123.837	0.380	143.837	0.417	154.899	0.500	179.366	316
0.235	98.791	0.259	106.663	0.314	124.152	0.380	144.217	0.417	155.316	0.500	179.866	317
0.235	99.026	0.259	106.922	0.314	124.466	0.380	144.596	0.417	155.732	0.500	180.366	318
0.235	99.260	0.259	107.180	0.314	124.780	0.379	144.976	0.416	156.149	0.500	180.866	319
0.234	99.494	0.259	107.439	0.314	125.094	0.379	145.355	0.416	156.565	0.500	181.366	320
0.234	99.729	0.258	107.697	0.314	125.407	0.379	145.734	0.416	156.981	0.499	181.865	321
0.234	99.963	0.258	107.956	0.313	125.721	0.379	146.113	0.416	157.396	0.499	182.364	322
0.234	100.196	0.258	108.214	0.313	126.034	0.379	146.491	0.416	157.812	0.499	182.863	323
0.234	100.430	0.258	108.472	0.313	126.347	0.378	146.870	0.415	158.227	0.499	183.362	324
0.233	100.663	0.258	108.729	0.313	126.660	0.378	147.248	0.415	158.642	0.499	183.861	325
0.233	100.897	0.257	108.987	0.313	126.973	0.378	147.626	0.415	159.057	0.499	184.359	326
0.233	101.130	0.257	109.244	0.312	127.285	0.378	148.004	0.415	159.472	0.498	184.858	327
0.233	101.363	0.257	109.501	0.312	127.597	0.378	148.381	0.415	159.887	0.498	185.356	328

(continued)

APPENDIX D LEARNING CURVE COEFFICIENTS AND

N	70%	Total	72%	Total	74%	Total	75%	Total	78%	Total	80%	Total	82%	Total
329	0.051	32.845	0.064	38.772	0.081	45.711	0.090	49.607	0.125	63.252	0.155	74.215	0.190	86.917
330	0.051	32.896	0.064	38.836	0.081	45.792	0.090	49.697	0.125	63.377	0.155	74.370	0.190	87.107
331	0.051	32.946	0.064	38.900	0.080	45.872	0.090	49.787	0.125	63.502	0.154	74.524	0.190	87.297
332	0.050	32.997	0.064	38.964	0.080	45.952	0.090	49.877	0.125	63.627	0.154	74.679	0.190	87.487
333	0.050	33.047	0.064	39.027	0.080	46.032	0.090	49.967	0.125	63.752	0.154	74.833	0.190	87.676
334	0.050	33.097	0.064	39.091	0.080	46.113	0.090	50.056	0.125	63.876	0.154	74.987	0.189	87.866
335	0.050	33.148	0.064	39.155	0.080	46.193	0.090	50.146	0.124	64.001	0.154	75.141	0.189	88.055
336	0.050	33.198	0.063	39.218	0.080	46.273	0.089	50.235	0.124	64.125	0.154	75.294	0.189	88.244
337	0.050	33.248	0.063	39.281	0.080	46.352	0.089	50.325	0.124	64.249	0.154	75.448	0.189	88.433
338	0.050	33.298	0.063	39.345	0.080	46.432	0.089	50.414	0.124	64.373	0.153	75.601	0.189	88.622
339	0.050	33.348	0.063	39.408	0.080	46.512	0.089	50.503	0.124	64.497	0.153	75.755	0.189	88.810
340	0.050	33.397	0.063	39.471	0.079	46.591	0.089	50.592	0.124	64.621	0.153	75.908	0.188	88.999
341	0.050	33.447	0.063	39.534	0.079	46.670	0.089	50.681	0.124	64.745	0.153	76.061	0.188	89.187
342	0.050	33.497	0.063	39.597	0.079	46.750	0.089	50.770	0.124	64.868	0.153	76.213	0.188	89.375
343	0.050	33.546	0.063	39.660	0.079	46.829	0.089	50.858	0.123	64.991	0.153	76.366	0.188	89.563
344	0.050	33.596	0.063	39.723	0.079	46.908	0.089	50.947	0.123	65.115	0.153	76.519	0.188	89.751
345	0.049	33.645	0.063	39.785	0.079	46.987	0.088	51.035	0.123	65.238	0.152	76.671	0.188	89.939
346	0.049	33.695	0.063	39.848	0.079	47.066	0.088	51.124	0.123	65.361	0.152	76.823	0.188	90.126
347	0.049	33.744	0.063	39.911	0.079	47.145	0.088	51.212	0.123	65.484	0.152	76.976	0.187	90.314
348	0.049	33.793	0.062	39.973	0.079	47.223	0.088	51.300	0.123	65.606	0.152	77.128	0.187	90.501
349	0.049	33.842	0.062	40.035	0.079	47.302	0.088	51.388	0.123	65.729	0.152	77.279	0.187	90.688
350	0.049	33.892	0.062	40.098	0.078	47.380	0.088	51.476	0.122	65.851	0.152	77.431	0.187	90.875
351	0.049	33.941	0.062	40.160	0.078	47.459	0.088	51.564	0.122	65.974	0.152	77.583	0.187	91.061
352	0.049	33.989	0.062	40.222	0.078	47.537	0.088	51.652	0.122	66.096	0.151	77.734	0.187	91.248
353	0.049	34.038	0.062	40.284	0.078	47.615	0.088	51.739	0.122	66.218	0.151	77.885	0.186	91.435
354	0.049	34.087	0.062	40.346	0.078	47.694	0.088	51.827	0.122	66.340	0.151	78.036	0.186	91.621
355	0.049	34.136	0.062	40.408	0.078	47.772	0.087	51.914	0.122	66.462	0.151	78.187	0.186	91.807
356	0.049	34.185	0.062	40.469	0.078	47.849	0.087	52.001	0.122	66.584	0.151	78.338	0.186	91.993
357	0.049	34.233	0.062	40.531	0.078	47.927	0.087	52.089	0.122	66.705	0.151	78.489	0.186	92.179
358	0.049	34.282	0.062	40.593	0.078	48.005	0.087	52.176	0.121	66.827	0.151	78.640	0.186	92.365
359	0.048	34.330	0.062	40.654	0.078	48.083	0.087	52.263	0.121	66.948	0.150	78.790	0.186	92.550
360	0.048	34.378	0.061	40.716	0.078	48.160	0.087	52.350	0.121	67.069	0.150	78.941	0.185	92.735
361	0.048	34.427	0.061	40.777	0.077	48.238	0.087	52.436	0.121	67.191	0.150	79.091	0.185	92.921
362	0.048	34.475	0.061	40.838	0.077	48.315	0.087	52.523	0.121	67.312	0.150	79.241	0.185	93.106
363	0.048	34.523	0.061	40.900	0.077	48.392	0.087	52.610	0.121	67.433	0.150	79.391	0.185	93.291
364	0.048	34.571	0.061	40.961	0.077	48.469	0.087	52.696	0.121	67.553	0.150	79.541	0.185	93.476
365	0.048	34.619	0.061	41.022	0.077	48.546	0.086	52.783	0.121	67.674	0.150	79.690	0.185	93.660
366	0.048	34.667	0.061	41.083	0.077	48.623	0.086	52.869	0.121	67.794	0.150	79.840	0.185	93.845
367	0.048	34.715	0.061	41.144	0.077	48.700	0.086	52.955	0.120	67.915	0.149	79.989	0.184	94.029
368	0.048	34.763	0.061	41.204	0.077	48.777	0.086	53.041	0.120	68.035	0.149	80.138	0.184	94.213
369	0.048	34.811	0.061	41.265	0.077	48.854	0.086	53.127	0.120	68.155	0.149	80.288	0.184	94.398
370	0.048	34.858	0.061	41.326	0.077	48.931	0.086	53.213	0.120	68.275	0.149	80.437	0.184	94.582
371	0.048	34.906	0.061	41.386	0.077	49.007	0.086	53.2929	0.120	68.395	0.149	80.585	0.184	94.765
372	0.048	34.954	0.060	41.447	0.076	49.083	0.086	53.385	0.120	68.515	0.149	80.734	0.184	94.949
373	0.047	35.001	0.060	41.507	0.076	49.160	0.086	53.470	0.120	68.635	0.149	80.883	0.184	95.133
374	0.047	35.049	0.060	41.568	0.076	49.236	0.086	53.556	0.120	68.755	0.148	81.031	0.183	95.316
375	0.047	35.096	0.060	41.628	0.076	49.312	0.085	53.641	0.119	68.874	0.148	81.180	0.183	95.499

CUMULATIVE TOTALS YN = Y1*(N)^(LOG L/ LOG 2)

84%	Total	85%	Total	87%	Total	89%	Total	90%	Total	92%	Total	N
0.233	101.595	0.257	109.758	0.312	127.909	0.377	148.759	0.414	160.301	0.498	185.854	**329**
0.233	101.828	0.257	110.015	0.312	128.221	0.377	149.136	0.414	160.715	0.498	186.352	**330**
0.232	102.060	0.257	110.271	0.312	128.533	0.377	149.513	0.414	161.129	0.498	186.849	**331**
0.232	102.292	0.256	110.528	0.312	128.845	0.377	149.890	0.414	161.543	0.497	187.347	**332**
0.232	102.525	0.256	110.784	0.311	129.156	0.377	150.266	0.414	161.956	0.497	187.844	**333**
0.232	102.756	0.256	111.040	0.311	129.467	0.376	150.643	0.413	162.370	0.497	188.341	**334**
0.232	102.988	0.256	111.296	0.311	129.778	0.376	151.019	0.413	162.783	0.497	188.838	**335**
0.231	103.219	0.256	111.551	0.311	130.089	0.376	151.395	0.413	163.196	0.497	189.335	**336**
0.231	103.451	0.255	111.807	0.311	130.399	0.376	151.771	0.413	163.609	0.497	189.831	**337**
0.231	103.682	0.255	112.062	0.310	130.710	0.376	152.147	0.413	164.022	0.496	190.327	**338**
0.231	103.913	0.255	112.317	0.310	131.020	0.376	152.522	0.412	164.434	0.496	190.824	**339**
0.231	104.144	0.255	112.572	0.310	131.330	0.375	152.897	0.412	164.846	0.496	191.320	**340**
0.231	104.374	0.255	112.827	0.310	131.640	0.375	153.272	0.412	165.259	0.496	191.815	**341**
0.230	104.605	0.255	113.082	0.310	131.949	0.375	153.647	0.412	165.670	0.496	192.311	**342**
0.230	104.835	0.254	113.336	0.309	132.259	0.375	154.022	0.412	166.082	0.495	192.807	**343**
0.230	105.065	0.254	113.590	0.309	132.568	0.375	154.397	0.412	166.494	0.495	193.302	**344**
0.230	105.295	0.254	113.844	0.309	132.877	0.374	154.771	0.411	166.905	0.495	193.797	**345**
0.230	105.525	0.254	114.098	0.309	133.186	0.374	155.145	0.411	167.316	0.495	194.292	**346**
0.230	105.755	0.254	114.352	0.309	133.495	0.374	155.519	0.411	167.727	0.495	194.787	**347**
0.229	105.984	0.254	114.606	0.309	133.804	0.374	155.893	0.411	168.138	0.495	195.281	**348**
0.229	106.213	0.253	114.859	0.308	134.112	0.374	156.267	0.411	168.549	0.494	195.776	**349**
0.229	106.442	0.253	115.112	0.308	134.420	0.373	156.640	0.410	168.959	0.494	196.270	**350**
0.229	106.671	0.253	115.365	0.308	134.728	0.373	157.014	0.410	169.370	0.494	196.764	**351**
0.229	106.900	0.253	115.618	0.308	135.036	0.373	157.387	0.410	169.780	0.494	197.258	**352**
0.229	107.129	0.253	115.871	0.308	135.344	0.373	157.760	0.410	170.190	0.494	197.752	**353**
0.228	107.357	0.253	116.123	0.308	135.651	0.373	158.133	0.410	170.600	0.494	198.245	**354**
0.228	107.586	0.252	116.376	0.307	135.959	0.373	158.505	0.410	171.009	0.493	198.739	**355**
0.228	107.814	0.252	116.628	0.307	136.266	0.372	158.878	0.409	171.419	0.493	199.232	**356**
0.228	108.042	0.252	116.880	0.307	136.573	0.372	159.250	0.409	171.828	0.493	199.725	**357**
0.228	108.270	0.252	117.132	0.307	136.880	0.372	159.622	0.409	172.237	0.493	200.218	**358**
0.228	108.497	0.252	117.384	0.307	137.186	0.372	159.994	0.409	172.646	0.493	200.711	**359**
0.228	108.725	0.252	117.635	0.306	137.493	0.372	160.366	0.409	173.054	0.493	201.204	**360**
0.227	108.952	0.251	117.887	0.306	137.799	0.372	160.737	0.409	173.463	0.492	201.696	**361**
0.227	109.179	0.251	118.138	0.306	138.105	0.371	161.109	0.408	173.871	0.492	202.188	**362**
0.227	109.406	0.251	118.389	0.306	138.411	0.371	161.480	0.408	174.280	0.492	202.680	**363**
0.227	109.633	0.251	118.640	0.306	138.717	0.371	161.851	0.408	174.688	0.492	203.172	**364**
0.227	109.860	0.251	118.891	0.306	139.023	0.371	162.222	0.408	175.096	0.492	203.664	**365**
0.227	110.086	0.251	119.141	0.305	139.328	0.371	162.592	0.408	175.503	0.492	204.156	**366**
0.226	110.313	0.250	119.392	0.305	139.633	0.371	162.963	0.408	175.911	0.491	204.647	**367**
0.226	110.539	0.250	119.642	0.305	139.939	0.370	163.333	0.407	176.318	0.491	205.138	**368**
0.226	110.765	0.250	119.892	0.305	140.244	0.370	163.703	0.407	176.725	0.491	205.630	**369**
0.226	110.991	0.250	120.142	0.305	140.548	0.370	164.073	0.407	177.132	0.491	206.121	**370**
0.226	111.217	0.250	120.392	0.305	140.853	0.370	164.443	0.407	177.539	0.491	206.611	**371**
0.226	111.443	0.250	120.641	0.304	141.157	0.370	164.813	0.407	177.946	0.491	207.102	**372**
0.225	111.668	0.249	120.891	0.304	141.462	0.370	165.183	0.407	178.352	0.490	207.592	**373**
0.225	111.893	0.249	121.140	0.304	141.766	0.369	165.552	0.406	178.759	0.490	208.083	**374**
0.225	112.119	0.249	121.389	0.304	142.070	0.369	165.921	0.406	179.165	0.490	208.573	**375**

(continued)

APPENDIX D LEARNING CURVE COEFFICIENTS AND

N	70%	Total	72%	Total	74%	Total	75%	Total	78%	Total	80%	Total	82%	Total
376	0.047	35.143	0.060	41.688	0.076	49.388	0.085	53.727	0.119	68.993	0.148	81.328	0.183	95.682
377	0.047	35.190	0.060	41.748	0.076	49.464	0.085	53.812	0.119	69.113	0.148	81.476	0.183	95.865
378	0.047	35.238	0.060	41.808	0.076	49.540	0.085	53.897	0.119	69.232	0.148	81.624	0.183	96.048
379	0.047	35.285	0.060	41.868	0.076	49.616	0.085	53.982	0.119	69.351	0.148	81.772	0.183	96.231
380	0.047	35.332	0.060	41.928	0.076	49.692	0.085	54.067	0.119	69.470	0.148	81.920	0.183	96.413
381	0.047	35.379	0.060	41.988	0.076	49.768	0.085	54.152	0.119	69.589	0.148	82.067	0.182	96.596
382	0.047	35.426	0.060	42.048	0.076	49.843	0.085	54.237	0.119	69.707	0.147	82.215	0.182	96.778
383	0.047	35.473	0.060	42.107	0.075	49.919	0.085	54.322	0.119	69.826	0.147	82.362	0.182	96.960
384	0.047	35.519	0.060	42.167	0.075	49.994	0.085	54.406	0.118	69.944	0.147	82.509	0.182	97.142
385	0.047	35.566	0.060	42.226	0.075	50.069	0.085	54.491	0.118	70.063	0.147	82.656	0.182	97.324
386	0.047	35.613	0.059	42.286	0.075	50.145	0.084	54.575	0.118	70.181	0.147	82.803	0.182	97.506
387	0.047	35.659	0.059	42.345	0.075	50.220	0.084	54.659	0.118	70.299	0.147	82.950	0.182	97.687
388	0.047	35.706	0.059	42.405	0.075	50.295	0.084	54.744	0.118	70.417	0.147	83.097	0.181	97.869
389	0.046	35.752	0.059	42.464	0.075	50.370	0.084	54.828	0.118	70.535	0.147	83.244	0.181	98.050
390	0.046	35.799	0.059	42.523	0.075	50.445	0.084	54.912	0.118	70.653	0.147	83.390	0.181	98.231
391	0.046	35.845	0.059	42.582	0.075	50.519	0.084	54.996	0.118	70.771	0.146	83.537	0.181	98.412
392	0.046	35.891	0.059	42.641	0.075	50.594	0.084	55.080	0.118	70.888	0.146	83.683	0.181	98.593
393	0.046	35.938	0.059	42.700	0.075	50.669	0.084	55.164	0.117	71.006	0.146	83.829	0.181	98.774
394	0.046	35.984	0.059	42.759	0.075	50.743	0.084	55.247	0.117	71.123	0.146	83.975	0.181	98.955
395	0.046	36.030	0.059	42.818	0.074	50.818	0.084	55.331	0.117	71.240	0.146	84.121	0.181	99.135
396	0.046	36.076	0.059	42.876	0.074	50.892	0.084	55.414	0.117	71.358	0.146	84.267	0.180	99.316
397	0.046	36.122	0.059	42.935	0.074	50.967	0.083	55.498	0.117	71.475	0.146	84.412	0.180	99.496
398	0.046	36.168	0.059	42.994	0.074	51.041	0.083	55.581	0.117	71.592	0.146	84.558	0.180	99.676
399	0.046	36.214	0.059	43.052	0.074	51.115	0.083	55.665	0.117	71.708	0.145	84.703	0.180	99.856
400	0.046	36.260	0.058	43.111	0.074	51.189	0.083	55.748	0.117	71.825	0.145	84.849	0.180	100.036
401	0.046	36.305	0.058	43.169	0.074	51.263	0.083	55.831	0.117	71.942	0.145	84.994	0.180	100.216
402	0.046	36.351	0.058	43.227	0.074	51.337	0.083	55.914	0.117	72.058	0.145	85.139	0.180	100.396
403	0.046	36.397	0.058	43.286	0.074	51.411	0.083	55.997	0.116	72.175	0.145	85.284	0.180	100.575
404	0.046	36.442	0.058	43.344	0.074	51.484	0.083	56.080	0.116	72.291	0.145	85.429	0.179	100.755
405	0.046	36.488	0.058	43.402	0.074	51.558	0.083	56.162	0.116	72.407	0.145	85.574	0.179	100.934
406	0.045	36.533	0.058	43.460	0.074	51.632	0.083	56.245	0.116	72.524	0.145	85.718	0.179	101.113
407	0.045	36.579	0.058	43.518	0.074	51.705	0.083	56.328	0.116	72.640	0.145	85.863	0.179	101.292
408	0.045	36.624	0.058	43.576	0.073	51.779	0.083	56.410	0.116	72.756	0.144	86.007	0.179	101.471
409	0.045	36.669	0.058	43.634	0.073	51.852	0.082	56.493	0.116	72.871	0.144	86.151	0.179	101.650
410	0.045	36.715	0.058	43.691	0.073	51.925	0.082	56.575	0.116	72.987	0.144	86.296	0.179	101.828
411	0.045	36.760	0.058	43.749	0.073	51.999	0.082	56.657	0.116	73.103	0.144	86.440	0.179	102.007
412	0.045	36.805	0.058	43.807	0.073	52.072	0.082	56.739	0.116	73.218	0.144	86.584	0.178	102.185
413	0.045	36.850	0.058	43.864	0.073	52.145	0.082	56.821	0.115	73.334	0.144	86.727	0.178	102.363
414	0.045	36.895	0.058	43.922	0.073	52.218	0.082	56.903	0.115	73.449	0.144	86.871	0.178	102.541
415	0.045	36.940	0.057	43.979	0.073	52.291	0.082	56.985	0.115	73.564	0.144	87.015	0.178	102.719
416	0.045	36.985	0.057	44.037	0.073	52.363	0.082	57.067	0.115	73.679	0.143	87.158	0.178	102.897
417	0.045	37.030	0.057	44.094	0.073	52.436	0.082	57.149	0.115	73.794	0.143	87.302	0.178	103.075
418	0.045	37.075	0.057	44.151	0.073	52.509	0.082	57.231	0.115	73.909	0.143	87.445	0.178	103.253
419	0.045	37.119	0.057	44.208	0.073	52.581	0.082	57.312	0.115	74.024	0.143	87.588	0.178	103.430
420	0.045	37.164	0.057	44.266	0.073	52.654	0.082	57.394	0.115	74.139	0.143	87.731	0.177	103.608
421	0.045	37.209	0.057	44.323	0.072	52.726	0.081	57.475	0.115	74.254	0.143	87.874	0.177	103.785
422	0.045	37.253	0.057	44.380	0.072	52.799	0.081	57.557	0.115	74.368	0.143	88.017	0.177	103.962

CUMULATIVE TOTALS YN = Y1*(N)^(LOG L/ LOG 2)

84%	Total	85%	Total	87%	Total	89%	Total	90%	Total	92%	Total	N
0.225	112.344	0.249	121.638	0.304	142.374	0.369	166.290	0.406	179.571	0.490	209.063	**376**
0.225	112.568	0.249	121.887	0.304	142.677	0.369	166.659	0.406	179.977	0.490	209.553	**377**
0.225	112.793	0.249	122.136	0.303	142.981	0.369	167.028	0.406	180.383	0.490	210.043	**378**
0.225	113.018	0.249	122.384	0.303	143.284	0.369	167.396	0.406	180.788	0.490	210.532	**379**
0.224	113.242	0.248	122.633	0.303	143.587	0.368	167.765	0.405	181.194	0.489	211.022	**380**
0.224	113.466	0.248	122.881	0.303	143.890	0.368	168.133	0.405	181.599	0.489	211.511	**381**
0.224	113.691	0.248	123.129	0.303	144.193	0.368	168.501	0.405	182.004	0.489	212.000	**382**
0.224	113.915	0.248	123.377	0.303	144.496	0.368	168.869	0.405	182.409	0.489	212.489	**383**
0.224	114.138	0.248	123.625	0.303	144.798	0.368	169.236	0.405	182.813	0.489	212.978	**384**
0.224	114.362	0.248	123.872	0.302	145.101	0.368	169.604	0.405	183.218	0.489	213.466	**385**
0.224	114.586	0.247	124.120	0.302	145.403	0.367	169.971	0.404	183.622	0.488	213.955	**386**
0.223	114.809	0.247	124.367	0.302	145.705	0.367	170.339	0.404	184.027	0.488	214.443	**387**
0.223	115.032	0.247	124.614	0.302	146.007	0.367	170.706	0.404	184.431	0.488	214.931	**388**
0.223	115.255	0.247	124.861	0.302	146.309	0.367	171.073	0.404	184.835	0.488	215.419	**389**
0.223	115.478	0.247	125.108	0.302	146.610	0.367	171.439	0.404	185.239	0.488	215.907	**390**
0.223	115.701	0.247	125.355	0.301	146.912	0.367	171.806	0.404	185.642	0.488	216.395	**391**
0.223	115.924	0.247	125.602	0.301	147.213	0.366	172.172	0.403	186.046	0.488	216.882	**392**
0.223	116.146	0.246	125.848	0.301	147.514	0.366	172.539	0.403	186.449	0.487	217.370	**393**
0.222	116.369	0.246	126.094	0.301	147.815	0.366	172.905	0.403	186.852	0.487	217.857	**394**
0.222	116.591	0.246	126.340	0.301	148.116	0.366	173.271	0.403	187.255	0.487	218.344	**395**
0.222	116.813	0.246	126.586	0.301	148.417	0.366	173.637	0.403	187.658	0.487	218.831	**396**
0.222	117.035	0.246	126.832	0.301	148.717	0.366	174.002	0.403	188.061	0.487	219.318	**397**
0.222	117.257	0.246	127.078	0.300	149.018	0.366	174.368	0.403	188.463	0.487	219.805	**398**
0.222	117.479	0.246	127.324	0.300	149.318	0.365	174.733	0.402	188.866	0.487	220.291	**399**
0.222	117.700	0.245	127.569	0.300	149.618	0.365	175.098	0.402	189.268	0.486	220.778	**400**
0.221	117.922	0.245	127.814	0.300	149.918	0.365	175.463	0.402	189.670	0.486	221.264	**401**
0.221	118.143	0.245	128.059	0.300	150.218	0.365	175.828	0.402	190.072	0.486	221.750	**402**
0.221	118.364	0.245	128.304	0.300	150.517	0.365	176.193	0.402	190.474	0.486	222.236	**403**
0.221	118.585	0.245	128.549	0.299	150.817	0.365	176.558	0.402	190.875	0.486	222.722	**404**
0.221	118.806	0.245	128.794	0.299	151.116	0.364	176.922	0.401	191.277	0.486	223.208	**405**
0.221	119.027	0.245	129.039	0.299	151.415	0.364	177.286	0.401	191.678	0.486	223.693	**406**
0.221	119.247	0.244	129.283	0.299	151.714	0.364	177.651	0.401	192.079	0.485	224.178	**407**
0.220	119.468	0.244	129.527	0.299	152.013	0.364	178.015	0.401	192.480	0.485	224.664	**408**
0.220	119.688	0.244	129.771	0.299	152.312	0.364	178.378	0.401	192.881	0.485	225.149	**409**
0.220	119.908	0.244	130.015	0.299	152.610	0.364	178.742	0.401	193.282	0.485	225.634	**410**
0.220	120.128	0.244	130.259	0.298	152.909	0.364	179.106	0.401	193.682	0.485	226.119	**411**
0.220	120.348	0.244	130.503	0.298	153.207	0.363	179.469	0.400	194.083	0.485	226.603	**412**
0.220	120.568	0.244	130.747	0.298	153.505	0.363	179.832	0.400	194.483	0.485	227.088	**413**
0.220	120.788	0.243	130.990	0.298	153.803	0.363	180.195	0.400	194.883	0.484	227.572	**414**
0.220	121.007	0.243	131.233	0.298	154.101	0.363	180.558	0.400	195.283	0.484	228.056	**415**
0.219	121.227	0.243	131.476	0.298	154.399	0.363	180.921	0.400	195.683	0.484	228.540	**416**
0.219	121.446	0.243	131.720	0.298	154.696	0.363	181.284	0.400	196.083	0.484	229.024	**417**
0.219	121.665	0.243	131.962	0.297	154.994	0.363	181.646	0.400	196.482	0.484	229.508	**418**
0.219	121.884	0.243	132.205	0.297	155.291	0.362	182.009	0.399	196.882	0.484	229.992	**419**
0.219	122.103	0.243	132.448	0.297	155.588	0.362	182.371	0.399	197.281	0.484	230.475	**420**
0.219	122.321	0.242	132.690	0.297	155.885	0.362	182.733	0.399	197.680	0.483	230.959	**421**
0.219	122.540	0.242	132.933	0.297	156.182	0.362	183.095	0.399	198.079	0.483	231.442	**422**

(continued)

APPENDIX D LEARNING CURVE COEFFICIENTS AND

N	70%	Total	72%	Total	74%	Total	75%	Total	78%	Total	80%	Total	82%	Total
423	0.045	37.298	0.057	44.436	0.072	52.871	0.081	57.638	0.114	74.483	0.143	88.160	0.177	104.139
424	0.044	37.342	0.057	44.493	0.072	52.943	0.081	57.719	0.114	74.597	0.143	88.302	0.177	104.316
425	0.044	37.387	0.057	44.550	0.072	53.015	0.081	57.800	0.114	74.711	0.143	88.445	0.177	104.493
426	0.044	37.431	0.057	44.607	0.072	53.087	0.081	57.881	0.114	74.825	0.142	88.587	0.177	104.670
427	0.044	37.475	0.057	44.664	0.072	53.159	0.081	57.962	0.114	74.939	0.142	88.729	0.177	104.846
428	0.044	37.519	0.057	44.720	0.072	53.231	0.081	58.043	0.114	75.053	0.142	88.872	0.176	105.023
429	0.044	37.564	0.057	44.777	0.072	53.303	0.081	58.124	0.114	75.167	0.142	89.014	0.176	105.199
430	0.044	37.608	0.056	44.833	0.072	53.375	0.081	58.205	0.114	75.281	0.142	89.156	0.176	105.375
431	0.044	37.652	0.056	44.890	0.072	53.447	0.081	58.285	0.114	75.395	0.142	89.298	0.176	105.551
432	0.044	37.696	0.056	44.946	0.072	53.518	0.081	58.366	0.114	75.508	0.142	89.439	0.176	105.727
433	0.044	37.740	0.056	45.002	0.072	53.590	0.080	58.446	0.113	75.622	0.142	89.581	0.176	105.903
434	0.044	37.784	0.056	45.058	0.071	53.661	0.080	58.527	0.113	75.735	0.142	89.723	0.176	106.079
435	0.044	37.828	0.056	45.115	0.071	53.733	0.080	58.607	0.113	75.848	0.141	89.864	0.176	106.254
436	0.044	37.872	0.056	45.171	0.071	53.804	0.080	58.687	0.113	75.962	0.141	90.005	0.176	106.430
437	0.044	37.915	0.056	45.227	0.071	53.876	0.080	58.767	0.113	76.075	0.141	90.147	0.175	106.605
438	0.044	37.959	0.056	45.283	0.071	53.947	0.080	58.848	0.113	76.188	0.141	90.288	0.175	106.781
439	0.044	38.003	0.056	45.339	0.071	54.018	0.080	58.928	0.113	76.301	0.141	90.429	0.175	106.956
440	0.044	38.046	0.056	45.395	0.071	54.089	0.080	59.008	0.113	76.413	0.141	90.570	0.175	107.131
441	0.044	38.090	0.056	45.450	0.071	54.160	0.080	59.087	0.113	76.526	0.141	90.710	0.175	107.306
442	0.044	38.133	0.056	45.506	0.071	54.231	0.080	59.167	0.113	76.639	0.141	90.851	0.175	107.481
443	0.043	38.177	0.056	45.562	0.071	54.302	0.080	59.247	0.113	76.751	0.141	90.992	0.175	107.655
444	0.043	38.220	0.056	45.618	0.071	54.373	0.080	59.327	0.112	76.864	0.141	91.132	0.175	107.830
445	0.043	38.264	0.056	45.673	0.071	54.443	0.080	59.406	0.112	76.976	0.140	91.273	0.174	108.004
446	0.043	38.307	0.056	45.729	0.071	54.514	0.080	59.486	0.112	77.089	0.140	91.413	0.174	108.179
447	0.043	38.350	0.055	45.784	0.071	54.584	0.079	59.565	0.112	77.201	0.140	91.553	0.174	108.353
448	0.043	38.394	0.055	45.839	0.071	54.655	0.079	59.645	0.112	77.313	0.140	91.693	0.174	108.527
449	0.043	38.437	0.055	45.895	0.070	54.725	0.079	59.724	0.112	77.425	0.140	91.833	0.174	108.701
450	0.043	38.480	0.055	45.950	0.070	54.796	0.079	59.803	0.112	77.537	0.140	91.973	0.174	108.875
451	0.043	38.523	0.055	46.005	0.070	54.866	0.079	59.882	0.112	77.649	0.140	92.113	0.174	109.049
452	0.043	38.566	0.055	46.060	0.070	54.936	0.079	59.961	0.112	77.760	0.140	92.253	0.174	109.223
453	0.043	38.609	0.055	46.116	0.070	55.007	0.079	60.040	0.112	77.872	0.140	92.392	0.174	109.396
454	0.043	38.652	0.055	46.171	0.070	55.077	0.079	60.119	0.112	77.984	0.140	92.532	0.173	109.570
455	0.043	38.695	0.055	46.226	0.070	55.147	0.079	60.198	0.111	78.095	0.139	92.671	0.173	109.743
456	0.043	38.738	0.055	46.281	0.070	55.217	0.079	60.277	0.111	78.206	0.139	92.811	0.173	109.916
457	0.043	38.780	0.055	46.335	0.070	55.287	0.079	60.356	0.111	78.318	0.139	92.950	0.173	110.090
458	0.043	38.823	0.055	46.390	0.070	55.356	0.079	60.434	0.111	78.429	0.139	93.089	0.173	110.263
459	0.043	38.866	0.055	46.445	0.070	55.426	0.079	60.513	0.111	78.540	0.139	93.228	0.173	110.436
460	0.043	38.908	0.055	46.500	0.070	55.496	0.078	60.591	0.111	78.651	0.139	93.367	0.173	110.608
461	0.043	38.951	0.055	46.554	0.070	55.566	0.078	60.670	0.111	78.762	0.139	93.506	0.173	110.781
462	0.043	38.994	0.055	46.609	0.070	55.635	0.078	60.748	0.111	78.873	0.139	93.645	0.173	110.954
463	0.042	39.036	0.055	46.663	0.070	55.705	0.078	60.826	0.111	78.984	0.139	93.783	0.173	111.126
464	0.042	39.079	0.054	46.718	0.069	55.774	0.078	60.905	0.111	79.095	0.139	93.922	0.172	111.299
465	0.042	39.121	0.054	46.772	0.069	55.843	0.078	60.983	0.111	79.205	0.138	94.060	0.172	111.471
466	0.042	39.163	0.054	46.827	0.069	55.913	0.078	61.061	0.111	79.316	0.138	94.199	0.172	111.643
467	0.042	39.206	0.054	46.881	0.069	55.982	0.078	61.139	0.110	79.426	0.138	94.337	0.172	111.815
468	0.042	39.248	0.054	46.935	0.069	56.051	0.078	61.217	0.110	79.537	0.138	94.475	0.172	111.987
469	0.042	39.290	0.054	46.990	0.069	56.120	0.078	61.295	0.110	79.647	0.138	94.613	0.172	112.159

CUMULATIVE TOTALS YN = Y1*(N)^(LOG L/ LOG 2)

84%	Total	85%	Total	87%	Total	89%	Total	90%	Total	92%	Total	N
0.218	122.759	0.242	133.175	0.297	156.479	0.362	183.457	0.399	198.478	0.483	231.925	423
0.218	122.977	0.242	133.417	0.297	156.775	0.362	183.818	0.399	198.877	0.483	232.408	424
0.218	123.195	0.242	133.659	0.296	157.072	0.361	184.180	0.399	199.275	0.483	232.891	425
0.218	123.413	0.242	133.901	0.296	157.368	0.361	184.541	0.398	199.674	0.483	233.374	426
0.218	123.631	0.242	134.142	0.296	157.664	0.361	184.902	0.398	200.072	0.483	233.856	427
0.218	123.849	0.242	134.384	0.296	157.960	0.361	185.263	0.398	200.470	0.482	234.339	428
0.218	124.067	0.241	134.625	0.296	158.256	0.361	185.624	0.398	200.868	0.482	234.821	429
0.218	124.284	0.241	134.867	0.296	158.552	0.361	185.985	0.398	201.266	0.482	235.303	430
0.217	124.502	0.241	135.108	0.296	158.847	0.361	186.346	0.398	201.663	0.482	235.785	431
0.217	124.719	0.241	135.349	0.295	159.143	0.361	186.706	0.398	202.061	0.482	236.267	432
0.217	124.936	0.241	135.590	0.295	159.438	0.360	187.067	0.397	202.458	0.482	236.749	433
0.217	125.153	0.241	135.831	0.295	159.733	0.360	187.427	0.397	202.856	0.482	237.231	434
0.217	125.370	0.241	136.071	0.295	160.028	0.360	187.787	0.397	203.253	0.482	237.712	435
0.217	125.587	0.241	136.312	0.295	160.323	0.360	188.147	0.397	203.650	0.481	238.194	436
0.217	125.804	0.240	136.552	0.295	160.618	0.360	188.507	0.397	204.047	0.481	238.675	437
0.217	126.020	0.240	136.792	0.295	160.913	0.360	188.866	0.397	204.443	0.481	239.156	438
0.216	126.237	0.240	137.032	0.295	161.207	0.360	189.226	0.397	204.840	0.481	239.637	439
0.216	126.453	0.240	137.272	0.294	161.502	0.359	189.585	0.396	205.236	0.481	240.118	440
0.216	126.669	0.240	137.512	0.294	161.796	0.359	189.945	0.396	205.633	0.481	240.599	441
0.216	126.885	0.240	137.752	0.294	162.090	0.359	190.304	0.396	206.029	0.481	241.079	442
0.216	127.101	0.240	137.992	0.294	162.384	0.359	190.663	0.396	206.425	0.480	241.560	443
0.216	127.317	0.239	138.231	0.294	162.678	0.359	191.022	0.396	206.821	0.480	242.040	444
0.216	127.533	0.239	138.471	0.294	162.971	0.359	191.380	0.396	207.217	0.480	242.520	445
0.216	127.748	0.239	138.710	0.294	163.265	0.359	191.739	0.396	207.612	0.480	243.000	446
0.215	127.964	0.239	138.949	0.293	163.558	0.358	192.097	0.395	208.008	0.480	243.480	447
0.215	128.179	0.239	139.188	0.293	163.852	0.358	192.456	0.395	208.403	0.480	243.960	448
0.215	128.394	0.239	139.427	0.293	164.145	0.358	192.814	0.395	208.798	0.480	244.440	449
0.215	128.609	0.239	139.665	0.293	164.438	0.358	193.172	0.395	209.194	0.480	244.919	450
0.215	128.824	0.239	139.904	0.293	164.731	0.358	193.530	0.395	209.588	0.479	245.399	451
0.215	129.039	0.238	140.143	0.293	165.024	0.358	193.888	0.395	209.983	0.479	245.878	452
0.215	129.254	0.238	140.381	0.293	165.316	0.358	194.245	0.395	210.378	0.479	246.357	453
0.215	129.468	0.238	140.619	0.293	165.609	0.358	194.603	0.395	210.773	0.479	246.836	454
0.214	129.683	0.238	140.857	0.292	165.901	0.357	194.960	0.394	211.167	0.479	247.315	455
0.214	129.897	0.238	141.095	0.292	166.193	0.357	195.317	0.394	211.561	0.479	247.794	456
0.214	130.111	0.238	141.333	0.292	166.486	0.357	195.674	0.394	211.955	0.479	248.272	457
0.214	130.326	0.238	141.571	0.292	166.778	0.357	196.031	0.394	212.350	0.479	248.751	458
0.214	130.540	0.238	141.808	0.292	167.070	0.357	196.388	0.394	212.743	0.478	249.229	459
0.214	130.753	0.238	142.046	0.292	167.361	0.357	196.745	0.394	213.137	0.478	249.708	460
0.214	130.967	0.237	142.283	0.292	167.653	0.357	197.102	0.394	213.531	0.478	250.186	461
0.214	131.181	0.237	142.521	0.292	167.944	0.356	197.458	0.394	213.924	0.478	250.664	462
0.214	131.394	0.237	142.758	0.291	168.236	0.356	197.814	0.393	214.318	0.478	251.142	463
0.213	131.608	0.237	142.995	0.291	168.527	0.356	198.171	0.393	214.711	0.478	251.620	464
0.213	131.821	0.237	143.232	0.291	168.818	0.356	198.527	0.393	215.104	0.478	252.097	465
0.213	132.034	0.237	143.469	0.291	169.109	0.356	198.883	0.393	215.497	0.478	252.575	466
0.213	132.248	0.237	143.705	0.291	169.400	0.356	199.238	0.393	215.890	0.477	253.052	467
0.213	132.461	0.237	143.942	0.291	169.691	0.356	199.594	0.393	216.283	0.477	253.529	468
0.213	132.673	0.236	144.178	0.291	169.981	0.356	199.950	0.393	216.675	0.477	254.007	469

(continued)

APPENDIX D LEARNING CURVE COEFFICIENTS AND

N	70%	Total	72%	Total	74%	Total	75%	Total	78%	Total	80%	Total	82%	Total
470	0.042	39.332	0.054	47.044	0.069	56.189	0.078	61.372	0.110	79.757	0.138	94.751	0.172	112.331
471	0.042	39.374	0.054	47.098	0.069	56.258	0.078	61.450	0.110	79.867	0.138	94.889	0.172	112.503
472	0.042	39.416	0.054	47.152	0.069	56.327	0.078	61.528	0.110	79.977	0.138	95.027	0.172	112.674
473	0.042	39.459	0.054	47.206	0.069	56.396	0.078	61.605	0.110	80.087	0.138	95.164	0.171	112.846
474	0.042	39.500	0.054	47.260	0.069	56.465	0.078	61.683	0.110	80.197	0.138	95.302	0.171	113.017
475	0.042	39.542	0.054	47.314	0.069	56.534	0.077	61.760	0.110	80.307	0.137	95.439	0.171	113.188
476	0.042	39.584	0.054	47.367	0.069	56.602	0.077	61.838	0.110	80.416	0.137	95.577	0.171	113.359
477	0.042	39.626	0.054	47.421	0.069	56.671	0.077	61.915	0.110	80.526	0.137	95.714	0.171	113.530
478	0.042	39.668	0.054	47.475	0.069	56.740	0.077	61.992	0.110	80.636	0.137	95.851	0.171	113.701
479	0.042	39.710	0.054	47.529	0.068	56.808	0.077	62.069	0.109	80.745	0.137	95.988	0.171	113.872
480	0.042	39.751	0.054	47.582	0.068	56.877	0.077	62.147	0.109	80.854	0.137	96.125	0.171	114.043
481	0.042	39.793	0.054	47.636	0.068	56.945	0.077	62.224	0.109	80.964	0.137	96.262	0.171	114.214
482	0.042	39.835	0.054	47.689	0.068	57.013	0.077	62.301	0.109	81.073	0.137	96.399	0.171	114.384
483	0.042	39.876	0.053	47.743	0.068	57.081	0.077	62.378	0.109	81.182	0.137	96.536	0.170	114.555
484	0.042	39.918	0.053	47.796	0.068	57.150	0.077	62.454	0.109	81.291	0.137	96.673	0.170	114.725
485	0.041	39.959	0.053	47.850	0.068	57.218	0.077	62.531	0.109	81.400	0.137	96.809	0.170	114.895
486	0.041	40.001	0.053	47.903	0.068	57.286	0.077	62.608	0.109	81.509	0.136	96.946	0.170	115.065
487	0.041	40.042	0.053	47.956	0.068	57.354	0.077	62.685	0.109	81.618	0.136	97.082	0.170	115.235
488	0.041	40.084	0.053	48.009	0.068	57.422	0.077	62.761	0.109	81.726	0.136	97.218	0.170	115.405
489	0.041	40.125	0.053	48.062	0.068	57.490	0.077	62.838	0.109	81.835	0.136	97.355	0.170	115.575
490	0.041	40.166	0.053	48.115	0.068	57.557	0.076	62.914	0.109	81.944	0.136	97.491	0.170	115.745
491	0.041	40.207	0.053	48.169	0.068	57.625	0.076	62.991	0.108	82.052	0.136	97.627	0.170	115.915
492	0.041	40.249	0.053	48.222	0.068	57.693	0.076	63.067	0.108	82.161	0.136	97.763	0.170	116.084
493	0.041	40.290	0.053	48.274	0.068	57.761	0.076	63.143	0.108	82.269	0.136	97.899	0.169	116.254
494	0.041	40.331	0.053	48.327	0.068	57.828	0.076	63.219	0.108	82.377	0.136	98.034	0.169	116.423
495	0.041	40.372	0.053	48.380	0.068	57.896	0.076	63.296	0.108	82.485	0.136	98.170	0.169	116.592
496	0.041	40.413	0.053	48.433	0.067	57.963	0.076	63.372	0.108	82.593	0.136	98.306	0.169	116.761
497	0.041	40.454	0.053	48.486	0.067	58.031	0.076	63.448	0.108	82.701	0.136	98.441	0.169	116.930
498	0.041	40.495	0.053	48.538	0.067	58.098	0.076	63.524	0.108	82.809	0.135	98.577	0.169	117.099
499	0.041	40.536	0.053	48.591	0.067	58.165	0.076	63.600	0.108	82.917	0.135	98.712	0.169	117.268
500	0.041	40.577	0.053	48.644	0.067	58.232	0.076	63.675	0.108	83.025	0.135	98.847	0.169	117.437
501	0.041	40.617	0.053	48.696	0.067	58.300	0.076	63.751	0.108	83.133	0.135	98.982	0.169	117.606
502	0.041	40.658	0.052	48.749	0.067	58.367	0.076	63.827	0.108	83.240	0.135	99.117	0.169	117.774
503	0.041	40.699	0.052	48.801	0.067	58.434	0.076	63.902	0.108	83.348	0.135	99.252	0.168	117.943
504	0.041	40.740	0.052	48.853	0.067	58.501	0.076	63.978	0.107	83.455	0.135	99.387	0.168	118.111
505	0.041	40.780	0.052	48.906	0.067	58.568	0.076	64.054	0.107	83.563	0.135	99.522	0.168	118.279
506	0.041	40.821	0.052	48.958	0.067	58.635	0.075	64.129	0.107	83.670	0.135	99.657	0.168	118.447
507	0.041	40.861	0.052	49.010	0.067	58.701	0.075	64.204	0.107	83.777	0.135	99.792	0.168	118.616
508	0.041	40.902	0.052	49.063	0.067	58.768	0.075	64.280	0.107	83.884	0.135	99.926	0.168	118.784
509	0.040	40.942	0.052	49.115	0.067	58.835	0.075	64.355	0.107	83.992	0.134	100.061	0.168	118.951
510	0.040	40.983	0.052	49.167	0.067	58.902	0.075	64.430	0.107	84.099	0.134	100.195	0.168	119.119
511	0.040	41.023	0.052	49.219	0.067	58.968	0.075	64.505	0.107	84.206	0.134	100.329	0.168	119.287
512	0.040	41.064	0.052	49.271	0.067	59.035	0.075	64.580	0.107	84.312	0.134	100.463	0.168	119.455
513	0.040	41.104	0.052	49.323	0.066	59.101	0.075	64.655	0.107	84.419	0.134	100.598	0.168	119.622
514	0.040	41.144	0.052	49.375	0.066	59.168	0.075	64.730	0.107	84.526	0.134	100.732	0.167	119.790
515	0.040	41.184	0.052	49.427	0.066	59.234	0.075	64.805	0.107	84.633	0.134	100.866	0.167	119.957

CUMULATIVE TOTALS YN = Y1*(N)^(LOG L/ LOG 2)

84%	Total	85%	Total	87%	Total	89%	Total	90%	Total	92%	Total	N
0.213	132.886	0.236	144.414	0.290	170.272	0.355	200.305	0.392	217.068	0.477	254.484	**470**
0.213	133.099	0.236	144.651	0.290	170.562	0.355	200.660	0.392	217.460	0.477	254.961	**471**
0.213	133.311	0.236	144.887	0.290	170.852	0.355	201.016	0.392	217.853	0.477	255.437	**472**
0.212	133.524	0.236	145.123	0.290	171.143	0.355	201.371	0.392	218.245	0.477	255.914	**473**
0.212	133.736	0.236	145.359	0.290	171.433	0.355	201.726	0.392	218.637	0.477	256.391	**474**
0.212	133.948	0.236	145.594	0.290	171.722	0.355	202.080	0.392	219.028	0.476	256.867	**475**
0.212	134.160	0.236	145.830	0.290	172.012	0.355	202.435	0.392	219.420	0.476	257.343	**476**
0.212	134.372	0.235	146.065	0.290	172.302	0.355	202.790	0.392	219.812	0.476	257.820	**477**
0.212	134.584	0.235	146.301	0.290	172.591	0.354	203.144	0.391	220.203	0.476	258.296	**478**
0.212	134.796	0.235	146.536	0.289	172.881	0.354	203.498	0.391	220.595	0.476	258.772	**479**
0.212	135.007	0.235	146.771	0.289	173.170	0.354	203.852	0.391	220.986	0.476	259.247	**480**
0.212	135.219	0.235	147.006	0.289	173.459	0.354	204.207	0.391	221.377	0.476	259.723	**481**
0.211	135.430	0.235	147.241	0.289	173.748	0.354	204.560	0.391	221.768	0.476	260.199	**482**
0.211	135.642	0.235	147.476	0.289	174.037	0.354	204.914	0.391	222.159	0.475	260.674	**483**
0.211	135.853	0.235	147.711	0.289	174.326	0.354	205.268	0.391	222.550	0.475	261.150	**484**
0.211	136.064	0.235	147.945	0.289	174.615	0.354	205.622	0.391	222.940	0.475	261.625	**485**
0.211	136.275	0.234	148.180	0.289	174.903	0.353	205.975	0.391	223.331	0.475	262.100	**486**
0.211	136.486	0.234	148.414	0.288	175.192	0.353	206.328	0.390	223.721	0.475	262.575	**487**
0.211	136.696	0.234	148.648	0.288	175.480	0.353	206.681	0.390	224.111	0.475	263.050	**488**
0.211	136.907	0.234	148.882	0.288	175.768	0.353	207.035	0.390	224.502	0.475	263.525	**489**
0.211	137.118	0.234	149.116	0.288	176.056	0.353	207.387	0.390	224.892	0.475	263.999	**490**
0.210	137.328	0.234	149.350	0.288	176.344	0.353	207.740	0.390	225.281	0.475	264.474	**491**
0.210	137.538	0.234	149.584	0.288	176.632	0.353	208.093	0.390	225.671	0.474	264.948	**492**
0.210	137.749	0.234	149.818	0.288	176.920	0.353	208.446	0.390	226.061	0.474	265.423	**493**
0.210	137.959	0.234	150.051	0.288	177.207	0.352	208.798	0.390	226.450	0.474	265.897	**494**
0.210	138.169	0.233	150.285	0.287	177.495	0.352	209.150	0.389	226.840	0.474	266.371	**495**
0.210	138.378	0.233	150.518	0.287	177.782	0.352	209.503	0.389	227.229	0.474	266.845	**496**
0.210	138.588	0.233	150.751	0.287	178.069	0.352	209.855	0.389	227.618	0.474	267.319	**497**
0.210	138.798	0.233	150.984	0.287	178.357	0.352	210.207	0.389	228.007	0.474	267.793	**498**
0.210	139.008	0.233	151.218	0.287	178.644	0.352	210.559	0.389	228.396	0.474	268.266	**499**
0.209	139.217	0.233	151.450	0.287	178.930	0.352	210.910	0.389	228.785	0.474	268.740	**500**
0.209	139.426	0.233	151.683	0.287	179.217	0.352	211.262	0.389	229.174	0.473	269.213	**501**
0.209	139.636	0.233	151.916	0.287	179.504	0.352	211.614	0.389	229.562	0.473	269.686	**502**
0.209	139.845	0.233	152.148	0.287	179.791	0.351	211.965	0.388	229.951	0.473	270.160	**503**
0.209	140.054	0.232	152.381	0.286	180.077	0.351	212.316	0.388	230.339	0.473	270.633	**504**
0.209	140.263	0.232	152.613	0.286	180.363	0.351	212.667	0.388	230.727	0.473	271.106	**505**
0.209	140.472	0.232	152.846	0.286	180.650	0.351	213.018	0.388	231.116	0.473	271.578	**506**
0.209	140.680	0.232	153.078	0.286	180.936	0.351	213.369	0.388	231.504	0.473	272.051	**507**
0.209	140.889	0.232	153.310	0.286	181.222	0.351	213.720	0.388	231.891	0.473	272.524	**508**
0.209	141.097	0.232	153.542	0.286	181.508	0.351	214.071	0.388	232.279	0.472	272.996	**509**
0.208	141.306	0.232	153.774	0.286	181.793	0.351	214.422	0.388	232.667	0.472	273.469	**510**
0.208	141.514	0.232	154.005	0.286	182.079	0.350	214.772	0.388	233.054	0.472	273.941	**511**
0.208	141.722	0.232	154.237	0.286	182.364	0.350	215.122	0.387	233.442	0.472	274.413	**512**
0.208	141.930	0.232	154.468	0.285	182.650	0.350	215.473	0.387	233.829	0.472	274.885	**513**
0.208	142.139	0.231	154.700	0.285	182.935	0.350	215.823	0.387	234.216	0.472	275.357	**514**
0.208	142.346	0.231	154.931	0.285	183.220	0.350	216.173	0.387	234.603	0.472	275.829	**515**

APPENDIX E TABLE OF RANDOM NUMBERS

52	06	50	88	53	30	10	47	99	37	66	91	35	32	00	84	57	07
37	63	28	02	74	35	24	03	29	60	74	85	90	73	59	55	17	60
82	57	68	28	05	94	03	11	27	79	90	87	92	41	09	25	36	77
69	02	36	49	71	99	32	10	75	21	95	90	94	38	97	71	72	49
98	94	90	36	06	78	23	67	89	85	29	21	25	73	69	34	85	76
96	52	62	87	49	56	59	23	78	71	72	90	57	01	98	57	31	95
33	69	27	21	11	60	95	89	68	48	17	89	34	09	93	50	44	51
50	33	50	95	13	44	34	62	64	39	55	29	30	64	49	44	30	16
88	32	18	50	62	57	34	56	62	31	15	40	90	34	51	95	26	14
90	30	36	24	69	82	51	74	30	35	36	85	01	55	92	64	09	85
50	48	61	18	85	23	08	54	17	12	80	69	24	84	92	16	49	59
27	88	21	62	69	64	48	31	12	73	02	68	00	16	16	46	13	85
45	14	46	32	13	49	66	62	74	41	86	98	92	98	84	54	33	40
81	02	01	78	82	74	97	37	45	31	94	99	42	49	27	64	89	42
66	83	14	74	27	76	03	33	11	97	59	81	72	00	64	61	13	52
74	05	81	82	93	09	96	33	52	78	13	06	28	30	94	23	37	39
30	34	87	01	74	11	46	82	59	94	25	34	32	23	17	01	58	73
59	55	72	33	62	13	74	68	22	44	42	09	32	46	71	79	45	89
67	09	80	98	99	25	77	50	03	32	36	63	65	75	94	19	95	88
60	77	46	63	71	69	44	22	03	85	14	48	69	13	30	50	33	24
60	08	19	29	36	72	30	27	50	64	85	72	75	29	87	05	75	01
80	45	86	99	02	34	87	08	86	84	49	76	24	08	01	86	29	11
53	84	49	63	26	65	72	84	85	63	26	02	75	26	92	62	40	67
69	84	12	94	51	36	17	02	15	29	16	52	56	43	26	22	08	62
37	77	13	10	02	18	31	19	32	85	31	94	81	43	31	58	33	51

Source: Excerpted from *A Million Random Digits with 100,000 Normal Deviates*, The Free Press, 1955, p. 7, with permission of the Rand Corporation.

APPENDIX F USING AB:POM

This technical appendix provides additional details as to the use of AB:POM. Specific program modules, such as Forecasting or Inventory, are illustrated in their respective chapters. The intent of this appendix is to discuss the overall program operations and to describe how the system may be run on your specific computer.

In this appendix, we first discuss (1) Hardware Requirements, then (2) the Main AB:POM Menu, (3) the Module Submenu Screen, (4) Entering/Editing data, and (5) Getting Started. This program is so user-friendly that, depending on your computer experience and skills, you may wish to go straight to the Getting Started section and proceed to the paragraphs called "Normal Startup."

HARDWARE REQUIREMENTS

AB:POM will work on any IBM or compatible personal computer. The programs themselves require less than 384K of available memory. The system has one 3.5-inch, 1.44-megabyte diskette. The programs also can be loaded onto a hard disk and run from there.

A printer is not required to run AB:POM. Of course, if you want a hard copy (printout), it is necessary to have a printer attached. No special features, characters, installation, or printer is required. It is possible to print the learning curve, Gantt charts, control charts, and linear programming graphs by running the DOS program GRAPHICS.EXE prior to starting up AB:POM and then pressing the **Prt Scn** key.

MAIN MENU

Program E.1 shows AB:POM's Main Menu, consisting of 19 individual application programs plus a **Help** command and an **Exit to DOS** command. Selections from this menu may be made by pressing the first letter (or highlighted letter) of each command on the screen or by moving the cursor to the program you want and then pressing the enter key.

If you request Help from this Main Menu, you may view four detailed Help screens. Program E.2 illustrates the program commands and how function keys may be used.

PROGRAM E.1 ■ The AB:POM Main Menu

```
Main Menu

Help                                Inventory
Decision Tables                     Simulation
Quality Control                     Material Requirements Planning
Forecasting                         Sizing, Lot
Linear Programming                  Aggregate Planning
Plant Location                      Job Shop Sequencing
Transportation                      Assignment
Operations Layout                   CPM/PERT Project Scheduling
Balancing, Assembly Line            Reliability
Waiting Line Models                 Configure
Experience (learning) Curves        Exit to DOS

INSTRUCTIONS
Use highlighted letter or point with
arrow keys and then press ENTER (↵) key
to select option or press ESC key to exit
```

PROGRAM E.2 ■ Optional Help Screen for Function Keys

```
Submenu Options

Submenu options appear on the last line of the data screen after a
module is chosen. The options are chosen by pressing the high-
lighted letter. When you press the ESC key while editing the data
the options will become available. It is also possible to access the
submenu options by using the function keys which are listed below.

  F1-Help-Displays the module or submodule help screen
  F2-New-Use this to start a new problem
  F3-Load-Use this to load a file from disk
  F4-Main-This returns to the module menu
  F5-Util-Customize colors, toggle sound, print to file, etc.
  F6-Quit-Exit AB:POM and go to DOS
  F7-Save-Save a problem/file on a disk
 *F8-Titl-Change the problem title
  F9-Prnt-Print the data or solution to a printer (or file)
F10-Run-Solve the problem

For most modules, ESC followed by the INSert key can be used to insert
```

THE MODULE SUBMENU SCREEN

The module submenu will appear after the module has been chosen.

Submenu Options

Each submenu will have the following six options, which can be selected by typing the highlighted (first) letter or the corresponding function key as shown in Program E.2.

Help (F1)

This option will present a brief description of the module, the data required for input, the output results, and the available options. It is worthwhile to look at this screen at least one time in order to be certain that there are no unsuspected differences between your assumptions and the assumptions of the program. The same help screen also can be accessed from the data screen, where it is perhaps most useful, because you will then be looking at the data to which the help screen is referring. You can examine the help screen at any time; the screen appears instantaneously and takes little time to read.

Create a New Data Set (F2)

Creating a new data set will be a frequently chosen option. After the create option is chosen, one of three types of screens will appear, depending on the module. For some modules (decision tables, forecasting, inventory plant location, project scheduling, and quality control), a model submenu will appear, indicating that different programs are available within the broad context of the module. The desired choice is made in the usual way—by using the first letter or point and shoot. After selecting a model, it will be possible to give the problem a title.

Load a Data Set from the Disk (F3)

If you have previously stored data on a disk (which may be the AB:POM program disk or any blank, formatted disk), it is possible to load the data into memory. If you choose the load data option, a screen will appear that contains the name of the drive, the name of the subdirectory (if there is one), and a list of the available files.

To load a file, simply type its name and then press **Return**. Standard DOS file names *without* extensions are legal. In other words, you may type in up to eight characters, but a period is illegal. You may preface the file name with a drive letter (with its colon). Examples of legal file names are **sample**, **test**, **b:sample**, **problem 1**. It does not matter whether you use uppercase or lowercase characters. DOS treats all characters as uppercase. You may type them as uppercase, lowercase, or mixed. The following are examples of illegal file names.

sample.1p The program will not allow you to type the period.

abcdefghij The name is too long; the program will issue an error message.

lpt1 This is a reserved DOS word.

After the file is loaded, you will be placed in the data screen and can edit or run the data.

Return to the Main Menu (F4)

The next option on the submenu list in Program E.2 is to return to the main menu. This option is not necessary if all of your problems come from the same module. However, if you have homework problems from more than one chapter, this is one way to go from module to module.

Utilities (F5)

If the utilities option is chosen, a new submenu will appear. The submenu options are again chosen in the normal fashion.

CUSTOMIZE COLORS. The first option allows you to create a custom color file. The colors of 13 different items can be changed (in the usual way). For example, to change the color of the boxes in AB:POM, keep pressing **b** until you are satisfied with the color. The colors of the two boxes on the screen change each time you press **b**.

If you have a monochrome monitor, it may take eight presses of a button in order for the shades to change. Be patient.

After you have made all of the desired color changes, you have a few additional choices to make. For example, you must decide whether or not you want to keep a permanent file of these colors; if you do want to save the colors, select the save colors option. (Once saved, these colors can be used by starting the program with **pom u**.) If you plan to use these colors one time only, select the quit option. If you want to cancel the changes and revert to the colors that you started the program with, pick the restore initial colors option.

DELETE A FILE. This option can be used to delete (erase) files from your diskette. If you choose this option, a list of your files for the module currently in use will appear, along with a prompt asking you for the name of the file you wish to delete. To erase a file, simply type the file name. This option should be used if you have trouble saving files because your diskette is full. Obviously, an option that erases files should be used with great care.

PRINT TO DISK FILE OR PRINTER TOGGLE SWITCH. It is possible to send the output to a file rather than to the printer. If this option is chosen, the program will request a name for the output file. All output will be sent to the file named until this option is toggled back to the printer. It is possible to use an extension (file.ext) for this file name.

TOGGLE FIX FORMAT ON. For most of the modules, you can fix the number of decimal places displayed on output by setting on the toggle for fixed number of places. This option must be used with care. (We demonstrate this option later in this section.)

ERROR BEEPS/SOUND OFF. Use this toggle to turn off or on the beep that alerts you when an error has occurred.

FUNCTION KEY DISPLAY OFF/ON. Use this toggle to turn off or on the function key display or the last row of the data screen. The function keys will work even when they are not displayed.

Exit (F6)

The last option on the submenu screen is the exit option. This is the option to choose when you have completed all of your work. The exit option will return control to DOS. If you wish to return to AB:POM from DOS after selecting this option, you must restart the system in the usual manner—by typing **pom** with any desired options.

(*Note:* If DOS is not on your diskette, the computer will issue a message stating that COMMAND.COM is missing. If you wish to continue working, you must insert a DOS diskette; otherwise, you can simply turn off the machine.)

ENTERING AND EDITING DATA

Character Data and Numerical Data

When entering names and numbers, simply type the name or number and then press one of the direction keys, the enter key, or a function key. If you make a mistake while editing, there are two other direction keys to consider: **Back Space** and **Del**, both of which will delete the last character typed.

A beep indicates that you have typed an illegal key while entering data. One of the following messages will appear.

- Typing a character when a number is required.
- Trying to enter a number larger than permitted.
- Trying to enter a name longer than permitted.
- Trying to enter more digits after the decimal than permitted.
- Trying to enter a character that is not permitted for this entry.

(*Note:* The format of numerical displays is handled by the program. Furthermore, any number less than .00001 is displayed as 0.)

Toggle Entries

As mentioned previously, you will not always be entering data. Some entries are toggled—that is, the allowable entries have been preset. For example, in assembly-line balancing, the time unit can be toggled. You can change seconds to minutes to hours and back to seconds again by moving the cursor to the top of the cell of the column with zeroes and pressing the space bar three times. The time unit will change each time the space bar is pressed. So, when the desired unit appears, simply go on to the next cell. Alternatively, you can call up a menu of all available options by pressing the **Enter** key.

While you are editing the data, the function keys shown on the bottom row of the data screen are available. Program E.2 tells what each function key does. Notice that function keys **F1** through **F6** correspond exactly to the menu options from the submenu. We now explain the four options we have not discussed.

Save **(F7)**: This option is similar to the load a data file option. When you choose this option, a screen will appear with the names of your data files, and you will be asked for the name under which to save the data.

If you give the file the name of an existing file, you will be warned about replacing the existing file. The existing file will be replaced by the more recent one if you press **y** (or **Y**) or **Return**. After entering the name, press **Return** to save the data. As before, it is possible to change the drive by using the **F1** key option. It also is possible to use the shell option in the set utilities option from the data screen to change the drive or the directory.

Titl **(F8)**: When you press **F8**, the top line of the data requests that you enter a new title. You will be permitted to enter a title up to 37 characters in length. The title is entered in the usual manner, and will appear at the top of the data after **Return**, a direction key, or a function key is pressed.

Prnt **(F9)**: This option will print the contents of the data or solution screen. The bottom lines and the outside box will not be printed. (It is possible to have everything printed character for character; use **Shift-PrtScn**.) The program prints to the LPT1 file, the standard printer file. If your printer is not attached to LPT1 (if, for example, you have a serial printer), you need to use the DOS MODE statement to redirect the output to the appropriate place; see your DOS manual for instructions. In one or two cases (most notably, linear programming and MRP), the output will not be exactly as it appears on the screen. Changes have been made to fit more than one screen's worth of data onto the printer.

If you have used the utility option, you can print to a file. Later, you can use a word processor to edit this file. In most cases, one of two things will happen if you press **F9** and your computer is not attached to a printer or your printer is not turned on: Either you will get an error message or the program will think that it is printing when it is not—which is harmless. It is also possible that the printer will keep trying to print every 30 seconds or so. You can stop this by pressing the **Esc** key.

Run **(F10)**: After you have entered all of the data, you can press **F10** to solve the problem. Answers will appear either in addition to the data or in place of the data. In either case, the function key bar at the bottom of the screen will change. In all modules, **F9** will be available to print the solution. In some modules, additional function keys for displaying more information will be defined. These definitions will appear in the chapters for those modules. After viewing or printing the solution, press any key to return to the data screen.

Formats for Data

All of the formats for the data are determined by the program. In general, the maximum value that can be input for a number is determined by the width of the field in which the number appears. For example, the largest possible number in a field with six spaces is 999,999. The field width also determines the number of places after the decimal. In most cases, this will not pose a problem. However, there will be occasions when the number of places after the decimal varies within a column, even though the screen would appear orderly if there were no variations.

There is a trade-off involved in the use of this option: In order to have neat columns, we must express the data in round numbers. In many cases, rounding poses no problem, but we advise you to use the **format** option with great care.

GETTING STARTED

Regardless of the configuration of your system, you should begin by making a backup copy of AB:POM. Because AB:POM is not copy-protected, it is very easy to copy with the DOS **copy *.*** or **diskcopy** command.

Normal Startup from a Disk Drive

In order to run AB:POM, simply follow the procedure below. The description that follows assumes that you have a standard disk drive system and are not using a hard drive.

1. Insert a DOS diskette into drive a: (usually the top drive or the left drive).
2. Turn on the computer.
3. When the A> prompt appears on the screen, insert the AB:POM diskette into drive a:.
4. Type **pom** with any options (described in the following section).

If you have trouble starting, try typing **go** (with any options) rather than **pom**.

(*Note:* If you use a version of DOS less than DOS 3.00, a prompt will appear after you have typed **pom**. The machine will ask you to input the run-time module path. In order to run the system, you must type a backslash (\ ) or the drive name in which AB:POM is running (usually drive a:). When AB:POM is in drive a:, the proper response to the prompt is to type **a:** followed by **Return** or **Enter**. Notice that the third character is a backslash, not a slash. On some machines, the backslash is not required. Alternately, it is possible to begin the program by typing **path** = \ prior to typing **pom**. The file GO.BAT will do this for you.)

Normal Startup from a Hard Drive

If you have a hard drive then the best way to run the system is to create a directory for AB:POM and run it from there. If a path is set it is possible to run AB:POM from any directory. To set the system up, perform the following steps:

1. From the C> prompt type **MD ABPOM**
2. Type **CD ABPOM**
3. Insert the 3.5″ AB:POM diskette into drive A: and type **COPY A:*.* C:**

Henceforth to use the AB:POM system

1. Boot the computer
2. Type **CD \ABPOM**
3. Type **POM** with any options

There is a file on the 3.5″ diskette named INSTALL that will perform the above steps. If you type INSTALL at the A:> prompt or type A:INSTALL at the C:> prompt with AB:POM in the A: drive then install will perform the steps above and create a directory named ABPOM on your C: drive and then copy all of the files from the AB:POM diskette to your drive.

Startup Options

The program starts with the command POM (or GO). The following options can be added.

DISK DRIVE FOR DATA. The letters a, b, c, d, and e can be used to specify which drive contains the data. (This can be changed from within the program also.) There is enough room on the program disk to store all your data files, if you so desire.

EXAMPLE

POM B will indicate to the program that the data files can be found on drive b:. The default drive is the drive from which AB:POM was started.

COLOR/MONITOR OPTIONS. The letter **m** can be used to indicate that the monitor is a monochrome (single-color monitor). The number 1 can be used to indicate that the monitor is a color monitor, colors should be used, and the background color should be black. The number 2 indicates a color monitor and a background color that allows shadowing. The letter **u** indicates that a user file of colors called COLOR.POM should be used. (This file can be created and/or changed from the utility menu within AB:POM.) If you do not choose a color option at the command line, the program will ask you for one.

EXAMPLES

POM M or POM m will use a monochrome monitor.

POM 1 will use default colors that include a black background.

POM 2 will use default colors that include a blue background and a shadowing effect.

POM U will look for the file COLOR.POM and use those colors.

NUMBER OF LINES ON THE SCREEN. The usual number of lines is 25 and this is the nicest display. However, if you use option H (high resolution), then 43 lines will be used (if your monitor allows this), and if you use option V (for VGA), then 50 lines will be used if your monitor allows this.

SOUND TOGGLE. If you start the program with the letter S, then the beeps made when errors occur will be silenced. This can be changed from within the program, using the utility option.

Combining Options. Options can be combined.

EXAMPLE

POM smb will turn off beeps, display everything in black/white and look for data on drive b:.

Formatting Procedures. POM F will change the formatting procedure of AB:POM. Typically, AB:POM allows nine spaces for numbers and decimal points. If this option is chosen, the number of places after the decimal is fixed. This makes for a neater display, but it can lead to roundoff problems. As explained in the earlier section on formatting, this option should be used with great care.

SOLUTIONS TO EVEN-NUMBERED PROBLEMS

Chapter 1

1.2 (a) 20 ornaments/hour.
(b) 26.7 ornaments/hour.
(c) 33.5%.

1.4

	LAST YEAR	THIS YEAR	% CHANGE
Labour	4.29	4.62	$\frac{.33}{4.29} = 7.7$
Capital	.10	.08	$\frac{-.02}{.1} = -20$
Energy	.50	.55	$\frac{.05}{.50} = 10$

Productivity of capital did drop, labour productivity increased as did energy (but only 10%, not 15%).

1.6 The business cycle impacts this number substantially, but for the economy as a whole probably less than 2%.

Chapter 2

2.2 (a) For a producer with high energy costs, major oil prices change the cost structure, result in higher selling prices, and, if the company is energy-inefficient compared to other producers, result in a change in competitive position.

Chapter 2 Supplement

S2.2 Major expansion; EMV = $250,000.

S2.4 8 cases.

S2.6 (a)

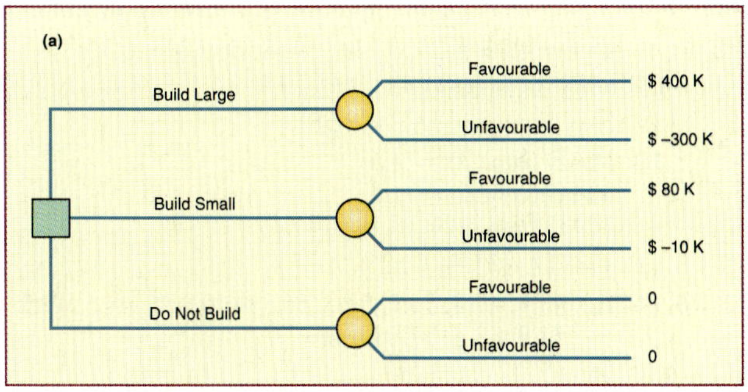

(b) Small plant with EMV = $26,000.
(c) EVPI = $134,000.

S2.8 (a) Max EMV = $11,700.
(b) EVPI = $13,200 − $11,700 = $1,500.

S2.10

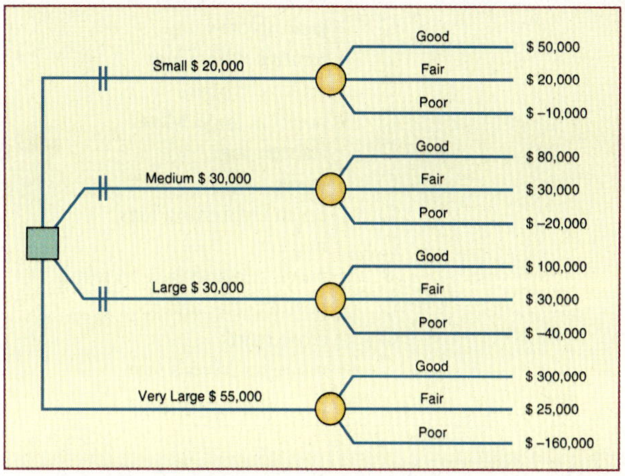

S2.12

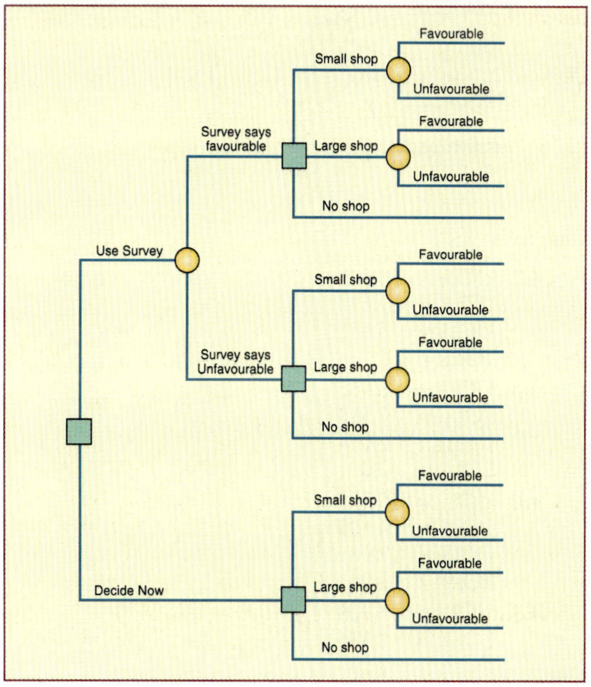

S2.14 No information and build large; $4,500.
S2.16 $12,000,000.

Chapter 3

3.2 Individual answer.

3.4 (a)

8′	↓	move to trunk
	O	open trunk
	O	loosen tire and jack
	O	remove tire and jack
8′	↓	move the tire and jack to wheel
	O	position jack
	□	inspect
	O	loosen wheel lugs
	O	jack-up car
	O	remove wheel lugs
	O	remove wheel
	O	position good wheel
	O	tighten lugs
	O	lower car
	O	finish tightening lugs
	□	inspect
8′	↓	move tire and jack to trunk
	O	position tire and jack
	O	close trunk
8′	↓	move to driver's seat

3.6

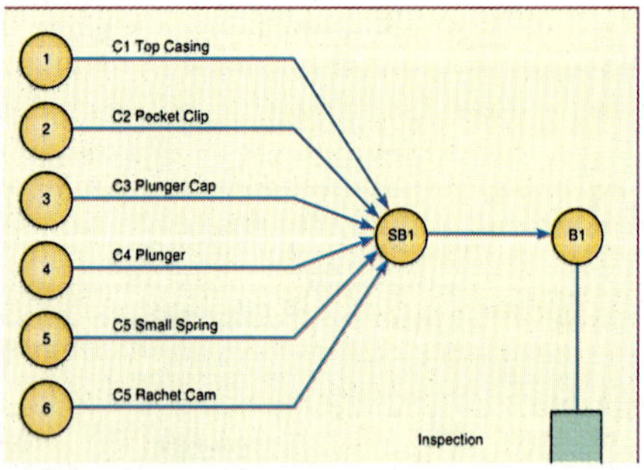

Chapter 4

4.2 $UCL_{\bar{\bar{x}}}$ = 52.308
$LCL_{\bar{\bar{x}}}$ = 47.692
UCL_R = 8.456
LCL_R = 0.0

4.4 $UCL_{\bar{\bar{x}}}$ = 8.483
$LCL_{\bar{\bar{x}}}$ = 7.517
UCL_R = 2.004
LCL_R = 0.0

4.6 $UCL_{\bar{\bar{x}}}$ = 515.595
$LCL_{\bar{\bar{x}}}$ = 504.405
UCL_R = 27.96
LCL_R = 2.04

4.8 $UCL_{\bar{\bar{x}}}$ = 3.728
$LCL_{\bar{\bar{x}}}$ = 2.336
UCL_R = 2.29
LCL_R = 0.0
The process is in control.

4.10 UCL_p = .0596
LCL_p = .0104

4.12 UCL_p = .0311 to .1636
LCL_p = 0.0 to .0364

4.14 $UCL_{\bar{\bar{x}}}$ = 64.54
$LCL_{\bar{\bar{x}}}$ = 62.36
UCL_R = 3.423
LCL_R = 0

4.16 UCL_p = .0581
LCL_p = 0

4.18 UCL_c = 33.4
LCL_c = 7

4.20

Fraction Defective	$P(x \leq 1)$
.01	.999
.10	.910
.20	.736
.40	.406
.60	.199
.80	.092
1.0	.040

4.22 The plan meets neither the products nor the consumers' requirement.

4.24 $UCL_{\bar{\bar{x}}}$ = 61.13
$LCL_{\bar{\bar{x}}}$ = 38.42
UCL_R = 41.62
LCL_R = 0.0
The process appears to be in control.

Chapter 4 Supplement

S4.2 5.45, 4.05.

S4.4 (a) .2743.
(b) .5.

S4.6 (a) .1587.
(b) .2347.
(c) .1587.

S4.8 (a) .0548.
(b) .6554.
(c) .6554.
(d) .2119.

Chapter 5

5.2 18.67, 16.67, 14, 14.33, 15.33, 17, 18.33, 19.33, 20.33, 21.33.

5.4 (a) 337; (b) 380; (c) 423.

5.6 2 year: 5, 5, 4.5, 7.5, 9.0, 7.5, 8.0, 10.5, 13.0.
4 year: 4.75, 6.25, 6.75, 7.50, 8.50, 9.00, 10.50.

5.8 Wtd. M.A. MAD = 2,312.
Exp. Smooth MAD = 2,581.

5.10 MAD ($\alpha = .3$) = 74.6.
MAD ($\alpha = .6$) = 51.8.
MAD ($\alpha = .9$) = 38.1 (best).

5.12 $y = 522 + 33.6x = 623$.

5.14 (a) 43.4, 47.4, 50.2, 53.7, 56.3 for $\alpha = .6$; 44.6, 49.5, 51.8, 55.6, 57.8 for $\alpha = .9$.
(b) 49, 52.7, 55.3.
(c) 45.8, 49.0, 52.2, 55.4, 58.6, 61.8.
(d) Trend with MAD = .6.

5.16 5, 5.4, 6.12, 5.90, 6.52, 7.82.

5.18 MAD = 3.98; $\beta = .8$ is better than $\beta = .2$.

5.20 $y = 5.26 + 1.11x$.
Period 7 demand = 13.03.

5.22 **(a)** Moving average forecast for February is 13.6667.
(b) Weighted moving average forecast for February is 13.16.
(c) MAD for Avg is 2.2.
MAD for Weighted Avg is 2.7.
(d) seasonality, causal variables such as advertising budget.

5.24 **(a)** $\hat{y} = 1 + 1x$; $r = .45$.
(b) $S_{yx} = 3.65$.

5.26 $y = .972 + .0035\,x$; $r^2 = 0.479$; $x = 350$; $y = 2.197$; $x = 800$; $y = 3.77$.

5.28 131.2 → 72.7 patients; 90.6 → 50.6 patients.

5.30 Fall = 270; Winter = 390; Spring = 189; Summer = 351.

5.32 **(a)** 1785.
(b) 1560.

5.34 **(a)** 17.00; 17.80; 18.04; 19.03; 18.83; 18.26; 18.61; 18.49; 19.19; 19.35; 18.48.
(b) 2.60.
(c) No, tracking signal exceeds 5 sigma at week 10.

5.36 **(a, b)**

WEEK	$\alpha = .1$ FORECAST	$\alpha = .6$ FORECAST
25	46.9	57.6

(c) On the basis of forecast and standard error of estimate, $\alpha = .6$ is better. But other α's should be tried.

5.38 Each answer will differ, but note the presence of both seasonal and trend factors.

5.40 150,000; 126,000; 120,000; and 207,000 for the four respective quarters.

Chapter 6

6.2 Assembly chart for a ballpoint pen.

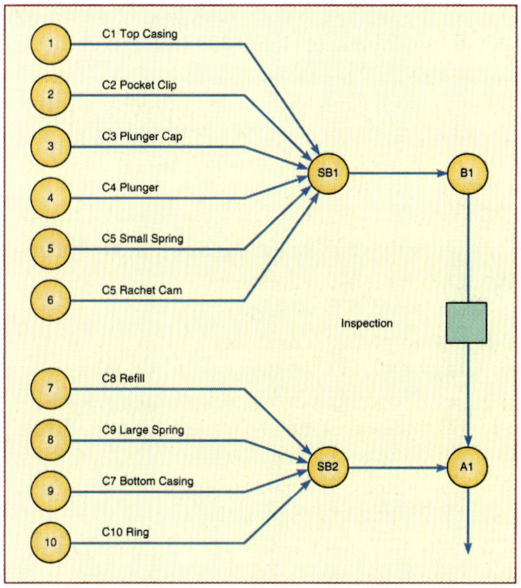

6.4

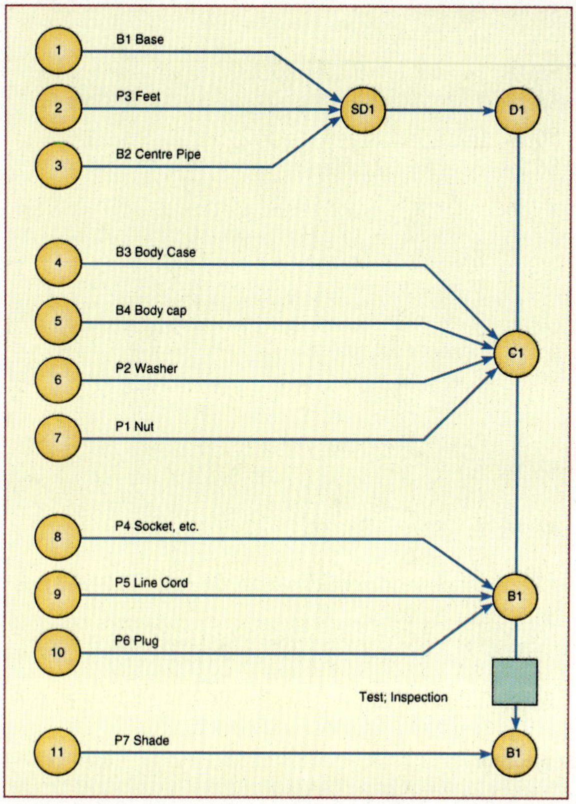

6.6 The lap top computer has contributed 30%, but sales are substantial, yielding 50% of the total contribution; conversely, the hand calculator has a high individual contribution, but only contributes 10% to the company's total contribution.

6.8 EMV of Proceed = \$49,500,000.
EMV of Do Value Analysis = \$55,025,000.
Therefore, Do Value Analysis.

6.10 EMV of Design A = \$875,000.
EMV of Design B = \$700,000.

Chapter 6 Supplement

S6.2 100 = profit at $x = 0$, $y = 10$.

S6.4 **(a)** $P = \$3{,}000$ at $x_1 = 75$, $x_2 = 75$ *or* $x_1 = 50$, $x_2 = 150$.
(b) Two solutions generate the same profit.

S6.6 **(a)** Minimize $x_1 + 2x_2$

$$x_1 + x_2 \geq 40$$
$$2x_1 + 4x_2 \geq 60$$
$$x_1 \leq 15$$

(b) Cost = 65¢ at $x_1 = 15$, $x_2 = 25$.
(c) 65¢.

S6.8 $x_1 = 200$, $x_2 = 0$, $P = \$18{,}000$.

S6.10 10 Alphas, 24 Betas, $P = \$55{,}200$.

S6.12 **(a)** $x_1 = 25.71$, $x_2 = 21.43$.
(b) Cost = \$68.57.

S6.14 Objective function, first and fifth constraints.

S6.16 **(a)** 26¢.
(b) $7.86.

S6.18 $x_1 = 60$, $x_2 = 90$, $P = \$3{,}930$.

S6.20 7,500 round, 5,000 square, cost = $115,000.

S6.22 **(e)** $x_1 = 8$, $x_2 = 4$, $P = \$60$.

S6.24 Basis for 1st tableau:
$A_1 = 80$
$A_2 = 75$
Basis for 2nd tableau:
$A_1 = 55$
$x_1 = 25$
Basis for 3rd tableau:
$x_1 = 14$
$x_2 = 33$
Cost = 221 at optimal solution.

S6.26 **(a)** x_1.
(b) A_1.

S6.28 **(a)** $22.50–$30.00.
(b) $5.00.
Shadow price holds within the range 210–280 hours.

S6.30 **(a)** $5.00–∞.
(b) –$5.00 is valid from 5,000–∞ hours.
(c) –$3.00 is valid from 0–20,000 tables.

S6.32 Minimize $6X1A + 5X1B + 3X1C + 8X2A + 10X2B + 8X2C + 11X3A + 14X3B + 18X3C$

Subject to:
$X1A + X2A + X3A = 7$
$X1B + X2B + X3B = 12$
$X1C + X2C + X3C = 5$
$X1A + X1B + X1C \leq 6$
$X2A + X2B + X2C \leq 8$
$X3A + X3B + X3C \leq 10$

S6.34 61 medical beds, 29 surgical beds, annual profit = $9,551,668.

Chapter 7

7.2 **(a)** 4,590 in excess capacity.
(b) 2,090 in excess capacity.

7.4 Design = 81,806.
Fabrication = 152,646.
Finishing = 62,899.

7.6 **(a)** $BEP_{\$} = \$125{,}000$.
(b) $BEP_{\$} = \$140{,}000$.

7.8 **(a)** Proposal A is best; $a = \$18{,}000$; $b = \$15{,}000$.
(b) Proposal B is best; $a = \$70{,}000$; $b = \$80{,}000$.

7.10 NPV = $19,800.

7.12 NPV = $1,764.

7.14 Present equipment = $1,000.
New equipment = 0.

7.16 **(a)** $100,000.
(b) 12,500 units.
(c) $350,000.

7.18 **(a)** Purchase two large ovens.
(b) Equal quality, equal capacity.
(c) Payments are made at end of each time period. And future interest rates are known.

7.20 BEP(x) = 25,000.

7.22 BEP($) = $7,584.83.
Daily meals = 9.

7.24 Payoff from small line equal $200,000; payoff from large line equals $133,000.

7.26 NPV for investment 1 = $17,127.
NPV for investment 2 = $25,532.
NPV for investment 3 = $18,962.

Chapter 8

8.2 GPE is best below 100,000; FMS is best between 100,000 and 300,000; DA is best above 300,000.

8.4 The optimum process will change with each additional 100,000 units.

Chapter 9

9.2 **(b)** Vancouver, 0–3570 units; Brampton, 3,571–24,999 units; New Glasgow, more than 25,000 units.
(c) Brampton.

9.4 Suburb B, rating = 6.35 but all are close.

9.6 Shopping is mall best.

9.8 Hyde Park with 54.5 points.

9.10 **(a)** Lyon, 3970; Bonn, 3915; The Hague, 3920.
(b) Lyon, 3730; Berlin, 3585; The Hague, 3840.
(c) Berlin, 3840; The Hague, 3840; Bonn, 3810.

Chapter 9 Supplement

S9.2 **(a)** A-1, 10; B-1, 30; C-2, 60; A-3, 40; C-3, 15.
(b) $1,775.

S9.4 Sarnia, $19,500.

S9.6 Solution is optimal.

S9.8 **(a)** Initial solution is degenerate.
(b) Cost = $2,750.

S9.10 W-A, 200; X-B, 100; X-C, 75; Y-C, 75; Dummy-A, 50.

S9.12 Fountainbleau is $1,530,000 vs. Dublin at a higher cost of $1,535,000.

S9.14 Campbell River with a cost of $17,400 is higher than Corner Brook with a cost of $17,250.

S9.16 A-1, 9; B-3, 8; C-1, 3; C-3, 7; D-1, 7; and D-2, 24.

Chapter 10

10.2 Yes, with AB:POM patient movement = 4,500 metres.

10.4 Layout #1, 600 = distance.
Layout #2, 602 = distance.

10.6 Layout #4, 609 = distance.
Layout #5, 372 = distance.

10.8 **(a)** Throughput of 3.75 people/hour possible.
(b) Medical exam—16 minutes.
(c) At least 5 per hour now.

10.10 Cycle time = 9.6 minutes; eight workstations with 63.8% efficiency is possible.

10.12 Station #1, tasks 1, 3; #2, task 5; #3, tasks 2, 4; #4, tasks 6, 8; #5, tasks 7, 9. Efficiency = 78%.

10.14 Cycle time = .5 minute/bottle. Possible assignments with four workstations yields efficiency = 90%.

10.16 Minimum (theoretical) = four stations. Efficiency = 80% with five stations. Several assignments with five are possible.

10.18 There are three alternatives each with an efficiency = 86.67%.

Chapter 10 Supplement

S10.2 (a) .5.
(b) .5.
(c) 1.
(d) .5.
(e) .05 hr.
(f) .1 hr.

S10.4 (a) .667.
(b) .667 min.
(c) 1.33.

S10.6 (a) .375.
(b) 1.6 hr.
(c) .225.

S10.8 (a) 2.25.
(b) .75.
(c) .857 min.
(d) .64 min.
(e) 42%, 32%, 24%.

S10.10 (a) 6 trucks.
(b) 12 min.
(c) .857.
(d) 54%.
(e) $1,728/day.
(f) Yes, save $3,096.

S10.12 (a) .666.
(b) 1.33.
(c) 10 sec.

S10.14 3, 2, 4 MDs, respectively.

S10.16 (a) .05.
(b) .743.
(c) .795.

Chapter 11

11.2

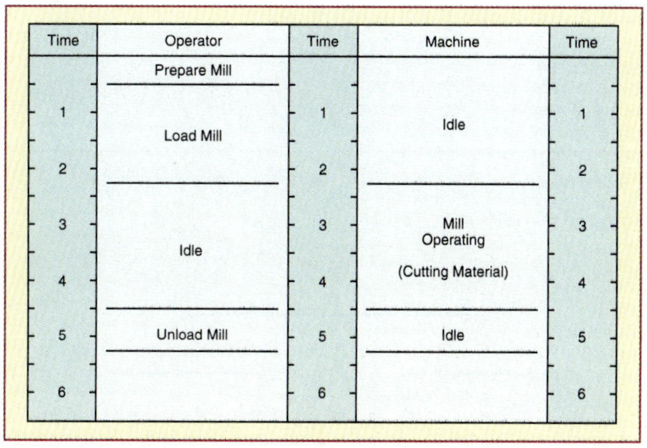

11.4 The first 10 steps are shown below. The remaining 10 steps are similar.

OPERATIONS CHART	SUMMARY					
PROCESS: CHANGE ERASER	SYMBOL	PRESENT LH	PRESENT RH	PROPOSED LH	PROPOSED RH	DIFF. LH	DIFF. RH
ANALYST:	O OPERATIONS	1	8				
DATE:	⇨ TRANSPORTS	3	8				
SHEET: 1 of 2	□ INSPECTIONS	1					
METHOD: PRESENT PROPOSED	D DELAYS	15	4				
REMARKS:	▽ STORAGE						
	TOTALS	20	20				

LEFT HAND	DIST.	SYMBOL	SYMBOL	DIST.	RIGHT HAND
1 Reach for pencil		⇨	D		Idle
2 Grasp pencil		O	D		Idle
3 Move to work area		⇨	⇨		Move to pencil top
4 Hold pencil		D	O		Grasp pencil top
5 Hold pencil		D	O		Remove pencil top
6 Hold pencil		D	⇨		Set top aside
7 Hold pencil		D	⇨		Reach for old eraser
8 Hold pencil		D	O		Grasp old eraser
9 Hold pencil		D	O		Remove old eraser
10 Hold pencil		D	⇨		Set aside old eraser

11.6 Individual solution.

11.8 The answer is similar to Solved Problem 11.1, but crew activities C and D become the limiting activities.

Chapter 11 Supplement

S11.2 Sample size of 166 is required.

S11.4 Six observations are required.

S11.6 Normal time = 5.565 min.
Allowance = 10%.
Std. time = 6.183.

S11.8 29.8 min.

S11.10 5.4 or 6.67 depending upon the observation deleted.

S11.12 82.35 seconds, 106 samples.

S11.14 (a) 47.55 min.
(b) 60 observations are required for element 4.

S11.16 336.

S11.18 .1092 min, or 6.55 sec.

Chapter 12

12.2 WARS costs increase by the amount of Tarleton's research.

12.4 Donna Inc.: 47.04.
Kay Corp.: 54.15.

Chapter 12 Supplement

S12.2 (a) 14.31 hr.
(b) $71,550.
(c) $947,250.

S12.4 (a) 80%.
(b) 3.51.
(c) 3.2, 2.98, 2.81.
(d) 21.5.

S12.6 (a) 72.2 hr.
(b) 60.55 hr.
(c) 41.47 hr.

S12.8 \$748,240 for fourth, \$709,960 for fifth, and \$679,942 for sixth.

S12.10 **(a)** 70 millicents/bit.
(b) 8.2 millicents/bit.

S12.12 26,755 hr.

S12.14 **(a)** 32.98 hr, 49.61 hr.
(b) Initial quote is high.

Chapter 13

13.2 A item is G2. B item is F3. All others = C.

13.4 7000.

13.6 **(a)** 78.
(b) 250.
(c) \$3,873.08.
(d) 64.
(e) 3.125 days.

13.8 Qty discount cost = \$41,436.25.

13.10 Total cost = total ordering cost + total holding cost.
Q = 25 TC = 1500
Q = 40 TC = 1230
Q = 50 TC = 1200
Q = 60 TC = 1220
Q = 100 TC = 1500
Small variations in order quantity will not have a significant impact on total cost.

13.12 **(a)** TSC + THC = \$1220.
(b) If we order EOQ = 60 units TSC + THC = \$1200.
(c) ROP = 24 units.

13.14 1217 units.

13.16 51 units, \$1,901.22.

13.18 TC = 753 @ 34 units.

13.20 Stock for demand = 3.

13.22 2809 units.

13.24 100 units of safety stock.

Chapter 13 Supplement

S13.2 0, 0, 0, 0, 0, 0, 0, 2, 0, 2.

S13.4 Profits = 20, −15, 20, 17.50, 20; average equals 12.50.

S13.6 Simulations will differ, depending on random numbers selected.

S13.8

Arrivals	*Arrival Time*	*Service Time*	*Departure Time*
1	11:01	3	11:04
2	11:04	2	11:06
3	11:06	2	11:08
4	11:07	1	11:09

S13.10 **(a, b)**

No. Cars	Prob.	Cum. Prob.	R.N. Interval
3 or less	0	0	—
4	.10	.10	01–10
5	.15	.25	11–25
6	.25	.50	26–50
7	.30	.80	51–80
8	.20	1.00	81–00
9 or more	0	—	—

(c) Average no. arrivals/hour = 105/15 = 7 cars.

S13.12 Each simulation will differ. Using random numbers from right-hand column of the random number table, reading top to bottom, in the order used, results in a \$9.20 cost. This is greater than the \$6.65 in Example S3.

S13.14 **(a)** 5 times.
(b) 6.95 times, yes.
(c) 7.16 heaters.

S13.16 Average demand is about 8.75, average lead time is 1.86, average end inventory = 6.50, average lost sales = 4.04.

S13.18 Average end inventory = 8.90; average lost sales = 3.41; total cost = \$488,568 or \$20,357/month. This new policy seems preferable.

S13.20 Here are the random-number intervals for the first two departments.

From	To	R.N. Interval
Initial exam	X-ray	01–45
	OR	46–60
	Observ.	61–70
	Out	71–00

From	To	R.N. Interval
X-ray	OR	01–10
	Cast	11–35
	Observ.	36–70
	Out	71–00

Each simulation will produce different results. Some will indeed show a person entering X-ray twice.

Chapter 14

14.2 **(a)**

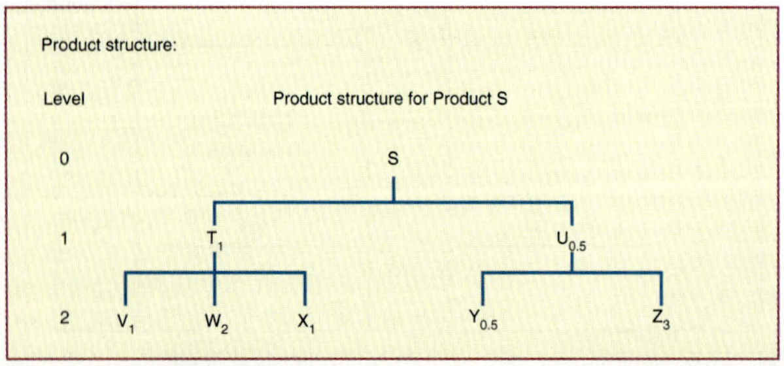

Gross material requirements plan:

Item		Week 1	2	3	4	5	6	7	8	Lead Time (wks)
S	Required date							100		
	Order release					100				2
T	Required date					100				
	Order release				100					1
U	Required date					50				
	Order release			50						2
V	Required date				100					
	Order release		100							2
W	Required date				200					
	Order release	200								3
X	Required date				100					
	Order release			100						1
Y	Required date			25						
	Order release	25								2
Z	Required date			150						
	Order release		150							1

(b) Net material requirements plan (only items S and T are shown):

Item		Week 1	2	3	4	5	6	7	8	Lead Time (wks)
S	Gross required							100		
	On hand							20		
	Net required							80		2
	Order receipt							80		
	Order release					80				
T	Gross required					80				
	On hand					20				
	Net required					60				1
	Order receipt					60				
	Order release				60					

14.4 **(a)** Gross material requirements plan:

		Week 1	2	3	4	5	6	7	8	9	10	11	12
X_1	Required date								50		20		100
	Order release							50		20		100	
B_1	Required date							50		20		100	
	Order release					50		20		100			
B_2	Required date							100		40		200	
	Order release					100		40		200			
A_1	Required date					50		20		100			
	Order release				50		20		100				
D	Required date					200		80		400			
	Order release				200		80		400				
E	Required date					100		40		200			
	Order release				100		40		200				
C	Required date				200	50	80	20	500				
	Order release	200	50	80	20	500							

(b) Net material requirements (planned order release) plan:

		Week 1	2	3	4	5	6	7	8	9	10	11	12
X_1	Required date										20		100
	Order release									20		100	
B_1	Required date											100	
	Order release									100			
B_2	Required date									20		200	
	Order release							20		200			
A_1	Required date									95			
	Order release								95				
D	Required date							40		400			
	Order release						40		400				
E	Required date							20		200			
	Order release						20		200				
C	Required date						30		400	100			
	Order release			30		400	100						

14.6 Net material requirements plan (only items A and H are shown):

		Week 1	2	3	4	5	6	7	8	9	10	11	12
A	Gross required								100		50		150
	On hand								0		0		0
	Net required								100		50		150
	Order receipt								100		50		150
	Order release							100		50		150	
H	Gross required									100		50	
	On hand									0		0	
	Net required									100		50	
	Order receipt									100		50	
	Order release								100		50		

14.8 (a) EOQ = 57.4 units.
Theoretical total cost: $1,723.42.
Actual total cost: $2,362.50.
(b) EOQ = 57.4 units.
Theoretical total cost: $1,723.42.
Actual total cost: $1,810.00.

14.10 (a) EOQ = $1,992.50.
(b) Lot-for-lot = $400.
(c) PPB cost = $220.

14.12 New master production schedule:

		Week 0	1	2	3	4	5	6	7	8	9	10
P	Gross required		0	0	30	40	10	70	40	10	30	60

Gross material requirements plan:

		Week 0	1	2	3	4	5	6	7	8	9	10
P	Required date				30	40	10	70	40	10	30	60
	Order release			30	40	10	70	40	10	30	60	
C	Required date			30	40	10	70	40	10	30	60	
	Order release		80			120			90			

Net material requirements plan:

		Week 0	1	2	3	4	5	6	7	8	9	10
P	Gross required	0	0	0	30	40	10	70	40	10	30	60
	On hand	20	20	20	20	0	0	0	0	0	0	0
	Net required				10	40	10	70	40	10	30	60
	Order receipt				10	40	10	70	40	10	30	60
	Order release			10	40	10	70	40	10	30	60	
C	Gross required			10	40	10	70	40	10	30	60	
	On hand	30	30	30	20			0			0	
	Net required	0	0	0	100			80			60	
	Order receipt				100			80			60	
	Order release			100			80			60		

14.14 The limit of 75 components per week constrains component production in weeks 4 and 7. Some production will need to be moved to weeks 2 and 5.

14.16 (a) Ten units are required for production, and ten for field service repair.

Components	Quantity
A	20
B	20
C	40
D	20
E	40
F	20
G	20
H	20

(b)

Components	Quantity
A	20
B	18
C	18
D	13
E	30
F	15
G	14
H	10

(c) Not shown here.

14.18 (a)

Requirements

	1	2	3	4	5	6	7	8	9	10	11	12
E.C.W.			40	100	80	70	20	25	70	80	30	50
W.C.W.		20	45	60	70	40	80	70	80	55		
F.W.			30	40	10	70	40	10	30	60		

Requirements Offset for Lead Times

	0	1	2	3	4	5	6	7	8	9	10	11	12
E.C.W.		40	100	80	70	20	25	70	80	30	50		
W.C.W.	20	45	60	70	40	80	70	80	55				
F.W.			30	40	10	70	40	10	30	60			

Receipts from Factory at Factory Warehouse

	0	1	2	3	4	5	6	7	8	9	10	11	12
Gross required	20	85	190	190	120	170	135	160	165	90	50		
On hand		80	95	5	15	95	25	90	30	65	75	25	
Planned receipt from Factory	100	100	100	200	200	100	200	100	200	100			

(b) Release all orders 2 weeks prior to the schedule above (the planned "Receipts from Factory" date).

If the schedule is late, as suggested above, then the initial order for receipt in week 3 should be for all requirements needed prior to that (i.e., weeks 0, 1, 2, and 3, for a total of 500 units). The release schedule would then be

	Week 1	2	3	4	5	6	7
Planned order release	500	200	100	200	100	200	100

Chapter 15

15.2 Cost = $53,320.
No, plan 2 is better.

15.4 Cost = $214,000 for plan B.

15.6 Plan D; $122,000.

15.8 Each answer you develop will differ.

15.10 Plan C, $92,000; Plan D, $82,300 assuming initial inventory = 0.

15.12 $11,790.

15.14 $1,186,810.

15.16 \$100,750.

15.18 \$88,150.

Chapter 16

16.2 **(a)** 1-D, 2-A, 3-C, 4-B.
(b) 40.

16.4

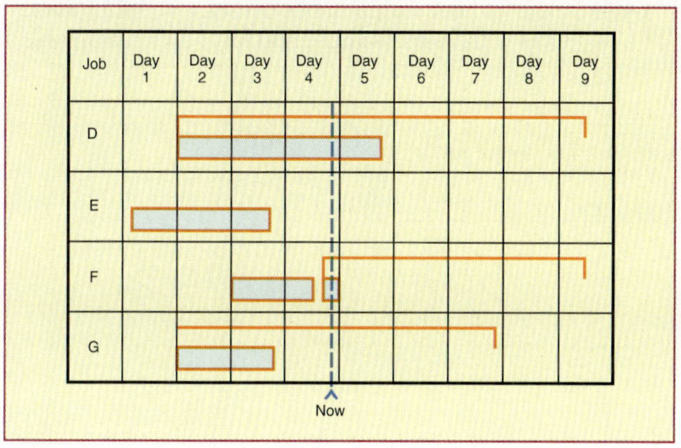

16.6 A-61 to 4; A-60 to 1; A-53 to 3; A-56 to 5; A-52 to 2; A-59 to 6; 150 hr.

16.8 1–2 P.M. on A; 2–3 P.M. on C; 3–4 P.M. on B; 4–5 P.M. on Independent; 75.5 rating.

16.10 **(a)** ABCDE.
(b) BADEC.
(c) EDABC.
(d) CBADE.
SPT is best.

16.12 DCAB sequence for critical ratio.

16.14 **(a)** A, B, C, D, E.
(b) C, A, B, E, D.
(c) C, D, E, A, B.
(d) B, A, E, D, C.
EDD is best on tardiness, SPT on other 2 measures.

16.16 D, B, A, C.

16.18 A, C, D, E, B.

16.20 4, 1, 2, 3, 5; makespan = 56 hr.

Chapter 17

17.2

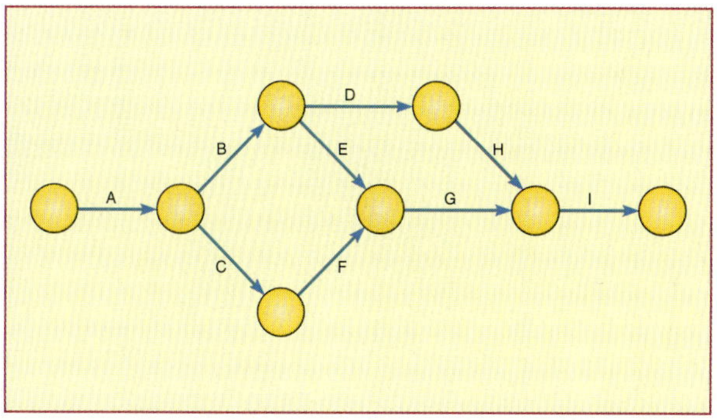

17.4

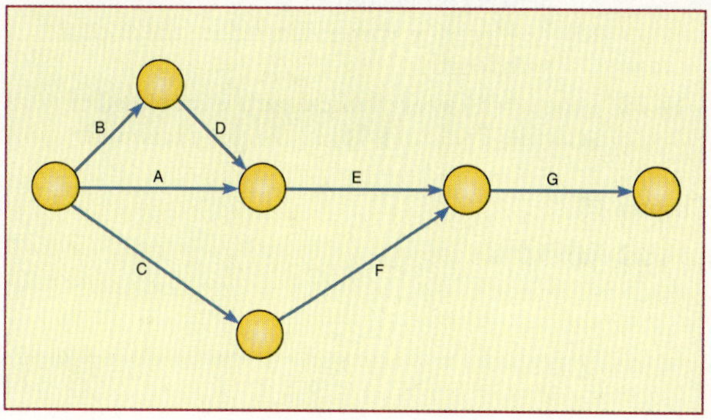

17.6

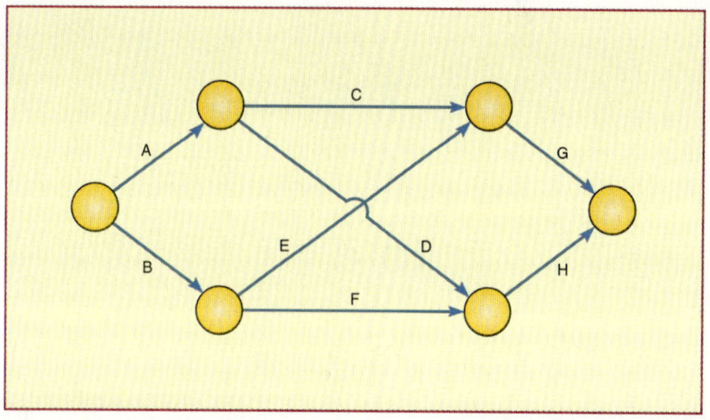

17.8 A, 5.83, 0.69.
B, 3.67, 0.11.
C, 2.00, 0.11.
D, 7.00, 0.11.
E, 4.00, 0.44.
F, 10.00, 1.78.
G, 2.17, 0.25.
H, 6.00, 1.00.
I, 11.00, 0.11.
J, 16.33, 1.00.
K, 7.33, 1.78.

17.10 .9463

17.12 **(a)** 15 (A, C, E).
(b) 2.

17.14 **(a)** 16 (A, D, G).
(b) \$12,300.
(c) D, 1 week for \$75.

17.16 A, C, E, H, I, K, M, N; 50 weeks.

17.18 **(a)** .0228.
(b) .3085.
(c) .8413.
(d) .9772.

17.20 **(a, b)** Critical path = A, B, J, K, L, M, R, S, T, U; time = 18.
(c) Transmissions and drive trains are not on the critical path; halving engine time reduces the

critical path by 2 days; speeding accessory delivery is not critical.
(d) Reallocating workers can reduce the critical path length.

17.22 Length = 34 weeks; critical path is composed of activities 11, 13, 14, 16, 17, 18, 19, 21, and 23.

Chapter 18

18.2 **(a)** 5.0%.
(b) .00001025 failures/unit-hr.
(c) .08979.
(d) 98.77.

18.4 $R_s = .8145$.

18.6 $R_p = .99925$.

18.8 $R_p = .984$.

18.10 $R = .7918$.

18.12 Cost without maintenance contract = \$1,255/week.
Cost with maintenance contract = \$1,395/week.

GLOSSARY

ABC analysis (p. 563) A method for dividing on-hand inventory into three classifications based on annual dollar volume.

Acceptable quality level (AQL) (p. 125) The quality level of a lot considered good.

Acceptance sampling (p. 123) A method of measuring random samples of lots or batches of products against predetermined standards.

Activity (p. 772) A task or a subproject in a CPM or PERT network that occurs between two events; a flow over time.

Activity charts (p. 484) A way of depicting studies and the resultant suggestions for improvement of utilization of an operator and a machine or some combination of operators (a crew) and machines.

Activity time estimate (p. 775) The time it takes to complete an activity in a PERT or CPM network.

Adaptive smoothing (p. 188) An approach to exponential smoothing forecasting in which the smoothing constant is automatically changed to keep errors to a minimum.

Aggregate planning (p. 682) An approach to determine the quantity and timing of production for the intermediate future (usually 3 to 18 months ahead).

Assembly chart (p. 228) A means of identifying the points of production where components flow into subassemblies and ultimately into a final product.

Assembly drawing (p. 227) An exploded view of the product, usually through a three-dimensional or isometric drawing.

Assembly line (p. 411) An approach that puts fabricated parts together at a series of workstations; used in repetitive processes.

Assembly-line balancing (p. 412) Obtaining output at each workstation on the production line so that it is nearly the same.

Assignable variations (p. 111) Variation in a production process that can be traced to specific causes.

Assignment method (p. 725) A special class of linear programming models that involves assigning tasks or jobs to resources.

Attribute inspection (p. 96) An inspection that classifies items as being either good or defective regardless of degree.

Automated guided vehicle (AGV) (p. 326) Electronically guided and controlled carts used to move materials.

Automated storage and retrieval system (ASRS) (p. 326) Computer-controlled warehouses that provide for the automatic placement of parts into and from designated places within the warehouse.

Automatic identification system (AIS) (p. 331) A system for transforming data into electronic form, for example, bar codes.

Average actual cycle time (p. 496) The arithmetic mean of the times for each element measured, adjusted for unusual influences for each element.

Average outgoing quality (AOQ) (p. 128) The percent defective in an average lot of goods inspected through acceptance sampling.

Backward scheduling (p. 719) A job shop scheduling technique in which the last operation on the routing is scheduled first.

Benchmarking (p. 85) Selecting a demonstrated standard of performance that represents the very best performance for a process or activity.

Beta probability distribution (p. 775) A mathematical distribution that may describe the activity time estimate distributions in a PERT network.

Bill of material (BOM) (pp. 223, 643) A listing of the components, their description, and the quantity of each required to make one unit of a product.

Bonus (p. 481) A monetary reward, usually in cash or stock options, given to management or executives in an organization.

Bottleneck (p. 736) An operation that limits output in the production sequence.

Breakdown maintenance (p. 817) Remedial maintenance that occurs when equipment fails and must be repaired on an emergency or priority basis.

Break-even analysis (p. 298) A means of finding the point, in dollars and units, at which costs equal revenues.

Buyer's risk (p. 126) The probability of a buyer's acceptance of a bad lot overlooked through sampling (a Type II error).

Can/CSA-ISO 9000 (p. 81) The European standard of quality adopted by the Canadian Standards Association.

Capacity (p. 292) The maximum output of a system in a given period.

Cause-and-effect diagram (p. 92) A chart designed to highlight possible quality problems and inspection points in a manufacturing process; also known as **Ishikawa diagram** or **Fish-bone chart**.

c-charts (p. 118) A quality control chart used to control the number of defects per unit of output.

Centre-of-gravity method (p. 350) A mathematical technique used for finding the best location for a single distribution point that services several stores or areas.

Central limit theorem (p. 113) The theoretical foundation for $\bar{x}$-charts that states that regardless of the distribution of the population of all parts or services, the distribution of x's will tend to follow a normal curve as the sample size grows large.

Closed-loop MRP system (p. 657) A system that provides feedback to the capacity plan, master production schedule, and production plan.

Coefficient of correlation (p. 184) A number measure, between –1 and +1, of the statistical relationship between variables.

Competitive advantage (p. 40) A unique advantage over competitors.

Computer-aided design (CAD) (p. 225, 323) Use of a computer to develop the geometry of a design.

Computer-aided manufacturing (CAM) (p. 323) The use of information technology to control machinery.

Computer-integrated manufacturing (CIM) (p. 327) A manufacturing system in which electronically controlled machines are integrated with robots, transfer machines, or automated guided vehicles to create a complete manufacturing system.

Computer numerical control (CNC) (p. 324) The control of machines via their own computer.

Configuration management (p. 228) A system by which a product's planned and changing components are accurately identified and for which control and accountability of change are maintained.

Consignment (p. 534) An arrangement whereby the supplier maintains title to the inventory.

Constraints (p. 241) Restrictions that limit the degree to which a manager can pursue an objective.

Consumer market survey (p. 163) A forecasting method that solicits input from customers or potential customers regarding their future purchasing plans.

Continuous process (p. 285) A product-oriented, high-volume, low-variety process.

Control chart (p. 94, 110) A graphical presentation of process data over time.

Control files (p. 721) All of the information in an MRP system pertaining to a particular order—the shop order master file and the shop order detail file.

Corner point method (p. 247) A method for solving graphical linear programming problems.

Corrective action reporting seminars (CARS) (p. 95) Integrative problem-solving model developed by Professor M. Piczak of Mohawk College.

CRAFT (Computer Relative Allocation of Facilities Technique) (p. 403) A computer program that systematically examines alternative departmental rearrangements to reduce total material-handling cost.

Critical path (p. 771) The computed longest time path(s) through a network.

Critical path analysis (p. 776) A network model for finding the shortest possible schedule for a series of activities. It usually employs PERT or CPM.

Critical path method (p. 770) A network technique using only one time factor per activity that enables managers to schedule, monitor, and control large and complex projects.

Critical ratio (CR) (p. 732) A sequencing rule that is an index number computed by dividing the time remaining until the due date by the work time remaining.

Crossover chart (p. 301) A chart depicting more than one process with costs for the possible volumes.

Cumulative probability distribution (p. 610) The accumulation of individual probabilities of a distribution.

Cycle counting (p. 567) A continuing audit of inventory records.

Cycle time (p. 414) The time the product is available at each workstation in assembly-line balancing.

Decision support system (DSS) (p. 332) A logical extension of MIS that helps managers model decision alternatives by allowing "what-if" analysis given certain financial or operating parameters.

Decision table (p. 55) A tabular means of analyzing decision alternatives and states of nature.

Decision tree (p. 59) A graphical means of analyzing decision alternatives and states of nature.

Degeneracy (p. 375) An occurrence in transportation models when there are too few squares or shipping routes being used so that tracing a closed path for each unused square becomes impossible. Degeneracy exists when the number of rows plus the number of columns minus one does not equal the number of occupied cells.

Delphi method (p. 162) A forecasting technique using a group process that allows experts to make forecasts.

Demand forecast (p. 162) A projection of a company's sales for each time period in the planning horizon.

Design for manufacturability and value engineering teams (p. 218) Teams charged with improvement of designs and specifications at the research, development, design, and production stages of product development.

Direct numerical control (DNC) (p. 324) A machine that is directly (hard) wired to a control computer that supplies the electronic instructions and controls.

Disaggregation (p. 697) The process of breaking the aggregate plan into greater detail.

Discrete probability distribution (p. 146) A frequency distribution in which outcomes are not continuous. Outcomes from the roll of a die are discrete, whereas temperatures (which can take on any fractional value) are considered continuous variables.

Distribution resource planning (DRP) (p. 662) A time-phased stock replenishment plan for all levels of a distribution network.

Double sampling (p. 123) A form of inspection that takes a small sample and if the resulting defects fall within a marginal acceptance level, a second sampling may be drawn; cumulative results determine rejection or acceptance of the lot.

Dummy activity (p. 774) An activity having no time, inserted into the network to maintain the logic of the network.

Dummy destinations (p. 375) Artificial destination points created in the transportation method of linear programming when the total supply is greater than the total demand; they serve to equalize the total demand and supply.

Dummy sources (p. 375) Artificial shipping source points created in the transportation method when total demand is greater than total supply in order to effect a supply equal to the excess of demand over supply.

Earliest due date (EDD) (p. 729) A priority scheduling rule that means the earliest due date job is performed next.

Economic forecasts (p. 162) Planning indicators, often provided by forecasting services, valuable in helping organizations prepare medium- to long-range forecasts.

Economic part period (p. 655) That period of time when the ratio of setup cost to holding cost is equal.

Effective capacity or utilization (p. 293) The maximum capacity a firm can expect to achieve given its product mix, methods of scheduling, maintenance, and standards of quality.

Efficiency (p. 293) A measure of actual output over effective capacity.

Electronic data interchange (EDI) (p. 532) A standardized data transmittal format for computerized communications between organizations.

Employee empowerment (p. 83, 476) Involving employees in every step of the production process.

Employee involvement (p. 83) Inclusion of employee(s) in every step of the process from product design to final packaging.

Engineering change notice (ECN) (pp. 228, 642) A correction or modification of an engineering drawing.

Engineering drawing (p. 222) A drawing that shows the dimensions, tolerances, materials, and finishes of a component.

Equally likely (p. 56) A criterion for decision making under certainty that assigns equal probability to each state of nature.

Ergonomics (p. 482) The study of work; in the United States, often called *human factors engineering*.

Event (p. 772) A point in time that marks the start or completion of a task or activity in a network.

Expected monetary value (EMV) (p. 57) The expected payout or value of a variable that has different possible states of nature, each with an associated probability.

Expected value (p. 147) A measure of central tendency and the weighted average of the values of the variable.

Expected value of perfect information (EVPI) (p. 58) The difference between the payoff under certainty and under risk.

Expected value under certainty (p. 58) The expected or average return.

Expert system (ES) (p. 332, 737) A computer program that mimics human logic and "solves" problems much as a human expert would.

Exponential smoothing (p. 169) A weighted moving-average forecasting technique in which data points are weighted by an exponential function.

Fabrication line (p. 411) A machine-paced, product-oriented facility for building components.

Factor-rating method (p. 345) A method of analysis used for solving location problems that allows managers to assign appropriate relative weights to a wide variety of qualitative and quantitative factors.

Failure (p. 812) The change in a product or system from a satisfactory working condition to a condition that is below an acceptable standard.

Finished goods inventory (p. 563) Inventory that's processing is complete and is awaiting shipment.

Finite scheduling (p. 737) An interactive computer technique that allows schedulers flexibility to handle any situation, including order, labour, or machine changes.

First-come, first-served (FCFS) (p. 729) A priority job scheduling rule by which the jobs are completed in the order in which they arrived.

First-in, first-out (FIFO) (p. 441) A queuing rule by which the first customers in line receive the first service—or, in an inventory system, by which the first inventory received is the first inventory used.

Fish-bone chart (p. 93) A schematic technique used to discover possible locations of quality problems in manufacturing; also known as an Ishikawa diagram or a cause-and-effect diagram.

Fixed costs (p. 298) Costs that continue even if no units are produced.

Fixed-period system (p. 589) A system that triggers inventory ordering on a uniform time frequency.

Fixed-position layout (p. 396) Addresses the layout requirements of stationary projects or large, bulky projects (such as ships or buildings).

Flexible manufacturing system (FMS) (p. 326) A system using an automated work cell controlled by electronic signals from a common centralized computer facility.

Flexible work week (p. 474) A work schedule that deviates from the normal or standard five 8-hour days (usually, four 10-hour days).

Flextime (p. 474) A system that allows employees, within limits, to determine their own work schedules.

Flow diagram (p. 484) A drawing used to analyze movement of people or material.

Focus forecasting (p. 189) Forecasting that tries a variety of computer models and selects the best one for the particular application.

Focussed factory (p. 406) A permanent facility to produce a product or component in a product-oriented facility.

Focussed work centre (p. 406) A permanent product-oriented arrangement of machines and personnel in what is ordinarily a process-oriented facility.

Forecasting (p. 160) The art and science of forecasting future events.

Forward scheduling (p. 719) Assumes that procurement of material and operations start as soon as the requirements are known.

Fuzzy logic (p. 333) A concept that deals with ambiguous and approximate information to make decisions.

Gain sharing (p. 481) A system of financial rewards to employees for improvements made in an organization's performance.

Gantt charts (p. 723, 767) Planning charts used to schedule resources and allocate time; developed by Henry L. Gantt in the late 1800s.

Goal statement (p. 34) A general statement of the results the organization wants to achieve.

Graphical/charting methods (p. 688) An aggregate planning technique that works with a few variables at a time to allow planners to compare projected capacity with existing capacity.

Gross material requirements plan (p. 646) A schedule that shows the total demand for an item (prior to subtraction of on-hand inventory and scheduled receipts) and when it must be ordered from suppliers or production must be started in order to meet its demand by a particular date.

Group technology (p. 224) A system that requires that components be identified by a coding system that specifies the type of processing and the parameters of the processing; it allows similar products to be processed together.

Holding cost (p. 572) The cost to keep or carry inventory in stock.

House of quality (p. 87) A graphic technique for defining the relationship between customer desires and a given product or service.

Incentive system (p. 481) An employee reward system based on individual or group productivity.

Industrial engineering (p. 6) Analytical approaches applied to the improvement of productivity in both manufacturing and service sectors.

Infant mortality (p. 817) The failure rate early in the life of a product or process.

Information sciences (p. 6) The systematic processing of data to yield information.

Input-output control (p. 722) A system that allows operations personnel to manage facility work flows, by tracking work added to a work centre and its work completed (in that work centre).

Inspection (p. 95) A means of ensuring that an operation is producing at the quality level expected.

Intangible costs (p. 346) A category of location costs that can be evaluated through weighting techniques.

Intermittent process (p. 284) A low-volume, high-variety process; also known as a process-oriented process.

Inventory (p. 562) A stored resource that is used to satisfy a current or future need.

Ishikawa diagram (p. 92) See **Fish-bone chart**.

ISO 9000 (p. 80) A set of quality standards developed by the European Community.

Iso-cost line approach (p. 250) An approach to solve a linear programming minimization problem graphically.

Iso-profit line method (p. 246) An approach to solving a linear programming maximization problem graphically.

Job design (p. 475) An approach that specifies the tasks that constitute a job for an individual or a group.

Job enlargement (p. 476) The grouping of a variety of tasks about the same skill level; horizontal enlargement.

Job enrichment (p. 476) A method of giving an employee more responsibility that includes some of the planning and control necessary for job accomplishment; vertical enlargement.

Job instructions (p. 228) A way of providing detailed instructions about how to perform a task.

Job lot (p. 399) A group or batch of parts processed together.

Job rotation (p. 476) A system in which an employee is moved from one specialized job to another.

Johnson's rule (p. 733) An approach that minimizes processing time for sequencing a group of jobs through two facilities and minimizes total idle time in the facilities.

Jury of executive opinion (p. 162) A forecasting technique that takes the opinion of a small group of high-level managers, often in combination with statistical models, and results in a group estimate of demand. The most widely used of all forecasting approaches.

Just-in-time (JIT) inventory (p. 568) The minimum inventory necessary to keep a perfect system running.

Just-in-time (JIT) purchasing (p. 533) Purchasing that reduces waste present at receiving and incoming inspection; it also reduces inventory, poor quality, and delay.

Kaizen (p. 83) The Japanese word for the ongoing process of incremental improvement.

Kanban or Kanban system (p. 570) The Japanese word for *card* that has come to mean "signal"; a Kanban system moves parts through production via a "pull" from a signal.

Keiretsu (p. 526) A Japanese word to describe subcontractors who become part of a company coalition.

Kit number (p. 644) See **Planning bill**.

Knowledge society (p. 18) A society in which much of the labour force has migrated from manual work to work based on knowledge.

Labour planning (p. 473) A means of determining staffing policies dealing with employment stability and work schedules.

Labour specialization (p. 475) The division of labour into unique ("special") tasks.

Labour standards (p. 485) The amount of time required to perform a job or part of a job.

Lead time (pp. 579, 645) In purchasing systems, the time between placing an order and receiving it; in production systems, it is the wait, move, queue, setup, and run times for each component produced.

Lean producers (p. 287) Repetitive producers who are world-class.

Lean production/lean manufacturing (p. 481) Using committed employees with ever-expanding responsibility in an effort to achieve zero waste, and 100% good product delivered on time every time. The concept implies expanding each employee's job to the maximum and enhancing each employee's responsibility. It is the opposite of some repetitive manufacturing, which removes responsibility and thinking from a job to simplify it to the maximum.

Learning curve (p. 546) The premise that people and organizations get better at their tasks as the tasks are repeated; sometimes called an experience curve.

Level material use (p. 740) The use of frequent, high-quality, small lot sizes for just-in-time production.

Level scheduling (level material scheduling) (p. 687) Mixing products so that each day's production meets the demand for that day. (Large/long production runs of the same product for inventory are not allowed.)

Limited, or finite, population (p. 439) A queuing system in which there are only a limited number of potential users of the service.

Linear decision rule (p. 696) An aggregate planning model that attempts to specify an optimum production rate and work-force level over a specific period.

Linear programming (LP) (p. 241) A mathematical technique designed to help production and operations managers in planning and decision making relative to the trade-off necessary to allocate resources.

Linear-regression analysis (p. 180) A straight-line mathematical model to describe the functional relationships between independent and dependent variables; common quantitative causal forecasting model.

Load reports (p. 658) A report for showing the resource requirements in a work centre for all work currently assigned there as well as all planned and expected orders.

Loading (p. 721) The assigning of jobs to work or processing centres.

Locational break-even analysis (p. 349) A cost-volume analysis to make an economic comparison of location alternatives.

Longest processing time (LPT) (p. 729) A priority rule that assigns the highest priority to those jobs with the longest processing time.

Lot-for-lot (p. 652) A lot-sizing technique producing exactly what was required to meet the plan.

Lot-sizing decisions (p. 652) The process of, or techniques used in, determining lot size.

Lot tolerance percent defective (LTPD) (p. 126) The quality level of a lot considered bad.

Low-level coding (p. 645) A system in a bill of material when an item is coded at the lowest level at which it occurs.

Maintenance (p. 812) All activities involved in keeping a system's equipment in working order.

Make-or-buy decision (p. 224, 523) The choice between producing a component or a service and purchasing it from an outside source.

Management coefficient model (p. 696) A formal planning model built around a manager's experience and performance; also known as Bowman's coefficient.

Management information system (MIS) (p. 331) A system dedicated to obtaining, formatting, manipulating, and presenting data as information to managers when needed.

Management process (p. 10) The application of planning, organizing, staffing, leading, and controlling to the achievement of objectives.

Management science (p. 6) A systematic approach to problem formulation and solution, typically utilizing interdisciplinary talents and making use of mathematical, behavioural, and computer skills.

Manufacturer's risk (p. 126) The probability of having a manufacturer's good lot rejected through sampling (a Type I error).

Marginal analysis (p. 591) When applied to inventory, a technique that determines the optimal stocking policy by taking into account marginal profit (MP) and marginal loss (ML).

Master production schedule (p. 641) A timetable that specifies what is to be made and when.

Material requirements planning (MRP) (p. 640) A dependent demand technique that uses bill of material, inventory, expected receipts, and a master production schedule to determine material requirements.

Material requirements planning II (MRP II) (p. 658) A system that allows, with MRP in place, inventory data to be augmented by other resource variables; in this case, MRP becomes *material resource planning*.

Materials management (p. 528) An approach that seeks efficiency of operations through the integration of all material acquisition, movement, and storage activities in the firm.

Maximax (p. 56) A criterion for decision making under uncertainty that finds an alternative that maximizes the maximum outcome or consequence; hence, an optimistic criterion.

Maximin (p. 56) A criterion for decision making under uncertainty that finds an alternative that maximizes the minimum outcome or consequence; hence, a pessimistic criterion.

Mean absolute deviation (MAD) (p. 171) One measure of the overall forecast error for a model; it is computed by taking the sum of the absolute values of the individual forecast errors and dividing by the number of periods of data (n).

Mean squared error (MSE) (p. 172) The average of the squared differences between the forecasted and observed values.

Mean time between failures (MTBF) (p. 815) The expected time between a repair and the next failure of a component, machine, process, or product.

Measured daywork (p. 481) A standard time system whereby employees are paid on the basis of the amount of standard time accomplished.

Merchandisers (p. 523) Buyers for retailers; buyers who are responsible for buying goods and services that can be resold for a profit.

Mission (p. 33) The purpose or rationale of an organization's activity.

Mixed strategy (p. 687) A planning strategy that uses two or more controllable variables to set a feasible production plan.

Model (p. 52) A representation of reality; it may be graphic, physical, or mathematical.

Modified distribution (MODI) method (p. 377) A method that computes improvement indices for each unused square without drawing all of the closed paths in a transportation system.

Modular bills (p. 644) Bills of material organized by major subassemblies or by product options.

Modules (p. 285) Parts or components of a product previously prepared, often in a continuous process.

Monte Carlo method (p. 608) A simulation technique that uses random elements when chance exists in their behaviour. The basis of this method is experimentation of the chance elements through random sampling.

Moving averages (p. 167) A forecasting method that uses an average of the *n* most recent periods of data to forecast the next period.

MRO (p. 563) Maintenance, repair, and operating systems.

Multiphase queuing system (p. 441) A system in which the customer receives services from several stations before exiting the system.

Multiple-channel queuing system (p. 441) A service system with one waiting line but with several servers.

Multiple regression (p. 186) A causal forecasting method with more than one independent variable.

Mutual commitment (p. 472) The concept that both management and employees strive to meet common objectives.

Mutual trust (p. 472) An atmosphere in which both management and employees operate with reasonable, documented employment policies that are honestly and equitably implemented.

Naive approach (p. 167) A forecasting technique that assumes demand in the next period is equal to demand in the most recent period.

Natural variations (p. 111) Variabilities that affect almost every production process to some degree and are to be expected; also known as common causes.

Negative exponential probability distribution (p. 442) A continuous probability distribution often used to describe the service time in a queuing system.

Negotiation strategies (p. 529) Approaches taken by purchasing personnel to develop contractual relationships with suppliers.

Net present value (p. 305) A means of determining the discounted value of a series of future cash receipts.

Network (p. 772) A sequence of activities defined by starting and ending events and the activities that occur between them.

Neural networks (p. 334) Computer programs modelled on the brain's meshlike network of interconnected cells and programmed to recognize patterns and to solve related problems.

Normal distribution (p. 149) A continuous probability distribution characterized by a bell-shaped curve, the parameters of which are the mean and the standard deviation.

Normal time (p. 496) The time, adjusted for performance, to complete a task observed during a time study.

Northwest-corner rule (p. 369) A systematic procedure in the transportation model where one starts at the upper left-hand cell of a table (i.e., the northwest corner) and systematically allocates units to shipping routes.

Numerical control (NC) (p. 324) The controlling of machines by computer programs on paper or magnetic tape.

Objective (p. 34) A specific statement of the tactical results the organization wants to achieve.

Objective function (p. 241) A mathematical expression in linear programming that maximizes or minimizes some quantity (usually profit or cost).

Office layout (p. 396) The grouping of workers, their equipment, and spaces/offices to provide for comfort, safety, and movement of information.

Operating characteristic (OC) curve (p. 124) A graph that describes how well an acceptance plan discriminates between good and bad lots.

Operations chart (p. 485) A chart depicting right- and left-hand motions.

Optimistic time (p. 775) The "best" activity completion time that could be obtained in a network plan.

Ordering cost (p. 572) The cost of the ordering process and its supplies and personnel.

Pareto charts (p. 89) Charts that organize errors, problems, or defects to help production personnel focus on problem solving efforts.

Part period balancing (PPB) (p. 655) An inventory ordering technique that balances setup and holding costs by changing the lot size to reflect requirements of the next lot size in the future.

Part-time status (p. 475) The status of an employee who works less than a normal week; less than 32 hours per week often classifies an employee as "part-time."

***p*-chart (p. 118)** A quality control chart that is used to control attributes.

Pegging (p. 652) In material requirements planning systems, tracing upward in the bill of material (BOM) from the component to parent item.

PERT/Cost (p. 785) A network technique that finds the least expensive method of shortening the entire project.

Pessimistic time (p. 775) The "worst" activity time that could be expected in a network activity.

Phantom bills (p. 644) Bills of material for components, usually assemblies, that exist only temporarily; they are never inventoried.

Physical sciences (p. 6) Physics, chemistry, biology, and other related sciences.

Piece rate (p. 481) A work system that assigns a standard time for each piece produced; the employee is paid on the basis of the number of pieces made.

Pivot column (p. 254) The column in a linear programming simplex table that indicates which variable will enter the solution next.

Pivot number (p. 254) The number at the intersection of the pivot row and the pivot column in a linear programming simplex table.

Pivot row (p. 254) The row in a linear programming simplex table that indicates which variable will leave the solution next.

Plan-Do-Check-Act (PDCA) Wheel (p. 94) Influential W. Edwards Deming model used in the total quality management (TQM) process.

Planning bill (p. 644) Paperwork created in order to assign an artificial parent to the bill of material. An artificial group of components issued together to facilitate production; not a complete subassembly; also known as a "kit" or "pseudo bill."

Planning files (p. 721) An item master file, a routing file, and a work centre master file in a material requirements planning system.

Poisson distribution (p. 439) An important discrete probability distribution that often describes the arrival rated in queuing theory; derived by Simeon Poisson in 1837.

Poka-yoke (p. 96) Literally translated, "foolproof"; it has come to mean a device or technique that ensures the production of a good unit every time.

Predetermined time standards (p. 501) An approach that divides manual work into small basic elements that have established and widely accepted times.

Preventive maintenance (p. 817) A plan that involves routine inspections, servicing, and keeping facilities in good repair to prevent failure.

Priority rules (p. 728) Rules that are used to determine the sequence of jobs in process-oriented facilities.

Probabilistic model (p. 587) A statistical model applicable when product demand or any other variable is not known, but can be specified by means of a probability distribution.

Probable time (p. 775) The most likely time to complete an activity in a PERT network.

Process chart (p. 90, 484) A chart using symbols to analyze the movement of people or material.

Process control (p. 324) The use of information technology to control a physical process.

Process focus (p. 284) A low-volume, high-variety process.

Process-oriented layout (p. 396) A layout that deals with low-volume, high-variety production; intermittent process; like machines and equipment are grouped together.

Process (or transformation) strategy (p. 284) The approach that an organization takes to transform resources into goods and services.

Product-by-value analysis (p. 220) A listing of products in descending order of their individual dollar contribution to the firm, as well as the *total annual* dollar contribution of the product.

Product development teams (p. 218) Teams charged with moving from market requirements for a product to achieving product success.

Product focus (p. 285) A product-oriented, high-volume, low-variety process.

Product-oriented layout (p. 396) A production process built around a product and seeking the best personnel and machine utilization via repetitive or continuous production.

Product strategy (p. 212) The selection, definition, and design of products.

Production (p. 4) The creation of goods and services.

Production and operations management (P/OM) (p. 4) Activities that relate to the creation of goods and services through the transformation of inputs to outputs.

Production order quantity model (p. 581) An economic order quantity technique applied to production orders.

Productivity (p. 15) The enhancement to the production process that results in a favourable comparison of the quantity of resources employed (inputs) to the quantity of goods and services produced (outputs).

Productivity variables (p. 18) The three factors critical to productivity improvement—labour, capital, and the arts and science of management.

Profit-sharing (p. 481) A system that provides for some part of the profit sharing to be distributed among employees.

Program Evaluation and Review Technique (PERT) (p. 770) A technique to enable managers to schedule, monitor, and control large and complex projects by employing three time estimates for each activity.

Project organization (p. 765) An organization formed to ensure that programs (projects) receive the proper management and attention.

Pseudo bill (p. 644) See **Planning bill**.

Pull system (p. 663) A distribution or production network driven by the top or end user level ordering more stock.

Purchasing (or procurement) (p. 522) The acquisition of goods and services.

Purchasing agent (p. 522) A person with legal authority to execute purchasing contracts on behalf of the firm.

Purchasing management (p. 527) The management of inventory, plus the transportation, availability of supply, and quality of suppliers.

Push system (p. 663) A distribution network in which orders are received from upstream locations (users) but are evaluated by the supplying location.

Qualitative forecasts (p. 162) Forecasts that incorporate important factors such as the decision maker's intuition, emotions, personal experiences, and value system.

Quality circle (p. 84) A group of employees meeting regularly with a facilitator to solve work-related problems in their work area; initiated by the Japanese in the 1970s.

Quality function deployment (QDF) (p. 87) Both (1) determining what will satisfy the customer and (2) translating those customer desires into the target design.

Quality loss function (p. 89) A mathematical function that identifies all costs connected with poor quality and shows how these costs increase as product quality moves from what the customer wants.

Quality-of-work-life (p. 472) Aims toward a job that is reasonably safe, is equitable in pay, and achieves an appropriate level of both physical and psychological requirements.

Quality robust (p. 89, 219) Said of products that are consistently built to specifications in spite of adverse conditions.

Quality robust design (p. 219) A design that yields a good product in spite of small variations in the production process.

Quantitative forecast (p. 162) An approach that employs one or more mathematical models that use historical data and/or causal variables to forecast demand.

Quantity discount (p. 583) A reduced price for items purchased in large quantities.

Queuing theory (p. 437) The body of knowledge about waiting lines.

Random number (p. 611) A series of digits that have been selected by a totally random process; all digits have an equal chance of occurring.

Random-number intervals (p. 611) A set of numbers to represent each possible value or outcome in a computer simulation.

Rated capacity (p. 293) A measure of the maximum usable capacity of a particular facility.

Raw material inventory (p. 563) Inventory that has been purchased, but not processed.

***R*-chart (p. 113)** A process control chart that tracks the "range" within a sample; indicates that a gain or loss in uniformity has occurred in a production process.

Reliability (p. 812) The probability that a machine part or product will function properly for a reasonable length of time.

Reorder point (p. 579) The inventory level (point) at which action is taken to replenish the stocked item.

Repetitive process (p. 285) A product-oriented production process that uses modules.

Retail/service layout (p. 396) An approach (often computerized) that allocates shelf space and responds to customer behaviour.

Revenue function (p. 298) An element in break-even analysis that increases by the selling price of each unit.

Robot (p. 325) A flexible machine with the ability to hold, move, or grab items that functions through electronic impulses that activate motors or switches.

Robust model (p. 578) A model that gives satisfactory answers even with substantial variation in the parameters.

Robust quality (p. 89, 219) Exists when a product can be produced to requirements even when minor variations occur in the production process.

Route sheet (p. 228) A listing of the operations necessary to produce the component with the material specified in the bill of material.

Safety stock (p. 580) Extra stock to allow for uneven demand; a buffer.

Sales force composite (p. 162) A forecasting technique based upon salespersons' estimates of expected sales.

Scheduling by simulation (p. 696) A computer model to find a minimum-cost combination for work-force size and production rate.

Search decision rule (p. 696) A pattern search algorithm that tries to find the minimum-cost combination of various force and production levels.

Self-directed team (p. 478) A group of empowered individuals working together to reach a common goal.

Sensitivity analysis (p. 258) An analysis that projects how much a solution might change if there were changes in the variables or input data.

Sequencing (p. 728) Determining the order in which jobs should be done at each work centre.

Sequential sampling (p. 124) An inspection system where units are randomly selected from a lot and tested one by one with a cumulative number of inspected pieces and defects recorded.

Service level (p. 587) The complement of the probability of a stockout.

Service sector (p. 17) That segment of the work force that includes trade, financial, education, legal, medical, and other professional occupations.

Setup cost (p. 572) The cost to prepare a machine or process for manufacturing an order.

Setup time (p. 572) The time required to prepare a machine or process for manufacturing an order.

Shadow price (p. 257) The value of one additional unit of a resource in the form of one more hour of machine time or labour time or other scarce resource in linear programming.

Shortest processing time (SPT) (p. 729) A priority job scheduling rule that assigns the shortest time job first.

Simplex method (p. 251) An algorithm developed by Dantzig for solving linear programming problems of all sizes.

Simulation (p. 607) The attempt to duplicate the features, appearance, and characteristics of a real system, usually a computerized model.

Single-channel queuing system (p. 441) A service system with one line and one server, e.g., a drive-in bank with one open teller.

Single-phase queuing system (p. 441) A system in which the customer receives service from only one station and then exits the system.

Single sampling (p. 123) A form of inspection that specifies a number of items to be sampled and an acceptable number of defects.

Slack time (p. 776) The amount of time an individual activity in a project management network can be delayed without delaying the entire project.

Smoothing constant (p. 169) The weighting factor used in an exponential smoothing forecast; a number between 0 and 1.

Source inspection (p. 96) Inspection at the supplier.

Source management (p. 527) An approach that seeks likely suppliers, develops their ability to produce, and negotiates acceptable relationships.

SPACECRAFT (p. 404) A three-dimensional layout system to minimize the cost of moving workers and materials.

Standard deviation (p. 148) A measure of dispersion or spread; the square root of the variance.

Standard error of the estimate (p. 183) A distribution within which samples of the process under study are expected to fall.

Standard for the Exchange of Product Data (STEP) (p. 323) A standard for the electronic exchange of product design information, used internationally.

Standard time (p. 497) A time-study adjustment to the total normal time; the adjustment provides allowances for personal needs, unavoidable work delays, and worker fatigue.

Standard work schedule (p. 474) Five $7^1/_2$-hour days in Canada.

Standards manuals (p. 228) Manuals that provide standard times for setup and information about speed, capacity, tolerance, and other pertinent data for each operation.

Statistical process control (SPC) (p. 93) A process used to monitor standards, making measurements and taking corrective action as a product or service is being produced.

Stepping-stone method (p. 370) An iterative technique for moving from an initial feasible solution to an optimal solution in the transportation method; it is used to evaluate the cost-effectiveness of shipping goods via transportation routes not currently in the system.

Strategy (p. 34) How an organization expects to achieve its missions and goals.

Suboptimize (p. 33) To operate at a level less than the best.

Supply management (p. 527) The control of long-term availability of high-dollar or critical purchases.

Surplus variable (p. 259) The amount over and above a required minimum level set on the right-hand side of a greater-than-or-equal-to constraint in a linear programming problem.

System (p. 32) An aggregation of interacting variables.

System nervousness (p. 652) A situation generated by frequent changes in the MRP system.

Tactical scheduling decisions (p. 682) Making monthly or quarterly plans that address fluctuating demands.

Taguchi technique (p. 89) A quality control technique that focusses on improving the product at the design stage.

Tangible costs (p. 346) Readily identifiable costs that can be measured with some precision.

Target-oriented quality (p. 89) A philosophy of continuous improvement to bring the product exactly on target.

Technological forecasts (p. 162) Long-term forecasts concerned with the rates of technological progress; such forecasts are critical in high-technology industries; usually performed by experts in each particular field.

Time-based competition (p. 220) Competition based on time; may take form of rapidly developing products and moving them to market or rapid product or service delivery.

Time fences (p. 652) A way of allowing a segment of the master schedule to be designated as "not to be rescheduled."

Time series (p. 163) A forecasting technique that uses a series of past data points to make a forecast.

Time standard team approach (p. 504) An approach to setting labour standards and labour rates whereby the union and management "agree to" the standards or rates.

Time study (p. 495) The timing of a sample of a worker's performance and using it to set a standard.

Total quality management (TQM) (p. 82) Management of an entire organization so that it excels in all aspects of products and services that are important to the customer.

Tracking signal (p. 187) A measurement of how well the forecast is predicting actual values.

Transaction processing system (p. 331) A system that processes the multitude of transactions that occur within and between firms.

Transportation method of LP (p. 693) A heuristic technique for solving a class of linear programming problems.

Transportation technique (or model) (p. 352) A linear programming technique that determines the best pattern of shipments from several points of demand to several destinations so as to minimize total production and transportation costs.

Trend projection (p. 176) A time-series forecasting method that fits a trend line to a series of historical data points and then projects the line into the future for forecasts.

Type I error (p. 126) Statistically, the probability of rejecting a good lot.

Type II error (p. 126) Statistically, the probability of accepting a bad lot.

Unlimited, or infinite, population (p. 439) A queuing situation in which a virtually unlimited number of people or items could request the services, or in which the number of customers or arrivals on hand at any given moment is a very small portion of potential arrivals.

Value analysis (p. 220) A review of products with long life cycles that takes place during the production process.

Variable costs (p. 298) Costs that vary with the volume of units produced; also known as direct costs.

Variable inspection (p. 96) As opposed to attribute inspection, the classifications of inspected items as falling on a continuum scale such as dimension size or strength.

Variance (p. 148) A number that reveals the overall spread or dispersion of the distribution.

Vertical integration (p. 524) Developing the ability to produce goods or services previously purchased by buying a supplier or distributor.

Virtual companies (p. 526) Companies that meet changing demands through flexible, fluid organizational boundaries by relying on a variety of supplier relationships.

Vision systems (p. 325) Using video cameras and computer technology in inspection roles.

Wagner-Whitin procedure (p. 656) A programming model for lot-size computation that assumes a finite time horizon beyond which there are no additional net requirements.

Waiting lines (p. 437) Queues; items or people in a line awaiting a service.

Warehouse layout (p. 396) A design that attempts to minimize total cost by addressing trade-offs between space and material handling.

Work cell (p. 405) A temporary product-oriented arrangement of machines and personnel in what is ordinarily a process-oriented facility.

Work-in-process inventory (p. 563) Inventory that has been only partially processed and is not completed.

Work order (p. 228) An instruction to make a given quantity of a particular item, usually to a given schedule.

Work sampling (p. 505) An estimate, via sampling, of the percentage of the time that a worker spends working on various tasks.

World-class firms (p. 43) Firms that compete successfully in the international arena.

World-class P/OM function (p. 44) See **World-class manufacturing**.

$\bar{x}$-chart (*x*-bar) (p. 113) A quality control chart for variables that indicates when changes occur in the central tendency of a production process.

Yield management (p. 699) The study of capacity allocation (such as airplane seats) in order to maximize profit or utilization.

NAME INDEX

Company Index

GENERAL INDEX

PHOTO CREDITS

pp. 2-3 Alcan Cable
p. 19 Joseph Pobereskin/Tony Stone Images
p. 37 Wajax Industries Limited
p. 51 Prentice Hall Archives
p. 53 Canadian Space Agency
p. 54 O & G Photography
p. 95 Bob Carroll
p. 108 (upper) and p. 109 American Iron & Steel Institute
p. 108 (lower) U.S.X. Corporation
p. 166 Xerox Tower of North American Centre, North York
p. 187 Northern Telecom/Prentice Hall Archives
p. 222 Orenda Aerospace Corporation
p. 225 Barrett and MacKay Photographers Inc.
p. 242 Thomas Kitchin/First Light
pp. 282-83 Hibernia Management and Development Co. Ltd.
p. 297 Bob Carroll
p. 298 Bob Carroll
p. 325 Canadian Space Agency
p. 342 Honda of Canada Mfg.
p. 396 National Public Relations (Toronto)
p. 410 Erin Elder/Maclean's
p. 470 (upper) Eaton School of Retailing
p. 470 (lower) Robert Karpa
p. 471 (upper) P. Austring
p. 471 (lower) Christopher Reardon
p. 477 Markham Stouffville Hospital
p. 504 Jean Heguy/First Light
p. 506 Bob Carroll
p. 765 Courtesy of Stadium Corporation of Ontario Limited. Skydome* ™ of Stadium Corporation of Ontario Limited

The Global Perspective of Heizer/Render/Forrester/Bailey, First Canadian Edition

Chapter 1 Production/Operations Management
World-class Profile: Alcan Cable, p. 2
Chapter section: The Productivity Challenge, p. 15
Comparison of Productivity in U.S., Japan, and Germany (Figure 1.5), p. 16
P/OM in Action: Does Canada Compete? p. 17
Critical Thinking Exercise: Canada second-lowest among G-7 nations in keeping educated people, p. 24

Chapter 2 P/OM Strategy and International Competition
World-Class Profile: Komatsu, p. 30
Whirlpool's global strategy (photo/caption), p. 35
P/OM in Action: Japan Flocks to Southeast Asia, p. 38
P/OM in Action: Strategy at Hong Kong's Johnson Electric Is Global, p. 41
Chapter section: International Issues in P/OM, p. 43
International firms (Table 2.1), p. 44
In-text quiz for identifying home of international firms (Table 2.2), p. 45
Characteristics of World-Class Firms (Table 2.3), p. 46

Chapter 3 Total Quality Management
World-Class Profile: Motorola, p. 76
Chapter section: International Quality Standards, p. 80
P/OM in Action: Sidus Systems Inc., p. 81
Chapter section: Achieving World-Class Standards, p. 98

Chapter 4 Statistical Quality Control
World-Class Profile: Acme Steel, p. 108
Chapter section: Achieving World-Class Standards, p. 130

Chapter 5 Forecasting
World-Class Profile: Tupperware International, p. 158
Chapter section: Achieving World-Class Standards, p. 190

Chapter 6 Product Strategy
World-Class Profile: Regal Marine, p. 210
Toyota and General Motors (opening quote/photo), p. 212
Hernia Repair at Canada's Shouldice Hospital (photo/caption), p. 213
Chapter section: Achieving World-Class Standards, p. 232

Chapter 6 Supplement: Linear Programming
Case: Quebec Wire Winding, p. 278

Chapter 7 Process Strategies and Capacity Planning
World-Class Profile: Hibernia Management and Development Company (HMDC), p. 282
Japan's National Bicycle (photo/caption), p. 294
Chapter section: Achieving World-Class Standards, p. 308

Chapter 8 State-of-the-Art Technology in P/OM
World-Class Profile: AT&T, pp. 318
P/OM in Action: Ford's Next World Car, p. 322
P/OM in Action: Benetton, The World's Fastest Clothing Manufacturer (Italy), p. 327
Chapter section: Achieving World-Class Standards, p. 333
P/OM in Action: Matsushita (Japan), p. 333

Chapter 9: Location Strategies
World-Class Profile: Federal Express,, p. 338
Motorola's Semi-conductor Plant, Aizu, Japan (photo/caption), p. 341
P/OM in Action: Canada Set for Bigger Share of Japanese Auto Investment, p. 342
Labour Costs in 17 Nations (Figure 9.2), p. 342
P/OM in Action: Norbord Industries Heads to Mississippi, p. 343
Deutsche Mark (cartoon), p. 344
P/OM in Action: Quality Coil Abandons Mexico, p. 344
Maquiladoras (photo/caption), p. 345
Volkswagen Worldwide Distribution (Figure 9.5), p. 351
Chapter section: Achieving World-Class Standards, p. 352
Volkswagen in Brazil (photo/caption), p. 353

Chapter 9 Supplement: Transportation Modelling
Australia's Brisbane Airport (photo/caption), p. 369
Transporting Recruits in the Thai Navy (photo/caption), p. 373
Critical Thinking Exercise: Irish Drug Distributor, Cahill May Roberts, p. 383

Chapter 10 Operations Layout Strategy
World-Class Profile: Pittsburgh Airport, p. 394
Chapter section: Achieving World-Class Standards, p. 416
P/OM in Action: Auto Disassembly Plants in Germany and Japan, p. 417
Critical Thinking Exercise: Japanese vs. American Offices, p. 424

Chapter 10 Supplement: Waiting-Line Models
P/OM in Action: The Culture of Queuing, p. 440
McDonald's in Moscow (photo/caption), p. 452
P/OM in Action: Time-Based Competition in Finland, p. 454

Chapter 11 Human Resource Strategy
World-Class Profile: The Learning Organization Trend, p. 470
P/OM in Action: How Mazda Picks Workers, p. 479
P/OM in Action: World Class Standards Are Tough (Volvo), p. 480
Disaster at Chernobyl (Ukraine) (photo/caption), p. 486
Chapter section: Achieving World-Class Standards, p. 485

Chapter 12 Purchasing Management and Just In Time
World-Class Profile: Boeing, p. 520
Jaguar suppliers (photo/caption), p. 525
P/OM in Action: The Dr. Jose Ignacio Lopez Escapade, p. 526
Chapter section: Keiretsu discussion, p. 526
AT&T supplier relations with Hitachi (photo/caption), p. 529
P/OM in Action: Shoemakers Leap into Mexico, p. 536
Chapter section: Achieving World-Class Standards, p. 538

Chapter 12 Supplement: Simulation
Samsung, Korea's giant manufacturer (opening quote/photo), p. 545

Chapter 13 Inventory Management and Just In Time Tactics
World-Class Profile: Harley Davidson, p. 560
Chapter section: Achieving World-Class Standards, p. 593

Chapter 14 Material Requirements Planning (MRP)
World-Class Profile: Collins Industries, p. 638
Nissan (photo/caption), p. 653
P/OM in Action: Fourth Shift Corp., p. 660
Chapter section: Achieving World-Class Standards, p. 663

Chapter 15 Aggregate Planning
World-Class Profile: Anheuser-Busch, p. 680
Chapter section: Achieving World-Class Standards, p. 699
Case: Andrew-Carter, Inc. (Canadian), p. 712

Chapter 16 Short-Term Scheduling Tactics
World-Class Profile: LTV, p. 716
Chapter section: Achieving World-Class Standards, p. 744

Chapter 17 Project Management
World-Class Profile: Bechtel in Kuwait, p. 762
Chapter section: Achieving World-Class Standards, p. 788
Case: Nigeria's Family Planning Centre, p. 805

Chapter 18 Maintenance and Reliability
World-Class Profile: Orlando Utilities Commission, p. 810
Chapter section: Achieving World-Class Standards, p. 823
Case: Worldwide Chemical, p. 829